W9-APN-638

THE
SCIENCE
OF GOOD
COOKING

THE SCIENCE OF GOOD COOKING

MASTER 50 SIMPLE CONCEPTS TO ENJOY A LIFETIME OF SUCCESS IN THE KITCHEN

THE EDITORS AT AMERICA'S TEST KITCHEN
AND GUY CROSBY, PhD

ILLUSTRATIONS BY MICHAEL NEWHOUSE
AND JOHN BURGOYNE

AMERICA'S
TEST KITCHEN

BROOKLINE, MASSACHUSETTS

America's Test Kitchen
17 Station Street, Brookline, MA 02445

Library of Congress Cataloging-in-Publication Data

The science of good cooking : master 50 simple concepts to enjoy a lifetime of success in the kitchen/ the editors at America's Test Kitchen and Guy Crosby ; illustrations by Michael Newhouse and John Burgoyne.
    p. cm.
Includes index.
ISBN 978-1-933615-98-1
1. Cooking. 2. Food. I. Crosby, Guy. II. America's Test Kitchen (Firm)
TX651.S375 2012
641.3--dc23
                        2012012807

Hardcover: US $40 / $51 CAN

Manufactured in the United States of America
10

Distributed by Penguin Random House Publisher Services
tel: 800-733-3000

EDITORIAL DIRECTOR: Jack Bishop
SCIENCE EDITOR: Guy Crosby, PhD
PROJECT EDITOR: Molly Birnbaum
TEST KITCHEN EXPERIMENT EDITOR: Dan Souza
DESIGN DIRECTOR: Amy Klee
ART DIRECTOR: Greg Galvan
ASSOCIATE ART DIRECTORS: Erica Lee, Matthew Warnick
DESIGNERS: Taylor Argenzio, Sarah Horwitch Dailey
COLOR ILLUSTRATIONS: Michael Newhouse
BLACK-AND-WHITE ILLUSTRATIONS: John Burgoyne
PHOTOGRAPHY: Daniel J. van Ackere
PRODUCTION DIRECTOR: Guy Rochford
SENIOR PRODUCTION MANAGER: Jessica Quirk
SENIOR PROJECT MANAGER: Alice Carpenter
PROJECT MANAGER: Kate Hux
WORKFLOW AND DIGITAL ASSET MANAGER: Andrew Mannone
PRODUCTION AND IMAGING SPECIALIST: Lauren Pettapiece
COPY EDITOR: Cheryl Redmond
PROOFREADER: Barbara Wood
SCIENCE PROOFREADER: Joanne Curran-Celentano, PhD
INDEXER: Elizabeth Parson

CONTENTS

PREFACE

Despite the saying about the cat, curiosity is what sets humans apart from other mammals. A hundred years ago, most cooks were working with a limited repertoire of recipes and ingredients, and they had plenty of first-hand experience to make those recipes work. Now we stand at the beginning of a new century, many of us keenly interested in the culinary arts, but without the years of practical experience that it takes to become a great cook.

What's the solution to this modern quandary? The answer reminds me a bit of my favorite physicist, Lawrence Krauss, who spends his time pondering the mysteries of the universe. In order to understand the cosmos and our place in it, he says, one has to ask how and why. Once the questions have been asked, we can conceive of experiments to prove or disprove our theorems.

All of that sounds rather familiar to everyone who works at America's Test Kitchen. We start every day by asking questions. Do bones add flavor to meat during cooking? What causes ice cream to turn icy in the freezer? Then we construct kitchen experiments to answer those questions in a manner that helps us, as home cooks, to produce more foolproof recipes, and better food.

To test our theory about the benefits of adding small pieces of frozen butter to eggs, we put 2-pound fishing weights on top of omelets. (The more tender omelet could not hold the weight.) To gauge the benefits of letting cooked meat rest, we sliced one roast as soon as it came out of the oven and measured 10 tablespoons of lost liquid; when we waited just 10 minutes to slice a second roast, the liquid lost was reduced to just 4 tablespoons. And does mixing method really matter when making brownies? We tested stirring gently (with some streaks of flour remaining), then stirred a second batch until all streaks were incorporated, and then finished with a third batch that was well mixed in a standing mixer. The brownies made with the lightest touch were perfect; the others were unpleasantly tough.

All of this is fun and interesting, but our real goal is to make you a better home cook. Understanding the difference between amylose and amylopectin (two types of starches) is of little use to cooks unless this information can be used to produce better mashed potatoes. (It can and does.) And understanding how heat is transferred from the outside of a roast to the inside is useful since it explains why a low oven is best when cooking large pieces of meat. (The outside won't overcook by the time the inside is done.)

This reminds me, of course, of the story of the Vermont storekeeper who was asked if he would have a particularly popular item back in stock before long.

"Nope," the old-timer replied.

"Why not?" the customer wanted to know.

"Moves too darn fast!"

That inexplicable logic is often like the science of cooking. At first it doesn't seem to make much sense but then, after a bit of thought, things come into focus. When you understand the language of science, cooking becomes clearer and you naturally make better choices in the kitchen. The next time you make pie dough, you might naturally replace half of the water with vodka. (It makes a more pliable dough that bakes up flaky.) Or you will know to brine beans or macerate sliced fruit.

Please enjoy this book. You will find the answers to most of your cooking questions, especially when it comes to "why"—the most important question of all.

Christopher Kimball
Founder and Publisher
America's Test Kitchen

WELCOME TO AMERICA'S TEST KITCHEN

This book has been tested, written, and edited by the folks at America's Test Kitchen, a very real 2,500-square-foot kitchen located just outside of Boston. It is the home of *Cook's Illustrated* magazine and *Cook's Country* magazine and is the Monday-through-Friday destination for more than three dozen test cooks, editors, food scientists, tasters, and cookware specialists. Our mission is to test recipes over and over again until we understand how and why they work and until we arrive at the "best" version.

We start the process of testing a recipe with a complete lack of conviction, which means that we accept no claim, no theory, no technique, and no recipe at face value. We simply assemble as many variations as possible, test a half-dozen of the most promising, and taste the results blind. We then construct our own hybrid recipe and continue to test it, varying ingredients, techniques, and cooking times until we reach a consensus. The result, we hope, is the best version of a particular recipe, but we realize that only you can be the final judge of our success (or failure). As we like to say in the

test kitchen, "We make the mistakes, so you don't have to."

All of this would not be possible without a belief that good cooking, much like good music, is indeed based on a foundation of objective technique. Some people like spicy foods and others don't, but there is a right way to sauté, there is a best way to cook a pot roast, and there are measurable scientific principles involved in producing perfectly beaten, stable egg whites. This is our ultimate goal: to investigate the fundamental principles of cooking so that you become a better cook. It is as simple as that.

You can watch us work (in our actual test kitchen) by tuning in to *America's Test Kitchen* (AmericasTestKitchen. com) or *Cook's Country from America's Test Kitchen* (CooksCountryTV.com) on public television, or by subscribing to *Cook's Illustrated* magazine (CooksIllustrated. com) or *Cook's Country* magazine (CooksCountry.com), which are each published every other month. We welcome you into our kitchen, where you can stand by our side as we test our way to the best recipes in America.

RECILES

CONTENTS

Pasta and Sauces

Rice, Grains, and Beans

Vegetables

Poultry

Fish and Shellfish

Eggs

Quick Breads, Biscuits, Pancakes, and Waffles

Yeast Breads, Rolls, and Pizza

Cookies and Brownies

Cakes

Pies, Tarts, and Fruit Desserts

Puddings, Custards, Soufflés, and Frozen Desserts

INTRODUCTION

What separates success from failure in the kitchen? It's the ability to think on your feet, to make adjustments as you cook. And, despite what you might think, a lifetime of experience isn't a prerequisite for being a good cook (although it does help).

Knowledge, however, is essential. The successful home cook understands the fundamental principles of good cooking and is able to apply them on the fly, almost without thinking.

But what are these principles and how do you learn them? At America's Test Kitchen we have spent 20 years investigating how cooking works—and why recipes sometimes don't. We've learned that without solid technique, good cooking is impossible.

Sure, there's artistry involved (the combination of ingredients, the presentation of the dish), but good cooking starts with good science. You must understand the basics—like the fact that gentle heat preserves moisture in meat, or salty marinades produce more tender meat than acidic marinades—before you get to the art.

So how do you learn these core cooking principles—and the simple science upon which they are based? Lots of practice is one way.

The observant cook will absorb and accumulate lifelong lessons in the kitchen and come to rely, probably unconsciously, on these principles at work.

But there's another way. Why not make a conscious effort to master these principles? Understanding the science that leads to success or failure in the kitchen is much simpler than you think. Trust us.

The Science of Good Cooking covers the 50 fundamental concepts that we think every good cook should know. We explain the science in simple, practical terms, so you really understand how these principles work and how you can apply them as you cook. Think of this book as an owner's manual for your kitchen.

We suggest you start by reading the following pages devoted to basic kitchen science before diving into the rest of the book. Make sure to consult the information about equipment, ingredients, and food safety in the Appendix, too.

One final word of advice: Be inquisitive in the kitchen. Think about what you're doing and why. That is the most important lesson science can teach anyone who wants to become a better cook.

THE SCIENCE OF MEASURING

A BRIEF HISTORY OF MEASURING

The science of cooking has come a long way in the past century, in part because measuring has become much more standardized and accurate. Until about 100 years ago, most recipes didn't call for specific measures. Even when they did, this information was only moderately helpful because home cooks did not own standardized measuring cups.

In colonial America, a recipe that called for 2 cups of flour assumed the cook would have a cup she used for measuring, but there was no guarantee that the cup used in Thomas Jefferson's kitchen held the same amount of flour as the cup used in George Washington's kitchen. It wasn't until the late 19th century that companies started to manufacture the type of standardized measuring cups and spoons we now take for granted.

So how did cooks get along without standardized measures? You might imagine that cooking before the advent of standardized measures was unreliable, but it wasn't. That's because the skill level of the home cook was quite high and the range of recipes prepared was quite narrow. Cooking was a specialized task, much like needlepoint or carpentry. It wasn't something you learned by reading a book. You learned from watching someone else (usually your mother). In addition, cooking was highly repetitive. You mastered a small set of recipes that relied on local ingredients and local traditions, and you made those same recipes over and over and over.

The publication of *The Boston Cooking-School Cook Book*, written in 1896 by Fannie Merritt Farmer (yes, that Fannie Farmer), marked a watershed moment in American cooking. Recipes in this best-selling book called for standardized measurements and future recipe writers followed suit. In the introduction, Fannie Farmer exhorted her readers to purchase true measuring cups: "Correct measurements are absolutely necessary to insure the best results. Good judgment, with experience, has taught some to measure by sight; but the majority need definite guides."

Fannie Farmer was a true believer in the power of science to improve home cooking. What she didn't see coming was the decline in experience that would make measurement by sight all but impossible for 99 percent of home cooks today. In addition, the explosion of recipe choices has meant that even experienced cooks find themselves preparing new recipes all the time. We source ingredients and recipes from around the world. For this model to work, accurate measurement is essential. How else would the modern American cook be able to make dishes as diverse as curries, stir-fries, tamales, and tiramisù?

MEASURING IS NOT AS SIMPLE AS IT SOUNDS

It's easy to understand that measuring matters, but many modern cooks don't comprehend that how they measure is just as important as the act of measuring itself. What's the point of measuring if you don't measure correctly?

Now, you might be thinking that it can't be that hard to measure, especially if you're using standardized measuring cups. But we ran the following experiment in the test kitchen to prove otherwise. We asked 18 cooks, all professionally trained, to measure 1 cup of flour using the same standardized measuring cup. We then weighed the flour they measured to see how much flour was in their "1 cup." Because of variations in measuring techniques, the weights of flour they obtained varied by 13 percent.

What makes this especially surprising is the fact that everyone in our test kitchen uses the same method for measuring flour. We dip the measuring cup into a container of flour and then sweep off the excess with a butter knife or icing spatula. (This method is known as the dip-and-sweep method.) If you measure flour by spooning the flour into a measuring cup, a technique that aerates the flour as you go, you might end up with 20 to 25 percent less flour.

So why would 18 cooks all using the same method for measuring flour get different results? We realized that how each person dips the cup into the flour affects the amount of flour that fits within. A forceful dip packs more flour into the cup than a gentle one.

PROFESSIONALS PREFER WEIGHT TO VOLUME

Recipes written for home cooks rely on volume (teaspoons, tablespoons, cups) for measurement. Recipes written for professionals generally list ingredients by weight. That's because weight involves no chance for operator error. Assuming the scale has been properly calibrated, 8 ounces of flour is 8 ounces of flour no matter how the flour is handled.

For this reason, we generally supply weights for key ingredients when we write our recipes. We always specify the weight of meat because the cooking time for a 12-ounce pork chop is different from the cooking time for an 8-ounce pork chop. Likewise, we list weights for fruits and vegetables when they are used in large quantity. Calling for 2 pounds of russet potatoes in a mashed potato recipe is much more accurate than calling for four russet potatoes, which can weigh as little as 7 ounces each (1¾ pounds total) or as much as 10 ounces each (2½ pounds total).

Weight is especially important when baking, which is why our recipes include both volume and weight measures for key baking ingredients, as does the chart below.

CONVERSIONS FOR INGREDIENTS COMMONLY USED IN BAKING

INGREDIENT	OUNCES	GRAMS
I cup all-purpose flour	5	142
I cup cake flour	4	113
I cup whole-wheat flour	5½	156
I cup granulated (white) sugar	7	198
I cup packed brown sugar (light or dark)	7	198
I cup confectioners' sugar	4	113
I cup cocoa powder	3	85
8 tablespoons butter (I stick, or ½ cup)	4	113

A WORD ABOUT METRIC CONVERSIONS

Though the recipes in this book were developed using standard United States measures, we know that cooks outside the United States use metric measures. The charts on page 450 offer equivalents for U.S. and metric measures.

Cooks using our recipes outside of the United States should also be aware that key ingredients are not always the same. Flour milled in the United Kingdom and elsewhere will feel and taste different from flour milled in the United States.

We recommend that all cooks, especially those using ingredients purchased outside of the United States, rely on their instincts when making our recipes. Refer to the visual cues provided. If the bread dough hasn't "come together in a ball," as described, you may need to add more flour—even if the recipe doesn't tell you so. You be the judge.

DRY VERSUS LIQUID MEASURES

HOW TO MEASURE

Here's how to measure dry and liquid ingredients.

DIP AND SWEEP *Dip the dry measuring cup into the container of flour (or sugar or cocoa) and sweep away the excess with a straight-edged object like the back of a butter knife or a small icing spatula.*

GET DOWN *Set the liquid measuring cup on a level surface and bend down to read the marking at eye level. Add the liquid until the bottom of the curved surface of the liquid, called the meniscus— not the edges of the meniscus, which can cling and ride up the walls of the measuring cup—is level with the desired measurement marking.*

Even though weight is a more accurate way to measure than volume, we know that most cooks will rely on measuring cups and spoons, not scales, when cooking. That's fine, but there are ways to increase your accuracy when using volume measures.

First and foremost, you should own and use three sets of measuring tools—dry measuring cups, liquid measuring cups, and measuring spoons. Here's what you need to know about each type of tool.

DRY MEASURING CUPS are generally made of metal or plastic and have long handles and flat tops that make it easy to sweep off excess flour or sugar. We recommend that you buy a set that includes ⅔- and ¾-cup measures as well as the standard ¼-, ⅓-, ½-, and 1-cup measures. Measure all dry ingredients (flour, sugar, chopped vegetables, herbs, etc.) in these cups. Don't measure liquid ingredients in these cups; you won't completely fill the cup (to prevent spills) or you will fill the cup and then spill some of the liquid as you work. Either way, the end result is a recipe with too little liquid.

LIQUID MEASURING CUPS are generally made of glass or plastic and are clear with markings on the side. All liquid measuring cups have handles and pour spouts. Because you're not filling the cup to the brim, liquids won't spill as you work.

Still not convinced you need both dry and liquid measuring cups? We ran another experiment to convince skeptics in the kitchen—and you. In addition to asking 18 cooks in our kitchen to measure 1 cup of flour with a dry measuring cup (where we found results varied by 13 percent), we asked the same cooks to measure 1 cup of flour in a liquid measuring cup and found the variation in the weight of the flour actually contained in the liquid measuring cup jumped to 26 percent. That's because there's no way to level off the flour in a liquid measuring cup.

Likewise, we asked these cooks to measure 1 cup of water (which should weigh 8.35 ounces) in both dry and liquid measuring cups. The measurements in the liquid measuring cups varied by 10 percent, based on different interpretations of when the water had reached the 1-cup marking. (To fill a liquid measuring cup we recommend placing it on the counter, bending down so that the cup's markings are at eye level, and then pouring liquid until the meniscus reaches the desired marking.) The measurements of water in the dry measuring cups varied much more— a whopping 23 percent.

The moral of the story: Measuring by weight is more accurate than measuring by volume, but if you use the right type of volume measure you can reduce the error rate.

In addition to dry measuring cups and liquid measuring cups, you need measuring spoons. (For more information about our top-rated measuring tools, see page 440.)

MEASURING SPOONS have handles and flat tops like dry measuring cups, so you can sweep off excess salt, spices, and other dry ingredients. These spoons are also used to measure small amounts of liquid. (You can't measure a tablespoon of soy sauce in a liquid measuring cup.) Yes, the liquid might spill, but there's really no other choice; work carefully and make sure to fill measuring spoons to the rim. We like oval rather than round spoons because they are easier to dip into narrow spice jars. You should own several sets of measuring spoons with a full complement of sizes— usually 1 tablespoon, 1 teaspoon, ½ teaspoon, ¼ teaspoon, and ⅛ teaspoon.

And memorize this now: 1 tablespoon equals 3 teaspoons. Forget this fact and you will invariably make mistakes when trying to scale recipes up or down. It also helps to remember that 4 tablespoons equal ¼ cup.

THE SCIENCE OF TIME AND TEMPERATURE

TIME CAN BE UNRELIABLE

Time is a useful measure when cooking, but many cooks make the mistake of giving it too much weight. All of our recipes include times as well as sensory cues to tell when a step in a recipe is complete. The times are guidelines meant to help you plan meals (will the roast take one hour or two hours?); they are not precise measures. Always rely on your five senses to determine if a step or recipe is completed. Does the food look like the description given? If a recipe says cook "until firm," then touch the food. Likewise, if a recipe says cook "until fragrant," then rely on that cue, rather than time, to determine when this step is complete.

So why is time such an unreliable measure? Variations in equipment and variations in ingredients. Heat output in grills and cooktops varies greatly. In addition, the weight and diameter of your cookware will affect cooking time.

Even your oven isn't as reliable as you think. How do we know this? We have more than two dozen ovens in our test kitchen and we keep an oven thermometer in each oven to tell us if they are properly calibrated. That is, are they reaching and holding the temperature set on the dial? With heavy use, we find that our ovens generally slip out of calibration in just a few months, so we get them serviced. The process will happen more slowly at home, but the odds are pretty good that your oven is not at 350 degrees Fahrenheit (to convert Fahrenheit to Celsius, see the table on page 450), even though that's what the dial says.

To prove the point, we gave 15 cooks in our test kitchen our top-rated oven thermometer and asked them to test their home ovens. After setting their ovens to 350 degrees and allowing a 30-minute preheating period, participants recorded the actual temperatures in the ovens. We found that the actual temperatures ranged from 300 to 390 degrees. A cake recipe designed to work in a 350-degree oven will behave much differently in a 300-degree oven or a 390-degree oven. Obviously, the cooking time will be affected, but how the cake rises and colors will also be impacted. So what should you do with this information?

First, do not assume your oven is accurate, which means that you should begin checking foods well before the time suggested in recipes. Second, buy an oven thermometer (see page 441 for our recommendation). A $6 investment could dramatically improve the quality of the food that comes out of your oven. Third, if your oven runs very hot or very cool (let's say it's off by 50 degrees), you might want to spend the money to have it calibrated by a professional.

It's important to note that some variation in oven temperature is expected. An oven does not simply heat up to the temperature set on the dial and then stay there. The heating elements are either on at full power or off—with no middle ground—in most ovens. To maintain the desired temperature, the heating element cycles within a manufacturer-determined tolerance, heating up and cooling down to temperatures just above and below the desired temperature. We've found that the temperature in the dead-center location of an electric oven preheated to 350 degrees cycled from a low of 335 degrees to a high of 361 degrees. We analyzed a gas oven and found the temperature ranged from 343 to 359 degrees.

The takeaway is simple: Don't make assumptions about your oven based on a single reading, and don't worry if any single temperature reading is 10 degrees too high or too low—that's normal. However, if your oven is always hot or always cold, and that deviation is 25 degrees or more, you have a problem.

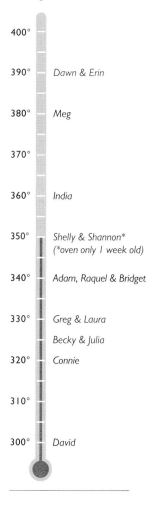

TESTING ACCURACY OF HOME OVENS

Fifteen test cooks set their home ovens to 350 degrees. Actual temperatures in these ovens ranged from 300 to 390 degrees.

400°

390° *Dawn & Erin*

380° *Meg*

370°

360° *India*

350° *Shelly & Shannon* (*oven only 1 week old)*

340° *Adam, Raquel & Bridget*

330° *Greg & Laura*

Becky & Julia

320° *Connie*

310°

300° *David*

TEMPERATURE ALWAYS MATTERS

CALIBRATING AN INSTANT-READ THERMOMETER

An instant-read thermometer is useful only if it's accurate. You should check the thermometer's accuracy when you buy it and then again periodically. Here's how:

MAKE AN ICY SLUSH *Put a mixture of ice and cold tap water in a drinking glass or bowl; allow this mixture to sit for two minutes so the temperature will stabilize. Put the probe in the slush, being careful not to touch the sides or bottom of the glass or bowl. If the temperature is not 32 degrees, then calibrate the thermometer by pressing the "calibrate" button to 32 degrees. If you have a dial-face thermometer, turn the dial to 32 degrees (the method differs from model to model; you may need to use pliers to turn a small knob on the back).*

While variations in equipment will affect cooking time, they are hard to track. How can you know if your skillet heats up faster than the ones we use in the test kitchen? Luckily, the other big variable in cooking time is easier to track.

The initial temperature of ingredients is a key factor in many recipes—and one that many cooks don't think about. Here's an extreme example of how temperature can affect cooking time.

If you start with two big steaks and grill one straight out of the refrigerator and let the other warm up on the counter, their cooking times will differ greatly. We actually ran this experiment with two 2-pound bottom round steaks, each 1½ inches thick. One steak was taken straight from the refrigerator to be cooked; it was 40 degrees when it went onto the grill and took 22 minutes to reach the desired internal temperature of 120 degrees. The second steak was wrapped in plastic and warmed in a bucket of water for one hour, until it was 70 degrees. When this steak was grilled, it took just 13 minutes to reach the same desired internal temperature of 120 degrees. The point of this exercise: Cold food cooks more slowly than room-temperature food. So when a recipe calls for a "chilled" or "room-temperature" ingredient, pay heed to these instructions.

In addition to affecting cooking time, the temperature of an ingredient will affect the quality of the finished recipe. If your butter is not well chilled, pie dough will turn out tough and leathery rather than tender and flaky. Eggs are much easier to separate when cold because the white is thicker when chilled. Here are some general assumptions and rules you should follow regarding the temperature of ingredients.

ROOM TEMPERATURE is generally considered to be about 70 degrees.

CHILLED (as in refrigerated) is generally considered to be 35 to 40 degrees. If the temperature inside your refrigerator is higher than 40 degrees, food is spoiling. If the temperature is 32 degrees or lower, food is freezing.

FROZEN is generally considered to be 0 to 10 degrees. The temperature inside your freezer should be 0 degrees.

FLOURS AND GRAINS are assumed to be at room temperature. If you store whole-grain flours and cornmeal in the freezer to prevent rancidity (which is a good idea if you won't use up these flours and grains within a few months), bring them to room temperature before baking with them. Cold flour will inhibit rise and yield dense baked goods. To quickly bring flour and grains to room temperature, spread them in a thin layer on a baking sheet and let sit for 30 minutes.

EGGS are assumed to be chilled unless otherwise noted. To bring eggs quickly to room temperature, place them (still in their shells) in a bowl of warm water for five minutes.

BUTTER is chilled unless otherwise noted. Softened butter should be between 60 and 68 degrees—see page 373 for more details. Do not attempt to soften butter in the microwave—you will end up melting some of it. Instead, set the butter on the counter, letting it slowly warm up. (This will take about an hour.) To speed up the process, unwrap the butter and cut it into chunks. Butter that has been melted and cooled should be still fluid and just warm to the touch, ideally 85 to 90 degrees.

MEAT, CHICKEN, AND FISH are chilled unless otherwise noted. Note that at temperatures above 40 degrees, bacteria will start to grow in all perishable foods, especially meat, chicken, and fish. (See page 448 for more on food safety.)

In order to track temperature, we strongly recommend that you invest in an instant-read thermometer (see page 441 for our recommendation). After good knives and cookware, a reliable thermometer might just be the most useful tool in any home kitchen.

USING TEMPERATURE TO GAUGE DONENESS

In addition to knowing the temperature of ingredients before cooking, we rely on temperature to determine when many foods are done cooking. Don't cut into food in order to determine if it's done. We prefer to use an instant-read thermometer. It is a much more foolproof way to tell if the holiday turkey is cooked through.

DONENESS TEMPERATURE FOR MEAT, POULTRY, AND FISH

Since the temperature of meat will continue to rise as it rests, an effect called carryover cooking, meat should be removed from the oven, grill, or pan when it's 5 to 10 degrees below the desired serving temperature. (For more on this phenomenon, see page 42.) Carryover cooking doesn't apply to poultry and fish (they don't retain heat as well as the dense muscle structure in meat), so they should be cooked to the desired serving temperatures. The following temperatures should be used to determine when to stop the cooking process.

INGREDIENT	TEMPERATURE
BEEF/LAMB	
Rare	115 to 120 degrees (120 to 125 degrees after resting)
Medium-Rare	120 to 125 degrees (125 to 130 degrees after resting)
Medium	130 to 135 degrees (135 to 140 degrees after resting)
Medium-Well	140 to 145 degrees (145 to 150 degrees after resting)
Well-Done	150 to 155 degrees (155 to 160 degrees after resting)
PORK	
Medium	140 to 145 degrees (145 to 150 degrees after resting)
Well-Done	150 to 155 degrees (155 to 160 degrees after resting)
CHICKEN	
White Meat	160 degrees
Dark Meat	175 degrees
FISH	
Rare	110 degrees (for tuna only)
Medium-Rare	125 degrees (for tuna or salmon)
Medium	140 (for white-fleshed fish)

DONENESS TEMPERATURES FOR VARIOUS FOODS

We rely on the measurement of temperature to tell when many other foods are done cooking, not just meat and poultry. Here's a partial list.

FOOD	DONENESS TEMPERATURE
Oil, for frying	325 to 375 degrees
Sugar, for caramel	350 degrees
Yeast bread, rustic and lean	200 to 210 degrees
Yeast bread, sweet and rich	190 to 200 degrees
Custard, for ice cream	180 degrees
Custard, for crème anglaise or lemon curd	170 to 180 degrees
Custard, baked (such as crème brûlée or crème caramel)	170 to 175 degrees
Cheesecake	150 degrees
Water, for bread baking	105 to 115 (sometimes)

TIPS FOR USING AN INSTANT-READ THERMOMETER

A thermometer must not only be properly calibrated but you must know how to use it. Here are a few tips for using a thermometer:

- Slide the probe deep into the center of the food, making sure that the tip does not exit the food.

- Avoid bones, cavities (in a turkey or chicken), and pan surfaces, all of which will throw off the reading.

- When taking the temperature of steaks, chops, and other relatively thin foods, use tongs to lift the food out of the pan (or off the grill) and slide the probe in through the side of the food.

- Take more than one reading, especially in large roasts and birds. We recommend measuring the temperature on either side of the breastbone and in both thighs on birds because one side of the bird can cook faster than the other, depending on how the bird was positioned in the oven.

- Don't forget about carryover cooking (see concept 4) when determining if meat is properly cooked.

THE SCIENCE OF HEAT AND COLD

HOW HEAT WORKS

So how exactly does cooking work? What's happening when food is placed over a hot fire—or the modern equivalents? First, a brief history of cooking.

The discovery of fire is among the most important events in human evolution. Fire not only protected humans against predators but it allowed our ancestors to cook their food. Why is this important? Before fire, our humanoid ancestors, like many other animals, spent most of the day grinding tough plant foods, through prolonged chewing, until they were small enough to swallow. (This is still how nonhuman primates spend their day.) In the thoroughly delightful *Catching Fire: How Cooking Made Us Human* (2009), Harvard primatologist Richard Wrangham links man's discovery of fire (which he believes was roughly 1.8 million years ago) with a dramatic increase in the size of the human brain. Cooking made it easier to digest high-quality proteins, especially meat, therefore the link between the advent of fire and human brain development. Cooking also made food tender, so eating was no longer an all-day activity. This "extra" time could now be used to hunt, to explore, and to build—simply put, to become human.

While it's easy to understand how cooking makes us human, few of us understand what's actually happening to food when it is heated. Heat is a form of energy. The term is used to describe the speed of molecules in a substance such as air or water. The higher the temperature, the faster the molecules are moving and the more energy, or heat, the molecules contain.

In order for this heat to be transferred from one substance to another, fast-moving molecules bump into slower-moving ones, causing them to pick up speed. The gaseous molecules in a fire, the metal atoms in a hot skillet, or the air molecules in a hot oven are bumping into the slow-moving molecules in the food (especially water molecules) and causing them to speed up.

A wide range of changes occurs once the molecules in food speed up. The food can change color, both by gases driven from hot food and through heat-induced chemical reactions. Water trapped between molecules can be freed and the food can lose moisture. Cell walls that give raw foods their integrity can break down, making foods more tender. The exact changes will depend on the food itself, the heat level, the type of heat, and the length of exposure to heat. One last thing: Heat makes many foods taste much better, but it can also spoil the taste of food when oils oxidize and bitter substances are released.

There are several types of heating that can occur when food is cooked. The most common—conduction, convection, and radiant heating—are described in detail in concept 1 on page 16. Most cooking methods, such as roasting, grilling, or frying, are really a combination of heating modes. For instance, a roast that is placed in a metal pan in the oven is being cooked by conduction (heat transferred from molecule to molecule within the food) as well as by convection (heat transferred by the hot air in the oven to the pan and then from the pan to the food) and radiant heat (the heat emitted by the heating element in the oven and absorbed by the food).

COOKING METHODS

Cookbook authors use a number of terms when referring to the specific way the food should be heated. It's helpful to understand these terms as you read through this (or any) cookbook.

METHOD	DEFINITION	DETAILS
Sauté	To cook foods in a thin film of hot oil in a skillet set on a hot burner.	Sautéing works best for flat, relatively thin foods, such as steaks, chops, and cutlets, as well as small items, such as chopped vegetables, shrimp, or scallops.
Roast	To cook foods in a pan in a hot oven.	Roasting works with a wide range of foods, from large cuts of meat and whole birds to sliced potatoes.
Fry	To cook in a significant quantity of hot oil in a skillet or pot set on a hot burner.	Food can be partially submerged in oil (shallow-frying or pan-frying) or completely submerged in oil (deep-frying). Deep-frying requires the use of a large pot and 1 to 2 quarts of oil. Shallow-frying generally employs a skillet and a modest amount of oil (about 1 cup). Many of the foods that are best for sautéing can also be fried; many fried foods are breaded or battered.
Boil	To cook foods in boiling liquid in a pot set on a hot burner.	At sea level, water boils at 212 degrees. The boiling point drops 2 degrees for every 1,000-foot increase in elevation. No matter the temperature, when a liquid boils, large bubbles energetically break the surface of the liquid at a rapid and constant pace. This cooking method is best with pasta, grains, and vegetables.
Simmer	To cook foods in liquid that is just below the boiling point in a pot set on a hot burner.	Depending on the desired intensity, the temperature of the liquid is generally between 180 and 205 degrees. When a liquid simmers, small bubbles gently break the surface of the liquid at a variable and infrequent rate. Many grains, including rice, are best simmered. Simmering is invaluable for stocks, soups, and sauces.
Poach	To cook foods in liquid that is well below the boiling point in a covered pot set on the stovetop.	Poaching is related to simmering; the temperature of the liquid is lower (no bubbles are breaking the surface) and the pot is generally covered to create a constant, gentle cooking environment. It's best used for delicate fish and fruits.
Steam	To cook foods that are suspended, generally in a basket, over simmering liquid in a covered pot set on a hot burner.	Steaming is an especially gentle cooking method. Unlike other moist-heat cooking methods, steaming does not wash away flavor. Steaming is an excellent choice for vegetables, fish, and delicate foods like dumplings.
Braise	To cook foods by first sautéing them and then adding liquid, covering the pan, and simmering.	Braising is ideal for tough cuts that require prolonged cooking to become tender, such as pot roast.
Stew	This is a subset of braising (food is sautéed, then simmered).	Stewing is generally reserved for recipes that involve small chunks of food, not entire roasts.
Grill	To cook foods on a grate set over a fire.	Although the term "grilling" is often used to describe the preparation of any food cooked over a fire, we generally reserve it for foods that cook quickly, such as steaks, cutlets, chops, vegetables, and seafood.
Grill-Roast	To cook foods on a grate set over a modest fire confined to a portion of the grill in a closed environment.	When the lid is placed on the grill, the cooking method resembles roasting, especially if the food is not positioned directly over the fire and thus won't brown too quickly. Best for thick, large cuts that require substantial cooking over moderate heat, such as a whole chicken or roast.
Barbecue	To cook foods on a grate set over a small, smoky fire confined to a portion of the grill in a closed environment.	When barbecuing, the setup is the same as with grill-roasting but the fire is smaller and wood is used to create smoky flavor in the food. Best for tough cuts that require prolonged cooking to become tender, such as brisket or ribs.

HOW COLD WORKS

Just as heat can change food, exposing food to cold temperatures can have a range of effects. Many naturally occurring processes stop in the cold. For instance, storage below 40 degrees can inhibit the activity of certain enzymes in peaches that normally break down pectin in its cell walls during the ripening process. If these enzymes are deactivated before the fruit is ripe, the pectin remains intact and the peaches will have a mealy texture. (To understand the practical effects of this process, see page 422.)

Of course, cold temperatures can be beneficial when storing other foods. Dairy products and meat will spoil much faster at temperatures above 40 degrees. (Note that the typical home refrigerator should be about 35 degrees.) These foods naturally contain bacteria, and at temperatures below 40 degrees the activity of these bacteria is suppressed. However, let these warm up a bit and they enter the danger zone, 40 to 140 degrees. Most bacteria will multiply at these temperatures, and that can cause spoilage of the food, or lead to food-borne illnesses if the food is consumed. Note that cooking often stops the activity of bacteria. (For more on this subject, see "Food Safety Basics" on page 448.)

THE DEEP FREEZE

WHY IS ICE SO HARD?
One last note about freezing: So why are ice cubes rock hard but ice cream is soft and scoopable, even though both are stored in the same freezer? Sugar (or any substance that dissolves in water) affects the freezing point of water. The more sugar added, the lower the freezing point. For more on this phenomenon, see page 189.

The moisture in food begins to freeze at temperatures below 32 degrees, and whether that moisture is in fruit, ice cream, or meat, it will form ice crystals. These crystals rupture cell walls and internal cell organelles in fresh foods, like fruits or vegetables, which release enzymes from their locked compartments. When thawed, these enzymes cause produce to develop off-flavors and turn brown and soggy.

In vegetables, these enzymes can be deactivated by blanching, or briefly boiling the foods. That's why the frozen broccoli you purchase at the supermarket is bright green (it has been cooked by the manufacturer). If you've tried to freeze fresh raw broccoli and then cook it, you know that it tastes sulfurous and has a mushy texture and off color.

Fruit cannot withstand precooking so manufacturers generally add sugar to reduce crystal size and thus limit the damage that these crystals can cause. Another trick used by manufacturers is to add ascorbic acid, which deactivates the enzymes that cause browning.

When freezing meat and other protein, the biggest issue is moisture loss. The ice crystals damage the cell structure and, as a result, frozen meat loses more moisture when cooked than meat that was never frozen. In addition, freezing causes moisture loss due to surface dehydration. To quantify this moisture loss, we cooked three 7-ounce samples of 85 percent lean ground beef—one fresh, one frozen and thawed once, and one frozen and thawed twice—over medium-high heat in a small skillet. We drained the cooked meat and measured the amount of liquid released, then repeated the tests with more batches of meat.

On average, the fresh ground meat lost ¾ teaspoon of liquid compared to 2 teaspoons for the once-frozen meat and 1 tablespoon for the twice-frozen meat. To put this in context, a burger made with 7 ounces of fresh ground meat will have an extra 1¼ teaspoons of juice compared to the same burger made with frozen meat. That's the difference between a juicy, tender burger and a dry, mealy one.

Another downside of freezing has to do with how your freezer works. Ideally, home freezers are set to 0 degrees and they maintain a constant temperature. However, that's not the case, especially if your freezer is opened and closed frequently. The reality is that foods are constantly warming up and then cooling down, which just accelerates the damage from ice crystals. Food that is encrusted in a layer of ice crystals, what is commonly called freezer burn, has suffered the ravages of constant freezing, thawing, and refreezing.

THE SCIENCE OF THE SENSES

THE FIVE TASTES

Cooking truly relies on the five senses: sight, smell, touch, taste, and sound. Does the chicken look properly browned? Does the cake feel firm to the touch? Is the consistency of the sauce smooth or lumpy? Does the garlic smell fragrant? Does the dish taste properly seasoned?

The sense of taste is worth some additional thought before we start cooking.

In grade school we learned that we experience four primary taste sensations: salty, sweet, bitter, and sour. (Bitter refers to the flavor sensation caused by foods like kale or eggplant, while sour refers to the flavor sensation caused by acidic foods such as limes or vinegar.)

In recent years, scientists have agreed that there is a fifth taste called umami. The "umami" taste is best described as "meaty" or "savory" and is produced by a common amino acid known as glutamate (also known as glutamic acid). Glutamate is present in relatively high amounts as free glutamate in certain fruits (like tomatoes), vegetables, and cheeses (especially Parmesan), and as part of most proteins, including meat and other dairy products. In mushrooms, the glutamate content is high enough to lend that familiar meaty flavor. Umami also works to make food more palatable in general. (See page 309 for a chart of glutamate levels in a variety of foods.)

The flavor enhancer monosodium glutamate (MSG), which is produced by growing a special type of bacteria on sugar or molasses and corn, captures the power of glutamates. In our kitchen tests, we have found that MSG bumps up the flavor of food. When we added MSG in the form of the supermarket product Accent to our beef and vegetable soup, tasters raved about the "rich," "ultra-beefy" results. (For more on glutamates, and MSG, see concept 35.)

HOW TASTE WORKS

The cells in our mouth that respond to taste are located in clusters of cells called tastebuds. Scientists used to believe that tastebuds were concentrated in specific regions of the tongue. In actuality, buds for the various tastes are evenly distributed all over the tongue as well as the mouth. But different individuals do taste things differently. This is due to a genetically predetermined effect that is directly related to the number of tastebuds each of us has.

Scientist Linda Bartoshuk, now with the Center for Taste and Smell at the University of Florida, found that one person can have up to 10 times as many tastebuds as another. This has obvious implications for taste—things seem sweeter, spicier, and more bitter to these "supertasters" than to regular or below-average tasters. Though more intense, the taste for a supertaster is not 10 times more intense because of mitigating factors—aroma, mouthfeel, and certain other aspects of a food that interfere with taste—but the difference can be up to three times as much.

So the next time you share a dish with a friend and she finds it much saltier or spicier than you do, don't worry. You don't have a lousy palate. Your friend probably just has more tastebuds.

While we can't do much about how our palates are hard-wired, every cook can adjust how we perceive flavors in a given dish by considering the balance among the five main tastes. For instance, researchers investigating methods for making bitter medications more palatable have discovered that salt can mask bitter flavors. According to one research group, for example, sodium ions can reduce the perceived bitterness of acetaminophen, the active ingredient in Tylenol, by more than 50 percent.

To see if salt might have the same effect on bitter-tasting foods, we performed a blind taste test of several, including coffee and eggplant, to which we either added salt or left as is. With the addition of ¼ teaspoon of salt per pint, the perceived bitterness of the coffee was cut in half. Salt also reduced the perceived bitterness of eggplant.

The tradition of salting eggplant, then, appears to serve two functions. The first, as we have found in kitchen tests, is that salt removes water and reduces the amount of oil eggplant will absorb. The second, as we discovered in the above tests, is that salt can mask bitterness. Indeed, when we had tasters sample previously salted and unsalted batches of sautéed eggplant, most claimed to detect a bitter background flavor in the unsalted batch that they didn't taste in the salted batch.

Likewise, we have noticed that very spicy dishes can seem less spicy when sugar is added. When developing a recipe for Thai-style chicken with basil we noticed that adding sugar to the recipe significantly toned down the heat of the chiles. It turns out that this phenomenon is the result of complex interactions in the brain that regulate our perception of flavor, pitting pain against pleasure. Compounds in chiles (mainly capsaicin) stimulate nerves (called trigeminals) surrounding the tastebuds to signal discomfort to the brain, in a process known as chemesthesis. Sugar, on the other hand, stimulates the tastebuds to signal pleasure. These signals are so enjoyable, scientists believe they overshadow the "pain" caused by chiles. Sugar also draws heat from the mouth when it dissolves in saliva, producing a mild cooling sensation.

So what does this mean, in practical terms? If you've added too much salt, sugar, or spice to a dish, the damage is usually done. In mild cases, however, the overpowering ingredient can sometimes be masked by the addition of another from the opposite end of the flavor spectrum. (Forget the potato trick listed in many cookbooks; adding potatoes to a salty soup does nothing to counter the salt—it just adds more bulk.)

In addition to fixing mistakes based on how the science of taste works, we often rely on the following seasoning strategies to make food taste better. (Remember to account for the reduction of liquids when seasoning a dish—a perfectly seasoned stew will likely taste too salty after several hours of simmering. Your best bet is to season with a light hand during the cooking process and then adjust the seasoning just before serving.)

SEASON WITH AN ACID In addition to grabbing the saltshaker to boost flavor in soups, stews, and sauces, try a drop of lemon juice or vinegar. Like salt, acid competes with bitter flavor compounds, reducing our perception of them as they "brighten" other flavors. Just a dash—⅛ teaspoon—can go a long way.

USE COARSE SALT WHEN SEASONING MEAT Use kosher salt—rather than table salt—when seasoning meat. Its larger grains distribute more easily and cling well to the meat's surface.

PEP UP—OR TONE DOWN—YOUR PEPPER When exactly you apply black pepper to meat—before or after searing—will affect the strength of its bite. If you want assertive pepper flavor, season meat after searing; keeping the pepper away from heat will preserve its volatile compounds. Alternatively, seasoning before cooking will tame pepper's punch.

SEASON COLD FOODS AGGRESSIVELY Chilling foods dulls their flavors, so it's important to compensate by seasoning generously—but judiciously. To keep from overdoing it, season with a normal amount of salt before chilling and then taste and add more salt as desired just before serving.

ADD HERBS AT THE RIGHT TIME Add hearty herbs like thyme, rosemary, oregano, sage, and marjoram to dishes early in the cooking process; this way, you give them time to release maximum flavor while ensuring that their texture will be less intrusive. Save delicate herbs like parsley, cilantro, tarragon, chives, and basil for the end, lest they lose their fresh flavor and bright color. (See concept 34 for more details on using herbs.)

ADD A LITTLE UMAMI Common pantry staples like soy sauce, Worcestershire sauce, and anchovies contain high levels of glutamates that can give a savory umami boost to a dish. Try mixing a teaspoon or two of soy sauce into chili or adding a couple of finely minced anchovies to a chicken braise. (See concept 35 for more information on cooking with glutamate-rich ingredients.)

THE SENSES OF GOOD COOKING

In addition to balancing the five tastes, good cooks will focus on aroma. Our tastebuds have a harder time detecting flavors in cold foods. That's why chilled soup must be aggressively seasoned. But cold soups also have almost no aroma, which is another reason that they require a heavier hand when seasoning. The aroma that wafts up to your nose from a piping-hot bowl of soup affects your perception of the flavor. Take away that aroma and the food does not seem as flavorful.

After all, aroma is an essential tool when it comes to perceiving flavor, as well as a cue for hunger and an important way to recognize when food goes bad. Without it, it's surprisingly difficult to tell the difference between strawberry and vanilla ice cream or pasta alla carbonara and pasta alla vodka without looking first.

While aroma and taste relate most directly to the enjoyment of food, don't neglect the other three senses. Food that looks attractive will probably taste better—or at least it will seem to taste better. To illustrate this principle, Frédéric Brochet, a researcher at the University of Bordeaux, asked a panel of wine experts to evaluate one white wine and one red wine. The experts relied on the adjectives you would expect to create two very different flavor profiles for each wine. Too bad the samples were both the same white wine, with one sample dyed red by the addition of a tasteless substance.

In the test kitchen, we've demonstrated this principle over and over in taste tests. Ask tasters to sample two chocolate puddings made with different brands of chocolate and they gush over the deeper, richer flavor of the darker (i.e., "more chocolaty-looking") sample. But taste the same puddings blindfolded and the results are much more mixed. We really do eat with our eyes.

Texture might be even more important than appearance. Soggy fried chicken or a dry, chewy steak isn't nearly as enjoyable as crisp fried chicken or a juicy, tender steak. Many of the concepts in this book are designed to create the optimal texture in the food being cooked.

Sound is probably the least important of the five senses to the eater, but the cook does have occasion to rely on sound. For example, you expect vegetables to sizzle when added to a hot pan, and if you don't hear this sound you know the pan is too cold.

WHY DO FOODS TASTE BETTER HOT?

The explanation is twofold: First, scientists have discovered that our ability to taste is heightened by microscopic proteins in our tastebuds that are extremely temperature-sensitive. These proteins, known as TRPM5 channels, perform far better at warm temperatures than at cooler ones. In fact, studies have shown that when food cooled to 59 degrees and below is consumed, the channels barely open, minimizing flavor perception. However, when food is heated to 98.5 degrees, the channels open up and TRPM5 sensitivity increases more than 100 times, making food taste markedly more flavorful.

Second, much of our perception of flavor comes from aroma, which we inhale as microscopic molecules diffuse from food. The hotter the food, the more energetic these molecules are, and the more likely they are to travel from the table to our nose.

The lessons? Dishes meant to be served hot should be reheated, and dishes served chilled (like gazpacho or potato salad) must be aggressively seasoned to make up for the flavor-dulling effects of cold temperatures.

THE SCIENCE OF TOOLS AND INGREDIENTS

THE PHYSICS OF COOKING

TOOLS THAT
TRANSFORM FOODS

Knives are not the only
tools used to physically
manipulate and change food.
Your kitchen is filled with
a wide range of tools that
mix, combine, whisk, stir,
grind, puree, blend, knead,
and whip. These tools can
perform a variety of tasks.
In some cases, the cook
supplies the energy, with his
or her arm; in other cases
electricity powers the tool.
A few examples:

• A balloon whisk incorporates air into chilled heavy
cream, turning a small
amount of liquid into a
mound of billowy foam.

• A spice grinder transforms
whole spices into a fine
powder, releasing flavorful
oils in the process.

• A meat pounder turns a
thick chicken breast into
a thin cutlet that will cook
much more quickly.

All of these examples show
how a tool can change a
single ingredient. But many
tools are meant to combine
several ingredients. The simplest example is a wooden
spoon used to turn water,
flour, and yeast into a dough.
The point here is foods
can change without being
heated (or chilled). As you
read through this book, you
will learn how the particular
mixing method can affect the
outcome in many recipes.

Changes in temperature can alter the flavor, texture, and appearance of foods, but they are not the only ways to "cook." Physical force is another way to transform foods. This includes everything from the force of a knife slicing through an onion to the power of a food processor blade pureeing ingredients into pesto.

We know that knives can change the appearance of foods, making them smaller, thinner, even more attractive. But as the knife blade cuts through food, it damages cell structure (much like cooking or freezing) and that can affect color, texture, and flavor as well.

For example, the way you cut an onion affects its flavor. To prove the point, we took eight onions and cut each two different ways: pole to pole (with the grain) and parallel to the equator (against the grain). We then smelled and tasted pieces from each onion cut each way. The onions sliced pole to pole were clearly less pungent in taste and odor than those cut along the equator.

Here's why: The intense flavor and acrid odor of onions are caused by substances called thiosulfinates, created when enzymes known as alliinases contained in the onion's cells interact with an amino acid called isoalliin that is also present in the vegetable. These reactions take place only when the onion's cells are ruptured and release the strong-smelling com-pounds. Cutting with the grain ruptures fewer cells than cutting against the grain, leading to the release of fewer alliinases and the cre-ation of fewer thiosulfinates. (See concept 31 for more information on using your knife to change the flavor of onions and garlic.)

Cutting can also affect cooked foods. You can see the muscle fibers on some steaks, espe-cially flank steak. Those long striations that run from end to end are actually muscle fibers. If you slice a grilled flank across the grain (that is, from side to side rather than end to end), you are in effect making these long muscle fibers much shorter and thus easier to chew.

UNDERSTANDING COMMON CUTTING TERMS

Professional cooks use a variety of terms to describe ways that foods can be cut. Here are the terms we use in this book.

CUT		DESCRIPTION
Chiffonade		To cut into very thin strips. Usually applies to fresh herbs, especially basil.
Chop	fine	To cut into ⅛- to ¼-inch pieces.
	medium	To cut into ¼- to ½-inch pieces.
	coarse	To cut into ½- to ¾-inch pieces.
Cut	crosswise	To cut across the food, perpendicular to its length
	lengthwise	To cut with the length of the food, from end to end.
	on the bias	To cut across the food with the knife held at a 45-degree angle to the food. Used for long, slender items such as asparagus and carrots.
Dice		To cut into uniform cubes with straight, even sides.
Julienne		To cut into matchstick-size pieces, usually 2 inches long and ⅛ inch thick.
Mince		To cut into ⅛-inch or smaller pieces.
Slice		To cut into flat pieces.
	thin	To cut into flat pieces ⅛ inch thick or less.

A COOK'S TOOLS

The exact tools used to heat, chill, chop, mix, or otherwise manipulate food will affect the final outcome. The Appendix in this book has much more information about equipment, but here are a few important things to keep in mind.

Cookware is made from a variety of metals, each with its own pros and cons. The ability of the metal to withstand and conduct heat will determine how well you can brown food, how easily food will burn, and how evenly the heat is distributed. Weight matters too. Buy a lightweight stainless steel pan and your stew meat will stick to the pot. Ease of cleaning varies, too.

In general, we reserve nonstick pans for delicate foods, such as fish and eggs, which are prone to sticking. We find that nonstick pans don't brown food as well as conventional pans. Also, there often are no browned bits left in the pan once something like a steak or chicken cutlet has been cooked, and thus nothing for the cook to use in building a pan sauce. Don't use a nonstick pan unless the recipe specifically calls for one.

Perhaps just as important as cookware material is the pan shape and size. Crowd four chicken breasts into a 10-inch pan and they will steam; space them out in a 12-inch pan and they will brown. Skillets should be measured from lip to lip to determine their size. Pots are generally measured by volume (2 quarts, 4 quarts, etc.). Use specified equipment in the specified size when following any recipe.

This admonishment applies to bakeware as well as cookware. If a recipe calls for 9-inch cake pans, don't use 8-inch pans. We've found this simple change will prolong the baking time (the batter is in a deeper layer in the smaller pans) and this can cause the bottom of the cake layers to burn by the time the middle is sufficiently baked. Even something as simple as the presence or absence of rims on the edges of a baking sheet can affect the outcome of a recipe. (See "Cookie Sheet Bake-Off" on page 414.)

MORE INFORMATION ABOUT TOOLS

EQUIPPING YOUR KITCHEN   *page 437*

COOKWARE MATERIALS   *page 444*

WHAT ABOUT NONSTICK PANS?   *page 445*

KNIFE BASICS   *page 446*

A COOK'S INGREDIENTS

The right equipment is key to good cooking, but so are the right ingredients. Even seemingly small ingredient changes can have a big effect on the final outcome. For instance, replace table salt with kosher salt and you have effectively reduced the salt level by half. That's because the coarse crystals of kosher salt "fluff up" when measured and you get far less salt in a teaspoon.

Bigger changes—such as replacing butter with shortening when making pie dough—have even larger effects. In this case, because butter is roughly 80 percent fat and 16 to 18 percent water it behaves differently in pie dough than vegetable shortening, which contains no water and is 100 percent fat. The chemistry of the fat crystals is different too, so the end product has a different texture—to say nothing of a different flavor.

So here's our best advice about substituting ingredients: Don't do it! Once you start changing the ingredients in a recipe, it's very hard to predict the outcome. This is especially true in baking recipes, where you can't judge the effect of the change until the dish is finished. In savory recipes, you can often taste as you go, and thus replacing parsley with another herb is a safer bet than replacing the cream with milk in a custard recipe.

Now, of course, we know there are times when substitutions are unavoidable; if you are already cooking, for instance, and realize you don't have an ingredient on hand. Refer to the Emergency Ingredient Substitutions chart on page 447 for a list of common substitutions that we have tested and can recommend in a pinch.

In addition, the "101" pages throughout the book will give you in-depth information on key ingredients. Refer to these pages for shopping, storage, and usage tips.

MORE INFORMATION ABOUT INGREDIENTS

FISH 101   *page 33*

MEAT 101   *page 41*

POULTRY 101   *page 87*

SALT 101   *page 113*

SHOPPING FOR BEEF 101   *page 141*

SHOPPING FOR PORK 101   *page 149*

EGGS 101   *page 175*

FLOUR 101   *page 357*

BUTTER 101   *page 373*

SWEETENERS 101   *page 421*

CHOCOLATE 101   *page 435*

Gentle Heat Prevents Overcooking

The discovery of fire—and, as a result, the invention of cooking—was a key step in human evolution. Heat kills germs that, if consumed, could cause illness. It makes food easier to chew and thus more palatable. It even changes some nutritional profiles, allowing our bodies to more readily absorb key vitamins and nutrients. But it's not all good. Too much heat can rob food of moisture, leaving it leathery, rubbery, and dry—especially large cuts of meat (such as prime rib, turkey, or ham) or delicate foods (like eggs or shrimp). Why? Let's start by understanding how heat works.

HOW HEAT WORKS

CONDUCTION *moves heat from the surface of the food to the center.*

CONVECTION *moves heat from the water or air to the food.*

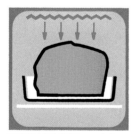

RADIANT HEAT *travels by high-energy waves and interacts directly with the exterior of the food, which heats the inside by conduction.*

HOW THE SCIENCE WORKS

Heat is a form of energy. The term is used to describe the speed of molecules in a substance such as air or water. The higher the temperature, the faster the molecules are moving and the more energy, or heat, the molecules contain. In order for this heat to be transferred from one item to another, fast-moving molecules bump into slower-moving ones, which then pick up speed. Therefore, heat always flows from a hot item—or region within a food—to a cold one.

There are several types of heating that occur in cooking. Conduction is the transfer of heat from a hotter to a colder region within a food—in effect, the movement of molecules inside a single substance. For example, the cold center of a roast beef becomes warmer as molecules in its exterior sections begin to pick up speed. Since water molecules are much smaller than fat or protein molecules, they are capable of moving quite fast and conduct much of the heat.

Convection is the transfer of heat from a hot liquid (like boiling water or frying oil), or a hot gas (like the air in an oven), to a food. In each case, heat is generated by an external source, such as a stovetop burner or the heating element in an oven. In most cooking applications, both conduction and convection are at work. There is one more important type of heating, however: Radiant heating is the transfer of heat by high-energy waves emitted from a remote object. One of the best examples is the sun on the surface of the earth. In cooking, radiant heating takes place most commonly in grilling, broiling, and even microwaving. Here, the waves of energy interact directly with the molecules in food, causing them to accelerate in speed and, therefore, become hotter.

Whether cooked by conduction, convection, or radiant heat, the outside of food always cooks faster than the inside. And if the temperature is too high, the outer layers may become overcooked by the time conduction moves the heat toward the center of the food. That's because the external moisture will evaporate (remember: heat puts small water molecules into motion), leaving the surface area vulnerable to becoming very dry. A greater difference in temperature between the food's edge and its center means that this will happen faster. Conversely, a smaller temperature difference within the food will help the exterior retain more moisture and produce more uniform cooking.

TEST KITCHEN EXPERIMENT

To demonstrate the effects of convection and conduction, we roasted two three-rib standing beef rib roasts. One was placed in a 450-degree oven, the other in a 250-degree oven. Prior to roasting, we trimmed the majority of visible fat from both roasts and weighed them. We set up probes to record temperatures within the meat at three places—the center, ¼ inch below the surface, and midway between these points. Both roasts were cooked until the center probe registered 125 degrees for medium-rare (this took just over two hours in the 450-degree oven and about three hours in the 250-degree oven). Both roasts were allowed to rest for 45 minutes, reweighed, sliced, and then sampled by tasters. We repeated the experiment two more times and the results below are the averages of the three tests.

THE RESULTS

Let's start with the taste-test results. The roast cooked in the 250-degree oven was noticeably juicier than the roast cooked in the 450-degree oven. Yes, the crust on the roast cooked in the hot oven was browner and crisper, but the majority of the meat was very dry and chalky—only the dead center of this roast boasted the tender, juicy texture we wanted. The exterior of the roast cooked at 250 degrees lacked a substantial crust, but the meat was moist and tender from the center all the way to the edge.

Weighing each roast before and after confirmed our tasters' impressions. The roast in the 250-degree oven lost 9.4 percent of its original weight. The roast cooked at 450 degrees shed 24.2 percent of its original weight, almost three times more than the slow-roasted beef. Put another way: The slow-roasted beef lost only 9 ounces of moisture during the roasting process while the high-temperature roasted beef lost 25 ounces. Since we had trimmed both roasts of exterior fat, these numbers represented moisture lost from the meat itself—no wonder the slow-roasted beef tasted so much juicier.

So if both roasts were cooked to the same internal temperature, why was the high-temperature roasted prime rib so much drier?

The answer lies in the relationship between convection and conduction, and their effect on moisture. In both ovens, hot air conveyed energy to the surface of the roasts, at which point the energy was absorbed and transferred, through conduction, to the center. In the 450-degree oven, the outer portions of the roast absorbed far more energy than did the outer layers of meat roasted in the cooler oven. More energy meant faster-moving water molecules and a greater amount of evaporation.

Moisture loss is proportional to meat temperature. The temperature probe inserted ¼ inch below the surface in the high-temperature roasted beef registered 189 degrees, indicating that almost all of the moisture had evaporated out of this part of the roast. The midpoint between the exterior and center of the roast registered 160 degrees—still seriously well-done, dry meat. In contrast, the temperature probes inserted in the same places in the roast cooked in the 250-degree oven never climbed above 146 degrees—indicating that the outer layers of this sample were losing much less moisture.

THE TAKEAWAY

For large roasts, where exterior meat can easily overcook and dry out before the center reaches the target temperature, low heat is the way to go. But sometimes moisture retention has a downside, such as a pale exterior. You may need to compensate with another cooking method (see concept 5).

THE EFFECT OF HEAT ON MOISTURE LOSS

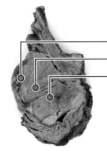

	ROASTED AT 450°	ROASTED AT 250°
Temperature at ¼" below surface	189°	146°
Temperature at midpoint	160°	135°
Temperature at center	125°	125°
Weight before roasting	6.34 lbs	5.98 lbs
Weight after roasting	4.8 lbs	5.42 lbs
Moisture loss	24.2%	9.38%

Big roasts (like prime rib, turkey, and ham) are especially prone to drying out when cooked in a hot oven. The bigger the roast, the bigger the heat differential between the center of the meat and the exterior. Also, turkey and ham are fairly lean, which just compounds the problem—there's very little fat to help moisten the dry meat. And turkey has the additional problem that the legs need to reach a higher internal temperature than the breast in order to break down their connective tissue and make them palatable. Keeping the oven temperature low reduces the heat differential and helps promote even cooking in these large cuts of meat. But, in each case, other strategies are used in conjunction with low oven temperature to ensure juicy, flavorful results.

PRIME RIB
SERVES 6 TO 8

A whole rib roast (aka prime rib) consists of ribs 6 through 12. Butchers tend to cut the roast in two. We prefer the cut further back on the cow, which is closest to the loin and less fatty. This cut is referred to as the first cut, the loin end, or sometimes the small end because the meat and ribs get larger as they move up toward the shoulder. When ordering a three-rib roast, ask for the first three ribs from the loin end—ribs 10 through 12.

1	(7-pound) first-cut beef rib roast, 3 ribs, set at room temperature for 3 hours, trimmed and tied with kitchen twine at both ends, twine running parallel to bone
1	tablespoon vegetable oil
	Salt and pepper

1. Adjust oven rack to lowest position and heat oven to 200 degrees. Pat roast dry with paper towels. Heat oil in large roasting pan over 2 burners set at medium-high heat. Place roast in pan and cook on all sides until nicely browned and about ½ cup fat has rendered, 6 to 8 minutes.

2. Remove roast from pan. Discard fat in pan. Set wire rack in pan, then set roast on rack. Season with salt and pepper.

3. Place roast in oven and roast until meat registers 125 degrees (for medium-rare), about 3½ hours (or about 30 minutes per pound). Remove roast from oven and tent with aluminum foil. Let rest for 20 minutes.

4. Remove twine and set roast on carving board, rib bones at 90-degree angle to board. Slice along bones to sever meat from bones. Set roast cut side down and carve meat across grain into ¾-inch-thick slices. Serve immediately.

✔ WHY THIS RECIPE WORKS

Prime rib is one of the largest cuts of meat the home cook will prepare. As the test kitchen experiment demonstrated, the difference between high-temperature roasting and low-temperature roasting is dramatic, with the roast shedding three times as much moisture when roasted at 450 degrees versus 250 degrees. (Here, we roast at an even lower temperature.) Unless you like tough, dry prime rib, low-temperature roasting is essential.

BROWN IT FIRST Low-temperature roasting will ensure a juicy roast but it does little for the exterior. That's why we start our recipe by browning the roast on the stovetop. If you have a heavy-duty roasting pan, you can brown the roast right in the roasting pan. This step will also render a fair amount of exterior fat.

ELEVATE ROAST To ensure even heating, we move the browned roast to a rack. This trick also ensures that the roast is elevated above any additional fat that is rendered during the long cooking time.

LET IT REST You've worked hard to retain all those juices, so don't be impatient and slice into the roast too soon. The meat needs time for the muscle fibers to relax. If you cut into the roast too soon, the muscle fibers won't be able to hold on to those juices, which will flood onto the carving board. (For more information on resting meat, see concept 3.)

SLOW-ROASTED TURKEY WITH GRAVY
SERVES 10 TO 12

Instead of drumsticks and thighs, you may use two (1½- to 2-pound) whole leg quarters. The recipe will also work with turkey breast alone; in step 2, reduce the butter to 1½ tablespoons, the salt to 1½ teaspoons, and the pepper to 1 teaspoon. If you are roasting kosher or self-basting turkey parts, season the turkey with only 1½ teaspoons salt.

TURKEY

3	onions, chopped
3	celery ribs, chopped
2	carrots, peeled and chopped
5	sprigs fresh thyme
5	garlic cloves, peeled and halved
1	cup low-sodium chicken broth
1	(5- to 7-pound) whole bone-in turkey breast, trimmed
4	pounds turkey drumsticks and thighs, trimmed
3	tablespoons unsalted butter, melted
1	tablespoon salt
2	teaspoons pepper

GRAVY

- 2 cups low-sodium chicken broth
- 3 tablespoons unsalted butter
- 3 tablespoons all-purpose flour
- 2 bay leaves

  Salt and pepper

1. FOR THE TURKEY: Adjust oven rack to lower-middle position and heat oven to 275 degrees. Arrange onions, celery, carrots, thyme, and garlic in even layer on rimmed baking sheet. Pour broth into baking sheet. Place wire rack on top of vegetables.

2. Pat turkey pieces dry with paper towels. Brush turkey pieces on all sides with melted butter and season with salt and pepper. Place breast skin side down and drumsticks and thighs skin side up on rack on vegetable-filled baking sheet, leaving at least ¼ inch between pieces.

3. Roast turkey pieces for 1 hour. Using 2 large wads of paper towels, turn turkey breast skin side up. Continue roasting until breast registers 160 degrees and thighs registers 175 degrees, 1 to 2 hours longer. Remove baking sheet from oven and transfer rack with turkey to second baking sheet. Allow pieces to rest for at least 30 minutes or up to 1½ hours.

4. FOR THE GRAVY: Strain vegetables and liquid from baking sheet through fine-mesh strainer set in 4-cup liquid measuring cup, pressing on solids to extract as much liquid as possible; discard solids. Add chicken broth to measuring cup (you should have about 3 cups liquid).

5. Melt butter in medium saucepan over medium-high heat. Add flour and cook, stirring constantly, until flour is dark golden brown and fragrant, about 5 minutes. Slowly whisk in broth mixture and bay leaves and gradually bring to boil. Reduce to simmer and cook, stirring occasionally, until gravy is thick and measures 2 cups, 15 to 20 minutes. Discard bay leaves. Off heat, season gravy with salt and pepper to taste. Cover to keep warm.

6. TO SERVE: Heat oven to 500 degrees. Place baking sheet with turkey in oven. Roast until skin is golden brown and crisp, about 15 minutes. Transfer turkey to carving board and let rest, uncovered, for 20 minutes. Carve and serve with gravy.

✓ WHY THIS RECIPE WORKS

Roasting a whole bird is a race to keep the white meat from drying out while the dark meat cooks through. A low oven temperature minimizes the temperature differential between the outer layers of the breast meat (just under the skin) and the center of the breast meat. However, this doesn't really solve the problem that dark meat is best cooked to an internal temperature of 175 degrees (in order to break down connective tissue and render excess fat), while lean white meat is best cooked to an internal temperature of 160 degrees (the temperature at which any pathogens have been killed and moisture loss has been minimized). Our solution: Forget about the whole bird and roast two leg quarters (separated into thighs and drumsticks) along with a whole turkey breast. The smaller dark-meat parts will reach 175 degrees at the same time the larger breast piece reaches 160 degrees.

ELEVATE THE BIRD   Placing the parts on a rack set inside a baking sheet promotes better air and heat circulation and ensures even cooking. Vegetables and herbs can be placed in the baking sheet and used to jump-start the gravy-making process.

FLIP THE BREAST   Even with the breast on a rack, the meat can cook unevenly. The solution is simple: Start the breast skin side down and then flip it skin side up partway through the roasting process.

CRISP THE SKIN   Forget about using high heat at the end of the roasting time to crisp up the skin—you end up just overcooking the outer layers of meat. Once the slow-roasted turkey comes up to temperature, we let it rest for at least 30 minutes (or up to 1½ hours) before returning the pieces to a 500-degree oven for 15 minutes. Letting the pieces rest lowers their internal temperature to about 130 degrees, so the meat won't dry out when it's put back in the hot oven to crisp the skin. Also, this method gives you time to use the pan drippings to create a rich gravy.

GLAZED SPIRAL-SLICED HAM
SERVES 12 TO 14, WITH LEFTOVERS

You can bypass the 90-minute soaking time, but the heating time will increase to 18 to 20 minutes per pound for a cold ham. If there is a tear or hole in the ham's inner covering, wrap it in several layers of plastic wrap before soaking it in hot water. Instead of using the plastic oven bag, the ham may be placed cut side down in the roasting pan and covered tightly with foil, but you will need to add 3 to 4 minutes per pound to the heating time. If using an oven bag, be sure to cut slits in the bag so it does not burst.

- 1 (7- to 10-pound) spiral-sliced bone-in half ham
- 1 large plastic oven bag
- 1 recipe glaze (recipes follow)

1. Leaving ham's inner plastic or foil covering intact, place ham in large container and cover with hot tap water; set aside for 45 minutes. Drain and cover again with hot tap water; set aside for another 45 minutes.

2. Adjust oven rack to lowest position and heat oven to 250 degrees. Unwrap ham; remove and discard plastic disk covering bone. Place ham in oven bag. Gather top of bag tightly so bag fits snugly around ham, tie bag, and trim excess plastic. Set ham cut side down in large roasting pan and cut 4 slits in top of bag with paring knife.

3. Bake ham until center registers 100 degrees, 1 to 1½ hours (about 10 minutes per pound).

4. Remove ham from oven and increase oven temperature to 350 degrees. Cut open oven bag and roll back sides to expose ham. Brush ham with one-third of glaze and return to oven until glaze becomes sticky, about 10 minutes (if glaze is too thick to brush, return to heat to loosen).

5. Remove ham from oven, transfer to carving board, and brush entire ham with another third of glaze. Let ham rest, loosely tented with aluminum foil, for 15 minutes. While ham rests, heat remaining third of glaze with 4 to 6 tablespoons of ham juices until it forms thick but fluid sauce. Carve and serve ham, passing sauce at table.

MAPLE-ORANGE GLAZE
MAKES 1 CUP, ENOUGH FOR ONE RECIPE SPIRAL-SLICED HAM

- ¾ cup maple syrup
- ½ cup orange marmalade
- 2 tablespoons unsalted butter
- 1 tablespoon Dijon mustard
- 1 teaspoon pepper
- ¼ teaspoon ground cinnamon

Combine all ingredients in small saucepan. Cook over medium heat, stirring occasionally, until mixture is thick, syrupy, and reduced to 1 cup, 5 to 10 minutes; set aside.

CHERRY-PORT GLAZE
MAKES 1 CUP, ENOUGH FOR 1 RECIPE SPIRAL-SLICED HAM

- ½ cup ruby port
- 1 cup packed dark brown sugar
- ½ cup cherry preserves
- 1 teaspoon pepper

Simmer port in small saucepan over medium heat until reduced to 2 tablespoons, about 5 minutes. Add remaining ingredients and cook, stirring occasionally, until sugar dissolves and mixture is thick, syrupy, and reduced to 1 cup, 5 to 10 minutes; set aside.

✔ WHY THIS RECIPE WORKS

When you purchase a ham at the supermarket it's fully cooked and technically ready to eat. What you're doing at home is "warming" the ham, not cooking it. The goal is to minimize the amount of time the ham spends in the oven (that is, unless you like leathery ham) and to get the center of this thick cut to heat up as quickly as possible. Using a low oven temperature (250 degrees) reduces the heat differential between the exterior and interior of the meat, but slow roasting isn't enough to ensure a juicy ham. The tricks outlined below help to cut the cooking time and moisture loss in half.

CHOOSE THE RIGHT HAM Bone-in hams with natural juices are the least processed of all the options at the supermarket. Boneless hams may seem like a good choice, but they contain several muscles that have been pressed together to look like ham and all that manipulation compromises the muscle structure, making them less able to hold on to natural juices. And while "water-added" ham might sound juicier, these hams taste awful and shed all that extra water in the oven. We do like the convenience of a spiral-cut ham, which makes serving a cinch.

GIVE THAT HAM A WARM BATH For serving, you need to warm the ham to 110 to 120 degrees—a process that takes a long time if you start with an ice-cold roast (35 to 40 degrees straight from the refrigerator). Instead, we found that soaking the wrapped ham in warm water for 90 minutes raises its internal temperature to 60 degrees and cuts total roasting time by an hour. Less time in the oven means less moisture loss.

BAKE IN AN OVEN BAG Roasting the ham in a plastic oven bag traps heat and further reduces cooking time. If you don't have an oven bag (we do recommending making a trip to the supermarket to get one), you can achieve a similar (if slightly less effective) result by wrapping the ham in foil before it goes into the oven.

LET IT REST Once the ham comes out of the oven, let it rest on the counter for at least 15 minutes. Two things are happening. The heat is continuing to move toward the center of the meat via conduction and the temperature in the center is creeping up to 110 or 120 degrees. Also, the resting period allows the muscle fibers to relax and retain more juices when the ham is carved. (For more on this phenomenon, see concept 3.)

Water is a much more efficient conductor of heat than air and is capable of cooking food very quickly. But because the action happens so fast, the risk of overcooking is quite high. The goal in boiling an egg is to get the proteins to coagulate (see concept 18) and turn from liquid to solid. However, the white starts to coagulate between 140 and 150 degrees, while the yolk doesn't start this process until the temperature reaches between 150 and 160. Since the heat takes longer to reach the yolk, the basic physics makes this process pretty tricky.

Boiling shrimp to make shrimp salad involves a similar process—the heat is shrinking the proteins, making them firmer and more palatable, but there's an added challenge: Ideally, the shrimp is also being flavored as it cooks.

In both cases, the solution turns out to be low-and-slow cooking. High heat increases the risk of overcooking because the window between perfection and overdone is so small, and because the outer layers (the egg whites or the outer parts of the shrimp) are cooking so much faster than the inner layers (the yolks or the middle of the shrimp). Lower the temperature of the water and you increase the window of time between perfectly cooked and overcooked, and you also reduce the temperature differential between the white and yolk, or between the exterior and interior of the shrimp.

HARD-COOKED EGGS
MAKES 6

Because these eggs are not boiled, this recipe is nearly foolproof. Just set the timer and you can be assured that the yolks will be set but not tinged with green. This recipe can be adjusted to make fewer or more hard-cooked eggs; just make sure to use a pan large enough to hold the eggs in a single layer. Very fresh eggs are the best choice for this recipe if you plan to make deviled eggs. As an egg ages, the cordlike strands that center the yolk weaken. If this happens, the yolk can end up close to the outer wall of the hard-cooked egg, making it likely you will tear the white when removing the yolk. Of course, this is not a concern in recipes like egg salad that call for dicing the hard-cooked eggs.

6 large eggs

1. Place eggs in medium saucepan in single layer and cover with 1 inch of water. Bring to boil over high heat. Remove pan from heat, cover, and let sit for 10 minutes.

2. Meanwhile, fill large bowl with 1 quart cold water and 1 tray of ice cubes. Pour off water from saucepan and gently shake pan back and forth to crack egg shells. Transfer eggs to ice-water bath with slotted spoon and let sit for 5 minutes. Peel and use as desired.

CLASSIC EGG SALAD
MAKES 2½ CUPS, ENOUGH FOR 4 SANDWICHES

6	hard-cooked eggs
¼	cup mayonnaise
2	tablespoons minced red onion
1	tablespoon minced fresh parsley
½	celery rib, chopped fine
2	teaspoons Dijon mustard
2	teaspoons lemon juice
¼	teaspoon salt
	Pepper

Cut peeled eggs into medium dice. Mix diced eggs with other ingredients in medium bowl, including pepper to taste. Serve. (Egg salad can be refrigerated in airtight container for 1 day.)

DEVILED EGGS
MAKES 1 DOZEN FILLED HALVES

To center the yolks, turn the carton of eggs on its side in the refrigerator the day before you plan to cook the eggs. For a nicer presentation, use a pastry bag fitted with a large star tip to pipe the filling into the egg whites.

6	hard-cooked eggs
2	tablespoons mayonnaise
1	tablespoon sour cream
½	teaspoon distilled white vinegar
½	teaspoon spicy brown mustard (such as Gulden's)
½	teaspoon sugar
⅛	teaspoon salt
⅛	teaspoon pepper

1. Slice peeled eggs in half lengthwise. Transfer yolks to fine-mesh sieve and use rubber spatula to press them through sieve into bowl. Add remaining ingredients, mashing mixture against sides of bowl until smooth.

2. Transfer mixture to zipper-lock plastic bag. Force mixture into 1 corner of bag and twist top of bag to keep filling in corner. Using scissors, snip about ½ inch off corner of bag.

3. Arrange whites on serving platter and squeeze bag to pipe filling into whites, mounding filling about ½ inch above whites. Serve immediately. (Unfilled whites and yolk mixture can be wrapped in plastic wrap and refrigerated separately for 2 days before assembling.)

✔ WHY THIS RECIPE WORKS

Hard-boiling an egg seems simple enough—you barely need a recipe. But because there's no way to watch the proteins cook under the brittle shell of an uncracked egg, the process is a crapshoot. You can't poke the egg with an instant-read thermometer. The classic method—cooking the eggs in a pot of boiling water for a precise period of time—doesn't account for variations in heat output of stoves or conductivity of pans or the different sizes of eggs. The difference between an undercooked egg (with a dark orange yolk that's soft in spots) and an overcooked egg (with a smelly green ring around the bright yellow yolk) can be just a few minutes.

TURN OFF THE HEAT Our solution to the boiled egg dilemma is to slow down the cooking process and rely on the residual heat in a covered pot of hot water to do the job safely and evenly. A pot of boiling water (at 212 degrees) contains a lot of heat that will be transferred to the eggs. Thus, an egg that's perfect after 10 minutes of boiling might be overcooked after 11 or 12 minutes. To avoid this problem, we start the eggs in cold water, gently raising their temperature as the water in the pot comes to a boil. Once the water boils, we remove the pot from the heat and throw on the cover. The eggs continue to cook as the temperature of the water drops. By the time the eggs are perfectly cooked (this takes 10 minutes with this method), the temperature of the water has dropped considerably and the water is transferring much less heat to the eggs, thus reducing the risk of overcooking.

SHOCK TO STOP THE COOKING PROCESS Once the eggs have been cooked off the heat for 10 minutes, we find it best to rapidly lower the temperature inside the egg, and thus prevent the sulfur smell and green ring. (The green ring is caused by excessive or prolonged heat; the iron in the yolk is reacting with the sulfur compounds in the white.) We accomplish this by transferring the eggs from the pot of hot water to a bowl of ice water. Shocking the eggs as soon as 10 minutes have elapsed ensures that the cooking process is halted.

CRACK BEFORE SHOCKING A perfectly cooked egg isn't good if you can't easily remove the shell. We find that draining off the cooking water, then sliding the eggs around the empty pan does a nice job of cracking the shells. When the cracked eggs are transferred to the ice-water bath, the water gets under the shells and helps loosen them further. (For more on this process, see page 386.) In addition, all those cracks make it easier for the ice-water bath to perform its primary function—that is, to quickly lower the internal temperature of the egg.

SHRIMP SALAD
SERVES 4

This recipe can also be prepared with large shrimp (26 to 30 per pound); the cooking time will be 1 to 2 minutes less. The shrimp can be cooked up to 24 hours in advance, but hold off on dressing the salad until ready to serve. The recipe can be easily doubled; cook the shrimp in a 7-quart Dutch oven and increase the cooking time to 12 to 14 minutes. Serve the salad on a bed of greens or on a buttered and grilled bun.

1	pound extra-large shrimp (21 to 25 per pound), peeled, deveined, and tails removed
5	tablespoons lemon juice (2 lemons), spent halves reserved
5	sprigs fresh parsley plus 1 teaspoon minced
3	sprigs fresh tarragon plus 1 teaspoon minced
1	teaspoon whole black peppercorns
1	tablespoon sugar
	Salt and pepper
¼	cup mayonnaise
1	small shallot, minced
1	small celery rib, minced

1. Combine shrimp, ¼ cup lemon juice, reserved lemon halves, parsley sprigs, tarragon sprigs, whole peppercorns, sugar, and 1 teaspoon salt with 2 cups cold water in medium saucepan. Place saucepan over medium heat and cook shrimp, stirring several times, until pink, firm to touch, and centers are no longer translucent, 8 to 10 minutes (water should be just bubbling around edge of pan and register 165 degrees). Remove pan from heat, cover, and let shrimp sit in broth for 2 minutes.

2. Meanwhile, fill medium bowl with ice water. Drain shrimp into colander; discard lemon halves, herbs, and spices. Immediately transfer shrimp to ice water to stop cooking and chill thoroughly, about 3 minutes. Remove shrimp from ice water and pat dry with paper towels.

3. Whisk together mayonnaise, shallot, celery, remaining 1 tablespoon lemon juice, minced parsley, and minced tarragon in medium bowl. Cut shrimp in half lengthwise and then cut each half into thirds; add shrimp to mayonnaise mixture and toss to combine. Season with salt and pepper to taste and serve. (Shrimp salad can be refrigerated overnight.)

SHRIMP SALAD WITH ROASTED RED PEPPER AND BASIL

Omit tarragon sprigs from cooking liquid. Replace celery, minced parsley, and minced tarragon with ⅓ cup thinly sliced jarred roasted red peppers, 2 teaspoons rinsed capers, and 3 tablespoons chopped fresh basil.

SHRIMP SALAD WITH AVOCADO AND ORANGE

Omit tarragon sprigs from cooking liquid. Replace celery, minced parsley, and minced tarragon with 4 halved and thinly sliced radishes; 1 large orange, peeled and cut into ½-inch pieces; ½ ripe avocado, cut into ½-inch pieces; and 2 teaspoons minced fresh mint.

SPICY SHRIMP SALAD WITH CORN AND CHIPOTLE

Substitute lime juice (3 limes; and save spent halves) for lemon juice and omit tarragon sprigs from cooking liquid. Replace celery, minced parsley, and minced tarragon with ½ cup cooked corn kernels, 2 tablespoons minced canned chipotle chile in adobo sauce, and 1 tablespoon minced fresh cilantro.

PRACTICAL SCIENCE FROZEN SHRIMP

When buying shrimp, go for frozen, unpeeled, and untreated.

Even the most basic market now sells several kinds of shrimp. We cooked more than 100 pounds to find out just what to look for (and avoid) at the supermarket.

FRESH OR FROZEN? Because nearly all shrimp are frozen at sea, you have no way of knowing when those "fresh" shrimp in the fish case were thawed (unless you are on very personal terms with your fishmonger). We found that the flavor and texture of thawed shrimp deteriorate after a few days, so you're better off buying frozen.

PEELED OR UNPEELED? If you think you can dodge some work by buying frozen shrimp that have been peeled, think again. Someone had to thaw those shrimp in order to remove their peel, and they can get pretty banged up when they are refrozen.

CHECK THE INGREDIENTS Finally, check the ingredient list. Frozen shrimp are often treated or enhanced with additives such as sodium metabisulfate, STPP (sodium tripolyphosphate), or salt to prevent darkening (which occurs as the shrimp ages) or to counter "drip loss," the industry term referring to the amount of water in the shrimp that is lost as it thaws. We have found that treated shrimp have a strange translucency and an unpleasant texture and suggest that you avoid them. Look for bags of frozen shrimp that list "shrimp" as the only ingredient.

SHRIMP SALAD WITH WASABI AND PICKLED GINGER

Omit tarragon sprigs from cooking liquid. Replace shallot, minced parsley, and minced tarragon with 2 thinly sliced scallions, 2 tablespoons chopped pickled ginger, 1 tablespoon toasted sesame seeds, and 2 teaspoons wasabi powder.

✔ WHY THIS RECIPE WORKS

Maybe it's a good thing that most shrimp salads are drowning in a sea of gloppy mayonnaise. The dressing might be bland, but at least it helps camouflage the sorry state of the rubbery, flavorless boiled shrimp. Fixing the dressing was easy (more potent ingredients, less mayonnaise), but getting the shrimp perfectly cooked (and adding some flavor in the process) required a bit more work.

START SHRIMP IN COLD WATER Classic recipes call for boiling water, white wine, lemon juice, herbs, and spices to create a court-bouillon to which the shrimp are then added. But despite all this work, the shrimp don't pick up much flavor. We take the same ingredients (cutting way back on the water and eliminating the wine, which overpowers the other flavors) and add the shrimp at the outset. The science here is simple. When the shrimp are added to boiling liquid, their proteins shrink and become firm. You can see this as the shrimp turn from translucent to opaque. In boiling water, this process happens almost instantly. Once the proteins have shrunk, there's less room for flavor molecules to be absorbed. When the shrimp are put in the broth at the beginning, they heat gently along with the broth and have more time to pick up flavor.

WARM, DON'T BOIL The proteins in shrimp start to shrink and toughen when the internal temperature reaches 120 degrees. We find bringing the internal temperature of shrimp to 140 degrees makes them pleasantly chewy but not tough. If you cook shrimp in boiling liquid (212 degrees), you pretty much guarantee that their internal temperature will rise above 140 degrees and the shrimp will turn rubbery. To prevent shrimp from overcooking, we heat the liquid to a simmer (no more than 165 degrees).

TAKE OFF HEAT, THEN SHOCK Once the cooking liquid reaches 165 degrees, we remove the pan from the heat, cover it, and let the shrimp finish cooking via conduction. This technique gives the shrimp about two minutes more of flavoring time, for a total of 10 to 12 minutes—far more than the two to three minutes shrimp spend cooking if directly added to boiling liquid. One last step—once the shrimp are done, we quickly transfer them to a bowl of ice water to stop the cooking process. Once chilled, the shrimp are ready to be dressed and served.

High Heat Develops Flavor

Gentle heat cooks food while minimizing moisture loss, but juiciness is not the only consideration when choosing a technique. High heat not only cooks a cut of meat but changes the flavor, too. (Think steak tartare versus a grilled steak.) Much of this change is related to the complex chemical interactions known as the Maillard reaction, named for the French scientist Louis-Camille Maillard, who first described the process in the early 1900s.

HOW THE SCIENCE WORKS

One hundred years after the Maillard reaction was first recognized, the principle is still not fully understood—the chemistry is that complicated. Simply put, in many foods, heat causes the amino acids (the building blocks of proteins) to react with certain types of sugars ("reducing sugars," like glucose and fructose) to create new, distinct flavor compounds. These compounds, called dicarbonyls, in turn react with more amino acids to form even more compounds, multiplying rapidly on both the surface of the cooking food and in the cooking vessel. Ultimately, very large molecules called melanoidin pigments, which are responsible for the deep brown hue on the crusts of roasted and grilled meats, are formed.

Depending on the specific amino acids or sugars present, different flavor compounds can be created. For example, cysteine, a sulfur-containing amino acid abundant in red meat, reacts with reducing sugars to form thiazoles and thiophenes, more complex compounds that are important components of "roasted meat" flavor. (This is one reason why a browned steak has a different flavor from a browned chicken breast.)

Temperature also affects the Maillard reaction. In general, this reaction occurs when the surface temperature exceeds 300 degrees. This seems high, but remember that because of the principles of conductive heat, the temperature of a piece of meat can vary greatly as it cooks. In the time it takes the center of a chilled thick steak to go from 35 to 80 degrees in the pan, the surface temperature can jump to 300 degrees.

Because the Maillard reaction becomes rapid at this high temperature, certain cooking methods don't brown foods. Food cooked in boiling water, for example, never browns because the surface temperature cannot exceed 212 degrees.

The presence of any moisture influences the Maillard reaction. Even with dry-heat cooking methods like sautéing or grilling, the surface moisture of food will steam—lowering the temperature, slowing the speed of the reaction, and thus reducing the amount of browning.

THE MAILLARD REACTION: HOW BROWNING OCCURS

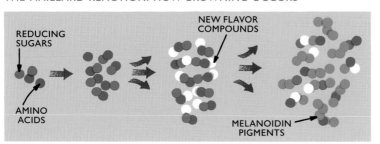

HIGH HEAT FOR BIG FLAVOR *When meat is heated, amino acids and reducing sugars (glucose and fructose) react to form new flavor compounds. In turn, these new compounds form yet more flavor compounds. This process keeps repeating itself until very large molecules called melanoidin pigments are created. These large molecules produce the brown colors (and flavors) associated with roasted and grilled meats.*

TEST KITCHEN EXPERIMENT

To demonstrate the effect of browning on flavor, we conducted the following experiment: We started with six chicken cutlets, which we patted dry with paper towels and seasoned with equal amounts of salt and pepper. We heated 1 tablespoon of vegetable oil in two 12-inch conventional skillets for three minutes. One pan was set over medium-low heat and the second pan over high heat. After the pans were heated for three minutes we recorded the temperature of the oil and added three cutlets to each pan. In each case, we cooked the chicken, flipping each piece once, until the temperature in the center reached 160 degrees, indicating that the chicken was fully cooked. We also tracked the surface temperature of the chicken as it cooked.

Once the chicken was cooked, we transferred it to a plate and added 1 cup of water to each pan. Using a wooden spoon, we scraped the browned bits in the pan loose and boiled the water until it had reduced to ½ cup. We poured the liquid into measuring cups and evaluated both the chicken and "sauce" for color and flavor. We repeated the experiment three times and compared the results.

THE RESULTS

Let's start with the visual observations. As you might expect, the chicken cooked over medium-low heat (the oil registered 240 degrees after preheating for three minutes) was very pale. Since there were almost no pan drippings in the pan set over medium-low heat, the "sauce" we created had almost no color. Tasters described the chicken as moist but bland and the sauce tasted like water.

The chicken cooked over high heat (the oil registered 420 degrees when the chicken was added) developed a nice golden exterior. During the cooking process, lots of browned bits (called fond) had formed in the pan and the "sauce" we made in this pan had a brown color and decent flavor. (Remember, we added only water.)

Cooking time had no relation to overall browning. The cutlets cooked over medium-low heat required about seven minutes to reach an internal temperature of 160 degrees. In contrast, the cutlets cooked over high heat required just five minutes to reach an internal temperature of 160 degrees. So browning was better in the sample that spent less—not more—time being heated.

While both samples were heated to the same internal temperature (160 degrees), the surface temperatures varied greatly. The surface temperature of the cutlets cooked over medium-low heat took an average of five minutes to reach their maximum of 300 degrees. In contrast, the surface temperature of the cutlets cooked over high heat raced ahead to over 300 degrees in about one minute and continued to climb to well over 400 degrees by the time the chicken was cooked through.

THE TAKEAWAY

Significant heat is required to jump-start the chemical reaction that causes food to brown. Absent the heat necessary to raise the surface temperature above 300 degrees, more cooking time won't really lead to more browning unless the food is cooked for a very long time. In the absence of other variables (such as other flavorful ingredients in the dish), well-browned food has a richer, more varied flavor profile than poorly browned food.

MORE HEAT = MORE BROWNING

COOKED OVER MEDIUM-LOW
The surface temperature of the chicken never exceeded 300 degrees and thus little browning occurred. The sauce made from the pan drippings was pale and bland.

COOKED OVER HIGH
The surface temperature of the chicken reached 440 degrees and thus a lot of browning occurred. The sauce made from the pan drippings was rich and brown.

One of the reasons stir-fries are appealing is that you can prepare a complete meal (with vegetables and protein) quickly in a single pan. This method relies on browning to impart flavor to both the protein and the vegetables. Choosing the right cooking vessel, using sufficient heat, and cooking food in small batches ensures that the pan remains hot enough to encourage the Maillard reaction.

STIR-FRIED BEEF WITH SNAP PEAS AND RED PEPPER
SERVES 4

To make slicing the meat easier, freeze it for 15 minutes. Serve with Simple White Rice (page 124).

SAUCE

- ½ cup low-sodium chicken broth
- ¼ cup oyster sauce
- 2 tablespoons dry sherry
- 1 tablespoon sugar
- 1 teaspoon cornstarch

BEEF STIR-FRY

- 2 tablespoons soy sauce
- 1 teaspoon sugar
- 1 (12-ounce) flank steak, trimmed, cut into 2-inch-wide strips with grain, and sliced thin across grain on slight bias
- 2 tablespoons vegetable oil
- 3 garlic cloves, minced
- 1 tablespoon grated fresh ginger
- 12 ounces sugar snap peas, strings removed
- 1 red bell pepper, stemmed, seeded, and cut into ¼-inch slices
- 2 tablespoons water

1. **FOR THE SAUCE:** Whisk all ingredients together in small bowl and set aside.

2. **FOR THE STIR-FRY:** Combine soy sauce and sugar in medium bowl. Add beef, toss well, and marinate for at least 10 minutes or up to 1 hour, stirring once. Meanwhile, combine 1 teaspoon oil, garlic, and ginger in small bowl.

3. Drain beef and discard liquid. Heat 1 teaspoon oil in 12-inch nonstick skillet over high heat until just smoking. Add half of beef in single layer, break up any clumps, and cook, without stirring, for 1 minute. Stir beef and continue to cook until browned, 1 to 2 minutes. Transfer beef

to clean bowl. Repeat with 1 teaspoon oil and remaining beef. Rinse skillet clean and dry with paper towels.

4. Add remaining 1 tablespoon oil to skillet and heat until just smoking. Add snap peas and bell pepper and cook, stirring frequently, until vegetables begin to brown, 3 to 5 minutes. Add water and continue to cook until vegetables are crisp-tender, 1 to 2 minutes longer. Clear center of skillet, add garlic mixture, and cook, mashing mixture into pan, until fragrant, 15 to 20 seconds. Stir mixture into vegetables. Return beef and any accumulated juices to skillet and stir to combine. Whisk sauce to recombine, add to skillet, and cook, stirring constantly, until thickened, about 30 seconds. Serve.

TERIYAKI STIR-FRIED BEEF WITH GREEN BEANS AND SHIITAKES
SERVES 4

To make slicing the meat easier, freeze it for 15 minutes. You can substitute 1 tablespoon of white wine or sake mixed with 1 teaspoon of sugar for the mirin. Serve with Simple White Rice (page 124).

SAUCE

- ½ cup low-sodium chicken broth
- 2 tablespoons soy sauce
- 2 tablespoons sugar
- 1 tablespoon mirin
- 1 teaspoon cornstarch
- ¼ teaspoon red pepper flakes

BEEF STIR-FRY

- 2 tablespoons soy sauce
- 1 teaspoon sugar
- 1 (12-ounce) flank steak, trimmed, cut into 2-inch-wide strips with grain, and sliced thin across grain on slight bias
- 2 tablespoons vegetable oil
- 3 garlic cloves, minced
- 1 tablespoon grated fresh ginger
- 8 ounces shiitake mushrooms, stemmed and cut into 1-inch pieces
- 12 ounces green beans, trimmed and halved
- ¼ cup water
- 3 scallions, cut into 1½-inch pieces, white and light green pieces quartered lengthwise

1. **FOR THE SAUCE:** Whisk all ingredients together in small bowl and set aside.

2. FOR THE STIR-FRY: Combine soy sauce and sugar in medium bowl. Add beef, toss well, and marinate for at least 10 minutes or up to 1 hour, stirring once. Meanwhile, combine 1 teaspoon oil, garlic, and ginger in small bowl.

3. Drain beef and discard liquid. Heat 1 teaspoon oil in 12-inch nonstick skillet over high heat until just smoking. Add half of beef in single layer, break up any clumps, and cook, without stirring, for 1 minute. Stir beef and continue to cook until browned, 1 to 2 minutes. Transfer beef to clean bowl. Repeat with 1 teaspoon oil and remaining beef. Rinse skillet clean and dry with paper towels.

4. Add remaining 1 tablespoon oil to skillet and heat until just smoking. Add mushrooms and cook until beginning to brown, about 2 minutes. Add green beans and cook, stirring frequently, until spotty brown, 3 to 4 minutes. Add water, cover, and continue to cook until green beans are crisp-tender, 2 to 3 minutes longer. Uncover, clear center of skillet, and add garlic mixture. Cook, mashing mixture into pan, until fragrant, 15 to 20 seconds. Stir mixture into vegetables. Return beef and any accumulated juices to skillet, add scallions, and stir to combine. Whisk sauce to recombine, add to skillet, and cook, stirring constantly, until thickened, about 30 seconds. Serve.

TANGERINE STIR-FRIED BEEF WITH ONION AND SNOW PEAS
SERVES 4

To make slicing the meat easier, freeze it for 15 minutes. Make sure to zest one of the tangerines before juicing them. Two oranges can be substituted for the tangerines. If available, substitute 1 teaspoon of toasted and ground Sichuan peppercorns for the red pepper flakes. Serve with Simple White Rice (page 124).

SAUCE

- ¾ cup tangerine juice (3 to 4 tangerines)
- 2 tablespoons soy sauce
- 1 tablespoon packed light brown sugar
- 1 teaspoon toasted sesame oil
- 1 teaspoon cornstarch

BEEF STIR-FRY

- 2 tablespoons soy sauce
- 1 teaspoon packed light brown sugar
- 1 (12-ounce) flank steak, trimmed, cut into 2-inch-wide strips with grain, and sliced thin across grain on slight bias
- 3 garlic cloves, minced

- 1 tablespoon grated fresh ginger
- 1 tablespoon black bean sauce
- 1 teaspoon grated tangerine zest
- ¼–½ teaspoon red pepper flakes
- 2 tablespoons vegetable oil
- 1 large onion, halved and cut into ½-inch wedges
- 10 ounces snow peas, strings removed
- 2 tablespoons water

1. FOR THE SAUCE: Whisk all ingredients together in small bowl and set aside.

2. FOR THE STIR-FRY: Combine soy sauce and sugar in medium bowl. Add beef, toss well, and marinate for at least 10 minutes or up to 1 hour, stirring once. Meanwhile, combine garlic, ginger, black bean sauce, tangerine zest, pepper flakes, and 1 teaspoon vegetable oil in small bowl.

3. Drain beef and discard liquid. Heat 1 teaspoon vegetable oil in 12-inch nonstick skillet over high heat until just smoking. Add half of beef in single layer, break up any clumps, and cook, without stirring, for 1 minute. Stir beef and continue to cook until browned, 1 to 2 minutes. Transfer beef to clean bowl. Repeat with 1 teaspoon vegetable oil and remaining beef. Rinse skillet clean and dry with paper towels.

4. Add remaining 1 tablespoon vegetable oil to skillet and heat until just smoking. Add onion and cook, stirring frequently, until beginning to brown, 3 to 5 minutes. Add snow peas and continue to cook until spotty brown, about

---

PRACTICAL SCIENCE SKILLET VS. WOK

On a Western stove, we prefer a skillet when stir-frying.

The skillet's flat-bottom design allows more of its surface area to come in direct contact with the flat burner of a Western stove. The wok, which is traditionally shaped with a conical bottom, was designed for pit-style stoves where flames come in contact with both the sides and the bottom of the pan. When a wok is placed on a Western stove, the heat from the flat burner does not reach the sides. On the same stove more of the skillet is in contact with the burner, allowing it to grow very hot. The wok, instead, heats inefficiently and its temperature drops precipitously when food is added. Since a hotter pan equals more browning, the choice of skillet or wok really matters.

To quantify their differences, we heated vegetable oil in a wok and a heavy 12-inch skillet over high heat on gas burners. Once the oil was smoking (at around 415 degrees), we added the same stir-fry ingredients to each pan. The wok's temperature plummeted dramatically, to 220 degrees at its center, rising only another 50 degrees over the course of cooking. The skillet's temperature dipped to 345 degrees, then recovered quickly, continuing to rise to almost 500 degrees. This higher heat translated to better browning and more flavor in the stir-fry prepared in the skillet.

2 minutes longer. Add water and cook until vegetables are crisp-tender, about 1 minute. Clear center of skillet, add garlic mixture, and cook, mashing mixture into pan, until fragrant, 15 to 20 seconds. Stir mixture into vegetables. Return beef and any accumulated juices to skillet and stir to combine. Whisk sauce to recombine, add to skillet, and cook, stirring constantly, until thickened, about 30 seconds. Serve.

✔ WHY THIS RECIPE WORKS

Stir-fries suffer from a number of common problems—including burned garlic and ginger and watery sauces—but the biggest problem is the meat, which is often steamed, bland, and tough. A 10-minute soy marinade adds flavor and helps the meat retain moisture. (The soy acts like a brine; see concept 13 for more information on this phenomenon.) A little sugar is mixed with the soy sauce to promote browning and the meat is drained before cooking so the excess marinade doesn't cause the meat to steam. Cooking the meat in two batches (rather than one) ensures that the pan remains plenty hot and that the beef browns nicely.

START WITH THE RIGHT CUT   Flank steak is the classic choice because it's relatively inexpensive and flavorful. We also like sirloin tip steaks and blade steaks. If using the latter, you will need to remove excess fat and gristle so start with 1 pound to compensate for the trimmings.

SLICE THIN, ACROSS THE GRAIN   Cutting the meat across the grain into thin strips ensures that it will be tender and easy to eat. Don't cut the meat with the grain. Cutting the meat across the grain shortens long, tough muscle fibers (most of which run from end to end on this oblong cut), dramatically diminishing chewiness. Thin slices will seem more tender than thick slices, so freeze the meat for 15 minutes before slicing it and make sure to use a sharp knife.

USE A BIG PAN   Piling food up in the skillet hampers browning. For maximum browning and flavor use a 12-inch skillet. We prefer a nonstick pan, which requires very little oil and keeps the stir-fry from becoming greasy.

COOK EVERYTHING IN BATCHES   The goal when stir-frying is to keep the temperature in the pan very hot. On a professional restaurant stove, this might not be much of a challenge, but at home it is. The meat is cooked in two batches so that each piece is in direct contact with the pan. Likewise, the vegetables are cooked in batches, with the slow-cooking vegetables (like mushrooms and onions) going into the pan before faster-cooking vegetables (like snow peas).

ADD THE GARLIC AND GINGER LAST   Many stir-fry recipes start by cooking the garlic and ginger. The idea, we think, is to flavor everything that subsequently goes into the pan. Sounds good, but the result is that the garlic and ginger often burn, imparting a scorched flavor to the dish. Instead, we add the garlic and ginger at the end of the cooking time, pushing the vegetables to the side of the pan and making a clearing in the middle for the garlic, ginger, and a little oil. Once the aromatics are fragrant (this will take 15 to 20 seconds), they are stirred back into the vegetables and the stir-fry is finished.

DON'T FORGET CORNSTARCH   A good stir-fry sauce starts with very potent ingredients. Some restaurants thicken their stir-fry sauces with so much cornstarch that the result is a pasty, gloppy stir-fry. Many home cooks don't bother with any cornstarch and their sauces are so watery they run off the food. We find that a little cornstarch (usually about 1 teaspoon for a typical stir-fry sauce) strikes just the right balance. Make sure to add the cornstarch to the sauce before it hits the pan. Cornstarch must be dispersed in cold or room-temperature liquids. If added to hot liquids or directly to the pan, the granules will swell quickly and form lumps.

PRACTICAL SCIENCE THE COLOR OF MEAT

Myoglobin is a protein that dictates the color of meat.

Why does meat change color when it cooks? Why is the ground beef you bring home from the market sometimes red on the outside but dark purple or brown on the inside?

The color in meat comes from a protein called myoglobin, which serves to store oxygen in muscle tissue. When the meat is freshly cut, this protein is deep purple. When the exterior of raw meat is exposed to oxygen (as it sits in its packaging, or in the butcher's display case), the protein will convert to oxymyoglobin, which is a striking bright red. Inside the meat, where less oxygen can penetrate, however, this protein will slowly convert to brown metmyoglobin. Color changes of this nature are purely cosmetic—they have no bearing on the meat's flavor or wholesomeness, except perhaps when meat turns brown with age. After all, the color of meat is also influenced by the age of the animal. The level of myoglobin increases with age, and with use. This is why the most-exercised parts of the animal (think chicken leg versus breast) is much darker in color.

Cooking, obviously, also changes the color of meat. As myoglobin is heated, the protein denatures and unfolds, and the portion of the molecule responsible for the color, called heme, is converted again to metmyoglobin, producing the gray color of cooked meat.

Grilling seems like the easiest way to brown food and encourage the development of flavor compounds associated with the Maillard reaction. Unlike the stovetop, where burner output and smoke are real challenges for the home cook, most grills are capable of maintaining high temperatures (well in excess of 500 degrees) and smoke is not a concern. In fact, with large, thick cuts, overbrowning is the bigger risk. (We've all incinerated something on the grill.) However, small cuts (like steaks, chops, or fish fillets) will cook very quickly on the grill, sometimes before the exterior has had time to brown sufficiently. The goal when preparing these foods for the grill is to remove excess moisture so that food can start to brown the instant it is placed on the grill.

GRILLED ARGENTINE STEAKS WITH CHIMICHURRI SAUCE
SERVES 6 TO 8

The chimichurri sauce can be made up to three days in advance. Our preferred steak for this recipe is strip steak, also known as New York strip. A less expensive alternative is a boneless shell sirloin steak (or top sirloin steak). When using a charcoal grill, we prefer wood chunks to wood chips whenever possible; substitute four medium wood chunks, unsoaked, for the wood chip packets. We like oak, but other types of wood chunks can be used.

CHIMICHURRI SAUCE
- ¼ cup hot water
- 2 teaspoons dried oregano
- 1 teaspoon salt
- 1⅓ cups parsley leaves
- ⅔ cup cilantro leaves
- 6 garlic cloves, minced
- ½ teaspoon red pepper flakes
- ¼ cup red wine vinegar
- ½ cup extra-virgin olive oil

STEAKS
- 1 tablespoon cornstarch
- 1½ teaspoons salt
- 4 (1-pound) boneless strip steaks, 1½ inches thick, trimmed
- 4 cups wood chips, soaked in water for 15 minutes and drained
  Pepper

1. FOR THE SAUCE: Combine water, oregano, and salt in small bowl and let sit until oregano is softened, about 15 minutes. Pulse parsley, cilantro, garlic, and pepper flakes in food processor until coarsely chopped, about 10 pulses.

Add water mixture and vinegar and pulse to combine. Transfer mixture to bowl and slowly whisk in oil until emulsified. Cover with plastic wrap and let stand at room temperature for at least 1 hour (if preparing sauce in advance, refrigerate and bring to room temperature before using).

2. FOR THE STEAKS: Set wire rack in rimmed baking sheet. Combine cornstarch and salt in small bowl. Pat steaks dry with paper towels and place on prepared baking sheet. Rub entire surface of steaks with cornstarch mixture and place steaks, uncovered, in freezer until very firm, about 30 minutes.

3. Using 2 large pieces of heavy-duty aluminum foil, wrap soaked chips in 2 foil packets and cut several vent holes in tops.

4A. FOR A CHARCOAL GRILL: Open bottom vent halfway. Light large chimney starter filled with charcoal briquettes (6 quarts). When top coals are partially covered with ash, pour evenly over grill. Place wood chip packets on coals. Set cooking grate in place, cover, and open lid vent halfway. Heat grill until hot and wood chips are smoking, about 5 minutes.

4B. FOR A GAS GRILL: Place wood chip packets on cooking grate. Turn all burners to high, cover, and heat until hot, about 15 minutes. Leave all burners on high.

5. Clean and oil cooking grate. Season steaks with pepper. Place steaks on grill, cover, and cook until beginning to brown on both sides, 4 to 6 minutes, flipping halfway through cooking.

6. Flip steaks and cook uncovered until well browned on first side, 2 to 4 minutes. Flip steaks and continue to cook until meat registers 115 to 120 degrees (for rare) or 120 to 125 degrees (for medium-rare), 2 to 6 minutes longer.

7. Transfer steaks to cutting board, tent loosely with foil, and let rest for 10 minutes. Cut each steak crosswise into ¼-inch slices. Transfer to serving platter and serve, passing chimichurri sauce separately.

✔ WHY THIS RECIPE WORKS

In Argentina, 2-pound steaks are grilled over a hardwood fire so they pick up a lot of smoke flavor. Because these steaks are so big, they spend plenty of time on the grill and emerge with a thick, flavorful browned crust. When translated to smaller American steaks, the method falters. Our goal was to devise a technique that would prolong the grill time (so the steaks could pick up more wood flavor) and maximize browning. We discovered that rubbing the steaks with a mixture of salt and cornstarch and then putting them in the freezer for 30 minutes accomplished both goals. The cornstarch-salt mixture wicked away moisture and the air inside a freezer is very dry, so moisture evaporates very quickly. Steaks treated this way started to brown as soon as they hit the grill. In addition, chilling the steaks in the freezer prolonged their total cooking time, which gave the steaks more time to pick up smoke flavor.

USE FREEZER AS DEHYDRATOR The freezer is a harsh environment for meat. Even when well wrapped, steaks can lose moisture and become covered with freezer burn. But we use this effect to our advantage. We found that steaks placed in the freezer for a short period of time emerged firmer and drier thanks to the evaporation of surface moisture. Rubbing the steaks with salt helps draw extra moisture to the surface, where it can evaporate. Adding some cornstarch to the rub absorbs moisture and promotes the development of an especially crisp crust on the grilled steaks. The starches in the cornstarch also enhance the browning by adding more "fuel" for the Maillard reaction.

MAKE SMOKE We use a lot of wood to produce sufficient smoke to flavor the steaks during the quick cooking time. Oak is the traditional choice for this recipe, but any wood will do. Placing the lid on the grill for the first few minutes of cooking time traps the smoke and helps jump-start the flavoring process. A charcoal grill does a much better job of producing smoke, although we did develop a workaround for a gas grill by placing the packets with the wood chips directly on the cooking grate.

PRACTICAL SCIENCE WILD VS. FARMED SALMON

We prefer wild Alaskan salmon to Norwegian farmed salmon.

Setting environmental and sustainability issues aside, we compared wild salmon fillets with farmed salmon fillets, noting variations in fattiness, flavor, aroma, and color. We tasted fresh wild Alaskan king salmon ($15.99 per pound), which is available year-round either fresh, frozen, or thawed, alongside fresh farmed salmon ($11.99 per pound) from Norway in a basic pan-fried application as well as in a salmon cake recipe.

Both raw and cooked, the wild salmon had a rosy-pink hue, while the farmed salmon was lighter pink. Wild salmon attain their color by absorbing a carotenoid called astaxanthin from a krill-based diet, while farmed salmon eat fish feed supplemented with various sources of astaxanthin to enhance their color.

The wild salmon exuded more oil in the pan than the farmed salmon but tasted leaner overall, with a buttery texture and a sweet, fresh flavor. The farmed salmon, which get less exercise and consume more fat than wild salmon, tasted "fishy," with "slimy, soft" flesh and a "musty, fatty" aftertaste. When mashed, seasoned, formed into cakes, and pan-fried, the differences remained. Tasters overwhelmingly preferred the wild salmon, which had a rich, full, but delicate flavor. In comparison, the farmed salmon had a "canned" flavor.

The flavor and texture of wild and farmed salmon will vary depending on a host of factors, including the species of salmon, the season, and the place of origin. In this particular instance, however, we found that the wild Alaskan salmon was preferable to the Norwegian farmed salmon.

BIG STEAKS NEED BIG SAUCE Steaks in Argentina are traditionally served with a tart herb-based sauce called chimichurri. The sharp, grassy flavors of the sauce are the perfect complement to the fatty, smoky beef. We make a traditional version of this sauce with parsley, cilantro, oregano, garlic, red wine vinegar, red pepper flakes, and salt—all emulsified with a fruity extra-virgin olive oil.

GRILLED SALMON FILLETS
SERVES 4

This recipe works best with salmon fillets but can also be used with any thick, firm-fleshed white fish, including red snapper, grouper, halibut, and sea bass (cook white fish to 140 degrees, up to 2 minutes longer per side). If you are using skinless fillets, treat the skinned side of each as if it were the skin side. Serve with lemon wedges, Almond Vinaigrette, or Olive Vinaigrette (recipes follow).

1   (1½- to 2-pound) skin-on salmon fillet,
    1½ inches thick
    Vegetable oil
    Salt and pepper
    Lemon wedges

1. Use sharp knife to remove any whitish fat from belly of salmon and cut fillet into 4 equal pieces. Place fillets skin side up on large plate lined with clean kitchen towel. Place second clean kitchen towel on top of fillets and press down to blot liquid. Refrigerate fish, wrapped in towels, while preparing grill, at least 20 minutes.

2A. FOR A CHARCOAL GRILL: Open bottom vent completely. Light large chimney starter two-thirds filled with charcoal briquettes (4 quarts). When top coals are partially covered with ash, pour evenly over half of grill. Set cooking grate in place, cover, and open lid vent completely. Heat grill until hot, about 5 minutes.

2B. FOR A GAS GRILL: Turn all burners to high, cover, and heat grill until very hot, about 15 minutes.

3. Clean cooking grate, then repeatedly brush grate with well-oiled paper towels until grate is black and glossy, 5 to 10 times. Lightly brush both sides of fish with oil and season with salt and pepper. Place fish skin side down on hot side of grill (if using charcoal) or turn all burners to medium (if using gas) with fillets diagonal to grate. Cover and cook without moving until skin is well browned and crisp, 3 to 5 minutes. (Try lifting fish gently with spatula after 3 minutes; if it doesn't cleanly lift off grill, continue to cook, checking at 30-second intervals, until it releases.)

4. Using 2 spatulas, flip fish and continue to cook, covered, until center is still translucent when checked with tip of paring knife and registers 125 degrees (for medium-rare), 2 to 6 minutes longer. Serve immediately with lemon wedges.

ALMOND VINAIGRETTE

MAKES ABOUT ½ CUP, ENOUGH FOR 1 RECIPE GRILLED SALMON FILLETS

⅓	cup whole almonds, toasted
1	small shallot, minced
4	teaspoons white wine vinegar
2	teaspoons honey
1	teaspoon Dijon mustard
⅓	cup extra-virgin olive oil
1	tablespoon cold water
1	tablespoon minced fresh tarragon
	Salt and pepper

Place almonds in zipper-lock bag and, using rolling pin, pound until no pieces larger than ½ inch remain. Combine pounded almonds, shallot, vinegar, honey, and mustard in medium bowl. Whisking constantly, drizzle in olive oil until emulsion forms. Add water and tarragon and whisk to combine, then season with salt and pepper to taste. Whisk to recombine before serving.

PRACTICAL SCIENCE DEAL WITH GRAY MATTER

The gray matter on salmon is rich in omega-3 fatty acids.

The gray portion of flesh just below the skin of salmon is a fatty deposit rich in omega-3 fatty acids and low in the natural pink pigments found in the rest of the fish. To get a handle on how the gray area affects flavor, we oven-roasted several fillets of salmon, then removed the gray portion from half of them and left it intact on the others. Only a few discerning tasters noted that the samples with the gray substance had an ever-so-slightly fishy flavor; most couldn't tell the difference. It's easy enough to remove the gray stuff by peeling off the skin of the cooked salmon and then scraping it away with the back of a knife, but the flavor difference is so minor that we don't think it's worth the hassle.

A TOUCH OF GRAY
The gray matter on the underside of salmon is rich in omega-3 fatty acids.

OLIVE VINAIGRETTE

MAKES ABOUT ½ CUP, ENOUGH FOR 1 RECIPE GRILLED SALMON FILLETS

½	cup pitted green or kalamata olives, chopped coarse
¼	cup extra-virgin olive oil
2	tablespoons minced fresh parsley
1	small shallot, minced
2	teaspoons lemon juice
	Salt and pepper

Combine all ingredients in bowl and season with salt and pepper to taste. Whisk to recombine before serving.

✔ WHY THIS RECIPE WORKS

We wanted grilled salmon with a tender interior and crisp skin, and we wanted each fillet to hold together on the grill. We prefer thicker salmon fillets, which can stand the heat of the grill for a little longer before the first turn. For moist, tender results, we cook the salmon to a perfect medium-rare—any longer and it begins to dry out.

COVER AND CHILL To prevent the fish from sticking and falling apart, we dry the fish's exterior by wrapping it in a clean kitchen towel and refrigerating it for 20 minutes. This removes more moisture than simply blotting the fish. With less moisture on the surface, the browning starts a bit faster. (When wet food is placed on a grill, much of the fire's energy is at first used to evaporate this moisture.)

SEASON THE GRILL To eliminate the risk of the fish sticking to the grill, you need a barrier between the fish and the cooking grate. We've noticed when oiling the grate that the oil vaporizes almost instantly, leaving behind a black, weblike residue. It turns out that as the oil heats up, its fatty-acid chains form polymers (that is, they stick together), creating that crisscross pattern over the surface of the metal. We've often observed the same phenomenon when seasoning a cast-iron pan with successive coatings of oil. A single layer of these polymers won't prevent sticking, but applying and heating oil repeatedly will build up a thick layer of them in a cast-iron pan and make it "nonstick." This same technique translates perfectly to the grill. We use tongs to rub oiled paper towels over the heated grate five to 10 times. When the grate is black and glossy you know you've built up a sufficient layer of polymers. The proteins in the fish are no longer in direct contact with the grill grate and cannot bond with it. Note that this effect is temporary and the grill must be reseasoned every time you want to cook fish.

Unlike other proteins, white fish and seafood, such as shrimp and scallops, have very little fat. As a result, overcooking can have disastrous results. The punishing heat used to encourage browning can cause delicate fish and seafood to become tough and dry. (Salmon has plenty of fat so this is less of a concern with this fish.) Because of this, we find it necessary to help the browning along— just turning the heat up or prolonging the cooking time simply isn't an option. We want the benefits that the Maillard reaction creates (that is, more flavor) but we don't want to risk ruining the fish or seafood in the process. We found that sugar and butter could both be used to speed up the browning process.

SKILLET-ROASTED FISH FILLETS
SERVES 4

Thick white fish fillets with a meaty texture, like halibut, cod, sea bass, or red snapper, work best in this recipe. If your fillets happen to come with skin, remove it. Because most fish fillets differ in thickness, some pieces may finish cooking before others—be sure to immediately remove any fillet that reaches 140 degrees. Serve the fish with lemon wedges or the relish (recipe follows).

4 (6- to 8-ounce) skinless white fish fillets,
   1 to 1½ inches thick
   Salt and pepper
½ teaspoon sugar
1 tablespoon vegetable oil
   Lemon wedges or relish (recipe follows)

1. Adjust oven rack to middle position and heat oven to 425 degrees. Dry fish thoroughly with paper towels and season with salt and pepper. Sprinkle very light dusting of sugar (about ⅛ teaspoon) evenly over 1 side of each fillet.

2. Heat oil in 12-inch ovensafe nonstick skillet over high heat until smoking. Place fillets in skillet, sugared sides down, and press down lightly to ensure even contact with pan. Cook until browned, 1 to 1½ minutes. Using 2 spatulas, flip fillets and transfer skillet to oven. Roast fillets until centers are just opaque and register 140 degrees, 7 to 10 minutes. Immediately transfer to serving plates and serve with lemon wedges, or relish spooned over each fillet.

ROASTED RED PEPPER, HAZELNUT, AND THYME RELISH
MAKES ABOUT 1½ CUPS, ENOUGH FOR 1 RECIPE SKILLET-ROASTED FISH FILLETS

Rubbing the warm, toasted hazelnuts in a kitchen towel is an easy way to remove their skins.

½ cup hazelnuts, toasted and skinned
½ cup jarred roasted red peppers, rinsed, patted dry, and chopped coarse
1 garlic clove, minced
½ teaspoon grated lemon zest plus 4 teaspoons juice
¼ cup extra-virgin olive oil
2 tablespoons minced fresh parsley
1 teaspoon minced fresh thyme
¼ teaspoon smoked paprika
   Salt and pepper

Pulse hazelnuts, roasted peppers, garlic, and lemon zest in food processor until finely chopped, 10 to 12 pulses. Transfer to bowl and stir in lemon juice, oil, parsley, thyme, and paprika. Season with salt and pepper to taste.

PRACTICAL SCIENCE
SUGAR JUMP-STARTS BROWNING

Add sugar for faster browning when cooking fish.

Fish begins to contract and dry out when its internal temperature reaches only 120 degrees and it is fully cooked at 140 degrees. Beyond this temperature, fish becomes dry and unpalatable. While the exterior of the fish will become hotter than 140 degrees, it won't really approach the 300 degrees necessary for the Maillard reaction to occur. Our challenge, then, was to get the fish to achieve flavorful browning at a lower temperature. Here's how we did it: When sugar (sucrose) is added to the wet surface of the fish and is exposed to the heat of the pan, it quickly breaks down into glucose and fructose. Fructose begins to rapidly caramelize at around 200 degrees—a temperature the exterior of the fish easily reaches within a minute or so of hitting the hot pan. Thus, a little bit of sugar sprinkled on a fillet will lead to faster browning, helping a good crust to form before the interior dries out.

WITH SUGAR   SUGAR-FREE

After just one minute, the fillet dusted with sugar is far more browned than the fillet without it.

FISH 101

STRUCTURE

The structure of fish is very different from that of meat or poultry: shorter muscle fibers, delicate connective tissue, and fat that is rich in unsaturated fatty acids. This combination makes fish more flaky and tender; it's important not to overcook it.

MUSCLE FIBERS

Why is meat so dense and fish so flaky? It has to do with the differences in the fibers of their flesh. Muscle fibers in meat are long and very thin—they can be as much as 10 centimeters in length. Fish, on the other hand, is constructed of very short bundles, up to 10 times shorter than the long muscle fibers in meat. This is why fish tends to flake—it is the flesh separating into its short fibers.

SKIN

Fish skin is thick and often rich—filled with connective tissue and fat. It is often covered with scales, a strong layer of protection, which vary in size and thickness, and are composed of the same form of calcium carbonate as mammals' teeth.

CONNECTIVE TISSUE

The connective tissue in fish is also quite different from that in meat. Compared with meat, fish muscle contains only a small fraction of connective tissue. Rather than running parallel with the muscle fibers, the small amount of connective tissue in fish sits in very thin sheets perpendicular to the muscle bundles. Fish collagen is much more fragile and much more easily converted to gelatin than that in meat. The connective tissue in most fish breaks down to gelatin at only 120 to 130 degrees. This, plus those short muscle fibers, explains why fish is always tender.

Because fish has almost no collagen, it never benefits from long cooking. In fact, many fish are delicious raw or lightly cooked. In any case, fish should never be cooked beyond 140 degrees.

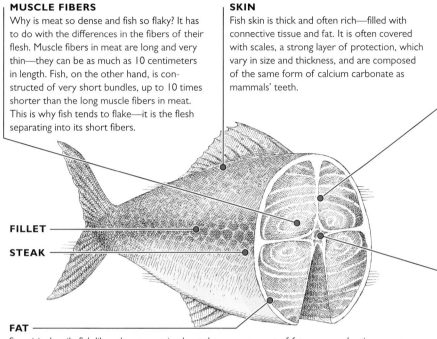

FILLET

STEAK

FAT

Surprisingly, oily fish like salmon contain about the same amount of fat per pound as ice cream. Good news: This fat is good for you. The fat in salmon—and all fish with dark flesh and a high oil content, such as mackerel, tuna, and anchovies—contains omega-3 fatty acids, which our bodies need to function properly. Because our bodies can't manufacture them, we have to get them from the food we eat. And some of the best sources of preformed omega-3s are fish and seafood.

BONES

Fish bones are delicate and distinctive, often consisting of a backbone and ribcage, with either bones leading out into fins, or many small pin bones supporting the connective tissue. Small bones in the flesh distract from the eating experience and are therefore best removed before cooking. However, cooking a whole fish on the bone can boost flavor and moisture.

BUYING

Whether it's a specialty seafood shop or a neighborhood supermarket, make sure the source is one with a high volume. High volume means high turnover, which ensures freshness. The store should smell like the sea, not fishy or sour.

The fish should be stored on ice or well refrigerated. If stored on ice, the fish shouldn't be sitting in water.

The flesh of fish should appear moist and shiny, not dull, and with even coloring. It should feel firm, not mushy. If possible, ask the fishmonger to press the flesh with a finger to confirm its texture.

Try to have the fishmonger slice steaks or fillets to order; it's best to avoid precut.

FREEZING FISH

How do the individually frozen fish from the freezer section compare to fresh fish sold at the fish counter? We gathered every type and brand of frozen fish we could find, defrosted them, and compared them to fresh fish. We found that doing a "quick thaw" by leaving the vacuum-sealed bags under cool running tap water for 30 minutes produced results identical to an overnight thaw in the refrigerator. We figured fresh fish would win by a landslide but found that with delicate, thin types of fish, like flounder or sole, it was almost impossible to tell the difference between fresh and frozen once cooked. (Be sure to thoroughly dry the fish before cooking.) For firm types of fish, like halibut, snapper, tilapia, and salmon, frozen versions were great when cooked beyond medium-rare. Cooked any less, they were dry and stringy. We don't recommend freezing cod, haddock, sea bass, tuna, or swordfish.

STORAGE

Fish stored at 32 degrees will keep twice as long as fish stored at the typical home refrigerator temperature of 40 degrees. To create the optimum storage conditions, place fish in a zipper-lock bag on ice (or cover with ice packs) and store it at the back of the refrigerator, where it's coldest. And remember to chill the fish immediately upon getting it home. If you live in a warm climate, you should consider keeping a cooler in your car trunk for transporting fish.

JUDGING DONENESS

An instant-read thermometer is a useful tool to check doneness in thick fillets, but with thin fillets you have to resort to a more primitive test—nicking the fish with a paring knife and then peeking into the interior to judge color and flakiness. White fish, such as cod, should be cooked to medium (140 degrees)—the flesh should be opaque but still moist and just beginning to flake; salmon is best cooked to medium-rare (125 degrees) with the center still translucent; and tuna is best when rare (110 degrees), with only the outer layer opaque and the rest of the fish translucent.

ENSURING EVEN COOKING

Fish fillets often come in odd-size pieces of uneven thickness. If your fillet has a thin, wide tailpiece, tuck it under before cooking to allow it to cook at the same rate as the thicker portion.

✔ WHY THIS RECIPE WORKS

There are two keys to cooking thick white fish fillets. First, a little sugar speeds the browning, thus creating more flavor. Second, a dual cooking method (starting on the stovetop and then transferring the fish, still in the skillet, to the oven) ensures even cooking.

START THICK Pan-roasting is the best way to cook fillets that are at least 1 inch thick. Thinner fillets can be cooked through on the stovetop.

SUGAR JUST ONE SIDE We find that searing one side of the fish is sufficient to develop the flavorful compounds associated with browning. Searing both sides of the fish yields tough, dry fillets. Sprinkling just ⅛ teaspoon of sugar on the side of the fish that is going to be seared makes a noticeable impact on browning without making the fish taste sweet.

LET THE OVEN DO THE WORK After the sugared side of the fish is seared (this will take just 60 to 90 seconds), flip the fillets over and put the skillet in a 425-degree oven to finish the cooking process. (The allover heat in the oven does a better job of cooking the fish evenly than the single-directional heat of the stovetop.) Higher oven temperatures will dry the fish out; at lower temperatures the fish won't brown as well.

PAN-SEARED SCALLOPS
SERVES 4

We recommend buying "dry" scallops, those without chemical additives. Dry scallops will look ivory or pinkish and feel tacky; wet scallops look bright white and feel slippery. If using wet scallops, soak them in a solution of 1 quart of cold water, ¼ cup of lemon juice, and 2 tablespoons of salt for 30 minutes before step 1, and do not season with salt in step 2. To remove the tendons from the scallops, simply peel away the small, rough-textured crescent-shaped tendon and discard. Serve the scallops with lemon wedges or a sauce (recipes follow). Prepare the sauce, if serving, while the scallops dry (between steps 1 and 2) and keep it warm while cooking them.

1½	pounds large sea scallops, tendons removed
	Salt and pepper
2	tablespoons vegetable oil
2	tablespoons unsalted butter
	Lemon wedges or sauce (recipes follow)

1. Place scallops on rimmed baking sheet lined with clean kitchen towel. Place second clean kitchen towel on top of scallops and press gently on towel to blot liquid. Let scallops sit at room temperature for 10 minutes while towels absorb moisture.

2. Sprinkle scallops on both sides with salt and pepper. Heat 1 tablespoon oil in 12-inch nonstick skillet over high heat until just smoking. Add half of scallops in single layer, flat side down, and cook, without moving, until well browned, 1½ to 2 minutes.

3. Add 1 tablespoon butter to skillet. Using tongs, flip scallops; continue to cook, using large spoon to baste scallops with melted butter (tilt skillet so butter runs to 1 side), until sides of scallops are firm and centers are opaque, 30 to 90 seconds longer (remove smaller scallops as they finish cooking). Transfer scallops to large plate and tent loosely with aluminum foil. Wipe out skillet with wad of paper towels and repeat cooking with remaining oil, scallops, and butter. Serve immediately with lemon wedges or sauce.

GINGER BUTTER SAUCE
MAKES ABOUT ¾ CUP, ENOUGH FOR 1 RECIPE
PAN-SEARED SCALLOPS

The richness of the cream and butter is balanced well by the bolder ingredients, like the cayenne and white wine vinegar, in this recipe.

½	cup dry white wine
2	tablespoons white wine vinegar
1	tablespoon grated fresh ginger
3	garlic cloves, minced
1	small shallot, minced
¼	cup heavy cream
12	tablespoons unsalted butter, cut into 12 pieces and chilled
½	teaspoon salt
	Pinch cayenne pepper

Combine wine, vinegar, ginger, garlic, and shallot in small saucepan and bring to boil over high heat. Lower heat to medium-high and simmer until mixture is reduced by half, about 5 minutes. Add cream and continue to simmer until mixture is reduced by half, 2 to 3 minutes longer. Strain mixture through fine-mesh strainer into small bowl; wipe out saucepan. Return mixture to saucepan set over medium heat. Whisk in 2 pieces of butter until melted. Continue adding butter, 2 pieces at a time, until all butter has been incorporated. Stir in salt and cayenne; cover and keep warm.

LEMON BROWNED BUTTER

MAKES ABOUT ¼ CUP, ENOUGH FOR I RECIPE
PAN-SEARED SCALLOPS

Watch the butter carefully, as it can go from brown to burnt quickly.

- 4 tablespoons unsalted butter, cut into 4 pieces
- I small shallot, minced
- I tablespoon minced fresh parsley
- ½ teaspoon minced fresh thyme
- 2 teaspoons lemon juice
  Salt and pepper

Heat butter in small saucepan over medium heat and cook, swirling pan constantly, until butter turns dark golden brown and has nutty aroma, 4 to 5 minutes. Add shallot and cook until fragrant, about 30 seconds. Remove pan from heat and stir in parsley, thyme, and lemon juice. Season with salt and pepper to taste. Cover to keep warm.

✔ WHY THIS RECIPE WORKS

A crisp, browned crust is the hallmark of a well-cooked scallop. In restaurants, they use powerful stoves and prepare just a few scallops at a time (for one order). At home, the burner output is weaker and you want to cook more scallops at once (at least enough to serve two people in each batch). We found that butter is the key to creating a flavorful browned crust as quickly as possible.

BUY BIG AND DRY It's much easier to brown big scallops (you have more time before they dry out). We recommend buying scallops that weigh at least an ounce each. Also, wicking away excess moisture with towels is key. We found it helpful to sandwich the scallops between two kitchen towels and leave them there for 10 minutes. Purchasing "dry" scallops that haven't been treated with a chemical solution also helps. If the scallops are sitting in a milky white solution, they are "wet." The chemical solution imparts an off-flavor to the scallops and makes it harder to get them really dry for sautéing. If you can, purchase scallops that appear sticky and dry—they taste better and will be easier to brown. If you can't find dry scallops in local markets, we recommend soaking wet scallops (see Practical Science sidebar on this page) to camouflage the off-flavor the chemical solution imparts. Make sure to blot the scallops well after they have been soaked and don't season them with salt before cooking. And if you are unsure whether your scallops are wet or dry, conduct this quick test: Place one scallop on a paper towel–lined, microwave-safe plate and microwave on high power for 15 seconds.

If the scallop is "dry," it will exude very little water. If it is "wet," there will be a sizable ring of moisture on the paper towel. (The microwaved scallop can be cooked as is.)

START WITH OIL, ADD BUTTER Butter contains milk proteins and the reducing sugar lactose that can enhance the Maillard reaction. We found that if we used butter alone to cook the scallops, it actually burned by the time the scallops were done. We had better luck when we heated oil in the pan, added the scallops, and then started basting them with butter about 90 seconds into the cooking time. Per our method, the scallops are flipped and continue cooking for another 30 to 90 seconds—just enough time for the butter to promote browning on the scallops without burning.

PRACTICAL SCIENCE
WHY SOME SCALLOPS SHOULD BE SOAKED

Mask the unpleasant flavor of STPP-treated scallops with lemon.

So-called wet scallops have been treated with sodium tripolyphosphate (STPP), which lends a disagreeable flavor. The scallops treated with STPP also contain much more moisture (that's the purpose of soaking the scallops in STPP and water—to add weight and "value" for the retailer). As a result, wet scallops tend to steam when cooked rather than brown. Could we get rid of the STPP by soaking the scallops in water?

We prepared three batches of wet scallops, soaking the first in a quart of water for 30 minutes, soaking the second for an hour, and leaving the third untreated. We then cooked each batch according to our recipe and sent them to a lab to be analyzed for STPP content.

The scallops soaked for 30 minutes had only about 10 percent less STPP than the untreated batch, and soaking for a full hour wasn't much better: Only about 11 percent of the STPP was removed. Tasters were still able to clearly identify an unpleasant chemical flavor in both soaked samples.

It turns out that the phosphates in STPP form a chemical bond with the proteins in scallops. The bonds are so strong that they prevent the STPP from being washed away, no matter how long the scallops are soaked. So, rather than try to remove the chemical taste from STPP-treated scallops, we masked it by soaking them in a solution of lemon juice, water, and salt for 30 minutes.

CHEMICAL COVER-UP
A lemon-flavored brine camouflages the off-taste of wet scallops.

Resting Meat Maximizes Juiciness

We've all had the impulse to slice and serve a piece of meat the second it exits the oven. After all, the internal temperature is just right. It looks beautiful. Why not? But as we've learned, heat causes a rapid exodus of water molecules from a piece of cooking meat and this can result in a dry, leathery texture. Resting, however, is an indispensable technique when it comes to maintaining maximum juiciness. Let's find out why.

HOW THE SCIENCE WORKS

Meat is mostly water. In fact, raw beef is about 75 percent water (the exact amount varies from cut to cut). The rest is protein and fat. Most of this water is referred to as "bound water" because the proteins in the meat trap the water molecules inside. As a result, a piece of raw beef will not shed liquid when you cut it up. However, if you slice into a just-cooked steak, suddenly a flood of juices will cover the cutting board. What's happening?

The protein that makes up muscle tissue in raw meat is similar to many bundles of wire, each surrounded by a covering of connective tissue. Each wire represents a single muscle cell called a muscle fiber. These fibers are made of many smaller structures called myofibrils, which in turn are made of protein molecules called actin and myosin. When red meat (as well as poultry) is heated, the linear protein molecules begin to chemically bond with each other, causing them to compress and contract, first in diameter and then in length. A single muscle fiber can shrink to as little as half of its original volume during the cooking process. When these proteins contract, they squeeze out part of the liquid trapped within their structures, which then moves into the spaces created between the shrinking myofibrils.

The process of muscle contraction explains why experienced chefs can determine the doneness of meat by pushing on it and judging the amount of resistance. The firmer the meat, the more shrinkage has occurred and the more cooked the meat will be. But the contraction process is at least partly reversible. If you allow cooked meat to rest, the proteins will relax, allowing some of the expelled moisture to move back in.

But back in where? Some of the proteins are doing more than shrinking when heated—they are dissolving. Resting allows the contracted proteins to relax and draw moisture back in where it is held by the dissolved proteins. As a result, rested meat will be able to hold on to more of its natural juices, making the meat seem less dry and more tender.

CROSS-SECTIONS OF A MUSCLE FIBER

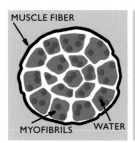

RAW *In raw meat, the majority of water is stored within individual muscle myofibrils.*

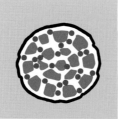

JUST COOKED *With intense heat, the water is squeezed out of the myofibrils into the spaces between.*

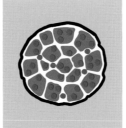

RESTED *While resting, some of the expelled water is reabsorbed by the relaxing myofibrils and fills the spaces once occupied by now-dissolved proteins.*

TEST KITCHEN EXPERIMENT

To demonstrate the effects of resting, we roasted five boneless pork loins, each weighing about 3.7 pounds, in a 400-degree oven until the internal temperature reached 140 degrees. One roast was cut crosswise into ½-inch-thick slices as soon as it came out of the oven. The other four roasts were tented with foil and allowed to rest for 10, 20, 30, and 40 minutes, respectively, before slicing. We collected any juices that accumulated during the resting period and separated them from juices that were lost during slicing. We repeated the experiment two more times and averaged the results.

THE RESULTS

The roasts that we sliced immediately after cooking shed an average of 10 tablespoons of liquid, both on the cutting board and on our serving platter. In contrast, the roasts that we allowed to rest for 10 minutes before carving shed an average of just 4 tablespoons of liquid. That's a 60 percent decrease in moisture loss by waiting 10 minutes to slice. The numbers continued to improve with extended resting time; the roasts that rested for 20, 30, and 40 minutes lost 2½ tablespoons, 1 tablespoon, and 2 teaspoons of juice, respectively.

Tasters described the roasts that had rested for at least 10 minutes as juicier and more tender, while the roasts sliced without resting were described as drier and tougher. Tasters could tell very little difference between roasts rested for 30 and 40 minutes.

THE TAKEAWAY

Resting helps meat hold on to moisture but there are a couple of caveats. While a longer resting time means more moisture reabsorption, the difference might not be significant enough to warrant the added time. For example, our 40-minute rested roasts retained a mere teaspoon more juices than the 30-minute roasts. The most dramatic decrease in moisture loss happens during the first 10 minutes of rest. The trick is to determine the optimal resting time.

The first consideration is the size of meat. While a big roast will still be hot after a 30-minute rest, a thin steak will be cold. Meat generally tastes best when it's above 100 degrees, so that limits how long to let meat rest.

The second factor to consider is cooking method. Two pieces of meat can be cooked to the same internal temperature while the surface temperature varies greatly. The more heat applied the bigger the difference between the two. As a result, meat cooked over high heat tends to benefit from a slightly longer resting period. The proteins at the surface are very hot and need more time to cool down, grabbing any available moisture that was not lost by evaporation.

SUGGESTED RESTING TIMES FOR MEAT

Here are some suggested resting times for various cuts of meat and poultry. Find the correct category for the cut you're preparing and then choose the shorter or longer time based on the cut's relative size. For instance, rest a small 2-pound beef tenderloin roast for 15 minutes but allow the full 30 minutes for a big prime rib.

BEEF	
Steaks	5 to 10 minutes
Roasts	15 to 30 minutes
LAMB	
Chops	5 to 10 minutes
Roasts	15 to 30 minutes
PORK	
Chops	5 to 10 minutes
Tenderloin	10 minutes
Roasts	15 to 30 minutes
CHICKEN	
Parts	5 to 10 minutes
Whole	15 to 20 minutes
TURKEY	
Parts	20 minutes
Whole	30 to 40 minutes

JUICES LOST WHEN ROASTS ARE SLICED AFTER COOKING

 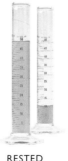   

| SLICED IMMEDIATELY | RESTED 10 MINUTES | RESTED 20 MINUTES | RESTED 30 MINUTES | RESTED 40 MINUTES |

The principle is the same across thousands of recipes: Meat and poultry should rest after cooking and before slicing or carving. This applies to any steak, chop, roast, or bird that has been roasted, grilled, broiled, or sautéed. We've chosen several simple recipes to illustrate this concept but resting is also a key step in the following recipes: Prime Rib (page 18), Roast Salted Turkey (page 110), and Roast Beef Tenderloin (page 59).

GRILLED FLANK STEAK WITH SPICE RUB
SERVES 4 TO 6

Flank steak is best when cooked medium-rare, or medium at most. It is very important for the meat to rest after it comes off the grill.

2	tablespoons ground cumin
2	tablespoons chili powder
1	tablespoon ground coriander
1	tablespoon kosher salt or 1½ teaspoons table salt
2	teaspoons pepper
½	teaspoon ground cinnamon
½	teaspoon red pepper flakes
1	(2½-pound) flank steak, trimmed

1A. FOR A CHARCOAL GRILL: Open bottom vent completely. Light large chimney starter filled with charcoal briquettes (6 quarts). When top coals are partially covered with ash, pour evenly over half of grill. Set cooking grate in place, cover, and open lid vent completely. Heat grill until hot, about 5 minutes.

1B. FOR A GAS GRILL: Turn all burners to high, cover, and heat grill until hot, about 15 minutes.

2. Clean and oil cooking grate. Combine spices and salt in a small bowl. Pat steak dry with paper towels and rub all over with spice mixture. Place steak directly on grill (hot side if using charcoal) and cook (covered if using gas) until well browned on first side, 4 to 7 minutes. Flip steak and continue to cook until meat registers 120 to 125 degrees (for medium-rare) or 130 to 135 degrees (for medium), 3 to 8 minutes. If necessary, slide steak to cooler part of grill (or lower heat on gas grill) to prevent spice rub from burning.

3. Transfer steak to cutting board, tent loosely with aluminum foil, and let rest for 10 minutes. Slice steak against grain on bias into ¼-inch-thick slices. Season with salt and pepper to taste, and serve immediately.

✔ WHY THIS RECIPE WORKS

Flank steak is a lean, relatively inexpensive cut, making it perfect for a quick weeknight dinner. However, flank steak can be tough if not handled correctly. What's the key to perfect flank steak? Not overcooking the meat, giving it a good rest, and slicing it properly.

RUB IN FLAVOR Marinades take time to work and all that liquid can slow down the browning process—which is an issue for such a thin steak that cooks quickly. We like the speed and ease of a spice rub. It flavors the steak instantly and helps create a really good crust on the steak when grilled. We've chosen a basic rub with Latin-inspired flavor but the basic formula can be varied endlessly. For fajitas (recipe follows), we lose the spice rub and simply season the steak with salt, pepper, and some fresh lime juice.

GIVE IT A REST Once the steak is done, transfer it to a cutting board, cover it loosely with foil (so it doesn't cool down excessively), and wait. Set a timer and come back 10 minutes later to start the slicing process. If you like, use the time to grill some vegetables to accompany the steak.

SLICE IT RIGHT It's important to slice the meat against the grain. On a flank steak, the grain runs from one rounded end to the other end, so you should slice across this steak. Slicing the meat across the grain shortens the long muscle fibers and diminishes chewiness in this cut. Cutting the meat into thin slices (about ¼ inch thick) also helps. Finally, angle the knife a bit to make each cut on the bias. Ideally, you will be holding the knife so that the blade forms a 45-degree angle with the cutting board. This technique produces wider, more attractive slices and likewise diminishes chewiness.

GRILLED BEEF FAJITAS
SERVES 4 TO 6

Flank steak is best when cooked medium-rare, or medium at most. It is also very important for the meat to rest after it comes off the grill. Use the time while the steak rests to grill the vegetables and warm the tortillas for this Tex-Mex classic. Serve with Fresh Guacamole (recipe follows), your favorite salsa, and/or sour cream.

1	(2- to 2½-pound) flank steak, trimmed
	Salt and pepper
¼	cup lime juice (2 limes)
1	large red onion, peeled and cut into ½-inch-thick rounds (do not separate rings)
2	large red or green bell peppers, cored, seeded, and cut into wedges
8–12	(6-inch) flour tortillas

IA. FOR A CHARCOAL GRILL: Open bottom vent completely. Light large chimney starter mounded with charcoal briquettes (7 quarts). When top coals are partially covered with ash, pour evenly over half of grill. Set cooking grate in place, cover, and open lid vent completely. Heat grill until hot, about 5 minutes.

IB. FOR A GAS GRILL: Turn all burners to high, cover, and heat grill until hot, about 15 minutes.

2. Clean and oil cooking grate. Pat steak dry with paper towels and sprinkle with lime juice, salt, and pepper. Place steak on grill (hot side if using charcoal) and cook (covered if using gas) until well browned on first side, 4 to 7 minutes. Flip steak and continue to cook until meat registers 120 to 125 degrees (for medium-rare) or 130 to 135 degrees (for medium), 3 to 8 minutes. Transfer steak to cutting board, tent loosely with aluminum foil, and let rest for 10 minutes.

3. While steak rests, place onion rounds and peppers (skin side down) on hot side of grill (if using charcoal) or turn all burners to medium (if using gas). Cook until tender and charred on both sides, 8 to 12 minutes, flipping every 3 minutes. Transfer onions and peppers to cutting board with beef.

4. Place tortillas in single layer on hot side of grill (if using charcoal) or turn all burners to low (if using gas). Cook until warm and lightly browned, about 20 seconds per side (do not grill too long or tortillas will become brittle). As tortillas are done, wrap them in kitchen towel or large sheet of foil.

5. Separate onion into rings and slice bell peppers into ¼-inch strips. Slice steak against grain on bias into ¼-inch-thick slices. Transfer beef and vegetables to serving platter and serve with warm tortillas.

FRESH GUACAMOLE

MAKES ABOUT 1½ CUPS, ENOUGH FOR 1 RECIPE GRILLED BEEF FAJITAS

The best guacamole recipe is a simple mixture of avocado, onion, garlic, chile, cilantro, and lime juice. For a pleasing texture, we mash some of the avocado while keeping the rest chunky.

2	small avocados
1	tablespoon minced red onion
1	small garlic clove, minced
½	small jalapeño chile, minced
2	tablespoons minced fresh cilantro
	Salt
1	tablespoon lime juice

1. Halve 1 avocado, remove pit, and scoop flesh into medium bowl. Using fork, mash lightly with onion, garlic, jalapeño, cilantro, and ⅛ teaspoon salt until just combined.

2. Halve and pit remaining avocado. Using dinner knife, carefully make ½-inch crosshatch incisions in flesh, cutting down to but not through skin. Using soup spoon, gently scoop flesh from skin; transfer to bowl with mashed avocado mixture. Sprinkle lime juice over and mix lightly with fork until combined but still chunky. Adjust seasoning with salt, if necessary, and serve. (Guacamole can be covered with plastic wrap, pressed directly onto surface of mixture, and refrigerated for up to 1 day. Return guacamole to room temperature, removing plastic wrap just before serving.)

✔ WHY THIS RECIPE WORKS

Though fajitas can be made with skirt steak, we prefer flank, which is incredibly tender when sliced thin and across the grain. As in our Grilled Flank Steak with Spice Rub recipe, it's imperative to let the meat rest after removing it from the grill—whether you spice it up or not.

AVOCADO EXTRACTION A key step in making fresh guacamole is removing the avocado flesh and dicing it without making a huge mess. To do this, first we slice the avocado in half lengthwise and remove the pit. Then we use a dish towel to hold it steady, making ½-inch crosshatch incisions in the flesh with a dinner knife, cutting down to but not through the skin. Separate the diced flesh from the skin using a spoon inserted between the skin and flesh, gently scooping out avocado cubes.

MAPLE-GLAZED PORK ROAST

SERVES 4 TO 6

In this recipe, the roast is coated with a sticky maple glaze as it rests. As the meat and glaze cool, the glaze will solidify a bit and create a burnished exterior on this simple roast. This dish is unapologetically sweet, so serve it with side dishes that take well to sweetness, such as garlicky sautéed greens, braised cabbage, or creamy polenta.

½	cup maple syrup, preferably grade B
⅛	teaspoon ground cinnamon
	Pinch ground cloves
	Pinch cayenne pepper
1	(2½-pound) boneless blade-end pork loin roast, tied at even intervals along length with 5 pieces butcher's twine
¾	teaspoon salt
½	teaspoon pepper
2	teaspoons vegetable oil

1. Adjust oven rack to middle position and heat oven to 325 degrees. Stir maple syrup, cinnamon, cloves, and cayenne together in measuring cup or small bowl; set aside. Pat roast dry with paper towels, then sprinkle evenly with salt and pepper.

2. Heat oil in 12-inch ovensafe skillet over medium-high heat until just beginning to smoke. Place roast fat side down in skillet and cook until well browned on all sides, 7 to 10 minutes, using tongs to turn roast. Transfer roast to large plate.

3. Reduce heat to medium and pour off fat from skillet. Add maple syrup mixture and cook until fragrant, about 30 seconds (syrup will bubble immediately). Off heat, return roast to skillet. Using tongs, roll to coat roast with glaze on all sides.

4. Place skillet in oven and roast until center of roast registers 140 degrees, 35 to 45 minutes, using tongs to roll and spin roast to coat with glaze twice during roasting time.

5. Using potholder (handle will be scorching hot), remove skillet from oven. Transfer roast to carving board and set skillet aside to cool slightly to thicken glaze, about 5 minutes. Being careful of hot handle, pour glaze over roast and let rest for 15 minutes longer. Snip twine off roast, cut into ½-inch slices, and serve immediately.

✔ WHY THIS RECIPE WORKS

Pork loin has very little fat and can be tough and dry if overcooked. The long resting time in this recipe ensures that the roast holds on to as much juice as possible while gently coming up to its final temperature of 150 degrees. (For more on the phenomenon of carry-over cooking, see concept 4.)

USE NATURAL PORK   Due to market demands, today's pork is bred to be 50 percent leaner than its counterpart in the 1950s and less fat means less flavor and moisture. The industry has addressed this issue by introducing a product called "enhanced pork"—meat injected with a solution of water, salt, and sodium phosphate. The idea is to both season the pork and prevent it from drying out. (The sodium phosphate increases the pH of the meat, which improves its water-retention abilities.) More than half of the fresh pork sold in supermarkets is now enhanced.

We've conducted countless tests comparing enhanced pork against natural pork and unilaterally prefer the latter. Natural pork has a better flavor and if cooked correctly, moisture isn't an issue. Also, we've found that enhanced pork often gives up much of the moisture added during the manufacturing process when the roast is sliced. In fact, in our tests with pork loins, enhanced roasts shed 50 percent more juices during slicing than natural roasts.

Manufacturers don't use the terms "enhanced" or "natural" on package labels, but if the pork has been enhanced it will have an ingredient list. Natural pork contains just pork and won't have an ingredient list.

Note that brining (see concept 11) can be a good option for natural pork in recipes where the pork can dry out. While natural pork sometimes benefits from brining, enhanced pork should never be brined; it's already pretty salty. In this recipe, the maple glaze keeps the pork plenty moist and there's no need to brine the meat.

TIE IT UP   Straight from the supermarket packaging, most pork loins will lie flat in the pan and cook unevenly. Tying the roast not only yields more attractive slices but also ensures that the roast will have the same thickness from end to end so that it cooks evenly. We like cotton or linen kitchen twine sold in most supermarkets, usually near the disposable baking pans.

PICK THE RIGHT MAPLE   Don't bother making this recipe with pancake syrup; only real maple syrup will do. The flavor of grade B maple syrup (sometimes called "cooking maple") is stronger and richer than grade A, but either will work in this recipe.

NONSTICK OR NOT?   A nonstick pan will be easier to clean, but this recipe can be tough on delicate nonstick surfaces. If using a traditional pan, let the pan cool completely and then bring a cup or two of water to a boil in the pan. The boiling water will loosen the glaze and make cleaning a snap. If using a nonstick pan, make sure to use tongs with nonstick-friendly nylon tips.

HANDLE WITH CARE   It's very economical to use the same pan to sear and cook the roast. However, the skillet will emerge from the oven with a scorching-hot handle. Make sure to use a very reliable oven mitt and consider leaving the mitt on the handle to remind yourself (and others in the kitchen) that the handle won't be safe to touch with bare hands for quite a while.

MEAT 101

STRUCTURE

What we call meat is actually muscle, taken from various parts of an animal. Whether it comes from a cow, pig, or lamb, meat consists primarily of muscle fibers, water, connective tissue, and fat.

MUSCLE FIBER

Each muscle contains thousands and thousands of individual muscle fibers that are very thin (even finer than human hair) and often several inches long. Each fiber is a single muscle cell composed of smaller units called myofibrils. The primary proteins in muscle fibers are called actin and myosin. Individual fibers are bundled together and wrapped in connective tissue—these are the thin strands visible as the "grain" in many cuts of meat.

WATER

Muscle fibers are saturated with water molecules. Lean meat is generally tender because of its high water content. (Most cuts contain about 75 percent water.) Most of the water is contained within the myofibrils that make up a single muscle cell. The remaining water is found in the spaces between individual muscle fibers. This water is especially prone to being lost when meat is cooked.

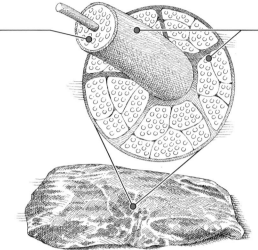

CONNECTIVE TISSUE

Bundles of muscle fibers are wrapped in a membranous, translucent film of protein that gives them structure and support. This thin, silvery film (which you can easily see when butchering a chuck roast or other cut with multiple muscles) also attaches muscles to the bone. Connective tissue is composed primarily of collagen, a sturdy protein that is quite tough to chew. Cuts from muscles that aren't used for mobility, such as the midsection, have very little collagen; however, muscles in the shoulder and hip area are filled with connective tissue, which must be broken down through prolonged cooking to make these cuts palatable.

FAT

Fat is produced and stored in a specialized form of connective tissue called adipose cells; the job of these cells is to store energy. There are two types of fat in most animals—the thick layer of fat that surrounds the muscles and the thin filaments that run through the muscles. The thick layer of fat that surrounds a steak, for instance, is generally removed during the butchering process so that only ¼ to ½ inch remains. The thin filaments of fat that run through the meat are called marbling and are a key factor in determining the flavor and perceived juiciness of a particular cut.

BUYING

For information on labeling and the purchase of various cuts of beef and pork, see "Shopping for Beef 101" on page 141 and "Shopping for Pork 101" on page 149.

STORAGE

REFRIGERATOR Keep meat in the coldest part of your refrigerator, generally in the back, where the temperature should be between 32 and 36 degrees. Place meat packages on plates to keep any condensation from dripping down onto other items in your refrigerator—this is especially important when defrosting meat.

FREEZER When meat is frozen, water vapor escapes from the food's surface, migrates through an air space in the package, and condenses on the inner surface of the package. The result is a piece of meat covered with ice crystals that can tear through the muscle tissue, what's commonly known as freezer burn. Freezer burn indicates a loss of moisture in the food and should be avoided. The food is still safe to eat, but the quality has suffered.

To prevent freezer burn, don't freeze meat in the store packaging. Wrap cuts individually in plastic (so they can be thawed separately) and then place each steak or chop in a large zipper-lock bag, pressing out all excess air. Defrost frozen meat according to the times below.

APPROXIMATE REFRIGERATOR DEFROSTING TIMES	
Thin steaks, chops, chicken breasts	8 to 12 hours
Thick steaks, chops, bone-in chicken parts, 1 pound ground beef	24 hours
Roasts, whole birds	5 hours per pound

SAFETY

There are two areas of concern when it comes to safely preparing meat: preventing cross-contamination that can occur before cooking (that is, transferring bacteria in meat to fruit, vegetables, or other foods that are not cooked) and proper cooking to kill any bacteria that may be present in the meat.

SAFER HANDLING Don't rinse meat before cooking. You aren't killing any bacteria and you may be spreading bacteria around your kitchen. To season meat without contaminating the salt box or pepper mill, mix a small amount of salt and pepper together in a small bowl and use this mixture to season the meat; discard any leftovers when you're done. After working with raw meat, wash all cutting boards, knives, kitchen surfaces, and your hands in hot, soapy water.

SAFER COOKING If safety were the only concern, you would cook all meat until well-done, or 160 degrees. Unfortunately, most cuts of meat are not very palatable when cooked this way. The risk of food-borne illness from steaks, roasts, and chops is fairly low because any bacteria present are located on the surface where the temperature will reach 160 degrees even if the internal temperature doesn't. Ground meat represents a much greater risk, especially if it is ground at a large beef processing facility. In that case, a single package of ground beef can contain meat from hundreds, if not thousands, of animals, increasing the odds of a problem. Buying beef that is ground to order at the market is a safer practice, as is grinding your own (see concept 14). Because of the risks associated with ground beef, you may want to cook it to 160 degrees.

Hot Food Keeps Cooking

You buy an expensive roast and monitor it carefully as it cooks. When the temperature in its center reaches 130 degrees—the standard published temperature for medium-rare beef—you take the roast out of the oven. Remembering that a roast needs to rest before slicing (see concept 3), you patiently wait. Five, 10, 15 minutes. After 20 minutes you begin to slice, only to find that the roast is a dull shade of gray and no longer pink at all. In fact, it appears to be cooked to medium, not medium-rare. What happened?

HOW THE SCIENCE WORKS

MOVEMENT OF HEAT

IN THE OVEN *Heat is hitting the exterior of the meat and moving by conduction toward the center.*

AT REST *Heat is rapidly exiting from the hot exterior but continuing to move toward the center, cooking the meat even further.*

Whether you enjoy your steak cooked rare, medium-rare, or well-done, most of us find the differences so significant that we send meat not cooked to our liking back to the kitchen when dining out. Since sending a steak back isn't an option when cooking at home, hitting the desired target spot-on is imperative. Five or 10 degrees can be the difference between meat that is pink and still juicy and meat that is gray and dry.

Unfortunately, judging when meat hits the desired target is tricky, in part because a big piece of meat doesn't have a single temperature. As we've learned, the exterior of the meat gets much hotter than the interior. Most recipes, however, are written based on the temperature in the dead center of the meat, far away from any bones (for more on bones and their effect on temperature, see concept 10). This makes sense: The internal temperature tells us when the entire roast is done. But what

many cooks don't understand is that because of how heat is transferred, food can continue to cook even after it has been removed from the heat source. This effect is called carryover cooking and is an important factor in determining when meat is ready to come out of the oven or off the grill.

As discussed in concept 1, conduction causes heat to move from a hotter to a cooler region within food. And as long as there is a difference in the temperature between the two regions—even after removing meat from the oven or off the grill—heat will continue to move from the surface to the center. This transfer will slow, and eventually stop, as internal and external temperatures approach each other and equal out. But this heat transfer can result in a significant 5- to 10-degree increase in the internal temperature of a large roast, bringing it from a perfect pink to a disappointing gray.

TEST KITCHEN EXPERIMENT

To demonstrate the effects of carryover cooking, we roasted four pork loins, varying both the internal temperature at which they were removed from the oven and the time allotted for carryover cooking. Two roasts were cooked until their internal temperature reached 140 degrees; we sliced one roast right away and let the other roast rest for 15 minutes before slicing, sticking a thermometer probe in its center so we could track its internal temperature during the resting period. The other two roasts were cooked to an internal temperature of 150 degrees; we sliced one of these roasts right away and let the other roast rest for 15 minutes before slicing, tracking its internal temperature as it rested as well.

THE RESULTS

Let's start with the two roasts cooked to 140 degrees. The roast that was sliced right away lost significantly more juice than the roast that was rested for 15 minutes (see concept 3). We also noted that the roast sliced right away was very pink—in fact, it seemed underdone. In contrast, the roast that rested for 15 minutes was perfectly cooked with just a faint tinge of pink. The temperature of this roast had risen to 150 degrees during the resting period, and those 10 degrees made a big difference.

The results were similar for the two roasts cooked to 150 degrees. The roast sliced right away seemed perfectly cooked but we lost a lot of juice to the carving board. The rested roast shed less juice but its internal temperature had risen to 160 degrees during the resting period and the meat was gray (no pink here).

In conclusion, we think lean pork is best served at 150 degrees. There are two ways to get there—cook to the desired temperature and slice immediately, or undercook the meat slightly and let carryover cooking do the rest of the work. The advantage to the second method is clear: The meat will also reabsorb moisture during this combination of resting and carryover cooking, resulting in a juicier, perfectly cooked roast.

THE TAKEAWAY

When it comes to red meat, including pork, judging doneness, even with a thermometer, involves some guesswork. That's because you aren't judging whether the food is ready to eat, but whether it will be ready to eat once it has rested. So how do you do this? There are two factors to keep in mind: the size of the roast and the heat level during cooking. A larger roast will absorb more heat than a thin steak and so there's more heat in the meat and a greater amount of carryover cooking that's possible. Likewise, meat cooked in a 400-degree oven absorbs more heat than meat cooked in a 200-degree oven, so carryover cooking is greater in a roast cooked in a hot oven.

To make this a bit easier, we've put together the following chart. Use the lower number in the "stop cooking" column when cooking large cuts or using a lot of heat; use the higher number in the "stop cooking" column for thin cuts or when using moderate heat. Note that in the test kitchen we generally cook beef to medium-rare and pork to medium.

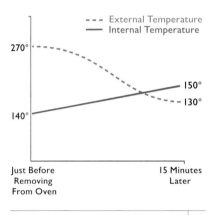

CHARTING TEMPERATURE OF MEAT

Just before the pork roast left the oven, its exterior registered 270 degrees while its interior had just reached 140 degrees. With time, however, the internal temperature continued to rise as the surface heat rapidly depleted. After 15 minutes, the internal temperature reached 150 degrees, surpassing the 130 degrees of the exterior.

ACCOUNTING FOR CARRYOVER COOKING

IF YOU WANT	STOP COOKING WHEN TEMPERATURE REACHES	SO FINAL SERVING TEMPERATURE IS
Rare Beef or Lamb	115° to 120°	125°
Medium-Rare Beef or Lamb	120° to 125°	130°
Medium Beef or Lamb	130° to 135°	140°
Well-Done Beef or Lamb	150° to 155°	160°
Medium Pork	140° to 145°	150°
Well-Done Pork	150° to 155°	160°

Carryover cooking can be a significant factor on the grill, especially when there is a big fire producing a lot of heat. In order not to overshoot doneness, grilled meats are generally pulled off the grill 5 to 10 degrees before they hit the ideal temperature. Since grill fires are so unpredictable, make sure to check the meat early. You can see the principle of carryover cooking at work in the following other meat recipes: Grilled Argentine Steaks with Chimichurri Sauce (page 29), Maple-Glazed Pork Roast (page 39), Pan-Seared Thick-Cut Pork Chops (page 57), and Slow-Roasted Pork Shoulder (page 66).

GRILL-ROASTED BEEF TENDERLOIN

SERVES 10 TO 12

Once trimmed, and with the butt tenderloin (the lobe at the large end of the roast) still attached, the roast should weigh 4½ to 5 pounds. If you purchase an already-trimmed tenderloin without the butt tenderloin attached, begin checking for doneness about five minutes early. When using a charcoal grill, we prefer wood chunks to wood chips whenever possible; substitute two medium wood chunks, soaked in water for one hour, for the wood chip packet (if using). Serve with Romesco Sauce (recipe follows).

1	(6-pound) beef tenderloin, trimmed, tail end tucked, and tied with kitchen twine at 2-inch intervals
1½	tablespoons kosher salt
2	cups wood chips, soaked in water for 15 minutes and drained (optional)
2	tablespoons olive oil
1	tablespoon pepper

1. Pat tenderloin dry with paper towels and rub with salt. Cover loosely with plastic wrap and let sit at room temperature for 1 hour.

2. Using large piece of heavy-duty aluminum foil, wrap soaked wood chips, if using, in foil packet and cut several vent holes in top.

3A. FOR A CHARCOAL GRILL: Open bottom vent halfway. Light large chimney starter filled with charcoal briquettes (6 quarts). When top coals are partially covered with ash, pour evenly over half of grill. Place wood chip packet, if using, on coals. Set cooking grate in place, cover, and open lid vent halfway. Heat grill until hot and wood chips are smoking, about 5 minutes.

3B. FOR A GAS GRILL: Place wood chip packet, if using, opposite primary burner. Turn all burners to high, cover, and heat grill until hot and wood chips are smoking, about 15 minutes. Leave primary burner on high and turn other burner(s) off. (Adjust primary burner as needed during cooking to maintain grill temperature of around 350 degrees.)

4. Clean and oil cooking grate. Rub tenderloin with oil and season with pepper. Place roast on hot side of grill and cook (covered if using gas) until well browned on all sides, 8 to 10 minutes, turning as needed. (If flare-ups occur, move roast to cooler side of grill until flames die down.)

5. Move roast to cooler side of grill, cover (position lid vent over meat if using charcoal), and cook until meat registers 115 to 120 degrees (for rare) or 120 to 125 degrees (for medium-rare), 15 to 30 minutes.

6. Transfer tenderloin to carving board, tent loosely with foil, and let rest for 15 minutes. Remove twine, cut into ½-inch-thick slices, and serve.

ROMESCO SAUCE

MAKES ABOUT 2 CUPS, ENOUGH FOR 1 RECIPE
GRILL-ROASTED BEEF TENDERLOIN

This sauce can be refrigerated in an airtight container for up to two days; bring to room temperature before serving and stir to combine.

1–2	slices hearty white sandwich bread, crusts removed, bread lightly toasted and cut into ½-inch pieces (½ cup)
3	tablespoons slivered almonds, toasted
1¾	cups jarred roasted red peppers, drained
1	small ripe tomato, cored, seeded, and chopped
2	tablespoons extra-virgin olive oil
1½	tablespoons sherry vinegar
1	large garlic clove, minced
¼	teaspoon cayenne pepper
	Salt

Process bread and almonds in food processor until nuts are finely ground, 10 to 15 seconds. Add red peppers, tomato, oil, vinegar, garlic, cayenne, and ½ teaspoon salt. Process, scraping down side of bowl as necessary, until mixture has texture similar to mayonnaise, 20 to 30 seconds. Season with salt to taste and transfer to serving bowl.

✔ WHY THIS RECIPE WORKS

This recipe is very simple. Start with an evenly shaped tenderloin, sear it on all sides to create a browned crust, and then cook the meat on a cool part of the grill. The cover turns the grill into an ovenlike environment that cooks the roast evenly.

SALT EARLY Salting the meat an hour before cooking improves its flavor. (For more on this phenomenon, see concept 12.)

TIE IT UP The key to cooking meat well generally starts at the supermarket: It's best to choose steaks or chops that are the same thickness so they are all done at the same time. But the thickness of a whole beef tenderloin varies dramatically, so shopping can't help here. In fact, the thick end can measure twice as large as the thin end. To promote even cooking, tuck the thin tail end back toward the center of the roast and tie the roast in 2-inch intervals to create a neat cylinder with a uniform thickness.

CREATE A TWO-LEVEL FIRE You can't simply throw a 5-pound roast over a roaring fire and cook it until well browned—that is, unless you like a bloody interior. Waiting for the interior to come up to the necessary temperature means that the exterior will blacken. The solution is what we call a two-level fire, with all the coals banked on one side of the grill. (On a gas grill, you can turn off some burners once the grill has been preheated.) You now have two cooking zones—one that is very hot and designed for browning, and another, more moderately heated area, where there's little browning but enough heat to keep cooking the interior of the meat.

SEAR, THEN ROAST To develop flavor (and jump-start the Maillard reaction), the roast is seared over the hot fire on all four sides. Once a browned crust has formed, the roast is moved to the cooler part of the grill and then roasted with the grill cover on. In effect, the grill becomes an oven. Searing then roasting also means that the roast is exposed to less heat during the crucial last stages of cooking, thus the window between perfectly cooked and over-cooked will be a bit longer since the roast is heating more gradually at this point in the cooking process.

LET IT REST To account for the effects of carryover cooking, we find it necessary to remove the tenderloin when it is 5 to 10 degrees below the ideal finished temperature. So, for a rare roast that should be 125 degrees when sliced, we remove the roast from the grill when the internal temperature is just 115 to 120 degrees. During the 15-minute resting time, the roast finishes cooking and the muscle fibers relax and are able to reabsorb most of the juices in the meat.

GRILLED RACK OF LAMB
SERVES 4 TO 6

We prefer the milder taste and bigger size of domestic lamb, but you may substitute lamb from New Zealand or Australia. Since imported racks are generally smaller, follow the shorter cooking times given in the recipe. While most lamb is sold frenched (meaning part of each rib bone is exposed), chances are there will still be some extra fat between the bones. Remove the majority of this fat, leaving an inch at the top of the small eye of meat. Also, make sure that the chine bone (along the bottom of the rack) has been removed to ensure that it will be easy to cut between the ribs after cooking. Ask the butcher to do it; it's very hard to cut off at home.

1	(13 by 9-inch) disposable aluminum pan (if using charcoal)
4	teaspoons olive oil
4	teaspoons minced fresh rosemary
2	teaspoons minced fresh thyme
2	garlic cloves, minced
2	(1½- to 1¾-pound) racks of lamb (8 ribs each), frenched and trimmed
	Salt and pepper

1A. FOR A CHARCOAL GRILL: Open bottom vent completely and place pan in center of grill. Light large chimney starter filled with charcoal briquettes (6 quarts). When top coals are partially covered with ash, pour into 2 even piles on either side of pan. Set cooking grate in place, cover, and open lid vent completely. Heat grill until hot, about 5 minutes.

1B. FOR A GAS GRILL: Turn all burners to high, cover, and heat grill until hot, about 15 minutes. Leave primary burner on high and turn other burner(s) off.

2. Clean and oil cooking grate. Combine 1 tablespoon oil, rosemary, thyme, and garlic in bowl. Pat lamb dry with paper towels, rub with remaining teaspoon oil, and season with salt and pepper. Place racks bone side up on cooler part of grill, with meaty side of racks very close to, but not quite over, hot coals or lit burner. Cover and cook until meat is lightly browned, faint grill marks appear, and fat has begun to render, 8 to 10 minutes.

3. Flip racks over, bone side down, and move to hotter parts of grill. Cook until well browned, 3 to 4 minutes. Brush racks with herb mixture. Flip racks bone side up and continue to cook until well browned, 3 to 4 minutes longer. Stand racks up and lean them against each other; continue to cook (over 1 hotter side of grill if using charcoal) until bottom is well browned and meat registers 120 to 125 degrees (for medium-rare) or 130 to 135 degrees (for medium), 3 to 8 minutes longer.

4. Transfer lamb to carving board, tent loosely with aluminum foil, and let rest for 15 minutes. Cut between ribs to separate chops and serve.

GRILLED RACK OF LAMB WITH SWEET MUSTARD GLAZE

Omit rosemary and add 3 tablespoons Dijon mustard, 2 tablespoons honey, and ½ teaspoon grated lemon zest to oil, thyme, and garlic. Reserve 2 tablespoons glaze, then brush racks as directed in step 3 and brush with reserved glaze while meat rests.

✔ WHY THIS RECIPE WORKS

Lamb and the grill have great chemistry. The intense heat of the coals produces a great crust and melts away the meat's abundance of fat, distributing flavor throughout, while imparting a smokiness that's the perfect complement to lamb's rich, gamy flavor. Because of the high heat of the sear, the outer surface of the lamb cooks far faster than the interior of the meat. Therefore, wait a good

15 minutes after the rack is removed from the grill before slicing between the rib bones and serving.

TRIM THE FAT The key to lamb's unique flavor and tenderness is its high proportion of fat, most of which covers one side of the rack like a cap. We know from experience that leaving on the fat leads to aggressive flare-ups over hot coals, virtually as soon as the lamb is placed on the grill. We don't want to remove all the fat because this would leave us with a dry rack with little flavor, though. Therefore, we leave a thin layer of fat over the loin and remove most of the fat between the bones. This means that we still have the superb lamb taste, but with less grease and fire.

BUILD A TWO-LEVEL FIRE In order to avoid charring the meat and causing way too many fat flare-ups, we build a modified two-level fire with no coals (or lit burners) in part of the grill. In a charcoal grill, we do this by piling the coals on either side of the grill and placing an aluminum pan directly between the two mounds. This way, the outer edges of the grill are the hottest, and we're able to cook the lamb more gently and evenly in the center. For a gas grill, we've found that it's possible to leave just one burner on high and turn the others off. When the lamb cooks over the pan (in a charcoal grill) or over the turned-off burners (in a gas grill), there's no chance of flare-ups.

REVERSE THE COOKING ORDER Traditionally, we sear lamb over high heat to develop flavor and browning and then finish cooking it at a gentler heat to promote tenderness and juiciness. Here, we found that searing first caused the ample fat to flare up on the grill, however. What to do? We reversed the order. Cooking lamb on the cooler part of the grill first allows the fat to render. Once that fat is sufficiently rendered, we move the racks to direct heat to brown the exterior. The result is a rack of lamb that is pink and juicy, with a well-browned crust that contrasts nicely with the lush, ultra-tender exterior. (And no towering inferno.)

USE A WET RUB Our goal in seasoning the lamb was to enhance its already-wonderful flavor without overwhelming it. We tried a number of things, including a marinade and a dry rub, but we found that the best option is a wet rub consisting of garlic and a couple of robust herbs (rosemary and thyme) mixed with a little oil (just enough to adhere the flavorings to the lamb without causing flare-ups). Brushed on the racks as they brown over the direct heat, the wet rub adds just the right note to the perfectly cooked meat.

The principle of carryover cooking is at work in most meat recipes, but the concept has applications in egg cookery, too. Many egg-based desserts that are baked, including cheesecake and crème brûlée, rely on a similar principle. (For more on these recipes, see concept 19.) In these recipes, there's a relatively narrow window between perfectly cooked and overcooked. In many instances, you purposely underbake the dessert slightly with the expectation that the eggs will continue to cook (and solidify) as the dessert cools. Pumpkin pie is a classic example—most recipes instruct the cook to bake the pie until the outer ring of filling is set but the center still jiggles a bit. If you continue to bake the pie until the center is set, the outer ring will be overcooked and curdled. Removing the pie before the center is set allows carryover cooking to finish the job gently. By the time the pie cools, the center will set up nice and firm. In egg cookery, a frittata is an easy way to see this principle at work.

ASPARAGUS, HAM, AND GRUYÈRE FRITTATA
SERVES 6 TO 8

A 12-inch ovensafe nonstick skillet is necessary for this recipe. Because broilers vary so much in intensity, watch the frittata carefully as it cooks.

12	large eggs
3	tablespoons half-and-half
½	teaspoon salt
¼	teaspoon pepper
2	teaspoons olive oil
8	ounces asparagus, trimmed and cut on bias into ¼-inch pieces
4	ounces ¼-inch-thick deli ham, cut into ½-inch cubes (¾ cup)
1	shallot, minced
3	ounces Gruyère cheese, cut into ¼-inch cubes (¾ cup)

1. Adjust oven rack 5 inches from broiler element and heat broiler. Whisk eggs, half-and-half, salt, and pepper together in medium bowl. Set aside.

2. Heat oil in 12-inch ovensafe nonstick skillet over medium heat until shimmering. Add asparagus and cook, stirring occasionally, until lightly browned and almost tender, about 3 minutes. Add ham and shallot and cook until shallot softens, about 2 minutes.

3. Stir Gruyère into eggs; add egg mixture to skillet and cook, using spatula to stir and scrape bottom of skillet,

until large curds form and spatula begins to leave a wake but eggs are still very wet, about 2 minutes. Shake skillet to distribute eggs evenly and cook without stirring to let bottom set, about 30 seconds.

4. Slide skillet under broiler and cook until surface is puffed and spotty brown, yet center remains slightly wet and runny when cut into with paring knife, 3 to 4 minutes. Using potholder (skillet handle will be hot), remove skillet from oven and let stand for 5 minutes to finish cooking; using spatula, loosen frittata from skillet and slide it onto platter or cutting board. Cut into wedges and serve.

LEEK, PROSCIUTTO, AND GOAT CHEESE FRITTATA
SERVES 6 TO 8

A 12-inch ovensafe nonstick skillet is necessary for this recipe. The goat cheese will crumble more easily if it is chilled.

12	large eggs
3	tablespoons half-and-half
	Salt and pepper
2	tablespoons unsalted butter
1	pound leeks, white and light green parts only, halved lengthwise, sliced thin, and washed thoroughly
3	ounces very thinly sliced prosciutto, cut into ½-inch-wide strips
¼	cup chopped fresh basil
4	ounces goat cheese, crumbled (1 cup)

1. Adjust oven rack 5 inches from broiler element and heat broiler. Whisk eggs, half-and-half, ½ teaspoon salt, and ¼ teaspoon pepper together in medium bowl. Set aside.

2. Melt butter in 12-inch ovensafe nonstick skillet over medium heat. Add leeks and ¼ teaspoon salt; reduce heat to low and cook, covered, stirring occasionally, until softened, 8 to 10 minutes.

3. Stir prosciutto, basil, and ½ cup goat cheese into eggs; add egg mixture to skillet and cook, using spatula to stir and scrape bottom of skillet, until large curds form and spatula begins to leave a wake but eggs are still very wet, about 2 minutes. Shake skillet to distribute eggs evenly and cook without stirring to let bottom set, about 30 seconds.

4. Distribute remaining ½ cup goat cheese evenly over frittata. Slide skillet under broiler and cook until surface is

puffed and spotty brown, yet center remains slightly wet and runny when cut into with paring knife, 3 to 4 minutes. Using potholder (skillet handle will be hot), remove skillet from oven and let stand for 5 minutes to finish cooking; using spatula, loosen frittata from skillet and slide it onto platter or cutting board. Cut into wedges and serve.

✔ WHY THIS RECIPE WORKS

In most egg recipes, the volume of ingredients is limited so heat conduction is fairly even. However, if you take 12 eggs and cook them in a large pan with several cups of vegetables, meat, and cheese to create a thick, hearty frittata, heat conduction starts to be a problem. The exterior of the frittata will set long before the interior. You can keep cooking the eggs, but because the bottom of the frittata is in direct contact with the hot pan it becomes tough and dry, and may even burn.

STIR AT FIRST Our first discovery was to stir the frittata from the outset. (Most recipes say to leave the eggs alone so they can set.) This helps promote even cooking and allows the large volume of eggs to set very quickly.

Once the eggs have actually set but still appear very wet, we stop stirring so a cohesive frittata can form.

TRY THE BROILER Rather than continuing to heat the frittata from the bottom up, we move the skillet to the broiler once the eggs have begun to set and allow the heat to cook the frittata from the top. After just three or four minutes under the broiler, the top browns and puffs, giving the appearance of a perfect frittata.

FINISH COOKING ON RACK Even though the top and bottom are nicely browned, the center of the 2-inch-thick frittata may still be runny. More time on the stovetop or under the broiler is not an option. Almost by luck, we realized that carryover cooking could solve the problem. After its time on both the stovetop and under the broiler, the pan is incredibly hot and hard to handle. Letting the frittata rest for five minutes on a cooling rack allows carryover cooking to firm up the center of the frittata without any risk of scorching the top or bottom. In addition, the pan cools a bit, so getting the frittata onto a serving platter is less daunting.

CARRYOVER COOKING AT WORK FISH

Carryover cooking can't always be used to the cook's advantage. For example, seared tuna needs to stay in the pan long enough to develop a good crust, but by the time that happens the interior is already rare (that is, perfectly cooked). You can't pull the tuna out of the pan any earlier, so our advice is to slice the fish as soon as it comes out of the pan. Unlike meat and poultry, which must rest before slicing, fish can be sliced immediately with no ill effects. Either way, fish won't lose juices like meat or poultry. So all you're doing by slicing immediately is speeding up the cooling process and thus preventing carryover cooking from having much of an effect.

PAN-SEARED SESAME-CRUSTED TUNA STEAKS
SERVES 4

If you plan to serve the fish with the sauce or salsa (recipes follow), prepare it before cooking the fish. Most members of the test kitchen staff prefer their tuna steaks rare to medium-rare; the cooking times given in this recipe are for tuna steaks cooked to these two degrees of doneness. For tuna steaks cooked medium, observe

the timing for medium-rare, then tent the steaks loosely with foil for five minutes before slicing. If you prefer tuna steaks cooked so rare that they are still cold in the center, try to purchase steaks that are 1½ inches thick and cook them according to the timing below for rare steaks. Bear in mind, though, that the cooking times below are estimates; check for doneness with an instant-read thermometer.

¾   cup sesame seeds
4   (8-ounce) tuna steaks, preferably yellowfin, about 1 inch thick
2   tablespoons vegetable oil
    Salt and pepper

1. Spread sesame seeds in shallow baking dish or pie plate. Pat tuna steaks dry with paper towel; rub 1 tablespoon oil over steaks, then sprinkle them with salt and pepper. Press both sides of each steak in sesame seeds to coat.

2. Heat remaining 1 tablespoon oil in 12-inch nonstick skillet over high heat until just beginning to smoke. Add tuna steaks and cook for 30 seconds without moving steaks. Reduce heat to medium-high and continue to

cook until seeds are golden brown, about 1½ minutes. Using tongs, flip tuna steaks carefully and cook, without moving them, until golden brown on second side and centers register 110 degrees (for rare), about 1½ minutes, or 125 degrees (for medium-rare), about 3 minutes. Cut into ¼-inch-thick slices and serve immediately.

GINGER-SOY SAUCE WITH SCALLIONS

MAKES ABOUT 1 CUP, ENOUGH FOR 1 RECIPE PAN-SEARED SESAME-CRUSTED TUNA STEAKS

If available, serve pickled ginger and wasabi, passed separately, with the tuna and this sauce.

¼	cup soy sauce
¼	cup rice vinegar
¼	cup water
1	scallion, sliced thin
2½	teaspoons sugar
2	teaspoons grated fresh ginger
1½	teaspoons toasted sesame oil
½	teaspoon red pepper flakes

Combine all ingredients in small bowl, stirring to dissolve sugar.

PRACTICAL SCIENCE
WHEN CARRYOVER COOKING MUST BE STOPPED

For rare tuna, slice the steak immediately after cooking.

These two tuna steaks were cooked in the same pan for the same amount of time. The piece on the left was cut immediately after it was removed from the pan; the center is rare. The piece on the right was placed on a plate and covered loosely with foil for 10 minutes before slicing; the center of this steak has cooked to medium because of carryover cooking. The heat that the steak has picked up from the pan continues to cook the tuna while it rests. If you want your tuna rare, slice the steak as soon as it is removed form the pan to release the internal heat.

SLICED 1 MINUTE AFTER COOKING   SLICED 10 MINUTES AFTER COOKING

AVOCADO-ORANGE SALSA

MAKES ABOUT 1 CUP, ENOUGH FOR 1 RECIPE PAN-SEARED SESAME-CRUSTED TUNA STEAKS

To keep the avocado from discoloring, prepare this salsa just before you cook the tuna steaks.

1	large orange
1	avocado, halved, pitted, and diced medium
2	tablespoons minced red onion
2	tablespoons minced fresh cilantro
4	teaspoons lime juice
1	small jalapeño chile, stemmed, seeded, and minced
	Salt

1. Cut ½ inch off top and bottom of orange. Set orange on cut side on cutting board. Working from top to bottom, cut away peel and pith in large strips, following contours of fruit. Remove flesh in wedge-shaped segments by cutting on both sides of white membrane; cut segments into ½-inch pieces.

2. Combine all ingredients, including salt to taste, in small bowl.

✔ WHY THIS RECIPE WORKS

Developing a crust is the main challenge when searing tuna. Restaurant chefs solve this problem by using extra-thick pieces of tuna. But most supermarkets don't sell 2-inch tuna steaks. If you want rare tuna (and you should), supermarket tuna steaks (usually about 1 inch thick) can stay in the pan for only three minutes. That's hardly enough time to create a crisp contrast to the tender interior.

HOT OIL, HOT PAN In order to create a crust as quickly as possible, the pan and the oil must be very hot. Make sure to heat the oil until it just begins to smoke. As with any fish recipe, a nonstick pan is essential.

SESAME SEEDS MAKE CRUNCHY CRUST Sesame seeds form a crunchy crust with a neutral flavor that doesn't overwhelm the fish. (When we tested peppercorns and other whole spices, tasters liked the results but complained that the tuna was now playing second fiddle.) Rubbing the fish with oil helps the sesame seeds to adhere.

Some Proteins Are Best Cooked Twice

While home cooks tend to think of recipes as either "stovetop" or "oven," it's different in restaurants. Professional chefs often move food back and forth from one heat source to the other—and not just for show. The stovetop is ideal for quick browning, but with heat from a single direction it's difficult to cook food evenly and preserve moisture. One solution is to open the oven.

HOW THE SCIENCE WORKS

When preparing meat and other proteins, we all struggle to balance flavor development with moisture retention. As a result, sometimes the use of two cooking methods is absolutely necessary. There are a couple of solutions to explore.

Sear and then roast is one. As we learned in the first concepts in this book, the high heat of the stovetop develops color and flavor, while the oven allows the meat's interior to come up to temperature with ease. Coupling these techniques prevents scorching and excess moisture loss.

After all, an oven is a relatively inefficient heat conductor. A 12-inch conventional skillet set over medium-high heat on a gas burner will reach 400 degrees in less than five minutes while an identical pan heated indirectly by the air of a 400-degree oven will take 30 minutes to reach the same temperature. As a result, cooking vessels in the oven are generally cooler than those on the stovetop, and a cooler vessel means less heat transfer and therefore less moisture loss.

While it's common to sear and then roast, it's also possible to flip the order. Both techniques accomplish the same thing, but when cooking very thick steaks and chops it makes sense to roast before the sear. Why?

Let's start with basic thermodynamics: When a 40-degree steak is placed in a 400-degree skillet, the temperature of the pan drops significantly. Until the temperature recovers to at least 300 degrees (necessary for rapid Maillard reaction), little browning will occur. Therefore, it can take more than four minutes per side to form a good crust on a cold, thick steak—during which time the meat beneath the surface is robbed of moisture as it swings way above 160 degrees. It's difficult to make the pan hotter than 450 degrees when cooking with oil due to its smoke point, but you can change the temperature of the meat.

Warming meat in an oven before searing accomplishes three things. The meat doesn't cool down a hot pan the way it would straight from the refrigerator. As a result, the pan stays hot enough for browning to commence almost immediately. Second, the oven-warming period evaporates some surface moisture, so there's less to be converted to steam before the browning process can begin. With less time in the pan, less heat is absorbed, and the meat just below the surface is not overcooked. Finally, the gentle heat of the slow warming stage in the oven activates enzymes called cathepsins, which produce more tender meat (see concept 6 for more on this topic).

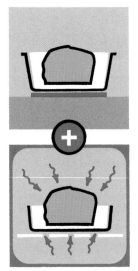

INTENSE HEAT FOR FLAVOR, GENTLE HEAT FOR MOISTURE

STOVETOP PLUS OVEN
The intense heat of the burner on a stovetop does allow quick development of flavor, but also more moisture loss. The slower, less efficient heat of the oven does not promote quick browning but helps to keep the meat moist and juicy.

TEST KITCHEN EXPERIMENT

To understand how cooking method affects moisture loss, we cooked boneless, skinless chicken breasts on the stovetop and compared moisture loss in these samples to moisture loss in identical breasts cooked to the same internal temperature, but seared on the stovetop and finished in the oven. We placed three 8-ounce breasts in a large skillet (nonstick, so we could see the results on the chicken, not the pan), set it over medium-high heat with 2 teaspoons of vegetable oil, and seared the chicken until it registered 160 degrees, flipping the breasts halfway through cooking. We also seared three more 8-ounce chicken breasts using the same method, but we transferred the skillet to a 400-degree oven after flipping. We repeated the tests and averaged the results.

THE RESULTS

First off, we noticed significant visual differences. The chicken on the stovetop was much darker in color (verging on burnt) than the chicken that spent half its time in the oven. This was due to the temperature of the skillet, which we tracked for both cooking methods. While the skillet that moved from the stovetop to the oven never got above 300 degrees, the skillet on the stovetop continued to climb to over 450 degrees. Interestingly, both samples reached 160 degrees in roughly 20 minutes. This is because while the bottom of the stovetop samples received intense heat from the skillet, the side not in contact with the pan received little heat. In contrast, the samples cooked partially in the oven absorbed moderate heat from all sides. So even though the oven was set to 400 degrees, the heat transfer on the stovetop was much more focused and efficient, thus the greater degree of browning. Browning, however, is only half the story.

When tasters sampled the chicken, they found samples cooked on the stovetop more flavorful. But tasters also noted that this chicken seemed drier and tougher than the chicken that finished cooking in the oven.

The before-and-after weights told the story here. Moisture loss was about 25 percent in

THE EFFECT OF COOKING METHOD ON MOISTURE LOSS IN CHICKEN BREASTS

	SEARED ON STOVETOP	SEARED ON STOVETOP, ROASTED IN OVEN
Weight before cooking	7.18 ounces	7.17 ounces
Weight after cooking	5.36 ounces	5.82 ounces
Moisture loss	25.35%	18.8%

the breasts cooked on the stovetop but 19 percent in those cooked partially on the stovetop and partially in the oven. These percentages translate into an extra tablespoon of juices in each of the combination-cooked breasts.

THE TAKEAWAY

Searing is a great way to add flavor because it delivers focused heat quickly and efficiently and thus promotes a lot of browning in a minimum of time. But it also causes a lot of moisture loss. Roasting small cuts yields food with spotty browning and flavor development but higher levels of moisture retention. Combining the methods offers the best of both worlds.

PRACTICAL SCIENCE DOES SEARING REALLY SEAL IN THE JUICES?

In a word: no. Instead, searing develops flavor through the Maillard reaction.

For centuries, professional cooks have been taught that searing meat "seals in juices." This simply isn't true. Searing meat adds a flavorful crust but it has nothing to do with juiciness.

To debunk this myth, we weighed six 1¼-inch-thick rib-eye steaks and divided them into two batches. We seared the first batch in a skillet over high heat until a brown crust formed, then transferred them to a wire rack set in a rimmed baking sheet and cooked them in a 275-degree oven until they reached an internal temperature of 125 degrees (or medium-rare). For the second batch, we reversed the order. We first placed the steaks on a wire rack set in a rimmed baking sheet and cooked them in the oven until they reached approximately 95 degrees, then we seared them until an equally well-browned crust developed and their interiors hit 125 degrees. We rested both sets for five minutes and reweighed them.

The steaks looked and tasted similar. Both batches were well browned and moderately juicy. We averaged the post-cooking weights for each batch, and then compared them with the average weight before cooking. Both sets of steaks lost nearly an identical amount of liquid: around 14 percent of their weight.

If searing truly sealed in juices, the steaks seared first (while raw) would have had more moisture trapped inside them than the steaks seared after cooking in the oven. Since this didn't happen, we can conclude that searing has nothing to do with moisture loss. In fact, juiciness is almost entirely determined by two factors: the fat content and the internal temperature of the meat when the cooking process ends. Fat makes meat seem moister. The internal temperature is so important because it is directly proportional to the degree to which muscle proteins shrink and release water.

Browning and then roasting is the ideal way to cook chicken parts, which are very thick and must be cooked to a fairly high internal temperature of 160 degrees to kill bacteria. Chicken parts need at least 20 minutes of cooking time, if not more. After all, the bones slow down the transfer of heat while the skin needs time to crisp (for more on cooking meat that contains bones, see concept 10). You could roast chicken parts entirely in the oven, but the skin won't become super-crisp. You need the stovetop for that. But if you cook bone-in parts solely on the stovetop, be prepared for a lot of splattering and fat. In this recipe, the blast of heat at the outset renders fat and crisps up the skin before the operation—skillet and all—is moved to the oven, where you can cook the chicken as long as necessary without the risk of splattering or scorching.

PAN-ROASTED CHICKEN BREASTS WITH SAGE-VERMOUTH SAUCE

SERVES 4

We prefer to split whole chicken breasts ourselves because store-bought split chicken breasts are often sloppily butchered. However, if you prefer to purchase split chicken breasts, try to choose 10- to 12-ounce pieces with skin intact. If using kosher chicken, do not brine in step 1, and season with salt as well as pepper. For more information on brining, see concept 11.

CHICKEN

½   cup salt
2   (1½-pound) bone-in whole chicken breasts, split through breastbone and trimmed
    Pepper
1   tablespoon vegetable oil

SAUCE

1   large shallot, minced
¾   cup low-sodium chicken broth
½   cup dry vermouth or dry white wine
4   fresh sage leaves, torn in half
3   tablespoons unsalted butter, cut into 3 pieces and chilled
    Salt and pepper

1. FOR THE CHICKEN: Dissolve salt in 2 quarts cold water in large container. Submerge chicken in brine, cover, and refrigerate for 30 minutes to 1 hour. Remove chicken from brine and pat dry with paper towels. Season chicken with pepper.

2. Adjust oven rack to middle position and heat oven to 450 degrees. Heat oil in 12-inch ovensafe skillet over medium-high heat until just smoking. Carefully lay chicken pieces skin side down in skillet and cook until well browned, 6 to 8 minutes. Flip chicken and continue to brown lightly on second side, about 3 minutes.

3. Flip chicken skin side down and transfer skillet to oven. Roast until chicken registers 160 degrees, 15 to 20 minutes.

4. Using potholder (skillet handle will be very hot), remove skillet from oven. Transfer chicken to serving platter and let rest while making sauce.

5. FOR THE SAUCE: Being careful of hot skillet handle, pour off all but 1 teaspoon fat from pan, add shallot, and cook over medium-high heat until softened, about 2 minutes. Stir in broth, vermouth, and sage, scraping up any browned bits. Bring to simmer and cook until liquid is slightly thickened and measures about ¾ cup, about 5 minutes. Stir in any accumulated chicken juices, return to simmer, and cook for 30 seconds.

6. Off heat, remove sage leaves and whisk in butter, 1 piece at a time. Season with salt and pepper to taste, spoon sauce over chicken, and serve.

PAN-ROASTED CHICKEN BREASTS WITH SWEET-TART RED WINE SAUCE

This sauce is a variation on the Italian sweet-sour combination called agrodolce.

Add 1 tablespoon sugar and ¼ teaspoon pepper along with chicken broth. Replace vermouth with ¼ cup each red wine and red wine vinegar and replace sage with 1 bay leaf.

PAN-ROASTED CHICKEN BREASTS WITH ONION AND ALE SAUCE

Brown ale gives this sauce a nutty, toasty, bittersweet flavor. Newcastle Brown Ale and Samuel Smith Nut Brown Ale are good choices.

Substitute ½ onion, sliced very thin, for shallot and cook onion until softened, about 3 minutes. Add 1 bay leaf and 1 teaspoon brown sugar along with chicken broth. Replace vermouth with brown ale and sage with 1 sprig fresh thyme. Add ½ teaspoon cider vinegar along with salt and pepper.

✔ WHY THIS RECIPE WORKS

Pan-roasting is a great way to cook chicken parts. In the oven, the skin never seems to crisp up enough. That's because chicken parts cook much faster than a whole bird. Our solution is simple: Brown chicken parts in a skillet until the fat has rendered and the skin is really crisp, then transfer the skillet to the oven so the chicken can finish cooking through.

START SKIN SIDE DOWN The skin benefits the most from the searing portion of the recipe, so make sure the chicken goes into the pan skin side down. You want to render as much fat as possible from the skin and jump-start the browning process—and the stovetop, rather than the oven, is the place to get this done.

PUT SKIN SIDE DOWN AGAIN Once the skin is browned, we flip the chicken and sear it lightly on the second side. We then flip the chicken skin side down and put the skillet in the oven. Keeping the skin in direct contact with the hot skillet ensures that the skin emerges crackling crisp from the oven. Once the hot skillet is placed in the oven the skillet will begin to cool down to the same temperature as the oven, slowing the cooking process and reducing the loss of moisture.

DON'T TOUCH THAT PAN Once the chicken is done, it can be set aside on a platter and you can prepare a pan sauce based on the flavorful browned bits in the pan. Just be careful—the skillet handle is very, very hot. Since most cooks are accustomed to holding the skillet handle when it sits on the stovetop, we suggest leaving a potholder on the handle to remind yourself of the risk. Just make sure the potholder is well away from the burner: You don't want to prevent one problem but cause another.

USE THE FOND The Maillard reaction is the source of deep flavors in meat (see concept 2). Some of the browned bits of meat end up sticking to the pan. The French call these browned bits fond, and they are a source of great flavor in quick pan sauces. Once the chicken has been removed from the pan, you can sauté an aromatic (shallot, garlic, or onion) and then add liquid (broth, wine, cider, or beer) and scrape the pan bottom with a wooden spoon to loosen those browned bits. The fond will dissolve into the sauce, adding complexity and depth. The liquid is reduced to concentrate the flavors of the sauce, and a little butter is whisked into the reduced sauce to give it some body.

ORANGE-HONEY GLAZED CHICKEN BREASTS
SERVES 4

We prefer to split whole chicken breasts ourselves because store-bought split chicken breasts are often sloppily butchered. However, if you prefer to purchase split chicken breasts, try to choose 10- to 12-ounce pieces with skin intact. When reducing the glaze in step 4, remember that the skillet handle will be hot; use a potholder. If the glaze looks dry during baking, add up to 2 tablespoons of juice to the pan. If your skillet is not ovensafe, brown the chicken breasts and reduce the glaze as instructed, then transfer the chicken and glaze to a 13 by 9-inch baking dish and bake (don't wash the skillet). When the chicken is fully cooked, transfer it to a plate to rest and scrape the glaze back into the skillet to be reduced.

1½	cups plus 2 tablespoons orange juice (4 oranges)
⅓	cup light corn syrup
3	tablespoons honey
1	tablespoon Dijon mustard
1	tablespoon distilled white vinegar
⅛	teaspoon red pepper flakes
	Salt and pepper
½	cup all-purpose flour
2	(1½-pound) whole bone-in chicken breasts, split through breastbone and trimmed
2	tablespoons vegetable oil
1	shallot, minced

1. Adjust oven rack to middle position and heat oven to 375 degrees. Whisk 1½ cups orange juice, corn syrup, honey, mustard, vinegar, pepper flakes, ⅛ teaspoon salt, and ⅛ teaspoon pepper together in medium bowl. Place flour in shallow dish. Pat chicken dry with paper towels

---

PRACTICAL SCIENCE WHY FRESH OJ TURNS SOUR

Don't squeeze OJ in advance.

Oranges contain a compound called limonoate A-ring lactone (LARL). When the cells are ruptured during the juicing process, LARL reacts with the juice to form a bitter compound called limonin. The heat used during the pasteurization process stops this reaction in store-bought juice. However, in freshly squeezed juice the reaction will continue unabated. When we tasted fresh orange juice against juice squeezed four hours earlier, tasters found the older juice much more bitter. So for recipes that call for fresh orange juice, it's best to squeeze the oranges at the last minute.

and season with salt and pepper. Working with 1 chicken breast at a time, coat chicken with flour, patting off excess.

2. Heat oil in ovensafe 12-inch skillet over medium heat until shimmering. Add chicken breasts skin side down; cook until well browned, 8 to 14 minutes, reducing heat if pan begins to scorch. Flip chicken skin side up and lightly brown other side, about 5 minutes. Transfer chicken to plate.

3. Pour off all but 1 teaspoon fat from pan. Add shallot and cook until softened, 1 to 2 minutes. Increase heat to high and add orange juice mixture. Simmer, stirring occasionally, until syrupy and reduced to 1 cup (heatproof spatula should leave slight trail when dragged through glaze), 6 to 10 minutes. Remove skillet from heat and tilt to one side so glaze pools in corner of pan. Using tongs, roll each chicken breast in pooled glaze to coat evenly and place skin side down in skillet.

4. Transfer skillet to oven and bake until chicken registers 160 degrees, 25 to 30 minutes, turning chicken skin side up halfway through cooking. Transfer chicken to platter and let rest for 5 minutes. Return skillet to high heat (be careful—handle will be very hot) and cook glaze, stirring constantly, until thick and syrupy, about 1 minute. Remove pan from heat and whisk in remaining 2 tablespoons orange juice. Spoon 1 teaspoon glaze over each breast and serve, passing remaining glaze at table.

APPLE-MAPLE GLAZED CHICKEN BREASTS

Substitute apple cider for orange juice and 2 tablespoons maple syrup for honey.

PRACTICAL SCIENCE
TIME LIMIT FOR FROZEN CHICKEN

Do not freeze chicken for more than two months.

We often store chicken breasts in the freezer. But then we read that storing chicken breasts in the freezer for longer than two months negatively affects tenderness. Ever the skeptics, we wanted to see for ourselves if this was true. So we bought six whole chicken breasts and split each one down the center. We immediately tested one breast from each chicken using a Warner-Bratzler shear device that measures tenderness by quantifying the force required to cut meat. We wrapped and froze the other breasts at 0 degrees (the temperature of the average home freezer). We tested three of the previously frozen breasts for tenderness after two months and the remaining three after three months. Our results confirmed it: Two-month-old chicken was nearly as tender as fresh chicken, while three-month-old chicken was about 15 percent tougher. We recommend freezing chicken wrapped in plastic and sealed in an airtight zipper-lock bag for no longer than two months.

PINEAPPLE–BROWN SUGAR GLAZED CHICKEN BREASTS

Substitute pineapple juice for orange juice and 2 tablespoons brown sugar for honey.

✔ WHY THIS RECIPE WORKS

This recipe is traditionally prepared entirely in the oven. The skin never really becomes crisp and the glaze does not adhere very well. Using the skillet accomplishes two things—it renders fat quickly from the skin so it becomes browned and crisp, and it allows the glaze to reduce and thicken both before and after the roasting portion of this recipe.

FLOUR THE CHICKEN In general, we don't flour meat before browning it. For instance, when browning meat for stew, we find that flour interferes with the complex taste of browned meat (instead you taste browned flour). In this recipe, however, the flour gives the chicken breasts a thin, crisp crust that serves as a good grip for the glaze.

REALLY RENDER THE FAT Cooking the chicken breasts skin side down over medium heat for 8 to 14 minutes gives the fat plenty of time to render and ensures that the skin will be crisp, even when glazed.

FORGET SUGARY GLAZES Most glazed chicken recipes rely on jam, honey, brown sugar, or maple syrup as the base for the glaze. The results are predictably sweet. We prefer using orange juice, which we reduce in the skillet once the chicken has been browned and set aside. A little honey, along with some Dijon mustard, vinegar, and red pepper flakes, creates a complex glaze with pantry ingredients. We also reserve some orange juice and add it to the finished glaze for a final hit of fresh orange flavor.

USE CORN SYRUP TO ADD MOISTURE While we dislike glazes that are all sweetener, we need something to thicken our glaze. A little honey helps, but adding more honey makes the glaze saccharine. We experimented with other sweeteners and tasters proclaimed corn syrup the winner. It turns out that corn syrup contains about half as much sugar as other sweeteners. Also, the sweeteners in corn syrup are mostly glucose and larger sugar molecules that are much less sweet than table sugar. An added benefit—when we added corn syrup to the glaze the chicken seemed moister. The concentrated glucose in corn syrup has an affinity for water, which means it helps to hold moisture in the glaze, making the overall dish seem juicier. That same glucose also thickens and adds a gloss to the glaze.

Most fish can be cooked completely on the stovetop. But if you have large halibut steaks, weighing 1¼ pounds and measuring 1½ inches thick, the exterior of the fish will dry and burn long before the interior comes up to 140 degrees, the temperature to which white fish are best cooked. A combination cooking method is ideal. We use a similar technique when preparing the Skillet-Roasted Fish Fillets on page 32.

PAN-ROASTED HALIBUT STEAKS
SERVES 4 TO 6

Prepare the vinaigrette (recipe follows) before cooking the fish. Even well-dried fish can cause the hot oil in the pan to splatter. You can minimize splattering by laying the halibut steaks in the pan gently and putting the edge closest to you in the pan first so that the far edge falls away from you. Make sure to cut off the cartilage at each end of the steaks to ensure that they will fit neatly in the pan and diminish the likelihood that the small bones located there will wind up on dinner plates.

2	(1¼-pound) skin-on full halibut steaks, 1¼ inches thick and 10 to 12 inches long
2	tablespoons olive oil
	Salt and pepper
1	recipe Chunky Cherry Tomato–Basil Vinaigrette (recipe follows)

1. Rinse halibut steaks, dry well with paper towels, and trim cartilage from both ends. Adjust oven rack to middle position and heat oven to 425 degrees. When oven reaches 425 degrees, heat oil in 12-inch ovenproof skillet over high heat until oil just begins to smoke.

2. Meanwhile, sprinkle both sides of halibut steaks with salt and pepper. Reduce heat to medium-high and swirl oil in pan to distribute; carefully lay steaks in pan and sear, without moving them, until spotty brown, about 4 minutes. (If steaks are thinner than 1¼ inches, check browning at 3½ minutes; thicker steaks of 1½ inches may require extra time, so check at 4½ minutes.) Off heat, flip steaks using 2 spatulas.

3. Transfer skillet to oven and roast until steaks register 140 degrees, flakes loosen, and flesh is opaque when checked with tip of paring knife, about 9 minutes (thicker steaks may take up to 10 minutes). Remove skillet from oven. Remove skin from cooked steaks and separate each quadrant of meat from bones by slipping spatula or knife gently between them. Transfer fish to warm platter and serve drizzled with vinaigrette.

CHUNKY CHERRY TOMATO–BASIL VINAIGRETTE
MAKES ABOUT 1½ CUPS, ENOUGH FOR 1 RECIPE PAN-ROASTED HALIBUT STEAKS

6	ounces cherry or grape tomatoes, quartered
¼	teaspoon salt
¼	teaspoon pepper
6	tablespoons extra-virgin olive oil
3	tablespoons lemon juice
2	shallots, minced
2	tablespoons minced fresh basil

Mix tomatoes with salt and pepper in medium bowl; let stand until juicy and seasoned, about 10 minutes. Whisk oil, lemon juice, shallots, and basil together in small mixing bowl, pour over tomatoes, and toss to combine.

✓ WHY THIS RECIPE WORKS

Halibut steaks this big will become very dry if cooked strictly on the stovetop. Roasting the fish produces moister results but there's not enough time for browning. The stovetop part of this recipe browns the fish and builds flavor, while the oven portion of the recipe finishes cooking the fish through while preserving as much moisture as possible.

BROWN JUST ONE SIDE   Even with its stint in the oven, we found that the fish dried out if we browned both sides. Instead, we browned just one side of the fish, flipped the steaks, and then immediately transferred the skillet to the oven, letting the second side brown more slowly in the oven, where the rate of moisture loss was lessened. Make sure to use two—not one—thin metal spatulas to flip the fish, and make sure to use 2 tablespoons of oil to prevent the fish from sticking.

MAKE A SEPARATE SAUCE   While beef steaks will create significant fond in a skillet, the proteins in fish don't create fond. Unlike beef, fish contains very little natural glucose, which is required to undergo the browning reaction with proteins. As a result, there's no benefit to making a pan sauce. We prefer to make something more potent, like a chunky vinaigrette. If you prefer, serve the pan-roasted fish with your favorite compound butter.

For steaks and chops in excess of 1½ inches we like this method because it raises the temperature of the meat before it is seared. Given the different final temperatures desired, 120 to 140 degrees for beef and 145 to 150 for pork, the steaks spend less time in the oven than the chops but the effect is the same.

PAN-SEARED THICK-CUT STRIP STEAKS
SERVES 4

Rib eye or filet mignon of similar thickness can be substituted for strip steaks. If using filet mignon, buying a 2-pound center-cut tenderloin roast and portioning it into four 8-ounce steaks yourself will produce more consistent results. If using filet mignon, increase the oven time by about five minutes. When cooking lean strip steaks (without an external fat cap) or filet mignon, add an extra tablespoon of oil to the pan.

2   (1-pound) boneless strip steaks, 1½ to 1¾ inches thick, trimmed
    Salt and pepper
1   tablespoon vegetable oil
1   recipe Red Wine–Mushroom Pan Sauce (optional) (recipe follows)

1. Adjust oven rack to middle position and heat oven to 275 degrees. Pat steaks dry with paper towels. Cut each steak in half vertically to create four 8-ounce steaks. Season steaks with salt and pepper; using hands, gently shape into uniform thickness. Place steaks on wire rack set in rimmed baking sheet; transfer baking sheet to oven. Cook until meat registers 90 to 95 degrees (for rare to medium-rare), 20 to 25 minutes, or 100 to 105 degrees (for medium), 25 to 30 minutes.

2. Heat oil in 12-inch skillet over high heat until smoking. Place steaks in skillet and sear until well browned and crusty, 1½ to 2 minutes, lifting once halfway through cooking to redistribute fat underneath each steak. (Reduce heat if fond begins to burn.) Using tongs, turn steaks over and cook until well browned on second side, 2 to 2½ minutes. Transfer steaks to clean wire rack and reduce heat under pan to medium. Use tongs to stand 2 steaks on their sides. Holding steaks together, return to skillet and sear on all edges until browned, about 1½ minutes. Repeat with remaining 2 steaks.

3. Return steaks to wire rack and let rest, loosely tented with aluminum foil, for about 10 minutes. If desired, cook sauce in now-empty skillet. Arrange steaks on individual plates and spoon sauce, if using, over steaks; serve.

RED WINE–MUSHROOM PAN SAUCE
MAKES ABOUT 1 CUP, ENOUGH FOR 1 RECIPE PAN-SEARED THICK-CUT STRIP STEAKS

Prepare all the ingredients for the pan sauce while the steaks are in the oven; the sauce can be cooked while the steaks are resting.

1   tablespoon vegetable oil
8   ounces white mushrooms, trimmed and sliced thin
1   small shallot, minced
1   cup dry red wine
½   cup low-sodium chicken broth
1   tablespoon balsamic vinegar

PRACTICAL SCIENCE THE BEST WAY TO WARM STEAKS BEFORE COOKING

Warm steaks in a 275-degree oven before searing. Excess moisture will evaporate, and the steaks will brown in half the time.

As we explored in "How the Science Works" on page 50, when a 40-degree steak is placed in a 400-degree skillet, the temperature of the pan drops significantly. Until the temperature in the pan recovers to at least 300 degrees, little browning can take place. While we can't make the pan much hotter, we can change the temperature of the meat. How?

Some cooks place a refrigerated steak on the counter to start raising its internal temperature. The theory is that with warmer meat, the middle can come up to temperature before a dry gray band of overcooked meat can develop under the crust during cooking, a problem with thick-cut steaks. But does a one- or two-hour warm-up at room temperature actually increase the internal temperature of steak enough to make a difference? (Keeping meat out longer is not advisable, since it puts it in the food safety "danger zone" as defined by the U.S. Department of Agriculture.) The short answer is no. A gray band appears as often as with a steak straight from the fridge.

We also tried warming the meat by submerging it in 120-degree water, enclosed in a zipper-lock bag, which brought the temperature of the meat up to 100 degrees after 30 minutes. But when this warm meat was seared in a preheated pan, it still took more than six minutes to brown both sides because the surface of the meat was covered with moisture and the heat of the pan simply turned it to steam.

We found that the best way to warm the steaks before searing is in a 275-degree oven for 20 to 30 minutes, or until the internal temperature is about 95 degrees. This way, the meat doesn't cool down a hot pan when added for a sear. In addition, this allows the tenderizing enzymes found in meat, called cathepsins, which are active in temperatures below 122 degrees, ample time to work (see concept 6). Also, the oven evaporates some surface moisture, so there's less to be converted to steam before the browning process can begin. We found steaks baked in the oven before being seared took half as much time to brown as those taken directly from the refrigerator.

1   teaspoon Dijon mustard
2   tablespoons unsalted butter, cut into 4 pieces
    and chilled
1   teaspoon minced fresh thyme
    Salt and pepper

Pour off fat from skillet in which steaks were cooked. Heat oil over medium-high heat until just smoking. Add mushrooms and cook, stirring occasionally, until beginning to brown and liquid has evaporated, about 5 minutes. Add shallot and cook, stirring frequently, until beginning to soften, about 1 minute. Increase heat to high; add wine and broth, scraping bottom of skillet with wooden spoon to loosen any browned bits. Simmer rapidly until liquid and mushrooms are reduced to 1 cup, about 6 minutes. Add vinegar, mustard, and any accumulated steak juices; cook until thickened, about 1 minute. Off heat, whisk in butter and thyme; season with salt and pepper to taste. Spoon sauce over steaks and serve immediately.

✔ WHY THIS RECIPE WORKS

When you're cooking a 1-inch steak, the most likely problem is the crust, not the interior, which is why starting with a cold piece of meat is an advantage. (It gives you more time for a crust to form.) But with a thick steak, the problem is just the opposite. It will take a long, long time for the interior of a mammoth 1¾-inch steak to reach 130 degrees. Warming the steaks in the oven jump-starts this process while minimizing internal moisture loss and promoting even cooking from edge to center.

COOK LOW AND SLOW FOR TENDERNESS We noticed that, in addition to being evenly cooked, steaks prepared this way were especially tender. It turns out that meat contains active enzymes called cathepsins, which break down connective tissues over time, increasing tenderness (a fact that is demonstrated to great effect in dry-aged meat). As the temperature of the meat rises, these enzymes work faster and faster until they reach 122 degrees, where all action stops. While our steaks are slowly heating up, the cathepsins are working overtime, in effect "aging" and tenderizing our steaks within half an hour. When thick steaks are cooked by conventional methods, their final temperature is reached much more rapidly, denying the cathepsins the time they need to properly do their job. (For more about cathepsins, see concept 6.)

SEAR ON THE SIDES While most recipes instruct the cook to sear steaks on both flat sides, we found it beneficial to sear the steaks on their edges as well. We use a pair of tongs to hold two steaks at a time on their edges in the pan. The extra browning adds flavor and doesn't overheat the steaks because the steaks are being rotated in the pan and don't spend very long in any one place.

PAN-SEARED THICK-CUT PORK CHOPS
SERVES 4

Buy chops of similar thickness so that they cook at the same rate. If using table salt, sprinkle each chop with ½ teaspoon salt. We prefer the flavor of natural chops over that of enhanced chops (which have been injected with a salt solution and various sodium phosphate salts to increase moistness and flavor), but if processed pork is all you can find, skip the salting step below.

4   (12-ounce) bone-in pork rib chops, 1½ inches
    thick, trimmed
    Kosher salt and pepper
1–2   tablespoons vegetable oil
1   recipe pan sauce (recipes follow)

1. Pat chops dry with paper towels. Using sharp knife, cut 2 slits, about 2 inches apart, through outer layer of fat and silverskin. Sprinkle entire surface of each chop with 1 teaspoon salt. Place chops on wire rack set in rimmed baking sheet and let stand at room temperature for 45 minutes. Meanwhile, adjust oven rack to middle position and heat oven to 275 degrees.

2. Season chops with pepper; transfer baking sheet to oven. Cook until chops (away from bone) register 120 to 125 degrees, 30 to 45 minutes.

3. Heat 1 tablespoon oil in 12-inch skillet over high heat until smoking. Place 2 chops in skillet and sear until well browned and crusty, 1½ to 3 minutes, lifting once halfway through cooking to redistribute fat underneath each chop. (Reduce heat if browned bits in pan bottom start to burn.) Using tongs, turn chops over and cook until well browned on second side, 2 to 3 minutes. Transfer chops to plate and repeat with remaining 2 chops, adding 1 tablespoon oil if pan is dry.

4. Reduce heat to medium. Use tongs to stand 2 pork chops on their sides. Holding chops together with tongs, return to skillet and sear sides of chops (with exception of bone side) until browned and chops register 145 degrees, about 1½ minutes. Repeat with remaining 2 chops. Let chops rest, tented loosely with aluminum foil, for 10 minutes while preparing sauce.

GARLIC AND THYME PAN SAUCE

MAKES ½ CUP, ENOUGH FOR 1 RECIPE
PAN-SEARED THICK-CUT PORK CHOPS

1	large shallot, minced
2	garlic cloves, minced
¾	cup low-sodium chicken broth
½	cup dry white wine
¼	teaspoon white wine vinegar
1	teaspoon minced fresh thyme
3	tablespoons unsalted butter, cut into 3 pieces and chilled
	Salt and pepper

Pour off all but 1 teaspoon fat from pan used to cook chops and return pan to medium heat. Add shallot and garlic and cook, stirring constantly, until softened, about 1 minute. Add broth and wine, scraping pan bottom to loosen browned bits. Simmer until reduced to ½ cup, 6 to 7 minutes. Off heat, stir in vinegar and thyme, then whisk in butter, 1 tablespoon at a time. Season with salt and pepper to taste and serve with chops.

CILANTRO AND COCONUT PAN SAUCE

MAKES ½ CUP, ENOUGH FOR 1 RECIPE
PAN-SEARED THICK-CUT PORK CHOPS

1	large shallot, minced
1	tablespoon grated fresh ginger
2	garlic cloves, minced
¾	cup coconut milk
¼	cup low-sodium chicken broth
1	teaspoon sugar
¼	cup minced fresh cilantro
2	teaspoons lime juice
1	tablespoon unsalted butter
	Salt and pepper

Pour off all but 1 teaspoon fat from pan used to cook chops and return pan to medium heat. Add shallot, ginger, and garlic and cook, stirring constantly, until softened, about 1 minute. Add coconut milk, broth, and sugar, scraping pan bottom to loosen browned bits. Simmer until reduced to ½ cup, 6 to 7 minutes. Off heat, stir in cilantro and lime juice, then whisk in butter. Season with salt and pepper to taste and serve with chops.

 WHY THIS RECIPE WORKS

The oven-then-searing method is especially beneficial with pork chops today because over the years they have become so lean. (Today's pork is at least 30 percent leaner than pork sold in the 1980s.) Overcooking pork, even slightly, yields tough results. And the window for doneness is quite narrow—lean pork chops are best cooked to 145 to 150 degrees. Also, because pork must be cooked to a higher internal temperature than beef, heat distribution is even more inequitable, especially in thick chops.

BUY BONE-IN RIB CHOPS You can generally find four different cuts of pork chops: sirloin, blade, center-cut, and rib loin. Sirloin chops, cut from the hip end of the pig, are tough, dry, and bland. For this recipe, we also decided against blade chops (cut from near the shoulder), which contain a fair amount of connective tissue and fat. Although the fat promises a juicy, flavorful chop, the connective tissue requires a long, moist cooking method to become tender. After comparing center-cut chops (cut from the center of the loin) and rib loin chops (cut from the rib section), we decided on the latter, preferring their meaty texture and slightly higher fat content. We opted to leave the bone in because it acts as an insulator and helps the chops cook gently while its fat helps to baste the meat as it cooks (see concept 10).

KEEP THEM FLAT Pork often comes covered with a thin membrane called silverskin. This membrane contracts faster than the rest of the meat, causing buckling and leading to uneven cooking. Cutting two slits about two inches apart in the silverskin around the edges of the chops prevents this problem. Make sure to cut through the fat and underlying silverskin.

SALT FOR FLAVOR Salting the pork chops draws out moisture via osmosis that, 45 minutes later, is pulled back into the meat, producing juicy, well-seasoned chops. Likewise this salt dissolves some of the meat proteins, making them more effective at holding moisture during cooking. (See concept 12 for more on salting meat.)

ROAST, THEN SEAR Cooking the salted chops in a gentle oven and then searing them in a smoking-hot pan has several advantages. First, chops cooked via this method are supremely tender because we keep them at a lower temperature for about 20 minutes longer than conventional sautéing or roasting methods do. This is in part because low-temperature enzymes called cathepsins (concept 6) are at work, breaking down proteins such as collagen and helping to tenderize the meat. Second, the gentle roasting dries the exterior of the meat, creating a thin, arid layer that turns into a gratifyingly crisp crust when seared.

Beef tenderloin is extremely tender but fairly bland. As a result, it's important to get a really good crust on the exterior. The problem is that it is very lean (that's why it's bland) and can easily dry out. Most cooks either sacrifice the browned crust (for a perfectly cooked interior) or live with a thick gray band of overcooked meat just below a nice brown crust. Baking then browning lets you have the best of both worlds—meat that is rosy pink from the edge to the center as well as a nice brown crust.

ROAST BEEF TENDERLOIN
SERVES 4 TO 6

Ask your butcher to prepare a trimmed center-cut Châteaubriand from the whole tenderloin, as this cut is not usually available without special ordering. If you are cooking for a crowd, this recipe can be doubled to make two roasts. Sear the roasts one after the other, wiping out the pan and adding new oil after searing the first roast. Both pieces of meat can be roasted on the same rack.

I	(2-pound) beef tenderloin center-cut Châteaubriand, trimmed
2	teaspoons kosher salt
I	teaspoon coarsely ground black pepper
2	tablespoons unsalted butter, softened
I	tablespoon vegetable oil
I	recipe flavored butter (recipes follow)

1. Using 12-inch lengths of twine, tie roast crosswise at 1½-inch intervals. Sprinkle roast evenly with salt, cover loosely with plastic wrap, and let stand at room temperature for 1 hour. Meanwhile, adjust oven rack to middle position and heat oven to 300 degrees.

2. Pat roast dry with paper towels. Sprinkle roast evenly with pepper and spread butter evenly over surface. Transfer roast to wire rack set in rimmed baking sheet. Roast until center of roast registers 125 degrees (for medium-rare), 40 to 55 minutes, or 135 degrees (for medium), 55 to 70 minutes, flipping roast halfway through cooking.

3. Heat oil in 12-inch skillet over medium-high heat until just smoking. Place roast in skillet and sear until well browned on 4 sides, 4 to 8 minutes. Transfer roast to carving board and spread 2 tablespoons flavored butter evenly over top of roast; let rest for 15 minutes. Remove twine and cut meat crosswise into ½-inch-thick slices. Serve, passing remaining flavored butter separately.

SHALLOT AND PARSLEY BUTTER
MAKES ABOUT ½ CUP, ENOUGH FOR I RECIPE ROAST BEEF TENDERLOIN

4	tablespoons unsalted butter, softened
½	shallot, minced
I	garlic clove, minced
I	tablespoon minced fresh parsley
¼	teaspoon salt
¼	teaspoon pepper

Combine all ingredients in medium bowl.

BLUE CHEESE AND CHIVE BUTTER
MAKES ABOUT ½ CUP, ENOUGH FOR I RECIPE ROAST BEEF TENDERLOIN

I½	ounces (¼ cup) mild blue cheese, room temperature
3	tablespoons unsalted butter, softened
⅛	teaspoon salt
2	tablespoons minced fresh chives

Combine all ingredients in medium bowl.

✓ WHY THIS RECIPE WORKS

Many recipes sear, then roast, beef tenderloin. But it takes a long time to sear a tenderloin straight from the refrigerator because a lot of surface moisture has to evaporate before any browning can occur. During this time, too much heat is transferred to the roast and you end up with a band of overcooked gray meat below the surface. Roasting the meat first ensures even cooking and evaporates surface moisture so that the searing time is just a few minutes.

BUY A CENTER-CUT ROAST A whole tenderloin is hard to handle. It's usually covered with a lot of fat and sinew and the meat varies widely in girth. For indoor cooking, we much prefer to buy a center-cut tenderloin, also called a Châteaubriand, because it's already trimmed and the thickness is the same from end to end. This 2-pound roast fits in a skillet and won't break the bank either.

USE SALT AND BUTTER To add flavor to this relatively bland cut, we apply salt an hour before cooking. The salt pulls juices out of the meat, then reverses the flow, drawing flavor deep into the meat (see concept 12). For richness, we slather the roast with softened butter before cooking, then cover it with a compound butter as it rests.

Slow Heating Makes Meat Tender

We've all had that magical restaurant moment: savoring a plate of meat, almost obscenely flavorful, so tender it's easily sliced with a butter knife. At home, on the other hand, we sometimes need to carve through bland roasts with a saw—even ones that are not overcooked. Are chefs buying better meat in restaurants? Or are they just cooking it differently?

HOW THE SCIENCE WORKS

As it turns out, many restaurant chefs use the same kind of meat available to us at home. But they use a secret weapon: time.

Aging is a technique used by many restaurants on primal cuts of beef to create more tender, flavorful meat. Dry-aging allows meat to sit undisturbed in a humid refrigerator ranging between 32 and 40 degrees for up to 30 days—during which time a significant portion of moisture is lost and the muscle proteins begin to break down. (For more information on dry-aging meat in a home refrigerator, see page 63.)

So why is dry-aged beef so much more tender? The results are largely due to enzymes. With the right temperature, and the correct amount of time, meat enzymes do their best work.

To rewind: Enzymes are a type of protein. In living animals, one of their functions is the turnover and reprocessing of other proteins around them. In meat, these enzymes continue to have the important role of catalyzing change—increasing the rates of chemical reaction, affecting food's consistency, texture, and color. Here, there are two important enzymes at work: calpains and cathepsins. Calpains break down the proteins that hold the muscle fibers in place. Cathepsins break apart a range of meat proteins, contracting filaments and supporting molecules, and can even weaken the collagen in the muscles' connective tissue (for more on collagen, see concept 7).

These crafty little enzymes have the ability to both impart a meatier, umami taste (encouraging the formation of amino acids and peptides as the muscle breaks down) and to tenderize (breaking down tough proteins with time)—that is, if the environment is right.

The activity level of these enzymes is largely based on temperature. The rate at which they break down the protein in a cut of meat held between 32 and 40 degrees is fairly slow, which is why a full 30 days of dry-aging is often needed. The rate becomes much faster as the temperature of the meat rises, though—right until it reaches 122 degrees. That's when everything comes to a halt.

So what can we do to simulate this process at home? We know that dry-aging creates tender, more flavorful meat. But most home cooks don't have the time, space, or energy to dry-age their own meat. Instead, we recommend roasting meat very slowly, purposely keeping the temperature below 122 degrees to encourage enzymatic activity for as long as possible. In contrast to the slow cooking methods used for tough cuts of meat (see concept 7), this technique is best for cuts of meat with little connective tissue, ones ideally cooked no further than medium. When slow-roasting cuts of meat at a low temperature, the cathepsins are given leave to work overtime, in effect "aging" the roast within a few hours. It's like dry-aging, only much faster.

ENZYMES AT WORK

BELOW 122 DEGREES
As the temperature in meat slowly rises, enzymes act like saws, breaking down muscle proteins at a faster and faster rate.

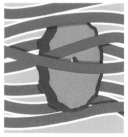

ABOVE 122 DEGREES
Heating enzymes above 122 degrees, however, changes their shape and eliminates their ability to break down muscle proteins.

TEST KITCHEN EXPERIMENT

To test the effects of enzymes active below 122 degrees, we cut one two-rib standing beef rib roast into two equal steaks. We cooked one in a sous vide water bath held at 120 degrees for two whole days (48 hours). We cooked the second in the same water bath—but just until its internal temperature hit 120 degrees, which took about two hours. We compared the two steaks for tenderness by tasting them, and every taster found the steak cooked for 48 hours to be more tender. We also devised a stress test: We cut a ¼-inch-thick, 4-inch-long cross-grain slice from the same part of each steak and suspended each vertically, holding them up with tongs. To the other end of the steak strips, we attached 2-pound weights and waited.

RESULTS

When we hung the slice of meat that had cooked for 48 hours, it tore in half quickly and easily—as soon as we let go of the weight. The second steak, however, didn't tear right away but hung there intact, stubbornly supporting the weight for 15 seconds.

THE TAKEAWAY

This experiment made it glaringly clear that internal temperature isn't the only factor in determining tenderness in meat. We cooked both samples of meat to the same temperature; the only difference was the length of time we held them there.

Enzymes called cathepsins do their best tenderizing work when held just below 122 degrees. We saw this to dramatic effect in the standing beef rib roast that cooked in a water bath at 120 degrees for 48 hours straight compared to the same cut cooked for only two hours. (We didn't cook the meat at 122 degrees exactly, as that's the temperature at which all enzymatic activity halts.) In the 48-hour sample, the enzymes had much more time to work their magic, which is why the

meat was so tender it fell apart immediately. The meat brought to temperature quickly did not benefit from the extra hours of enzymatic activity and was much less tender as a result. (This is not to say that the home cook should spend two days cooking a steak. Even an hour of enzymatic activity makes a difference.)

It's important to note that even though the cathepsin enzymes weaken the collagen in connective tissue, the collagen does not begin to break down into gelatin until the temperature reaches 140 degrees—and even then, it happens at a slow rate (see concept 7). So the longer cooking time at 120 degrees does not produce a more tender cut of meat because of an extended period of heat-induced collagen breakdown. Instead, it must be due to the action of the enzymes alone.

PUTTING ENZYMES TO THE TEST WITH SOUS VIDE

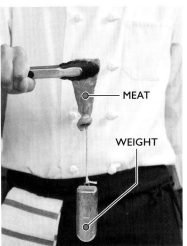
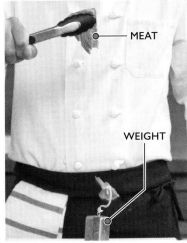

SHORT BATH, STRONG MEAT *We took a slice of the roast cooked to just 120 degrees (for about two hours) and attached a 2-pound weight with a piece of twine. Because the enzymes in the meat had little time to work, this sample was tough, and it held the weight for 15 seconds before tearing in half.*

LONG SOAK, TENDER CUT *When we tied a 2-pound weight to a slice of the meat that had cooked at 120 degrees for 48 hours straight, the meat didn't hold for a second. The enzymes had worked their magic with time, and the beef was so delicate it tore in half immediately.*

This method is designed for slightly tough cuts of meat with little connective tissue. Low-temperature tenderizing is not necessary when preparing supremely tender cuts like the tenderloin. However, slightly tougher (and less expensive) roasts from the round or sirloin really benefit from this technique. While enzymes active at this low temperature do weaken collagen, a key component of the connective tissue, they are more effective on muscle proteins. There are better ways to tenderize collagen-heavy meats (see concept 7).

SLOW-ROASTED BEEF
SERVES 6 TO 8

We don't recommend cooking this roast past medium. Open the oven door as little as possible and remove the roast from the oven while taking its temperature. If the roast has not reached the desired temperature in the time specified in step 3, heat the oven to 225 degrees for five minutes, shut it off, and continue to cook the roast to the desired temperature. For a smaller (2½- to 3½-pound) roast, reduce the amount of kosher salt to 3 teaspoons and pepper to 1½ teaspoons. For a 4½- to 6-pound roast, cut in half crosswise before cooking to create two smaller roasts. Slice the roast as thin as possible.

- 1   (3½- to 4½-pound) boneless eye-round roast, trimmed
- 4   teaspoons kosher salt
- 2   teaspoons plus 1 tablespoon vegetable oil
- 2   teaspoons pepper

1. Sprinkle all sides of roast evenly with salt. Wrap with plastic wrap and refrigerate for 18 to 24 hours.

2. Adjust oven rack to middle position and heat oven to 225 degrees. Pat roast dry with paper towels; rub with 2 teaspoons oil and sprinkle all sides evenly with pepper. Heat remaining tablespoon oil in 12-inch skillet over medium-high heat until starting to smoke. Sear roast until browned on all sides, about 12 minutes. Transfer roast to wire rack set in rimmed baking sheet. Roast until meat registers 115 degrees (for medium-rare), 1¼ to 1¾ hours, or 125 degrees (for medium), 1¾ to 2¼ hours.

3. Turn oven off; leave roast in oven, without opening door, until center of roast registers 130 degrees (for medium-rare) or 140 degrees (for medium), 30 to 50 minutes longer. Transfer roast to carving board and let rest for 15 minutes. Slice meat crosswise as thin as possible and serve.

✔ WHY THIS RECIPE WORKS

For an inexpensive slow-roasted beef recipe, we transform a bargain cut into a tender, juicy roast by salting the meat a full day before roasting. The salt penetrates the meat where it dissolves some of the muscle proteins, making it easier for the enzymes to break them down. In addition, the soluble proteins hold moisture, which helps to prevent the meat from drying out. (For more on salting, see concept 12.) We then cook the meat at a very low temperature, which allows the meat's enzymes to act as natural tenderizers, breaking down its tough muscle proteins.

CHOOSE FROM A LOW-COST LINEUP Not all bargain cuts have the potential to taste like a million bucks—or look like it when carved and served on a plate. We tried the eye-round roast, chuck eye, top round, and bottom round rump. While the chuck eye was too fatty, the top round an odd, uneven shape, and the bottom round rump too tough to carve, we loved the eye-round roast for its good flavor, relative tenderness, and uniform shape, which means even cooking and good looks on the plate.

SALT EARLY We tried salting the roast for four, 12, and 24 hours. Because the process of diffusion causes salt to travel from areas of higher to lower concentration, the full 24 hours gave it the most time to penetrate deep into the meat and season the roast evenly (though as few as 18 hours is effective). The salt dissolves some of the proteins, too, making it easier for the enzymes to break them down.

SEAR, THEN ELEVATE A roast cooked entirely in a cool oven will have a soft, pallid exterior. A quick sear in a hot skillet develops a flavorful crust on the meat and is an essential first step in this recipe. Rather than placing the roast directly in a roasting pan, we elevate the roast on a rack set inside a rimmed baking sheet. The rack allows the oven heat to circulate evenly around the meat and prevents the bottom crust from steaming in the oven (which would happen if the roast was set directly in a pan).

UTILIZE CARRYOVER COOKING It's important to shut the oven off before the internal temperature of the roast reaches 122 degrees; in this recipe we stop at 115 degrees. This allows the oven to cool while the roast continues to cook, just more slowly. Like carryover cooking (see concept 3), this allows the process of conduction to continue to cook the meat, preserving tenderness and juiciness, even when the external heat source is no longer active. The roast takes another 30 to 50 minutes to slowly climb from 115 to a final temperature of 130 degrees for medium-rare, and much of this time the internal temperature is still below 122 so the cathepsins are continuing to make the roast more tender.

INEXPENSIVE GRILL-ROASTED BEEF WITH GARLIC AND ROSEMARY

SERVES 6 TO 8

A pair of kitchen shears works well for punching the holes in the aluminum pan. We prefer a top sirloin roast, but you can substitute a top round or bottom round roast. Start this recipe the day before you plan to grill so the salt rub has time to flavor and tenderize the meat.

6	garlic cloves, minced
2	tablespoons minced fresh rosemary
4	teaspoons kosher salt
1	tablespoon pepper
1	(3- to 4-pound) top sirloin roast
1	(13 by 9-inch) disposable aluminum roasting pan

1. Combine garlic, rosemary, salt, and pepper in bowl. Sprinkle all sides of roast evenly with salt mixture, wrap with plastic wrap, and refrigerate for 18 to 24 hours.

2A. FOR A CHARCOAL GRILL: Open bottom vent halfway. Light large chimney starter half filled with charcoal briquettes (3 quarts). When top coals are partially covered with ash, pour evenly over one-third of grill. Set cooking grate in place, cover, and open lid vent halfway. Heat grill until hot, about 5 minutes.

2B. FOR A GAS GRILL: Turn all burners to high, cover, and heat grill until hot, about 15 minutes.

PRACTICAL SCIENCE DRY-AGING STEAK AT HOME

Wrapping steaks in cheesecloth and storing them in the fridge for four days gives them a meatier flavor and a tender texture.

To try replicating the results of commercial dry-aging at home, we bought rib-eye and strip steaks ($10.99 per pound) and stored them in the back of the refrigerator, where the temperature is coldest. Since home refrigerators are less humid than the commercial units used for dry-aging, we wrapped the steaks in cheesecloth to allow air to pass through while also preventing excessive dehydration. We checked them after four days (the longest we felt comfortable storing raw beef in a home fridge).

Their edges looked appropriately dried out, so we pan-seared the home-aged steaks and tasted them alongside a batch of the same commercially dry-aged cuts costing $19.99 per pound. Our findings? Sure enough, four days of dry-aging in a home fridge gave the steaks a comparably meatier flavor and tender texture. As long as you remember to wrap the meat in plenty of cheesecloth, place it on a wire rack for air circulation, and store it in the coldest part of the fridge, you can skip shelling out extra money for commercially aged beef.

---

3. Clean and oil cooking grate. Place roast on grill (hot side if using charcoal) and cook (covered if using gas) until well browned on all sides, 10 to 12 minutes, turning as needed. (If flare-ups occur, move roast to cooler side of grill until flames die down.)

4. Meanwhile, punch fifteen ¼-inch holes in center of disposable pan in area roughly same size as roast. Once browned, place beef in pan over holes and transfer pan to cool side of grill (if using charcoal) or turn primary burner to medium and turn other burner(s) off (if using gas). Cover and cook until meat registers 120 to 125 degrees (for medium-rare) or 130 to 135 degrees (for medium), 40 minutes to 1 hour, rotating pan halfway through cooking.

5. Transfer meat to wire rack set in rimmed baking sheet, tent loosely with aluminum foil, and let rest for 20 minutes. Transfer meat to carving board, slice thin against grain, and serve.

✔ WHY THIS RECIPE WORKS

This recipe translates our slow-roasting method from the oven to the grill. The trick is to create enough heat on the grill in order to sear the roast—but not so much that the roast cooks too quickly, finishing before the cathepsins have had time to do their work.

KEEP THE HEAT DOWN Traditional recipes for grill-roasting sear the meat over the hot side of the grill, then move it to the cooler side, where it cooks at a gentler pace. To ensure an evenly cooked, pink, tender interior, we adjusted that approach in two ways: First, we minimized the heat output by using only half a chimney's worth of coals—just enough to give the meat a good sear. (To replicate this effect on a gas grill, we turn the heat down after searing.) Second, we shielded the seared roast from excess heat by placing it in a disposable aluminum pan when we moved it to the grill's cooler side. Both measures help keep the roast below 122 degrees for as long as possible.

PUNCH HOLES It's important to punch holes in the disposable aluminum roasting pan. Without them, the juices that exude from the meat as it cooks on the grill will pool around the roast and turn its underside boiled and gray, ruining any crust achieved from searing. The addition of a dozen or so small escape channels in the bottom of the pan allows the liquid to drain away and leaves the meat perfectly pink with a crisp, flavorful crust.

THINK THIN When slicing this roast beef to serve, peel off wafer-thin slices of the rosy meat with your knife. (A slicing knife is ideal for this task.) Cutting extra-thin slices will make the meat seem even more tender.

Cook Tough Cuts Beyond Well-Done

Tough cuts of meat don't have to be unpalatable. They can become meltingly tender … if cooked to death. This seems contradictory to most meat cookery, where more time in the oven yields drier, chewier results. What's going on?

HOW THE SCIENCE WORKS

As we saw on page 41, meat mainly consists of four components: muscle fiber, connective tissue, fat, and lots of water. The fibers, which are long, thin, and bundled together in elongated groups, create the "grain" of the meat. Though small in young animals, muscle fibers grow with both age and exercise. They are generally tender because of their high water content, which is around 75 percent. In cooking, the strands of muscle fiber begin to shrink, first in diameter between 104 and 145 degrees, and then in length above 145 degrees, expelling moisture as they contract, like wringing out a wet towel. The rate of moisture loss becomes significant around 140 degrees, however, when the connective tissue surrounding the muscle fibers begins to tighten as well, squeezing the fibers even more firmly. This is why tender cuts are best cooked to rare or medium-rare before this process really gets underway.

The connective tissue surrounding the fiber bundles is a membranous, translucent covering that consists of cells and protein filaments and provides both structure and support to muscles. Collagen is the predominant protein in connective tissue and is found in everything from a cow's muscle tendons to its hooves. In contrast to the muscle fibers, collagen is composed of three protein chains tightly wound together in a triple-stranded helix

and, therefore, is almost unchewable when raw. In cooking, this sturdy protein remains largely unaffected when heated to temperatures lower than 140 degrees. It's only when the meat exceeds this temperature that collagen begins to relax, unwinding into individual strands. When held at this temperature—or, ideally, one a bit higher (preferably 160 to 180 degrees)—for an extended period of time, the triple helix of collagen unwinds to form gelatin, a single-stranded protein able to retain up to 10 times its weight in moisture, tenderize meat, and add a thick richness to the sauces of braised dishes. The conversion of collagen to gelatin is both temperature- and time-dependent; the longer the food is held in the ideal temperature range the more collagen will break down.

Extended cooking destroys lean cuts with little collagen (like pork tenderloin) because as the muscle fibers contract, they steadily give up their juices and become drier and tougher with time. Therefore, cuts with little collagen should be cooked with moisture preservation in mind, with a final cooking temperature no higher than 130 degrees for beef or 150 degrees for pork. But collagen-rich cuts are too tough to eat when cooked to rare or medium-rare. Extended cooking actually improves the texture of tough cuts with lots of sinuous collagen (like beef brisket), because it allows the abundant collagen to transform into gelatin, retaining significantly more moisture, and the tightened muscle fibers to relax a bit, drawing moisture back inside the meat.

FROM COLLAGEN TO GELATIN

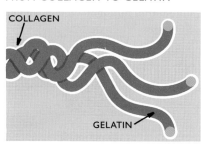

MELTING DOWN *At temperatures above 140 degrees, the triple helix of collagen unwinds to form three strands of gelatin.*

TEST KITCHEN EXPERIMENT

To demonstrate the slow rate at which collagen melts into gelatin, we cleaved 1 pound of oxtail (an almost obscenely collagen-rich cut of meat) into rough ½-inch pieces (chopping through the bone). Placing these pieces in one large saucepan, we filled the pan with just enough water (dyed dark brown for visibility) to cover the meat. We brought the liquid to a simmer on the stovetop, covered the pot, and cooked it in a 325-degree oven for three hours. Along the way, every 30 minutes we removed ¼ cup of the braising liquid, put it in a separate cup, and transferred it to the fridge to cool and set. After they were all fully chilled, we examined the samples to see how they changed.

THE RESULTS

While the 30-minute sample showed little change from the control (¼ cup liquid reserved prior to cooking), the one-hour sample was slightly thickened. The two-hour sample turned to a fragile jelly that could be inverted onto a plate but quickly lost its structure. The three-hour sample had turned from a liquid to a firm jelly that held sharp edges when inverted onto a plate.

THE TAKEAWAY

The collagen in meat can produce enough gelatin to turn water into Jell-O. That's because gelatin can hold up to 10 times its weight in moisture. But as this experiment shows, the conversion of collagen to gelatin is a slow process. The temperature of the oxtail exceeded 140 degrees—the temperature at which collagen begins to unwind into individual strands of gelatin—rather quickly since the oxtail and water mixture was brought to a simmer on the stovetop. However, collagen's conversion to gelatin is dependent not only on temperature but also on time. That's why the one-hour sample failed to hold its shape when chilled. Even with such small pieces of oxtail, more collagen was still being converted to gelatin after two hours of cooking—as demonstrated by the firmer texture of the sample that was taken out of the pot after three hours of cooking and then chilled.

So, when cooking collagen-rich cuts, take your time. Well-done meat has already lost most of its natural moisture. The goal now is to maximize the conversion of collagen to gelatin, and this takes time—a lot of time!

MELTING OXTAIL COLLAGEN INTO GELATIN

AFTER ONE HOUR
After one hour of braising, little of the oxtail's collagen had melted into gelatin and then seeped into the surrounding liquid. When we chilled a sample of the braising liquid to see how much it would set, we were left with a mushy soup.

AFTER TWO HOURS
After two hours of braising, the chunks of oxtail began to break down. A sample of the braising liquid, now containing more gelatin, became much firmer (though still a bit mushy) when chilled.

AFTER THREE HOURS
After three hours of braising, the oxtail was in shreds, and enough collagen had turned to gelatin to produce a veritable Jell-O mold when a sample of the braising liquid was chilled.

Collagen-rich cuts contain a lot of gelatin and that gelatin can make tough cuts of meat especially moist and tender. But you can't rush this process. A tough pork butt should be roasted for at least five hours.

SLOW-ROASTED PORK SHOULDER WITH PEACH SAUCE
SERVES 8 TO 12

Add more water to the roasting pan as necessary during the last hours of cooking to prevent the fond from burning. Serve the pork with the accompanying peach sauce or with cherry sauce or a sweet-tart chutney (recipes follow).

PORK ROAST

1	(6- to 8-pound) bone-in pork butt (also known as Boston butt)
1/3	cup kosher salt
1/3	cup packed light brown sugar
	Pepper

PEACH SAUCE

10	ounces frozen peaches, cut into 1-inch chunks, or 2 fresh peaches, peeled, pitted, and cut into 1/2-inch wedges
2	cups dry white wine
1/2	cup granulated sugar
1/4	cup plus 1 tablespoon rice vinegar
2	sprigs fresh thyme
1	tablespoon whole-grain mustard

1. FOR THE PORK ROAST: Using sharp knife, cut slits 1 inch apart in crosshatch pattern in fat cap of roast, being careful not to cut into meat. Combine salt and sugar in bowl. Rub salt mixture over entire pork shoulder and into slits. Wrap roast tightly in double layer of plastic wrap, place on rimmed baking sheet, and refrigerate for 12 to 24 hours.

2. Adjust oven rack to lowest position and heat oven to 325 degrees. Unwrap roast and brush any excess salt mixture from surface. Season roast with pepper. Set V-rack in large roasting pan, spray with vegetable oil spray, and place roast on rack. Add 1 quart water to roasting pan.

3. Cook roast, basting twice during cooking, until meat is extremely tender and roast near (but not touching) bone registers 190 degrees, 5 to 6 hours. Transfer roast to carving board and let rest, tented loosely with aluminum foil, for 1 hour. Transfer liquid in roasting pan to fat separator and let stand for 5 minutes. Pour off 1/4 cup jus and set aside; discard fat and reserve remaining jus for another use.

4. FOR THE SAUCE: Bring peaches, wine, sugar, 1/4 cup vinegar, 1/4 cup defatted jus, and thyme sprigs to simmer in small saucepan; cook, stirring occasionally, until reduced to 2 cups, about 30 minutes. Stir in remaining 1 tablespoon vinegar and mustard. Remove thyme sprigs, cover, and keep warm.

5. Using sharp paring knife, cut around inverted T-shaped bone until it can be pulled free from roast (use clean kitchen towel to grasp bone). Using serrated knife, slice roast. Serve, passing sauce separately.

SLOW-ROASTED PORK SHOULDER WITH CHERRY SAUCE

Substitute 10 ounces fresh or frozen pitted cherries for peaches, red wine for white wine, and red wine vinegar for rice vinegar and add 1/4 cup ruby port along with defatted jus. Increase granulated sugar to 3/4 cup, omit thyme sprigs and mustard, and reduce mixture to 1 1/2 cups.

FENNEL-APPLE CHUTNEY
MAKES ABOUT 2 CUPS, ENOUGH FOR 1 RECIPE SLOW-ROASTED PORK SHOULDER

1	tablespoon olive oil
1	large fennel bulb, stalks discarded, bulb halved, cored, and cut into 1/4-inch pieces
1	onion, chopped fine
2	Granny Smith apples, peeled, cored, and cut into 1/2-inch pieces
1	cup rice vinegar
3/4	cup sugar
2	teaspoons grated lemon zest
1	teaspoon salt
1/2	teaspoon red pepper flakes

Heat oil in medium saucepan over medium heat until shimmering. Add fennel and onion and cook until softened, about 10 minutes. Add apples, vinegar, sugar, lemon zest, salt, and pepper flakes. Bring to simmer and cook until thickened, about 20 minutes. Let cool to room temperature, about 2 hours or overnight. Serve with pork.

GREEN TOMATO CHUTNEY

MAKES ABOUT 2 CUPS, ENOUGH FOR 1 RECIPE
SLOW-ROASTED PORK SHOULDER

2	pounds green tomatoes, cored and cut into 1-inch pieces
¾	cup sugar
¾	cup distilled white vinegar
1	teaspoon coriander seeds
1	teaspoon salt
½	teaspoon red pepper flakes
2	teaspoons lemon juice

Bring tomatoes, sugar, vinegar, coriander seeds, salt, and pepper flakes to simmer in medium saucepan. Cook until thickened, about 40 minutes. Let cool to room temperature, about 2 hours or overnight. Stir in lemon juice just before serving with pork.

RED BELL PEPPER CHUTNEY

MAKES ABOUT 2 CUPS, ENOUGH FOR 1 RECIPE
SLOW-ROASTED PORK SHOULDER

1	tablespoon olive oil
1	red onion, chopped fine
4	red bell peppers, stemmed, seeded, and cut into ½-inch pieces
1	cup white wine vinegar
½	cup plus 2 tablespoons sugar
2	garlic cloves, peeled and smashed
1	(1-inch) piece ginger, peeled, sliced into thin coins, and smashed
1	teaspoon yellow mustard seeds
1	teaspoon salt
½	teaspoon red pepper flakes

Heat oil in medium saucepan over medium heat until shimmering. Add onion and cook until softened, about 7 minutes. Add bell peppers, vinegar, sugar, garlic, ginger, mustard seeds, salt, and pepper flakes. Bring to simmer and cook until thickened, about 40 minutes. Let cool to room temperature, about 2 hours or overnight. Serve with pork.

✓ WHY THIS RECIPE WORKS

This is a slow, slow roast. Not only do we let the roast sit with a mixture of salt and sugar overnight; we cook it for almost six hours straight. But don't let that intimidate you. This roast is the definition of tender when it finally emerges from the oven. And don't worry: This cut has so much fat, it's almost impossible to overcook.

USE BONE-IN PORK BUTT Instead of the lean, center-cut loin, our choice for roasting is pork butt (also known as Boston butt). This shoulder roast packs plenty of intramuscular fat that melts and bastes the meat during cooking, and it's available with or without the bone. We prefer bone-in for two reasons: First, bone conducts heat poorly and, in effect, acts as an insulator against heat. This means that the meat surrounding it stays cooler and the roast cooks at a slower, gentler pace. Second, bones have a large percentage of the meat's connective tissue attached to them, which eventually breaks down to gelatin and helps the roast retain moisture. (For more on bones, see concept 10.) This cut may take a long time to cook, but it's also inexpensive, loaded with flavorful intramuscular fat, and boasts a thick fat cap that renders to a bronze, baconlike crust.

LET SALTY-SWEET RUB SIT For super-tender meat and a deeply browned crust, our roast pork shoulder takes time—about 24 hours total—but the results are worth the wait. We rub our roast with a mixture of salt and sugar and let it rest overnight. The salt enhances juiciness and seasons the meat throughout, while the sugar caramelizes to create a crackling-crisp, salty-sweet crust.

SET OVEN TO SLOW Cooking pork slowly (at 325 degrees for five to six hours) pushes the meat well beyond its "done" mark into the 190-degree range. In lean cuts, this well-done temperature would result in a devastatingly dry piece of meat. But because there is so much collagen and fat in this roast, the high temperature encourages intramuscular fat to melt, collagen to break down and tenderize the meat, and the fat cap to render and crisp. Most importantly, gelatin formed from the collagen holds tightly on to the moisture, producing a juicy, not dry, roast.

PLACE IN A V-RACK When the pork is cooked directly in the pan, the dark layer of drippings burns quickly thanks to its high sugar content, and therefore these usually flavorful bits of fond are not ideal to be made into a sauce. This is easily fixed with a V-rack and a quart of water poured into the bottom of the pan. Once the roast is perched higher up, its fat drips down and mixes with the water to create a significant amount of jus, with no burning.

Barbecuing is the traditional slow-cooking method used with ribs, pulled pork, and brisket on the grill. Here we're taking the concept of cooking slow and low to a high final temperature—breaking down muscle fiber and melting collagen as we go—and moving it outdoors. Because the goal is to impart as much smoke flavor as possible, a long cooking time over a relatively low fire is required.

BARBECUED PULLED PORK
SERVES 8

Pulled pork can be made with a fresh ham or picnic roast, although our preference is for Boston butt. Preparing pulled pork requires little effort, but lots of time. Plan on 10 hours from start to finish: three hours with the spice rub, one hour to come to room temperature, three hours on the grill, two hours in the oven, and one hour to rest. Hickory is the classic choice when it comes to supplying the smoke in this recipe. Four medium wood chunks, soaked in water for one hour, can be substituted for the wood chip packets on a charcoal grill. Serve the pulled pork on plain white bread or warmed buns with the classic accompaniments of dill pickle chips and coleslaw. You will need a disposable aluminum roasting pan as well as heavy-duty aluminum foil and a brown paper grocery bag.

1	(6- to 8-pound) bone-in pork roast, preferably pork butt (also known as Boston butt), trimmed
¾	cup Dry Rub for Barbecue (recipe follows)
4	cups wood chips, soaked in water for 15 minutes and drained
1	(13 by 9-inch) disposable aluminum roasting pan
2	cups barbecue sauce (recipes follow)

1. Pat pork dry with paper towels, then massage dry rub into meat. Wrap meat in plastic wrap and refrigerate for at least 3 hours or up to 3 days.

2. At least 1 hour prior to cooking, remove roast from refrigerator, unwrap, and let sit at room temperature. Using 2 large pieces of heavy-duty aluminum foil, wrap soaked chips in 2 foil packets and cut several vent holes in tops.

3A. FOR A CHARCOAL GRILL: Open bottom vent halfway. Light large chimney starter three-quarters filled with charcoal briquettes (4½ quarts). When top coals are partially covered with ash, pour evenly over half of grill. Place wood chip packets on coals. Set cooking grate in place, cover, and open lid vent halfway. Heat grill until hot and wood chips are smoking, about 5 minutes.

3B. FOR A GAS GRILL: Place wood chip packets over primary burner. Turn all burners to high, cover, and heat grill until hot and wood chips are smoking, about

15 minutes. Turn primary burner to medium-high and turn off other burner(s). (Adjust primary burner as needed to maintain grill temperature of 300 to 325 degrees.)

4. Set roast in disposable pan, place on cool side of grill, and cook for 3 hours. During final 20 minutes of cooking, adjust oven rack to lower-middle position and heat oven to 325 degrees.

5. Wrap disposable pan with heavy-duty foil and cook in oven until meat is fork-tender, about 2 hours.

6. Carefully slide foil-wrapped pan with roast into brown paper bag. Crimp end shut and let rest for 1 hour.

7. Transfer roast to carving board and unwrap. Separate roast into muscle sections, removing fat, if desired, and tearing meat into shreds with your fingers. Place shredded meat in large bowl and toss with 1 cup barbecue sauce. Serve, passing remaining sauce separately.

DRY RUB FOR BARBECUE
MAKES ABOUT 1 CUP

You can adjust the proportions of spices in this all-purpose rub or add or subtract a spice, as you wish. Extra rub can be stored in an airtight container for several weeks.

¼	cup paprika
2	tablespoons chili powder
2	tablespoons ground cumin
2	tablespoons packed dark brown sugar
2	tablespoons salt
1	tablespoon dried oregano
1	tablespoon granulated sugar
1	tablespoon black pepper
1	tablespoon white pepper
1–2	teaspoons cayenne pepper

Combine all ingredients in small bowl.

WESTERN SOUTH CAROLINA BARBECUE SAUCE
MAKES 2 CUPS

The sauce can be refrigerated in an airtight container for up to four days.

1	tablespoon vegetable oil
½	cup finely chopped onion
2	garlic cloves, minced
½	cup cider vinegar

½ cup Worcestershire sauce

1 tablespoon dry mustard

1 tablespoon packed dark brown sugar

1 tablespoon paprika

1 teaspoon salt

1 teaspoon cayenne pepper

1 cup ketchup

Heat oil in small saucepan over medium heat. Add onion and cook, stirring occasionally, until softened, 5 to 7 minutes. Stir in garlic and cook until fragrant, about 30 seconds. Stir in vinegar, Worcestershire, mustard, sugar, paprika, salt, and cayenne, bring to simmer, and stir in ketchup. Cook over low heat until thickened, about 15 minutes.

EASTERN NORTH CAROLINA
BARBECUE SAUCE
MAKES ABOUT 2 CUPS

This sauce can be refrigerated in an airtight container for up to four days.

1 cup distilled white vinegar

1 cup cider vinegar

1 tablespoon sugar

1 tablespoon red pepper flakes

1 tablespoon hot sauce

Salt and pepper

Mix all ingredients together in bowl and season with salt and pepper to taste.

MID–SOUTH CAROLINA MUSTARD SAUCE
MAKES ABOUT 2½ CUPS

The sauce can be refrigerated in an airtight container for up to four days.

1 cup cider vinegar

1 cup vegetable oil

6 tablespoons Dijon mustard

2 tablespoons maple syrup or honey

4 teaspoons Worcestershire sauce

1 teaspoon hot sauce

Salt and pepper

Mix all ingredients together in bowl and season with salt and pepper to taste.

 **WHY THIS RECIPE WORKS**

Slow-cooked pulled pork is a summertime favorite; however, many barbecue procedures demand the regular attention of the cook for eight hours or more. We wanted to find a way to make moist, fork-tender pulled pork without the marathon cooking time and constant attention to the grill. A combination of cooking at a relatively low heat on the grill and then in the oven creates a well-done, tender, and smoky pork roast that goes well with many geographical variants of a traditional sauce.

RUB IN THE SPICES As with any other aspect of barbecuing, there is considerable controversy over not only what is the best combination of spices, but how to combine them, and even how to apply them. There are some who say the spices should be ground together with a mortar and pestle, others who resort to the convenience of grinding them in an electric coffee grinder or spice mill, and finally those who simply buy the individual spices off the shelf, mix them in a bowl, and call it done. It's your call, but most longtime barbecuers favor the last method; while home-ground spices have more pungent flavors, they are, to put it simply, also a lot more work. For an even simpler method, you can follow the example of those who just layer one spice over another directly on the meat.

PUT IN THE OVEN TO FINISH We cook the roast first on the grill to absorb smoky flavor (from wood chips—no smoker required). We use a moderate amount of charcoal—more than a typical low-and-slow method, but less than what we use for other large roasts, which could give it too much char. We then finish the pork in the oven at a relatively low temperature for two hours. This method produces almost the same results as the traditional barbecue, but in considerably less time and with much less effort. Placing the roast in a disposable pan shields it from the heat source on the grill, so there's no risk of scorching the meat. The pan also makes it easy to get the meat from the grill into the oven.

PAPER BAG IT Don't forget the bag! Allowing the pork to rest for an hour inside a paper grocery sack allows time for the flavorful juices to be reabsorbed. In addition, it produces a steaming effect that helps break down any remaining tough collagen. The result is a much more savory and succulent roast.

TOSS WITH THE SAUCE Almost all traditional pulled pork recipes involve tossing the shredded meat in a sauce—and that's precisely where the agreement ends. Even in the Carolinas, tastes don't fall across state lines, ranging from a tangy combination of vinegar and peppers, the introduction of tomatoes or ketchup, or even tomatoes and brown sugar. We play with a few options here.

BARBECUED BEEF BRISKET

SERVES 8 TO 10

Two medium wood chunks, soaked in water for one hour, can be substituted for the wood chip packet on a charcoal grill.

1	(5- to 6-pound) beef brisket, flat cut, fat trimmed to ⅓ to ½ inch
⅔	cup salt
½	cup plus 2 tablespoons sugar
2	cups wood chips, soaked in water for 15 minutes and drained
3	tablespoons kosher salt
2	tablespoons pepper
1	(13 by 9-inch) disposable aluminum roasting pan (if using charcoal) or 1 disposable aluminum pie plate (if using gas)

1. Using sharp knife, cut slits in fat cap, spaced 1 inch apart, in crosshatch pattern, being careful not to cut into meat. Dissolve table salt and ½ cup sugar in 4 quarts cold water in large container. Submerge brisket in brine, cover, and refrigerate for 2 hours.

2. Using large piece of heavy-duty aluminum foil, wrap soaked chips in foil packet and cut several vent holes in top.

3. Combine remaining 2 tablespoons sugar, kosher salt, and pepper in bowl. Remove brisket from brine and pat dry with paper towels. Transfer to rimmed baking sheet and rub salt mixture over entire brisket and into slits.

4A. FOR A CHARCOAL GRILL: Open bottom vent halfway. Arrange 3 quarts unlit charcoal banked against 1 side of grill and disposable pan filled with 2 cups water on empty side of grill. Light large chimney starter two-thirds filled with charcoal (4 quarts). When top coals are partially covered with ash, pour on top of unlit charcoal to cover one-third of grill with coals steeply banked against side of grill. Place wood chip packet on top of coals. Set cooking grate in place, cover, and open lid vent halfway. Heat grill until hot and wood chips begin to smoke, about 5 minutes.

4B. FOR A GAS GRILL: Place wood chip packet directly on primary burner. Place disposable aluminum pie plate filled with 2 cups water on other burner(s). Turn all burners to high, cover, and heat grill until hot and wood chips

begin to smoke, about 15 minutes. Turn primary burner to medium and turn other burner(s) off. (Adjust primary burner as needed during cooking to maintain grill temperature between 250 and 300 degrees.)

5. Line rimmed baking sheet with foil and set wire rack in baking sheet. Clean and oil cooking grate. Place brisket fat side down on cool side of grill, as far away from coals and flames as possible with thickest side facing coals and flames. Loosely tent meat with foil or build foil shield (see opposite page). Cover (position lid vent over meat if using charcoal) and cook for 3 hours. Transfer brisket to prepared baking sheet.

6. Adjust oven rack to middle position and heat oven to 325 degrees. Roast brisket until tender and meat registers 195 degrees, about 2 hours.

7. Transfer brisket to carving board, tent loosely with foil, and let rest for 30 minutes. Cut brisket against grain into long, thin slices and serve.

PRACTICAL SCIENCE TWO CUTS OF BRISKET

There are two smaller roasts in every whole brisket.

Cut from the cow's breast section, a whole brisket is a boneless, coarse-grained cut composed of two smaller roasts: the flat (or first) cut and the point (or second) cut. The knobby point cut (A) overlaps the rectangular flat cut (B). The point cut has more marbling and fat, and the flat cut's meat is lean and topped with a thick fat cap. Our recipe calls for the widely available flat cut. Make sure that the fat cap isn't overtrimmed and is ⅓ to ½ inch thick.

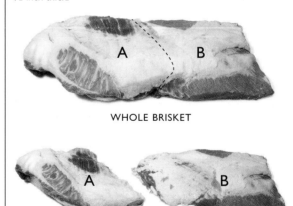

WHOLE BRISKET

POINT CUT   FLAT CUT

✓ WHY THIS RECIPE WORKS

In researching recipes for barbecued brisket, we found cooks could agree on one thing: slow cooking (for up to 12 hours) for the purpose of tenderizing. That seemed like a lot of time, though. We wanted to figure out a way to make cooking this potentially delicious cut of meat less daunting and less time-consuming, and we wanted to trade in a professional smoker for a backyard grill. Brining the brisket seasoned it throughout and allowed the meat to remain juicy even after hours on the grill. It's a necessary step because brisket, unlike other frequently slow-roasted cuts, does not contain a lot of intramuscular fat. Most of its fat is on the outside of the cut; the interior is relatively lean, but with lots of connective tissue. Therefore, the extra moisture extracted from the brine is key (see concept 11 for more on the science of brining).

PICK ONE CUT OF BRISKET   Cut from the cow's breast section, a whole brisket is a boneless, coarse-grained cut composed of two smaller roasts: the flat (or first) cut and the point (or second) cut. The knobby point cut overlaps the rectangular flat cut. The point cut has more marbling and fat, and the flat cut's meat is lean and topped with a thick fat cap. Our recipe calls for the widely available flat cut, which is more prone to dryness because it is so lean, with very little marbling to keep the interior moist. Make sure that the fat cap isn't overtrimmed and is ⅓ to ½ inch thick. If using the point cut, which has substantially more fat and, as a result, more moisture when cooked, you should omit the step of brining.

CHOOSE THE RIGHT WOOD   When using a charcoal grill, we prefer wood chunks to wood chips whenever possible; substitute two medium wood chunks, soaked in water for one hour, for the wood chip packet. We prefer hickory wood chunks to smoke our brisket. Pecan, maple, oak, or fruitwoods such as apple, cherry, and peach also work well. It is best to avoid mesquite, which turns bitter during the long process of barbecuing. Use wood chunks that are about the size of a tennis ball.

BURN IT DOWN   In our tests, we had trouble figuring out how to maintain a low temperature in the grill without frequently refueling. But then we realized that fire can burn down as well as up. We layer unlit briquettes on the bottom of our grill and add 4 quarts of hot coals on top. The result? A fire that burns consistently in the optimal 300-degree range for about three hours. We then transfer the brisket to the oven to finish cooking.

USE A FOIL SHIELD   If your brisket is smaller than 5 pounds or the fat cap has been removed, or if you are using a small charcoal grill, it may be necessary to build a foil shield in order to keep the brisket from becoming too dark. To do this, make two ½-inch folds on the long side of an 18 by 20-inch piece of heavy-duty aluminum foil to form a reinforced edge. Place the foil on the center of the cooking grate, with the reinforced edge over the hot side of the grill. Position the brisket fat side down over the cool side of the grill so that it covers about half of the foil. Pull the foil over the brisket to loosely tent it.

PRACTICAL SCIENCE   WHY IS BRISKET PINK?

The pink layer beneath the surface of barbecued meat is called the smoke ring.

In the competitive barbecue world, championship brisket always contains a thick smoke ring—the ¼-inch pink layer just beneath the meat's surface. Often mistaken for underdone meat, smoke rings—which don't affect taste—occur in most barbecued meats. Smoke rings are caused by reactions that occur when meat is cooked for a long time at a low temperature in a closed chamber (i.e., barbecued). Despite the name, only one compound in smoke plays a role in the ring. The color of meat comes from a protein called myoglobin. When raw meat is freshly cut, this protein is a deep purple. When the iron atom in myoglobin binds to oxygen, it is a striking bright red. In cooked meat, this iron atom is oxidized and turns gray. In barbecuing, however, this iron atom binds to the nitric oxide of the smoke, which dissolves in the moisture on the surface of the meat to create new compounds similar to the nitrites that keep deli meats pink. We found that placing a pan of water in the grill added enough moisture to guarantee a proper smoke ring.

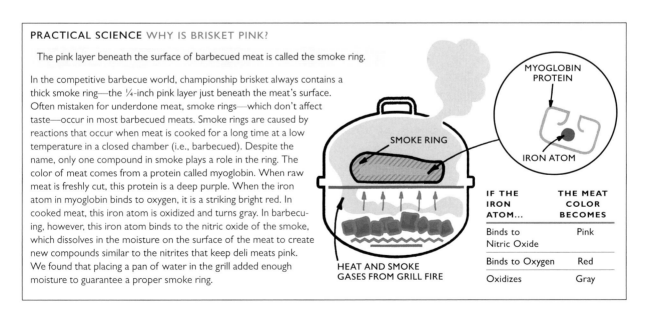

IF THE IRON ATOM...	THE MEAT COLOR BECOMES
Binds to Nitric Oxide	Pink
Binds to Oxygen	Red
Oxidizes	Gray

Braising is the technique that involves slowly simmering food in a small amount of liquid (generally at 180 to 190 degrees) in a tightly covered pot, or sealed in foil. The closed lid allows the meat not only to cook in the evenly heated liquid, but also to more easily reach a collagen-melting temperature due to the power of steam. Braising is ideal for collagen-heavy meats like brisket. We will cover this technique in more depth in concept 8.

ONION-BRAISED BEEF BRISKET
SERVES 6 TO 8

This recipe requires a few hours of unattended cooking. It also requires advance preparation. After cooking, the brisket must stand overnight in the braising liquid that later becomes the sauce; this helps to keep the brisket moist and flavorful. Good accompaniments to braised brisket include mashed potatoes and buttered egg noodles. Matzo meal or potato starch can be substituted for the flour.

1	(4- to 5-pound) beef brisket, flat cut, fat trimmed to ¼ inch
	Salt and pepper
	Vegetable oil
2½	pounds onions, halved and sliced ½ inch thick
1	tablespoon packed brown sugar
3	garlic cloves, minced
1	tablespoon tomato paste
1	tablespoon paprika
⅛	teaspoon cayenne pepper
2	tablespoons all-purpose flour
1	cup low-sodium chicken broth
1	cup dry red wine
3	bay leaves
3	sprigs fresh thyme
2	teaspoons cider vinegar

1. Adjust oven rack to lower-middle position and heat oven to 300 degrees. Line 13 by 9-inch baking dish with two 24-inch-long sheets of 18-inch-wide heavy-duty aluminum foil, positioning sheets perpendicular to each other and allowing excess foil to extend beyond edges of pan. Pat brisket dry with paper towels. Place brisket fat side up on cutting board; using dinner fork, poke holes in meat through fat layer about 1 inch apart. Season both sides of brisket with salt and pepper.

2. Heat 1 teaspoon oil in large skillet over medium-high heat until oil just begins to smoke. Place brisket, fat side up, in skillet (brisket may climb up sides of pan); weight brisket with heavy Dutch oven or cast-iron skillet and cook until well browned, about 7 minutes. Remove Dutch oven; using tongs, flip brisket and cook on second side without weight until well browned, about 7 minutes longer. Transfer brisket to platter.

3. Pour off all but 1 tablespoon fat from pan (or, if brisket was lean, add enough oil to fat in skillet to equal 1 tablespoon); stir in onions, sugar, and ¼ teaspoon salt and cook over medium-high heat, stirring occasionally, until onions are softened, 10 to 12 minutes. Add garlic and cook, stirring frequently, until fragrant, about 1 minute; add tomato paste and cook, stirring to combine, until paste darkens, about 2 minutes. Add paprika and cayenne and cook, stirring constantly, until fragrant, about 1 minute. Add flour and cook, stirring constantly, until well combined, about 2 minutes. Add broth, wine, bay leaves, and thyme, stirring to scrape up browned bits from pan; bring to simmer and simmer for 5 minutes to fully thicken.

4. Pour sauce and onions into foil-lined baking dish. Nestle brisket, fat side up, in sauce and onions. Fold foil extensions over and seal (do not tightly crimp foil because foil must later be opened to test for doneness). Place in oven and cook until fork slips easily in and out of meat, 3½ to 4 hours (when testing for doneness, open foil with caution as contents will be steaming). Carefully open foil and let brisket cool at room temperature, 20 to 30 minutes.

5. Transfer brisket to large bowl; set fine-mesh strainer over bowl and strain sauce over brisket. Discard bay leaves and thyme from onions and transfer onions to small bowl. Cover both bowls with plastic wrap, cut vents in plastic, and refrigerate overnight.

6. About 45 minutes before serving, adjust oven rack to lower-middle position; heat oven to 350 degrees. While oven heats, transfer cold brisket to carving board. Scrape off and discard any fat from surface of sauce, then heat sauce in medium saucepan over medium heat until warm, skimming any fat on surface with wide shallow spoon (you should have about 2 cups sauce without onions; if necessary, simmer sauce over medium-high heat until reduced to 2 cups). Slice brisket against grain into ¼-inch-thick slices and place slices in 13 by 9-inch baking dish. Stir reserved onions and vinegar into warmed sauce and season with salt and pepper to taste. Pour sauce over brisket slices, cover baking dish with foil, and bake until heated through, 25 to 30 minutes. Serve immediately.

SAME-DAY ONION-BRAISED BEEF BRISKET

After removing brisket from oven in step 4, reseal foil and let brisket sit at room temperature for 1 hour. Transfer brisket to carving board and continue with straining, defatting, and reheating sauce and slicing meat; omit step of returning brisket to oven once reheated sauce is poured over it.

✔ WHY THIS RECIPE WORKS

The brisket in this recipe—a lean, collagen-heavy cut—is cooked until it is well-done, sealed with its braising liquid in an oven for a very long time. Unlike with slow-roasting, the steam generated in its sealed foil package helps the meat reach a higher temperature relatively quickly. This melts the collagen and keeps the meat moist, despite its lack of fat. Leaving the brisket in its sauce overnight, and then slicing the following day, helps to restore some of the moisture lost in the cooking process, as well as prevent the tender meat from shredding under the knife.

BUY THE RIGHT CUT A whole beef brisket weighs up to 12 pounds. It is usually sold in two pieces, the flat (or first) cut and the point cut. The flat cut is leaner and thinner, with a rectangular shape and an exterior fat cap. It is more commonly available at supermarkets than the point cut, which has an oblong, irregular shape and contains large interior pockets of fat.

We found the point cut to be marginally more flavorful but, more important, much less prone to drying out, thanks to all that extra fat. Unfortunately, more than a few tasters found the point cut too fatty to enjoy, and it was next to impossible to carve it into neat slices. All in all, it seemed a better cut for barbecuing than braising.

The flat cut is easier to sear and to slice, provided it has cooled. Butchers usually trim away some or all of the fat cap, but try to find one with at least ¼ inch of fat in place, as it will help to keep the meat moist during cooking. If the fat cap is very thick and untrimmed in places, cut it down to a thickness of about ¼ inch. A flat-cut brisket roast usually weighs between 4 and 5 pounds, though butchers occasionally cut them into smaller 2- to 3-pound roasts. You can substitute two of these smaller cuts if that is all that is available, although the cooking time may vary.

USE HEAVY-DUTY FOIL For this braise, we use 18-inch-wide heavy-duty aluminum foil to seal in the brisket as it cooks. It's important to create a tight seal around the meat, so that it can cook in the even heat of the simmering liquid, but also in the heat of the steam collecting in the closed container. Be careful not to crimp the foil too tightly when you enclose the brisket—you will need to open it later when checking for doneness.

CHICKEN OR BEEF? Though many recipes call for the use of beef broth in the braising liquid of brisket, we've found most canned beef broths to taste salty and artificial. In testing this recipe, we found that testers preferred chicken to beef broth for its cleaner flavor. To boost the flavor of this sauce, we add red wine.

REST OVERNIGHT We find it's preferable to leave the brisket in the refrigerator overnight. Not only does it produce a juicier, tenderer brisket, but it also allows you to slice the meat without it falling apart or shredding. This is perfect if you're cooking brisket for a crowd: Making this dish a day ahead reduces the stress of timing in the kitchen and the neatly sliced brisket creates a much more elegant spread on the serving platter. (Though in a pinch, it's possible to make and serve this brisket the same day. See Same-Day Onion-Braised Beef Brisket, above.)

FINISH THE SAUCE While we were testing this recipe, a debate sprang up in the test kitchen over the proper thickness of the finished sauce. "Gravy" enthusiasts wanted a thick sauce that would cling to the meat, while their opponents backed a thinner, more natural jus. But everyone agreed that too much flour, stirred into the skillet while building the sauce, resulted in a sauce that was overly pasty; just 2 tablespoons were enough to give it the proper body. To further thicken the sauce, we put it back on the stove to simmer while slicing the finished brisket. Just before serving, we add a couple of teaspoons of cider vinegar to brighten the flavor.

PRACTICAL SCIENCE HOW TO STORE BAY LEAVES

Keep bay leaves in the freezer to prolong freshness.

Given that most soups and stews call for just one or two bay leaves, the jar of bay leaves in your kitchen is likely pretty old. Does it matter? To find out, we ran tests with a freshly opened jar of bay leaves, with bay leaves that had been opened for three months and stored in their original jar (the jar was of course kept closed), and with bay leaves that had been sealed in a zipper-lock storage bag and stored in the freezer for three months. Two bay leaves of each were simmered in 2 cups of canned chicken broth and tasted for herbal potency. We were amazed by the amount of flavor loss in the leaves that had been left in their original, opened container in the pantry. Enough flavor loss, in fact, that the package of freshly opened bay leaves tasted nearly twice as flavorful. The good news is that there is a way to retain much of the bay flavor. The frozen leaves put out great, assertive bay flavor and aroma, nearly as good as the leaves from the freshly opened jar.

Tough Cuts Like a Covered Pot

When roasting, grilling, or sautéing meat, our goal is usually to develop flavor through browning and avoid moisture loss by not overcooking. But as we learned in concept 7, collagen-heavy cuts can be handled differently: We can cook them until they are very, very well-done. Slow-roasting, barbecuing, and braising are three possible choices, but in many ways braising—which cooks the meat in a covered pot—is the most reliable and versatile choice.

HOW THE SCIENCE WORKS

ON THE STOVE *Heat is unevenly distributed and concentrated on the bottom of the pot.*

IN THE OVEN *Heat is evenly distributed, with no hot spots.*

When we braise, we generally begin by searing a cut of meat to develop color and flavor but then partially submerge it in liquid and seal the pot, cooking with gentle heat until the meat is so tender it can be sliced with a butter knife. Braising works best with fatty cuts rich in collagen, such as short ribs, chuck roasts, or chicken thighs.

This technique coaxes the same tenderizing effects out of tough cuts as slow-roasting and barbecuing do (see concept 7). But it has some advantages over these dry-heat methods as well.

First, it offers even, steady cooking. Because the cooking liquid maintains a temperature no higher than boiling water, or 212 degrees, braising provides an unflappably low-and-slow heat source as the meat is cooked to well-done. As with slow-roasting or barbecuing, this cooking method melts collagen into gelatin, producing juicy, tender meat, but without the worry that one part of the meat will cook too fast or too slow.

Second, because we cover our pot while braising, steam is generated within. This provides a secondary heat source and, in many cases, shortens the cooking time when compared to slow-roasting or barbecuing.

Finally, the liquid used to braise tough cuts of meat picks up flavor and depth and becomes a concentrated, succulent sauce.

It's possible to braise in a covered pot on the stove, but we find that the direct heat of the burner is intense, specific, and entirely too efficient. It can cook the meat quickly and unevenly as well as affect the consistency of the braising liquid, breaking down added starch (like flour) on the bottom of the pan, creating a too-thin sauce. The oven, however, uses indirect and less efficient heat (see concept 1). This translates to gentle, even cooking in the closed environment of a covered pot and allows for a silky and luxurious sauce.

Three cooking methods fall under the broad banner of braising: pot-roasting, stewing, and braising itself. *Pot roasts* are large cuts of meat cooked partly submerged in liquid. *Stews* consist of smaller pieces, swimming in liquid. The term "braise" is reserved for everything else.

TEST KITCHEN EXPERIMENT

To demonstrate the effects of braising on moisture, we set up a test designed to simulate cooking meat with liquid in a covered pot. We placed five 200-gram samples of beef chuck, along with measured amounts of broth, in individual vacuum-sealed bags to eliminate the possibility of evaporation. We then submerged the bags in water held at 190 degrees (the low-end temperature of a typical braise) for 1½ hours. We then removed the bags from the water, weighed the beef, and measured the liquid in each bag.

THE RESULTS

We found that the weight of the meat decreased (losing an average of 25 grams, or 12.5 percent of its weight) during cooking. When we measured the liquid in each bag, we found it had increased by an average of 25 grams.

THE TAKEAWAY

It's a common misconception that braising adds moisture to meat as it cooks. However, this experiment demonstrates that moisture is being pulled out of the meat and into the surrounding liquid—not the other way around. So why, then, does braised meat seem so moist? Gentle cooking helps break down the meat's connective tissue and collagen into gelatin, which lubricates and tenderizes the muscle fibers. The resulting soft, tender texture is perceived as moist.

MEASURING MOISTURE IN MEAT BEFORE AND AFTER BRAISING

BEFORE BRAISING

AFTER BRAISING

We weighed our samples of beef chuck before and after braising in vacuum-sealed bags and found that the meat lost 25 grams of liquid on average, proving that braising does not retain moisture.

PRACTICAL SCIENCE THE BEST PLACE TO BRAISE

Braising a stew in the oven, rather than on the stove, helps to make a nice, thick sauce.

In many instances, the test kitchen favors braising stews in the oven instead of on top of the stove. A good example is the oven-braised Daube Provençal (page 82). For testing purposes, we cooked one daube in a 350-degree oven and simmered another on the stove. Both stews produced moist, tender meat in 2½ hours, but the textures of the braising liquids differed dramatically. The stovetop stew produced a thin sauce more like soup, while the oven-braised daube yielded a silky and luxurious sauce.

Why so different? At moderate temperatures, the flour in a braising liquid gradually absorbs water, thus thickening the sauce. If the liquid gets too hot, however, the starch breaks down and loses its thickening properties, resulting in a thinner sauce. Because stovetop cooking heats from the bottom only, the flour closest to the heat source loses its thickening ability.

Daubes were traditionally cooked in a covered urn-shaped pot (called a *daubière*). The pot was placed in the fireplace—away from direct flame—on a bed of hot embers with more embers piled into the indentations in the lid. The result? Even heat from above and below that gently simmered the stew. So oven-braising is not only more effective than stovetop simmering, it's also more authentic.

In pot-roasting, we turn large cuts of tough (read cheap), nearly unpalatable meat into a tender, rich, flavorful main course. The meat is partially submerged in liquid in a closed pot and cooked in the gentle heat of the oven. When finished, the roast should be so tender that it can be "sliced" with a dull knife. Our classic recipe begins by browning the meat on the stovetop to develop flavor; our easy recipe skips this step.

CLASSIC POT ROAST
SERVES 6 TO 8

For pot roast, remember to add only enough water to come halfway up the sides of the roast, and begin checking the roast for doneness after only two hours. Mashed or boiled potatoes are good accompaniments.

1	(3½-pound) boneless beef chuck-eye roast, trimmed
	Salt and pepper
2	tablespoons vegetable oil
1	onion, chopped
1	small carrot, chopped
1	small celery rib, chopped
2	garlic cloves, minced
2	teaspoons sugar
1	cup low-sodium chicken broth
1	cup beef broth
1	sprig fresh thyme
1–1½	cups water
¼	cup dry red wine

1. Adjust oven rack to middle position and heat oven to 300 degrees. Pat beef dry with paper towels; season with salt and pepper.

2. Heat oil in Dutch oven over medium-high heat until shimmering but not smoking. Brown beef thoroughly on all sides, reducing heat if fat begins to smoke, 8 to 10 minutes. Transfer to large plate; set aside. Reduce heat to medium; add onion, carrot, and celery to pot and cook, stirring occasionally, until beginning to brown, 6 to 8 minutes. Add garlic and sugar; cook until fragrant, about 30 seconds. Add chicken and beef broths and thyme, scraping bottom of pan with wooden spoon to loosen browned bits. Return beef and any accumulated juices to pot; add enough water to come halfway up sides of beef. Place large piece of aluminum foil over pot and cover tightly with lid; bring liquid to simmer over medium heat, then transfer pot to oven. Cook, turning roast every 30 minutes, until fully tender and fork slips easily in and out of meat, 3½ to 4 hours.

3. Transfer roast to carving board; tent with foil to keep warm. Allow liquid in pot to settle about 5 minutes; skim fat off surface with wide spoon and discard thyme sprig. Boil over high heat until reduced to about 1½ cups, about 8 minutes. Add red wine and reduce again to 1½ cups, about 2 minutes. Season with salt and pepper to taste.

4. Slice meat against grain into ½-inch-thick slices, or pull apart into large pieces; transfer meat to serving platter and pour about ½ cup sauce over meat. Serve, passing remaining sauce separately.

✔ WHY THIS RECIPE WORKS
In this recipe, we brown the chuck-eye roast over medium-high heat to develop both color and flavor. We cover the pot first with foil, and then with the lid, in order to create as tight a seal as possible. This prevents liquid from escaping (in the form of steam) through the cracks of a loose-fitting lid as we gently simmer the pot roast in the oven. With the meat submerged halfway, we cook it until it is very well-done to create a tender, succulent roast.

CHOOSE A CHUCK EYE We recommend chuck eye for this pot roast. This boneless roast is cut from the center of the first five ribs. It is very tender and juicy, though it does contain a healthy amount of fat. The chuck 7-bone and top blade roasts also work for this pot roast, though they are thinner cuts and will likely require an hour less cooking time. If you use the top blade, be sure to tie it with twine before cooking.

COOK UNTIL DONE, AND THEN SOME We cook this pot roast until it's very well-done—to an internal temperature of about 210 degrees, the point at which the fat and connective tissue are really melting well. Simply bringing the meat to this temperature does not achieve the desired fall-apart-tender pot roast. But we found that if you leave the pot roast to cook at that same internal temperature for a full hour longer, the roast will be so tender that a fork poked into its center will be met with no resistance, nearly disappearing into the flesh.

USE A MAGIC TEMPERATURE We began pot-roasting in an oven set to 250 degrees, and then tested roasts at higher temperatures to see if it would be possible to reduce the cooking time. Heat levels above 350 degrees boiled the meat to a stringy, dry texture because the exterior overcooked before the interior was cooked and tender. The magic oven temperature turned out to be 300 degrees—just enough heat to keep the meat at a low simmer while high enough to shave a few minutes off the cooking time.

REDUCE, REDUCE, REDUCE Some recipes thicken the pot roast sauce with a mixture of butter and flour or a slurry of cornstarch mixed with a little braising liquid. Both techniques make the sauce more gravylike than we prefer, as well as diluting the flavor. We like to remove the roast from the pot and reduce the liquid until the flavors are well concentrated and the texture is more substantial.

EASY POT ROAST

SERVES 6 TO 8

Chilling the whole cooked pot roast overnight improves its flavor and makes it moister and easier to slice.

1	(3½- to 4-pound) boneless beef chuck-eye roast, pulled apart at seams and trimmed
	Kosher salt and pepper
2	tablespoons unsalted butter
2	onions, halved and sliced thin
1	large carrot, peeled and chopped
1	celery rib, chopped
2	garlic cloves, minced
2–3	cups beef broth
¾	cup dry red wine
1	tablespoon tomato paste
1	bay leaf
1	sprig fresh thyme plus ¼ teaspoon minced
1	tablespoon balsamic vinegar

1. Season pieces of meat with 1 tablespoon salt, place on wire rack set in rimmed baking sheet, and let stand at room temperature for 1 hour.

2. Adjust oven rack to lower-middle position and heat oven to 300 degrees. Melt butter in Dutch oven over medium heat. Add onions and cook, stirring occasionally, until softened and beginning to brown, 8 to 10 minutes. Add carrot and celery; continue to cook, stirring occasionally, about 5 minutes. Add garlic and cook until fragrant, about 30 seconds. Stir in 1 cup broth, ½ cup wine, tomato paste, bay leaf, and thyme sprig; bring to simmer.

3. Pat beef dry with paper towels and season with pepper. Using 3 pieces of kitchen twine, tie each piece of meat into loaf shape for even cooking.

4. Nestle meat on top of vegetables. Cover pot tightly with large piece of aluminum foil and cover with lid; transfer pot to oven. Cook beef until fully tender and paring knife easily slips in and out of meat, 3½ to 4 hours, turning meat halfway through cooking.

5. Transfer roasts to carving board and tent loosely with foil. Strain liquid through fine-mesh strainer into 4-cup liquid measuring cup. Discard bay leaf and thyme sprig. Transfer vegetables to blender. Let liquid settle for 5 minutes, then skim off fat; add beef broth to bring liquid amount to 3 cups. Add liquid to blender and blend until smooth, about 2 minutes. Transfer sauce to medium saucepan and bring to simmer over medium heat.

6. Meanwhile, remove twine from roasts and slice against grain into ½-inch-thick slices. Transfer meat to serving platter. Stir remaining ¼ cup wine, minced thyme, and vinegar into gravy and season with salt and pepper to taste. Spoon half of gravy over meat; pass remaining gravy separately.

TO MAKE AHEAD: Pot roast can be made up to 2 days ahead. Follow recipe through step 4, then transfer cooked roasts to large bowl. Strain and defat liquid and add beef broth to bring liquid amount to 3 cups; transfer liquid and vegetables to bowl with roasts, let cool for 1 hour, cover with plastic wrap, cut vents in plastic, and refrigerate overnight or up to 48 hours. One hour before serving, adjust oven rack to middle position and heat oven to 325 degrees. Slice roasts as directed, place in 13 by 9-inch baking dish, cover tightly with foil, and bake until heated through, about 45 minutes. Blend liquid and vegetables, bring gravy to simmer, and finish as directed.

PRACTICAL SCIENCE LOW-TEMPERATURE BROWNING

The flavorful browning of the Maillard reaction can take place at low temperatures, too.

When meat is seared at a very high temperature, the Maillard reaction rapidly kicks in, rendering the exterior deeply browned and flavorful. (For more on this, see concept 2.) But can browning take place at lower temperatures in the moist, closed environment of a braise, where the temperature can never rise above the boiling point of water, 212 degrees?

We cooked two pot roasts: one that we seared before adding a small amount of liquid to the pot, and the other that we placed directly in the pot with the liquid without searing. Surprisingly, we found that the dry part of the two roasts that sat above the liquid had a similar level of browning, and the unseared roast tasted nearly as good as the seared one.

What was going on? In the searing heat of a 500-degree pan, the Maillard reaction quickly produces countless new flavor compounds that improve taste. But as it turns out, given enough time, browning can also occur at temperatures as low as 160 degrees.

Our Easy Pot Roast (above) cooks for a good 3½ hours. This is ample time for lots of new flavor compounds to be created on the dry top part of the meat. Though these compounds won't be as plentiful or richly flavorful as when browning occurs at higher temperatures, in some cases we feel that we can skip the sear.

✔ WHY THIS RECIPE WORKS

This recipe veers away from "classic"—instead of first browning the meat, as we do with most braises in order to develop flavor, we coax out some of the browning effects through an extended cooking time in the oven. To promote this low-temperature browning, we use minimal amounts of liquid in the braise. (See "Low-Temperature Browning," page 77.) We also compensate for this lack of a flavorful sear by using intense flavors in the pot—tomato paste, beef broth, red wine, sautéed mirepoix. We finish the sauce with even bolder flavors—vinegar and more wine.

SPLIT IT IN TWO Before cooking, we divide the roast in two, peeling it apart at the seams and removing any excess fat. The pesky globs of interior fat that stubbornly refuse to render are a common problem in pot roasts. In addition, we found that halving the beef increases the total surface area that can brown while the meat cooks in the covered pot.

SALT AHEAD We salt the meat an hour before beginning to cook. Salting draws moisture out of the meat, forming a shallow brine that, over time, migrates back into the meat to season it throughout rather than just on the exterior (see concept 12). While many brines take hours and hours, we find that salting just one hour before cooking makes a big difference—especially with the additional exposed surface area that comes with splitting the roast in two. When cooking, this technique—along with the additions of beef broth and the glutamate-rich tomato paste (see concept 35)—really brings out the meaty flavors.

PUREE THE GRAVY FOR FLAVOR By the time the pot roast is cooked until it's well-*well*-done, the vegetables have broken down and started to thicken the gravy. We coax out the last of their flavor by tossing them in the blender with the cooking liquid, which we have already defatted. This is a similar flavor-enhancing technique to that in the Classic Pot Roast recipe (page 76) because for each we use no thickeners—here we simply puree the sauce rather than reduce it. Just before serving, we add balsamic vinegar and wine for a brighter flavor.

BRAISING AT WORK SHORT RIBS AND CHICKEN THIGHS

Braising bone-in cuts like short ribs and chicken parts has the potential to yield extreme flavor (for more on bones and flavor see concept 10), but also an excess of fat. We try a variety of methods to reduce the amount of fat while maintaining the intensity of flavor in these meaty braises, including removing the bones and chicken skin, and defatting the sauce before serving.

BRAISED BONELESS BEEF SHORT RIBS
SERVES 6

In this recipe, we use boneless short ribs—or we remove the bones ourselves. Make sure the ribs are at least 4 inches long and 1 inch thick. If boneless ribs are unavailable, substitute 7 pounds of bone-in beef short ribs at least 4 inches long with 1 inch of meat above the bone. We recommend a bold red wine such as Cabernet Sauvignon. Serve with buttered egg noodles, mashed potatoes, or roasted potatoes.

3½ pounds boneless short ribs, trimmed
   Kosher salt and pepper
2 tablespoons vegetable oil
2 large onions, sliced thin
1 tablespoon tomato paste
6 garlic cloves, peeled
2 cups red wine
1 cup beef broth
4 large carrots, peeled and cut into 2-inch pieces
4 sprigs fresh thyme
1 bay leaf
¼ cup cold water
½ teaspoon unflavored gelatin

1. Adjust oven rack to lower-middle position and heat oven to 300 degrees. Pat beef dry with paper towels and season with 2 teaspoons salt and 1 teaspoon pepper. Heat 1 tablespoon oil in Dutch oven over medium-high heat until smoking. Add half of beef and cook, without moving, until well browned, 4 to 6 minutes. Turn beef over and continue to cook on second side until well browned, 4 to 6 minutes longer, reducing heat if fat begins to smoke. Transfer beef to medium bowl. Repeat with remaining 1 tablespoon oil and remaining meat.

2. Reduce heat to medium, add onions, and cook, stirring occasionally, until softened and beginning to brown, 12 to 15 minutes. (If onions begin to darken too quickly, add 1 to 2 tablespoons water to pot.) Add tomato paste and cook, stirring constantly, until it browns on sides and

bottom of pan, about 2 minutes. Add garlic and cook until fragrant, about 30 seconds. Increase heat to medium-high, add wine, and simmer, scraping bottom of pan with wooden spoon to loosen browned bits, until reduced by half, 8 to 10 minutes. Add broth, carrots, thyme, and bay leaf. Add beef and any accumulated juices to pot; cover and bring to simmer. Transfer pot to oven and cook, using tongs to turn meat twice during cooking, until fork slips easily in and out of meat, 2 to 2½ hours.

3. Put water in small bowl and sprinkle gelatin on top; let stand for at least 5 minutes. Using tongs, transfer meat and carrots to serving platter and tent with aluminum foil. Strain cooking liquid through fine-mesh strainer into fat separator or bowl, pressing on solids to extract as much liquid as possible; discard solids. Let liquid settle for 5 minutes and strain off fat. Return cooking liquid to Dutch oven and cook over medium heat until reduced to 1 cup, 5 to 10 minutes. Remove from heat and stir in gelatin mixture; season with salt and pepper to taste. Pour sauce over meat and serve.

BRAISED BEEF SHORT RIBS WITH GUINNESS AND PRUNES

Substitute 1 cup Guinness (or other full-flavored porter or stout) for red wine and omit 8- to 10-minute reduction time in step 2. Add ⅓ cup pitted prunes to pot along with broth.

PRACTICAL SCIENCE A REAL MELTING POT

Bone-in short ribs render exponentially more fat than boneless.

Although we expected that bone-in short ribs would exude more fat than their boneless counterparts, we were shocked by the dramatic difference—1½ cups versus ¼ cup (six times as much)! No wonder most short rib recipes call for letting the fat solidify overnight in the fridge. (For more on bones, see concept 10.)

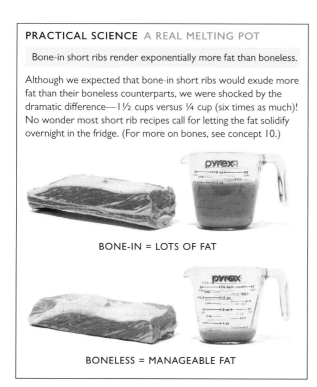

BONE-IN = LOTS OF FAT

BONELESS = MANAGEABLE FAT

✔ WHY THIS RECIPE WORKS

We begin with boneless short ribs in order to reduce the amount of fat rendered during the braising process, which can be monumental (see "A Real Melting Pot," below). This allows us to simply defat the sauce at the end of cooking and serve, rather than chill the ribs overnight in order to solidify the fat for easy removal the following day. (The latter method is commonly used in short rib recipes.) This does mean that without the bones, there is less connective tissue available to melt down into gelatin and the sauce can be a bit thin. We stir ½ teaspoon of gelatin into the strained sauce to give it the proper viscosity and suppleness.

SIZE DOES MATTER Butchers typically divide the ribs into sections about 10 inches square and 3 to 5 inches thick. Cutting the ribs between the bones and into lengths between 2 and 6 inches yields what butchers call "English" style, a cut typically found in European braises. Cutting the meat across the bone yields the "flanken" cut, more typically found in Asian cuisines. We focus on the widely available English-style short ribs but find that the smallest (about 2 inches) are too short; once braised, they shrink into pieces resembling stew meat. At the other extreme, the 6- to 8-inchers are fairly unwieldy to brown in the pan. We split the difference and settle on 4-inch-long ribs.

BROWN WELL The first step in most braises is browning the meat. Searing adds color and flavor due to the Maillard reaction (see concept 2). But here, searing also rids the ribs of some of their excess fat by rendering.

FLAVOR ACTION To jump-start the flavor of our sauce, we reduce the wine right over the browned aromatics, which adds an intensity and depth. Still in need of more liquid for the braise, however, we find that beef broth offers a nice flavor balance to the wine.

CHICKEN PROVENÇAL
SERVES 4

This dish is often served with rice or slices of crusty bread, but soft polenta is also a good accompaniment. Be sure to use niçoise olives here; other olives are too potent.

8	(5- to 7-ounce) bone-in chicken thighs, trimmed
	Salt
1	tablespoon extra-virgin olive oil
1	small onion, chopped fine
6	garlic cloves, minced
1	anchovy fillet, rinsed and minced
⅛	teaspoon cayenne pepper
1	cup dry white wine
1	(14.5-ounce) can diced tomatoes, drained

I	cup low-sodium chicken broth
2½	tablespoons tomato paste
I½	tablespoons minced fresh thyme
I	teaspoon minced fresh oregano
I	teaspoon herbes de Provence (optional)
I	bay leaf
I½	teaspoons grated lemon zest
½	cup pitted niçoise olives
I	tablespoon chopped fresh parsley

1. Adjust oven rack to lower-middle position and heat oven to 300 degrees. Season both sides of chicken with salt. Heat 1 teaspoon oil in Dutch oven over medium-high heat until shimmering. Add 4 chicken thighs, skin side down, and cook without moving until skin is crisp and well browned, about 5 minutes. Using tongs, turn chicken pieces and brown on second side, about 5 minutes longer; transfer to large plate. Add remaining 4 chicken thighs to pot and repeat, then transfer to plate and set aside. Discard all but 1 tablespoon fat from pot.

2. Add onion to fat in Dutch oven and cook, stirring occasionally, over medium heat until browned, about 4 minutes. Add garlic, anchovy, and cayenne; cook, stirring constantly, until fragrant, about 1 minute. Add wine and scrape up browned bits from bottom of pot. Stir in tomatoes, broth, tomato paste, thyme, oregano, herbes de Provence, if using, and bay leaf. Remove and discard skin from chicken thighs, then submerge chicken in liquid and add accumulated chicken juices to pot. Increase heat to high, bring to simmer, cover, and transfer pot to oven; cook until chicken offers no resistance when poked with tip of paring knife but still clings to bones, about 1¼ hours.

3. Using slotted spoon, transfer chicken to serving platter and tent with aluminum foil. Discard bay leaf. Set Dutch oven over high heat, stir in 1 teaspoon lemon zest, bring to boil, and cook, stirring occasionally, until slightly thickened and reduced to 2 cups, about 5 minutes. Stir in olives and cook until heated through, about 1 minute. Meanwhile, mix remaining ½ teaspoon zest with parsley. Spoon sauce over chicken, drizzle chicken with remaining 2 teaspoons oil, sprinkle with parsley mixture, and serve.

CHICKEN PROVENÇAL WITH SAFFRON, ORANGE, AND BASIL

Add ⅛ teaspoon saffron threads with wine in step 2. Substitute orange zest for lemon zest and 2 tablespoons chopped fresh basil for parsley.

✔ WHY THIS RECIPE WORKS

Chicken Provençal represents the best of rustic peasant food— bone-in chicken simmered slowly in a tomatoey, garlicky herb broth that is flavorful enough to mop up with thick slices of crusty bread. To achieve our ideal, we start with bone-in, skin-on chicken thighs and brown them in olive oil to develop rich flavor and leave behind browned bits in the pan. Because dark meat has more connective tissue than white meat, we are able to braise the chicken thighs for a long time—until they reach 210 degrees—rendering them tender and juicy and not at all dry.

START WITH THIGHS   Chicken thighs are a favorite for braising. Unlike drumsticks and wings, they are easy to handle and eat. And unlike breasts, which are very lean, dark meat thighs contain collagen and fat because there is more connective tissue surrounding these heavily used muscles. The collagen and fat render in the long cooking time to create a juicy, tender braise.

DITCH THE SKIN   The chicken skin is a necessary cushion between the meat and pan when browning, and so we leave it on to begin. After all, it's important to deeply brown the chicken thighs in order to render more fat and therefore add more chicken flavor in the dish. We discard the skin after browning the thighs, as it turns flabby and inedible during the long braising time.

AUGMENT WITH OLIVE OIL   We use less rather than more olive oil while browning the chicken thighs in the beginning of this recipe—just 1 teaspoon. This allows more chicken fat to be rendered and then kept as we continue the braise, resulting in more chicken flavor in the final dish. But we do drizzle two additional teaspoons of extra-virgin olive oil over the finished results for its added fruity flavor. Olive oil, after all, is a staple of southern France, where this dish originated.

TASTE FOR SEASONING   As for seasonings, the combination of the dried herbs referred to as herbes de Provence (lavender, marjoram, basil, fennel seeds, rosemary, sage, summer savory, and thyme) originally seemed like a shoo-in. But we found that when used alone, these dried herbs were too strong, giving the sauce a flavor that bordered on medicinal. Instead, we prefer fresh thyme, oregano, parsley, and a bay leaf, with a teaspoon of the dried blend as an optional item. A pinch of cayenne balances the sweet tomatoes and a teaspoon of minced anchovies, which are rich in glutamates and nucleotides (for more on glutamates and nucleotides, see concept 35), makes the sauce taste richer and fuller. Finally, lemon zest adds a light touch.

CHICKEN PAPRIKASH
SERVES 4

In this rendition of the Hungarian classic, the natural juices of chicken, bell peppers, onion, and tomatoes are released during the braising process and then enriched with sour cream to create a dish that's especially comforting in cold weather. Serve with buttered egg noodles; rice or mashed potatoes are also good options.

8	(5- to 7-ounce) bone-in chicken thighs, trimmed
	Salt and pepper
1	teaspoon vegetable oil
1	large onion, halved and sliced thin
1	large red bell pepper, stemmed, seeded, halved widthwise, and cut into thin strips
1	large green bell pepper, stemmed, seeded, halved widthwise, and cut into thin strips
3½	tablespoons paprika
1	tablespoon all-purpose flour
¼	teaspoon dried marjoram
½	cup dry white wine
1	(14.5-ounce) can diced tomatoes, drained
⅓	cup sour cream
2	tablespoons minced fresh parsley

1. Adjust oven rack to lower-middle position and heat oven to 300 degrees. Pat chicken dry with paper towels and season with salt and pepper. Heat oil in Dutch oven over medium-high heat until shimmering. Add 4 chicken thighs, skin side down, and cook without moving them until skin is crisp and well browned, about 5 minutes. Using tongs, flip chicken and brown on second side, about 5 minutes. Transfer to large plate. Add remaining 4 chicken thighs to pot and repeat, then transfer to plate and set aside. Discard all but 1 tablespoon fat from pot.

2. Add onion to fat left in Dutch oven and sauté over medium heat until softened, 5 to 7 minutes. Add bell peppers and sauté until onions are browned and peppers are softened, about 3 minutes. Stir in 3 tablespoons paprika, flour, and marjoram and cook, stirring constantly, until fragrant, about 1 minute. Add wine, scraping pot bottom with wooden spoon to loosen brown bits. Stir in tomatoes and 1 teaspoon salt. Remove and discard skin from chicken thighs, then nestle chicken under onion and peppers, and add accumulated juices to pot. Bring to simmer, cover, and place pot in oven. Cook until chicken offers no resistance when poked with tip of paring knife, but still clings to bone, about 1¼ hours. (Stew can be cooled to room temperature, covered, and refrigerated for up to 3 days. Bring to simmer over medium-low heat before proceeding.)

3. Combine sour cream and remaining ½ tablespoon paprika in small bowl. Remove chicken from pot and place portion on each plate. Stir few tablespoons of hot sauce into sour cream to temper, and then stir mixture back into remaining peppers and sauce. Ladle peppers and enriched sauce over chicken, sprinkle with parsley, and serve immediately.

✔ WHY THIS RECIPE WORKS

Chicken paprikash is an easy-to-make braise with succulent chicken, a balance of heat, spice, and aromatics, and a rich, flavorful sauce with paprika at center stage. To get to this goal, we pared down the usual mile-long ingredient list. Sautéing a handful of aromatics and vegetables in the fond led to a rich base for our sauce, which we enhanced with paprika twice: once while sautéing the vegetables to let its flavor bloom, then once again when adding sour cream to finish the dish.

DITCH THE SKIN Just as for Chicken Provençal, we ditch the skin after browning to prevent the accumulation of excess fat and a greasy sauce. To do this, grasp the skin from one end of the browned and cooled chicken thighs and simply pull to separate it from the meat.

CHOOSING YOUR PAPRIKA The brilliant red powder we call "paprika" comes from the dried pods (fruit) of the plant species *Capisicum annuum L.*, the family of peppers that ranges from sweet bells to the very hottest chiles. Several varieties of this clan are used to produce paprika and as a result there are many different kinds of paprika. We found that chicken paprikash is best flavored with Hungarian sweet paprika. Other sweet paprikas can deliver good results, but don't use hot paprika in this dish.

TEMPER, TEMPER If sour cream is added directly to the pot it can curdle—especially when added to a hot sauce made acidic with tomatoes. The tomato acid neutralizes some of the electrical charges on the proteins in sour cream (mostly proteins called casein), causing them to be more prone to clump together (coagulate) and separate (curdle). Tempering the sour cream (stirring some of the hot liquid from the stew pot together with the sour cream in a small bowl, then adding the warmed mixture to the pot) helps to prevent curdling, however. This is because the addition of a small amount of the warm liquid dilutes the proteins in the sour cream and gradually brings them all up to temperature. Any extra fat in the cooking liquid also helps to coat the proteins and prevent them from clumping.

In stews, we use small, boneless chunks of meat rather than the big hunks typical in pot roasts. We cook stews with a generous amount of liquid, alongside a lot of big vegetable pieces—and, as with most braises, we do this in a covered pot. Again, we like to use the oven to simmer our stews evenly and gently, maintaining the well-done temperature of the meat until its collagen melts, tough muscle fibers break down, and fat renders, leaving us with a tender, flavorful stew. These two recipes offer bold riffs on the classic beef stew. For a more traditional beef stew, see Best Beef Stew on page 310.

DAUBE PROVENÇAL
SERVES 4 TO 6

Serve this French beef stew with buttered egg noodles or boiled potatoes.

- ¾ ounce dried porcini mushrooms, rinsed
- 2 cups water
- 1 (3½-pound) boneless beef chuck-eye roast, pulled apart at seams, trimmed, and cut into 2-inch pieces
- 1 teaspoon salt
- 1 teaspoon pepper
- 4 tablespoons olive oil
- 5 ounces salt pork, rind removed
- 4 carrots, peeled and cut into 1-inch pieces
- 2 onions, halved and sliced ⅛ inch thick
- 4 garlic cloves, sliced thin
- 2 tablespoons tomato paste
- ⅓ cup all-purpose flour
- 1 (750-ml) bottle red wine
- 1 cup low-sodium chicken broth
- 4 (2-inch) strips orange zest, cut lengthwise into thin strips
- 1 cup pitted niçoise olives
- 3 anchovy fillets, rinsed and minced
- 5 sprigs fresh thyme, tied together with kitchen twine
- 2 bay leaves
- 1 (14.5-ounce) can whole tomatoes, drained and cut into ½-inch pieces
- 2 tablespoons minced fresh parsley

1. Cover mushrooms with 1 cup water in small bowl, cover, and microwave until steaming, about 1 minute. Lift mushrooms from liquid with fork and chop into ½-inch pieces (you should have about ¼ cup). Strain liquid through paper towel–lined fine-mesh strainer into medium bowl. Set mushrooms and liquid aside.

2. Adjust oven rack to lower-middle position and heat oven to 300 degrees. Pat beef dry and season with salt and pepper. Heat 2 tablespoons oil in Dutch oven over medium-high heat until shimmering. Add half of beef and cook without moving until well browned, about 2 minutes per side. Transfer meat to medium bowl. Repeat with remaining 2 tablespoons oil and remaining meat.

3. Reduce heat to medium and add salt pork, carrots, onions, garlic, and tomato paste to now-empty pot; cook, stirring occasionally, until light brown, about 2 minutes. Stir in flour and cook, stirring constantly, about 1 minute. Slowly add wine, scraping bottom of pot to loosen browned bits. Add broth, remaining 1 cup water, and beef with any accumulated juices. Increase heat to medium-high and bring to simmer. Stir in mushrooms and their liquid, orange zest, ½ cup olives, anchovies, thyme, and bay leaves, arranging beef so it is completely covered by liquid; partially cover pot and place in oven. Cook until fork inserted in beef meets little resistance (meat should not be falling apart), 2½ to 3 hours.

4. Discard salt pork, thyme, and bay leaves. Add tomatoes and remaining ½ cup olives and cook over medium-high heat until heated through, about 1 minute. Cover pot and let stew sit, about 5 minutes. Using large spoon, skim excess fat from surface of stew. Stir in parsley and serve.

TO MAKE AHEAD: Once salt pork, thyme, and bay leaves are removed in step 4, daube can be cooled and refrigerated in airtight container for up to 4 days. Before reheating, skim hardened fat from surface and then continue with recipe.

✓ WHY THIS RECIPE WORKS

Daube Provençal, also known as daube Niçoise, has all the elements of the best French fare: tender beef, a luxurious sauce, and complex flavors. But it usually ends up as beef stew with a few misplaced ingredients. We wanted to translate the flavors of Provence to an American home kitchen, with ingredients that marry into a robust but unified dish. We start with our reliable set of techniques for turning tough but flavorful beef into a tender stew and then add briny niçoise olives, bright tomatoes, floral orange peel, and the regional flavors of thyme and bay. A few anchovies add complexity without a fishy taste, and salt pork contributes rich body.

SUPER-SIZE IT We began by cutting the chuck roast into 1-inch cubes, a standard size for beef stew. But because we cook this stew for longer than normal—a time that allows the full bottle of wine to mellow and the sauce to become thick and flavorful—the meat was drying out and losing its distinct character. The 1½-inch pieces that we use in our Hungarian Beef Stew (below) and Best Beef Stew (page 310) seemed too small as well. But by cutting the chuck roast into super-sized 2-inch chunks, we end up with not only a complex sauce but tender beef, too.

ACTIVATE FLOUR POWER Instead of using a traditional roux, which we found made a thin, greasy-looking sauce, we sprinkle flour into the pot to cook with the vegetables and tomato paste. We also increase the usual amount of flour—to ⅓ cup, which is a little more than most recipes contain. This helps to create a braising liquid that thickens to the consistency of a luxurious sauce.

HUNGARIAN BEEF STEW
SERVES 6

Serve the stew over boiled potatoes or buttered egg noodles.

1	(3½- to 4-pound) boneless beef chuck-eye roast, pulled apart at seams, trimmed, and cut into 1½-inch pieces
	Salt and pepper
⅓	cup paprika
1	cup jarred roasted red peppers, rinsed and patted dry
2	tablespoons tomato paste
1	tablespoon distilled white vinegar
2	tablespoons vegetable oil
4	large onions, chopped fine
4	large carrots, peeled and cut into 1-inch rounds
1	bay leaf
1	cup beef broth, warmed
¼	cup sour cream (optional)

1. Adjust oven rack to lower-middle position and heat oven to 325 degrees. Season meat evenly with 1 teaspoon salt and let stand for 15 minutes. Process paprika, roasted peppers, tomato paste, and 2 teaspoons vinegar in food processor until smooth, 1 to 2 minutes, scraping down sides as needed.

2. Combine oil, onions, and 1 teaspoon salt in Dutch oven; cover and set over medium heat. Cook, stirring occasionally, until onions soften but have not yet begun to brown, 8 to 10 minutes. (If onions begin to brown, reduce heat to medium-low and stir in 1 tablespoon water.)

3. Stir in paprika mixture; cook, stirring occasionally, until onions stick to bottom of pot, about 2 minutes.

Add beef, carrots, and bay leaf; stir until beef is well coated. Using rubber spatula, scrape down sides of pot. Cover pot and transfer to oven. Cook until meat is almost tender and surface of liquid is ½ inch below top of meat, 2 to 2½ hours, stirring every 30 minutes. Remove pot from oven and add enough beef broth so that surface of liquid is ¼ inch from top of meat (beef should not be fully submerged). Return covered pot to oven and continue to cook until fork slips easily in and out of beef, about 30 minutes longer.

4. Using large spoon, skim fat off surface; stir in remaining teaspoon vinegar. If using sour cream, stir few tablespoons of hot sauce into sour cream to temper it, and then stir mixture back into pot. Remove bay leaf, season with salt and pepper to taste, and serve. (Stew, minus optional sour cream, can be refrigerated for up to 2 days. Stir sour cream into reheated stew just before serving.)

✓ WHY THIS RECIPE WORKS
The Americanized versions of Hungarian goulash served in the United States bear little resemblance to the traditional dish. Mushrooms, green peppers, and most herbs have no place in the pot and sour cream is not authentic to the dish. We wanted the real deal—a simple dish of tender braised beef packed with paprika flavor. Though we don't add liquid to the stew itself (for more on covered pot cooking without liquid, see concept 9), a bit of broth added near the end thins out the stewing liquid to just the right consistency.

MAKE PAPRIKA CREAM To achieve the desired level of spicy intensity, we create our own version of paprika cream, a condiment common in Hungarian cooking but hard to find in the United States. Pureeing the paprika with roasted red peppers, tomato paste, and vinegar imparts vibrant paprika flavor without any grittiness. Do not substitute hot, half-sharp, or smoked Spanish paprika for the sweet paprika; they will compromise the flavor of the dish.

SKIP THE SEAR, NOT THE FLAVOR Most stews begin by browning meat on the stovetop to boost flavor. They also call for lots of added liquid. Like our Easy Pot Roast recipe (page 77), this recipe skips the sear and goes into a moderate 325-degree oven. Over time, the dry top layer of meat will begin to brown, forming new flavor compounds. (See "Low-Temperature Browning," page 77.) We stir the meat every 30 minutes to expose new surfaces and promote as much of the slow browning to take place as possible.

A Covered Pot Doesn't Need Liquid

In concept 8, we looked at covered pot cooking with liquid. But just because the vessel is closed, that doesn't mean the options are, too. You don't need added liquid to effectively cook a cut of meat in a closed pot. Sometimes it's best to do it completely dry.

HOW THE SCIENCE WORKS

Cooking *en cocotte*, or casserole-roasting, is a common cooking method in France that is typically used for chicken and lamb. The approach is simple: Place a seasoned piece of meat in a pot, scatter in a small handful of chopped vegetables, cover, and bake. This technique has many similarities to braising: It utilizes a covered pot, low oven temperature, and extended cooking time to yield tender, flavorful meat. But the big difference is when cooking en cocotte, no liquid is added. Instead, juices are drawn from the meat into the pot. These juices eventually create a moist-heat environment, so that the meat cooks gently—in effect, braising in its own juices. The result is unbelievably tender and flavorful meat undiluted by additional liquid.

Unlike braising, where tough, fatty cuts are generally cooked until they are tender and falling off the bone, cooking en cocotte begins with lean, naturally tender cuts, such as a whole chicken or pork loin. The meat is cooked until it is just done, which is why we take the temperature of the meat to ensure it is not overcooked or undercooked.

We cook en cocotte in a low-temperature oven to retain moisture, help break down whatever tough muscle fibers are present, as well as to intensify the flavors of the meat. In our kitchen testing, we found that temperatures of 325 to 375 degrees produced decent results, but even lower temperatures—around 250 degrees—yielded incredibly tender meat, thanks to the gentle heat and longer cooking time. Sure, some of these low-temperature versions take up to an hour and 45 minutes to cook, but it's worth it for the rich, concentrated flavors. (For more on the benefits of cooking with gentle heat, see concept 1.)

While cooking en cocotte resembles braising, it's probably more helpful to think of it as an alternative to roasting, where the emphasis is on moisture retention rather than browning. In order to maximize moisture retention, it's important to let meat cooked this way rest before carving or slicing (see concept 3). Use the remaining concentrated liquid left in the pot as the basis for an easy-to-prepare sauce that further enhances the flavor and juiciness of the meat.

THE BENEFITS OF "DRY" BRAISING

DRY ENVIRONMENT *In a dry, covered pot with no added liquid, the juices that come out of the chicken create a moist heat environment and are retained for a sauce, undiluted by other flavors.*

TEST KITCHEN EXPERIMENT

To understand how effective cooking en cocotte is at preserving moisture in meat, we devised the following test: We cooked two whole chickens, one en cocotte in a covered Dutch oven and the other in an uncovered baking dish—both in 250-degree ovens, the temperature at which we cook our French Chicken in a Pot (page 86). To determine moisture loss, we weighed the birds before and after cooking and collected the liquid that settled in the cooking vessels. Both birds were raised up on wire racks to eliminate any potential reabsorption of expelled juices. We ran this test three times and averaged the results.

THE RESULTS

The chickens cooked in the open baking dish lost 11 percent of their moisture compared to roughly 7.5 percent moisture loss in the en cocotte samples. While these numbers are telling in and of themselves, they become all the more impressive when we factor in the amount of liquid recovered in the bottom of each cooking vessel. While there was almost 3 ounces of liquid in the Dutch oven on average, there was just 1 ounce in the open baking dish. If you serve the liquid in the cooking vessel with the chicken, you can mitigate some of the moisture loss that occurred during cooking. Assuming that this liquid makes it back onto the dinner plate, the difference

between the two cooking methods becomes even starker. With the recovered liquid added to the equation, the chickens cooked in the open baking dish lost 9.5 percent of their initial moisture on average while the chickens cooked in the covered Dutch oven lost just 3.5 percent of their initial moisture.

THE TAKEAWAY

It did not come as a surprise that the chickens roasted in open vessels lost more moisture than those roasted in a closed pot. This difference is likely due to the greater evaporative moisture loss for the exposed birds. (It's important to note, too, that if we had cooked the uncovered birds at a higher temperature, which is how we normally roast chicken, they would have lost even more moisture due to evaporation.) But what makes the results of this experiment dramatic is when you factor in the liquid remaining in the pan, because that is one of the reasons—if not the best reason— to cook en cocotte: the built-in sauce. While the low oven temperature in our en cocotte method is partially responsible for supremely moist poultry and meat, it's the pot's tight-fitting lid that allows us to trap the meat juices and mitigate total moisture loss by using these juices to produce a rich jus.

WHAT REMAINS: JUICES RETAINED WHEN ROASTING VS. EN COCOTTE

ROASTED
A chicken cooked in an open baking dish loses a good deal of moisture; only 28 grams of juices remain in the dish.

EN COCOTTE
A chicken cooked in a covered pot loses some moisture, but 74 grams of juices remain in the pot after cooking.

Chicken in a pot, or poulet en cocotte, is a Parisian bistro classic. The dish features a whole chicken baked with a smattering of vegetables in a covered pot. We brown it, cover it—no liquid added!—and cook it in a low-temperature oven. At first glance, this chicken is nothing to rave about. After all, it has pale, soft skin unlike the crisp exterior of roasted poultry. But the first time we tried this dish, one bite confirmed it was special indeed—the meat was incredibly tender and juicy, with a rich, soul-satisfying flavor.

FRENCH CHICKEN IN A POT
SERVES 4

You will need at least a 6-quart Dutch oven with a tight-fitting lid. If you choose not to serve the skin with the chicken, simply remove it before carving. The amount of jus varies depending on the size of the chicken; season it with ¼ teaspoon of lemon juice for every ¼ cup.

1	(4½- to 5-pound) whole chicken, giblets discarded
	Salt and pepper
1	tablespoon olive oil
1	small onion, chopped
1	small celery rib, chopped
6	garlic cloves, peeled
1	bay leaf
1	sprig fresh rosemary (optional)
½–1	teaspoon lemon juice

1. Adjust oven rack to lowest position and heat oven to 250 degrees. Pat chicken dry with paper towels, tuck wings behind back, and season with salt and pepper. Heat oil in Dutch oven over medium heat until just smoking. Add chicken breast side down; scatter onion, celery, garlic, bay leaf, and rosemary sprig, if using, around chicken. Cook until breast is lightly browned, about 5 minutes. Using wooden spoon inserted into cavity of bird, flip chicken breast side up and cook until chicken and vegetables are well browned, 6 to 8 minutes.

2. Off heat, place large sheet of aluminum foil over pot and cover tightly with lid. Transfer pot to oven and cook chicken until breast registers 160 degrees and thighs register 175 degrees, 1 hour 20 minutes to 1 hour 50 minutes.

3. Transfer chicken to carving board, tent with foil, and let rest for 20 minutes. Meanwhile, strain chicken juices from pot through fine-mesh strainer into fat separator, pressing on solids to extract liquid; discard solids. Let juices settle for 5 minutes, then pour into saucepan and set over low heat. Carve chicken, adding any accumulated juices to saucepan. Season with lemon juice, salt, and pepper to taste. Serve chicken, passing sauce separately.

✓ WHY THIS RECIPE WORKS

The method for our French chicken in a pot is simple: Place a seasoned chicken in a pot, brown it, scatter in some vegetables, cover, and bake. When done right, this dish forgoes crispy skin for unbelievably tender, succulent meat and rich flavor. The key is a dry cooking environment and our main challenge is to minimize the humidity in the pot so that it doesn't dilute the flavor of the meat as it cooks. By cooking the chicken by itself in a tightly sealed pot—with few added vegetables in order to prevent the extra liquid and steam that come from large chunks—we get the concentrated flavor we seek. Cooking the bird at a low 250 degrees ensures the breast meat doesn't dry out. Finally, we add a small amount of aromatics, lightly browned to remove some of their moisture, for extra flavor.

BROWN FIRST We sear the chicken over medium heat in order to cause browning, instigate the Maillard reaction, and, as a result, build flavor. (For more on this, see concept 2.) Though often browning is used as a technique to build flavor in the crust of the meat or chicken itself, many cooks will choose to discard the skin of this chicken before serving. Therefore, the real flavor comes in the potent jus that will be left in the pot once the chicken is done.

PROTECT THE WINGS Tucking the wings of a chicken behind the back will keep them out of the way and prevent the wingtips from burning. To do this, simply twist the wing behind the back and close the joints of the wing tightly. The tension of the closed, tucked wing will help to keep it in place.

FOIL IT It's important to add a sheet of aluminum foil over the pot before placing on its lid. This will help to create the tightest seal possible and prevent any steam from escaping from the pot as the chicken cooks.

COOK BREAST SIDE UP We found it necessary to cook the chicken breast side up in the covered pot. Because the dark meat is resting on the bottom of the pot, where heat transfer is best, it will cook faster than the white meat above. As a result, by the time the breast meat reaches 160 degrees (a temperature beyond which the meat will dry out), the dark meat has raced ahead to 175 degrees (the temperature at which it is no longer tough).

STRAIN AND SERVE After transferring the chicken to a carving board and tenting it with foil to rest, strain the chicken juices from the pot through a fine-mesh strainer. We don't strain the sauce purely for textural and aesthetic reasons: It makes a more intensely flavored jus, too. By straining the sauce and pressing on the aromatics, we release the essence of onion, carrot, celery, and garlic into the sauce. Now we just need a little lemon juice for brightness, and it's ready to serve.

POULTRY 101

STRUCTURE

Chicken, turkey, and other poultry have the same basic structure as other meats. We eat muscles that consist of muscle fibers, fat, and connective tissue (see page 41). As with other animals, the location and function of poultry muscles will affect the amount of fat and connective tissue. In poultry, the differences between various "cuts" are especially dramatic—white meat and dark meat look and taste quite different and cook differently, too.

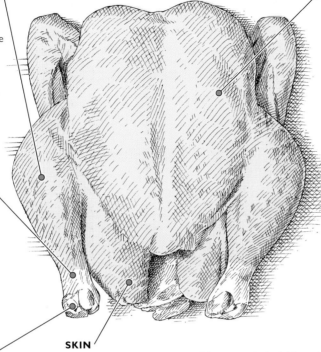

DARK MEAT
The thighs and legs consist primarily of dark muscle cells, which make up what are known as "slow-twitch" fibers and are necessary for long, continuous activity. Dark muscle cells rely on oxygen in the blood to convert stored fat into energy. This metabolic process requires the help of several agents, including the protein myoglobin, a red pigment that stores oxygen in muscle cells.

COLLAGEN
All animal tissue contains some collagen, the sheets of connective tissue that hold muscle fibers together. However, the collagen level in white meat chicken is less than 2 percent; dark meat chicken contains as much as 8 percent collagen, which makes the legs and thighs a much better choice for slow-cooking methods like braising, which can convert all that tough collagen into tender gelatin (see page 64).

BONES
Bones insulate the meat and thus slow down the rate of cooking. They also provide flavor—see concept 10.

WHITE MEAT
The breast consists primarily of white muscle cells, which make up what are known as "fast-twitch" fibers and are necessary for quick bursts of energy. White muscle cells rely on carbohydrates stored in the muscle for energy and do not need the myoglobin in the blood to supply the necessary oxygen. While this energy can be generated quickly, it cannot be sustained, and therefore white meat cells are abundant only in muscles that see little or no activity. Birds that rarely fly (such as chickens or turkeys) have an especially high proportion of white cells in their breast muscles; in contrast, ducks and birds that fly long distances have relatively few white cells in their breast muscles—thus the darker color of their breast meat.

SKIN
The skin is the primary source of fat in most birds. Additional fat lies just under the skin—it is visible as yellow clumps, especially near the neck and tail end of the bird. The dark meat also contains some intramuscular fat—generally more than twice as much as the white meat.

BUYING

FRESHNESS Some poultry has a sell-by date (usually 12 to 14 days after processing), but this date is more for stores (to ensure that they aren't selling old birds) and should not be considered a use-by date for the consumer. Cook or freeze poultry within a day of its purchase.

SIZE Whole chickens can weigh as little as 1 pound or as much as 8 pounds; likewise, whole turkeys can range in size from 10 to 25 pounds. Turkeys are easy to shop for since the nomenclature is the same no matter the size. When shopping for chicken, the same bird can be labeled differently depending on age and size at time of slaughter.

APPROXIMATE WEIGHT OF VARIOUS CHICKEN SIZES	
Cornish hens	1 to 1½ pounds
Poussins	1 to 2 pounds
Broiler/fryers	3 to 5 pounds
Roasters	5 to 8 pounds

PROCESSING Simply put, buy a natural bird. When it comes to chicken, we prefer air-chilled versus water-chilled birds. The latter method (which soaks the bird in 34-degree water after slaughtering) causes the bird to absorb water. If you see the phrase "contains up to 4% retained water" on the label, you know the bird was water-chilled. Besides the fact that you're paying for the water, the water dilutes the chicken flavor and makes it hard to crisp up the skin during cooking.

Turkeys can be injected with a salt-based solution to increase perceived juiciness. If in doubt, look for the words "basted" or "self-basting" and check to see if there's an ingredient label—if the turkey has been injected you should see a list of ingredients. While we prefer to brine or salt natural turkeys (see concepts 11 and 12), a self-basting bird, such as a frozen Butterball, is the best option if you're going to skip these steps.

STORAGE

REFRIGERATOR Keep chicken in the coldest part of your refrigerator, generally in the back, where the temperature should be between 32 and 36 degrees. Place chicken packages on plates to keep any condensation from dripping down onto other items in your refrigerator—this is especially important when defrosting poultry.

FREEZER Poultry is especially prone to freezer burn. Wrap all food, including birds, tightly with plastic wrap before freezing, making sure to press the wrap directly against the surface of the food to minimize exposure to air. However, given the odd shape of most birds (either whole or in parts), expect some freezer burn. Since freezer burn increases with storage time, use frozen poultry within a month or two. Allow 24 hours to defrost a whole chicken and three to four days to defrost a turkey in the refrigerator.

Roasting en cocotte can produce just as wonderful results for pork as it does for chicken. You will need a cut that will fit in a Dutch oven—and something boneless will be easier to work with. Also, since this method won't break down much collagen, a cut that will be tender when cooked through is essential. A pork loin is the best cut for the job. After browning the meat, we cook it in a low-temperature oven with minimal aromatics for an incredibly juicy, tender roast.

PORK ROAST EN COCOTTE WITH APPLES AND SHALLOTS
SERVES 4 TO 6

Leaving a ¼-inch-thick layer of fat on top of the roast is ideal; if your roast has a thicker fat cap, trim it back to be about ¼ inch thick. You can find herbes de Provence in most large grocery stores; however, 1 teaspoon each of dried thyme, dried rosemary, and dried marjoram can be substituted.

1	(2½- to 3-pound) boneless pork loin roast, trimmed and tied at 1½-inch intervals
1	tablespoon herbes de Provence
	Salt and pepper
3	tablespoons vegetable oil
8	shallots, peeled and quartered
1	pound Golden Delicious or Granny Smith apples, peeled, cored, and cut into ½-inch-thick wedges
¼	teaspoon sugar
1	tablespoon unsalted butter

1. Adjust oven rack to lowest position and heat oven to 250 degrees. Pat pork dry with paper towels, sprinkle herbes de Provence evenly over pork, and season with salt and pepper.

2. Heat 2 tablespoons oil in Dutch oven over medium-high heat until just smoking. Brown pork well on all sides, 7 to 10 minutes, reducing heat if pot begins to scorch. Transfer pork to large plate.

3. Add remaining 1 tablespoon oil to pot and heat over medium heat until shimmering. Add shallots and cook, stirring often, until golden, about 3 minutes. Stir in apples and sugar and cook, stirring often, until golden, 5 to 7 minutes.

4. Off heat, nestle pork, along with any accumulated juices, into pot. Place large sheet of aluminum foil over pot and press to seal, then cover tightly with lid. Transfer pot to oven and cook until roast registers 140 degrees, 35 to 55 minutes.

5. Remove pot from oven. Transfer pork to cutting board, tent loosely with foil, and let rest for about 20 minutes. Stir butter into apple-shallot mixture, season with salt and pepper to taste, and cover to keep warm.

6. Remove twine, slice pork thin, and transfer to serving platter. Spoon apple-shallot mixture over pork and serve.

☑ WHY THIS RECIPE WORKS

As with chicken, we found that browning the pork was an essential step in developing deep flavor. Unfortunately, lean pork doesn't have as much flavor as a good-quality bird. Our solution is to add shallots and apples to the pot. Rubbing the roast with herbes de Provence adds another layer of flavor.

PICK THE RIGHT ROAST Buying the right pork loin will make all the difference in this recipe because the pork needs to fit inside the pot. Look for a 2½- to 3-pound pork loin roast that is wide and short and steer clear of those that are long and narrow. A roast that is 7 to 8 inches long and 4 to 5 inches wide is perfect. We prefer a roast cut from the blade end; however, a center-cut roast (which is more common) works just fine.

MAKE APPLE "SAUCE" Since fruit is a traditional pairing with pork, we add apples to the mix. Knowing that the apples would compete with the pork for space in the pot, preventing it from browning evenly, and that the liquid they release would dull the flavor of the meat, we remove the browned pork to a plate and cook the apples separately on the stovetop. This allows some of their juices to evaporate. We then add the pork back to the pot to let the dish finish in the oven—leaving us with a rustic, chunky applesauce to accompany our pork.

LET IT REST Remove this pork roast from the oven when it reaches 140 to 145 degrees and let it rest, tented with foil, for 20 minutes. This rest time allows the pork to keep cooking, reaching the desired temperature of 150 degrees (for more on carryover cooking, see concept 4), and for the muscle fibers to relax so the meat will retain more of its juices (for more on resting, see concept 3).

Fish is well suited to a variety of preparations, from pan-searing, baking, and steaming to grilling and oven-roasting. Some types of fish have a high fat content and some are quite lean, but they all have one trait in common: They tend to cook fairly quickly. Since the whole premise of cooking en cocotte is to slow down cooking to concentrate flavor, we were skeptical that this technique would successfully translate to fish. But by not searing the fish, we found that we got just what we wanted: perfectly cooked, moist salmon that flaked apart into large buttery chunks.

SALMON EN COCOTTE WITH LEEKS AND WHITE WINE

SERVES 4

To ensure uniform pieces of fish that cook at the same rate, we prefer to buy a whole center-cut fillet and cut it into evenly sized individual fillets ourselves. If buying individual fillets, make sure they are the same size and thickness. If the fillets are thicker or thinner than 1¼ inches, you may need to adjust the cooking time slightly. If you can find only skin-on fillets, be sure to remove the skin before cooking or the sauce will be greasy; have the fishmonger do this for you, or see the instructions that follow the recipe. You can substitute arctic char or cod fillets for the salmon.

1	(1¾- to 2-pound) skinless salmon fillet, about 1½ inches at thickest part
	Salt and pepper
2	tablespoons extra-virgin olive oil
2	leeks, white and light green parts only, halved lengthwise, sliced thin, and washed thoroughly
2	sprigs fresh thyme
2	garlic cloves, minced
½	cup dry white wine
2	tablespoons unsalted butter, cut into 2 pieces

1. Adjust oven rack to lowest position and heat oven to 250 degrees. Trim any whitish fat from belly of fillet, then cut fish into 4 equal pieces. Pat salmon dry with paper towels and season with salt and pepper.

2. Heat oil in Dutch oven over medium-low heat until shimmering. Add leeks, thyme, and pinch salt, cover, and cook until softened, 8 to 10 minutes. Stir in garlic and cook until fragrant, about 30 seconds. Remove pot from heat.

3. Lay salmon, skinned side down, on top of leeks. Place large sheet of aluminum foil over pot and press to seal, then cover tightly with lid. Transfer pot to oven and cook until salmon is opaque and flakes apart when gently prodded with paring knife, 25 to 30 minutes.

4. Transfer fish to serving platter and tent loosely with foil. Stir wine into leeks in pot and simmer over medium-high heat until slightly thickened, about 2 minutes. Off heat, whisk in butter and season with salt and pepper to taste. Spoon sauce over salmon and serve.

SALMON EN COCOTTE WITH CELERY AND ORANGE

Add 2 thinly sliced celery ribs and 1 teaspoon minced orange zest along with garlic in step 2. Substitute ½ cup orange juice for wine, and add 1 orange, peeled and segmented, when thickening sauce in step 4.

✓ WHY THIS RECIPE WORKS

In this recipe, we take evenly cut fillets of salmon and cook them slowly, en cocotte in the oven. By eliminating the sear and adding leeks with their delicate, onionlike sweetness, as well as wine and butter, we achieve a flavorful, moist piece of fish.

CUT FISH YOURSELF It's important to have uniform pieces of fish so that they will cook evenly en cocotte. To guarantee this, we begin with a whole center-cut fillet that we cut ourselves into four individual servings. (That said, if only individual fillets are available, just be sure that they are of even size and thickness.)

REMOVE THE SKIN We remove the skin so that the actual flesh of the fish will pick up the flavors of the aromatics. Removing the skin also makes our final sauce less greasy. Starting at one end of the fillet, slide the knife between the skin and flesh, until you can grab hold of the skin with a paper towel. Holding the skin firmly, continue to cut the flesh from the skin until it is completely removed.

SKIP THE SEAR Here, we find that there is no discernible advantage to searing the fish before cooking it en cocotte. To streamline the process, we simply place the raw fish on top of the softened leeks and let it cook undisturbed.

BUTTER IT UP After removing the salmon from the pot we add a healthy dose of white wine to the leeks and simmer the mixture until it reduces slightly. Then we whisk in some butter to add richness before spooning this simple sauce over the salmon.

Bones Add Flavor, Fat, and Juiciness

In our grandparents' era, meat was generally cooked on the bone. But as a result of today's demand for convenience, boneless cuts have gradually replaced bone-in options in many markets. It's true, boneless cuts cook faster and are easier to carve and serve, but are we losing something in the process? Should we consider buying and cooking bone-in chops, steaks, and roasts more often? Well, yes.

HOW THE SCIENCE WORKS

Bones have the ability to make juicier, more flavorful roasts, chops, steaks, and ribs. Anyone who has experienced the pleasure of ending a meal by gnawing on a meat-stripped bone intuitively knows the value of bones. Here's the science.

The main structural material of bone is calcium phosphate, an insoluble rigid inorganic compound. But bone also contains a lot of connective tissue. In fact, collagen, the primary protein in connective tissue, comprises about 40 percent of bone. So, given enough cooking time, bones can be made to yield a significant amount of moisture-holding gelatin. As we learned in concept 7, when collagen converts to gelatin good things happen. Veal bones, being high in connective tissue, are frequently used to make the most luscious stocks. Some stocks yield so much gelatin that they actually gel when cooled. (For more on this, see the Test Kitchen Experiment on page 65.)

Second, although calcium phosphate is a good heat-conducting substance alone, bone is very porous and thus a relatively poor conductor of heat. This means that the meat located next to the bone doesn't cook as quickly as the rest of the roast—a phenomenon that helps to prevent overcooking and moisture loss and contributes to a noticeably juicier end product. This is why whenever you cut into any bone-in cut of meat, you'll notice that the rarest part is right next to the bone.

In addition, bones are lined with fat, a crucial source of flavor. For example, take barbecue, a popular cooking method for many bone-in cuts. A good number of flavor compounds found in smoke vapor are fat-soluble, and since there is extra fat in the roast or the ribs—courtesy of the bones—the meat is likely to absorb and retain more flavor from the smoke. In addition, as the fat melts during the cooking process, it bastes the meat, increasing the perceived juiciness.

And it doesn't end there. Bones actually add flavor directly to the meat. Here, the credit goes to the marrow, where blood cells are made, which is rich in fat and other flavorful substances. While bone-in cuts cook, the marrow's flavor compounds slowly migrate through the porous bone into the surrounding meat.

All in all, choosing a bone-in cut has a lot of advantages.

ANATOMY OF A STEAK

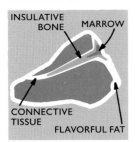

INSULATIVE BONE   MARROW

CONNECTIVE TISSUE   FLAVORFUL FAT

T-BONE *A T-shaped bone in the center of a steak extends the cooking time, provides connective tissue for juiciness, and fat and marrow for flavor.*

TEST KITCHEN EXPERIMENT

We've long known that the fat and connective tissue that surround bones lend moisture and richness to bone-in meats, while the mere presence of bones slows cooking and limits evaporation of juices. But it seemed to us that there must be other reasons why bone-in meat tastes better than the boneless kind. So when two meat experts suggested that some flavor might migrate from the rich marrow at the center of bones through the porous bone itself and right into the meat, our curiosity was piqued. We devised a test to see if this theory made any sense.

To fabricate a neutral-flavored pork substitute, we made a big batch of mashed potatoes and seasoned it with 8 percent butter and 1 percent salt by weight, amounts that mimic the fat and salt found in a pork roast. Mashed potatoes also contain nearly the same amount of moisture as raw meat. Then we formed the potatoes into two equal-size oblong shapes on a baking sheet. Next we scraped three pork rib bones clean of all fat and connective tissue, so that the only flavor would be from the marrow, and placed these bones on top of one of the "roasts." To create a control, we left the other mashed-potato "roast" alone. Then we cooked both of our imitation roasts in a 425-degree oven for 1½ hours. After a 20-minute rest, we compared the plain sample to the one with bones.

THE RESULTS

In a blind taste test, a majority of tasters found that the sample cooked with bones tasted noticeably meaty.

THE TAKEAWAY

As bones are heated, they expel moisture, salt, amino acids, and nucleotides (the last two being responsible for the "meatiness" that tasters detected) from the richly flavored marrow. (For more information on nucleotides, see concept 35.) Since those water-soluble flavor molecules must penetrate through a thick layer of bone to reach the meat, the diffusion process is slow and the amount of flavor contributed is not enormous— but it is detectable. When coupled with the considerable moisture- and flavor-enhancing benefits of the fat and connective tissue around the bones, the process certainly provides another good reason to opt for bone-in cuts of meat.

BONE-IN MASHED-POTATO "ROAST"

Crazy as it sounds, our imitation roast proved that some flavor from the bone can migrate into the meat—or potatoes, in this test.

OUR FAVORITE BONE-IN CUTS: PORK

CUTS	DESCRIPTION	COOKING METHOD
Center Rib Roast	Often referred to as the pork equivalent of prime rib or rack of lamb, this roast consists of a single muscle with a protective fat cap. It is from the top rib section of the animal and may be cut with anywhere from five to eight ribs.	It is juicy and flavorful, mild and fairly lean. Best when roasted (see page 95) or grilled.
Rib Chops	Our favorite chops are cut from the rib section of the loin. Rib chops can be distinguished by the section of rib bone running along one side.	With a relatively high fat content, this cut is flavorful and unlikely to dry out during cooking. Best when pan-seared (see page 57) or grilled (see page 107).
Blade Chops	Cut from the shoulder end of the loin, these chops can be difficult to find at the market. They can be fatty and tough, though they have good flavor and juiciness.	Best when braised.
St. Louis–Style Spareribs	This narrow, rectangular rack is cut close to the belly of the pig. It has been trimmed of skirt steak and excess cartilage.	Best when barbecued (see page 97).

We cook bone-in chops and steaks in part because of the insulating power of their ribs. The bones slow down the cooking process, giving the cook more time to infuse the meat with such flavors as smoke from the grill. Not only that, but the bones can serve as a shield, protecting tender meats from high heat and making it easier to cook your chops and steaks to the correct temperature without drying them out.

GRILL-SMOKED PORK CHOPS
SERVES 4

When using a charcoal grill, we prefer wood chunks to wood chips whenever possible; substitute two medium wood chunks, soaked in water for one hour, for the wood chip packet. Grate the onion on the large holes of a box grater.

SAUCE

½   cup ketchup
¼   cup molasses
2   tablespoons grated onion
2   tablespoons Worcestershire sauce
2   tablespoons Dijon mustard
2   tablespoons cider vinegar
1   tablespoon packed light brown sugar

CHOPS

2   cups wood chips, soaked in water for 15 minutes
     and drained
4   (12-ounce) bone-in pork rib chops, 1½ inches
     thick, trimmed
2   teaspoons salt
2   teaspoons pepper
1   (13 by 9-inch) disposable aluminum roasting pan
     (if using charcoal)

1. FOR THE SAUCE: Bring all ingredients to simmer in small saucepan over medium heat and cook, stirring occasionally, until reduced to about 1 cup, 5 to 7 minutes. Transfer ½ cup sauce to small bowl and set aside remaining sauce for serving.

2. FOR THE CHOPS: Using large piece of heavy-duty aluminum foil, wrap soaked chips in foil packet and cut several vent holes in top. Pat pork chops dry with paper towels. Use sharp knife to cut 2 slits about 1 inch apart through outer layer of fat and connective tissue. Season each chop with ½ teaspoon salt and ½ teaspoon pepper.

Place chops side by side, facing in same direction, on cutting board with curved rib bone facing down. Pass 2 skewers through loin muscle of each chop, close to bone, about 1 inch from each end, then pull apart to create 1-inch space between each.

3A. FOR A CHARCOAL GRILL: Open bottom vent halfway and place roasting pan in center of grill. Light large chimney starter filled with charcoal briquettes (6 quarts). When top coals are partially covered with ash, pour into 2 even piles on either side of roasting pan. Place wood chip packet on coals. Set cooking grate in place, cover, and open lid vent halfway. Heat grill until hot and wood chips are smoking, about 5 minutes.

3B. FOR A GAS GRILL: Place wood chip packet over primary burner. Turn all burners to high, cover, and heat grill until hot and wood chips are smoking, about 15 minutes. Turn all burners to medium. (Adjust burners as needed during cooking to maintain grill temperature between 300 and 325 degrees.)

4. Clean and oil cooking grate. Place skewered chops bone side down on grill (over pan if using charcoal). Cover and cook until meat registers 120 degrees, 28 to 32 minutes.

5. Remove skewers from chops, tip chops onto flat side, and brush surface of each with 1 tablespoon sauce. Transfer chops, sauce side down, to hotter parts of grill (if using charcoal) or turn all burners to high (if using gas) and cook until browned on first side, 2 to 6 minutes. Brush top of each chop with 1 tablespoon sauce, flip, and continue to cook until browned on second side and meat registers 145 degrees, 2 to 6 minutes longer.

6. Transfer chops to serving platter, tent loosely with foil, and let rest for 5 to 10 minutes. Serve, passing reserved sauce separately.

✔ WHY THIS RECIPE WORKS
For great grill-smoked pork chops with rosy-pink, ultra-moist meat we use bone-in chops because bones add flavor to the meat as it cooks and contain connective tissue and fat that break down to lend suppleness. What's more, the porous structure of a bone acts as an insulator, slowing down heat penetration. We use this to our advantage by resting the chops on their bones instead of laying them flat. To keep them from toppling over, we spear them together with skewers, then stand them upright in the center of the grill with bone, not meat, touching the grill.

PICK BIG CHOPS   We use chops at least 1½ inches thick for this recipe. The larger chops mean more meat and more bone, which gives us more time on the grill to really infuse the meat with smoke before it grows leathery and dry. It's important that every chop is of the same thickness so that they all cook evenly to the same temperature.

GRATE ON THE BOX   We like the flavor of onions in our sauce but don't like the crunch when they are added in chunks. Therefore, we grate rather than mince the onions. To do this, we use the large holes of a box grater.

SKEWER AND STACK   Not only does skewering and stacking the chops on the grill insulate the meat and therefore slow down the cooking time (allowing us to infuse the meat with more smoky flavor), but it's an excellent technique for space management. Cooking for a crowd? This will help.

COOK LOW TO HIGH   We begin cooking these chops at a lower heat. This mimics the reversed low-and-slow cooking method we wrote about in concept 5 and allows the enzymes present and active in meat under 122 degrees to create tender, juicy chops (for more on enzymes, see concept 6). After the chops spend about 30 minutes at this lower temperature, we apply a few coats of sauce and then achieve a beautiful crust by searing them over high heat.

GRILLED PORTERHOUSE OR T-BONE STEAKS
SERVES 4 TO 6

Be sure to buy steaks that are at least 1 inch thick.

2   (1¾-pound) porterhouse or T-bone steaks,
    1 to 1½ inches thick, trimmed
2   teaspoons salt
2   teaspoons pepper
1   recipe Chive Butter (optional) (recipe follows)

1. Season entire surface of each steak with 1 teaspoon salt and let sit at room temperature for 1 hour. Pat steaks dry with paper towels and season each with 1 teaspoon pepper.

2A. FOR A CHARCOAL GRILL: Open bottom vent completely. Light large chimney starter three-quarters filled with charcoal briquettes (4½ quarts). When top coals are partially covered with ash, pour evenly over half of grill. Set cooking grate in place, cover, and open lid vent completely. Heat grill until hot, about 5 minutes.

2B. FOR A GAS GRILL: Turn all burners to high, cover, and heat grill until hot, about 15 minutes. Leave primary burner on high and turn other burner(s) to low.

OUR FAVORITE BONE-IN CUTS: BEEF

CUTS	DESCRIPTION	COOKING METHOD
T-Bone Steak	The T-shaped bone in this steak, which comes from the short loin, separates the long, narrow strip of top loin and a small piece of tenderloin. Since it contains both cuts of meat, the T-bone is really two steaks in one, with different textures and flavors in each.	The size, shape, and bone make indoor cooking tricky; grilling is the best option (see above).
Porterhouse Steak	The porterhouse steak is cut farther back in the animal than the T-bone and is really just a huge T-bone steak with a larger tenderloin section.	Like the T-bone, the porterhouse has well-balanced flavor and texture, and is also best when grilled (see above).
Rib Roast, First Cut	This cut consists of ribs 9 through 12, toward the back of the rib section, closer to the loin of the animal, and contains the large rib-eye muscle. The clearest way to indicate what you want when you order a rib roast is to ask for the "first four ribs from the loin end."	Extremely tender and flavorful, it's best when roasted in a low oven (see page 18) or grill-roasted.
Beef Ribs	These large ribs come from the top half of the animal and are cut from rib bones 6 through 12—the home to prime rib. These ribs are often very large (about 8 inches long) and can be sold in smaller slabs with just three or four bones.	Rib cuts have excellent beefy flavor. We like them best when barbecued (see page 96).
Short Ribs	These meaty ribs can be cut from various locations on the cow, although they commonly come from the underside of the animal. Often each rib bone has been separated and cut crosswise so that a large chunk of meat is attached to one side of the bone.	Inexpensive and rich, these ribs can be tough without prolonged cooking. Best when braised (see page 78), although they can be butterflied and grilled.

3. Clean and oil cooking grate. Place steaks on hot side of grill with tenderloin sides (smaller side of T-bone) facing cool side of grill. Cook (covered if using gas) until dark crust forms, 6 to 8 minutes. (If steaks start to flame, move them to cooler side of fire and/or extinguish flames with squirt bottle of water.) Flip steaks and turn so that tenderloin sides are facing cool side of grill. Continue to cook (covered if using gas) until dark brown crust forms on second side, 6 to 8 minutes longer.

4. Brush with butter, if using, and transfer steaks to cool side of grill with bone side facing hot side of grill. Cover grill and continue to cook until meat registers 115 to 120 degrees (for rare) or 120 to 125 degrees (for medium-rare), 2 to 4 minutes longer, flipping halfway through cooking.

5. Transfer steaks to cutting board, tent loosely with aluminum foil, and let rest for 10 minutes. Cut strip and tenderloin pieces off bones, then cut each piece crosswise into ¼-inch slices. Serve.

CHIVE BUTTER

MAKES ABOUT 6 TABLESPOONS, ENOUGH FOR I RECIPE
GRILLED PORTERHOUSE OR T-BONE STEAKS

4   tablespoons unsalted butter, melted
2   tablespoons minced shallot
I   garlic clove, minced
I   tablespoon minced fresh chives
     Salt and pepper

Combine all ingredients in medium bowl and season with salt and pepper to taste.

✓ WHY THIS RECIPE WORKS

For a grilled steak that sports a dark (but not blackened) crust, smoky aroma, and deep grilled flavor, we first sear the meat directly over a hot fire, then gently finish cooking it over indirect heat. Since a T-bone is really two steaks—a tender New York strip steak on one side of the bone and a buttery, quicker-cooking tenderloin on the other, we position the meat so that the tenderloin always faces the cooler side of the grill, which prevents that portion from becoming overcooked and dry.

PICK FROM TWO TYPES OF T-BONE   Both T-bone and porterhouse steaks contain a strip steak and a tenderloin steak connected by a T-shaped bone (see illustration, page 90). The strip steak section is a bit chewy, with a noticeable grain, while the tenderloin, a long, cylindrical muscle, is the most tender meat on the cow but has a less beefy flavor. The porterhouse is really just a huge T-bone steak with a larger tenderloin section and is cut farther back in the animal than the T-bone steak. Technically, a T-bone must have a tenderloin portion at least ½ inch across, and a porterhouse's tenderloin usually measures at least 1¼ inches across. Both types are well balanced for texture and flavor, and either will work here.

TIME TO SEASON   Though in Florence, Italy, where they are known for the *bistecca alla fiorentina*, a huge T-bone grilled over an oak fire, they season the steaks after they're cooked, we like to salt the meat an hour before. This enables the salt to penetrate the meat's interior, boosting the flavor from crust to bone. Be sure to remove any accumulated moisture on the surface of the steaks with paper towels before grilling, though. If left in place, this moisture can cause the steaks to steam rather than develop a crust.

USE TWO LEVELS OF HEAT   On a charcoal grill, we create a two-level fire by piling the lit coals on only one side of the grill. (It's important to stack these coals in an even layer; if they are uneven, large flare-ups may occur, causing the steaks to blacken.) On a gas grill, we keep the primary burner on high and turn the others to low. This allows us to sear the meat on the grill's hotter side and then gently finish cooking the steak's interior using indirect heat on the other side, avoiding large flare-ups.

SHIELD THE TENDERLOIN   After discovering the ease of cooking steaks on these two levels of heat, we still encountered one problem. Though tasters were impressed with the crust and the steaks' grilled flavor, they found the coveted tenderloin section to be somewhat tough and dry. The solution: Position the meat so that the tenderloin faces the cooler side of the grill, with the bone between the tenderloin and the fire. This allows the delicate tenderloin to cook at a slightly slower rate and stay tender and juicy, shielded from the higher heat by the bone.

When cooking bone-in roasts, the bones add flavor and moisture to the meat with their added fat and connective tissue. The bone marrow adds an unmistakable meaty flavor, too.

GRILL-ROASTED BONE-IN PORK RIB ROAST
SERVES 6 TO 8

When using a charcoal grill, we prefer wood chunks to wood chips whenever possible; substitute one medium wood chunk, soaked in water for one hour, for the wood chip packet.

1	(4- to 5-pound) bone-in center-cut pork rib roast, tip of chine bone removed, fat trimmed to ¼-inch thickness
4	teaspoons kosher salt
1	cup wood chips, soaked in water for 15 minutes and drained
1½	teaspoons pepper

1. Pat roast dry with paper towels. Using sharp knife, cut slits in surface fat layer, spaced 1 inch apart, in cross-hatch pattern, being careful not to cut into meat. Season roast with salt. Wrap with plastic wrap and refrigerate for at least 6 hours or up to 24 hours.

2. Using large piece of heavy-duty aluminum foil, wrap soaked chips in foil packet and cut several vent holes in top.

3A. FOR A CHARCOAL GRILL: Open bottom vent halfway. Light large chimney starter filled with charcoal briquettes (6 quarts). When top coals are partially covered with ash, pour into steeply banked pile against side of grill. Place wood chip packet on coals. Set cooking grate in place, cover, and open lid vent halfway. Heat grill until hot and wood chips are smoking, about 5 minutes.

3B. FOR A GAS GRILL: Place wood chip packet over primary burner. Turn all burners to high, cover, and heat grill until hot and wood chips are smoking, about 15 minutes. Turn primary burner to medium-high and turn off other burner(s). (Adjust primary burner as needed during cooking to maintain grill temperature around 325 degrees.)

4. Clean and oil cooking grate. Unwrap roast and season with pepper. Place roast on grate with meat near, but not over, coals and flames and bones facing away from coals and flames. Cover (position lid vent over meat if

using charcoal) and cook until meat registers 140 degrees, 1¼ to 1½ hours.

5. Transfer roast to carving board, tent loosely with foil, and let rest for 30 minutes. Carve into thick slices by cutting between ribs. Serve.

✔ WHY THIS RECIPE WORKS

Grilling a bulky cut of meat like a pork rib roast may sound difficult, but it's not. We found that a tender, quick-cooking center-cut rib roast and a simple salt rub were all that we needed for a juicy grilled roast with a thick mahogany crust. We grill it over indirect heat (on the cooler side of the grill) so it can cook through slowly, adding a packet of soaked wood chips (or a single soaked wood chunk) for a subtle tinge of smoke flavor. After little more than an hour on the grill, our roast is tender and juicy, with plenty of rich, deep flavor.

CHOOSE YOUR CUTS There are three possible cuts from the loin section of the animal—the best cuts for a roast such as this. There is the blade-end roast (sometimes called the rib end), the center-cut rib roast, and the confusingly named center-cut loin roast. We like the center-cut rib roast for its flavor and simplicity: Because the meat is a single muscle attached along one side to the bones, there is no need to tie the roast for tidy presentation. If you buy a blade-end roast (sometimes called a "rib-end roast"), tie it into a uniform shape with kitchen twine at 1-inch intervals; this step is unnecessary with a center-cut rib roast. For easier carving, ask the butcher to remove the tip of the chine bone and to cut the remainder of the chine bone between each rib.

COOK ON TWO LEVELS We use a two-level fire here, cooking the roast on the cool side. It's important to position the roast away (but not too far away) from the coals or flames with the bones facing away from the fire. After an hour a mahogany crust develops—no high-temperature sear needed.

GIVE A LONG REST We let this roast rest for a full 30 minutes after it finishes on the grill, allowing the meat to reabsorb some of the juices lost in cooking as its muscle fibers relax (see concept 3), as well as employing the principle of carryover cooking (see concept 4). In this case, we remove the roast from the heat when it registers 140 degrees; it will reach 145 to 150 degrees as it rests.

The thin layers of meat and thick layers of connective tissue and fat lining the bones make beef and pork ribs a somewhat tricky yet potentially magnificent dish. Cooking ribs low and slow—in the oven, on the grill, or with both—imbues the meat with the flavors of fat and smoke, creating a baconlike crust and tender flesh with just a bit of chew.

TEXAS-STYLE BARBECUED BEEF RIBS
SERVES 4

It is important to use beef ribs with a decent amount of meat, not bony scraps; otherwise, the rewards of making this recipe are few. When using a charcoal grill, we prefer wood chunks to wood chips whenever possible; substitute two medium wood chunks, soaked in water for one hour, for the wood chip packet.

- 4 teaspoons chili powder
- 2 teaspoons salt
- 1½ teaspoons pepper
- ½ teaspoon cayenne pepper
- 4 (1¼-pound) beef rib slabs, trimmed
- 2 cups wood chips, soaked in water for 15 minutes and drained
- 1 recipe Barbecue Sauce for Texas-Style Beef Ribs (recipe follows)

1. Combine chili powder, salt, pepper, and cayenne in bowl. Pat ribs dry with paper towels, rub evenly with spice mixture, and let sit at room temperature for 1 hour.

2. Using large piece of heavy-duty aluminum foil, wrap soaked chips in foil packet and cut several vent holes in top.

3A. FOR A CHARCOAL GRILL: Open bottom vent halfway. Light large chimney starter one-third filled with charcoal briquettes (2 quarts). When top coals are partially covered with ash, pour into steeply banked pile against 1 side of grill. Place wood chip packet on coals. Set cooking grate in place, cover, and open lid vent halfway. Heat grill until hot and wood chips are smoking, about 5 minutes.

3B. FOR A GAS GRILL: Place wood chip packet over primary burner. Turn all burners to high, cover, and heat grill until hot and wood chips are smoking, about 15 minutes. Turn primary burner to medium and turn other burner(s) off. (Adjust primary burner as needed during cooking to maintain grill temperature between 250 and 300 degrees.)

4. Clean and oil cooking grate. Place ribs meat side down on cool side of grill (ribs may overlap slightly). Cover (position lid vents over meat if using charcoal) and cook for 1 hour.

5. If using charcoal, remove cooking grate and add 20 new briquettes; set cooking grate in place. Flip ribs meat side up and rotate racks. Cover (position lid vents over meat if using charcoal) and continue to cook until meat begins to pull away from bone, 1¼ to 1¾ hours longer.

6. Transfer ribs to cutting board, tent loosely with aluminum foil, and let rest for 5 to 10 minutes. Cut ribs between bones and serve, passing sauce separately.

BARBECUE SAUCE FOR TEXAS-STYLE BEEF RIBS
MAKES ABOUT 1¾ CUPS

This is a simple, vinegary dipping sauce quite unlike the sweet, thick barbecue sauces found in the supermarket. The sauce can be refrigerated in an airtight container for up to four days.

- 2 tablespoons unsalted butter
- ¼ cup finely chopped onion
- 1½ teaspoons chili powder
- 1 garlic clove, minced
- 2 cups tomato juice
- ¾ cup distilled white vinegar
- 2 tablespoons Worcestershire sauce
- 2 tablespoons molasses
- 1 teaspoon minced chipotle chile in adobo sauce
- ½ teaspoon dry mustard mixed with
  1 tablespoon water
  Salt and pepper

1. Melt butter in small saucepan over medium heat. Add onion and cook, stirring occasionally, until softened, 2 to 3 minutes. Stir in chili powder and garlic and cook until fragrant, about 30 seconds. Add tomato juice, ½ cup vinegar, Worcestershire, molasses, chipotle, mustard mixture, ½ teaspoon salt, and ¼ teaspoon pepper. Bring to simmer and cook over medium heat, stirring occasionally, until slightly thickened and reduced to 1½ cups, 30 to 40 minutes.

2. Off heat, stir in remaining ¼ cup vinegar and season with salt and pepper to taste. Let cool to room temperature before serving.

✔ WHY THIS RECIPE WORKS
Good beef ribs are all about intense meat flavor—not just smoke and spice. We found that the juiciest meat with the most flavor was obtained by leaving the fat and membrane on the back of the ribs in place. The fat not only bastes the ribs as they cook but also renders to a crisp, baconlike texture.

FIND THE BEEF   In Texas, excellent beef ribs are the secret handshake between experienced grillers. With a low price tag and availability at nearly every butcher's counter (they are the scrap bones from trimming rib-eye steaks), beef ribs manage to maintain a cool, cultlike obscurity. Be careful when you're shopping for beef ribs, however— some ribs will yield poor results when barbecued. We prefer partial slabs (with three or four bones) that are very meaty.

RUB THAT SPICE   We found that only a small amount (2 teaspoons for each rack) of a simple mixture of salt, pepper, cayenne, and chili powder worked best to bring out the flavors of the meat. Though we tested rubbing on the spice far in advance, as well as aging the ribs in the refrigerator for up to two days, the best flavor comes from leaving the ribs at room temperature for just an hour.

MAINTAIN THE TEMPERATURE   To turn our grill into a backyard smoker, we make a slow, even fire with a temperature in the range of 250 to 300 degrees. A couple of hours of slow cooking are enough to render some of the fat and make the ribs juicy, tender, and slightly toothy. If the temperature is any higher, too much fat will render and the meat will turn dry and stringy. If it's any lower, the fat won't render and the meat will stay tough, the ribs never achieving that signature roasted beefy flavor.

PAIR WITH SAUCE   For a real Texas-style barbecue sauce, we pull together the usual ingredients (vinegar, onion, and molasses) with dry mustard and chipotle chile for spiciness. Worcestershire sauce adds depth and tomato juice provides tangy flavor and helps thin out the sauce.

MEMPHIS-STYLE BARBECUED SPARERIBS
SERVES 4 TO 6

Don't remove the membrane that runs along the bone side of the ribs; it prevents some of the fat from rendering and is authentic to this style of ribs.

2	(2½- to 3-pound) racks St. Louis–style spareribs, trimmed
1	recipe Spice Rub (recipe follows)
¾	cup wood chips, soaked in water for 15 minutes and drained
½	cup apple juice
3	tablespoons cider vinegar
1	(13 by 9-inch) disposable aluminum roasting pan (if using charcoal) or disposable aluminum pie plate (if using gas)

Pile coals on one side. Place lid vent on other side. Don't peek.

Barbecue experts have plenty of theories as to exactly what goes on inside a covered grill, but agreement is hard to come by. We wanted to see if we could scientifically determine the best way to lay a fire. What really is the best way to arrange the coals to secure evenly, thoroughly barbecued meat?

We drilled holes into our kettle grill so we could snake thermocouples from a computer data recorder to the fire.

We outfitted a Weber kettle grill with five temperature probes, four around the edges of the grill and one in the center. Through holes drilled in the lid, we attached probes—or thermocouples—to a computer data recorder that would measure the temperature inside the grill every minute for up to two hours. After running more than a dozen tests over six weeks, we arrived at some answers.

Because barbecue is by definition slow cooking over low heat, the high temperatures produced by so-called direct heat (cooking directly over a pile of coals) are unacceptable. What's wanted is indirect heat, and, in a kettle grill, you can produce indirect heat in one of two ways: by banking two piles of coals on opposite sides of the grill or by banking one pile on one side.

The computer data showed that splitting the coals between two sides produced worrisome temperature spikes—unacceptable if the goal was to maintain a near-constant temperature. Also, the temperatures within the grill showed significant variation.

If anything, we expected the variation in heat distribution with the single-banked coals to be even worse. With the exception of the probe placed directly over the fire, however, the probes in this case produced temperature readings that were within a few degrees of each other. This was surprising considering that one probe was about twice the distance from the fire as the other three. This was also good news, as it meant that a large part of the cooking area was being held at a pretty constant temperature. The single-banked method also showed almost no heat spikes and held the temperature between the ideal (for barbecue) 250 and 300 degrees for the longest period of time.

The results of these tests, then, seemed clear: For barbecuing, it's best to have a single pile of coals rather than two piles, because one source of heat produces steady, evenly distributed heat, while two sources produce greater temperature variation.

But this wasn't the only thing we learned. Barbecue experts often recommend placing the lid vent away from the fire. Was it really part of the reason why the pile of banked coals was providing even, steady heat? Sure enough, when we placed the open vent directly over the fire, the fire burned hotter and faster. In this position, a direct convection current was formed inside the egg-shaped Weber kettle. When the vent was placed away from the fire, a more diffuse convection current ensured a more even distribution of heat. Also important: the degree to which we opened the lid vent. When it was open completely, the fire burned much hotter, and less evenly. The vent is best kept partially cracked.

Finally, when you open the lid to check on the progress of your barbecue, you lose all of the even heat distribution that you have worked so hard to establish. Resist the temptation to peek.

1. Rub each side of each rack of ribs with 2 tablespoons spice rub. Let ribs sit at room temperature for 1 hour.

2. Using large piece of heavy-duty aluminum foil, wrap soaked chips in foil packet and cut several vent holes in top. Combine apple juice and vinegar in small bowl and set aside.

3A. FOR A CHARCOAL GRILL: Open bottom vent halfway. Place roasting pan filled with 2 cups water on 1 side of grill and arrange 15 unlit charcoal briquettes on other side of grill. Light large chimney starter one-third filled with charcoal briquettes (2 quarts). When top coals are partially covered with ash, pour on top of unlit briquettes to cover half of grill. Place wood chip packet on coals. Set cooking grate in place, cover, and open lid vent halfway. Heat grill until hot and wood chips are smoking, about 5 minutes.

3B. FOR A GAS GRILL: Place wood chip packet directly on primary burner. Place disposable pie plate filled with 2 cups water on other burner(s). Turn all burners to high, cover, and heat grill until hot and wood chips are smoking, about 15 minutes. Turn primary burner to medium-high and turn other burner(s) off. (Adjust primary burner as needed during cooking to maintain grill temperature between 250 and 275 degrees.)

4. Clean and oil cooking grate. Place ribs meat side down on cool side of grill over water-filled pan. Cover (position lid vents over meat if using charcoal) and cook for 1½ hours, brushing each rack with 2 tablespoons apple juice mixture and flipping and rotating racks halfway through cooking. During final 20 minutes of cooking, adjust oven rack to lower-middle position and heat oven to 300 degrees.

5. Set wire rack in rimmed baking sheet and add enough water to cover bottom of pan. Transfer ribs to prepared rack and brush top of each slab with 2 tablespoons apple juice mixture. Roast for 1 hour.

6. Brush ribs with remaining apple juice mixture and continue to roast until meat is tender but not falling off bones (internal temperature should be 195 to 200 degrees), 1 to 2 hours. Transfer ribs to cutting board, tent loosely with foil, and let rest for 15 minutes. Slice ribs between bones and serve.

SPICE RUB
MAKES ABOUT ½ CUP, ENOUGH FOR 1 RECIPE
MEMPHIS-STYLE BARBECUED SPARERIBS

For less spiciness, reduce the cayenne to ½ teaspoon.

- 2 tablespoons paprika
- 2 tablespoons packed light brown sugar
- 1 tablespoon salt
- 2 teaspoons chili powder
- 1½ teaspoons pepper
- 1½ teaspoons garlic powder
- 1½ teaspoons onion powder
- 1½ teaspoons cayenne pepper
- ½ teaspoon dried thyme

Combine all ingredients in bowl.

✔ WHY THIS RECIPE WORKS

In Memphis, ribs get flavor from a spice rub and a thin, vinegary liquid—called a mop—that is basted on the ribs as they cook. To keep the meat moist on the grill, we stow a pan of water underneath the cooking grate on the cooler side of the grill, where it absorbs heat and works to keep the temperature stable. Last, we transfer the ribs to the oven to cook through until tender.

MOP IT UP For the mop, we combine apple juice and cider vinegar and brush it on the ribs while they cook on the grill. This helps to cool down the meat and prevent interior moisture from evaporating.

RUB THE RIGHT WAY Many experts claim that the spice rub must be applied to the ribs 24 hours in advance. But the thinness of the meat on the bones here means that the rub doesn't have all that far to travel. Applying the rub right before cooking gives us all the flavor we need. (Note that when making ribs in the oven, as in the next recipe, we do think it's worth applying the spice rub well in advance.)

MAKE SMOKE WITHOUT FIRE Before settling on the dual cooking method of grill to oven, we tried roasting the ribs before searing them on the grill. This didn't work. We were left with overly wet, soft-textured ribs with little spice and a superficial smoke flavor. Why? Research revealed the first serious misstep: exposing ribs to smoke after they cook. Smoke contains both water-soluble and fat-soluble flavor compounds. As traditional dry-rub ribs cook, the water-soluble compounds dissolve in the meat's surface moisture and get left behind as it evaporates. Fat-soluble compounds dissolve in the rendering fat, which then spreads through the meat, lubricating the muscle fibers and depositing smoke flavor as it goes. The problem is, if the ribs start cooking in the oven, much of the fat renders and drips out of the meat before it even gets to the grill.

COOK TO TEMP While wet ribs are pretty forgiving, dry-rub ribs are more exacting and have a very small window during which they are perfectly cooked. The foolproof solution? A thermometer. Pull the ribs out of the oven when the thickest section reaches 195 degrees. At this temperature, the meat will turn out consistently tender with a good bit of satisfying chew.

OVEN-BARBECUED SPARERIBS
SERVES 4

You will need a baking stone, a sturdy baking sheet with a 1-inch rim, and a wire cooling rack that fits inside. It's fine if the ribs overlap slightly on the rack. For this recipe, we find it best to coat the ribs with the spice rub at least eight hours ahead of cooking. Use caution when opening the crimped foil to add the juice: Hot steam and smoke will billow out. Serve with barbecue sauce, if desired.

6	tablespoons yellow mustard
2	tablespoons ketchup
3	garlic cloves, minced
3	tablespoons packed brown sugar
1½	tablespoons kosher salt
1	tablespoon sweet paprika
1	tablespoon chili powder
2	teaspoons pepper
½	teaspoon cayenne pepper
2	(2½- to 3-pound) racks St. Louis–style spareribs, trimmed, membrane removed, and each rack cut in half
¼	cup finely ground Lapsang Souchong tea leaves (from about 10 tea bags, or ½ cup loose tea leaves ground to powder in spice grinder)
½	cup apple juice

1. Combine mustard, ketchup, and garlic in bowl; combine sugar, salt, paprika, chili powder, pepper, and cayenne in separate bowl. Spread mustard mixture in thin, even layer over both sides of ribs; coat both sides with spice mixture, then wrap ribs in plastic wrap and refrigerate for 8 to 24 hours.

2. Transfer ribs from refrigerator to freezer for 45 minutes. Adjust oven racks to lowest and upper-middle positions (at least 5 inches below broiler). Place baking stone on lower rack; heat oven to 500 degrees. Sprinkle ground tea evenly over bottom of rimmed baking sheet; set wire rack in baking sheet. Place ribs meat side up on rack and cover with heavy-duty aluminum foil, crimping edges tightly to seal. Place baking sheet on stone and roast ribs for 30 minutes, then reduce oven temperature to 250 degrees, leaving oven door open for 1 minute to cool. While oven is open, carefully open 1 corner of foil and pour apple juice into bottom of baking sheet; reseal foil. Continue to roast until meat is very tender and begins to pull away from bones, about 1½ hours. (Begin to check ribs after 1 hour; leave loosely covered with foil for remaining cooking time.)

3. Remove foil and carefully flip racks bone side up;

place baking sheet on upper-middle rack. Turn on broiler; cook ribs until well browned and crispy in spots, 5 to 10 minutes. Flip ribs meat side up and cook until second side is well browned and crispy, 5 to 7 minutes more. Let cool for at least 10 minutes before cutting into individual ribs. Serve with barbecue sauce, if desired.

✓ WHY THIS RECIPE WORKS

We wanted to replicate the deep, rich flavor and fork-tender texture of barbecued ribs indoors. To do this, we rejected stovetop smokers in favor of the oven, which better contained the smoke and was able to accommodate the ribs in one batch.

BUY THE RIGHT RIBS There are three types of pork ribs. Spareribs, from near the pig's fatty belly, are an acceptable choice but need a fair amount of trimming at home. Baby back ribs are smaller, leaner ribs from the adult pig's back, which dry out too quickly in this recipe. For outdoor barbecue, we favor St. Louis–style spareribs—pork spareribs trimmed of skirt meat and excess cartilage—and here we found no reason to change.

REMOVE THE MEMBRANE For this recipe, we like to remove the thin membrane lining the concave side of the rib rack. This way, the ribs are easier to manipulate and smoke penetrates both sides of the rack directly. Insert the handle of a spoon between the membrane and ribs to loosen. Then grasp the membrane with a paper towel and pull away gently.

MAKE YOUR OWN SMOKER You can crowd ribs into an indoor smoker, but we prefer our roomier makeshift version: Spread tea leaves on a rimmed baking sheet, place a wire cooling rack on top, followed by the ribs and heavy-duty foil in order to trap the smoke. A baking stone gets the tea smoking quickly.

TIME FOR TEA To replace the wood chips of a stovetop smoker, we sprinkle ground Lapsang Souchong tea leaves underneath the ribs, which add a rich smokiness to the meat. After all, Chinese cooks smoke a variety of foodstuffs over smoldering black tea. The leaves won't burn in the oven, but "roasting" is enough to unlock their flavor. We grind the leaves to a fine power in order to maximize their surface area and give the ribs a deeper flavor.

ROAST HOT AND COLD We begin by roasting at high heat before lowering the temperature to 250 degrees. The high heat, however good for smoke, can make the ribs inedibly tough. Therefore, we quick-freeze them before cooking. Then they can withstand high heat and quickly absorb smoke without toughening. After the ribs are fork-tender, we pass them under the high heat of the broiler to turn the wet exterior into a chewy, crispy crust.

Bones are great for adding flavor to meat, but they can do more. Traditionally, stocks are made by simmering bones (as well as meat and vegetables) for hours and hours on the stove, the cooking time coaxing their deep, rich flavors into the broth. We harness the power of chicken bones in our chicken stocks and soups, using some timesaving techniques to avoid being stuck in the kitchen all day for a simple chicken soup.

QUICK CHICKEN STOCK
MAKES ABOUT 8 CUPS

If you use a cleaver, you will be able to cut up the chicken parts quickly. A chef's knife or kitchen shears will also work. To defat hot stock, we recommend using a ladle or fat separator. Alternatively, you can refrigerate the stock and then simply remove the hardened fat with a spoon.

I	tablespoon vegetable oil
4	pounds whole chicken legs or backs and wingtips, cut into 2-inch pieces
I	onion, chopped
8	cups boiling water
½	teaspoon salt
2	bay leaves

1. Heat oil in stockpot or Dutch oven over medium-high heat until shimmering. Add half of chicken pieces and cook until lightly browned, about 5 minutes per side. Transfer cooked chicken to bowl and repeat with remaining chicken pieces; transfer to bowl with first batch. Add onion and cook, stirring frequently, until onion is translucent, 3 to 5 minutes.

2. Return chicken to pot. Reduce heat to low, cover, and cook until chicken releases its juices, about 20 minutes. Increase heat to high and add boiling water, salt, and bay leaves. Bring to boil, then reduce heat to low, cover, and simmer slowly until stock is rich and flavorful, about 20 minutes, skimming foam off surface if desired.

3. Strain stock through fine-mesh strainer; discard solids. Before using, defat stock. (Stock can be refrigerated for up to 4 days or frozen for up to 6 months.)

✓ WHY THIS RECIPE WORKS
Restaurant chefs adhere to time-consuming, involved routines for making chicken stock. Bones, meat, and mirepoix (onions, carrots, and celery) are first oven-roasted or sautéed on the stovetop. A bouquet garni (a bundle of several fresh herbs) and water are added, and the stock simmers, uncovered, for hours, with the cook periodically skimming off impurities. Finally, the stock is strained, cooled, and defatted. This method is fine for cooks with the inclination to spend all day tending a simmering pot, and it does produce very fine results. But most home cooks don't want (or need) to follow such a complicated regimen. We simplify the process by using small pieces and fewer vegetables, and we subject the chicken to some browning and a solid sweat before bringing the stock to a boil and letting it simmer for only 20 minutes.

HACK THE CHICKEN Many recipes throw whole chicken parts into the pot. We found that cutting the parts into small chunks (a cleaver is perfect for this task) releases the chicken flavor in a shorter amount of time since more surface area of the meat is exposed. This also exposes more bone marrow, key for both flavor and a thicker consistency.

BROWN FIRST Most stock recipes dump the chicken and water into the pot at the same time. We found that browning the chicken creates a ton of flavor that would otherwise take hours to eke out.

DON'T SKIP THE ONIONS Though carrots and celery aren't vital for a flavorful stock, onions certainly are. We sauté one chopped onion before returning the chicken to the pot.

SWEAT IT OUT Cooking the browned onion and chicken pieces in a covered pot in their own juices (a process called sweating) further speeds along the release of flavor. A 20-minute sweat before adding the water is key to this recipe.

CLASSIC CHICKEN NOODLE SOUP
SERVES 6 TO 8

Make sure to reserve the chicken breast pieces until step 2; they should not be browned. Be sure to reserve 2 tablespoons of chicken fat for sautéing the aromatics in step 4; however, if you prefer not to use chicken fat, vegetable oil can be substituted.

STOCK

I	tablespoon vegetable oil
I	(4-pound) whole chicken, breast removed, split, and reserved; remaining chicken cut into 2-inch pieces
I	onion, chopped
8	cups boiling water
I	teaspoon salt
2	bay leaves

SOUP

2	tablespoons chicken fat, reserved from making stock, or vegetable oil

1	onion, chopped
1	large carrot, peeled and sliced ¼ inch thick
1	celery rib, sliced ¼ inch thick
½	teaspoon dried thyme
3	ounces egg noodles
¼	cup minced fresh parsley
	Salt and pepper

1. FOR THE STOCK: Heat oil in Dutch oven over medium-high heat until shimmering. Add half of chicken pieces and cook until lightly browned, about 5 minutes per side. Transfer cooked chicken to bowl and repeat with remaining chicken pieces; transfer to bowl with first batch. Add onion and cook, stirring frequently, until onion is translucent, 3 to 5 minutes. Return chicken pieces to pot. Reduce heat to low, cover, and cook until chicken releases its juices, about 20 minutes.

2. Increase heat to high; add boiling water, reserved chicken breast pieces, salt, and bay leaves. Reduce heat to medium-low and simmer until flavors have blended, about 20 minutes.

3. Remove breast pieces from pot. When cool enough to handle, remove skin from breasts, then remove meat from bones and shred into bite-size pieces; discard skin and bones. Strain stock through fine-mesh strainer; discard solids. Allow liquid to settle, about 5 minutes, then skim off fat; reserve 2 tablespoons, if desired.

4. FOR THE SOUP: Heat reserved chicken fat in Dutch oven over medium-high heat. Add onion, carrot, and celery and cook until softened, about 5 minutes. Add thyme and reserved stock and simmer until vegetables are tender, 10 to 15 minutes.

5. Add noodles and reserved shredded chicken and cook until just tender, 5 to 8 minutes. Stir in parsley, season with salt and pepper to taste, and serve. (After skimming broth in step 3, shredded chicken, strained stock, and fat can be refrigerated in separate containers for up to 2 days.)

CLASSIC CHICKEN SOUP WITH ORZO AND SPRING VEGETABLES

Substitute 1 leek, quartered lengthwise, sliced thin crosswise, and washed thoroughly, for onion and ½ cup orzo for egg noodles. Along with orzo, add 4 ounces trimmed asparagus, cut into 1-inch lengths, and ¼ cup fresh or frozen peas. Substitute 2 tablespoons minced fresh tarragon for parsley.

CLASSIC CHICKEN SOUP WITH SHELLS, TOMATOES, AND ZUCCHINI

Add 1 diced zucchini to pot with onion, carrot, and celery in step 4, increasing cooking time to 7 minutes. Add 1 tomato, cored, seeded, and chopped, to pot along with stock in step 4. Substitute 1 cup small shells or macaroni for egg noodles and simmer until pasta is just tender. Substitute ¼ cup minced fresh basil for parsley and serve with grated Parmesan, if desired.

✔ WHY THIS RECIPE WORKS

While the stock for our Classic Chicken Noodle Soup is similar to our Quick Chicken Stock in that both are, well, quick, there are some important differences. We use a whole chicken so that we will have some white meat for the soup. We remove the breast and reserve it for use later in the recipe. The rest of the bird is cut into small pieces and browned and sweated per our stock-making method.

USE BROTH FOR FLAVOR Once the onion and hacked-up chicken have been browned and sweated, it's time to add the water and bay leaves. At this point in the recipe, we also add the split breast and let it simmer for just 20 minutes. This ensures that the white meat for the soup won't overcook.

RESERVE THAT CHICKEN FAT Reserve 2 tablespoons of the chicken fat skimmed from the broth. We use this fat to sauté the aromatics for the soup, which imparts an excellent chicken flavor.

COOK PASTA RIGHT IN BROTH Egg noodles (cooked right in the broth so they soak up the chicken flavor), celery, carrot, onion, thyme, and parsley round out our classic recipe.

PRACTICAL SCIENCE HOW BEST TO COOL SOUP

Let your soup cool for an hour before placing it in the fridge.

For safety reasons, the U.S. Food and Drug Administration (FDA) recommends cooling liquids to 70 degrees within the first two hours after cooking and 40 degrees within four hours after that.

The easiest method to cool soup is to put the hot pot straight in the refrigerator. When we tried this, the boiling soup cooled from 212 degrees to 40 degrees in a total time of four hours and 15 minutes. However, the fridge's temperature rose to nearly 50 degrees, which is unsafe for everything else being stored in there. We found that by letting the soup cool to 85 degrees on the counter (which took only an hour) before transferring it to the fridge, we could bring it down to 40 degrees in a total time of four hours and 30 minutes (well within the FDA's recommended range), and the fridge never got above 40 degrees. You can speed up the process even further by dividing the soup into smaller containers.

Brining Maximizes Juiciness in Lean Meats

Why are some turkeys dry as sawdust while others boast meat that's firm, juicy, and well seasoned? The answer is brining. Soaking a turkey (or a chicken or even lean pork) in a brine—a solution of salt water—provides it with a plump cushion of seasoned moisture that will sustain it throughout cooking, which translates into moist meat, especially in the breast.

HOW THE SCIENCE WORKS

MOVEMENT OF SALT AND WATER IN A BRINE

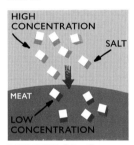

DIFFUSION *Salt will move from an area of greater concentration (the brine) to an area of lesser concentration (the meat).*

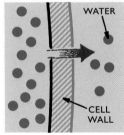

OSMOSIS *Water moves across cell walls from areas with a higher concentration of water (the brine) to areas of lower concentration (the meat).*

Brining relies on two scientific principles—diffusion and osmosis—that sound complicated but are actually quite easy to understand. They depend on a simple concept: Nature likes things to be kept in balance.

If you remember basic biology, meat is made mostly of muscle fibers, which are individual cells. These cells allow certain molecules to flow in and out in order to keep things in balance. Small molecules (like salt) will naturally move from an area of greater concentration to an area of lesser concentration by a process called diffusion. The salt molecules in a typical brine are more concentrated than inside the muscle cells so the salt diffuses into the muscle cells.

When water moves across cell membranes, however, the process is called osmosis. In brining, the dissolved salts, sugars, amino acids, and proteins inside the muscle cells create a more concentrated environment (one with less water) than that of the brine. In order to maintain a balance, water travels from a less concentrated to a more concentrated environment. Therefore, water flows into the muscle cells, causing the meat to pick up "water weight" as it soaks. (The concentration of salt in a brine is important. If it is too high, then water will be drawn out of the meat instead of

traveling in. If it is too low, the movement of water into the meat will be very slow.)

It's intuitive that this added water would make brined meat juicer. But why can't we just soak our meat in a bucket of plain water? How exactly is the salt working?

It all comes down to the reshaping of protein molecules in the meat—a task taken on by the salt in the brine. This reshaping helps the proteins to hold on to the added water, even after the meat is cooked.

But let's take a step back: Salt is made up of two ions, sodium and chloride, which are oppositely charged. Proteins, such as those in meat, are large molecules that contain a mosaic of charges, negative and positive. When proteins are placed in a solution containing salt, they readjust their shape to accommodate the opposing charges. This rearrangement of the protein molecules creates gaps that fill up with water. More than that: The salt actually dissolves some of the proteins, forming a gel capable of holding on to even more water.

This rearrangement of the protein molecules has an additional effect. It compromises the structural integrity of the meat, reducing overall toughness. So, in addition to being juicier, brined meat should be more tender, too.

TEST KITCHEN EXPERIMENT

To tease out the relative effects of osmosis and diffusion, we conducted the following experiment: We soaked one 2½-pound center-cut boneless pork loin (which we trimmed of fat and silverskin) in plain water and a second 2½-pound trimmed loin in a brine made with 3 quarts of cold water and ¾ cup of table salt for four hours, measuring the weight of the loins before and after soaking. We then roasted these samples, along with a third 2½-pound pork loin taken straight from the package and trimmed. We repeated this test three more times, cooking a total of 12 pork loins, and then averaged the results.

THE RESULTS

Before we even turned on the oven, we noticed a big difference between the pork loins soaked in plain water and the loins soaked in the brine. The water-soaked pork absorbed about 0.5 percent of its weight in water (a little over ½ ounce), whereas the brined pork absorbed almost three times that amount. It was clear that the brine was doing something and the weigh-in after roasting confirmed its effect. The loins taken straight from the package and the loins soaked in water showed little difference, each losing about 19 percent of their original weight. The brined pork shed only 14.1 percent of its starting weight, nearly 25 percent less than the other two samples.

When our tasters sampled each pork loin, they found the brined pork to be noticeably juicier. It was also well seasoned. (Perhaps even too well seasoned. We used a higher ratio of salt to water in our experiment than we do in our Grill-Roasted Pork Loin recipe, page 106.) In separate tests, we had our food lab analyze sodium content in a variety of brined foods. We found that brining adds about ⅛ teaspoon of salt per serving in pork or poultry. This is roughly the amount of seasonings found in a kosher chicken (which is salted during processing) or enhanced pork (which has been injected with a sodium solution by the manufacturer to increase juiciness).

THE TAKEAWAY

Brining pork and other lean proteins accomplishes three things. The salt in the brine changes the structure of the proteins in the meat so that they are able to both absorb and hold on to more moisture, resulting in juicier meat when cooked. This change in the protein structure also makes the meat more tender. Finally, unlike salt sprinkled on the surface of meat just before cooking, the salt in a brine penetrates deeper into the meat and produces meat that is especially well seasoned.

WEIGHT OF PORK LOINS BEFORE AND AFTER ROASTING

	BEFORE	AFTER	DIFFERENCE
Control	2.35 pounds	1.92 pounds	18.4%
Soaked in plain water	2.42 pounds	1.94 pounds	19.7%
Brined in salt water	2.49 pounds	2.14 pounds	14.1%

Note: Numbers represent average of 12 samples, four of each type.

BRINING FORMULA FOR POULTRY AND PORK

MEAT	COLD WATER	TABLE SALT*	TIME**
CHICKEN*			
1 (3- to 8-pound) Whole Chicken	2 quarts	½ cup	1 hour
2 (3- to 8-pound) Whole Chickens	3 quarts	¾ cup	1 hour
4 pounds Bone-In Chicken Pieces	2 quarts	½ cup	½ to 1 hour
Boneless, Skinless Chicken Breasts (up to 6 breasts)	1½ quarts	3 tablespoons	½ to 1 hour
TURKEY*			
1 (12- to 17-pound) Whole Turkey	2 gallons	1 cup	6 to 12 hours
1 (18- to 24-pound) Whole Turkey	3 gallons	1½ cups	6 to 12 hours
Bone-In Turkey Breast	1 gallon	½ cup	3 to 6 hours
PORK*			
Bone-In Pork Chops (up to 6)	1½ quarts	3 tablespoons	½ to 1 hour
Boneless Pork Chops (up to 6)	1½ quarts	3 tablespoons	½ to 1 hour
1 (2½- to 6-pound) Boneless Roast	2 quarts	¼ cup	1 to 1½ hours

* The large clusters of crystals in kosher salt dissolve quickly in water, making this salt a good option for brining. Each brand has a different crystal size (unlike table salt, which has a standard crystal size). To use Morton kosher salt, increase amounts in this chart by 50 percent. To use Diamond Crystal kosher salt, double amounts in this chart. It is possible to add sugar (in equal amounts to salt) to brines for chicken and pork to promote browning.

** Do not brine longer than recommended or foods will become overly salty.

*** Don't brine kosher chickens or turkeys, self-basting turkeys (such as frozen Butterballs), or enhanced pork (injected with sodium solution).

Lean turkey and chicken are prime candidates for brining. The dark meat in birds tastes best when cooked to an internal temperature of 175 degrees—the point at which the fat and connective tissue have melted and the meat becomes tender. However, lean white breast meat will be incredibly dry when cooked to this temperature. Brining, in effect, adds moisture to the breast meat so it won't be so dry, even if it's overcooked.

ROASTED BRINED TURKEY
SERVES 10 TO 12

This recipe is designed for a natural turkey, not treated with salt or chemicals. If using a self-basting turkey (such as a frozen Butterball) or kosher turkey, do not brine in step 1, and season with salt after brushing with melted butter in step 5. Resist the temptation to tent the roasted turkey with foil while it rests on the carving board. Covering the bird will make the skin soggy. If making gravy, see our Giblet Pan Gravy recipe on page 110.

1	cup salt
1	(12- to 14-pound) turkey, neck, giblets, and tailpiece removed and reserved for gravy
2	onions, chopped coarse
2	carrots, peeled and chopped coarse
2	celery ribs, chopped coarse
6	sprigs fresh thyme
3	tablespoons unsalted butter, melted
1–1½	cups water
1	recipe Giblet Pan Gravy (see page 110)

1. Dissolve salt in 2 gallons cold water in large container. Submerge turkey in brine, cover, and refrigerate or store in very cool spot (40 degrees or less) for 6 to 12 hours.

2. Set wire rack in rimmed baking sheet. Remove turkey from brine and pat dry, inside and out, with paper towels. Place turkey on prepared wire rack. Refrigerate, uncovered, for at least 8 hours or overnight.

3. Adjust oven rack to lowest position and heat oven to 400 degrees. Line V-rack with heavy-duty aluminum foil and poke holes in foil. Set V-rack in roasting pan and spray foil with vegetable oil spray.

4. Toss half of onions, half of carrots, half of celery, and thyme with 1 tablespoon melted butter in bowl and place inside turkey. Tie legs together with kitchen twine and tuck wings behind back. Scatter remaining vegetables in pan.

5. Pour water over vegetable mixture in pan. Brush turkey breast with 1 tablespoon melted butter, then place turkey breast side down on V-rack. Brush with remaining 1 tablespoon butter.

6. Roast turkey for 45 minutes. Remove pan from oven. Using 2 large wads of paper towels, turn turkey breast side up. If liquid in pan has totally evaporated, add another ½ cup water. Return turkey to oven and roast until breast registers 160 degrees and thighs register 175 degrees, 50 minutes to 1 hour.

7. Remove turkey from oven. Gently tip turkey so that any accumulated juices in cavity run into pan. Transfer turkey to carving board and let rest, uncovered, for 30 minutes. Carve turkey and serve with gravy.

✔ WHY THIS RECIPE WORKS
A roast turkey benefits from brining more than chicken or even pork because it is so lean and because it so big. With such a long roasting time, there's no way to keep the breast juicy without the help of a brine. However, brining alone won't keep a turkey moist.

BRINE, THEN DRY Brining adds moisture to the meat but also the skin, where it can cause problems. Make sure to pat the bird dry with paper towels once it comes out of the brine. Air-drying the brined bird in the refrigerator (a technique used to make Peking duck so crispy) is worth the advance planning.

KEEP THE STUFFING SEPARATE A stuffed bird is very difficult to cook properly. By the time the stuffing reaches a safe temperature (165 degrees), the white meat is way overcooked. The easiest solution is to bake the stuffing in a separate dish, but we did devise a more complicated recipe that cooks some of the stuffing inside the bird to soak up poultry flavor (see recipe on page 116).

FLIP THE BIRD Starting the bird breast side down shields the white meat from oven heat and helps solve the fundamental problem with cooking any bird—dark meat should be heated to a higher internal temperature than white meat. To crisp the skin on the breast, turn the bird breast side up for the second half of the roasting.

ROAST ON A RACK Cooking the turkey in a V-rack allows heat to circulate around the bird and promotes even cooking. Line the rack with foil so the metal bars of the rack don't tear the turkey skin. Cutting slits in the foil allows the turkey juices to drip into the roasting pan and mix with vegetables that will be used to enrich the gravy.

LET IT REST When cooked meat and poultry are sliced right away, juices flood the carving board. The bigger the roast, the longer it should rest. While a 4-pound beef roast might be ready to carve after 15 minutes, a big bird should rest for at least half an hour, if not longer. (For more details on the science of resting, see concept 3.)

CLASSIC ROAST CHICKEN
SERVES 2 TO 3

This recipe is designed for a natural chicken, not treated with salt or chemicals. If using a kosher chicken, do not brine; it already contains a good amount of sodium. We recommend using a V-rack to roast the chicken. If you don't have a V-rack, set the bird on a regular roasting rack and use balls of aluminum foil to keep the roasting chicken propped up on its side.

½   cup salt
½   cup sugar
1   (3-pound) whole chicken, giblets discarded
2   tablespoons unsalted butter, softened
1   tablespoon olive oil
    Pepper

1. Dissolve salt and sugar in 2 quarts cold water in large container. Submerge chicken in brine, cover container with plastic wrap, and refrigerate for 1 hour.

2. Adjust oven rack to lower-middle position, place roasting pan on rack, and heat oven to 400 degrees. Coat V-rack with vegetable oil spray and set aside. Remove chicken from brine and pat dry with paper towels.

3. Using your fingers, gently loosen center portion of skin covering each side of breast and place butter under skin, directly on meat in center of each side of breast. Gently press on skin to distribute butter over meat. Tuck wings behind back. Rub skin with oil, season with pepper, and place chicken wing side up on prepared V-rack. Place V-rack in preheated roasting pan and roast for 15 minutes.

4. Remove roasting pan from oven and, using 2 large wads of paper towels, rotate chicken so that opposite wing side is facing up. Return roasting pan to oven and roast for another 15 minutes.

5. Using 2 large wads of paper towels, rotate chicken again so that breast side is facing up and continue to roast until breast registers 160 degrees and thighs register 175 degrees, 20 to 25 minutes longer. Transfer chicken to carving board and let rest for 15 minutes. Carve chicken and serve.

✔ WHY THIS RECIPE WORKS

Adding sugar to the brine encourages browning, which can be an issue with a quick-cooking roast chicken. Soaking poultry in a brine makes the skin soggy (no surprise) and will slow down its browning and crisping. With roast turkey, the cooking time is so long that the skin will eventually dry out and crisp. A roast chicken cooks much more quickly; the sugar compensates for the negative effects brining has on poultry skin.

BLOT DRY   Make sure to thoroughly dry the bird after brining; excess moisture will cause the skin to steam and become flabby.

BUTTER THE MEAT, NOT THE SKIN   Because a chicken cooks so fast, brushing the bird with melted butter isn't a good idea. The moisture in the butter can soften poultry skin and there isn't enough time for it to crisp up. Instead, put the butter where it does the most good—directly on top of the lean breast meat. Use your fingers to loosen the skin from the breast meat and smear softened butter directly onto the meat on either side of the breastbone. You can flavor this butter with herbs, garlic, or grated citrus zest, if desired.

OIL THE EXTERIOR   To help the skin crisp, we do rub a little oil on the exterior of the bird. While butter is 16 to 18 percent water and 80 percent fat, oil is 100 percent fat and won't soften poultry skin.

ELEVATE AND FLIP   To promote even cooking, it's essential to roast a chicken in a V-rack, which allows heat to circulate around the bird. Placing the V-rack in a preheated roasting pan jump-starts the browning of the skin. Turning the bird two times as it cooks helps protect the white meat from overcooking and crisps the entire exterior of the bird.

PRACTICAL SCIENCE THE BASICS OF BRINING

Pay attention to the type of salt and the container options.

Successful brining is easy but depends on paying attention to a few details. The type of salt used in the brine will affect the quantity that you use. (See page 113 for more information about substituting one type of salt for another.) Likewise, you'll want to make sure that you've got the right container on hand for the job. Zipper-lock bags work well for chicken breasts and chops, but for whole birds and roasts you'll need something larger. In the test kitchen we use heavy-duty Cambro containers, and for a really big job—like a turkey—you may need a cooler. In that case, keep the brine cold with ice packs. Last, for optimal results, don't forget to make sure the salt is fully dissolved in the water before adding the meat.

Lean pork cuts from the loin and rib are good candidates for brining. By the time these cuts reach the proper internal temperature (150 degrees), much of their moisture has been expelled. With so little fat, these cuts will be leathery and tough. Brining allows you to cook lean pork while keeping it tender and juicy.

GRILL-ROASTED PORK LOIN
SERVES 4 TO 6

We find that the blade-end roast is a bit more flavorful than the center-cut roast, but either works well in this recipe. To make sure the roast doesn't dry out during cooking, look for one covered with a layer of fat on one side that is at least ⅛ inch thick. Because the diameter of pork loins varies significantly from one to another, start checking the internal temperature of the loin after 30 minutes of grilling time. When using a charcoal grill, we prefer wood chunks to wood chips whenever possible; substitute two medium wood chunks, soaked in water for one hour, for the wood chip packet. This recipe is intended for natural pork; if the pork is enhanced (injected with a salt solution), do not brine.

¼	cup salt
1	(2½- to 3-pound) boneless blade-end or center-cut pork loin roast, trimmed and tied at 1½-inch intervals
2	tablespoons olive oil
1	tablespoon pepper
2	cups wood chips, soaked in water for 15 minutes and drained

1. Dissolve salt in 2 quarts water in large container. Submerge pork loin in brine, cover, and refrigerate for 1 to 1½ hours. Remove pork from brine and pat dry with paper towels. Rub pork loin with oil and coat with pepper. Let sit at room temperature for 1 hour.

2. Using large piece of heavy-duty aluminum foil, wrap soaked chips in foil packet and cut several vent holes in top.

3A. FOR A CHARCOAL GRILL: Open bottom vent halfway. Light large chimney starter three-quarters filled with charcoal briquettes (4½ quarts). When top coals are partially covered with ash, pour evenly over half of grill. Place wood chip packet on coals. Set cooking grate in place, cover, and open lid vent halfway. Heat grill until hot and chips are smoking, about 5 minutes.

3B. FOR A GAS GRILL: Place wood chip packet over primary burner. Turn all burners to high, cover, and heat grill until hot and chips are smoking, about 15 minutes. Leave primary burner on medium-high and turn off other burner(s). (Adjust primary burner as needed to maintain grill temperature between 300 and 350 degrees.)

4. Clean and oil cooking grate. Place pork loin on hot side of grill, fat side up, and cook (covered if using gas) until well browned on all sides, 10 to 12 minutes, turning as needed. Move loin to cool side of grill, positioning roast parallel with and as close as possible to heat. Cover (position lid vent over roast if using charcoal) and cook for 20 minutes.

5. Rotate roast 180 degrees, cover, and continue to cook until center of meat registers 140 degrees, 10 to 30 minutes longer, depending on thickness of roast.

6. Transfer roast to carving board, tent loosely with foil, and let rest for 15 minutes. Remove twine, cut roast into ½-inch-thick slices, and serve.

✔ WHY THIS RECIPE WORKS
Brining adds moisture to lean pork loin but proper cooking is essential, too. Here it's important to build a two-level fire, first searing the pork over the hot flames and then roasting it, covered, on the cooler side of the grill. Be sure to remove the pork before it's completely done: Carryover cooking (concept 4) will do its work.

CHOOSE YOUR CUT   Butchers typically cut and merchandise a loin roast in three sections. Closest to the shoulder is the blade end (blade refers to the shoulder blade). Moving down the back of the pig you find the center cut, which is the most expensive—comparable to a beef prime rib when sold bone-in. The third and last section is called the sirloin. Here the loin muscle tapers off and rests above the tenderloin. When the sirloin section is cut into roasts or chops, part of the tenderloin is included. The tenderloin muscle can be purchased separately as a boneless roast, but it should not be confused with the larger loin roast, which is what we prefer here. After testing them all, the blade roast was favorably compared by our tasters to the dark meat of chicken. The fatty pockets that separate the different muscles add moisture and flavor. The center-cut roast has a milder flavor, but it was also well liked by tasters in this recipe.

UNDERCOOK IT, THEN LET IT REST   While a pork loin that is properly cooked to an internal temperature of 145 degrees will still be moist, a roast cooked to an internal temperature of 160 degrees will be tough and leathery, even if it has been brined. Our solution is simple: As soon as the meat reaches an internal temperature of 140 degrees, remove it from the grill. Tent the roast with foil as it rests and don't carve the meat for 15 minutes. During this time, the internal temperature will gently climb to 145 to 150 degrees and there's no risk of overcooking the meat.

GRILLED PORK CHOPS
SERVES 4

Rib loin chops are our top choice for their big flavor and juiciness. The spice rub adds a lot of flavor for very little effort, but the chops can also be seasoned with pepper alone just before grilling. This recipe is intended for natural pork; if the pork is enhanced (injected with a salt solution), do not brine, and add 2 teaspoons of salt to the spice rub or the pepper.

- 3   tablespoons salt
- 3   tablespoons sugar
- 4   (12-ounce) bone-in pork rib or center-cut chops, 1½ inches thick, trimmed
- 1   recipe Basic Spice Rub for Pork Chops (recipe follows) or 2 teaspoons pepper

1. Dissolve salt and sugar in 1½ quarts cold water in large container. Submerge chops in brine, cover, and refrigerate for 30 minutes to 1 hour. Remove chops from brine and pat dry with paper towels. Rub chops with spice rub (or season with pepper).

2A. FOR A CHARCOAL GRILL: Open bottom vent completely. Light large chimney starter filled with charcoal briquettes (6 quarts). When top coals are partially covered with ash, pour two-thirds evenly over grill, then pour remaining coals over half of grill. Set cooking grate in place, cover, and open lid vent completely. Heat grill until hot, about 5 minutes.

2B. FOR A GAS GRILL: Turn all burners to high, cover, and heat grill until hot, about 15 minutes. Leave primary burner on high and turn off other burner(s).

3. Clean and oil cooking grate. Place chops on hotter side of grill and cook (covered if using gas) until browned on both sides, 4 to 8 minutes. Move chops to cool side of grill, cover, and continue to cook, turning once, until meat registers 145 degrees, 7 to 9 minutes longer. Transfer chops to serving platter, tent loosely with aluminum foil, and let rest for 5 to 10 minutes. Serve.

BASIC SPICE RUB FOR PORK CHOPS
MAKES ¼ CUP, ENOUGH FOR 1 RECIPE GRILLED PORK CHOPS

- 1   tablespoon ground cumin
- 1   tablespoon chili powder
- 1   tablespoon curry powder
- 2   teaspoons packed brown sugar
- 1   teaspoon pepper

Combine all ingredients in bowl.

✔ WHY THIS RECIPE WORKS

During our testing, we discovered a few simple secrets to the juiciest, most flavorful pork chops. Choose tender and flavorful bone-in rib or center-cut chops and brine them to pump up their flavor and lock in their moisture. Use a heavy hand with the pepper or apply a quick spice rub before the chops are put on the grill. Finally, cook the chops over high heat until browned and then move them to a cooler part of the grill to allow the chops to cook through without burning the exterior.

PUMP UP THE FLAVOR   Although rib chops are flavorful on their own, we wanted to see if we could boost their flavor by using a spice rub. We tried two types of rub: wet and dry. The wet rubs, made with spices and a liquid, gave the chops good flavor but also caused their exteriors to turn syrupy. We prefer the dry rubs, which combine potent dried spices with sugar to create big flavor and a crisp crust. With the addition of the brine, these chops not only have big flavor but are well seasoned throughout.

PRACTICAL SCIENCE BRINING FROZEN MEAT

It's possible to combine the thawing and brining of frozen meat.

Submerging small portions of frozen meat in a bucket of cold water speeds up the defrosting process. For recipes where the first step is brining, we wondered if we could combine these two steps into one. Testing with chicken parts and pork chops, we found that this method works well as long as the meat is fully defrosted when the brining time has elapsed. This won't be a problem for pork chops or chicken parts, which need an hour to defrost. Just brine these small cuts for one hour—the upper time limit listed in the chart on page 103. However, a 2½-pound boneless pork roast should be thawed in plain water for one hour and then brined for the 1½ hours recommended on page 103. Likewise, a whole chicken should be thawed in plain water for two hours and then brined for one hour.

Salt Makes Meat Juicy and Skin Crisp

Brining is an excellent technique to prevent chalky, dried-out meat. But sometimes we prefer a different way to season. After all, the added moisture of a brine makes it difficult to get the bronzed, crispy poultry skin that we love. In some cases, we lose the water and turn to straight salt. Here's why.

HOW THE SCIENCE WORKS

Salting poultry fulfills many of the same roles as brining. The salt, which slowly penetrates the bird's flesh, helps to break down proteins and retain moisture. But salting is different from brining—in more ways than the presence of a bucket of water.

Poultry naturally contains some salt and lots of water, which normally coexist in a happy balance. But when salt is applied directly to the meat, it starts by drawing the moisture out to the surface of the bird via osmosis (for more on this, see concept 11). On the surface, this moisture dissolves the applied salt in an effort to restore balance.

But wouldn't drawing all that water out of the chicken make the situation worse, simply causing the meat to dry out? At first, yes.

If you cook a chicken very soon after salting, the juices that traveled to the exterior would simply evaporate in the oven. With a little time, however, the surface moisture forms a super-concentrated brine with the salt it has dissolved. At first this draws even more moisture to the surface in an effort to further dilute the salt. But because salt diffuses from a higher concentration to a lower concentration, the dissolved salt will eventually move into the chicken.

Once inside the bird, the salt accomplishes two things. First, it causes some muscle proteins to swell, making room for more liquid. Second, it dissolves other proteins, which then act like a sponge to soak up and hold moisture. As the surface concentration of salt decreases and the internal concentration of dissolved salt and protein increases, the moisture on the surface of the bird is gradually drawn back inside as well—another attempt to strike balance. This process takes time. After all, we are essentially "brining" the birds using their own juices instead of a bucket of water. There is no net gain or loss.

Now here's the key: After the salt we've applied causes the moisture to migrate back within the bird, we are left with a drier surface area. This means we more rapidly obtain a high outer temperature and, as a result, there is better browning and a supremely crispy skin.

SALT AND WATER

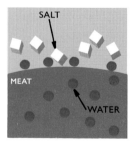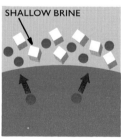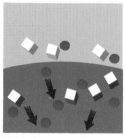

A TRIP FOR TWO *When salt is applied to the exterior of the bird, it draws water from within to the surface, creating a shallow brine. With time, however, first the salt and then the water begin to move back into the bird. This gives us a moist, tender bird after cooking, while the dry surface helps to promote crisp skin.*

TEST KITCHEN EXPERIMENT

To tease out the relative effects of brining and salting on muscle fibers and skin, we ran the following experiment: We started with three bone-in, skin-on chicken breasts; we brined one for one hour in a solution of ¼ cup of table salt and 1 quart of water, seasoned another with ¾ teaspoon of kosher salt and left it uncovered in the fridge for 18 hours, and took a third straight from the package and seasoned it with salt just prior to cooking. We roasted the breasts in a 450-degree oven until their internal temperature hit 160 degrees. We tasted the meat of each breast and inspected the skin for color and crispness. We repeated this experiment three times and had similar results each time.

THE RESULTS

Tasters found the brined and salted samples to be equally juicy and well seasoned, while the untreated sample was seasoned only at the very surface and the meat was noticeably drier. The salted and untreated samples had equally browned, crispy, shattering skin, while the skin on the brined breast was paler and a bit soggy. To help illustrate the dramatic difference in texture, we removed the skin from each breast and balanced it on an overturned glass bowl. Even without any added weight, the brined skin immediately slumped around the curve, while the salted skin remained flat as a board.

THE TAKEAWAY

Salting poultry allows us to reap the benefits of brining as it breaks down proteins and helps to retain moisture within the meat—as well as its added bonus of leaving the chicken with a drier surface area. This means we get well-seasoned meat and easily crisped skin. While brining is equally effective at helping the meat retain moisture, all that water does negatively impact the crispness of the skin.

CHICKEN SKIN: SALTED VS. BRINED

SALTED SKIN
The skin of a salted bird is crisp and bronze.

BRINED SKIN
The skin of a brined bird is softer and paler.

NOT ALL KOSHER SALT IS THE SAME

Unlike table salt, kosher salt is fairly easy to spread and won't clump, so it is a must in our salted turkey recipes. But the two leading brands of kosher salt are not the same. Because of its more open crystal structure, a teaspoon of Diamond Crystal actually contains less salt than a teaspoon of Morton kosher salt. Use this reference guide to convert measurements.

*3 teaspoons Diamond Crystal kosher salt =
2¼ teaspoons Morton kosher salt =
1½ teaspoons table salt*

Adding salt to poultry acts as a shallow but concentrated brine: Over time, the salt migrates into the meat, just as it does with our brining technique (see concept 11). Once inside, the salt changes the structure of the muscle fibers so that the meat is able to hold more moisture, even in a hot oven. Not only that, it pulls moisture away from the surface of the bird, resulting in a crispier skin.

ROAST SALTED TURKEY

SERVES 10 TO 12

This recipe is designed for a natural turkey that hasn't been treated with salt or other ingredients. If using a self-basting turkey (such as a frozen Butterball) or kosher turkey, do not salt in step 1, and season with salt after brushing with melted butter in step 5. This recipe was developed and tested using Diamond Crystal kosher salt. If you have Morton kosher salt, which is denser than Diamond Crystal, use only 2¼ teaspoons of salt in the cavity, 2¼ teaspoons of salt for each half of the breast, and 1 teaspoon of salt per leg. Table salt is too fine and is not recommended for this recipe. Serve with Giblet Pan Gravy.

1	(12- to 14-pound) turkey, neck, giblets, and tailpiece removed and reserved for gravy
4	tablespoons kosher salt
1	(5-pound) bag ice cubes
4	tablespoons unsalted butter, melted
3	onions, chopped coarse
2	carrots, peeled and chopped coarse
2	celery ribs, chopped coarse
6	sprigs fresh thyme
1	cup water
1	recipe Giblet Pan Gravy (recipe follows)

1. Use your fingers or thin wooden spoon handle to gently loosen skin covering breast, thighs, drumsticks, and back; avoid breaking skin. Rub 1 tablespoon salt evenly inside cavity of turkey, 1 tablespoon salt under skin of each side of breast, and 1½ teaspoons salt under skin of each leg. Wrap turkey tightly with plastic wrap and refrigerate for at least 24 hours or up to 48 hours.

2. Remove turkey from refrigerator. Rinse off any excess salt between meat and skin and in cavity, then pat dry, inside and out, with paper towels. Add ice to two 1-gallon zipper-lock bags until each is half full. Place bags in roasting pan and lay turkey breast side down on top of ice. Add ice to two 1-quart zipper-lock bags until each is one-third full; place 1 bag of ice in large cavity of turkey and other bag in neck cavity. (Make sure that ice touches breast only,

not thighs or legs.) Keep turkey on ice for 1 hour (pan should remain on counter).

3. Meanwhile, adjust oven rack to lowest position and heat oven to 425 degrees. Line V-rack with heavy-duty aluminum foil, poke several holes in foil, and spray foil with vegetable oil spray.

4. Remove turkey from ice and pat dry with paper towels (discard ice). Tuck tips of drumsticks into skin at tail to secure and tuck wings behind back. Brush turkey breast with 2 tablespoons melted butter.

5. Set V-rack in pan, then scatter vegetables and thyme into pan and pour water over vegetable mixture. Place turkey breast side down on V-rack. Brush turkey with remaining 2 tablespoons melted butter.

6. Roast turkey for 45 minutes. Remove pan from oven (close oven door to retain oven heat) and reduce oven temperature to 325 degrees. Using 2 large wads of paper towels, rotate turkey breast side up; continue to roast until breast registers 160 degrees and thighs register 175 degrees, 1 to 1½ hours longer. Transfer turkey to carving board and let rest, uncovered, for 30 minutes. Carve turkey and serve with gravy.

GIBLET PAN GRAVY

MAKES ABOUT 6 CUPS

Complete step 1 up to a day ahead, if desired. Begin step 3 once the bird has been removed from the oven and is resting on a carving board.

1	tablespoon vegetable oil
	Reserved turkey giblets, neck, and tailpiece
1	onion, chopped
4	cups low-sodium chicken broth
2	cups water
2	sprigs fresh thyme
8	sprigs fresh parsley
3	tablespoons unsalted butter
¼	cup all-purpose flour
1	cup dry white wine
	Salt and pepper

1. Heat oil in Dutch oven over medium heat until shimmering. Add giblets, neck, and tailpiece and cook until golden and fragrant, about 5 minutes. Stir in onion and cook until softened, about 5 minutes. Reduce heat to low, cover, and cook until turkey parts and onion release their juices, about 15 minutes. Stir in broth, water, thyme, and parsley, bring to boil, and adjust heat to low. Simmer, uncovered, skimming any impurities that may rise to surface, until broth is rich and flavorful, about 30 minutes longer. Strain broth into large container and reserve giblets. When cool enough to handle, chop giblets. Refrigerate giblets and broth until ready to use. (Broth can be stored in refrigerator for up to 1 day.)

2. While turkey is roasting, return reserved turkey broth to simmer in saucepan. Melt butter in separate large saucepan over medium-low heat. Add flour and cook, whisking constantly (mixture will froth and then thin out again), until nutty brown and fragrant, 10 to 15 minutes. Vigorously whisk all but 1 cup of hot broth into flour mixture. Bring to boil, then continue to simmer, stirring occasionally, until gravy is lightly thickened and very flavorful, about 30 minutes longer. Set aside until turkey is done.

3. When turkey has been transferred to carving board to rest, spoon out and discard as much fat as possible from pan, leaving caramelized herbs and vegetables. Place pan over 2 burners set on medium-high heat. Return gravy to simmer. Add wine to pan of caramelized vegetables, scraping up any browned bits. Bring to boil and cook until reduced by half, about 5 minutes. Add remaining 1 cup turkey broth, bring to simmer, and cook for 15 minutes; strain pan juices into gravy, pressing as much juice as possible out of vegetables. Stir reserved giblets into gravy and return to boil. Season with salt and pepper to taste, and serve.

SIMPLE CRANBERRY SAUCE
MAKES 2¼ CUPS

If you've got frozen cranberries, do not defrost them before use; just pick through them and add about two minutes to the simmering time.

1	cup sugar
¾	cup water
¼	teaspoon salt
1	(12-ounce) bag cranberries, picked through

Bring sugar, water, and salt to boil in medium saucepan, stirring occasionally to dissolve sugar. Stir in cranberries; return to boil, then reduce to simmer and cook until saucy and slightly thickened, and about two-thirds of berries have popped open, about 5 minutes. Transfer to bowl, let cool to room temperature, and serve. (Cranberry sauce can be refrigerated for up to 1 week.)

✓ WHY THIS RECIPE WORKS

Brining is our go-to technique when we want moist, well-seasoned turkey. But with refrigerator space at a premium around the holidays, we look to salting as a space-saving alternative. Here, we carefully separate the skin from the meat and rub the meat thoroughly with kosher salt. Though the results are not quite as moist as with a brined turkey, we've discovered that salting and refrigerating the turkey for up to 48 hours results in a bird that is well seasoned throughout, with a wonderful natural turkey texture and flavor.

MASSAGE THE SALT Because the skin is very high in water-impenetrable fat we've found that it is most effective to apply the salt underneath the skin and in direct contact with the meat. We like to use our fingers or the handle of a wooden spoon to separate the skin from the meat.

TAKE YOUR TIME Though salting is effective, it's not always quick. If the salted bird sits for only 12 hours, the result is a salty crust and bland inner meat. If the salt sits for 72 or even 96 hours, we find that the birds turn out overly salty, with a jerkylike appearance. But turkeys salted for 24 to 48 hours are the perfect compromise: Most of the meat ends up nicely seasoned and is pretty moist. Make sure to rinse away excess salt before roasting to avoid salty pockets, especially in the deep valleys between the thighs and breast. Blot up the excess moisture to ensure crisp, brown skin.

ICE DOWN THE BREAST Ideally, the turkey breast should be cooked to 160 degrees and the thighs to 175 degrees, but these two temperatures are hard to achieve simultaneously, even when the bird is roasted breast side down (giving it some protection from the direct heat of the oven). Since we find that dryness in turkey meat is often concentrated in the lean breast, our solution is to ice the breast before the turkey goes into the oven. This way, the breast meat starts at a lower temperature than the dark meat, and we are able to remove the turkey when the dark meat is thoroughly cooked but the breast isn't overdone. To do this, place the bags of ice in a roasting pan and lay the turkey breast side down on top. Also place bags of ice inside both the large cavity and the neck area. It may look strange, but it sure does work.

DO ONE FLIP Repeatedly rotating a hot turkey is ultimately not worth it for the minimal extra browning provided. Still, one flip protects the delicate breast meat during the first half of the cooking time and results in meat that is moister—and that is worth the bother.

SPICE-RUBBED PICNIC CHICKEN
SERVES 8

If you plan to serve the chicken later on the same day that you cook it, refrigerate it after it has cooled, then let it come back to room temperature before serving. If using large chicken breasts (about 1 pound each), cut each breast into three pieces.

3	tablespoons packed brown sugar
2	tablespoons chili powder
2	tablespoons paprika
1	tablespoon salt
2	teaspoons pepper
¼–½	teaspoon cayenne pepper
5	pounds bone-in chicken pieces (split breasts cut in half, drumsticks, and/or thighs), trimmed

1. Set wire rack in rimmed baking sheet. Combine sugar, chili powder, paprika, salt, pepper, and cayenne in bowl.

2. Using sharp knife, make 2 or 3 short slashes into skin of each piece of chicken, taking care not to cut into meat. Coat chicken with spice mixture, gently lifting skin to distribute spice mixture underneath but leaving it attached to chicken. Transfer chicken skin side up to prepared wire rack (if desired, secure skin of each breast piece with 2 or 3 toothpicks placed near edges of skin). Tent chicken loosely with aluminum foil and refrigerate for at least 6 hours or up to 24 hours.

3. Adjust oven rack to middle position and heat oven to 425 degrees. Roast chicken until smallest piece registers 140 degrees, 15 to 20 minutes. Increase oven temperature to 500 degrees and continue roasting until chicken is browned and crisp and breast pieces register 160 degrees, 5 to 8 minutes longer. (Smaller pieces may cook faster than larger pieces. Remove pieces from oven as they reach correct temperature.) Continue to roast thighs and/or drumsticks until they register 175 degrees, about 5 minutes longer. Transfer chicken to wire rack and let cool completely before refrigerating or serving.

✔ WHY THIS RECIPE WORKS

Cold barbecued chicken is a picnic classic with a host of problems, namely, sticky sauce, flabby skin, and dry meat. In addition to solving those problems, we want the flavor and appeal of great barbecued chicken—without turning on the grill. To start, we replace the sauce with a dry rub; by rubbing the spice mixture all over the chicken, even under the skin, we achieve the robust barbecue flavor we prefer, and the skin is noticeably less soggy. We also salt the chicken instead of brining it, allowing both the salt and spices to penetrate the meat for even deeper flavor. We roast the chicken at 425 degrees before cranking up the heat to 500 to really crisp the skin.

SLASH THE SKIN Chicken breasts and thighs possess some excess fat that never quite renders properly, no matter how long the chicken cooks. Right out of the oven, the fat is mildly annoying; the coagulated mess you bite into the next day, however, is disgusting. To solve this, first trim the chicken pieces. And then slit the skin with a sharp knife (being careful not to cut into the flesh). This provides escape hatches for the melting fat during roasting.

SALT OVER AND UNDER It's important to apply the salty spice rub both on and beneath the skin. This ensures that neither the exterior nor the interior will be bland.

CHILL OUT We like to place the chicken pieces directly on the rack they'll be cooked on and let the whole pan air-dry in the refrigerator overnight. This allows the spice flavor to penetrate the meat alongside the salt, while also drying out the skin, which will help it to crisp in the oven.

PIN DOWN On the breast pieces, we use toothpicks to secure the skin, which otherwise shrinks considerably in the oven, leaving the meat exposed and prone to drying out. We think the extra effort is justified, but you can omit this step.

PRACTICAL SCIENCE CHICKEN SAFETY

> Raw chicken can harbor bacteria. Handle and cook with care.

Although the exact figures are a matter of debate, you should assume that the poultry you buy is contaminated with dangerous bacteria. Unlike beef, chicken meat can actually harbor harmful bacteria such as salmonella within, as well as on the surface. At home, you have two goals: to prevent the bacteria from contaminating other foods and to kill any bacteria present in poultry by thorough cooking.

SAFER HANDLING Don't rinse poultry before cooking. You aren't killing any bacteria and you may be spreading bacteria around your kitchen. To season poultry without contaminating the salt box or pepper mill, mix a small amount of salt and pepper together in a small bowl and use this mixture to season the bird; discard any excess when you're done. After working with raw poultry, wash all cutting boards, knives, kitchen surfaces, and your hands well in hot, soapy water.

SAFER COOKING Cooking poultry to 160 degrees will kill bacteria. Make sure to take the temperature of a whole bird in several places. The thickest part of the thigh is the last part to come up to temperature. Note that we recommend cooking white meat to 160 degrees; above 165 degrees, it becomes dry. Dark meat has the best texture when cooked to an internal temperature of 175 degrees.

SALT 101

STRUCTURE

Salt may well be the most important ingredient in cooking. It is one of our five basic tastes, a nutrient our body cannot live without. It adds an essential depth of flavor to food, and we add it to almost every single dish. Salt has the ability to change the molecular makeup of food and is used to preserve and to add moisture to meat. It occurs naturally, is made from evaporated seawater or obtained from rock deposits, and its cubic crystal shape can vary in size depending on how quickly and where the evaporation takes place. Salt's two basic ions—sodium and chloride—are small, nimble ions with positive and negative charges, respectively, that can easily penetrate food.

SALT CRYSTALS
Alternating sodium and chloride ions (right) are held together by electrostatic attraction so that they form a cubic crystal structure (below).

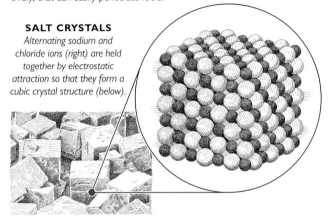

HOW MUCH SALT IS IN THAT TEASPOON?

Given the various crystal and particle sizes and shapes, some brands of salt pack a lot less into every teaspoon when compared with regular table salt. The simple formula is:

*1 teaspoon table salt =
1 ½ teaspoons Morton kosher salt =
2 teaspoons Diamond Crystal kosher salt.*

But to find out just how much less salt we might be using depending on the brand, we sent nine salts to a laboratory to determine the exact weight of 1 teaspoon of each. As we learned, a teaspoon of Maldon sea salt contains only half the amount of salt that's in a teaspoon of Morton table salt. The numbers on the far right in the table below indicate how many teaspoons of each brand are needed to equal 1 teaspoon of table salt.

BRAND	AMOUNT OF SALT IN 1 TSP.	AMOUNT TO EQUAL 1 TSP. TABLE SALT
Maldon Sea Salt	3.55 grams	2 teaspoons
Diamond Crystal Kosher Salt	3.60 grams	2 teaspoons
Espirit du Sel Fleur de Sel	5.30 grams	1⅓ teaspoons
Light Grey Celtic Sea Salt	5.66 grams	1¼ teaspoons
Morton Coarse Kosher Salt	5.80 grams	1¼ teaspoons
Fleur de Sel de Camargue	5.90 grams	1¼ teaspoons
Morton Salt (noniodized)	7.15 grams	1 teaspoon
Morton Iodized Salt	7.15 grams	1 teaspoon
La Baleine Sea Salt	7.25 grams	1 teaspoon

BUYING

Whether mined from underground salt deposits or obtained by evaporating seawater, salt in its most basic form is the same: sodium chloride. What distinguishes one salt from another is texture, size, and mineral content. These qualities can affect how a salt tastes (although only when salt is used as a garnish for food) as well as how it interacts with other foods.

TABLE SALT Table salt, also known as common salt, consists of tiny, uniformly cube-shaped crystals created during rapid vacuum evaporation. It usually includes anti-caking agents that help it pour smoothly. Fine-grain table salt dissolves easily, making it our go-to for most applications, both sweet and savory. (Avoid iodized salt, which can impart a subtle chemical flavor.) The anti-caking agents are insoluble in water so common table salt does not produce a clear solution.

KOSHER SALT Coarse-grain kosher salt is raked during the evaporation process to yield flaky aggregates of cubic crystals originally used for koshering meat. Unlike table salt, kosher salt doesn't contain any additives. Kosher salt is our top choice for seasoning meat. The large grains distribute easily and cling well to the meat's surfaces. The two major brands of kosher salt—Morton and Diamond Crystal—work equally well; however, their particle sizes differ considerably, and this makes a difference when measuring by volume (see chart, below).

SEA SALT Sea salt is the product of seawater evaporation—a time-consuming, expensive process that yields irregularly shaped, mineral-rich flakes that vary in color but only slightly in flavor. The presence of impurities in sea salt can produce crystal shapes other than cubes. Don't bother cooking with pricey sea salt; we've found that mixed into food, it doesn't taste any different from table salt. Instead, we use it as a "finishing salt," where its delicate crunch stands out. Texture—not exotic provenance—is the main consideration when buying sea salt. Look for brands boasting large, flaky crystals, such as Maldon Sea Salt.

USING

SAFE SEASONING To avoid contaminating our salt box when seasoning raw meat, poultry, or fish, we mix fresh ground pepper and salt (a ratio of 1 part pepper to 4 parts kosher salt is ideal) in a small bowl or ramekin. This way we can keep reaching into the bowl without having to constantly wash our hands. (Just be sure to discard the leftovers.)

AVOID OVERSALTING Why do some recipes include a specific amount of salt and then instruct that you "season to taste"? It helps to prevent oversalting. Because slight variations in ingredients and cooking times affect the saltiness of a dish, it's best to hold back on fully seasoning until the very end.

SALT HIGH Ever notice that some chefs season food by sprinkling it from a good foot above the counter? Is this just kitchen theatrics, or is there a reason behind this practice? We sprinkled chicken breasts with salt and ground black pepper from different heights—4 inches, 8 inches, and 12 inches—and found the higher the starting point, the more evenly the seasoning was distributed. And the more evenly the seasoning is distributed, the better food tastes. So go ahead and add a little Jamie Oliver flourish the next time you season.

Salt doesn't have to work alone. A rub made with salt and baking powder guarantees super-crisp skin in poultry. Why? Baking powder is composed of an alkali (a chemical compound that generates hydroxide ions when dissolved in water) and mild acids. The alkali in this case is baking soda, and more than half of the acids present are formulated to be released only when heated. Before cooking, then, the baking powder acts as a mild alkali, prodding some of the proteins and fat in the chicken skin to break down, as well as speeding up the dehydration of the skin. The combination of a more alkaline environment and weakened protein and fat accelerates the Maillard reaction during roasting for crisper, more flavorful skin. An overnight rub works best for a plain roast bird. A one-hour rub dries out the skin on birds we brush with a sticky glaze.

CRISP ROAST CHICKEN
SERVES 3 TO 4

The recipe requires salting the chicken for at least 12 hours. The sheet of foil between the roasting pan and V-rack will keep drippings from burning and smoking.

1	(3½- to 4-pound) whole chicken, giblets discarded
1½	teaspoons salt
1	teaspoon baking powder
½	teaspoon pepper

1. Place chicken breast side down on counter. Insert tip of sharp knife to make four 1-inch incisions along back of chicken. Using your fingers, gently loosen skin covering breast and thighs. Using metal skewer, poke 15 to 20 holes in fat deposits on top of breast and thighs. Tuck wings behind back.

PRACTICAL SCIENCE SKIN CONDITIONING

Baking powder helps to make poultry skin crisp and brown.

To demonstrate the effects of our advanced salting method, we removed two pieces of skin from two chickens. One piece was left au naturel while the other was conditioned with a rub of baking powder and salt and allowed to dry out overnight in the refrigerator. We then roasted the two pieces of skin and found that the conditioned skin was both crisper and browner than the untreated skin.

AU NATUREL
Soft and soggy

CONDITIONED
Crisp and brown

---

2. Combine salt, baking powder, and pepper in bowl. Pat chicken dry with paper towels and sprinkle evenly all over with salt mixture. Rub in mixture with hands, coating entire surface evenly. Set chicken breast side up in V-rack set in rimmed baking sheet and refrigerate, uncovered, for 12 to 24 hours.

3. Adjust oven rack to lowest position and heat oven to 450 degrees. Using paring knife, poke 20 holes about 1½ inches apart in 16 by 12-inch piece of aluminum foil. Place foil loosely in roasting pan. Flip chicken breast side down and set V-rack in prepared pan on top of foil. Roast chicken for 25 minutes.

4. Remove pan from oven. Using 2 large wads of paper towels, rotate chicken breast side up. Continue to roast until breast registers 135 degrees, 15 to 25 minutes.

5. Increase oven temperature to 500 degrees. Continue to roast chicken until skin is golden brown and crisp, breast registers 160 degrees, and thighs register 175 degrees, 10 to 20 minutes. Transfer chicken to carving board and let rest for 20 minutes. Carve and serve immediately.

✔ WHY THIS RECIPE WORKS
We modify our basic roast chicken recipe here to produce even crisper skin. By mixing baking powder with the salt rub, we create an alkaline environment that helps to speed up the Maillard reaction and produce a browner poultry skin. The baking powder helps to dehydrate the chicken skin and also reacts with the proteins and fat in chicken skin to produce a crunchier texture.

PICK THE RIGHT CHICKEN We almost always use a high-quality chicken from Bell & Evans. But we tested this recipe using a regular supermarket brand, and the skin did not brown as much and the meat tasted bland. When we read the label—"Contains up to 4 percent retained water"—we understood why. Unlike Bell & Evans chickens, which are air-chilled soon after slaughtering in order to cool to a safe temperature, most supermarket birds are submerged in a 34-degree chlorinated water bath. According to the USDA's Agricultural Research Service, chickens can absorb up to 12 percent of this additional moisture; the amount drops to about 4 percent by the time they are sold. Air-chilled chickens, however, are not exposed to water and do not absorb additional moisture, which helps with their concentrated flavor and better browning of their skin.

PUNCH HOLES Soggy chicken skin is often caused by poorly rendered fat, which accumulates under the skin with nowhere to go. The excess fat and juices need an escape route. We poke holes in the fat deposits of each breast and thigh. (Look for yellow pockets of fat under the skin, which will look opaque rather than translucent.)

LOOSEN THE SKIN Sometimes holes aren't enough: To allow fat to flow freely from the roasting chicken, we separate the skin from the meat over much of the bird. To do this, run your hand between the meat and the skin (making sure not to tear it). Also, cut a few holes near the back of the bird to provide extra-large channels for the rendering fat to drip down and escape.

USE A HOT OVEN We cook this bird in a relatively hot oven: 450 degrees for the majority, and then 500 for the last few minutes to really crisp up the skin. Starting the chicken breast side down and flipping it midway through cooking protects the meat and cooks it gently enough to keep it tender and juicy.

PROTECT WITH A FOIL SHIELD Though the high heat can cause these escaped juices to burn, creating clouds of smoke, we can fix this by placing a sheet of aluminum foil with holes punched in it under the chicken to shield the rendered fat from the direct oven heat.

GLAZED ROAST CHICKEN
SERVES 4 TO 6

For best results, use a 16-ounce can of beer. A larger can will work, but avoid using a 12-ounce can, as it will not support the weight of the chicken. A vertical poultry roaster can be used in its place, but we recommend only using a model that can be placed in a roasting pan. Taste your marmalade before using it; if it is overly sweet, reduce the amount of maple syrup in the glaze by 2 tablespoons.

CHICKEN

1	(6- to 7-pound) whole chicken, giblets discarded
2½	teaspoons salt
1	teaspoon baking powder
1	teaspoon pepper
1	(16-ounce) can beer

GLAZE

1	teaspoon cornstarch
1	tablespoon water, plus extra as needed
½	cup maple syrup
½	cup orange marmalade
¼	cup cider vinegar
2	tablespoons unsalted butter
2	tablespoons Dijon mustard
1	teaspoon pepper

1. FOR THE CHICKEN: Place chicken breast side down on counter. Insert tip of sharp knife to make four 1-inch incisions along back of chicken. Using your fingers, gently loosen skin covering breast and thighs. Using metal skewer, poke 15 to 20 holes in fat deposits on top of breast and thighs. Tuck wings behind back.

2. Combine salt, baking powder, and pepper in bowl. Pat chicken dry with paper towels and sprinkle evenly all over with salt mixture. Rub in mixture with hands, coating entire surface evenly. Set chicken, breast side up, on wire rack set in rimmed baking sheet and refrigerate, uncovered, for 30 minutes to 1 hour. Meanwhile, adjust oven rack to lowest position and heat oven to 325 degrees.

3. Open beer can and pour out (or drink) about half of liquid. Spray can lightly with vegetable oil spray and place in middle of roasting pan. Slide chicken over can so drumsticks reach down to bottom of can, chicken stands upright, and breast is perpendicular to bottom of pan. Roast chicken until skin starts to turn golden and breast registers 140 degrees, 1¼ to 1½ hours. Carefully remove chicken and pan from oven and increase oven temperature to 500 degrees.

4. FOR THE GLAZE: While chicken cooks, stir cornstarch and water together in bowl until no lumps remain. Bring syrup, marmalade, vinegar, butter, mustard, and pepper to simmer in medium saucepan over medium-low heat and cook, stirring occasionally, until reduced to ¾ cup, 6 to 8 minutes. Slowly whisk in cornstarch mixture; return to simmer and cook for 1 minute. Remove pan from heat.

5. When oven has come to temperature, place 1½ cups water in bottom of pan and return chicken to oven. Roast until entire chicken skin is browned and crisp, breast registers 160 degrees, and thighs register 175 degrees, 24 to 30 minutes. Check chicken halfway through roasting; if top is becoming too dark, place 7-inch square piece of foil over neck and wingtips of chicken to prevent burning and continue to roast (if pan begins to smoke and sizzle, add additional ½ cup water to pan).

6. Brush chicken with ¼ cup glaze and continue to roast until browned and sticky, about 5 minutes. (If glaze has become stiff, return to low heat to soften.) Carefully remove chicken from oven, transfer chicken, still on can, to carving board, and brush with ¼ cup glaze. Let rest for 20 minutes.

7. While chicken rests, strain juices from pan through fine-mesh strainer into fat separator; allow liquid to settle for 5 minutes. Whisk ½ cup juices into remaining ¼ cup glaze in saucepan and set over low heat. Using 2 large wads of paper towels, carefully lift chicken off can and onto carving board. Carve chicken, adding any accumulated juices to sauce. Serve, passing sauce separately.

✔ WHY THIS RECIPE WORKS

Glazed roast chicken sounds simple but actually presents a host of troubles, as the problems inherent in roasting chicken (dry breast meat, flabby skin, big deposits of fat under the skin) are compounded by the glaze (won't stick to the meat, burns in patches, introduces moisture to already flabby skin). We wanted an evenly glazed chicken with crisp skin and moist meat. To dehydrate the skin enough for the glaze to stick, we separate it from the meat and poke holes in the fat deposits to allow rendered fat to escape, then rub the skin with salt and baking powder. Resting the roasted bird before blasting it with heat results in burnished skin.

ROAST VERTICAL   While vertically roasting a chicken is a technique usually associated with the grill, we use it here to help us glaze the entire bird evenly. Though we could use a vertical roaster, there's a simpler answer: a beer can. After allowing the chicken to rest with its rub for an hour, straddle the chicken on top of a can of beer (after pouring out, or drinking, about half). Place it in a roasting pan, and put it in the oven. This will reduce any awkward flipping, allow you to glaze every nook and cranny with ease, and let the fat drip freely from the bird.

USE BEER CAN OR VERTICAL ROASTER   Because the interiors of beer cans are coated with an epoxy that contains bisphenol A (BPA), which some studies have linked to cancer and other harmful health effects, we wondered if cooking a chicken on an open can was really a good idea. To test this, we roasted two whole birds, one set on an open beer can containing 6 ounces of beer and the other on a stainless steel vertical roaster with the same amount of beer poured into the reservoir. After roasting the chickens, we collected their drippings and stripped each carcass, grinding the meat and skin to create homogeneous samples. We sent the samples to a lab to be evaluated.

In each chicken, the BPA measured less than 20 micrograms per kilogram, leading us to believe that the beer can cooking method is safe. (The Food and Drug Administration's current standard for exposure is 50 micrograms per kilogram of body weight for adults, or 3,400 micrograms per day for a 150-pound person.) For those who have any remaining concerns, there is always the vertical roaster, which works just as well as a low-tech option.

REDUCE THE GLAZE   Most glazed chicken recipes call for a watery glaze that slowly reduces and thickens as the bird cooks—a hindrance when you're trying to crisp up the skin. Instead, we reduce the glaze on the stovetop before applying it to the bird. This way, we can wait to apply it until the very end, when it won't ruin the texture of the skin. We thicken the glaze with cornstarch to help it adhere to the bird.

OLD-FASHIONED STUFFED ROAST TURKEY
SERVES 10 TO 12

This recipe is designed for a natural turkey, not treated with salt or chemicals. If using a self-basting turkey (such as a frozen Butterball) or kosher turkey, do not salt in step 1. This recipe was developed and tested using Diamond Crystal kosher salt. If you have Morton kosher salt, which is denser than Diamond Crystal, use only 2¼ teaspoons of salt in the cavity, 1 teaspoon of salt for each half of the breast, and 1 teaspoon of salt per leg. Table salt is not recommended for this recipe for salting the turkey because it is too fine. Look for salt pork that is roughly equal parts fat and lean meat. Serve with Giblet Pan Gravy (page 110), if desired. The bread for the stuffing can be toasted up to one day in advance. If you prefer, replace the Classic Herb Stuffing with the Dried Fruit and Nut Stuffing on the opposite page.

TURKEY

1	(12- to 14-pound) turkey, neck, giblets, and tailpiece removed and reserved for gravy
3	tablespoons plus 2 teaspoons kosher salt
2	teaspoons baking powder
1	(36-inch) square cheesecloth, folded into quarters

CLASSIC HERB STUFFING

1½	pounds hearty white sandwich bread, cut into ½-inch cubes (12 cups)
4	tablespoons unsalted butter
1	onion, chopped fine
2	celery ribs, minced
1	teaspoon salt
1	teaspoon pepper
2	tablespoons minced fresh thyme
1	tablespoon minced fresh marjoram
1	tablespoon minced fresh sage
1½	cups low-sodium chicken broth
2	large eggs
12	ounces salt pork, cut into ¼-inch-thick slices and rinsed
1	recipe Giblet Pan Gravy (page 110)

1. FOR THE TURKEY: Use your fingers or thin wooden spoon handle to gently loosen skin covering breast, thighs, drumsticks, and back; avoid breaking skin. Rub 1 tablespoon salt evenly inside cavity of turkey, 1½ teaspoons salt under skin of each side of breast, and 1½ teaspoons salt under skin of each leg. Wrap turkey tightly with plastic wrap and refrigerate for at least 24 hours or up to 48 hours.

2. FOR THE STUFFING: Adjust oven rack to lowest position and heat oven to 250 degrees. Spread bread cubes in single layer on rimmed baking sheet; bake until edges have dried but centers are slightly moist (cubes should yield to pressure), about 45 minutes, stirring several times during baking. (Bread can be toasted up to 1 day in advance.) Transfer dried bread to large bowl.

3. While bread dries, melt butter in 12-inch skillet over medium-high heat. Add onion, celery, salt, and pepper and cook, stirring occasionally, until vegetables are softened and lightly browned, 5 to 7 minutes. Stir in thyme, marjoram, and sage and cook until fragrant, about 1 minute. Add vegetable mixture to bowl with dried bread; add 1 cup broth and toss until evenly moistened (you should have about 12 cups stuffing).

4. Remove turkey from refrigerator and pat dry, inside and out, with paper towels. Using metal skewer, poke 15 to 20 holes in fat deposits on top of breast halves and thighs, 4 to 5 holes in each deposit. Tuck wings behind back.

5. Increase oven temperature to 325 degrees. Combine remaining 2 teaspoons kosher salt and baking powder in bowl. Sprinkle surface of turkey with salt mixture and rub in mixture with hands, coating entire surface evenly. Line turkey cavity with cheesecloth, pack with 4 to 5 cups stuffing, and tie ends of cheesecloth together. Cover remaining stuffing with plastic wrap and refrigerate. Using kitchen twine, loosely tie turkey legs together. Place turkey breast side down in V-rack set in roasting pan and drape salt pork slices over back.

6. Roast turkey until breast registers 130 degrees, 2 to 2½ hours. Remove pan from oven (close oven door to retain oven heat) and increase oven temperature to 450 degrees. Transfer turkey in V-rack to rimmed baking sheet. Remove and discard salt pork. Using 2 large wads of paper towels, rotate turkey breast side up. Cut twine binding legs and remove stuffing bag; empty into reserved stuffing in bowl. Pour drippings from roasting pan into fat separator and reserve for gravy, if making.

7. Once oven has come to temperature, return turkey in V-rack to pan and roast until skin is golden brown and crisp, breast registers 160 degrees, and thighs register 175 degrees, about 45 minutes, rotating pan halfway through roasting. Transfer turkey to carving board and let rest, uncovered, for 30 minutes.

8. While turkey rests, reduce oven temperature to 400 degrees. Whisk eggs and remaining ½ cup broth from stuffing recipe together in bowl. Pour egg mixture over stuffing and toss to combine, breaking up any large chunks; spread stuffing into buttered 13 by 9-inch baking dish. Bake until stuffing registers 165 degrees and top is golden brown, about 15 minutes. Carve turkey and serve with stuffing and gravy.

DRIED FRUIT AND NUT STUFFING
MAKES ABOUT 12 CUPS

Dried cranberries can be substituted for the raisins.

1½	pounds hearty white sandwich bread, cut into ½-inch cubes (12 cups)
4	tablespoons unsalted butter
1	onion, chopped fine
2	celery ribs, minced
1	teaspoon salt
1	teaspoon pepper
2	tablespoons minced fresh thyme
1	tablespoon minced fresh marjoram
1	tablespoon minced fresh sage
1	cup raisins
1	cup dried apples, chopped fine
1	cup walnuts, chopped coarse
1½	cups low-sodium chicken broth
3	large eggs

1. Adjust oven rack to lowest position and heat oven to 250 degrees. Spread bread cubes in single layer on rimmed baking sheet; bake until edges have dried but centers are slightly moist (cubes should yield to pressure), about 45 minutes, stirring several times during baking. (Bread can be toasted up to 1 day in advance.) Transfer dried bread to large bowl and increase oven temperature to 325 degrees.

2. While bread dries, melt butter in 12-inch skillet over medium-high heat. Add onion, celery, salt, and pepper and cook, stirring occasionally, until vegetables are softened and lightly browned, 5 to 7 minutes. Stir in thyme, marjoram, and sage and cook until fragrant, about 1 minute. Add vegetable mixture, raisins, dried apples, and walnuts to bowl with dried bread; add 1 cup broth and toss until evenly moistened (you should have about 12 cups stuffing).

3. Use stuffing as directed in Old-Fashioned Stuffed Roast Turkey, adding eggs and remaining ½ cup broth in step 8.

✔ WHY THIS RECIPE WORKS

Stuffing a turkey generally complicates the matter of properly cooking the bird; still, we couldn't help but wonder if there was a way to have it all—juicy meat, burnished skin, richly flavored stuffing, and drippings suitable for gravy. For crisp skin, we opt to salt the bird rather than brine it, and using a minimal amount of salt ensures the gravy won't be too salty. Unlike in the Roast Salted Turkey recipe (page 110), we also rub the skin with a mixture of baking powder and salt for crispier skin. As in the Crisp Roast Chicken recipe (page 114), we poke holes in the skin to help render the fat.

SALT GENTLY In the past, we've used as many as 5 tablespoons of salt on the bird, but this makes it impossible to create a gravy from the drippings without rinsing off some salt. Therefore, we lower the total amount of salt used here to 3 tablespoons. This allows for a gravy made from the drippings that won't make tasters wince but still allows for juicy and tender meat when roasted wisely.

DRAPE WITH SALT PORK Inspired by the once-popular technique of barding, or wrapping lean meat with fattier meat, we drape the turkey with pieces of salt pork. The salt pork enhances the turkey without making its presence too clear. To fix the problem of smoking in the oven, we remove the salt pork and drain the drippings from the roasting pan before cranking up the heat and returning the bird to the oven.

V-RACK IT A V-rack is important for two reasons. First, the rack holds the turkey in position during roasting and keeps it from rolling to one side or the other. Second, it elevates the meat above the roasting pan, allowing air to circulate and promoting even cooking and browning. If you don't own a V-rack, cooking grates from a gas stove can be used to create a makeshift roasting rack. Wrap two stove grates with aluminum foil and then use a paring knife or skewer to poke holes in the foil so that juices can drip down into the pan as the bird roasts. Place the grates in the roasting pan, leaning them against the sides of the pan so that the bottoms of the grates meet to create a V shape. Roast the turkey as usual.

COOK LOW, THEN HIGH Starting the turkey in a low oven and then cranking up the heat allows us to cook the large turkey evenly, yielding breast meat that is moist and tender. We crank the temperature to 450 to give it a final blast of skin-crisping heat and bring the center up to temperature.

STUFF, THEN UNSTUFF To solve the age-old stuffing dilemma (getting the stuffing to reach a safe 165 degrees while not overcooking the white meat), we remove the stuffing (moistened with broth and no eggs, which would cause the stuffing to be too firm too early) from the turkey when the meat is nearly cooked through. Because it is saturated with turkey juices, we are able to mix this stuffing with the remaining stuffing (the portion that didn't fit in the bird) so that every bite of stuffing is infused with turkey flavor. We add eggs to this mix, and then cook all of it together in a baking dish until it's crisped up and at a safe temperature. The timing works well because the stuffing can crisp up while the turkey rests.

BUTTERFLIED TURKEY WITH CRANBERRY-MOLASSES GLAZE
SERVES 10 TO 12

If using a self-basting turkey or kosher turkey, do not salt in step 1. Table salt is not recommended for this recipe because it is too fine. If you have a V-rack that, when inverted, still fits into your roasting pan, place the turkey on that rather than on the onions.

TURKEY

- 1 (12- to 14-pound) turkey, neck, giblets, and tailpiece discarded
  Kosher salt and pepper
- 2 teaspoons baking powder
- 2 large onions, halved

GLAZE

- 3 cups apple cider
- 1 cup frozen or fresh cranberries
- ½ cup molasses
- ½ cup cider vinegar
- 1 tablespoon Dijon mustard
- 1 tablespoon grated fresh ginger
- 2 tablespoons unsalted butter, cut into 2 pieces and chilled

1. FOR THE TURKEY: Using kitchen shears, cut along both sides of backbone to remove it. Flatten breastbone and tuck wings underneath. Use your fingers or thin wooden spoon handle to gently loosen skin covering breast, thighs, drumsticks, and back; avoid breaking skin. Using metal skewer, poke 15 to 20 holes in fat deposits on top of breast and thighs, 4 to 5 holes in each deposit. Rub bone side of turkey evenly with 2 teaspoons salt and 1 teaspoon pepper. Flip turkey skin side up and rub 1 tablespoon salt evenly under skin. Tuck wings under turkey.

Push legs up to rest on lower portion of breast and tie legs together with kitchen twine.

2. Combine 1 tablespoon salt, 1 teaspoon pepper, and baking powder in bowl. Pat skin side of turkey dry with paper towels. Sprinkle surface of turkey with salt mixture and rub in mixture with hands, coating entire surface evenly. Transfer turkey to roasting pan, skin side up. Place 1 onion half under each breast and thigh to elevate turkey off bottom of roasting pan. Allow turkey to stand at room temperature for 1 hour.

3. Adjust oven rack to lower-middle position and heat oven to 275 degrees. Roast turkey until breast registers 160 degrees and thighs register 175 degrees, 2½ to 3 hours. Remove pan from oven and allow turkey to rest in pan for at least 30 minutes or up to 1½ hours. Thirty minutes before returning turkey to oven, increase oven temperature to 450 degrees.

4. FOR THE GLAZE: While turkey rests, bring cider, cranberries, molasses, vinegar, mustard, and ginger to boil in medium saucepan. Cook, stirring occasionally, until reduced to 1½ cups, about 30 minutes. Strain mixture through fine-mesh strainer into 2-cup liquid measuring cup, pressing on solids to extract as much liquid as possible. Discard solids (you should have about 1¼ cups glaze). Transfer ½ cup glaze to small saucepan and set aside.

5. Brush turkey with one-third of glaze in measuring cup, transfer to oven, and roast for 7 minutes. Brush on half of remaining glaze in measuring cup and roast additional 7 minutes. Brush on remaining glaze in measuring cup and roast until skin is evenly browned and crisp, 7 to 10 minutes. Transfer turkey to carving board and let rest for 20 minutes.

6. While turkey rests, remove onions from pan and discard. Strain liquid from pan into fat separator (you should have about 2 cups liquid). Allow liquid to settle for 5 minutes, then pour into saucepan with reserved glaze, discarding any remaining fat. Bring mixture to boil and cook until slightly syrupy, about 10 minutes. Remove pan from heat and whisk in butter. Carve turkey and serve, passing sauce separately.

BUTTERFLIED TURKEY WITH APPLE-MAPLE GLAZE

Substitute ½ cup dried apples for cranberries and ½ cup maple syrup for molasses.

☑ WHY THIS RECIPE WORKS

In this recipe, we butterfly the turkey so that all the skin is facing up in the oven, and thus much easier to crisp. The setup also makes it much easier to glaze the turkey because the bird is now flat. We use a combination of salt and baking powder to create crackling skin. We don't add the glaze until late in the cooking process in order to maintain that crisp, browned exterior.

BUTTERFLY THE BIRD Using kitchen shears, cut through the bones on either side of the backbone, staying as close as possible to the backbone, which you should remove and discard. Flip turkey over and press down firmly with the heels of your hands to flatten the breastbone.

CRISP SKIN AND SEASONED MEAT We rub this bird with a combination of salt and baking powder to ensure moist, tender meat and crisp skin. The salt helps dehydrate the skin, while the baking powder creates a more alkaline environment that promotes browning and helps break down proteins to produce a crunchier texture. To promote crispness, we loosen the skin from the bird's thighs and breasts and poke holes in the fat deposits with a skewer; the loosening helps air to circulate around the skin, which dries it out, while the poking creates escape channels for the rendered fat.

FASHION A ROASTING RACK Our butterflied turkey fits in a large roasting pan but needs to be elevated to brown properly. You can easily raise it by placing four onion halves cut side down in the pan. Place one onion half under each breast and thigh to elevate the turkey off the bottom of the pan.

COOK LOW AND SLOW We roast the bird slowly and gently in a low oven (for more on gentle heat, see concept 1) before blasting it with high heat at the very end (for more on high heat, see concept 2). We've found that this is the best way to get evenly cooked meat and a nicely browned exterior.

GET THE GLAZE RIGHT A glossy, tangy-sweet glaze is the perfect complement to a beautifully bronzed turkey, but it often pools at the bottom of the roasting pan and prevents the skin from crisping. The solution to avoiding soggy skin is a simple matter of timing: Adding the glaze at the outset of cooking leads to predictably flabby skin, but brushing it on toward the very end of cooking works great. Molasses serves as the sticky base of our glaze, but we first thin it out with apple cider and cider vinegar and then thicken it with some cranberries (which contain a natural thickener called pectin).

Salty Marinades Work Best

Marinating is often regarded as a cure-all for bland, chewy meat. Years of testing have taught us that while many marinades can bump up flavor, most will never turn a tough cut tender. Well, not without the right ingredient. What's the secret to a marinade that can add complexity to steak, chicken, and pork and enhance juiciness? You guessed it: salt.

HOW THE SCIENCE WORKS

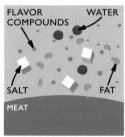

START THE SOAK
When marinating, meat is immersed in a solution of water, flavor compounds, fat, and, most important, salt.

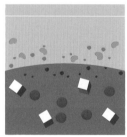

AFTER THE MARINADE
With time, the water and salt penetrate to the center of the meat while the fat and fat-soluble flavor compounds remain on the surface.

A marinade is a seasoned, traditionally acidic liquid in which we soak meat before (and sometimes after) cooking. On one level, marinating is about getting as much of the soaking liquid flavors as possible into (and on) a piece of meat. But the effectiveness of a marinade really rests on salt, a key ingredient that plays much the same role here as it does in brining (see concept 11). After all, soaking meat in a saltwater solution is a way to create more juiciness. To pump up flavor as well as moisture, our marinades combine both approaches, with soaking liquids that contain not only lots of flavorings but so much salt you might even call them "brinerades." (We do.)

As in a brine, salt in a marinade affects meat in four ways. It restructures the protein molecules in the meat, creating gaps that fill with water to increase juiciness, as well as loosening the bundles of muscle fibers, making them more tender and easier to bite through and chew. In addition, the salt dissolves some of the muscle proteins, which act like a sponge to soak up and hold moisture within the gaps. Salt also seasons the meat, enhancing its inherent flavors. And, finally, while the salt is doing its work, osmosis causes water to move across cell walls from areas with a lower concentration of dissolved substances (the marinade) to areas of higher concentration (the meat).

Along with salt, it's important to use ample amounts of strong, potent flavors in marinades. We can look at this on a molecular level: In a marinade, the salt will bind to the muscle proteins in meat, increasing the electric charge of these proteins and making them less attractive to electrically neutral flavor molecules. So whatever flavors do enter the meat, we want them to pack a punch. Furthermore, most flavor molecules in herbs and spices are fat-soluble—yet the water in meat repels fat-soluble flavors. This means that there is very little flavor contribution from herbs and spices in marinades except on the surface of meat, and we must use as many water-soluble flavors in our marinades as we can. (The characteristic flavor compounds of onion and garlic, for example, are water-soluble, allowing them to passively migrate into meat along with the water.)

We also gravitate toward flavor potentiators in our marinades, like the water-soluble glutamates found in ingredients like soy sauce, which enter meat in a manner similar to salt. Though also characterized as salt, glutamates are not the same as sodium chloride. In the meat, glutamates provide umami flavor (see concept 35) but play no role in holding moisture. Sodium chloride, also present in soy sauce, is responsible for increased juiciness.

Oil is often a component of marinades, too, because it dissolves some of the fat-soluble flavors and helps them to cling to the surface of meat and even penetrate exposed fat.

But just as important as what you include in a marinade is what you leave out, most notably, acids. Commonly thought to tenderize, acids in fact can make meat mushy. To tenderize meat, you have to break down muscle fiber and collagen, the connective tissues that make meat tough, thus increasing the meat's ability to retain moisture and become easier to chew. While acidic ingredients like citrus juice, vinegar, yogurt, buttermilk, and wine do weaken muscle tissue, their impact is confined to the meat's surface. And if left too long, acids break down protein too much, turning the outermost layer of meat mushy, not tender. (Acid can also make meat tough. For more, see "Why Does Acid Make Meat Tough and Dry?," page 132.)

So with proper timing and ingredients, marinating can infuse flavor and juiciness into meat. But after all this work, just how much flavor will a marinade impart? We hit the test kitchen to find out.

TEST KITCHEN EXPERIMENT

To test the reach of the flavor compounds in a marinade, we marinated boneless, skinless chicken breasts in four different marinades (based on soy, yogurt, red wine, and lemon and garlic, and all made without added salt) for 18 hours. (We used zipper-lock bags and pressed out the air to ensure full contact between the chicken and the marinade.) Afterward, we wiped off the excess marinade and baked the chicken breasts in a 300-degree oven until they reached 160 degrees, along with unmarinated breasts as a control. After the breasts rested for five minutes, we trimmed off the outer 3 millimeters of flesh (which is how far we could see the colorful marinades penetrated) and tasted the remaining chicken.

THE RESULTS

An overwhelming majority of tasters could discern little or no difference among the various chicken breasts. For all we could tell, none of them had been marinated. Most tasters did find the soy-marinated chicken breasts to be juicier than the other samples, however.

THE TAKEAWAY

Contrary to popular belief, marinades do most of their work on the surface of meat or just below. Even with prolonged contact, marinades don't travel very far. Oil-soluble flavors, like most in our marinades, are incapable of deeply penetrating water-filled meat. Only the salt in the soy sauce traveled far enough for our tasters to discern a difference. Acting as a brine (see concept 11), the soy marinade created a more tender and juicier piece of meat.

THE SHORT JOURNEY OF A MARINADE

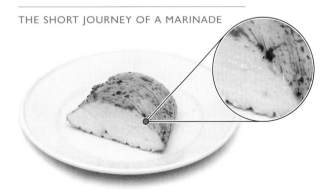

Though soaked in a soy-based mixture for 18 hours, the chicken did not absorb the dark-colored flavor compounds any deeper than a few millimeters from the surface. When we cut off the exterior, tasters confirmed that salt had an impact on the interior, but they could not detect any other flavors from the marinade.

Shrimp cook so quickly that developing flavor can be tricky. As a result, marinating is especially important. Here, we use thick, almost pastelike marinades—a mixture of salt, oil, and aromatics—that really cling to the individual shrimp and impart the optimal flavor. The very high concentration of salt works its magic in two ways. First, it quickly enters the flesh of the shrimp, helping them to retain valuable juices during cooking. Second, it forces the flavors from aromatics such as garlic and ginger into the oil. This is called the "salting out" effect, in which the high concentration of salt forces even water-soluble compounds out of the water into the oil. The oil in the mix distributes those flavor compounds evenly over the flesh (not just the parts in direct contact with the garlic) for shrimp that taste better than ever.

SPANISH-STYLE GARLIC SHRIMP
SERVES 6

Serve the shrimp with crusty bread for dipping. The dish can be served directly from the skillet (make sure to use a trivet) or, for a sizzling effect, transferred to an 8-inch cast-iron skillet that's been heated for 2 minutes over medium-high heat. We prefer the slightly sweet flavor of dried chiles in this recipe, but ¼ teaspoon of sweet paprika can be substituted. If sherry vinegar is unavailable, use 2 teaspoons of dry sherry and 1 teaspoon of distilled white vinegar.

14	garlic cloves, peeled
1	pound large shrimp (26 to 30 per pound), peeled, deveined, and tails removed
½	cup olive oil
½	teaspoon salt
1	bay leaf
1	(2-inch) piece mild dried chile, such as New Mexican, roughly broken, seeds included
1½	teaspoons sherry vinegar
1	tablespoon minced fresh parsley

1. Mince 2 garlic cloves and toss with shrimp, 2 tablespoons olive oil, and salt in medium bowl. Let shrimp marinate at room temperature for 30 minutes.

2. Meanwhile, using flat side of chef's knife, smash 4 garlic cloves. Heat smashed garlic with remaining 6 tablespoons olive oil in 12-inch skillet over medium-low heat, stirring occasionally, until garlic is light golden brown, 4 to 7 minutes. Remove pan from heat and allow oil to cool to room temperature. Using slotted spoon, remove smashed garlic from skillet and discard.

3. Thinly slice remaining 8 garlic cloves. Return skillet to low heat and add sliced garlic, bay leaf, and chile.

Cook, stirring occasionally, until garlic is tender but not browned, 4 to 7 minutes. (If garlic has not begun to sizzle after 3 minutes, increase heat to medium-low.) Increase heat to medium-low; add shrimp with marinade to pan in single layer. Cook shrimp, undisturbed, until oil starts to gently bubble, about 2 minutes. Using tongs, flip shrimp and continue to cook until almost cooked through, about 2 minutes longer. Increase heat to high and add vinegar and parsley. Cook, stirring constantly, until shrimp are cooked through and oil is bubbling vigorously, 15 to 20 seconds. Serve immediately.

✔ WHY THIS RECIPE WORKS
We wanted a garlic shrimp recipe that would make six good-size appetizer portions of wonderfully sweet and tender shrimp, infused with deep garlic flavor and not drenched in oil. First, we chose a large pan to accommodate the shrimp in one layer in a reduced amount of oil. Then, to get the intense flavor we wanted, we added garlic in three ways—including in a marinade, which uses both oil and salt.

USE GARLIC THREE WAYS We add lots of garlic to this recipe to make sure its heady aroma and flavor share equal billing with the tender shrimp. We use minced cloves in a marinade, smash whole cloves and brown them in the cooking oil (removing them before the shrimp are added), and then add slices to the oil right before the shrimp. (For more on garlic, see concept 31.)

CHOOSE THE RIGHT CHILE The authentic choice here is the slightly sweet cascabel chile, which is traditionally used in the kinds of *gambas al ajillo* you will order at a Spanish tapas restaurant. The best substitute is the New Mexican chile (aka California chile, chile Colorado, or dried Anaheim chile), which is far more widely available

---

PRACTICAL SCIENCE MARINADE SUPERHEROES

Oil and salt are key components in our marinade.

We found that omitting either the oil or the salt from our marinade significantly reduced garlic flavor in the cooked shrimp. Why? Oil protects and stabilizes allicin, the compound in garlic that is responsible for its characteristic flavor. Allicin is produced when garlic is cut or crushed, and it quickly degrades into less flavorful compounds when exposed to air. Once in oil, however, the allicin dissolves and is protected from air. There's one more advantage to oil—it coats the shrimp and delivers flavor evenly, not just in areas directly in contact with the minced garlic. But allicin is one of those unique small molecules that is soluble in both oil and water. So allicin will migrate into the shrimp along with water from the marinade. Salt contributes to the process by speeding things up, drawing water containing allicin out of the garlic at a faster rate than allicin would migrate on its own.

and has the same bright freshness as the cascabel. The last resort is sweet paprika. You won't have any trouble finding it, but its slightly stale flavor cannot compare with the complex taste of whole dried chiles. Chiles also provide another advantage in pastes and rubs. The principal oil-soluble pungent flavor compounds in chiles are not as volatile as those in most herbs and spices, so they evaporate less quickly from the hot surface of meat and seafood. (For more on chiles, see concept 32.)

COOK LOW AND SLOW The heat is low and the cooking time relatively slow for this dish so that we can cook the shrimp in a single layer and flip them only once. If we were to reduce the cooking time by using a higher heat, it would be almost impossible to move fast enough to flip all the shrimp without some of them becoming woefully overcooked. Low and slow guarantees tender, well-cooked shrimp. It also helps to guarantee that more of the volatile flavor molecules stay on the shrimp rather than evaporate into the air.

STIR-FRIED SHRIMP WITH SNOW PEAS AND RED BELL PEPPER IN HOT AND SOUR SAUCE
SERVES 4

Serve this stir-fry with Simple White Rice (page 124).

SAUCE

3	tablespoons sugar
3	tablespoons distilled white vinegar
1	tablespoon Asian chili-garlic sauce
1	tablespoon dry sherry or Chinese rice cooking wine
1	tablespoon ketchup
2	teaspoons toasted sesame oil
2	teaspoons cornstarch
1	teaspoon soy sauce

SHRIMP STIR-FRY

1	pound extra-large shrimp (21 to 25 per pound), peeled, deveined, and tails removed
3	tablespoons vegetable oil
1	tablespoon grated fresh ginger
2	garlic cloves (1 minced, 1 sliced thin)
½	teaspoon salt
1	large shallot, sliced thin
8	ounces snow peas or sugar snap peas, strings removed
1	red bell pepper, stemmed, seeded, and cut into ¾-inch pieces

1. FOR THE SAUCE: Whisk all ingredients together in small bowl and set aside.

2. FOR THE STIR-FRY: Combine shrimp with 1 tablespoon oil, ginger, minced garlic, and salt in medium bowl. Let shrimp marinate at room temperature for 30 minutes.

3. Combine sliced garlic with shallot in small bowl. Heat 1 tablespoon oil in 12-inch nonstick skillet over high heat until just smoking. Add snow peas and bell pepper and cook, stirring frequently, until vegetables begin to brown, 1½ to 2 minutes. Transfer vegetables to medium bowl.

4. Heat remaining 1 tablespoon oil over high heat until just smoking. Add shallot mixture and cook, stirring frequently, until just beginning to brown, about 30 seconds. Add shrimp, reduce heat to medium-low, and cook, stirring frequently, until shrimp are light pink on both sides, 1 to 1½ minutes. Stir sauce to recombine and add to skillet; return to high heat and cook, stirring constantly, until sauce is thickened and shrimp are cooked through, 1 to 2 minutes. Return vegetables to skillet, toss to combine, and serve.

STIR-FRIED SICHUAN-STYLE SHRIMP WITH ZUCCHINI, RED BELL PEPPER, AND PEANUTS
SERVES 4

Note that this recipe is spicy and not for the timid. If you can find a Chinese long pepper, use it in place of the jalapeño. Broad bean chili paste is also referred to as chili bean sauce or horse bean chili paste. If you can't find it, increase the amount of Asian chili-garlic sauce by 1 teaspoon. Sichuan peppercorns, available at Asian markets and some supermarkets, have purplish-red husks and shiny black seeds; it is preferable to buy them with the seeds removed, as it's the husk that provides the aromatic, gently floral fragrance (and the notable numbing effect on the tongue). Serve with Simple White Rice (recipe follows).

SAUCE

2	tablespoons dry sherry or Chinese rice cooking wine
1	tablespoon broad bean chili paste
1	tablespoon Asian chili-garlic sauce
1	tablespoon distilled white vinegar or Chinese black vinegar
2	teaspoons soy sauce
2	teaspoons chili oil or toasted sesame oil
1	teaspoon sugar
1	teaspoon cornstarch
½	teaspoon Sichuan peppercorns, toasted and ground (optional)

SHRIMP STIR-FRY

 1   pound extra-large shrimp (21 to 25 per pound), peeled, deveined, and tails removed
 3   tablespoons vegetable oil
 2   garlic cloves (1 minced, 1 sliced thin)
 ½   teaspoon salt
 ½   cup dry-roasted peanuts
 1   jalapeño chile, stemmed, halved, seeded, and sliced thin on bias
 1   small zucchini, cut into ¾-inch dice
 1   red bell pepper, stemmed, seeded, and cut into ¾-inch dice
 ½   cup fresh cilantro leaves

1. FOR THE SAUCE: Whisk all ingredients together in small bowl and set aside.

2. FOR THE STIR-FRY: Combine shrimp with 1 tablespoon oil, minced garlic, and salt in medium bowl. Let shrimp marinate at room temperature for 30 minutes.

3. Combine sliced garlic, peanuts, and jalapeño in small bowl. Heat 1 tablespoon oil in 12-inch nonstick skillet over high heat until just smoking. Add zucchini and bell pepper and cook, stirring frequently, until zucchini is tender and well browned, 2 to 4 minutes. Transfer vegetables to medium bowl.

4. Add remaining 1 tablespoon oil to skillet and heat until just smoking. Add peanut mixture and cook, stirring frequently, until just beginning to brown, about 30 seconds. Add shrimp, reduce heat to medium-low, and cook, stirring frequently, until shrimp are light pink on both sides, 1 to 1½ minutes. Stir sauce to recombine and add to skillet. Return to high heat and cook, stirring constantly, until sauce is thickened and shrimp are cooked through, 1 to 2 minutes. Return vegetables to skillet, add cilantro, toss to combine, and serve.

SIMPLE WHITE RICE
SERVES 4

You will need a saucepan with a tight-fitting lid for this recipe. (For more information on cooking rice, see concept 30.)

 1½   cups long-grain white rice
  1   tablespoon unsalted butter or vegetable oil
 2¼   cups water
  1   teaspoon salt

1. Place rice in colander or fine-mesh strainer and rinse under cold running water until water runs clear. Place strainer over bowl and set aside.

2. Melt butter in large saucepan over medium heat. Add rice and cook, stirring constantly, until grains become chalky and opaque, 1 to 3 minutes. Add water and salt, increase heat to high, and bring to boil, swirling pot to blend ingredients. Reduce heat to low, cover, and simmer until all liquid is absorbed, 18 to 20 minutes. Off heat, remove lid and place kitchen towel folded in half over saucepan; replace lid. Let stand for 10 to 15 minutes. Fluff rice with fork and serve.

☑ WHY THIS RECIPE WORKS

Our typical high-heat stir-fry technique, which works well with chicken, beef, and pork, doesn't fly with quick-cooking shrimp. (The different muscle structure of shrimp requires cooking to an internal temperature about 20 degrees lower than meat to avoid overcooking.) Here, we modify our technique to produce plump, juicy, well-seasoned shrimp in a balanced, flavorful sauce. For our sauce, the heavily soy-based brews we turn to for meat stir-fries are a poor match with the shrimp. Sweeter or spicier sauces flavored with garlic and chiles are better suited, and they reduce to a consistency that tightly adheres to the shellfish.

PEEL THE SHRIMP Chinese stir-fries often work around the problem of tough shrimp by cooking them shell-on to protect their delicate flesh, but neither crunching into shrimp shells nor peeling them at the table appeals to us. We use other methods for tender shrimp; make sure that your shrimp are peeled, deveined, and tails removed.

USE A SKILLET, NOT A WOK To keep the pan good and hot throughout the process of this recipe, we use a large, shallow nonstick skillet. (On a Western range, a skillet heats more efficiently than a wok and provides maximum surface area for evaporation. See "Skillet vs. Wok," page 27.)

REVERSE THE ORDER Traditionally, stir-fry recipes call for browning meat over high heat—often in batches—before removing and then adding the vegetables and aromatics. It's only at the end that you return the protein to the pan. Here, however, we start out cooking the vegetables over high heat. We remove them and then turn the heat down before adding the shrimp. This way the shrimp, which have a very small window of time before they're overcooked on high heat, are cooked slowly and remain tender and juicy. Once the shrimp are cooked through, we return the vegetables to the pan.

Marinades containing oil, salt, and aromatics work wonders with beef, too. The salt acts as a brine, adding tenderness and seasoning, while the oil helps to intensify the flavors of the fat-soluble spices and herbs.

BEEF STROGANOFF
SERVES 4

Steak tips, also known as flap meat, are sold as whole steak, cubes, and strips. To ensure uniform pieces that cook evenly, we prefer to purchase whole steak tips and cut them ourselves. You can substitute 1½ pounds of blade steak for the steak tips; if using, cut each steak in half lengthwise and remove the gristle that runs down the center before cooking. Since blade steak yields smaller strips of meat, reduce the cooking time in step 3 by several minutes. If the mushrooms are larger than 1 inch, cut them into six even wedges. Serve the stroganoff over buttered egg noodles.

1¼	pounds sirloin steak tips, trimmed and cut lengthwise (with grain) into 4 equal pieces
2	teaspoons soy sauce
1	pound white mushrooms, trimmed and quartered
1	tablespoon dry mustard
2	teaspoons hot water
1	teaspoon sugar
	Salt and pepper
1	tablespoon vegetable oil
1	onion, chopped fine
4	teaspoons all-purpose flour
2	teaspoons tomato paste
1½	cups beef broth
⅓	cup plus 1 tablespoon white wine or dry vermouth
½	cup sour cream
1	tablespoon minced fresh parsley or dill

1. Using fork, poke each piece of steak 10 to 12 times. Place in baking dish; rub both sides evenly with soy sauce. Cover with plastic wrap and refrigerate for at least 15 minutes or up to 1 hour.

2. While meat marinates, place mushrooms in medium bowl, cover, and microwave until mushrooms have decreased in volume by half, 4 to 5 minutes (there should be as much as ¼ cup liquid in bowl). Drain mushrooms and set aside; discard liquid. Combine mustard, water, sugar, and ½ teaspoon pepper in small bowl until smooth paste forms; set aside.

3. Pat steak pieces dry with paper towels and season with pepper. Heat oil in 12-inch skillet over medium-high heat until just smoking. Place steak pieces in skillet and cook until browned on all sides and meat registers 125 to 130 degrees, 6 to 9 minutes. Transfer meat to large plate and set aside while cooking sauce.

4. Add mushrooms, onion, and ½ teaspoon salt to skillet and cook until vegetables begin to brown and dark bits form on bottom of pan, 6 to 8 minutes. Add flour and tomato paste and cook, stirring constantly, until onions and mushrooms are coated, about 1 minute. Stir in beef broth, ⅓ cup wine, and mustard paste and bring to simmer, scraping bottom of pan to loosen browned bits. Reduce heat to medium and cook until sauce has reduced slightly and begun to thicken, 4 to 6 minutes.

5. While sauce is reducing, slice steak pieces against grain into ¼-inch-thick slices. Stir meat and any accumulated juices into thickened sauce and cook until beef has warmed through, 1 to 2 minutes. Remove pan from heat and let any bubbles subside. Stir in sour cream and remaining tablespoon wine; season with salt and pepper to taste. Sprinkle with parsley and serve.

PRACTICAL SCIENCE
CUTTING OUT CURDLING IN CULTURED DAIRY

With all of its fat, crème fraîche will not curdle when heated in dishes like beef stroganoff.

Dishes like beef stroganoff, chicken paprikash, and many of the Moroccan stews known as tagines wouldn't be complete without a little sour cream or yogurt stirred in at the end. However, these cultured dairy products are sensitive to heat and can easily curdle if the stew is too hot or reheated. We wondered if another dairy product would provide a more suitable tang.

We stirred dollops of whole-milk yogurt, full-fat sour cream, and crème fraîche (which boasts much more fat) into water that we brought to just a simmer (185 degrees). After letting the samples sit for 10 seconds, we examined the liquid for signs of curdling.

Both the yogurt and the sour ream mixtures quickly curdled, while the crème fraîche mixture remained perfectly creamy.

Curdling occurs when excessive heat causes the whey proteins in dairy to denature (unfold) and bind with casein proteins, forming clumps of larger proteins. The greater amount of butterfat in crème fraîche (30 to 40 percent, versus 18 to 20 percent and roughly 4 percent in sour cream and yogurt, respectively) protects against this process by more thoroughly coating the proteins and preventing them from binding together. Plus, with more fat, crème fraîche has far fewer proteins to bind together in the first place. It's now our go-to dairy product for hot dishes; in fact, we found that crème fraîche is so resistant to curdling that it can withstand reheating. Feel free to replace sour cream in any heated sauce with an equal amount of crème fraîche.

✔ WHY THIS RECIPE WORKS

For a beefy stroganoff recipe, we substitute sirloin steak tips for traditional tenderloin. Marinating the meat in soy sauce makes it as tender as tenderloin. Pan-roasting the meat in larger pieces develops rich flavor, and letting it rest before cutting it into strips preserves its juiciness. Adding just a touch of sour cream to the sauce completes our ideal beef stroganoff recipe, by providing body and tang without overwhelming the other flavors.

USE A FLAVORFUL CUT Traditionally, tenderloin—a buttery, tender cut—is used in beef stroganoff. But tenderloin also lacks a beefy flavor. Instead, we like to use sirloin steak tips (also known as "flap meat"), which have an intensely beefy taste. While not tough, their texture is a far cry from tenderloin, which is why we use a marinade, too.

POKE FOR FASTER ABSORPTION Poking holes in the meat allows the marinade to penetrate more deeply and contributes to a more tender texture.

MAKE A SIMPLE MARINADE We marinate the flap meat in soy sauce, which is so salty it works just like a brine, breaking down proteins in meat and helping the meat to retain more juices, as well as loosening the bundles of muscle fibers, making them easier to bite through and chew. Soy sauce also contains glutamate, which boosts meaty flavor (see concept 35).

SEAR BIG PIECES, THEN SLICE We pan-sear large pieces of meat and cut them into strips only after they have browned and left their flavorful fond in the pan. This way there is enough time to allow the meat to develop rich, dark fond without overcooking. Moreover, we can let it rest before slicing, further improving juiciness.

MICROWAVE MUSHROOMS Our recipe calls for a pound of white mushrooms. It can take up to 20 minutes for all their moisture to evaporate and they finally brown in the pan. Microwaving the mushrooms before putting them in the pan reduces the process to a mere 6 to 8 minutes.

BUILD FLAVOR While many contemporary recipes call for ketchup, we like to use just a bit of tomato paste stirred in after the onions and mushrooms brown, which brings subtle depth to the sauce. In addition, we use a paste made of dry mustard bloomed in warm water and seasoned with sugar and black pepper to give a little kick and bring other flavors into focus. White wine adds brightness, allowing the beef and mushrooms to shine through.

TEMPER THE SOUR CREAM The acidity of sour cream causes its casein proteins to become so unstable that exposure to even a little heat makes them clump. For this reason, we temper the sour cream by adding it when the sauce is off the heat.

STEAK TACOS
SERVES 4 TO 6

For a spicier dish, add the seeds from the chiles. In addition to the toppings suggested below, try serving the tacos with Sweet and Spicy Pickled Onions (recipe follows), thinly sliced radishes or cucumber, or salsa. Warm tortillas over the medium flame of a gas burner (until slightly charred, 30 seconds per side), in a dry skillet over medium-high heat (until softened and speckled with brown spots, 20 to 30 seconds per side), or in two foil-wrapped stacks in a 350-degree oven (for five minutes).

HERB PASTE

½	cup fresh cilantro leaves
3	garlic cloves, chopped coarse
3	scallions, chopped coarse
1	jalapeño chile, stemmed, seeds reserved, and chopped coarse
½	teaspoon ground cumin
¼	cup vegetable oil
1	tablespoon lime juice

STEAK

1	(1½- to 1¾-pound) flank steak, trimmed and cut lengthwise (with grain) into 4 equal pieces
1	tablespoon kosher salt
½	teaspoon sugar
½	teaspoon pepper
2	tablespoons vegetable oil

TACOS

12	(6-inch) corn tortillas, warmed
	Fresh cilantro leaves
	Minced white or red onion
	Lime wedges

1. FOR THE HERB PASTE: Pulse cilantro, garlic, scallions, jalapeño, and cumin in food processor until finely chopped, 10 to 12 pulses, scraping down sides of bowl as necessary. Add oil and process until mixture is smooth and resembles pesto, about 15 seconds, scraping down sides of bowl as necessary. Transfer 2 tablespoons herb paste to medium bowl; whisk in lime juice and set aside.

2. FOR THE STEAK: Using dinner fork, poke each piece of steak 10 to 12 times on each side. Place in large baking dish; rub all sides of steak pieces evenly with salt and then coat with remaining herb paste. Cover with plastic wrap and refrigerate for at least 30 minutes or up to 1 hour.

3. Scrape herb paste off steak and sprinkle all sides of pieces evenly with sugar and pepper. Heat oil in 12-inch nonstick skillet over medium-high heat until just smoking. Place steak in skillet and cook until well browned, about 3 minutes. Flip steak and sear until second side is well browned, 2 to 3 minutes. Using tongs, stand each piece on 1 cut side and cook, turning as necessary, until all cut sides are well browned and meat registers 125 to 130 degrees, 2 to 7 minutes. Transfer steak to cutting board and let rest for 5 minutes.

4. FOR THE TACOS: Using sharp chef's knife or carving knife, slice steak pieces against grain into thin slices. Transfer sliced steak to bowl with herb paste–lime juice mixture and toss to coat. Season with salt to taste. Spoon small amount of sliced steak into center of each warm tortilla and serve, passing toppings separately.

SWEET AND SPICY PICKLED ONIONS
MAKES ABOUT 2 CUPS

To make this dish spicier, add the reserved chile seeds with the vinegar.

1	red onion, sliced thin (1½ cups)
1	cup red wine vinegar
⅓	cup sugar
2	jalapeño chiles, stemmed, seeds reserved, and cut into thin rings
¼	teaspoon salt

Place onion in medium heatproof bowl. Bring vinegar, sugar, jalapeños, and salt to simmer in small saucepan over medium-high heat, stirring occasionally, until sugar dissolves. Pour vinegar mixture over onion, cover loosely, and let cool to room temperature, about 30 minutes. Once cool, drain and discard liquid. (Pickled onions can be refrigerated in airtight container for up to 1 week.)

✓ WHY THIS RECIPE WORKS
Steak tacos are great on the grill, but we wanted to bring them indoors for those times when grilling outside isn't an option. Cutting the beef into long pieces and pan-searing all four sides gave us the browned exterior and crisp edges characteristic of grilled meat. A paste of oil, cilantro, scallions, garlic, and jalapeño applied to the meat and scraped off just before cooking gave our steak taco recipe a flavor boost without sacrificing browning.

STAKE OUT THE STEAK Traditional Mexican recipes typically call for skirt or flank steak for taco meat, both of which come from the belly of the cow. We also tried blade steak, which comes from the shoulder, and steak tips, from the sirloin of the animal. Flank steak, however, turned out to be the best choice; it has a nice beefy flavor and, when sliced thin against the grain, is quite tender.

QUARTER AND SEAR In order to maximize flavor, we cut the steak lengthwise with the grain into four long strips, about 2½ inches wide and 1 inch thick. Because the strips are relatively thick, we are able to brown them on four sides rather than just two, which gives us even more exposed edges to become crisp and super-flavored.

SALT AND MARINADE We slather our steak with a wet pestolike paste made of cilantro, scallions, garlic, and jalapeños. When coupled with salt, this oil-based marinade provides plenty of fat-soluble cumin-chile flavor on the surface as well as penetrating water-soluble flavors from the garlic, flavoring it throughout. We reserve some of the fresh marinade to toss with the steak after it is sliced.

GRILLED BEEF KEBABS WITH LEMON AND ROSEMARY MARINADE
SERVES 4 TO 6

If you can't find sirloin steak tips, sometimes labeled "flap meat," substitute 2½ pounds of blade steak; if using, cut each steak in half to remove the gristle. You will need four 12-inch metal skewers for this recipe. If you have long, thin pieces of meat, roll or fold them into approximate 2-inch cubes before skewering.

MARINADE
1	onion, chopped
⅓	cup beef broth
⅓	cup vegetable oil
3	tablespoons tomato paste
2	tablespoons minced fresh rosemary
6	garlic cloves, chopped
2	teaspoons grated lemon zest
2	teaspoons salt
1½	teaspoons sugar
¾	teaspoon pepper

BEEF AND VEGETABLES
2	pounds sirloin steak tips, trimmed and cut into 2-inch chunks
1	large zucchini or summer squash, halved lengthwise and sliced 1 inch thick
1	large red or green bell pepper, stemmed, seeded, and cut into 1½-inch pieces
1	large red or sweet onion, peeled, halved lengthwise, each half cut into 4 wedges and each wedge cut crosswise into thirds

We prefer thick, whole steak tips with a longitudinal grain.

Beef labeled "steak tips" can be cut from various muscles of the cow and turned into cubes, strips, or steaks. Our favorite kind is cut into a steak that boasts a coarse, longitudinal grain. Butchers call this form of steak tips "flap meat" or "sirloin tips." Look for pieces that range from 1 to 1½ inches thick.

SKIP THE STRIPS
Don't buy meat that's been cut into strips or cubes—you can't tell what you're buying.

GO FOR WHOLE
Look for whole steak with a coarse, longitudinal grain labeled "sirloin tips" or "flap meat."

1. FOR THE MARINADE: Place all ingredients in blender and process until smooth, about 45 seconds. Transfer ¾ cup marinade to large bowl and set aside.

2. FOR THE BEEF AND VEGETABLES: Place remaining marinade and beef in 1-gallon zipper-lock bag and toss to coat; press out as much air as possible and seal bag. Refrigerate for at least 1 hour or up to 2 hours, flipping bag every 30 minutes.

3. Add zucchini, bell pepper, and onion to bowl with reserved marinade and toss to coat. Cover and let sit at room temperature for at least 30 minutes.

4. Remove beef from bag and pat dry with paper towels. Thread beef tightly onto two 12-inch metal skewers, rolling or folding meat as necessary to maintain 2-inch cubes. Thread vegetables onto two 12-inch metal skewers, in alternating pattern of zucchini, pepper, and onion.

5A. FOR A CHARCOAL GRILL: Open bottom vent completely. Light large chimney starter mounded with charcoal briquettes (7 quarts). When top coals are partially covered with ash, pour evenly over grill. Set cooking grate in place, cover, and open lid vent completely. Heat grill until hot, about 5 minutes.

5B. FOR A GAS GRILL: Turn all burners to high, cover, and heat grill until hot, about 15 minutes. Leave primary burner on high and turn other burner(s) to medium-low.

6. Clean and oil cooking grate. Place beef skewers on grill (directly over coals if using charcoal or over hotter side of grill if using gas). Place vegetable skewers on grill (near edge of coals but still over coals if using charcoal or over cooler side of grill if using gas). Cook (covered if using gas), turning skewers every 3 to 4 minutes, until beef skewers are well browned and register 120 to 125 degrees (for medium-rare) or 130 to 135 degrees (for medium), 12 to 16 minutes. Transfer beef skewers to platter and tent loosely with aluminum foil. Continue cooking vegetable skewers until tender and lightly charred, about 5 minutes longer; serve with beef skewers.

WHY THIS RECIPE WORKS

Well-marbled steak tips, with their beefy flavor and tender texture, proved to be the best choice for our grilled beef kebabs. To the beef's marinade, we added salt for moisture, oil for flavor, and sugar for browning. For even more depth, we used tomato paste, a host of seasonings and herbs, and beef broth. We chose three grill favorites for the vegetables: peppers, onions, and zucchini. Grilling the beef kebabs and vegetables separately allowed us to cook the vegetables at a lower temperature while the beef seared over the hotter area.

POWER UP THE MARINADE As we've learned, most of the flavors in a marinade do not penetrate to the center of the meat, no matter how long you soak it. But research has shown that salt—ordinary table salt as well as sodium glutamates, the naturally occurring flavor enhancers found in many foods—are the exception, traveling far into meat chunks and ramping up taste as they go. With this in mind, we created a turbo-charged marinade with three key ingredients: salt, tomato paste, and beef broth. Tomato paste is full of glutamates, which enhance that meaty flavor. And when we used beef broth instead of only water, tasters raved about the new depth of flavor. This is because many commercial broths contain yeast extract, a powerhouse of not one but two kinds of flavor enhancers: glutamates and nucleotides. The latter works in synergy with the naturally occurring glutamates in meat to ramp up savory taste by as much as 20-fold (for more on glutamates, see concept 35).

PICK THE RIGHT CUT We tried five different cuts of meat for this recipe, from pricey tenderloin to bottom round. After cutting them all into big, 2-inch pieces and cooking them on the grill, we discovered that the tenderloin was a waste of money, as tasters found it bland, and the bottom round was too chewy. The more marbled cuts—skirt steak, blade steak, and steak tips—all boasted respectable flavor, but the looser-grained steak tips outdid the others in both beefiness and tender texture.

PUREE THE SAUCE We mix our marinade up in a blender so that the flavors are optimally combined. No blender? Don't worry. A food processor will work as well.

As we've seen, a salt-based marinade will make meat juicier but the flavors of the marinade are mostly confined to the exterior. Even prolonged marinating doesn't really help. Marinating meat for a short time before cooking, and then using the marinade again after cooking, yields meat that is juicy and well flavored in every bite. The quick premarinade does the tenderizing work of a brine, while the postmarinade—often done while the meat rests—heightens the flavor.

CLASSIC MARINADE FOR STEAKS
MAKES ABOUT 1 CUP, ENOUGH TO MARINATE
4 TO 6 INDIVIDUAL STEAKS OR ONE 2-POUND STEAK

½   cup soy sauce
⅓   cup vegetable oil
¼   cup Worcestershire sauce
2   tablespoons packed dark brown sugar
2   tablespoons minced fresh chives
4   garlic cloves, minced
1½   teaspoons pepper
2   teaspoons balsamic vinegar

1. Combine soy sauce, oil, Worcestershire, sugar, chives, garlic, and pepper in medium bowl. Remove ¼ cup marinade and combine with vinegar in small bowl; set aside.

2. Place remaining marinade and steaks in 1-gallon zipper-lock bag; press out as much air as possible and seal bag. Refrigerate for 1 hour, flipping bag after 30 minutes to ensure that steaks marinate evenly.

3. Remove steaks from marinade, letting any excess marinade drip back into bag. Discard bag and marinade. Grill steaks as desired.

4. Transfer steaks to shallow pan and pour reserved marinade over top. Tent loosely with aluminum foil and let rest for 10 minutes, turning meat halfway through resting. Slice steaks or serve whole, passing reserved marinade if desired.

MOLE MARINADE FOR STEAKS
MAKES ABOUT 1 CUP, ENOUGH TO MARINATE
4 TO 6 INDIVIDUAL STEAKS OR ONE 2-POUND STEAK

½   cup soy sauce
⅓   cup vegetable oil
2   tablespoons packed dark brown sugar
4   minced chipotle chiles in adobo sauce
4   garlic cloves, minced
4   teaspoons cocoa

1½   teaspoons dried oregano
1   teaspoon pepper
2   tablespoons lime juice

1. Combine soy sauce, oil, sugar, chipotle, garlic, cocoa, oregano, and pepper in medium bowl. Remove ¼ cup marinade and combine with lime juice in small bowl; set aside.

2. Place remaining marinade and steaks in 1-gallon zipper-lock bag; press out as much air as possible and seal bag. Refrigerate for 1 hour, flipping bag after 30 minutes to ensure that steaks marinate evenly.

3. Remove steaks from marinade, letting any excess marinade drip back into bag. Discard bag and marinade. Grill steaks as desired.

4. Transfer steaks to shallow pan and pour reserved marinade over top. Tent loosely with aluminum foil and let rest for 10 minutes, turning meat halfway through resting. Slice steaks or serve whole, passing reserved marinade if desired.

SOUTHEAST ASIAN MARINADE FOR STEAKS
MAKES ABOUT 1 CUP, ENOUGH TO MARINATE
4 TO 6 INDIVIDUAL STEAKS OR ONE 2-POUND STEAK

⅓   cup soy sauce
⅓   cup vegetable oil
2   tablespoons packed dark brown sugar
2   tablespoons fish sauce
2   tablespoons red curry paste
2   tablespoons grated fresh ginger
4   garlic cloves, minced
2   tablespoons lime juice

1. Combine soy sauce, oil, sugar, fish sauce, curry paste, ginger, and garlic in medium bowl. Remove ¼ cup marinade and combine with lime juice in small bowl; set aside.

2. Place remaining marinade and steaks in 1-gallon zipper-lock bag; press out as much air as possible and seal bag. Refrigerate for 1 hour, flipping bag after 30 minutes to ensure that steaks marinate evenly.

3. Remove steaks from marinade, letting any excess marinade drip back into bag. Discard bag and marinade. Grill steaks as desired.

4. Transfer steaks to shallow pan and pour reserved marinade over top. Tent loosely with aluminum foil and let rest for 10 minutes, turning meat halfway through resting. Slice steaks or serve whole, passing reserved marinade if desired.

MOJO MARINADE FOR STEAKS

MAKES ABOUT 1 CUP, ENOUGH TO MARINATE
4 TO 6 INDIVIDUAL STEAKS OR ONE 2-POUND STEAK

½   cup soy sauce
⅓   cup vegetable oil
2   tablespoons packed dark brown sugar
6   garlic cloves, minced
2   tablespoons minced fresh cilantro
1   teaspoon grated orange zest plus 2 tablespoons
    juice
1   teaspoon pepper
½   teaspoon ground cumin
½   teaspoon dried oregano
2   teaspoons white vinegar

1. Combine soy sauce, oil, sugar, garlic, cilantro, orange zest, pepper, cumin, and oregano in medium bowl. Remove ¼ cup of marinade and combine with orange juice and vinegar in small bowl; set aside.

2. Place remaining marinade and steaks in 1-gallon zipper-lock bag; press out as much air as possible and seal bag. Refrigerate for 1 hour, flipping bag after 30 minutes to ensure that steaks marinate evenly.

3. Remove steaks from marinade, letting any excess marinade drip back into bag. Discard bag and marinade. Grill steaks as desired.

4. Transfer steaks to shallow pan and pour reserved marinade over top. Tent loosely with aluminum foil and let rest for 10 minutes, turning meat halfway through resting. Slice steaks or serve whole, passing reserved marinade if desired.

HONEY-MUSTARD MARINADE FOR STEAKS

MAKES ABOUT 1 CUP, ENOUGH TO MARINATE
4 TO 6 INDIVIDUAL STEAKS OR ONE 2-POUND STEAK

½   cup soy sauce
⅓   cup vegetable oil
3   tablespoons Dijon mustard
2   tablespoons minced fresh tarragon
4   garlic cloves, minced
4   teaspoons honey
1½   teaspoons pepper
1   teaspoon cider vinegar

1. Combine soy sauce, oil, mustard, tarragon, garlic, honey, and pepper in medium bowl. Remove ¼ cup marinade and combine with vinegar in small bowl; set aside.

2. Place remaining marinade and steaks in 1-gallon zipper-lock bag; press out as much air as possible and seal bag. Refrigerate for 1 hour, flipping bag after 30 minutes to ensure that steaks marinate evenly.

3. Remove steaks from marinade, letting any excess marinade drip back into bag. Discard bag and marinade. Grill steaks as desired.

4. Transfer steaks to shallow pan and pour reserved marinade over top. Tent loosely with aluminum foil and let rest for 10 minutes, turning meat halfway through resting. Slice steaks or serve whole, passing reserved marinade if desired.

✔ WHY THIS RECIPE WORKS

These five marinade recipes for steaks use bright, intense flavors combined with the salty power of soy sauce to create marinades excellent for their ability to impart flavor and improve texture in the steaks. The salt in soy sauce acts much like a brine, helping the meat retain moisture during cooking and making it more tender. But to add more depth of flavor, we needed additional seasonings. We found them in the international section of the supermarket, with ingredients as diverse as red curry paste, Dijon mustard, and chipotle chiles.

SEND ALL CUTS TO SOAK   While the looser-textured skirt, flank, and sirloin tip steaks absorb the marinade better than the thicker rib-eye, strip, and blade steaks, all of these cuts benefit from the one-hour precooking marinade and the 10-minute postcooking marinade. This is one case where double dipping is a good thing.

ADD ACID AT THE END   We add the acidic component of these marinades to the amount that we reserve for the cooked steak at rest. As we've learned, the acid can break down the meat, causing it to become tough and dry and not at all tender. But because it imparts great flavor, it is included in the second marinade, when it can no longer do any harm.

DOUSE THEN SLICE   Once the beef is pulled off the grill, we dip the entire steak into the reserved marinade, flipping it once to ensure an even coating. If we slice the beef before it goes for a second run in the marinade, the flavors can be too intense.

GRILLED LEMON-PARSLEY CHICKEN BREASTS
SERVES 4

The chicken should be marinated for no less than 30 minutes and no more than one hour. Serve with a simply prepared vegetable or use in a sandwich or salad.

6	tablespoons olive oil
2	tablespoons lemon juice
I	tablespoon minced fresh parsley
I¼	teaspoons sugar
I	teaspoon Dijon mustard
	Salt and pepper
2	tablespoons water
3	garlic cloves, minced
4	(6- to 8-ounce) boneless, skinless chicken breasts, trimmed

1. Whisk 3 tablespoons oil, 1 tablespoon lemon juice, parsley, ¼ teaspoon sugar, mustard, ¼ teaspoon salt, and ¼ teaspoon pepper together in bowl and set aside for serving.

2. Whisk remaining 3 tablespoons oil, remaining 1 tablespoon lemon juice, remaining 1 teaspoon sugar, 1½ teaspoons salt, ½ teaspoon pepper, water, and garlic together in bowl. Place marinade and chicken in 1-gallon zipper-lock bag and toss to coat; press out as much air as possible and seal bag. Refrigerate for at least 30 minutes or up to 1 hour, flipping bag every 15 minutes.

3A. FOR A CHARCOAL GRILL: Open bottom vent completely. Light large chimney starter filled with charcoal briquettes (6 quarts). When top coals are partially covered with ash, pour evenly over half of grill. Set cooking grate in place, cover, and open lid vent completely. Heat grill until hot, about 5 minutes.

3B. FOR A GAS GRILL: Turn all burners to high, cover, and heat grill until hot, about 15 minutes. Leave primary burner on high and turn off other burner(s).

4. Clean and oil cooking grate. Remove chicken from bag, allowing excess marinade to drip off. Place chicken on cooler side of grill, smooth side down, with thicker sides facing coals and flames. Cover and cook until bottom of chicken just begins to develop light grill marks and is no longer translucent, 6 to 9 minutes.

5. Flip chicken and rotate so that thinner sides face coals and flames. Cover and continue to cook until chicken is opaque and firm to touch and registers 140 degrees, 6 to 9 minutes longer.

6. Move chicken to hot side of grill and cook until dark grill marks appear on both sides and chicken registers 160 degrees, 2 to 6 minutes longer.

7. Transfer chicken to cutting board, tent loosely with aluminum foil, and let rest for 5 to 10 minutes. Slice each breast on bias into ¼-inch-thick slices and transfer to individual plates. Drizzle with reserved sauce and serve.

GRILLED CHIPOTLE-LIME CHICKEN BREASTS

Substitute lime juice for lemon juice and use 1 extra teaspoon juice in reserved sauce. Substitute minced chipotle chile in adobo sauce for mustard and cilantro for parsley.

GRILLED ORANGE-TARRAGON CHICKEN BREASTS

Substitute orange juice for lemon juice and tarragon for parsley. Add ¼ teaspoon grated orange zest to reserved sauce.

✓ WHY THIS RECIPE WORKS
Because they have no skin and little fat, plain boneless chicken breasts invariably turn out dry and leathery when grilled. A common solution—marinating them in bottled salad dressings, which are laden with acid, sweeteners, stabilizers, and gums—often imparts off-flavors. We wanted grilled chicken breasts that would come off the grill juicy and flavorful, and we wanted to look beyond bottled salad dressing to get there. We use a homemade marinade and then drizzle a separate, reserved vinaigrette on top for the optimal combination of texture and flavor.

MAKE A TWO-LEVEL FIRE Cooked over a hot, single-level fire as many recipes suggest, the outer layers of chicken breasts turn into black shoe leather before the inside reaches the requisite 160 degrees. But we found that by using a two-level fire and cooking the chicken, covered, over the cooler side of the grill until almost done (140 degrees) and finishing with a quick sear, we are rewarded with perfectly cooked breasts.

ACID TO FINISH Originally, we used a marinade that included olive oil, lemon juice, garlic, salt, pepper, and a bit of sugar. But with this combination, we found that the acid of the lemon juice caused the exterior of the chicken breasts to turn white. In our finished dish, we reduce the amount of lemon juice in the marinade and use a complementary vinaigrette after cooking to amp up the flavors.

CHICKEN FAJITAS
SERVES 4 TO 6

You can use red, yellow, orange, or green bell peppers in this recipe. The chicken tenderloins can be reserved for another use or marinated and grilled along with the breasts. When you head outside to grill, bring a clean kitchen towel in which to wrap the tortillas and keep them warm. The chicken and vegetables have enough flavor on their own, but accompaniments (guacamole, salsa, sour cream, shredded cheese, and lime wedges) can be offered at the table.

6	tablespoons vegetable oil
⅓	cup lime juice (3 limes)
I	jalapeño chile, stemmed, seeded, and minced
I½	tablespoons minced fresh cilantro
3	garlic cloves, minced
I	tablespoon Worcestershire sauce
I½	teaspoons packed brown sugar
	Salt and pepper
I½	pounds boneless, skinless chicken breasts, tenderloins removed, trimmed, pounded to ½-inch thickness
I	large red onion, peeled and cut into ½-inch-thick rounds (do not separate rings)
2	large bell peppers, quartered, stemmed, and seeded
8–12	(6-inch) flour tortillas

I. Whisk ¼ cup oil, lime juice, jalapeño, garlic, Worcestershire, sugar, 1 teaspoon salt, and ¾ teaspoon pepper together in bowl. Reserve ¼ cup marinade and set aside. Add 1 teaspoon salt to remaining marinade. Place marinade and chicken in 1-gallon zipper-lock bag and toss to coat; press out as much air as possible and seal bag. Refrigerate for at least 15 minutes, flipping bag halfway through marinating. Brush both sides of onion rounds and peppers with remaining 2 tablespoons oil and season with salt and pepper.

2A. FOR A CHARCOAL GRILL: Open bottom vent completely. Light large chimney starter filled with charcoal briquettes (6 quarts). When top coals are partially covered with ash, pour coals over two-thirds of grill, leaving remaining one-third empty. Set cooking grate in place, cover, and open lid vent completely. Heat grill until hot, about 5 minutes.

2B. FOR A GAS GRILL: Turn all burners to high, cover, and heat grill until hot, about 15 minutes. Leave primary burner on high and turn other burner(s) to medium.

3. Clean and oil cooking grate. Remove chicken from bag, allowing excess marinade to drip off. Place chicken

on hotter side of grill, smooth side down. Cook (covered if using gas) until well browned on first side, 4 to 6 minutes. Flip and continue to cook until chicken registers 160 degrees, 4 to 6 minutes longer. Transfer chicken to cutting board, tent loosely with aluminum foil, and let rest for 5 to 10 minutes.

4. While chicken cooks, place onion rounds and peppers (skin side down) on cooler side of grill and cook until tender and charred on both sides, 8 to 12 minutes, flipping every 3 minutes. Transfer onion and peppers to cutting board with chicken.

5. Working in 2 or 3 batches, place tortillas in single layer on cooler side of grill. Cook until warm and lightly browned, about 20 seconds per side (do not grill too long or tortillas will become brittle). As tortillas are done, wrap in kitchen towel or large sheet of foil.

6. Separate onion into rings and place in medium bowl. Slice peppers into ¼-inch strips and place in bowl with onion. Add 2 tablespoons reserved marinade and toss to combine. Slice each breast on bias into ¼-inch-thick slices, place in second bowl, and toss with remaining 2 tablespoons reserved marinade.

7. Transfer chicken and vegetables to serving platter and serve with warmed tortillas.

PRACTICAL SCIENCE WHY DOES ACID MAKE MEAT TOUGH AND DRY?

Acid and tough meat? It all comes down to the isoelectric point.

A common misconception is that acidic marinades are the key for making meat tender. But acidic marinades can easily take it too far, making meat mushy (see page 121) or tough and dry. Why?

A protein molecule normally contains many positive and negative charges. These electrical charges determine how proteins interact with each other. Often, there are more positive or more negative charges, which cause the protein molecules to repel each other, keeping them far apart. But sometimes these electrical charges completely balance each other out. This moment of balance is called the isoelectric point. And while being in balance sounds like a good thing, when proteins hit the isoelectric point, they pack closer together, squeezing out any excess liquid. And this squeezing, as we know, can make the meat tough and dry.

But what causes proteins to reach the isoelectric point? You guessed it: acid. Most chicken proteins, for example, are slightly acidic, with a pH between 6.0 and 6.5. The isoelectric point of all muscle proteins, however, occurs at a pH of 5.2.

The marinades that we offer here contain very little acid or use an acidic marinade for a very short period of time. With these proportions, there is not enough acid present (or enough time) to lower the pH of chicken much below 6.0. But if there are a lot of acidic ingredients in a marinade, and it is left on a piece of chicken for a long time, the risk is high that the pH of the chicken will drop to the isoelectric point, causing the proteins to pack together and the meat to become tough and dry.

WHY THIS RECIPE WORKS

We quickly realized that the separate components of the best chicken fajita recipe would require special handling. Unlike many of our marinades, in which we avoid acid in order to prevent mushy meat, here we use a high-acid mixture—but only briefly. A 15-minute soak in this lime-saturated marinade gives a bright tang.

KEEP TIME IN CHECK Though marinating often takes some time, here it's important not to let the minutes get away from you. If the chicken breasts soak in the high-acid marinade for more than 15 minutes, they will begin to "cook" in the acid, like a "chicken ceviche" of sorts.

ADD A SMOKY DEPTH While we began experimenting with a marinade that included lime juice, vegetable oil, garlic, salt, and pepper, we felt that it lacked smokiness and depth. What to add? We finally stumbled upon an unlikely candidate: Worcestershire sauce, which is made with molasses, anchovies, tamarind, onion, garlic, and other seasonings. Worcestershire sauce has some of the characteristics of umami, the fifth taste sensation often equated with "meaty" or simply "delicious." A mere tablespoon of Worcestershire was plenty to add another layer of saltiness and smoke without revealing its true identity. (Later, a bit of brown sugar helped to round out the salty flavors in the marinade, and minced jalapeño and cilantro added freshness.)

MAKE A TWO-LEVEL FIRE The chicken needs blazing-hot coals to cook correctly while the vegetables, which are prone to burning, require more moderate heat in order for them to brown nicely as well as cook though without char. To allow the chicken and vegetables to cook side by side, we create a two-level fire by first placing coals over two-thirds of the grill. (On a gas grill, we heat the entire grill on high, and then turn down the other burner(s) to medium before cooking commences.)

WRAP IT UP As for the flour tortillas, 8- to 10-inch rounds yield too much excess tortilla; small (but not dainty) 6-inch tortillas are the perfect size. Heating each side of the tortillas for 20 brief seconds on the cooler side of the grill allows them to puff up and lose their raw, gummy texture. Quickly wrapping the warmed tortillas in a clean kitchen towel or foil prevents them from becoming dry and brittle.

MARINATING AT WORK BUTTERMILK BRINING

When buttermilk is mixed with salt and used as a marinade for fried chicken, the results are impressive. Buttermilk contains lactic acid, which activates the cathepsin enzymes naturally present in meat, as it penetrates mostly the outer layers of the chicken. These enzymes break down proteins into smaller molecules, tenderizing the meat. (As we've learned, strong acids such as wine and vinegar can break down so many proteins that the meat turns mushy. But the lactic acid in buttermilk is too weak to have this effect.) Just as in a traditional brine, the salt helps change the protein structure of meat so that it can retain more moisture as it cooks, producing noticeably juicier results. See concept 17 for more information about the science of frying.

in two batches. Follow the recipe, frying the chicken four pieces at a time and keeping the first batch warm in a 200-degree oven while the second batch is cooking. If you want to produce a slightly healthier version of this recipe, you can remove the skin from the chicken before soaking it in the buttermilk. The chicken will be slightly less crunchy. If you have leftovers, they crisp up and reheat nicely—put them in a 375-degree oven for 10 to 15 minutes. For this recipe, cut a whole chicken into eight pieces—two drumsticks, two thighs, and two breast halves cut in half crosswise.

1	cup plus 6 tablespoons buttermilk
1	tablespoon salt
1	whole chicken (about 3½ pounds), cut into 8 pieces, giblets discarded, wings and back reserved for stock
3	cups all-purpose flour
2	teaspoons baking powder
¾	teaspoon dried thyme
½	teaspoon pepper
¼	teaspoon garlic powder
4–5	cups peanut oil, vegetable oil, or vegetable shortening

EXTRA-CRUNCHY FRIED CHICKEN
SERVES 4

Keeping the oil at the correct temperature is essential to producing crunchy fried chicken that is neither too brown nor too greasy. Use a candy/deep-fry thermometer to check the temperature of the oil before you add the chicken. If you cannot find a chicken that weighs 3½ pounds or less, or if you don't have a pan that is 11 inches in diameter, you will have to fry the chicken

1. Whisk together 1 cup buttermilk and salt in large bowl until salt is dissolved. Add chicken pieces to bowl and stir to coat; cover bowl and refrigerate for at least 1 hour or up to overnight.

2. Whisk flour, baking powder, thyme, pepper, and garlic powder together in large bowl. Add remaining 6 tablespoons buttermilk; with your fingers rub flour and buttermilk together until buttermilk is evenly incorporated into flour and mixture resembles coarse wet sand.

3. Working in batches of 2, drop chicken pieces into flour mixture and turn to thoroughly coat, gently pressing flour mixture onto chicken. Shake excess flour from each piece of chicken and transfer to wire rack set over rimmed baking sheet.

4. Heat oil (it should measure ¾ inch deep) in Dutch oven over medium-high heat until it reaches 375 degrees. Place chicken pieces skin side down in oil, cover, and fry until deep golden brown, 8 to 10 minutes. Remove lid after 4 minutes and lift chicken pieces to check for even browning; rearrange if some pieces are browning faster than others. (At this point, oil should be about 300 degrees. Adjust burner, if necessary, to regulate temperature of oil.) Turn chicken pieces over and continue to fry, uncovered, until chicken pieces are deep golden brown on second side, 6 to 8 minutes longer. (At this point, to keep chicken from browning too quickly, adjust burner to maintain oil temperature of about 315 degrees.) Using tongs, transfer chicken to paper towel–lined plate; let stand for 5 minutes to drain. Serve.

✔ WHY THIS RECIPE WORKS

There's no arguing the point: Making even the simplest fried chicken is a kitchen production. So when you do go to the trouble, the recipe had better deliver. With a quick buttermilk brine to season the meat, keep it moist, and tenderize it, and with a simple coating of buttermilk-moistened flour that fries up to a deeply bronzed, crisp, and crunchy crust, this recipe will please the cook and diners alike.

CUT THE CHICKEN INTO SMALL PIECES It's important that each piece of chicken be the same size. This way, no one leg or breast will cook faster—or slower than the others. You have two options: Buy one cut-up whole chicken (about 3 pounds), or cut one whole chicken into six pieces yourself (two drumsticks, two thighs, and two breast halves). Save the wings for stock (see page 100), and cut each breast piece in half to yield eight pieces.

USE A BUTTERMILK BRINERADE Most fried chicken recipes dip the chicken in buttermilk, though mainly for flavor reasons—the acidity of the buttermilk adds a gentle tang that balances the richness of the fried coating. But we've built on that idea and turned the buttermilk soak into a buttermilk brine. A heavily salted marinade keeps the chicken moist and well seasoned with a flavor far deeper than the typical water brine can deliver. The lactic acid present in the buttermilk helps to tenderize the outer layers of the meat, while the salt penetrates to the center for a juicy, well-seasoned bird. An hour's soak seasons the meat to the bone.

We experimented with the brinerade by cooking four batches of chicken side by side. Three of them soaked for an hour, one in a solution of buttermilk and salt, one in only buttermilk, and one in a plain saltwater solution. The fourth was not soaked at all. All of the chicken was dredged in flour before frying. The unsoaked chicken was dry and tough. The saltwater-soaked chicken was moist but a bit rubbery. The chicken soaked in plain buttermilk, while tender, was not terribly moist. Only the chicken soaked in salted buttermilk came out both tender and moist.

ADD BAKING POWDER, BUTTERMILK After trying everything from Melba toast to pancake batter for the crunchy coating, we found a completely unexpected method for rolling the chicken in a starchy coating. We started with a classic flour coating—and added a few enhancements. First, a little baking powder. (As the chicken fries, the baking powder releases carbon dioxide, leavening the crust and increasing its surface area, keeping it light and crisp.) And then, buttermilk. We noticed that the flour stuck better to the chicken as we battered the last piece. That's because some buttermilk had dripped off the chicken and mixed with the flour to form large clumps, which when fried made the coating especially crunchy.

FRY (RELATIVELY) SHALLOW Although it's not uncommon for fried chicken to be deep-fried, here we use a relatively shallow-frying technique (though not as shallow as for our Easier Fried Chicken, page 135). But because the chicken cooks in a fair amount of fat, we call on a Dutch oven—a large one, so as to fit all the chicken without layering—as the cooking vessel rather than a skillet. With the chicken parts only partially submerged in oil, the cooking time is longer than if they were fully submerged, but this suits slow-cooking bone-in chicken pieces just fine.

COVER IT UP Covering the pot during the first half of cooking helps ensure that the interior meat will be done at the same time as the exterior crust. It also contains the spatter-prone oil and helps keep the oil hot so the coating is less greasy. As an added bonus, using the lid makes the meat moister because the chicken cooks through faster and, therefore, doesn't have time to dry out.

MIND THE TEMPERATURE   When you prepare the oil for frying, make sure you heat it to just about 375 degrees. When the chicken is added, the temperature of the oil will drop. If it drops too far, and for too long, it becomes difficult to obtain that crunchy, bronzed crust. So it's important to monitor the temperature while the chicken is frying, keeping it between 300 and 315 degrees. (To learn more about the dynamics of frying, see concept 17.)

EASIER FRIED CHICKEN
SERVES 4

A whole 4-pound chicken, cut into eight pieces, can be used instead of the chicken parts. Skinless chicken pieces are also an acceptable substitute, but the meat will come out slightly drier. If using large chicken breasts (about 1 pound each), cut each breast into three pieces. If using smaller breasts (10 to 12 ounces each), cut each breast into two pieces. A Dutch oven with an 11-inch diameter can be used in place of the straight-sided sauté pan.

1¼	cups buttermilk
	Salt and pepper
1	teaspoon garlic powder
1	teaspoon paprika
¼	teaspoon cayenne pepper
	Dash hot sauce
3½	pounds bone-in chicken pieces (split breasts cut in half, drumsticks, and/or thighs), trimmed
2	cups all-purpose flour
2	teaspoons baking powder
1¾	cups vegetable oil

1. Whisk 1 cup buttermilk, 1 tablespoon salt, 1 teaspoon pepper, ¼ teaspoon garlic powder, ¼ teaspoon paprika, pinch cayenne, and hot sauce together in large bowl. Add chicken and turn to coat. Cover and refrigerate for at least 1 hour or up to overnight.

2. Adjust oven rack to middle position and heat oven to 400 degrees. Set wire rack in rimmed baking sheet. Whisk flour, baking powder, 1 teaspoon salt, 2 teaspoons pepper, remaining ¾ teaspoon garlic powder, remaining ¾ teaspoon paprika, and remaining cayenne together in large bowl. Add remaining ¼ cup buttermilk to flour mixture and mix with fingers until combined and small clumps form. Working with 1 chicken piece at a time, dredge in flour mixture, pressing mixture onto pieces to form thick, even coating. Place dredged chicken on large plate, skin side up.

3. Heat oil in 11-inch straight-sided sauté pan over medium-high heat until it registers 375 degrees. Carefully place chicken in pan, skin side down, and fry until golden brown, 3 to 5 minutes. (Adjust heat as necessary to maintain oil at 375 degrees.) Carefully flip and continue to fry until golden brown on second side, 2 to 4 minutes longer. Transfer chicken to prepared wire rack and bake until breast pieces register 160 degrees and thighs and drumsticks register 175 degrees, 15 to 20 minutes. (Smaller pieces may cook faster than larger pieces. Remove pieces from oven as they reach correct temperature.) Let chicken rest for 5 minutes before serving.

✔ WHY THIS RECIPE WORKS

Is it possible to achieve fried chicken with a crisp crust without resorting to a quart of oil? To find an easier way to fry chicken, we started with our standard procedure of soaking the chicken in a salt and buttermilk brine and then dredging it in seasoned flour (along with a little baking powder, which keeps the crust light and crisp due to the carbon dioxide released by the powder during frying). A dual-method cooking technique leaves us with perfect fried chicken, without all the messy work.

FRY FIRST   While our standard fried chicken recipe calls for about 5 cups of oil, we wanted to significantly reduce the volume of oil for an easier, less messy frying experience. We began with 1¾ cups of oil, but found that the temperature of the oil dropped significantly after the chicken was added and only climbed back up to the necessary heat level when we cranked the stove up to high. Now we had a new problem: burnt patches on the parts of the chicken in direct contact with the bottom of the pan. To fix this, each chicken piece could not spend more than 3 or 4 minutes without being flipped—not enough time to cook them through. The solution? Combine a fast, early fry with a second technique: baking.

BAKE LATER   We found that the radiant, circulating heat of the oven was just the ticket to replace the even heating of a deep, hot oil bath, allowing the quickly shallow-fried chicken to brown and cook through properly. We start by frying the chicken on the stovetop until it forms a light brown crust, and then finish it in a hot oven (perched on a wire rack set in a sheet pan to prevent burnt spots and promote air circulation all around the meat) to both cook it through and deepen its color. Though we were worried that there wouldn't be enough fat left on the surface of the chicken after its initial fry to fully permeate the crust as it dehydrated, as in traditionally fried chicken, we found that 15 minutes in the oven was all it took to give our shallow-fried chicken a golden-brown crust that was crisp and craggy.

Grind Meat at Home for Tender Burgers

We don't like to eat all of our beef in big slabs or cuts. Sometimes only a burger will do. So far we've learned about the molecular level of whole cuts of beef. But what happens when we grind them up?

HOW THE SCIENCE WORKS

Ground meat is a staple ingredient in many American homes. We use it for burgers, pasta sauce, meatballs, and meatloaves. We often buy it straight from the supermarket. But it's also possible to grind it at home. And for the ultimate burgers, we find that's the best option. Why? Let's start with the mechanics of ground beef.

As we've learned, whole standard cuts of beef are composed of the many long muscle fibers that make up muscle tissue, bundled within protective sheaths of connective tissue like electrical wires encased in plastic. Individual muscle fibers can be a few to tens of centimeters long, making them difficult to bite through when held together with connective tissue. But grinding meat dramatically reduces the length of muscle fibers and cuts connective tissue into pieces that are easier to chew. Grinding also releases soluble sticky proteins, which hold together the now-tiny pieces of meat.

The size of these ground pieces of meat is important. When it comes to burgers, we don't want to grind the meat too fine, as this will produce rubbery, dense results, or too coarse, which will leave gristly bits in burgers that fall apart as they cook. And when we use fresh ground meat as opposed to store-bought packages, the size of the grind, as well as how tightly we pack our meat together, is something we can control. This gives us the ability to create different textures in our finished dish (see Test Kitchen Experiment, page 137).

Using fresh ground meat also allows us to control the type of meat we use. This is important because different cuts of meat differ in flavor and levels of connective tissue and fat, variables that greatly influence a final dish.

It's possible to buy meat from grocers who grind in-house, but many markets purchase bulk packages of ground beef from beef-processing plants. Sometimes this is then reground and supplemented with meat scraps before being packed into smaller parcels. Understanding this is important from both a consumer choice standpoint and a health standpoint. In the United States, most preground beef comes from any of about a dozen processing plants, which means that preground beef can contain meat from hundreds of different cattle. Because the act of grinding meat mixes what was once on the outside (including any bacterial contamination) with the inside (which is sterile), when the meat from many animals is combined, one cut with harmful bacteria can contaminate large amounts of ground meat rather than tainting only a small batch. (Preground beef has been recalled on several occasions for this very reason.) Alternatively, consuming freshly ground meat is safer because the meat is coming from a single animal.

Grinding beef at home isn't hard to do. All it takes is a food processor (and access to a freezer). For the small amount of extra time it takes, grinding your own meat allows you to control what kind of meat you use and how finely ground you want it for the most desirable texture and taste.

THE EFFECTS OF GRINDING

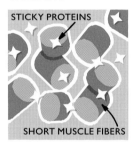

CUT DOWN TO SIZE

Grinding meat reduces the size of muscle fibers and connective tissue, making meat easier to chew, and releases sticky proteins, which help to bind the meat together.

TEST KITCHEN EXPERIMENT

To test whether freshly ground beef would make for more tender burgers, we ran the following experiment: We made three sets of burger patties, one with store-bought 90 percent lean ground chuck and two with flap meat that we ground ourselves in the food processor (we ground one batch to mimic the texture of the store-bought meat; the other we ground moderately coarse in the manner we prefer—see "Getting the Perfect Grind," below). After cooking all three sets of burgers to medium-rare, we let them rest for five minutes and then dropped a large Dutch oven on each patty from 6 inches above the counter. We repeated the test three times.

THE RESULTS

Messy. The burgers reacted very differently to the weight of the Dutch oven. The one made from the dense store-bought ground meat remained intact (though somewhat flattened) and did not ooze any liquid at all. The burger made from the beef we ground to mimic the store-bought texture spread a bit but did not release any of its juices. The looser, more coarsely home-ground burger, however, flattened like a pancake, spewing its moist interior all over the board.

THE TAKEAWAY

One important variable in ground beef is the texture of the grind. Because we could control the texture of the meat we ground ourselves, we were able to construct a looser, more tender burger with our coarse-ground meat. Because we could not control the size of the grind in the burger patty made from store-bought meat, it was much denser, tougher, and ultimately much more resilient when smashed. (In this case, resilience is not a good thing!) A second variable in ground beef is the choice of cut. Because we could choose to grind flap meat, a cut with more fat and flavor than chuck, both of our home-ground burgers tasted richer and more flavorful (no matter how they smashed) than the store-bought.

SMASHING BURGERS: HOME-GROUND AND STORE-BOUGHT

To test the difference between burgers made with home-ground and store-bought meat, we dropped a Dutch oven on top of each patty from 6 inches above.

HOME-GROUND
The burger made from meat we ground to perfection at home was much more tender, and therefore splattered and smushed much more under the weight of the falling Dutch oven.

STORE-BOUGHT
The burger made from store-bought ground meat cooked up dense and tough and remained relatively solid when smashed with a heavy Dutch oven.

PRACTICAL SCIENCE GETTING THE PERFECT GRIND

Under- and overprocessed meat will produce burgers with unpleasant textures.

Underprocessed meat will lead to gristly bits in the finished burgers and patties that don't hold together. Overprocessed meat becomes rubbery and dense as it cooks. Perfectly ground meat contains pieces that are fine enough to ensure tenderness but coarse enough that the patty will stay loose.

| UNDERPROCESSED | OVERPROCESSED | GROUND TO PERFECTION |

For the ultimate burger, one modeled after a classic drive-in or a juicy pub-style option, we prefer to grind our own meat. This gives us control over the type of meat and the size of our grind. If store-bought ground meat is your only option, however, see our Well-Done Burger recipe (page 144).

BEST OLD-FASHIONED BURGERS
MAKES 4 BURGERS

Sirloin steak tips are also sold as flap meat. Flank steak can be used in its place. This recipe yields juicy medium to medium-well burgers. It's important to use very soft buns. If doubling the recipe, process the meat in three batches in step 2. Because the cooked burgers do not hold well, fry four burgers and serve them immediately before frying more, or cook them in two pans. Extra patties can be frozen for up to two weeks. Stack the patties, separated by parchment, and wrap them in three layers of plastic wrap. Thaw burgers in a single layer on a baking sheet at room temperature for 30 minutes before cooking.

10	ounces sirloin steak tips, trimmed and cut into 1-inch chunks
6	ounces boneless beef short ribs, trimmed and cut into 1-inch chunks
	Kosher salt and pepper
1	tablespoon unsalted butter
4	soft hamburger buns
½	teaspoon vegetable oil
4	slices American cheese
	Thinly sliced onion
1	recipe Classic Burger Sauce (recipe follows)

1. Place beef chunks on baking sheet in single layer, leaving ½ inch of space around each chunk. Freeze meat until very firm and starting to harden around edges but still pliable, 15 to 25 minutes.

2. Pulse half of meat in food processor until coarsely ground, 10 to 15 pulses, stopping and redistributing meat around bowl as necessary to ensure beef is evenly ground. Transfer meat to baking sheet, overturning processor bowl and without directly touching meat. Repeat grinding with remaining meat. Spread meat over baking sheet and inspect carefully, discarding any long strands of gristle or large chunks of hard meat or fat.

3. Gently separate ground meat into 4 equal mounds. Without picking meat up, with your fingers gently shape each mound into loose patty ½ inch thick and 4 inches in diameter, leaving edges and surface ragged. Season top of each patty with salt and pepper. Using spatula, flip patties and season other side. Refrigerate while toasting buns.

4. Melt ½ tablespoon butter in 12-inch skillet over medium heat. Add bun tops, cut side down, and toast until light golden brown, about 2 minutes. Repeat with remaining ½ tablespoon butter and bun bottoms. Set buns aside and wipe out skillet with paper towels.

5. Return skillet to high heat; add oil and heat until just smoking. Using spatula, transfer burgers to skillet and cook without moving for 3 minutes. Using spatula, flip burgers over and cook for 1 minute. Top each patty with slice of cheese and continue to cook until cheese is melted, about 1 minute longer.

6. Transfer patties to bun bottoms and top with onion. Spread about 1 tablespoon of burger sauce on each bun top. Cover burgers and serve immediately.

CLASSIC BURGER SAUCE
MAKES ABOUT ¼ CUP, ENOUGH FOR 1 RECIPE BEST OLD-FASHIONED BURGERS

2	tablespoons mayonnaise
1	tablespoon ketchup
½	teaspoon sweet pickle relish
½	teaspoon sugar
½	teaspoon distilled white vinegar
¼	teaspoon pepper

Whisk all ingredients together in bowl.

✔ WHY THIS RECIPE WORKS

Classic drive-in burgers used to mean freshly ground high-quality beef, but today fast-food burgers are nothing more than tasteless, mass-produced patties. We wanted to bring back the original—an ultra-crisp, ultra-browned, ultra-beefy burger perfect with melted cheese and a tangy sauce. We learned that freshly ground beef, loosely packed, was essential. Topped with a sweet and tangy sauce, cheese, and a few thin slices of onion, this burger recaptures the flavor and texture that started a nationwide craze.

COMBINE TWO KINDS OF MEAT We use a combination of sirloin steak tips and boneless beef short ribs for this burger. Though this makes our technique a bit more complicated, we find it's worth it. We choose sirloin steak tips for their beefy flavor, and the short ribs add an element of fat and provide some much-needed juiciness.

FREEZE FIRST Most home cooks don't own a meat grinder, but don't worry: A food processor will work. When meat gets too warm, however, it can end up being smeared in the processor instead of evenly chopped. That's why it's important to cut the meat into chunks and chill them in the freezer before processing. This way they will be chopped, not pulverized, and cook up just as perfectly tender (with as crisp a crust) as those ground in an official meat grinder. Be careful not to grind the meat too small, or leave it too large. (See "Getting the Perfect Grind," page 137).

KEEP HANDS OFF We struggled with rubbery meat when developing this recipe and discovered that collagen was the culprit. As the collagen proteins are heated past 140 degrees, they begin to squeeze the meat, causing it to become dense and rubbery. (At 140 degrees, the collagen will also begin to unravel, turning the meat from tough to tender, but this process takes hours—far longer than the mere minutes burgers spend on the griddle.) The more these proteins come in contact with each other, the more shrinkage and tightening will take place. The key to a tender burger is to keep it as loosely packed as possible. In fact, we hardly touch the meat at all. After letting it fall directly onto a baking sheet after grinding, we separate the ground meat and gently press it into four patties without lifting it up. Keep your hands off the burgers!

KEEP NOOKS AND CRANNIES Because our burgers are so loosely packed with home-ground meat, there are many nooks and crannies on their surfaces as they cook. This allows juices to bubble up through their porous surface

and drip back down, basting the burgers as they cook. The finished result is juicy with a substantial, crisp crust.

TOP IT OFF This style of burger is often served with a tangy and sweet Thousand Island–style dressing. We replicate this by adding relish, sugar, and white vinegar to a mayo and ketchup base: a great foil for the juicy, salty burger. We like American cheese, a classic choice that will fill the cracks and crevices in the patty with gooey cheese and won't compete against the other flavors. Garnishing simply with onions—in lieu of "the works")—keeps the flavor of the beef at center stage.

JUICY PUB-STYLE BURGERS
SERVES 4

Sirloin steak tips are also sold as flap meat. When stirring the butter and pepper into the ground meat and shaping the patties, take care not to overwork the meat or the burgers will become dense. For the best flavor, season the burgers aggressively just before cooking. The burgers can be topped as desired or with one of the test kitchen's favorite combinations (recipes follow).

2	pounds sirloin steak tips, trimmed and cut into ½-inch chunks
4	tablespoons unsalted butter, melted and cooled slightly
	Salt and pepper
1	teaspoon vegetable oil
4	large hamburger buns, toasted and buttered

1. Place beef chunks on baking sheet in single layer. Freeze meat until very firm and starting to harden around edges but still pliable, 15 to 25 minutes.

2. Place one-quarter of meat in food processor and pulse until finely ground into ¹/₁₆-inch pieces, about 35 pulses, stopping and redistributing meat around bowl as necessary to ensure beef is evenly ground. Transfer meat to baking sheet, overturning processor bowl and without directly touching meat. Repeat grinding with remaining 3 batches of meat. Spread meat over baking sheet and inspect carefully, discarding any long strands of gristle or large chunks of hard meat or fat.

3. Adjust oven rack to middle position and heat oven to 300 degrees. Drizzle melted butter over ground meat and add 1 teaspoon pepper. Gently toss with fork to combine. Divide meat into 4 lightly packed balls. Gently flatten into patties ¾ inch thick and about 4½ inches in diameter. Refrigerate patties until ready to cook. (Patties can be refrigerated for up to 1 day.)

PRACTICAL SCIENCE
WHEN TO SALT FRESH-GROUND

> Do not salt your meat before grinding it up.

We thought that we could improve the flavor of our burgers by salting the meat before grinding it, but we found the burgers ended up very dense. What was going on? We know that when exposed to a strong concentration of salt, meat proteins will dissolve. This breakdown is desirable in steak or chops—the action of dissolving the protein allows the meat to hold on to more moisture, making it juicier when cooked. In our burgers, however, the dissolved meat proteins act as a sort of glue, binding the ground bits together very tightly to create a rubbery, almost sausagelike texture. So while you may be tempted to add salt to the meat before grinding, we recommend waiting until you've formed the patties. (Note the exception in our Well-Done Burger recipe, page 144, which includes a tenderizing panade.) Salting just the exterior will maintain the tender, open structure you're after.

GLUED TOGETHER
The meat for this patty was salted before it was ground, leading to a dense, rubbery texture.

LOOSENED UP
Salt just on its exterior helped this patty maintain the loose structure we wanted.

4. Season 1 side of patties with salt and pepper. Using spatula, flip patties and season other side. Heat oil in 12-inch skillet over high heat until just smoking. Using spatula, transfer burgers to skillet and cook without moving for 2 minutes. Using spatula, flip burgers over and cook for 2 minutes longer. Transfer patties to rimmed baking sheet and bake until burgers register 125 degrees (for medium-rare) or 130 degrees (for medium), 3 to 6 minutes.

5. Transfer burgers to plate and let rest for 5 minutes. Transfer to buns, add desired toppings, and serve.

PUB-STYLE BURGER SAUCE
MAKES ABOUT 1 CUP, ENOUGH FOR 1 RECIPE
JUICY PUB-STYLE BURGERS

¾   cup mayonnaise
2   tablespoons soy sauce
1   tablespoon packed dark brown sugar
1   tablespoon Worcestershire sauce
1   tablespoon minced fresh chives
1   garlic clove, minced
¾   teaspoon pepper

Whisk all ingredients together in bowl.

JUICY PUB-STYLE BURGERS WITH CRISPY SHALLOTS AND BLUE CHEESE

Heat ½ cup vegetable oil and 3 thinly sliced shallots in medium saucepan over high heat; cook, stirring frequently, until shallots are golden, about 8 minutes. Using slotted spoon, transfer shallots to paper towel–lined plate, season with salt, and let drain until crisp, about 5 minutes. (Cooled shallots can be stored at room temperature for up to 3 days.) Top each burger with 1 ounce crumbled blue cheese before transferring to oven. Top with crispy shallots just before serving.

JUICY PUB-STYLE BURGERS WITH SAUTÉED ONION AND SMOKED CHEDDAR

Heat 2 tablespoons vegetable oil in 12-inch skillet over medium-high heat until just smoking. Add 1 thinly sliced onion and ¼ teaspoon salt; cook, stirring frequently, until softened and lightly browned, 5 to 7 minutes. Top each burger with 1 ounce grated smoked cheddar cheese before transferring to oven. Top with onions just before serving.

✔ WHY THIS RECIPE WORKS

Few things are as satisfying as a thick, juicy pub-style burger. But avoiding the usual gray band of overcooked meat is a challenge. We wanted a patty that was well seared, juicy, and evenly rosy from center to edge. We found grinding our own meat in the food processor to be a must. Sirloin steak tips are the right cut for the job. They offer a supremely beefy flavor without gristly sinew.

CUT INTO SMALLER PIECES   Though for our Best Old-Fashioned Burgers (see page 138) we cut the meat into 1-inch chunks, we found that in these heftier, pub-size burgers, the patties broke apart when flipped in the pan. The solution? Cutting the meat into small ½-inch chunks before grinding and lightly packing the meat to form patties gives the burgers just enough structure to hold their shape in the skillet.

ADD STRAIGHT FAT   Instead of adding another cut of meat with more fat (as we do in our Best Old-Fashioned Burgers), here we add straight fat. A little melted butter, which solidifies as it hits the cold meat, creates pinhead-size particles of fat strewn throughout the patties. The butter acts as lubrication and adds a little more moisture, improving the burgers' flavor and juiciness. Also, and even better, the dairy proteins and sugar (lactose) in the butter boost the browning on the burgers' exteriors.

USE TWO COOKING METHODS   Using a standard cooking method for these burgers—preheating a skillet over high heat and then cooking the patties to medium-rare for about four minutes on each side—doesn't work. The meat is marred by a thick band of gray meat that no extra fat can help. Instead we use a two-method cooking technique, first searing the burgers over the high heat of a skillet to produce a great crust and then sticking them in the gentle, ambient heat of the oven to finish. (For more on two-method cooking, see concept 5.)

TRANSFER TO COLD PAN   While the two-method cooking technique is important, it makes only a small change in the finished product without an important element: the cold baking sheet. When we simply transferred the burgers in the hot skillet to the oven to finish, the bottom of the burgers cooked too quickly. But if placed on a cold sheet pan in a 300-degree oven, the burgers emerge after three to six minutes with perfect interiors—juicy and rosy throughout.

SHOPPING FOR BEEF 101

PRIMAL CUTS

Eight different cuts of beef are sold at the wholesale level. From this first series of cuts, known in the trade as primal cuts, a butcher (usually at a meat-packing plant in the Midwest but sometimes on-site at your market) will make the retail cuts that you bring home from the market.

CHUCK/SHOULDER

The chuck (or shoulder) runs from the neck down to the fifth rib. There are four major muscles in this region, and meat from the chuck tends to be flavorful and fairly fatty, which is why ground chuck makes the best hamburgers. Chuck also contains a fair amount of connective tissue, so when the meat is not ground it generally requires a long cooking time to become tender.

RIB

The rib section extends along the back of the animal from the sixth to the twelfth rib. The prime rib comes from this area, as do rib-eye steaks. Rib cuts have excellent beefy flavor and are quite tender.

SHORT LOIN

The short loin (also called the loin) extends from the last rib back through the midsection of the animal to the hip area. It contains two major muscles—the tenderloin and the shell. The tenderloin is extremely tender (it is positioned right under the spine) and has a quite mild flavor. This muscle may be sold whole as a roast or sliced crosswise into steaks, called filet mignon. The shell is a much larger muscle and has a more robust beef flavor as well as more fat. Strip steaks (also called shell steaks) come from this muscle and are a test kitchen favorite. Two steaks from the short loin area contain portions of both the tenderloin and shell muscles. These steaks are called the T-bone and porterhouse, and both are excellent.

BRISKET/SHANK, PLATE, AND FLANK

Moderately thick boneless cuts are removed from the three primal cuts that run along the underside of the animal. The brisket is rather tough and contains a lot of connective tissue. The plate is rarely sold at the retail level (it is used to make pastrami). The flank is a leaner cut that makes an excellent steak when grilled.

ROUND

Roasts and steaks cut from the round are usually sold boneless and are quite lean and can be tough. Again, we generally prefer cuts from other parts of the cow, although top round can be roasted with some success.

SIRLOIN

The sirloin contains relatively inexpensive cuts that are sold as both steaks and roasts. We find that sirloin cuts are fairly lean and tough. In general, we prefer other parts of the animal, although top sirloin makes a decent roast.

GRADING

The U.S. Department of Agriculture assigns different quality grades to beef, but most of the meat available to consumers is confined to just three: Prime, Choice, and Select. Grading is strictly voluntary on the part of the meat packer. If meat is graded, the meat should bear a USDA stamp indicating the grade, though it may not be visible to the consumer. To grade meat, inspectors evaluate color, grain, surface texture, and fat content and its distribution.

Our blind tasting of all three grades of strip steaks produced predictable results: Prime ranked first for its tender, buttery texture and rich, beefy flavor. Next came Choice, with good meaty flavor and a little more chew. The tough and stringy Select steak followed, with flavor that was barely acceptable. Our advice: When you're willing to splurge, go for Prime steak (which in our sampling cost $6 more per pound than the Choice meat), but a Choice steak that exhibits a moderate amount of marbling is a fine, affordable option. Just steer clear of Select-grade steak.

PRIME
Prime meat is heavily marbled with intra-muscular fat. About 2 percent of graded beef is considered Prime.

CHOICE
The majority of graded beef is Choice. It is generally moderately marbled with intramuscular fat.

SELECT
Select beef has little marbling, which can make Select meats drier, tougher, and less flavorful than the two higher grades.

GRAIN-FED VS. GRASS-FED

Most U.S. beef is raised on grain but grass-fed beef is becoming an increasingly popular option. Grain-fed beef is generally considered to be richer and fattier, while grass-fed beef is leaner, chewy, and more gamy—or at least that's the conventional wisdom.

In our taste tests, we pitted grain-fed and grass-fed rib-eye steaks and strip steaks against each other. We found differences among the various strip steaks to be quite small. The grain-fed rib eyes had a milder flavor compared to the nutty, complex flavor of the grass-fed beef, but our tasters' preferences were evenly split. The texture of all samples was similar.

A Panade Keeps Ground Meat Tender

Let's put the big, juicy, home-ground burgers aside. After all, it's relatively easy to keep a rare burger tender and moist (see concept 14). It's when ground beef is cooked through that the meat, no matter how lovingly handled, turns gray and you're left with a dinner of dense, dry hockey pucks. But sometimes you need to fully cook beef: like the occasionally well-done burger (for kids, especially), not to mention in dishes like meatloaf or meatballs. So how do you cook ground beef until well-done? It's amazing what a simple bread-and-milk paste can do to help.

HOW THE SCIENCE WORKS

A panade is a mixture of starch and liquid. It can be simple (white bread and regular milk), or it can be complex (panko or saltines; buttermilk or yogurt or even added gelatin). But it always has the same set of goals: to keep ground meat moist and tender, and to help meatballs and meatloaf hold their shape. How does it work?

As we learned in concept 14, meat is made of long fibers of protein that run parallel to each other, producing bundled strands encased in sheaths of connective tissue. The length of individual muscle fibers can range from several to tens of centimeters. The collection of long fibers encased in tough connective tissue shrinks during cooking and therefore can be difficult to bite through. But when meat is ground and mixed, these proteins are cut into much smaller pieces. In the process, they exude a sticky mass of soluble proteins that glue the whole lot of it together in a tangled web. Upon cooking, this web of proteins can shrink as much as 25 percent, squeezing out excess moisture and, as a result, making burgers and meatballs that are dry and tough.

But all is not lost. That's where the panade comes in. This mixture, most commonly of bread and milk, works in two ways. First, its liquid adds moisture to the ground meat. Second, the molecules of starch in the bread actually get in the way of the meat proteins, preventing them from interconnecting too strongly.

In addition, starches from the bread absorb liquid from the milk to form a gel that coats and lubricates the protein molecules in the meat, much in the same way as fat, keeping them moist and preventing them from linking together and shrinking into a tough matrix.

Starch from bread works in the same way as cornstarch when it is used to thicken a sauce or gravy. Starch granules absorb water and swell with heat, making the liquid thick and viscous. It takes little cornstarch to thicken a sauce, and so it also takes relatively little panade to keep ground meat from becoming tough and dry. Although plain water will work, milk adds more depth of flavor by contributing protein and lactose, a sugar, which combine to produce extra browning and flavor via the Maillard reaction.

POWER OF PANADE

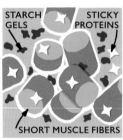

STARCH GELS · STICKY PROTEINS · SHORT MUSCLE FIBERS

ADDED STARCH GEL *The molecules of starch combine with the milk in the panade to create a gel that lubricates the ground meat proteins, preventing them from interconnecting too strongly, which would leave us with a tough and dry finished dish.*

TEST KITCHEN EXPERIMENT

To test the effects of a panade in ground meat, we mixed up two batches of burger meat. One batch contained 12 ounces of 90 percent lean ground beef, half a slice of white bread, 1 tablespoon of milk, and ½ teaspoon of salt while the other had only the meat and salt. We made four 3-ounce (85-gram) patties from each batch and sealed each burger individually in an airtight bag. We then placed all of the burgers in a temperature-controlled hot water bath set to 160 degrees (the temperature of a well-done burger) and let them cook for 30 minutes (ample time for the burgers to reach 160 degrees throughout). After letting them cool for five minutes, we opened the bags and recorded the amount of liquid that had pooled around the burgers.

THE RESULTS

The burgers with the bread and milk panade lost 4.5 grams of liquid on average, or just over 5 percent of their weight. The patties made without panade shed twice that amount: 9 grams of liquid, or almost 11 percent of their weight.

THE TAKEAWAY

The goal when cooking ground meat is to minimize moisture loss, even when the meat is cooked to well-done. Without a panade, the meat proteins create a dense web that contracts when the meat is cooked. As a result, ground meat without a panade will expel a lot of moisture. The addition of a panade cuts this moisture loss in half. The mixture of starch and milk forms a gel-like substance that coats the meat proteins and prevents them from interconnecting too strongly. In addition, the milk adds more moisture to the equation so the end results are juicier and more tender.

MOISTURE LOSS IN WELL-DONE BURGERS

PANADE   NO PANADE

We cooked burgers made with and without a panade and poured the liquid shed by each batch into graduated cylinders. The panade-less burgers lost twice as much liquid as burgers made with a panade, and less liquid in the vial means more juice in the burgers.

PRACTICAL SCIENCE SHOPPING FOR GROUND BEEF

Our favorite preground beef is chuck, with ground sirloin coming in a close second.

Today, many supermarkets classify ground beef by fat levels alone, and this means that the meat can come from anywhere on the animal. This is different from the old-fashioned approach to grinding, when butchers ground specific primal cuts and labeled them as such. The U.S. Department of Agriculture defines ground beef as ground fresh and/or frozen beef from primal cuts and trimmings containing no more than 30 percent fat. Therefore, ground beef can be made from a variety of cuts, and fat levels vary from 70 to 95 percent lean. But this doesn't help us understand the difference among ground chuck, sirloin, and round.

Ground chuck frequently ranks tops in our taste tests. Cut from the shoulder, ground chuck ranges from 15 to 20 percent fat and has been described by our tasters as having a "rich" flavor and a "tender" and "moist" texture. Ground sirloin comes in a close second. Cut from the midsection of the animal near the hip, ground sirloin usually ranges in fat content from 7 to 10 percent. Our tasters have described it as "tender and tasty." Ground round has a fat content ranging from 10 to 20 percent and comes from the rear upper leg and rump of the cow. Our tasters have described it as "gristly" and "lacking beef flavor," rejecting it in most recipes as lean and tough. While chuck is great for burgers, and sirloin ideal for bolognese, we sometimes recommend a combination (see Glazed All-Beef Meatloaf, page 145). Other times, our instructions are to purchase a certain percentage lean—in this case, whatever is available at your market.

Given the real food-safety issues surrounding ground beef from the supermarket, we recognize that many backyard cooks (and test cooks) grill their burgers to medium-well and beyond—especially when kids are around (the minimum temperature to kill all bacteria is 160 degrees). Instead of accepting the usual tough, desiccated hockey pucks with diminished beefy flavor, we use a simple panade (just a mixture of white bread and milk) to retain moisture and juiciness so our well-done burgers are truly done well.

WELL-DONE BURGERS
SERVES 4

Adding bread and milk to the beef creates burgers that are juicy and tender even when well-done. For cheeseburgers, follow the optional instructions below.

1	slice hearty white sandwich bread, crust removed, cut into ¼-inch pieces
2	tablespoons whole milk
2	teaspoons steak sauce
1	garlic clove, minced
¾	teaspoon salt
¾	teaspoon pepper
1½	pounds 80 percent lean ground chuck
6	ounces sliced cheese (optional)
4	hamburger rolls, toasted

1. Mash bread and milk in large bowl with fork until homogeneous. Stir in steak sauce, garlic, salt, and pepper. Using hands, gently break up meat over bread mixture and toss lightly to distribute. Divide meat into 4 portions and lightly toss 1 portion from hand to hand to form ball, then lightly flatten ball with fingertips into ¾-inch-thick patty. Press center of patty down with fingertips until it is about ½ inch thick, creating slight depression. Repeat with remaining portions.

2A. FOR A CHARCOAL GRILL: Open bottom vent completely. Light large chimney starter filled with charcoal briquettes (6 quarts). When top coals are partially covered with ash, pour evenly over half of grill. Set cooking grate in place, cover, and open lid vent completely. Heat grill until hot, about 5 minutes.

2B. FOR A GAS GRILL: Turn all burners to high, cover, and heat grill until hot, about 15 minutes.

3. Clean and oil cooking grate. Place burgers on grill (on hot side if using charcoal) and cook, without pressing on them, until well browned on first side, 2 to 4 minutes.

Flip burgers and cook for 3 to 4 minutes for medium-well or 4 to 5 minutes for well-done, adding cheese, if using, about 2 minutes before reaching desired doneness and covering grill to melt cheese.

4. Transfer burgers to serving platter, tent loosely with aluminum foil, and let rest for 5 to 10 minutes before serving on rolls.

WELL-DONE BACON-CHEESEBURGERS

Most bacon burgers simply top the burgers with bacon. We also add bacon fat to the ground beef, which adds juiciness and unmistakable bacon flavor throughout the burger.

Cook 8 slices bacon in skillet over medium heat until crisp, 7 to 9 minutes. Transfer bacon to paper towel–lined plate and set aside. Reserve 2 tablespoons fat and refrigerate until just warm. Add reserved bacon fat to beef mixture. Include optional cheese and top each burger with 2 slices bacon before serving.

PRACTICAL SCIENCE TO DENT OR NOT TO DENT?

Dimple your burgers cooked on the grill or under the broiler.

To prevent hamburgers from puffing up during cooking, we sometimes recommend making a slight depression in the center of the patty before placing it on the heat. Meat inflates upon cooking when its connective tissue, or collagen, shrinks at temperatures higher than 140 degrees. The result is a round burger that does a poor job of holding on to toppings. If burgers are cooked on a grill or under a broiler, a dimple is in order because the meat is exposed to direct heat not only from below or above, but also on its sides. As a result, the edges of the patty shrink, cinching the hamburger like a belt, compressing its interior up and out. There's no need to dimple burgers that are cooked in a hot pan, since the sides of the burger are exposed to far less heat.

DIMPLED FOR GRILL AND BROILER

NOT DIMPLED FOR SKILLET

WHY THIS RECIPE WORKS

While developing a recipe for well-done hamburgers that would still be tender and moist, we opted to pack the patties with a very basic panade, a paste made from bread and milk that's often used to keep meatloaf and meatballs moist.

PICK YOUR GROUND CHUCK   We work with supermarket ground beef here—nothing fancy. What type is best? Supermarkets sell beef according to the ratio of lean meat to fat, the three most common categories being 80 percent lean (usually from the chuck, or front shoulder), 85 percent (usually from the round, or hind legs), and 90 percent (usually from the sirloin). Our testers prefer the fattier 80 percent lean: The well-done chuck burgers are noticeably moister than the inedible versions we tried with the leaner sirloin.

SEASON AGGRESSIVELY   To punch up the flavor in our well-done hamburger recipe, we add minced garlic and tangy steak sauce. This contributes to a deep, meaty flavor.

DON'T OVERWORK   It's important not to overwork these burger patties—too much handling can result in a rubbery burger. Aggressively grinding meat as they do in the supermarket, often multiple times, releases too many soluble proteins that act as a glue to stick the proteins together to form a dense, rubbery mass.

USE HIGH HEAT   While cooking our burgers over a medium fire would ensure a juicier, more tender burger, it would be a burger without that flavorful sear. We cook these burgers over high heat to create great flavor. The panade helps to stem the moisture loss along the way.

PANADES AT WORK MEATLOAF, MEAT SAUCE, MEATBALLS

When making loaves, sauces, and balls with ground meat, our panades are often tweaked from the traditional white bread and milk combination. This can range from using saltines or panko as the bread, and yogurt or buttermilk instead of milk. In a clever twist, we've found that adding baking powder as part of the panade can leaven meat just as it does bread, creating delicate and juicy Swedish meatballs.

GLAZED ALL-BEEF MEATLOAF
SERVES 6 TO 8

We suggest you use 1 pound of ground chuck and 1 pound of ground sirloin for the ground beef, though you may substitute any 85 percent lean ground beef. Handle the meat gently; it should be thoroughly combined but not pastelike. To avoid using the broiler, glaze the loaf in a 500-degree oven; increase the cooking time for each interval by two to three minutes.

MEATLOAF

- 3 ounces Monterey Jack cheese, shredded (¾ cup)
- 1 tablespoon unsalted butter
- 1 onion, chopped fine
- 1 celery rib, chopped fine
- 2 teaspoons minced fresh thyme
- 1 garlic clove, minced
- 1 teaspoon paprika
- ¼ cup tomato juice
- ½ cup low-sodium chicken broth
- 2 large eggs
- ½ teaspoon unflavored gelatin
- ⅔ cup crushed saltines (about 16)
- 2 tablespoons minced fresh parsley
- 1 tablespoon soy sauce
- 1 teaspoon Dijon mustard
- ¾ teaspoon salt
- ½ teaspoon pepper
- 2 pounds 85 percent lean ground beef

GLAZE

- ½ cup ketchup
- ¼ cup cider vinegar
- 3 tablespoons packed light brown sugar
- 1 teaspoon hot sauce
- ½ teaspoon ground coriander

1. FOR THE MEATLOAF: Adjust oven rack to middle position and heat oven to 375 degrees. Spread cheese on plate and place in freezer until ready to use. Fold piece of heavy-duty aluminum foil to form 10 by 6-inch rectangle. Center foil on wire rack and place rack in rimmed baking sheet. Poke holes in foil with skewer about ½ inch apart. Spray foil with vegetable oil spray and set aside.

2. Melt butter in 10-inch skillet over medium-high heat; add onion and celery and cook, stirring occasionally, until beginning to brown, 6 to 8 minutes. Add thyme, garlic, and paprika and cook, stirring constantly, until fragrant, about 1 minute. Reduce heat to low and add tomato juice. Cook, scraping bottom of skillet with wooden spoon to loosen any browned bits, until thickened, about 1 minute. Transfer mixture to bowl and set aside to cool.

3. Whisk broth and eggs in large bowl until combined. Sprinkle gelatin over liquid and let stand for 5 minutes. Stir in saltines, parsley, soy sauce, mustard, salt, pepper, and onion mixture. Crumble frozen cheese into coarse powder and sprinkle over mixture. Add ground beef; mix gently with hands until thoroughly combined, about 1 minute. Transfer meat to foil rectangle and shape into 10 by 6-inch oval about 2 inches high. Smooth top and edges of meatloaf with moistened spatula. Bake until meatloaf registers 135 to 140 degrees, 55 to 65 minutes. Remove meatloaf from oven and turn on broiler.

4. FOR THE GLAZE: While meatloaf cooks, combine glaze ingredients in small saucepan; bring to simmer over medium heat and cook, stirring, until thick and syrupy, about 5 minutes. Spread half of glaze evenly over cooked meatloaf with rubber spatula; place under broiler and cook until glaze bubbles and begins to brown at edges, about 5 minutes. Remove meatloaf from oven and spread evenly with remaining glaze; place back under broiler and cook until glaze is again bubbling and beginning to brown, about 5 minutes more. Cool meatloaf for about 20 minutes before slicing.

PRACTICAL SCIENCE HOW GELATIN MIMICS VEAL

The collagen in veal converts to gelatin with ease. Adding powdered gelatin mimics the effects.

Many traditional meatloaf recipes call for three different meats (beef, pork, and veal), and each one has a core function. Beef contributes assertive beefiness, while pork adds dimension with flavor and extra fattiness. With veal, it's mostly about the gelatin—a viscous substance with natural water-retaining qualities that help keep a meatloaf moist and unctuous. Gelatin is formed when collagen, the protein in a cow's connective tissue, breaks down during cooking. Collagen is naturally present in cows of all ages, but the collagen in calves (the source of veal) is more loosely structured—and therefore converts to gelatin more easily and quickly—than the collagen in an adult cow. In our all-beef meatloaf, we successfully replicated the gelatinous qualities of veal by adding powdered gelatin.

So how does it work? Gelatin is a pure protein that suspends water in a meshlike, semisolid matrix similar to a cotton ball that has absorbed and trapped water. In fact, gelatin can hold as much as 10 times its own weight in water. By slowing down the movement of liquids, gelatin has a stabilizing effect, making it harder for water and other liquids to be forced out, essentially fencing them in. In meatloaf, then, gelatin helps by (1) decreasing the amount of liquid leaking from the meat as the other proteins coagulate and (2) improving the textural feel by making the liquids more viscous even when very hot—sort of a transitional state between liquid and solid. That viscosity translates to a luxuriant texture in the mouth—much like reduced stock, or demi-glace—and the perception of greater richness, as if we had added more fat.

WHY THIS RECIPE WORKS

For a tender, moist, and light meatloaf, a combination of ground beef, pork, and veal (known as meatloaf mix) is usually the way to go. But sometimes we can't find meatloaf mix or don't have it on hand. For an all-beef loaf that's just as good as one made with meatloaf mix, we recommend using equal parts ground chuck and sirloin, which provide just the right balance of juicy, tender meat and assertive beefy flavor. (Simply using 85 percent lean ground beef works, too.) A panade along with frozen, grated cheese adds moisture as well as fat.

ADD A PANADE We use saltines as the bread for our panade, delivering a well-seasoned, tender loaf with good moisture. Instead of milk, which does little to tone down beef's naturally liver-y flavor, we use chicken broth, which adds savory notes to the loaf. Powdered gelatin rounds out the panade, replacing what was lost in the ground veal of a meatloaf mix, and giving our version a luxurious smoothness.

USE FROZEN CHEESE We add cheese to this meatloaf for its flavor, moisture, and binding quality. We don't want little pockets of cheese that ooze unappealing liquid when the loaf is cut, though. Therefore, the method to break down the cheese for this recipe is critical. Dicing and shredding leaves those undesirable hot pockets of cheese. Grated cheese proves superior, and freezing the grated cheese keeps it crumbly.

BIND WITH EGGS While the additions of frozen, grated cheese and a panade made of saltines, chicken broth, and gelatin are important steps toward binding the meatloaf together, more is required. We also add 2 large eggs to the mix. The eggs, which solidify as they cook, hold in moisture and add body to the meatloaf.

BAKE FREE-FORM Allowing meatloaf baked in a loaf pan to stew in its own juices makes for a greasy mess. We ditch the loaf pan and bake the meatloaf "free-form" on a raised rectangle we make from aluminum foil set atop a wire cooling rack. Setting the meatloaf on this raised surface not only allows the fat to drain away, preventing the meatloaf from tasting greasy, it also encourages allover browning, which adds a layer of flavor. (Because the bigger surface area and browning invite moisture loss, we add a panade.)

GLAZE LATE The almost-finished meatloaf needs its crowning glory—a glaze. But applied at the beginning of cooking, the glaze mixes unappealingly with the liquids seeping out of the loaf. Finishing with the glaze produces better results, especially when placing the loaf briefly under the broiler.

SIMPLE ITALIAN-STYLE MEAT SAUCE
SERVES 8 TO 10

High-quality canned tomatoes will make a big difference in this sauce. We recommend Hunt's and Muir Glen diced tomatoes, and Tuttorosso and Muir Glen crushed tomatoes. If using dried oregano, add the entire amount with the canned tomato liquid in step 2.

4	ounces white mushrooms, trimmed and halved if small or quartered if large
1	slice hearty white sandwich bread, torn into quarters
2	tablespoons whole milk
	Salt and pepper
1	pound 85 percent lean ground beef
1	tablespoon olive oil
1	large onion, chopped fine
6	garlic cloves, minced
1	tablespoon tomato paste
¼	teaspoon red pepper flakes
1	(14.5-ounce) can diced tomatoes, drained with ¼ cup juice reserved
1	tablespoon minced fresh oregano or 1 teaspoon dried
1	(28-ounce) can crushed tomatoes
¼	cup grated Parmesan cheese, plus extra for serving
2	pounds spaghetti or linguine

1. Pulse mushrooms in food processor until finely chopped, about 8 pulses, scraping down sides as needed; transfer to bowl. Add bread, milk, ½ teaspoon salt, and ½ teaspoon pepper to now-empty food processor and pulse until paste forms, about 8 pulses. Add ground beef and pulse until mixture is well combined, about 6 pulses.

2. Heat oil in large saucepan over medium-high heat until just smoking. Add onion and mushrooms and cook until vegetables are softened and well browned, 6 to 12 minutes. Stir in garlic, tomato paste, and pepper flakes and cook until fragrant and tomato paste starts to brown, about 1 minute. Stir in reserved tomato juice and 2 teaspoons oregano, scraping up any browned bits. Stir in meat mixture and cook, breaking up any large pieces with wooden spoon, until no longer pink, about 3 minutes, making sure that meat does not brown.

3. Stir in diced tomatoes and crushed tomatoes, bring to gentle simmer, and cook until sauce has thickened and flavors meld, about 30 minutes. Stir in Parmesan and remaining 1 teaspoon oregano and season with salt and

pepper to taste. (Sauce can be refrigerated for up to 2 days or frozen for up to 1 month.)

4. Meanwhile, bring 8 quarts water to boil in 12-quart pot. Add pasta and 2 tablespoons salt and cook, stirring often, until al dente. Reserve ½ cup cooking water, then drain pasta and return it to pot. Add 1 cup sauce and reserved cooking water to pasta and toss to combine. Serve, topping individual portions with more sauce and passing Parmesan separately.

✔ WHY THIS RECIPE WORKS

Simmering a meat sauce all day does two things: It concentrates flavors as the liquid reduces slowly over the three- to four-hour cooking time; and it breaks down the meat, giving it a soft, lush texture. For a quick meat sauce that tastes as if it had simmered all day, we use a few tricks: Instead of browning the meat, we brown mushrooms to give the sauce flavor without drying it out. We blend a panade into the meat before cooking, to keep it tender. Finally, for good tomato flavor, we add tomato paste to the browned vegetables in our meat sauce recipe and deglaze the pan with a little tomato juice before adding canned tomatoes.

TEACH AN OLD PANADE NEW TRICKS We use a basic panade in this sauce (white bread, whole milk). Even though it's for a sauce and not a compact construction like a burger, meatball, or meatloaf, the goal is the same: producing tender, juicy meat. Here, we mix the beef and panade in a food processor in order to help ensure that the starch is well dispersed so that all the meat reaps its benefits. The food processor also breaks the meat into tiny pieces that cook up supple and tender. When we skipped this step, the meat was chunkier—more like chili than a good sauce.

USE FLAVOR ENHANCERS We ramp up flavor in this quick sauce in a few ways. First: mushrooms. Basic white ones (browned in the pan with an onion) are enough to impart a real beefy taste. We also add tomato paste and Parmesan cheese, which are rich in glutamates (see concept 35) and add an umami, or savory, taste, along with liberal amounts of red pepper flakes and fresh oregano.

GRIND THE MUSHROOMS, TOO We process the mushrooms in a food processor until finely chopped before browning them in a pan. After all, we want the beefy flavor that the mushrooms add to the sauce but are not interested in their squishy texture. This way, the mushrooms blend right in with the ground beef.

DEGLAZE WITH JUICE We save some tomato juice from the drained diced tomatoes to deglaze the pan after browning the mushrooms. This (plus a bit of tomato paste) gives the sauce's tomato flavor a boost.

CLASSIC SPAGHETTI AND MEATBALLS FOR A CROWD
SERVES 12

If you don't have buttermilk, you can substitute 1 cup of plain yogurt thinned with ½ cup of milk. Grate the onion on the large holes of a box grater. You can cook the pasta in two separate pots if you do not have a pot large enough to cook all of the pasta together. The ingredients in this recipe can be reduced by two-thirds to serve four.

MEATBALLS
2¼	cups panko bread crumbs
1½	cups buttermilk
1½	teaspoons unflavored gelatin
3	tablespoons water
2	pounds 85 percent lean ground beef
1	pound ground pork
6	ounces thinly sliced prosciutto, chopped fine
3	large eggs
3	ounces Parmesan cheese, grated (1½ cups)
6	tablespoons minced fresh parsley
3	garlic cloves, minced
1½	teaspoons salt
½	teaspoon pepper

SAUCE
3	tablespoons extra-virgin olive oil
1	large onion, grated
6	garlic cloves, minced
1	teaspoon dried oregano
½	teaspoon red pepper flakes
3	(28-ounce) cans crushed tomatoes
6	cups tomato juice
6	tablespoons dry white wine
	Salt and pepper
½	cup minced fresh basil
3	tablespoons minced fresh parsley
	Sugar
3	pounds spaghetti
2	tablespoons salt
	Grated Parmesan cheese

1. FOR THE MEATBALLS: Adjust oven racks to lower-middle and upper-middle positions and heat oven to 450 degrees. Line 2 rimmed baking sheets with aluminum foil, set wire racks in baking sheets, and spray racks with vegetable oil spray.

2. Combine bread crumbs and buttermilk in large bowl and let sit, mashing occasionally with fork, until smooth paste forms, about 10 minutes. Meanwhile, sprinkle gelatin over water in small bowl and allow to soften for 5 minutes.

3. Mix ground beef, ground pork, prosciutto, eggs, Parmesan, parsley, garlic, salt, pepper, and gelatin mixture into bread-crumb mixture using hands. Pinch off and roll mixture into 2-inch meatballs (about 40 meatballs total) and arrange on prepared racks. Bake until well browned, about 30 minutes, switching and rotating baking sheets halfway through baking.

4. FOR THE SAUCE: While meatballs bake, heat oil in Dutch oven over medium heat until shimmering. Add onion and cook until softened and lightly browned, 5 to 7 minutes. Stir in garlic, oregano, and pepper flakes and cook until fragrant, about 30 seconds. Stir in crushed tomatoes, tomato juice, wine, 1½ teaspoons salt, and ¼ teaspoon pepper, bring to simmer, and cook until thickened slightly, about 15 minutes.

5. Remove meatballs from oven and reduce oven temperature to 300 degrees. Gently nestle meatballs into sauce. Cover, transfer to oven, and cook until meatballs are firm and sauce has thickened, about 1 hour. (Sauce and meatballs can be cooled and refrigerated for up to 2 days. To reheat, drizzle ½ cup water over sauce, without stirring, and reheat on lower-middle rack of 325-degree oven for 1 hour.)

6. Meanwhile, bring 10 quarts water to boil in 12-quart pot. Add pasta and salt and cook, stirring often, until al dente. Reserve ½ cup cooking water, then drain pasta and return it to pot.

7. Gently stir basil and parsley into sauce and season with sugar, salt, and pepper to taste. Add 2 cups sauce (without meatballs) to pasta and toss to combine. Add reserved cooking water as needed to adjust consistency. Serve, topping individual portions with more tomato sauce and several meatballs and passing Parmesan separately.

✔ WHY THIS RECIPE WORKS
Making spaghetti and meatballs to serve a crowd can try the patience of even the toughest Italian grandmother. We sought an easier way and found that roasting our meatballs on a wire rack, rather than frying them in batches, makes our recipe faster and cleaner. Adding some powdered gelatin to a mix of ground chuck and ground pork serves to plump the meatballs and lends them a soft richness.

USE A MEAT COMBO Though we tried making these meatballs with beef alone—using 85 percent lean ground beef (anything less fatty would almost certainly produce a

SHOPPING FOR PORK 101

PRIMAL CUTS

Five different cuts of pork are sold at the wholesale level. From this first series of cuts, known in the trade as primal cuts, a butcher (usually at a meat-packing plant in the Midwest but sometimes on-site at your market) will make the retail cuts that you bring home from the market.

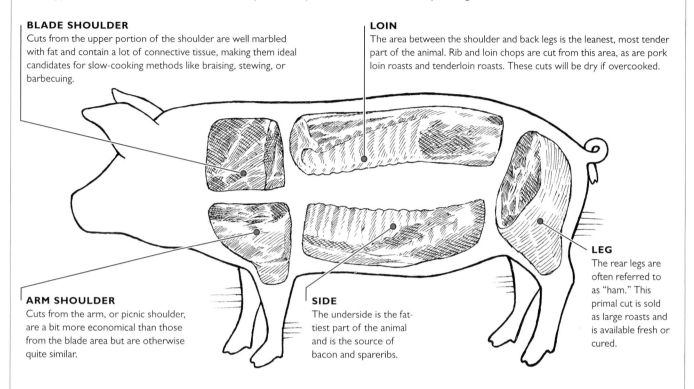

BLADE SHOULDER
Cuts from the upper portion of the shoulder are well marbled with fat and contain a lot of connective tissue, making them ideal candidates for slow-cooking methods like braising, stewing, or barbecuing.

LOIN
The area between the shoulder and back legs is the leanest, most tender part of the animal. Rib and loin chops are cut from this area, as are pork loin roasts and tenderloin roasts. These cuts will be dry if overcooked.

ARM SHOULDER
Cuts from the arm, or picnic shoulder, are a bit more economical than those from the blade area but are otherwise quite similar.

SIDE
The underside is the fattiest part of the animal and is the source of bacon and spareribs.

LEG
The rear legs are often referred to as "ham." This primal cut is sold as large roasts and is available fresh or cured.

THE OTHER WHITE MEAT

The pork sold today bears little resemblance to the pork our grandparents consumed. New breeding techniques and feeding systems have slimmed down the modern pig, which contains a third less fat than it did 30 years ago. As you might imagine, leaner pork is not as flavorful and is prone to drying out as it cooks. Old-fashioned heritage breeds, however, are making a comeback. These breeds are touted as being fattier, juicier, and far more flavorful. In addition to fat content, heritage breeds often have a higher pH and darker color than modern pork.

When we tasted 100 percent Berkshire pork, a heritage breed, against standard supermarket pork we found the differences to be astounding. The Berkshire meat had a rich crimson color and a smoky, intense pork flavor. It was also very tender and juicy. The pale supermarket pork was bland and chewy in comparison. Other heritage breeds (including Duroc) failed to impress our tasters, but if you can find Berkshire pork we recommend buying it.

ENHANCED OR NOT?

Because modern pork is so lean and therefore somewhat bland and prone to dryness if overcooked, many producers now inject their fresh pork products with a sodium solution. So-called "enhanced" pork is now the only option at many supermarkets, especially when buying lean cuts like the tenderloin. (To be sure, read the label; if the pork has been enhanced it will have an ingredient label.)

Enhanced pork is injected with a solution of water, salt, sodium phosphates, sodium lactate, potassium lactate, sodium diacetate, and varying flavor agents, generally adding 7 to 15 percent extra weight. While enhanced pork does cook up juicier (it has been pumped full of water!), we find the texture almost spongy and the flavor is often unpleasantly salty. We prefer the genuine pork flavor of natural pork and prefer to brine lean cuts (see concept 11) to keep them juicy. Note that enhanced pork loses six times more moisture when frozen and thawed compared to natural pork—yet another reason to avoid enhanced pork.

NITRITES VS. NITRATES

Cured pork products, such as bacon, often contain nitrites and/or nitrates. While nitrites and nitrates are virtually identical, only nitrites have been shown to form carcinogenic compounds called nitrosamines when heated in the presence of proteins, like those in pork.

So should you buy "nitrate-free" or "nitrite-free" bacon? These products are generally brined with salt, a bacterial lactic acid starter culture, and celery juice (which is sometimes listed as "natural flavor"). The problem is that celery juice contains a high level of nitrate, which is converted to the problematic nitrite by the bacteria in the starter culture. While technically these products can be labeled "no nitrates or nitrites added," the compounds are naturally formed during production.

When we analyzed various brands of bacon, we found that regular bacon actually contained lower levels of nitrites and nitrates than some brands labeled "no nitrites or nitrates added." All the bacon we tested fell well within federal standards for these compounds, but if you want to avoid nitrites and nitrates you need to avoid bacon and other processed pork products altogether.

dry, bland meatball)—we found that replacing some of the beef with ground pork (we like a 2:1 ratio best) makes for a markedly richer, meatier taste.

PICK PANKO For this panade we use panko, super-crunchy Japanese bread crumbs that hold on to meat juices and keep the meatballs from getting tough, along with buttermilk, which adds more flavor to meatballs than regular milk. One cup of plain yogurt thinned with half a cup of milk can be substituted for the buttermilk.

GRATE THE ONION TO REDUCE CRUNCH We grate the onion for this sauce on the large holes of a box grater. This allows us to have the onion taste without the big crunch.

BUILD FLAVOR We chop up some prosciutto, which is packed with glutamates (see concept 35) that enhance savory flavor, and mix it in with the meat for an extra-meaty flavor. Parmesan, too, adds lots of glutamates.

ADD GELATIN We pondered adding veal to these meatballs because veal has lots of gelatin and could add suppleness to the dish. While the veal did add suppleness, another problem arose, though: Ultra-lean veal is usually ground very fine, and these meatballs lacked the pleasantly coarse texture of the beef-and-pork batch. Instead, we add 1½ teaspoons of powdered gelatin moistened in a little water to the meatballs. Works like a charm.

FLAVOR THE SAUCE Because we roast our meatballs in the oven, there are no pan drippings to add flavor to the sauce. This is why we drop the roasted meatballs into the simple marinara sauce and braise them together in the oven for an hour. With time, the rich flavor of the browned meat infiltrates the sauce. One problem we found with this technique, however, was that as the meatballs absorb the liquid around them, the sauce can overreduce in the oven. To combat this, we swap almost half of the crushed tomatoes in our marinara recipe for an equal portion of tomato juice, leaving us with a full-bodied, but not sludgy, sauce.

SWEDISH MEATBALLS
SERVES 4 TO 6

The traditional accompaniments for Swedish meatballs are lingonberry preserves and Swedish Pickled Cucumbers (recipe follows). If you can't find lingonberry preserves, cranberry preserves may be used. For a slightly less sweet dish, omit the brown sugar in the meatballs and reduce the brown sugar in the sauce to 2 teaspoons. A 12-inch slope-sided skillet can be used in place of the sauté pan— use 1½ cups of oil for frying instead of 1¼ cups. Serve the meatballs with mashed potatoes, boiled red potatoes, or egg noodles.

MEATBALLS

1	large egg
¼	cup heavy cream
1	slice hearty white sandwich bread, crusts removed, torn into 1-inch pieces
8	ounces ground pork
¼	cup grated onion
1½	teaspoons salt
1	teaspoon packed brown sugar
1	teaspoon baking powder
⅛	teaspoon ground nutmeg
⅛	teaspoon ground allspice
⅛	teaspoon pepper
8	ounces 85 percent lean ground beef
1¼	cups vegetable oil

SAUCE

1	tablespoon unsalted butter
1	tablespoon all-purpose flour
1½	cups low-sodium chicken broth
1	tablespoon packed brown sugar
½	cup heavy cream
2	teaspoons lemon juice
	Salt and pepper

1. FOR MEATBALLS: Whisk egg and cream together in bowl. Stir in bread and set aside. Meanwhile, using stand mixer fitted with paddle, beat pork, onion, salt, sugar, baking powder, nutmeg, allspice, and pepper on high speed until smooth and pale, about 2 minutes, scraping down bowl as necessary. Using fork, mash bread mixture until no large dry bread chunks remain; add mixture to mixer bowl and beat on high speed until smooth and homogeneous, about 1 minute, scraping bowl as necessary. Add beef and mix on medium-low speed until just incorporated, about 30 seconds, scraping down bowl as necessary. Using moistened hands, form generous tablespoon of meat mixture into 1-inch round meatball; repeat with remaining mixture to form 25 to 30 meatballs.

2. Heat oil in 10-inch straight-sided sauté pan over medium-high heat until edge of meatball dipped in oil sizzles (oil should register 350 degrees on instant-read thermometer), 3 to 5 minutes. Add meatballs in single layer and fry, flipping once halfway through cooking, until lightly browned all over and cooked through, 7 to 10 minutes. (Adjust heat as needed to keep oil sizzling but not smoking.) Using slotted spoon, transfer browned meatballs to paper towel–lined plate.

3. FOR SAUCE: Pour off and discard oil in pan, leaving any browned bits behind. Return pan to medium-high heat and melt butter. Add flour and cook, whisking constantly, until flour is light brown, about 30 seconds. Slowly whisk in broth, scraping bottom of pan with wooden spoon to loosen any browned bits. Add sugar and bring to simmer. Reduce heat to medium and cook until sauce is reduced to about 1 cup, about 5 minutes. Stir in cream and return to simmer.

4. Add meatballs to sauce and simmer, turning occasionally, until heated through, about 5 minutes. Stir in lemon juice, season with salt and pepper to taste, and serve.

TO MAKE AHEAD: Meatballs can be fried and then frozen for up to 2 weeks. To continue with recipe, thaw meatballs in refrigerator overnight and proceed from step 3, using clean pan.

SWEDISH PICKLED CUCUMBERS
MAKES 3 CUPS, ENOUGH FOR 1 RECIPE SWEDISH MEATBALLS

Kirby cucumbers are also called pickling cucumbers. If these small cucumbers are unavailable, substitute 1 large American cucumber. Serve the pickles chilled or at room temperature.

3	small Kirby cucumbers (1 pound), sliced into ⅛- to ¼-inch-thick rounds
1½	cups distilled white vinegar
1½	cups sugar
1	teaspoon salt
12	whole allspice berries

Place cucumber slices in medium heatproof bowl. Bring vinegar, sugar, salt, and allspice to simmer in small saucepan over high heat, stirring occasionally to dissolve sugar. Pour vinegar mixture over cucumbers and stir to separate slices. Cover bowl with plastic wrap and let sit for 15 minutes. Uncover and cool to room temperature, about 15 minutes.

TO MAKE AHEAD: Pickles can be refrigerated in their liquid in airtight container for up to 2 weeks.

✔ WHY THIS RECIPE WORKS
Most of us know Swedish meatballs as lumps of flavorless ground beef or pork covered in heavy gravy that congeals as it sits. But when done right these main-course meatballs are melt-in-your-mouth tender, substantial yet delicate. To achieve the right texture, we combine beef, pork, a panade (a mixture of bread, egg, and cream), and a surprise ingredient, baking powder, which keeps the meatballs delicate and juicy.

STRIVE FOR SPRINGY While Italian meatballs are ideally moist and almost fall-apart tender, that's not at all what we want in Swedish meatballs. We want them to be springy. Therefore, we still use both pork and beef, but we use cream (rather than milk) and egg along with bread for a small amount of panade. The extra fat from the cream and egg coats the starch granules, reducing the extent of hydration and swelling so the structure is springy rather than loose. The egg protein also adds both structure and springiness.

LIGHTEN WITH BAKING POWDER We don't end our textural quest there, though. With the mixture of pork and beef, as well as our creamy panade, our meatballs still turned out a bit dry and dense. We wanted to lighten them up. Thinking of other ingredients used elsewhere to do just that, we turned to baking powder. Can it leaven a meatball the way it leavens bread? Indeed. We use a single teaspoon of baking powder to help produce meatballs with the ideal moistness, substance, and lightness.

GRATE ONIONS Just as we do in our recipe for Classic Spaghetti and Meatballs for a Crowd (page 148), we grate the onion on a box grater here. This way we have the taste of onion without its crunch.

MIX THE PORK, NOT THE BEEF We add a bit of sausagelike springiness by whipping the pork in a stand mixer along with the salt, baking powder, and seasonings until an emulsified paste forms before adding the panade and the ground beef. We whip the pork and not the beef because the pork has a higher fat content and less robust muscle structure. Whipping it finely distributes the fat into the lean meat, thus guaranteeing a juicy finished product.

USE FOND FOR FLAVOR For the gravy, we wanted a light cream sauce instead of a heavy brown one. To get this, we add a bit of cream to our stock to lighten it up and a splash of lemon juice for bright flavor. We make it in the same pan that we use for the meatballs, scraping up the browned bits, or fond, for extra flavor.

PICKLE QUICKLY Swedish pickled cucumbers are a traditional accompaniment to these meatballs. Here, we heat the vinegar with the sugar, salt, and allspice before pouring it over the cucumbers. The warm vinegar (a mild acid) with dissolved salt and sugar not only adds seasoning but quickly draws moisture out of the cucumbers, creating a texture that is more like a pickle than a crisp cucumber.

Create Layers for a Breading That Sticks

Chicken breasts and pork chops: They're simple, good for you, and sometimes, just so boring. One way to mix it up is to add a flavorful coating. After all, there's little better than a breaded cutlet or chop—if done right. Here, we explore how to get a coating to stick to meat when baked in the oven (à la Shake 'N Bake) or when pan-fried in a little oil.

HOW THE SCIENCE WORKS

A crisp crust. A crunchy coating. Officially, it's called bound breading. But however we refer to that crackling, starchy layer that comes on top of many chicken breasts and pork chops, it generally consists of three things: flour (or some flourlike substance); an egg wash (or something like it); and bread crumbs (sometimes toasted), ground cereal, or crushed crackers.

The problem, however, lies in creating a bound breading that is both texturally pleasing and will not fall off the meat. Too often coatings are mushy, unevenly browned, and flaking off of the cutlet or chop. Why is it so hard to get breading to stick to protein?

To understand why some breadings adhere and others do not, we must examine what is happening on the surface of the meat. One of the principal reasons breadings fail to adhere is excess moisture. As the breaded meat is cooked, surface moisture rapidly turns to steam, forcing the coating to separate from the meat as the steam tries to escape. (This is why it is essential to thoroughly dry your meat before applying a coating.) Conversely, the presence of sticky proteins, which we first learned about in concept 14 in relation to ground meat, can help keep coatings in place. Most of the recipes that follow incorporate a simple step, such as pounding or cutting the meat, to encourage the release of these soluble, sticky proteins.

Getting the meat dry but sticky helps, but using a three-layer coating is paramount to creating a good bound breading. First comes flour (or cornstarch). The initial coating of starch will absorb any remaining moisture on the surface of the meat, creating a tacky base coat when combined with the sticky meat proteins that acts as a glue for the breading. Next comes an egg wash (or similar liquid coating). The proteins in the eggs are also sticky, especially when lightly mixed at room temperature, when they begin the process of unraveling and, as a result, are better able to bind with the layer of flour beneath. And finally, the third layer consists of bread crumbs (or something similar) to provide the textural majority of the crust. A short rest after applying the bread crumbs helps to ensure a strong bond with the egg proteins, which will then have time to penetrate into the honeycomb structure of the bread.

The proportions of the layers are important: Too much flour can act as a barrier between the meat proteins and the egg wash layer. Likewise, the egg wash should not be too heavy and thick, or it will separate from the meat due to the combination of its own weight and the steam escaping during cooking. (To combat this, oil is often added to the egg wash to act as a "thinner.")

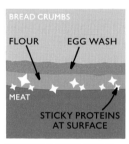

LAYERS OF BREADING

BREAD CRUMBS

FLOUR   EGG WASH

MEAT

STICKY PROTEINS
AT SURFACE

BREADING THAT STICKS
To make a breaded coating that sticks to meat when it is cooked, layering is important. The flour, egg wash, and bread crumbs adhere to one another as they are applied, especially with help from the presence of sticky meat proteins, which act like a natural glue.

TEST KITCHEN EXPERIMENT

The standard breading procedure calls for dipping food in flour, beaten egg, and then bread crumbs. Is it really necessary to do all three? To find out, we made three batches of breaded boneless pork chops, coating one with just panko bread crumbs, a second with egg and panko, and a third with the full breading trifecta. We baked all of the chops in a 400-degree oven until they registered 140 degrees, let them rest for five minutes, and examined their coatings. We repeated the test three times.

THE RESULTS

Even before we popped the pork into the oven, we noticed some differences among the three batches. We noted that it was incredibly difficult to get a sufficient amount of panko to stick to the naked chops—it just kept falling back into the bowl. The egg and panko sample fared better but was still sparsely coated compared to the pork with flour, egg, and panko. Post-baking, these differences were even more dramatic.

THE TAKEAWAY

The standard procedure for breading—flour, egg, and bread crumbs—still holds … literally. The sticky proteins present on the surface of the pork adhere to the flour, creating a tacky base that acts like glue. Next the egg proteins are likewise sticky and able to bind to the bread crumbs, which give the coating a nice texture and heft. Without the flour, the egg and bread-crumb layers simply slide off. Without the egg, the crumbs have nothing to which to stick. A proper breading requires all three ingredients.

GETTING BREADING TO STICK

JUST PANKO
We coated (or tried to coat) our first pork chop with panko bread crumbs alone. The coating was patchy because the crumbs did not stick well to the meat.

EGG AND PANKO
A coating of egg and then panko was more successful, but it was still impossible to get a good, full breaded coating to stick.

FLOUR, EGG, AND PANKO
The addition of flour made all the difference. The pork chop coated in flour, egg, and then panko had a full, unblemished coating that held up well before and after cooking.

PRACTICAL SCIENCE MAKE-AHEAD BREAD CRUMBS

It's possible to make bread crumbs ahead of time and store them in the freezer for up to a month.

Homemade bread crumbs add crunch to everything from chicken cutlets to casseroles, but we wondered if we could save time and money by grinding homemade crumbs in advance (when we happen to have stale bread on hand) and freezing them for later use. We ground crumbs two ways—fine and coarse—and toasted some batches before putting them in the freezer and left others as is. All crumbs were stored in plastic zipper-lock bags to prevent them from picking up moisture or unwanted flavors in the freezer. All of the crumbs were fine at the one-month mark but after two months in the freezer they had lost most of their flavor.

With crumbs in the freezer, you will need to convert recipes that call for bread slices processed into crumbs. Use the chart below to figure out how much of your freezer stash you should use.

I LARGE SLICE (1.5 OZ.) SANDWICH BREAD	FROZEN CRUMBS	FROZEN TOASTED CRUMBS
Finely processed	⅔ cup	⅓ cup plus I tablespoon
Coarsely processed	I cup	⅔ cup

A combination of techniques—including pounding, flouring, using an egg wash and fresh bread crumbs, and a turn in either the frying pan or the oven—helps us to achieve a range of flavorful and crisp breaded crusts.

CRISP BREADED CHICKEN CUTLETS
SERVES 4

If you'd rather not prepare fresh bread crumbs, use panko, the extra-crisp Japanese bread crumbs. The chicken is cooked in two batches because the crust is noticeably crisper if the pan is not overcrowded.

4   (6- to 8-ounce) boneless, skinless chicken breasts, tenderloins removed, trimmed
    Salt and pepper
3   slices hearty white sandwich bread, torn into quarters
¾   cup all-purpose flour
2   large eggs
1   tablespoon plus ¾ cup vegetable oil
    Lemon wedges

1. Cover chicken breasts with plastic wrap and pound to even ½-inch thickness with meat pounder. Pat chicken dry with paper towels and season chicken with salt and pepper.

2. Adjust oven rack to middle position and heat oven to 200 degrees. Set wire rack in rimmed baking sheet. Pulse bread in food processor to coarse crumbs, about 10 pulses; transfer to shallow dish or pie plate. Place flour in second dish. Lightly beat eggs and 1 tablespoon oil together in third dish.

3. Working with 1 cutlet at a time, dredge in flour, shaking off excess, then coat with egg mixture, allowing excess to drip off. Coat all sides of cutlet with bread crumbs, pressing gently so that crumbs adhere; transfer to prepared wire rack and let sit for 5 minutes.

4. Heat 6 tablespoons oil in 10-inch nonstick skillet over medium-high heat until shimmering. Place 2 cutlets in skillet and cook until deep golden brown and crisp on first side, about 3 minutes. Flip cutlets, reduce heat to medium, and continue to cook until deep golden brown and crisp on second side and meat feels firm when pressed gently, about 3 minutes longer. Drain cutlets briefly on paper towel–lined plate, then transfer to clean wire rack set in baking sheet and keep warm in oven. Pour off all oil left in skillet and wipe out with paper towels. Repeat with remaining 6 tablespoons oil and remaining 2 cutlets. Serve with lemon wedges.

DEVILED CRISP BREADED CHICKEN CUTLETS

Rub each breast with generous pinch cayenne before dredging in flour. Lightly beat 3 tablespoons Dijon mustard, 1 tablespoon Worcestershire sauce, and 2 teaspoons minced fresh thyme into eggs along with oil.

CRISP BREADED CHICKEN CUTLETS WITH PARMESAN (CHICKEN MILANESE)

Though Parmesan is the traditional cheese to use in this dish, feel free to substitute Pecorino Romano cheese if you prefer a stronger, tangier flavor. The cheese is quite susceptible to burning, so be sure to keep a very close eye on the cutlets as they cook.

Substitute ¼ cup finely grated Parmesan cheese for an equal amount of bread crumbs.

✔ WHY THIS RECIPE WORKS
Most chicken cutlets offer a thin, uneven, pale crust; we wanted a thick, crisp, flavorful coating that wouldn't fall off. To do this, we pounded the chicken to release sticky proteins, used flour to absorb moisture, eggs to help it adhere, and fresh bread crumbs for a subtly sweet flavor and light, crisp texture.

POUND FOR EVEN THICKNESS When cooked as is, the thin tip of the chicken cutlet and the more plump opposite end will cook at different rates. It's an easy fix, though: All you have to do is pound the breast to a uniform ½ inch to ensure the cutlets will cook evenly. (Use a meat pounder or the bottom of a small pan.) But don't pound it any thinner than ½ inch; if you do, the chicken can overcook before the breading is sufficiently browned. Pounding also encourages the release of sticky meat proteins.

BLOT DRY Even if every other step in the process of breading your cutlets is in place, a moist piece of chicken can ruin it all. We find that if there is even a tiny bit of moisture on the breast, the breading will peel off the finished cutlets in sheets because the moisture (now steam) will try to escape, forcing aside whatever is in its path.

EGG WASH WITH OIL While it's possible to use an egg wash with just egg, beaten eggs alone are thick and viscous and tend to form too heavy a layer on the meat, making the breading too thick. Thinning the egg with oil, water, or both is a common practice that allows excess egg to slide off the meat more easily, leaving a thinner, more delicate, and tenderer coat. Though all three techniques work, thinning the egg with just oil helps the breading to brown a bit more deeply without adding more moisture, which makes it our pick.

MAKE YOUR OWN CRUMBS We tested fresh bread crumbs, dry bread crumbs, and Japanese panko crumbs in this recipe. The dry bread crumbs had an unmistakably stale flavor, while the panko crumbs rated well for their shattering crispness and wheaty flavor. But the fresh bread crumbs, with their mild, subtly sweet flavor and light, crisp texture, swept the test. We recommend using premium sliced sandwich bread to make the crumbs; it's the sweetest. Simply tear the slices into rough pieces and pulse them in the food processor until the desired size.

LET 'EM REST Yes, we all want to get the chicken into the pan, and then our mouths, as soon as we can. But it's important to wait—just a few minutes. Letting the chicken rest for five minutes after breading will help everything to solidify. It takes a little time for the egg proteins to unravel and intermingle with the sticky meat proteins and porous bread crumbs to ensure a strong bond among all three.

USE ENOUGH OIL For even, thorough browning, it's important for the oil to reach one-third to one-half of the way up the sides of the food being cooked. Because it's also important for the breading to brown gently and evenly, the oil should not be as hot as it is for a sauté, in which there is no breading and instant browning is critical. In the test kitchen we put pure olive oil up against vegetable oil, and top billing went to the vegetable oil for its light, unobtrusive presence.

BATCH COOK FOR BROWNING Even though four cutlets will fit comfortably in a 12-inch skillet on the stove, the breading tends to get greasy and will brown unevenly due to the accumulation of too much steam. Therefore, we recommend using a 10-inch skillet and cooking only two at a time. This will result in cutlets with a crisp, well-browned crust every time. It's worth the minimal extra time and effort.

CHICKEN KIEV
SERVES 4

To make butterflying the chicken easier, freeze it for 15 minutes.

HERB BUTTER

8	tablespoons unsalted butter, softened
1	tablespoon lemon juice
1	tablespoon minced shallot
1	tablespoon minced fresh parsley
½	teaspoon minced fresh tarragon
⅜	teaspoon salt
⅛	teaspoon pepper

CHICKEN

4	slices hearty white sandwich bread, torn into quarters
2	tablespoons vegetable oil
	Salt and pepper
4	(8-ounce) boneless, skinless chicken breasts, tenderloins removed, trimmed
1	cup all-purpose flour
3	large eggs
1	teaspoon Dijon mustard

1. FOR THE HERB BUTTER: Mix all ingredients in medium bowl with rubber spatula until thoroughly combined. Form into 3-inch square on sheet of plastic wrap; wrap tightly and refrigerate until firm, about 1 hour.

2. FOR THE CHICKEN: Adjust oven rack to lower-middle position and heat oven to 300 degrees. Pulse bread in food processor to coarse crumbs, about 10 pulses; transfer to large bowl. Add oil, ⅛ teaspoon salt, and ⅛ teaspoon pepper and toss until crumbs are evenly coated. Spread crumbs on rimmed baking sheet and bake until golden brown and dry, about 25 minutes, stirring twice during baking. Let cool to room temperature.

3. Slice each chicken breast horizontally, stopping ½ inch from edges so halves remain attached. Open chicken like a book. Pound between 2 sheets of plastic wrap to even ¼-inch thickness with meat pounder. Pound outer perimeter to ⅛ inch. Unwrap herb butter and cut it into 4 rectangular pieces. Pat chicken dry with paper towels, place on counter, and season with salt and pepper. Position breasts cut side up and place 1 piece of butter in center of bottom half of each breast. Roll bottom edge of chicken over butter, then fold in sides and continue rolling to form a neat, tight bundle, pressing on seam to seal. Repeat with remaining butter and chicken. Refrigerate chicken, uncovered, to allow edges to seal, about 1 hour.

4. Adjust oven rack to middle position and heat oven to 350 degrees. Set wire rack in rimmed baking sheet. Combine flour, ¼ teaspoon salt, and ⅛ teaspoon pepper in shallow dish. Lightly beat eggs and mustard together in second shallow dish. Place bread crumbs in third shallow dish. Working with 1 chicken bundle at a time, dredge in flour, shaking off excess, then coat with egg mixture, allowing excess to drip off. Coat all sides of chicken bundle with bread crumbs, pressing gently so that crumbs adhere. Place on prepared wire rack.

5. Bake chicken until center of bundles registers 160 degrees, 40 to 45 minutes. Let rest for 5 minutes before serving.

TO MAKE AHEAD: Unbaked, breaded chicken Kiev can be refrigerated overnight and baked the next day or frozen for up to 1 month. To cook frozen chicken Kiev, increase the baking time to 50 to 55 minutes (do not thaw chicken).

✓ WHY THIS RECIPE WORKS

Chicken Kiev has developed a reputation as bad banquet fare. We wanted to bring this dish back to its roots as an elegant dish of crisply breaded chicken packed with a flavorful herb butter. A new rolling technique and some time in the fridge helped us avoid a few typical roadblocks. Toasting the bread crumbs prior to coating the chicken allows us to skip the step of pan-frying so we can cook the chicken entirely in the oven.

POUND, FILL, AND ROLL   While many recipes call for making a slit in the chicken and then sliding the butter in, we find that it's almost impossible to prevent the butter from leaking out while cooking in the hot oil. Our solution? First, we butterfly the breasts lengthwise and then pound them to a uniform ¼ inch. Flattened, these cutlets resemble teardrops; placing the butter just above the tapered end, we proceed as if wrapping up a burrito. To make sure the fat edges do not come undone, we pound them to ⅛ inch.

FILL WITH BUTTER   Traditional recipes stuff the Kievs with butter spiked with nothing more than parsley and chives. We prefer the more aromatic minced shallots over chives and a small amount of minced tarragon for a hint of sweetness. A squeeze of lemon juice tames the rich butter with a bit of acidity.

CHILL THE CUTLETS FOR A GOOD SEAL   Breading the filled cutlets can be treacherous. Right after they have been filled, the chicken bundles want to unravel, and handling them too much can do just that. But if you leave the unbreaded chicken bundles (uncovered) in the fridge for an hour, the edges will begin to stick together, nearly gluing shut and providing a much sturdier base for breading. This is further proof that sticky meat proteins really work.

EGG WASH WITH MUSTARD   We add another layer of flavor to the Kiev in a surprising place: the egg wash. A teaspoon of Dijon mustard adds an excellent flavor boost.

TOAST THE BREAD CRUMBS   Toasting the bread crumbs before using them to coat the chicken transforms this recipe. This simple step eliminates messy frying and makes this dish truly company-friendly. Make sure to bake the chicken bundles on a wire rack set inside a rimmed baking sheet so that the heat hits them evenly all around.

CRUNCHY BAKED PORK CHOPS
SERVES 4

If the pork is enhanced (injected with a salt solution), do not brine in step 1, and season with salt in step 4.

	Salt and pepper
4	(6- to 8-ounce) boneless pork chops, ¾ to 1 inch thick, trimmed
4	slices hearty white sandwich bread, torn into 1-inch pieces
2	tablespoons vegetable oil
1	small shallot, minced
3	garlic cloves, minced
2	tablespoons grated Parmesan cheese
2	tablespoons minced fresh parsley
½	teaspoon minced fresh thyme
¼	cup plus 6 tablespoons all-purpose flour
3	large egg whites
3	tablespoons Dijon mustard
	Lemon wedges

1. Adjust oven rack to middle position and heat oven to 350 degrees. Dissolve 3 tablespoons salt in 1½ quarts cold water in large container. Submerge chops in brine, cover, and refrigerate for 30 minutes to 1 hour. Remove chops from brine and thoroughly pat dry with paper towels.

2. Meanwhile, pulse bread in food processor until coarsely ground, about 8 pulses (you should have about 3½ cups crumbs). Transfer crumbs to rimmed baking sheet and add oil, shallot, garlic, ¼ teaspoon salt, and ¼ teaspoon pepper. Toss until crumbs are evenly coated with oil. Bake until deep golden brown and dry, about 15 minutes, stirring twice during baking. (Do not turn off oven.) Let cool to room temperature. Add crumbs to Parmesan, parsley, and thyme. (Bread-crumb mixture can be prepared up to 3 days in advance.)

3. Place ¼ cup flour in shallow dish. In second shallow dish, whisk egg whites and mustard until combined; add remaining 6 tablespoons flour and whisk until almost smooth, with pea-size lumps remaining.

4. Increase oven temperature to 425 degrees. Spray wire rack with vegetable oil spray and set in rimmed baking sheet. Season chops with pepper. Dredge 1 pork chop in flour; shake off excess. Using tongs, coat with egg mixture; let excess drip off. Coat all sides of chop with bread-crumb mixture, pressing gently so that thick layer of crumbs adheres to chop. Transfer breaded chop to prepared wire rack and repeat with remaining 3 chops.

5. Bake until chops register 145 degrees, 17 to 25 minutes. Let rest on rack for 5 minutes before serving with lemon wedges.

TO MAKE AHEAD: Breaded chops can be frozen for up to 1 week. Do not thaw before baking; simply increase cooking time in step 5 to 35 to 40 minutes.

CRUNCHY BAKED PORK CHOPS WITH PROSCIUTTO AND ASIAGO CHEESE

Omit salt added to bread-crumb mixture in step 2. Before breading, place ⅛-inch-thick slice Asiago cheese (about ½ ounce) on top of each chop. Wrap each chop with thin slice prosciutto, pressing on prosciutto so that cheese and meat adhere to one another. Proceed with recipe from step 4, being careful when handling chops so that cheese and meat do not come apart during breading.

✔ WHY THIS RECIPE WORKS

When done right, baked breaded pork chops are the ultimate comfort food—tender cutlets surrounded by a crunchy coating that crackles apart with each bite. But use a packaged supermarket breading and you get a thin, sandy crust. Make your own breading and you have different problems: a soggy, patchy crust that won't stick to the meat. We combat this with a batterlike egg wash, a flavorful mix of ingredients for the crust, and time in the oven rather than on top of the stove.

USE FRESH BREAD CRUMBS Forget dusty, stale-tasting packaged crumbs. Fresh crumbs, made from good-quality sandwich bread, are a must. Pretoasting the crumbs ensures that they will be plenty crunchy by the time the pork is done. Don't skip the toasting step. If you do, you must choose between a less-than-crunchy coating and overcooked pork.

MAKE BATTERLIKE COATING Most recipes dust the chops with flour, dip them in beaten eggs, and then coat with crumbs. The result is a soft crust that has a greater propensity to peel away when baked. (Pan-frying does a better job of fusing crumbs to meat.) Our solution is to replace the beaten whole eggs with a batterlike mixture of egg whites, flour, and mustard. The fat in the yolks can make the crumbs soft, so we get rid of them. Adding flour and mustard to the egg whites turns the typically liquid-y wash into a Spackle-like paste that really sticks to the chops and holds on to the crumbs.

BAKE ON A RACK Oven-baked items need a hot oven in order to crisp the coating. But no matter how hot the oven, the side of the food resting against the baking sheet will never crisp up. Elevating the chops on a baking sheet allows any moisture shed by the chops to drip harmlessly away and permits heat to circulate around the chops, ensuring that the coated chops brown on all sides.

BRINE THE CHOPS You might be tempted to skip the brining step when preparing these chops. Don't. Center-cut chops are quite lean, and left untreated they will be very dry and chewy, even when cooked to medium (an internal temperature of 145). The salt in the brine changes the structure of the muscle proteins and allows them to hold on to more moisture when exposed to heat. (For more on brining, see concept 11.)

CRISPY PAN-FRIED PORK CHOPS
SERVES 4

We prefer natural to enhanced pork (pork that has been injected with a salt solution to increase moistness and flavor) for this recipe. Don't let the chops drain on the paper towels for longer than 30 seconds, or the heat will steam the crust and make it soggy. You can substitute ¾ cup of store-bought cornflake crumbs for the whole cornflakes. If using crumbs, omit the processing step and mix the crumbs with the cornstarch, salt, and pepper.

⅔	cup cornstarch
I	cup buttermilk
2	tablespoons Dijon mustard
I	garlic clove, minced
3	cups cornflakes
	Salt and pepper
8	(3- to 4-ounce) boneless pork chops, ½ to ¾ inch thick, trimmed
⅔	cup vegetable oil
	Lemon wedges

I. Place ⅓ cup cornstarch in shallow dish. In second shallow dish, whisk buttermilk, mustard, and garlic until combined. Process cornflakes, ½ teaspoon salt, ½ teaspoon pepper, and remaining ⅓ cup cornstarch in food processor until cornflakes are finely ground, about 10 seconds. Transfer cornflake mixture to third shallow dish.

2. Adjust oven rack to middle position and heat oven to 200 degrees. Set wire rack in rimmed baking sheet. Cut 1/16-inch-deep slits on both sides of chops, spaced ½ inch apart, in crosshatch pattern. Season chops with salt and pepper. Dredge 1 chop in cornstarch; shake off excess. Using tongs, coat with buttermilk mixture; let excess drip off. Coat with cornflake mixture; gently pat off excess. Transfer coated chop to prepared wire rack and repeat with remaining 7 chops. Let coated chops stand for 10 minutes.

3. Heat ⅓ cup oil in 12-inch nonstick skillet over medium-high heat until shimmering. Place 4 chops in skillet and cook until golden brown and crisp, 2 to 5 minutes. Carefully flip chops and continue to cook until second side is golden brown, crisp, and chops register 145 degrees, 2 to 5 minutes longer. Transfer chops to paper towel–lined plate and let drain for 30 seconds on each side. Transfer to clean wire rack set in rimmed baking sheet, then transfer to oven to keep warm. Discard oil in skillet and wipe clean with paper towels. Repeat process with remaining oil and pork chops. Serve with lemon wedges.

CRISPY PAN-FRIED PORK CHOPS WITH LATIN SPICE RUB

Combine 1½ teaspoons ground cumin, 1½ teaspoons chili powder, ¾ teaspoon ground coriander, ⅛ teaspoon ground cinnamon, and ⅛ teaspoon red pepper flakes in bowl. Omit pepper and coat chops with spice rub after seasoning with salt in step 2.

CRISPY PAN-FRIED PORK CHOPS WITH THREE-PEPPER RUB

Combine 1½ teaspoons pepper, 1½ teaspoons white pepper, ¾ teaspoon coriander, ¾ teaspoon ground cumin, ¼ teaspoon red pepper flakes, and ¼ teaspoon ground cinnamon in bowl. Omit pepper and coat chops with spice rub after seasoning with salt in step 2.

✔ WHY THIS RECIPE WORKS

A breaded coating can be just the thing to give lean, bland pork chops a flavor boost—but not when it turns gummy and flakes off the meat. Using boneless chops is fast and easy. Forgoing the traditional flour, egg wash, and bread crumbs, we use cornstarch, buttermilk, and cornflakes for a light crust with a craggy, crunchy texture.

LOSE THE BONE To keep this dish fast and easy, we forgo bone-in pork chops for boneless loin chops. Shallow-frying these thin chops takes just a few minutes per side.

GO FOR LIGHT AND CRISPY Unlike in the Crunchy Baked Pork Chops recipe (page 156), here we don't want a thick, batterlike crust. Instead, we're shooting for an ultra-light and crispy coating. To do this, we use cornstarch, which releases sticky starch as it absorbs water and forms an ultra-crisp sheath when exposed to heat and fat.

DIP IN BUTTERMILK We substitute buttermilk for an egg wash because cornstarch absorbs liquid less readily than flour and raw egg is already less available to be soaked up because it is so bound up in its protein. Buttermilk, instead, brings a nice subtle tang. Adding a dollop of mustard and a little minced garlic perks up its flavor even more.

ADD STARCH TO CORNFLAKES Traditionally, bound breading necessitates the use of bread crumbs. But with buttermilk as our wash, bread crumbs absorb too much liquid and no longer remain crunchy. After experimenting with Ritz crackers, Melba toasts, and Cream of Wheat, we settled on finely ground cornflakes. The crisp flakes, which are engineered to retain their crunch in liquid, are a popular way to add craggy texture to oven-fried chicken so it's not a surprise that they work here, too. We also add cornstarch to the cornflakes before dredging the chops. Once swollen, the starch granules work their magic, turning the flakes even crispier in the hot fat.

SCORE FOR STICKY PROTEINS Making shallow cuts in the chops' surface releases sticky meat proteins that dampen the cornstarch and help the coating adhere.

REST TO SOLIDIFY BREADING As in our Crisp Breaded Chicken Cutlets recipe (page 154), it's important to let the pork rest after breading and before cooking. Here, we let the chops sit for 10 minutes before hitting the oil. This way, the breading has a chance to solidify and will remain intact during the cooking process.

PRACTICAL SCIENCE WHERE BREADED COATINGS GO WRONG

The use of cornstarch and buttermilk helps keep the breading on a juicy pork chop.

The components of a traditional breading—flour, beaten egg, and bread crumbs—present special challenges when applied to juicy pork chops. Here's how we ensured a crust that stays put and packs plenty of crunch in our Crispy Pan-Fried Pork Chops (page 157).

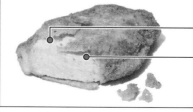

	PROBLEM	SOLUTION
	Gummy patches under the coating	We swap flour—the usual breading base coat—for cornstarch.
	Breading pulls away	Instead of the typical egg wash, which puffs up when cooked and contributes to a heavier coating that can pull away from the meat, we use buttermilk as the second layer. It makes for a lighter shell that clings nicely to the chops.

PORK SCHNITZEL
SERVES 4

The 2 cups of oil called for in this recipe may seem like a lot, but this amount is necessary to achieve a wrinkled texture on the finished cutlets. To ensure ample cooking space, a large Dutch oven is essential. If you don't have an instant-read thermometer to gauge the oil's temperature, place a fresh (not dry) bread cube in the oil and start heating; when the bread is deep golden brown, the oil is ready. The hard-cooked egg, capers, parsley, and lemon are the traditional garnish, although the egg can be omitted.

PORK

- 7   slices hearty white sandwich bread, crusts removed, cut into ¾-inch cubes
- ½   cup all-purpose flour
- 2   large eggs
- 1   tablespoon plus 2 cups vegetable oil
- 1   (1¼-pound) pork tenderloin, trimmed and cut on angle into 4 equal pieces
       Salt and pepper

GARNISHES

-      Lemon wedges
- 2   tablespoons minced fresh parsley
- 2   tablespoons capers, rinsed
- 1   Hard-Cooked Egg (page 21), yolk and white separated and passed separately through fine-mesh strainer (optional)

1. Place bread cubes on large plate. Microwave on high power for 4 minutes, stirring well halfway through cooking. Microwave on medium power until bread is dry and few pieces start to lightly brown, 3 to 5 minutes longer, stirring every minute. Process dry bread in food processor to very fine crumbs, about 45 seconds. Transfer bread crumbs to shallow dish (you should have about 1¼ cups crumbs). Spread flour in second shallow dish. Beat eggs with 1 tablespoon oil in third shallow dish.

2. Working with 1 piece at a time, place pork, with 1 cut side down, between 2 sheets of parchment paper or plastic wrap and pound to even thickness between ⅛ and ¼ inch. Pat cutlets dry with paper towels and season with salt and pepper. Working with 1 cutlet at a time, dredge cutlets thoroughly in flour, shaking off excess, then coat with egg mixture, allowing excess to drip back into dish to ensure very thin coating, and coat evenly with bread crumbs, pressing on crumbs to adhere. Place breaded cutlets in single layer on wire rack set on baking sheet; let coating dry for 5 minutes.

3. Heat remaining 2 cups oil in large Dutch oven over medium-high heat until it registers 375 degrees. Lay 2 cutlets, without overlapping, in pan and cook, shaking pan continuously and gently, until cutlets are wrinkled and light golden brown on both sides, 1 to 2 minutes per side. Transfer cutlets to paper towel–lined plate and flip cutlets several times to blot excess oil. Repeat with remaining cutlets. Serve with garnishes.

✔ WHY THIS RECIPE WORKS

Pork schnitzel is often a soggy, greasy affair. But when done right, it features an irresistible combination of light bread-crumb coating and tender, juicy meat. Unlike in other recipes in this concept, here we want our breaded coating to be puffy. For remarkably tender texture and mild flavor, we use pounded medallions of pork tenderloin, homemade bread crumbs, and some arm strength.

CHOICE CUTS   Most schnitzel recipes call for boneless pork chops, pounded thin. However, pork chops have very compact muscle fibers, which means that pounding them into thin cutlets is laborious. It also means that once cooked, the pork has a dry, mealy texture. We use pork tenderloin instead. Pounded thin and fried, cutlets made from the tenderloin are remarkably tender with a mild flavor similar to veal.

MICROWAVE BREAD CRUMBS   Using raw homemade bread crumbs can result in a pork cutlet that is overcooked before the crumbs are crisp, with a too coarsely textured crust. We found that microwaving the bread cubes first on high power, then medium, and giving them a whirl in the food processor produces super-fine, dry bread crumbs that fry up extra-crisp.

USE ARM POWER   Wiener schnitzel's signature attribute is a wrinkled, puffy exterior. When the pan is shaken, gently but continuously, the ample hot oil will heat the eggs in the coating very quickly, solidifying the proteins, creating a barrier that captures steam and begins to puff. The shaking sends the hot oil over the top of the cutlets, speeding up the setting process and enhancing the puff.

Good Frying Is All About Oil Temperature

You can get French fries pretty much anywhere: at fast-food chains, served with ketchup squeezed from a plastic pouch; at baseball stadiums, doused with chili and cheese; at high-end bistros, sprinkled with truffle oil and sea salt. They're one of America's favorite foods. So why do we never make them at home? Many of us avoid frying because of the grease. But we shouldn't be so skittish. When done right, frying isn't difficult. It all comes down to the temperature of the oil.

WHAT HAPPENS WHEN A POTATO HITS HOT OIL?

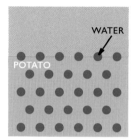

RAW *Before hitting the oil, the potato holds moisture evenly spaced within.*

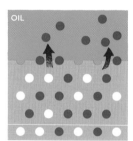

FRYING *While frying in hot oil, the moisture turns to steam and exits, leaving holes in its wake.*

AFTER *The craters on the surface fill with oil, helping to create a crisp brown crust. The amount of oil absorbed is directly proportional to the amount of water lost.*

HOW THE SCIENCE WORKS

When we fry food, it is generally in oil held between 325 and 375 degrees. This way when we place potatoes, chicken, or shrimp in the pot, their surface moisture immediately turns to steam. (We've all seen the bubbles produced as soon as we place food into hot fat. The oil isn't boiling … that's moisture escaping.)

Though it seems counterintuitive, frying is a dry-heat cooking method. As the steam flees the frying food, leaving tiny craters in its wake, a small amount of oil moves in to take its place. And as the food cooks, its outermost coating of starch (because we generally fry starchy food, or nonstarchy food battered in starch) dries out, becoming porous and crispy, with lots of oil clinging to the newly formed crust.

The high temperature is important here: If the oil isn't hot enough, the moisture will not turn to steam, the outer edge will not dry out, and the trademark brown and crispy crust will not form. After all, flavor-producing browning reactions, such as caramelization (concept 27) and the Maillard reaction (concept 2), do not take place rapidly until temperatures of at least 300 degrees. And if the crisp crust containing sufficient amounts of hot oil does not materialize, there is nothing keeping the moisture in the food being fried from migrating to the outer edges, and the result is a limp and soggy

end product. (This is why we often fry in batches. Dumping large amounts of food into hot oil significantly lowers the temperature of the oil and guarantees soggy fries.)

A crisp crust is not only more flavorful, but it will help prevent fried food from tasting greasy. Believe it or not, the oil temperature while frying is only part of the reason food can taste greasy. In fact, the hotter the oil, the greater the moisture loss and the amount of oil absorbed (see "Giving Fat the Cold Shoulder," page 165). But oil absorption during frying is really a secondary cause of greasiness in fried food. It turns out that most fried foods absorb oil after they are cooked, when oil on the surface is able to penetrate the crust. A nice crisp crust doesn't prevent a potato from absorbing oil, but it does prevent it from growing limp and seeming greasy.

Keep in mind that it's possible for oil to get too hot. When oil temperature climbs above 400 degrees, the exterior of the food can burn before the interior is cooked through. Even if the interior does cook through, excessive heat can cause excessive moisture loss and the food becomes tough. Perhaps the biggest impact of excess heat is on the quality of the oil. Before we take a look at this phenomenon, let's turn to the basic science of fats and oils.

Although the terms are often used interchangeably, by definition, a fat is solid at room temperature while an oil is liquid. Fresh frying oil is composed of more than 98 percent triglycerides, which are made of three fatty acids chemically bonded to a molecule of glycerol. Triglycerides that are high in saturated fatty acids, such as those in meat, are solid at room temperature, while those that are high in unsaturated fatty acids, such as from plants, are liquids. When fats and oils are heated, and then put in contact with food, two things can happen: The triglycerides can react with water from the food to form additional free fatty acids and glycerol, and the unsaturated fatty acids can be oxidized by the air. Both of these reactions limit the useful lifetime of frying oil by causing it to smoke at a lower and lower temperature. This smoke point, or temperature at which the oil begins to emit unwelcome smoke, changes from oil to oil, depending on how quickly it breaks down to free fatty acids (see "Smoke Points of Fats and Oils," page 163). The amount of these free fatty acids in the oil is an indication of the suitability of the oil for high-temperature frying—or, where its smoke point falls. Every oil will eventually start to smoke during normal use. And the more you use an oil, the lower the smoke point becomes.

So now we know about the importance of oil temperature. But where to begin in the kitchen? French fries are always a good bet.

TEST KITCHEN EXPERIMENT

To determine the ideal temperature of the oil in which to cook French fries, we ran the following experiment: We cut russet potatoes into ¼-inch-thick fries and fried batches of them in oil at 275 degrees, 325 degrees, and 400 degrees.

THE RESULTS

There were some significant differences. First off, cooking times varied widely. While the 400-degree fries were torched after just a few minutes in the hot oil, the ones fried at 275 degrees remained blond after a full 10 minutes in the pot. The fries cooked at 325 degrees landed in the middle, developing a golden brown crust in about six minutes. Exterior appearance aside, the real story lay on the inside of the fries. After letting the fries cool for a minute, we sliced them in half in the name of autopsy. Once again, the fries cooked at 325 degrees were perfect, featuring a core of fluffy, just-cooked potato surrounded by a substantial, crispy crust. The 275-degree sample was moist throughout (and that included the super-soggy crust), while the fries from the 400-degree pot had a small ring of overcooked potato surrounding a completely raw center.

THE TAKEAWAY

The temperature of the oil makes a big difference. Our French fries cooked at 400 degrees browned far too quickly, verging on burnt before the inside of the potato could cook at all. Our French fries cooked at 275 degrees, on the other hand, cooked through completely, but a crust was never able to form, and they grew limp and floppy. The magic temperature is 325 degrees: The heat is high enough to turn the water in the potato immediately to steam, to dry out the outer edge, and to form a brown, crispy crust, all the while cooking the potato for a moist and creamy center, too. Be sure to monitor the temperature of your oil!

OIL TEMPERATURE AND THE COLOR OF FRENCH FRIES

TOO LIGHT
The crust is pale when cooked in 275-degree oil.

PERFECT
The magic number for a crisp crust is 325 degrees.

TOO BROWN
Fries cook too fast (almost burnt) at 400 degrees.

When we fry potatoes, we're looking for crispy, brown crusts and tender, moist interiors. We achieve this by using hot (but not too hot) oil and techniques developed to control potato starch. Taking our knowledge of the science of frying to the next level, we even explore a counterintuitive method and begin some of our French fries in cold oil. More information on the theories behind another popular fried food—chicken—can be found in concept 13.

CLASSIC FRENCH FRIES
SERVES 4

Flavoring the oil with a few tablespoons of bacon fat gives the fries a mild, meaty flavor, but omitting it will not affect the final texture of the fries. The oil will bubble up when you add the fries, so be sure you leave at least 3 inches of room between the oil and the top of your pot. We prefer peanut oil for frying, but vegetable oil can be substituted. You will need at least a 7-quart Dutch oven for this recipe.

2½	pounds russet potatoes, peeled and cut lengthwise into ¼-inch-thick fries
2	tablespoons cornstarch
3	quarts peanut oil
¼	cup bacon fat, strained (optional)
	Kosher salt

1. Rinse cut potatoes in large bowl under cold running water until water turns clear. Cover with cold water and refrigerate for 30 minutes or up to 12 hours.

2. Pour off water, spread potatoes onto kitchen towels, and thoroughly dry. Transfer potatoes to large bowl and toss with cornstarch until evenly coated. Transfer potatoes to wire rack set in rimmed baking sheet and let rest until fine white coating forms, about 20 minutes.

3. Meanwhile, heat peanut oil and bacon fat, if using, in Dutch oven over medium heat to 325 degrees. Set wire rack in rimmed baking sheet, line rack with triple layer of paper towels, and set aside.

4. Add half of potatoes, handful at a time, to hot oil and increase heat to high. Fry, stirring with wire skimmer or slotted spoon, until potatoes start to turn from white to blond, 4 to 5 minutes. (Oil temperature will drop about 75 degrees during this frying.) Using skimmer or slotted spoon, transfer fries to prepared wire rack. Return oil to 325 degrees and repeat with remaining potatoes. Let fries cool for at least 10 minutes.

5. Increase heat under Dutch oven to high and heat oil to 350 degrees. Set second wire rack in second rimmed baking sheet and line with triple layer of paper towels. Add half of fries, handful at a time, to hot oil and fry until golden brown and puffed, 2 to 3 minutes; transfer to prepared wire rack. Return oil to 350 degrees and repeat with remaining fries. Season fries with salt to taste, and serve immediately.

✓ WHY THIS RECIPE WORKS

Homemade French fries—with their crisp exteriors, airy interiors, and earthy, sweet flavor—are a revelation. When you start with fresh potatoes and cook them in batches in hot peanut oil, the results are hard to beat. We find that coating the potatoes with a little cornstarch creates a shatteringly crisp crust.

PRACTICAL SCIENCE WHEN IS FRYER OIL AT ITS BEST?

Save a cup of used oil to mix with fresh oil when frying. The fried food will be crisper and more evenly golden.

In deep-frying, the first batch is never the best. Food writer Russ Parsons explains in *How to Read a French Fry* that fry oil has five stages: break-in (too fresh to fry well), fresh, optimum, degrading (on the way to spoiling), and runaway (dark, smelly, and prone to smoking). Food fried in optimum oil is golden and crisp. Break-in and fresh oil yield paler, less crisp food. Degrading and runaway oil produce dark, greasy food with rancid odors.

Why? Oil that is too fresh can't penetrate the barrier of moisture that surrounds food as it fries. Over time, as the oil continues to be exposed to heat, it breaks down, producing slippery, soaplike compounds that can penetrate the water barrier. This increased contact between oil and food promotes browning and crispness. (During repeated use, the level of free fatty acid increases from about 0.03 to 0.05 percent in fresh oil to 8 to 10 percent in runaway oil.)

With this in mind, we wondered if we could create optimum oil by mixing used and new. We fried shrimp, fish, and French fries in fresh oil and in a mixture of fresh oil and oil that had been used once to make French fries (and then strained through a coffee filter to remove any solids). We found that food fried in the mix of new and used oil was crisper and more uniformly golden than food fried in fresh oil.

So save a cup or two of used oil to mix with fresh the next time you fry (we found that a ratio of 1 cup of used oil to 5 cups of fresh oil worked best). Once the oil has cooled, filter it through a strainer lined with a few layers of cheesecloth or paper coffee filters and place it in the refrigerator (or freezer; see "Storing Used Frying Oil," page 164) in an airtight container. Stored in this fashion, the oil should be good for two or three uses. But it's important to remember that frying oil can transfer flavors from food to food. As a rule, discard oil in which fish was fried; multiple batches of chicken or potatoes may be cooked in the same oil, but oil used for doughnuts should only be used for doughnuts. The oil should also be kept clean when frying; skim away any detritus and keep salt and/or water out of the oil. And, last, pay keen attention to oil temperature: If the oil reached the smoke point during frying it will impart an off-flavor to foods, so don't try to reuse it.

START WITH RUSSETS Obviously, a good French fry requires the right potato. Should it be starchy or waxy? (For more on potatoes, see concept 25.) We tested two of the most popular waxy (low-starch/high-moisture) potatoes, and neither was even close to ideal, both being too watery. During the frying, water evaporated inside the potato, leaving hollows that would fill with oil, so the finished fries were greasy. Next we tested the starchy potato most readily available nationwide, the russet. This potato turned out to be ideal. Its high-starch/low-moisture levels allow the starch granules on the outer layers of the potato to swell and explode, releasing a starch molecule called amylose that later turns into an excellent crust. It fries up with all the qualities that we were looking for.

RINSE WELL Because these are such starchy potatoes, it is important to rinse off the surface after you cut the potato into fries. (For more on controlling starches in potatoes, see concept 26.) To do this, simply put the cut fries in a bowl, place the bowl in the sink, and run cold water into it, swirling with your fingers until the water runs clear. This might seem like an unimportant step, but it makes a real difference. When potatoes are fried by the classical method, any excess sugars left on the surface of the potatoes will brown too quickly during the first frying stage before the potatoes can be fried to a crispy crust in the second stage. Rinsing removes the sugars.

HOT POTATO, COLD POTATO Refrigerating the potatoes in a bowl of ice water for at least 30 minutes means that when the potatoes first enter the hot oil, they are nearly frozen. This allows a slow, thorough cooking of the inner potato pulp and a finished batch of fries with crispier crusts and great coloration.

PEEL AND CUT Our preference is to peel potatoes for French fries. The skin keeps the potato from forming those little airy blisters that we love. Peeling the potato also allows home cooks to see—and remove, if they want—any imperfections. The best way to uniformly cut fries is to start by trimming a thin slice from each side of the potato. Once the potato is "squared," you can slice it into ¼-inch planks and then cut each plank into ¼-inch fries.

USE CORNSTARCH As soon as we discovered that many fast-food French fries are covered in a thin layer of starch-based coating before they are fried, we decided to try it ourselves. The result? After testing cornstarch, potato starch, and arrowroot, we saw an immediate improvement in the crispiness of our fries. It turns out that the added starch is absorbing some of the surface moisture on the potatoes to form a gel-like coating. This coating releases the starch molecule amylose that turns into a shatteringly crisp crust when heated in oil. Our preference is cornstarch. Just 2 tablespoons provides a flavorless coating that guarantees crisp fries.

PICK YOUR FAT What is the right fat for making perfect French fries? To find out, we experimented with lard, vegetable shortening, canola oil, corn oil, and peanut oil. Lard and shortening make great fries, but we figured that many cooks won't want to use these saturated fat–laden products. We moved on to canola oil, the ballyhooed oil of the '90s, now used in a blend by McDonald's, which produces 9 million pounds of finished fries a day. But we were unhappy with the results: bland, almost watery fries. Corn oil was the most forgiving oil in the test kitchen. But we found that a potato fried in peanut oil is light, and the flavor is rich but not dense. The earthy flavor of the potato is there but is not overbearing. There was still something missing, though: the high flavor note, which is supplied by the animal fat in lard. We tried a dollop of strained bacon grease in peanut oil, about 1 generous tablespoon per quart of oil. The meaty flavor came through, but without its nasty baggage. At last, an equivalent to lard.

FRY TWICE First, we par-fry the potatoes at a relatively low temperature to release their rich and earthy flavor. The potatoes are then quick-fried at a higher temperature until nicely browned. The garden-variety cookbook recipe calls for par-frying at 350 degrees and final frying at 375 to 400 degrees. But we found these temperatures to be far too aggressive. We prefer an initial frying at 325 degrees, with the final frying at 350 degrees. Lower temperatures allow for easier monitoring; with higher temperatures, the fries can get away from the cook.

PRACTICAL SCIENCE
SMOKE POINTS OF FATS AND OILS

Smoke points vary in different fats and oils.

FATS & OILS	SMOKE POINT (DEGREES FAHRENHEIT)*
Coconut Oil	385
Extra-Virgin Olive Oil**	410
Peanut Oil	446
Corn Oil	455
Canola Oil	457
Lard	464

Data from the Institute of Shortening and Edible Oils

* The smoke point of all fats and oils varies from sample to sample depending on how it has been refined and processed.

** Data from the California Olive Oil Council. The smoke point of filtered olive oils can be higher, though all vary widely by source.

REST BETWEEN BATCHES After 10 minutes' rest between the first and second fry, the starches on the exterior of the blanched fries form a thin film. This helps the potatoes to become crisp once they are fried again.

USE A SKIMMER If you peek into a restaurant kitchen, you'll see chefs working over steaming stockpots or vats of bubbling oil using shallow, woven wire baskets on long handles to retrieve blanched vegetables, French fries, and thin-skinned wontons. Suffice it to say that most chefs wouldn't part with their "spiders," as they are called, which effortlessly scoop out multiple handfuls of food with one swoop and leave all the hot cooking oil, water, or broth behind. We highly recommend using one here.

EASIER FRENCH FRIES
SERVES 3 TO 4

Flavoring the oil with a few tablespoons of bacon fat gives the fries a mild, meaty flavor, but omitting it will not affect the final texture of the fries. We prefer peanut oil for frying, but vegetable oil can be substituted. This recipe will not work with sweet potatoes or russets. Serve with ketchup or a dipping sauce (recipes follow), if desired. You will need at least a 6-quart Dutch oven for this recipe.

2½	pounds Yukon Gold potatoes, dried, sides squared off, and cut lengthwise into ¼-inch-thick fries
6	cups peanut oil
¼	cup bacon fat, strained (optional)
	Kosher salt

1. Set wire rack in rimmed baking sheet, line rack with triple layer of paper towels, and set aside. Combine potatoes, oil, and bacon fat, if using, in Dutch oven. Cook over high heat until oil has reached rolling boil, about 5 minutes. Continue to cook, without stirring, until potatoes are limp but exteriors are beginning to firm, about 15 minutes.

2. Using tongs, stir potatoes, gently scraping up any that stick, and continue to cook, stirring occasionally, until golden and crisp, 5 to 10 minutes longer. Using skimmer or slotted spoon, transfer fries to prepared wire rack. Season with salt to taste, and serve immediately.

BELGIAN-STYLE DIPPING SAUCE
MAKES ABOUT ½ CUP, ENOUGH FOR 1 RECIPE
EASIER FRENCH FRIES

In Belgium, mayonnaise-based dipping sauces for fries are standard. Hot sauce gives this dipping sauce a bit of a kick.

5	tablespoons mayonnaise
3	tablespoons ketchup
1	garlic clove, minced
½–¾	teaspoon hot sauce
¼	teaspoon salt

Whisk all ingredients together in small bowl.

CHIVE AND BLACK PEPPER DIPPING SAUCE
MAKES ABOUT ½ CUP, ENOUGH FOR 1 RECIPE
EASIER FRENCH FRIES

5	tablespoons mayonnaise
3	tablespoons sour cream
2	tablespoons minced fresh chives
1½	teaspoons lemon juice
¼	teaspoon salt
¼	teaspoon pepper

Whisk all ingredients together in small bowl.

PRACTICAL SCIENCE STORING USED FRYING OIL

Keep used frying oil in the freezer. The cold temperature slows oxidation and helps prevent rancidity.

What is the best way to store used frying oil so that it doesn't taste fishy and stale when reused? A cool, dark cupboard is fine for the short term, since exposure to air and light hastens oil's rate of oxidative rancidification and the creation of off-flavors and odors. But for long-term storage (beyond one month), the cooler the storage temperature the better. We fried chicken in vegetable oil and then divided the oil (strained first) among three containers and stored them in various locations: in a cool, dark cupboard; in the refrigerator; and in the freezer. Two months later, we sautéed chunks of white bread in each sample and took a taste. Sure enough, the oil from the cupboard had turned fishy and unpleasant and the refrigerated sample only somewhat less so, while the oil kept in the freezer tasted remarkably clean. Why? Though an absence of light is important, very cold temperatures are the most effective at slowing oxidation and the production of peroxides, which are the source of rancid oil's unpleasant taste and smell. That's why storing oil in the super-cold, dark freezer is your best bet for keeping it fresh.

✔ WHY THIS RECIPE WORKS

When we wanted a French fry recipe with half the oil and no double-frying, we tried submerging the potatoes in cold oil before frying them over high heat until browned. With lower-starch potatoes like Yukon Golds, the result was a crisp exterior and a creamy interior.

START COLD To find a cooking method that would mimic the results of double-fried French fries, we were inspired by food writer Jeffrey Steingarten, who was in turn inspired by a method attributed to Michelin-starred French über-chef Joël Robuchon. In this recipe, Robuchon skips rinsing and soaking, and instead submerges potatoes in room-temperature, or "cold," oil and fries them over high heat until browned. Surprisingly, it works. How? This method gives the potato interior an opportunity to soften and cook through before the exterior needs to start crisping. In effect, the potatoes are parcooking as the oil gradually heats up, mimicking the first phase of double-frying. Once the oil is hot, the exterior of the potatoes will crisp and brown, mimicking the second phase of double-frying.

USE YUKON GOLDS When we made these fries with russet potatoes, which we prefer in our Classic French Fries (page 162), we found our finished results to be slightly tough. We thought this might be because of the russets' starchiness. Starchiness is an asset for the typical double-fry method—the starch granules from the outermost layers of the potato swell, burst, and release amylose that solidifies into a crisp crust. However, with a longer cooking time, too many starch granules were bursting, leading to an overly thick crust that was more leathery than crisp. If starchy potatoes were the problem, why not start with a less starchy spud? We sliced up a couple of pounds of Yukon Golds, which also have more water than russets, and proceeded with our working recipe. And these worked well, really well. These Easier French Fries made with Yukon Golds have a crisp exterior—well within the ballpark of double-fried fries—with none of the toughness of russets, and a creamy interior. Clearly, the moister, less starchy composition of the Yukon Golds can better withstand the long cooking time of this approach. Plus, Yukon Golds have such a thin skin that they can be used unpeeled, making the recipe even easier.

DON'T RINSE For this recipe it's not necessary to rinse the potatoes. But why? For one, we use a lower-starch potato so there will be less sugars (which come from the breakdown of starch) on the surface to brown, and the lower frying temperatures also slow down browning more than they do crisping, making sure our fries don't over-brown before they are fully cooked.

DON'T STIR/STIR In the conventional deep-fry approach, sticking can be addressed by stirring the potatoes throughout cooking, but with our method the Yukons (which soften significantly during the early part of cooking) are so fragile that any disturbance causes them to break apart. We found that not touching the spuds for 20 minutes after putting them in the pot will allow enough of a crust to form so that we can then stir them with no ill effect. We also determined that thinner ¼-inch fries are less likely to stick (and we like their greater ratio of crispy crust to creamy interior).

PRACTICAL SCIENCE
GIVING FAT THE COLD SHOULDER

Surprisingly, starting out in cold oil does not make a greasier fry.

Our easier approach to cooking French fries does not preheat the oil and calls for one prolonged frying instead of the quicker double-dip in hot oil used in the classic method. But does the lengthy exposure to oil lead to a greasier fry?

We prepared two batches of fries using Yukon Gold potatoes, our preferred spud for the cold-start method. We cooked one batch the conventional way, heating 3 quarts of peanut oil to 325 degrees and frying 2½ pounds of potatoes until just beginning to color, removing them, increasing the oil temperature to 350 degrees, then returning the potatoes to the pot to fry until golden brown. Total exposure to oil: less than 10 minutes. The second batch we cooked according to our working method, submerging 2½ pounds of spuds in 6 cups of cold oil and cooking over high heat for about 25 minutes, with the oil temperature never rising above 280 degrees. We then sent samples from each batch to an independent lab to analyze the fat content.

Our cold-start spuds contained about one-third less fat than spuds deep-fried twice the conventional way: 13 versus 20 percent.

Fries absorb oil two ways. As the potatoes cook, they lose moisture near their surface, which is replaced by oil. Then, as they cool after being removed from the hot grease, oil from their exterior gets pulled in. Because our cold-start method cooks the fries more gently, less moisture is lost (but enough so the fries stay crisp) and less oil is absorbed during frying. Plus, this approach exposes the spuds to just one cool-down, versus the two cooling-off periods of the classic method, so less oil gets absorbed after cooking as well.

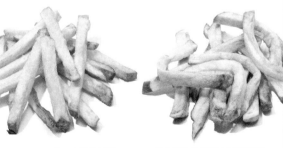

COLD OIL METHOD	DOUBLE-FRY METHOD
13% fat	*20% fat*

Shrimp tempura should be light and crisp. But with a tricky batter and quick cooking time, a perfect first (or second, or third) batch can be elusive. We use hot oil (even hotter than the oil we use for our Classic French Fries, page 162) and a surprising technique for our batter to produce great tempura on the first (and every) try.

SHRIMP TEMPURA
SERVES 4

Do not omit the vodka; it is critical for a crisp coating. You will need at least a 7-quart Dutch oven. Be sure to begin mixing the batter when the oil reaches 385 degrees (the final temperature should be 400 degrees). It is important to maintain a high oil temperature throughout cooking. Jumbo (16 to 20) or extra-large (21 to 25) shrimp may be substituted. Fry smaller shrimp in three batches, reducing the cooking time to 1 ½ to 2 minutes per batch. When cooking shrimp for tempura, the underside tends to shrink more than the top, causing the shrimp to curl tightly and the batter to clump. To prevent this, we make two shallow cuts on the shrimp's underside.

3	quarts vegetable oil
1 ½	pounds colossal shrimp (8 to 12 per pound), peeled and deveined, tails left on
1 ½	cups all-purpose flour
½	cup cornstarch
1	cup vodka
1	large egg
1	cup seltzer water
	Kosher salt
1	recipe dipping sauce (recipes follow)

1. Adjust oven rack to upper-middle position and heat oven to 200 degrees. Set wire rack in rimmed baking sheet. Heat oil in Dutch oven over medium-low heat to 385 degrees.

2. While oil heats, make 2 shallow cuts about ¼ inch deep and 1 inch apart on underside of each shrimp. Whisk flour and cornstarch together in large bowl. Whisk vodka and egg together in second large bowl. Whisk seltzer water into egg mixture.

3. When oil reaches 385 degrees, pour liquid mixture into bowl with flour mixture and whisk gently until just combined (it is OK if small lumps remain). Submerge half of shrimp in batter. Using tongs, remove shrimp from batter 1 at a time, allowing excess batter to drip off, and carefully place in oil (temperature should now be at 400 degrees). Fry, stirring with chopstick or wooden skewer to prevent sticking, until light brown, 2 to 3 minutes. Using slotted spoon, transfer shrimp to paper

towel–lined plate and sprinkle with salt. Once paper towels absorb excess oil, place shrimp on prepared wire rack and place in oven.

4. Return oil to 400 degrees, about 4 minutes, and repeat with remaining shrimp. Serve immediately with dipping sauce.

PRACTICAL SCIENCE
BOOZE FOR A BETTER BATTER

> The addition of vodka keeps gluten formation in check.

The batter for shrimp tempura is devilishly hard to get right, easily turning thick and heavy if you overmix even slightly or let it sit too long. Even when a first batch came out light and crisp, subsequent batches were progressively thicker and greasier. In the past, we've guaranteed success with another finicky foodstuff—pie crust (see concept 44)—by replacing some of the water with vodka. Would the same swap in tempura batter lead to a coating immune to overmixing and resting?

We fried two batches of shrimp in two different batters. The first batter contained one egg, 1 ½ cups of flour, ½ cup of cornstarch, and 2 cups of seltzer water. In the second, we replaced 1 cup of the seltzer water with 1 cup of vodka.

The vodka-batter shrimp was identical from the first batch to the second, turning out light and crisp each time. The shrimp dipped in the batter without vodka came out heavier and greasier in the second batch. When water and flour are mixed, the proteins in the flour form gluten, which provides structure—but it takes just a few too many stirs (or minutes of sitting) to develop too much gluten. Because vodka is about 60 percent water and 40 percent alcohol (which does not combine with protein to form gluten), it makes the batter fluid and keeps gluten formation in check no matter how much you stir or allow it to sit.

JUST RIGHT
A surprise ingredient and the right technique keep our coating crisp and airy.

TOO PUFFY
Whisking whipped egg white into the batter creates a balloonlike coating.

TOO THICK
Overmixed batter fries into a thick, breadlike coating.

TOO THIN
Undermixed batter remains thin, contributing to overcooked shrimp.

GINGER-SOY DIPPING SAUCE

MAKES ABOUT ¾ CUP, ENOUGH FOR
1 RECIPE SHRIMP TEMPURA

¼   cup soy sauce
3   tablespoons mirin
1   teaspoon sugar
1   teaspoon toasted sesame oil
1   scallion, sliced thin
2   teaspoons grated fresh ginger
1   garlic clove, minced

Whisk all ingredients together in medium bowl.

CHILE AÏOLI DIPPING SAUCE

MAKES ABOUT ¾ CUP, ENOUGH FOR
1 RECIPE SHRIMP TEMPURA

Sriracha, an Asian chili sauce made with garlic and chiles, adds both heat and flavor to this sauce.

½   cup mayonnaise
2   tablespoons Sriracha sauce
2   tablespoons lime juice
1   tablespoon grated fresh ginger
¼   teaspoon soy sauce

Whisk all ingredients together in medium bowl.

TEPPANYAKI MUSTARD DIPPING SAUCE

MAKES ABOUT ¾ CUP, ENOUGH FOR
1 RECIPE SHRIMP TEMPURA

This dipping sauce gets its zesty bite from mustard, ginger, and horseradish.

3   tablespoons mayonnaise
2   tablespoons Dijon mustard
2   teaspoons lime juice
2   teaspoons prepared horseradish
2   teaspoons soy sauce
1   teaspoon grated fresh ginger

Whisk all ingredients together in medium bowl.

✔ WHY THIS RECIPE WORKS

Many fried foods, including shrimp tempura, are coated with a starchy batter (usually made with flour) and then fried. When done right, the shrimp is perfectly cooked and tender, while the batter fries to a crisp, light shell. But undermix tempura batter by a hair and it will be too thin and won't provide enough of a barrier for the shrimp against the hot oil. Overmix and you wind up with a coating so thick it would be more at home on a corn dog. We wanted a foolproof recipe that landed us between the extremes. Using hot oil and a surprising batter recipe, which includes vodka, did the trick. These shrimp emerge from the oil light and crisp, batch after batch.

STRAIGHTEN THOSE SHRIMP When cooking shrimp for tempura, the underside tends to shrink more than the top, causing the shrimp to curl tightly and the batter to clump up and cook unevenly inside the curl. Here's a way to alleviate the problem: After peeling and deveining a shrimp, hold it on its back on the cutting board. Using the tip of a paring knife, make two ¼-inch-deep incisions on the underside about 1 inch apart.

COMBINE FLOUR AND CORNSTARCH In our first attempts at this batter we used only flour, which forms gluten when mixed with water, giving structure to the coating. But there is a thin line between just enough and too much gluten here, and after the first batch of frying the flour batter can become thick and doughy. A batter made solely with cornstarch, which does not form gluten, is tough as Styrofoam. Mixing the two starches together, though, greatly improves the structure of the batter.

USE SELTZER AND VODKA When we use ice water in a tempura batter, it slows down the development of gluten—until it warms up. Searching for an alternative, we swapped the water for effervescent seltzer water, hoping that its multitude of bubbles would make our batter even more delicate and lacy. It produced the desired effect, and then some. As it turns out, seltzer, with a pH of 4, is slightly more acidic than regular tap water, enough to slow down gluten development (a pH of 5 to 6 is optimal for gluten formation). Even with this, though, the batter was easy to overmix and thickened too much as it sat. The solution? Vodka. While water contributes to gluten, alcohol doesn't. (For more on the phenomenon, see concept 44.) A mixture of half vodka and half seltzer slows the gluten development and helps to create the perfect crust.

MAKE BATTER AT LAST MINUTE Because gluten develops even without stirring, a batter left sitting will thicken with every second that passes. Make the batter at the very last minute, reducing the time it sits and ensuring the lightest, laciest tempura possible.

Fat Makes Eggs Tender

Scrambled eggs should be a dreamy mound of big, soft, wobbling curds. They should be cooked enough to hold their shape when cut but soft enough to eat with a spoon. An omelet must be firm enough to roll or fold, but the eggs should still be tender and soft. The reality is that all too often both dishes turn out dry, tough, or rubbery. Overcooking is one culprit, but the eggs need some help—in the form of fat—to ensure that they remain soft and tender, even when fully set.

HOW THE SCIENCE WORKS

We call them scrambled eggs, no doubt because of the mixing that occurs before the eggs are cooked, but this recipe relies on a process called coagulation and could rightly be called "coagulated eggs." Cooking causes the egg proteins to denature (unfold) and form a latticed gel. As a result, eggs transition from a liquid to a semisolid you can pick up with a fork. Coagulation also explains how eggs thicken custards, puddings, and sauces.

To understand what's really happening, you have to start with the notion that eggs actually contain distinct elements—the whites and the yolks—that behave quite differently. The whites, which represent about two-thirds of the total volume in an egg, are 88 percent water, 11 percent protein, and 1 percent minerals and carbohydrates. The yolks are 50 percent water, 34 percent lipids (fats and related elements), and 16 percent protein.

When eggs are heated, the water they contain turns to steam. At the same time, the protein strands are unfolding, sticking to each other, and eventually forming a latticed network. Ideally, these proteins form a loose network that's capable of holding on to the water in the eggs, which will make the cooked eggs tender and fluffy. However, with continued cooking, these cross-linked proteins form very tight bonds that squeeze out too much liquid, and the end result is tough, dry eggs.

Most scrambled egg recipes call for some sort of dairy, usually milk. The fat in the milk coats the proteins and slows down the coagulation process. The water in the dairy provides additional moisture, which helps keep scrambled eggs tender. This added liquid also produces more steam, which translates into fluffier, lighter scrambled eggs.

The science of omelets is similar but the technique used to prevent overcoagulation is different. While scrambled eggs should be fluffy, an omelet is more compact (so it can be rolled or folded). Thus, there's no need for additional liquid or steam. In fact, adding dairy to eggs causes problems when making an omelet—the extra liquid prolongs the cooking time and toughens the omelet. We turned to small cubes of butter, which contains lots of fat and very little liquid. The fat in the butter coats the egg proteins and produces an omelet that is set but still tender. Frozen butter works even better because it doesn't melt as quickly and disperses more evenly throughout the egg.

HOW PROTEINS CHANGE WHEN EGGS COOK

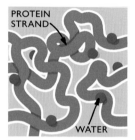

RAW *In raw eggs, globular protein strands are tangled and interspersed with water molecules.*

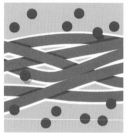

COOKED WITHOUT FAT *Cooking causes the protein strands to align and bond together. Continued cooking can cause the strong bonds to squeeze out the water molecules.*

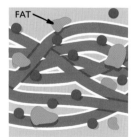

COOKED WITH FAT *Fat slows down this process, keeping eggs fluffy and moist.*

TEST KITCHEN EXPERIMENT

To demonstrate the effect of fat on eggs, we cooked up a batch of our Perfect French Omelet recipe (page 173), which uses two whole eggs, one yolk, and a half tablespoon of cubed frozen butter to make each omelet. We prepared two omelets using this recipe, so that we would have one omelet for tasting and one omelet for testing.

We also prepared the recipe without the frozen butter, again making one omelet for tasting and one for testing. All omelets were prepared as follows: We preheated an 8-inch skillet over low heat for 10 minutes, added the eggs, increased the heat to medium-high, and stirred with chopsticks until small curds formed. Off the heat, we smoothed the eggs into an even layer, covered the skillet, and allowed residual heat to finish the cooking. For both the omelets with and without butter, we rolled the omelets up like cigars, tasted one, and placed a 2-pound lead fishing sinker on the middle of the other. We repeated this test three times.

THE RESULTS

While our tasters' reactions said a lot (everyone found the omelets with butter to be more tender than the ones without butter), the lead sinkers told the story best. The heavy 2-pound weights easily crushed the omelets that contained butter. On the other hand, the samples without butter showed only a slight depression. Why the dramatic difference?

Since the eggs in the butter-less omelets contained little fat to interfere with coagulation, the latticed protein network was able to form tighter bonds. These tighter bonds resulted in a tougher, more resilient omelet—great for supporting a lot of weight, but not for eating.

As the frozen butter cubes melted in the omelets made with butter, the fat prevented the protein strands in the eggs from forming tight bonds. The result was an omelet that held its shape but was still very tender.

THE TAKEAWAY

An omelet needs enough structure to allow for rolling or folding, but too much will result in rubbery eggs. Added fat, in the form of frozen butter, coats protein strands, producing a looser network and more tender omelet.

TESTING TENDERNESS OF EGGS

OMELET COOKED WITHOUT BUTTER
Without fat from butter, the omelet cooks up tough and sturdy enough to support a 2-pound weight.

OMELET COOKED WITH BUTTER
The fat in the butter makes the omelet noticeably more tender and too delicate to support a 2-pound weight.

PRACTICAL SCIENCE SALT EGGS BEFORE COOKING

Don't wait to salt your scrambled eggs. Salting before cooking gives us tender, moist curds.

Some sources suggest waiting to salt scrambled eggs until just before serving. The danger, they suggest, is that salt beaten into the raw eggs can make them watery. To find out if there's merit to this idea, we salted beaten eggs one minute before cooking and another batch right after scrambling.

Our tasters disliked the eggs salted after scrambling, finding them rubbery and firm. By comparison, the eggs salted prior to cooking were tender and moist. (With these results in hand, we wondered if salting the beaten eggs an hour before cooking would make them even more tender. It didn't; they were nearly identical to eggs salted just before cooking.)

The science here is pretty simple. Salt affects the electrical charge on the protein molecules in the eggs, reducing the tendency of the proteins to bond with each other. A weaker protein network means eggs are less likely to overcoagulate and will cook up tender, not tough.

Cooking turns liquid eggs into a semisolid. The goal is to get the eggs set but to keep them moist and tender. Dairy is an essential addition to ensure that the eggs coagulate but still remain tender—we often choose half-and-half. The fat in the half-and-half coats the egg proteins and keeps them from overcoagulating and squeezing out too much liquid. The water in the half-and-half adds moisture to the eggs and produces extra steam, which results in scrambled eggs that are especially light and fluffy.

PERFECT SCRAMBLED EGGS
SERVES 4

It's important to follow visual cues, as pan thickness will affect cooking times. If using an electric stove, heat one burner on low heat and a second on medium-high heat; move the skillet between burners when it's time to adjust the heat. If you don't have half-and-half, substitute 8 teaspoons of whole milk and 4 teaspoons of heavy cream. To dress up the dish, add 2 tablespoons of minced fresh parsley, chives, basil, or cilantro or 1 tablespoon of minced fresh dill or tarragon to the eggs after reducing the heat to low.

8   large eggs plus 2 large yolks
¼   cup half-and-half
     Salt and pepper
1   tablespoon unsalted butter, chilled

1. Beat eggs, yolks, half-and-half, ¼ teaspoon salt, and ¼ teaspoon pepper with fork until eggs are thoroughly combined and color is pure yellow; do not overbeat.

2. Melt butter in 10-inch nonstick skillet over medium-high heat (butter should not brown), swirling to coat pan. Add egg mixture and, using heatproof rubber spatula, constantly and firmly scrape along bottom and sides of skillet until eggs begin to clump and spatula leaves trail on bottom of pan, 1½ to 2½ minutes. Reduce heat to low and gently but constantly fold eggs until clumped and just slightly wet, 30 to 60 seconds. Immediately transfer eggs to warmed plates and season with salt to taste. Serve immediately.

✔ WHY THIS RECIPE WORKS
Adding salt and half-and-half to the raw eggs before beating them lightly are key steps toward creating great scrambled eggs. With these additions, as well as a dual-heat cooking method, we've discovered the route to perfect—glossy, fluffy, wobbly—scrambled eggs.

BEAT LIGHTLY   For uniform texture, it's important to beat the eggs before cooking them. That said, you can overdo. Some recipes suggest whipping the eggs with an egg beater or electric mixer. We found that overbeating causes premature coagulation of the egg proteins. When overbeaten eggs are then cooked, they turn out tough. For a smooth yellow color and no streaks of white, we whip eggs with a fork and stop once large bubbles form.

WHAT KIND OF DAIRY?   We tested milk, half-and-half, and heavy cream while making these scrambled eggs. Milk produced slightly fluffier, cleaner-tasting curds, but they were particularly prone to weeping. Heavy cream, on the other hand, rendered the eggs very stable but dense, and some tasters found their flavor just too rich. Everyone agreed that ¼ cup of half-and-half fared best. The benefit of the dairy is threefold: First, the water it contains (80 percent in half-and-half) interrupts the protein network and dilutes the molecules, thereby raising the temperature at which the eggs coagulate and providing a greater safety net against overcooking (and disproving the classic French theory that adding the dairy at the end of cooking is best). Second, as the water in the dairy vaporizes, it provides lift (just as in a loaf of baking bread), which causes the eggs to puff up. And third, the fat in the dairy also raises the coagulation temperature by coating and insulating part of

---

FORMULA FOR PERFECT SCRAMBLED EGGS

Half-and-half adds liquid that turns to steam when eggs are cooked, thus helping them cook into soft, fluffy mounds. You need 1 tablespoon of half-and-half for each serving of eggs. In addition to varying the half-and-half to match the number of eggs, you will need to vary the seasonings, pan size, and cooking time. Here's how to do that.

SERVINGS	EGGS	HALF-AND-HALF	SEASONINGS	BUTTER	PAN SIZE	COOKING TIME
1	2 large, plus 1 yolk	1 tablespoon	pinch salt pinch pepper	¼ tablespoon	8 inches	30-60 seconds over medium-high, 30-60 seconds over low
2	4 large, plus 1 yolk	2 tablespoons	⅛ teaspoon salt ⅛ teaspoon pepper	½ tablespoon	8 inches	45-75 seconds over medium-high, 30-60 seconds over low
3	6 large, plus 1 yolk	3 tablespoons	¼ teaspoon salt ⅛ teaspoon pepper	¾ tablespoon	10 inches	1-2 minutes over medium-high, 30-60 seconds over low

each protein molecule so that they cannot stick together as tightly.

ADD YOLK To boost the egg flavor and minimize the dairy tones of our scrambled eggs, we add more yolks to the mix. There's no need to overdo it, though: Two extra yolks per eight eggs balance the flavor nicely. Even better, the high proportion of fat and emulsifiers in the yolks further raises the coagulation temperature, helping to stave off overcooking.

CHOOSE THE RIGHT PAN Pan size is important when scrambling eggs. If the skillet is too large, the eggs spread out in too thin a layer and overcook. A smaller pan forces you to mound the eggs on top of each other, which traps steam and ensures tender, fluffy eggs.

FORGET LOW AND SLOW Since overcoagulation is a danger, many cooks use low or moderate heat for scrambling eggs. That's a big mistake. Getting the pan hot is crucial for generating the steam that creates moist, puffy curds. But cooking on high heat alone can easily cause overcooking. As a result, we use a dual-heat method. First, cook the eggs over medium-high heat, scraping the eggs with a spatula to form large curds and prevent any spots from overcooking. As soon as the spatula just leaves a trail in the pan with minimal raw egg filling in the gap (about two minutes in), drop the heat to low and switch to a gentle folding motion to keep from breaking up the larger curds. When the eggs look cooked through but still glossy (about 45 seconds later), slide them onto a plate to stop the cooking process. The result? Fluffy and tender; a failsafe method for perfect scrambled eggs.

HEARTY SCRAMBLED EGGS WITH BACON, ONION, AND PEPPER JACK CHEESE

SERVES 4 TO 6

Note that you'll need to reserve 2 teaspoons of bacon fat to sauté the onion. After removing the cooked bacon from the skillet, be sure to drain it well on paper towels; otherwise, the eggs will be greasy.

12	large eggs
6	tablespoons half-and-half
¾	teaspoon salt
¼	teaspoon pepper
4	slices bacon, cut into ½-inch pieces
1	onion, chopped
1	tablespoon unsalted butter
1½	ounces pepper Jack or Monterey Jack cheese, shredded (⅓ cup)
1	teaspoon minced fresh parsley (optional)

1. Beat eggs, half-and-half, salt, and pepper with fork in medium bowl until thoroughly combined.

2. Cook bacon in 12-inch nonstick skillet over medium heat, stirring occasionally, until crisp, 5 to 7 minutes. Using slotted spoon, transfer bacon to paper towel–lined plate; discard all but 2 teaspoons bacon fat. Add onion to skillet and cook, stirring occasionally, until lightly browned, 2 to 4 minutes; transfer onion to second plate.

3. Wipe out skillet with paper towels. Add butter to now-empty skillet and melt over medium heat, swirling to coat pan. Pour in egg mixture. With heatproof rubber spatula, stir eggs constantly, slowly pushing them from side to side, scraping along bottom and sides of skillet, and lifting and folding eggs as they form curds (do not overscramble or curds formed will be too small). Cook until large curds form but eggs are still very moist, 2 to 3 minutes. Off heat, gently fold in onion, pepper Jack, and half of bacon until evenly distributed; if eggs are still underdone, return skillet to medium heat for no longer than 30 seconds. Divide eggs among individual plates, sprinkle with remaining bacon and parsley, if using, and serve.

HEARTY SCRAMBLED EGGS WITH SAUSAGE, SWEET PEPPER, AND CHEDDAR CHEESE

SERVES 4 TO 6

We prefer sweet Italian sausage here, especially for breakfast, but you can substitute spicy sausage if desired.

12	large eggs
6	tablespoons half-and-half
¾	teaspoon salt
¼	teaspoon pepper
1	teaspoon vegetable oil
8	ounces sweet Italian sausage, casings removed, sausage crumbled into ½-inch pieces
1	red bell pepper, stemmed, seeded, and cut into ½-inch cubes
3	scallions, white and green parts separated, both sliced thin on bias
1	tablespoon unsalted butter
1½	ounces sharp cheddar cheese, shredded (⅓ cup)

1. Beat eggs, half-and-half, salt, and pepper with fork in medium bowl until thoroughly combined.

2. Heat oil in 12-inch nonstick skillet over medium heat until shimmering. Add sausage and cook until beginning to brown but still pink in center, about 2 minutes. Add bell pepper and scallion whites; continue to cook, stirring occasionally, until sausage is cooked through and pepper is beginning to brown, about 3 minutes. Spread mixture in single layer on medium plate; set aside.

3. Wipe out skillet with paper towels. Add butter to now-empty skillet and melt over medium heat, swirling to coat pan. Pour in egg mixture. With heatproof rubber spatula, stir eggs constantly, slowly pushing them from side to side, scraping along bottom and sides of skillet, and lifting and folding eggs as they form curds (do not overscramble or curds formed will be too small). Cook until large curds form but eggs are still very moist, 2 to 3 minutes. Off heat, gently fold in sausage mixture and cheddar until evenly distributed; if eggs are still underdone, return skillet to medium heat for no longer than 30 seconds. Divide eggs among individual plates, sprinkle with scallion greens, and serve immediately.

HEARTY SCRAMBLED EGGS WITH ARUGULA, SUN-DRIED TOMATOES, AND GOAT CHEESE
SERVES 4 TO 6

Rinsing and patting the sun-dried tomatoes dry prevents them from making the eggs greasy.

12	large eggs
6	tablespoons half-and-half
¾	teaspoon salt
¼	teaspoon pepper
2	teaspoons olive oil
½	onion, chopped fine
⅛	teaspoon red pepper flakes
5	ounces baby arugula (5 cups), cut into ½-inch-wide strips
1	tablespoon unsalted butter
¼	cup oil-packed sun-dried tomatoes, rinsed, patted dry, and chopped fine
3	ounces goat cheese, crumbled (¾ cup)

1. Beat eggs, half-and-half, salt, and pepper with fork in medium bowl until thoroughly combined.

2. Heat oil in 12-inch nonstick skillet over medium heat until shimmering. Add onion and pepper flakes and cook

until onion has softened, about 2 minutes. Add arugula and cook, stirring gently, until arugula begins to wilt, 30 to 60 seconds. Spread mixture in single layer on medium plate; set aside.

3. Wipe out skillet with paper towels. Add butter to now-empty skillet and melt over medium heat, swirling to coat pan. Pour in egg mixture. With heatproof rubber spatula, stir eggs constantly, slowly pushing them from side to side, scraping along bottom and sides of skillet, and lifting and folding eggs as they form curds (do not overscramble or curds formed will be too small). Cook until large curds form but eggs are still very moist, 2 to 3 minutes. Off heat, gently fold in arugula mixture and sun-dried tomatoes until evenly distributed; if eggs are still underdone, return skillet to medium heat for no longer than 30 seconds. Divide eggs among individual plates, sprinkle with goat cheese, and serve immediately.

✓ WHY THIS RECIPE WORKS

When vegetables are added to scrambled eggs, they can become oversaturated and weep. Adding lots of cooked sausage or bacon as well as cheese just complicates matters further. Here's how to keep hearty scrambled eggs tender and moist—but not soggy.

PRECOOK ADD-INS We found that precooking vegetables drives off excess moisture that can ruin scrambled eggs. If you're adding bacon or sausage to eggs, they need to be cooked to render excess fat, which can then be used to cook the vegetables and boost their flavor. Also, folding these cooked ingredients (as well as cheese) into the nearly finished eggs reduces the risk of weeping.

HALF-AND-HALF IS ESSENTIAL Removing some liquid from the scrambled eggs also compensates for any liquid left in the add-on ingredients. To accomplish this, we use a smaller amount of half-and-half—with its higher percentage of fat and lower water content—than the milk used in most scrambled egg recipes.

LOWER THE HEAT Finally, reducing the heat to medium provides a greater margin of error and reduces the risk of overcoagulation. As a result of these changes, hearty scrambled eggs—loaded with vegetables, meat, and cheese—will be a bit less fluffy than plain scrambled eggs (less heat generates less steam), but at least they won't weep.

Unlike scrambled eggs, which should be cooked until they are just set, an omelet requires cooking the eggs a bit further. After all, the omelet needs be rolled (for the traditional French version) or folded (for a diner-style version). This extra cooking pretty much guarantees tough, rubbery eggs. We found that cubes of butter coat the egg proteins with plenty of fat and do so without adding much water. Freezing the butter cubes ensures that they melt slowly enough to disperse evenly through the eggs, just at the point when the eggs are beginning to coagulate.

PERFECT FRENCH OMELETS
MAKES 2

Because making omelets is such a quick process, make sure to have all your ingredients and equipment at the ready. If you don't have skewers or chopsticks to stir the eggs in step 3, try the handle of wooden spoon. Warm the plates in a 200-degree oven.

- 2 tablespoons unsalted butter, cut into 2 pieces
- ½ teaspoon vegetable oil
- 6 large eggs, chilled
  Salt and pepper
- 2 tablespoons shredded Gruyère cheese
- 4 teaspoons minced fresh chives

1. Cut 1 tablespoon butter in half. Cut remaining 1 tablespoon butter into small pieces, transfer to small bowl, and place in freezer while preparing eggs and skillet, at least 10 minutes. Meanwhile, heat oil in 8-inch nonstick skillet over low heat for 10 minutes.

2. Crack 2 eggs into medium bowl and separate third egg; reserve egg white for another use and add yolk to bowl. Add ⅛ teaspoon salt and pinch pepper. Break egg yolks with fork, then beat eggs at moderate pace, about 80 strokes, until yolks and whites are well combined. Stir in half of frozen butter cubes.

3. When skillet is fully heated, use paper towels to wipe out oil, leaving thin film on bottom and sides of skillet. Add ½ tablespoon of reserved butter to skillet and heat until melted. Swirl butter to coat skillet, add egg mixture, and increase heat to medium-high. Use 2 chopsticks or wooden skewers to scramble eggs, using quick circular motion to move around skillet, scraping cooked egg from side of skillet as you go, until eggs are almost cooked but still slightly runny, 45 to 90 seconds. Turn off heat (remove pan from heat if using electric burner) and smooth eggs into even layer using heatproof rubber spatula. Sprinkle omelet with 1 tablespoon Gruyère and 2 teaspoons chives. Cover skillet with tight-fitting lid and let sit for 1 minute for runnier omelet or 2 minutes for firmer omelet.

4. Heat skillet over low heat for 20 seconds, uncover, and, using rubber spatula, loosen edges of omelet from skillet. Place folded square of paper towel on warmed plate and slide omelet out of skillet onto paper towel so that omelet lies flat on plate and hangs about 1 inch off paper towel. Roll omelet into neat cylinder and set aside. Return skillet to low heat and heat 2 minutes before repeating instructions for second omelet starting with step 2. Serve.

✔ WHY THIS RECIPE WORKS
The added fat from the frozen butter helps produce a tender omelet, but there are a few other key steps in this recipe.

LOSE A WHITE Our recipe starts with six large eggs (enough for two omelets) but we discard two egg whites along the way. We found that the amount of butter needed to keep the proteins in three eggs from toughening

---

PRACTICAL SCIENCE EGG SAFETY

The risk of salmonella can be removed by cooking eggs to 160 degrees or buying pasteurized eggs.

The Egg Safety Center estimates that one in every 10,000 to 20,000 eggs is contaminated by salmonella bacteria. Salmonella, if present, can be on the outside of the egg shell or inside the egg if the hen that laid it was infected. There are two ways to reduce the risk.

SAFER COOKING Salmonella is destroyed at 160 degrees. Eggs that have just barely set, or are still runny, have not reached this temperature. Eggs that are fully set and dry, as they are when hard-cooked or used in a frittata, have reached this temperature.

SAFER SHOPPING Pasteurized eggs are whole eggs that have been put through a heating process that kills bacteria but does not cook the eggs themselves. Once cracked open, pasteurized eggs do have a slightly different appearance and consistency, but for the most part we found that they performed on par with standard eggs in applications in which pasteurized eggs might be beneficial (such as mayonnaise); we had less success using them in cakes and cookies. Note that the majority of eggs pasteurized in the United States are liquid eggs already removed from the shell.

resulted in a very rich omelet. Removing a single white from the equation allows us to use less butter and keeps our cheesy omelet from becoming too rich.

BREAK UP EGGS, DON'T BEAT 'EM   Many sources suggest beating eggs with a whisk or even an electric mixer. We found that such tough treatment unravels egg proteins and causes them to cross-link when cooked. The end result is tough eggs. You want the yolks and whites to be fully combined before you start cooking, so some beating of the eggs is a must. We found that a fork does the job nicely and reduces the risk of overbeating. Once the eggs look well combined, stop beating. This will take about 80 strokes.

STIR GENTLY AS EGGS SET   Stirring the eggs as they set breaks the coagulating eggs into small curds that produce a more refined omelet with a silkier texture. We found the usual tool for cooking eggs in a nonstick skillet—a rubber spatula—wasn't up to the job. The smaller tines of a fork break the curds into much smaller bits. Unfortunately, a fork will scratch the nonstick surface. We get excellent results with nonstick-friendly wooden chopsticks or bamboo skewers. The handle of a wooden spoon can be used if you don't have either chopsticks or skewers.

PUT A LID ON IT   Preheating the skillet over 10 minutes (see "Preheat Your Omelet Pan Slowly," right) ensured that the heat was evenly distributed across the pan surface and reduced the risk of an overcooked, tough omelet. But we still had trouble getting the eggs furthest from the heat source to cook fully. By the time they did, often the bottom of the omelet had become tough. The solution is quite simple: Once the eggs are set but still runny, slide the pan off the heat, smooth the eggs into an even layer with a spatula, add the cheese and chives, then cover the pan. After a minute or two (depending on whether you like a runnier or firmer omelet), the residual heat trapped by the lid will have gently cooked through the top layer of eggs, and since the pan is off the heat there's no danger that the bottom of the omelet will become tough.

SLIDE AND ROLL   The traditional way to remove an omelet from the pan is to give the skillet a quick jerk in order to fold the omelet over. You then slide it out of the pan, tilting the skillet so that the remaining flap of eggs rolls over neatly. Sounds good, but this method has a high failure rate. For an easier approach, we tried slipping the omelet onto a plate, then using our fingers to roll it. The eggs are still pretty hot, so we prefer to line the plate with a paper towel, which can be used to roll the omelet into a neat cylinder without burning your fingertips.

PRACTICAL SCIENCE
PREHEAT YOUR OMELET PAN SLOWLY

Preheat your omelet pan over low heat for even cooking.

While developing our omelet recipe, we found that the way we preheated the pan before adding the eggs was critical to achieving a creamy omelet with a uniformly golden exterior. Instead of preheating over medium-high heat for two or three minutes (the most common approach), we preheated the pan over low heat for a full 10 minutes.

On a gas stove, a high flame licks up the sides of the pan, creating hot spots at the outer edges of the pan bottom. These hot spots, in turn, can lead to brown splotches on your omelet. Preheating the low-and-slow way ensures that the heat is more evenly distributed.

Preheating over low heat has another advantage: It gives you a wider window for adding your eggs. Over high heat, it takes just 30 seconds for the pan to go from an acceptable 250 degrees to an egg-toughening 300 degrees. (Note: Preheating an omelet pan is one case in which electric stoves show an edge over gas. Because of their wide, flat heating elements, electric stoves do not produce hot spots in the pan, even over a high setting. However, we still recommend preheating over low heat to allow plenty of time for adding your eggs.)

MEDIUM-HIGH = SPOTTY

LOW = UNIFORM

To demonstrate the importance of preheating over the correct (low) temperature, we spread a layer of grated Parmesan cheese over the bottom of two pans, then heated one over medium-high heat and the other one over low heat. Cheese heated over medium-high heat browned on the edges, while the cheese heated over low heat melted to an even, uniform color.

EGGS 101

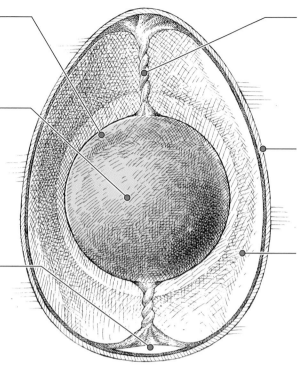

VITELLINE
This membrane contains and protects the yolk. It weakens as the egg ages, causing the yolk to break more easily. This is why fresh eggs are easier to separate than older eggs.

YOLK
Most of the egg's vitamins and minerals, as well as all of the fat and half of the protein, are found in the yolk. It also contains lecithin, a powerful emulsifier (lecithin is the emulsifying agent that makes it possible to make mayonnaise and hollandaise sauce). The yolk is firmer when cold and thus less likely to break; for this reason, separate eggs when chilled.

AIR CELL
The void at the wide end of the egg results from contraction as the interior cools after the egg is laid. This space increases in size as the egg ages and moisture inside the egg evaporates through the shell.

CHALAZAE
These whitish cords extend from each pole end and center the yolk. As an egg ages, the chalazae weaken and the yolk can become off center. We often strain sauces and custards (such as Crème Brûlée, on page 180) so the chalazae don't mar their texture and appearance.

SHELL
The shell and inner membrane keep the contents in place and keep out bacteria. The shell is permeable and over time the contents of an egg can evaporate. Never use an egg with a cracked or split shell.

WHITE
The white, also called the albumin, is made of protein and water and is divided into thick and thin layers, with the thickest layer closest to the yolk. A slight cloudiness indicates extreme freshness. As eggs age, the white becomes thinner and clearer.

BUYING

FRESHNESS Egg cartons are marked with both a sell-by date and a pack date. The pack date is the day the eggs were graded and packed, which is generally within a week of being laid but, legally, may be as much as 30 days later. The pack date is printed on egg cartons as a three-number code just below the sell-by date and it runs consecutively from 001, for January 1, to 365, for December 31. The sell-by date is the legal limit until which eggs may be sold and is within 30 days of the pack date. In short, a carton may be up to two months old by the sell-by date. Even so, according to the USDA, eggs are still fit for consumption for an additional three to five weeks past the sell-by date if refrigerated. We tasted two- and three-month-old eggs and found them palatable. At four months, the white was loose and the yolk tasted of the refrigerator, though it was still edible. Our advice? Use your discretion. If the eggs smell odd or display discoloration, pitch them. Older eggs also lack the structure-lending properties of fresh eggs, so beware when baking.

COLOR The shell's hue depends on the breed of the chicken. The run-of-the-mill Leghorn chicken produces the typical white egg. Brown-feathered birds, such as Rhode Island Reds, produce *café au lait*–colored eggs. Our tests proved that shell color has no effect on flavor or nutritional value.

FARM-FRESH AND ORGANIC In our taste tests, farm-fresh eggs were standouts. The large yolks were bright orange and sat high above the comparatively small whites. Their flavor was rich and complex. The organic eggs followed in second place, while eggs from hens raised on a vegetarian diet came in third and standard supermarket eggs last. Differences were easily detected in egg-based dishes but not in cakes or cookies.

EGG SIZES Eggs vary in size, which will make a difference in recipes. We use large eggs in our recipes. If you do the math, you can substitute one size for another. For instance, four jumbo eggs are equivalent to five large eggs (both weigh 10 ounces).

STORING

REFRIGERATOR If your refrigerator has an egg tray on the door, don't use it. Eggs should be stored on the shelf, where the temperature is below 40 degrees. The average door temperature in our test kitchen refrigerators is closer to 45 degrees.

Eggs are also best stored in their protective cardboard carton; when removed they may absorb flavors from other foods. The egg carton also helps maintain humidity, which is ideally 70 to 80 percent, and thus slows down evaporation of the eggs' contents.

FREEZER Extra whites can be frozen, but in our tests we found their rising properties compromised: Angel food cake didn't rise quite as well and meringues baked up deflated and a bit gummy. Frozen whites are best used in recipes that call for small amounts (like an egg wash) or recipes that don't depend on whipping the egg whites (such as an omelet). Yolks, however, can't be frozen as is; the water forms ice crystals that disrupt the protein network. Adding sugar syrup (2 parts sugar to 1 part water) allows yolks to be frozen. Stir a scant ¼ teaspoon of syrup per yolk into yolks before freezing. Defrost and use in custards.

APPROXIMATE WEIGHTS OF VARIOUS EGG SIZES

MEDIUM	LARGE	EXTRA-LARGE	JUMBO
1.75 ounces	2.00 ounces	2.25 ounces	2.50 ounces

Gentle Heat Guarantees Smooth Custards

When it comes to baked desserts, eggs are key. They add richness to baked custards (like crème brûlée), custard pies (including pumpkin), and cheesecakes, as well as help them all to thicken and set. Heat unlocks the power of eggs but can also take it too far.

HOW THE SCIENCE WORKS

THE EFFECTS OF HEAT ON EGGS

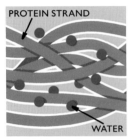

GENTLE HEAT *Careful cooking keeps the network of egg proteins loose and smooth.*

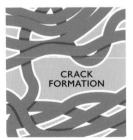

HIGH HEAT *Fast cooking can cause egg proteins to clump together, pull apart, and separate from the liquid surrounding them.*

As with scrambled eggs and omelets, we use whole eggs when baking custardy desserts. In concept 18, we learned about coagulation. As the temperature in eggs rises, the proteins in both the white and the yolk become active. They begin to move about, running into each other, breaking the delicate bonds that hold them as coiled-up balls. Once unfurled, they are able to bond with the other proteins likewise whirling around them, creating a weblike structure that becomes increasingly opaque and solid with time.

The temperatures at which the egg white and the yolk coagulate are different—whites begin to thicken at 140 to 150 degrees and yolks at 150 to 160 degrees. This difference makes egg cookery a two-tiered task and is why when we cook an egg "over easy," the white is solid while the yolk is still a gooey orange liquid. When baking custardy desserts, we use whole eggs mixed with many other ingredients (which often affect how rapidly the egg proteins uncoil and bond together) but that doesn't make the technique any less delicate.

Cooking egg custards requires very careful control of temperatures. When exposed to too much heat, the egg proteins will coagulate too much. They will form stronger bonds with the surrounding proteins, making clumps and lumps and separating from the liquid surrounding them. This is called curdling. Curdling is the enemy of egg-based desserts that are supposed to entice us with their smooth and creamy texture.

To combat this risk, we cook custardlike desserts low and slow. In a hot oven, pumpkin pie will leap from not yet set to overcooked in a heartbeat. And, because of the principles of conduction (see concept 1), the edges will cook much faster than the center. We generally bake custards in a low oven in order to mitigate the heat differential between the exterior of a pie or cheesecake and the interior. A low oven temperature also slows down the rate of cooking, thereby increasing the window of time when a dessert is perfectly cooked.

In addition to a low-temperature oven, we sometimes bake delicate egg-based desserts in a water bath, also known as a *bain-marie*. The ramekin or springform pan is placed in a roasting pan filled with water. Because the water never reaches a temperature higher than that of boiling water, or 212 degrees, the water further slows down cooking in these desserts.

Finally, for custards that are prepared on the stovetop, we temper eggs, or heat them very gently by mixing them with a small amount of hot liquid, in order to slow the rate of cooking.

TEST KITCHEN EXPERIMENT

To demonstrate the effects of a water bath on egg-based baked desserts, we prepared two identical cheesecakes and baked one directly on the rack and the other in a water bath, both in a 325-degree oven. Both cheesecakes were removed from the oven when their centers reached 147 degrees.

THE RESULTS

The cake that had been baked in a water bath was even-colored and smooth; the other cake was browned and cracked. A quick comparison of the temperature at the edges of the cakes confirmed what we suspected: Upon removal from the oven, the cake that had had the benefit of a water bath was 184 degrees at the edge, whereas the cake baked without the water bath had climbed to 213 degrees.

THE TAKEAWAY

A water bath is commonly called for in the baking of cheesecakes and custards to guarantee evenly cooked, smooth results. Why? Our experiment showed that the cheesecake baked in a water bath was 30 degrees cooler at the edges than the cake baked without a water bath. Although in both cases the oven had been set to 325 degrees, a water bath cannot exceed 212 degrees, as this is the temperature at which water converts to steam. Plus, the water takes time to heat up, so most water baths never exceed 190 degrees in a 325-degree oven. This even, gentle heat moderates the temperature around the perimeter of the pan, preventing overheating (and overcooking) at the edges. The cheesecake baked in the water bath also had an even, uncracked surface. By moderating the temperature of the cheesecake, the water bath prevented the cheesecake top from inflating like a soufflé. In addition, the water bath added considerable moisture to the oven (more than 4 cups of water evaporated from the bath during cooking). The added moisture helped to keep the top of the cake supple, which discouraged cracking. This is in opposition to the cake baked directly on the rack, in which the egg proteins coagulated so rapidly under the unmitigated heat that they clumped together, creating a lumpy texture and pulling apart the surface of the cake.

A WATER BATH PREVENTS UNEVEN COOKING

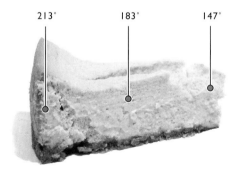

213°   183°   147°

184°   158°   147°

BAKED WITHOUT A WATER BATH
The direct heat of the oven caused the edges to heat far faster than the center. As a result, the edges of the cheesecake are overcooked. Also, the direct heat causes the egg proteins to clump together and pull apart.

BAKED IN A WATER BATH
The gentle, even heat of a water bath allowed the egg proteins to cook slowly and evenly, resulting in a cheesecake with a smooth, supple texture, even at the edges.

We use water baths in order to cook delicate custards and custardy cakes slowly and evenly throughout. After all, the water in a water bath never reaches more than 212 degrees. We nestle the ramekins or cake pan in the bath (so that the water comes at least halfway up its sides) in order to moderate the temperature around the perimeter and prevent overcooking around the edge.

SPICED PUMPKIN CHEESECAKE
SERVES 12 TO 16

This cheesecake is good on its own, but either Brown Sugar Whipped Cream or Brown Sugar and Bourbon Whipped Cream (recipes follow) is a great addition. When cutting the cake, have a pitcher of hot tap water nearby; dipping the blade of the knife into the water and wiping it clean with a kitchen towel after each cut helps make neat slices.

CRUST

9	whole graham crackers, broken into rough pieces
3	tablespoons sugar
½	teaspoon ground ginger
½	teaspoon ground cinnamon
¼	teaspoon ground cloves
6	tablespoons unsalted butter, melted

FILLING

1⅓	cups (9⅓ ounces) sugar
1	teaspoon ground cinnamon
½	teaspoon ground ginger
¼	teaspoon ground nutmeg
¼	teaspoon ground cloves
¼	teaspoon ground allspice
½	teaspoon salt
1	(15-ounce) can unsweetened pumpkin puree
1½	pounds cream cheese, cut into 1-inch chunks and softened
1	tablespoon vanilla extract
1	tablespoon lemon juice
5	large eggs, room temperature
1	cup heavy cream
1	tablespoon unsalted butter, melted

1. FOR THE CRUST: Adjust oven rack to lower-middle position and heat oven to 325 degrees. Pulse crackers, sugar, ginger, cinnamon, and cloves in food processor until crackers are finely ground, about 15 pulses. Transfer crumbs to medium bowl, drizzle with melted butter, and mix with rubber spatula until evenly moistened. Empty crumbs into

9-inch springform pan and, using bottom of ramekin or dry measuring cup, press crumbs firmly and evenly into pan bottom, keeping sides as clean as possible. Bake crust until fragrant and browned around edges, about 15 minutes. Let crust cool completely on wire rack, about 30 minutes. When cool, wrap outside of pan with two 18-inch square pieces of heavy-duty aluminum foil and set springform pan in roasting pan. Bring kettle of water to boil.

2. FOR THE FILLING: Whisk sugar, cinnamon, ginger, nutmeg, cloves, allspice, and salt together in small bowl; set aside. Line baking sheet with triple layer of paper towels. Spread pumpkin on paper towels in roughly even layer and pat puree with several layers of paper towels to wick away moisture.

3. Using stand mixer fitted with paddle, beat cream cheese on medium speed until broken up and slightly softened, about 1 minute. Scrape down bowl, then beat in sugar mixture in 3 additions on medium-low speed until combined, about 1 minute, scraping down bowl after each addition. Add pumpkin, vanilla, and lemon juice and beat on medium speed until combined, about 45 seconds; scrape down bowl. Reduce speed to medium-low, add eggs, 1 at a time, and beat until incorporated, about 1 minute. Reduce speed to low, add cream, and beat until combined, about 45 seconds. Give filling final stir by hand.

4. Being careful not to disturb baked crust, brush inside of pan with melted butter. Pour filling into prepared pan and smooth top with rubber spatula. Set roasting pan on oven rack and pour enough boiling water into roasting pan to come about halfway up sides of springform pan. Bake cake until center is slightly wobbly when pan is shaken and cake registers 150 degrees, about 1½ hours. Set roasting pan on wire rack, then run paring knife around cake. Let cake cool in roasting pan until water is just warm, about 45 minutes. Remove springform pan from water bath, discard foil, and set on wire rack; continue to let cool until barely warm, about 3 hours. Wrap with plastic wrap and refrigerate until chilled, at least 4 hours.

5. To unmold cheesecake, wrap hot kitchen towel around pan and let stand for 1 minute. Remove sides of pan. Slide thin metal spatula between crust and pan bottom to loosen, then slide cake onto serving platter. Let cheesecake sit at room temperature for about 30 minutes before serving. (Cake can be made up to 3 days in advance; however, crust will begin to lose its crispness after only 1 day.)

PUMPKIN-BOURBON CHEESECAKE WITH GRAHAM-PECAN CRUST

Reduce graham crackers to 5 whole crackers, process ½ cup chopped pecans with crackers, and reduce butter to 4 tablespoons. In filling, omit lemon juice, reduce vanilla extract to 1 teaspoon, and add ¼ cup bourbon along with heavy cream.

BROWN SUGAR WHIPPED CREAM
MAKES ABOUT 2½ CUPS

Refrigerating the mixture in step 1 gives the brown sugar time to dissolve. This whipped cream pairs well with Spiced Pumpkin Cheesecake or with any dessert that has lots of nuts, warm spices, or molasses, like gingerbread, pecan pie, or pumpkin pie.

1	cup heavy cream, chilled
½	cup sour cream
½	cup packed (3½ ounces) light brown sugar
⅛	teaspoon salt

1. Using stand mixer fitted with whisk, whip heavy cream, sour cream, sugar, and salt until combined. Cover with plastic wrap and refrigerate until ready to serve, at least 4 hours or up to 1 day, stirring once or twice during chilling to ensure that sugar dissolves.

2. Before serving, using stand mixer fitted with whisk, whip mixture on medium-low speed until foamy, about 1 minute. Increase speed to high and whip until soft peaks form, 1 to 3 minutes.

BROWN SUGAR AND BOURBON WHIPPED CREAM

Add 2 teaspoons bourbon to cream mixture before whipping.

✔ WHY THIS RECIPE WORKS

Adding pumpkin, with all of its extra liquid, to a cheesecake makes everything more challenging. An unusual method to remove moisture from pumpkin (which includes paper towels) and the use of a water bath ensure that our Spiced Pumpkin Cheesecake has a velvety texture.

PREBAKE THE CRUST We use crumbled graham crackers for the crust, as we do in our New York–Style Cheesecake recipe (page 182). Here we add butter and sugar and a bit of ground cinnamon and ginger to them in order to complement the spices in the filling. Also, as with our New York cheesecake, we prebake the crust. This way a sturdy, crisp, buttery crust forms. (Without prebaking, the crust becomes a pasty, soggy layer beneath the filling.)

DRY YOUR CANNED PUMPKIN Anyone who has prepared fresh pumpkin for pumpkin pie can attest to the fact that cutting, seeding, peeling, and cooking it can take hours and is not time and effort well spent. We prefer opening a can, which takes only a few seconds. But pumpkin in any form is filled with liquid. We could remove some of the moisture by cooking, as we do in our Pumpkin Pie (page 184). But that involves frequent stirring, a cooking period, and waiting for it to cool. An easier way? Paper towels. Spread the pumpkin on a baking sheet lined with paper towels and then press additional paper towels on the surface to wick away more moisture. In seconds, the pumpkin will shed enough liquid to yield a cheesecake with a lovely texture, and the paper towels will peel away almost effortlessly. Removing this moisture allows us to add heavy cream to the mix, which gives us a cheesecake that is smooth and lush.

PICK YOUR EGGS While cheesecake recipes can take various amounts of eggs in different configurations (whole eggs, egg whites, or egg yolks for a range of textures), we prefer simply using five whole eggs here. This produces a satiny, creamy, unctuous cheesecake.

PRACTICAL SCIENCE LEAK-PROOFING SPRINGFORM PANS

Another option to prevent water from seeping into your springform pan is to place it within a larger cake pan in your water bath.

We'd love to find a springform pan that doesn't let moisture seep in when you place it in a water bath, but so far a less-than-watertight seal seems unavoidable on pans with removable bottoms. Our solution has always been to wrap the pan with a double layer of aluminum foil. But steam from the water bath can condense inside the foil, so that the pan still sits in liquid. There is a better way to address the problem: placing the springform pan inside a slightly larger metal pan or pot—a 10 by 3-inch cake pan or deep-dish pizza pan is ideal—before lowering it into the bath. The slight gap between the pans isn't wide enough to prevent the water from insulating the springform pan, and there is zero danger of exposing the cheesecake to water, since any moisture that condenses on the sides of the pan rapidly evaporates. If you bake cheesecakes regularly, this method is worth the minimal expense.

FLAVOR IT UP   Our Spiced Pumpkin Cheesecake is flavored with lemon juice, salt, and vanilla extract to start. But we also add sweet, warm cinnamon and sharp, spicy ground ginger alongside small amounts of cloves, nutmeg, and allspice. In unison, these spices provide a deep, resounding flavor but not an overspiced burn.

GIVE IT A BATH   In a springform pan, a cheesecake can be baked either directly on the oven rack like a regular cake or in a water bath like a delicate custard. Because we bake this cheesecake at 325 degrees, a water bath is needed for even cooking on the edges and the center (for more on this, see Test Kitchen Experiment, page 177). For the water bath, the pan must be wrapped in a double layer of foil to prevent leakage (or placed within another pan, see "Leak-Proofing Springform Pans," page 179). The water, which moderates the cooking temperature and protects the edges of the cake, should come halfway up the sides of the springform pan. The extra humidity in the air due to the steaming water helps to reduce the level of evaporation from the cake, for a better, moister cheesecake after it exits the oven.

PRACTICAL SCIENCE CHOOSING VANILLA BEANS

Vanilla beans are a key component of crème brûlée. We tested five brands.

We tested five brands of vanilla beans sourced from Madagascar (the world's largest producer)—three mail-order beans and two from the supermarket—wondering if the tides had turned since we rated them more than a decade ago. At that time, we couldn't recommend any supermarket samples, finding them dried out and hardened, with few seeds and even less flavor.

To assess the differences, we sliced open a pod from each brand and scraped out the seeds. We then used the seeds in an uncooked cream cheese frosting and simmered both seeds and pods in dairy for use in a simple crème anglaise and in the base of our Vanilla Ice Cream.

This time around, in a surprising reversal, we found the supermarket beans not only improved, but also slightly better than the mail-order ones. While some variation can be expected from any agricultural product, most of the differences among beans likely came from how much of the flavor compound vanillin was developed during the curing process. For Madagascar beans, this involves dipping the pods in hot water to halt all growth, drying them in the sun, and placing them (wrapped in cloth and straw mats) in wooden boxes to sweat overnight. This cycle is repeated until a manufacturer decides that the beans are ready to be moved to holding rooms, where they rest until they're shriveled, brown, and fragrant—an indication that they're ready for sorting.

Bottom line: Although all of the brands were acceptable, we recommend splurging on our winner, McCormick Madagascar Vanilla Beans (at $15.99 for two, they're more costly than the mail-order brands), when you want moist, seed-filled pods with complex flavor that tasters called exceptionally "robust" and "vivid."

CRÈME BRÛLÉE
SERVES 8

Separate the eggs and whisk the yolks after the cream has finished steeping; if left to sit, the surface of the yolks will dry and form a film. A vanilla bean gives the custard the deepest flavor, but 2 teaspoons of vanilla extract, whisked into the yolks in step 4, can be used instead. While we prefer turbinado or Demerara sugar for the caramelized sugar crust, regular granulated sugar will work, too, but use only 1 scant teaspoon on each ramekin or 1 teaspoon on each shallow fluted dish.

1	vanilla bean
4	cups heavy cream
2/3	cup (4 2/3 ounces) granulated sugar
	Pinch salt
12	large egg yolks
8–12	teaspoons turbinado or Demerara sugar

1. Adjust oven rack to lower-middle position and heat oven to 300 degrees.

2. Cut vanilla bean in half lengthwise. Using tip of paring knife, scrape out seeds. Combine vanilla bean and seeds, 2 cups cream, granulated sugar, and salt in medium saucepan. Bring mixture to boil over medium heat, stirring occasionally to dissolve sugar. Off heat, let steep for 15 minutes.

3. Meanwhile, place kitchen towel in bottom of large baking dish or roasting pan; set eight 4- or 5-ounce ramekins (or shallow fluted dishes) on towel (they should not touch each other). Bring kettle of water to boil.

4. After cream has steeped, stir in remaining 2 cups cream. Whisk egg yolks in large bowl until uniform. Whisk about 1 cup cream mixture into yolks until combined; repeat with 1 cup more cream mixture. Add remaining cream mixture and whisk until evenly colored and thoroughly combined. Strain mixture through fine-mesh strainer into large liquid measuring cup or bowl; discard solids in strainer. Divide mixture evenly among ramekins.

5. Set baking dish on oven rack. Taking care not to splash water into ramekins, pour enough boiling water into dish to reach two-thirds up sides of ramekins. Bake until centers of custards are just barely set and register 170 to 175 degrees, 30 to 35 minutes (25 to 30 minutes for shallow fluted dishes), checking temperature about 5 minutes before recommended minimum time.

6. Transfer ramekins to wire rack and let cool to room temperature, about 2 hours. Set ramekins on baking sheet,

cover tightly with plastic wrap, and refrigerate until cold, at least 4 hours.

7. Uncover ramekins; if condensation has collected on custards, blot moisture with paper towel. Sprinkle each with about 1 teaspoon turbinado sugar (1½ teaspoons for shallow fluted dishes); tilt and tap each ramekin to distribute sugar evenly, dumping out excess sugar. Ignite torch and caramelize sugar. Refrigerate ramekins, uncovered, to rechill, 30 to 45 minutes; serve.

ESPRESSO CRÈME BRÛLÉE

Crush the espresso beans lightly with the bottom of a skillet.

Substitute ¼ cup lightly crushed espresso beans for vanilla bean. Whisk 1 teaspoon vanilla extract into yolks in step 4 before adding cream.

MAKE-AHEAD CRÈME BRÛLÉE

Reduce egg yolks to 10. After baked custards cool to room temperature, wrap each ramekin tightly in plastic wrap and refrigerate for up to 4 days. Proceed with step 7.

✔WHY THIS RECIPE WORKS

Crème brûlée is all about the contrast between the crisp sugar crust and the silky custard underneath. But too often the crust is either stingy or rock-hard, and the custard is heavy and tasteless. We found that the secret to a soft, supple custard is using egg yolks rather than whole eggs, and a water bath for gentle, even cooking. For the crust, we use crunchy turbinado sugar and a propane or butane torch (which work better than the broiler) for caramelizing the sugar. Because the blast of heat inevitably warms the custard beneath the crust, we chill our crèmes brûlées once more before serving.

START WITH HEAVY CREAM   There is no point cutting corners here. We tried this crème brûlée with half-and-half (with a fat content of around 10 percent), whipping cream (30 percent fat), and heavy cream (36 percent fat). The half-and-half was far too lean, and the custard was watery and lightweight. The whipping cream custard was an improvement, but still a bit loose. Heavy cream makes a custard that is thick but not overbearing, luxurious but not death-defying. In short: everything we want.

USE YOLKS ONLY   Firm custards, like crème caramel, are made with whole eggs, which help the custard to achieve a clean-cutting quality. Crème brûlée is richer and softer—with a puddinglike, spoon-clinging texture—in part because of the exclusive use of yolks. Using 4 cups of heavy cream, we played with the number of yolks here. The custard

refuses to set with as few as six; eight is better, though still slurpy. With 12, however, the custard has a lovely lilting texture, a glossy, luminescent look, and the richest flavor.

PICK VANILLA BEANS   We prefer the use of a vanilla bean, rather than vanilla extract, in this custard. The downside to starting with cold ingredients (as we do to prevent any curdling eggs) is that it becomes almost impossible to extract the flavor of a vanilla bean. We solve this problem with a hybrid technique: We scald half the cream, along with the sugar (to dissolve) and vanilla bean, and let it sit for 15 minutes to extract the flavor of the vanilla. Later, we add the cold cream to lower the temperature before mixing in the eggs. You end up with the tiny black flecks of vanilla bean seeds in the final dish, but don't worry, it's only added flavor. (It's possible to use vanilla extract, but a bean is far better.)

COOL THE CREAM   Even though we warm some of the cream to better extract the flavor of the vanilla, it's important to lower the temperature before adding the eggs. Cold-started custard and scalded-cream custard display startling differences. As we've learned, eggs respond favorably to cooking at a slow, gentle pace. If heated quickly, they set only just shortly before they enter the overcooked zone, leaving a very narrow window between just right and overdone. If heated gently, however, they begin to thicken the custard at a lower temperature and continue to do so gradually. Therefore, cooling the cream before adding the eggs gives us more time to develop a perfectly textured crème brûlée before we enter the danger zone of overcooked eggs. Because the cream is not straight-from-the-fridge cold, the baking time is nicely reduced.

BATHE THE RAMEKINS   We use a large baking dish for our water bath (or bain-marie, which prevents the custard from overcooking while the center saunters to the finish line), one that can hold all of the ramekins comfortably. (The ramekins must not touch and should be at least ½ inch away from the sides of the dish.) Line the bottom of the pan with a kitchen towel to protect the floors of the ramekins from the heat of the dish.

PICK THE BEST SUGAR   For the crackly caramel crust, we prefer Demerara and turbinado sugars, which are both coarse light brown sugars. They are better than brown sugar, which is moist and lumpy, and granulated sugar, because it can be difficult to distribute evenly over the custards. Don't use a broiler to caramelize; it's an almost guaranteed fail with its uneven heat. A torch accomplishes the task efficiently. (And be sure to refrigerate the finished crèmes brûlées—the brûlée can warm up the custard, ruining an otherwise perfect dish.)

Though we often use water baths to help our custards bake gently, sometimes just the oven is fine. For silky cakes and pies without rough edges and jiggly centers, we set our ovens low—very low. This helps the eggs to cook slowly and evenly. It also expands the window of opportunity before our desserts are cracked, rough, and woefully overcooked.

NEW YORK–STYLE CHEESECAKE
SERVES 12 TO 16

For the crust, chocolate wafers can be substituted for graham crackers; you will need about 14 wafers. The flavor and texture of the cheesecake are best if the cake is allowed to sit at room temperature for 30 minutes before serving. When cutting the cake, have a pitcher of hot tap water nearby; dipping the blade of the knife into the water and wiping it clean with a kitchen towel after each cut helps make neat slices. Serve with Fresh Strawberry Topping (recipe follows) if desired.

CRUST

- 8 whole graham crackers, broken into rough pieces
- 1 tablespoon sugar
- 5 tablespoons unsalted butter, melted

FILLING

- 2½ pounds cream cheese, cut into 1-inch chunks and softened
- 1½ cups (10½ ounces) sugar
- ⅛ teaspoon salt
- ⅓ cup sour cream
- 2 teaspoons lemon juice
- 2 teaspoons vanilla extract
- 6 large eggs plus 2 large yolks
- 1 tablespoon unsalted butter, melted

1. FOR THE CRUST: Adjust oven rack to lower-middle position and heat oven to 325 degrees. Process graham cracker pieces in food processor to fine crumbs, about 30 seconds. Combine graham cracker crumbs and sugar in medium bowl, add melted butter, and toss with fork until evenly moistened. Empty crumbs into 9-inch springform pan and, using bottom of ramekin or dry measuring cup, press crumbs firmly and evenly into pan bottom, keeping sides as clean as possible. Bake crust until fragrant and beginning to brown around edges, about 13 minutes. Let crust cool in pan on wire rack while making filling.

2. FOR THE FILLING: Increase oven temperature to 500 degrees. Using stand mixer fitted with paddle, beat cream cheese on medium-low speed until broken up and slightly softened, about 1 minute. Scrape down bowl. Add ¾ cup sugar and salt and beat on medium-low speed until combined, about 1 minute. Scrape down bowl, then beat in remaining ¾ cup sugar until combined, about 1 minute. Scrape down bowl, add sour cream, lemon juice, and vanilla, and beat on low speed until combined, about 1 minute. Scrape down bowl, add egg yolks, and beat on medium-low speed until thoroughly combined, about 1 minute. Scrape down bowl, add whole eggs, 2 at a time, beating until thoroughly combined, about 1 minute, and scraping bowl between additions.

3. Being careful not to disturb baked crust, brush inside of pan with melted butter and set pan on rimmed baking sheet to catch any spills in case pan leaks. Pour filling into cooled crust and bake for 10 minutes; without opening oven door, reduce temperature to 200 degrees and continue to bake until cheesecake registers about 150 degrees, about 1½ hours. Let cake cool on wire rack for 5 minutes, then run paring knife around cake to loosen from pan. Let cake continue to cool until barely warm, 2½ to 3 hours. Wrap tightly in plastic wrap and refrigerate until cold, at least 3 hours. (Cake can be refrigerated for up to 4 days.)

4. To unmold cheesecake, wrap hot kitchen towel around pan and let stand for 1 minute. Remove sides of pan. Slide thin metal spatula between crust and pan bottom to loosen, then slide cake onto serving platter. Let cheesecake sit at room temperature for about 30 minutes before serving. (Cheesecake can be made up to 3 days in advance; however, crust will begin to lose its crispness after only 1 day.)

FRESH STRAWBERRY TOPPING
MAKES ABOUT 6 CUPS

This accompaniment to cheesecake is best served the same day it is made.

- 2 pounds strawberries, hulled and sliced lengthwise ¼ to ⅛ inch thick (3 cups)
- ½ cup (3½ ounces) sugar
  Pinch salt
- 1 cup strawberry jam
- 2 tablespoons lemon juice

1. Toss berries, sugar, and salt in medium bowl and let sit until berries have released juice and sugar has dissolved, about 30 minutes, tossing occasionally to combine.

2. Process jam in food processor until smooth, about 8 seconds, then transfer to small saucepan. Bring jam to simmer over medium-high heat and simmer, stirring frequently, until dark and no longer frothy, about 3 minutes. Stir in lemon juice, then pour warm liquid over strawberries and stir to combine. Let cool, then cover with plastic wrap and refrigerate until cold, at least 2 hours or up to 12 hours.

✔ WHY THIS RECIPE WORKS

A rejection of the Ben and Jerry school of everything-but-the-kitchen-sink concoctions, the ideal New York cheesecake is timeless in its adherence to simplicity. It is a tall, toasty-skinned, dense affair, a classic cheesecake with bronzed top and lush interior. After giving it a quick blast in a hot oven, we bake it low and slow for even cooking and a lovely graded texture.

MAKE A HOMEMADE CRUST   Though some New York–style cheesecakes have pastry crusts, we find they become soggy beneath the filling. Our preference? Graham crackers. Store-bought graham cracker crumbs don't taste nearly as good as crumbs you grind in the food processor from real graham crackers. We enrich ours with butter and sugar and press them into place in a springform pan with the bottom of a ramekin. Prebaking keeps this crust from becoming soggy.

USE ROOM-TEMPERATURE CHEESE   A New York cheesecake should be one of great stature. When we made one with 2 pounds (four bars) of cream cheese, it was not tall enough. Therefore, we fill the springform pan to the very top with an added half-pound. It's important that the cream cheese is at least moderately soft so that it can fully incorporate into the batter and you aren't left with a piece of cake containing small nodules of unmixed cream cheese amid an otherwise smooth bite. Simply cutting the cheese into chunks and letting them stand while preparing the crust and assembling the other ingredients—30 to 45 minutes—makes mixing easier.

CHOOSE THE RIGHT DAIRY   Cream cheese alone as the filling of a cheesecake makes for a pasty cake—much like a bar of cream cheese straight from its wrapper. Additional dairy loosens up the texture of the cream cheese, giving the cake a smoother, more luxurious texture. Although some recipes call for large amounts of sour cream, we use

only ⅓ cup so that the cake has a nice tang but won't end up tasting sour and acidic.

MIX WHOLE EGGS AND YOLKS   In this cheesecake, eggs do a lot of work. They help to bind, making the cake cohesive and giving it structure. Whole eggs alone are often called for in softer, airier cheesecakes. But recipes for New York cheesecakes tend to include additional yolks, which add fat and emulsifiers, and less water than whole eggs, to help produce a velvety, lush texture. We use six eggs plus two yolks, a combination that produces a dense but not heavy, firm but not rigid, perfectly rich cake.

FLAVOR, PLEASE   We keep the flavor of this cake simple. Lemon juice is a great addition, perking things up without adding a distinctively lemon flavor (no zest!). Just a bit of salt (cream cheese already contains sodium chloride) and a couple of teaspoons of vanilla extract round out the flavors well.

GO HIGH TO LOW   There are many ways to bake a cheesecake—in a moderate oven, in a low oven, in a water bath, or in the New York fashion, in which the cake bakes at 500 degrees for about 10 minutes and then at 200 degrees for about an hour and a half. This super-simple, no-water-bath (no leaking pans, layers of foil prophylactics, or boiling water), dual-temperature baking method produces a lovely graded texture—soft and creamy at the center and firm and dry at the periphery. It also yields the attractive nut-brown surface that we're after.

PREVENT CRACKS   Some cooks use the crack to gauge when a cheesecake is done. But we say if there's a crack it's already overdone. The best way to prevent a cheesecake from cracking is to use an instant-read thermometer to test its doneness. Take the cake out of the oven when it reaches 150 degrees to avoid overbaking. Higher temperatures cause the cheesecake to rise so much that the delicate network of egg proteins tears apart as the center shrinks and falls during cool-down.

SEPARATE AND COOL   During baking is not the only time a cheesecake can crack. There is a second opportunity outside the oven. A perfectly good-looking cake can crack as it sits on the cooling rack. The cake shrinks during cooling and will cling to the sides of the springform pan. If the cake clings tenaciously enough, the delicate egg structure splits at its weakest point, the center. To avoid this type of late cracking, cool the cheesecake for only a few minutes, then free it from the sides of the pan with a paring knife before allowing it to cool fully.

PUMPKIN PIE
SERVES 8

Use the Foolproof Baked Pie Shell on page 380. If candied yams are unavailable, regular canned yams can be substituted. When the pie is properly baked, the center 2 inches of the pie should look firm but jiggle slightly. The pie finishes cooking with residual heat; to ensure that the filling sets, let it cool at room temperature and not in the refrigerator. Do not cool this fully baked crust; the crust and filling must both be warm when the filling is added.

I	cup heavy cream
I	cup whole milk
3	large eggs plus 2 large yolks
I	teaspoon vanilla extract
I	(15-ounce) can unsweetened pumpkin puree
I	cup candied yams, drained
¾	cup (5¼ ounces) sugar
¼	cup maple syrup
2	teaspoons grated fresh ginger
I	teaspoon salt
½	teaspoon ground cinnamon
¼	teaspoon ground nutmeg
I	recipe Foolproof Baked Pie Shell (page 380), partially baked and still warm

I. Adjust oven rack to lowest position, place rimmed baking sheet on rack, and heat oven to 400 degrees. Whisk cream, milk, eggs and yolks, and vanilla together in bowl. Bring pumpkin, yams, sugar, maple syrup, ginger, salt, cinnamon, and nutmeg to simmer in large saucepan and cook, stirring constantly and mashing yams against sides of pot, until thick and shiny, 15 to 20 minutes.

2. Remove saucepan from heat and whisk in cream mixture until fully incorporated. Strain mixture through fine-mesh strainer into bowl, using back of ladle or spatula to press solids through strainer. Whisk mixture, then pour into warm prebaked pie crust.

3. Place pie on heated baking sheet and bake for 10 minutes. Reduce oven temperature to 300 degrees and continue to bake until edges of pie are set and center registers 175 degrees, 20 to 35 minutes longer. Let pie cool on wire rack to room temperature, about 4 hours. Serve.

✔ WHY THIS RECIPE WORKS

Too many pumpkin pie recipes result in a grainy custard in a soggy crust. For our pumpkin pie recipe, we avoid this outcome by drying out the pumpkin puree (with yams added for complex flavor) on the stovetop before whisking in dairy and eggs. The hot filling lets the creamy custard firm up quickly in the oven, preventing it from both curdling and soaking into the crust.

PREBAKE PIE SHELL Prebaking the pie crust is an essential step here. If we skipped it, and instead poured the pie filling straight into the raw dough, we would end up with a soggy, sad crust when the pie finally exited the oven. This is because the filling is very wet, and the crust needs that extra alone time in the oven to crisp up before coming in contact with all the extra moisture. (For more on pie crust, see concept 44.)

PUT HOT FILLING IN WARM CRUST If you're tempted to bake the pie crust way ahead of time, don't. It's imperative that the pie crust is warm when you add the hot filling. If it is not, the pie will become soggy. Using a hot filling in a warm crust allows the custard to firm up quickly in the oven, preventing it from soaking into the crust and turning it soggy. This is even true if you let the filling cool to room temperature. Keep that crust warm!

COOK THE PUMPKIN To maximize flavor, we concentrate the pumpkin's liquid rather than remove it, and we've found it best to do this on the stove. This is an added bonus for the spices that we add to the filling as well. Cooking the fresh ginger and spices along with the pumpkin puree intensifies their taste—the direct heat blooms their flavors (see concept 33). In addition, cooking minimizes the mealy texture in this pie where pumpkin is the star.

SUPPLEMENT WITH YAMS When we used solely pumpkin puree, we craved more flavor complexity. Therefore, we experimented with roasted sweet potatoes, which added a surprisingly deep flavor without a wholly recognizable taste. In an effort to streamline this technique, we tried adding canned sweet potatoes—commonly labeled as yams—instead. They were a hit. The yams add a complex flavor that complements the pumpkin.

ADD EXTRA YOLKS Our goal with this pie was to eliminate the grainy texture that plagues most custard in favor of a creamy, sliceable, not-too-dense pie. We start with a balance of whole milk and cream, and firm up the mixture with eggs. We don't simply add whole eggs, though—that just makes the pie too eggy. Because the whites are filled with much more water than the yolks, we exchange some whole eggs for the yolks alone.

Don't forget to pass the mixed filling through a fine-mesh strainer to remove any stringy bits. This will ensure the ultimate smooth texture.

TURN OVEN HIGH TO LOW Most pumpkin pie recipes call for a high oven temperature to expedite cooking time. But as we've learned, baking any custard at high heat has its dangers. Once the temperature of custard rises above 185 degrees it curdles, turning the filling coarse and grainy. This is why we cannot bake the pie at 425 degrees, as most recipes suggest. Lowering the temperature to 350 only provided us with a curdled and overcooked pie at the edges that was still underdone in the center. But baking at a low 300 degrees would mean leaving the pie in the oven for two hours. What to do? As with our New York–Style Cheesecake (page 182) we combine the two techniques, blasting the pie for 10 minutes on high heat and then baking it at 300 degrees for the rest of the baking time. This lessens the cooking time exponentially and leaves us with a creamy pie fully and evenly cooked from edge to center.

TEMPERING AT WORK CHEESECAKE AND ICE CREAM

Another technique we use to cook eggs gently and slowly for our stovetop custards is tempering. Tempering is the act of gradually increasing the temperature of a sensitive ingredient—in this case, eggs—to prevent it from curdling once added to a hot liquid. This is done by adding a small portion of the hot component (the base for lemon curd, for example) to the cooler ingredient (eggs) and stirring it in before adding the now-warmed ingredient to the rest of the hot component.

LEMON CHEESECAKE
SERVES 12 TO 16

When cutting the cake, have a pitcher of hot tap water nearby; dipping the blade of the knife into the water and wiping it clean with a kitchen towel after each cut helps make neat slices.

CRUST

5	ounces Nabisco Barnum's Animals Crackers or Social Tea Biscuits
3	tablespoons sugar
4	tablespoons unsalted butter, melted

FILLING

1¼	cups (8¾ ounces) sugar
1	tablespoon grated lemon zest plus ¼ cup juice (2 lemons)
1½	pounds cream cheese, cut into 1-inch chunks and softened
4	large eggs, room temperature
2	teaspoons vanilla extract
¼	teaspoon salt
½	cup heavy cream
1	tablespoon unsalted butter, melted

LEMON CURD

⅓	cup lemon juice (2 lemons)
2	large eggs plus 1 large yolk
½	cup (3½ ounces) sugar
2	tablespoons unsalted butter, cut into ½-inch pieces and chilled
1	tablespoon heavy cream
¼	teaspoon vanilla extract
	Pinch salt

1. FOR THE CRUST: Adjust oven rack to lower-middle position and heat oven to 325 degrees. Process cookies in food processor to fine crumbs, about 30 seconds (you should have about 1 cup). Add sugar and pulse 2 or 3 times to incorporate. Add melted butter in slow, steady stream while pulsing; pulse until mixture is evenly moistened and resembles wet sand, about 10 pulses. Empty crumbs into 9-inch springform pan and, using bottom of ramekin or dry measuring cup, press crumbs firmly and evenly into pan bottom, keeping sides as clean as possible. Bake crust until fragrant and golden brown, 15 to 18 minutes. Let cool on wire rack to room temperature, about 30 minutes. When cool, wrap outside of pan with two 18-inch square pieces of heavy-duty aluminum foil and set springform pan in roasting pan. Bring kettle of water to boil.

2. FOR THE FILLING: While crust is cooling, process ¼ cup sugar and lemon zest in food processor until sugar is yellow and zest is broken down, about 15 seconds, scraping down bowl as needed. Transfer lemon-sugar mixture to small bowl and stir in remaining 1 cup sugar.

3. Using stand mixer fitted with paddle, beat cream cheese on low speed until broken up and slightly softened, about 5 seconds. With mixer running, add lemon-sugar mixture in slow, steady stream; increase speed to medium and continue to beat until mixture is creamy and smooth, about 3 minutes, scraping down bowl as needed. Reduce speed to medium-low and beat in eggs, 2 at a time, until incorporated, about 30 seconds, scraping down bowl well after each addition. Add lemon juice, vanilla, and salt and mix until just incorporated, about 5 seconds. Add cream and mix until just incorporated, about 5 seconds longer. Give filling final stir by hand.

4. Being careful not to disturb baked crust, brush inside of pan with melted butter. Pour filling into prepared pan and smooth top with rubber spatula. Set roasting pan on oven rack and pour enough boiling water into roasting pan to come halfway up sides of pan. Bake cake until center jiggles slightly, sides just start to puff, surface is no longer shiny, and cake registers 150 degrees, 55 minutes to 1 hour. Turn off oven and prop open oven door with potholder or wooden spoon handle; allow cake to cool in water bath in oven for 1 hour. Transfer pan to wire rack. Remove foil, then run paring knife around cake and let cake cool completely on wire rack, about 2 hours.

5. FOR THE LEMON CURD: While cheesecake bakes, heat lemon juice in small saucepan over medium heat until hot but not boiling. Whisk eggs and yolk together in medium bowl, then gradually whisk in sugar. Whisking constantly, slowly pour hot lemon juice into eggs, then return mixture to saucepan and cook over medium heat, stirring constantly with wooden spoon, until mixture is thick enough to cling to spoon and registers 170 degrees, about 3 minutes. Immediately remove pan from heat and stir in cold butter until incorporated. Stir in cream, vanilla, and salt, then pour curd through fine-mesh strainer into small bowl. Place plastic wrap directly on surface of curd and refrigerate until needed.

6. When cheesecake is cool, scrape lemon curd onto cheesecake still in springform pan. Using offset spatula, spread curd evenly over top of cheesecake. Cover tightly with plastic and refrigerate for at least 4 hours or up to 1 day. To unmold cheesecake, wrap hot kitchen towel around pan and let stand for 1 minute. Remove sides of pan. Slide thin metal spatula between crust and pan bottom to loosen, then slide cake onto serving platter and serve. (Cake can be made up to 3 days in advance; however, the crust will begin to lose its crispness after only 1 day.)

GOAT CHEESE AND LEMON CHEESECAKE WITH HAZELNUT CRUST

The goat cheese gives this cheesecake a distinctive tang and a slightly savory edge. Use a mild-flavored goat cheese.

For crust, process generous ⅓ cup hazelnuts, toasted, skinned, and cooled, in food processor with sugar until finely ground and mixture resembles coarse cornmeal, about 30 seconds. Add cookies and process until mixture is finely and evenly ground, about 30 seconds. Reduce melted butter to 3 tablespoons. For filling, reduce cream cheese to 1 pound and beat 8 ounces room-temperature goat cheese with cream cheese in step 3. Omit salt.

TRIPLE-CITRUS CHEESECAKE

For filling, reduce lemon zest to 1 teaspoon and lemon juice to 1 tablespoon. Process 1 teaspoon grated lime zest and 1 teaspoon grated orange zest with lemon zest in step 2. Add 1 tablespoon lime juice and 2 tablespoons orange juice to mixer with lemon juice in step 3. For curd, reduce lemon juice to 2 tablespoons and heat 2 tablespoons lime juice, 4 teaspoons orange juice, and 2 teaspoons grated orange zest with lemon juice in step 5. Omit vanilla.

✓ WHY THIS RECIPE WORKS

We love cheesecake it in its unadulterated form, but sometimes the fresh flavor of citrus can take it to a refreshing new level. We aimed to develop a creamy cheesecake with a bracing but not overpowering lemon flavor. The use of animal rather than graham crackers, lemon zest, heavy cream, lemon curd, and—of course— a water bath helps us to achieve the ultimate lemon cheesecake. In addition: This cheesecake has a crowning layer of lemon curd, which in turn demonstrates the power of tempering at work.

USE ANIMAL CRACKERS Most cheesecakes have sweet and spicy graham cracker crusts that remain crunchy under the weight of the cheesy filling. But here the strong molasses taste of the graham crackers overwhelms the lemon flavor. We experimented with several kinds of more neutral-flavored crumb crusts and found that we liked the one made with animal crackers best.

PROCESS ZEST FOR FLAVOR Zest offers a nice balance of lemon flavor, but it comes with a hitch: The fibrous texture of the zest can mar the creamy smoothness of the filling. To solve this, we process the zest and ¼ cup of sugar together before adding them to the cream cheese. This produces a wonderfully potent lemon flavor by breaking down the zest and releasing its oils. Don't process all the sugar, though; that would wreak havoc with its crystalline structure (necessary for aerating the cream cheese) as well as meld it with the oils from the lemon zest, creating a strangely dense cake.

BAKE IN A BATH Like our Spiced Pumpkin Cheesecake (page 178), this cheesecake is baked in a water bath in a 325-degree oven. But here we turn the oven off and leave the cake in the oven for an additional hour with the door ajar. This technique of cooking at a very slow crawl so as not to overcook the eggs gives us a foolproof creamy consistency in our cheesecake from edge to center. We cook our cheesecake until it reaches 150 degrees in the center; this accounts for the fact that the edges, which generally cook faster, have already reached 170 degrees.

CHILL THE CAKE If the cheesecake is not thoroughly chilled, it will not hold its shape when sliced. After four hours in the refrigerator (and preferably longer), the cheesecake has set up. The fat in cream cheese has a relatively low softening temperature, and the high proportion of cream cheese to eggs makes it difficult for the egg proteins alone to provide enough structure when the cheesecake is warm. The solution is to ensure the cream cheese is cold enough to be firm. Likewise, the curd will firm up only when the cheesecake is thoroughly chilled. Only then can the cake be sliced neatly.

USE ACID To make a creamy curd with a silken texture, acid is key. Here, we get it from the lemon juice. The acid changes the electrical charge of the egg proteins, causing them to denature and eventually form a gel (see "How Does Acid Affect the Texture of Eggs?," right).

TIME TO TEMPER Like other stovetop custards, lemon curd combines eggs with hot liquid. To heat the eggs gently, we temper them, or slowly whisk in the hot liquid before putting the eggs on the stove. On the stove, we stir the mixture constantly (this motion reduces the amount that the egg proteins will bond so that our end product is a sauce rather than a solid mass) until it reaches 170 degrees. Be careful not to overcook the curd. While we want to get the maximum thickening power from the heat, we don't want so much that the eggs will curdle.

COLD BUTTER COOLS DOWN CURD Once the curd reaches 170 degrees, immediately remove the pan from the heat and stir in cold cubed butter, which cools the curd and prevent curdling and overcooking. The butter also helps to create a smoother emulsion. (For more on emulsions, see concept 36.)

PRACTICAL SCIENCE
HOW DOES ACID AFFECT THE TEXTURE OF EGGS?

Acids neutralize some of the negative electrical charges of egg proteins, causing them to form a gel.

When testing our Lemon Cheesecake recipe, we wondered how a high proportion of eggs in the presence of a relatively small amount of liquid could produce the creamy silken texture of lemon curd, while the same proportion of eggs and cream, for example, would simply scramble. What was the difference?

We suspected it had something to do with the strength of the acid. So we did a little experiment to test this hypothesis. We placed an egg in each of three separate pans over medium heat and added 2 tablespoons of rice wine vinegar to one pan, 2 tablespoons of lemon juice to the second pan, and the same amount of water to the third pan. The egg stirred with weaker vinegar cooked quickly and remained pale yellow and very creamy. The egg stirred with stronger lemon juice turned a more lemony yellow, took longer to cook, and, though it also remained creamy, formed a more solid gel than the egg cooked with vinegar. The egg stirred with plain water took almost twice as long to cook as the first egg and contained distinctly coagulated bits of bright yellow egg—just like scrambled eggs.

Egg proteins are tangled chains of amino acids. Each chain carries an abundance of negative electrical charges, which cause the chains to repel each other. Applying heat causes each protein chain to unravel, exposing more balanced electrical charges, at which point the chains are inclined to bond together and form clumps of protein. In the process of clumping, the amino acid molecules squeeze out any liquid that comes between them. This is known, as we've learned, as curdling.

Introducing an acid to the egg proteins neutralizes some of their negative electrical charges. Consequently, when the proteins are heated and unwind they do so at a lower temperature. However, the altered electrical charges on the proteins cause them to form a weak, soft gel. This creates a layer of liquid trapped between the weakly bonded ribbons of protein, like a sandwich, producing the effect that we pleasantly experience with our lemon curd. ("Curd" is a misnomer in this case.) The vinegar created a similar but different effect because different acids have different degrees of ability to alter the charge on the proteins depending on the strength of the acid. Thus, the stronger acid in lemon juice, while encouraging an egg to cook and form a solid, keeps the solid moist and creamy.

VANILLA ICE CREAM
MAKES ABOUT 1 QUART

Two teaspoons of vanilla extract can be substituted for the vanilla bean; stir the extract into the cold custard in step 3. An instant-read thermometer is critical for the best results. Using a prechilled metal baking pan and working quickly in step 4 will help prevent melting and refreezing of the ice cream and will speed the hardening process. If using a canister-style ice cream machine, be sure to freeze the empty canister for at least 24 hours and preferably 48 hours before churning. For self-refrigerating ice cream machines, prechill the canister by running the machine for five to 10 minutes before pouring in the custard.

1	vanilla bean
1¾	cups heavy cream
1¼	cups whole milk
½	cup plus 2 tablespoons sugar
⅓	cup light corn syrup
¼	teaspoon salt
6	large egg yolks

1. Place 8- or 9-inch square metal baking pan in freezer. Cut vanilla bean in half lengthwise. Using tip of paring knife, scrape out vanilla seeds. Combine vanilla bean, seeds, cream, milk, ¼ cup plus 2 tablespoons sugar, corn syrup, and salt in medium saucepan. Heat over medium-high heat, stirring occasionally, until mixture is steaming steadily and registers 175 degrees, 5 to 10 minutes. Remove saucepan from heat.

2. While cream mixture heats, whisk yolks and remaining ¼ cup sugar together in bowl until smooth, about 30 seconds. Slowly whisk 1 cup heated cream mixture into egg yolk mixture. Return mixture to saucepan and cook over medium-low heat, stirring constantly, until mixture thickens and registers 180 degrees, 7 to 14 minutes. Immediately pour custard into large bowl and let cool until no longer steaming, 10 to 20 minutes. Transfer 1 cup custard to small bowl. Cover both bowls with plastic wrap. Place large bowl in refrigerator and small bowl in freezer and cool completely, at least 4 hours or up to 24 hours. (Small bowl of custard will freeze solid.)

3. Remove custards from refrigerator and freezer. Scrape frozen custard from small bowl into large bowl of custard. Stir occasionally until frozen custard has fully dissolved. Strain custard through fine-mesh strainer and transfer to ice cream machine. Churn until mixture resembles thick soft-serve ice cream and registers about 21 degrees, 15 to 25 minutes. Transfer ice cream to frozen baking pan and press plastic wrap onto surface. Return to freezer until firm around edges, about 1 hour.

4. Transfer ice cream to airtight container, pressing firmly to remove any air pockets, and freeze until firm, at least 2 hours. Serve. (Ice cream can be stored for up to 5 days.)

✔ WHY THIS RECIPE WORKS
While you might not think of heat and eggs when making ice cream, eggs give homemade ice cream its silky texture. But heat the eggs and cream incorrectly and you get ice cream with odd lumps and awful eggy flavor. The quicker it freezes, the smoother the ice cream, so we speed up the freezing time of our homemade Vanilla Ice Cream recipe by starting with a colder base. Supplementing the sugar with corn syrup gives us ice cream that freezes faster, remains hard at home-freezer temperatures, and is free of large ice crystals.

TEMPER THE EGGS Because we are making this custard on the stovetop, as we do for Lemon Curd (see page 185), the techniques of a water bath or a low-temperature oven are not available to help us cook the eggs gently. Instead, we temper them by adding 1 cup of the hot cream mixture to the yolks, slowly whisking away. This not only warms the eggs up gently, it also dilutes the proteins so they are less likely to bond so tightly that they curdle when cooking on the stovetop.

COOK TO 180 DEGREES Though on their own, egg yolks begin to solidify around 150 degrees, the other ingredients that we add to this custard change the temperature of coagulation. For example, milk dilutes the proteins as well as introduces some fat, both of which raise the temperature at which eggs coagulate because in their presence the proteins don't bump into each other as readily. Sugar slows down protein unfolding as well. So together, the extra ingredients in our custard base raise the coagulation temperature of egg yolks to around 180 degrees. This is why it's so important to cook the custard until it reaches that point. Below that temperature, the egg proteins will not have uncoiled enough to form sufficient bonds to create the solid gel structure we need. (Make sure to strain the custard before freezing to remove any little bits that may have curdled along the way.)

SUPER-CHILL THE CUSTARD Smooth ice cream isn't technically less icy than "icy" ice cream. Instead, its ice crystals are so small that our tongues can't detect them. One way to encourage the creation of small ice crystals is to freeze the ice cream base as quickly as possible. Fast freezing, along with agitation, causes the formation of thousands of tiny seed crystals, which in turn promote the formation of more tiny crystals. Speed is such an important factor in ice cream making that commercial producers as well as restaurant kitchens spend tens of thousands of dollars on super-efficient "continuous batch" churners. The best of these can turn a 40-degree custard base (the coldest temperature it can typically achieve in a refrigerated environment) into soft-serve ice cream in 24 seconds. Our canister-style machine, on the other hand, takes roughly 35 minutes. No wonder our ice creams had always been so icy!

To combat this, we start with a colder base. After letting the hot custard cool for a few minutes, we pop 1 cup of it into the freezer and let the rest of the custard chill in the fridge overnight. The next day we mix the two together and churn the blend (now a cool 30 degrees) in our machine for a much smoother result.

COMBAT ICINESS WITH CORN SYRUP   One key to our ice cream's smoothness was to replace some of the sugar with corn syrup. (This was after trying other ice-crystal-reducing ingredients—condensed and evaporated milk, cornstarch, gelatin, pectin, and nonfat dry milk—to no avail.) This sweetener has a twofold effect: First, it is made up of glucose molecules and large tangled chains of starch that interrupt the flow of water molecules in a custard base. Since the water molecules can't move freely, they are less likely to combine and form large crystals as the ice cream freezes. Second, corn syrup creates a higher freezing point in ice cream than granulated sugar does. Since the water in ice cream made with corn syrup freezes at a higher temperature it is less likely to thaw and refreeze. This makes the ice cream less susceptible to the temperature shifts inevitable in a home freezer. These shifts cause constant thawing and refreezing, which creates large crystals even in the smoothest ice cream. Our ice cream stays smooth for nearly a week—far longer than most homemade ice creams do.

HARDEN FAST   But we don't stop there. For creamier results, we also needed to figure out a way to get our already-churned ice cream to freeze faster than it had in the past. With no way to make our freezer colder, we took a different route. Instead of scraping our churned ice cream into a tall container before placing it in the freezer, we spread it into a thin layer in a chilled square metal baking pan (metal conducts heat faster than glass or plastic). In an hour's time, the ice cream firms up significantly and can easily be scooped and transferred to an airtight container.

PRACTICAL SCIENCE ROLE OF SUGAR IN FREEZING

The addition of sugar to a frozen dessert makes it harder for water molecules to form ice crystals for smoother, creamier results.

When we freeze water it turns into a hard, impenetrable block of ice. Why, when we freeze our ice cream base, does it remain soft and smooth enough to scoop? It all comes down to the sugar.

A microscopic view of a frozen dessert—like ice cream, sherbet, sorbet, or granita—would reveal small grains of ice lubricated with sugar, fat, and bubbles of air. The simple churning of an ice cream machine can add lots of air, sometimes as much as doubling the volume. The other piece of the chemical puzzle—the transformation of the ice cream from liquid to solid—is more complicated. Sugar, it turns out, is the mediating factor between the two. Water freezes at 32 degrees, but the addition of sugar makes it harder for water molecules to form ice crystals and thus lowers the freezing temperature of the mixture. The higher the sugar concentration (that is, the more sugar there is in proportion to water), the greater this effect will be. As the temperature of the ice cream mixture drops below 32 degrees, some water starts to freeze into solid ice crystals, but the remaining water and sugar, which are in syrup form, remain unfrozen. As more water freezes, the sugar concentration in the remaining syrup increases, making it less and less likely to freeze.

Unfrozen sugar, corn syrup, or sugar syrup allows frozen desserts to be scooped straight from the freezer. (Without the sugar, they would be as hard as ice.) Sugar also reduces the size of the ice crystals, physically interfering with their growth. Smaller ice crystals translate into a less grainy texture. Sugar, then, not only makes ice cream sweet but also makes it smooth and scoopable, as you can see in the photos below of sherbet made with various amounts of sugar. For more on freezing and the role of sugar, see page 411.

NO SUGAR ADDED
Sherbet is hard and icy.

1 CUP SUGAR ADDED
Sherbet is somewhat softer.

2 CUPS SUGAR ADDED
Sherbet is smooth and creamy.

Starch Keeps Eggs from Curdling

So now we know that we can use low-temperature ovens, water baths, and tempering to prevent curdled eggs in baked desserts. But there are other cooking methods and recipes where we need to combat curdled eggs. For a wide range of dishes (from quiche to soup to pastry cream) our magic ingredient is … starch.

HOW THE SCIENCE WORKS

As we've learned, the proteins in raw egg whites and yolks are long chains of amino acids coiled up in balls. When cooked, they unfurl and then bond together to form a solid network, or gel, with all the water in which they were once floating now trapped inside.

Increasing temperature is one way to make the egg proteins uncoil and bond, also known as coagulation. The rate at which the proteins coagulate is directly related to the amount of heat introduced. If egg proteins are blasted with too much heat, then the rate of uncoiling and bonding increases to the point that the newly formed network is so extensive and strong that water is actually squeezed right out of its tight molecular web. This is called curdling.

There are various ingredients that can affect the rate of coagulation. Dairy dilutes the egg proteins, preventing them from bumping into each other and bonding so easily, thus raising the temperature at which they coagulate. Sugar also raises the coagulation temperature, but it does so by slowing down the unfolding of the proteins. (This is why custards must be cooked to 180 degrees, rather than about 150 degrees, the temperature at which eggs on their own coagulate. The added ingredients push the temperature a full 30 degrees higher. For more on the effect of sugar in eggs, see concept 21.)

Stirring also affects the strength of the protein network. Constant stirring on the stovetop is required for puddings and pastry cream to prevent overcooking and burning, but it also reduces the extent to which the proteins bond into a solid mass. This means that stirred custards form thinner custard sauces, while oven-cooked custards form solid gels (for example, Creamy Chocolate Pudding, page 196, versus Deep-Dish Quiche Lorraine, page 192).

But what we'll concentrate on here is starch. Cornstarch and, in some cases, flour are ingredients that affect how readily egg proteins will coagulate, and therefore the temperature of coagulation. When added to eggs and cooked, starch granules release spindly threads of amylose that interfere with the cross-linking of proteins, increasing the temperature at which the eggs coagulate. This plays an important role in the stabilization of egg proteins when they're heated, helping to prevent the clumping and curdling of eggs in creamy custards for quiche, and to keep the wisps of raw egg added to a hot soup feathery and fine. This also allows us to cook our pastry creams and puddings for much longer, and to a higher temperature, than we could without added starch, while still avoiding curdling the eggs. As a result, pudding becomes thick enough to mound on a spoon and pastry cream is thick enough to slice through in a tart.

WHEN STARCH IS ADDED TO EGGS

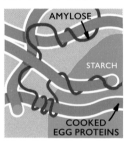

AMYLOSE

STARCH

COOKED EGG PROTEINS

EGGS AND STARCH *When egg proteins are mixed with large starch granules, the starch releases strands of amylose, which coat the proteins, helping to prevent tight links from forming as the eggs are cooked.*

TEST KITCHEN EXPERIMENT

To show the importance of adding starch to eggs for stability, we ran a simple experiment based on the classic French pastry cream. This recipe calls for heating 2 cups of half-and-half with 6 tablespoons of sugar and tempering this mixture into five egg yolks beaten with 3 tablespoons of cornstarch and 2 tablespoons of sugar. Once tempered, the mixture is brought to a full boil and cooked until thickened. We made one batch following the recipe, and then made the recipe again, this time omitting the cornstarch. We repeated both of these attempts twice and compared the results.

THE RESULTS

The pastry cream made with cornstarch thickened into a creamy, smooth, puddinglike consistency with nary a trace of curdled egg. The starchless pastry cream broke into two phases, becoming a thin, watery base with bits of curdled egg throughout. Comparing a spoonful of each was telling, but the difference was particularly drastic when we used a pastry brush to paint a thin layer of each onto a black board. The pastry cream made with starch gave us a smooth, full stroke, while the pastry cream without starch brushed chunky and thin.

THE TAKEAWAY

When the eggs in pastry cream are heated, the granules of starch from the added cornstarch release threads of amylose, which then coat the egg proteins and prevent them from linking too tightly, too quickly—something that can result in curdled eggs and, in this case, a broken pastry cream.

The lesson? Starch is an important element in a diverse range of recipes, from pastry cream to chocolate pudding, quiche to hot and sour soup. In all of these recipes the eggs are exposed to high heat and/or prolonged heat and they will curdle if you forget the starch.

ADD STARCH FOR CREAMY, NOT CURDLED, PASTRY CREAM

STARCH
Our pastry cream made with starch was creamy and smooth.

NO STARCH
Our pastry cream without starch was thin and broken.

PAINTING WITH PASTRY CREAM

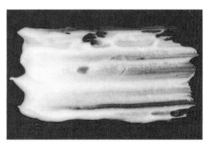

STARCH *When painted across a black board, our starchy pastry cream made a full, clear stroke.*

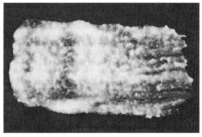

NO STARCH *When we painted with our starchless cream, however, the stroke appeared broken and splotchy.*

The rich, eggy custard of quiche is laden with additional fillings—from bacon to onions to cheese. As we've learned, custards are delicate, and these add-ons have the potential to wreak havoc. Cornstarch, with its ability to interfere with the clumping and curdling of egg proteins, is a lifesaver.

DEEP-DISH QUICHE LORRAINE
SERVES 8 TO 10

To prevent the crust from sagging during blind-baking, make sure it overhangs the pan's edge and use plenty of pie weights (3 to 4 cups). Be sure to use a cake pan with at least 2-inch-tall straight sides. To reheat the whole quiche, place it on a rimmed baking sheet on the middle rack of a 325-degree oven for 20 minutes; slices can be reheated in a 375-degree oven for 10 minutes. This recipe uses a total of nine eggs; one egg is separated and the white is used for the crust, while the yolk is used in the filling.

CRUST

1¾	cups (8¾ ounces) all-purpose flour
½	teaspoon salt
12	tablespoons unsalted butter, cut into ½-inch pieces and chilled
3	tablespoons sour cream
4–6	tablespoons ice water
1	large egg white, lightly beaten

CUSTARD FILLING

8	slices thick-cut bacon, cut into ¼-inch pieces
2	onions, chopped fine
1½	tablespoons cornstarch
1½	cups whole milk
8	large eggs plus 1 large yolk
1½	cups heavy cream
½	teaspoon salt
¼	teaspoon pepper
⅛	teaspoon ground nutmeg
⅛	teaspoon cayenne pepper
6	ounces Gruyère cheese, shredded (1½ cups)

1. FOR THE CRUST: Process flour and salt in food processor until combined, about 3 seconds. Add butter and pulse until butter is size of large peas, about 10 pulses.

2. Combine sour cream and ¼ cup ice water in small bowl. Add half of sour cream mixture to flour mixture; pulse 3 times. Repeat with remaining sour cream mixture. Pinch dough with fingers; if dough is floury, dry, and does not hold together, add 1 to 2 tablespoons more ice water and pulse until dough forms large clumps and no dry flour remains, 3 to 5 pulses.

3. Turn dough out onto counter and flatten into 6-inch disk; wrap disk in plastic wrap and refrigerate until firm but not hard, 1 to 2 hours, before rolling. (Dough can be refrigerated for up to 1 day; let stand at room temperature for 15 minutes before rolling.)

4. Cut two 16-inch lengths of aluminum foil. Arrange foil pieces, perpendicular to each other, in 9-inch round cake pan, pushing them into corners and up sides of pan; press overhang against outside of pan. Spray foil lightly with vegetable oil spray.

5. Roll out dough on generously floured counter to 15-inch circle about ¼ inch thick. Roll dough loosely around rolling pin and unroll into prepared cake pan. Working around circumference, ease dough into pan by gently lifting edge of dough with 1 hand while pressing into pan bottom with other. Trim any dough that extends more than 1 inch over edge of pan. Patch any cracks or holes with dough scraps as needed. Refrigerate any remaining dough scraps. Refrigerate dough-lined pan until dough is firm, about 30 minutes, then freeze for 20 minutes.

6. Adjust oven rack to lower-middle position and heat oven to 375 degrees. Line dough with foil or parchment paper and fill completely with pie weights, gently pressing weights into corners of shell. Bake on rimmed baking sheet until exposed edges of dough are beginning to brown but bottom is still light in color, 30 to 40 minutes. Carefully remove foil and pie weights. If any new holes or cracks have formed in dough, patch with reserved scraps. Return shell to oven and bake until bottom is golden brown, 15 to 20 minutes longer. Remove shell from oven and brush interior with egg white. Set aside while preparing filling. Reduce oven temperature to 350 degrees.

7. FOR THE CUSTARD FILLING: Cook bacon in 12-inch skillet over medium heat until crisp, 5 to 7 minutes. Transfer to paper towel–lined plate and discard all but 2 tablespoons bacon fat from skillet. Return to medium heat, add onions, and cook, stirring frequently, until softened and lightly browned, about 12 minutes. Set aside to cool slightly.

8. Whisk cornstarch and 3 tablespoons milk together in large bowl to dissolve cornstarch. Whisk in remaining milk, eggs, egg yolk, cream, salt, pepper, nutmeg, and cayenne until smooth.

9. Scatter onions, bacon, and cheese evenly over crust. Gently pour custard mixture over filling. Using fork, push filling ingredients down into custard and drag gently through custard to dislodge air bubbles. Gently tap pan on counter to dislodge any remaining air bubbles.

10. Bake until top of quiche is lightly browned, toothpick inserted in center comes out clean, and center registers 170 degrees, 1¼ to 1½ hours. Transfer to wire rack and let stand until cool to touch, about 2 hours.

11. When ready to serve, use sharp paring knife to remove any crust that extends beyond edge of pan. Lift foil overhang from sides of pan and remove quiche from pan; gently slide thin-bladed spatula between quiche and foil to loosen, then slide quiche onto serving plate. Cut into wedges. Serve warm or at room temperature.

DEEP-DISH QUICHE WITH LEEKS AND BLUE CHEESE

Omit bacon and onions. Melt 1 tablespoon unsalted butter in 12-inch skillet over medium heat. Add 4 large leeks, white and light green parts only, halved lengthwise, sliced ¼ inch thick, and washed thoroughly; cook until softened, 10 to 12 minutes. Increase heat to medium-high; continue to cook, stirring constantly, until leeks are beginning to brown, about 5 minutes. Transfer leeks to plate lined with triple layer of paper towels; press with double layer of paper towels to remove excess moisture. Increase salt in filling to 1 teaspoon. Substitute 1½ cups crumbled blue cheese for Gruyère; scatter blue cheese and sautéed leeks evenly over crust before adding custard. Reduce baking time to 1 to 1¼ hours.

DEEP-DISH QUICHE WITH SAUSAGE, BROCCOLI RABE, AND MOZZARELLA

Be sure to use supermarket-style low-moisture mozzarella in this variation; fresh mozzarella will make for a too-wet filling.

Omit bacon and onions. Cook 8 ounces hot or sweet Italian sausage, casings removed, in 12-inch skillet over medium heat, breaking sausage into ½-inch pieces, until no longer pink, 5 to 7 minutes. Transfer to paper towel–lined plate and discard all but 2 tablespoons fat from skillet. Return skillet to medium heat, add 8 ounces broccoli rabe, trimmed and cut into ½-inch pieces, and cook until slightly softened, about 6 minutes. Transfer rabe to plate lined with triple layer of paper towels; press with double layer of paper towels to remove excess moisture. Increase salt in filling to 1 teaspoon. Substitute 1½ cups shredded whole-milk mozzarella cheese for Gruyère; scatter mozzarella, cooked sausage, and broccoli rabe evenly over crust before adding custard. Reduce baking time to 1 to 1¼ hours.

✓ WHY THIS RECIPE WORKS

There's nothing wrong with classic quiche, but sometimes we crave a thick-crusted quiche brimming with a luxuriously creamy custard and a healthy dose of perfectly suspended fillings. To make this work, we change our bakeware, use a generous amount of crust, and mitigate the curdling effects of onions in the filling with cornstarch.

CHANGE THE BAKEWARE For us, a real quiche is a tall quiche. But to get a good and tall quiche, we need to use a lot of custard. And a lot of custard does not fit in a traditional tart pan. We could use a springform pan, but the custard has a tendency to leak through the thin gap between the springform's base and ring, not to mention that fitting the pastry dough up the exceptionally tall sides without tearing takes some practice. This is why we use a 9 by 2-inch round cake pan. It's tall enough to contain all the custard we want and won't leak.

PREVENT LEAKS For extra insurance against leaks and tearing, we employ three tricks for baking a quiche in a cake pan. First, we line the pan with a foil "sling" to help extract the pastry from this mold. Second, we roll out a 15-inch round of pastry and drape a generous amount of dough up and over the sides of the pan. This helps to anchor the crust in place, preventing it from sagging or shrinking when prebaked. And, third, we glaze the baked crust with an egg-white wash before adding the filling, which helps seal any would-be cracks. Rich with butter, supremely flaky, and strong enough to resist turning soggy, this crust is the perfect bowl for the satiny custard.

MAKE THE CUSTARD We wanted a quivering, barely set pudding for our quiche custard. But like all gels, custard is a delicate matter, and its success depends on just the right ratio of eggs to liquid (including any excess moisture exuded by watery ingredients like onions), plus gentle, even heat. Too few eggs and the custard is loose and runny, while too many lend it a scrambled-egg flavor and rubbery chew. We settle on eight whole eggs plus the extra yolk left over from sealing the crust and 3 cups of dairy.

USE CORNSTARCH The tricky part comes with adding the fillings: bacon, onions, and cheese. When onions enter the equation, the acids they release alter the electrical charges on the egg proteins, causing them to clump together so tightly that they squeeze out the moisture held between them. Starch granules in cornstarch interfere with this clumping by acting as a barrier between the proteins, which prevents them from squeezing out liquid and results in a smooth and creamy custard. Thanks to the cornstarch, this quiche can hold a full 2 cups of onions with no ill effects.

Cornstarch is a traditional thickener in hot and sour soup, but it can do more than thicken. Cornstarch is the reason we can get our egg, dropped carefully into the finished soup, to form perfect wisps.

HOT AND SOUR SOUP
SERVES 6 TO 8

To make slicing the pork chop easier, freeze it for 15 minutes. We prefer the distinctive flavor of Chinese black vinegar; look for it in Asian supermarkets. If you can't find it, a combination of red wine vinegar and balsamic vinegar approximates its flavor. This soup is very spicy. For a less spicy soup, omit the chili oil altogether or add only 1 teaspoon.

7	ounces extra-firm tofu, drained
¼	cup soy sauce
1	teaspoon toasted sesame oil
3½	tablespoons cornstarch
1	(6-ounce) boneless pork chop, ½ inch thick, trimmed and cut into 1 by ⅛-inch matchsticks
3	tablespoons plus 1 teaspoon cold water
1	large egg
6	cups low-sodium chicken broth
1	(5-ounce) can bamboo shoots, sliced lengthwise into ⅛-inch-thick strips
4	ounces shiitake mushrooms, stemmed and sliced ¼ inch thick
5	tablespoons Chinese black vinegar or 1 tablespoon red wine vinegar plus 1 tablespoon balsamic vinegar
2	teaspoons chili oil
1	teaspoon ground white pepper
3	scallions, sliced thin

1. Place tofu in paper towel–lined pie plate, top with heavy plate, and weight with 2 heavy cans. Let tofu drain until it has released about ½ cup liquid, about 15 minutes.

2. Whisk 1 tablespoon soy sauce, sesame oil, and 1 teaspoon cornstarch together in medium bowl. Add pork to bowl, toss to coat, and let marinate for at least 10 minutes or up to 30 minutes.

3. Combine 3 tablespoons cornstarch with 3 tablespoons water in small bowl. Mix remaining ½ teaspoon cornstarch with remaining 1 teaspoon water in second small bowl. Add egg and beat with fork until combined.

4. Bring broth to boil in large saucepan over medium-high heat. Reduce heat to medium-low, add bamboo shoots and mushrooms, and simmer until mushrooms are just tender, about 5 minutes. While broth simmers, cut tofu into ½-inch cubes. Add tofu and pork, with its marinade, to pan, stirring to separate any pieces of pork that stick together. Continue to simmer until pork is no longer pink, about 2 minutes.

5. Stir cornstarch mixture to recombine, then add to soup and increase heat to medium-high. Cook, stirring occasionally, until soup thickens and turns translucent, about 1 minute. Stir in vinegar, chili oil, pepper, and remaining 3 tablespoons soy sauce and turn off heat.

6. Without stirring soup, use soup spoon to slowly drizzle very thin streams of egg mixture into pot in circular motion. Let soup sit for 1 minute, then return saucepan to medium-high heat. Bring soup to gentle boil, then immediately remove from heat. Gently stir soup once to evenly distribute egg. Ladle soup into bowls, top with scallions, and serve.

✔ WHY THIS RECIPE WORKS
Authentic versions of this soup call for ingredients like mustard pickle, pig's-foot tendon, and dried sea cucumber. To get an authentically spicy, rich, and complex version that uses only ingredients from our local supermarket, we create a "hot" side for our soup using two heat sources—a full teaspoon of distinctive, penetrating white pepper and a little chili oil. To create the "sour" side, we prefer Chinese black vinegar but find a combination of balsamic and red wine vinegar to be an acceptable substitute. Cornstarch pulls triple duty here, going into our slurry to thicken the soup, into the marinade to keep the meat tender when it is cooked, and getting beaten with the egg to keep the egg light, wispy, and cohesive.

TOSS PORK WITH CORNSTARCH In addition to its role as thickener, cornstarch is believed by many Chinese cooks to play the part of protein tenderizer. We tested this theory by preparing two batches of soup, adding cornstarch to a simple soy sauce marinade for one julienned pork chop and omitting it in the marinade for another. The cornstarch-marinated pork was noticeably more tender. The cornstarch clings to and coats the meat during cooking, creating a protective sheath that slows the loss of moisture, thus preventing our moist, tender pork from becoming dry, chalky pork jerky.

BUILD HOT AND SOUR FLAVOR   The heat in hot and sour soup traditionally comes not from fresh chiles but from ground white peppercorns. Unlike chiles, pepper delivers direct spiciness but doesn't leave a lingering burn in its wake. We layer this with chili oil—a bit unconventional for this recipe, but a great support of the white-hot heat of the pepper, laying the groundwork for the opposing flavor of vinegar. The traditional vinegar, or sour component, in this soup is Chinese black vinegar, which is made from toasted rice. Looking for a more easily obtainable substitute, we settled on a combination of fruity balsamic and robust red wine vinegar.

PICK YOUR VEGGIES   Almost all authentic hot and sour soups start with reconstituted dried wood ear mushrooms and lily buds. Wood ear mushrooms, also known as tree ear or cloud ear, offer snappy texture but little else. We tried swapping in commonly available dried porcini and shiitake mushrooms, but their woodsy notes had a negative influence on the flavor equilibrium. Fresh, mild shiitake mushrooms are a better choice. Lily buds, or golden needles, are the dried buds of the tiger lily flower. Tangy, mildly crunchy canned bamboo shoots closely approximate the musky, sour flavor of lily buds and add textural variety (a crisp foil for the fluffy wisps of egg).

PRESS THE TOFU   As for the tofu, we had one basic question: Must it be pressed? The answer was a simple yes. Spongelike tofu is full of water, and weighting it beneath a heavy plate yields firmer, cleaner-tasting cubes.

STABILIZE THE EGG   After the pork is cooked and the soup thickened, beaten egg is drizzled in to create another complementary texture: fine, feathery shreds. But if the egg doesn't set immediately, it can blend into the soup and muddy the appearance of the broth. To make this step foolproof, we use vinegar in the soup, and cornstarch with the egg. The vinegar, which neutralizes some of the electrical charges on the egg proteins so they will combine and bond together, instantly coagulates the egg, helping it to form visible feathery threads rather than disperse so quickly that the individual proteins are almost invisible in the hot soup. The added cornstarch is the miracle worker: The cornstarch molecules stabilize the liquid proteins, preventing them from contracting excessively in the hot liquid.

To add the egg, make sure to turn off the heat so the surface of the soup is calm, and then use a spoon to drizzle egg onto the surface in a thin stream. Let it sit for 1 minute. Then turn the heat back on and stir gently to finish cooking, breaking it into light, soft ribbons.

PRACTICAL SCIENCE   TOASTED SESAME OIL

Toasted sesame oil is used as a flavoring agent, rather than a cooking oil.

Also referred to as dark or Asian sesame oil, toasted sesame oil is produced from deeply roasted sesame seeds, which give it a dark brown color and rich, perfumed flavor. It should not be confused with cold-pressed sesame oil, which is produced from raw seeds and has a very light color and little aroma or flavor. Whereas cold-pressed sesame oil may be used interchangeably with other vegetable oils—indeed, even to cook foods—toasted sesame oil, which has a low smoke point (it burns easily), is used not to cook foods but as a flavoring agent to give them a distinctive character. Because toasted sesame oil is particularly prone to damage from heat and light, it should be purchased only in tinted glass bottles and stored in the refrigerator.

PRACTICAL SCIENCE   THE FLAVOR OF SCALLIONS

White and green areas of scallions differ in texture and flavor.

Color aside, is there a difference between the green and white parts of the scallion?

To find out, we began by tasting raw scallions. Tasters described distinctly different flavor profiles for the white and green parts. The white section has a delicate, sweet taste similar to shallots, while the green portion has grassy notes and a peppery bite. When we used the raw scallions in salsa, tasters were still able to identify the same distinguishing characteristics; which scallion parts worked better depended on individual taste. Finally, we cooked scallions in a pork stir-fry. Tasters didn't notice major flavor differences, but the textures varied: The whites softened nicely while the greens wilted, taking on a limp texture that some tasters didn't like.

So if texture is an issue, cook only the white part and reserve the green portion to use as a garnish. When it comes to using the scallions raw, choose the white part for mild flavor and add the green for a strong, peppery taste.

And how do scallions get their flavor? As with onions (see concept 31), when scallions are chopped, enzymes within their cells are able to come in contact with sulfur-bearing amino acids to produce their familiar oniony flavor. But don't chop them in advance. That spry scallion bite that adds mild green onion sweetness to soups, salads, and the like is supplanted by a dull, soapy flavor when the scallions are prechopped and left to await sprinkling or simmering.

In stovetop custards and creams, we often temper our eggs, or slowly whisk a small amount of hot liquid into the cold eggs before putting the mixture on the stove, to more gradually bring them up to temperature. We also add a thickener. Cornstarch, as we've seen, is effective. But sometimes, as in our Pastry Cream, flour works, too. Flour, which is about 75 percent wheat starch, is similar to cornstarch, though less concentrated. We simply need to use a little bit more.

CREAMY CHOCOLATE PUDDING
SERVES 6

We prefer this recipe made with 60 percent bittersweet chocolate (our favorite brands are Ghirardelli Bittersweet Chocolate Baking Bar and Callebaut Intense Dark Chocolate). Using a chocolate with a higher cacao percentage will result in a thicker pudding. Low-fat milk (1 percent or 2 percent) may be substituted for the whole milk with a small sacrifice in richness. Do not use skim milk as a substitute.

2	teaspoons vanilla extract
½	teaspoon instant espresso powder
½	cup (3½ ounces) sugar
3	tablespoons Dutch-processed cocoa
2	tablespoons cornstarch
¼	teaspoon salt
3	large egg yolks
½	cup heavy cream
2½	cups whole milk
4	ounces bittersweet chocolate, chopped fine
5	tablespoons unsalted butter, cut into 8 pieces

1. Stir together vanilla and espresso in bowl; set aside. Whisk sugar, cocoa, cornstarch, and salt together in large saucepan. Whisk in egg yolks and cream until fully incorporated, making sure to scrape corners of saucepan. Whisk in milk until incorporated.

2. Place saucepan over medium heat; cook, whisking constantly, until mixture is thickened and bubbling over entire surface, 5 to 8 minutes. Cook for 30 seconds longer, remove from heat, add chocolate and butter, and whisk until melted and fully incorporated. Whisk in vanilla mixture.

3. Strain pudding through fine-mesh strainer into bowl. Place lightly greased parchment paper against surface of pudding and place in refrigerator to cool, at least 4 hours. Serve. (Pudding can be refrigerated for up to 2 days.)

✔ WHY THIS RECIPE WORKS

Homemade chocolate pudding often suffers from either lackluster chocolate flavor, caused by a dearth of chocolate, or a grainy texture, caused by too much cocoa butter. We were after chocolate pudding that tasted deeply of chocolate and was thickened to a perfectly silky, creamy texture. We found that using a moderate amount of bittersweet chocolate in combination with unsweetened cocoa and espresso powder helped us achieve maximum chocolate flavor, while cornstarch proved the right thickener. Salt and vanilla enhance the chocolate flavor even more.

USE THE RIGHT DAIRY Though most pudding recipes call for only milk, we find that swapping out a half a cup of milk for heavy cream adds a lush creaminess that we love.

ADD EGGS FOR RICHNESS A pudding made with cornstarch only is a hollow affair, not as texturally dense and creamy as we prefer. Adding eggs lends richness and body. Here, we use three egg yolks and no whites.

MAKE IT SILKY As we developed our pudding recipe, we found that there was a limit to how much bittersweet chocolate we could add before the texture turned gritty—but that we could continue to add chocolate in the form of cocoa powder without affecting smoothness. Why should this be the case? The culprit in causing grittiness, it turns out, is cocoa butter—and solid chocolate has far more of it than cocoa powder. Chocolate is manufactured so that its fat remains solid at room temperature but literally melts in the mouth. When melted chocolate is allowed to resolidify, however, the crystalline structure of its cocoa butter is reorganized. It becomes more stable and melts much more slowly at close to body temperature. If present in high enough amounts, this more stable form of cocoa butter can create the grainy texture we detected in the pudding. Cocoa powder adds more chocolate flavor without increasing the overall amount of cocoa butter in the pudding.

THICKEN WITH CHOCOLATE Using chocolate with a higher cacao percentage will result in a thicker pudding. This is because chocolate with a higher cacao percentage has more cocoa butter and cocoa solids, both of which act as thickeners, just as more fat in heavy cream makes it much thicker than milk. The cocoa solids suspended in the fat also add to the thickening effect, just as a slurry of flour in water is thicker than plain water. For all these reasons, make sure to use bittersweet chocolate in this recipe.

FLAVOR WITH ESPRESSO POWDER A little bit of coffee flavor in our chocolate pudding serves to reinforce, but not compete with, the flavor of the chocolate, enhancing its roasted undertones.

PASTRY CREAM

MARKES ABOUT 2 CUPS

This Pastry Cream can be used with the Boston Cream Cupcakes recipe on page 407.

- 2 cups half-and-half
- 6 large egg yolks, room temperature
- ½ cup (3½ ounces) sugar
  Pinch salt
- ¼ cup (1¼ ounces) all-purpose flour
- 4 tablespoons unsalted butter, cut into 4 pieces and chilled
- 1½ teaspoons vanilla extract

1. Heat half-and-half in medium saucepan over medium heat until just simmering. Meanwhile, whisk egg yolks, sugar, and salt together in medium bowl until smooth. Add flour to yolk mixture and whisk until incorporated. Remove half-and-half from heat and, whisking constantly, slowly add ½ cup to yolk mixture to temper. Whisking constantly, return tempered yolk mixture to half-and-half in saucepan.

2. Return saucepan to medium heat and cook, whisking constantly, until mixture thickens slightly, about 1 minute. Reduce heat to medium-low and continue to simmer, whisking constantly, for 8 minutes.

3. Increase heat to medium and cook, whisking vigorously, until bubbles burst on surface, 1 to 2 minutes. Remove saucepan from heat; whisk in butter and vanilla until butter is melted and incorporated. Strain pastry cream through fine-mesh strainer set over medium bowl. Press lightly greased parchment paper directly on surface and refrigerate until set, at least 2 hours or up to 24 hours.

✔ WHY THIS RECIPE WORKS

We prefer to use half-and-half as the dairy in our pastry cream. It gives us a nice, full taste without feeling either too light or too rich. Combined with flour as a thickening agent and the body-adding power of butter, half-and-half gives us a lush and fool-proof custard sauce.

TEMPER THE EGGS Add a portion of the heated dairy to the cold eggs to gently raise their temperature before cooking on the stove—a method that reduces the risk of curdling. (For more on tempering, see concept 19.)

HEAT FULLY Pastry cream is an anomaly among custards. Although overheating a typical custard can lead to curdling, it's vital to bring pastry cream almost to a boil. Doing so sets the eggs and activates (gelatinizes) the starch, thereby ensuring the proper consistency.

As a typical custard heats, the egg proteins unravel and intertwine, eventually forming cross-links that can result in coagulation, or even curdling. Why is pastry cream different? Because it contains starch, which affects texture in two ways. First, the starch interferes with the cross-linking of egg proteins, thus delaying coagulation. But the main reason that pastry cream must be heated even more is an enzyme in the egg yolks called amylase. If left unchecked, amylase can break down the starch and make the pastry cream runny. Whether spread into a tart shell, sandwiched between cake layers, or piped into éclairs, pastry cream must be both creamy and stiff. The starch in pastry cream allows the mixture to be brought almost to a boil, which destroys the amylase in the egg yolks, at the same time keeping the eggs from scrambling. When it's hot enough, three or four bubbles will burst on the surface, its temperature will read 200 degrees on an instant-read thermometer, and it will appear thick and glossy.

PRACTICAL SCIENCE FLOUR OR CORNSTARCH? A THICKENER FACE-OFF

Flour is a less potent thickener than cornstarch, but when it comes to our Pastry Cream, a much more reliable one.

When developing this pastry cream recipe, too often we found that the custard, which is made by heating half-and-half with egg yolks and cornstarch, failed to thicken properly. Would flour be more reliable?

We made multiple batches of pastry cream thickened with 3 tablespoons of cornstarch according to our recipe, and another set thickened with 4 tablespoons of flour (a less potent thickener than cornstarch), which we cooked longer to remove the floury taste.

The flour-thickened batches of pastry cream set up and held perfectly every time, while those containing cornstarch occasionally did not set at all or even thinned out once they had thickened.

When starch is heated in water, its granules absorb water, swell, and eventually burst, releasing a starch molecule called amylose that diffuses throughout the solution, trapping additional water and forming a gelatinous network. Because cornstarch is a pure starch, it contains far more amylose than flour (which is only about 75 percent starch), giving it maximum thickening power. But its purity makes cornstarch finicky. If a custard such as pastry cream isn't heated enough, an enzyme in the yolks called amylase can weaken the starch gels so the custard never fully sets up. If the custard is heated too much, the starch granules can burst. And even if it does thicken properly, overwhisking the mixture can break the bonds of the starch gels and thin it out. Flour, on the other hand, contains proteins and lipids that dilute its capacity to form starch gels, so that more of it is needed for thickening. But these other components also act as binders, keeping water trapped and ensuring that liquid not only thickens, but stays that way.

Whipped Egg Whites Need Stabilizers

One of the greatest feats of culinary magic is taking a few egg whites and whipping them into a billowy mound of cloudlike foam that fills the entire bowl. A range of recipes—from soufflés to angel food cake to lemon meringue pie—rely on whipped egg whites. How does beating transform a few tablespoons of liquid into several cups of foam? Let's find out.

HOW THE SCIENCE WORKS

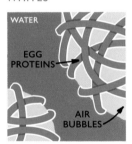

INSIDE WHIPPED EGG WHITES

WHEN WHIPPED *Air bubbles whipped into the egg whites are coated with the unfurled egg proteins to make a foam.*

Egg whites are different from egg yolks, and while we mix the two together for scrambled eggs, omelets, and many baked desserts, we just as often split them up and use each separately. Sometimes we need just the yolks, such as for ice cream, which is dense and rich, but here we explore using the whites alone.

The most common way to use egg whites is to beat them, changing their structure from a liquid to a voluminous foam. As an egg white is beaten, its proteins unfold and bond to create a meshlike network that coats and reinforces the surface of the air bubbles produced in a sea of water (remember, egg whites are composed of about 90 percent water). These unfurled proteins actually increase the viscosity of the water immediately surrounding the air bubbles, enhancing their stability. As the whites are beaten further, more air bubbles form and more proteins bond to coat and reinforce them. Eventually the whole mix will puff up and take on the firm texture of shaving cream. The trick here is to neither underbeat the whites (the mixture will not be stable) nor overbeat them (the foam will become too rigid and will rupture, squeezing out the liquid contained in the whites).

Though this seems simple, things can easily go astray. If any fats, oils, or emulsifiers (for example, a bit of the yolk) get in the mix they can compromise the success of an egg-white foam, because these substances will coat the proteins, preventing them from unfolding and bonding. Fats and oils also take up valuable space on the surface of the air bubbles created when whipping egg whites, which disrupts and weakens the network of protective proteins, causing the foam to collapse very quickly and resulting in a soggy, deflated mass.

As a rule, whipped egg-white foams are temporary things. Whether the foam is raw or cooked, the water surrounding the air bubbles will eventually succumb to the force of gravity and begin to drain away, causing the foam to separate and release its liquid. Our goal is to delay this as long as possible.

We've seen the role of starch when it comes to stabilizing fully cooked eggs and preventing a curdled mess (concept 20). But when we isolate and whip egg whites, a different kind of stabilization is called for. Two ingredients help.

The first is sugar, which slows the drainage of moisture from the film surrounding the air bubbles in egg foams, helping the whites to remain stable as well as achieve maximum volume. Here, the timing is key.

In the early stage of whipping, the proteins have not completely unfurled and linked together, so the air bubbles that ultimately give the foam its volume can't hold a firm shape. Sugar, however, interferes with the ability of proteins to cross-link. If it's added too early, fewer proteins will bond and trap air, resulting in a foam that is less voluminous. If, on the other hand, you beat the egg whites until they are very thick and dense, the sugar added at this stage will have less water to dissolve in, giving the finished meringue a gritty texture and a tendency to form drops of sugar syrup during baking. The key is to add sugar only when the whites have been whipped enough to gain some volume but still have enough free water left in them to dissolve the sugar completely. The right moment? Just before the soft peak stage, when the foam is frothy and bubbly but not quite firm enough to hold a peak.

The second stabilizing ingredient is cream of tartar, an acid that alters the electric charge on the proteins of the egg whites, in turn reducing the interactions between protein molecules. Because this delays the formation of the foam, whipping takes longer but also results in a much more stable foam.

TEST KITCHEN EXPERIMENT

To demonstrate the effects of adding cream of tartar to egg whites when whipping them to stiff peaks, we devised the following test: We beat eight batches of four egg whites in a stand mixer (starting on low speed to unravel the egg proteins and finishing on high to incorporate significant air) until they achieved stiff peaks. In half the batches we included ¼ teaspoon of cream of tartar before whipping, while the others were left plain. We transferred the fluffy eggs to funnels set over beakers and collected exuded water for 60 minutes, long enough to see significant results.

THE RESULTS

The whites whipped without any stabilizers lost 23 mL of liquid on average. The whites stabilized with cream of tartar lost less than half that amount, about 10 mL on average.

THE TAKEAWAY

While our egg foams made with and without a stabilizer did not look different—both were light and fluffy foams holding stiff peaks—they released a drastically different amount of liquid with time. Why is this important? Beating air into egg whites transforms them from a liquid to a foam. But whipped egg whites can revert, at least partially, to their liquid state over time. This is what is happening when the meringue topping on a pie "weeps"—the egg foam is breaking down and becoming soft and wet.

The addition of cream of tartar changed the electric charges of the egg-white proteins,

CREAM OF TARTAR STABILIZES WHITES

UNSTABILIZED
Whipped with no stabilizer, these egg whites oozed liquid.

STABILIZED
Cream of tartar helped these egg whites to hold on to much more liquid.

delaying their ability to link together and therefore creating a stronger network around the air bubbles of the foam. This stronger network is better able to withstand gravity and hold moisture within. Keeping whipped egg whites stable is important in a variety of recipes. If your egg whites are not stabilized (with cream of tartar or sugar), they can lose a large amount of liquid while baking, causing gritty, weepy meringues or baked goods that deflate disastrously in the oven.

The addition of sugar stabilizes whipped egg whites in two ways. First, it slows the unfolding of egg proteins, delaying the formation of foam and protecting against overwhipping. Second, sugar dissolves in the liquid surrounding the air bubbles in an egg foam, forming a thick and viscous syrup that is slow to drain. (If the liquid drains too quickly, the air bubbles, and therefore the foam, will collapse.) Here, we look at the stabilizing effect of sugar when used alone in our Meringue Cookies and when combined with other ingredients in our Bittersweet Chocolate Mousse Cake.

MERINGUE COOKIES
MAKES ABOUT 48 SMALL COOKIES

Meringues may be a little soft immediately after being removed from the oven but will stiffen as they cool. To minimize stickiness on humid or rainy days, allow the meringues to cool in a turned-off oven for an additional hour (for a total of two hours) without opening the door, then transfer them immediately to airtight containers and seal.

¾	cup (5¼ ounces) sugar
2	teaspoons cornstarch
4	large egg whites
¾	teaspoon vanilla extract
⅛	teaspoon salt

1. Adjust oven racks to upper-middle and lower-middle positions and heat oven to 225 degrees. Line 2 baking sheets with parchment paper. Combine sugar and cornstarch in small bowl.

2. Using stand mixer fitted with whisk, beat egg whites, vanilla, and salt together on high speed until very soft peaks start to form (peaks should slowly lose their shape when whisk is removed), 30 to 45 seconds. Reduce speed to medium and slowly add sugar mixture in steady stream down side of mixer bowl (process should take about 30 seconds). Stop mixer and scrape down bowl. Increase speed to high and beat until glossy and stiff peaks have formed, 30 to 45 seconds.

3. Working quickly, place meringue in pastry bag fitted with ½-inch plain tip or large zipper-lock bag with ½ inch of corner cut off. Pipe meringues into 1¼-inch-wide mounds about 1 inch high on baking sheets, 6 rows of 4 meringues on each sheet. Bake for 1 hour, switching and rotating baking sheets halfway through baking. Turn off oven and let meringues cool in oven for at least 1 hour. Remove meringues from oven, immediately transfer from baking sheet to wire rack, and let cool to room temperature. (Meringues can be stored in airtight container for up to 2 weeks.)

CHOCOLATE MERINGUE COOKIES

Gently fold 2 ounces finely chopped bittersweet chocolate into meringue mixture at end of step 2.

TOASTED ALMOND MERINGUE COOKIES

Substitute ½ teaspoon almond extract for vanilla extract. In step 3, sprinkle meringues with ⅓ cup coarsely chopped toasted almonds and 1 teaspoon coarse sea salt (optional) before baking.

ORANGE MERINGUE COOKIES

Stir 1 teaspoon grated orange zest into sugar mixture in step 1.

ESPRESSO MERINGUE COOKIES

Stir 2 teaspoons instant espresso powder into sugar mixture in step 1.

PRACTICAL SCIENCE
TWIN STABILIZERS—SUGAR AND CORNSTARCH

Sugar and cornstarch stabilize, without being too sweet.

We wanted meringue cookies that were less sweet than the traditional kind, but when we cut back on sugar, our cookies collapsed in the oven. What was going on? In their raw state, the tiny bubbles that form a meringue get their structure from two things: the cross-linking of egg-white proteins and the water that occupies virtually all the space between the bubbles. As a meringue bakes, its moisture slowly evaporates, weakening its structure. At the same time, the egg-white protein ovalbumin is becoming stronger by bonding with other proteins, providing additional structure for the foam. Because sugar has a tendency to hold on to water molecules, if there is not enough sugar in the meringue, the water evaporates too quickly, causing the cookies to collapse before the ovalbumin has time to strengthen. We found that cornstarch, which shares the water-clinging property of sugar, could perform the same role in our recipe, allowing us to cut back on sweetness without compromising structure.

SUGAR WITHDRAWAL
Removing too much sugar causes meringues to collapse in the oven.

FORTIFIED FOAM
Replacing a little sugar with cornstarch helps meringues keep their shape while baking.

✔ WHY THIS RECIPE WORKS

A classic meringue cookie may have only two basic ingredients—egg whites and sugar—but it requires precise timing. Otherwise, you'll end up with a meringue that's as dense as Styrofoam or weepy, gritty, and cloyingly sweet. A great meringue cookie should emerge from the oven glossy and white, with a shatteringly crisp texture that dissolves instantly in your mouth. The key to glossy, evenly textured meringue is adding the sugar at just the right time—when the whites have been whipped enough to gain some volume and strength but still have enough free water left in them for the sugar to dissolve completely. Surprisingly, we find that cream of tartar is not necessary here. The sugar and cornstarch are stabilizers enough.

PICK FRANCE There are three types of meringue: Italian, in which a hot sugar syrup is poured into the egg whites as they are beaten; Swiss, which heats the whites with the sugar; and French, in which egg whites are whipped with sugar alone. For this recipe, French is best. We find that it's the simplest of the meringues, and we prefer the results in comparison, for example, to the dense and candylike cookies made by the Italian method.

ADD SUGAR Pay attention to your egg whites as you beat them. You don't want to add the sugar too early, when it will interfere with the cross-linking proteins, or too late, when there isn't enough water in which the sugar can dissolve, resulting in a gritty, weeping meringue. Add the sugar just before the soft peak stage, when the whites have gained some volume but still have enough water for the sugar to dissolve. Adding the sugar in a slow stream down the side of the bowl of a running stand mixer helps distribute the sugar more evenly, which creates a smoother meringue.

USE CORNSTARCH When tasting traditional recipes, we found the majority of them to be too sweet. But when we cut back on the amount of sugar, it produced disastrous results. The meringues with less sugar started collapsing and shrinking in the oven. Why? Turns out sugar stabilizes in both the mixing bowl and the oven. Without sufficient sugar, the meringues lose moisture too rapidly as they bake, causing them to collapse. We solve this problem with a bit of cornstarch (see "Twin Stabilizers—Sugar and Cornstarch," left).

PIPE THE COOKIES To guarantee uniform shape and proper even cooking, it's essential to pipe the cookies rather than use a spoon. A pastry bag produces perfectly shaped meringues; a zipper-lock bag with a corner cut off works nearly as well.

TURN OFF YOUR OVEN Traditionally, meringues are baked at a low temperature and then left in the turned-off oven, sometimes for as long as overnight. The idea is to completely dry out the cookies while allowing them to remain snow white. We tried baking ours at 175 degrees, but our ovens had trouble maintaining this temperature. An hour in a 225-degree oven followed by another hour in the turned-off oven produces perfectly cooked meringues every time.

BITTERSWEET CHOCOLATE MOUSSE CAKE
MAKES ONE 9-INCH CAKE, SERVING 12 TO 16

If the sugar is lumpy you should crumble it with grease-free fingers. Any residual fat from butter or chocolate might hinder the whipping of the whites. If you like, dust the cake with confectioners' sugar just before serving or top slices with a dollop of lightly sweetened whipped cream.

12	tablespoons unsalted butter, cut into 12 pieces
12	ounces bittersweet chocolate, chopped
1	ounce unsweetened chocolate, chopped
8	large eggs, separated
1	tablespoon vanilla extract
⅛	teaspoon salt
⅔	cup packed (4⅔ ounces) light brown sugar

1. Adjust oven rack to lower-middle position and heat oven to 325 degrees. Grease 9-inch springform pan, line with parchment paper, grease parchment, and flour pan. Wrap bottom and sides of pan with large sheet of aluminum foil.

2. Melt butter and chocolates in large heatproof bowl set over saucepan filled with 2 quarts barely simmering water, stirring occasionally, until smooth. Remove from heat and let mixture cool slightly, then whisk in egg yolks and vanilla. Set chocolate mixture aside, reserving hot water, covered, in saucepan.

3. Using stand mixer fitted with whisk, whip egg whites and salt on medium speed until frothy, about 30 seconds. Add ⅓ cup sugar, increase speed to high, and whip until combined, about 30 seconds. Add remaining ⅓ cup sugar and continue to whip until soft peaks form when whisk is lifted, about 2 minutes longer. Using whisk, stir about one-third of beaten egg whites into chocolate mixture to lighten it, then fold in remaining egg whites in 2 additions using whisk. Gently scrape batter into prepared springform pan, set pan in large roasting pan, then pour hot water from saucepan into roasting pan to depth of 1 inch. Carefully slide roasting pan into oven and bake until cake has risen, is firm around edges, center has just set, and center registers about 170 degrees, 45 to 55 minutes.

4. Remove springform pan from water bath, discard foil, and let cool on wire rack for 10 minutes. Run thin-bladed paring knife between sides of pan and cake to loosen; let cake cool in pan on wire rack until barely warm, about 3 hours, then wrap pan in plastic wrap and refrigerate until thoroughly chilled, at least 8 hours. (Cake can be refrigerated for up to 2 days.)

5. To unmold cake, remove sides of pan. Slide thin metal spatula between cake and pan bottom to loosen, then invert cake onto large plate, peel off parchment, and reinvert onto serving platter. To serve, use sharp, thin-bladed knife, dipping knife in pitcher of hot water and wiping blade before each cut.

✔ WHY THIS RECIPE WORKS

This recipe combines the techniques of using sugar to stabilize the egg whites and a water bath to cook the cake gently and evenly (see concept 19). It's important to whip the egg whites well before folding them into the chocolate mixture. The Bittersweet Chocolate Mousse Cake is nothing without stable, voluminous egg whites.

PREPARE THE PAN To keep the cake from sticking, be sure to butter, flour, and then line the bottom of the springform pan with parchment paper. We also wrap the outside of the pan with foil to prevent leakage when in the water bath. (See "Leak-Proofing Springform Pans," page 179, for an alternative to wrapping the pan in foil.)

USE LOTS OF YOLKS Butter and egg yolks are the ingredients that give this cake its melt-in-your-mouth texture. Twelve tablespoons is the perfect amount of butter. Any more makes the cake unpalatably greasy; less makes it dry. As for the egg yolks, we made cakes using as few as four and as many as 10. The 10-yolk version remained a little too damp in the middle, even when thoroughly baked. Eight is the magic number.

PICK BROWN SUGAR When we tried using light brown sugar rather than granulated, we knew we were on to something good. The flavor was fabulous, with just the right amount of sweetness and a tiny hint of smokiness from the molasses. Brown sugar offers an additional bonus, too: The molasses in brown sugar is slightly acidic, eliminating the need for cream of tartar (another acid) to

stabilize the egg whites. When beaten together, the whites and brown sugar turn into a glossy, perfect meringue.

FOLD IN THE FOAM After beating the egg whites, we fold them into the batter for our cake. But if the meringue is not the proper consistency, this can be problematic. Delicate egg whites beaten with nothing added to them will collapse under the weight of the chocolate, giving the cake a dense, bricklike structure. Beating the egg whites further, until they are almost rigid, will just make the cake unappealingly dry. Beating them less will only make the cake more dense. But adding the sugar to the egg whites as they are being beaten will create a thicker, more stable egg foam. This method will produce a creamy meringue that holds up well when folded into the chocolate mixture, creating a baked mousse cake that is moist, rich, and creamy. Because the egg whites are only beaten to soft peaks—and no further—we add the sugar a bit earlier in the process, as compared to recipes where egg whites are beaten to stiff peaks. We use a similar technique in the Angel Food Cake recipe on page 204.

BAKE IN A WATER BATH Baking the mousse cake on its own in an oven set to the standard temperature for cakes (350 degrees) turns it into a giant mushroom that collapses after cooking. A more gentle heat level (300 degrees) causes the outside of the cake to be overdone while the center remains raw. The solution? A water bath. A mousse cake baked in a water bath in a 325-degree oven rises evenly and has a velvety, creamy texture throughout. The extra step is worth the effort.

PRACTICAL SCIENCE
THE EASIEST WAY TO SEPARATE AN EGG

It is easier to separate cold eggs than room-temperature eggs.

Many baking recipes call for bringing eggs to room temperature before they are separated. But this can be a tricky business, as the warm yolk can easily fall into the white (a recipe for failure if you are looking for fluffy, whipped whites). Separating each egg over a smaller bowl before adding the yolk or white to another bowl is always a safe measure, but we have found that we have much better luck when we separate the eggs while they are still chilly from the fridge. Yolks are more taut and less apt to break into the whites when cold. If a recipe calls for the eggs to be brought to room temperature, simply separate the eggs while cold, cover both bowls with plastic wrap (make sure the wrap touches the surface of the eggs to keep them from drying out), and let sit on the counter until they've lost their chill.

Cream of tartar, also known as potassium bitartrate, or potassium acid tartrate, is a powdered byproduct of the winemaking process and, along with baking soda, is one of the two main ingredients in baking powder. Cream of tartar's acidic nature lowers the pH of egg whites, altering the electric charge on the proteins and encouraging them to unfold, thus creating more volume, greater stability, and a glossier appearance. We use it here to help stabilize egg whites in pies, cakes, and soufflés.

LEMON MERINGUE PIE
SERVES 8

For the best flavor, use freshly squeezed lemon juice; don't use bottled lemon juice. Be sure that the filling is cool when spreading the meringue onto the pie. This pie should be served the same day that it is prepared.

FILLING

1½   cups water
1   cup (7 ounces) sugar
¼   cup cornstarch
⅛   teaspoon salt
6   large egg yolks
1   tablespoon grated lemon zest plus ½ cup juice (3 lemons)
2   tablespoons unsalted butter, cut into 2 pieces

1   recipe Foolproof Single-Crust Pie Dough for Custard Pies (page 381), fully baked and cooled

MERINGUE

¾   cup (5¼ ounces) sugar
⅓   cup water
3   large egg whites
¼   teaspoon cream of tartar
     Pinch salt
¼   teaspoon vanilla extract

1. FOR THE FILLING: Bring water, sugar, cornstarch, and salt to simmer in large saucepan over medium heat, whisking constantly. When mixture starts to turn translucent, whisk in egg yolks, 2 at a time. Whisk in lemon zest and juice and butter. Return mixture to brief simmer, then remove from heat.

2. Pour filling into baked and cooled pie crust. Lay sheet of plastic wrap directly on surface of filling and refrigerate pie until filling is cold, about 2 hours.

3. FOR THE MERINGUE: Adjust oven rack to middle position and heat oven to 400 degrees. Bring sugar and water to vigorous boil in small saucepan over medium-high heat. Once syrup comes to rolling boil, cook for 4 minutes (mixture will become slightly thickened and syrupy). Remove from heat and set aside while beating whites.

4. Using stand mixer fitted with whisk, whip whites, cream of tartar, and salt on medium-low speed until foamy, about 1 minute. Increase speed to medium-high and whip until soft peaks form, about 2 minutes. With mixer running, slowly pour hot syrup into whites (avoid pouring syrup onto whisk or it will splash). Add vanilla and beat until meringue has cooled and becomes very thick and shiny, 3 to 6 minutes.

5. Using rubber spatula, mound meringue over filling, making sure meringue touches edges of crust. Use spatula to create peaks all over meringue. Bake until peaks turn golden brown, about 6 minutes. Transfer to wire rack and let cool to room temperature. Serve.

✔ WHY THIS RECIPE WORKS

We wanted our Lemon Meringue Pie recipe to produce a tall and fluffy topping, so we make the meringue with a hot sugar syrup and add a bit of cream of tartar to the egg whites before beating them. This technique ensures that the meringue is cooked through and stable enough to be piled high on top of the filling.

ADD GRAHAM CRACKERS TO CRUST   To promote browning and really crisp the crust, we roll our Foolproof Single-Crust Pie Dough for Custard Pies (page 381) in graham cracker crumbs. Not only does this help the texture of our crust, but it adds a wonderful graham flavor to complement the lemon pie without masking the character of the dough itself. It's important to note that the crust is fully baked and cooled before it is filled and chilled.

MAKE THE RIGHT FILLING   The filling for our Lemon Meringue Pie is a close relative of lemon curd (see page 185), but because you need so much more of it to fill a pie shell it's diluted with water (all lemon juice would be too intense) and stabilized with cornstarch (so you can slice cleanly through the thick filling).

PICK ITALIAN   Rather than simply beating egg whites with raw sugar (the French method), here we pour hot sugar syrup into the whites as they are beaten (the Italian method). The hot syrup cooks the whites and helps transform them into a soft, smooth meringue that is stable enough to resist weeping during its short time in the oven. With a French meringue, the bottom portion often doesn't cook through and weeping is a greater risk.

BAKE, DON'T BROIL   While some recipes throw the pie under the broiler, a hot oven greatly reduces the risk of burning the meringue.

ANGEL FOOD CAKE
SERVES 10 TO 12

Do not use all-purpose flour. Our tasters unflatteringly compared a cake made with it to Wonder Bread. If your angel food cake pan does not have a removable bottom, line the bottom of the pan with parchment paper. In either case, do not grease the pan (or the paper).

1	cup plus 2 tablespoons (4½ ounces) cake flour
¼	teaspoon salt
1¾	cups (12¼ ounces) sugar
12	large egg whites
1½	teaspoons cream of tartar
1	teaspoon vanilla extract

1. Adjust oven rack to lower-middle position and heat oven to 325 degrees. Whisk flour and salt together in bowl. Process sugar in food processor until fine and powdery, about 1 minute. Reserve half of sugar in small bowl. Add flour mixture to food processor with remaining sugar and process until aerated, about 1 minute.

2. Using stand mixer fitted with whisk, whip egg whites and cream of tartar on medium-low speed until foamy, about 1 minute. Increase speed to medium-high, slowly add reserved sugar, and whip until soft peaks form, about 6 minutes. Add vanilla and mix until incorporated.

3. Sift flour mixture over egg whites in 3 additions, folding gently with rubber spatula after each addition until incorporated. Scrape mixture into ungreased 12-cup tube pan.

4. Bake until toothpick inserted in center comes out clean and cracks in cake appear dry, 40 to 45 minutes. Let cake cool completely in pan, upside down, about 3 hours. Run knife around edge of cake to loosen, then gently tap pan upside down on counter to release cake. Turn cake right side up onto platter and serve.

✓ WHY THIS RECIPE WORKS

Unlike other cakes, angel food cake uses no oil or butter—you don't even grease the cake pan. It doesn't call for baking soda or baking powder, either, relying solely on beaten egg whites for its dramatic height. To make angel food cake, you whip egg whites with sugar and cream of tartar—stabilizing ingredients, as we know—until soft peaks form, fold in flour and flavorings, and bake.

GRIND SUGAR EXTRA-FINE Granulated or confectioners' sugar will make acceptable but somewhat heavy cakes. For an extraordinary angel food cake, process granulated sugar in the food processor until powdery. It will dissolve much faster, so it won't deflate the egg whites.

KEEP YOLKS AT BAY We stirred ½ teaspoon of egg yolk into a dozen whites, just to see what would happen. The eggs turned white and frothy with whipping, but even after 25 minutes, they failed to form peaks. Lesson learned: Separate eggs with care.

FLUFF WITH FLOUR Some recipes call for sifting the flour and/or sugar as many as eight times. What a pain! We tried skipping sifting altogether, but the resulting cake was squat. Ultimately, we figured out that by processing the flour (with half the sugar) in the food processor to aerate it, we could get away with sifting just once.

FOLD GENTLY Use a rubber spatula to gently turn or "fold" the flour and egg whites over one another until they are thoroughly combined. Add the flour in three batches so you don't deflate the whites.

COOL UPSIDE DOWN Invert the cooked cake until it is completely cool, about 3 hours. If you don't have a pan with feet, invert it over the neck of a bottle. Angel food cakes cooled right side up can be crushed by their own weight.

GRAND MARNIER SOUFFLÉ WITH GRATED CHOCOLATE
SERVES 6 TO 8

Make the soufflé base and immediately begin beating the whites before the base cools too much. Once the whites have reached the proper consistency, they must be used at once. Do not open the oven door during the first 15 minutes of baking time; as the soufflé nears the end of its baking, you may check its progress by opening the oven door slightly. (Be careful; if your oven runs hot, the top of the soufflé may burn.) Confectioners' sugar is a nice finishing touch, but be ready to serve the soufflé immediately.

3	tablespoons unsalted butter, softened
¾	cup (5¼ ounces) sugar
2	teaspoons sifted cocoa
5	tablespoons (1½ ounces) all-purpose flour
¼	teaspoon salt
1	cup whole milk
5	large eggs, separated
3	tablespoons Grand Marnier
1	tablespoon grated orange zest
⅛	teaspoon cream of tartar
½	ounce bittersweet chocolate, finely grated

1. Adjust oven rack to upper-middle position and heat oven to 400 degrees. Grease 1½-quart soufflé dish with 1 tablespoon butter. Combine ¼ cup sugar and cocoa in small bowl and pour into prepared dish, shaking to coat bottom and sides of dish evenly. Tap out excess and set dish aside.

2. Whisk flour, ¼ cup sugar, and salt together in small saucepan. Gradually whisk in milk, whisking until smooth and no lumps remain. Bring mixture to boil over high heat, whisking constantly, until thickened and mixture pulls away from sides of pan, about 3 minutes. Scrape mixture into medium bowl; whisk in remaining 2 tablespoons butter until combined. Whisk in egg yolks until incorporated; stir in Grand Marnier and orange zest.

3. Using stand mixer fitted with whisk, whip egg whites, cream of tartar, and 1 teaspoon sugar on medium-low speed until foamy, about 1 minute. Increase speed to medium-high and whip whites to soft, billowy mounds, about 1 minute. Gradually add half of remaining sugar and whip until glossy, soft peaks form, about 30 seconds; with mixer still running, add remaining sugar and whip until just combined, about 10 seconds.

4. Using rubber spatula, immediately stir one-quarter of whipped whites into soufflé base to lighten until almost no white streaks remain. Scrape remaining whites into base and fold in whites, along with grated chocolate, with whisk until mixture is just combined. Gently pour mixture into prepared dish and run your index finger, about ½ inch from side of dish, through mixture, tracing circumference to help soufflé rise properly. Bake until surface of soufflé is deep brown, center jiggles slightly when shaken, and soufflé has risen 2 to 2½ inches above rim, 20 to 25 minutes. Serve immediately.

PRACTICAL SCIENCE
DO COPPER BOWLS MAKE A DIFFERENCE?

Copper bowls help make whipped egg whites stable, and more.

While testing our soufflé recipe, we decided to find out whether copper bowls are better for whisking egg whites and discovered that they do have a contribution to make: The final baked soufflé has a greater volume, its flavor is less eggy, and it has a crust that has a beautiful light golden color.

Why? When egg whites are whipped in a copper bowl, the copper ions combine with conalbumin, an egg-white protein, and as a result slow the coagulation process. This means that the foam takes longer to whip and therefore is more stable. Because the egg foam is more stable, it can better tolerate expansion in the oven. More specifically, the copper of the bowl binds with sulfur atoms contained within some of the egg proteins. And since the eggy flavor comes from the breakdown of these proteins (and the resulting release of sulfur-containing compounds), a soufflé made in a copper bowl is more stable and tastes less eggy. These copper and sulfur bonds also reflect light in a way that allows us to see a golden yellow color in the crust. That said, very good results can also be achieved in stainless steel bowls, so copper is nice, but not necessary.

WHY THIS RECIPE WORKS

We wanted our Grand Marnier Soufflé to be airy and light, yet still taste creamy. Knowing the finicky reputation of soufflés, we wanted it to be reliable, too. Because of the soufflé's airy texture, we knew that we needed to increase its stability. We found that building the soufflé base on a bouillie (a paste made from flour and milk), enhanced with butter and egg yolks, gives us the richness we wanted without harming the soufflé's texture. And no surprise here: Whipping the egg whites with both cream of tartar and granulated sugar serves to enhance the soufflé's stability.

MAKE A BASE The base for this soufflé, into which the beaten egg whites are eventually folded, provides flavor and additional moisture to help it all rise. We prepared a blind taste test with three different base options: béchamel, a classic French sauce made with butter, flour, and milk; pastry cream; and bouillie, a paste made from flour and milk. The bouillie soufflé had the creamiest, richest texture.

WHIP IT RIGHT The technique used to beat egg whites is crucial to a successful soufflé. The objective is to create a strong, stable foam that rises well and is not prone to collapse during either folding or baking. As we've learned, adding sugar to the egg whites as they are whipped enhances their stability. This makes them more resilient to a heavy hand during the folding and less apt to fall quickly after being pulled from the oven. Most of the sugar must be added after the eggs have become foamy and should be added gradually. If it's added all at once, the soufflé will be uneven, with a shorter rise, and a bit of an overly sweet taste. Don't forget the cream of tartar; it makes for a more stable soufflé with a bigger rise.

FOLD IT OVER When combining the voluminous whipped egg whites with the dense batter, vigorous stirring will get you nowhere, quick. The technique we use is called folding. The goal is to incorporate the light egg whites with the heavy batter without deflating the foam.

GIVE A QUICK SWIPE Our Grand Marnier Soufflé relies on little beyond eggs, milk, and a little flour for structure and benefits from the following technique: After pouring the batter into the dish, trace a circle in the batter with your finger, ½ inch from the edge of the dish. This breaks the surface tension and helps the ultra-light soufflé achieve a high, even rise.

DO NOT OVERCOOK Most important: Never overcook a soufflé. It should be very creamy in the middle and firm around the outside, almost like a pudding cake. Don't wait until the center is completely solid; it will be too late. The center should not be liquid-y, but it should still be quite loose and very moist. Once you can smell a soufflé baking in the oven, it's about ready to come out.

Starch Helps Cheese Melt Nicely

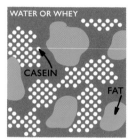

COLD CHEESE *The casein proteins are clustered together amid water and droplets of fat.*

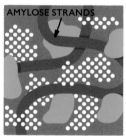

MELTED CHEESE, WITH STARCH *The casein clusters separate and flow but are prevented from forming clumps by strands of amylose from the starch.*

BROKEN CHEESE *If cheese is melted without starch, the casein proteins can regroup into large clusters with a gritty texture. These clusters also cause fat droplets to pool together.*

We eat a lot of cheese. Sometimes we serve it cold, on top of crackers or alone on a plate. But we often use it in cooking—sandwiched between slices of bread and grilled, or baked into pasta. And when heated, cheese melts. This important characteristic defines dishes from macaroni and cheese to lasagna.

HOW THE SCIENCE WORKS

Before we explore the science of melting cheese, let's start with how cheese is made. All cheeses start with milk. This can be any kind of milk, typically cow, sheep, or goat's milk. Each type of milk has different flavor characteristics and a different amount of protein, which translates into a very different texture in cheese. Goat's milk, for example, has much less of the protein casein, the solid component that gives cheese its structure, which is why goat cheese is usually soft and creamy compared to cow's milk cheeses like cheddar.

Most cheese also contains an enzyme called rennet that traditionally comes from the stomach of a very young calf. Rennet is important because unlike other enzymes (like those present in meat, for example; see concept 6), it breaks down only one of the proteins in milk—casein. Not only that, rennet does not break casein proteins down into many different pieces, but only at one specific point, which allows these now-clipped proteins to bond together into a gel, also known as the curd.

The final ingredient is microbes, or bacteria, which further break down proteins slowly over time. This process creates the distinctive flavor compounds that make cheddar cheese sharp or give Limburger its strong odor.

When making cheese, these three ingredients are combined. First, bacteria are added to milk, converting the milk's sugar to lactic acid. This acidification then causes the milk proteins to form a weak gel. Then, the rennet enzymes work to curdle the casein proteins, separating the resulting gelled curds (which will become the cheese) from the watery whey. With time, enzymes from the bacteria (both present in the milk, and added) ripen and intensify the flavors of the cheese.

Some cheese is ready immediately after it is made (ricotta and mozzarella). Other types (cheddar and Parmesan) are aged so the bacteria have time to develop more complex flavors.

When heated, cheese doesn't melt in the true sense, not like an ice cube. Instead, the casein proteins, which have bonded together in the presence of rennet, begin to break apart. These protein molecules separate and flow, like molten plastic, which gives the appearance of melting.

Relatively young cheeses, such as fontina and mozzarella, have a high moisture content and a weaker protein structure, allowing the protein molecules to separate and flow at lower temperatures. This higher moisture content means these cheeses have less of a tendency to "break" and are less likely to become greasy when they melt. (Cheeses "break" when the hot flowing protein network loses moisture and forms even stronger bonds between protein molecules, recombining into big clumps that squeeze out fat like a sponge.) On the other hand, aged cheeses, such as Gruyère and cheddar, have less moisture and a stronger protein network. This means they melt at higher temperatures, needing more heat to break apart the tightly bonded proteins, which must happen before they can flow. Once melted, the more developed protein structures in these cheeses begin to regroup, making small clumps that separate from the remaining mass of cheese, leaving behind a gritty texture and the occasional pool of fat. (The fat content of cheese varies widely—from 13 percent in ricotta to 33 percent in cheddar.)

When cheeses break and form unseemly clumps, they can ruin the texture of our creamy pasta sauces made with melted cheese. We solve this by adding starch. The starch (generally flour or cornstarch) holds apart the tiny clusters of protein molecules as the cheese melts. This prevents the proteins from recombining and forming even larger clusters that eventually would become big clumps of cheese.

TEST KITCHEN EXPERIMENT

To prove the value in adding starch to cheeses that don't naturally melt well, we made batches of a classic roux-thickened cheese sauce (like that used for macaroni and cheese) with and without flour. For the floured version we made a roux with 2 tablespoons of butter and 3 tablespoons of all-purpose flour, whisked in 2½ cups of milk, and then, off the heat, slowly added 8 ounces of shredded cheddar cheese. For the comparison batch we simply brought the butter and milk to a simmer and added the cheese off the heat. We repeated the test three times.

THE RESULTS

Ignoring the obvious difference in thickness between the two sauces, it was clear what role the flour was playing. The flourless sauce quickly broke into clumpy curds of cheese that clung to the whisk, while the traditional sauce emulsified to a smooth, creamy consistency.

MEASURING CHEESE

We prefer to weigh cheese when cooking. You can use cup measures, but note that different graters will produce more or less volume from the same piece of cheese. To obtain the most accurate measure, cheese should be lightly packed into a measuring cup.

PARMESAN AND OTHER HARD CHEESES	
Fine holes of box grater	I ounce = ½ cup
Rasp-style grater	I ounce = ¾ cup
CHEDDAR, MOZZARELLA, AND OTHER SEMISOFT CHEESES	
Large holes of box grater	I ounce = ¼ cup
BLUE CHEESE, FETA, AND GOAT CHEESE	
Crumbled by hand	I ounce = ¼ cup

THE TAKEAWAY

To avoid the clumpy, lumpy mess of a broken cheese sauce, a sauce that would ruin a good macaroni and cheese, starch is a necessary addition. When combined with melting cheese, starch granules release elongated threads of amylose, which then wrap around the casein proteins, preventing them from squeezing out fat and recombining into unpleasant curds. The lesson? Don't forget to add flour!

It's important to note that we add starch to melting cheeses in a number of different ways. This may mean starting with a roux (flour and butter) when making a cheese sauce for a dish like Classic Macaroni and Cheese (page 208). Other techniques include tossing shredded cheese with cornstarch for dishes like fondue. We also like to combine easily melted cheeses (relatively young cheeses like fontina, Monterey Jack, and mozzarella) with cheeses that don't melt so well (aged varieties like Gruyère and cheddar). In dishes like Four-Cheese Lasagna (page 209), this strategy gives us the benefit of better texture from the young cheese, and the deeper flavor of the aged cheese.

USING STARCH TO MAKE CREAMY CHEESE SAUCE

WITHOUT STARCH *A cheese sauce made without starch is gritty and clumps on the tines of a whisk.*

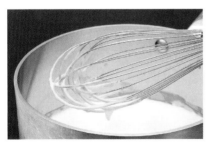

WITH STARCH *A cheese sauce made with starch, on the other hand, is smooth and creamy—no broken clumps here.*

Adding starch to cheese as it melts helps to prevent clumping—an enemy of rich and creamy cheese sauces. Making a béchamel, or béchamel-like sauce, which contains a healthy amount of butter, milk, and flour, is a great way to stabilize the cheese as well as add flavor and substance to the dish. But it can be even simpler: Just a bit of starchy pasta water can do wonders.

CLASSIC MACARONI AND CHEESE
SERVES 6 TO 8

It's crucial to cook the pasta until tender—just past the al dente stage. Whole, low-fat, and skim milk all work well in this recipe. The recipe may be halved and baked in an 8-inch square broiler-safe baking pan. If desired, offer hot sauce at the table.

6	slices hearty white sandwich bread, torn into quarters
5	tablespoons unsalted butter, plus 3 tablespoons cut into 6 pieces and chilled
1	pound elbow macaroni
	Salt
6	tablespoons all-purpose flour
1½	teaspoons dry mustard
¼	teaspoon cayenne pepper (optional)
5	cups milk
8	ounces Monterey Jack cheese, shredded (2 cups)
8	ounces sharp cheddar cheese, shredded (2 cups)

1. Pulse bread and 3 tablespoons chilled butter in food processor to coarse crumbs, about 10 pulses; set aside.

2. Adjust oven rack to lower-middle position and heat broiler. Bring 4 quarts water to boil in large pot. Add pasta and 1 tablespoon salt and cook, stirring often, until tender; drain pasta.

3. Melt remaining 5 tablespoons butter in now-empty pot over medium-high heat. Add flour, mustard, 1 teaspoon salt, and cayenne, if using, and cook, whisking constantly, until mixture becomes fragrant and deepens in color, about 1 minute. Gradually whisk in milk; bring mixture to boil, whisking constantly. Reduce heat to medium and simmer, whisking occasionally, until thickened, about 5 minutes. Off heat, slowly whisk in cheeses until completely melted. Add pasta to sauce and cook over medium-low heat, stirring constantly, until mixture is steaming and heated through, about 6 minutes.

4. Transfer mixture to 13 by 9-inch broiler-safe baking dish and sprinkle with bread-crumb mixture. Broil until topping is deep golden brown, 3 to 5 minutes. Let casserole cool for 5 minutes before serving.

CLASSIC MACARONI AND CHEESE WITH HAM AND PEAS

Add 8 ounces deli ham, sliced ¼ inch thick and cut into 1-inch pieces, and 1 cup frozen peas to cheese sauce along with pasta.

CLASSIC MACARONI AND CHEESE WITH KIELBASA AND MUSTARD

Add 1 finely chopped onion to melted butter in step 3 and cook until softened and lightly browned, 5 to 7 minutes. Add flour to onion and continue with recipe, reducing salt in sauce to ½ teaspoon. Add 8 ounces kielbasa, quartered lengthwise and sliced ½ inch thick, and 4 teaspoons whole-grain Dijon mustard to cheese sauce along with pasta.

✔ WHY THIS RECIPE WORKS

For a classic, old-fashioned macaroni and cheese, we took no shortcuts. This family favorite should boast tender pasta in a smooth, creamy sauce with great cheese flavor. Two types of cheese are better than one: Monterey Jack melts nicely, while sharp cheddar supplies the flavor. We bind the macaroni and cheese with a béchamel sauce, or a mixture of flour, butter, and milk. As we've learned, the flour stabilizes the cheese.

BIND IT UP Most macaroni and cheese recipes use either eggs or starch to stabilize the sauce. The eggs are great, and we've used them on occasion ourselves, but you need to add evaporated milk to prevent the eggs from curdling and the end result is very, very rich. For everyday mac and cheese, we think the flour route (through the use of a béchamel) is better.

CREATE A ROUX Béchamel is a white sauce made by cooking flour and butter to create a light roux. We use 5 tablespoons of butter and 6 tablespoons of flour (pretty close to a 1:1 ratio), along with a bit of powdered mustard and cayenne (optional). Milk (any kind) is gradually whisked in, and the béchamel is cooked until it thickens. Let the binding begin!

USE CHEESE AND PASTA EQUALLY For this recipe, we found that two types of cheese were better than one. We tried Parmesan, Gruyère, and some aged cheddars but were not pleased with their grainy texture and potent flavor. On the other hand, the incredibly mild, soft cheeses like mascarpone and ricotta contributed no flavor at all. We prefer sharp cheddar for flavor and Monterey Jack for creaminess. And how much to use? We find that 1 pound of cheese to 1 pound of pasta is the perfect ratio—just the right texture and flavor, and easy to remember, too.

MAKE PASTA ON THE STOVETOP It's difficult to get the timing right for macaroni and cheese baked in the oven. Either the pasta is overcooked or it needs more time; and the sauce ends up breaking from being overbaked. It's easier to cook the pasta on the stovetop and thus easier not to ruin the cheese sauce, too.

COOK UNTIL JUST PAST AL DENTE The trick is to cook the pasta just past al dente before adding it to the sauce. If cooked less, the pasta releases starch into the sauce and makes it gritty. If cooked until very tender, the noodles won't absorb the sauce. Boiled until just past al dente, however, the noodles retain structure to stand up to the heat of the sauce for a few minutes without turning mushy, and the cheese can fill every nook and cranny.

GET THE "BAKED" LOOK Toasted bread crumbs, even when applied to mac and cheese made on the stovetop, give the dish a baked look that we love. Place fresh buttered bread crumbs atop your batch of macaroni and cheese and place it under the broiler. The broiler will concentrate the heat right on the bread crumbs, turning them a deep, golden brown. This only takes a few minutes—just enough for the crumbs to sink into the cheese sauce and seem baked right in.

PRACTICAL SCIENCE MELTING CHEESE

Moisture, fat, and age affect the way different cheeses melt.

Government regulations allow Jack cheese to have 5 percent more total moisture than cheddar cheese, while cheddar has more fat. Age also has a profound effect on how a cheese behaves when melted. Monterey Jack is never aged for more than a few months, but cheddar can be aged for years.

What does this difference in age mean for cheese sauce? Cheddar, particularly older cheddar, is gritty because casein, the primary protein in cheese, becomes more strongly bonded together as the cheese ages. Monterey Jack is creamy because the casein structure is more loosely bonded and therefore better able to retain fat and moisture. The combination of young Jack cheese and moderately aged cheddar gives you good texture and flavor in a dish like Classic Macaroni and Cheese.

HOW CHEESE MELTS *When cheddar is melted, right, the fat separates from the cheese. Monterey Jack, left, has a higher moisture content and looks creamier when melted, with less separation.*

Note that some pasta brands contain only 12 no-boil noodles per package; this recipe requires 15 noodles. Whole milk is best in the sauce, but skim and low-fat milk also work. Supermarket-brand cheeses work fine in this recipe. The Gorgonzola may be omitted, but the flavor of the lasagna won't be as complex. It's important to not overbake the lasagna. Once the sauce starts bubbling around the edges, uncover the lasagna and turn the oven to broil. If your lasagna dish is not broiler-safe, brown the lasagna at 500 degrees for about 10 minutes.

6	ounces Gruyère cheese, shredded (1½ cups)
2	ounces Parmesan cheese, grated fine (1 cup)
12	ounces (1½ cups) part-skim ricotta cheese
1	large egg
2	tablespoons plus 2 teaspoons minced fresh parsley
¼	teaspoon pepper
3	tablespoons unsalted butter
1	shallot, minced
1	garlic clove, minced
⅓	cup all-purpose flour
2½	cups whole milk
1½	cups low-sodium chicken broth
½	teaspoon salt
1	bay leaf
	Pinch cayenne pepper
15	no-boil lasagna noodles
8	ounces fontina cheese, shredded (2 cups)
3	ounces Gorgonzola cheese, finely crumbled (¾ cup)

1. Place Gruyère and ½ cup Parmesan in large heatproof bowl. Combine ricotta, egg, 2 tablespoons parsley, and pepper in medium bowl. Set both bowls aside.

2. Melt butter in medium saucepan over medium heat. Add shallot and garlic and cook, stirring often, until shallot is softened, about 2 minutes. Add flour and cook, stirring constantly, until thoroughly combined, about 1½ minutes; mixture should not brown. Gradually whisk in milk and broth; increase heat to medium-high and bring to boil, whisking often. Stir in salt, bay leaf, and cayenne, reduce heat to medium-low, and simmer until sauce thickens and measures 4 cups, about 10 minutes, stirring occasionally and making sure to scrape bottom and corners of pan.

3. Discard bay leaf. Gradually whisk ¼ cup sauce into ricotta mixture. Pour remaining sauce over Gruyère mixture and stir until smooth.

4. Adjust oven rack to upper-middle position and heat oven to 350 degrees. Pour 2 inches of boiling water into 13 by 9-inch broiler-safe baking dish. Slip noodles into water, 1 at a time, and soak until pliable, about 5 minutes, separating noodles with tip of sharp knife to prevent sticking. Remove noodles from water and place in single layer on clean kitchen towels; discard water. Dry dish and spray lightly with vegetable oil spray.

5. Spread ½ cup sauce evenly over bottom of dish. Arrange 3 noodles in single layer on top of sauce. Spread ½ cup ricotta mixture evenly over noodles and sprinkle with ½ cup fontina and 3 tablespoons Gorgonzola. Spoon ½ cup sauce over top. Repeat layering of noodles, ricotta mixture, fontina, Gorgonzola, and sauce 3 more times. For final layer, arrange remaining 3 noodles on top and cover completely with remaining sauce. Sprinkle with remaining ½ cup Parmesan.

6. Cover dish tightly with aluminum foil that has been sprayed with oil spray and bake until edges are just bubbling, 25 to 30 minutes, rotating dish halfway through baking. Remove foil and turn oven to broil. Broil lasagna until surface is spotty brown, 3 to 5 minutes. Cool lasagna for 15 minutes, then sprinkle with remaining 2 teaspoons parsley and serve.

✓ WHY THIS RECIPE WORKS

Cheese lasagna offers an elegant alternative to meat-laden, red-sauce lasagna. But some cheese lasagna is just heavy and bland, due to the use of plain-tasting cheeses. And even those with good cheese flavor can have soupy, dry, or greasy textures. We wanted a robust cheese lasagna with great structure, creamy texture, and maximum flavor. For the best cheese flavor, we settled on a combination of fontina, Parmesan, Gorgonzola, and Gruyère cheeses—plus a surprise fifth addition. We found that making the white sauce (a béchamel) with a high ratio of flour to butter created a thick binder that provided enough heft to keep the lasagna layers together.

MAKE VELOUTÉ HYBRID Though our béchamel, with its high flour-to-butter ratio, did a great job binding, using all milk in the sauce left us with a bland flavor that dulled the overall cheesiness of the dish. The solution lies in the classic French sauce called velouté, which is the same sauce as béchamel except the milk is replaced by chicken broth, or basically a roux-thickened broth. We replace 1½ cups of the milk with chicken broth to balance the richness of the sauce and bring forward the cheese flavor. For more complexity, we add shallot and a garlic clove. A bay leaf and a pinch of cayenne add backbone without overshadowing the other components.

MIX AGED CHEESES INTO SAUCE To counter the recurring problem of all the cheese causing the lasagna to bake up with pools of unseemly grease on the surface and a slightly curdled texture, we take a cue from the Swiss. Classic fondue recipes include a starch when melting cheese in order to keep it from becoming oily and gritty. This is why we incorporate the Gruyère into the béchamel sauce, which contains a significant amount of flour. The starch helps to trap oil and keep it from pooling on top of the lasagna. Gruyère, an aged cheese with less moisture and a stronger protein network, produces the most oil when cooked, which is why it is the best choice to mix into the sauce.

USE A FIFTH CHEESE The real secret of a great four-cheese lasagna is a fifth cheese. Who knew? While ricotta doesn't add much flavor, it gives the lasagna body without making the dish heavy and starchy.

SOAK THOSE NOODLES For this recipe, we presoak no-boil lasagna noodles for five minutes before layering them with the other ingredients, which shortens the lasagna's baking time. We have tried—and failed—in the past to substitute regular boiled lasagna noodles for no-boil noodles. Recipes using no-boil noodles need more liquid, and substituting regular boiled noodles leads to soupy lasagna. However, since the no-boil noodles for this

---

PRACTICAL SCIENCE A GOOD WAY TO STORE CHEESE

Store cheese wrapped in two layers: waxed or parchment paper, and aluminum foil.

Storing cheese presents a conundrum: As it sits, it releases moisture. If this moisture evaporates too quickly, the cheese dries out. But if the moisture is trapped on the cheese's surface, it encourages mold. Specialty cheese paper avoids this problem with a two-ply construction that lets cheese breathe without drying out, but it usually requires mail-ordering. To find a more accessible method, we single- and double-wrapped cheddar, Brie, and fresh goat cheese in various ways, refrigerated the cheeses for six weeks, and monitored them for mold and dryness. Cheeses single-wrapped in plastic—whether cling wrap or zipper-lock bags—were the first to show mold. However, cheeses shrouded in waxed or parchment paper alone lost moisture and dried out. The best method: waxed or parchment paper loosely wrapped with aluminum foil. Both papers wick moisture away, while the foil cover traps just enough water to keep the cheese from drying out. Wrapped this way, even super-perishable goat cheese kept for about a week, and the Brie and cheddar were almost like new more than a month later. Cheese paper extended the life of these cheeses by only a few days more.

lasagna are first soaked in hot water and the sauce isn't so watery, we wondered if this finding would still hold true.

We used regular boiled noodles in this recipe, and the lasagna looked fine—no excessive soupiness. Unfortunately, the lasagna tasted too starchy and heavy. The regular lasagna noodles were so thick and bulky that they overpowered the delicate balance of pasta to sauce, adding excessive starchiness to the dish.

When we compared the actual weight of each type of pasta, we found that an uncooked regular lasagna noodle weighed almost twice as much as a no-boil noodle. So for creamy, delicate lasagnas (where fresh noodles are traditionally used), thinner, no-boil noodles are not only faster than regular dried lasagna noodles—they are also better.

BAKE LOW AND HIGH   Another technique to minimize the time in the oven for our delicate lasagna is to employ a low-heat/high-heat method. We bake the lasagna, covered, at 350 degrees until it just starts to bubble around the edges. We then remove the cover and quickly broil the lasagna to brown the top.

SPAGHETTI WITH PECORINO ROMANO AND BLACK PEPPER (CACIO E PEPE)
SERVES 4 TO 6

For a slightly less rich dish, substitute half-and-half for the heavy cream. Do not adjust the amount of water for cooking the pasta; the amount used is critical to the success of the recipe. Make sure to stir the pasta frequently while cooking so that it doesn't stick to the pot. Draining the pasta water into the serving bowl warms the bowl and helps keeps the dish hot until it is served.

6	ounces Pecorino Romano cheese, 4 ounces grated fine (2 cups) and 2 ounces grated coarse (1 cup)
1	pound spaghetti
	Salt
2	tablespoons heavy cream
2	teaspoons extra-virgin olive oil
1½	teaspoons pepper

1. Place finely grated Pecorino in medium bowl. Set colander in large bowl.

2. Bring 2 quarts water to boil in large pot. Add pasta and 1½ teaspoons salt and cook, stirring often, until al dente. Drain pasta into prepared colander, reserving cooking water. Pour 1½ cups cooking water into liquid measuring cup and discard remainder. Return drained pasta to now-empty bowl.

3. Slowly whisk 1 cup reserved cooking water into finely grated Pecorino until smooth, then whisk in heavy cream, oil, and pepper. Gradually pour cheese mixture over pasta and toss to combine. Let pasta rest for 1 to 2 minutes, tossing frequently and adding remaining cooking water as needed to adjust consistency. Serve, passing coarsely grated Pecorino separately.

✔ WHY THIS RECIPE WORKS
With just three main ingredients (cheese, pepper, and pasta), this Roman dish makes a delicious and quick pantry supper. But in versions we tried, the creamy sauce quickly turned into clumps of solidified cheese. For a smooth, intensely cheesy sauce that wouldn't separate once tossed with the pasta, we whisked some of the pasta cooking water with the grated cheese. Swapping out butter for cream further ensured a smooth sauce. Even after sitting on the table for a full five minutes, there wasn't a clump in sight.

START WITH GOOD CHEESE   High-quality ingredients are essential in this dish, most importantly, imported Pecorino Romano. Imported Pecorino Romano is a hard, aged sheep's milk cheese with a distinctively pungent, salty flavor that bears almost no resemblance to domestic cheeses simply labeled "Romano." (These wan stand-ins are made with cow's milk and lack the punch of the real deal.)

PAY ATTENTION TO STARCH   Even finely grated, cheese can still clump. Starch helps. In a hard lump of Pecorino, the fat, protein, and water (the three main components of cheese) are locked into position by the solid structure of the cheese. But when the cheese is heated, the proteins can fuse together. The starch from the semolina-infused pasta water, however, coats the cheese and prevents the proteins from sticking. (Make sure to use the correct amount of water for your pasta: 2 quarts of water for a pound of pasta, rather than the usual 4 quarts. This volume will get the optimal concentration of starch in the liquid.)

CREAM HELPS, TOO   Starch on its own can't completely prevent the cheese from clumping. But there is another factor that affects how proteins and fat interact: emulsifiers. Milk, cream, and fresh cheeses have special molecules called lipoproteins that can associate with both fat and protein, acting as a sort of liaison between the two and keeping them from separating. But as cheese ages, the lipoproteins break down, losing their emulsifying power. No wonder Pecorino Romano, aged for at least eight months, forms clumps. How to get an infusion of lipoproteins? Add milk or cream. When we replace the traditional butter with the same amount of cream, the cheese forms a light, perfectly smooth sauce that coats the spaghetti.

Salting Vegetables Removes Liquid

Vegetables, especially summer vegetables like tomatoes and zucchini, are made up of mostly water. When cooking, the biggest challenge is dealing with all this liquid. (After all, no one wants a soggy slaw.) We often employ salt to remove liquid from vegetables before using them in recipes.

HOW THE SCIENCE WORKS

THE EFFECT OF SALT ON VEGETABLE CELLS

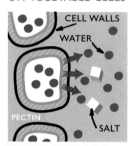

WHILE SALTING *Salt draws water out of vegetable cells via osmosis.*

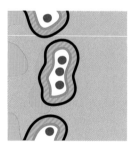

AFTER SALTING *When water exits a vegetable, its cells lose pressure and begin to collapse. Pectin, the glue that holds cells together, likewise begins to weaken.*

Edible plants include both fruits and vegetables. Technically fruits are the reproductive parts of the plant (those containing seeds), while vegetables are everything else (roots, stems, and leaves). The culinary definition of vegetables, however, expands to include some seeded specimens like tomatoes and cucumbers.

Plants, like animals, are made up of countless numbers of cells. Plant cells contain a wide array of proteins, enzymes, sugars, and color pigments. Each one is surrounded by a tough cell wall made mostly of cellulose, which gets thicker with age. (That's one reason why raw veggies are so crunchy.) Pectin, a water-soluble polysaccharide, is also present in the cell walls and in between cells, acting like a glue to hold them together. And, like most everything we eat, vegetables are filled with water.

Unlike cooking meat, where we want to preserve as much moisture as possible, with vegetables we want the water out. However counterintuitive it may seem, we reach the opposite goal for meat and vegetables with the same ingredient … salt.

When salt is applied to vegetables, it creates a higher ion concentration at the surface than exists deep within the cells. To equalize the concentration levels, the water within the cells is drawn out through the permeable cell walls. This is called osmosis, an important process in brining (concept 11) and marinating

(concept 13). When salting meat, the trick is to wait until the meat reabsorbs that liquid along with some water. When salting vegetables, we often wick that moisture (and most of the salt) away.

This removal of water is important when making slaws and salads; the excess liquid can dilute a dressing, causing the vegetables to swim in a flavorless pool of juice. But the exodus of water plays another role in the preparation of vegetables—it can radically change their texture. When salt draws water out of vegetable cells, the cells lose pressure (called turgor pressure) and begin to collapse, like a balloon letting out air. This means that the texture of these vegetables becomes softer and less crisp.

But that's not the only way salt affects the texture of vegetables. Much of the strength of pectin, the glue that holds the cells together, comes from the presence of calcium and magnesium ions within the molecules. These ions are part of the pectin structure, but they also act as links, holding the pectin molecules together. When raw vegetables are salted, or salt is added to the cooking water, the sodium ions in the salt replace the calcium and magnesium ions in the pectin. This causes the pectin—and therefore the cell walls of vegetables—to weaken and is another reason why your broccoli florets or head of cabbage will soften with salt.

TEST KITCHEN EXPERIMENT

To show the drastic effect that salt can have on raw vegetables, we tossed three 1-pound batches of whole napa cabbage leaves with 2½ tablespoons of kosher salt each. We then placed the cabbage leaves in colanders set over bowls and let them sit. After one hour, we collected and then measured the exuded liquid. As a control we left a fourth batch of cabbage unsalted. We repeated the experiment three times.

THE RESULTS

Over the course of an hour, the batches of salted cabbage lost, on average, more than 2 tablespoons of water each. Not surprisingly, the control batch lost no moisture during this time.

Even more impressive than the numbers was the visual difference between the salted and unsalted cabbage. While the control stayed firm and crisp, the salted samples became soft and flexible, easily drooping when held with a pair of tongs.

THE TAKEAWAY

When we salt vegetables like cabbage, the effect is clear: We lose a lot of moisture, the

WITH SALT, CABBAGE WILTS

When we applied salt to napa cabbage, the leaves became soft and limp, wilting when held by a pair of tongs. The unsalted cabbage leaves (like the one on top) held straight as a board.

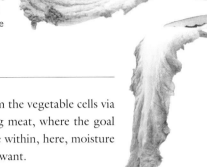

salt drawing water from the vegetable cells via osmosis. Unlike salting meat, where the goal is to keep the moisture within, here, moisture loss is exactly what we want.

We salt cabbage (and other vegetables) and then drain away that extra moisture before adding the dressing for our salads and slaws. This way, when we do add the creamy dressing of a buttermilk coleslaw, for example, the excess liquid does not seep out into the salad and dilute the flavor. Though the limp cabbage may not look appealing, it will create a far better final product. In fact, the salted, wilted cabbage leaves will draw back some of the added dressing in order to restore turgor pressure, thereby enhancing the flavor.

PRACTICAL SCIENCE SALTING CAN ALSO MAKE VEGETABLES TASTE BETTER

Salt unlocks flavor in vegetables, but only in recipes where the salt and liquid released are not discarded.

To determine if the length of time we salted our vegetables affected flavor, we made two batches of Creamy Gazpacho Andaluz (page 219). For the first, we salted the tomatoes, cucumber, onion, and green bell pepper and let them sit for one hour before pureeing these ingredients with their accumulated juices in a blender. For the second batch, we skipped the salting step but stirred in the equivalent amount of salt after we pureed the vegetables. The results? The vegetables that were salted for one hour before pureeing produced gazpacho with fuller, more complex flavor.

To experience a food's flavors, our tastebuds must be exposed to its flavor molecules. But many of the flavor molecules in fruits and vegetables are not only trapped within their cell walls, they are tightly bound to proteins that also make them inaccessible to our tastebuds. Blending or even vigorous chewing releases some of the flavor molecules. But for maximum flavor extraction, salting the vegetables and letting them sit for an hour works best. (This works only in recipes that use the liquid released by the application of salt.) With time, the salt draws flavor compounds out of the cell walls while simultaneously forcing the proteins to separate from these molecules, producing a more intensely flavored soup. Simply seasoning the soup before serving will not have the same effect.

Vegetable salads can be easy to prepare, but hard to make well. If the veggies release liquid after the dressing has been applied, this can result in a diluted sauce, one that is too thin and bland and not appetizing at all. To prevent this, we salt our vegetables before the dressing is applied, encouraging them to release their liquid ahead of time, which we then discard before adding the dressing. The salt also makes the vegetables softer and more appealing to eat.

CREAMY BUTTERMILK COLESLAW
SERVES 4

If you are planning to serve the coleslaw immediately, rinse the salted cabbage in a large bowl of ice water, drain it in a colander, pick out any ice cubes, then pat the cabbage dry before dressing.

½   head red or green cabbage, cored and shredded (6 cups)
     Salt
1   carrot, peeled and shredded
½   cup buttermilk
2   tablespoons mayonnaise
2   tablespoons sour cream
1   small shallot, minced
2   tablespoons minced fresh parsley
½   teaspoon cider vinegar
½   teaspoon sugar
¼   teaspoon Dijon mustard
⅛   teaspoon pepper

1. Toss shredded cabbage and 1 teaspoon salt in colander or large-mesh strainer set over medium bowl. Let stand until cabbage wilts, at least 1 hour or up to 4 hours. Rinse cabbage under cold running water. Press, but do not squeeze, to drain; pat dry with paper towels. Place wilted cabbage and carrot in large bowl.

2. Stir buttermilk, mayonnaise, sour cream, shallot, parsley, vinegar, sugar, mustard, ¼ teaspoon salt, and pepper together in small bowl. Pour dressing over cabbage and toss to combine; refrigerate until chilled, about 30 minutes. (Coleslaw can be refrigerated for up to 3 days.)

BUTTERMILK COLESLAW WITH SCALLIONS AND CILANTRO

Omit mustard, substitute 1 tablespoon minced fresh cilantro for parsley and 1 teaspoon lime juice for cider vinegar, and add 2 thinly sliced scallions to dressing.

✔ WHY THIS RECIPE WORKS
We wanted a recipe for buttermilk coleslaw that would produce a salad with crisp, evenly cut pieces of cabbage lightly coated with a flavorful buttermilk dressing that would cling to the cabbage instead of collecting in the bottom of the bowl. We found that salting and draining the cabbage removed excess water. For a dressing that was both hefty and tangy, we combined buttermilk, mayonnaise, and sour cream.

SHRED THE CABBAGE   The tough, squeaky leaves and compact core of a cabbage head require both a sharp knife and a good game plan. It is best to quarter and core the cabbage, then disassemble each quarter into stacks containing several layers of cabbage. These stacks can then be either laid flat on a cutting board and sliced with a chef's knife or rolled and pushed into the feeder tube of a food processor fitted with the shredding disk.

SALT THE CABBAGE, TOO   To combat a weepy dressing, we salt the cabbage. As the salt and cabbage sit, moisture is drawn out of the cabbage cells. To eliminate

---

PRACTICAL SCIENCE
WHEN GOOD BUTTERMILK GOES BAD

Opened buttermilk can last up to three weeks, but the taste is best when used fresh.

Since buttermilk always smells sour, how do we know when it has gone bad? When we asked this question of the folks at the dairy farm that produces the buttermilk we use in the test kitchen, they told us to consume their product within five to seven days after opening. However, guidelines from agricultural programs at various universities extend that period to two weeks. Then there's our experience, which has shown that refrigerated buttermilk won't turn truly bad (signified by the growth of blue-green mold) until at least three weeks after opening. That it can last this long is not surprising, since buttermilk is high in lactic acid, which is hostile to the growth of harmful bacteria and mold. That said, we wondered if the flavor of buttermilk changes the longer it's stored. To find out, we held a series of tastings, comparing pancakes made with freshly opened buttermilk with those made with buttermilk that had been refrigerated for one week, two weeks, and three weeks. We found that as time went on, the pancakes tasted increasingly bland.

Here's why: The bacteria in buttermilk produce lactic acid and diacetyl, a flavor compound that gives buttermilk its characteristic buttery aroma and taste (diacetyl is also the dominant flavor compound in butter). As time passes, the buttermilk continues to ferment and becomes more acidic. The abundance of acid kills off virtually all of the bacteria that produce the buttery-tasting diacetyl. So three-week-old buttermilk will retain its tartness (from lactic acid) but lose much of its signature buttery taste, giving it less dimension. The good news is that there is a way to prolong the shelf life and preserve the flavor of buttermilk: Freeze it.

---

excess salt and water, the now-wilted cabbage needs a quick rinse and towel dry. (Left unrinsed and undried, the salty moisture trapped within the thatch of shredded cabbage ruins both the flavor and the texture of the coleslaw.) A mere teaspoon of salt is enough to draw the moisture out of the cabbage.

BULK UP BUTTERMILK We like to bulk up the buttermilk in our dressing so that it will cling to the cabbage without losing its distinctively Southern twang. Mayonnaise gives the dressing good heft and adhesiveness while sour cream reinforces the characteristic zip of the buttermilk. Together, they give us a dressing that adheres well to the cabbage without tasting overly potent or losing its bite.

CREAMY DILL CUCUMBER SALAD
SERVES 4

Fresh dill is essential to the flavor of this salad; do not substitute dried.

3	cucumbers (2 pounds), peeled, halved lengthwise, seeded, and sliced ¼ inch thick
1	small red onion, sliced very thin
1	tablespoon salt
1	cup sour cream
3	tablespoons cider vinegar
1	teaspoon sugar
¼	cup minced fresh dill

1. Toss cucumbers and onion with salt in colander set over large bowl. Weight cucumbers with gallon-size zipper-lock bag filled with water; let drain for 1 to 3 hours. Rinse and pat dry.

2. Whisk remaining ingredients together in medium bowl. Add cucumbers and onion; toss to coat. Serve chilled.

YOGURT-MINT CUCUMBER SALAD
SERVES 4

3	cucumbers (2 pounds), peeled, halved lengthwise, seeded, and sliced ¼ inch thick
1	small red onion, sliced very thin
	Salt and pepper
1	cup plain low-fat yogurt

2	tablespoons extra-virgin olive oil
¼	cup minced fresh mint
1	garlic clove, minced
½	teaspoon ground cumin

1. Toss cucumbers and onion with 1 tablespoon salt in colander set over large bowl. Weight cucumbers with gallon-size zipper-lock bag filled with water; let drain for 1 to 3 hours. Rinse and pat dry.

2. Whisk together yogurt, oil, mint, garlic, cumin, and salt and pepper to taste in medium bowl. Add cucumbers and onion; toss to coat. Serve chilled.

PRACTICAL SCIENCE BUYING CUCUMBERS

A genetic difference keeps American cucumbers crisper in the presence of a softening enzyme than the seedless English.

Supermarkets carry two kinds of slicing cucumbers: seedless English and standard American. To assess which we prefer, we tasted them grated in a yogurt sauce, salted in a salad, and plain. We found that the American cucumbers had the crisper texture and the more concentrated cucumber flavor, while the English variety were much milder and more watery.

It turns out that cucumbers contain a "softening" enzyme that breaks down cell walls when the vegetable is cut open. Due to genetic differences between the English and American varieties, as well as differences in how they are grown (English cucumbers are almost exclusively raised in greenhouses, while most American kinds grow outdoors), English cucumbers have weaker cell walls that are more easily broken down by the enzyme. Weak cells lead to less-than-crisp texture and flavor that leaks out. And salting cucumbers (which we regularly do for salads) makes the problem worse.

What about the seedless advantage? We'd rather suffer the minor inconvenience of seeding our own cukes than have to wade through watery salads.

WEAK AND SOGGY
English cucumbers have a weak cellular structure that turns them mushy when cut and salted.

STRONG AND CRISP
Regular American cukes retain their crunch with the same treatment.

SESAME-LEMON CUCUMBER SALAD
SERVES 4

3 cucumbers (2 pounds), peeled, halved lengthwise, seeded, and sliced ¼ inch thick
1 tablespoon salt
¼ cup rice vinegar
1 tablespoon lemon juice
2 tablespoons toasted sesame oil
2 teaspoons sugar
⅛ teaspoon red pepper flakes, plus more to taste
1 tablespoon sesame seeds, toasted

1. Toss cucumbers with salt in colander set over large bowl. Weight cucumbers with gallon-size zipper-lock bag filled with water; let drain for 1 to 3 hours. Rinse and pat dry.

2. Whisk remaining ingredients together in medium bowl. Add cucumbers; toss to coat. Serve chilled or at room temperature.

SWEET-AND-TART CUCUMBER SALAD
SERVES 4

Based on a common Thai relish served with sautés, this salad is also great with grilled salmon or grilled chicken breasts.

3 cucumbers (2 pounds), peeled, halved lengthwise, seeded, and sliced ¼ inch thick
½ red onion, sliced very thin
1 tablespoon salt
½ cup rice vinegar
2½ tablespoons sugar
2 small jalapeño chiles, seeded and minced (or more, to taste)

1. Toss cucumbers and onion with salt in colander set over large bowl. Weight cucumbers with gallon-size zipper-lock bag filled with water; drain for 1 to 3 hours. Rinse and pat dry.

2. Bring ⅔ cup water and vinegar to boil in small non-reactive saucepan over medium heat. Stir in sugar to dissolve; reduce heat and simmer for 15 minutes. Let cool to room temperature.

3. Meanwhile, mix cucumbers, onion, and jalapeños together in medium bowl. Pour dressing over cucumber mixture; toss to coat. Serve chilled.

✔ WHY THIS RECIPE WORKS

Cucumbers can make a cool, crisp salad, but often they turn soggy from their own moisture. For a good cucumber salad that doesn't swim in liquid, we found that weighting salted cucumbers forced more water from them than salting alone. After many tests, we determined that one to three hours worked best: Even after 12 hours, the cucumbers gave up no more water than they had after three hours. (Three hours is best, but one will work in a pinch.) For a bit of zip, we like pairing cucumbers with onion— and found that salting and draining the onion along with the cucumbers removes its sharp sting. Whether we dress them with a lively vinaigrette or rich, creamy dressing, our cucumbers retain maximum crunch.

SEED, SALT, AND WEIGHT To prepare the cucumbers for these salads, first peel them, halve them lengthwise, and scoop out the seeds (which are more watery than the flesh and can add an unappealing texture). After slicing them into ¼-inch half rounds, place them in a colander set over a large bowl. Adding 1 tablespoon of salt helps to remove the water from the vegetables. Weighing them down with a gallon-size zipper-lock bag filled with water and letting them drain for one to three hours removes the most liquid, preventing a soggy finished salad.

SALT LESS Though some people extol the virtues of salting cucumbers with much more salt than you would use to season the salad, rinsing off the excess before serving, we don't agree. We've found that even after rinsing the heavily salted cucumbers and blotting with paper towels, the salad is overly salty. Instead, we prefer to salt the cucumbers with just 1 tablespoon of salt and let them sit, weighted down, for a few hours. We still rinse the cucumbers, but this smaller amount of salt is easily removed, leaving us with perfectly seasoned cucumbers.

PRACTICAL SCIENCE VINEGAR SEDIMENT

Don't worry: Vinegar with a cloudy, slimy sediment at the bottom is still usable.

Nearly all commercially made vinegar will last indefinitely in an unopened bottle. Once the vinegar is exposed to air, however, harmless "vinegar bacteria" may start to grow. These bacteria cause the formation of a cloudy sediment that is nothing more than harmless cellulose, a complex carbohydrate that does not affect the quality or flavor of the vinegar. We confirmed this with a side-by-side comparison of freshly opened bottles of vinegar and those with sediment (strained before tasting).

The Vinegar Institute carried out storage studies of vinegar and determined that the shelf life of opened vinegar stored in a dark cabinet at room temperature is "almost indefinite." To deal with the unsightly sediment, simply strain the vinegar through a coffee filter set inside a fine-mesh strainer before using it.

Everyone knows tomatoes are juicy. What are the best strategies for dealing with all this liquid? Salt can help to remove excess moisture and prevent the waterlogging of such baked dishes as tarts and stuffed tomatoes, and it can play an instrumental role in helping to coax the flavor out of the cells.

TOMATO AND MOZZARELLA TART

SERVES 6 TO 8

Thawing the frozen puff pastry in the refrigerator overnight will help prevent cracking while unfolding it. Be sure to use low-moisture supermarket mozzarella sold in block form, not fresh water-packed mozzarella.

2 (9½ by 9-inch) sheets puff pastry, thawed
1 large egg, beaten
2 ounces Parmesan cheese, grated (1 cup)
1 pound plum tomatoes, cored and cut crosswise into ¼-inch-thick slices
  Salt and pepper
2 garlic cloves, minced
2 tablespoons extra-virgin olive oil
8 ounces whole-milk mozzarella cheese, shredded (2 cups)
2 tablespoons chopped fresh basil

1. Adjust oven rack to lower-middle position and heat oven to 425 degrees. Line rimmed baking sheet with parchment paper. Dust counter with flour and unfold both pieces of puff pastry onto counter. Brush 1 short edge of 1 sheet of pastry with egg and overlap with second sheet by 1 inch, forming 18 by 9-inch rectangle. Press to seal edges, then use rolling pin to smooth seam. Cut two 1-inch-wide strips from long side of dough and two more from short side. Transfer large piece of dough to prepared baking sheet and brush with egg. Attach long dough strips to long edges of dough and short strips to short edges, then brush dough strips with egg. Sprinkle Parmesan evenly over shell. Using fork, uniformly poke holes in shell all over. Bake for 13 to 15 minutes, then reduce oven temperature to 350 degrees. Continue to bake until golden brown and crisp, 13 to 15 minutes longer. Transfer to wire rack; increase oven temperature to 425 degrees.

2. While shell bakes, place tomato slices in single layer on double layer of paper towels and sprinkle evenly with ½ teaspoon salt; let stand for 30 minutes. Place another double layer of paper towels on top of tomatoes and press firmly to dry tomatoes. Combine garlic, olive oil, and pinch each salt and pepper in small bowl; set aside.

3. Sprinkle mozzarella evenly over baked shell. Shingle tomato slices widthwise on top of cheese (about 4 slices per row); brush tomatoes with garlic oil. Bake until shell is deep golden brown and cheese is melted, 15 to 17 minutes. Let cool on wire rack for 5 minutes. Sprinkle with basil, slide onto cutting board or serving platter, cut into pieces, and serve.

TO MAKE AHEAD: Tart shell can be prebaked through step 1, cooled to room temperature, wrapped in plastic wrap, and kept at room temperature for up to 2 days before being topped and baked with mozzarella and tomatoes.

SUN-DRIED TOMATO AND MOZZARELLA TART

Replacing the plum tomatoes with sun-dried tomatoes turns this into an appetizer you can make any time of year.

Substitute ½ cup oil-packed sun-dried tomatoes, drained, rinsed, and chopped fine, for plum tomatoes.

TOMATO AND MOZZARELLA TART WITH PROSCIUTTO

Place 2 ounces thinly sliced prosciutto in single layer on top of mozzarella before arranging tomato slices.

PRACTICAL SCIENCE
THE TALE OF THE SOGGY TART

Three steps are necessary to prevent a soggy tart: salt, an egg wash, and some Parmesan.

If you neglect to salt the tomatoes and brush the dough with egg wash, the baked tart will be soggy and limp. If you take both of these precautions (and add a layer of grated Parmesan), individual slices will be firm and dry and have enough structural integrity to hold their shape.

SOGGY
Without salted, drained tomatoes, Parmesan, or an egg wash, this is one soggy tart.

FIRM
After implementing our three precautions, this tart can be held firmly in one hand.

✔ WHY THIS RECIPE WORKS

Falling somewhere in between pizza and quiche, a tomato and mozzarella tart shares the flavors of both but features problems unique unto itself. For starters, the moisture in the tomatoes almost guarantees a soggy pastry crust. Also, tomato tarts are often short on flavor. We set out to develop a recipe that could easily be made at home with a solid bottom crust and great vine-ripened flavor. The best results came from using a two-step baking method, "waterproofing" the crust with egg wash, layering cheese to prevent sogginess, and, of course, salting the sliced tomatoes to remove excess juices.

SALT AND DRAIN A combination of salting and draining on paper towels (with some pressing at the end) extracts much of the moisture from sliced tomatoes destined for a tart. We begin with plum tomatoes here, rather than beefsteak tomatoes, because they have less liquid.

FORM THE PUFF PASTRY CRUST We transform store-bought puff pastry sheets into a rectangular crust with a thin border to contain the topping (tomatoes easily slip off a flat sheet of anything). To do this, we brush egg along one edge of one sheet of puff pastry and overlap it with the second sheet of dough by 1 inch, pressing to seal them together. With a rolling pin, we smooth out the seam. The dough should measure about 18 by 9 inches. (You can use a pizza cutter to trim the edges straight.) Next, we cut two 1-inch strips from the long side of the dough, and then two 1-inch strips from the short side. After brushing the dough with an egg wash, we gently press the thin strips onto the outer edges of the dough—one per side, creating a well-fitting border. Brushing the strips with more egg wash secures them in place.

PREBAKE THE CRUST We prebake the crust at two different heat levels: a high temperature for initial lift and browning, then a lower temperature to dry out the shell for maximum sturdiness. Starting out at 425 degrees (and held there until puffed and light golden, about 15 minutes) and finishing at 350 degrees (and held there until well browned, 15 minutes longer), the crust emerges flaky yet rigid enough for us to hold it aloft while grasping just one end.

WATERPROOF THE DOUGH The first lines of defense against a soggy tart are a thick coat of egg and a layer of Parmesan cheese applied to the entire tart before prebaking begins. The egg wash creates a deflective but not impermeable layer on the delicate crust. But the Parmesan melts into a solid (and delicious, nutty-tasting) fatty layer that liquid rolls right off, like rain off a duck's back. With these layers intact, we can add mozzarella and tomatoes and still end up with a firm, crisp tart, even hours after baking.

STUFFED TOMATOES WITH PARMESAN, GARLIC, AND BASIL
SERVES 6

Make sure not to use tomatoes that are too ripe, as they will not hold their shape.

6	firm, ripe large tomatoes (8 ounces each), ⅛ inch sliced off stem end, cored, and seeded
1	teaspoon kosher salt
1	slice hearty white sandwich bread, torn into quarters
3	tablespoons plus 1 teaspoon olive oil
1½	ounces Parmesan cheese, grated (¾ cup)
⅓	cup shredded fresh basil
2	garlic cloves, minced
	Pepper

1. Line baking sheet with double layer of paper towels. Sprinkle inside of each tomato with salt and place upside down on baking sheet. Let sit to remove excess moisture, about 30 minutes.

2. Meanwhile, adjust oven rack to upper-middle position and heat oven to 375 degrees. Line bottom of 13 by 9-inch baking dish with aluminum foil; set aside. Pulse bread in food processor to coarse crumbs, about 10 pulses. Toss with 1 tablespoon olive oil, Parmesan, basil, and garlic in small bowl; season with pepper to taste.

3. Pat inside of each tomato dry with paper towels. Arrange tomatoes in single layer in prepared baking dish. Brush top cut edges of tomatoes with 1 teaspoon oil. Mound stuffing into tomatoes (about ¼ cup per tomato) and drizzle with remaining 2 tablespoons oil. Bake until tops are golden brown and crisp, about 20 minutes. Serve immediately.

STUFFED TOMATOES WITH GOAT CHEESE, OLIVES, AND OREGANO

Substitute 3 ounces crumbled goat cheese (¾ cup) for Parmesan, omit basil, and add 3 tablespoons minced fresh parsley, 1½ teaspoons minced fresh oregano, and 3 tablespoons chopped black olives to bread-crumb mixture in step 2.

✔ WHY THIS RECIPE WORKS

Most stuffed tomatoes are mealy and bland, with a stuffing of waterlogged, tasteless bread. We were after ripe, sun-drenched summer tomatoes filled with garden-fresh herbs, garlicky bread crumbs, and sharp cheese. To combat sogginess, we salt and drain the tomatoes prior to stuffing. We use homemade bread crumbs as a base for a stuffing that also includes olive oil, cheese, garlic, and fresh basil. We generously fill the tomatoes and bake for just 20 minutes for tender tomatoes topped with a crisp, golden crust.

SALT THOSE TOMATOES Rather than letting the tomato juices make the filling runny when baked, we remove these juices before stuffing by salting the interior. After salting, the water passes through the cells' semipermeable membranes, moving from the inside of the cells to the outside, in effect draining the tomato of its excess juices.

DRY THEM, TOO After salting the tomatoes, we place them upside down on a pile of paper towels. Not only does the salt help to remove the liquid, but the paper towels, too, draw even more moisture from the tomatoes. Placing the tomatoes upside down helps to speed up this process.

MAKE HOMEMADE CRUMBS Homemade bread crumbs are better for both flavor and texture in this dish. Store-bought crumbs can be gritty and dry, and don't absorb the remaining tomato moisture very well. The homemade crumbs, on the other hand, absorb the juices yet still provide an interesting chew and crunch.

USE POTENT SEASONINGS There isn't a lot of space in a tomato, so a little filling has to have big flavor. Choose other ingredients (besides the bread) carefully. In addition to the crumbs, we like a potent cheese, garlic, fresh herbs, and even olives.

PRACTICAL SCIENCE
REMOVE GREEN SPROUTS FROM GARLIC

Green sprouts in garlic can taste bitter and harsh.

Many a culinary student has been told to remove any green shoots from cloves of garlic because they are thought to have a bitter taste that persists even when the garlic is cooked. To test the validity of this advice, we used raw garlic in aïoli and cooked garlic in pasta with olive oil and tried each recipe with the shoots removed before mincing the garlic as well as with the shoots left in. In the aïoli, tasters could clearly identify a more bitter, unpleasant taste in the batch made with the shoots left in; the batch without the shoots still had the bite that you expect from garlic, but it was less harsh. The pasta made with the shoots had a harsh, somewhat metallic aftertaste that, once established, tainted every bite that followed.

Why? The sprouts contain stronger, more bitter-tasting compounds than those found in the clove, and they tend to persist even after cooking. We recommend removing the sprouts when cooking with garlic.

USE A MODERATE OVEN If a tomato spends too much time in the oven, it will shrivel. But if the temperature is too high, the stuffing will burn while the tomato remains raw-tasting inside. We compromise: 375 degrees for 20 minutes leaves us with a tender tomato and a lovely golden crust on top.

CREAMY GAZPACHO ANDALUZ
SERVES 4 TO 6

For ideal flavor, allow the gazpacho to sit in the refrigerator overnight before serving. Red wine vinegar can be substituted for the sherry vinegar. Although we prefer to use kosher salt in this soup, half the amount of table salt can be used. Serve the soup with additional extra-virgin olive oil, sherry vinegar, ground black pepper, and diced vegetables for diners to season and garnish their own bowls as desired.

3	pounds tomatoes, cored
1	small cucumber, peeled, halved lengthwise, and seeded
1	green bell pepper, stemmed, halved, and seeded
1	small red onion, peeled and halved
2	garlic cloves, peeled and quartered
1	small serrano chile, stemmed and halved lengthwise Kosher salt and pepper
1	slice hearty white sandwich bread, crust removed, torn into 1-inch pieces
½	cup extra-virgin olive oil, plus extra for serving
2	tablespoons sherry vinegar, plus extra for serving
2	tablespoons minced fresh parsley, chives, or basil

1. Coarsely chop 2 pounds tomatoes, half of cucumber, half of bell pepper, and half of onion and place in large bowl. Add garlic, serrano, and 1½ teaspoons salt and toss to combine.

2. Cut remaining tomatoes, cucumber, and bell pepper into ¼-inch dice and place in medium bowl. Mince remaining onion and add to diced vegetables. Toss with ½ teaspoon salt and transfer to fine-mesh strainer set over medium bowl. Let drain for 1 hour. Transfer drained diced vegetables to medium bowl and set aside, reserving exuded liquid (there should be about ¼ cup; discard extra liquid).

3. Add bread pieces to exuded liquid and soak for 1 minute. Add soaked bread and any remaining liquid to coarsely chopped vegetables and toss thoroughly to combine.

4. Transfer half of vegetable-bread mixture to blender and process for 30 seconds. With blender running, slowly drizzle in ¼ cup oil and continue to blend until completely

smooth, about 2 minutes. Strain soup through fine-mesh strainer into large bowl, using back of ladle or rubber spatula to press soup through strainer. Repeat with remaining vegetable-bread mixture and ¼ cup oil.

5. Stir vinegar, parsley, and half of diced vegetables into soup and season with salt and pepper to taste. Cover and refrigerate overnight or for at least 2 hours to chill completely and develop flavors. Serve, passing remaining diced vegetables, oil, vinegar, and pepper separately.

✔ WHY THIS RECIPE WORKS

The gazpacho popular in Andalusia, the southern region of Spain, is creamy and complex, with the bright flavor of naturally ripened vegetables. The key to fresh tomato flavor is salting the tomatoes and letting them sit to release more flavor. This is also true for the other vegetables—cucumber, bell pepper, and onion (see "Salting Can Also Make Vegetables Taste Better," page 213). For added flavor, we soak the bread, which we use to thicken the soup, in the exuded vegetable juices. A final dash of olive oil and sherry vinegar further brightens the flavor of our soup. A diced-vegetable garnish lends a fresh finish.

SOAK THAT BREAD True old-world gazpacho is more concept than precise recipe. Centuries ago, Spanish field-workers cobbled together leftover odds and ends— yesterday's bread, almonds, garlic, olive oil, water—and mashed it all together into a humble potage. (Even the etymology of gazpacho is fuzzy, though most authorities suggest it derives from words for "fragments," "remainder," and "soaked bread.") Needless to say, the bread is an important ingredient. It adds body—and authenticity. We soak our bread not in water, the liquid traditionally used to soften the bread, but in the exuded liquid from the salted vegetables to add even more flavor to the soup.

DRIZZLE OIL SLOWLY The trick to a smooth soup with a fully blended texture is all in how you add the olive oil. Go slow. It's important to drizzle the oil slowly in order for it to emulsify (see concept 36).

TIME TO DEVELOP FLAVORS Chilling the soup not only gets it to the right (and refreshing) temperature, but the time it takes to chill the soup helps to develop flavor. The soup should be chilled for at least two hours, but overnight is best.

SALTING AT WORK EGGPLANT

Eggplants are filled with both air pockets and water. Diced and cooked as is, they will absorb large amounts of the cooking medium—usually oil—resulting in a greasy mess. It's important to remove the liquid before cooking, allowing the eggplant to brown under high heat and collapse the air bubbles so that excessive amounts of oil are not absorbed. We do this with salt. Salting and then draining the eggplant is traditional, but we take it one step further and use the microwave. Salting draws out the moisture and microwaving causes the liquid to evaporate rapidly, resulting in a dehydrated vegetable ready for deep caramelization in a pan.

CAPONATA
MAKES 3 CUPS

Serve caponata spooned over slices of toasted baguette or alongside grilled meat or fish. Adjust the vinegar as necessary, depending on the acidity of your tomatoes and what you are serving with the caponata. To allow the steam released by the eggplant to escape, remove the plate from the microwave immediately. Although the test kitchen prefers the complex flavor of V8 vegetable juice, tomato juice can be substituted. Caponata is best made a day in advance to allow the flavors to meld.

1½	pounds eggplant, cut into ½-inch pieces
¾	teaspoon kosher salt
¾	cup V8 juice
¼	cup red wine vinegar, plus extra for seasoning
¼	cup minced fresh parsley
2	tablespoons packed light brown sugar
3	anchovy fillets, rinsed and minced
8	ounces tomatoes, cored, seeded, and cut into ½-inch pieces
¼	cup raisins
2	tablespoons minced black olives
5	teaspoons extra-virgin olive oil, plus extra 1 teaspoon if needed
1	celery rib, cut into ¼-inch pieces
1	small red bell pepper, stemmed, seeded and cut into ¼-inch pieces
1	small onion, chopped fine
¼	cup pine nuts, toasted

1. Toss eggplant and salt together in bowl. Line surface of large plate with double layer of coffee filters and lightly spray with vegetable oil spray. Spread eggplant in even layer over coffee filters. Microwave until eggplant is dry and shriveled to one-third its size but is not brown, 8 to 15 minutes. (If microwave has no turntable, rotate plate after 5 minutes.) Remove eggplant from microwave and immediately transfer to paper towel–lined plate.

2. Meanwhile, whisk V8 juice, vinegar, parsley, sugar, and anchovies together in medium bowl. Stir in tomatoes, raisins, and olives.

3. Heat 1 tablespoon oil in 12-inch nonstick skillet over medium-high heat until shimmering. Add eggplant and cook, stirring occasionally, until edges are browned, 4 to 8 minutes, adding up to 1 teaspoon oil if pan appears dry. Transfer to bowl and set aside.

4. Add remaining 2 teaspoons oil to now-empty skillet and heat until shimmering. Add celery and bell pepper and cook, stirring occasionally, until softened and edges are spotty brown, 2 to 4 minutes. Add onion and continue to cook until vegetables are browned, about 4 minutes longer.

5. Reduce heat to medium-low and stir in eggplant and V8 juice mixture. Bring to simmer and cook until vegetable juices are thickened and coat vegetables, 4 to 7 minutes. Transfer to serving bowl and let cool to room temperature. Taste and season with up to 1 teaspoon additional vinegar, if necessary. Sprinkle with pine nuts before serving. (Caponata can be refrigerated for up to 1 week.)

✔ WHY THIS RECIPE WORKS

This classic Sicilian dish, featuring a mix of sautéed vegetables (primarily tomatoes and eggplant) and accented with anchovies, capers, and pine nuts, can turn out greasy thanks to the spongy nature of eggplants, which causes them to soak up oil. For a balanced and boldly flavored caponata with eggplant that doesn't turn to oil-soaked mush, we like to salt and then microwave rather than just salt and drain the eggplant. Though an unexpected move, it turns out to be critical for drying out the eggplant sufficiently.

SALT AND MICROWAVE Eggplant is essentially a sponge, consisting of a maze of tiny air pockets ready to absorb anything, especially the medium it's cooked in. It's also packed with water. Both of these properties make it troublesome to cook. When it is sautéed, for example, the air pockets will suck up any oil in the pan, forcing the cook to keep adding oil to prevent sticking or burning. Meanwhile, the moisture inside turns to steam. This one-two punch transforms the eggplant into oil-soaked mush before it has a chance to caramelize. The classic technique of salting and draining the eggplant isn't enough for this dish. Instead, we dehydrate the eggplant faster and more effectively by cutting it into small cubes, salting it, and sticking it in the microwave. After all, the microwave works by causing the water molecules in food to oscillate rapidly and generate steam. Food left in the microwave will transition from merely heating up to actually dehydrating. Coffee filters (rather than paper towels, which can contain dyes that are not microwave-safe) absorb the released liquid and prevent the newly dried eggplant from turning into mush.

SAUTÉ SEPARATELY We sauté our eggplant separately so that it won't be affected by the moisture shed by the other vegetables as they cook. As for the other vegetables, we sauté the celery, bell pepper, and onion in order to develop their flavors. We don't add the fresh tomatoes until close to the end of cooking because a long cooking time would rob them of their fresh taste. Adding them right before taking the pan off the heat would give the caponata a texture like salsa, however. We strike the perfect balance by gently simmering the tomatoes with the browned eggplant and other ingredients for a handful of minutes at the very end of cooking. About five minutes over medium-low heat incorporates the tomatoes' sweet juiciness while preserving their bright freshness.

PRACTICAL SCIENCE
A CURE FOR WHAT AILS EGGPLANT

Eggplant can be mushy and greasy without our surprising solution: salt and a microwave.

To rid the eggplant of excess moisture and collapse the air pockets that make it soak up oil like a sponge, we came up with a novel solution: salting it and then heating it in the microwave. The salt pulls out liquid from inside the eggplant at the same time the microwave causes it to steam. In addition, the microwave helps to collapse the weakened cell walls in the eggplant, making it less spongy. To keep the eggplant from poaching in the liquid it releases, we set it on a layer of coffee filters. By absorbing all of that liquid, the filters also help to maintain a super-high salt concentration on the exterior of the eggplant, which causes even more unwanted moisture to be drawn out.

RAW DEAL
Without pretreatment, the raw eggplant looks good but cooks up oily and mushy.

MICROWAVE MAGIC
Salted, microwaved eggplant isn't as pretty, but the shrunken cubes soak up far less oil.

GOTTA HAVE V8 Alongside the fresh tomatoes, we also add some V8 juice to this dish in order to achieve the deep tomato flavor that makes a great caponata so memorable. A small amount is just enough to provide another layer of tomato flavor, while still allowing the fresh tomatoes to shine.

BUILD FLAVOR Traditional caponata has a sweet and sour finish that helps distinguish it from the stewed eggplant specialty from France, ratatouille. Brown sugar adds a sweet note, while we prefer red wine vinegar for the sour. It provides just the right degree of bracing tartness. Customary inclusions of raisins and olives are also a must. After trying a dozen different olive varieties, we find that almost any olive will work. A few anchovy fillets deepen the overall flavor of the dish, and a scattering of toasted pine nuts provides an aromatic crunch. Together, these ingredients give us well-balanced, authentic caponata that tastes great as an appetizer, a relish, or just straight from the bowl.

PASTA ALLA NORMA
SERVES 4

Ricotta salata is traditional, but French feta, Pecorino Romano, and Cotija (a firm, crumbly Mexican cheese) are acceptable substitutes. We prefer kosher salt because it clings best to the eggplant. If using table salt, reduce salt amounts by half. Use the smaller amount of red pepper flakes for a milder sauce.

1½	pounds eggplant, cut into ½-inch pieces
	Kosher salt
¼	cup extra-virgin olive oil
4	garlic cloves, minced
2	anchovy fillets, rinsed and minced
¼–½	teaspoon red pepper flakes
1	(28-ounce) can crushed tomatoes
6	tablespoons chopped fresh basil
1	pound ziti, rigatoni, or penne
3	ounces ricotta salata, shredded (1½ cups)

1. Toss eggplant with 1 teaspoon salt in large bowl. Line surface of large plate with double layer of coffee filters and lightly spray with vegetable oil spray. Spread eggplant in even layer over coffee filters; wipe out and reserve bowl. Microwave eggplant, uncovered, until dry to touch and slightly shriveled, about 10 minutes, tossing halfway through cooking. Let cool slightly.

2. Transfer eggplant to now-empty bowl, drizzle with 1 tablespoon oil, and toss gently to coat; discard coffee filters and reserve plate. Heat 1 tablespoon oil in 12-inch nonstick skillet over medium-high heat until shimmering. Add eggplant and cook, stirring every 1½ to 2 minutes (more frequent stirring may cause eggplant pieces to break apart), until well browned and fully tender, about 10 minutes. Transfer eggplant to now-empty plate and set aside. Let skillet cool slightly, about 3 minutes.

3. Heat 1 tablespoon oil, garlic, anchovies, and pepper flakes in now-empty skillet over medium heat. Cook, stirring often, until garlic turns golden but not brown, about 3 minutes. Stir in tomatoes, bring to simmer, and cook, stirring occasionally, until slightly thickened, 8 to 10 minutes. Add eggplant and continue to cook, stirring occasionally, until eggplant is heated through and flavors meld, 3 to 5 minutes longer. Stir in basil and remaining 1 tablespoon oil and season with salt to taste.

4. Meanwhile, bring 4 quarts water to boil in large pot. Add pasta and 2 tablespoons salt and cook, stirring often, until al dente. Reserve ½ cup cooking water, then drain pasta and return it to pot. Add sauce to pasta and toss to combine. Add reserved cooking water as needed to adjust consistency. Serve immediately, passing ricotta salata separately.

✓ WHY THIS RECIPE WORKS
To create a bold, complex Pasta alla Norma without a lot of work, we came up with a few strategies. As we do for our Caponata (page 220), we salt and then microwave the eggplant to rid it of as much liquid as possible, enabling us to deeply caramelize the vegetable in only a little bit of oil. When developing this recipe, we tried many different types of eggplant: portly globe eggplant; smaller, more svelte Italian eggplant; and slender, lavender-colored Chinese eggplant. All worked, but in the end we prefer globe eggplant, which has a tender yet resilient texture and far fewer seeds than other varieties, including Italian eggplant. Cut into cubes, it retains its shape even after sautéing.

BUILD A QUICK SAUCE For the sauce, we prefer using canned crushed tomatoes for their thick texture and added cohesion. We season the sauce with garlic, which is cooked using residual heat to prevent burning. A little bit of red pepper flakes adds a suggestion of heat, a generous dose of chopped basil brings fresh flavor, and a tablespoon of extra-virgin olive oil stirred in at the end with the basil gives the sauce rich, round, fruity notes. Two anchovy fillets, minced, give the sauce a deep, savory flavor without any trace of fishiness. We don't add the eggplant until the very end to prevent it from becoming mushy.

CHOOSE THE RIGHT CHEESE Ricotta salata is a firm, tangy Italian sheep's milk cheese that bears little resemblance to the moist ricotta sold in tubs. It is an essential component of traditional pasta alla Norma. If you can't find it in the market, consider substituting French feta (which is milder but tangy, a close cousin to ricotta salata in flavor and texture), Pecorino Romano (which is hard and dry, with a slightly more assertive aroma and flavor than ricotta salata), or Cotija (a Mexican cow's milk cheese that is firm yet crumbly and less complex than ricotta salata).

SALTING AT WORK ZUCCHINI AND SUMMER SQUASH

Like cabbage, tomatoes, and eggplant, zucchini and summer squash benefit from salting before being cooked. (After all, zucchini is almost 95 percent water.) Here, the salt draws water out of slices of squash to prevent a gratin swimming in water, and from shredded zucchini (minus the seeds) to avoid a watery sauté.

SUMMER VEGETABLE GRATIN
SERVES 6 TO 8

Buy zucchini and summer squash of roughly the same diameter. While we like the visual contrast zucchini and summer squash bring to the dish, you can also use just one or the other. A similarly sized broiler-safe gratin dish can be substituted for the 13 by 9-inch baking dish. Serve the gratin alongside grilled fish or meat and accompanied by bread to soak up any flavorful juices.

6	tablespoons extra-virgin olive oil
1	pound zucchini, sliced ¼ inch thick
1	pound yellow summer squash, sliced ¼ inch thick
2	teaspoons salt
1½	pounds tomatoes, cored and sliced ¼ inch thick
2	onions, halved and sliced thin
¾	teaspoon pepper
2	garlic cloves, minced
1	tablespoon minced fresh thyme
1	slice hearty white sandwich bread, torn into quarters
2	ounces Parmesan cheese, grated (1 cup)
2	shallots, minced
¼	cup chopped fresh basil

1. Adjust oven rack to upper-middle position and heat oven to 400 degrees. Brush 13 by 9-inch baking dish with 1 tablespoon oil and set aside. Line 2 baking sheets with triple layer of paper towels and set aside.

2. Toss zucchini and summer squash slices with 1 teaspoon salt in large bowl; transfer to colander. Let drain until zucchini and squash release at least 3 tablespoons liquid, about 45 minutes. Arrange slices on 1 prepared baking sheet and cover with another triple layer of paper towels. Firmly press each slice to remove as much liquid as possible.

PRACTICAL SCIENCE KEEP THE SEEDS

The seeds and jelly contain most of the tomato's glutamate. For our gratin, we think twice before discarding them.

At first we thought that removing the seeds and jelly from the tomatoes would help to cure the problem of too much liquid in this gratin. This is a common practice intended to improve the texture of a finished dish. But we found it affects the flavor, too.

To test this, we prepared two gratins, one made with intact tomatoes and another where the tomato seeds and jelly had been removed. We found that the gratin with the intact tomatoes had a decidedly richer, deeper flavor than its stripped-down counterpart.

According to a study published in the *Journal of Agricultural and Food Chemistry*, that's because the seeds and jelly actually contain three times the amount of flavor-enhancing glutamic acid as the flesh. (Also called glutamate, this is the compound that supplies the savory quality known as umami in many foods; see concept 35.) Sometimes removing seeds is necessary (as in our Stuffed Tomatoes recipe, page 218), but it's generally a last resort. The next time a recipe calls for removing the seeds from tomatoes, you may want to ignore the instructions. You'll be saving time.

3. Place tomato slices in single layer on second prepared baking sheet, sprinkle evenly with ½ teaspoon salt, and let stand for 30 minutes. Cover with double layer of paper towels and press firmly to dry tomatoes.

4. Meanwhile, heat 1 tablespoon oil in 12-inch nonstick skillet over medium heat until shimmering. Add onions, remaining ½ teaspoon salt, and ¼ teaspoon pepper. Cook, stirring occasionally, until onions are softened and dark golden brown, 20 to 25 minutes. Set onions aside.

5. Combine garlic, 3 tablespoons oil, remaining ½ teaspoon pepper, and thyme in small bowl. In large bowl, toss zucchini and summer squash in half of oil mixture, then arrange in prepared baking dish. Arrange caramelized onions in even layer over squash. Slightly overlap tomato slices in single layer on top of onions. Spoon remaining garlic-oil mixture evenly over tomatoes. Bake until vegetables are tender and tomatoes are starting to brown on edges, 40 to 45 minutes.

6. Meanwhile, process bread in food processor until finely ground, about 10 seconds. (You should have about 1 cup crumbs.) Combine bread crumbs, remaining 1 tablespoon oil, Parmesan, and shallots in medium bowl. Remove baking dish from oven and increase heat to 450 degrees. Sprinkle bread-crumb mixture evenly on top of tomatoes. Bake gratin until bubbling and cheese is lightly browned, 5 to 10 minutes. Sprinkle with basil and let sit for 10 minutes before serving.

SUMMER VEGETABLE GRATIN WITH ROASTED PEPPERS AND SMOKED MOZZARELLA

You can use store-bought roasted red peppers or make your own. If using store-bought, rinse and pat the peppers dry before using.

Substitute 1 cup shredded smoked mozzarella for Parmesan and 3 roasted red peppers, cut into 1-inch pieces, for summer squash (do not salt roasted peppers).

✔ WHY THIS RECIPE WORKS

Layering summer's best vegetables into a gratin can lead to a memorable side dish—or a soggy mess. We wanted a simple Provençal-style vegetable gratin, where a golden brown, cheesy topping provides a rich contrast to the fresh, bright flavor of the vegetables. The typical combination of tomatoes, zucchini, and summer squash made the cut (eggplant was too mushy and bell peppers took on a steamed flavor). To eliminate excess moisture, we bake the casserole uncovered after salting the vegetables. We move the tomatoes to the top gratin layer, which allows them to roast and caramelize. We build flavor by tossing the zucchini and tomatoes with homemade garlic-thyme oil.

SALT AND SLICE The zucchini, summer squash, and tomatoes all get the salt treatment here. The squash is sliced and placed in a colander, then patted dry and pressed to remove excess liquid. The tomatoes are placed directly on paper towels and salted; they are too delicate to be tossed in the colander like the squash.

CARAMELIZE THE ONION To add complexity, we insert a layer of caramelized onions between the zucchini/squash and tomato layers.

BAKE HOT AND UNCOVERED For this gratin, we use a big dish and a fairly shallow layer of vegetables to prevent liquid from pooling and collecting among the veggies as they bake. By cooking the gratin at a relatively high temperature without a foil covering, we are likewise helping excess liquid to evaporate.

FINISH WITH CHEESY CRUMBS Homemade crumbs are key here, giving much better flavor and texture to the dish. We add cheese and shallots to punch up the flavors.

SAUTÉED SHREDDED ZUCCHINI WITH GARLIC AND LEMON
SERVES 4

The bread-crumb topping adds a nice textural contrast to this recipe, but you may omit it if you prefer.

TOPPING

- 2 slices hearty white sandwich bread, torn into quarters
- 2 tablespoons unsalted butter

ZUCCHINI

- 5 zucchini, halved lengthwise, seeded, and shredded
   Salt and pepper
- 4 teaspoons extra-virgin olive oil, plus extra for drizzling
- 1 small garlic clove, minced
- 1–2 teaspoons lemon juice

1. **FOR THE TOPPING:** Pulse bread in food processor to coarse crumbs, about 10 pulses. Melt butter in 12-inch nonstick skillet over medium-high heat. Add bread crumbs and cook, stirring frequently, until golden brown, about 3 minutes. Transfer to small bowl; set aside.

2. **FOR THE ZUCCHINI:** Toss zucchini with 1½ teaspoons salt in large bowl. Transfer to colander and let drain for 5 to 10 minutes. Place zucchini in center of kitchen towel and wring out excess moisture, in batches if necessary.

3. Place zucchini in medium bowl and separate any large clumps. Combine 2 teaspoons oil with garlic in small bowl. Add to zucchini and toss to combine.

4. Heat remaining 2 teaspoons oil in 12-inch nonstick skillet over high heat until just smoking. Add zucchini in even layer and cook, without stirring, until bottom layer browns, about 2 minutes. Stir well, breaking up any clumps with tongs, then cook until bottom layer browns, about 2 minutes more. Off heat, season with lemon juice and salt and pepper to taste. Sprinkle with topping, drizzle with olive oil, and serve immediately.

SAUTÉED SHREDDED ZUCCHINI WITH TOMATOES AND BASIL

Omit bread-crumb topping. Combine 3 diced plum tomatoes, 2 tablespoons chopped fresh basil, 2 teaspoons extra-virgin olive oil, 1 teaspoon balsamic vinegar, 1 minced garlic clove, and ¼ teaspoon salt in small bowl and set aside. Omit garlic in step 3 and replace lemon juice with tomato mixture in step 4. Transfer to serving platter, sprinkle with ¼ cup grated Parmesan, and serve immediately, drizzling with additional olive oil if desired.

SAUTÉED SHREDDED ZUCCHINI WITH SPICED CARROTS AND ALMONDS

Omit bread-crumb topping. Follow steps 2 and 3 as directed, omitting garlic, then heat 1 tablespoon extra-virgin olive oil in 12-inch nonstick skillet over medium heat until shimmering. Add 2 grated carrots and cook, stirring occasionally, until tender, about 5 minutes. Add ½ teaspoon ground coriander and ¼ teaspoon red pepper flakes and cook, stirring constantly, until fragrant, about 30 seconds. Add grated zucchini and ½ cup golden raisins to skillet, spread into even layer, and cook as directed. Add ½ cup sliced toasted almonds and toss to combine before seasoning with lemon juice, salt, and pepper.

SAUTÉED SHREDDED ZUCCHINI WITH PEAS AND HERBS

Omit bread-crumb topping and lemon juice. Follow steps 2 and 3 as directed, omitting garlic, then heat 2 teaspoons oil in 12-inch nonstick skillet over medium heat until shimmering. Add finely chopped whites from 1 bunch scallions and cook, stirring, until softened and beginning to brown, about 3 minutes. Increase heat to high, add zucchini, and cook as directed. Once browned, add 1 cup thawed frozen peas and ½ cup heavy cream and cook, stirring, until cream is mostly reduced, about 2 minutes. Off heat, stir in 2 tablespoons minced fresh dill or mint and thinly sliced scallion greens and season with salt and pepper to taste. Serve with lemon wedges.

☑ WHY THIS RECIPE WORKS

Because zucchini is so watery, it often cooks up soggy and bland. We wanted to find a way to make sautéed zucchini with concentrated flavor and appealing texture. The secret is to remove water using more than one method: salting and draining as well as shredding and squeezing.

SHRED, SALT, AND WRING DRY The first step is to seed the zucchini. The seeds and core should be discarded to avoid a soupy, steamy mess when sautéed. Next, we shred the zucchini on the large holes of a box grater. Then we toss the shreds with salt and drain them in a colander. After draining, we wring them out to dry in a kitchen towel. The shredding cuts way down on the time the zucchini needs to drain—five minutes as opposed to the 30 minutes needed for whole slices.

OIL BEFORE COOKING To avoid a slightly clumpy, tangled texture to the zucchini, which can make it tricky to distribute flavorful ingredients evenly, the key is to toss the raw shreds of zucchini with olive oil before adding them to the pan.

BROWN AND BREAK To cook zucchini, we crank up the heat and minimize the stirring. This way the zucchini browns nicely, and we can break up the clumps, somewhat like making hash browns.

Green Vegetables Like It Hot–Then Cold

Many older recipes boil green vegetables too long and the result is a pile of mushy, army-green broccoli or peas. Barely cooking these vegetables, however, results in the opposite problem. They look great but taste raw and woody. How do you cook these vegetables so they are tender and still brilliantly colored? It's all about a high-heat blanch followed by an ice-cold shock.

HOW THE SCIENCE WORKS

TWO STEPS FOR TENDER, BRIGHT VEGETABLES

BLANCH *A quick blanch in boiling water cooks the vegetables until just tender, brightening their colors at the same time.*

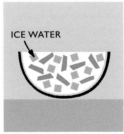

SHOCK *Tossing the vegetables in ice water stops the cooking, preventing them from becoming mushy and drab.*

When vegetables are cooked, they can change drastically—especially in terms of texture. Heat immediately weakens the cells that hold water, causing liquid to leak out and the vegetable to become limp. Pectin, the soluble glue that reinforces the cell walls and holds the cells together, breaks down and dissolves, leaving a suddenly softer piece of produce behind. Not all vegetables are meant to be eaten raw, so this change is often a welcome one.

Besides texture, heat also affects the color of vegetables. Green vegetables get their bright color from chlorophyll, a complex molecule that contains a magnesium ion at its center. When chlorophyll is heated, however, it loses this magnesium ion. This loss results in a dull, olive-green hue—familiar to all of us who have eaten drab stalks of overcooked broccoli.

The process of color change is accelerated in the presence of acids, which occur naturally in plants. Acids release hydrogen ions, which actually come in and replace chlorophyll's magnesium ions, a change that produces a dull-colored molecule called pheophytin. This is why the pH of the water (the levels of which change drastically between "hard" and "soft" water) used to boil your green veggies can affect their color—not to mention the use of acid-based dressings.

So what's the home cook to do? Well, move fast. We recommend cooking vegetables as quickly as possible in order to soften their texture but not compromise their appearance. Blanching (that is, cooking quickly in a pot of boiling, salted water) is the preferred method for cooking broccoli, green beans, snow peas, and other green vegetables. It's important not to skimp on the amount of water in the pot—a lot of water means that the added vegetables won't lower the temperature too much, allowing them to cook rapidly. In addition to adding flavor, salt weakens pectin, helping to speed the softening of the vegetables before the chlorophyll has time to change.

Interestingly, a dip in boiling water actually brightens the color of green vegetables before causing it to dull: In raw vegetables, the pockets of air in the plant refract, and therefore dim, the color of chlorophyll. But as soon as the peas or beans hit the water, some of the air contained between their cells expands and bubbles off, bringing the cell walls closer together and causing the plant tissue to become more transparent, producing a brighter green color.

After blanching, we then "shock" these vegetables in a bowl of ice water. This abruptly halts the cooking process, preventing any further transformation of the chlorophyll and leaving us with crisp-tender vegetables with brilliant color.

TEST KITCHEN EXPERIMENT

To determine the importance of not only blanching green vegetables, but also shocking them in ice water, we set up a simple test: We took two 1-pound batches of broccoli spears and blanched each for four minutes in a pot of boiling, salted water. After removing the broccoli from the pot, we then shocked one batch in ice water and let the other batch simply sit in an empty bowl. After three minutes, we drained the batch in the ice water and then examined them both for changes in color, texture, and taste.

THE RESULTS

Not surprisingly, the difference was big. The broccoli that had been shocked in ice water was firmer in texture and had a brighter green color. The broccoli that had been left to sit in the bowl grew mushy and olive drab. Because they were boiled in salted water (our preferred method for blanching), both samples were relatively well seasoned.

THE TAKEAWAY

When cooking green vegetables so that they remain bright and tender, not brown and mushy, the ability to abruptly stop the cooking process through the use of an ice bath is necessary.

Why? Blanching vegetables in boiling, salted water for four minutes first begins to break down the cell structure of the broccoli, beans, or peas. The pectin within starts to break down and dissolve, and therefore the texture of that veggie moves from tough toward tender. Likewise, the heat evaporates some of the excess air within the vegetable cells, enhancing its color from a muted green to an emerald green. This is all good.

But as we learned in concept 4, cooking doesn't always stop when the food leaves the pot (or oven, or pan). According to the principles of carryover cooking, unless cooked vegetables receive an ice-water bath immediately after exiting the pot of boiling water, they will continue to cook. When our blanched broccoli was placed in a bowl (without an ice bath), the individual stalks were hot and as they sat piled together they shared their heat, continuing to cook. The result is that the cell structures continue to degrade, turning the vegetables mushier by the minute. It also gives more time for the chlorophyll, responsible for color, to lose its magnesium ion and fade into a drab olive green. In an ice bath, however, the heat that is already inside the vegetables will reverse direction and flow into the cold water, preventing further cooking. The cold water surrounding the vegetables also stops the heat from transferring from one piece to another.

THE EFFECTS OF HEAT ON TEXTURE

RAW STALK
A raw piece of broccoli is tough in texture and light green in color.

BLANCHED AND SHOCKED
Once blanched, the broccoli is tender and bright green. The shock keeps it that way.

BLANCHED ALONE
Broccoli that is blanched and then left to sit becomes soft and mushy, with an olive-drab hue.

HOW LONG SHOULD YOU COOK THAT VEGETABLE?

VEGETABLE	PREPARATION	BOILING TIME	STEAMING TIME
Asparagus	Tough ends snapped off and discarded	2 to 4 minutes	3 to 5 minutes
Broccoli	Florets cut into 1- to 1½-inch pieces, stalks peeled and cut into ¼-inch pieces	2 to 4 minutes	4 to 6 minutes
Brussels Sprouts	Stem ends trimmed, discolored leaves removed, and halved through stems	6 to 8 minutes	7 to 9 minutes
Green Beans	Ends trimmed	3 to 5 minutes	6 to 8 minutes
Snap Peas	Strings removed	2 to 4 minutes	4 to 6 minutes
Snow Peas	Strings removed	2 to 3 minutes	4 to 6 minutes

We often blanch and shock small green vegetables like peas and beans. The quick turn in boiling, salted water cooks them just enough to lose their raw edge but keeps them crisp and bright green. It's a technique that can be used for a quick sauté, a casserole, or even to help plan ahead.

BLANCHED SUGAR SNAP PEAS
SERVES 6

See the following recipes for seasoning ideas.

- 1   pound sugar snap peas, strings removed
- 1   teaspoon salt

1. Fill large bowl with ice water and set aside. Bring 6 cups water to boil in large saucepan. Add peas and salt and cook until peas are crisp-tender, 1½ to 2 minutes.

2. Drain peas, transfer to bowl with ice water, drain again, and pat dry. (Peas can be set aside for up to 1 hour.)

SUGAR SNAP PEAS WITH LEMON, GARLIC, AND BASIL
SERVES 6

Keep a close eye on the garlic, as it can go from soft to brown quickly during cooking.

- 2   tablespoons olive oil
- 1½   teaspoons grated lemon zest plus 1 tablespoon juice
- 1   garlic clove, minced
- 1   recipe Blanched Sugar Snap Peas
- 2   tablespoons chopped fresh basil
     Salt and pepper

Heat oil over medium heat in 10-inch skillet until shimmering. Add zest and garlic and cook until garlic is soft but not browned, about 2 minutes. Add peas, lemon juice, and basil and toss to combine. Cook until just heated through, 1 to 1½ minutes. Season with salt and pepper to taste, and serve immediately.

SUGAR SNAP PEAS WITH HAM AND MINT
SERVES 6

Do not use sliced deli ham for this recipe.

- 1   tablespoon unsalted butter
- 3   ounces country ham or smoked ham, cut into ¼-inch pieces
- 1   recipe Blanched Sugar Snap Peas
- 2   tablespoons minced fresh mint
     Salt and pepper

Melt butter over medium heat in 10-inch skillet. Add ham and cook for 1 minute. Add peas and mint and toss to combine. Cook until just heated through, 1 to 1½ minutes. Season with salt and pepper to taste, and serve immediately.

✔ WHY THIS RECIPE WORKS

We wanted to determine a cooking method that would highlight the crisp texture and sweet flavor of sugar snap peas. Blanching them in salted water produces peas with excellent flavor and texture. Shocking them in ice water prevents shriveling and puckering and sets their color, too.

BLANCH AND SHOCK A sweet, crisp cross between the snow pea and the green garden pea, the sugar snap is completely edible, pod and all. Because raw sugar snaps taste chalky and flat, the peas should be eaten cooked, but just barely. They taste best when they are still quite crisp, which takes some heat, some liquid, and a little time. Blanching yields peas with excellent taste and texture. Adding salt to the water helps to season the peas and speed up the softening before the bright color fades. Shocking in

---

PRACTICAL SCIENCE TO COVER, OR NOT TO COVER

Contrary to popular belief, an uncovered pot is not necessary when blanching green vegetables.

Blanching involves briefly dunking fruits or vegetables in boiling water to set color, flavor, and texture. Some sources say that to successfully blanch green vegetables, the lid must be kept off of the pot to allow the acids they contain to evaporate, rather than trapping them in the cooking water and turning the vegetables brown.

To examine the validity of this claim, we blanched batches of broccoli, green beans, and broccoli rabe in both covered and uncovered pots. After blanching, the pH (acid) level of the water in both pots was identical for each vegetable. Moreover, all of the vegetables were bright green, and the covered and uncovered batches tasted exactly the same. The simple truth is that the acids in vegetables are not volatile, so they can't escape with the steam. The bottom line: When it comes to blanching, it makes not a whit of difference whether you cover the pot or not.

ice water stops the cooking, helps to set the bright color, and prevents further softening from residual heat.

DRY AND FINISH   Once the peas have been shocked in ice water, they can be dried with paper towels and then sautéed briefly with flavorful ingredients. Don't cook them too long—just about a minute to warm them up. Also, add the lemon juice at the very end so the acid doesn't have time to dull the color.

SAUTÉED PEAS WITH SHALLOT AND MINT
SERVES 4

Do not thaw the peas before cooking. Regular frozen peas can be used in place of baby peas; increase the cooking time in step 2 by one to two minutes. Add the lemon juice right before serving; otherwise, the peas will turn brown.

2	teaspoons olive oil
1	small shallot, minced
1	garlic clove, minced
3	cups frozen baby peas
¼	cup low-sodium chicken broth
¼	teaspoon sugar
¼	cup minced fresh mint
1	tablespoon unsalted butter
2	teaspoons lemon juice
	Salt and pepper

1. Heat oil in 12-inch skillet over medium-high heat until shimmering. Add shallot and cook, stirring frequently, until softened, about 2 minutes. Add garlic and cook, stirring frequently, until fragrant, about 30 seconds.

2. Stir in peas, broth, and sugar. Cover and cook until peas are bright green and just heated through, 3 to 5 minutes. Add mint and butter and toss to combine. Off heat, stir in lemon juice. Season with salt and pepper to taste, and serve immediately.

SAUTÉED PEAS WITH LEEKS AND TARRAGON

Substitute 1 small leek, white and light green parts only, halved lengthwise, cut into ¼-inch pieces, and washed thoroughly, for shallot and increase cooking time in step 1 to 3 to 5 minutes (leek should be softened). Substitute heavy cream for broth, 2 tablespoons minced fresh tarragon for mint, and white wine vinegar for lemon juice.

✔ WHY THIS RECIPE WORKS

Frozen peas have already been blanched during processing, so the keys to making a good and easy-to-prepare side dish from them are to avoid overcooking as they are heated and to pair the peas with ingredients that don't require much preparation. We found that five minutes of simmering was all that was needed to produce bright, tender green peas.

CHOOSE PETITE PEAS   We've always been big fans of frozen peas. Individually frozen right after being shucked from the pod, they are often sweeter and fresher-tasting than the shuck-'em-yourself "fresh" peas that may have spent days in storage. (Sugars in just-picked peas convert to starches over time.) Frozen peas have already been blanched. This stops the process of starch conversion, sets the color of the peas, and cooks them so that they are tender enough to eat. We've seen two varieties in the freezer aisle: regular frozen peas and bags labeled "petite peas" (or sometimes "petit pois" or "baby sweet peas"). To see if there is a difference, we tasted each type with butter. Tasters unanimously favored the smaller peas for their sweeter flavor and creamier texture. Regular peas were by no means unacceptable but had tougher skins and mealier interiors. Since both varieties are available for the same price, we're going with the petite peas from now on.

USE A SKILLET   You do need to reheat frozen peas—and flavor them in the process. A skillet, rather than the usual saucepan, lets you spread out the peas so they heat quickly and don't lose their color or texture.

ADD SUGAR AND BUTTER   A smidge of sugar helps bring out the sweetness of these peas. Finishing them with a bit of butter adds body and richness without drowning them in fat.

ULTIMATE GREEN BEAN CASSEROLE
SERVES 10 TO 12

This recipe can be halved and baked in a 2-quart (or 8-inch square) baking dish. If making a half batch, decrease the cooking time of the sauce in step 3 to about six minutes (reducing it to 1¾ cups) and the baking time in step 4 to 10 minutes.

TOPPING

4	slices hearty white sandwich bread, torn into quarters
2	tablespoons unsalted butter, softened
¼	teaspoon salt
⅛	teaspoon pepper
3	cups canned fried onions (about 6 ounces)

BEANS AND SAUCE

- 2 pounds green beans, trimmed and halved crosswise

  Salt and pepper
- 3 tablespoons unsalted butter
- 1 pound white mushrooms, trimmed and broken into ½-inch pieces
- 3 garlic cloves, minced
- 3 tablespoons all-purpose flour
- 1½ cups low-sodium chicken broth
- 1½ cups heavy cream

1. FOR THE TOPPING: Pulse bread, butter, salt, and pepper in food processor until mixture resembles coarse crumbs, about 10 pulses. Transfer to large bowl and toss with onions; set aside.

2. FOR THE BEANS AND SAUCE: Adjust oven rack to middle position and heat oven to 425 degrees. Fill large bowl with ice water. Line baking sheet with paper towels. Bring 4 quarts water to boil in Dutch oven. Add beans and 2 tablespoons salt. Cook beans until bright green and crisp-tender, about 6 minutes. Drain beans in colander, then plunge immediately into ice water to stop cooking. Spread beans on prepared baking sheet to drain.

3. Melt butter in now-empty Dutch oven over medium-high heat. Add mushrooms, garlic, ¾ teaspoon salt, and ⅛ teaspoon pepper and cook until mushrooms release moisture and liquid evaporates, about 6 minutes. Add flour and cook for 1 minute, stirring constantly. Stir in broth and bring to simmer, stirring constantly. Add cream, reduce heat to medium, and simmer until sauce is thickened and reduced to 3½ cups, about 12 minutes. Season with salt and pepper to taste.

4. Add green beans to sauce and stir until evenly coated. Arrange in even layer in 3-quart (or 13 by 9-inch) baking dish. Sprinkle with topping and bake until top is golden brown and sauce is bubbling around edges, about 15 minutes. Serve immediately.

TO MAKE AHEAD: Store bread-crumb topping in refrigerator for up to 2 days and combine with onions just before cooking. Combine beans and cooled sauce in baking dish, cover with plastic wrap, and refrigerate for up to 24 hours. To serve, remove plastic wrap and heat casserole in 425-degree oven for 10 minutes, then add topping and bake as directed.

✔ WHY THIS RECIPE WORKS

Green bean casserole is a classic, but we wanted a fresher spin that skipped the frozen green beans, condensed soup, and canned onions. Using fresh green beans was an obvious place to start, and blanching them is the first step toward preserving their color and texture. In place of canned soup, we made a mushroom variation of the classic French velouté sauce (traditionally made by thickening white stock with a roux).

USE FRESH BEANS Using canned beans for a dish that requires baking is a nonstarter. Frozen beans are better, but for the best results you must blanch and shock fresh beans. Blanching prevents overcooking and also seasons them nicely.

FORGET CANNED SOUP Rather than the traditional condensed canned soup, we build a real sauce—but with as little work as possible. Using the same pot in which we blanched our beans, we sauté a pound of white button mushrooms (broken, not sliced, for a chunkier texture) and then make a thick roux. (We found fancier mushrooms, like dried porcini, were not worth the added effort.) We finish the sauce with chicken broth and cream, which is rich but not over the top, giving this sauce the perfect balance of savory and creamy.

COMPROMISE ON THE TOPPING Of all the places to use a convenience product, it's the topping (not the beans or the filling). Though we tried to recreate the taste and texture of the canned fried onions, we couldn't do it in a way that was worth the time and effort. Instead, we toss the canned fried onions with fresh bread crumbs and butter. This is an easy way to make them seem homemade.

BAKE FAST To keep the beans from turning mushy in the oven, spread them out in a big dish and bake quickly in a hot oven—just long enough to heat everything up and brown the crumbs on top.

MAKE-AHEAD BLANCHED GREEN BEANS
SERVES 4

Make sure to undercook the beans slightly; they will continue to soften when reheated in the recipes that follow.

- 1 pound green beans, trimmed
- 1 teaspoon salt

Bring 2½ quarts water to boil in large saucepan over high heat. Add green beans and salt, return to boil, and cook until beans are bright green and crisp-tender, 3 to 4 minutes. Meanwhile, fill large bowl with ice water. Drain beans, then transfer immediately to ice-water bath. When beans no longer feel warm to touch, drain beans again, then dry thoroughly with paper towels. Transfer beans to large zipper-lock bag and refrigerate until ready to use, up to 3 days.

GREEN BEANS WITH SAUTÉED SHALLOTS AND VERMOUTH
SERVES 4

The amount of shallots in this recipe may seem like a lot, but they cook down.

- 4   tablespoons unsalted butter
- 5   ounces shallots, sliced thin
- I   recipe Make-Ahead Blanched Green Beans
      Salt and pepper
- 2   tablespoons dry vermouth

1. Melt 2 tablespoons butter in 8-inch skillet over medium heat. Add shallots and cook, stirring frequently, until golden brown, fragrant, and just crisp around edges, about 10 minutes. Set aside.

2. Heat beans and ¼ cup water in 12-inch skillet over high heat and cook, tossing frequently with tongs, until beans are warmed through, 1 to 2 minutes. Season with salt and pepper to taste and transfer to serving platter.

3. Return shallots to high heat, stir in vermouth, and bring to simmer. Whisk in remaining 2 tablespoons butter, 1 tablespoon at a time; season with salt and pepper to taste. Top beans with shallots and sauce and serve immediately.

GREEN BEANS WITH BUTTERED BREAD CRUMBS AND ALMONDS
SERVES 4

An equal amount of chopped walnuts or pecans can be substituted for the almonds.

- I   slice hearty white sandwich bread, crust removed and bread torn into 1½-inch pieces
- 2   tablespoons sliced almonds, crumbled by hand into ¼-inch pieces
- 2   garlic cloves, minced
- 2   teaspoons minced fresh parsley
- I   recipe Make-Ahead Blanched Green Beans
      Salt and pepper
- 4   tablespoons unsalted butter

1. Process bread in food processor to fine crumbs, 20 to 30 seconds (you should have about ¼ cup bread crumbs). Transfer bread crumbs to 12-inch nonstick skillet, add almonds, and toast over medium-high heat, stirring constantly, until golden brown, about 5 minutes. Off heat, add garlic and parsley and toss with hot crumbs. Season with salt and pepper to taste, transfer to small bowl, and set aside. (Do not wash skillet.)

2. Heat beans and ¼ cup water in now-empty skillet over high heat and cook, tossing frequently with tongs, until beans are warmed through, about 1 to 2 minutes. Season with salt and pepper to taste and transfer to platter.

3. Melt butter in now-empty skillet over medium-high heat, add bread-crumb mixture, and cook, stirring frequently, until fragrant, about 1 to 2 minutes. Top beans with buttered crumb mixture and serve immediately.

✔ WHY THIS RECIPE WORKS
Green beans are a classic side when entertaining but we wanted a recipe that would alleviate some of the typical last-minute cooking frenzy. For green beans that could be cooked ahead of time and given a quick finishing touch before serving, we found blanching to be the best method, as it guaranteed evenly cooked, well-seasoned beans with a crisp texture. Once the beans were blanched and cooled, we refrigerated them for up to three days. On the day of serving, we simply tossed them in a hot skillet with a little water to warm them through quickly. To dress up the green beans, we came up with a few simple butter sauces.

BLANCH FIRST   When we developed this recipe, we tried blanching, steaming, and braising our green beans and concluded that blanching (immersing them briefly in boiling water) was the way to go for two reasons. First, blanched beans cook more evenly than steamed ones, and second, they are easier to salt as they cook, which means they become more deeply seasoned.

SHOCK SECOND   If the finished, dressed beans are to arrive at the table with a properly crisp-tender texture, it is especially important not to overcook them. Shocking the beans in ice water halts their cooking abruptly and completely. After that the beans can be refrigerated.

REHEAT WITH THE SAUCE   As we developed the butter sauces, we reheated plenty of chilled beans and learned a thing or two in the process. Most important is to add a little bit of water to the pan with the beans. This small amount comes to a boil quickly and evaporates almost completely, helping to heat the beans through in just a minute or two.

All Potatoes Are Not Created Equal

You might think one potato is pretty much the same as the next. But bake a russet potato and a red potato and the two will emerge from the oven completely different—one light and fluffy, the other creamy and dense. All potatoes are not created equal. Let's find out why.

HOW THE SCIENCE WORKS

The average supermarket might contain four or five different varieties of potatoes, while a farmers' market will have dozens more. (There are more than 200 different species of potato in the world!) Each of these nubby tubers is different from the next, but all varieties do share some general traits.

Potatoes consist mainly of two things: starch and moisture (along with small amounts of sugar, fiber, minerals, and protein). The density of each particular potato correlates to the amount of starch, and the starch content in potatoes can range from 16 percent to 22 percent. Less starch, and you get a firm, waxy potato, like the Red Bliss or French Fingerling. More starch can give varieties such as russet a crumbly, mealy texture. In the middle is Yukon Gold. The amount of starch in a potato affects many things, including its fluffiness and ability to hold its shape.

Starch occurs within the cells of potatoes as microscopic granules. When potatoes are cooked the granules absorb water from within the potato and swell like balloons, causing the cells that contain them to expand, separate, and eventually burst. With continued cooking, many of the swollen granules will also burst and, as a result, release some of the entrapped starch. So, more starch translates to more burst potato cells. This, in turn, translates to a potato that falls apart when cooked. And that is exactly what happens when you boil russet potatoes.

But this can actually be a good a thing, especially when making mashed potatoes. In addition to being easier to mash, cooked russets, with all their burst cells, will soak up more liquid than sturdy Red Bliss. That's because russets contain about 25 percent more starch than Red Bliss, and that starch has the capacity to soak up more liquid even after cooking.

It's important to note that there are two kinds of starch molecules—amylose and amylopectin—and they behave quite differently. Amylose molecules, which are shaped like long chains, easily escape from the swollen starch granules when cooked. As a result, granules with more amylose can suck up more liquid—just what you want when adding dairy to make mashed potatoes. This explains why russet potatoes, which have a high amount of starch (and a higher percentage of amylose), are the best choice for mashing.

In contrast, amylopectin molecules have a much larger, highly branched shape that holds together when cooked and helps the potato remain intact. Varieties with a higher percentage of amylopectin and much less of amylose, such as Red Bliss, are the best choice for boiling. That's because these potatoes are less likely to absorb liquid and are also able to retain their shape when cooked. For the same reasons, Red Bliss are a poor choice when making mashed potatoes; they are physically harder to mash than russets and can't absorb liquid as well.

POTATO STARCHES

RUSSET CELLS *Russet potatoes contain more starch granules. This higher starch content causes the cells to separate and cell walls to burst during cooking, forming fluffier potatoes that absorb more liquid.*

RED BLISS CELLS *Red Bliss potatoes contain fewer starch granules. The lower starch content allows the cells to remain together and intact rather than bursting, so they absorb less liquid.*

TEST KITCHEN EXPERIMENT

To illustrate the significant differences in density and starch makeup among common potato varieties, we cooked ½-inch cubes of three types of potato—Red Bliss, Yukon Gold, and russet—in water dyed dark blue with food coloring. After letting the cooked potatoes cool, we cut them open and examined how far the blue coloring had traveled.

THE RESULTS

The russets absorbed the dye to their very core, while Red Bliss exhibited only a thin blue line around the very exterior. The Yukon Golds sat right in the middle, with more penetration than the Red Bliss, but less than the russets.

THE TAKEAWAY

Here, the most important factor at work is the ratio of starch to moisture. Because russets have a higher percentage of starch than the other varieties, they are denser (see "Sink or Swim," page 239). Therefore, when we cook them, their starch granules have a greater propensity to absorb liquid, swell, and cause the potato cells to separate from each other and even burst. This means that they are better able to absorb liquid (including blue dye) and is why we generally use russets for mashed potatoes. Red Bliss potatoes, on the other hand, have less starch, and because there is more room, there is therefore less pressure for the individual potato cells to separate and burst during cooking. This means that there is less ability for them to absorb liquid (like blue dye) and is why we prefer them for dishes in which potatoes keep their shape, like French Potato Salad, page 235. As you can probably guess, Yukon Golds fall right in the middle.

The second factor is the ratio of the two starches amylose and amylopectin. Russets not only have more starch, but they also have a higher percentage of amylose, the long chains of starch that separate from the swollen granules when exposed to heat. This results in a fluffier-textured potato when cooked and is another reason why the blue dye penetrated to the center of our russet potatoes. Red Bliss have less total starch, as well as a high ratio of amylopectin, which helps hold the potato tightly together when exposed to heat. Again, Yukon Golds fall right in the middle, with a balance of the two starches, and as a result, a middling amount of blue-dyed liquid was able to enter the sample.

Our conclusion? Because each type of potato has a different ratio of starch to moisture and a different ratio of amylose to amylopectin, and each behaves in different ways when exposed to water and heat, it's important to pay attention to what kind of potato you choose for different recipes.

POTATOES COOKED IN BLUE WATER

How much liquid, dyed blue, do potatoes actually absorb?

RED BLISS
Low-starch potatoes absorbed little water.

YUKON GOLDS
Moderately starchy spuds began to absorb a small amount of water.

RUSSETS
Starchy potatoes absorbed the most water.

The simplest way to see how potato varieties differ is to boil them for salad. Here we offer two options—a classic American-style potato salad with crumbly, cohesive chunks of peeled potatoes bound with mayonnaise as well as a French-style recipe with slices of skin-on potatoes dressed with a garlicky, herby vinaigrette.

ALL-AMERICAN POTATO SALAD
SERVES 4 TO 6

Note that this recipe calls for celery seeds, not celery salt; if only celery salt is available, use the same amount but omit the addition of salt in the dressing. When testing the potatoes for doneness, simply taste a piece; do not overcook the potatoes or they will become mealy and will break apart. The potatoes must be just warm, or even fully cooled, when you add the dressing. If the potato salad seems a little dry, add up to 2 tablespoons more mayonnaise.

2	pounds russet potatoes, peeled and cut into ¾-inch cubes
	Salt and pepper
2	tablespoons distilled white vinegar
1	celery rib, chopped fine
½	cup mayonnaise
3	tablespoons sweet pickle relish
2	tablespoons minced red onion
2	tablespoons minced fresh parsley
¾	teaspoon dry mustard
¾	teaspoon celery seeds
2	Hard-Cooked Eggs (page 21), peeled and cut into ¼-inch cubes (optional)

1. Place potatoes in large saucepan and add water to cover by 1 inch. Bring to boil over medium-high heat; add 1 tablespoon salt, reduce heat to medium, and simmer, stirring once or twice, until potatoes are tender, about 8 minutes.

2. Drain potatoes and transfer to large bowl. Add vinegar and, using rubber spatula, toss gently to combine. Let stand until potatoes are just warm, about 20 minutes.

3. Meanwhile, in small bowl, stir together celery, mayonnaise, relish, onion, parsley, mustard, celery seeds, ½ teaspoon salt, and ¼ teaspoon pepper. Using rubber spatula, gently fold dressing and eggs, if using, into potatoes. Cover with plastic wrap and refrigerate until chilled, about 1 hour; serve. (Potato salad can be refrigerated for up to 1 day.)

WHY THIS RECIPE WORKS
Classic potato salad is too often blanketed in a mayonnaise-rich dressing that results in bland flavor. We were looking for flavorful, tender potatoes punctuated by crunchy bits of onion and celery. We found that russets soaked up the most flavor, especially with a bit of vinegar added to them while hot. A conservative hand with the mayonnaise in the dressing and some unexpected seasonings give this salad a boost.

USE RUSSETS The truth is you can use most potato varieties to make potato salad. The decision depends on what traits are most important to you. If you want chunks of potatoes that will hold their shape, then red potatoes are best. If you want potatoes that will soak up the flavors of the dressing (and don't mind a slightly crumbly texture), then russets are best. We find many potato salads to be quite bland. Adding more dressing doesn't solve the problem—the dressing just pools at the bottom of the bowl. We think russets, which absorb moisture much better than red potatoes, are the best choice for a classic American potato salad. We find their starchy texture a welcome plus—the salad is more cohesive than one made with red potatoes.

PRACTICAL SCIENCE START IN COLD WATER

Should you cook potatoes starting in cold water? In a word: yes. It makes for a speedier cooking time and better potato texture.

Many cookbook authors suggest starting potatoes in cold, rather than boiling, water. The theory: Because potatoes take a while to cook, their exteriors tend to become mushy by the time their interiors cook through. Starting the potatoes in cold water allows their temperature to gradually increase, preventing excess softening of the exterior. We put the theory to the test by preparing plain whole unpeeled boiled potatoes, mashed potatoes (made with whole unpeeled potatoes), and potato salad (made with potatoes that were peeled and cut into ¾-inch cubes) both ways—started in boiling water and kept at a simmer, and started in cold water that was brought to a boil and lowered to a simmer—to see if one method was indeed better than the other.

Once the cubed potato pieces were cooled and tossed with mayonnaise and seasonings for the potato salad and the whole potatoes were peeled, pressed through a ricer, and combined with half-and-half and melted butter for the mashed potatoes, no differences between the two samples could be detected. In the case of the plain boiled whole potatoes, we did notice that the samples started in boiling water were softer on the exterior than on the interior. These boiled potatoes weren't terrible, but they weren't as good as the ones started in cold water.

In addition to slightly better texture in one test, the potatoes started in cold water were ready a few minutes earlier. Yes, the potatoes added to boiling water spent less time in the pot, but we had to wait for the water to boil before we could cook the potatoes. The bottom line is that starting the potatoes in cold water yields slightly better results in some applications and is always faster.

SEASON WHEN HOT We've found that the best time to add seasoning is when the potatoes are still warm. This maximizes flavor and is why we add the vinegar as soon as the potatoes are drained. (Don't add the mayo then, though. You don't want the dressing to turn oily and thin.)

DRESS WELL When developing this recipe, we knew that we wanted a classic mayonnaise-based dressing, but we decided to investigate some variations as well. We substituted buttermilk, sour cream, and yogurt for half of the mayo in different tests but found that unadulterated mayonnaise was preferred by tasters. Along with the mayonnaise, we add celery for crunch, and red onion for color and flavor. Pickle relish requires no preparation and gives the potato salad a subtle sweetness. Celery seeds, which have fallen out of general favor as a seasoning, provide an underlying complexity and depth, and dry mustard gives the salad an added pungency.

MINIMIZE MIXING Make the dressing in a separate bowl from the potatoes. Adding the dressing ingredients one by one to the cooked potatoes leads to excess mixing, which turns the salad to mush. It's important to add the dressing after it's already been mixed.

FRENCH POTATO SALAD WITH DIJON MUSTARD AND FINES HERBES
SERVES 6

If fresh chervil isn't available, substitute an additional ½ tablespoon of minced parsley and an additional ½ teaspoon of tarragon. For best flavor, serve the salad warm.

2	pounds small red potatoes, cut into ¼-inch-thick slices
2	tablespoons salt
I	garlic clove, peeled and threaded on skewer
¼	cup olive oil
1½	tablespoons champagne vinegar or white wine vinegar
2	teaspoons Dijon mustard
½	teaspoon pepper
I	small shallot, minced
I	tablespoon minced fresh chervil
I	tablespoon minced fresh parsley
I	tablespoon minced fresh chives
I	teaspoon minced fresh tarragon

I. Place potatoes and salt in large saucepan and add water to cover by 1 inch; bring to boil over high heat, then reduce heat to medium. Lower skewered garlic into simmering water and partially blanch, about 45 seconds. Immediately run garlic under cold running water to stop cooking; remove garlic from skewer and set aside. Continue to simmer potatoes, uncovered, until tender but still firm, about 5 minutes. Drain potatoes, reserving ¼ cup cooking water. Arrange hot potatoes close together in single layer on rimmed baking sheet.

2. Mince garlic. Whisk garlic, reserved potato cooking water, oil, vinegar, mustard, and pepper in small bowl until combined. Drizzle dressing evenly over warm potatoes; let stand for 10 minutes.

3. Toss shallot and herbs in small bowl. Transfer potatoes to large serving bowl; add shallot-herb mixture and mix gently with rubber spatula to combine. Serve immediately.

TO MAKE AHEAD: Follow recipe through step 2, cover with plastic wrap, and refrigerate. Before serving, bring salad to room temperature, then add shallot and herbs.

PRACTICAL SCIENCE
KEEPING POTATO SALAD SAFE

Mayonnaise won't spoil your potato salad. The potatoes will.

Mayonnaise has gotten a bad reputation, being blamed for spoiled potato salads and upset stomachs after many summer picnics and barbecues. You may think that switching from a mayonnaise-based dressing to a vinaigrette will protect your potato salad (and your family) from food poisoning. Think again.

The main ingredients in mayonnaise are raw eggs, vegetable oil, and an acid (usually vinegar or lemon juice). The eggs used in commercially made mayonnaise have been pasteurized to kill salmonella and other bacteria. Its high acidity is another safeguard: Because bacteria do not fare well in acidic environments, the lemon juice or vinegar inhibits bacterial growth. Mayonnaise, even when homemade, is rarely the problem unless it contains very little acid. It's the potatoes that are more likely to go bad.

The bacteria usually responsible for spoiled potato salad are *Bacillus cereus* and *Staphylococcus aureus* (commonly known as staph). Both are found in soil and dust, and they thrive on starchy, low-acid foods like rice, pasta, and potatoes. If they find their way into your potato salad via an unwashed cutting board or contaminated hands, they can wreak havoc on your digestive system.

Most food-borne bacteria grow well at temperatures between 40 and 140 degrees Fahrenheit. This is known as the temperature danger zone, and if contaminated food remains in this zone for too long, the bacteria can produce enough toxins to make you sick. The U.S. Food and Drug Administration recommends refrigerating food within two hours of its preparation, or one hour if the room temperature is above 90 degrees. Heat from the sun is often what causes the trouble at summer picnics.

Although the high acid content of the vinaigrette for our French Potato Salad might slow bacterial growth, it's best to play it safe and follow the FDA's guideline. Don't leave the salad out for more than two hours; promptly refrigerate any leftovers.

FRENCH POTATO SALAD WITH ARUGULA, ROQUEFORT, AND WALNUTS

Omit herbs and toss dressed potatoes with ½ cup chopped toasted walnuts, 1 cup crumbled Roquefort cheese, and 3 ounces baby arugula, torn into bite-size pieces along with shallot in step 3.

FRENCH POTATO SALAD WITH FENNEL, TOMATO, AND OLIVES

When chopping the fennel fronds for this variation, use only the delicate wispy leaves, not the tough, fibrous stems to which they are attached.

Trim stalks and fronds from 1 small fennel bulb; coarsely chop and reserve ¼ cup fronds. Halve bulb lengthwise; using paring knife, core 1 half of bulb, reserving second half for another use. Cut half crosswise into very thin slices. Omit chervil, chives, and tarragon and increase parsley to 3 tablespoons. Toss dressed potatoes with fennel, 1 peeled, seeded, and diced tomato, and ¼ cup quartered oil-cured pitted black olives along with shallot and parsley in step 3.

FRENCH POTATO SALAD WITH RADISHES, CORNICHONS, AND CAPERS

Omit herbs and substitute 2 tablespoons minced red onion for shallot. Toss dressed potatoes with 2 thinly sliced red radishes, ¼ cup rinsed capers, and ¼ cup thinly sliced cornichons along with red onion in step 3.

PRACTICAL SCIENCE
WHY ARE MY POTATOES GREEN?

Cut off the green patches from your potatoes. They are an indication of a toxic alkaloid and can cause illness.

The green patches found on some potatoes are caused by prolonged exposure to light or improper storage. This discoloration is produced by chlorophyll and is usually an indication of increased levels of a naturally occurring toxic alkaloid called solanine. Ingesting solanine can lead to gastrointestinal distress, so if you discover green patches when peeling your potatoes, make sure to cut off up to an inch below the affected areas. Also, make sure to store potatoes in a well-ventilated, dark, dry, cool place. If left on the counter, potatoes will begin to turn green in as little as one week.

✔ WHY THIS RECIPE WORKS

French potato salad should be pleasing not only to the eye but also to the palate. The potatoes (small red potatoes are traditional) should be tender but not mushy, and the flavor of the vinaigrette should penetrate the relatively bland potatoes. To eliminate torn skins and broken slices, a common pitfall in boiling skin-on red potatoes, we sliced the potatoes before boiling them. Then, to evenly infuse the potatoes with the garlicky mustard vinaigrette, we spread the warm potatoes out on a sheet pan and poured the vinaigrette over the top. Gently folding in fresh herbs just before serving helped keep the colors and flavors of the herbs bright and vibrant. It helped to keep the potatoes intact, too.

SLICE AND BOIL Slicing the potatoes before cooking them prevents the ugliness of torn skin and broken potato flesh in the finished salad. (Not to mention saving our hands from burning on the hot potatoes as we try to slice.) The already sliced potatoes emerge from the water after a quick cooking time unbroken and with their skins intact. They have a clean (not starchy) taste, are evenly cooked, and hold together perfectly. We still boil potatoes whole and in their skins for mashed potatoes because the starch retained produces a thick, creamy sauce. But here we prefer ¼-inch slices.

RAMP UP THE VINEGAR We pump up the flavor of this salad by using 3 parts oil to 1 part vinegar, rather than the tamer 4 parts oil in many classic vinaigrette recipes. Bland potatoes can handle the extra acid. We love the sharp flavor notes added by champagne vinegar but find that white wine vinegar works well, too.

SAVE SOME COOKING WATER Dressing potatoes with vinaigrette can yield a dry salad. Some recipes add chicken stock or wine. We take a cue from Julia Child and use some of the potato water. It's nicely seasoned and readily available.

BLANCH THE GARLIC Raw garlic is too strong and pungent a flavor for this more delicate potato salad. Blanching the garlic clove before adding it to the dressing tones it down.

SPREAD AND DRESS After the potatoes have been thoroughly drained, spread them out on a rimmed baking sheet and drizzle them evenly with the vinaigrette. Spreading out the potatoes this way allows them to cool off a bit, preventing residual cooking and potential mushiness. It also allows us to get the warm potatoes to soak up the vinaigrette without damaging the slices by tossing them.

While different potato varieties yield different textures in salad, the same thing holds true when it comes to boiling and mashing. Use one kind of potato to create the ultimate creamy, smooth puree and another for rustic, chunky "smashed" potatoes.

CLASSIC MASHED POTATOES
SERVES 4

Russet potatoes make fluffier mashed potatoes, but Yukon Golds have an appealing buttery flavor and can be used.

2   pounds russet potatoes
8   tablespoons unsalted butter, melted
I   cup half-and-half, warmed
     Salt and pepper

1. Place potatoes in large saucepan and add cold water to cover by 1 inch. Bring to boil over high heat, reduce heat to medium-low, and simmer until potatoes are just tender (paring knife can be slipped in and out of potatoes with little resistance), 20 to 30 minutes. Drain.

2. Set ricer or food mill over now-empty saucepan. Using potholder (to hold potatoes) and paring knife, peel skins from potatoes. Working in batches, cut peeled potatoes into large chunks and press or mill into saucepan.

3. Stir in butter until incorporated. Gently whisk in half-and-half, add 1½ teaspoons salt, and season with pepper to taste. Serve.

GARLIC MASHED POTATOES

Avoid using unusually large garlic cloves, which will not soften adequately during toasting. For chunky mashed potatoes, use a potato masher, decrease the half-and-half to ¾ cup, and mash the garlic to a paste with a fork before you add it to the potatoes.

Toast 22 unpeeled garlic cloves (about 3 ounces, or ⅔ cup), covered, in 8-inch skillet over low heat, shaking pan frequently, until cloves are dark spotty brown and slightly softened, about 22 minutes. Off heat, let sit, covered, until fully softened, 15 to 20 minutes. Peel cloves and, with paring knife, cut off woody root end; set aside. Press or mill garlic along with potatoes in step 2.

MASHED POTATOES WITH SMOKED CHEDDAR AND GRAINY MUSTARD

After stirring butter into potatoes in step 3, season with 1¼ teaspoons salt and ½ teaspoon pepper. Add ¾ cup grated smoked cheddar cheese and 2 tablespoons whole-grain mustard with half-and-half and stir until just combined. Serve immediately.

MASHED POTATOES WITH SMOKED PAPRIKA AND TOASTED GARLIC

While potatoes are simmering, toast 1 teaspoon smoked paprika in 8-inch skillet over medium heat, stirring frequently, until fragrant, about 2 minutes. Transfer to small bowl; set aside. Melt 8 tablespoons butter in small saucepan over medium-low heat. Add 3 minced garlic cloves, reduce heat to low, and cook, stirring frequently, until garlic begins to brown, 12 to 14 minutes. Remove saucepan from heat immediately and set aside for 5 minutes (garlic will continue to brown). Pour butter-garlic mixture through fine-mesh strainer; reserve butter and set toasted garlic aside. Rice or mill potatoes as directed, then stir butter into potatoes until just incorporated. Season potatoes with toasted paprika, 1½ teaspoons salt, and ½ teaspoon pepper. Add warm half-and-half and stir until just combined. Serve immediately, sprinkling with reserved toasted garlic.

☑ WHY THIS RECIPE WORKS

Many people would never consider consulting a recipe when making mashed potatoes, instead adding chunks of butter and spurts of cream until their conscience tells them to stop. Little wonder then that mashed potatoes made this way are consistent only in their mediocrity. We wanted mashed potatoes that were perfectly smooth and creamy, with great potato flavor and plenty of buttery richness every time. We use russet potatoes, boil them whole for optimal texture and flavor, and tweak the temperature and order of the addition of butter and dairy for a smooth, velvety mash.

START WITH RUSSETS Russets have an earthy potato flavor coupled with a mild sweetness. They are starchy and fluffy and do the best job of absorbing butter and cream.

BOIL, THEN PEEL The usual method of peeling, cutting into chunks, and boiling potatoes isn't nearly as good as boiling the potatoes in their skins. Peeling and cutting before simmering increases the surface area through which the potatoes lose soluble substances such as starch, proteins, and flavor compounds to the cooking water. The greater surface area also enables lots of water molecules to bind with the potatoes' starch molecules. Combine these two effects and you've got bland, watery mashed potatoes. When boiled whole and unpeeled, the potatoes absorb less water so they can absorb more cream and butter. Their potato flavor is much stronger, too—not washed out.

PROTECT YOUR HANDS Yes, it's a pain to peel hot potatoes, but it's worth it. You can handle the job by first holding the hot potato with a potholder, and peel the potato skins using a paring knife. Or you can cut each boiled potato in half and use a spoon to scoop the flesh away from the skins.

RICE OR MILL There is more than one way to mash potatoes. We prefer a ricer or a food mill, both of which yield a much smoother mash than a potato masher. After the cooked potatoes have been drained and peeled, process them back into the still-warm saucepan so they don't cool off.

USE HOT BUTTER Adding butter and dairy to the mix is more complicated than you might think. Two things are important: the order in which they are added to the potatoes, and the temperature of the butter. The water in the half-and-half, when stirred into the potatoes before the butter, works with the starch in the potatoes to make the dish gluey and heavy. When the butter is added before the half-and-half, however, the fat coats the starch granules and released starch molecules, inhibiting their interaction with the water in the half-and-half added later and thereby yielding silkier, creamier potatoes. The benefit of using melted butter is that, as a liquid, it coats the starch molecules quickly and easily. This buttery coating not only affects the interaction of the starch molecules with the half-and-half, it also affects the starch molecules' interaction with each other. All in all, it makes for smoother, more velvety mashed potatoes. (Don't forget to warm the half-and-half, too, so the potatoes don't get cold.)

SMASHED POTATOES
SERVES 4 TO 6

White potatoes can be used instead of red, but the dish won't be as colorful. We prefer to use small potatoes, 2 inches in diameter, in this recipe. Try to get potatoes of equal size; if that's not possible, test the larger potatoes for doneness. If only larger potatoes are available, increase the cooking time by about 10 minutes.

- 2 pounds small red potatoes
  Salt and pepper
- 1 bay leaf
- 4 ounces cream cheese, softened
- 4 tablespoons unsalted butter, melted
- 3 tablespoons minced fresh chives (optional)

1. Place potatoes in large saucepan and add cold water to cover by 1 inch. Add 1 teaspoon salt and bay leaf. Bring to boil over high heat, then reduce heat to medium-low and simmer gently until paring knife can be inserted into potatoes with no resistance, 35 to 45 minutes. Reserve ½ cup cooking water, then drain potatoes. Return potatoes to pot, discard bay leaf, and let potatoes sit in pot, uncovered, until surfaces are dry, about 5 minutes.

2. While potatoes dry, whisk cream cheese and butter in medium bowl until smooth and fully incorporated. Add ¼ cup reserved cooking water, chives, if using, ½ teaspoon salt, and ½ teaspoon pepper. Using rubber spatula or back of wooden spoon, smash potatoes just enough to break skins. Fold in cream cheese mixture until most of liquid has been absorbed and chunks of potatoes remain. Add more cooking water as needed, 1 tablespoon at a time, until potatoes are slightly looser than desired (potatoes will thicken slightly with sitting). Season with salt and pepper to taste; serve immediately.

GARLIC-ROSEMARY SMASHED POTATOES

Add 2 peeled garlic cloves to potatoes in saucepan along with salt and bay leaf in step 1. Melt 4 tablespoons butter in 8-inch skillet over medium heat. Add 1 minced garlic clove and ½ teaspoon minced fresh rosemary and cook until just fragrant, about 30 seconds; substitute butter-garlic mixture for melted butter, adding cooked garlic cloves to cream cheese along with butter-garlic mixture. Omit chives.

SMASHED POTATOES WITH BACON AND PARSLEY

Cook 6 slices bacon, cut lengthwise in half then crosswise into ¼-inch pieces, in 10-inch skillet over medium heat until crisp, 5 to 7 minutes. Using slotted spoon, transfer bacon to paper towel–lined plate; reserve 1 tablespoon fat. Substitute bacon fat for 1 tablespoon melted unsalted butter, 2 tablespoons minced fresh parsley for chives, and reduce salt added to cream cheese mixture to ¼ teaspoon. Sprinkle potatoes with cooked bacon before serving.

✔ WHY THIS RECIPE WORKS

Bold flavors and a rustic, chunky texture make smashed potatoes a satisfying side dish that pairs well with a range of entrées. We were after a good contrast of textures, with chunks of potato bound by a rich, creamy puree. Low-starch, high-moisture red potatoes are the best choice for smashing since their compact structure holds up well under pressure, maintaining its integrity, and their red skins provide nice contrasting color. For the best chunky texture, we smashed the potatoes, which we had cooked whole in salted water with a bay leaf, with a rubber spatula or the back of a wooden spoon. Giving the potatoes a few minutes to dry ensured the skins weren't too slippery, making the job even easier. A combination of cream cheese, melted butter, and a little reserved potato cooking water gave our potatoes a unified creamy consistency.

CHOOSE RED   The classic mashed potatoes are perfectly silky. But a newer style—simply "smashed" with the skin on—is an appealing option, especially for simpler weeknight meals. When the goal is a rustic, chunky smash, red potatoes are best. They have the thinnest skin (other varieties have pretty tough skin) and their structure is compact enough to hold up when smashed—in this case (as in French potato salad), you want a potato with some integrity.

COOK 'EM WHOLE   As we do for our Classic Mashed Potatoes (page 237), we cook these potatoes whole. Cut into chunks, they absorb too much water and the result is a soggy texture and washed-out potato flavor. Additions to the cooking water like salt and a bay leaf (and, for a variation, garlic) penetrate the thin skins easily to flavor the potatoes.

SMASH WISELY   Potato mashers and forks are too tough on potatoes. A wooden spoon breaks them up without reducing them to a smooth puree.

USE CREAM CHEESE   We liked the idea of tangy sour cream as the dairy element but we weren't wild about the texture of the finished dish—the potatoes needed more body. In the end, we had the best results with cream cheese. It adds plenty of tang and makes the potatoes creamy. A little butter is necessary, and mixing the butter and cream together before adding them to the potatoes reduces the chance of overworking the potatoes and making them gluey.

RESERVE COOKING WATER   As we often do with pasta, we reserve a bit of the salty cooking water to adjust the consistency of the smash. It keeps the finished dish from being too dry (you need some liquid, but more dairy, like cream or half-and-half, will dull the tang of the cream cheese). The water reinforces the salty flavor but doesn't dull the tang.

PRACTICAL SCIENCE SINK OR SWIM

The different ratios of starch in Red Bliss, Yukon Gold, and russet potatoes can be seen when the potatoes are placed in salted water.

To determine the difference in density of potato varieties, we mixed up an 11 percent salt solution and split it among three containers. We then added a Red Bliss, Yukon Gold, and russet potato, respectively. The Red Bliss floated to the top of the container, the russet sank like a rock, and the Yukon Gold stayed suspended right in the middle of the container. What does this tell us? Density correlates to starch content in potatoes so russets are the highest in starch, and Red Bliss are the least starchy. Yukon Golds have a starch content between these two.

RED BLISS

RUSSET

YUKON GOLD

Potato Starches Can Be Controlled

Potatoes contain a great deal of starch. Sometimes these starches work against us, causing gluey mashed potatoes. Other times the surplus starch is exactly what we need for crisp, browned home fries. We don't leave our results up to chance, however. Taking control of the starches in potatoes is easy: Use simple steps to either remove or activate starch, depending on the dish.

HOW THE SCIENCE WORKS

We learned in concept 25 that anywhere between 16 and 22 percent of a raw potato's weight is made up of starch. We also learned that there are two types of starch molecules: amylose and amylopectin, which act in different ways. Because each variety of potato has different amounts of starch and moisture, this means that some potatoes are best for mashing (the fluffy varieties such as russet) and others for boiling and retaining their shape (the less dense, waxy Red Bliss). In addition to choosing the best potato for the job, there are things that we can do to help control the starches in potatoes, enhancing or eliminating them with different techniques as we cook.

When we cook potatoes, the starch granules within the potato cells are greatly affected. These granules begin to absorb water when the temperature of the potato hits 140 degrees. They swell intensely by 160 degrees. The danger here is that the starch granules can rupture if they get too hot and absorb too much water. And when they burst, they spill out a sticky gel made of amylose. If the potato cells holding these burst starch granules also explode, this released amylose will no doubt turn potatoes into a gluey mess. This becomes a significant problem when the temperature reaches 180 degrees. At this point, pectin, which acts as a glue surrounding the cells and within the cell walls, begins to break down,

becomes water-soluble, and dissolves, causing the cells to separate and the cell walls to break open, releasing the gel. Overcooked potatoes, because a large percentage of their starch granules have exploded, produce a great deal of sticky gel, making them extremely gluey, even if they are easy to mash. (These starch granules can also explode if the potatoes are overworked after cooking.)

To prevent a gluey dish, we often remove starch by rinsing it off of the cut potatoes either before, during, or after cooking. Rinsing helps remove some of the free starch that has escaped from the potato's starch granules. With less starch, the potatoes are less inclined to become gluey and thick when cooked, and we're left with mashed potatoes, for example, with a lighter, silkier texture.

Sometimes, however, we want to use this excess starch to our advantage. We can do this by activating the starch granules—in a controlled setting. This can be as simple as stirring or using the food processor. We use techniques like this to manipulate texture for dishes that are meant to have a more sticky, tacky texture (like some kinds of mashed potatoes), or to promote browning by activating extra starch on the surface of a slice of potato going in to roast (the starch will convert to sugar and form a nicely browned crust).

POTATO STARCH GRANULES

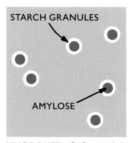

UNCOOKED *Before cooking, the potato starch amylose is held within the starch granules.*

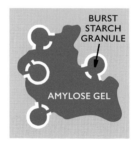

COOKED *When cooked (or, more often, overcooked), these starch granules swell with water and then burst, releasing the amylose, which forms a gluey gel.*

TEST KITCHEN EXPERIMENT

To demonstrate that how you handle a potato once it is cooked can be just as important as which potato variety you choose, we mashed batches of potatoes in two different ways. First, we made a batch of mashed potatoes by gently folding warm milk and butter into a bowl of russets that we had processed with a ricer. For the other batch, we used the fast action of a food processor blade to puree the ingredients into the potatoes for 30 seconds. We repeated the test three times.

THE RESULTS

While the folded batch of mashed potatoes was fluffy, the sample out of the food processor was sticky, a sign of burst starch granules. Tasters unanimously preferred the folded potatoes, which were described as "light." Tasters found the potatoes made in the food processor to be "too thick" and "gluey."

THE TAKEAWAY

Because potatoes have so much starch, which can drastically alter the texture of the finished dish, it's important to handle them with care.

As our experiment shows, the texture of potatoes run through a food processor is sticky and gummy—and, unless we're making Aligot (page 244), this is everything we don't want in a classic mashed potato dish. Why is the texture so different? Because a food processor, with its sharp blade, is a full-contact tool, using one is an especially rough method of creaming a vegetable. It slices through many—if not all—of the already-expanded starch granules and cells in the potatoes, causing them to burst and release the sticky amylose strands. This creates a gel that turns the potato dish into a substance closer to glue than mashed potatoes.

The potatoes we barely touched, however, kept their starch granules and cells intact. Without the rough handling, the starch granules were not punctured or split, and a good deal of the amylose remained within the intact cells, allowing us to finish with a light and fluffy mashed potato.

In conclusion: The method of handling your potatoes will affect the texture of your final dish. Pay careful attention to how much—or how little—you process your spuds. It could mean the difference between a puddle of glue and a dish so fluffy it resembles a cloud.

STICKY VERSUS FLUFFY MASHED POTATOES

BEATEN IN A FOOD PROCESSOR *The mashed potatoes made in a food processor were so violently handled that the majority of their starch granules burst, causing them to be so sticky they clung to a spatula like glue.*

GENTLY MADE BY HAND *The mashed potatoes run through a ricer and then folded by hand were processed very lightly, making sure the majority of their starch granules remained intact and resulting in fluffy potatoes.*

To control the levels of sticky starch glue released from potatoes in such recipes as Mashed Potatoes and Root Vegetables (below) and Potato Roesti (page 243), we rinse it away. This helps prevent the finished dishes from becoming heavy and dense.

MASHED POTATOES AND ROOT VEGETABLES
SERVES 4

Russet potatoes will yield a slightly fluffier, less creamy mash, but they can be used in place of the Yukon Gold potatoes if desired. Rinsing the potatoes in water reduces starch and helps prevent the mashed potatoes from becoming gluey. It is important to cut the potatoes and root vegetables into evenly sized pieces so they cook at the same rate. This recipe can be doubled and cooked in a large Dutch oven. If doubling, increase the cooking time in step 2 to 40 minutes.

4	tablespoons unsalted butter
8	ounces carrots, parsnips, turnips, or celery root, peeled, carrots or parsnips cut into ¼-inch-thick half-moons, turnips or celery root cut into ½-inch dice (about 1½ cups)
1½	pounds Yukon Gold potatoes, peeled, quartered lengthwise, and cut crosswise into ¼-inch-thick slices, rinsed and well drained
⅓	cup low-sodium chicken broth
	Salt and pepper
¾	cup half-and-half, warmed
3	tablespoons minced fresh chives

1. Melt butter in large saucepan over medium heat. Add root vegetables and cook, stirring occasionally, until butter is browned and vegetables are dark brown and caramelized, 10 to 12 minutes. (If after 4 minutes vegetables have not started to brown, increase heat to medium-high.)

2. Add potatoes, broth, and ¾ teaspoon salt and stir to combine. Cook, covered, over low heat (broth should simmer gently; do not boil), stirring occasionally, until potatoes fall apart easily when poked with fork and all liquid has been absorbed, 25 to 30 minutes. (If liquid does not gently simmer after a few minutes, increase heat to medium-low.) Remove pan from heat, remove lid, and allow steam to escape for 2 minutes.

3. Gently mash potatoes and root vegetables in saucepan with potato masher (do not mash vigorously). Gently fold in warm half-and-half and chives. Season with salt and pepper to taste; serve immediately.

MASHED POTATOES AND ROOT VEGETABLES WITH BACON AND THYME

Cook 4 slices bacon, cut into ½-inch pieces, in large saucepan over medium heat until crisp, 5 to 7 minutes. Using slotted spoon, transfer bacon to paper towel–lined plate; set aside. Pour off all but 2 tablespoons fat from pan. Add 2 tablespoons butter to pan and continue with step 1, cooking root vegetables in bacon fat mixture instead of butter. Substitute 1 teaspoon minced fresh thyme for chives and fold reserved bacon into potatoes along with thyme.

MASHED POTATOES AND ROOT VEGETABLES WITH PAPRIKA AND PARSLEY

This variation is particularly nice with carrots.

Toast 1½ teaspoons smoked or sweet paprika in 8-inch skillet over medium heat until fragrant, about 30 seconds. Substitute parsley for chives and fold toasted paprika into potatoes along with parsley.

✔ WHY THIS RECIPE WORKS
Root vegetables like carrots, parsnips, turnips, and celery root can add an earthy, intriguing flavor to mashed potatoes, but despite being neighbors in the root cellar, root vegetables contain more water (80 percent to 92 percent) than russet potatoes (about 79 percent), the test kitchen's first choice for mashing. Root vegetables also have less starch (between 0.2 percent and 6.2 percent wet weight) than potatoes (about 16 to 22 percent). Finally, many root vegetables are either noticeably sweet or slightly bitter—traits that can overwhelm mild potatoes. So knowing that treating root vegetables and potatoes the same way can create a bad dish, adding up to a watery, lean, or saccharine mash, we played with the ratio, caramelized the root vegetables, and braised them all in chicken broth. But to avoid a gluey texture we hit the sink.

USE THE RIGHT RATIO You need to use far fewer root vegetables than you think for this recipe. The usual 1:1 ratio of root vegetables to potatoes in other recipes proves to be too thin because of the extra moisture in the root vegetables. We found that a 1:3 ratio is much better.

BROWN, BABY, BROWN Because we use fewer root vegetables, however, it's imperative to enhance their flavor. Browning them in butter (not oil) does the job.

MAKE IT A ONE-POT WONDER With the vegetables being browned in one pot, why dirty a second pot just to boil the potatoes? We add the raw potatoes to the pot with the browned root vegetables and braise them.

We prefer chicken stock to water as the liquid for extra flavor. Once they are tender, we mash the root veggies and potatoes right in the butter.

RINSE AWAY STARCH   When boiling peeled chunks of russets, you wash away the excess starch as part of the cooking process. Braising, however, means the finished dish will contain all that starch. Switching to Yukon Golds helps, but to further cut down on starch you need to rinse the sliced potatoes before adding them to the pot. (Rinsing will even make russets an acceptable—if slightly less fluffy—choice.)

USE HALF-AND-HALF   After cooking the root vegetables, the butter is already in the pot, so we just need to add the dairy. As usual, we prefer half-and-half.

POTATO ROESTI
SERVES 4

The test kitchen prefers a roesti prepared with potatoes that have been cut with the large shredding disk of a food processor. It is possible to use a box grater to cut the potatoes, but they should be cut lengthwise, so you are left with long shreds. It is imperative to squeeze the potatoes as dry as possible. A well-seasoned cast-iron skillet can be used in place of the nonstick skillet. With the addition of fried eggs, bacon, or cheese, roesti can be turned into a light meal for two.

1½	pounds Yukon Gold potatoes, peeled and shredded
1	teaspoon cornstarch
	Salt and pepper
4	tablespoons unsalted butter

1. Place potatoes in large bowl and fill with cold water. Using hands, swirl to remove excess starch, then drain.

2. Wipe bowl dry. Place half of potatoes in center of kitchen towel. Gather ends together and twist as tightly as possible to expel maximum moisture. Transfer potatoes to bowl and repeat process with remaining potatoes.

3. Sprinkle cornstarch, ½ teaspoon salt, and pepper to taste over potatoes. Using hands or fork, toss ingredients together until well blended.

4. Melt 2 tablespoons butter in 10-inch nonstick skillet over medium heat. Add potato mixture and spread into even layer. Cover and cook for 6 minutes. Remove cover and, using spatula, gently press potatoes down to form round cake. Cook, occasionally pressing on potatoes to shape into uniform round cake, until bottom is deep golden brown, 4 to 6 minutes longer.

5. Shake skillet to loosen roesti and slide onto large plate. Add remaining 2 tablespoons butter to skillet and swirl to coat pan. Invert roesti onto second plate and slide it, browned side up, back into skillet. Cook, occasionally pressing down on cake, until bottom is well browned, 7 to 9 minutes. Remove pan from heat and allow cake to cool in pan for 5 minutes. Transfer roesti to cutting board, cut into 4 pieces, and serve immediately.

POTATO ROESTI WITH FRIED EGGS AND PARMESAN
SERVES 2 AS A MAIN COURSE

Slide 2 fried eggs onto finished roesti, sprinkle with ½ cup grated Parmesan cheese, and season with salt to taste.

POTATO ROESTI WITH BACON, ONION, AND SHERRY VINEGAR
SERVES 2 AS A MAIN COURSE

Cook 3 chopped slices bacon in 10-inch skillet over medium-high heat until crisp, 5 to 7 minutes. Transfer bacon to paper towel–lined plate and pour off all but 1 tablespoon fat from skillet. Add 1 thinly sliced large onion to skillet, season with salt and pepper, and cook until onion is softened, about 5 to 7 minutes, topping finished roesti with bacon and onion and sprinkling with sherry vinegar to taste before serving.

CHEESY POTATO ROESTI
SERVES 2 AS A MAIN COURSE

While not traditional, sharp cheddar, Manchego, Italian fontina, and Havarti cheeses are each a good match for this potato dish.

Sprinkle ½ cup shredded Gruyère or Swiss cheese over roesti in step 5 about 3 minutes before fully cooked on second side.

✔ WHY THIS RECIPE WORKS
Roesti—a broad, golden brown cake of simply seasoned grated potatoes fried in butter—is hugely popular in Switzerland. We set out to master a stateside recipe with a crunchy, crisp exterior encasing a tender, creamy interior; one with good potato flavor, rich with butter. The goal here is to control the starch and the moisture, which tend to make roesti heavy and gluey. Some roesti are made with cooked potatoes, which makes these issues easier to control. However, we wanted a weeknight recipe that could be made with no advance planning so raw potatoes were a must. Rinsing and wringing out the potatoes helps.

SHRED, RINSE, AND SQUEEZE Excess starch and moisture in the potatoes will cause roesti to cook up gummy in the middle. The best way to remove both the excess starch and moisture is to shred the raw potatoes (we like the flavor of Yukon Golds best), rinse them, and then squeeze them dry in a kitchen towel. Even without rinsing, you can extract ¼ cup of liquid from 1½ pounds of potatoes.

ADD A LITTLE CORNSTARCH While rinsing away starch helps reduce gumminess, if you remove too much starch the potato cake isn't cohesive and it will fall apart when sliced. Our solution is simple: Rinse the potatoes and then add a little cornstarch along with the salt and pepper. (This is much easier than trying to extract some of the potato starch from the rinsing liquid, as recommended in other recipes.) The added cornstarch also helps to crisp and brown the exterior of the potatoes.

COVER AT THE OUTSET Since you're using raw potatoes, you need to make sure they are fully cooked by the time the exterior of the roesti is browned. Using the cover for the first few minutes traps steam and actually yields a lighter potato cake than leaving the cover off the whole time. (Loosely packing the potatoes into the pan is important—you need to give the steam a way to exit the roesti.)

DO THE FLIP While certain expert chefs may think nothing of flipping over a piping-hot skillet to turn a potato roesti out onto a plate, it can be a scary endeavor for mere mortals. A slipped grip or faltering wrist can send dinner crashing to the floor. Fortunately, there is a safer and less intimidating way to turn something over in a large skillet. Working with two plates, slide whatever you wish to flip onto one plate and top it with the other. Then, holding the two plates together, flip them over and slide the inverted food back into the pan to finish cooking.

ACTIVATING STARCHES AT WORK ALIGOT, ROASTED POTATOES, HOME FRIES

We don't always want to rid our dishes of starches. Sometimes we want to activate them—for cheesy mashed potatoes with an elastic texture, or roasted potato slices with great exterior browning. Some recipes call for manipulation to develop the starches in potatoes. By stirring, or simply roughing up the surface of our potatoes, we make the starch work to our advantage.

FRENCH-STYLE MASHED POTATOES WITH CHEESE AND GARLIC (ALIGOT)
SERVES 6

The finished potatoes should have a smooth and slightly elastic texture. White cheddar can be substituted for the Gruyère.

2	pounds Yukon Gold potatoes, peeled, cut into ½-inch-thick slices, rinsed well, and drained
	Salt and pepper
6	tablespoons unsalted butter
2	garlic cloves, minced
1–1½	cups whole milk
4	ounces mozzarella cheese, shredded (1 cup)
4	ounces Gruyère cheese, shredded (1 cup)

I. Place potatoes in large saucepan, add cold water to cover by 1 inch, and add 1 tablespoon salt. Partially cover saucepan and bring potatoes to boil over high heat. Reduce heat to medium-low and simmer until potatoes are tender and just break apart when poked with fork, 12 to 17 minutes. Drain potatoes and dry saucepan.

2. Transfer potatoes to food processor. Add butter, garlic, and 1½ teaspoons salt and pulse until butter is melted and incorporated into potatoes, about 10 pulses. Add 1 cup milk and continue to process until potatoes are smooth and creamy, about 20 seconds, scraping down sides halfway through processing.

3. Transfer potato mixture to saucepan and set over medium heat. Stir in cheeses, 1 cup at a time, until incorporated. Continue to cook potatoes, stirring vigorously, until cheese is fully melted and mixture is smooth and elastic, 3 to 5 minutes. If mixture is difficult to stir and seems thick, stir in 2 tablespoons milk at a time (up to ½ cup) until potatoes are loose and creamy. Season with salt and pepper to taste. Serve immediately.

✓ WHY THIS RECIPE WORKS
Aligot is French cookery's intensely rich, cheesy take on mashed potatoes. These potatoes get their elastic, satiny texture through prolonged, vigorous stirring—which can easily go awry and lead to a gluey, sticky mess. We monitor our stirring with caution to release just the right amount of starch for increasing the elasticity of the cheese.

START WITH YUKON GOLDS Russets have an earthy flavor we like in mashed potatoes, but with all the stirring this recipe requires they can be way too gluey. The Yukon Golds have good flavor, but a little less starch, so they are not as sticky or tacky in the finished dish. After making aligot with different potatoes, we found medium-starch Yukon Golds to be the clear winner.

CHUNK AND BOIL In the test kitchen, we've found that how you cook the potatoes for a regular mash is critical to their final texture. To avoid glueyness, we've gone so far as to steam as well as rinse the spuds midway through cooking to rid them of excess amylose, the starch in potatoes that turns them tacky. But because the potatoes are stirred so vigorously later (rough handling also bursts the granules that contain amylose, and the potato cells, releasing the starch into the mix), such treatment doesn't matter. It's fine to peel and boil the potatoes in chunks.

GET OUT THE FOOD PROCESSOR We use a food processor to "mash" our potatoes here. It most closely approximates the super-smooth puree produced by a tamis, a drum-size sieve, which is the traditional French tool used for this dish.

GO EASY ON BUTTER AND DAIRY This recipe needs less butter and lower-fat dairy (milk is fine) than regular mashed potatoes because of all the fat that will be supplied by the cheese. We add the butter (and garlic) to the mix in the food processor. Once the potato starches are coated with fat, we add the milk. The coating of butter helps to make the starch more compatible with the fatty cheeses so the starch molecules are better able to combine with the proteins. If milk is added first, the starch becomes so wet it resists interaction with the fatty cheese.

ADD TWO TYPES OF CHEESE The authentic cheese in aligot is *tome fraîche*, a spongy and elastic cow's milk cheese not easily found in the United States. To replace this with something more readily available, we end up with two cheeses. Mozzarella gives the dish stretch, and Gruyère gives it a nutty flavor.

But is it the cheese alone that gives this dish its stretch? No. As it turns out, there is something different about the starch in potatoes that makes it possible to form the super stretch of aligot. Unlike the starch from other plants, the molecules in potato starch contain a small number of negative electrical charges. When combined with cheese proteins, parts of which contain positive electrical charges, an electrical bond between the two is created. Therefore, when curly amylose molecules bond with cheese proteins, the combination becomes very springy and stretchy.

STIR, STIR, STIR Stirring is the key to aligot, but it's tricky. Too much and the aligot turns so rubbery that it is reminiscent of chewing gum. Too little and the cheese doesn't truly marry with the potatoes for that essential elasticity. Three to five minutes is the magic number. During this time the amylose, released from the starch molecules, is binding with the proteins from the melted cheese, enhancing its stretch without causing glueyness.

CRISP ROASTED POTATOES
SERVES 4 TO 6

The steps of parcooking the potatoes before roasting and tossing the potatoes with salt and oil until they are coated with starch are the keys to developing a crisp exterior and creamy interior. The potatoes should be just undercooked when they are removed from the boiling water.

2½	pounds Yukon Gold potatoes, cut into ½-inch-thick slices
	Salt and pepper
5	tablespoons olive oil

1. Adjust oven rack to lowest position, place rimmed baking sheet on rack, and heat oven to 450 degrees. Place potatoes and 1 tablespoon salt in Dutch oven, add cold water to cover by 1 inch. Bring to boil over high heat, then reduce heat and gently simmer until exteriors of potatoes have softened but centers offer resistance when poked with paring knife, about 5 minutes. Drain potatoes well and transfer to large bowl.

2. Drizzle potatoes with 2 tablespoons oil and sprinkle with ½ teaspoon salt; using rubber spatula, toss to combine. Repeat with 2 tablespoons oil and ½ teaspoon salt and continue to toss until exteriors of potato slices are coated with starchy paste, 1 to 2 minutes.

3. Working quickly, remove baking sheet from oven and drizzle remaining 1 tablespoon oil over surface. Carefully transfer potatoes to baking sheet and spread into even layer (place end pieces skin side up). Bake until bottoms of potatoes are golden brown and crisp, 15 to 25 minutes, rotating baking sheet after 10 minutes.

4. Remove baking sheet from oven and, using metal spatula and tongs, loosen potatoes from pan and carefully flip each slice. Continue to roast until second side is golden and crisp, 10 to 20 minutes longer, rotating baking sheet as needed to ensure potatoes brown evenly. Season with salt and pepper to taste, and serve immediately.

✓ WHY THIS RECIPE WORKS

For roasted potatoes with the crispiest exterior and creamiest interior, we had to find the right spud, the right shape, and the right cooking method. Parcooking is key, as gently simmering the potatoes draws starch and sugar to the surface and washes away the excess quickly. In the oven, the starch and sugar will harden into a crisp shell, especially after we rough up the surface of the potatoes, which helps to speed up evaporation during roasting, making the crusts even crisper.

YUKON GOLDS ARE BEST Most recipes rely on long cooking times for crisp roasted potatoes, yielding tough, leathery exteriors and dried-out, mealy interiors. With the goal of creating a really crisp roast potato with a creamy interior, we tested different types of potatoes. For velvety interiors, the ideal potato has high moisture and low starch. But the ideal potato for a crisp exterior has low moisture and high starch. Russets and red potatoes give either the exterior or the interior too much weight. Yukon Golds are the perfect compromise choice—enough moisture so the interior is creamy, enough starch for a crispy exterior.

CUT INTO DISKS We cut our potatoes into disks rather than chunks because the disks have much more surface area for maximum browning. They also flip easily, and we can be sure that each side will sit flush against the pan.

PARCOOK THE POTATOES For a potato to brown and crisp, two things need to happen, both of which depend on moisture. First, starch granules in the potatoes must absorb water and swell, releasing some of their amylose. Second, some of the amylose must break down into glucose, a type of sugar. Once the moisture evaporates on the surface of the potato, the amylose hardens into a plasticlike shell, yielding crispness, and the glucose darkens, yielding an appealing brown color. In the dry heat of the oven, this is a lengthy process because the starch granules swell slowly, releasing little amylose. In contrast, parboiled potatoes are swimming in the requisite moist heat, releasing lots of amylose on the surface of the potato. By the time parcooked spuds get transferred to the oven, they are ready to begin browning and crisping almost immediately.

HANDLE ROUGHLY Potatoes that are parcooked brown faster in the oven. But potatoes that are parcooked and "roughed up" by being tossed vigorously with salt and oil brown even faster. It's all a matter of surface area. Browning or crisping can't begin until the surface moisture evaporates and the temperature rises. The parcooked, roughed-up slices—riddled with tiny dips and mounds, the salt causing added friction—have more exposed surface area than the smooth raw slices and thus more escape routes for moisture.

USE HOT OVEN, HOT BAKING SHEET Preheat the baking sheet used for the potatoes along with the oven. This allows for a shorter roasting time. A shorter time in the oven allows more retention of moisture in the potato innards, resulting in a creamier texture.

PRACTICAL SCIENCE JUST SCRATCH THE SURFACE

Roughing up slices of potatoes allows for more moisture evaporation, and better crusts.

While developing our recipe for Crisp Roasted Potatoes, we discovered that parcooked potato slices browned faster in the oven than raw slices. When we subsequently "roughed up" the parcooked slices by tossing them vigorously with salt and oil, they browned faster still. The explanation? It's all a matter of surface area. Browning or crisping can't begin until the surface moisture evaporates. The parcooked, roughed-up slices—riddled with tiny dips and mounds—have more exposed surface area than the smooth raw slices and thus more escape routes for moisture. If you have trouble getting your head around two potato slices of identical width having vastly different surface areas, think of it this way: Five square miles of Colorado's mountain region will have far more exposed surface area than 5 square miles of the Kansas plains. (Just try walking them both.)

ROUGHED-UP SURFACE = FAST EVAPORATION

SMOOTH SURFACE = SLOW EVAPORATION

HOME FRIES
SERVES 6 TO 8

Don't skip the baking soda in this recipe. It's critical for home fries with just the right crisp texture.

3½	pounds russet potatoes, peeled and cut into ¾-inch dice
½	teaspoon baking soda
3	tablespoons unsalted butter, cut into 12 pieces
	Kosher salt and pepper
	Pinch cayenne pepper
3	tablespoons vegetable oil
2	medium onions, cut into ½-inch dice
3	tablespoons minced fresh chives

1. Adjust oven rack to lowest position, place rimmed baking sheet on rack, and heat oven to 500 degrees.

2. Bring 10 cups water to boil in Dutch oven over high heat. Add potatoes and baking soda. Return to boil and cook for 1 minute. Drain potatoes. Return potatoes to Dutch oven and place over low heat. Cook, shaking pot occasionally, until any surface moisture has evaporated, about 2 minutes. Remove from heat. Add butter, 1½ teaspoons salt, and cayenne; mix with rubber spatula until potatoes are coated with thick starchy paste, about 30 seconds.

3. Remove preheated baking sheet from oven and drizzle with 2 tablespoons oil. Transfer potatoes to baking sheet and spread into even layer. Roast for 15 minutes. While potatoes roast, combine onions, remaining tablespoon oil, and ½ teaspoon salt in bowl.

4. Remove baking sheet from oven. Using thin, sharp metal spatula, scrape and turn potatoes. Clear about 8 by 5-inch space in center of baking sheet and add onion mixture. Roast for 15 minutes.

5. Scrape and turn again, mixing onions into potatoes. Continue to roast until potatoes are well browned and onions are softened and beginning to brown, 5 to 10 minutes longer. Stir in chives and season with salt and pepper to taste. Serve immediately.

✔ WHY THIS RECIPE WORKS

Despite the cozy image conjured by the name, few people actually make home fries at home. That's probably because producing the perfect dish—a mound of golden-brown potato chunks with crisp exteriors and moist, fluffy insides dotted with savory onions and herbs—calls for more time, elbow grease, and stovetop space than most cooks care to devote to the project. We simplify our home fries with a super-fast precook in boiling water (with baking soda!), and some time in a hot oven.

CHOOSE RUSSETS When developing this recipe, we tested the three main kinds of potatoes: waxy, low-starch red-skinned spuds; all-purpose, medium-starch Yukon Golds; and floury, high-starch russets (see concept 25). Tasters almost universally rejected the texture of the red-skinned potatoes as too waxy for home fries. Though some praised the creaminess of the Yukon Golds, the majority preferred the earthy flavor of russets. After all, the higher starch content of russets does make for a crustier exterior—especially when manipulated.

PARBOIL WITH BAKING SODA A very quick jaunt in boiling water—with baking soda—is the secret to the success of these home fries. Because the russets are so starchy, if they are cooked all the way through before going against high heat, they will absorb all the oil before beginning to brown. The short blanch (just 1 minute) is an effective way to break down just the very exterior of the potato. This is possible because of the baking soda, which speeds up the softening process (see "Baking Soda for Brown Crusts," below) and therefore exaggerates the differences in doneness between the exterior and the interior of the potatoes. The thin outer layer of blown-out, starchy potato will brown thoroughly in the oven, while the raw middle will stay moist.

SALT THE EXTERIOR Tossing the drained parcooked potato chunks with butter and salt before placing them on the baking sheet helps with the browned exterior. The coarse salt roughs up the surface of the potatoes so that moisture evaporates faster, leading to better browning.

ROAST IN THE OVEN These home fries might as well be called home-roasted potatoes, because we do just that. Unable to ignore the fact that the oven is best for large batches, we choose high-temperature roasting over making many batches in a skillet.

PRACTICAL SCIENCE
BAKING SODA FOR BROWN CRUSTS

Creating an alkaline environment in which to boil potatoes helps to later brown the crust.

While developing a potato salad recipe, we discovered that adding vinegar to the cooking water creates an acidic environment that slows the breakdown of the pectin that holds potato cells together, resulting in a firm, intact texture. So when our home fries required a thin outer layer of mush that would brown thoroughly in the oven, we took the opposite approach: We created an alkaline environment by adding a little bit of baking soda to the water. After just one minute in the pot, the exteriors of the potatoes became so soft that they were mushy—but the interiors remained raw. This led to potatoes that more readily crisped on the outside when roasted but didn't dry out on the inside.

How could just ½ teaspoon of baking soda added to 10 cups of water be so powerful? It's because alkaline baking soda triggers a chain reaction that literally unzips the backbone of the pectin molecules and causes them to fall apart. This requires only enough alkali to raise the pH of the water high enough to start the reaction, after which it becomes self-sustaining.

BOILED WITH BAKING SODA (pH 8.1)

BOILED WITH VINEGAR (pH 3)

Precooking Makes Vegetables Firmer

Almost any vegetable can be roasted (in a pan or in the oven)—even green vegetables. High heat is a must to develop flavor, but sometimes it's not sufficient to produce a well-cooked finished dish. As we learned in concept 5, many meats benefit from the use of two cooking methods. Sometimes vegetables are just the same.

HOW THE SCIENCE WORKS

A GENTLE START AFFECTS THE PECTIN IN VEGETABLES

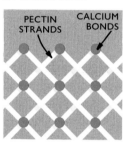

GENTLE START, HOT FINISH *When first cooked at a low temperature, vegetable cells maintain a strong pectin network due to the work of the enzyme pectin methylesterase, which causes the pectin to link with calcium ions.*

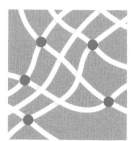

HIGH HEAT ALONE *When cooked in an open vessel on high heat, this enzyme is not active, and the pectin network within vegetable cells is more prone to breaking down.*

Cooks have known for centuries that browning makes food taste better. But for some reason, vegetables have rarely received this treatment. Their small size makes them challenging to work with (you can't really roast them on a spit), but modern ovens have made roasting almost any vegetable a cinch. The problem is that vegetables are very high in water, and when browned in a hot oven, there is a significant loss of moisture by evaporation. This concentrates flavor but can leave you with a batch of wrinkled, dry carrots.

To combat this, we turn to the same technique we learned in concept 5: the use of two cooking methods. To get our vegetables tender while not expelling liquid, we first steam them, often by covering the pan with foil or a lid. It's only after this initial cooking that we then turn up the heat.

This precooking stage is especially important in vegetables like potatoes, sweet potatoes, carrots, Brussels sprouts, asparagus, and cauliflower—vegetables that can actually become firm and stay firm during cooking if they are subjected to a short time in the oven at lower heat. This persistent firmness helps to prevent excess moisture loss, keeping the vegetables tender and moist even when subjected to high heat. Why? It all comes down to enzymes. Not unlike the enzymes we learned about in concept 6, which actively work to break down the tough connective tissue in proteins when held at a temperature under 122 degrees, these vegetables contain an enzyme that becomes most active between 120 and 160 degrees. This enzyme, called pectin methylesterase, causes the pectin in the cell walls to more readily link with calcium ions, which are already present in the vegetable's structure. This link causes the pectin to become stronger, making the vegetable much less prone to breaking down. This is important because when we uncover the veggies to begin browning, more moisture evaporates. Precooking can keep vegetables firm and tender even as they become well caramelized.

Before we start cooking, let's address an important distinction. Many meat and vegetable recipes include a step where the ingredients are either caramelized or browned. Lots of people—even professional chefs—use "caramelize" and "brown" interchangeably, but if you look at the science behind these flavor-boosting techniques, they're related but actually quite different (though both, of course, lead to a literal browning of the food).

Caramelization describes the chemical reactions that take place when sugar is heated to the point that its molecules begin to break apart and generate hundreds of new flavor, color, and aroma compounds. Consider crème brûlée—after being exposed to high heat, the sugar atop the custard turns golden brown, with rich, complex flavors. Many vegetables are high in natural sugars—especially onions, carrots, and squash. In high heat, once most of their surface moisture has evaporated, a similar process to the one for crème brûlée takes place, and their natural sugars begin to caramelize.

As for browning, the process involves the interaction of not just sugar molecules and heat but also proteins and their breakdown products, amino acids—and is called the Maillard reaction (see concept 2). Browning creates a tremendous number of flavors and colors, but they're not the same as those created by caramelization because protein is involved. Meats and bread benefit from browning, but since vegetables contain little or no protein they technically caramelize.

TEST KITCHEN EXPERIMENT

To determine the effects of precooking vegetables, we devised a simple test. We cooked three 500-gram batches of carrots cut into ¾-inch dice. One batch was cooked uncovered in a 425-degree oven for one hour. The second batch was covered for 15 minutes and then uncovered for 45 minutes in a 425-degree oven. The third batch was cooked in a sealed bag in a water bath at 150 degrees for 30 minutes, and then roasted uncovered in a 425-degree oven for 45 minutes. We weighed the carrots before and after cooking. We repeated the experiment two more times and averaged the results.

THE RESULTS

The carrots roasted uncovered came out of the oven looking wrinkled and small. They lost an average of 305 grams, or 62 percent of their weight. The carrots covered and then uncovered in the oven were also wrinkled, but less so, and lost an average of 293 grams, or 60 percent of their weight. The carrots first cooked in the water bath came from the oven looking relatively firm. They lost 260 grams on average, or 53 percent of their weight.

THE TAKEAWAY

It was no surprise that the carrots roasted uncovered in a hot oven lost the most water weight. They were brought to temperature quickly and began caramelizing (and losing water via evaporation) almost immediately. On the opposite end, the carrots precooked in the low-temperature water bath lost the least amount of water weight when later roasted uncovered in the oven. For the sample that technically cooked the longest of all three, this was no small feat and had everything to do with enzymes. Because these carrots were held at a temperature optimal for the activation of the enzyme pectin methylesterase, they had the most time to reap the benefits, becoming persistently firm and therefore able to retain more moisture.

But the real story comes with the middle results. We don't expect home cooks to use the extra pots and take the extra time to precook vegetables in a water bath. Instead, we recommend cooking vegetables, including carrots, first covered with foil and then uncovered in the oven. This gentle start is less effective than actual precooking, but it does keep the vegetables at a lower temperature for a longer period of time. This allows the enzyme pectin methylesterase to help keep the vegetables' flesh firmer and less prone to water loss. When we roast carrots this way (especially when they're cut into larger chunks, like our Roasted Carrots, page 252), the finished results are tender, flavorful roasted veggies without the dry, leathery texture.

WEIGHING CARROTS: GENTLE START VS. HIGH HEAT

RAW CARROTS *We took two batches of cubed carrots that weighed exactly the same and then cooked them in two different ways.*

GENTLE START VS. HIGH HEAT *Our carrots started under foil (left) retained more water (and weight) than those cooked straight under high heat (right).*

Instead of placing vegetables straight into a hot oven without any protection, we cover our pans of chopped, thick cauliflower, sweet potatoes, Brussels sprouts, and carrots with aluminum foil. This way, the vegetables steam in the oven at a lower temperature for a short amount of time, retaining moisture and acquiring some persistent firmness before we remove the foil and let them brown.

ROASTED CAULIFLOWER
SERVES 4 TO 6

This dish stands well on its own, drizzled with extra-virgin olive oil, but it can also be prepared with a sauce (recipes follow).

1	head cauliflower (2 pounds)
¼	cup extra-virgin olive oil
	Salt and pepper

1. Adjust oven rack to lowest position and heat oven to 475 degrees. Trim outer leaves off cauliflower and cut stem flush with bottom. Cut head into 8 equal wedges through center core. Place wedges cut side down on aluminum foil– or parchment paper–lined rimmed baking sheet. Drizzle with 2 tablespoons oil and season with salt and pepper to taste. Gently rub seasonings and oil into cauliflower. Gently flip cauliflower and repeat on second cut side with remaining 2 tablespoons oil, salt, and pepper.

2. Cover baking sheet tightly with foil and cook for 10 minutes. Remove foil and continue to roast until bottoms of cauliflower pieces are golden, 8 to 12 minutes. Remove baking sheet from oven and, using spatula, carefully flip wedges. Return baking sheet to oven and continue to roast until cauliflower is golden all over, 8 to 12 minutes longer. Season with salt and pepper to taste, and serve immediately.

PRACTICAL SCIENCE
TAKING THE SIDE OF ALUMINUM FOIL

The shiny and dull sides of aluminum foil work the same.

Aluminum foil is made by passing two layers of foil through a rolling mill at the same time. The side in contact with the rolling mill comes out shiny, while the other side is dull. To see if one side heats faster than the other, we ran a series of kitchen tests. In one test, mashed potatoes covered with foil heated up a bit faster when the shiny side was facing the food rather than the heat source, but the differences were so slight that we concluded that foil works the same, whether the shiny or dull side is touching the food.

SHERRY VINEGAR–HONEY SAUCE WITH ALMONDS
MAKES ENOUGH FOR 1 RECIPE ROASTED CAULIFLOWER

Both regular and golden raisins work well here.

1	tablespoon extra-virgin olive oil
¼	cup raisins
2	large garlic cloves, minced
¼	cup water
3	tablespoons sherry vinegar
2	tablespoons honey
¼	cup sliced almonds, toasted
2	tablespoons minced fresh parsley
	Salt and pepper
1	tablespoon minced fresh chives

Heat oil in 8-inch skillet over medium-high heat until shimmering. Add raisins and garlic and cook, stirring constantly, until garlic is fragrant, about 1 minute. Reduce heat to medium and add water, vinegar, and honey. Simmer until lightly syrupy, 4 to 6 minutes. Stir in almonds, parsley, and salt and pepper to taste. Drizzle sauce over roasted cauliflower and garnish with chives before serving.

SOY-GINGER SAUCE WITH SCALLION
MAKES ENOUGH FOR 1 RECIPE ROASTED CAULIFLOWER

If using this sauce, use vegetable oil to roast the cauliflower instead of olive oil.

2	teaspoons vegetable oil
1	tablespoon grated fresh ginger
2	garlic cloves, minced
¼	cup water
2	tablespoons soy sauce
2	tablespoons mirin
1	tablespoon rice vinegar
1	teaspoon toasted sesame oil
1	scallion, sliced thin

Heat oil in 8-inch skillet over medium-high heat until shimmering. Add ginger and garlic and cook until fragrant, about 1 minute. Reduce heat to medium-low and add water, soy sauce, mirin, and vinegar. Simmer until slightly syrupy, 4 to 6 minutes. Drizzle sauce and sesame oil over roasted cauliflower and garnish with scallion before serving.

CURRY-YOGURT SAUCE WITH CILANTRO
MAKES ENOUGH FOR I RECIPE ROASTED CAULIFLOWER

If using this sauce, use vegetable oil to roast the cauliflower instead of olive oil.

- I tablespoon vegetable oil
- I shallot, minced
- 2 teaspoons curry powder
- ¼ teaspoon red pepper flakes
- ⅓ cup water
- ¼ cup plain whole-milk yogurt
- 2 tablespoons minced fresh cilantro
- I teaspoon lime juice
  Salt and pepper

Heat oil in small skillet over medium-high heat until shimmering. Add shallot and cook until softened, about 2 minutes. Stir in curry powder and pepper flakes; cook until fragrant, about 1 minute. Remove from heat and whisk in water, yogurt, cilantro, lime juice, and salt and pepper to taste. Drizzle sauce over roasted cauliflower before serving.

✔ WHY THIS RECIPE WORKS

We wanted to add flavor to cauliflower without drowning it in a heavy blanket of cheese sauce, so we developed a roasted cauliflower recipe that gave us cauliflower with a golden, nutty exterior and sweet interior. We discovered that steaming (in a covered sheet pan) followed by roasting produces nicely caramelized cauliflower with a creamy texture. Though the cauliflower is excellent on its own, we also developed some simple sauces to dress it up.

CUT BIG WEDGES Roasting makes cauliflower creamy and brings out the sweet, nutty notes. If the cauliflower is cut too small, however, the florets will disintegrate into small pieces and burn. Cutting the cauliflower through the core (so that each fat wedge has some of the core) keeps the florets attached to each other. It also ensures that each piece will lie flat—and that translates to maximum color and flavor through caramelization.

OIL WELL Cauliflower wedges have lots of nooks and crannies. If you skimp on the oil, the cauliflower can dry out and become leathery. Also, the oil promotes good browning.

OVEN-STEAM, THEN ROAST Straight-up roasting causes cauliflower to shed its moisture rapidly within the first few minutes of cooking. Covering the baking sheet with foil, however, traps this moisture and adds just enough steam to cook the cauliflower gently, keeping the florets firm and moist enough to withstand the next 20 minutes of roasting and preventing them from becoming dry and leathery.

FLIP WITH CARE Turn cauliflower just once (to minimize chances of breakage) and use a spatula to get under each wedge and flip it over.

ROASTED SWEET POTATOES
SERVES 4 TO 6

Note that this recipe calls for starting the potatoes in a cold oven. Choose potatoes that are as even in width as possible; trimming the small ends prevents them from burning. If you prefer not to peel the potatoes, just scrub them well before cutting.

- 3 pounds sweet potatoes, ends trimmed, peeled, rinsed, and cut into ¾-inch-thick rounds
- 2 tablespoons vegetable oil
  Salt and pepper

1. Toss potatoes in large bowl with oil, 1 teaspoon salt, and pepper to taste until evenly coated. Line rimmed baking sheet with aluminum foil and coat with vegetable oil spray. Arrange potatoes in single layer on baking sheet and cover tightly with foil. Adjust oven rack to middle position and place potatoes in cold oven. Turn oven to 425 degrees and cook potatoes for 30 minutes.

2. Remove baking sheet from oven and carefully remove top piece of foil. Return potatoes to oven and roast, uncovered, until bottom edges of potatoes are golden brown, 15 to 25 minutes.

3. Remove baking sheet from oven and, using thin metal spatula, flip potato slices over. Continue to roast until bottom edges of potatoes are golden brown, 18 to 22 minutes longer. Remove from oven, let cool for 5 to 10 minutes, and serve.

ROASTED SWEET POTATOES WITH MAPLE-THYME GLAZE

Whisk ¼ cup maple syrup, 2 tablespoons melted unsalted butter, and 2 teaspoons minced fresh thyme together in small bowl. Follow recipe as directed through step 2. After removing baking sheet from oven in step 3, brush potatoes with half of maple syrup glaze, flip slices over with thin metal spatula, and brush with remaining glaze. Return potatoes to oven and proceed as directed.

ROASTED SWEET POTATOES WITH SPICED BROWN SUGAR GLAZE

Heat ¼ cup packed light brown sugar, 2 tablespoons apple juice, 2 tablespoons unsalted butter, ¼ teaspoon ground cinnamon, ¼ teaspoon ground ginger, and ⅛ teaspoon ground nutmeg in small saucepan over medium heat. Cook, stirring constantly, until butter has melted and sugar is dissolved, 2 to 4 minutes. Follow recipe as directed through step 2. After removing baking sheet from oven in step 3, brush potatoes with half of spice glaze, flip slices over with thin metal spatula, and brush with remaining glaze. Return potatoes to oven and proceed as directed.

✔ WHY THIS RECIPE WORKS

Too often, roasted sweet potatoes turn out starchy and wan. We wanted a method that gave us potatoes with a nicely caramelized exterior, a smooth, creamy interior, and an earthy sweetness. A two-step cooking method is key: We begin the sliced sweet potato rounds in a cold oven, covered in foil. Only after they cook for 30 minutes do we remove the foil and let them brown and crisp.

USE THICK ROUNDS The thin tips of wedges can burn. Big rounds are the same thickness throughout, though. And with rounds, there are just two sides to brown, rather than three.

COLD START, FINISH SWEET In developing this recipe, we noticed that the lower the oven temperature, the less the potatoes browned, but the sweeter they became. Why? The starch in sweet potatoes is converted into sugars between 135 and 170 degrees. Once the internal temperature of the potato exceeds 170 degrees, no further conversion occurs. Thus, the lower the oven temperature, the longer the potatoes will stay within this range and the sweeter the finished results will be. Therefore, we cover our potatoes with foil and start them in a cold oven to maximize their time in the "sweet zone."

REMOVE THE FOIL After 30 minutes, remove the foil to get the browning really going. Roast the potatoes uncovered, turning once. Don't worry, they won't stick: Greased foil on the bottom of the pan makes it easy to flip 'em.

ROASTED CARROTS
SERVES 4 TO 6

While cutting the carrots into uniformly sized pieces is key for even cooking, it's the large size of the pieces that makes this recipe work, so make sure not to cut them too small.

1½	pounds carrots, peeled
2	tablespoons unsalted butter, melted
	Salt and pepper

1. Adjust oven rack to middle position and heat oven to 425 degrees. Cut the carrots in half crosswise, then into halves or quarters lengthwise if necessary to create uniformly sized pieces. In large bowl, combine carrots with butter, ½ teaspoon salt, and ¼ teaspoon pepper and toss to coat. Transfer carrots to aluminum foil– or parchment paper–lined rimmed baking sheet and spread in single layer.

2. Cover baking sheet tightly with foil and cook for 15 minutes. Remove foil and continue to cook, stirring twice, until carrots are well browned and tender, 30 to 35 minutes. Transfer to serving platter, season with salt and pepper to taste, and serve.

PRACTICAL SCIENCE STORING SWEET POTATOES

Storing sweet potatoes in the refrigerator can cause them to develop a tough interior, even when cooked for long periods of time.

We normally store sweet potatoes away from light at a cool room temperature, but we wondered if storing them in the refrigerator would have any detrimental effects. We bought a case of sweet potatoes and divided it into two batches. We stored each batch for four weeks, one at room temperature (in a cabinet, between 55 and 65 degrees) and one in the refrigerator (between 34 and 38 degrees). After four weeks, we removed the sweet potatoes from the refrigerator and allowed them to come to room temperature before cutting both batches of potatoes into pieces and roasting them in a 400-degree oven for 45 minutes. We tasted them to see if we could spot any differences.

Both batches of potatoes looked the same coming out of storage, but cooking them told a different story. While the room-temperature potatoes were creamy and soft all the way through, the refrigerated potatoes remained hard at the center. To see if another cooking method would produce different results, we repeated the test, this time boiling sliced potatoes for 40 minutes. The outcome was the same: The refrigerated potatoes had tough centers.

It turns out that the development of a hard core in sweet potatoes is the result of chilling and then warming. During the chilling stage, the sweet potatoes' cell walls become more permeable, allowing the calcium ions located between the cells to enter into the cell walls. Warming the sweet potatoes to room temperature activates the enzyme called pectin methylesterase (the same enzyme that kicks into high gear during precooking). This enzyme alters pectin in a way that allows it to react with calcium ions, strengthening the pectin molecules in the cells' walls so that they can't be broken down—even by prolonged cooking. In effect, the same thing happens when sweet potatoes are refrigerated as when many vegetables are precooked, but at a slower pace.

ROASTED CARROTS AND FENNEL
WITH TOASTED ALMONDS AND LEMON

Reduce amount of carrots to 1 pound. Add 1 small fennel bulb, stalks discarded, halved, cored, and sliced ½ inch thick, to bowl with carrots and roast as directed. Toss vegetables with ¼ cup toasted sliced almonds, 2 teaspoons minced fresh parsley, and 1 teaspoon lemon juice before serving.

ROASTED CARROTS AND PARSNIPS
WITH ROSEMARY

Reduce amount of carrots to 1 pound. Add 8 ounces peeled parsnips, halved crosswise and cut lengthwise if necessary to create even pieces, and 1 teaspoon chopped fresh rosemary to bowl with carrots and roast as directed. Toss vegetables with 2 teaspoons minced fresh parsley before serving.

✔ WHY THIS RECIPE WORKS

Roasting carrots draws out their natural sugars and intensifies their flavor—if you can prevent them from coming out dry, shriveled, and jerkylike. We avoid dirtying a second pan by precooking the carrots (which we butter and season) right on the baking sheet, covered with foil.

BATONS BROWN BEST Cutting carrots to a uniform size is the key to evenly cooked results. If you have large carrots (over 1 inch in diameter), you can do this by halving them crosswise, then quartering each section lengthwise to create a total of eight pieces. With medium carrots (½ inch to 1 inch in diameter), halve them crosswise, then halve the wider section lengthwise to create a total of three pieces. If you have small carrots (less than ½ inch in diameter), simply halve them crosswise and leave the sections whole.

COVER TO TRAP MOISTURE Roasted carrots can dry out and become tough. They contain more pectin than any other vegetable. We've found that keeping their internal temperature between 120 and 160 degrees for as long as possible converts the pectin to a heat-stable form that reinforces cell walls and keeps moisture in (see Test Kitchen Experiment, page 249). To prevent the carrots' internal temperature from climbing too quickly, we start them in the oven under foil.

ROASTED BRUSSELS SPROUTS
SERVES 6 TO 8

If you are buying loose Brussels sprouts, select those that are about 1½ inches long. Quarter Brussels sprouts longer than 2½ inches; don't cut sprouts shorter than 1 inch.

2¼   pounds Brussels sprouts, trimmed and halved
3   tablespoons olive oil
1   tablespoon water
    Salt and pepper

1. Adjust oven rack to upper-middle position and heat oven to 500 degrees. Toss Brussels sprouts, oil, water, ¾ teaspoon salt, and ¼ teaspoon pepper in large bowl until sprouts are coated. Transfer sprouts to rimmed baking sheet and arrange so cut sides are facing down.

2. Cover sheet tightly with aluminum foil and cook for 10 minutes. Remove foil and continue to cook until Brussels sprouts are well browned and tender, 10 to 12 minutes longer. Transfer to serving platter, season with salt and pepper to taste, and serve.

ROASTED BRUSSELS SPROUTS WITH
GARLIC, RED PEPPER FLAKES, AND PARMESAN

While Brussels sprouts roast, heat 3 tablespoons olive oil in 8-inch skillet over medium heat until shimmering. Add 2 minced garlic cloves and ½ teaspoon red pepper flakes; cook until garlic is golden and fragrant, about 1 minute. Remove from heat. After transferring Brussels sprouts to platter, toss with garlic oil and season with salt and pepper to taste. Sprinkle with ¼ cup grated Parmesan cheese before serving.

ROASTED BRUSSELS SPROUTS WITH
BACON AND PECANS

While Brussels sprouts roast, cook 4 slices bacon in 10-inch skillet over medium heat until crisp, 7 to 10 minutes. Using slotted spoon, transfer bacon to paper towel–lined plate and reserve 1 tablespoon bacon fat. Finely chop bacon. After transferring sprouts to platter, toss with 2 tablespoons olive oil, reserved bacon fat, chopped bacon, and ½ cup finely chopped toasted pecans. Season with salt and pepper to taste, and serve.

ROASTED BRUSSELS SPROUTS WITH
WALNUTS AND LEMON

Transfer roasted Brussels sprouts to platter and toss with ⅓ cup finely chopped toasted walnuts, 3 tablespoons melted unsalted butter, and 1 tablespoon lemon juice. Season with salt and pepper to taste, and serve.

✔ WHY THIS RECIPE WORKS

Brussels sprouts don't have to taste overly bitter or sulfurous. Like other members of the crucifer family (which also includes broccoli, cabbage, and mustard greens), Brussels sprouts are rich in flavor precursors that react with the vegetable's enzymes to produce pungent new compounds when the sprouts are cut, cooked, and even eaten. But when the sprouts are handled just right, this pungency takes on a nutty sweetness. We steam and then roast these sprouts on one pan in the oven. They emerge with tender, sweet insides and caramelized exteriors.

ARRANGE CUT SIDE DOWN We make sure to arrange the halved Brussels sprouts cut side down on the baking sheet. This flat surface is optimal for browning and, as a result, extra flavor.

WATER AND FOIL THE SPROUTS We toss these sprouts with a tablespoon of water along with olive oil and seasonings before putting them in the oven. Covered in foil, each halved sprout acts like its own little steam chamber, holding on to a tiny bit of water to finish cooking its interior even as its outside begins to brown.

PECTIN STABILIZATION AT WORK PAN-ROASTED VEGETABLES

As we do for oven-roasted vegetables, we often precook vegetables before letting them brown on top of the stove. This method is especially appealing when pan-roasting quick-cooking vegetables such as asparagus. (Note that the oven is really the best choice for denser, larger vegetables like cauliflower and sweet potatoes.) Here we take one very simple step—briefly putting a lid on our pan of asparagus—to keep the spears firm and moist before letting them begin to brown.

PAN-ROASTED ASPARAGUS
SERVES 4 TO 6

This recipe works best with asparagus that is at least ½ inch thick near the base. If using thinner spears, reduce the covered cooking time to three minutes and the uncovered cooking time to five minutes. Do not use pencil-thin asparagus; it cannot withstand the heat and overcooks too easily.

- 1 tablespoon olive oil
- 1 tablespoon unsalted butter
- 2 pounds thick asparagus, trimmed
    Salt and pepper
- ½ lemon (optional)

1. Heat oil and butter in 12-inch skillet over medium-high heat. When butter has melted, add half of asparagus to skillet with tips pointed in one direction; add remaining spears with tips pointed in opposite direction. Using tongs, distribute spears evenly (spears will not quite fit into single layer); cover and cook until asparagus is bright green and still crisp, about 5 minutes.

2. Uncover and increase heat to high; season asparagus with salt and pepper to taste. Cook until spears are tender and well browned along one side, 5 to 7 minutes, using tongs to occasionally move spears from center of pan to edge of pan to ensure all are browned. Transfer asparagus to serving dish, adjust seasonings with salt and pepper, and, if desired, squeeze lemon half over spears. Serve immediately.

PAN-ROASTED ASPARAGUS WITH
TOASTED GARLIC AND PARMESAN

Heat 2 tablespoons olive oil in 12-inch skillet, add 3 thinly sliced garlic cloves, and cook over medium heat, stirring occasionally, until garlic is crisp and golden but not dark brown, about 5 minutes. Using slotted spoon, transfer garlic to paper towel–lined plate. Follow recipe, adding butter to oil already in skillet. After transferring asparagus to serving dish, sprinkle with 2 tablespoons grated Parmesan and toasted garlic. Season with lemon juice, salt, and pepper to taste, and serve immediately.

PAN-ROASTED ASPARAGUS WITH
RED ONION AND BACON

Cook 4 slices bacon, cut into ¼-inch pieces, in 12-inch skillet over medium heat until crisp, 5 to 7 minutes. Using slotted spoon, transfer bacon to paper towel–lined plate; set aside. Pour off all but 1 tablespoon fat from pan. Return skillet to medium-high heat and add 1 large red onion, halved and sliced thin. Cook, stirring occasionally, until edges darken and onion begins to soften, about 3 minutes. Add 2 tablespoons balsamic vinegar and 1 tablespoon maple syrup to skillet and cook until liquids reduce and cling to onions, about 2 minutes. Transfer onions to bowl, season with salt and pepper to taste, and cover to keep warm. Top cooked asparagus with onion mixture and bacon before serving.

PAN-ROASTED ASPARAGUS WITH
RED PEPPERS AND GOAT CHEESE

Heat 1 tablespoon olive oil in 12-inch skillet over medium-high heat until shimmering. Add 2 red bell peppers, stemmed, seeded, and cut into ¼-inch-wide strips, and cook, stirring occasionally, until skins begin to blister, 4 to 5 minutes. Transfer peppers to bowl, season with salt and pepper to taste, and cover to keep warm. Top cooked asparagus with peppers, 1 cup crumbled goat cheese, ¼ cup toasted pine nuts, and 2 tablespoons minced fresh mint before serving.

PAN-ROASTED ASPARAGUS WITH
WARM ORANGE-ALMOND VINAIGRETTE

Heat 2 tablespoons olive oil in 12-inch skillet over medium heat until shimmering. Add ¼ cup slivered almonds and cook, stirring frequently, until golden, about 5 minutes. Add ½ cup orange juice and 1 teaspoon minced fresh thyme, increase heat to medium-high, and simmer until thickened, about 4 minutes. Off heat, stir in 2 tablespoons minced shallot, 2 tablespoons sherry vinegar, and salt and pepper to taste. Transfer vinaigrette to small bowl. Wipe out skillet and follow recipe, cooking asparagus in same pan. After transferring asparagus to serving dish, pour vinaigrette over and toss to combine. Season with salt and pepper to taste, and serve immediately.

✔ WHY THIS RECIPE WORKS

Pan-roasting is a simple stovetop cooking method that delivers crisp, evenly browned asparagus without the fuss of having to rotate each spear individually. To help the asparagus release moisture, which encourages caramelization and better flavor, we parcook it, covered, with butter and oil before browning it. The water evaporating from the butter helps to steam the asparagus, producing bright green, crisp-tender spears that remain firm and juicy even when browned.

STEAM THEN BROWN We found that steaming before sautéing produces better results than just sautéing. That's because the raw asparagus is dry and waxy and the sugars necessary for the browning reaction are locked up inside the plant's tough cell walls. Cooking is required to release these sugars. Adding liquid and covering the pan for the first few minutes of cooking is a step in the right direction, but for better browning we simply use butter (which is 16 to 18 percent water, as opposed to olive oil, which is 100 percent fat) as the cooking medium. That small amount of water starts steaming the asparagus, which then begins to release its own moisture to help the process. A crowded pan also helps maximize the effect of the steam that is generated.

ARRANGE CAREFULLY We fit all of the asparagus spears into the pan with careful arrangement. A better fit and better browning are possible with half of the spears pointed in one direction and the other half pointed in the opposite direction. We found that tasters preferred the spears to be browned only on one side, and bright green on the other. Therefore, only the occasional toss is enough to ensure that all the spears become partially browned.

PRACTICAL SCIENCE STORING ASPARAGUS

The best way to store asparagus is trimmed, standing upright in a glass, with a bit of water, in the refrigerator.

To determine how to best maintain asparagus's bright color and crisp texture, we tested refrigerating spears in the plastic bag we'd bought them in, enclosed in a paper bag, wrapped in a damp paper towel, and with the stalk ends trimmed and standing up in a small amount of water. After three days the results were clear. Those left in the plastic bag had become slimy, while the paper bag and towel bunches had shriveled tips and limp stalks. However, the bunch stored in water looked as good as fresh and retained its firm texture. To store asparagus this way, trim the bottom ½ inch of the stalks and stand the spears upright in a glass. Add enough water to cover the bottom of the stalks by 1 inch and place the glass in the refrigerator. Asparagus stored this way should remain relatively fresh for about four days; you may need to add a little more water every few days. Retrim the very bottom of the stalks before using.

Don't Soak Beans–Brine 'Em

Dried beans defy most of the rules of cooking. For something so small, they sure do require a lot of cooking. And while the active work is minimal, it can be frustrating when a considerable investment of time yields subpar results. You want beans to be creamy, with soft skins. But often the skins are still tough despite hours of cooking. Or worse, the beans have exploded and formed a starchy mass. What to do?

HOW THE SCIENCE WORKS

Dried beans may not play a central role in the American diet, but they are among the most important foodstuffs on the planet because they are high in protein and fiber, inexpensive, and shelf-stable for years. Legumes (a group that includes dried peas and lentils as well as beans) are basically embryonic plants surrounded by hard seed coats. The seed coat is mostly carbohydrates and contains a significant amount of fiber. The seed itself is rich in protein and starch.

Eating dried beans requires planning and patience since they are best soaked overnight and then gently simmered for several hours. Gentle simmering allows the beans to absorb water gradually and keeps them from exploding. Rushing this process causes the starches to swell unevenly and the skins to burst. The starches can make beans sticky and gummy. Our solution to this problem is simple—we use the oven to cook most bean recipes. The heat is more evenly distributed than it is on the stovetop (see concept 1), so there's no risk of the beans on the bottom of the pot cooking too quickly. Also, it's much easier to maintain a gentle simmer in the oven; many stovetops run too hot, even on low.

We also have found that soaking the beans overnight starts the hydration process. As a result, soaked beans cook up faster than unsoaked beans (as much as 45 minutes faster), and, more important, they seem to absorb water more evenly so the end result is a creamier texture. A quick soak (covering the beans with boiling water for an hour) is better than nothing.

But even with soaking and gentle cooking, we find that beans still have trouble. Yes, their interiors are creamy but their skins are not. Soaking the beans in salted water (in effect, brining them) is the key to beans that cook up with tender skins. Why? As the beans soak, the sodium ions replace some of the calcium and magnesium ions in the skins. Because calcium and magnesium ions form links between pectin molecules, they are responsible for creating strong cells that are tightly bound together. When they are replaced by sodium ions, the pectin weakens, leading to a softer texture. During soaking, the sodium ions will filter only partway into the beans, so their greatest effect is on the cells in the outermost part of the beans.

When brined beans are cooked (preferably with a little salt), the result is tender skins. And, as we will see in the Test Kitchen Experiment, getting the skins to soften reduces the number of beans that explode during the cooking process, which is the key to beans that cook up creamy rather than starchy.

BRINING BEANS

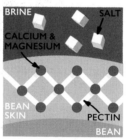

BEFORE BRINING *Before beans are brined, the strong pectin molecules in the beans' skin are tightly bound by calcium and magnesium ions.*

WHILE BRINING *When beans are brined, sodium replaces the calcium and magnesium ions, causing the gluelike pectin network to more readily break down, softening the skin and preventing exploding legumes.*

TEST KITCHEN EXPERIMENT

To determine the value of soaking—and cooking—beans in water seasoned with salt, we started with four 1-cup samples of dried black beans. We soaked two samples of beans for 24 hours in 2 quarts of cold water mixed with 1 ½ tablespoons of table salt. After draining and rinsing these beans, we cooked one sample in 5 cups of water mixed with ½ teaspoon of table salt, and the other in 5 cups of plain water. (To cook all samples, we first brought the beans and water to a simmer in a medium saucepan on the stovetop, and then baked them, with the cover on, in a 325-degree oven for one hour.) We soaked the other two samples for 24 hours in 2 quarts of cold water without any salt. We then cooked one sample in salted water and the other in unsalted water. After all of the beans were cooked, we compared the results. We repeated the test three times.

THE RESULTS

The beans that were brined for 24 hours and cooked in salted water remained completely intact and were the clear winners in a side-by-side comparison with the other three samples. The beans that were brined and cooked in

---

PRACTICAL SCIENCE
HARD WATER = HARD BEANS

Avoid cooking your beans in hard water. But if you have no choice, be sure to add salt.

How does the mineral content of water affect bean texture? To find out, we compared a batch of dried white beans soaked and cooked in mineral-free distilled water with a batch prepared with tap water containing dissolved minerals. The beans cooked in this hard tap water came out with tougher skins. This is because two of the minerals in tap water, magnesium and calcium, are enemies of beans. If given the chance, each will bind together pectin molecules in the cell walls of the bean skins, lending reinforcement that creates harder, tougher skins. But you don't need distilled water to prevent this; salt will do (see "How the Science Works").

---

unsalted water were largely intact, with a small percentage having skins that began to burst. In contrast, the two samples that were soaked in plain water, rather than brined, yielded far inferior results. Many of the beans that were soaked in plain water, and then cooked in salted water, burst in the process. And every single one of the beans that were soaked in plain water and then cooked in unsalted water burst while cooking. Yes, not a single bean in this last sample remained intact.

THE TAKEAWAY

While soaking beans in water can help to tenderize, allowing us to greatly reduce the cooking time, the skins of the beans can remain tough even after the legumes themselves are fully cooked. Beans with tough skins have a tendency to burst in the process of cooking, spilling their starchy innards into the pot and finishing with a sticky, unappealing texture. The answer? Salt.

Our test revealed that adding salt to the cooking water only helped to soften the skins a bit. Brining the beans for 24 hours did a much better job of giving us cooked beans with tender skins, ones that were more pliable and did not burst while cooking. And for maximum tenderness and the fewest burst beans, it's best to brine beans and then cook them with a little salt. During the brine and simmer, the sodium ions replace some of the calcium and magnesium ions (which are responsible for bonding with the pectin to keep the cells in bean skins strongly bound), causing the skins to soften considerably. For most recipes (including the ones found here) we recommend brining the beans ahead of time, and then cooking them with salt, or a salty ingredient such as pancetta, chicken broth, or Parmesan.

THE EFFECT OF SALT ON SKIN

BRINED, COOKED WITH SALT
Elastic skins remained intact.

BRINED, COOKED WITH NO SALT
Only a few skins broke.

SOAKED, COOKED WITH SALT
Many beans began to explode.

SOAKED, COOKED WITH NO SALT
With no salt all beans blew.

Recipes for bean dishes come from all over the world. We find that there is a common denominator, however: No matter the finished product, dried beans can be difficult to cook. To guarantee a finished dish with good texture and not too long a cooking time, we often soak our beans in salted water—a brine—overnight. This softens their skins, paving the way for a perfectly cooked batch of beans, whether the finished product is a stew, a soup, a salad, or a bowl of rice and beans.

HEARTY TUSCAN BEAN STEW
SERVES 8

We prefer the creamier texture of beans soaked overnight for this recipe. If you are pressed for time you can quick-soak your beans. In step 1, combine the salt, water, and beans in a Dutch oven and bring to a boil over high heat. Remove the pot from the heat, cover, and let stand for one hour. Drain and rinse the beans and proceed with step 2. If pancetta is unavailable, substitute four slices of bacon.

	Salt and pepper
1	pound dried cannellini beans (2½ cups), picked over and rinsed
1	tablespoon extra-virgin olive oil, plus extra for drizzling
6	ounces pancetta, cut into ¼-inch pieces
1	large onion, chopped
2	carrots, peeled and cut into ½-inch pieces
2	celery ribs, cut into ½-inch pieces
8	garlic cloves, peeled and crushed
4	cups low-sodium chicken broth
3	cups water
2	bay leaves
1	pound kale or collard greens, stemmed and chopped into 1-inch pieces
1	(14.5-ounce) can diced tomatoes, drained
1	sprig fresh rosemary
8	(1¼-inch-thick) slices rustic white bread, broiled until golden brown on both sides and rubbed with garlic clove (optional)

1. Dissolve 3 tablespoons salt in 4 quarts cold water in large bowl or container. Add beans and soak at room temperature for at least 8 hours or up to 24 hours. Drain and rinse well.

2. Adjust oven rack to lower-middle position and heat oven to 250 degrees. Heat oil and pancetta in Dutch oven over medium heat. Cook, stirring occasionally, until pancetta is lightly browned and fat has rendered, 6 to 10 minutes. Add onion, carrots, and celery and cook,

stirring occasionally, until vegetables are softened and lightly browned, 10 to 16 minutes. Stir in garlic and cook until fragrant, about 1 minute. Stir in broth, water, bay leaves, and soaked beans. Increase heat to high and bring to simmer. Cover pot, transfer to oven, and cook until beans are almost tender (very center of beans will still be firm), 45 minutes to 1 hour.

3. Remove pot from oven and stir in kale and tomatoes. Return pot to oven and continue to cook until beans and greens are fully tender, 30 to 40 minutes longer.

4. Remove pot from oven and submerge rosemary in stew. Cover and let stand for 15 minutes. Discard bay leaves and rosemary and season stew with salt and pepper to taste. If desired, use back of spoon to press some beans against side of pot to thicken stew. Serve over toasted bread, if desired, and drizzle with additional olive oil.

✔ WHY THIS RECIPE WORKS
We wanted to convert rustic Tuscan bean soup into a hearty stew. Determined to avoid tough, exploded beans in our stew, we soak the beans overnight in salted water to soften the skins. To complete our stew, we like other traditional Tuscan flavors, including pancetta, kale, lots of garlic, and a sprig of rosemary.

USE BROTH AND WATER While you could make this soup with all water (as Tuscans often do), we find a mix of chicken broth and water adds more richness to the finished stew.

GO SLOW AND STEADY The traditional version of this recipe is made by cooking the beans in a wine flask set in the dying embers of a fire overnight. Our low oven (250 degrees) replicates this gentle cooking method. Once everything is in the pot and brought to a simmer, we cover the pot and shove it into the oven for 1¼ to 1¾ hours. (Cooking time will vary depending on the exact variety and age of the beans.)

ADD GREENS AND TOMATOES LATER If added at the outset, the kale will become limp and gray. We add it late in the cooking process to preserve its color. We also wait to add the tomatoes because their acidity, which causes the pectin in beans to be less soluble, actually strengthens the cell walls, preventing the beans from softening.

STEEP AND DISCARD ROSEMARY We love the flavor of rosemary but it can quickly become medicinal. Rather than mincing the rosemary and adding it with the aromatic vegetables, we simply steep a sprig in the finished stew for 15 minutes—this infuses the broth with a delicate, not overpowering, herbal aroma. (For more on herbs, see concept 34.)

HEARTY MINESTRONE
SERVES 6 TO 8

If you are pressed for time you can quick-soak your beans. In step 1, combine the salt, water, and beans in a Dutch oven and bring to a boil over high heat. Remove the pot from the heat, cover, and let stand for one hour. Drain and rinse the beans and proceed with the recipe. Cannellini beans are our first choice for this soup, but navy or great Northern beans will also work. We prefer pancetta, but bacon can be used. To make this soup vegetarian, substitute vegetable broth for chicken broth and 2 teaspoons of olive oil for the pancetta. Parmesan rind is added for flavor but can be replaced with a 2-inch chunk of the cheese. In order for the starch from the beans to thicken the soup, it is important to maintain a vigorous simmer in step 3.

	Salt and pepper
8	ounces dried cannellini beans (1¼ cups), picked over and rinsed
3	ounces pancetta, cut into ¼-inch pieces
1	tablespoon extra-virgin olive oil, plus extra for serving
2	celery ribs, cut into ½-inch pieces
1	carrot, peeled and cut into ½-inch pieces
2	small onions, cut into ½-inch pieces
1	zucchini, cut into ½-inch pieces (1 cup)
½	small head green cabbage, halved, cored, and cut into ½-inch pieces (2 cups)
2	garlic cloves, minced
⅛–¼	teaspoon red pepper flakes
8	cups water
2	cups low-sodium chicken broth
1	Parmesan cheese rind plus grated Parmesan for serving
1	bay leaf
1½	cups V8 juice
½	cup chopped fresh basil

1. Dissolve 1½ tablespoons salt in 2 quarts cold water in large bowl or container. Add beans and soak at room temperature for at least 8 hours or up to 24 hours. Drain beans and rinse well.

2. Heat pancetta and oil in Dutch oven over medium-high heat. Cook, stirring occasionally, until pancetta is lightly browned and fat has rendered, 3 to 5 minutes. Add celery, carrot, onions, and zucchini and cook, stirring frequently, until vegetables are softened and lightly browned, 5 to 9 minutes. Stir in cabbage, garlic, ½ teaspoon salt, and pepper flakes to taste and continue to cook until cabbage

starts to wilt, 1 to 2 minutes longer. Transfer vegetables to rimmed baking sheet and set aside.

3. Add soaked beans, water, broth, Parmesan rind, and bay leaf to Dutch oven and bring to boil over high heat. Reduce heat and simmer vigorously, stirring occasionally, until beans are fully tender and liquid begins to thicken, 45 minutes to 1 hour.

4. Add reserved vegetables and V8 juice to pot and cook until vegetables are soft, about 15 minutes. Discard bay leaf and Parmesan rind, stir in basil, and season with salt and pepper to taste. Serve with additional oil and grated Parmesan. (Soup can be refrigerated for up to 2 days. Reheat it gently and add basil just before serving.)

☑ WHY THIS RECIPE WORKS
We wanted a minestrone with fresh, bright flavors that didn't have to rely on market-fresh vegetables like the best Italian versions. First, we begin with a manageable list of supermarket vegetables for our base. Slowly layering flavors, salt-soaking dried beans, and adding a surprising ingredient—vegetable juice—gives us a complex soup with a good, hearty texture.

BUILD THE FLAVOR BASE Our first step in building a soup with great flavor is to brown the vegetables to help them develop sweetness. First we sauté the zucchini and aromatics, and then add the cabbage and garlic and cook them just until the cabbage wilts and the garlic releases its aroma before adding the water and chicken broth.

RELEASE THE STARCH To give the soup some body we simmer the beans so that they release some of their starches and thicken the soup. Though their coats may look smooth and unbroken as they simmer, starches are continually being released into the water through a section of their seed coat called the hilum. These starches absorb the hot liquid and eventually burst, releasing the molecule amylose, which acts as a thickener.

REMOVE THE VEGGIES But simmering the beans vigorously turns the vegetables to mush. To keep the vegetables vibrant in this dish, we remove them from the pot after sautéing, and then add them back to the pot after the beans have simmered.

GIVE ME A V8 For the tomato element of this soup, we tried supermarket tomatoes, which did nothing for the flavor. We also tried canned products. These provided brighter flavor, but tasters dismissed the diced tomatoes as too thick and chunky and the crushed ones as only marginally better. Our solution? Tomato juice ensured consistent tomato flavor in every spoonful. But then we tried V8, which instantly boosts the vegetable factor and creates depth through an arsenal of vegetal flavors.

CUBAN BLACK BEANS AND RICE

SERVES 6 TO 8

It is important to use lean—not fatty—salt pork. If you can't find it, substitute six slices of bacon. If using bacon, decrease the cooking time in step 4 to eight minutes. You will need a Dutch oven with a tight-fitting lid for this recipe.

	Salt
1	cup dried black beans, picked over and rinsed
2	cups low-sodium chicken broth
2	cups water
2	large green bell peppers, stemmed, seeded, and halved
1	large onion, halved at equator and peeled, root end left intact
1	head garlic, 5 cloves minced, rest of head halved at equator with skin left intact
2	bay leaves
1½	cups long-grain white rice
2	tablespoons olive oil
6	ounces lean salt pork, cut into ¼-inch pieces
4	teaspoons ground cumin
1	tablespoon minced fresh oregano
2	tablespoons red wine vinegar
2	scallions, sliced thin
	Lime wedges

1. Dissolve 1½ tablespoons salt in 2 quarts cold water in large bowl or container. Add beans and soak at room temperature for at least 8 hours or up to 24 hours. Drain and rinse well.

2. In Dutch oven, stir together drained beans, broth, water, 1 bell pepper half, 1 onion half (with root end), halved garlic head, bay leaves, and 1 teaspoon salt. Bring to simmer over medium-high heat, cover, and reduce heat to low. Cook until beans are just soft, 30 to 35 minutes. Using tongs, remove and discard pepper, onion, garlic, and bay leaves. Drain beans in colander set over large bowl, reserving 2½ cups bean cooking liquid. (If you don't have enough bean cooking liquid, add water to equal 2½ cups.) Do not wash out Dutch oven.

3. Adjust oven rack to middle position and heat oven to 350 degrees. Place rice in large fine-mesh strainer and rinse under cold running water until water runs clear, about 1½ minutes. Shake strainer vigorously to remove all excess water; set rice aside. Cut remaining bell peppers and onion into 2-inch pieces and pulse in food processor until broken into rough ¼-inch pieces, about 8 pulses, scraping down bowl as necessary; set vegetables aside.

4. In now-empty Dutch oven, heat 1 tablespoon oil and salt pork over medium-low heat and cook, stirring frequently, until lightly browned and fat has rendered, 15 to 20 minutes. Add remaining 1 tablespoon oil, chopped peppers and onion, cumin, and oregano. Increase heat to medium and continue to cook, stirring frequently, until vegetables are softened and beginning to brown, 10 to 15 minutes longer. Add minced garlic and cook, stirring constantly, until fragrant, about 1 minute. Add rice and stir to coat, about 30 seconds.

5. Stir in beans, reserved bean cooking liquid, vinegar, and ½ teaspoon salt. Increase heat to medium-high and bring to simmer. Cover and transfer to oven. Cook until liquid is absorbed and rice is tender, about 30 minutes. Fluff with fork and let rest, uncovered, for 5 minutes. Serve, passing scallions and lime wedges separately.

VEGETARIAN CUBAN-STYLE BLACK BEANS AND RICE

Substitute water for chicken broth and omit salt pork. Add 1 tablespoon tomato paste with vegetables in step 4 and increase amount of salt in step 5 to 1½ teaspoons.

✓ WHY THIS RECIPE WORKS

Beans and rice is a familiar combination the world over, but Cuban black beans and rice is unique in that the rice is cooked in the inky concentrated liquid left over from cooking the beans, which lends the grains extra flavor. For our own superlative version, we brine our beans and reserve a portion of the sofrito (the traditional combination of garlic, bell pepper, and onion) to simmer with our beans and infuse them with flavor.

FLAVOR THE BEANS AS THEY COOK The traditional recipe has three parts—cook the beans, cook the sofrito, and then combine the sofrito and beans with the rice to finish cooking. Our version begins with brining the beans and then cooking them partway. A sofrito adds depth but we found we needed more. Our twofold solution: Adding some vegetables to the pot of beans as they cook and using a mixture of chicken broth and water gives flavor to the beans as well as to the cooking liquid (which is later used to cook the rice).

MAKE THE SOFRITO The sofrito is commonly pureed before adding it to the beans and rice mixture, but this muddies the texture and eliminates the possibility of browning the vegetables for flavor. Instead, we chop the onion and peppers small (or pulse them in a food processor). Then we sauté them with some cumin and oregano in the rendered fat from salt pork until they're golden brown and packed with flavor. This sofrito is the backbone of our black beans and rice.

PREVENT SCORCHED RICE Many recipes suffer from rice that is scorched on the bottom of the pan and undercooked on top. What to do? First, we remove excess starch from the rice by rinsing it in water (for more on this, see concept 30). This helps prevent the individual rice grains from clumping and becoming sticky. We then move the entire operation into the oven. The even heat from the oven helps to cook the rice perfectly from top to bottom.

BRIGHTEN FLAVORS When we put the pot in the oven (with the rice, beans, and liquid) we add a splash of red wine vinegar for brightness. We finish the dish with scallions and lime, which are important additions, because they really bring the flavors to life.

LENTIL SALAD WITH OLIVES, MINT, AND FETA
SERVES 4 TO 6

French green lentils, or lentilles du Puy, are our first choice for this recipe, but it works with any type of lentil except red or yellow. Brining helps keep the lentils intact, but if you don't have time, they'll still taste good without it. The salad can be served warm or at room temperature.

I	cup lentils, picked over and rinsed
	Salt and pepper
6	cups water
2	cups low-sodium chicken broth
5	garlic cloves, lightly crushed and peeled
I	bay leaf
5	tablespoons extra-virgin olive oil
3	tablespoons white wine vinegar
½	cup coarsely chopped pitted kalamata olives
½	cup minced fresh mint
I	large shallot, minced
I	ounce feta cheese, crumbled (¼ cup)

I. Place lentils and 1 teaspoon salt in bowl. Cover with 4 cups warm water (about 110 degrees) and soak for 1 hour. Drain well. (Drained lentils can be refrigerated for up to 2 days before cooking.)

2. Adjust oven rack to middle position and heat oven to 325 degrees. Place drained lentils, 2 cups water, broth,

garlic, bay leaf, and ½ teaspoon salt in medium saucepan. Cover and bake until lentils are tender but remain intact, 40 minutes to 1 hour. Meanwhile, whisk oil and vinegar together in large bowl.

3. Drain lentils well; remove and discard garlic and bay leaf. Add drained lentils, olives, mint, and shallot to dressing and toss to combine. Season with salt and pepper to taste. Transfer to serving dish, sprinkle with feta, and serve.

LENTIL SALAD WITH HAZELNUTS AND GOAT CHEESE

Substitute red wine vinegar for white wine vinegar and add 2 teaspoons Dijon mustard to dressing in step 2. Omit olives and substitute ¼ cup minced fresh parsley for mint. Substitute 2 ounces crumbled goat cheese for feta and sprinkle with ⅓ cup coarsely chopped toasted hazelnuts before serving.

✓ WHY THIS RECIPE WORKS
The most important step in making a lentil salad is perfecting the cooking of the lentils so they maintain their shape and firm-tender bite. Two things help. The first is to brine the lentils in warm salt water. With brining, the lentils' skins soften, which leads to fewer blowouts. The second step is to cook the lentils in the oven, which heats them gently and uniformly. Once we had perfectly cooked lentils, all we had left to do was to pair the earthy legumes with a tart vinaigrette and boldly flavored mix-ins.

BRINE FASTER We brine our lentils to soften their outer shells and make them less likely to burst. Given the smaller size of lentils (as opposed to beans), you don't need to brine them overnight. (In fact, most recipes don't even soak lentils. But soaking does help them to cook faster and yields creamier results.) We cut down on the time even more by brining our lentils in warm water (because heat speeds up all chemical reactions).

USE THE OVEN While cooking our lentils in the oven, rather than on the stove, increases the cooking time from 30 minutes to one hour, the results are worth the wait. With the gentle, even heat of the oven, the result is creamy lentils with intact skins.

MAKE A TART VINAIGRETTE For the finished salad, we toss our lentils with a tart vinaigrette—using less than a 2:1 ratio of oil to vinegar versus our usual dressing ratio of three or even four to one. We dress the lentils when warm and add in some vibrantly flavored mix-ins: feta, olives, and mint; or hazelnuts and goat cheese. These additions brighten and balance the rich, earthy flavor of the lentils.

Baking Soda Makes Beans and Grains Soft

One of the reasons why many people shy away from dried beans is that they just take so long to cook. We've seen how soaking and salting can reduce cooking time and yield better results. But that's not the only path toward faster, better beans. Creating an alkaline cooking environment with the introduction of baking soda can cut time in the kitchen as well.

HOW THE SCIENCE WORKS

Baking soda, or sodium bicarbonate, is most often used as a leavening agent for baked goods (see concept 42). But its role in the kitchen doesn't end there. When added to a pot of cooking beans, baking soda can do wonders—resulting in more tender legumes in significantly less time.

How? Baking soda is an alkali (also known as a "base"). And when added to a pot of boiling water and beans, it creates an alkaline environment. This environment causes a chemical reaction that actually forces the beans' pectin to break down into smaller water-soluble fragments. The breakdown of pectin causes the cell walls within the beans to weaken, allowing water to be absorbed at a faster rate. And this means that beans become tender and cook more quickly. But it's important to use baking soda sparingly, as too much can lend a bitter, soapy flavor to the beans.

In addition, baking soda can be used to set the color of black beans, preventing them from turning a grayish-purple color when cooked. The coating of black beans contains anthocyanins (colored pigments) that change color with alterations in pH: A more alkaline broth makes them darker; a more acidic broth makes them lighter. We've found that a very small amount of baking soda (a mere ⅛ teaspoon) added at the outset sets the color of the beans without producing any unpleasant aftertaste.

If you find yourself with a pot of beans that will not soften after the recommended cooking time—even with baking soda—your water may be the culprit. Mineral deposits in pots and green rings in porcelain sinks or tubs are signs of "hard water," or water rich with calcium, magnesium, and other ions, which can prevent beans from softening. As we learned in concept 28, calcium and magnesium ions are capable of bonding pectin molecules together, creating stronger cell walls. As a result, beans absorb water much more slowly.

Finally, the same science can be used to shorten the cooking time for grains like polenta, or cornmeal. The goal when cooking dried beans and dried corn is essentially the same. In a bean, water has to penetrate the hard outer skin (through a very specific region called the hilum) in order to gelatinize the starch within. In cornmeal, the water has to penetrate the cell walls within the endosperm, the starchy part of the kernel. Corn cells, like bean cells, contain a lot of pectin. So when the alkaline sodium bicarbonate is present, the pectin breaks down, weakening the corn's structure and allowing water to enter and gelatinize the starch in less than half the time.

WHEN BAKING SODA IS ADDED TO BEANS

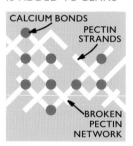

CALCIUM BONDS

PECTIN STRANDS

BROKEN PECTIN NETWORK

WITH SODA *Baking soda creates an alkaline environment when cooking beans (and grains), which causes the pectin strands to break down, weakening the cell walls. Weaker cell walls mean beans (and grains) cook quickly.*

TEST KITCHEN EXPERIMENT

To tease out the effects of pH when cooking legumes, we filled three pots, each with 5 cups of water. To one we added 1 percent baking soda by weight to turn it alkaline (about 8 on the pH scale) and to another we added enough citric acid to increase its acidity to 3. We left the third pot untreated so that it registered a neutral pH of 7. We stirred a cup of black beans into each pot, brought them all to a simmer, covered the pots, and put them in the same 350-degree oven to cook. We removed all three pots from the oven when the beans in the alkaline water had turned tender, or about 45 minutes. We repeated the test three times.

THE RESULTS

When the beans in the alkaline environment turned tender, the others were far behind. The beans in the plain water had only slightly softened after 45 minutes. We returned this pot to the oven and they required another 15 minutes of cooking time, an hour in total. Those in the acidic water were still rock-hard after 45 minutes. They required a total cooking time of one hour and 45 minutes to soften fully.

At the 45-minute mark, we removed some beans from each pot and placed them on the counter. We then applied a 5-pound weight on top. The beans cooked with baking soda were incredibly tender and squished down beautifully. The beans cooked in a neutral environment squished slightly but were still hard.

The beans cooked with acid were rock-hard; the weight barely made a difference.

THE TAKEAWAY

What was happening? It turns out that an alkaline environment starts a chemical reaction that causes the cell structure of legumes to break down. When we add baking soda to a pot of cooking beans, it results in tender beans in less time.

On the flip side, adding acid causes the cell structure of legumes to remain firm. If there is too much acid in the pot, the beans may never soften enough to be ready to eat. This means that you should be careful when cooking beans with acidic ingredients, especially tomatoes, citrus juices, and vinegar. We find it is best to add citrus juices and vinegars at the end of the cooking process—when the beans are already softened. (This also preserves the flavor of these acidic ingredients.) Tomatoes generally need some cooking time, so we often add tomatoes (including all canned tomato products) partway through the cooking process, after the beans have softened considerably.

The lesson? Along with brining and soaking (see concept 28), baking soda can work wonders on beans, saving you up to an hour of cooking time. Just be sure not to add more than a pinch—too much and the beans can end up tasting soapy and unpleasant.

EFFECTS OF 5-POUND WEIGHT ON COOKED BEANS

COOKED WITH ACID
After 45 minutes of cooking in water spiked with citric acid, these beans remained hard.

COOKED IN PLAIN WATER
At the 45-minute mark, these beans cooked in plain water had begun to soften but needed more time to fully cook.

COOKED WITH BAKING SODA
After 45 minutes of cooking in water spiked with a little baking soda, these beans were soft and tender.

Just a pinch of baking soda can cut the cooking time of beans and grains by as much as half. We add this alkaline ingredient to a diverse set of recipes—from baked beans to hummus, black bean soup to creamy polenta—to vastly reduce the hours spent in the kitchen. As long as you don't use too much baking soda, no one will guess the secret to these faster-cooking recipes.

BOSTON BAKED BEANS
SERVES 4 TO 6

Liquids evaporate faster in the oven in heavy cast-iron Dutch ovens than in lighter pots. If you're using a heavy pot, increase the water in step 2 to 4½ cups.

1	pound dried navy beans (about 2½ cups), picked over and rinsed
1	tablespoon baking soda
6	ounces salt pork, rind removed, cut into ¼-inch pieces
1	onion, chopped fine
3	cups water
5	tablespoons packed dark brown sugar
5	tablespoons molasses
2	tablespoons Worcestershire sauce
4	teaspoons Dijon mustard
2	teaspoons cider vinegar
	Salt and pepper

1. Adjust oven rack to middle position and heat oven to 350 degrees. Bring 3 quarts water, beans, and baking soda to boil in Dutch oven over high heat. Reduce heat to medium-high and simmer briskly for 20 minutes. Drain beans in colander. Rinse beans and pot.

2. Cook salt pork in now-empty pot over medium heat, stirring occasionally, until browned, about 10 minutes. Add onion and cook until softened, about 5 minutes. Stir in water, beans, sugar, ¼ cup molasses, Worcestershire, 1 tablespoon mustard, vinegar, and ¼ teaspoon pepper and bring to boil. Cover, transfer to oven, and cook until beans are nearly tender, about 1½ hours.

3. Remove lid and continue to bake until beans are completely tender, about 30 minutes longer. Stir in remaining 1 tablespoon molasses and remaining 1 teaspoon mustard. Season with salt and pepper to taste. Serve. (Beans can be refrigerated for up to 4 days.)

✔ WHY THIS RECIPE WORKS

We love authentic Boston baked beans but don't always have the five to six hours they require. To get the same creamy texture fast, we first simmer dried beans with a little baking soda. The soda jump-starts their softening, allowing us to shave the baking time down to two hours. We boost the flavor with well-browned salt pork, rich dark brown sugar, and beefy Worcestershire; a little Dijon mustard and cider vinegar add the requisite tang.

COOK SLOW AND LOW, BUT FAST Authentic Boston baked beans are not about fancy seasonings; they are about developing intense flavor by means of the judicious employment of canonical ingredients (beans, pork, molasses, mustard, and sometimes onion) and a slow, five-hour cooking time. We found that briskly simmering the beans in water, draining them, and then using them to make baked beans is faster than the traditional method that simply cooks dried beans with all the other ingredients at a very gentle simmer. Just boiling them for 45 minutes saves several hours of baking time. But adding a little baking soda to the water cuts the boiling time for the beans down to 20 minutes. The alkaline soda breaks down the pectin in the cell walls of the skin, allowing our beans to become tender in record time. We use a lot of soda here (more

---

PRACTICAL SCIENCE
HOW TO ELIMINATE GAS FROM BEANS

Precooked, quick-soaked beans produce the least amount of gas.

For some, the greatest obstacle to preparing beans is not the lack of a good recipe but an aversion to the discomfort associated with digestion. The creation of unwanted intestinal gas begins with the arrival of small chains of carbohydrates (called oligosaccharides) into the large intestine. People cannot digest these molecules efficiently, but bacteria residing at the end of the gut do, and they produce gas as a byproduct. Some sources say that presoaking or precooking beans alleviates gas production by removing these carbohydrates. We decided to put these theories to the test by measuring the amount of one of the most prevalent small carbohydrates in black beans, stachyose.

Our results gave the theories some credence. Beans soaked overnight in water and then cooked and drained showed a 28 percent reduction in stachyose. The quick-soak method, pouring boiling water over dried beans and soaking them for an hour, was more effective, removing 42.5 percent of the stachyose once these beans were cooked. Though these results were encouraging, we thought we could do better. We tried several recommended ingredients that are purported to "neutralize" the offending compounds as beans cook: epazote, kombu (giant kelp), bay leaves, and baking soda. None of these seemed to do much in the pot, though it is possible that they act only during digestion.

Our conclusion: Though the quick-soak method can produce more broken beans in the finished dish, if beans cause you significant discomfort, this approach was the most effective at reducing the amount of the offending compounds.

than in other bean recipes), but most of it is washed down the drain with the simmering liquid. After the partially cooked beans are rinsed to remove any remaining traces of soda, they're ready to be baked with the other ingredients.

ADD POTENT SEASONINGS The combination of dark brown sugar, molasses, Worcestershire, Dijon (which is better than the usual brown mustard), cider vinegar, and pepper gives our beans their characteristic rich flavor. Because the beans have been precooked and thus are already partially softened, it's OK to add acidic ingredients at the outset of the baking time.

UNCOVER AND FINISH We remove the lid from the pot for the final 30 minutes of cooking. This helps to thicken up the consistency of our "sauce." We finish the beans with an additional tablespoon of molasses and a teaspoon of mustard to reinforce these flavors.

ULTIMATE HUMMUS
MAKES ABOUT 2 CUPS

It's possible to use canned beans instead of dried beans for this recipe. Replace the dried chickpeas with one 15-ounce can of chickpeas, rinsed. (If using canned chickpeas, we recommend Pastene.) Exchange the cooking liquid for tap water.

½ cup dried chickpeas, picked over and rinsed
⅛ teaspoon baking soda
3 tablespoons lemon juice
6 tablespoons tahini
2 tablespoons extra-virgin olive oil, plus extra
   for drizzling
1 small garlic clove, minced
½ teaspoon salt
¼ teaspoon ground cumin
   Pinch cayenne pepper
1 tablespoon minced fresh cilantro or parsley

1. Place beans in large bowl, cover with 1 quart water, and soak overnight. Drain. Bring 1 quart water, beans, and baking soda to boil in large saucepan over high heat. Reduce heat to low and simmer gently, stirring occasionally, until beans are tender, about 1 hour. Drain, reserving ¼ cup bean cooking water, and cool.

2. Combine cooking water and lemon juice in small bowl or measuring cup. Whisk together tahini and 2 tablespoons oil in second small bowl. Set aside 2 tablespoons chickpeas for garnish.

3. Process remaining chickpeas, garlic, salt, cumin, and cayenne in food processor until almost fully ground, about 15 seconds. Scrape down bowl with rubber spatula. With processor running, add lemon juice mixture in steady stream. Scrape down bowl and continue to process for 1 minute. With processor running, add tahini mixture in steady stream; continue to process until hummus is smooth and creamy, about 15 seconds, scraping down bowl as needed.

4. Transfer hummus to serving bowl, sprinkle reserved chickpeas and cilantro over surface, cover with plastic wrap, and let stand until flavors meld, at least 30 minutes. Drizzle with extra olive oil and serve. (Hummus can be refrigerated for up to 5 days; refrigerate garnishes separately. When ready to serve, stir in approximately 1 tablespoon warm water if texture is too thick.)

✓ WHY THIS RECIPE WORKS
We wanted hummus with a light, silky-smooth texture and balanced flavor profile. In theory, the best way to guarantee a creamy texture is to remove the chickpeas' tough skins, but we couldn't find an approach that wasn't tedious or futile. The food processor, while it couldn't remove all the graininess when we pureed the chickpeas alone, did produce the desired texture when we used it to make an emulsion (much like a mayonnaise). Earthy cumin, a pinch of cayenne, lemon juice, and garlic keep the flavors in balance.

SOAK AND SODA You want chickpeas to break down completely and you want this to happen quickly. Soaking the beans and then gently simmering them is the best cooking method. Adding a little baking soda ensures that they break down when pureed—no tough skins here.

MAXIMIZE SMOOTHNESS Grind the cooked chickpeas with garlic, salt, and spices, and then add lemon juice and water. This two-step process, along with adding the water mixture slowly, produces a smoother puree than just dumping everything into the food processor at once.

EMULSIFY To keep the oil and water together, we found it best to mix the olive oil and tahini together and then drizzle them into the chickpea puree. We add the oil slowly so that it doesn't break, using the same principles as for making a vinaigrette (see concept 36).

ADD MORE TAHINI Tahini is a thick paste made from ground sesame seeds. We use a hefty 6 tablespoons, three times the amount usually found in other recipes. It turns out that different brands vary significantly in fat content as well as flavor, with some carrying bitter off-tastes. Tasters appreciated the nutty flavor and silken texture that a good tahini lent to the dip. We prefer Joyva Sesame Tahini and Krinos Tahini.

BLACK BEAN SOUP
SERVES 6

Dried beans tend to cook unevenly, so be sure to taste several beans to determine their doneness in step 1. For efficiency, you can prepare the soup ingredients while the beans simmer and the garnishes while the soup simmers. Though you do not need to offer all of the garnishes listed below, do choose at least a couple; garnishes are essential for this soup, as they add not only flavor but texture and color as well.

BEANS

5	cups water, plus extra as needed
1	pound dried black beans (2½ cups), picked over and rinsed
4	ounces ham steak, trimmed
2	bay leaves
⅛	teaspoon baking soda
1	teaspoon salt

SOUP

3	tablespoons olive oil
2	large onions, chopped fine
1	large carrot, peeled and chopped fine
3	celery ribs, chopped fine
½	teaspoon salt
5–6	garlic cloves, minced
½	teaspoon red pepper flakes
1½	tablespoons ground cumin
6	cups low-sodium chicken broth
2	tablespoons cornstarch
2	tablespoons water
2	tablespoons lime juice

GARNISHES

Lime wedges
Minced fresh cilantro
Red onion, diced fine
Avocado, halved, pitted, and diced
Sour cream

1. FOR THE BEANS: Place 4 quarts cold water in large bowl or container. Add beans and soak at room temperature for at least 8 hours or up to 24 hours. Drain and rinse well.

2. Place 5 cups water, soaked beans, ham, bay leaves, and baking soda in large saucepan with tight-fitting lid. Bring to boil over medium-high heat. Using large spoon, skim foam from surface as needed. Stir in salt, reduce heat to low, cover, and simmer briskly until beans are tender, 1 to 1½ hours (if after 1½ hours beans are not tender, add 1 cup more water and continue to simmer until tender); do not drain beans. Discard bay leaves. Remove ham steak, cut into ¼-inch cubes, and set aside.

3. FOR THE SOUP: Heat oil in Dutch oven over medium-high heat until shimmering. Add onions, carrot, celery, and salt and cook, stirring occasionally, until vegetables are soft and lightly browned, 12 to 15 minutes. Reduce heat to medium-low, add garlic, pepper flakes, and cumin, and cook, stirring constantly, until fragrant, about 3 minutes. Stir in beans, bean cooking liquid, and chicken broth. Increase heat to medium-high and bring to boil, then reduce heat to low and simmer, uncovered, stirring occasionally, to blend flavors, about 30 minutes.

4. Ladle 1½ cups beans and 2 cups liquid into food processor or blender, process until smooth, and return to pot. Stir cornstarch and water in small bowl until combined, then gradually stir half of cornstarch mixture into soup. Bring to boil over medium-high heat, stirring occasionally, to fully thicken. If soup is still thinner than desired once boiling, stir remaining cornstarch mixture to recombine and gradually stir mixture into soup; return to boil to fully thicken. Off heat, stir in lime juice and reserved ham; ladle soup into bowls and serve immediately, passing garnishes separately. (Soup can be refrigerated for up to 4 days. If necessary, thin it with additional chicken broth when reheating.)

PRACTICAL SCIENCE
GETTING THE BEST FROM CANNED BEANS

Simmer canned beans in soups for the best results.

Dried beans are always our first choice in soups because they soak up the flavor of the broth so readily. But if you're going to use canned beans in soups, don't shortchange their cooking time. Even though canned beans are fully cooked, we found that beans simmered for 30 minutes in Tuscan white bean soup as well as black bean soup tasted much better than beans simmered for just five minutes in these dishes.

In a recipe that calls for one pound of dried beans, substitute 58 ounces of canned beans. Make sure to drain and rinse the beans well and be prepared to radically reduce the amount of liquid. A long simmer gives canned beans time to pick up flavors from the broth, but they aren't going to absorb nearly as much liquid as dried beans.

BLACK BEAN SOUP WITH CHIPOTLE CHILES

The addition of chipotle chile in adobo—smoked jalapeños packed in a seasoned tomato-vinegar sauce—makes this a spicier, smokier variation on Black Bean Soup.

Omit pepper flakes and add 1 tablespoon minced canned chipotle chile in adobo sauce plus 2 teaspoons adobo sauce along with chicken broth in step 2.

✔ WHY THIS RECIPE WORKS

For a black bean soup recipe full of sweet, spicy, smoky flavors, we went with dried beans, which release flavor into the broth as they cook, unlike canned beans. Adding baking soda to the pot as the beans cooked saved time. We found that we didn't need from-scratch stock; we maximized flavor by using a mixture of store-bought chicken broth and the bean cooking water flavored with ham and bay leaves.

MAKE IT SMOOTH AND BLACK When making black bean soup, you want the beans to break down so that a portion of the soup can be pureed. So getting the beans fully cooked is important. And when you puree the beans, you don't want them to lose their black color; the resulting soup would be an unattractive purple-gray. The alkaline baking soda solves both problems. Soaking the beans reduces the cooking time. Because the beans are cooked until they break down, there's no benefit to brining them.

PICK HAM STEAK Cooking the beans with a ham hock (and bay leaves) is traditional, but we wanted more meat for the soup. We tested salt pork, slab bacon, and ham steak and liked the latter best. It adds smoky pork flavor to the beans and broth, and the meat can be reserved, diced, and stirred into the soup just before serving.

USE A SOFRITO A flavorful black bean soup needs a base of sautéed aromatic vegetables. We like garlic, cumin, and red pepper flakes along with the usual onion, celery, and carrot.

PUREE SOME OF THE BEANS To get a soup with some body, we puree only part of the soup—this way it's smooth and chunky at the same time. Beans absorb water differently and different stoves cook at different rates; to get the texture just right we found it best to adjust the soup at the end with a cornstarch slurry. Make sure to disperse the cornstarch in cold water. Hot water will immediately wet the surface of the starch granules, causing them to stick together before they can disperse, and the clusters of granules that stick together will remain dry in the center.

FINISH WITH LIME AND GARNISH Without an array of colorful garnishes, even the best black bean soup might be dull. Sour cream and diced avocado offset the soup's heat, while red onion and minced cilantro contribute freshness and color. Finally, wedges of lime accentuate the bright flavor of the juice that's already in the soup.

CREAMY PARMESAN POLENTA
SERVES 4

Coarse-ground degerminated cornmeal such as yellow grits (with grains the size of couscous) works best in this recipe. Avoid instant and quick-cooking products, as well as whole-grain, stone-ground, and regular cornmeal. Do not omit the baking soda—it reduces the cooking time and makes for a creamier polenta. If the polenta bubbles or sputters even slightly after the first 10 minutes, the heat is too high and you may need a flame tamer. For a main course, serve the polenta with a topping (recipes follow) or with a wedge of rich cheese (like Gorgonzola) or a meat sauce.

7½   cups water
     Salt and pepper
     Pinch baking soda
1½   cups coarse-ground cornmeal
4   ounces Parmesan cheese, grated (2 cups),
     plus extra for serving
2   tablespoons unsalted butter

1. Bring water to boil in large saucepan over medium-high heat. Stir in 1½ teaspoons salt and baking soda. Slowly pour cornmeal into water in steady stream, while stirring back and forth with wooden spoon or rubber spatula. Bring mixture to boil, stirring constantly, about 1 minute. Reduce heat to lowest possible setting and cover.

2. After 5 minutes, whisk polenta to smooth out any lumps that may have formed, about 15 seconds. (Make sure to scrape down sides and bottom of pan.) Cover and continue to cook, without stirring, until grains of polenta are tender but slightly al dente, about 25 minutes longer. (Polenta should be loose and barely hold its shape but will continue to thicken as it cools.)

3. Remove from heat, stir in Parmesan and butter, and season with pepper to taste. Let stand, covered, for 5 minutes. Serve, passing extra Parmesan separately.

WILD MUSHROOM AND ROSEMARY TOPPING
MAKES ENOUGH FOR 1 RECIPE CREAMY PARMESAN POLENTA

If you use shiitake mushrooms, they should be stemmed.

2   tablespoons unsalted butter
2   tablespoons olive oil
1   small onion, chopped fine
2   garlic cloves, minced
2   teaspoons minced fresh rosemary
1   pound wild mushrooms (such as cremini,
     shiitake, or oyster), trimmed and sliced
⅓   cup low-sodium chicken broth
     Salt and pepper

1. Heat butter and oil in 12-inch nonstick skillet over medium-high heat until shimmering. Add onion and cook, stirring frequently, until onion softens and begins to brown, 5 to 7 minutes. Stir in garlic and rosemary and cook until fragrant, about 30 seconds longer.

2. Add mushrooms and cook, stirring occasionally, until juices release, about 6 minutes. Add broth and salt and pepper to taste; simmer briskly until sauce thickens, about 8 minutes. Spoon mushroom mixture over individual portions of polenta and serve.

SAUTÉED CHERRY TOMATO AND FRESH MOZZARELLA TOPPING
MAKES ENOUGH FOR 1 RECIPE CREAMY PARMESAN POLENTA

Don't stir the cheese into the sautéed tomatoes or it will melt prematurely and turn rubbery.

3   tablespoons extra-virgin olive oil
2   garlic cloves, peeled and sliced thin
     Pinch red pepper flakes
     Pinch sugar
1½   pounds cherry tomatoes, halved
     Salt and pepper
6   ounces fresh mozzarella cheese, cut into
     ½-inch cubes (1 cup)
2   tablespoons shredded fresh basil

Heat oil, garlic, pepper flakes, and sugar in 12-inch nonstick skillet over medium-high heat until fragrant and sizzling, about 1 minute. Stir in tomatoes and cook until they just begin to soften, about 1 minute. Season with salt and pepper to taste and remove from heat. Spoon tomato mixture over individual portions of polenta, top with mozzarella, sprinkle with basil, and serve.

BROCCOLI RABE, SUN-DRIED TOMATO, AND PINE NUT TOPPING
MAKES ENOUGH FOR 1 RECIPE CREAMY PARMESAN POLENTA

½   cup oil-packed sun-dried tomatoes, chopped coarse
3   tablespoons extra-virgin olive oil
6   garlic cloves, minced
½   teaspoon red pepper flakes
     Salt
1   pound broccoli rabe, trimmed and cut into
     1½-inch pieces
¼   cup low-sodium chicken broth
3   tablespoons pine nuts, toasted

Heat sun-dried tomatoes, oil, garlic, pepper flakes, and ½ teaspoon salt in 12-inch nonstick skillet over medium-high heat, stirring frequently, until garlic is fragrant and slightly toasted, about 1½ minutes. Add broccoli rabe and broth, cover, and cook until rabe turns bright green, about 2 minutes. Uncover and cook, stirring frequently, until most of broth has evaporated and rabe is just tender, 2 to 3 minutes. Season with salt to taste. Spoon broccoli rabe mixture over individual portions of polenta, sprinkle with pine nuts, and serve.

✔ WHY THIS RECIPE WORKS

If you don't stir polenta almost constantly, it forms intractable lumps. Is there a way to get creamy, smooth polenta with rich corn flavor, but without the fussy process? Taking a cue from dried bean recipes, which use baking soda to help break down the tough bean skins and accelerate cooking, we added a pinch to our polenta. The baking soda helped soften the cornmeal's cell walls within the endosperm, which cut the cooking time in half and eliminated the need for stirring.

ADD A PINCH OF SODA Because corn, like beans, contains pectin, baking soda can work its magic in much the same way. Just a pinch of baking soda greatly reduces the cooking time by helping to break down the pectin and allowing water to enter and gelatinize the starch with ease.

Be sure not to add too much baking soda—it can turn the polenta gluey and lend it a strange, toasted, chemical flavor. Just a pinch is all that is needed to start the breakdown of pectin. Once the reaction starts it is self-perpetuating, like a string of dominos.

USE THE LID Since we're not fans of being chained to the kitchen stove, stirring a pot of polenta constantly for up to an hour, our goal was to cut down on the amount of stirring in our polenta recipe. We stumbled upon the answer when in the midst of cooking one day we were called away from the kitchen. We threw a lid on the polenta and turned the flame down to low. When we returned a half-hour later, we didn't find a clumpy, burnt-on-the-bottom mess as we feared. Instead we discovered a perfectly creamy polenta. The low-heat, covered method had cooked the polenta so gently and evenly that the result was lump-free, even without vigorous stirring. We found that one stir right after the cornmeal goes in and another five minutes later are all we need.

FINISH WITH CHEESE AND BUTTER A full 2 cups of Parmesan plus a pair of butter pats stirred in at the last minute give this humble mush enough nutty tang and richness to make it a satisfying dish, with or without a topping—and with the barest amount of effort.

PRACTICAL SCIENCE THE BEST CORNMEAL FOR POLENTA

We prefer coarse-ground, degerminated cornmeal for polenta.

In the supermarket, cornmeal can be labeled anything from yellow grits to corn semolina. Forget the names. When shopping for the right product to make polenta there are three things to consider: "instant" or "quick-cooking" versus the traditional style, degerminated or full-grain meal, and grind size. Instant and quick-cooking cornmeals are parcooked and comparatively bland—leave them on the shelf. Though we love the full-corn flavor of whole-grain cornmeal, it remains slightly gritty no matter how long you cook it. We prefer degerminated cornmeal, in which the hard hull and germ are removed from each kernel (check the back label or ingredient list to see if your cornmeal is degerminated; if it's not explicitly labeled as such, you can assume it's whole grain).

As for grind, we found coarser grains brought the most desirable and pillowy texture to our Creamy Parmesan Polenta. However, grind coarseness can vary dramatically from brand to brand since there are no standards to ensure consistency. One manufacturer's "coarse" may be another's "fine." Here's how to identify the optimal coarsely ground texture.

TOO FINE
The super-fine grains of quick-cooking cornmeal speed the cooking process but lack corn flavor.

STILL TOO FINE
Regular cornmeal (such as Quaker's) has a similarly sandlike texture that also cooks up gluey.

JUST RIGHT
A coarser cut, about the size of couscous, retains a soft but hearty texture after cooking.

Rinsing (Not Soaking) Makes Rice Fluffy

Cooking rice is easy, but cooking rice well isn't. Many competent cooks claim they can't cook rice at all. It scorches. It's mushy. The rice is sticky when they want it fluffy. Convenience products, like converted or instant rice, are supposed to take some of the guesswork out of the process, but their texture and flavor make them poor options. Once you understand how rice works, though, you will realize that cooking it well is not hard.

HOW THE SCIENCE WORKS

THE STRUCTURE OF A GRAIN OF RICE

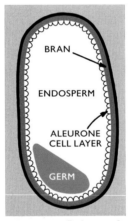

RICE GRAIN *Each grain of brown rice contains the outer bran and aleurone cell layer, which are removed when milling for white rice. All types of rice contain the endosperm.*

Rice is a seed from the plant known as *Oryza sativa*. When harvested, rice is covered by a protective husk. After the husk is removed, we're left with brown rice, which is composed of three parts: the bran (which encloses a layer of cells called the aleurone layer, which is rich in oil and enzymes), the germ, and the endosperm. For several thousand years, whole-grain rice has been parboiled and then milled in order to remove the bran and germ, leaving only the starchy endosperm. Parboiled, polished rice (known simply as white rice) is the most common form called for in recipes.

Like potatoes or pasta, the main challenge when cooking rice is figuring out how to control the starches. However, while potatoes or pasta are often cooked in lots of water to wash away excess starch, rice requires a more precise cooking method. If you boil and drain rice, you end up washing away its delicate flavor and the grains turn soggy and bloated. Rice is best cooked with a measured amount of liquid in a covered pot. The cover ensures that the liquid doesn't evaporate but instead eventually gets absorbed by the rice. (If too much water evaporates, the rice will burn before it becomes tender.)

Starch granules, which are the primary component of rice, tend not to absorb water when held at room temperature. As you heat rice in water, however, the energy from the rapidly moving water molecules begins to loosen the bonds between the starch molecules, allowing the water to seep in. This in turn causes the starch granules to swell and release some gummy starch molecules that then act like a glue to hold the grains together. The rice softens and becomes sticky, or "starchy."

Like potatoes (see concept 26), rice contains two kinds of starch molecules: amylose and amylopectin. The amount of amylose and the protein content of the starch granules determine the textural properties of the rice—from separate and fluffy to sticky and gummy—when it is cooked. Though there are exceptions, rice with higher amylose and protein content (like long-grain rice) cooks into grains that are separate, light, and fluffy. Rice with a lower amylose and protein content (like Arborio) cooks into grains that are moist and tender, with a greater tendency to cling together.

As a result of the differences in the amylose and protein content, the starch granules in long-grain rice swell and gelatinize at a much higher temperature (158 degrees) than the granules in medium-grain rice (144 degrees). Starch granules that gelatinize at a lower temperature release more amylose, even though they have a lower amylose content. The higher amount of released amylose causes the grains to cling together.

Long-grain rice contains about 22 percent amylose and 8.5 percent protein, and the grains are four to five times longer than they are wide. Long-grain rice needs the most water for cooking and, when cooked, remains as separate grains that harden as they cool (because of the higher amylose content). We prefer long-grain rice for dishes like pilaf.

Medium-grain rice contains about 18 percent amylose and 6.5 percent protein, and the grains are two to three times longer than they are wide. This rice needs a bit less water to cook than long-grain rice and cooks up tender and somewhat clingy. Medium-grain rices like Arborio are perfect for dishes like risotto, as they can be creamy but not sticky.

Short-grain contains about 15 percent amylose and 6 percent protein and the grains are almost round. This rice needs the least amount of water and can be quite sticky and tender when cooked. Short-grain rice is ideal for dishes like sushi, in which the grains need to stick together.

TEST KITCHEN EXPERIMENT

To determine the value of soaking rice in water before cooking, which is a technique purported to help rice cook faster and better, we devised a simple test: Some recipes call for soaking brown rice for three hours, so that's just what we did. We soaked one batch of brown rice, then cooked it according to our recipe (page 273), but with a slightly reduced amount of water. We made another batch of rice that had not been soaked (but was rinsed before cooking) using the same recipe with the correct amount of liquid. We repeated the test using long-grain white rice and basmati rice.

THE RESULTS
Every single variety of rice that had been soaked was overcooked and bloated, with grains that tended to blow out.

THE TAKEAWAY
To be frank, soaking was a waste of time. Even with brown rice, which, with its bran, germ, and aleurone layers intact, can take two to three times longer to cook than white rice, the results were overly tender and unpleasant. Soaking caused the rice to absorb too much water, which in turn caused the starch granules to swell as soon as the heat was applied.

Does that mean that there's no place for water in the world of rice preparation? Not necessarily. We find that the extra step of rinsing long-grain white or basmati rice in several changes of water is indispensable for a pilaf with distinct, separate grains. Rinsing washes away starches on the surface of these grains that helps them cook up lighter and fluffier. What about rinsing brown rice? Our tests showed no benefit (or harm). Because the bran is still intact, brown rice doesn't have starch on its exterior. So rinsing doesn't accomplish anything—except for wasting time and water.

SOAKING RICE CAN CAUSE BLOWOUTS WHEN COOKED

SOAKED	UNSOAKED AND RINSED
This bloated rice overcooked.	*This rice cooked perfectly.*

When making rice pilaf, we add just enough water so that when it is fully absorbed the rice is tender and perfectly cooked. A covered pot is essential here. Without a tight lid, the water will evaporate from the pot before being absorbed by the rice, and the rice will burn before it is fully cooked.

SIMPLE RICE PILAF
SERVES 6

You will need a saucepan with a tight-fitting lid for this recipe. You can substitute basmati rice for the long-grain white rice.

- 2 cups long-grain white rice
- 3 tablespoons unsalted butter or vegetable oil
- 1 small onion, chopped fine
- 3 cups water
- 1 teaspoon salt
-    Pepper

1. Place rice in colander or fine-mesh strainer and rinse under cold running water until water runs clear. Place strainer over bowl and set aside.

2. Melt butter in large saucepan over medium heat. Add onion and cook until softened but not browned, about 4 minutes. Add rice and cook, stirring constantly, until grains become chalky and opaque, 1 to 3 minutes. Add water, salt, and pepper to taste, increase heat to high, and bring to boil, swirling pot to blend ingredients. Reduce heat to low, cover, and simmer until all liquid is absorbed, 18 to 20 minutes. Off heat, remove lid and place kitchen towel folded in half over saucepan; replace lid. Let stand for 10 to 15 minutes. Fluff rice with fork and serve.

RICE PILAF WITH CURRANTS AND PINE NUTS

Add 2 minced garlic cloves, ½ teaspoon ground turmeric, and ¼ teaspoon ground cinnamon to softened onion and cook until fragrant, about 30 seconds. When rice is off heat, before covering saucepan with towel, sprinkle ¼ cup currants over top of rice (do not mix in). When fluffing rice with fork, toss in ¼ cup toasted pine nuts.

WHY THIS RECIPE WORKS

Rice pilaf should be fragrant and fluffy, perfectly steamed, and tender. While recipes for rice pilaf abound, none seem to agree on the best method for guaranteeing these results; many espouse rinsing the rice and soaking it overnight, but we wondered if this was really necessary for a simple rice dish. For the best pilaf, we start with long-grain white rice (though basmati rice is even better if you have it on hand). We find that an overnight soak isn't necessary (see Test Kitchen Experiment, page 271), but rinsing the rice before cooking gives us beautifully separated grains. Sautéing the rice in butter for just a minute gives our pilaf great flavor.

THE RIGHT RICE Pilaf should be light and fluffy so you want to use long-grain rice. Long-grain white rice is neutral in flavor, providing a backdrop for other foods. Nonetheless, higher-quality white rice offers a pleasingly chewy al dente texture and a slightly buttery natural flavor of its own. The buttery notes are caused by a naturally occurring flavor compound, 2-acetyl-1-pyrroline, and higher levels lend an almost popcornlike taste. Basmati rice, which can be used instead of long-grain white rice, is prized for its nutty flavor and sweet aroma. Indian basmati, unlike American-grown basmati, is aged for a minimum of a year, though often much longer, before being packaged. Aging dehydrates the rice, which translates into grains that, once cooked, expand greatly, and more so than any other long-grain rice. American-grown basmati is not aged and hence doesn't expand as much as Indian-grown rice. When shopping, make sure that the label indicates that the basmati rice has been aged. The only "bad" choice of rice for this recipe is converted rice, which is steam-treated before packaging. This gelatinizes the starch in the center of the grain and removes some of the starch from the rice exterior, making the rice less likely to become starchy or sticky when cooked. The result is "bouncy" rice, with an assertive flavor our tasters don't like.

USE LESS WATER The conventional ratio of 2 parts water to 1 part rice makes rice too sticky and soft. We find the right ratio to be 3 parts water to 2 parts rice, which also takes into account the effects of rinsing the rice before cooking.

SAUTÉ THE RICE Sautéing the rice in butter develops the nutty notes in the rice and helps the individual grains to maintain their integrity. Also this step gives us the chance to sauté an onion (or another flavorful ingredient) first.

BRING TO A BOIL, REDUCE HEAT Once the rice looks translucent around the edges, add the water and salt, bring to a boil, reduce the heat to the lowest setting, and cover the pot. The rice should be tender (and with all the water absorbed) after 18 to 20 minutes.

STEAM OFF THE HEAT After boiling, the rice will be a bit heavy. To lighten it up, we slide a towel under the lid and let the pot sit off the heat for 10 to 15 minutes. The towel absorbs some of the moisture in the pot and helps produce rice that is nice and fluffy. Just fluff with a fork (to separate the grains) and serve.

For slow-cooking rice dishes, even a tight cover might not solve all the problems. You need to even out the cooking of the rice so the bottom won't scorch. Moving the operation to the oven does this.

BROWN RICE
SERVES 4 TO 6

To minimize any loss of water through evaporation, cover the saucepan and use the water as soon as it reaches a boil. An 8-inch ceramic baking dish with a lid may be used instead of the baking dish and aluminum foil. To double the recipe, use a 13 by 9-inch baking dish; the baking time does not need to be increased.

1½	cups long-grain, medium-grain, or short-grain brown rice
2⅓	cups water
2	teaspoons unsalted butter or vegetable oil
½	teaspoon salt

1. Adjust oven rack to middle position and heat oven to 375 degrees. Spread rice in 8-inch square baking dish.

2. Bring water and butter to boil, covered, in medium saucepan. Once boiling, immediately stir in salt and pour water over rice in baking dish. Cover baking dish tightly with 2 layers of aluminum foil. Transfer baking dish to oven and bake rice until tender, about 1 hour.

3. Remove baking dish from oven and uncover. Fluff rice with fork, then cover dish with kitchen towel and let rice stand for 5 minutes. Uncover and let rice stand for 5 minutes longer. Serve immediately.

CURRIED BAKED BROWN RICE WITH TOMATOES AND PEAS

Increase butter to 2 tablespoons and melt in 10-inch non-stick skillet over medium heat. Add 1 minced small onion and cook until translucent, about 3 minutes. Add 1 minced garlic clove, 1 tablespoon grated fresh ginger, 1½ teaspoons curry powder, and ¼ teaspoon salt and cook until fragrant, about 1 minute. Add one 14.5-ounce can drained diced tomatoes and cook until heated through, about 2 minutes. Set aside. Substitute vegetable broth for water and reduce amount of salt to ⅛ teaspoon. After pouring broth over rice, stir tomato mixture into rice and spread rice and tomato mixture into even layer. Bake as directed, increasing baking time to 70 minutes. Before covering baking dish with kitchen towel, stir in ½ cup thawed frozen peas.

BAKED BROWN RICE WITH PARMESAN, LEMON, AND HERBS

Increase butter to 2 tablespoons and melt in 10-inch nonstick skillet over medium heat. Add 1 minced small onion and cook until translucent, about 3 minutes; set aside. Substitute low-sodium chicken broth for water and reduce salt to ⅛ teaspoon. Stir onion mixture into rice after adding broth. Cover and bake rice as directed. After removing foil, stir in ½ cup grated Parmesan, ¼ cup minced fresh parsley, ¼ cup chopped fresh basil, 1 teaspoon grated lemon zest, ½ teaspoon lemon juice, and ⅛ teaspoon pepper. Cover dish with kitchen towel and proceed as directed.

BAKED BROWN RICE WITH SAUTÉED MUSHROOMS AND LEEKS

Substitute low-sodium chicken broth for water and reduce amount of salt to ⅛ teaspoon; bake as directed. When rice has about 10 minutes baking time remaining, melt 1 tablespoon unsalted butter with 1 tablespoon olive oil in 12-inch nonstick skillet over medium-high heat. Add 1 leek, white part only, sliced into ¼-inch-thick rings, and cook, stirring occasionally, until wilted, about 2 minutes. Add 6 ounces cremini mushrooms, trimmed and sliced ¼ inch thick, and ¼ teaspoon salt and cook, stirring occasionally, until moisture has evaporated and mushrooms are browned, about 8 minutes. Stir in 1½ teaspoons minced fresh thyme and ⅛ teaspoon pepper. After removing kitchen towel, stir in mushroom-leek mixture and 1½ teaspoons sherry vinegar; serve immediately.

✓ WHY THIS RECIPE WORKS

Brown rice should have a nutty, gutsy flavor and more textural personality—slightly sticky and just a bit more chewy—than white rice. To achieve this ideal, we stayed close to the water-to-rice ratio established in our Simple Rice Pilaf (page 272), settling on 2⅓ cups water to 1½ cups rice. But unlike our white rice method, here we cooked the rice in the oven to approximate the controlled, indirect heat of a rice cooker. A couple of teaspoons of butter or oil added to the cooking water added mild flavor while allowing the earthy, nutty flavor of the rice to take center stage.

MOVE IT TO THE OVEN Brown rice doesn't require more water (just an extra tablespoon compared to white rice) but it does need a lot more time to soften. Brown rice is a whole-grain rice with the hull intact (white rice has had this hull removed). This hull is the reason it takes just about twice as long to cook brown rice as white rice. Moving the cooking to the oven allows the rice to be cooked more gently and evenly, reducing the risk of the bottom layer of rice burning, which frequently happens if brown rice is cooked on the stovetop.

USE LESS WATER Most recipes for brown rice cooked on the stovetop prevent scorching by upping the amount of water (usually to a 2:1 ratio). But this can result in very soggy, overcooked rice. We find that using less water (and then trapping the moisture in a covered baking dish) yields a much better product. Boiling water before adding it to the rice (instead of using cold tap water) keeps the oven time to one hour. A tight seal on the baking dish is paramount—this is why we use the two layers of foil.

ADD A LITTLE FAT AND SALT Make sure to season the rice before it goes into the oven. A little bit of added fat gives mild flavor while keeping the rice fluffy.

FLUFF AND LET REST After the rice comes out of the oven, fluff the rice in order to separate the grains, and then cover the dish with a clean towel to absorb some moisture.

MEXICAN RICE
SERVES 6 TO 8

Because the spiciness of jalapeños varies from chile to chile, we try to control the heat by removing the ribs and seeds (the source of most of the heat) from those chiles that are cooked in the rice. It is important to use an ovensafe pot about 12 inches in diameter so that the rice cooks evenly and in the time indicated. The pot's depth is less important than its diameter; we've successfully used both a straight-sided sauté pan and a Dutch oven. Whichever type of pot you use, it should have a tight-fitting, ovensafe lid. Vegetable broth can be substituted for the chicken broth.

2	tomatoes, cored and quartered
1	white onion, peeled and quartered
3	jalapeño chiles, 2 stemmed, seeded, and minced, 1 stemmed and minced
2	cups long-grain white rice
⅓	cup vegetable oil
4	garlic cloves, minced
2	cups low-sodium chicken broth
1	tablespoon tomato paste
1½	teaspoons salt
½	cup minced fresh cilantro
	Lime wedges

PRACTICAL SCIENCE SEEDING HOT CHILES

A melon baller can be effective when seeding jalapeños.

Using a knife to remove the seeds and ribs from a hot chile pepper takes a very steady hand. Fortunately there is a safer and equally effective alternative.

First, cut the chile in half with a knife. Then, starting opposite the stem end, run the edge of a small melon baller scoop down the inside of the chile, scraping up seeds and ribs. Finally, cut off the core with the scoop. (For more on chiles, see concept 32.)

1. Adjust oven rack to middle position and heat oven to 350 degrees. Process tomatoes and onion in food processor until smooth, about 15 seconds, scraping down bowl if necessary. Transfer mixture to liquid measuring cup; you should have 2 cups (if necessary, spoon off excess so that volume equals 2 cups).

2. Place rice in large fine-mesh strainer and rinse under cold running water until water runs clear, about 1½ minutes. Shake rice vigorously in strainer to remove excess water.

3. Heat oil in ovensafe 12-inch straight-sided sauté pan or Dutch oven over medium-high heat for 1 to 2 minutes. Drop 3 or 4 grains rice in oil; if grains sizzle, oil is ready. Add rice and cook, stirring frequently, until rice is light golden and translucent, 6 to 8 minutes. Reduce heat to medium, add garlic and seeded minced jalapeños, and cook, stirring constantly, until fragrant, about 1½ minutes. Stir in pureed tomatoes and onion, chicken broth, tomato paste, and salt, increase heat to medium-high, and bring to boil. Cover pan and transfer to oven; bake until liquid is absorbed and rice is tender, 30 to 35 minutes, stirring well halfway through cooking.

4. Stir in cilantro and reserved minced jalapeño with seeds to taste. Serve immediately, passing lime wedges separately.

MEXICAN RICE WITH CHARRED TOMATOES, CHILES, AND ONION
SERVES 6 TO 8

For this variation, the vegetables are charred in a cast-iron skillet, which gives the finished dish a deeper color and a slightly toasty, smoky flavor. A cast-iron skillet works best for toasting the vegetables; a traditional or even a nonstick skillet will be left with burnt spots that are difficult to remove, even with vigorous scrubbing. Vegetable broth can be substituted for the chicken broth. Include the ribs and seeds when mincing the third jalapeño.

2 tomatoes, cored

I white onion, peeled and quartered

6 garlic cloves, unpeeled

3 jalapeño chiles, 2 stemmed, halved, and seeded,
  I stemmed and minced

2 cups long-grain white rice

⅓ cup vegetable oil

2 cups low-sodium chicken broth

I tablespoon tomato paste

1½ teaspoons salt

½ cup minced fresh cilantro
  Lime wedges

1. Heat 12-inch cast-iron skillet over medium-high heat for about 2 minutes. Add tomatoes, onion, garlic, and halved jalapeños and toast, using tongs to turn them frequently, until vegetables are softened and almost completely blackened, about 10 minutes for tomatoes and 15 to 20 minutes for other vegetables. When cool enough to handle, trim root ends from onion and halve each piece. Remove skins from garlic and mince. Mince jalapeños.

2. Adjust oven rack to middle position and heat oven to 350 degrees. Process toasted tomatoes and onion in food processor until smooth, about 15 seconds, scraping down bowl if necessary. Transfer mixture to liquid measuring cup; you should have 2 cups (if necessary, spoon off any excess so that volume equals 2 cups).

3. Place rice in large fine-mesh strainer and rinse under cold running water until water runs clear, about 1½ minutes. Shake rice vigorously in strainer to remove excess water.

4. Heat oil in ovensafe 12-inch straight-sided sauté pan or Dutch oven over medium-high heat, 1 to 2 minutes. Drop 3 or 4 grains rice in oil; if grains sizzle, oil is ready. Add rice and cook, stirring frequently, until rice is light golden and translucent, 6 to 8 minutes. Reduce heat to medium, add toasted minced garlic and toasted minced jalapeños, and cook, stirring constantly, until fragrant, about 1½ minutes. Stir in pureed tomatoes and onion, chicken broth, tomato paste, and salt, increase heat to medium-high, and bring to boil. Cover pan and transfer to oven; bake until liquid is absorbed and rice is tender, 30 to 35 minutes, stirring well halfway through cooking.

5. Stir in cilantro and reserved minced jalapeño with seeds to taste. Serve immediately, passing lime wedges separately.

✓ WHY THIS RECIPE WORKS

Rice cooked the Mexican way is a flavorful pilaf-style dish, but we've had our share of soupy or greasy versions. With a whole host of ingredients in the pot it can be hard to get the rice to cook through evenly on the stovetop. Not to mention that excess stirring causes the rice to be extra starchy. We move the pot to the oven to solve both of these problems.

RINSE AND FRY   Rinsing the rice washes away excess starch that can make this dish gummy. Frying the rice in ⅓ cup of oil imparts a rich, toasted flavor. Note that some recipes deep-fry the rice, but we found that this was unnecessary. Likewise, simply sautéing the rice in a tablespoon of oil didn't impart the necessary richness.

USE TWO TYPES OF TOMATOES   Most recipes use fresh tomatoes and we found out why—the versions with canned tomatoes tasted overcooked and too tomatoey. We did like the richer color of the versions made with canned tomatoes; we got this by adding a tablespoon of tomato paste. To further guarantee the right flavor, color, and texture, we stir the rice midway through cooking to reincorporate the tomato mixture.

ADD FLAVOR, TEXTURE   We found pureeing the tomatoes into a pulp was best—and that we could puree the onion with the tomatoes as well. We prefer to mince garlic and chiles and sauté them in the pot with the rice, before adding the tomatoes and onion, to develop their flavor. We also cook in chicken broth for richer flavor.

FINISH FRESH   While many traditional recipes consider fresh cilantro and minced jalapeño optional, in our book they are mandatory. The raw herbs and pungent chiles complement the richer tones of the cooked tomatoes, garlic, and onion. A squirt of fresh lime illuminates the flavor even further.

PRACTICAL SCIENCE USING HERBS STEMS

Cilantro stems have great flavor but avoid parsley stems.

Can you use cilantro and parsley stems when cooking? We asked tasters to eat the herbs by the sprig, from the tender leaf to the fat tip of the stem. While the parsley leaves were fresh and herbal, we were surprised by how intense the flavor became as we traveled down the stems. By the time we reached the stem ends, tasters were complaining (loudly) about bitterness. Cilantro, however, was another story. Sure, the leaves were tasty, but the great flavor found in the stems caught us all off guard. Sweet, fresh, and potent, the flavor intensified as we traveled down the stem but never became bitter. The moral? If a recipe calls for cilantro and a slightly crunchy texture isn't an issue, use the stems as well as the leaves. But when it comes to parsley—unless you'll be using the herb in a soup or stew where its strong flavor won't be out of place—be picky and use just the leaves.

Traditional risotto recipes call for constant stirring while the rice cooks. Stirring releases the starches in the rice, helping to create that iconic creamy sauce. We've revamped the traditional recipe to drastically reduce the stirring time, but still achieve the firm yet tender texture by not rinsing the rice, and flooding it with water.

NO-FUSS RISOTTO WITH PARMESAN AND HERBS
SERVES 6

This more hands-off method requires precise timing, so we strongly recommend using a timer.

5	cups low-sodium chicken broth
1½	cups water
4	tablespoons unsalted butter
1	large onion, chopped fine
	Salt and pepper
1	garlic clove, minced
2	cups Arborio rice
1	cup dry white wine
2	ounces Parmesan cheese, grated (1 cup)
2	tablespoons minced fresh parsley
2	tablespoons minced fresh chives
1	teaspoon lemon juice

1. Bring broth and water to boil in large saucepan over high heat. Reduce heat to medium-low to maintain gentle simmer.

2. Melt 2 tablespoons butter in Dutch oven over medium heat. Add onion and ¾ teaspoon salt and cook, stirring frequently, until onion is softened, 5 to 7 minutes. Add garlic and stir until fragrant, about 30 seconds. Add rice and cook, stirring frequently, until grains are translucent around edges, about 3 minutes.

3. Add wine and cook, stirring constantly, until fully absorbed, 2 to 3 minutes. Stir 5 cups hot broth mixture into rice; reduce heat to medium-low, cover, and simmer until almost all liquid has been absorbed and rice is just al dente, 16 to 19 minutes, stirring twice during cooking.

4. Add ¾ cup hot broth mixture and stir gently and constantly until risotto becomes creamy, about 3 minutes. Stir in Parmesan. Remove pot from heat, cover, and let stand for 5 minutes. Stir in remaining 2 tablespoons butter, parsley, chives, and lemon juice. To loosen texture of risotto, add remaining broth mixture to taste. Season with salt and pepper to taste, and serve immediately.

NO-FUSS RISOTTO WITH CHICKEN AND HERBS
SERVES 6

This more hands-off method requires precise timing, so we strongly recommend using a timer.

5	cups low-sodium chicken broth
2	cups water
1	tablespoon olive oil
2	(12-ounce) bone-in split chicken breasts, trimmed and cut in half crosswise
4	tablespoons unsalted butter
1	large onion, chopped fine
	Salt and pepper
1	garlic clove, minced
2	cups Arborio rice
1	cup dry white wine
2	ounces Parmesan cheese, grated (1 cup)
2	tablespoons minced fresh parsley
2	tablespoons minced fresh chives
1	teaspoon lemon juice

1. Bring broth and water to boil in large saucepan over high heat. Reduce heat to medium-low to maintain gentle simmer.

2. Heat oil in Dutch oven over medium heat until just starting to smoke. Add chicken, skin side down, and cook without moving until golden brown, 4 to 6 minutes. Flip chicken and cook second side until lightly browned, about

---

PRACTICAL SCIENCE DON'T RINSE RICE WHEN YOU WANT A CREAMY CONSISTENCY

Are you making risotto or rice pudding? Don't rinse your rice. Rinsing is for dishes where individual grains are desired.

Do you always need to rinse rice? In the test kitchen, we recommend rinsing long-grain white rice when we want separate, distinct grains. That's because rinsing flushes away excess starch that would otherwise absorb water and swell, causing grains to stick together. To see if this was also true for other types of white rice, we gathered up three of the most common kinds called for in our recipes and cooked them, rinsed and unrinsed, in a few typical applications: We cooked medium-grain Arborio rice in risotto, medium-grain rice in rice pudding, and steamed long-grain basmati plain. After side-by-side tastings, we confirmed that for steamed basmati rice, where individual grains are desired, rinsing improves the result. But for creamy dishes like risotto and rice pudding, rinsing compromises the texture of the finished dish. The bottom line: If you want a sticky, creamy texture, don't rinse your rice.

2 minutes. Transfer chicken to saucepan of simmering broth and cook until chicken registers 160 degrees, 10 to 15 minutes. Transfer to large plate.

3. Melt 2 tablespoons butter in now-empty Dutch oven over medium heat. Add onion and ¾ teaspoon salt and cook, stirring frequently, until onion is softened, 5 to 7 minutes. Add garlic and stir until fragrant, about 30 seconds. Add rice and cook, stirring frequently, until grains are translucent around edges, about 3 minutes.

4. Add wine and cook, stirring constantly, until fully absorbed, 2 to 3 minutes. Stir 5 cups hot broth mixture into rice; reduce heat to medium-low, cover, and simmer until almost all liquid has been absorbed and rice is just al dente, 16 to 19 minutes, stirring twice during cooking.

5. Add ¾ cup hot broth mixture to risotto and stir gently and constantly until risotto becomes creamy, about 3 minutes. Stir in Parmesan. Remove pot from heat, cover, and let stand for 5 minutes.

6. Meanwhile, remove and discard skin and bones from chicken and shred meat into bite-size pieces. Gently stir shredded chicken, remaining 2 tablespoons butter, parsley, chives, and lemon juice into risotto. To loosen texture of risotto, add remaining broth mixture to taste. Season with salt and pepper to taste, and serve immediately.

☑ WHY THIS RECIPE WORKS

Classic risotto can demand half an hour of stovetop tedium for the best creamy results. Our goal was five minutes of stirring, tops. Typical recipes dictate adding the broth in small increments after the wine has been absorbed (and stirring constantly after each addition), but we add most of the broth at once and cover the pan, allowing the rice to simmer until almost all the broth is absorbed (stirring just twice).

DON'T STIR We have rethought this recipe to reduce stirring to a bare minimum. Flooding the rice with most of the liquid at the outset and then using the lid to help the rice cook evenly is our unique trick here. (But be sure to measure the liquid with care; success is dependent on the correct ratios and volumes.) We don't rinse the Arborio rice; we want that extra starch to help make our risotto creamy. (Traditionally, it's the stirring that causes the rice to release its starch and create the creamy "sauce.") Stirring also prevents sticking or scorching, but by flooding the rice and then bringing that liquid to a boil, we're letting the natural jostling of the rice take the place of stirring— our rice doesn't burn, and we get a great creamy sauce.

USE A DUTCH OVEN We swap out the saucepan for a Dutch oven, which has a thick, heavy bottom, deep sides, and tight-fitting lid—perfect for trapping and distributing heat as evenly as possible. Also, its wider surface area means there's less differential in cooking rates between top and bottom; the rice is spread out in a thinner layer in the pot.

COOK WITH RESIDUAL HEAT We stir the rice twice in the first 16 to 19 minutes of cooking to help release some starch and build our sauce. After a second addition of broth, we stir the pot constantly until the risotto is creamy, which takes just three minutes. We then remove the pot from the heat, throw on the cover, and wait for five minutes. Without sitting over a direct flame, the heavy Dutch oven maintains enough residual heat to finish off the rice to a perfect al dente—thickened, velvety, and just barely chewy. Adding the Parmesan cheese before the off-heat "cooking" helps to build this creamy sauce.

FINISH WITH FLAVOR Just before serving, we stir in extra butter to make the sauce velvety and add herbs and a squeeze of lemon.

PRACTICAL SCIENCE
WHAT RICE IS BEST FOR RISOTTO?

There are many different types of rice, but for risotto, Arborio is best.

The stubby, milky grains of Arborio rice, once grown exclusively in Italy, are valued for their high starch content and the subsequent creaminess they bring to risotto.

Arborio, the classic choice for risotto, is different from other types of white rice for a couple of reasons. First, it contains roughly 19 to 21 percent amylose (as opposed to 22 percent of amylose in long-grain white rice). But more importantly, the desirable "bite" in risotto is due to a defect in Arborio rice called chalk. During maturation, the starch structures at the grain's core deform, making for a firm, toothy center when cooked.

Italian rice comes in four grades: *superfino, fino, semifino,* and *commune.* The top two grades include Arborio (the most widely available), Carnaroli, and Vialone Nano. (There are even more varieties, like Baldo and the newly developed quick-cooking Poseidone, but they can be difficult to find outside of Italy.)

In a side-by-side tasting of Arborio, Carnaroli, and Vialone Nano, tasters were split evenly between the Arborio and Carnaroli; those liking firmer rice grains chose Arborio, and those liking softer, creamier rice chose Carnaroli. Vialone was deemed too soft and had a pasty texture; the grains lacked a firm center. On a whim, we also tried an Arborio *integrale,* or whole-grain (brown) Arborio. While it did take nearly twice as long to cook and was not quite as creamy as fully processed white Arborio, some tasters appreciated its nutty taste and chewy texture.

To find the best Arborio rice brand, we cooked up batches of Parmesan risotto with two domestically grown brands of Arborio rice and four Italian imports; all brands are widely available in supermarkets. To our surprise, the winning rice hailed not from the Boot, but from the Lone Star State: RiceSelect Arborio Rice.

Slicing Changes Garlic and Onion Flavor

Garlic and onions are key components of countless savory recipes. Most cooks understand that cooking tames the harsh notes in garlic and onions and brings out their sweetness. What most cooks don't understand is that the method by which garlic and onions are prepared on the cutting board is important, too.

HOW THE SCIENCE WORKS

Garlic and onions belong to the same botanical family (called alliums) that also includes shallots and leeks. Unlike many other foods with potent flavors (think aged cheese or fresh basil), garlic and onions have almost no aroma. Sure, the papery skin keeps some of the strong compounds in garlic and onions from reaching our noses, but it turns out that these compounds are not really activated until the cell structure is disturbed. That is, until you slice into garlic or onions they don't really smell.

When the cells of a garlic clove are ruptured, an odorless sulfur-containing amino acid is released and immediately comes into contact with an enzyme called alliinase. The reaction of the two eventually produces a new compound commonly called allicin, which is responsible for garlic's familiar scent and characteristic fiery flavor. The more a garlic clove is broken down, the more enzymes are released, and the more allicin—and therefore more flavor—is produced. But be careful: As soon as you cut the garlic, the allicin will start to build and build until its flavor becomes overwhelmingly strong. So if a recipe calls for chopped raw garlic we suggest you avoid advance preparation of your cloves. (Fortunately, when garlic is cooked the very

pungent allicin is converted to a variety of more mellow-tasting compounds.)

Onions glean their intense flavor and acrid odor from sulfur-containing substances similar to allicin, called thiosulfinates, which are created when the same enzyme alliinase interacts with an odorless sulfur-containing amino acid, similar to the one in garlic, released when the onion's cells are ruptured. (Unlike garlic, onions also contain an enzyme called LF synthase, which is responsible for forming the tear-causing compound propanethial S-oxide.) Like garlic, these pungent sulfur compounds are converted to milder-tasting sulfonate and sulfide compounds by cooking.

We've found that there is a way to control the levels of strong-smelling compounds that are released from garlic and onions—at least to an extent. It's all about how you cut them up. For garlic, you can control the bite by cutting it into thin slices rather than finely mincing it. (That said, in many recipes we want more garlic flavor to be distributed evenly throughout a dish, so we do mince it, even though mincing produces more garlic flavor than slicing.) For onions, we've found that slicing them through the root end (rather than crosswise) gives us pieces with clearly less pungency in taste and odor.

WHAT HAPPENS WHEN YOU SLICE ONION OR GARLIC

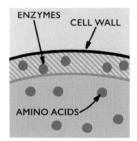

BEFORE SLICING *Enzymes and amino acids are stored in separate sections of the onion and garlic cells.*

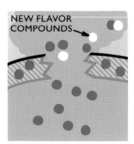

AFTER SLICING *When cell walls are ruptured (often by a knife), the enzymes and amino acids react with each other to create new compounds responsible for the characteristic onion or garlic flavor.*

TEST KITCHEN EXPERIMENT

Knowing that the way that onions are cut determines the amount of thiosulfinates (the compounds that give onions their flavor and aroma) released, we devised an experiment to illustrate the relationship between ruptured onion cells and thiosulfinate production. To do this, we relied on the antioxidant properties of thiosulfinates to prevent enzymatic browning, an oxidation reaction that takes place in peeled potatoes left out too long.

First, we pureed and strained a pound of potatoes to produce what was essentially potato juice. To half of the juice we added an onion that had been "minced" in the food processor—a violent method that bursts lots of cells. And to the other half we added an onion that we'd minced by hand with a sharp knife (producing far fewer ruptured cells). We left both samples to sit overnight in the refrigerator (alongside a bowl of potato juice without any onion) and then examined their color.

THE RESULTS

The plain potato juice had turned the color of strong black tea because of oxidation. The potato juice spiked with hand-minced onion was slightly lighter in color, like a weaker cup of tea, and had a strong onion smell. Clearly, hand-chopping the onion had released thiosulfinates (we could smell them), but not enough to keep the potato juice from oxidizing. The potato juice spiked with the onion "minced" in a food processor was pale yellow and had a much stronger onion aroma than the sample spiked with the hand-minced onion. Not only did the battered and bruised onion pieces create a stronger onion aroma, but we could see that this rough handling of the onion had created more thiosulfinates, which had protected the potato juice from oxidizing even after an overnight stay in the refrigerator.

THE TAKEAWAY

The lesson? Take care with the manner in which you chop your onions. The more you chop the onions, the more flavorful thiosulfinates you will release. Precisely sliced onions

with a minimum of bruising will have a far less pungent flavor than onions you manhandle in the food processor. For this reason, it's important to use a sharp knife (it will cut more cleanly through an onion and cause less bruising). If your cutting board is covered with juices by the time you've finished mincing an onion, your knife is not sharp enough and you're likely creating an excess of onion flavor.

Not only is proper technique essential when preparing onions (as well as garlic), but it is important to understand that more chopping equals more cellular damage, which equals more flavor. For instance, slicing onions produces a milder onion flavor than mincing them. There are recipes where a single onion needs to provide a lot of flavor and should be evenly dispersed throughout the dish. In these cases, we will generally mince the onion. In recipes with several onions, such as onion soup, we often slice the onions to keep their flavor from overwhelming the dish. The same exact principle applies to garlic.

HARNESSING THE POWER OF ONIONS

When potato juice sits overnight, it oxidizes and turns black. The potent flavor compounds in onions (thiosulfinates) prevent oxidation. We mixed onions processed in two ways with this juice and compared the results.

Precisely chopping onions by hand released fewer potent flavor compounds, which in turn created less protection against oxidation in what became the dark brown potato juice.

CHOPPED ONIONS

HIGHLY OXIDATED POTATO JUICE

Manhandling onions in a food processor released a great amount of potent flavor compounds, which created more protection against oxidation in the potato juice and kept it from turning brown.

PROCESSED ONIONS

MINIMALLY OXIDATED POTATO JUICE

We use garlic in many ways, manipulating its pungent flavor depending on what will work best in the finished dish. These flavor-enhancing (or -minimizing) techniques range from mincing to poaching and sautéing. Other recipes that rely on garlic include Spanish-Style Garlic Shrimp (page 122) and Garlic Mayonnaise (page 317).

GARLIC-POTATO SOUP
SERVES 6

A garnish is essential to add texture to this soup. We like Garlic Chips, but crisp bacon bits, fried leeks, or croutons are good options, too. A potato masher can be used instead of an immersion blender to mash some of the potatoes right in the pot, though the consistency will not be as creamy. If leeks are not available, substitute an equal amount of yellow onion. The test kitchen prefers the soup made with chicken broth, but vegetable broth can be substituted.

3	tablespoons unsalted butter
1	leek, white and light green parts only, halved lengthwise, chopped small, and washed thoroughly
3	garlic cloves, minced, plus 2 whole heads garlic, outer papery skins removed and top third of heads cut off and discarded
6–7	cups low-sodium chicken broth
2	bay leaves
	Salt and pepper
1½	pounds russet potatoes, peeled and cut into ½-inch cubes
1	pound red potatoes (unpeeled), cut into ½-inch cubes
½	cup heavy cream
1½	teaspoons minced fresh thyme
¼	cup minced fresh chives
1	recipe Garlic Chips (recipe follows)

1. Melt butter in Dutch oven over medium heat. Add leeks and cook until soft (do not brown), 5 to 8 minutes. Stir in minced garlic and cook until fragrant, about 1 minute. Add garlic heads, 6 cups broth, bay leaves, and ¾ teaspoon salt. Partially cover pot and bring to simmer over medium-high heat. Reduce heat and simmer until garlic is very tender when pierced with tip of knife, 30 to 40 minutes. Add russet potatoes and red potatoes and continue to simmer, partially covered, until potatoes are tender, 15 to 20 minutes.

2. Discard bay leaves. Remove garlic heads from pot and, using tongs or paper towels, squeeze at root end until cloves slip out of their skins into bowl. Using fork, mash garlic to smooth paste.

3. Stir cream, thyme, and half of mashed garlic into soup. Heat soup until hot, about 2 minutes. Taste soup and add remaining garlic paste if desired.

4. Using immersion blender, process soup until creamy, with some potato chunks remaining. Alternatively, transfer 1½ cups potatoes and 1 cup broth to blender or food processor and process until smooth. (Process more potatoes for thicker consistency.) Return puree to pot and stir to combine, adjusting consistency with up to 1 cup more broth if necessary. Season with salt and pepper to taste, sprinkle with chives and Garlic Chips, and serve.

GARLIC CHIPS
MAKES ABOUT ¼ CUP

3	tablespoons olive oil
6	garlic cloves, sliced thin lengthwise
	Salt

Heat oil and garlic in 10-inch skillet over medium-high heat. Cook, turning frequently, until light golden brown, about 3 minutes. Using slotted spoon, transfer garlic to paper towel–lined plate. Season with salt to taste.

PRACTICAL SCIENCE
MANIPULATING GARLIC'S FLAVOR

The method of preparation and cooking affects garlic's flavor.

As we've learned, the method of cutting garlic can affect its taste. Cooking also affects flavor intensity. Garlic is sharpest when raw. When it's heated to about 150 degrees, its enzymes are destroyed and no new flavor is produced, but the flavor molecules that have been produced are transformed by the heat to more mellow-tasting sulfur compounds. This is why toasted or roasted garlic has a mellow, slightly sweet flavor. But be careful; garlic browned (or overbrowned) at very high temperatures (300 to 350 degrees) results in a bitter flavor. (Garlic Chips are the exception, since they are mellowed first, then crisped, which creates a sweet flavor with only hints of bitterness.)

GARLIC	FLAVOR
Roasted Whole Head	Very mild, sweet, caramel-like
Toasted Whole Clove	Mellow and nutty
Slivered and Sautéed	Mellow
Minced and Sautéed	Full and rounded
Pressed and Sautéed	Very robust, harsh
Raw Paste	Sharp and fiery

✔ WHY THIS RECIPE WORKS

This soup is a classic: Simple and economical, both chunky and smooth, it is modeled after the French potage Parmentier. We use a combination of two different kinds of potatoes and garlic cooked in three ways to maximize flavor.

PICK TWO POTATOES Choosing the right potato was the first step in developing our Garlic-Potato Soup. We like peeled russets for the way they break down and thicken the broth, but we find that adding red potatoes to the mix ramps up the potato flavor. (For more on the differences in potato varieties, see concept 25.)

USE GARLIC THREE WAYS The key to getting the garlic right proved to be not quantity but cooking technique. Finding that sautéed garlic was too harsh and poached was too mild, we settled on incorporating garlic in two ways: We sauté three cloves in the pot before adding the broth (the base of our soup), and we poach two whole heads of garlic in the broth, then squeeze out the softened pods, mash them, and add them back to the soup. Finally, we top the soup with Garlic Chips, which have a toasty, pleasantly bitter flavor to push our soup over the top.

ADD LEEKS, CREAM, AND THYME Leeks are a natural partner for potatoes, especially when paired with cream (which our tasters favored over half-and-half and milk) and fresh thyme (added at the end of cooking for maximum flavor).

MAKE IT SMOOTH AND CHUNKY In the lexicon of French cookery, there are three classifications for soup: *consommé* describes a clear, brothy soup; *soupe* refers to a thick, chunky, stewlike mixture; and *potage* is a hybrid of consommé and soupe, being at once partly chunky and partly smooth. For this country-style soup, we adopt the texture of a potage. We puree a portion of the soup to a creamy, smooth consistency and leave the remaining chunks untouched.

CAESAR SALAD
SERVES 4 TO 6

If you can't find ciabatta, a similar crusty, rustic loaf of bread can be substituted. A quarter-cup of Egg Beaters may be substituted for the egg yolks. Since anchovy fillets vary in size, more than six fillets may be necessary to yield 1 tablespoon of minced anchovies. The easiest way to turn garlic cloves into a paste is to grate them on a rasp-style grater.

PRACTICAL SCIENCE TEMPERING GARLIC'S BITE

Soak minced garlic in lemon juice for a nice, mellow flavor.

In our Caesar dressing, every little detail counts—especially the strong flavor of raw garlic. In the past, we've found that cloves minced well in advance end up tasting harsh in the final dish. Would letting the grated garlic in our recipe sit for just 10 minutes while we prepared the rest of the salad ingredients have the same effect? And could steeping it in lemon juice for the same amount of time—a practice recommended by an old French wives' tale—actually mellow it out?

We made three batches of Caesar dressing: In the first, we grated the garlic and immediately combined it with the other dressing ingredients. In the second, we soaked the grated garlic in lemon juice for 10 minutes before proceeding. In the third, we let the grated garlic rest for 10 minutes on its own before combining it with the other components.

Tasters found the garlic grated in advance without steeping tasted the harshest of the three. The other two preparations—grated garlic soaked in lemon juice and grated garlic immediately mixed into the dressing—tasted milder, with the lemon juice–soaked sample making for a particularly well-balanced dressing.

Raw garlic's harsh flavor comes from a compound called allicin, which forms as soon as the clove's cells are ruptured and continues to build as it sits. The citric acid in lemon juice hastens the conversion of harsh-tasting allicin to more mellow compounds called thiosulfinates, disulfides, and trisulfides—the same milder-tasting compounds that form when garlic is heated. And since soaking the garlic is easy to do while preparing the other ingredients, it's a step we think is worthwhile.

CROUTONS

2	garlic cloves, peeled
5	tablespoons extra-virgin olive oil
½–¾	loaf ciabatta, cut into ¾-inch cubes (5 cups)
¼	cup water
¼	teaspoon salt
2	tablespoons finely grated Parmesan cheese

SALAD

2–3	tablespoons lemon juice
2	large egg yolks
6	anchovy fillets, rinsed, patted dry, minced, and mashed to paste with fork (1 tablespoon)
½	teaspoon Worcestershire sauce
5	tablespoons canola oil
5	teaspoons extra-virgin olive oil
1½	ounces Parmesan cheese, grated fine (¾ cup) Pepper
2–3	romaine lettuce hearts (12 to 18 ounces), cut into ¾-inch pieces, rinsed, and dried

1. Grate garlic on rasp-style grater or press through garlic press. Measure out ½ teaspoon garlic paste for croutons and ¾ teaspoon garlic paste for dressing (discard remaining garlic). Combine 1 tablespoon oil and ½ teaspoon garlic paste in small bowl; set aside. Whisk 2 tablespoons lemon juice and ¾ teaspoon garlic paste together in large bowl. Let stand for 10 minutes.

2. **FOR THE CROUTONS:** Place bread cubes in large bowl. Sprinkle with water and salt. Toss, squeezing gently so bread absorbs water. Place remaining ¼ cup oil and soaked bread cubes in 12-inch nonstick skillet. Cook over medium-high heat, stirring frequently, until browned and crisp, 7 to 10 minutes.

3. Remove skillet from heat and push croutons to sides of skillet to clear center; add garlic-oil mixture to clearing and cook with residual heat of pan, 10 seconds. Sprinkle with Parmesan; toss until garlic and Parmesan are evenly distributed. Transfer croutons to bowl; set aside.

4. **FOR THE SALAD:** Whisk egg yolks, anchovies, and Worcestershire into garlic–lemon juice mixture. While whisking constantly, drizzle canola oil and olive oil into bowl in slow, steady stream until fully emulsified. Add ½ cup Parmesan and pepper to taste; whisk until incorporated.

5. Add romaine to dressing and toss to coat. Add croutons and mix gently until evenly distributed. Taste and season with up to 1 tablespoon remaining lemon juice. Serve immediately, passing remaining ¼ cup Parmesan separately.

✓ WHY THIS RECIPE WORKS

For our Caesar Salad, we wanted crisp-tender romaine lettuce tossed with a creamy, garlicky dressing boasting a pleasing salty undertone, with crunchy, savory croutons strewn throughout. To start, we cut the extra-virgin olive oil in the dressing with canola oil, which made for a less harsh flavor, and we used egg yolks instead of a whole egg to add richness. A garlic paste steeped in lemon juice, a double layer of Parmesan, and a novel method to make croutons round out our classic salad.

MAKE A PASTE Well aware that the dressing's flavor depends on how the garlic is prepared, we worked our way through a series of tests—everything from finely chopping the cloves with salt to rubbing whole cloves around the interior of the serving bowl. Ultimately, we prefer the flavor of the garlic transformed into a pulp on a rasp-style grater. The fine paste virtually disappears into the dressing, suffusing it with a robust (though far from aggressive) flavor, especially when we steep it in lemon juice for a few minutes before introducing the rest of the dressing ingredients. (See "Tempering Garlic's Bite," page 281.)

ADD WATER FOR NOVEL CROUTONS To get our croutons perfect (brown and crunchy, yet still tender and not parched within), we sprinkle the bite-size bread cubes with a little water and salt and cook them in an oiled nonstick skillet. The result? Croutons that are perfectly tender at the center, and browned and crunchy as could be around the edges. Water gelatinizes the starch in the bread, simultaneously breaking some of it down to glucose. As it cooks, the gelatinized starch turns crispy on the exterior but remains tender within. And the glucose? Like all sugars, it hastens browning—a good thing when it comes to croutons.

MINCE THOSE ANCHOVIES When making anchovy paste, start with whole fish. The deep flavor of good-quality oil-packed fillets is a must in this recipe. The fishier, flatter taste of commercial anchovy paste won't do. And be sure to mash them up well. Even small bits of anchovy can be distracting in Caesar salad. Finely slice the fillets and mash with a fork to create a paste that contributes savory—not fishy—flavor.

PASTA WITH GARLIC AND OIL
SERVES 4

It pays to use high-quality extra-virgin olive oil in this dish.

1	pound spaghetti
	Salt
6	tablespoons extra-virgin olive oil
12	garlic cloves, minced
3	tablespoons minced fresh parsley
2	teaspoons lemon juice
¾	teaspoon red pepper flakes
1	ounce Parmesan cheese, grated (½ cup)

1. Bring 4 quarts water to boil in large pot. Add pasta and 1 tablespoon salt and cook, stirring often, until al dente. Reserve ⅓ cup cooking water, then drain pasta.

2. Meanwhile, heat 3 tablespoons oil, two-thirds of garlic, and ½ teaspoon salt in 10-inch nonstick skillet over low heat. Cook, stirring constantly, until garlic foams and is sticky and straw-colored, about 10 minutes. Off heat, add remaining garlic, parsley, lemon juice, pepper flakes, and 2 tablespoons reserved cooking water.

3. Transfer drained pasta to warm serving bowl. Add garlic mixture, remaining 3 tablespoons oil, and remaining reserved cooking water to pasta and toss to combine. Season with salt to taste and serve immediately, passing Parmesan separately.

✔ WHY THIS RECIPE WORKS

Nothing sounds easier than pasta with olive oil and garlic, but too often this Italian pantry classic, aglio e olio, turns out oily or rife with burnt garlic. For deep, mellow garlic flavor, we cooked most of the garlic over low heat; a modest amount of raw garlic added at the end brought in some potent fresh garlic flavor. Extra-virgin olive oil and reserved pasta cooking water helped to keep our pasta saucy. A splash of lemon juice and a sprinkling of red pepper flakes added some brightness and heat to this simple, yet complex-flavored dish.

WORK FOR MELLOW GARLIC FLAVOR This recipe relies on a lot of garlic. The secret is to sauté it very slowly over low heat for 10 minutes. The garlic should not brown but become golden. To do this, we start the garlic in cold oil, as it's much easier to cook it slowly and therefore prevent the heavy browning that causes the garlic to taste acrid and one-dimensional.

FINISH WITH FRESH GARLIC The remaining garlic is added along with the red pepper flakes to bloom its flavor but preserve punch. Adding some pasta cooking water at the same time stops the cooking process so that the garlic doesn't begin to sauté.

USE BOLD SEASONINGS Red pepper flakes are a must in this dish, as are fresh parsley, lemon juice, and coarse salt. Parmesan is optional, but a great (if nontraditional) addition. Reserve some of the olive oil to toss into the finished dish. This will preserve the fruity flavor of the extra-virgin olive oil.

PRACTICAL SCIENCE
CLOUDY WITH A CHANCE OF MUSHINESS

Cloudy pasta water generally means the pasta will be mushy.

Cloudy pasta water isn't necessarily an indication that you've overcooked the noodles. It can be a visual cue that the pasta has a weak structure and breaks down too much as it cooks, resulting in a mushy texture. Even though we kept a close eye on both pots, our favorite spaghetti, from De Cecco, cooked up firm and springy and left the water relatively clear, while the low-ranking Montebello noodles, boiled for the same amount of time, swam in cloudy, starchy water and were soft.

CLEARER WATER = FIRM PASTA

CLOUDIER WATER = WEAK PASTA

PRACTICAL SCIENCE WHAT MAKES GOOD PASTA?

Great pasta texture all comes down to the maintenance of the extruder and the die, as well as the drying process.

When it comes to taste, you can't really tell the difference between different brands of pasta. We tasted eight top brands tossed with just olive oil and tasters struggled to find differences. Flavor differences were even harder to tease out when we ran the same tasting but tossed each brand with tomato sauce.

Texture, however, was another matter. None of the samples were unacceptable, but regardless of how vigilantly we tracked their doneness, some noodles cooked up sticky and gummy, while the best spaghettis were springy and firm. Because these pastas were made with 100 percent semolina, it couldn't be the fault of the ingredients. Could the way the dough was processed also affect the texture?

To form pasta into shapes, most dough is passed through the holes of a die. All dies were originally made with bronze blocks, which give the noodles' surface a rough-hewn appearance that some manufacturers still prefer; they claim that sauce clings better to the coarse, craggy exterior. Meanwhile, other pasta producers, including both American brands in our lineup, have switched to Teflon-coated dies, mostly for cosmetic reasons. Because it's nonstick, Teflon reduces the surface tension of the dough extrusion and, as a result, produces smoother, shinier noodles. We found that sauce clung equally well to noodles made by both types of dies—but could bronze dies be responsible for producing the firmer texture we noticed in some of the spaghettis? As it turned out, no. While our favorite pasta was produced by bronze dies, so were our two least favorite brands, assailed for having "mushy," "soft" texture "with no spring in the bite."

The more important distinction is not the material of the die, but how well the extruder and the die have been maintained. The heat, friction, and pressure applied to the dough wear down and loosen the extruder parts over time. When this happens, the machine is no longer able to press the dough with enough force to make perfectly compact strands of spaghetti, and the texture of the noodles suffers. Based on our results, we could only assume that some extruders were in better shape than others.

The other major processing step is drying the noodles. Drying times and temperatures range widely among brands: Some companies dry their pasta low (95 to 100 degrees) and slow (over the course of many hours, or even days) in drying rooms, claiming that it preserves flavor. Others, including Barilla and Ronzoni, place the noodles in special ultra-high-temperature (UHT) ovens and crank the heat to 190 degrees or higher, which gets the job done faster. The high heat cross-links some of the gluten strands and can strengthen the pasta. But UHT drying tends to cook out some of the pasta's flavor, an effect we noticed in the slightly duller taste of these two UHT-dried brands.

Ultimately, we liked six of the eight samples enough to recommend them. But one pasta, De Cecco, stood out for particularly good texture—the result, we could only assume, of balancing all the variables most successfully.

When onions caramelize, a complex series of chemical reactions takes places. Heat causes water molecules to separate from the onions' sugar molecules. As they cook, the dehydrated sugar molecules react with each other to form new molecules that produce new colors, flavor, and aromas. (This is the same series of reactions that occurs when granulated sugar is heated to make caramel.) We use this reaction to our advantage in flavorful dips and soups.

BACON, SCALLION, AND CARAMELIZED ONION DIP
MAKES ABOUT 1½ CUPS

This recipe uses half a recipe of Caramelized Onions. Leftovers can be used in a number of dishes, including omelets and pizza.

3	slices bacon, cut into ¼-inch pieces
¾	cup sour cream
½	cup Caramelized Onions (recipe follows)
2	scallions, minced
½	teaspoon cider vinegar
	Salt and pepper

1. Cook bacon in 8-inch skillet over medium heat until crisp, 5 to 7 minutes. Transfer to paper towel–lined plate and set aside.

2. Combine sour cream, caramelized onions, scallions, vinegar, and bacon in medium bowl. Season with salt and pepper to taste, and serve. (Dip can be refrigerated for up to 3 days.)

CARAMELIZED ONIONS
MAKES 1 CUP

If the onions are sizzling or scorching in step 2, reduce the heat. If the onions are not browning after 15 to 20 minutes, raise the heat.

1	tablespoon unsalted butter
1	tablespoon vegetable oil
1	teaspoon packed light brown sugar
½	teaspoon salt
2	pounds onions, halved and sliced through root end into ¼-inch-thick pieces
1	tablespoon water
	Pepper

1. Heat butter and oil in 12-inch nonstick skillet over high heat and stir in sugar and salt. Add onions and stir to coat. Cook, stirring occasionally, until onions begin to soften and release some moisture, about 5 minutes.

Salt onions as soon as they go into the sauté pan. The salt draws out moisture, helping them to cook up tender and well seasoned.

When is the best time to salt onions? We have experienced a dilemma in the test kitchen about this very question—each cook has a different opinion on the appropriate salting time when sautéing onions. Putting aside any preconceived notions, we set out to get to the bottom of this simple but vexing issue.

We started by sautéing 1 cup of diced onions in oil in a medium skillet over medium heat. After six minutes of frequent stirring, the onions were beautifully golden. After removing the onions from the skillet, we added ½ teaspoon salt. Tasters loved the caramelized flavor but commented on the crunchiness of the onions. They also pointed out that the onions weren't seasoned throughout—only on the surface.

Next, we kept the stove on the same setting and sautéed a second cup of diced onions, this time adding ½ teaspoon of salt at the outset. After six minutes, the onions were not as brown as the first batch had been so we cooked them a few more minutes until they were golden brown. When we tasted these onions, they were meltingly tender and well seasoned. The salt had drawn out their liquid, causing them to soften as they cooked. But the liquid also caused the onions to brown more slowly, tacking a few extra minutes onto the cooking time. So the controversy is over: Salt onions when they go into the sauté pan, leaving them over the heat for as long as necessary for decent browning.

2. Reduce heat to medium and cook, stirring frequently, until onions are deeply browned and slightly sticky, about 40 minutes longer.

3. Off heat, stir in water. Season with pepper to taste. (Onions can be refrigerated for up to 1 week.)

✓ WHY THIS RECIPE WORKS
Onion dip is an old favorite, but we wanted a recipe that went beyond stirring powdered onion soup mix into sour cream and mayonnaise. For a more modern, grown-up take, we start with caramelized onions, which lend our dip a sweet, more complex flavor. We discovered several keys to making caramelized onions that weren't burnt, gummy, bland, or greasy. We incorporate complementary flavors to give the dip more heft. Bacon adds a smokiness that perfectly balances the sweet onions, while fresh minced scallions reinforce the onion flavor and add a touch of color.

PICK THE RIGHT ONION What is the best onion to caramelize? We tasted all types in caramelized form before we decided on our favorite. In the end, we prefer yellow onions, which strike a good balance between savory and sweet, with a mild onion flavor and beautiful color. Other options in the produce aisle are white onions, Spanish onions, red onions, and Vidalia onions. White onions were controversial in the test kitchen—some described them as sugary and mellow while others found them too sweet and one-dimensional. Spanish onions have a deep and complex flavor but can seem a bit harsh. Red onions turn very dark when caramelized and can be pleasantly sweet despite their sticky and jammy consistency. Finally, Vidalia onions are the sweetest sample but have a chalky and gummy texture when caramelized.

CHOOSE THE RIGHT PAN We tried caramelizing our onions on top of the stove, uncovered, in a regular skillet, a nonstick skillet, and a Dutch oven. The high sides of the Dutch oven encourage condensation, causing the reduction and caramelization process to take about 15 minutes longer with no discernible difference in flavor or texture. The low-sided skillets caramelize the onions more quickly. When it comes to choosing between regular and nonstick, we prefer the slippery nonstick surface. This pan is easier to clean, and the flavorful juices do not cling to the pan but are instead forced to mingle with the onions.

START HIGH Starting our onions over high heat for five minutes jump-starts caramelization by causing them to quickly release their moisture. We then lower the heat to medium and continue to cook the onions to a perfect caramel brown. We add salt and sugar to the onions at the outset to help draw moisture out. A combination of vegetable oil and butter is preferred as it results in clean, well-defined onion flavor lightly tempered with the rich taste of butter.

FINISH WITH WATER One tablespoon of water added at the end of cooking gathers up the drops of caramelized onion juice from around the edges of the pan without diminishing the flavor or texture of the onions.

BEST FRENCH ONION SOUP
SERVES 6

Use a Dutch oven with at least a 7-quart capacity for this recipe. Sweet onions, such as Vidalia or Walla Walla, will make this recipe overly sweet. Use broiler-safe crocks and keep the rim of the bowls 4 to 5 inches from the heating element to obtain a proper gratinée of melted, bubbly cheese. If using ordinary soup bowls, sprinkle the toasted bread slices with Gruyère and return them to the broiler until the cheese melts, then float them on top of the soup.

SOUP

4 pounds onions, halved and sliced through root end into ¼-inch-thick pieces
3 tablespoons unsalted butter, cut into 3 pieces
  Salt and pepper
2 cups water, plus extra for deglazing
½ cup dry sherry
4 cups low-sodium chicken broth
2 cups beef broth
6 sprigs fresh thyme, tied with kitchen twine
I bay leaf

CHEESE CROUTONS

I small baguette, cut into ½-inch slices
8 ounces shredded Gruyère cheese (2 cups)

I. **FOR THE SOUP:** Adjust oven rack to lower-middle position and heat oven to 400 degrees. Generously spray inside of Dutch oven with vegetable oil spray. Add onions,

---

PRACTICAL SCIENCE WHY SLOW-COOK ONIONS?

Slow-cooking onions helps to develop a complex, sweet flavor.

Invariably, the first step in any soup or sauce recipe is "Heat oil over low heat and cook onions until soft but not browned." But why not accelerate the process by turning up the heat? And is "precooking" in oil even necessary?

We made three batches of tomato sauce and tasted them side by side. In the first, we slow-cooked the onions for 10 minutes in oil over low heat before adding the tomatoes; in the second, we cooked the onions in oil over high heat for 8 minutes; in the last batch, we dumped the onions and tomatoes into the oil all at once.

The wisdom of the ages proved correct: The sauce with gently cooked onions was strongly preferred by the majority of tasters, who praised its "rich," "round, sweet flavor." The sauce with onions cooked over high heat was deemed "sharp" and "flat," while the sauce made with raw onions was even more "thin-tasting."

Onions contain different types of sulfur molecules. Chopping and low heat release the enzyme alliinase, which zeroes in on some of these molecules, breaking them in half and producing pungent compounds that, over time, transform into sweeter-tasting disulfides and trisulfides. The longer the exposure to low heat, the more such molecules are produced—and the greater complexity the onions can add to a sauce. High heat, on the other hand, deactivates the enzymes, so that fewer of these flavor molecules are produced.

Slowly cooking the raw onions in oil or butter is also important to better flavor. Cooking onions in water (or watery substances like tomatoes) triggers the release of smelly and unpleasant-tasting sulfur compounds (boiled onions, anyone?). But when fat coats the onions during cooking, it protects against the reaction with water, so that fewer of these objectionable molecules can form. The bottom line: Take the time to slow-cook onions in fat. The added complexity is worth it.

butter, and 1 teaspoon salt. Cook, covered, for 1 hour (onions will be moist and slightly reduced in volume). Remove pot from oven and stir onions, scraping bottom and sides of pot. Return pot to oven with lid slightly ajar and continue to cook until onions are very soft and golden brown, 1½ to 1¾ hours longer, stirring onions and scraping bottom and sides of pot after 1 hour.

2. Carefully remove pot from oven (leave oven on) and place over medium-high heat. Cook onions, stirring frequently and scraping bottom and sides of pot, until liquid evaporates and onions brown, 15 to 20 minutes (reduce heat to medium if onions brown too quickly). Continue to cook, stirring frequently, until bottom of pot is coated with dark crust, 6 to 8 minutes, adjusting heat as necessary. (Scrape any browned bits that collect on spoon back into onions.) Stir in ¼ cup water, scraping pot bottom to loosen crust, and cook until water evaporates and pot bottom has formed another dark crust, 6 to 8 minutes. Repeat process of deglazing 2 or 3 more times, until onions are very dark brown. Stir in sherry and cook, stirring frequently, until sherry evaporates, about 5 minutes.

3. Stir in 2 cups water, chicken broth, beef broth, thyme, bay leaf, and ½ teaspoon salt, scraping up any final bits of browned crust on bottom and sides of pot. Increase heat to high and bring to simmer. Reduce heat to low, cover, and simmer for 30 minutes. Remove and discard herbs and season with salt and pepper to taste.

PRACTICAL SCIENCE ODORS BE GONE

Remove strong odors from cutting boards with baking soda.

We wondered what was the best way to remove strong odors, such as onion and garlic, from cutting boards.

The dishwasher is the best way to clean plastic cutting boards, but often you can't wait two hours to reuse a malodorous board. To find the best way to remove odors without a dishwasher, we cut a large onion and made garlic paste out of raw minced garlic on each of four cutting boards. When they were nice and smelly, we used a different odor-removal method on each board before immediately washing it with hot, soapy water: spraying with a mixture of 1 tablespoon of bleach and 1 gallon of water; scrubbing with a paste of 1 tablespoon of baking soda and 1 teaspoon of water; spraying with distilled white vinegar; and doing nothing more than washing with hot, soapy water.

After the boards were wiped dry, we sliced apples on each one. Tasters were required not only to taste the apples for off-flavors but to sniff the boards as well. The results? Only the baking soda paste–treated cutting board was odor-free; the other boards suffered from varying degrees of sulfurous odors and allium flavors. Tasters were nearly unanimous in finding the apples cut on the baking soda board "fine," with "no off-flavors." So the next time you stink up your cutting board, scrub it with a baking soda paste and follow up by washing it with hot, soapy water.

---

4. FOR THE CHEESE CROUTONS: While soup simmers, arrange baguette slices in single layer on rimmed baking sheet and bake until bread is dry, crisp, and golden at edges, about 10 minutes. Set aside.

5. TO SERVE: Adjust oven rack 7 to 8 inches from broiler element and heat broiler. Set 6 broiler-safe crocks on rimmed baking sheet and fill each with about 1¾ cups soup. Top each bowl with 1 or 2 baguette slices (do not overlap slices) and sprinkle evenly with Gruyère. Broil until cheese is melted and bubbly around edges, 3 to 5 minutes. Let cool for 5 minutes before serving.

TO MAKE AHEAD: Onions can be prepared through step 1, cooled in pot, and refrigerated for up to 3 days before proceeding with recipe. Soup can be prepared through step 3 and refrigerated for up to 2 days.

QUICKER FRENCH ONION SOUP

This variation uses a microwave for the initial cooking of the onions, which dramatically reduces the cooking time. The soup's flavor, however, will not be quite as deep as with the stovetop method. If you don't have a microwave-safe bowl large enough to accommodate all of the onions, microwave in a smaller bowl in 2 batches.

Combine onions and 1 teaspoon salt in large bowl and cover with large plate (plate should completely cover bowl and not rest on onions). Microwave for 20 to 25 minutes until onions are soft and wilted, stirring halfway through cooking. (Use oven mitts to remove bowl from microwave and remove plate away from you to avoid steam.) Drain onions (about ½ cup liquid should drain off) and proceed with step 2, melting butter in Dutch oven before adding wilted onions.

✔WHY THIS RECIPE WORKS
We found that the secret to a rich onion soup is caramelizing the onions a full 2½ hours in the oven and then deglazing the pot several times with a combination of water, chicken broth, and beef broth. For the classic crouton topping, we toast the bread before floating it in the soup to ward off sogginess, and we sprinkle the toasts with just a modest amount of nutty Gruyère to keep its flavor from overwhelming the soup.

HOW TO SLICE ONIONS Onions are best when sliced pole to pole, with the grain. This way, the onions have more presence and retain some shape. As in our Caramelized Onions recipe (page 284), we prefer using yellow onions here. Red onions bleed out to produce a dingy-looking soup. White onions are too mild, and Vidalia onions make the broth candy-sweet. Yellow onions, on the other hand, offer just the sweet and savory notes we're after.

CARAMELIZE IN THE OVEN Our soup recipe is inspired by a friend visiting from France name Henri Pinon. He patiently cooked 3 pounds of onions in butter over very low heat until they were golden brown (which took about 90 minutes). He then deglazed the pot with water and recaramelized the onions again over a dozen times. The finished soup was phenomenal but took hours and hours at the stove. We shortened this method by using the oven. Four pounds of onions squeezed into a Dutch oven and cooked slowly and evenly, covered, in the oven effectively build flavor all the while. After a beginning hour-long stint in the oven, we move the lid to be ajar and finish them for another 1½ to 1¾ hours.

DEGLAZE ON THE STOVETOP Most French onion soup recipes call for deglazing—loosening the flavorful dark brown crust, or fond, that forms on the bottom of the pot—only once, if at all. The secret to our recipe is to deglaze the pot at least three times. We do this on the stovetop. (Be careful: The pot will be very hot.) The stovetop deglazing process will take 45 to 60 minutes.

USE TWO BROTHS While Henri used only water for his broth, we prefer using both chicken broth and beef broth along with the water. The broths add complexity, helping us to build as many layers of flavor as possible.

PRACTICAL SCIENCE CUTTING ONIONS FOR NO MORE TEARS

We tested 20 common methods used to reduce tears while cutting onions. Protective eye gear turned out to be the best.

We compiled more than 20 ideas from reader correspondence, books, and conversations with colleagues all aimed at reducing our tears while cutting onions. Why not put them to the test? Our tests, which are detailed in this chart along with their results, range from common sense to comical. Overall, the two general methods that we found worked best were to protect our eyes or to introduce a flame near the cut onions. The flame, which can be produced by either a lit candle or a gas burner, changes the activity of sulfuric propanethial S-oxide (see page 278) by completely oxidizing it and probably deteriorating it as well. Two people, intense criers both, tried each method several times and rated its effectiveness on a scale of 1 to 10, 10 being the most effective and 1 being the least.

METHOD	RESULTS	EFFECTIVENESS
Wear contact lenses	Almost no tears onion after onion, but useless if you don't wear contacts	10
Wear ski or swimming goggles	Very effective, although it makes you look like a kitchen burglar	9
Burn a candle near the cutting board	Easy to do, and it worked pretty well	6.5
Place cutting board near a lit gas burner	Worked as well as a candle, but not terribly practical	6.5
Refrigerate whole onion for 8 hours	Chilled onions; some tears	5
Refrigerate quartered onion for 8 hours	Even colder onions; some tears	5
Freeze onions for 30 minutes	Coldest onions; some tears	5
Hold a slice of bread in your mouth	Looked silly; didn't work consistently	5
Balance a slice of onion on your head	Talk about looking silly, but since it forces you to tilt your head up, your eyes are averted from the fumes and the tears do slow down a little	5
Hold a lit-and-put-out match in your teeth	Looked silly, but it worked better than the unlit match	4
Slice onions under a running faucet	Onion slices washed off the board; so frustrating the tears didn't matter	3
Trim off ends and microwave for 1 minute	Onions began to cook; minor tear reduction	3
Hold a toothpick in your teeth	Looked silly; we cried a lot	2
Work underneath an exhaust fan	Not at all effective under a home exhaust	2
Tie a scarf around nose and mouth	Looked silly; minor tear reduction	1
Soak onions in ice water for 30 minutes	Wet onions; lots of tears	1
Blanch onions for 1 minute	Slimy onions; lots of tears	1
Wipe cutting board with vinegar	Vinegary onions; lots of tears	1
Slice onions next to a running faucet	Didn't work; lots of tears	1
Slice onions in plastic bag opened at ends	Awkward and dangerous because bag obstructs view; didn't stop the tears	1
Hold an unlit match in your teeth	Looked silly; we cried a lot	1
Leave root end of onion intact	Didn't work	1

Chile Heat Resides in Pith and Seeds

When it comes to cooking with fresh chiles, it sometimes feels like you're playing roulette. Who hasn't mistakenly cooked a dish that's way too hot? Chiles add depth and complexity to countless dishes, but how can you use them more reliably?

HOW THE SCIENCE WORKS

We admit that chiles are confusing. Part of the problem is the sheer number of varieties. The fact that the same chile often has a different name when it's dried doesn't help either.

Chiles are sold in two basic forms—fresh and dried. Fresh chiles can range in color from green to red, yellow, or orange. As with bell peppers, green chiles are picked before they are ripe while red, orange, and yellow chiles are picked when they are fully matured. Dried chiles are red, brown, or black. Generally picked when they, too, are fully ripe, the dried versions tend to have more concentrated and complex flavors than fresh chiles.

All chiles get their heat from a group of chemical compounds call capsaicinoids, the best known being capsaicin. Most of the capsaicin is concentrated in the inner whitish pith, with progressively smaller amounts in the seeds and the flesh (see Test Kitchen Experiment on opposite page). When eating chiles, we have the ability to detect a very small amount of capsaicin—an amount that can cause a painful burning on the tongue and a short-lived inflammation of the mouth. We detect this spiciness in a manner similar to the way we detect taste. It involves receptors in the mouth and is known as "chemesthesis," or the perception of pain, touch, and heat. For aficionados of spicy foods, of course, this pain is often perceived as pleasure.

Varieties of chiles have a wide range of heat. Some chile varieties are 10 or even 100 times hotter than others. Even the same variety can produce specimens with a wide range of heat levels. Chiles grown in sunny, arid weather undergo a lot of stress, and stressed chiles produce more capsaicin than chiles grown in temperate climates. In fact, we measured the amount of capsaicin and dihydrocapsaicin, the two compounds responsible for the majority of the heat, in five similar-looking jalapeños and found that some jalapeños were 10 times hotter than other samples. We can measure this heat (also called pungency), rating it in something called Scoville units, which were traditionally determined by extracting the compound that produces chile heat with alcohol and adding it in tiny drops to a sugar solution until the heat is just detectable by sensory panelists. Today, more sophisticated analytical instruments are used.

So how do you figure out which chiles are hot and which are fairly mild? Forget anything you've heard about appearance being an indicator of chile heat. Small chiles, for example, have no more heat than larger ones. And "corking" (the white striations visible on the skin of some chiles) also has no correlation to heat. It helps to understand the general traits of various chile varieties. For instance, serranos are generally hotter than jalapeños. But even armed with this knowledge, be aware that heat levels will still vary considerably.

INSIDE A CHILE

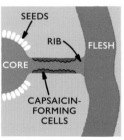

FLESH TO CORE *A chile's heat comes from capsaicin, a chemical compound produced mainly in the inner white pith, or rib, rather than in the seeds or flesh. The seeds absorb capsaicin from the rib.*

TEST KITCHEN EXPERIMENT

To determine where most of the capsaicinoids—the chemical compounds that give their "heat" (or pungency) to chiles and the best known of which is capsaicin—reside, we devised a simple experiment. Donning rubber gloves, we separated the outer green-colored flesh, the inner whitish pith (also known as the membranes or ribs), and the seeds from 40 jalapeños. We then sent the lot to our food lab.

THE RESULTS

As it turned out, there were just 5 milligrams of capsaicin per kilogram of green jalapeño flesh (not enough to really make much impact on the human tongue), 73 mg per kg in the seeds, and an impressive 512 mg per kg in the pith.

THE TAKEAWAY

The pith is the hot spot. The reason the seeds registered more heat than the flesh is simply that they are embedded in the pith; they are essentially guilty—or hot—by association. If you want to carefully mete out the fire in salsa or chili, do it by means of the pith. The seeds will just be along for the ride.

Our method for controlling chile heat is to remove the seeds and ribs from all fresh chiles. We then mince, chop, or puree the colored, fleshy portion of the chiles and use them as directed in recipes. Just before serving, we add a portion of the seeds and ribs if we think the dish needs more punch. When working with dried chiles, we break off the stem to open up the chiles and then brush out the seeds. Dried chiles are generally quite intense and we don't usually reserve their seeds for later use.

WHERE THE HEAT OF JALAPEÑOS RESIDES

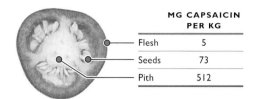

	MG CAPSAICIN PER KG
Flesh	5
Seeds	73
Pith	512

COMMON FRESH CHILES

For many cooks, fresh chiles are a bit of a mystery. And it's no wonder: The same chile can go by different names in different parts of the country and can range from green to red, depending on when it was harvested. To ensure that you're buying the chile called for in a recipe, it's a good idea to look at a photo before shopping. Whatever the variety, you should choose chiles with tight, unblemished skin and flesh that's firm to the touch.

	APPEARANCE	FLAVOR	HEAT	SUBSTITUTIONS
Poblano	Large, triangular; green to red-brown	Crisp, vegetal	🌶	Anaheim, bell pepper
Anaheim	Large, long, skinny; yellow-green to red	Mildly tangy, vegetal	🌶🌶	Poblano
Jalapeño	Small, smooth, shiny; green or red	Bright, grassy	🌶🌶	Serrano
Serrano	Small; dark green	Bright, citrusy	🌶🌶🌶	Jalapeño
Bird's Eye	Narrow and petite; bright red	Rich, fruity	🌶🌶🌶	Serrano
Habanero	Bulbous; bright orange to red	Deeply floral, fruity	🌶🌶🌶🌶	Double dose of Thai Bird's Eye

COMMON DRIED CHILES

Just as dried fruit has a more concentrated taste than its fresh counterpart, chiles gain a more intense character when dried. Because they're allowed to ripen on the plant, many chiles taste sweeter dried than fresh. For dried chiles with the best flavor, buy ones that are pliable and smell slightly fruity.

	APPEARANCE	FLAVOR	HEAT	SUBSTITUTIONS
Ancho	Wrinkly; dark red	Rich, with raisiny sweetness	🌶	Mulato
Mulato	Wrinkly; deep brown	Very smoky, with hints of licorice and dried cherry	🌶	Ancho
Chipotle	Wrinkly; brownish red	Smoky, chocolaty, with tobacco-like sweetness	🌶🌶	None
Cascabel	Small, round; reddish brown	Nutty, woodsy	🌶🌶	New Mexican
New Mexican	Smooth; brick red	Slightly acidic, earthy	🌶🌶	Cascabel
Arbol	Smooth; bright red	Bright with smoky undertones	🌶🌶🌶	Pequin
Pequin	Small, round; deep red	Bright, citrusy	🌶🌶🌶	Arbol

To control the heat of fresh and dried chiles in chilis and stir-fries, we remove the seeds, as well as the whitish pith (also called the ribs), when working with fresh chiles. The pith and seeds contain the majority of the capsaicin, the compound responsible for that spicy kick. We do the same thing in our Mexican Rice (page 274).

WHITE CHICKEN CHILI
SERVES 6 TO 8

Adjust the heat in this dish by adding the minced ribs and seeds from the jalapeño as directed in step 6. If Anaheim chiles cannot be found, add an additional poblano and jalapeño to the chili. Serve this chili with sour cream, tortilla chips, and lime wedges.

3	pounds bone-in split chicken breasts or thighs, trimmed
	Salt and pepper
I	tablespoon vegetable oil, plus extra as needed
3	jalapeño chiles
3	poblano chiles, stemmed, seeded, and cut into large pieces
3	Anaheim chiles, stemmed, seeded, and cut into large pieces
2	onions, cut into large pieces
6	garlic cloves, minced
I	tablespoon ground cumin
I ½	teaspoons ground coriander
2	(15-ounce) cans cannellini beans, rinsed
3	cups low-sodium chicken broth
3	tablespoons lime juice (2 limes)
¼	cup minced fresh cilantro
4	scallions, sliced thin

1. Season chicken with 1 teaspoon salt and ¼ teaspoon pepper. Heat oil in Dutch oven over medium-high heat until just smoking. Add chicken, skin side down, and cook without moving until skin is golden brown, about 4 minutes. Using tongs, flip chicken and lightly brown on other side, about 2 minutes. Transfer chicken to plate; remove and discard skin.

2. While chicken is browning, remove and discard ribs and seeds from 2 jalapeños, then mince jalapeños and set aside. Pulse half of poblanos, Anaheims, and onions in food processor until consistency of chunky salsa, 10 to 12 pulses, scraping down bowl halfway through. Transfer mixture to medium bowl. Repeat with remaining poblanos, Anaheims, and onions; combine with first batch (do not wash food processor).

3. Pour off all but 1 tablespoon fat from Dutch oven (adding additional vegetable oil if necessary) and reduce heat to medium. Add minced jalapeños, chile mixture, garlic, cumin, coriander, and ¼ teaspoon salt. Cover and cook, stirring occasionally, until vegetables have softened, about 10 minutes. Remove pot from heat.

4. Transfer 1 cup cooked vegetable mixture to now-empty food processor. Add 1 cup beans and 1 cup broth and process until smooth, about 20 seconds. Add vegetable-bean mixture, remaining 2 cups broth, and chicken breasts to Dutch oven and bring to boil over medium-high heat. Reduce heat to medium-low and simmer, covered, stirring occasionally, until chicken registers 160 degrees (175 degrees if using thighs), 15 to 20 minutes (40 minutes if using thighs).

5. Transfer chicken to large plate. Add remaining beans to pot and continue to simmer, uncovered, until beans are heated through and chili has thickened slightly, about 10 minutes.

6. Mince remaining jalapeño, reserving and mincing ribs and seeds, and set aside. When cool enough to handle, shred chicken into bite-size pieces, discarding bones. Stir shredded chicken, lime juice, cilantro, scallions, and remaining minced jalapeño (with seeds if desired) into chili and return to simmer. Season with salt and pepper to taste and serve.

✔ WHY THIS RECIPE WORKS

White chicken chili is a fresher, lighter cousin of the thick red chili most Americans know and love. Its appeal is not surprising. First, because the recipe uses chicken rather than beef, many folks appreciate it for being healthier. Next, because there are no tomatoes to mask the other flavors, the chiles, herbs, and spices take center stage. Unlike red chili, which uses any combination of dried chiles, chili powders, and cayenne pepper, white chicken chili gets its backbone from fresh green chiles. We use bone-in, skin-on chicken pieces, three kinds of chiles, and pureed vegetables to make our version filled with flavor and great texture.

BROWN BONE-IN CHICKEN When it came time to choose our chicken, we experimented with ground chicken, chicken thighs, and chicken breasts. Ground chicken was moist but spongy, thighs were flavorful but tended to compete with the flavors of the fresh chiles, and boneless, skinless breasts contributed very little flavor to the chili at all. We had the best luck with bone-in, skin-on breasts (though thighs came in a close second). We brown them in the pot to help develop fond and render their fat, which we like to save to cook with the aromatics later. Discard the skin after browning; if left on, it will be soggy and floppy after stewing.

USE THREE CHILES We use a combination of poblano, Anaheim, and jalapeño chiles in order to achieve vibrant chile flavor. Jalapeños are small, smooth-skinned, forest-green chiles that provide heat and a bitter, green bell pepper–like flavor. Anaheims are long, medium-green, mildly spicy chiles with an acidic, lemony bitterness. Poblanos are large, heart-shaped, blackish-green chiles that are mild to medium-hot and pack a rich, vegetal, slightly sweet flavor.

PUREE THE VEGETABLES When it comes to the vegetables, we start by pulsing the seeded chiles in a food processor in order to chop them up. We cook them along with the onions, garlic, and spices in a covered pot to help soften them. Once they're cooked, we puree the chiles and onions (along with some canned beans and broth) to thicken the chili and to evenly distribute the chile flavor.

POACH THE CHICKEN After we return the pureed chile-onion mixture to the pot and add a bit more broth, we poach the browned chicken in the liquid and later, once slightly cooled, we shred it. The remaining white beans are heated through during this time.

FINISH WITH SEASONINGS This chili is finished with one more minced jalapeño, with its ribs and seeds minced separately and added to taste, giving us control over the level of spiciness. We also top the chili with lime juice, cilantro, and scallions for a bright, colorful finish.

PRACTICAL SCIENCE
KEEPING THE FRESHNESS IN FRESH CHILES

The best way to keep chiles fresh for weeks is in a brine.

Fresh chiles like jalapeños and serranos have a relatively brief shelf life in the refrigerator. We tried four different refrigerator storage methods to see if any would help these chiles keep their crisp texture and fresh flavor longer. We sealed whole chiles in a plastic bag; left them loose in the crisper drawer; sliced them in half (to allow liquid to penetrate) and stored them in plain white vinegar; and sliced them in half and submerged them in a brine solution (1 tablespoon of salt per cup of water). In both the bag and the crisper, the chiles began to soften and turn brown in a week. Storing in vinegar was also not ideal; after about a week, the chiles began tasting more pickled than fresh. The brine-covered chiles, however, retained their crispness, color, and bright heat for several weeks and, after a quick rinse to remove excess brine, were indistinguishable from fresh chiles when we sampled them raw and in salsa. After a month they began to soften, but they remained perfectly usable in cooked applications for several more weeks.

ULTIMATE BEEF CHILI
SERVES 6 TO 8

A 4-pound chuck-eye roast, well trimmed of fat, can be substituted for the steak. Because much of the chili flavor is held in the fat of this dish, refrain from skimming fat from the surface. Dried New Mexican, mulato, or guajillo chiles make a good substitute for the anchos; each dried arbol may be replaced with ⅛ teaspoon cayenne. If you prefer not to work with any whole dried chiles, the anchos and arbols can be replaced with ½ cup of commercial chili powder and ¼ to ½ teaspoon of cayenne pepper, though the texture of the chili will be slightly compromised. Good choices for condiments include diced avocado, finely chopped red onion, chopped cilantro, lime wedges, sour cream, and shredded Monterey Jack or cheddar cheese.

8	ounces (1¼ cups) dried pinto beans, picked over and rinsed
	Salt
6	dried ancho chiles, stemmed, seeded, and torn into 1-inch pieces
2–4	dried arbol chiles, stemmed, seeded, and split into 2 pieces
3	tablespoons cornmeal
2	teaspoons dried oregano
2	teaspoons ground cumin
2	teaspoons cocoa
2½	cups low-sodium chicken broth
2	onions, cut into ¾-inch pieces
3	small jalapeño chiles, stemmed, seeded, and cut into ½-inch pieces
3	tablespoons vegetable oil
4	garlic cloves, minced
1	(14.5-ounce) can diced tomatoes
2	teaspoons molasses
3½	pounds blade steak, ¾ inch thick, trimmed and cut into ¾-inch pieces
1	(12-ounce) bottle mild lager, such as Budweiser

1. Combine 4 quarts water, beans, and 3 tablespoons salt in Dutch oven and bring to boil over high heat. Remove pot from heat, cover, and let stand for 1 hour. Drain and rinse well.

2. Adjust oven rack to lower-middle position and heat oven to 300 degrees. Place anchos in 12-inch skillet set over medium-high heat; toast, stirring frequently, until flesh is fragrant, 4 to 6 minutes, reducing heat if chiles begin to smoke. Transfer to food processor and let cool. Do not wash out skillet.

3. Add arbols, cornmeal, oregano, cumin, cocoa, and ½ teaspoon salt to food processor with toasted anchos; process until finely ground, about 2 minutes. With processor running, slowly add ½ cup broth until smooth paste forms, about 45 seconds, scraping down bowl as necessary. Transfer paste to small bowl. Place onions in now-empty processor and pulse until roughly chopped, about 4 pulses. Add jalapeños and pulse until consistency of chunky salsa, about 4 pulses, scraping down bowl as necessary.

4. Heat 1 tablespoon oil in Dutch oven over medium-high heat. Add onion mixture and cook, stirring occasionally, until moisture has evaporated and vegetables are softened, 7 to 9 minutes. Add garlic and cook until fragrant, about 1 minute. Add chile paste, tomatoes, and molasses; stir until chile paste is thoroughly combined. Add remaining 2 cups broth and drained beans; bring to boil, then reduce heat to simmer.

5. Meanwhile, heat 1 tablespoon oil in 12-inch skillet over medium-high heat until shimmering. Pat beef dry with paper towels and sprinkle with 1 teaspoon salt. Add half of beef and cook until browned on all sides, about 10 minutes. Transfer meat to Dutch oven. Add half of beer to skillet, scraping up browned bits from bottom of pan, and bring to simmer. Transfer beer to Dutch oven. Repeat with remaining 1 tablespoon oil, remaining steak, and remaining beer. Stir to combine and return mixture to simmer.

6. Cover pot and transfer to oven. Cook until meat and beans are fully tender, 1½ to 2 hours. Let chili stand, uncovered, for 10 minutes. Stir well, season with salt to taste, and serve. (Chili can be refrigerated for up to 3 days.)

☑ WHY THIS RECIPE WORKS

Our goal in creating an "ultimate" beef chili was to determine which of the "secret ingredients" recommended by chili experts around the world were spot-on—and which were expendable. We discarded ground beef for blade steaks, used a combination of dried and fresh chiles, and brined our beans for legumes that stayed creamy for the duration of cooking.

CHOOSE YOUR MEAT   After deciding to use diced—not ground—beef, we began by testing six different cuts of beef for our chili: flap meat, brisket, chuck-eye roast, skirt steak, blade steak, and short ribs. Though the short ribs were extremely tender, some tasters felt that they tasted too much like pot roast. The brisket was wonderfully beefy but lean and a bit tough. The clear winner was blade steak, favored for its tenderness and rich flavor. Chuck-eye roast is a good second option.

BRINE THE BEANS   It's important to brine your beans in order to get them to cook quickly, with a lasting tender and creamy texture (see concept 28). We use a quick brine here because beans are not the central focus and, after all, the rest of the recipe takes a fair amount of work. The timing works out perfectly, though: By the time the beans are done brining (one hour), the rest of the work is done.

SEED, TOAST, AND PUREE   For complex chile flavor, we trade in the commercial chili powder in favor of ground dried ancho and arbol chiles; for a grassy heat, we add fresh jalapeños. We toast the anchos to develop their flavor and seed all our chiles to control the heat. We include oregano, cumin, cocoa, salt, and cornmeal (which thickens the chili).

ADD FLAVOR AND TEXTURE   Beer and chicken broth outperformed red wine, coffee, and beef broth as the liquid component. To balance the sweetness of our pot, light molasses beat out other offbeat ingredients (including prunes and Coca-Cola). For the right level of thickness, flour and peanut butter didn't perform as promised; instead, a small amount of ordinary cornmeal sealed the deal, providing just the right consistency in our ultimate beef chili.

STIR-FRIED THAI BEEF WITH CHILES AND SHALLOTS
SERVES 4

If you cannot find blade steaks, use flank steak. Because flank steak requires less trimming, you will need only about 1¾ pounds. To prepare the flank steak, first cut the steak with the grain into 1½-inch-wide strips, then cut the strips against the grain into ¼-inch-thick slices. To make slicing the steak easier, freeze it for 15 minutes. White pepper lends this stir-fry a unique flavor; black pepper is not a good substitute. Serve with steamed jasmine rice.

BEEF STIR-FRY
- 1   tablespoon fish sauce
- 1   teaspoon packed light brown sugar
- ¾   teaspoon ground coriander
- ⅛   teaspoon ground white pepper
- 2   pounds blade steak, trimmed and cut crosswise into ¼-inch-thick strips

SAUCE AND GARNISH
- 2   tablespoons fish sauce
- 2   tablespoons rice vinegar
- 2   tablespoons water

1   tablespoon packed light brown sugar
1   tablespoon Asian chili-garlic sauce
3   garlic cloves, minced
3   tablespoons vegetable oil
3   serrano or jalapeño chiles, stemmed, seeded, and sliced thin
3   shallots, peeled, quartered, and layers separated
½   cup fresh mint leaves, large leaves torn into bite-size pieces
½   cup fresh cilantro leaves
⅓   cup dry-roasted peanuts, chopped
    Lime wedges

1. FOR THE STIR-FRY: Combine fish sauce, sugar, coriander, and white pepper in large bowl. Add beef and toss well to combine; marinate for 15 minutes.

2. FOR THE SAUCE AND GARNISH: Stir together fish sauce, vinegar, water, sugar, and chili-garlic sauce in small bowl until sugar dissolves and set aside. In second small bowl, mix garlic and 1 teaspoon oil together and set aside.

3. To prepare stir-fry, heat 2 teaspoons oil in 12-inch nonstick skillet over high heat until just smoking. Add one-third of beef to skillet in even layer. Cook, without stirring, until well browned, about 2 minutes, then stir and continue cooking until beef is browned around edges and no longer pink in center, about 30 seconds. Transfer beef to medium bowl. Repeat with 4 teaspoons oil and remaining meat, in 2 batches.

4. Reduce heat to medium, add remaining 2 teaspoons oil to skillet, and swirl to coat. Add serranos and shallots and cook, stirring frequently, until beginning to soften, 3 to 4 minutes. Clear center of skillet, add garlic-oil mixture, and cook, mashing garlic into pan, until fragrant, 15 to 20 seconds. Stir garlic into chile mixture. Add fish sauce mixture to skillet, increase heat to high, and cook until slightly reduced and thickened, about 30 seconds.

5. Return beef and any accumulated juices to skillet and toss well to combine and coat with sauce. Stir in half of mint and cilantro. Serve immediately, sprinkling each serving with peanuts and remaining herbs, and passing lime wedges separately.

✔ WHY THIS RECIPE WORKS

Traditional Thai-style beef relies on obscure ingredients like galangal, palm sugar, and dried prawns and requires hours of prep plus deep-frying. We wanted to use easily available ingredients and spend minimal time cooking. We settled on inexpensive blade steak, which offers beefy flavor and tenderness when fully cooked.

With a marinade made of fish sauce, white pepper, coriander, and a little light brown sugar, the beef needed to marinate for only 15 minutes to develop full flavor. To add heat, we introduced an easily controlled heat source—Asian chili-garlic sauce—that also contributed toasty, garlicky flavors.

USE A SALTY MARINADE   We replace our usual stir-fry marinade base—soy sauce—with the equally salty fermented fish sauce that is traditional in Thai chile beef. (For more on the effect of salt in marinades, see concept 13.) The fish sauce simulates the briny flavors of the dried shrimp and shrimp paste listed in many original recipes. To this, we add a little light brown sugar, coriander, and white pepper, which is deeply spicy and penetrating, with a somewhat gamy flavor.

STIR-FRY WELL   As with all of our stir-fries, we cook our ingredients in a predictable order. First, we cook the beef in batches to maximize browning (see concept 2), then add the vegetables (in this case the chiles and shallots), and finish with the garlic (to keep it from scorching). For a Thai dish like this one, we want our sauce to contain salty, sweet, spicy, and sour notes. To that end we use salty fish sauce and sweet brown sugar. Rice vinegar gives us a sour note and the spice comes from the chiles. Thai stir-fries are often finished with fresh herbs (we use cilantro and mint here) and something crunchy (we use peanuts).

CONTROL THE HEAT   We remove the seeds and ribs from the chiles in order to control the level of heat, and then cut the chiles into strips. We add another layer of heat to the mix with the Asian chile-garlic sauce, which provides a complex mix of spicy, toasty, and garlicky flavors. The use of two types of heat gives us the opportunity to control the spice level even more.

PRACTICAL SCIENCE DON'T FREEZE FRESH CHILES

If you have chiles that are on the verge of spoiling, use them up or store them in a brine. But don't bother freezing.

In the test kitchen, we know that fresh chile peppers will last about a week when properly stored in a humid crisper drawer. We also know that we can store them in a brine (see "Keeping the Freshness in Fresh Chiles," page 291). The next question: Could freezing them prolong their life even further? To find out, we froze whole jalapeños and poblano chiles. Two weeks later, we compared batches of frozen and fresh chiles—the jalapeños in salsa, and the poblanos straight up. Texturewise, the thawed frozen peppers were markedly inferior; their once-crisp flesh turned mushy and waterlogged. The flavor of the poblanos had weakened, and the jalapeños' "fresh, grassy" flavor and "building heat" were all but gone. Therefore, use up those chiles before they go bad or stick them in a brine. Freezing is not the way to go.

Bloom Spices to Boost Their Flavor

Spices are a mystery to many American home cooks. We use them in baking recipes like gingerbread but not so much in savory cooking, with the exception of barbecuing (where spice rubs are essential) and some regional cuisines (such as Tex-Mex or Cajun). Part of the problem is how we buy spices (those old jars of ground spices in your pantry probably aren't very good) and part of the problem is not understanding how spices actually work.

HOW THE SCIENCE WORKS

WHEN SPICES ARE BLOOMED

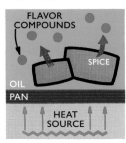

IN HOT OIL *When fat-soluble spices are heated in oil, many of their flavor compounds are released into the surrounding solution, heightening the flavors of both the spices and the oil.*

Spices are generally berries, plant seeds, roots, or bark. When dried, their flavor intensifies, and they can be sold in "whole" form or in powders (called ground spices). Cloves, for example, are dried flower buds. They can be bought whole—the pungent little buds are often used to flavor roasts or mulled drinks. They can also be bought ground and added to spice cakes or cookies.

What unites all spices is their common use as flavoring agents. They have been used in cooking for tens of thousands of years. But they were not viewed as simple ingredients alone: Spices have long been hot commodities, highly sought after and valued for their use in religious rituals and medicine, as well as cooking. The desire for more spices (both larger quantities and a greater variety) spurred a trade system that began in the Middle East around 2000 BC and expanded throughout the world.

But why do spices have so much flavor? The flavor of spices comes mainly from their aroma, which we detect from the volatile molecules they release into the air. Spices have a high proportion of these flavor molecules, which is why they are incredibly potent—in fact, spices in their naked form are almost impossible to ingest alone.

Most spices glean their flavors from a host of different flavor compounds, the mixture giving them character and complexity.

Take black peppercorns. Their unique taste and aroma come from volatile oils called terpenes, which contribute notes of turpentine, clove, and citrus; and pyrazines, which provide earthy, roasty, green vegetable aromas. Peppercorns also contain the heat-bearing compound piperine, which provides that familiar sharp bite and has the added effect of perking up our tastebuds.

Spices generally fall into three categories: those with water-soluble flavor compounds, those with fat-soluble flavor compounds, and those that form new flavor molecules when exposed to dry heat alone. This means that flavors able to dissolve into water are better able to penetrate meat via brinerades (see concept 13), while those able to dissolve into fat can do much more in oil-based marinades (like the one used for Spanish-Style Garlic Shrimp, page 122). Other spices benefit simply from toasting in a dry skillet. (See chart, page 301, for more on individual spices.) But what really makes a difference in the flavor (and intensity of flavor) of spices is the way we use heat.

We can directly apply heat to spices, as when we toast spices or when the spice rub applied to the outside of a cut of meat hits the grill. Toasting a spice whole brings its aromatic oils to the surface, contributing to a stronger, more complex aroma. Toasting certain spices like cumin and coriander also brings about Maillard reactions (see concept 2) between sugars and amino acids, producing potent flavor molecules such as pyrazines. We find it's best to toast spices before grinding them, as grinding releases moisture and aromatic oils into the air, subsequently leaving the spice with less to give when toasted.

We can also cook spices in fat, a process called blooming. This works for spices that are fat-soluble and intensifies the flavors of both ground and whole spices. (We usually discard the pungent whole spices before the dish is served.) When we bloom spices, the fat-soluble flavor molecules are released from a solid state into solution form, where they mix and interact, thereby producing an even more complex flavor. Like most substances, these flavor molecules dissolve faster and to a greater extent in a hot solvent (such as fat or oil) than a cold one. But be careful: If the oil or butter is too hot, the spices can scorch.

TEST KITCHEN EXPERIMENT

In order to determine whether blooming spices and some herbs in oil (as opposed to just water) truly produces more flavorful results, we designed the following experiment: We steeped 50 grams of crushed red pepper flakes separately in 100 grams of canola oil and 100 grams of water, both held at a constant 200 degrees, for 20 minutes. We then strained out the pepper flakes and tasted the water and oil on white rice. We also sent samples of the water and oil to an independent lab to test for capsaicin content (the compound responsible for the heat in pepper flakes) using a technique called high-performance liquid chromatography (HPLC). Finally, we repeated the test with thyme leaves and measured the concentration of their main flavor compound, thymol, to demonstrate the effect of oil blooming on woody herbs. We repeated this test three times.

THE RESULTS

First up, the taste results. For both the pepper flakes and thyme, the oil infusion was far more flavorful than the water sample when tasted on plain white rice. There was no contest, and the lab provided the numbers to prove it. The pepper flake–infused water registered an average of 1113 Scoville Heat Units (SHU), while the pepper-infused oil doubled that number at 2233 SHU. The results for thyme were even more dramatic: The water contained 19.4 parts per million (ppm) of thymol, a tenth as much as the thyme-infused oil with an average of 197 ppm of thymol.

THE TAKEAWAY

While we used some heavy science to quantify our experiment, the takeaway is a no-brainer. For more flavor, many spices (and some herbs) should be bloomed in oil. This requires no extra work. Simply add the spices (or herbs) to the fat in the pan before the liquid goes into the pot. For instance, when making chili, let the spices cook with the onions and garlic before adding the liquid, rather than adding the spices along with the liquid as many recipes do.

And what are some other ways we accentuate the flavor of spices? Grinding, for one. Buying whole spices and then grinding them ourselves keeps them fresher longer and intensifies their aroma and taste. If you buy already ground spices, be sure to replace them every year (whole spices retain their flavor for up to two years). In addition to blooming, we also toast spices in a dry pan. The heat brings the spice's aromatic oils to the surface.

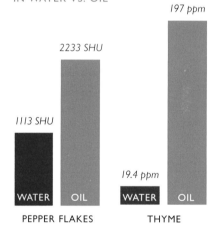

MEASURING FLAVOR COMPOUNDS WHEN SPICES ARE BLOOMED IN WATER VS. OIL

*Capsaicin was tested for using HPLC and reported in Scoville Heat Units (SHU).
**Thymol was tested for using HPLC and reported in parts per million (ppm).

Blooming spices before incorporating them into a dish is an easy step that helps to draw out maximum aroma, boosts flavor, and brings our finished dishes up to the next level. Here, we bloom spices in chili, curry, blackened fish, and pepper-crusted steaks.

SIMPLE BEEF CHILI WITH KIDNEY BEANS
SERVES 8 TO 10

Good choices for condiments include diced fresh tomatoes, diced avocado, sliced scallions, finely chopped red onion, minced fresh cilantro, sour cream, and/or shredded Monterey Jack or cheddar cheese. If you are a fan of spicy food, consider using a little more of the red pepper flakes or cayenne—or both. The flavor of the chili improves with age; if possible, make it the day before you plan to serve it.

2	tablespoons vegetable oil
2	onions, chopped fine
I	red bell pepper, stemmed, seeded, and cut into ½-inch pieces
6	garlic cloves, minced
¼	cup chili powder
I	tablespoon ground cumin
2	teaspoons ground coriander
I	teaspoon red pepper flakes
I	teaspoon dried oregano
½	teaspoon cayenne pepper
2	pounds 85 percent lean ground beef
2	(15-ounce) cans red kidney beans, rinsed
I	(28-ounce) can diced tomatoes, drained with juice reserved
I	(28-ounce) can tomato puree
	Salt
	Lime wedges

1. Heat oil in Dutch oven over medium heat until shimmering but not smoking. Add onions, bell pepper, garlic, chili powder, cumin, coriander, pepper flakes, oregano, and cayenne and cook, stirring occasionally, until vegetables are softened and beginning to brown, about 10 minutes. Increase heat to medium-high and add half of beef. Cook, breaking up pieces with spoon, until no longer pink and just beginning to brown, 3 to 4 minutes. Add remaining beef and cook, breaking up pieces with spoon, until no longer pink, 3 to 4 minutes.

2. Add beans, tomatoes, tomato puree, and ½ teaspoon salt; bring to boil, then reduce heat to low and simmer, covered, stirring occasionally, for 1 hour. Remove cover and continue to simmer for 1 hour longer, stirring occasionally (if chili begins to stick to bottom of pot, stir in ½ cup water and continue to simmer), until beef is tender and chili is dark, rich, and slightly thickened. Season with salt to taste. Serve with lime wedges and condiments, if desired. (Chili can be refrigerated for up to 2 days.)

BEEF CHILI WITH BACON AND BLACK BEANS

Cook 8 slices bacon, cut into ½-inch pieces, in Dutch oven over medium heat, stirring frequently, until browned, about 8 minutes. Pour off all but 2 tablespoons fat, leaving bacon in pot. Substitute bacon fat in Dutch oven for vegetable oil and canned black beans for canned kidney beans.

✔ WHY THIS RECIPE WORKS
With the goal of developing a no-fuss chili that would taste far better than the sum of its parts, we discovered that adding the chili powder to the pan with the aromatics boosted its potency. We enhanced the flavor with additional spices and chose beef without too much (or too little) fat. Cooking the chili with the lid on for half the simmering time resulted in a rich, thick consistency.

ADD SPICES EARLY Unlike our Ultimate Beef Chili recipe (page 291), this chili is the definition of simple. And to get great flavor from easily accessible ingredients, we have to take steps to get the most mileage from jarred spices. Many chili recipes call for the spices to be added after the beef has been browned, but we knew that sometimes ground spices taste better when they get direct contact with the cooking oil. We tested this by cooking three pots of chili—one with the ground spices added before the beef, one with the spices added after the beef, and a third in which we toasted the spices in a separate dry skillet and added them to the pot after the beef. The batch made with spices added after the beef tasted weak. The batch made with the spices toasted in a separate pan was better, but in this case toasting the spices subdued the flavor because some of the volatile flavor molecules vaporized. The clear favorite was the batch made with spices added directly to the pot before the meat. In fact, the best results come with the spices added at the outset of cooking to develop their fat-soluble flavors fully through the power of blooming.

HELP THE CHILI POWDER Commercial chili powder is typically 80 percent ground dried red chiles with the rest a mix of garlic powder, onion powder, oregano, ground cumin, and salt. To boost flavor, we increase the amount of chili powder from the typical recipe, add more cumin and oregano, and toss in some cayenne. The trio of aromatics—onions, red bell pepper, garlic—helps, too.

LEAN, BUT NOT TOO LEAN We tried using beef with different levels of fat for this chili. Pools of orange oil floated to the top of the chili made with ground chuck (80 percent lean beef). At the other end of the spectrum, the chili made with 90 percent lean beef was a tad bland—not bad, but not as full-flavored as the chili made with 85 percent lean beef, our final choice. Be sure not to overbrown the beef when you add it to the pot—it will get tough if you brown it too much. Just cook until it loses its raw pink color.

TWO TOMATOES We tried batches of chili made with water (too watery), chicken broth (too chicken-y and dull), beef broth (too metallic), wine (too acidic), and no liquid at all except for that in the tomatoes (beefy-tasting and by far the best). When we tried beer, we were surprised to find that it subdues that great beefy flavor. Tomato puree gives the chili body, and diced tomatoes give it heft.

DON'T WAIT ON BEANS Most chili recipes add beans toward the end of cooking, the idea being to let them heat through without causing them to fall apart. But this method often makes for beans that are bland orbs floating in a sea of highly flavorful chili. We prefer adding the beans along with the tomatoes. The more time the beans spend in the pot, the better they taste.

INDIAN CURRY WITH POTATOES, CAULIFLOWER, PEAS, AND CHICKPEAS
SERVES 4 TO 6

This curry is moderately spicy when made with one chile. For more heat, use the larger amount of chiles. For a mild curry, do not add the chile's ribs and seeds. (For more on chiles, see concept 32.) The onions can be pulsed in a food processor. You can substitute 2 teaspoons of ground coriander, ½ teaspoon of pepper, ¼ teaspoon of ground cardamom, and ¼ teaspoon of ground cinnamon for the garam masala. In addition to the suggested condiments, serve with Simple Rice Pilaf (page 272) and plain whole-milk yogurt.

2	tablespoons sweet or mild curry powder
1½	teaspoons garam masala
1	(14.5-ounce) can diced tomatoes
¼	cup vegetable oil
2	onions, chopped fine
12	ounces red potatoes, cut into ½-inch pieces
3	garlic cloves, minced
1	tablespoon grated fresh ginger
1–1½	serrano chiles, stemmed, seeds reserved, minced
1	tablespoon tomato paste
½	head cauliflower (1 pound), cored and cut into 1-inch florets
1	(15-ounce) can chickpeas, rinsed
1¼	cups water
	Salt
1½	cups frozen peas
¼	cup heavy cream or coconut milk

CONDIMENTS
    Onion Relish (recipe follows)
    Cilantro-Mint Chutney (recipe follows)

1. Toast curry powder and garam masala in small skillet over medium-high heat, stirring constantly, until spices darken slightly and become fragrant, about 1 minute. Transfer to small bowl and set aside. Pulse tomatoes in food processor until coarsely chopped, 3 to 4 pulses.

2. Heat 3 tablespoons oil in Dutch oven over medium-high heat until shimmering. Add onions and potatoes and cook, stirring occasionally, until onions are caramelized and potatoes are golden brown on edges, about 10 minutes. (Reduce heat to medium if onions darken too quickly.)

3. Reduce heat to medium. Clear center of pot and add remaining 1 tablespoon oil, garlic, ginger, serrano, and tomato paste and cook, stirring constantly, until fragrant, about 30 seconds. Add reserved toasted spices and cook, stirring constantly, about 1 minute. Add cauliflower and cook, stirring constantly, until spices coat florets, about 2 minutes longer.

4. Add tomatoes, chickpeas, water, and 1 teaspoon salt. Increase heat to medium-high and bring mixture to boil, scraping bottom of pot with wooden spoon to loosen browned bits. Cover and reduce heat to medium. Simmer briskly, stirring occasionally, until vegetables are tender, 10 to 15 minutes.

5. Stir in peas and cream and continue to cook until heated through, about 2 minutes. Season with salt to taste, and serve immediately, passing condiments separately.

PRACTICAL SCIENCE PURCHASING SPICES

Buy spices whole and grind them at home.

How should we purchase spices? In most cases, purchasing whole spices and grinding them is preferable to buying ground spices. Whole spices have a longer shelf life (about twice that of ground spices), and most fresh-ground spices also have superior aroma and taste. Black pepper is one spice we never buy preground. As soon as peppercorns are cracked, they begin losing the volatile compounds that give them their bold aroma and subtle flavor; soon enough, all that's left is the more stable, nonvolatile piperine, which gives that sensation of "hotness" but little else. Whether whole or ground, spices should be bought in the smallest quantities available. It also pays to check the expiration date.

ONION RELISH
MAKES ABOUT 1 CUP

If using a regular yellow onion, increase the sugar to 1 teaspoon.

    1   Vidalia onion, diced fine
    1   tablespoon lime juice
    ½   teaspoon sugar
    ½   teaspoon paprika
    ⅛   teaspoon salt
         Pinch cayenne pepper

Combine all ingredients in medium bowl. (Relish can be refrigerated for up to 1 day.)

CILANTRO-MINT CHUTNEY
MAKES ABOUT 1 CUP

    2   cups fresh cilantro leaves
    1   cup fresh mint leaves
    ⅓   cup plain whole-milk yogurt
    ¼   cup finely chopped onion
    1   tablespoon lime juice
    1½   teaspoons sugar
    ½   teaspoon ground cumin
    ¼   teaspoon salt

Process all ingredients in food processor until smooth, about 20 seconds, scraping down sides of bowl halfway through. (Chutney can be refrigerated for up to 1 day.)

✔ WHY THIS RECIPE WORKS
Vegetable curries can be complicated affairs, with lengthy ingredient lists and fussy techniques meant to compensate for the lack of meat. We wanted a curry we could make on a weeknight in less than an hour—without sacrificing flavor or overloading the dish with spices. Toasting store-bought curry powder in a skillet turned it into a flavor powerhouse, and a few pinches of garam masala added even more spice flavor.

TOAST AND BLOOM We toast curry powder and garam masala—which includes such warm spices as black pepper, cinnamon, coriander, and cardamom—in a dry skillet to explode their flavors for this curry. Why is toasting so beneficial? When added to a simmering sauce, the spices can be heated to only 212 degrees. In a dry skillet, temperatures can exceed 500 degrees, heightening flavors exponentially. (But be aware that you can overdo the toasting and burn the spices.) Curry powder and garam masala likewise benefit from an initial dry toasting because the heat induces the formation of Maillard reaction products, which greatly boost flavor. (These reactions do not occur as readily when the spices are bloomed in oil.) Add the toasted spices to the pot with the onions and aromatics so that the spices can bloom even further in the added oil.

SUPERCHARGE THE BASE As the onions caramelize with the other ingredients, fond (flavorful dark bits) develops in the bottom of the pan, mimicking the phenomenon that occurs when browning meat. We add garlic, ginger, and a minced fresh chile for heat. Tomato paste, though inauthentic, adds sweetness, helps browning, and even gives us a meaty flavor (see concept 35).

BROWN THE POTATOES Potatoes can be bland. We like them oven-roasted but that takes time; we found we could brown them along with the onions. We wondered if we could intensify the flavor of the other vegetables as well. An Indian cooking method called *bhuna* involves sautéing the spices and main ingredients together to enhance and meld flavors. This technique works well with the cauliflower used in this recipe, helping to develop a richer, more complex flavor. This method also works with other sturdy vegetables, including green beans and eggplant.

ADD LIQUID A combination of water and pureed canned tomatoes, along with a splash of cream or coconut milk, allows the delicate vegetables and fragrant spices to shine.

GRILLED BLACKENED RED SNAPPER
SERVES 4

Striped bass, halibut, or grouper can be substituted for the snapper; if the fillets are thicker or thinner than ¾ inch, they will have slightly different cooking times. Serve the fish with lemon wedges or Rémoulade (recipe follows).

    2   tablespoons paprika
    2   teaspoons onion powder
    2   teaspoons garlic powder
    ¾   teaspoon ground coriander
    ¾   teaspoon salt
    ¼   teaspoon pepper
    ¼   teaspoon cayenne pepper
    ¼   teaspoon white pepper
    3   tablespoons unsalted butter
    4   (6- to 8-ounce) red snapper fillets, ¾ inch thick

1. Combine paprika, onion powder, garlic powder, coriander, salt, pepper, cayenne, and white pepper in bowl. Melt butter in 10-inch skillet over medium heat. Stir in spice mixture and cook, stirring frequently, until fragrant and spices turn dark rust color, 2 to 3 minutes. Transfer mixture to pie plate and let cool to room temperature. Use fork to break up any large clumps.

2A. FOR A CHARCOAL GRILL: Open bottom vent completely. Light large chimney starter three-quarters filled with charcoal briquettes (4½ quarts). When top coals are partially covered with ash, pour evenly over half of grill. Set cooking grate in place, cover, and open lid vent completely. Heat grill until hot, about 5 minutes.

2B. FOR A GAS GRILL: Turn all burners to high, cover, and heat grill until hot, about 15 minutes.

3. Clean cooking grate, then repeatedly brush grate with well-oiled paper towels until black and glossy, 5 to 10 times.

4. Meanwhile, pat fillets dry with paper towels. Using sharp knife, make shallow diagonal slashes every inch along skin side of fish, being careful not to cut into flesh. Place fillets skin side up on large plate. Using your fingers, rub spice mixture in thin, even layer on top and sides of fish. Flip fillets over and repeat on other side (you should use all of spice mixture). Refrigerate until needed.

5. Place fish skin side down on grill (hot side if using charcoal) with fillets diagonal to grate. Cook until skin is very dark brown and crisp, 3 to 5 minutes. Carefully flip fish and continue to cook until dark brown and beginning to flake and center is opaque but still moist, about 5 minutes longer. Serve.

RÉMOULADE

MAKES ABOUT ½ CUP, ENOUGH FOR 1 RECIPE GRILLED
BLACKENED RED SNAPPER

The rémoulade can be refrigerated for up to three days.

½	cup mayonnaise
1½	teaspoons sweet pickle relish
1	teaspoon hot sauce
1	teaspoon lemon juice
1	teaspoon minced fresh parsley
½	teaspoon capers, rinsed
½	teaspoon Dijon mustard
1	small garlic clove, minced
	Salt and pepper

Pulse all ingredients in food processor until well combined but not smooth, about 10 pulses. Season with salt and pepper to taste. Transfer to serving bowl.

✓ WHY THIS RECIPE WORKS

Blackened fish is usually prepared in a cast-iron skillet, but it can lead to a relentlessly smoky kitchen. We thought we'd solve this issue by throwing our fish on the grill, but this introduced a host of new challenges, including curled fillets that stuck to the grill and spices that tasted raw and harsh. Scoring the skin of our fish, cleaning our grill thoroughly, and creating a rich spice rub gives us a well-cooked red snapper dish with a great crust and the proper depth and richness of flavor.

MAKE BLACKENING RUB After sampling six store-bought Cajun spice rubs, we found that mixing our own delivers superior results. We add coriander, which can take the heat and gives the spice rub a bright floral note. We also use garlic and onion powders, and sweet paprika, cayenne pepper, black pepper, white pepper, and salt.

BLOOM IN BUTTER Yes, the spices will get plenty of heat on the grill. But sautéing them in butter releases additional flavors; they turn several shades darker (bright red to dark, rusty brown) and you can smell the difference. After they cool, we break apart the clumps and apply a thin layer to the fish. By the time the fish is cooked, the spices are blackened.

FLATTEN FILLETS Skin-on fillets will buckle when grilled because the skin shrinks back, pulling the flesh along with it. The fillets remain flat if the skin is scored first, which prevents it from contracting more quickly than the flesh. Use a sharp knife to make shallow slits in the skin before applying the rub, and make sure not to cut too deep, into the flesh.

CATCH AND RELEASE Blackening fish indoors makes no sense at home; you don't have enough ventilation. We bring our recipe out to the grill. But to prevent the fish from sticking to the grill, we have to take some preventive measures. First, we chill the fish. At room temperature, the fillets will become floppy and will stick more readily to the grill. Second, we heat the grill, scrape the grate clean with a brush, and wipe it with oil-dipped paper towels at least five times, until the grates are black and glossy. To cook, place the fish diagonal to the grill grate with skin side facing down. And to flip? Slide one spatula underneath the fillet to lift, while using another to help support the fish as it's flipped.

PEPPER-CRUSTED FILETS MIGNONS
SERVES 4

To crush the peppercorns, spread half of them on a cutting board, place a skillet on top, and, pressing down firmly with both hands, use a rocking motion to crush the peppercorns beneath the "heel" of the skillet. Repeat with the remaining peppercorns. While heating the peppercorns in oil tempers much of their pungent heat, this recipe is still pretty spicy. If you prefer a very mild pepper flavor, drain the cooled peppercorns in a fine-mesh strainer in step 1, toss them with 5 tablespoons of fresh oil, add the salt, and proceed. Serve with Blue Cheese and Chive Butter (recipe follows).

5   tablespoons black peppercorns, crushed
5   tablespoons plus 2 teaspoons olive oil
1   tablespoon kosher salt
4   (7- to 8-ounce) center-cut filets mignons,
    1½ to 2 inches thick

1. Heat peppercorns and 5 tablespoons oil in small saucepan over low heat until faint bubbles appear. Continue to cook at bare simmer, swirling pan occasionally, until pepper is fragrant, 7 to 10 minutes. Remove from heat and set aside to cool. When mixture is room temperature, add salt and stir to combine. Rub steaks with oil and pepper mixture, thoroughly coating top and bottom of each steak with peppercorns. Cover steaks with plastic wrap and press gently to make sure peppercorns adhere; let stand at room temperature for 1 hour.

PRACTICAL SCIENCE
DON'T TOAST YOUR PEPPERCORNS

Black pepper loses its characteristic bite when toasted.

We often recommend toasting whole spices before grinding them to intensify their taste, but what about black pepper? We took two batches of Kalustyan's (our favorite brand of peppercorns); toasted one in a dry skillet and left the other alone; and tasted each plain, ground over scrambled eggs, and crushed and pan-seared in steak *au poivre*. The untoasted pepper won every test. While tasters noted that the flavor of the toasted pepper was smokier, it lacked the pungency of the untoasted pepper. This is because pepper's piquancy comes from a volatile molecule called piperine. When pepper is heated, piperine is converted to less pungent molecules (called isomers). Without piperine, pepper has no bite, and without bite, pepper has no purpose.

---

2. Meanwhile, adjust oven rack to middle position, place baking sheet on oven rack, and heat oven to 450 degrees. When oven reaches 450 degrees, heat remaining 2 teaspoons oil in 12-inch skillet over medium-high heat until just smoking. Place steaks in skillet and cook, without moving, until dark brown crust has formed, 3 to 4 minutes. Using tongs, turn steaks and cook until well browned on second side, about 3 minutes. Transfer steaks to hot baking sheet in oven. Roast until meat registers 115 to 120 degrees (for rare), 120 to 125 degrees (for medium-rare), or 130 to 135 degrees (for medium), 3 to 7 minutes. Transfer steaks to wire rack and let rest, tented loosely with aluminum foil, for 5 minutes before serving.

BLUE CHEESE AND CHIVE BUTTER
MAKES ABOUT ½ CUP, ENOUGH FOR 1 RECIPE PEPPER-CRUSTED FILETS MIGNONS

1½   ounces (¼ cup) mild blue cheese, room
     temperature
3   tablespoons unsalted butter, softened
⅛   teaspoon salt
2   tablespoons minced fresh chives

Combine all ingredients in medium bowl. While steaks are resting, spoon 1 to 2 tablespoons butter onto each one.

✓ WHY THIS RECIPE WORKS
Black peppercorns can give mild-tasting filet mignon a welcome flavor boost. But they can also create a punishing blast of heat. For pepper-crusted filets mignons with a crust that wouldn't overwhelm the meat, we mellowed the peppercorns' heat by gently simmering them in olive oil.

REVERSE ENGINEER In this recipe we're using the same principles of blooming to convert the natural irritant in peppercorns (piperine) into more complex, less harsh flavor molecules. This means that we're increasing overall flavor and complexity, while reducing the level of heat. How? As peppercorns age, the piperine is converted into closely related molecules (called isomers) that have different flavor characteristics and that are less irritating to the nose and throat. Left sitting at room temperature in your cupboard, the peppercorns may take months to undergo this reaction, but the hot oil serves as a catalyst, driving the conversion at hundreds of times its natural speed, as well as vaporizing some of the piperine, quickly tempering the pepper's pungency. As a bonus, piperine and its isomers are oil-soluble, so that during the simmer some of the remaining pepper heat and flavor leach out of the peppercorns into the surrounding oil. This oil can then be discarded to further reduce the heat of the dish.

COAT AND PRESS We use a two-step process to create a well-browned and attractive pepper crust: First, we rub the raw steaks with a paste of the cooked cracked peppercorns, oil, and salt; then we press the paste into each steak using a sheet of plastic wrap to ensure it stays put. The paste not only adds flavor to the meat but also draws out the meat's own beefy flavor. Adding salt to the rub makes it easy to season the steaks at the same time the crust is applied. The one-hour rest gives the salt time to do its work (see concept 12).

SEAR, THEN ROAST Here we sear the steaks in order to get them to brown and become flavorful (see concept 2) and then let them finish cooking in the oven on a preheated baking sheet (see concept 5). This is partly to ensure even cooking of the steaks, but also to limit the time the pepper crust is being seared—you don't want it to burn.

REST AND SAUCE Be sure to let the steaks rest before serving (concept 3). If you like, spoon the compound Blue Cheese and Chive Butter over the steaks as they rest.

PRACTICAL SCIENCE COMMON SPICES AND HOW TO USE THEM

It can be difficult to keep all the spices in your cupboard straight. Knowing their solubility and the best way to buy them can help.

SPICE	BEST TO BUY	SOLUBLE IN	HOW TO USE
Cardamom	Whole	Oil	Whole cardamom consists of a green seed pod that holds about 20 small black seeds. Since the flavor resides in the seeds, it is necessary to crush whole pods before using them.
Cayenne Pepper	Ground	Oil	Originally made from cayenne peppers, this spice is now made from a variety of ground dried chiles. Cayenne pepper is rich with volatile oils, making it susceptible to flavor loss within a few months.
Chili Powder	Ground	Oil	Because chili powder is a blend of spices (generally 80 percent ground dried chiles with garlic powder, oregano, and cumin), it should be bloomed in hot oil to bring out its complex flavors.
Cinnamon	Ground	Oil	Cinnamon is one of the few spices we prefer to buy ground. Save whole cinnamon sticks for infusing flavor into hot liquids.
Cloves	Ground	Oil	Cloves are potent and should be used sparingly. Because whole cloves are difficult to grind, we buy them ground. Reserve whole cloves for infusing flavor into hot liquids (that include fat or alcohol, in which cloves are soluble) or for inserting into ham.
Coriander	Whole	Oil	Coriander is the seed of the plant that produces the herb cilantro. Coriander is sold whole and ground, but whole seeds provide a more vibrant, complex flavor. Toasting whole coriander seeds helps to release their aroma.
Cumin	Whole	Oil	Cumin is the highly aromatic spice that comes from a plant in the parsley family. If time allows, we like to toast whole cumin seeds and then grind them; this gives the spice a more complex peppery flavor than when purchased ground.
Curry Powder	Ground	Oil	Curry powder is a blend of spices. Most formulas include cardamom, chiles, cumin, fennel, fenugreek, nutmeg, and turmeric, which gives curry its characteristic yellow color. For general cooking, we prefer a mild curry powder; hot curry powder, which contains more chiles, can be overpowering. Curry should be sautéed in hot oil to bloom its flavor.
Nutmeg	Whole	Oil	Nutmeg is the dried seedlike kernel of an evergreen tree. It loses its aroma when ground, so it's best to buy whole nutmegs and grate them when needed. Just keep in mind that a little goes a long way.
Paprika	Ground	Oil	Paprika is a fine powder made by grinding dried red peppers. We prefer the complexity of sweet paprika, especially brands from Hungary and Spain, which have a slightly fuller flavor than domestic varieties.
Saffron	Whole	Water and Oil	Saffron, the world's most expensive spice, is the hand-harvested stigma of a type of crocus. To release flavor, crush saffron threads with your fingers before adding them to a dish. Use sparingly; too much will impart a metallic taste.

Not All Herbs Are for Cooking

Herbs often mean the difference between a good dish and a great one. Sure, sometimes they serve little purpose, like when they're used as a garnish on a restaurant plate. But they shouldn't be an afterthought. Herbs play a critical role in the kitchen in many dishes, and knowing how to handle them is key.

HOW THE SCIENCE WORKS

Herbs are plants or parts of plants used in cooking to add flavor rather than substance. Basil, rosemary, parsley, and oregano might all grow in the same patch in your garden but in the kitchen these herbs require different treatment. We think it helps to divide the world of herbs into two camps.

Some herbs have a hearty, almost woody texture. The leaves are sturdy and the stems can be tough. This group includes rosemary, oregano, sage, thyme, and marjoram. In addition, these herbs are quite potent. A little bit goes a long way. For these reasons, these herbs are best cooked. They often go into the pot along with the aromatics. Cooking gives these herbs time to soften and permeate a dish with their flavors. These herbs are potent enough that dried forms are acceptable in long-simmering dishes like soups, stews, and chili.

Other herbs have a delicate leafy texture. The stems are tender, even edible. This group includes basil, parsley, cilantro, dill, mint, chives, and tarragon. These herbs are subject to wilting and discoloration. Also, it often requires a significant amount of these herbs to have an impact on a dish. You can easily finish a pound of pasta with several tablespoons of minced parsley, but do the same thing with oregano and the effect is overwhelming. For these reasons, these herbs are best used to finish dishes or used raw in sauces. While heartier herbs are still good to use when dried, delicate herbs like parsley lose much of their oomph.

Why the difference in flavor and flavor duration in these herbs? The principal flavor compounds in herbs and spices can be divided into a few categories: hydrocarbons, aldehydes, ketones, and phenols. The flavor of most herbs and spices is due to a combination of these classes of molecules, although a few of them owe their flavor to just one or two dominant compounds. The heartiness of an herb or spice is dependent on the volatility or stability of its flavor compounds. The delicate herbs lose flavor compounds during cooking or drying. The flavor of dill, for example, is lost because a number of its aroma compounds, such as the hydrocarbon phellandrene, are not stable under the conditions of cooking and drying. In contrast, the dominant flavor compounds in oregano are relatively nonvolatile, chemically stable phenols, such as carvacrol and thymol, while rosemary contains the stable ketones cineole and camphor. Thus, the hearty herbs contain "hardy" flavor compounds, while the delicate herbs contain "delicate" compounds.

The flavors of fresh herbs are transmitted in a few ways. Chopping is one. The knife ruptures the herb's cells, releasing flavor molecules. Bruising, or muddling, is another. Heating is the third way. We cook heartier herbs so they release their flavors over a long period of time. Delicate herbs are best added at the end.

COOKING WITH HEARTY AND DELICATE HERBS

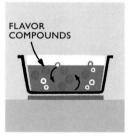

FLAVOR COMPOUNDS

HEARTY HERBS *Heartier herbs like rosemary and oregano have more stable flavor compounds that remain in the dish when cooked.*

DELICATE HERBS *Delicate herbs like basil, parsley, and cilantro contain volatile flavor compounds that quickly disperse when cooked.*

TEST KITCHEN EXPERIMENT

Dried herbs are more convenient to use than fresh because they require no more prep than a twist of the lid. Some cooks swear by the convenience of dried herbs. Others refuse to use dried herbs—ever. We decided to look into the matter more thoroughly and purchased fresh and dried versions of basil, chives, dill, oregano, parsley, rosemary, sage (in coarsely crumbled, rubbed, and ground forms), tarragon, and thyme. Then we cooked our way through 24 recipes (including marinades, sauces, and braises), making each with fresh and dried herbs and comparing differences in flavor.

THE RESULTS

In all but one application, fresh herbs were preferred over dry. A common criticism of dried herbs was that they tasted "dusty" and "stale," while fresh herbs tasted "clean" and "bright." Many of the subtleties and nuances of fresh herbs seemed to be lost with drying.

THE TAKEAWAY

The good news is that there were a few instances in which some dried herbs were passable, mainly in recipes involving fairly long cooking times (20 minutes plus) and a good amount of moisture. Chili stood out as the one dish that was better when made with a dried herb (oregano) than with fresh. Dried rosemary, sage, and thyme also fared reasonably well in some applications. In other tests, we found that dried bay leaf and marjoram will work just fine in similar preparations. The flavor compounds in these herbs are relatively stable at high temperatures, helping them maintain their flavor even through the drying process. Those herbs that we unofficially classify as delicate (basil, chives, dill, parsley, and tarragon) seemed to have lost most of their flavor when dried; we preferred fresh forms of these herbs in every test.

There is sometimes the misconception that dried herbs are less potent than fresh. But depending on the variety, fresh herb leaves are 80 to 90 percent water. With drying, water is lost and, consequently, so are weight and volume. The volatile essential oils that give an herb its characteristic flavor and aroma are left closer to the surface. Because of this water loss, ounce for ounce, dried herbs are more potent than fresh. Our testing—in which we used only newly purchased jars of herbs—indicated that using 1 part dried herb to 3 parts fresh came closest to producing flavors of equal strength. However, if the herb is ground, like sage, 1 part dried ground to 4 parts fresh was the more suitable ratio.

If using dried herbs, keep in mind that the flavorful oils should be released before the herbs are added to the food. Place the dried herbs in a mesh strainer and push down on them with your fingertips as you shake the strainer back and forth over a bowl. And don't forget: In all recipes that use herbs raw (like pesto, see page 304) or to finish a dish, you must use fresh herbs—no substitutions will work.

SIZING UP HERBS

TYPES OF HERBS	WHOLE LEAVES PER ½ OUNCE	FINELY MINCED LEAVES PER ½ OUNCE
Rosemary, Thyme	½ cup	2–2½ tablespoons
Basil, Cilantro, Dill, Mint, Parsley, Tarragon	¾ cup	3 tablespoons
Chives	No whole leaves	4 tablespoons
Marjoram, Oregano, Sage	¾ cup	5 tablespoons

We use milder herbs to add fresh, bright flavor to dishes through-
out this book. For more recipes, see Grilled Argentine Steaks with
Chimichurri Sauce (page 29), Hearty Minestrone (page 259), and
French Potato Salad with Dijon Mustard and Fines Herbes (page 235).

CLASSIC BASIL PESTO
MAKES ENOUGH FOR 1 POUND OF PASTA

Basil usually darkens in homemade pesto, but you can boost the
green color a little by adding the optional parsley. Pecorino Romano
cheese gives the pesto a sharper flavor than Parmesan. When adding pesto to cooked pasta it is important to include 3 or 4 tablespoons of the pasta cooking water for proper consistency and even
distribution.

3   garlic cloves, unpeeled
¼   cup pine nuts
2   cups fresh basil leaves
2   tablespoons fresh parsley leaves (optional)
7   tablespoons extra-virgin olive oil
    Salt and pepper
¼   cup finely grated Parmesan cheese or Pecorino
    Romano cheese

1. Toast garlic in 8-inch skillet over medium heat, shaking pan occasionally, until softened and spotty brown,
about 8 minutes; when cool enough to handle, remove and
discard skins. While garlic cools, toast nuts in now-empty
skillet over medium heat, stirring often, until golden and
fragrant, 4 to 5 minutes.

PRACTICAL SCIENCE STORING BASIL

The best way to store basil is wrapped in a damp paper towel,
in an unsealed zipper-lock bag, in the refrigerator.

When making pesto, storing leftover basil won't be an issue—the
large bunches available at the supermarket will be easily used up.
But what about those occasions when only two or three leaves
are needed to season a dish? We wondered how long we could
keep leftover basil and what would be the best way to store it.

   Since leaving basil out on the counter wasn't an option (it
wilted within hours) we were stuck with refrigerator storage,
which is about 15 degrees colder than the recommended temperature for basil. We tested storing basil in unsealed zipper-lock
bags (to prevent buildup of moisture, which can cause basil to
turn black), both plain and wrapped in damp paper towels (our
preferred method for most leafy greens). After three days in the
refrigerator, both samples were still green and perky. But after
one week, only the towel-wrapped basil still looked and tasted
fresh. Don't be tempted to rinse basil until just before you need
to use it; when we performed the same tests after rinsing, the
shelf life was decreased by half.

---

2. Place basil and parsley, if using, in 1-gallon zipper-
lock bag. Pound bag with flat side of meat pounder or rolling pin until all leaves are bruised.

3. Process garlic, nuts, herbs, oil, and ½ teaspoon salt
in food processor until smooth, about 1 minute, scraping down bowl as needed. Transfer mixture to small bowl,
stir in Parmesan, and season with salt and pepper to taste.
(Pesto can be refrigerated for up to 3 days in bowl with
plastic wrap or thin layer of oil covering surface.)

✓ WHY THIS RECIPE WORKS

Our goal in developing our pesto was to heighten the basil and
subdue the garlic flavors so that each major element balanced the
other. We started with plenty of fresh basil and pounded to bruise
it and release flavorful oils. To tame the raw garlic edge, we toasted
it, toasting the nuts as well to give them more intense flavor. And
we used a food processor to combine the ingredients in our pesto
quickly and easily.

TOAST THE GARLIC   The biggest problem with most
pesto recipes is an abundance of garlic flavor. It's harsh and
bitter. But if you don't use enough garlic, the sauce lacks

PRACTICAL SCIENCE BRIGHTER, GREENER PESTO

To prevent darkening basil and a drab-looking pesto, blanch.

To find out if pesto can be prevented from darkening by blanching the basil before adding it to the food processor, we made
two batches of pesto: one with fresh basil and one with blanched
leaves. The pesto made with fresh basil started to darken as soon
as we scooped it out of the food processor, but the blanched
batch stayed bright green even after sitting for a few hours on
the counter. When we sampled the sauces, tasters found them
virtually identical in flavor. After an entire week in the refrigerator,
the blanched-basil pesto was still a brilliant green, as was a sample
that we froze for three weeks and then thawed.

   Here's why blanching works: Cutting, processing, or bruising
releases enzymes within the basil leaf that promote rapid oxidation, darkening its bright green color. Blanching (dunking the
leaves in boiling water for 20 to 30 seconds, then plunging them
into ice water) inactivates those enzymes, so the color holds fast.

   If you're making a limited quantity of pesto to use right away,
blanching is hardly worth the trouble. But if you're transforming a
bumper crop into a year's worth of pesto, the process will ensure
vivid color that lasts.

BLANCHED = BRIGHT   UNBLANCHED = DULL

oomph. Toasting is a guaranteed way to control the garlic flavor; you bring out its sweetness and dial back the harshness (see concept 31). To do this, leave the peel on the garlic and cook in a dry skillet until spotty brown. Once the garlic cools, remove the skin to reveal cloves that have been lightly cooked.

TOAST THE NUTS, TOO   Toasting nuts brings out their aromatic oils, contributing to a stronger, more complex flavor and aroma. If you decide to toast more than the requisite ¼ cup for this recipe—more than 1 cup—oven-toast the nuts on a roomy, rimmed baking sheet. The oven offers not only more space than a skillet but also more even heat than the stove, with less need for stirring.

BRUISE THE HERBS   Bruising the herbs is an important step for this pesto because it releases the basil's full range of herbal and anise flavor notes in a way that the chopping action of the food processor alone cannot accomplish. Bruising the basil leaves in a zipper-lock bag with a meat pounder helps to make for a mellow, full-tasting pesto.

ADD PARSLEY TO KEEP THE PESTO GREEN   A little parsley doesn't really affect flavor, but it can help keep basil fresh-looking.

USE EXTRA-VIRGIN OLIVE OIL   In raw sauces like pesto, or Salsa Verde (recipe follows), you can really taste the oil used. Therefore, this isn't the place to skimp. Use the good stuff for the best flavor.

SALSA VERDE
MAKES 1½ CUPS

Salsa verde is excellent with grilled or roasted meats, fish, or poultry; poached fish; boiled or steamed potatoes; or sliced tomatoes. It is also good on sandwiches. This recipe can be easily cut in half.

2–3	slices hearty white sandwich bread, lightly toasted and cut into ½-inch pieces (1½ cups)
1	cup extra-virgin olive oil
¼	cup lemon juice (2 lemons)
4	cups parsley leaves (2 bunches)
¼	cup capers, rinsed
4	anchovy fillets, rinsed
1	garlic clove, minced
¼	teaspoon salt

Process bread, oil, and lemon juice in food processor until smooth, about 10 seconds. Add parsley, capers, anchovies, garlic, and salt and pulse until finely chopped (mixture should not be smooth), about 5 pulses. Transfer to serving bowl. (Salsa verde can be refrigerated for up to 2 days.)

LEMON-BASIL SALSA VERDE

Replace 2 cups parsley with 2 cups fresh basil leaves, increase garlic to 2 cloves, and add 1 teaspoon grated lemon zest.

✔ WHY THIS RECIPE WORKS

Despite its innate simplicity, salsa verde can easily go wrong. In fact, many of the recipes we tested were overly potent and harsh, leaving tasters with puckered lips and raging garlic breath. The texture was problematic, too; all of those first salsas separated into pools of oil and clumps of parsley. Processing chunks of toasted bread with oil and lemon juice—not vinegar—in a food processor created a smooth base. We then added the remaining ingredients: anchovies for a touch of complexity, capers for brininess, a little garlic for bite, and parsley to make the sauce "verde." For a variation, we replaced half of the parsley with fragrant basil.

PICK FLAT-LEAF PARSLEY   Some parsley is curly, some is flat. What's the difference? Though curly and flat-leaf parsley have the same Latin name—*Petroselinum crispum*—they are far from identical. Curly parsley is the old-fashioned corsage propped up next to your steak, a flouncy garnish. Beyond that—being practically flavorless—it's not much use. Even so, restaurants often favor curly parsley for chopping because its upright carriage and drier nature make the going easier. Flat-leaf, on the other hand, with its big green flavor, deserves the same culinary status of any fresh herb. Salsa verde depends on it. So shop wisely: Go for the big taste, forget the frills.

TOAST YOUR BREAD   Bread buffers some of the strong flavors of this salsa and helps to make the sauce less puckery. Also, processing bread with the oil and lemon juice gives the sauce a smoother texture and keeps the oil from separating into pools. Airy, moist breads produce gummy sauces, however. The ideal choice is firm, dry bread with a tight crumb. But don't go out and buy bread just for salsa verde. Fifteen seconds in the toaster will dry out even the squishiest of breads.

ADD SOUR AND SALTY   Among olives, capers, cornichons, and combinations thereof, capers alone were the top choice for their salty, pungent bite. As for the acidic component, fresh lemon juice narrowly won out over an array of vinegars. The lemon juice nicely accents the fresh, clean flavor of the parsley. Lemon juice is also less harsh than most vinegars. The anchovy fillets are mandatory, adding a welcome complexity (but not fishiness) to the sauce.

Heartier herbs stand up to long cooking and can be effectively infused into oils. We use herbs like oregano and rosemary in other recipes throughout this book, like Hearty Tuscan Bean Stew (page 258), Cuban Black Beans and Rice (page 260), and Inexpensive Grill-Roasted Beef with Garlic and Rosemary (page 63).

MARINARA SAUCE
MAKES ENOUGH FOR I POUND OF PASTA

Chianti or Merlot work well for the dry red wine. We like a smoother marinara, but if you prefer a chunkier sauce, give it just three or four pulses in the food processor in step 4.

2   (28-ounce) cans whole tomatoes
3   tablespoons extra-virgin olive oil
I   onion, chopped fine
2   garlic cloves, minced
2   teaspoons minced fresh oregano or
    ½ teaspoon dried
⅓   cup dry red wine
3   tablespoons chopped fresh basil
    Salt and pepper
    Sugar

I. Pour tomatoes and juice into strainer set over large bowl. Open tomatoes with hands and remove and discard seeds and fibrous cores; let tomatoes drain excess liquid, about 5 minutes. Remove ¾ cup tomatoes from strainer and set aside. Reserve 2½ cups tomato juice and discard remainder.

2. Heat 2 tablespoons oil in 12-inch skillet over medium heat until shimmering. Add onion and cook until softened and lightly browned, 5 to 7 minutes. Stir in garlic and oregano and cook until fragrant, about 30 seconds.

3. Stir in strained tomatoes and increase heat to medium-high. Cook, stirring often, until liquid has evaporated, tomatoes begin to stick to bottom of pan, and brown fond forms around pan edges, 10 to 12 minutes. Stir in wine and cook until thick and syrupy, about 1 minute. Stir in reserved tomato juice, scraping up any browned bits. Bring to simmer and cook, stirring occasionally, until sauce is thick, 8 to 10 minutes.

4. Transfer sauce and reserved tomatoes to food processor and pulse until slightly chunky, about 8 pulses. Return sauce to now-empty skillet, stir in basil and remaining 1 tablespoon oil, and season with salt, pepper, and sugar to taste.

✔ WHY THIS RECIPE WORKS

For a multidimensional marinara sauce that would take less than an hour to prepare, we chose canned whole tomatoes. We added flavor by browning the tomatoes and included a minced onion and red wine. We cooked hearty dried oregano to draw out its flavor but saved delicate fresh basil for the finish.

COOK OREGANO WITH AROMATICS We add the oregano with the garlic to bloom its flavor, similar to the way we handle spices. (See concept 33.) Oregano is a hearty herb, able to survive the longer cooking time of this sauce. This recipe works with either fresh or dried oregano. (For more on dried herbs, see Test Kitchen Experiment, page 303.)

DRAIN AND BROWN THE TOMATOES Crushed, pureed, and diced tomatoes offer the ultimate ease in sauce making: Open can, dump contents into pan. But all three options have downsides. Pureed tomatoes go into the can already cooked, which imparts a stale, flat flavor to the final sauce. Crushed tomatoes are generally packed in tomato puree; same problem. With canned diced tomatoes, the problem is texture, not flavor. In the past, we've learned that manufacturers treat diced tomatoes with calcium chloride to keep them from turning to mush and losing their shape. That's fine for many dishes, but for recipes in which a smooth consistency is desired, calcium chloride does its job too well, making the tomatoes harder to break down—and the resulting sauces oddly granular. The only choice left, then, is canned whole tomatoes. (While whole tomatoes are also treated with calcium chloride, the chemical has direct contact with a much smaller percentage of the tomato.) The big drawback of using whole tomatoes in this sauce is that they have to be cut up. Chopping them on the cutting board makes a mess. Our solution is to dump the tomatoes into a strainer over a bowl and then hand crush them, removing the hard core and any stray bits of skin. We sauté the tomato meats until they glaze the bottom of the pan. Only then do we add the tomato liquid, a step that, by essentially deglazing the pan, adds crucial flavor to the sauce.

ADD WINE AND REDUCE We like a nice dry wine for this sauce. Wines with a heavy oak flavor rated lower than those with little to no oak presence. (Chianti and Merlot scored particularly high marks with tasters.) The wine adds flavor, but we cook it down to get rid of the majority of alcohol. (For more on cooking with wine, see concept 37.)

FRESH BASIL COMES LAST The basil is added at the end to preserve its color and flavor. It adds a floral aroma that complements the sauce's careful balance of sweet and acidic flavors.

GRILLED POTATOES WITH GARLIC AND ROSEMARY
SERVES 4

This recipe works best with small potatoes that are about 1 ½ inches in diameter. If using medium potatoes, 2 to 3 inches in diameter, cut them into quarters. If the potatoes are larger than 3 inches in diameter, cut each potato into eighths. Since the potatoes are first cooked in the microwave, use wooden skewers.

¼	cup olive oil
9	garlic cloves, minced
1	teaspoon minced fresh rosemary
	Salt and pepper
2	pounds small red potatoes, halved and skewered
2	tablespoons minced fresh chives

1. Heat oil, garlic, rosemary, and ½ teaspoon salt in 8-inch skillet over medium heat until sizzling, about 3 minutes. Reduce heat to medium-low and continue to cook until garlic is light blond, about 3 minutes. Pour mixture through fine-mesh strainer into small bowl; press on solids. Measure 1 tablespoon solids and 1 tablespoon oil into large bowl and set aside. Discard remaining solids but reserve remaining oil.

2. Place skewered potatoes in single layer on large plate and poke each potato several times with skewer. Brush with 1 tablespoon strained oil and season with salt. Microwave until potatoes offer slight resistance when pierced with paring knife, about 8 minutes, turning halfway through cooking. Transfer potatoes to baking sheet coated with 1 tablespoon strained oil. Brush with remaining 1 table-spoon strained oil and season with salt and pepper.

3A. FOR A CHARCOAL GRILL: Open bottom vent completely. Light large chimney starter filled with char-coal briquettes (6 quarts). When top coals are partially covered with ash, pour two-thirds evenly over grill, then pour remaining coals over half of grill. Set cooking grate in place, cover, and open lid vent completely. Heat grill until hot, about 5 minutes.

3B. FOR A GAS GRILL: Turn all burners to high, cover, and heat grill until hot, about 15 minutes. Turn all burners to medium-high.

4. Clean and oil cooking grate. Place potatoes on grill (hotter side if using charcoal) and cook (covered if using gas) until grill marks appear, 3 to 5 minutes, flipping half-way through cooking. Move potatoes to cooler side of grill

(if using charcoal) or turn all burners to medium-low (if using gas). Cover and continue to cook until paring knife slips in and out of potatoes easily, 5 to 8 minutes longer.

5. Remove potatoes from skewers and transfer to bowl with reserved garlic-oil mixture. Add chives, season with salt and pepper to taste, and toss until thoroughly coated. Serve.

✔ WHY THIS RECIPE WORKS

Grilled potatoes are a summer classic, but we wanted to put a new spin on this dish by adding rosemary and garlic. Unfortunately, we found it was difficult to add garlic and rosemary flavors to plain grilled potatoes. Our solution came in infusing the flavors of garlic and rosemary into olive oil, and using the oil to flavor the potatoes. We finally had it—tender grilled potatoes infused with the smoky flavor of the grill and enlivened with the bold flavors of garlic and rosemary.

MAKE AN INFUSED OIL We wanted the potent flavors of garlic and rosemary on our grilled potatoes, but we didn't want the garlic or herb to burn when exposed to the high heat of the grill. We solve this problem by cooking the garlic and rosemary in olive oil, to release their full flavor before straining and discarding them. This way, when we brush the potatoes with this oil a few times throughout the cooking process, the potatoes drink that flavor right in. This is a much more effective way to flavor the potatoes than simply tossing them with chopped rosemary at the end of cooking, as many recipes do. It's important to note that garlic in olive oil should not be kept for more than a few days, even if it's made with roasted garlic. This is because garlic can harbor the fatally toxic botulism bacteria. As the University of California at Davis cautions, even roasting garlic does not kill the bacteria's spores.

MICROWAVE, THEN GRILL We cook our potatoes in two stages. First: Pierce, salt, and precook in the microwave. Precooking—rather than parboiling—helps to keep their texture firmer and skins saltier. Second: Grill. Skewering potatoes makes them easier to handle throughout the process. This two-step process means that there are multiple chances to flavor the potatoes—before they go into the microwave, before they go onto the grill, and after they finish cooking.

FLAVOR AND SERVE For one last hit of flavor, we toss these potatoes with chives just before serving. This adds some color and a bit of allium flavor, too. Chives are best used just before serving because their flavor and color are so delicate.

Glutamates, Nucleotides Add Meaty Flavor

Even when the ingredients are properly cooked, some stews, soups, and sauces fail to deliver. All the components seem to be in place, but the flavor is a bit dull. The sauce, broth, or gravy isn't as savory, as meaty, as robust, or as complex as it could be. What's missing? Flavor enhancers.

HOW THE SCIENCE WORKS

In grade school, we learned that we experience four primary taste sensations: salty, sweet, bitter, and sour. But what gives food a savory, meaty flavor? Japanese physical chemistry professor Kikunae Ikeda answered this question in 1909 when he extracted a white compound from giant sea kelp used to give Japanese broths a savory and meaty flavor, even in the absence of meat.

Ikeda identified the substance as glutamate and named the taste effect it produced umami, which translates as "delicious" or "savory." Like foods that contain the other four basic tastes—salty, sweet, bitter, and sour—foods containing umami have been found to stimulate different receptor proteins in the mouth. The receptor for glutamate was discovered by molecular biologists only as recently as 2000, confirming that umami is one of the five basic tastes. When American cooks describe a soup, stew, or sauce as "full," "meaty," or "robust," they are likely describing umami without realizing it. A wide variety of foods, everything from Parmesan cheese to tomato paste, contain glutamates (see chart on opposite page).

Glutamates are a type of amino acid, the same molecules that build proteins. We've learned that amino acids play a role in the browning of meat (see concept 2). But amino acids play a larger role than that when it comes to flavor in foods that contain glutamates, like mushrooms and tomatoes, and even more so in foods where the proteins have begun to break down, like aged cheese and soy sauce.

So how do these naturally occurring glutamates compare to monosodium glutamate (MSG), which is used as a flavor enhancer in countless prepared products from packaged broth to frozen dinners? MSG is simply the sodium salt form of naturally occurring glutamate, produced by growing bacteria on cane molasses and ammonia. Only the salt forms of the amino acid glutamic acid, called glutamates, produce the sensation of umami. MSG is believed to enhance the response of our tastebuds, especially to meats and proteins.

MSG has gotten somewhat of a bad rap in the press, in part because of "Chinese restaurant syndrome." The term was coined in the late 1960s, when people complained of headaches and digestive upset after eating Chinese food and suspected MSG was the cause. However, numerous studies failed to find a link between MSG and these symptoms. Some experts suggest that bacteria growing on room-temperature cooked rice was the culprit. Given the prevalence of MSG in the American food supply today, there is no evidence that this additive causes medical problems.

As pure substances, glutamates, including MSG, produce a relatively weak umami taste. But when tasted in combination with naturally occurring substances called nucleotides—especially inosinate and guanylate, which are found in meat, seafood, and dried mushrooms—the sensation of umami is greatly magnified. When glutamates and nucleotides

GLUTAMATES AND NUCLEOTIDES ON THE TONGUE

GLUTAMATES ALONE
We taste meaty, savory glutamates when they interact with a particular kind of taste receptor on the tongue.

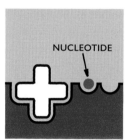

WITH NUCLEOTIDES
Nucleotides change the shape of the glutamate taste receptor, however, allowing the receptor to send stronger signals to the brain.

are present at equal levels in food the strength of umami taste is as much as 20 to 30 times greater than for glutamates alone.

Interestingly, when nucleotides and glutamates are combined in cooking, there is no chemical reaction between the two. Instead, the nucleotides affect the taste receptors on the human tongue, altering the shape of the glutamate receptors and allowing them to send stronger signals to the brain. If tasting the umami of glutamates were like lifting a heavy box, the addition of nucleotides give us handles, making the box exponentially easier to pick up off the ground.

TEST KITCHEN EXPERIMENT

To determine the flavor value of adding glutamates, nucleotides, or glutamates and nucleotides together to foods as we cook, we designed a blind taste test. First, we got our hands on pure forms of both sodium glutamate (MSG powder) and nucleotides (inosinate powder). Using four equal samples of warm tap water, we left one untouched, added 0.3 percent by weight MSG powder to one, 0.3 percent by weight inosinate powder to another, and both MSG and inosinate (each 0.15 percent by weight) to the last.

THE RESULTS

We had 21 people taste the four identical-looking samples. Our tasters rated each sample on a scale from zero to 10, zero being the least savory, meatlike, or umami, and 10 being the most. While tasters found the plain water not savory (zero), the inosinate-only sample moderately savory (an average of five), and the MSG-only sample to be likewise moderately savory (an average of five), the inosinate-MSG sample was considered very savory (10).

THE TAKEAWAY

For years now we've added glutamate-rich ingredients like soy sauce and Parmesan cheese to everything from sauces to stews to boost a rich meatiness. The amino acid glutamate in these ingredients stimulates our tongue's taste receptors, increasing the perception of umami, or savoriness. But it turns out that glutamate also plays well with others and can have a synergistic effect when paired with certain nucleotides. One such nucleotide, called inosinate, has the ability to amplify the perception of umami and is readily found in chicken, pork, anchovies, and many kinds of seafood. A classic example of umami synergy is Caesar salad, which combines the glutamates found in Parmesan cheese with the inosinate in anchovies.

We don't recommend buying powdered forms of MSG and inosinate to add to your soup, stew, or salad, of course. But combining ingredients rich in glutamates (like tomatoes, aged cheese, and cured meat) with ingredients rich in nucleotides (including beef, sardines, and mushrooms) can heighten the savory, umami taste in countless dishes without turning your kitchen into a science lab.

GLUTAMATES AND NUCLEOTIDES IN COMMON FOODS

This chart shows milligrams of glutamates and nucleotides per 100 grams (3½ ounces). The information comes from the Umami Information Center and was published in *Food Technology* (2009).

GLUTAMATES		NUCLEOTIDES	
Kombu (kelp)	2240	Dried Bonito Flakes	700
Marmite	1900	Anchovies	300 (+4300 mg glutamates)
Parmigiano-Reggiano	1680	Chicken	288
Vegemite	1400	Pork	262
Nori (seaweed)	1378	Sardines	193 (+300 mg glutamates)
Soy Sauce	1100	Tuna	188
Fish Sauce	950	Dried Shiitake Mushrooms	150
Oyster Sauce	900	Beef	94 (+100 mg glutamates)
Tomato Paste*	556	Shrimp	92 (+45 mg glutamates)
Cured Ham	340	Dried Morel Mushrooms	40
Tomatoes	246	Nori	13
Garlic*	112	Dried Oyster Mushrooms	10
Onions*	102	Dried Porcini Mushrooms	10
Green Tea Extract	32	Snow Crab	9
Red Wine*	12.2	Sea Urchin	2

Food Chemistry (1988) by Geoffrey R. Skurray and Nicholas Pucar

There are many stews, soups, and sauces that rely on ingredients rich in glutamates and/or nucleotides to build flavor. The three recipes that follow were specifically engineered with this principle in mind. But Daube Provençal on page 82 and Chicken Provençal on page 79, among others, also depend on potent flavor enhancers.

BEST BEEF STEW
SERVES 6 TO 8

Use a good-quality medium-bodied wine, such as a Côtes du Rhône or Pinot Noir, for this stew. Try to find beef that is well marbled with white veins of fat. Meat that is too lean will come out slightly dry. Look for salt pork that is roughly 75 percent lean.

2	garlic cloves, minced
4	anchovy fillets, rinsed and minced
1	tablespoon tomato paste
1	(4-pound) boneless beef chuck-eye roast, pulled apart at seams, trimmed, and cut into 1½-inch pieces
2	tablespoons vegetable oil
1	large onion, halved and sliced ⅛ inch thick
4	carrots, peeled and cut into 1-inch pieces
¼	cup all-purpose flour
2	cups red wine
2	cups low-sodium chicken broth
4	ounces salt pork, rinsed
2	bay leaves
4	sprigs fresh thyme
1	pound Yukon Gold potatoes, cut into 1-inch pieces
1½	cups frozen pearl onions, thawed
2	teaspoons unflavored gelatin
½	cup water
1	cup frozen peas, thawed
	Salt and pepper

1. Adjust oven rack to lower-middle position and heat oven to 300 degrees. Combine garlic and anchovies in small bowl; press with back of fork to form paste. Stir in tomato paste and set aside.

2. Pat meat dry with paper towels. (Do not season.) Heat 1 tablespoon vegetable oil in Dutch oven over high heat until just starting to smoke. Add half of beef and cook until well browned on all sides, about 8 minutes. Transfer beef to large plate. Repeat with remaining beef and remaining 1 tablespoon vegetable oil, leaving second batch of meat in pot after browning.

3. Reduce heat to medium and return first batch of beef to pot. Add onion and carrots to Dutch oven and stir to combine with beef. Cook, scraping bottom of pot to loosen any browned bits, until onion is softened, 1 to 2 minutes. Add garlic mixture and cook, stirring constantly, until fragrant, about 30 seconds. Add flour and cook, stirring constantly, until no dry flour remains, about 30 seconds.

4. Slowly add wine, scraping bottom of pot to loosen any browned bits. Increase heat to high and allow wine to simmer until thickened and slightly reduced, about 2 minutes. Stir in broth, salt pork, bay leaves, and thyme. Bring to simmer, cover, transfer to oven, and cook for 1½ hours.

5. Remove pot from oven; remove and discard bay leaves and salt pork. Stir in potatoes, cover, return to oven, and cook until potatoes are almost tender, about 45 minutes.

6. Using large spoon, skim any excess fat from surface of stew. Stir in pearl onions; cook over medium heat until potatoes and onions are cooked through and meat offers little resistance when poked with fork (meat should not be falling apart), about 15 minutes. Meanwhile, sprinkle gelatin over water in small bowl and let sit until gelatin softens, about 5 minutes.

7. Increase heat to high, stir in softened gelatin mixture and peas; simmer until gelatin is fully dissolved and stew is thickened, about 3 minutes. Season with salt and pepper to taste; serve.

✔ WHY THIS RECIPE WORKS

This recipe uses evenly cut chunks of chuck-eye roast—one of the cheapest, beefiest cuts in the supermarket—which we brown and gently simmer in a rich broth. We flavor this broth with glutamate-rich ingredients like salt pork and tomato paste, and thicken it with gelatin. Beef and anchovies are also a good source of nucleotides that work synergistically with glutamates.

CUT YOUR OWN MEAT Using packaged "stew meat" from the supermarket is a nonstarter here; the jumble of scraggly bits and large chunks from all over the cow (some of which are too lean to be stewed) is impossible to cook evenly. We prefer chuck-eye roast, which can turn meltingly tender when properly cooked. To ensure consistent texture and flavor, trim and cut the meat yourself. First, pull apart the roast at its major seams (marked by lines of fat and silverskin). Then, with a sharp chef's knife or boning knife, trim off the thick layers of fat and silverskin. Slice the meat into even, stew-ready chunks.

BUILD FLAVOR We build flavor a number of ways in this stew—from browning to using glutamate- and nucleotide-rich ingredients in the sauce. We also sauté the aromatics. Caramelizing the onion and carrots (rather than just adding them raw to the broth, as many other recipes suggest) helps to start the stew off with as much flavor as possible. We like to leave the meat in the pot while the vegetables sauté, as the residual heat helps the vegetables to cook faster and more evenly.

FISH FOR MEATIER FLAVOR To boost meaty flavor in food, we often add ingredients high in glutamate. This common amino acid is the building block for MSG and occurs naturally in foods from mushrooms to cheese, tomatoes, and fish. Thus it wasn't exactly a surprise that the addition of two such glutamate-rich ingredients—tomato paste and salt pork—to our beef stew intensified its savory taste. But when we added a third ingredient, anchovies, the beefy flavor seemed to increase exponentially. This is because anchovies also contain compounds called nucleotides, which scientists have found to have a synergistic effect on glutamate, heightening its meaty taste 20- to 30-fold.

STAGGER THE VEGETABLES We stagger the addition of vegetables to the stew in order to prevent overcooking. Medium-starch Yukon Gold potatoes, which aren't as starchy as russets and therefore won't break down too easily and turn the stew grainy, are added 1½ hours into the stewing time. Pearl onions are added 45 minutes later, and a handful of frozen peas are added at the very end.

QUICK BEEF AND VEGETABLE SOUP
SERVES 6

Choose whole sirloin steak tips over ones that have been cut into small pieces, often labeled for stir-fries. If sirloin steak tips are unavailable, substitute blade or flank steak, removing any hard gristle or excess fat. White mushrooms can be used in place of the cremini. Feel free to add 1 cup of frozen peas, frozen corn, or frozen cut green beans during the last five minutes of cooking. For a heartier soup, add 10 ounces of red potatoes, cut into ½-inch pieces (2 cups), during the last 15 minutes of cooking.

1	pound sirloin steak tips, trimmed and cut into ½-inch pieces
2	tablespoons soy sauce
1	teaspoon vegetable oil
1	pound cremini mushrooms, trimmed and quartered
1	large onion, chopped
2	tablespoons tomato paste
1	garlic clove, minced
½	cup red wine
4	cups beef broth
1¾	cups low-sodium chicken broth
4	carrots, peeled and cut into ½-inch pieces
2	celery ribs, cut into ½-inch pieces
1	bay leaf
1	tablespoon unflavored gelatin
½	cup cold water
2	tablespoons minced fresh parsley
	Salt and pepper

1. Combine beef and soy sauce in medium bowl. Let sit for 15 minutes.

2. Heat oil in Dutch oven over medium-high heat until just smoking. Add mushrooms and onion and cook, stirring frequently, until onion is browned, 8 to 12 minutes. Transfer vegetables to bowl.

3. Add beef and cook, stirring occasionally, until liquid evaporates and meat starts to brown, 6 to 10 minutes. Add tomato paste and garlic to pot and cook, stirring constantly, until aromatic, about 30 seconds. Stir in wine, scraping bottom of pot with wooden spoon to loosen browned bits, and cook until liquid reduces and becomes syrupy, 1 to 2 minutes.

4. Add beef broth, chicken broth, carrots, celery, bay leaf, and browned mushrooms and onion to pot and bring to boil. Reduce heat to low, cover, and simmer until vegetables and meat are tender, 25 to 30 minutes. Remove from heat and remove and discard bay leaf.

5. Meanwhile, sprinkle gelatin over cold water in small bowl and let sit until gelatin softens, about 5 minutes. Add gelatin mixture to pot with soup and stir until completely dissolved. Stir in parsley, season with salt and pepper to taste, and serve.

✓ WHY THIS RECIPE WORKS
For a beef and vegetable soup that we could make in just an hour, we turned to quick-cooking, richly flavored sirloin steaks tips and doctored store-bought broth with a few of the test kitchen's favorite ingredients for accentuating meatiness: mushrooms, tomato paste, soy sauce, and red wine. To give our quick version the rich texture of a long-simmered soup, we added a tablespoon of gelatin softened in cold water, which provided the body typically lent by gelatin released from the beef bones in a traditional recipe.

PICK THE RIGHT BEEF We love the fall-apart tenderness of the shin meat in the traditional recipe for this soup. But it takes hours to break down those tougher muscle fibers into anything remotely tender. We wanted to find a cut of meat that had the same textural characteristics of the shin meat but would cook in a quarter of the time. We cooked through various cuts and discovered that those with a loose, open grain—including hanger steak, flank steak, sirloin steak tips (or flap meat), and blade steak—had a shredded texture that fooled our tasters into thinking we had cooked the meat for hours. Of these four cuts, sirloin steak tips offer the best balance of meat flavor and tenderness. Just be careful how you cut the steaks: If the meat is cut too large, the soup will seem more like a stew. If you use too many small pieces, it will resemble a watery chili. For six generous bowls of soup, you will need 1 pound of sirloin tip steaks cut into ½-inch pieces.

USE A SALTY MARINADE Soy sauce is especially high in glutamates. Because of this, we feared that it might overpower the soup. But to our surprise, it enhanced the beef flavor. This is also why soy sauce is a favorite in test kitchen marinades (see concept 13). Like a brine, the salt in soy sauce diffuses into the meat, allowing the individual muscle fibers to retain moisture while cooking. When we marinate the beef cubes with soy sauce for just 15 minutes, the flavor of the meat improves, and the texture becomes softer and juicier.

CREATE A POWERFUL BASE While sirloin steak tips cook up with the right texture and good flavor, they don't flavor the broth. This is why we use a flavorful combination of broths—both chicken and beef. We also brown the glutamate-rich onions and mushrooms to kick-start flavor development.

ADD MORE GLUTAMATES Once the veggies are browned, we remove them from the pot and then brown the beef. Tomato paste, garlic, and red wine add more meaty notes, especially when we brown the tomato paste and garlic with the beef and deglaze the pot with red wine. We now add the broth along with carrots, celery, bay leaf, and the browned mushrooms and onions.

ADD POWDERED GELATIN The classic slow-simmering approach allows the gelatin in the beef bones to give the stock (and the eventual soup) great body. Since our recipe uses a boneless cut, we produce a similar effect by stirring some gelatin (which we soften in cold water) into the finished soup.

PASTA WITH CREAMY TOMATO SAUCE
SERVES 4

High-quality canned tomatoes will make a big difference in this sauce.

3	tablespoons unsalted butter
I	small onion, chopped fine
I	ounce thinly sliced prosciutto, minced
I	bay leaf
	Salt and pepper
	Pinch red pepper flakes
3	garlic cloves, minced
¼	cup oil-packed sun-dried tomatoes, rinsed, patted dry, and chopped coarse
2	tablespoons tomato paste
6	tablespoons dry white wine
2	cups plus 2 tablespoons crushed tomatoes (from one 28-ounce can)
I	pound penne, fusilli, or other short, tubular pasta
½	cup heavy cream
¼	cup chopped fresh basil
	Grated Parmesan cheese

1. Melt butter in medium saucepan over medium heat. Add onion, prosciutto, bay leaf, ¼ teaspoon salt, and pepper flakes and cook, stirring occasionally, until onion is softened and lightly browned, 5 to 7 minutes. Stir in garlic, increase heat to medium-high, and cook until fragrant, about 30 seconds. Add sun-dried tomatoes and tomato paste and cook, stirring constantly, until slightly darkened, 1 to 2 minutes. Add ¼ cup wine and cook, stirring often, until liquid has evaporated, 1 to 2 minutes.

2. Stir in 2 cups crushed tomatoes and bring to simmer. Reduce heat to low, partially cover, and simmer gently, stirring occasionally, until sauce is thickened, 25 to 30 minutes. Discard bay leaf.

3. Meanwhile, bring 4 quarts water to boil in large pot. Add pasta and 1 tablespoon salt and cook, stirring often, until al dente. Reserve ½ cup cooking water, then drain pasta and return it to pot.

4. Stir cream, remaining 2 tablespoons wine, and remaining 2 tablespoons crushed tomatoes into sauce and season with salt and pepper to taste. Add sauce and basil to pasta and toss to combine. Add reserved cooking water as needed to adjust consistency. Serve immediately, passing Parmesan separately.

✔ WHY THIS RECIPE WORKS

Cream gives a basic tomato sauce richness and body but it also tends to deaden the flavor of the tomatoes. Our challenge was to ramp up the savory, meaty notes in the tomato sauce so that it could stand up to the richness and sweetness imparted by the cream.

CONCENTRATE TOMATO FLAVOR Adding potent sources of tomato flavor (both tomato paste and sun-dried tomatoes) is a step in the right direction. Tomatoes are rich in glutamates and these concentrated forms of tomatoes are particularly good flavor enhancers. Adding an onion to the sauce helps, as does some minced prosciutto. (Yes, some actual meat does help develop meaty flavors.) After sautéing the onions until golden, we add the tomato paste and sun-dried tomatoes and cook them to maximize their impact.

ADD WHITE WINE FOR ACIDITY Cream can make sauces heavy. Adding a splash of white wine to the sautéed aromatics and then letting it reduce provides a welcome brightness to the sauce. It also helps balance the sweetness of the tomatoes (and the cream).

CRUSH THOSE TOMATOES With the flavor base set, it's time for the tomatoes. The cream melds best with a smooth sauce; rather than starting with whole or diced tomatoes and then pureeing the finished sauce, we found that crushed tomatoes gave the sauce the perfect consistency and there was no need to get out the food processor. Brands of crushed tomatoes vary greatly so choose carefully; look for a brand that lists fresh tomatoes, not tomato puree, as the first ingredient. (Some puree is fine—it adds body, but it shouldn't be the dominant source of tomato flavor because it does have a cooked, not terribly fresh flavor.)

SAVE THE CREAM Cooking the cream can bring out its sweet notes and throw off the balance of the sauce. Simply stir ½ cup of cream into the finished sauce. Also, we found that reserving 2 tablespoons each of the tomatoes and wine adds another layer of tomato flavor and some needed acidity that helps balance the richness of the cream.

PRACTICAL SCIENCE CHOOSING THE RIGHT CANNED TOMATOES

Tomatoes, packed with glutamates, add great flavor to many dishes. We often use canned tomatoes, which come in several forms.

Unlike most kinds of canned produce, which pale in comparison to their fresh counterparts, a great can of tomatoes offers flavor almost as intense as ripe, in-season fruit. For this reason it's one of the most important staples in our pantry. We rely on canned tomatoes for everything from pasta sauce to chili to soups and stews. We even use them to make a quick salsa when good fresh tomatoes are in short supply.

WHOLE TOMATOES When big, bright chunks of tomatoes are what we're after, we reach for canned whole tomatoes and cut them ourselves. Good canned whole tomatoes balance sweetness and acidity. Some brands treat the tomatoes with calcium chloride, which is added by manufacturers to maintain a firmness that we prefer. Our favorite brands are Muir Glen Organic Whole Peeled Tomatoes and Hunt's Whole Plum Tomatoes.

DICED TOMATOES Great diced canned tomatoes start with the tomatoes themselves. Some companies experiment constantly to grow not only the best-tasting varieties but also the firmest fruit, with thick "walls" that will stand up to mechanical dicing. Others choose to use thin-walled tomatoes and cook them longer for a softer consistency, which our tasters did not care for. After peeling, the tomatoes are machine-diced and canned. The juice is handled separately, heated and treated with calcium chloride (a firming agent), salt, and citric acid (to boost bright flavor and lower the pH). The juice is then added to the cans, which are sealed, heat-sterilized, and rapidly cooled to prevent the tomatoes from overcooking. The timing and temperatures of these steps can mean the difference between preserving fresh flavor and boiling it to death. Our preferred brand is Hunt's Diced Tomatoes.

CRUSHED TOMATOES The value of using crushed tomatoes depends greatly upon the brand. Texture is important. We prefer cans of crushed tomatoes containing actual tomato pieces and a fair amount of liquid. Fresh tomato taste is another essential. How the tomatoes are processed (either at a low temperature for a longer time, or a high temperature for a shorter time) makes a difference. So does the topping: Crushed canned tomatoes are topped with either tomato puree or juice. Puree is cooked, and so the more puree, the less fresh tomato flavor. We prefer Tuttorosso Crushed Tomatoes in Thick Puree with Basil. Muir Glen Organic Crushed Tomatoes with Basil came in a close second in our tasting.

TOMATO PUREE In the family of canned tomato products, tomato puree is often overlooked in favor of whole peeled or diced tomatoes. The reason is clear: While whole and diced tomatoes offer a passable substitute for fresh tomatoes (they are simply skinned and processed), tomato puree is cooked and strained, removing all seeds and all illusions of freshness. That's not to say that tomato puree doesn't have a place; it's just more suited to long-cooked dishes where the thick, even texture of puree is important and fresh tomato flavor is not.

TOMATO PASTE Tomato paste is the backbone of many of our recipes, providing deep, rich tomato flavor. Even in some non-tomato-based recipes, like beef stew, the paste acts as our secret ingredient. Because it's naturally full of glutamates, which stimulate tastebuds just like salt and sugar, it brings out subtle depths and savory notes. Our preferred brand is Goya Tomato Paste.

Emulsifiers Make Smooth Sauces

Vinaigrette seems simple because it requires only two ingredients: oil and vinegar. But salad greens dressed with a broken vinaigrette can be harsh and bristling in one bite, dull and oily in the next. The best vinaigrettes are ones that stay together—at least long enough for you to dress and eat the salad.

HOW THE SCIENCE WORKS

Vinaigrette relies on the principle of emulsification. An emulsion is a combination of two liquids that don't ordinarily mix, such as oil and vinegar. The only way to mix them is to whisk so strenuously that one of the two ingredients breaks down into tiny droplets—eventually so tiny that they remain separated by the other liquid. The two fluids are now effectively one.

The liquid in the droplet form is called the dispersed phase (vinegar in a simple water-in-oil vinaigrette) because the droplets are dispersed throughout the emulsion. The liquid that surrounds the droplets is the continuous phase (oil in a simple water-in-oil vinaigrette). Depending on how it's formed, it's possible to make emulsions in which the oil is either the dispersed phase or the continuous phase. Because the continuous phase forms the surface of the emulsion, that's what the mouth and tongue feel and taste first. This explains why mayonnaise, which is as much as 80 percent oil, doesn't taste greasy, because lemon juice is in the continuous phase.

Unfortunately, as soon as you stop mixing oil and vinegar, many of these tiny dispersed droplets will start to find each other and coalesce. When enough vinegar droplets find each other, the emulsion breaks and the vinegar and oil separate. If you drizzle a broken vinaigrette over salad greens, the salad will taste too oily or sour depending on the leaf.

Many emulsions contain an agent called an emulsifier, which helps the vinegar and oil combine into a unified sauce and stay that way. Egg yolk, which contains lecithin, a phospholipid, is one example. Here's how it works: The lecithin molecule has two ends. One end is attracted to water (hydrophilic), while the other end is repelled by water (hydrophobic) but is compatible with oil. When egg yolks are added along with the vinegar in a simple vinaigrette, however, the emulsion changes: It is now an oil-in-water emulsion, or more stable with the oil droplets suspended in vinegar, rather than the other way around. This is because the hydrophilic ends of lecithin dissolve in the vinegar while the exposed hydrophobic ends form a shield around droplets of oil. This is why mayonnaise can form an emulsion of oil droplets suspended in vinegar or lemon juice. Another commonly used emulsifier is mustard. The emulsifying component in mustard is a complex polysaccharide that is less effective than the lecithin found in egg yolks.

BREAKING OIL AND VINEGAR

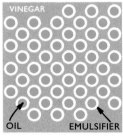

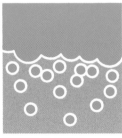

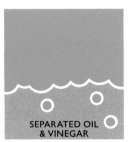

EMULSIFIED *When oil and vinegar are emulsified, tiny droplets of oil are surrounded by an added emulsifier and dispersed in vinegar.*

BREAKING *With time, however, the droplets of oil begin to find each other and coalesce.*

BROKEN *Eventually the oil and vinegar separate into distinct liquids, resulting in a broken vinaigrette.*

Emulsifiers are important in recipes far more diverse than the vinaigrettes and mayonnaise recipes found in this concept. Many classic French sauces, including béarnaise and hollandaise, rely on emulsifiers. Pan sauces likewise rely on this concept; swirling cold butter rather than softened butter into a finished sauce ensures a smoother, more emulsified result. Another common ingredient in emulsified sauces is cornstarch, which acts by thickening and making it more difficult for the dispersed droplets to move about and coalesce. Even cakes need emulsifiers. Pound cake, for example, relies on the proper emulsification of eggs.

TEST KITCHEN EXPERIMENT

To tease out the relative effectiveness of three common emulsifiers (mustard, egg yolk, and mayonnaise), we created three vinaigrettes, using three stand mixers fitted with the whisk attachment to ensure that ingredients received the same amount of whisking. We added ¼ cup of vinegar to the bowl of each mixer, then added 1 tablespoon of Dijon mustard to one, an egg yolk to the second, and 1 tablespoon of mayonnaise to the third. With the mixers running on medium-high speed, we drizzled ¾ cup of oil into each over the course of 30 seconds. We tracked all blended samples at 15-minute intervals. As a control, we made a fourth vinaigrette in a stand mixer with no emulsifier, just vinegar and oil.

THE RESULTS

The vinaigrette made with the egg yolk was clearly the most stable. It was still emulsified more than three hours after being mixed. The vinaigrette made with mayonnaise showed signs of separation after 1½ hours, while the one with mustard started to break apart after only 30 minutes. The control began separating immediately and was almost completely separated after the first 15-minute interval.

And the taste? The egg yolk gave the dressing an eggy flavor that tasters didn't like. (And adding raw egg to salad dressing isn't for everyone.) The mayonnaise didn't add much flavor, but it did impart a slight creaminess tasters liked. The mustard dressing tasted best.

THE TAKEAWAY

Sauces that require the seamless blending of liquid ingredients that normally don't blend should be made with an emulsifier, such as egg yolks, mayonnaise, or mustard. In addition to

KEEPING TRACK OF EMULSIFIERS IN VINAIGRETTES

	15 MINUTES	30 MINUTES	60 MINUTES
NO EMULSIFIER			
MUSTARD			
MAYONNAISE			
EGG YOLK			

stability, a good emulsifier will bring something else to a vinaigrette—or, at the very least, will cause no harm. Egg yolks are a very potent emulsifier but their flavor isn't always appropriate. Mayonnaise is a (slightly weaker) emulsifier because it contains egg yolks; it can be used to stabilize a dressing without adding eggy flavor. Mustard is a decent emulsifier but its primary advantage is flavor.

The egg yolks in mayonnaise are a very potent emulsifier. The mustard isn't quite as strong but adds great flavor. A little of each emulsifier yields a smooth, flavorful dressing, provided the dressing is properly prepared. We found that the way the oil and vinegar are combined can also affect the stability of the emulsion.

FOOLPROOF VINAIGRETTE

MAKES ABOUT ¼ CUP, ENOUGH TO DRESS 8 TO 10 CUPS OF LIGHTLY PACKED GREENS

Red or white wine vinegar or champagne vinegar will work in this recipe. It is important to use high-quality ingredients. This vinaigrette works with nearly any greens (as do the walnut and herb variations). For a hint of garlic flavor, rub the inside of the salad bowl with a clove of garlic before adding the lettuce.

1	tablespoon wine vinegar
1½	teaspoons minced shallot
½	teaspoon regular or light mayonnaise
½	teaspoon Dijon mustard
⅛	teaspoon salt
	Pepper
3	tablespoons extra-virgin olive oil

1. Combine vinegar, shallot, mayonnaise, mustard, salt, and pepper to taste in small nonreactive bowl. Whisk until mixture is milky in appearance and no lumps of mayonnaise remain.

2. Place oil in small measuring cup so that it is easy to pour. Whisking constantly, very slowly drizzle oil into vinegar mixture. If pools of oil are gathering on surface as you whisk, stop addition of oil and whisk mixture well to combine, then resume whisking in oil in slow stream. Vinaigrette should be glossy and lightly thickened, with no pools of oil on its surface. (Vinaigrette can be refrigerated for up to 2 weeks.)

HERB VINAIGRETTE

Add 1 tablespoon minced fresh parsley or chives and ½ teaspoon minced fresh thyme, tarragon, marjoram, or oregano to vinaigrette just before use.

WALNUT VINAIGRETTE

Substitute 1½ tablespoons roasted walnut oil and 1½ tablespoons regular olive oil for extra-virgin olive oil.

LEMON VINAIGRETTE

This is best for dressing mild greens.

Substitute lemon juice for vinegar, omit shallot, and add ¼ teaspoon finely grated lemon zest and pinch sugar along with salt and pepper.

BALSAMIC-MUSTARD VINAIGRETTE

This is best for dressing assertive greens.

Substitute balsamic vinegar for wine vinegar, increase mustard to 2 teaspoons, and add ½ teaspoon minced fresh thyme along with salt and pepper.

✔ WHY THIS RECIPE WORKS

Modern recipes often call for 4 parts oil to 1 part vinegar. We found this formula yields a bland, greasy dressing. It turns out that slack attention to mixing (modern recipes tend to favor the dump-and-stir or dump-and-shake method) has bumped up the oil-to-vinegar ratio to mitigate the effects of an improperly emulsified dressing. The 3:1 ratio found in classic French cookbooks is correct. Yes, you need to work a bit more slowly when adding the oil, but the result is a bright, vibrant dressing. Both the mustard and mayonnaise help to keep the dressing emulsified for hours.

WHISK RATHER THAN SHAKE In kitchen tests, we found that vinaigrette recipes that call for shaking ingredients together in a jar or dumping the vinegar and oil into a bowl and whisking them together separated very quickly and tasted harsh—because the vinegar and oil weren't fully emulsified. In contrast, the classic technique (slowly whisking the oil into the dressing) yields a dressing that tastes smoother and stays emulsified longer. Oil and vinegar don't typically mix since vinegar is 95 percent water. Using mayonnaise as the emulsifier added to the vinegar, followed by the addition of the oil with vigorous whisking, breaks the oil into very tiny droplets that more easily disperse in the vinegar and are more likely to form a stable emulsion. Also, the smaller the droplets the more stable the emulsion.

ADD SEASONINGS TO VINEGAR Salt won't dissolve in oil, so for even seasoning add the salt (and other seasonings and the emulsifiers) to the vinegar.

SCALE DRESSING; DON'T OVERDRESS If you follow the 3:1 ratio of oil to vinegar, you can make as much or as little dressing as you need. One-quarter cup of dressing is the right amount to dress 8 to 10 cups of lightly packed greens, enough salad for four people. The vinaigrette should lightly coat the salad greens and there shouldn't be so much dressing that some collects at the bottom of the bowl.

The emulsifying power of egg yolks turns liquid oil into a thick, creamy sauce. This is true in vinaigrette and is even more apparent in mayonnaise, which contains 2.3 parts oil dispersed into 1 part egg yolk–lemon juice.

AÏOLI (GARLIC MAYONNAISE)
MAKES ABOUT ¾ CUP

Use this sauce as a condiment for meats, fish, and vegetables or sandwiches. If necessary, remove the green germ in the garlic before pressing or grating it; the germ will give the aïoli a bitter flavor. If you do not have regular olive oil, use a blend of equal parts extra-virgin olive oil and vegetable oil. Ground white pepper is preferred because it's not as visible as black pepper, but either can be used. To make "regular" mayonnaise, simply omit the garlic.

1	garlic clove, peeled
2	large egg yolks
4	teaspoons lemon juice
⅛	teaspoon sugar
	Salt
	Ground pepper, preferably white
¾	cup olive oil

1. Press garlic through garlic press or grate very fine on rasp-style grater. Measure out 1 teaspoon garlic; discard remaining garlic.

2. Process garlic, egg yolks, lemon juice, sugar, ¼ teaspoon salt, and pepper to taste in food processor until combined, about 10 seconds. With processor running, gradually add oil in slow, steady stream (process should take about 30 seconds); scrape down bowl with rubber spatula and process for 5 seconds longer. Season with salt and pepper to taste, and serve. (Aïoli can be refrigerated in airtight container for 3 days.)

ROSEMARY-THYME AÏOLI

Serve this aïoli with roasted and grilled meats or grilled vegetables.

Add 1 teaspoon minced fresh rosemary and 1 teaspoon minced fresh thyme to food processor along with garlic.

✓ WHY THIS RECIPE WORKS

Aïoli is a quick emulsion sauce that by tradition is the centerpiece of a simple supper of cooked vegetables and potatoes and steamed fish. When it's made badly, the overwhelming impression is one of garlic: bitter, sharp, and long-lasting. We found that fine, evenly minced garlic maintained the smooth texture of the sauce and prevented oversize garlic bombs that exploded in the mouth.

GET THE GARLIC RIGHT Garlic gives aïoli its personality but it can be a bully. We scale back the amount of garlic used in a traditional recipe and use a garlic press or rasp grater to break it down into a very fine mince. (Don't use more than 1 teaspoon.)

PICK THE RIGHT OIL We found that the peppery, fruity flavor of extra-virgin olive oil was too overpowering for mayonnaise. Tasters preferred regular olive oil, which has been stripped of much of its flavor during processing. If you do not have regular olive oil, use a blend of equal parts extra-virgin olive oil and vegetable oil.

WHISK EGGS AND LEMON JUICE To keep the mayonnaise from breaking, we found it necessary to whisk the egg yolks and lemon juice thoroughly. The yolks contain liquid and fat that must first be emulsified before the oil is added.

PROCESS WELL When we tried blending the sauce, the emulsion became way too thick. Whisking by hand worked beautifully, but after four minutes, our arms grew tired. The food processor, which pulls the sauce together in just 30 seconds, is our top choice. You can certainly make mayonnaise by hand—French cooks have for centuries. But since you're dispersing a lot of oil in a little bit of egg yolks and lemon juice, you have to whisk the oil into exceedingly tiny droplets in order to make a stable emulsion. If using a whisk, plan on adding the oil in a very, very slow stream—the process will take at least four minutes of constant whisking.

PRACTICAL SCIENCE EMULSIFYING EGG BEATERS

If you don't want to consume raw eggs, pick Egg Beaters.

Egg Beaters is one of the only pasteurized egg options available to most consumers, but we doubted its ability to serve as a substitute for real eggs in something like mayonnaise. Real egg yolks contain the emulsifying agent lecithin, which helps thicken mayonnaise, whereas Egg Beaters is made from egg whites and therefore contains no lecithin. We gave it a whirl in our Garlic Mayonnaise, replacing the two egg yolks with ¼ cup of Egg Beaters. The result? An incredibly thick emulsion, albeit slightly less rich-tasting than the real thing.

Encouraged, we went on to make Egg Beaters–based hollandaise sauce and Caesar dressing, both with great success. We prepared a classic crème brûlée, swapping in the Egg Beaters for the prescribed 12 large yolks. The custard was remarkably creamy but unacceptably dull.

How does this product work? The secret is the use of vegetable gums. Unlike lecithin, which forms a barrier around water droplets, making it difficult for them to separate, gums simply add viscosity, helping mixtures coalesce. So if you're concerned about consuming raw egg yolks, Egg Beaters can work. Just don't swap it for large quantities of yolks, as in custards.

Speed Evaporation When Cooking Wine

Wine is a key ingredient in countless recipes. It adds depth, complexity, and acidity to everything from stews to sauces. There's a popular misconception that the alcohol cooks off when heated. The truth is more complicated.

HOW THE SCIENCE WORKS

COOKING WITH WINE

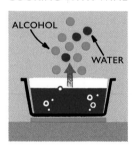

WINE AND WATER *When simmering a mixture of water and wine, alcohol molecules are a major component of the vapor in the beginning.*

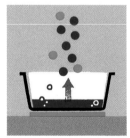

WATER AND WINE *After simmering for a while, water molecules compose the majority of vapor. It is impossible to get rid of all the alcohol unless all of the liquid evaporates.*

Archeological evidence indicates that wine was first produced from grapes 8000 years ago. Today, we drink red, white, and rosé wine, as well as fortified wines like sherry and vermouth. The alcohol content in the average non fortified wine ranges from 10 to 14 percent.

To make wine, first grapes are crushed to free their juices, which include water, sugars, and some acids. Sometimes winemakers add additional yeast for fermentation, but a strain of yeast that grows naturally on the skin of grapes ferments the sugars in grapes, turning them to ethyl alcohol. Fermentation also helps to create new aromatic molecules within the mixture, giving wine some of its familiar flavors. Once these sugars are converted to alcohol, the new wine is set to age, allowing the slow procession of chemical reactions to impart even more, and more complex, flavor. Fortified wines like sherry and vermouth are simply wines fortified with extra alcohol (their alcohol content generally ranges from 18 to 20 percent).

Distilled spirits, such as whiskey and brandy, are made in a fashion similar to wine—at least to begin. But yeast cannot survive in an environment too saturated with alcohol, and it dies when the alcohol percentage reaches 20 percent. Therefore, spirits, which have alcohol contents ranging from 40 to 70 percent, undergo a process called distillation in which a moderately alcoholic liquid is heated and the alcohol and aroma vapors are collected and then condensed.

While alcohol is a key component in wine and spirits, it's not always a desired component

in a finished recipe. For instance, you wouldn't want to serve steak Diane with uncooked brandy—the alcohol content would be overwhelming. Cooking certainly reduces the alcohol content in wine and spirits, but it rarely eliminates it. In most recipes, wine is used in conjunction with broth or another water-based ingredient. When alcohol and water mix, they form a solution called an azeotrope—a mixture of two different liquids that behaves as if it were a single compound. Even though alcohol evaporates at a lower temperature than water, the vapors coming off of an alcohol-water azeotrope will contain both alcohol and water—they become inextricably mixed.

Initially an equal mixture of alcohol and water will begin to boil at about 173 degrees (which is even a little lower than the boiling point of pure alcohol) and the vapor will consist of about 95 percent alcohol. Gradually the temperature of the boiling liquid increases and the vapor becomes richer in water. Eventually, as the temperature of the liquid begins to approach the boiling point of pure water (212 degrees), more and more water evaporates, along with a smaller and smaller amount of alcohol. But unless you keep cooking until all the azeotropic mixture evaporates, the alcohol content of the liquid will remain at about 5 percent of the initial alcohol content no matter how long you simmer the mixture.

As a cook, you can employ various strategies to maximize evaporation in dishes with alcohol. One way is to reduce the alcohol before adding any other water-based ingredients to the mix. High heat, a wide pot, and cooking uncovered will remove more alcohol than low heat, a narrow saucepan, and cooking with a cover. Another way to quickly reduce the amount of alcohol in a liquid is to ignite the vapors that lie above the pan, a technique known as flambéing. (This technique works better with high-alcohol spirits than with wine.) But the degree to which a flambé will remove alcohol depends partly on the heat added to the liquid underneath. We found that brandy ignited over high heat retains 29 percent of its original alcohol concentration, while brandy flamed in a cold pan holds 57 percent, nearly twice as much alcohol. In the case of a flambé, the addition of heat (not just the flame from a match) can make a significant difference in the strength of the finished sauce. In practical terms, this mean that steak Diane, which is cooked on the stovetop, will lose more alcohol than cherries jubilee, in which flaming liquid is poured over ice cream.

TEST KITCHEN EXPERIMENT

In order to settle the debate about how much alcohol remains in a wine-based reduction sauce we had to get technical. We wanted to know if it made a difference whether we reduced the wine alone before adding broth, or if we could get similar results by skipping this step and combining the wine and broth from the outset. We made two different sauces: For one we reduced 2 cups of red wine with 14.5 percent alcohol by volume (abv) to 1 cup, added 1 cup of store-bought chicken broth, and reduced this mixture to 1 cup; for the second we combined 2 cups of 14.5 percent abv red wine with 1 cup of store-bought chicken broth and reduced the mixture to 1 cup. Both sauces took roughly 15 minutes to reach their final volume. We repeated the test three times, tasted each, and sent portions to an independent lab for analysis of the remaining ethanol.

THE RESULTS

Even though we started with identical amounts of both ingredients, and the reductions took roughly the same amount of time, both our tasters and the lab found quite a difference between the samples. Tasters overwhelmingly found the sample where we first reduced the wine to be less "boozy"-tasting than the batches where we combined both liquids right off the bat. And the lab was able to quantify what we tasted. The former samples averaged a very low .175 percent abv, while the latter samples averaged a moderate 1.55 percent abv—over eight times as much!

THE TAKEAWAY

While neither sauce contained a large quantity of alcohol after cooking, the disparity between the samples—and our ability to taste the difference—makes it significant. If your goal is to make a sauce with strong wine flavor but without the bite of alcohol, it pays to reduce the wine alone before adding other liquids.

It's important to note that these results are specific to this experiment, where we used wide skillets and medium-high heat to rapidly reduce the sauces—a method that is highly efficient at evaporation. A 1992 study published in the *Journal of the American Dietetic Association* found that the amounts of alcohol retained in the entirety of various cooked recipes ranged considerably—from 4 to 60 percent—depending on the dish. For example, the alcohol retained in Pot Roast Milano, which simmered at 185 degrees for 2½ hours, amounted to 4 to 6 percent abv, while that retained in Orange Chicken Burgundy, simmered at 185 degrees for 10 minutes, ranged from 10 to 60 percent. Cooking temperature and time, as well as additional ingredients that can absorb liquid, will greatly impact final alcohol content.

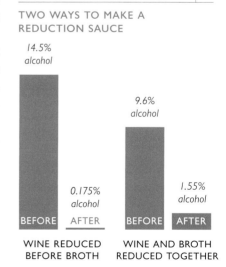

TWO WAYS TO MAKE A REDUCTION SAUCE

14.5% alcohol

9.6% alcohol

0.175% alcohol

1.55% alcohol

BEFORE AFTER

BEFORE AFTER

WINE REDUCED BEFORE BROTH

WINE AND BROTH REDUCED TOGETHER

Wine adds great flavor and depth to a whole range of dishes. When stewing our pot roast, we deal with the wine before it goes into the pot, reducing the amount of alcohol to prevent a boozy sauce. When poaching, we use a small amount of wine to help cook perfect fillets of salmon and then to create a flavorful sauce.

FRENCH-STYLE POT ROAST
SERVES 6 TO 8

A medium-bodied, fruity red wine, such as a Côtes du Rhône or Pinot Noir, is best for this recipe. The gelatin lends richness and body to the finished sauce; don't omit it. Serve this dish with boiled potatoes, buttered noodles, or steamed rice.

I	(4- to 5-pound) boneless beef chuck-eye roast, pulled apart at seams and trimmed
	Kosher salt and pepper
I	(750-ml) bottle red wine
10	sprigs fresh parsley plus 2 tablespoons minced
2	sprigs fresh thyme
2	bay leaves
3	slices thick-cut bacon, cut into ¼-inch pieces
I	onion, chopped fine
3	garlic cloves, minced
I	tablespoon all-purpose flour
2	cups beef broth
4	carrots, peeled and cut on bias into 1½-inch pieces
2	cups frozen pearl onions, thawed
¾	cup water
3	tablespoons unsalted butter
2	teaspoons sugar
10	ounces white mushrooms, trimmed, halved if small and quartered if large
I	tablespoon unflavored gelatin

1. Season pieces of meat with 2 teaspoons salt, place on wire rack set in rimmed baking sheet, and let rest at room temperature for 1 hour.

2. Meanwhile, bring wine to simmer in large saucepan over medium-high heat. Cook until reduced to 2 cups, about 15 minutes. Using kitchen twine, tie parsley sprigs, thyme sprigs, and bay leaves into bundle.

3. Pat beef dry with paper towels and season generously with pepper. Tie 3 pieces of kitchen twine around each piece of meat to keep it from falling apart.

4. Adjust oven rack to lower-middle position and heat oven to 300 degrees. Cook bacon in Dutch oven over medium-high heat, stirring occasionally, until crisp, 6 to 8 minutes. Using slotted spoon, transfer bacon to paper towel–lined plate and reserve. Pour off all but 2 tablespoons fat; return Dutch oven to medium-high heat and heat until fat begins to smoke. Add beef to pot and brown on all sides, 8 to 10 minutes total. Transfer beef to large plate and set aside.

5. Reduce heat to medium; add onion and cook, stirring occasionally, until beginning to soften, 2 to 4 minutes. Add garlic, flour, and reserved bacon; cook, stirring constantly, until fragrant, about 30 seconds. Add reduced wine, broth, and herb bundle, scraping bottom of pot to loosen browned bits. Return roast and any accumulated juices to pot; increase heat to high and bring liquid to simmer, then place large sheet of aluminum foil over pot and cover tightly with lid. Set pot in oven and cook, using tongs to turn beef every hour, until fork slips easily in and out of meat, 2½ to 3 hours, adding carrots to pot after 2 hours.

6. While meat cooks, bring pearl onions, ½ cup water, butter, and sugar to boil in large skillet over medium-high heat. Reduce heat to medium, cover, and cook until onions are tender, 5 to 8 minutes. Uncover, increase heat to medium-high, and cook until all liquid evaporates, 3 to 4 minutes. Add mushrooms and ¼ teaspoon salt; cook, stirring occasionally, until vegetables are browned and glazed, 8 to 12 minutes. Remove from heat and set aside. Sprinkle gelatin over remaining ¼ cup water in small bowl and let sit until gelatin softens.

7. Transfer beef to carving board; tent with foil to keep warm. Let braising liquid settle, about 5 minutes; using large spoon, skim fat from surface. Remove herb bundle and stir in onion-mushroom mixture. Bring liquid to simmer over medium-high heat and cook until mixture is slightly thickened and reduced to 3¼ cups, 20 to 30 minutes. Season sauce with salt and pepper to taste. Add softened gelatin and stir until completely dissolved.

8. Remove twine from roasts and discard. Slice meat against grain into ½-inch-thick slices. Divide meat among warmed bowls or transfer to platter; arrange vegetables around meat, pour sauce over top, and sprinkle with minced parsley. Serve immediately.

TO MAKE AHEAD: Follow recipe through step 7, skipping step of softening and adding gelatin. Place meat back in pot, let cool to room temperature, cover, and refrigerate for up to 2 days. To serve, slice beef and arrange in 13 by 9-inch baking dish. Soften gelatin as directed in step 6. Bring sauce to simmer and stir in softened gelatin until completely dissolved. Pour warm sauce over meat, cover with foil, and bake in 350-degree oven until heated through, about 30 minutes.

✔ WHY THIS RECIPE WORKS

How do you use an entire bottle of wine in a stew recipe that calls for covered cooking and not end up with a sauce that's too boozy? You deal with the wine before it goes into the pot.

USE A NEW METHOD *Boeuf à la mode*—"beef in the latest fashion"—is a classic French recipe that dates to a time when a multiday recipe was the rule rather than the exception. Although boeuf à la mode bears some similarity to American pot roast, this elegant French dish relies heavily on wine for flavor, adds collagen-rich veal and pork parts for body, and has a separately prepared mushroom-onion garnish. Today's grain-fed beef gets little exercise and has much more marbling than the leaner, grass-fed beef eaten in France when this recipe was created. Therefore, we are able to simplify this dish and skip the traditional larding and marinating of the beef, and yet still produce a tender pot roast in a suave, rich wine sauce with great body.

SALT THE BEEF We take the usual pot roast cut (chuck-eye roast) and split it in half to expose (and remove) excess fat so we can guarantee an especially refined final product. We then salt the meat for an hour to ramp up the meaty quotient. This works by drawing moisture out of the meat and forming a shallow brine. Over time, the salt migrates back into the meat, seasoning it throughout rather than just on the exterior. (See concept 12 for more details on salting.)

REDUCE THE WINE In all of the classic recipes, the meat is marinated in a mixture of red wine and large-cut mirepoix (carrots, onions, and celery) for a significant period of time, up to three days in some cases. Testing various lengths of time, we found that the effect was superficial unless we were willing to invest at least two full days. Even then, the wine flavor penetrated only the outer part of the meat, and the vegetables didn't really add much. Frankly, the meat picked up so much wine flavor during the hours-long braising time that marinating didn't seem worth the effort. In fact, we felt that the meat picked up too much wine flavor as it cooked, tasting sour and harsh. We fixed this problem by cooking the wine before braising the beef. When we combined the reduced wine with the beef broth and used this mixture as the braising liquid, we knew we'd got it right. The wine tastes complex and fruity, not sour and astringent. Reducing the wine before using it in this recipe also cuts the alcohol content in the final dish.

PUT IT IN THE OVEN We cook this pot roast, covered, in the oven and use foil to maintain a good seal. The steam that collects in the pot helps to cook the meat slowly and evenly. (See concept 8 for more on this phenomenon.)

MAKE IT THICK AND GLOSSY Compared with regular pot roast braising liquid, which is flavorful but relatively thin and brothy, the sauce that accompanies boeuf à la mode is richer and more akin to a sauce that might be found on a steak at a fine restaurant. Adding some flour to the sautéed onion and garlic helps with the overall consistency, but the sauce still needs body. Instead of adding pork rind, split calves' feet, or veal bones, we go straight to the source: powdered gelatin. Adding powdered gelatin after the sauce has finished reducing gives us the results we want: a rich and velvety sauce, on par with the best classic recipes out there.

PRACTICAL SCIENCE DEALCOHOLIZED WINES

> If substituting dealcoholized wine, we prefer the brand Fre.

To see how dealcoholized wine performs in the kitchen, we sampled both red and white versions of two national brands, Ariel and Fre. Neither brand had the complexity of real wine, but the Fre red and white beverages were a step up from mere grape juice. To find out what factors might contribute to the differences between the brands, we looked into how each producer removes alcohol from wine. Ariel uses a cold filtration process, repeatedly passing the wine along meshlike membranes to remove the alcohol. The resulting alcohol-free syrup is then diluted with water. Fre wines, on the other hand, are produced with a technique known as the "spinning-cone" method, in which the wine cascades down spinning cone-shaped cylinders in a thin stream. Nitrogen gas is sprayed over this thin layer of wine to prevent any of the flavor compounds from becoming volatile and escaping. When the wine is subsequently heated to remove the alcohol, the nitrogen shield protects the flavors of the wine. In the end, the alcohol is reduced from 10 to 12 percent to .3 to .5 percent. Since some liquid evaporates in the process, a small amount of unfermented grape juice is added to the wine. Though sweet, wines that are dealcoholized with the spinning-cone method retain distinct wine aromas and flavors.

To see how dealcoholized Fre would stand up to the real deal in cooking, we sautéed chicken cutlets and made our Daube Provençal (page 82). While all tasters could easily detect the sweet and less acidic notes of the dealcoholized wine in both dishes, most thought it was still quite acceptable. When we added some lemon juice or wine vinegar to cut the sweetness, both dishes got near universal compliments. If you want to avoid wine with alcohol, the only national brand we found that uses the spinning-cone method is Fre, which is made by Sutter Home.

If you don't have dealcoholized wine on hand and really want to avoid cooking with alcohol, we found that broth can work in sauces or stews that don't rely heavily on wine for flavor. (This includes simple pan sauces with wine but excludes dishes like French-Style Pot Roast or Daube Provençal that call for an entire bottle of wine.) Replace the wine with an equal amount of broth and add a little red wine vinegar, white wine vinegar, or lemon juice just before serving to mimic the acidity of the wine. For every ½ cup of broth added, use ½ teaspoon of vinegar or lemon juice.

POACHED SALMON WITH HERB AND CAPER VINAIGRETTE
SERVES 4

To ensure uniform pieces of fish that cook at the same rate, buy a whole center-cut fillet and cut it into four pieces. If a skinless whole fillet is unavailable, remove the skin yourself or follow the recipe as directed with a skin-on fillet, adding three to four minutes to the cooking time in step 2. This recipe will yield salmon fillets cooked to medium-rare.

2   lemons
2   tablespoons minced fresh parsley, stems reserved
2   tablespoons minced fresh tarragon, stems reserved
1   large shallot, minced
½   cup dry white wine
½   cup water
1   (1¾- to 2-pound) skinless salmon fillet, about 1½ inches thick
2   tablespoons capers, rinsed and chopped
2   tablespoons extra-virgin olive oil
1   tablespoon honey
     Salt and pepper

1. Line plate with paper towels. Cut top and bottom off 1 lemon, then cut into eight to ten ¼-inch-thick slices. Cut remaining lemon into 8 wedges and set aside. Arrange lemon slices in single layer across bottom of 12-inch skillet. Scatter herb stems and 2 tablespoons minced shallot evenly over lemon slices. Add wine and water to skillet.

2. Use sharp knife to remove any whitish fat from belly of salmon and cut fillet into 4 equal pieces. Place salmon fillets in skillet, skinned side down, on top of lemon slices. Set pan over high heat and bring liquid to simmer. Reduce heat to low, cover, and cook until sides are opaque but center of thickest part of fillet is still translucent when cut into with paring knife, or until fillet registers 125 degrees (for medium-rare), 11 to 16 minutes. Remove pan from heat and, using spatula, carefully transfer salmon and lemon slices to prepared plate and tent loosely with aluminum foil.

3. Return pan to high heat and simmer cooking liquid until slightly thickened and reduced to 2 tablespoons, 4 to 5 minutes. Meanwhile, combine minced parsley and tarragon, remaining minced shallot, capers, oil, and honey in medium bowl. Strain reduced cooking liquid through fine-mesh strainer into bowl with herb mixture, pressing on solids to extract as much liquid as possible. Whisk to combine and season with salt and pepper to taste.

4. Season salmon with salt and pepper. Using spatula, carefully lift and tilt salmon fillets to remove lemon slices. Place salmon on serving platter or individual plates and spoon vinaigrette over top. Serve, passing lemon wedges separately.

PRACTICAL SCIENCE BENEFITS OF BELLY FAT

Belly fat helps keep salmon moist.

A center-cut salmon fillet typically tapers down on one side to the fattier belly of the fish. The belly's fattiness helps keep this section of the fish moist, despite its thinner profile. The belly area is sometimes covered with a chewy white membrane, which should be trimmed away before cooking. We also like to neaten up any ragged edges that can dry out and fray during cooking.

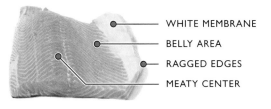

WHITE MEMBRANE
BELLY AREA
RAGGED EDGES
MEATY CENTER

PRACTICAL SCIENCE
QUICK FIX FOR CORKED WINES

The acrid taste of corked wine can be lessened with plastic wrap—but not enough to make the wine drinkable.

The chemical culprit responsible for a "corked," or tainted, bottle of wine—which will have an unmistakable musty smell and acrid taste—is TCA (2,4,6-trichloroanisole). TCA is produced when fungi naturally present in the cork encounter chlorophenols—ironically a product of the chlorine bleaching process used to sterilize cork. While TCA is harmless to health, it renders wine undrinkable.

It never occurred to us that there might be a way to salvage the wine, but with a little digging, we actually found a quirky recommendation: Submerge a ball of plastic wrap in the wine and let it sit for a while. As odd as it sounds, the theory behind the suggestion makes sense: The polyethylene material attracts the TCA, effectively removing it from the wine.

With nothing to lose, we tracked down four corked bottles, poured half of each into a jar with a loose wad of plastic wrap, sealed the lids, and soaked them for 10 minutes, shaking each sample occasionally. When we sipped the treated wines, we found that the nasty "dirty-socks" odor and bitterness from the TCA were indeed greatly reduced. But we also noticed that the plastic had absorbed many of the desirable aromatic compounds, leaving the wines tasting flat and muted—and still unfit for drinking or cooking. Your best bet: Return the tainted wine for a refund.

✔ WHY THIS RECIPE WORKS

The classic poaching method calls for submerging salmon completely in liquid in a deep pan. This method makes sense in a restaurant where the poaching liquid is used over and over again. But at home it seems wasteful. Plus, all that liquid causes flavor to leach out of the fish. We reinvent poached fish in this recipe to preserve flavor and moisture; we also make a sauce in the process.

USE LESS LIQUID Rather than poaching fish in a big pot of wine and water, which has to be flavored with a ton of herbs and aromatic vegetables, we cut way back on the liquid. This keeps more flavor in the fish. And with so little liquid in the pot we need just a couple of shallots and a few herbs to flavor the water and wine.

BOOST THE WINE Because we're using less liquid, the salmon isn't totally submerged as it cooks. Therefore it relies on steam to deliver heat and flavor. With our original ratio of wine to liquid, and at such a low temperature, not enough steam was being created to efficiently cook the parts of the fish sticking out above the liquid. But then we remembered that adding alcohol to water lowers the boiling temperature. The higher the concentration of

alcohol, the more vapor will be produced as the liquid is heated. More vapor, in turn, means better heat transfer, which leads to faster cooking, even at temperatures below a simmer. We also know that alcohol can increase the rate at which proteins denature. Therefore, by using more alcohol in the cooking liquid, we can cook the fish faster and at a lower temperature. The results? A piece of salmon that is perfectly cooked.

TURN LIQUID INTO SAUCE We were happy to discover that the super-concentrated poaching liquid was the foundation for a beurre blanc, and therefore we didn't have to make a separate sauce. This classic French sauce is made by reducing wine flavored with vinegar, shallots, and herbs and then finishing it with butter. But since a few tablespoons of butter per serving push this dish out of the "everyday" category, we offer a vinaigrette-style variation in which we use olive oil instead of butter.

REMOVE THE SKIN This recipe calls for skinless fillets so that the flavors of the poaching liquid can be easily absorbed by the flesh. If you're able to purchase only skin-on fillets, they will work in this recipe but you won't want to serve the soggy skin. To remove it, transfer the cooked fillets to paper towels and let cool slightly. Gently slide a thin spatula between the flesh and skin and use the fingers of your free hand to help separate the skin. In the process, you can also remove the unattractive gray portion of the flesh that is found next to the skin, but you may not want to. While this tissue occasionally has a slightly fishy flavor, it is rich in omega-3 fatty acids and well worth eating.

Flambés do not have to be scary. The classic Crêpes Suzette uses the high-heat flambé technique to reduce the boozy nature of the sauce, and to provide deeper, better flavor.

CRÊPES SUZETTE
SERVES 6

To allow for practice, the recipe yields about 16 crêpes; only 12 are needed for the dish. We prefer crêpes made with whole milk, but skim milk or 1 percent or 2 percent low-fat milk can also be used. Before flambéing, be sure to roll up long shirtsleeves, tie back long hair, and turn off the exhaust fan and any lit burners.

CRÊPES

1½	cups whole milk
1½	cups (7½ ounces) all-purpose flour
3	large eggs
½	cup water
5	tablespoons unsalted butter, melted, plus extra for pan
3	tablespoons sugar
2	tablespoons cognac
½	teaspoon salt

ORANGE SAUCE

¼	cup cognac
1	tablespoon finely grated orange zest plus 1¼ cups juice (3 oranges)
6	tablespoons unsalted butter, cut into 6 pieces
¼	cup sugar
2	tablespoons orange liqueur, such as triple sec

1. FOR THE CRÊPES: Process all ingredients in blender until smooth, about 10 seconds. Transfer to bowl.

2. Brush bottom and sides of 10-inch nonstick skillet lightly with melted butter and heat skillet over medium heat. Pour in scant ¼ cup batter in slow, steady stream, twirling skillet slowly until bottom is evenly covered. Cook crêpe until it starts to lose its opaqueness and turns spotty light golden brown on bottom, 30 seconds to 1 minute, loosening edge with rubber spatula. Gently slide spatula underneath edge of crêpe, grasp edge with fingertips, and flip crêpe. Cook until dry on second side, about 20 seconds.

3. Transfer cooked crêpe to wire rack, inverting so spotted side is facing up. Return pan to heat, brush pan lightly with butter, and heat for 10 seconds before repeating with remaining batter. As crêpes are done, stack on wire rack.

(Cooked crêpes can be refrigerated, wrapped in plastic wrap, for up to 3 days; bring them to room temperature before proceeding with recipe.)

4. FOR THE ORANGE SAUCE: Adjust oven rack to lower-middle position and heat broiler. Heat 3 tablespoons cognac in 12-inch broiler-safe skillet over medium heat just until warmed through, about 5 seconds. Off heat, wave lit match over pan until cognac ignites, then shake pan to distribute flames.

5. When flames subside, add 1 cup orange juice, butter, and 3 tablespoons sugar and simmer over high heat, stirring occasionally, until many large bubbles appear and mixture

---

PRACTICAL SCIENCE THE BEST WAYS TO FLAMBÉ

Here are some tips to help you flambé without any fear.

Flambéing is more than just tableside theatrics: As dramatic as it looks, igniting alcohol actually helps develop a deeper, more complex flavor in sauces, thanks to flavor-boosting chemical reactions that occur only at the high temperature reached in flambéing. But accomplishing this feat at home can be daunting. Here are some tips for successful—and safe—flambéing at home.

BE PREPARED Turn off the exhaust fan, tie back long hair, and have a lid ready to smother dangerous flare-ups.

USE PROPER EQUIPMENT A pan with flared sides (such as a skillet) rather than straight sides will allow more oxygen to mingle with the alcohol vapors, increasing the chance that you'll spark the desired flame. If possible, use long wooden chimney matches, and light the alcohol with your arm extended to full length.

IGNITE WARM ALCOHOL If the alcohol becomes too hot, the vapors can rise to dangerous heights, causing large flare-ups once lit. Inversely, if the alcohol is too cold, there won't be enough vapors to light at all. We found that heating alcohol to 100 degrees Fahrenheit (best achieved by adding alcohol to a pan off the heat, then letting it heat from five to 10 seconds) produced the most moderate, yet long-burning flames.

LIGHT THE ALCOHOL OFF THE HEAT If using a gas burner, be sure to turn off the flame to eliminate accidental ignitions near the side of the pan. Removing the pan from the heat also gives you more control over the alcohol's temperature.

IF A DANGEROUS FLARE-UP SHOULD OCCUR Simply slide the lid over the top of the skillet (coming in from the side of, rather than over, the flames) to put out the fire quickly. Let the alcohol cool down and start again.

IF THE ALCOHOL WON'T LIGHT If the pan is full of other ingredients, the potency of the alcohol can be diminished as it becomes incorporated. For a more foolproof flame, ignite the alcohol in a separate small skillet or saucepan; once the flame has burned off, add the reduced alcohol to the remaining ingredients.

---

reduces to thick syrup, 6 to 8 minutes (you should have just over ½ cup sauce). Transfer sauce to small bowl; do not wash skillet. Stir remaining ¼ cup orange juice, orange zest, orange liqueur, and remaining 1 tablespoon cognac into sauce; cover to keep warm.

6. To assemble, fold each crêpe in half, then fold into quarters. Arrange 9 folded crêpes around edge of now-empty skillet, with rounded edges facing inward, overlapping as necessary to fit. Arrange remaining 3 crêpes in center of pan. Sprinkle crêpes evenly with remaining 1 tablespoon sugar. Broil until sugar caramelizes and crêpes turn spotty brown, about 5 minutes. (Watch crêpes constantly to prevent scorching; turn pan as necessary.) Carefully remove pan from oven and pour half of sauce over crêpes, leaving some areas uncovered. Transfer crêpes to individual plates and serve immediately, passing extra sauce separately.

☑ WHY THIS RECIPE WORKS

This classic recipe for crêpes flambéed with an orange-cognac sauce is certainly dramatic but the reality is often disappointing. The sauce can fail to ignite, which makes the dish too boozy. And even if the sauce does flambé, the crêpes are too soggy. Finally, we wanted to make this dish for a small crowd rather than an individual, as is the custom when this dish is made tableside in a restaurant.

BLEND AND GO   Classic crêpe recipes generally call for resting the batter (made with eggs, milk, melted butter, flour, and sugar) for several hours so that the gluten can relax. (For more on gluten, see concept 39.) We found that skipping this step yielded sturdier crêpes more capable of standing up to the sauce, plus we saved two hours of waiting time. To maximize gluten development we simply throw all the batter ingredients into a blender. A splash of cognac and a dash of salt give our crêpes additional flavor.

DON'T BUY A CRÊPE PAN   There's no need to invest in a special crêpe pan; a buttered nonstick pan works just fine for this recipe. Use a pastry brush to ensure an even, light coating of fat. Use a dry measuring cup with a ¼-cup capacity to portion the batter. When you're ready to go, tilt the buttered and heated nonstick skillet slightly to the right and begin pouring in a scant ¼ cup of batter. Continue tilting the pan slowly, in a counterclockwise motion, until a thin, even crêpe is formed. Loosen the edge with a heatproof rubber spatula and, with fingertips on the top side, grab the edge and flip. The first few may not come out perfectly (or even be usable at all). Here, practice really does make perfect.

FLAMBÉ FIRST   For a foolproof flambé that doesn't create a frightening fireball or, conversely, doesn't burn at all, we ignite the alcohol (cognac) alone in the skillet before building the sauce. We then enrich a reduction of butter, sugar, and orange juice with additional orange juice, orange zest, and triple sec.

BROIL THE CRÊPES   Before saucing, we sprinkle our crêpes with sugar and broil them, forming a crunchy, sugary barrier that provides partial protection from the sauce, so our crêpes don't turn soggy.

PRACTICAL SCIENCE   IS FLAMBÉ JUST FOR SHOW?

Flambéing improves the flavor of a sauce by removing much of the alcohol and reconfiguring the molecules as a result of the high heat.

A flambé looks impressive and is easy enough to execute, but we wondered if it really improves the flavor of a sauce and, if so, why. Blind taste tests quickly revealed that flambéing a sauce did indeed improve its flavor: A flamed sauce was richer and sweeter than a sauce that had not been ignited. To get a handle on why it was better, we looked into the scientific principles involved.

A flambé is the ignition of the alcohol vapor that lies above the pan, a reaction that generates significant amounts of heat. To measure this heat, we used an infrared thermometer and discovered that the temperature at the surface of the cognac—the base of this particular sauce—quickly climbed past 500 degrees. Curious to know whether the high heat served to remove all of the alcohol from the pan, we sent samples of the flambéed cognac as well as the completed sauce to a food lab for alcohol analysis. Tests revealed that the flambé removed 79 percent of the alcohol from the cognac. (The simmering of the sauce that followed the flambé removed almost all of the remaining alcohol.) So the flambé was removing most of the alcohol, but what effect was the high heat having on flavor?

Many of the great, flavor-boosting chemical reactions of cooking require high heat. Reactions involving sugar, such as caramelization and browning, occur at temperatures higher than 300 degrees. Because the surface had reached above 500 degrees, we noticed some of this type of flavor development. A simmered cognac, in contrast, maintains a steady temperature of about 180 degrees at its surface and therefore develops none of that extra flavor. Another benefit of the flambé is that at very high heat, molecules can absorb enough energy to isomerize, or change shape. The consequences of this reconfiguration might include improved solubility and changed flavor perception. The mystery was solved. A flambéed sauce burns off most of its alcohol and gains flavor from several high-heat cooking reactions. The result is a sauce with a hint of alcohol and great depth.

More Water Makes Chewier Bread

Bread. It's ironic that something so simple seems so complicated to modern cooks. In many cases, the ingredient list for bread recipes consists of just flour, water, salt, and yeast. And the method and required equipment should not be daunting. After all, they were baking bread in ancient Egypt.

HOW THE SCIENCE WORKS

WHEN WATER AND FLOUR COMBINE

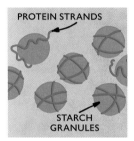

WITHOUT WATER *When flour is dry, the starch's protein strands are lifeless and unmoving.*

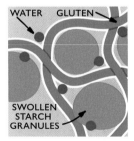

WATER ADDED *When flour and water are combined, the protein strands change shape and link together to form gluten.*

Let's start with the ingredients.

Yeast is a living organism. Its function in bread dough is to consume sugars and starches present in the flour and then convert them into carbon dioxide and alcohol, which gives the finished loaf its lift and flavor. This process is known as fermentation.

The two most common forms of yeast in the grocery store are active dry and instant. They are similar in appearance and origins but are processed differently: Active dry yeast is dried at higher temperatures, which kills more of the exterior yeast cells (this is why it requires an initial activation in warm water), whereas instant, or rapid-rise, yeast is dried at more gentle temperatures (so it can be added directly to the dry ingredients). As a result, substituting equal amounts of one for the other will not provide the same results. (See "Substituting Active Dry Yeast for Instant," page 329.)

Yeast is important, but bread would be nothing without the combination of flour and water. Though it may look like nothing more than white powder, flour is a complex substance made mostly of starch and lesser amounts of proteins (see "Flour 101," page 357). With the proper treatment, it provides the structure and texture of breads of all kinds.

The role of flour in bread begins when it is combined with water and yeast—the first step of bread making. The wheat proteins in flour are unmoving and lifeless when dry but begin to change shape when they come in contact with water, a process called hydration. During hydration, the individual protein molecules, which consist of the loosely coiled glutenin and the more tightly wound gliadin (see concept 39), begin to link up with one another to form long, elastic chains called gluten. These strands of gluten combine to form a membranelike network. The network engulfs swollen starch granules and gas bubbles, stretching as the dough rises and then bakes, giving the finished loaf its structure and chew.

The amount of water added to your flour and yeast is important: The more water in a dough, the stronger and more extensible the gluten strands. If the gluten strands are strong and extensible, they can support the starch granules and gas bubbles that hydrate and swell as the dough rises and bakes, giving you an airier bread with good chew. During baking, the water within the dough turns to steam, creating hollow pockets as moisture rushes to escape. Extra water also creates a looser dough, which allows the steam bubbles to expand more easily. In a drier dough, gas bubbles have a harder time forming and are more likely to collapse. Getting those gas bubbles to hold their shape until the dough has risen and set in the oven is the key to creating an open, airy crumb.

TEST KITCHEN EXPERIMENT

We wanted to see and taste the differences in bread made with varying quantities of water so we designed a simple experiment. We started with our recipe for a rustic Italian bread, which has a hydration level of about 68 percent (for more on percent hydration, see "Calculating Baker's Percentage," page 328), and tried both increasing and decreasing the amount of water in the recipe. For simplicity's sake, and to eliminate unwanted variables, we skipped using a biga (see concept 40) and made the doughs using a straight mixing method. Along with the original recipe, we tested the following hydration levels: 50 percent, 60 percent, 75 percent, and 80 percent.

THE RESULTS

While even the 60 and 75 percent hydrated doughs showed significant differences, the extremes were most illustrative. The 50 percent hydrated loaf featured a tight, fine crumb with small air pockets—and showed little spread and expansion. On the other hand, the dough with 80 percent water had a loose, open crumb with large, irregular holes, and the bread baked up very flat and wide. In the middle of these outer limits, the original recipe featured moderate-size holes and good volume and height. Because the levels of flour, yeast, and salt were the same for all of our breads, ignoring the texture, tasters found the flavor of each loaf to be identical.

THE TAKEAWAY

The ratio of water to flour is important when making bread dough. When flour hits water, the individual wheat proteins begin to change shape, connecting to form strands of gluten. Gluten is responsible for creating the network within a dough that gives bread its structure. Too little water, and a strong gluten network cannot form. Without a strong gluten network, the gas bubbles created within the dough cannot hold and rise, making the finished product a dense loaf with too tight a crumb, as we saw in our bread with 50 percent hydration. Too much water, on the other hand, can dilute and weaken the gluten, likewise hindering a bread's ability to rise, as in the loaf with 80 percent hydration.

We vary the hydration of our doughs depending on our desired end product, however. Our Pizza Bianca (page 328), which does not need a high rise, is a bread that we want to be extraordinarily chewy. Therefore, we hydrate it at 90 percent. Our Olive-Rosemary Bread (page 334), on the other hand, is best with a moderate chew, medium-sized holes, and a nice rise. We hydrate this loaf at 63 percent. No matter what kind of crumb and rise you desire, it always pays to measure your ingredients well. Too much water or flour can drastically alter the texture of your bread.

HOW WATER AFFECTS BREAD TEXTURE

50 PERCENT HYDRATION
This loaf had the smallest ratio of water to flour, resulting in a weak gluten network. As a result, the loaf was small and dense with a tight crumb.

68 PERCENT HYDRATION
With a typical hydration level of 68 percent, this loaf rose and expanded well, possessing modest-size holes.

80 PERCENT HYDRATION
This loaf had the greatest ratio of water to flour, causing the gluten network to be weak and diluted. Therefore, the loaf is flat and wide with large air pockets.

The ratio of water to flour plays a large role in the finished texture and chew of any loaf of bread or pizza. More water helps the gluten network within the dough to become stretchy and elastic, allowing it to hold more gas bubbles as the bread bakes. We use an extremely high percentage of water in our Pizza Bianca and a lower but still high percentage of water in our Almost No-Knead Bread to create the chewy, bubbly textures that we desire. Our Pizza Bianca is so hydrated, in fact, that it is impossible to roll out. Instead, we simply pour it into a pan and press to fit.

PIZZA BIANCA
SERVES 6 TO 8

If you don't have a stand mixer, you can mix the dough by hand. To do this, stir the wet and dry ingredients together with a stiff rubber spatula until the dough comes together and looks shaggy. Transfer the dough to a clean counter and knead by hand to form a smooth, round ball, 15 to 25 minutes, adding additional flour, if necessary, to prevent the dough from sticking to the counter. Proceed with the recipe as directed. If you don't have a baking stone, bake the pizza on an overturned and preheated rimmed baking sheet set on the lowest oven rack. This recipe was developed using an 18 by 13-inch baking sheet. Smaller baking sheets can be used, but because the pizza will be thicker, baking times will be longer. Place a damp kitchen towel under the mixer and watch it at all times during kneading to prevent it from wobbling off the counter. Handle the dough with lightly oiled hands to prevent sticking. Resist flouring your fingers or the dough might stick further. Serve the pizza by itself as a snack, or with soup or salad as a light entrée.

3	cups (15 ounces) all-purpose flour
1⅔	cups water, room temperature
1¼	teaspoons table salt
1½	teaspoons instant or rapid-rise yeast
1¼	teaspoons sugar
5	tablespoons extra-virgin olive oil
1	teaspoon kosher salt
2	tablespoons fresh rosemary leaves

1. Using stand mixer fitted with dough hook, mix flour, water, and table salt together on low speed until no areas of dry flour remain, 3 to 4 minutes, scraping down bowl as needed. Turn off mixer and let dough rest for 20 minutes.

2. Sprinkle yeast and sugar over dough. Knead on low speed until fully combined, 1 to 2 minutes. Increase mixer speed to high and knead until dough is glossy and smooth and pulls away from sides of bowl, 6 to 10 minutes.

(Dough will pull away from sides only while mixer is on. When mixer is off, dough will fall back to sides.)

3. Using fingers, coat large bowl with 1 tablespoon oil, rubbing excess oil from fingers onto blade of rubber spatula. Using oiled spatula, transfer dough to prepared bowl and pour 1 tablespoon oil over top. Flip dough over once so that it is well coated with oil; cover bowl tightly with plastic wrap and let dough rise at room temperature until nearly tripled in volume and large bubbles have formed, 2 to 2½ hours. (Dough can be refrigerated for up to 24 hours. Bring dough to room temperature, 2 to 2½ hours, before proceeding with step 4.)

PRACTICAL SCIENCE
CALCULATING BAKER'S PERCENTAGE

> Quantify the ratio of water to flour with baker's percentage.

So how do you figure out how much water is actually in a particular bread recipe? Professional bakers rely on a method called "baker's percentage." It presents the quantity of each ingredient as a percentage by weight of the amount of flour, which is always set at 100 percent. One advantage of the system: It allows for easy conversion from pounds and ounces to kilograms and grams (or vice versa). And once weights are calculated, scaling recipes up or down is a simple matter of multiplication or division.

Perhaps the most important part of a baker's percentage formula is the weight of the water (or other liquid) relative to the weight of the flour, since hydration level helps the baker predict the texture of the crumb. (Generally speaking, the more water in the dough, the more open the crumb.) Sandwich-bread dough with a typical 60 percent hydration (the weight of the liquid is 60 percent of the weight of the flour), for example, yields a loaf with a denser, closed crumb, whereas the 80 percent hydration level of a rustic Italian loaf such as ciabatta (the weight of the liquid is 80 percent of the weight of the flour) is responsible for its airy crumb and large, irregular holes.

To calculate the hydration level of a conventional recipe, first weigh the flour and water or other liquid. Divide the weight of the water by the weight of the flour and then multiply the result by 100. For example, a recipe containing 1¼ cups of water (10 ounces) and 3 cups of all-purpose flour (15 ounces) will have a 67 percent (10/15 x 100 = 67) hydration level, indicating a moderately airy crumb.

BREAD TYPE	BAKER'S PERCENTAGE
Pizza Bianca (page 328)	90%
Whole-Wheat Sandwich Bread (page 341)	85%
Rosemary Focaccia (page 340)	84%
Rustic Dinner Rolls (page 336)	72%
Almost No-Knead Bread (page 330)	70%
Olive-Rosemary Bread (page 334)	63%
New York–Style Thin-Crust Pizza (page 344)	63%

4. One hour before baking, adjust oven rack to middle position, place baking stone on rack, and heat oven to 450 degrees. Coat rimmed baking sheet with 2 tablespoons oil. Using rubber spatula, turn dough out onto prepared baking sheet along with any oil in bowl. Using fingertips, press dough out toward edges of baking sheet, taking care not to tear it. (Dough will not fit snugly into corners. If dough resists stretching, let it relax for 5 to 10 minutes before trying to stretch it again.) Let dough rest until slightly bubbly, 5 to 10 minutes. Using dinner fork, poke surface of dough 30 to 40 times and sprinkle with kosher salt.

5. Bake until golden brown, 20 to 30 minutes, sprinkling rosemary over top and rotating baking sheet halfway through baking. Using metal spatula, transfer pizza to cutting board. Brush dough lightly with remaining 1 tablespoon oil. Slice and serve immediately.

✔ WHY THIS RECIPE WORKS

With no cheese or sauce—just a gloss of olive oil and flakes of salt—Pizza Bianca looks more like focaccia than pizza. But its crisp exterior and chewy, bubbly middle make us forget all about nomenclature. In some ways, this is the simplest bread imaginable because it does not involve shaping it into a loaf… just stretching the dough into a pan. Therefore, the dough can be very, very wet.

ADD WATER To achieve its chewy, bubbly texture, our recipe for Pizza Bianca calls for 9 parts water to 10 parts flour—an almost 30 percent higher level of hydration than in most other pizza dough. Water aids the development of gluten, the network of cross-linked proteins that gives bread its internal structure and chew. Up to a point, the more water in the dough, the stronger and more elastic the gluten strands and the chewier the bread. These strands, in turn, help to support the gas bubbles formed as the dough bakes, preventing them from bursting and creating an open, airy crust.

MIX, REST, AND KNEAD We let the dough rest for 20 minutes before kneading. This rest time, called autolyse, allows gluten to develop and therefore cuts down drastically on the kneading time. (See concept 39 for more on autolyse.) Instead of a half-hour of kneading in the mixer, now we need less than 10 minutes.

PRESS THE DOUGH Because this recipe is traditionally baked in a pan, it is easy to avoid handling the wet dough; simply pour it onto a well-oiled baking sheet. Shaping is easy: Press the dough from its middle toward the edges of the pan. It's important, however, to stop pressing the dough if it is resisting. Give it a little rest: Resting allows the large gluten molecules to relax (like straightening curly hair) and stretch more easily.

USE A BAKING STONE Most pizza kitchens are equipped with stone- or tile-lined ovens that supply the steady, dry, intense heat necessary to make pizzas with crisp, crackerlike crusts. Baking stones (also called pizza stones) were created to simulate these conditions in the home oven.

Home ovens, whether electric or gas, are furnished with thermostats that switch on and off to maintain the oven's internal temperature. This, along with the opening and closing of the oven door, causes the temperature to fluctuate, which can be damaging to baked goods that require extremely high heat. Our Pizza Bianca requires such an environment, so we turn to the baking stone. Preheating the oven with a baking stone for an hour evens out the heat in the oven, and the stone's ability to absorb, retain, and radiate heat insulates the pizza from temperature swings that may occur during baking.

Baking stones intended for home use are usually made from clay or terra cotta. When purchasing, be sure to look for the thickest possible stone. Thickness is indicative of a stone's ability to retain heat.

PRACTICAL SCIENCE
SUBSTITUTING ACTIVE DRY YEAST FOR INSTANT

To substitute active dry yeast for instant, use 25 percent more of it. To substitute instant for active dry, use 25 percent less.

When substituting active dry yeast for instant (also called rapid-rise) yeast, it's important to compensate for the "dead weight" of the inactive yeast cells. To compensate for the greater quantity of inactive yeast cells in the active dry yeast, simply use 25 percent more of it (for example, if the recipe calls for 1 teaspoon of instant yeast, use 1¼ teaspoons of active dry). The inverse holds true as well—use about 25 percent less instant yeast in a recipe that calls for active dry. Also, don't forget to dissolve active dry yeast in a portion of the water from the recipe, heated to 110 degrees (be careful, as fermentation slows above 120 degrees, and all the yeast cells will die at 140 degrees). Then let it stand for five minutes before adding it to the remaining wet ingredients. Skip this step if using instant yeast in recipes that call for active dry.

ALMOST NO-KNEAD BREAD
MAKES I LARGE ROUND LOAF

You will need at least a 6-quart Dutch oven for this recipe. An enameled cast-iron Dutch oven with a tight-fitting lid yields the best results, but the recipe also works in a regular cast-iron Dutch oven or heavy stockpot. Check the knob on your Dutch oven lid, as not all are ovensafe to 500 degrees; look for inexpensive replacement knobs from the manufacturer of your Dutch oven (or try using a metal drawer handle from a hardware store). This dough rises best in a warm kitchen that is at least 68 degrees.

3	cups (15 ounces) all-purpose flour
1½	teaspoons salt
¼	teaspoon instant or rapid-rise yeast
¾	cup plus 2 tablespoons water, room temperature
6	tablespoons mild-flavored lager, room temperature
I	tablespoon white vinegar

I. Whisk flour, salt, and yeast together in large bowl. Add water, beer, and vinegar. Using rubber spatula, fold mixture, scraping up dry flour from bottom of bowl, until shaggy ball forms. Cover bowl with plastic wrap and let sit at room temperature for at least 8 hours or up to 18 hours.

2. Lay 18 by 12-inch sheet of parchment paper inside 10-inch skillet and spray with vegetable oil spray. Transfer dough to lightly floured counter and knead by hand 10 to 15 times. Shape dough into ball by pulling edges into middle. Transfer loaf, seam side down, to prepared skillet and spray surface of dough with oil spray. Cover loosely with plastic wrap and let rise at room temperature until doubled in size, about 2 hours. (Dough should barely spring back when poked with knuckle.)

3. Thirty minutes before baking, adjust oven rack to lowest position, place Dutch oven (with lid) on rack, and heat oven to 500 degrees. Lightly flour top of dough and, using sharp serrated knife or single-edge razor blade, make one 6-inch-long, ½-inch-deep slash along top of dough. Carefully remove pot from oven and remove lid. Pick up loaf by lifting parchment overhang and lower into pot (let any excess parchment hang over pot edge). Cover pot and place in oven. Reduce oven temperature to 425 degrees and bake, covered, for 30 minutes. Remove lid and continue to bake until crust is deep golden brown and loaf registers 210 degrees, 20 to 30 minutes longer. Carefully remove loaf from pot; transfer to wire rack, discard parchment, and let cool to room temperature, about 2 hours, before slicing and serving. (Bread is best eaten on day it is baked but will keep wrapped in double layer of plastic wrap and stored at room temperature for up to 2 days. To recrisp crust, place unwrapped bread in 450-degree oven for 6 to 8 minutes.)

PRACTICAL SCIENCE BREAD LIKES A HUMID OVEN

Steam is key when baking bread with a nice, crisp crust. A Dutch oven holds steam well, or you can add steam to the oven yourself.

A major breakthrough in the no-knead bread recipe first published in the *New York Times* was to bake the bread in a preheated Dutch oven, which creates the dramatic open-crumbed structure and the shatteringly crisp crust that was previously attainable only in a professional bakery. How does this work?

First, as the loaf heats it gives off steam to create a very humid environment inside the Dutch oven. Since moist air transfers heat much more efficiently than dry air, the loaf heats much more rapidly. This in turn causes the air bubbles inside to expand much faster, leading to a more open crumb structure. As a test, we baked two loaves of bread, one in a Dutch oven and the other on a preheated baking stone. After one minute in the oven, the surface temperature of the Dutch oven–baked loaf had risen past 200 degrees, while the other loaf had reached only 135 degrees.

Steam contributes to a great loaf in several other ways. As steam condenses onto the surface of the baking bread, it keeps the crust soft, allowing the bread to continue to expand until the crust dries. (A dry crust is much harder to expand.) It also causes the starches to form a thin sheath that eventually dries out, giving the finished loaf a shiny crust that stays crisp. Finally, once the crust dries and gets very hot, sugar molecules caramelize and react with proteins to form the wonderful flavor and dark brown color of crusty bread.

Many recipes suggest adding water or ice cubes to the oven; the problem is home ovens cannot retain moisture in the way a professional steam-injected oven can. With its thick walls, small internal volume, and heavy lid, a Dutch oven is the ideal environment to create and trap steam.

For regular bread baking, with loaves baking on a rimmed baking sheet, our usual approach to creating steam in a home oven is to pour boiling water into a preheated loaf pan placed on the oven's bottom rack, but the water doesn't continue to boil for very long. Inspired by the superheated stones used to generate steam in Swedish saunas, we've come up with a more effective approach: using lava rocks. These irregularly shaped rocks (available at many hardware stores for use in gas grills) have a lot of surface area for absorbing and retaining heat, maximizing the amount of steam produced when boiling water is introduced. To do this, place a wide pan filled with lava rocks on the bottom oven rack, and pour about ¼ cup of boiling water into the rocks once they are preheated. Keep the oven door closed for one minute to create steam. When you place the bread in the oven, pour another ¼ cup of water over the rocks, and bake as usual.

WHY THIS RECIPE WORKS

In 2006, New York Times *writer Mark Bittman published a recipe developed by Jim Lahey of the Sullivan Street Bakery in Manhattan that promised to shake up the world of home baking: It allowed the average cook to bake bread that looked like it had been produced in a professional bakery and involved no kneading at all. However, as we baked loaf after loaf, we found two big problems: The dough deflated when carried to the pot, causing misshapen loaves, and it lacked flavor. To give the dough more strength, we lower the hydration and add the bare minimum of kneading time to compensate.*

DON'T KNEAD—MUCH   The original no-knead bread has a hydration level of 85 percent (see "Calculating Baker's Percentage," page 328), while most rustic breads max out at around 80 percent hydration, and standard sandwich breads hover between 60 percent and 75 percent hydration. This high level of water, along with the long rest, helps to form the gluten strands and, in effect, takes the place of kneading (see concept 39). Here, we cut back on the water in order to make the dough easier to handle. But with a lower level of hydration the gluten strands are not rearranged to the same degree as they are in the original recipe and need some help. This is why we knead our "no-knead" dough. Fifteen seconds is all it takes.

ADD VINEGAR AND BEER   Two ingredients proved key to help boost the loaf's flavor: vinegar and beer. Bottled vinegars are generally 5 percent solutions of acetic acid—the same acid produced by bacteria during dough fermentation. The addition of 1 tablespoon of distilled white vinegar adds tang. Bread's unique flavor comes during fermentation, when yeast produces alcohol, carbon dioxide, and sulfur compounds. These three elements are present together in another location—a bottle of beer. We choose lager over other types of beer because most non-lager beers undergo a process called "top fermentation," whereby yeast floats on top of the wort (grain mashed in hot water), which is exposed to oxygen and kept warm. Oxygen and warmth persuade yeast to produce spicy, astringent flavor compounds called phenols and fruity, floral compounds called esters that are desirable in beer but not in bread. Lagers, on the other hand, undergo "bottom fermentation," where the yeast is kept submerged in the low-oxygen environment at the bottom of the wort at colder temperatures, which causes the yeast to produce fewer phenols and esters, but more sulfur compounds, so that the breadier yeast and sulfur flavors come forward.

BAKE IN TWO HOT OVENS   We bake this bread in a preheated Dutch oven. Be careful of the knobs. The manufacturers of our favorite Dutch ovens (the 7¼-Quart Round French Oven by Le Creuset) and our Best Buy Dutch oven (the 6.5-Quart Cast Iron Dutch Oven by Tramontina) recommend against heating the pots to this temperature due to the phenolic (black) knobs used on the lids. But there is a simple solution. The knobs on both lids are secured with a single screw that is easily removed. Once the knob is removed, you can replace it with an inexpensive all-metal drawer handle purchased from a hardware store.

PRACTICAL SCIENCE BAKE UNTIL IT IS DONE

Internal temperature can be less useful than appearance.

We commonly advise checking the internal temperature of a loaf of bread before making the decision to pull it from the oven. A properly baked loaf should register a temperature between 195 and 210 degrees on an instant-read thermometer, depending upon the type of bread. But is internal temperature by itself sufficient proof that bread is fully baked?

We placed temperature probes in the center of two loaves of rustic Italian bread and monitored them as they baked. Halfway into the baking time, the internal temperature of the loaves had already passed 200 degrees, and they reached the optimal 210 degrees a full 15 minutes before the end of the recommended baking time. We pulled one loaf from the oven as soon as it neared 210 degrees and left the other in the oven for the recommended baking time. (The temperature of the longer-baked loaf never rose above 210, because the moisture it contains, even when fully baked, prevents it from going past the boiling point of water, or 212 degrees.) The differences between the two loaves were dramatic: The loaf removed early had a pale, soft crust and a gummy interior, while the loaf that baked for the full hour had a nicely browned, crisp crust and a perfectly baked crumb.

The takeaway? Internal temperature is less useful than appearance as a sign of a well-baked loaf.

210 BUT HALF-BAKED

210 AND FULLY BAKED

Rest Dough to Trim Kneading Time

Part therapy, part exercise, kneading is the most enjoyable part of the bread-making process. But many bakers make the mistake of overdoing it, especially when they rely on mixers. Yes, kneading is an important step, necessary in order to develop structure in the bread. But too much kneading robs the dough of flavor and alters its texture. The solution is as simple as taking a break during the mixing process.

HOW GLUTEN FORMS DURING AUTOLYSE

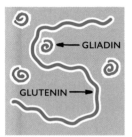

FLOUR *The two proteins in flour are gliadin and glutenin. When flour and water are combined, these proteins come together in a random matrix.*

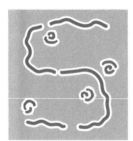

AUTOLYSE *While the dough rests before kneading, the flour proteins begin to break down.*

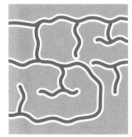

KNEADING *After autolyse, the broken flour proteins are easy to align into an organized network by kneading.*

HOW THE SCIENCE WORKS

The ultimate goal of making bread dough is to create gluten, a strong network of cross-linked proteins that traps gas bubbles and stretches as the dough bakes, creating the bubbly, chewy crumb structure that is the signature of any good loaf. How does it work?

To really understand gluten we need to begin with the proteins in flour: glutenin and gliadin. Glutenin is a very large, loosely coiled protein while gliadin is a much smaller and tightly coiled sphere. Glutenin provides most of the strength and elasticity of the dough, allowing it to bounce back after it has been stretched. Gliadin provides its stretch.

When water and flour first mix, the glutenin and gliadin form in a random, disorganized matrix of gluten that is initially very weak. In order to strengthen this network, these proteins need to be aligned next to each other so that they can better link together. Imagine the proteins as coiled-up balls of yarn you are trying to tie together into one longer piece, which you'll then sew together into a wider sheet. In their coiled state, it's not possible to tie them together; first you have to untangle and straighten them out. This straightening out and aligning is usually accomplished by kneading. As the matrix of proteins are kneaded, disorganized weaker bonds are pulled apart and reattached into straight, strong, orderly sheets of gluten.

And it's important for this gluten network to be very strong, especially in rustic breads with a fair amount of water. If not, the loaves spread sideways in the oven rather than rising up.

Kneading develops gluten but at some point more kneading is counterproductive. Too much kneading causes the dough to become warm and turn from a wheaty tan color to a grayish white, producing loaves with a sickly pallor and expired flavors. Overmixing and overheating are difficult to do by hand, but easy when using an electric mixer. The action of the dough hook creates heat through friction and also kneads excessive air into the dough, bleaching it of flavor and color in a process known as oxidation. (When properly kneaded, dough should have a smooth, almost shiny appearance. If you pull the dough, it should feel very stretchy and quickly spring back into place.) We don't want to give up the easy, quick option of our stand mixer. But how do we prevent overmixing the dough?

Autolyse. Developed by French bread-making authority Raymond Calvel in the 1970s, autolyse (pronounced AUTO-lees, also called autolysis in the U.S.) is a technique in which flour and water are first mixed together and then allowed to rest before being kneaded. (We often add yeast along with the flour and water. Though it's not traditionally part of autolyse, we find that the early addition does not make a significant change.) Autolyse makes a significant difference in both the flavor and structure of many breads. Why?

Autolyse occurs after the random matrix of proteins has come together, but before the sheets of gluten have formed and aligned. While the mixture rests, naturally occurring enzymes (known as proteases) break down the disorganized bonds of gluten, acting like scissors, cutting the coiled-up proteins into smaller segments that are easier to straighten and align during kneading. This is why dough that has undergone autolyse requires much less kneading than freshly made dough. When this rested dough is then kneaded, the gluten is positioned to form a stronger, more organized network more quickly. And the less time the dough is kneaded in the stand mixer, the better.

While kneading by hand can be a gratifying process, most of our recipes call for a stand mixer simply because it's easier. (And in cases where the dough is extremely wet and loose—as in Pizza Bianca (page 328)—working it by hand is virtually impossible.) Machine-kneading is rougher; it links gluten strands together only to tear them apart. Hand-kneading is gentler, producing gluten that, once formed, stays together, which can ultimately lead to chewier texture. But gluten develops no matter how you mix the dough. And we've found the differences aren't dramatic enough to lock away our stand mixer and revert to hand-kneading. Yes, hand-kneading can deliver ever so slightly better results, but it's more work and there's the risk of adding too much flour as you work the dough on the counter.

TEST KITCHEN EXPERIMENT

Just how much kneading time does an autolyse period really save? To find out, we made two batches of a simple rustic Italian bread. For one loaf we mixed flour, water, yeast, and salt together in a stand mixer with a dough hook and kneaded it on low speed until the dough completely cleared the bowl and clung to the hook. For the second, we mixed only the flour, water, and yeast until just combined, and then let the mixture sit for 20 minutes before adding the salt and kneading. We repeated the test two more times, measuring the time it took for the dough to cling to the hook, not the bowl, and averaged the results.

THE RESULTS

The results painted a clear picture. The doughs that were given the 20-minute respite took an average of about five minutes less kneading (about 10 minutes versus more than 15) to clear the bowl. This significant decrease in kneading time translated into bread with better crumb color, aroma, and wheat flavor.

THE TAKEAWAY

During autolyse, naturally occurring enzymes begin to break down the bonds of gluten, turning the long and coiled glutenin and gliadin proteins into smaller pieces. These smaller pieces of protein are much easier to organize and align during kneading than they would be if the autolyse were skipped. The result? For the mixture of water, flour, and yeast that we let rest, a full five minutes was shaved from our kneading time, preventing overmixing and unnecessary oxidation, which dulls the natural flavor and color of wheat. (Be sure not to add salt during autolyse. See "Hold the Salt—Temporarily," page 334.)

The lesson? Let your dough rest. Autolyse does not reduce the overall time it takes to make a loaf of bread, but it gives you a better-tasting, better-looking loaf of bread. And it will reduce wear and tear on your stand mixer.

AUTOLYSE AT WORK

WITHOUT A REST *The dough without a rest was far from ready after 10 minutes of kneading.*

AFTER 20-MINUTE REST *The dough that was allowed to rest for 20 minutes pulled away from the side of the bowl, finished with kneading, after 10 minutes.*

A brief rest after mixing together the ingredients for our doughs shortens the kneading time on recipes ranging from Olive-Rosemary Bread to Rustic Dinner Rolls. We also use this technique with Pizza Bianca (page 328), Rosemary Focaccia (page 340), and New York–Style Thin-Crust Pizza (page 344).

OLIVE-ROSEMARY BREAD
MAKES 2 LARGE LOAVES

If you don't have a stand mixer, you can mix the dough by hand. To do this, stir the wet and dry ingredients together with a stiff rubber spatula until the dough comes together and looks shaggy. Transfer the dough to a clean counter and knead by hand to form a smooth, round ball, 15 to 25 minutes, adding additional flour, if necessary, to prevent the dough from sticking to the counter. Proceed with the recipe as directed. If you don't have a baking stone, bake the bread on an overturned and preheated rimmed baking sheet set on the lowest oven rack. Almost any variety of brined or oil-cured olives works in this recipe, although we prefer a mix of both green and black olives.

1¾	cups water, room temperature
2	tablespoons honey
2	teaspoons instant or rapid-rise yeast
3½	cups (19¼ ounces) bread flour, plus extra as needed
½	cup (2¾ ounces) whole-wheat flour
2	teaspoons salt
2	tablespoons minced fresh rosemary
1½	cups olives, pitted, rinsed, and chopped coarse

1. Whisk water, honey, and yeast together in bowl of stand mixer fitted with dough hook. Add bread flour and whole-wheat flour to bowl and mix on low speed until cohesive dough is formed, about 3 minutes; cover bowl tightly with plastic wrap and let sit at room temperature for 20 minutes.

2. Make well in center of dough and add salt and rosemary. Knead dough on low speed for 5 minutes, scraping down bowl and dough hook as needed. Increase speed to medium and continue to knead until dough is smooth and slightly tacky, about 1 minute. If dough is very sticky, add 1 to 2 tablespoons bread flour and continue mixing for 1 minute. Transfer dough to lightly floured counter and press into 12 by 6-inch rectangle, with long side facing you. Press olives evenly into dough, then roll dough toward you into firm cylinder, keeping roll taut by tucking it under itself as you go. Turn loaf seam side up and roll cylinder into coil. Transfer dough, spiral side up, to large, lightly greased bowl,

cover tightly with plastic wrap, and let rise at room temperature until it increases in size by 50 percent, about 1 hour.

3. Spray rubber spatula or bowl scraper with vegetable oil spray. Fold partially risen dough over itself by gently lifting and folding edge of dough toward middle. Turn bowl 90 degrees; fold again. Turn bowl again; fold once more. Cover with plastic and let rise for 30 minutes. Repeat folding, replace plastic, and let rise until doubled in size, about 30 minutes.

4. Transfer dough to lightly floured counter, being careful not to deflate. Divide dough in half, loosely shape each piece into ball, and let rest for 15 minutes. Flip each ball over and, starting from top, roll dough toward you into firm oval shape. Using palms, roll each oval (seam side down) from center outward until 12-inch loaf is formed.

PRACTICAL SCIENCE
HOLD THE SALT—TEMPORARILY

Salt hinders autolyse. Wait to add it to bread dough.

Salt is an important component of dough because it strengthens gluten to help form chewy bread. But does it hinder autolyse? We wondered if adjusting when we added salt to bread dough could help speed things along.

We prepared two simple doughs. In the first, we combined the flour, water, yeast, and salt with a bread starter called a biga (see concept 40 for more on starters) all at once before resting; in the second, we withheld the salt for 15 minutes.

We found that briefly omitting the salt hastened gluten development by an hour. After just 15 minutes, the unsalted dough was already pliant and smooth, while the salted dough was still gluey and stiff. Why? Salt inhibits both the ability of flour to absorb water and the activity of the enzymes that break down proteins to begin the process of forming gluten. If allowed to rest without salt, the flour is able to get a jump on gluten development by absorbing as much water as it can and letting its enzymes work sooner to develop gluten networks.

15-MINUTE REST, WITH SALT
Dough is sticky and stiff.

15-MINUTE REST, WITHOUT SALT
Dough is supple and smooth.

Poke any olives that fall off into bottom seam, then pinch seam closed. Transfer each loaf, seam side down, to 12 by 6-inch piece of parchment and cover with plastic. Let rise until doubled in size, 1 to 1½ hours. (Dough should barely spring back when poked with knuckle.)

5. One hour before baking, adjust oven rack to lower-middle position, place baking stone on rack, and heat oven to 450 degrees. Slide parchment with loaves onto pizza peel. Using sharp serrated knife or single-edge razor blade, make one 3½-inch-deep slash on diagonal along top of each fully risen loaf, starting and stopping about 1 inch from ends. Spray loaves with water and slide parchment with loaves onto baking stone. Bake for 15 minutes, spraying loaves with water twice more during first 5 minutes of baking time. Reduce oven temperature to 375 degrees and continue to bake until crust is deep golden brown and loaves register 210 degrees, 25 to 30 minutes. Transfer loaves to wire rack, discard parchment, and let cool to room temperature, about 2 hours, before slicing and serving. (Bread can be wrapped in double layer of plastic wrap and stored at room temperature for up to 3 days. Wrapped with additional layer of aluminum foil, bread can be frozen for up to 1 month. To recrisp crust, thaw bread at room temperature, if frozen, and place unwrapped bread in 450-degree oven for 5 to 10 minutes.)

PRACTICAL SCIENCE
TURN THE DOUGH, DON'T PUNCH IT

Turning the dough creates a coarser crumb with better chew.

Most bread recipes call for punching down the dough between the first and second rises. Despite its name, punching down is best accomplished by pressing down gently on the dough. This process exposes the yeast to new food sources, which keeps it going strong longer. Punching also "degasses" the bread, resulting in a loaf with a fairly fine crumb—perfect for sandwich bread, but not a rustic loaf. To create a coarser crumb with better chew, we discovered that turning the dough (gently folding it over onto itself between the first and second rises) reactivates the yeast without pressing out as much air. (For more information, see "Turn the Dough Gently," page 340.)

PUNCHED
Bread bakes up with a tight, more regular crumb better suited to sandwich bread.

TURNED
Bread bakes up with a coarse, open crumb and chewy texture better suited to rustic bread.

☑ WHY THIS RECIPE WORKS:

Olive-rosemary bread is a basic Italian rustic loaf flavored with olives and the subtle perfume of rosemary. It should have a coarse crumb, chewy interior, and thick, burnished crust. But this hearty loaf is about as elusive as it is perfect. At home, it's too easy to bake loaves that are more like sandwich bread than rustic breads, with a soft crumb and thin crust. And the olives are either forced into the dough early on and mixed to the point of disintegration or added at the very end as a sparse afterthought. To perfect our home version, we first turn to the bread recipe, and then work on the olive distribution plan.

ADD A LITTLE HONEY We add a bit of honey to our bread dough to add sweetness and help bring out the savory flavor of the olives. Replacing some bread flour with whole-wheat flour gives a nuttier flavor, too. Because we add these flavors, this means that the dough doesn't need to ferment overnight like many other simple rustic breads.

PRESS THE OLIVES Pitting the olives against the stand mixer isn't a fair match. The olives and dough are like oil and water—resisting each other and leaving the olives to smear against the outside of the dough and the bottom of the bowl. We found success in rolling the olives into the dough before the first rise, pressing them into the rolled-out dough as if making cinnamon rolls. This gives us a nicely textured loaf with evenly dispersed olives. As for what kind of olives to use, any variety will do. Olive preference is highly subjective. We tend to prefer a mix.

USE MORE ROSEMARY Rosemary is often perceived as being brutish; if used excessively, it can easily overpower a dish with its piney harshness. But we soon realized that this herb behaves differently when baked into bread—its flavor is as fleeting as the little specks are invisible. We use a whopping 2 tablespoons in order to get a demure background flavor to complement the bright, fruity olives.

LET IT REST The autolyse (allowing the mixture of flours, water, and yeast to rest so that the flour has more time to absorb the water) is instrumental for more efficient kneading in this recipe. It takes 20 minutes, but this is 20 minutes we don't mind adding. Turning the dough during the first rise also drastically improves its elasticity and strength, which results in larger holes in the bread and a heartier chew (see "Turn the Dough, Don't Punch It").

SLASH AND SPRAY Slashing the risen loaf with a sharp paring knife or razor allows the crust to expand, preventing the bread from splitting in the oven. Misting the loaf right before it goes into the oven delays the formation of a crust, allowing the bread to fully expand without tearing or splitting. The steam also promotes the formation of a crispy, glossy crust.

RUSTIC DINNER ROLLS
MAKES 16 ROLLS

If you don't have a stand mixer, you can mix the dough by hand. To do this, stir the wet and dry ingredients together with a stiff rubber spatula until the dough comes together and looks shaggy. Transfer the dough to a clean counter and knead by hand to form a smooth, round ball, 15 to 25 minutes, adding additional flour, if necessary, to prevent the dough from sticking to the counter. Proceed with the recipe as directed. Because this dough is sticky, keep your hands well floured when handling it.

1½   cups plus 1 tablespoon water, room temperature
2   teaspoons honey
1½   teaspoons instant or rapid-rise yeast
3   cups plus 1 tablespoon (16½ ounces) bread flour, plus extra as needed
3   tablespoons whole-wheat flour
1½   teaspoons salt

1. Whisk water, honey, and yeast together in bowl of stand mixer until well combined, making sure no honey sticks to bottom of bowl. Transfer bowl to stand mixer fitted with dough hook. Add bread flour and whole-wheat flour and mix on low speed until cohesive dough is formed, about 3 minutes; cover bowl tightly with plastic wrap and let sit at room temperature for 30 minutes.

2. Sprinkle salt evenly over dough and knead on low speed for 5 minutes, scraping down bowl and dough hook as needed. Increase speed to medium and continue to knead until dough is smooth and slightly tacky, about 1 minute. If dough is very sticky, add 1 to 2 tablespoons flour and continue mixing for 1 minute. Transfer dough to large, lightly greased bowl; cover tightly with plastic and let rise at room temperature until doubled in size, about 1 hour.

3. Spray rubber spatula or bowl scraper with vegetable oil spray. Fold partially risen dough over itself by gently lifting and folding edge of dough toward middle. Turn bowl 90 degrees; fold again. Rotate bowl again and fold once more. Cover with plastic and let rise for 30 minutes. Repeat folding, replace plastic, and let dough rise until doubled in size, about 30 minutes longer.

4. Grease two 9-inch round cake pans. Transfer dough to floured counter and sprinkle top with more flour. Using bench scraper, cut dough in half and gently stretch each half into 16-inch log. Cut each log into 8 equal pieces and dust top of each piece with more flour. With floured hands,

gently pick up each piece and roll in palms to coat with flour, shaking off excess. Arrange rolls in prepared pans, placing 1 in center and 7 spaced evenly around edges, with long side of each roll running from center of pan to edge and making sure cut side faces up. Loosely cover pans with lightly greased plastic and let rolls rise until doubled in size, about 30 minutes. (Dough should barely spring back when poked with knuckle.)

5. Thirty minutes before baking, adjust oven rack to middle position and heat oven to 500 degrees. Spray rolls lightly with water, bake until tops of rolls are brown, about 10 minutes, then remove them from oven. Reduce oven temperature to 400 degrees; using kitchen towels or oven mitts, invert rolls from both cake pans onto rimmed baking sheet. When rolls are cool enough to handle, turn them right side up, pull apart, and space evenly on baking sheet. Continue to bake until rolls develop deep golden brown crust and sound hollow when tapped on bottom, 10 to 15 minutes, rotating sheet halfway through baking. Transfer rolls to wire rack and let cool to room temperature, about 1 hour, before serving. (Rolls can be placed in zipper-lock bag and stored at room temperature for up to 3 days. Wrapped with aluminum foil before placing in bag, rolls can be frozen for up to 1 month. To recrisp crust, thaw rolls at room temperature, if frozen, and place unwrapped rolls in 450-degree oven for 6 to 8 minutes.)

✔ WHY THIS RECIPE WORKS
The remarkably crisp crust of European-style dinner rolls keeps them in the domain of professionals, who use steam-injected ovens to expose the developing crust to moisture. We wanted a reliable recipe for rustic dinner rolls with a crisp crust and chewy crumb as good as any from an artisanal bakery. But when we tasted our first batch, we found a dense, bland crumb beneath a leathery crust. The flavor was easy to improve—we add whole-wheat flour for earthiness and honey for sweetness. A little extra yeast improves the crumb slightly, but making the dough wetter and letting it sit for 30 minutes (a process called autolyse) are the best fixes.

USE A WET DOUGH Our first tests left us with unimpressive dinner rolls. As a result, we began playing with hydration (see concept 38) to fix the dense crumb. After all, during baking, the water within the dough turns to steam, which then rushes to escape, making hollow pockets within. The more water, the airier the crumb. Determining that our original recipe gave us a dough with 60 percent hydration, we assembled several batches of dough with varying amounts of water. Sure enough, increasing hydration opened the crumb considerably.

Working our way up, we found about 72 percent hydration to be optimal; more than that and the dough started to get too wet to shape into rolls.

ADD HONEY AND WHEAT As in our Olive-Rosemary Bread (page 334), we swap some bread flour for whole wheat and add a bit of honey. This gives us rolls with subtle earthiness and just enough sweetness to leave the rolls' savory profile intact.

HANDLE GENTLY Using more water improves the finished rolls but also makes the dough extremely sticky, oozy, and hard to shape. In fact, the very process of forming rolls sometimes causes the delicate dough to deflate, making its texture too dense. To solve this problem, we forgo shaping altogether and instead use a bench scraper to divide the dough into rough (but equal) pieces. With less handling, these rolls retain far more of the open texture we take such pains to achieve. But to keep the soft dough from spreading and baking into a squat shape we begin by crowding them in a cake pan, coated lightly with flour. To keep the spots that rest against each other from staying soft, we remove the rolls from the oven halfway through baking, pull them apart, and return them to the oven spaced out on a baking sheet. With this two-stage baking method, they finish uniformly golden and crisp.

PRACTICAL SCIENCE
A HOT OVEN MEANS MORE RISE

Baking rolls in a hot oven means they will rise higher.

Cranking up the heat when the rolls go into the oven maximizes what professional bakers call "oven spring," the rapid rise in volume that all yeasted dough experiences when it first hits a hot oven. The higher this initial lift, the higher the finished bread.

HIGHER HEAT = HIGHER RISE   **LOWER HEAT = LESS LIFT**

START HIGH For a shatteringly crisp crust, we start the rolls at a higher temperature, then reduce the heat to finish them. This initial blast of heat makes all the difference between a so-so crust and one with real crackling crispness. It has another advantage, too—boosting the oven spring (the rise that yeasted dough experiences when it first hits the heat of the oven), so the crumb is even airier than before. Misting the rolls with water before baking (mimicking steam-injected ovens) makes the crust even crisper.

PRACTICAL SCIENCE FREEZE AND BAKE DOUGH

Freeze bread dough between the first and second rises for the best results.

For most of us, fresh-baked bread is a treat rather than an everyday event, since mixing the dough and allowing it to rise (or "proof") typically takes at least four hours (around three hours for the first rise and one hour for the second). But what about freezing the dough ahead of time? We froze dough for a rustic white loaf at three separate junctures: immediately after mixing, after the first rise (just before the dough was divided and shaped into loaves), and after forming the loaves and letting them rise the final time. Several weeks later, we thawed the dough in the refrigerator overnight and then baked it.

TOO SOON
Freezing the dough just after mixing killed too many of the yeast cells before they had a chance to ferment—a process that creates more complex flavor compounds and releases the carbon dioxide that makes dough rise. In addition, freezing before the first rise reduced gluten development, so the loaf didn't have enough structure to fully expand. The result: a small, squat loaf with bland flavor.

TOO LATE
Dough frozen late in the game—after the second rise—was overproofed: As the already fully risen dough slowly thawed, the random remaining viable yeast cells continued to produce gas in some parts of the dough but not in others, weakening this structure. The result: a misshapen loaf that collapsed during baking.

JUST RIGHT
Freezing the dough between the first and second rises was the best strategy. The first rise ensured that enough yeast had fermented for the dough to develop complex flavors and some rise. The remaining viable yeast cells then finished the job as the dough thawed and then rose for the second time.

Time Builds Flavor in Bread

Why do breads from artisan bakers taste so good? Sure, these bakers probably have access to great flour and very good water. And, yes, their skill level and professional equipment no doubt contribute to the tangy, complex flavor of their breads. But expert bakers know that really good flavor comes simply from waiting. Stretching the bread-making process over two days isn't any more work but it can yield fantastic bread with much better flavor.

HOW THE SCIENCE WORKS

In bread baking, we follow a basic set of steps. After mixing and kneading comes fermentation, also known as the first rise.

Fermentation is arguably the oldest of cooking techniques. Even the early hunters and gatherers must have noticed that meat and berries tasted and smelled quite different a few days after collection. Louis Pasteur made the seminal discovery that the changes in food over time often result from the metabolic activity of microbes. Pasteur was observing the action of yeast, which converts sugars to ethyl alcohol and releases carbon dioxide gas as a byproduct. And as we know, an important component of bread is yeast.

During fermentation, the gluten, which was worked hard during kneading, will relax and become more stretchable and supple. Meanwhile, the live yeast cells will begin to go to work, reacting with the sugars produced from the breakdown of starch, releasing carbon dioxide and ethyl alcohol. This releasing of the carbon dioxide into the relaxed, elastic dough is like slowly blowing air into a balloon. The bread is ready for its next step—shaping—when it has doubled in size. (The yeast doesn't stop its work after the first rise, however. It continues to produce carbon dioxide during the second rise, and during baking the heat causes a last rise, called oven spring, which lasts until all of the yeast is killed.)

Fermentation not only allows the yeast to give the dough its lofty rise but also produces a multitude of aromatic molecules that contribute to the flavor of the bread. If the fermentation happens too quickly in a warm room, however, the yeast can produce an excess of unpleasant sour-smelling volatile acids. To combat this, and to produce bread with deep flavor, we like to use two different techniques: pre-ferments and cool fermentation.

Pre-ferments—often known as sponges or starters—are made before the bread dough itself is even put together. In a sponge, for example, yeast, water, and flour are mixed together and left to ferment for a few hours. The sponge is then combined with more water and flour and any other ingredients in the recipe for the final dough. This dough is then kneaded and left to sit for its first rise.

In contrast to a sponge, a starter consists of a portion of dough saved from the last time bread was made. The classic example is sourdough starter, which many cooks save in a crock in their refrigerator. To begin the bread-making process with a starter, the baker adds water and flour to the starter and then lets the

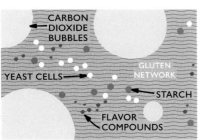

FERMENTATION IN BREAD DOUGH

CARBON DIOXIDE BUBBLES

YEAST CELLS

GLUTEN NETWORK

STARCH

FLAVOR COMPOUNDS

FERMENTATION *With time, the yeast produces flavor compounds in bread dough, as well as carbon dioxide, which helps it to rise.*

mixture sit and ferment. Whereas the sponge is added in its entirety to the ingredients for the final dough, a small portion of the starter is put back in the crock and saved for the next round of baking. Pre-ferments are great for recipes with minimal ingredients because they boost the flavor in bread dramatically. With a lengthy rest, long carbohydrate chains, starches, and other polysaccharides that have little taste break down into a multitude of sugars, acids, and alcohol with lots of flavor.

Cool fermentation, on the other hand, is all about temperature and is why we often recommend letting bread dough rise overnight in the refrigerator. This takes longer then letting bread rise on a warm counter. But there are many positive effects. First, it reduces the size of the gas bubbles that are created as the dough rises. (The larger the bubbles in the dough prior to baking the more open and puffy the final dough will be.) But aside from producing finer, tighter gas bubbles, cold fermentation has the added benefit of creating more flavorful dough. Why? Because at lower temperatures yeast produces less carbon dioxide and more of the initial side products of fermentation: flavorful sugars, alcohol, and acids.

TEST KITCHEN EXPERIMENT

To determine the rate at which yeast converts sugars to ethyl alcohol and releases carbon dioxide during fermentation, we made the basic yeasted dough for our waffles (see page 348) using milk, butter, flour, sugar, salt, two eggs, and 1½ teaspoons of instant yeast. We split the batter into two batches and then fashioned a simple respirometer, using a test tube and balloon, for each of them. We left one out at room temperature and placed one in the refrigerator.

THE RESULTS

Within a short period of time (three hours), the room-temperature batter had produced enough carbon dioxide to inflate the (semipermeable) balloon, indicating healthy yeast activity. But after 18 hours, the batter was spent and no longer produced carbon dioxide, causing the balloon to deflate. The refrigerated batter produced carbon dioxide at a very slow but steady rate. Even after 18 hours, the batter was still producing enough carbon dioxide to partially fill the balloon.

THE TAKEAWAY

Yeast plays two roles: providing leavening and flavor. When yeast is left out at room temperature, it grows quickly, leavening the batter—or dough—rapidly. In this case, however, the yeast is spent, and therefore no longer providing and making flavor, after 18 hours.

Cool fermentation takes place in the refrigerator. And refrigerating the dough allows the yeast to leaven at a slow and steady pace, producing flavor along the way. You get to the same place (a fully risen dough) but because the journey has taken so much longer, more flavorful compounds are created in the process. Not only does this cool fermentation provide more flavor in our finished product, but it gives the cook more time and flexibility to move the dough or batter along to its next step when you want.

COOL FERMENTATION TAKES MORE TIME, ADDS MORE FLAVOR

ON THE COUNTER

IN THE REFRIGERATOR

AFTER 3 HOURS
The batter quickly produces enough carbon dioxide to fill the balloon.

AFTER 18 HOURS
Yeast cells have died and the balloon has collapsed.

AFTER 3 HOURS
The batter produces a little carbon dioxide to partially fill the balloon.

AFTER 18 HOURS
The batter continues to produce carbon dioxide at a steady rate.

Both of these recipes rely on a sponge made the day before the bread is baked to build flavor.

ROSEMARY FOCACCIA

MAKES TWO 9-INCH ROUND LOAVES

If you don't have a baking stone, bake the bread on an overturned and preheated rimmed baking sheet set on the lowest oven rack.

SPONGE

½	cup (2½ ounces) all-purpose flour
⅓	cup water, heated to 110 degrees
¼	teaspoon instant or rapid-rise yeast

DOUGH

2½	cups (12½ ounces) all-purpose flour
1¼	cups water, heated to 110 degrees
1	teaspoon instant or rapid-rise yeast
	Kosher salt
¼	cup extra-virgin olive oil
2	tablespoons minced fresh rosemary

1. FOR THE SPONGE: Combine flour, water, and yeast in large bowl and stir with wooden spoon until uniform mass forms and no dry flour remains, about 1 minute. Cover bowl tightly with plastic wrap and let stand at room temperature for at least 8 hours or up to 24 hours. Use immediately or store in refrigerator for up to 3 days (allow to stand at room temperature for 30 minutes before proceeding with recipe).

2. FOR THE DOUGH: Stir flour, water, and yeast into sponge with wooden spoon until uniform mass forms and no dry flour remains, about 1 minute. Cover with plastic and let rise at room temperature for 15 minutes.

3. Sprinkle 2 teaspoons salt over dough; stir into dough until thoroughly incorporated, about 1 minute. Cover with plastic and let rise at room temperature for 30 minutes. Spray rubber spatula or bowl scraper with vegetable oil spray. Fold partially risen dough over itself by gently lifting and folding edge of dough toward middle. Turn bowl 90 degrees; fold again. Turn bowl and fold dough 6 more times (for total of 8 folds). Cover with plastic and let rise for 30 minutes. Repeat folding, turning, and rising 2 more times, for total of three 30-minute rises.

4. One hour before baking, adjust oven rack to upper-middle position, place baking stone on rack, and heat oven to 500 degrees. Gently transfer dough to lightly floured counter. Lightly dust top of dough with flour and divide it in half. Shape each piece of dough into 5-inch round by gently tucking under edges. Coat two 9-inch round cake pans with 2 tablespoons oil each. Sprinkle each pan with ½ teaspoon salt. Place round of dough in 1 pan, top side down; slide dough around pan to coat bottom and sides with oil, then flip dough over. Repeat with second piece of dough. Cover pans with plastic and let rest for 5 minutes.

5. Using fingertips, press dough out toward edges of pan, taking care not to tear it. (If dough resists stretching, let it relax for 5 to 10 minutes before trying to stretch it again.) Using dinner fork, poke entire surface of dough 25 to 30 times, popping any large bubbles. Sprinkle rosemary evenly over top of dough. Let dough rest in pans until slightly bubbly, 5 to 10 minutes.

6. Place pans on baking stone and lower oven temperature to 450 degrees. Bake until tops are golden brown, 25 to 28 minutes, rotating pans halfway through baking. Transfer pans to wire rack and let cool for 5 minutes. Remove loaves from pans and return to rack. Brush tops with any oil remaining in pans. Cool for 30 minutes before serving. (Leftover bread can be wrapped in double layer of plastic wrap and stored at room temperature for 2 days. Wrapped with additional layer of aluminum foil, bread can be frozen for up to 1 month.)

PRACTICAL SCIENCE TURN THE DOUGH GENTLY

Delicately folding the dough helps the bread to rise and improves flavor.

We rely on turning to build flavor and structure in bread dough as it rises. Turning involves delicately folding the dough over several times as it rises. A plastic bowl scraper is perfect for this job, but a rubber spatula will work, too. Just coat the scraper or spatula lightly with vegetable oil to keep it from sticking to the dough. Slide the scraper under the edge of the dough and lift and fold the dough toward the center of the bowl. Turn the bowl 90 degrees and repeat the process. Turn the bowl 90 degrees one more time and fold. When you're done, the dough should be shaped roughly like a square. In general, you will want to re-cover the bowl with plastic wrap, let it rise, and repeat the turning process 30 minutes later. (The exact timing will vary from recipe to recipe.)

Turning gently stretches the dough and builds strength as any wayward sheets of gluten—the protein that gives baked goods structure—are brought into alignment. In addition, turning the dough rids the dough of excess carbon dioxide, which otherwise inhibits yeast activity, to ensure maximum flavor and rise. We strongly recommend that you take a minute to turn the dough as it rises.

WHY THIS RECIPE WORKS

Focaccia can easily disappoint when it turns out heavy and thick. We wanted a light, airy loaf, crisp-crusted and topped with just a smattering of herbs. To start, a sponge (a mixture of flour, water, and yeast that rests for at least eight hours) gives us the flavor benefits of a long fermentation with minimal effort. But loaves with a sponge alone are not tender and airy enough. Because vigorous kneading develops too much gluten, we use a gentler approach— and a lot of oil in the pan.

BEGIN WITH THE BIGA A brush of fruity olive oil and heady seasonings give focaccia an addictive savory edge, but that doesn't mean a thing if the dough itself lacks flavor. The biggest key here is fermentation—the process by which long chains of carbohydrates with little taste convert to sugars, alcohol, acids, and carbon dioxide. And like many other organic processes, it's most effective over a long period of time. To get the benefits of long fermentation with minimal effort, we use a "pre-ferment" (also known as a sponge, or *biga* in Italian): a mixture of flour, water, and a small amount of yeast that rests overnight before being incorporated into a dough either in place of or along with more yeast. Time is the main factor here. That little bit of yeast in the biga grows as the hours go by, and the flavor that slowly develops is stronger and more complex than you would get by simply adding yeast to flour and water and kneading. With a biga, our focaccia dough holds plenty of flavor—with or without toppings added.

USE A LOT OF WATER As we've learned, a dough with a higher level of hydration is more capable of expanding without tearing, promoting the formation of larger bubbles (see concept 38). A high proportion of water to flour and a long resting process let the natural enzymes in the wheat replicate the effect of kneading. We use a higher level of hydration here in our focaccia—84 percent—to help open up the crumb structure.

REST AND FOLD As for our Almost No-Knead Bread (page 330), we don't knead our focaccia, per se. But we do fold it. (See "Turn the Dough Gently," opposite.) To prevent squat loaves of bread, we turn the dough while it rises. A standard no-knead dough develops structure gradually because the individual gluten clusters are relatively slow to combine into larger units. But gently turning the dough over itself at regular intervals accomplishes three things: It brings the wheat proteins into closer proximity with one another, keeping the process going at maximum clip; it aerates the dough, replenishing the oxygen that the yeasts consume during fermentation; and it elongates and redistributes the bubbles. After turning our dough three times

in the process, we end up with a well-risen focaccia with a tender, moist crumb.

KEEP THE OIL IN THE PAN Olive oil is a key ingredient in focaccia, but we find that if added straight to the dough, it can turn the bread dense and cakelike. (Just as with shortbread, fat "shortens" the dough by blocking gluten's ability to form continuous networks.) Instead, we bake the bread in round cake pans, where a few tablespoons of oil coating the exterior can be contained. After swirling the bottom in the oil and some coarse salt, we flip the dough, gently stretch it into the pan's edges, and let it rest for just a few extra minutes before sliding it onto the hot pizza stone. This focaccia has a crackly, crisp bottom, a deeply browned top, and an interior that is open and airy.

POKE AND SPRINKLE With a dinner fork, poke the dough surface 25 to 30 times. This will pop large bubbles of air and allow any extra gas to escape. Then sprinkle the dough with a healthy dose of minced fresh rosemary.

WHOLE-WHEAT SANDWICH BREAD
MAKES TWO 8-INCH LOAVES

If you don't have a stand mixer, you can mix the dough by hand. To do this, stir the wet and dry ingredients together along with the soaker and sponge with a stiff rubber spatula until the dough comes together and looks shaggy. Transfer the dough to a clean counter and knead by hand to form a smooth, round ball, 15 to 25 minutes, adding additional flour, if necessary, to prevent the dough from sticking to the counter. Proceed with the recipe as directed. If you don't have a baking stone, bake the bread on an overturned and preheated rimmed baking sheet set on the lowest oven rack.

SPONGE

  2   cups (11 ounces) bread flour

  1   cup water, heated to 110 degrees

 ½   teaspoon instant or rapid-rise yeast

SOAKER

  3   cups (16½ ounces) whole-wheat flour

 ½   cup wheat germ

  2   cups whole milk

DOUGH

  6   tablespoons unsalted butter, softened

 ¼   cup honey

  2   tablespoons instant or rapid-rise yeast

  2   tablespoons vegetable oil

  4   teaspoons salt

1. FOR THE SPONGE: Combine flour, water, and yeast in large bowl and stir with wooden spoon until uniform mass forms and no dry flour remains, about 1 minute. Cover bowl tightly with plastic wrap and let sit at room temperature for at least 8 hours or up to 24 hours.

2. FOR THE SOAKER: Combine flour, wheat germ, and milk in separate large bowl and stir with wooden spoon until shaggy mass forms, about 1 minute. Transfer dough to lightly floured counter and knead by hand until smooth, 2 to 3 minutes. Return soaker to bowl, cover tightly with plastic, and refrigerate for at least 8 hours or up to 24 hours.

3. FOR THE DOUGH: Tear soaker apart into 1-inch pieces and place in bowl of stand mixer fitted with dough hook. Add sponge, butter, honey, yeast, oil, and salt and mix on low speed until cohesive mass starts to form, about 2 minutes. Increase speed to medium and knead until dough is smooth and elastic, 8 to 10 minutes. Transfer dough to lightly floured counter and knead by hand to form smooth, round ball, about 1 minute. Place dough in large, lightly greased bowl. Cover tightly with plastic and let rise at room temperature for 45 minutes.

4. Gently press down on center of dough to deflate. Spray rubber spatula or bowl scraper with vegetable oil spray; fold partially risen dough over itself by gently lifting and folding edge of dough toward middle. Turn bowl 90 degrees; fold again. Turn bowl and fold dough 6 more times (total of 8 folds). Cover tightly with plastic and allow to rise at room temperature until doubled in size, about 45 minutes.

5. Grease two 8½ by 4½-inch loaf pans. Transfer dough to well-floured counter and divide in half. Press 1 piece of dough into 17 by 8-inch rectangle, with short side facing you. Roll dough toward you into firm cylinder, keeping roll taut by tucking it under itself as you go. Turn loaf seam side up and pinch it closed. Place loaf seam side down in prepared pan, pressing gently into corners. Repeat with second piece of dough. Cover loaves loosely with greased plastic and let rise at room temperature until nearly doubled in size, 1 to 1½ hours (top of loaves should rise about 1 inch over lip of pan).

6. One hour before baking, adjust oven racks to middle and lowest positions, place baking stone on middle rack, place empty loaf pan or other heatproof pan on bottom rack, and heat oven to 400 degrees. Bring 2 cups water to boil on stovetop. Using sharp serrated knife or single-edge razor blade, make one ¼-inch-deep slash lengthwise down center of each loaf. Working quickly, pour boiling water into empty loaf pan in oven and set loaves in pans on baking stone. Reduce oven temperature to 350 degrees. Bake until crust is dark brown and loaves register 200 degrees, 40 to 50 minutes, rotating loaves front to back and side to side halfway through baking. Transfer pans to wire rack and let cool for 5 minutes. Remove loaves from pans, return to rack, and let cool to room temperature, about 2 hours, before slicing and serving. (Bread can be wrapped in double layer of plastic wrap and stored at room temperature for up to 3 days. Wrapped with additional layer of aluminum foil, bread can be frozen for up to 1 month.)

WHY THIS RECIPE WORKS

To bump up the whole-wheat flavor, we soak the whole-wheat flour in milk overnight to soften the flour and reduce its bitter notes. Adding some wheat germ further ramps up the wheat flavor. We use a biga (a combination of bread flour, water, and yeast left overnight in the refrigerator) to develop a full range of unique flavors. Three final tweaks give our bread even more character: using honey instead of white sugar, cutting back on the fat, and swapping some of the butter for vegetable oil.

UP THE AMOUNT OF WHOLE WHEAT Most recipes for whole-wheat sandwich bread lead to one of two pitfalls. They either pay lip service to being "whole wheat," yielding loaves containing so little of the whole-grain stuff that they resemble the fluffy, squishy bread you find at the supermarket, or they call for so much whole wheat that the loaves bake up coarse and dense, crumbling as soon as you slice into them. (The challenge when making whole-wheat bread is that the very thing that gives it character and distinguishes it from white bread—the presence of bran—is also an impediment to gluten development.) We wanted a sandwich bread with a full-blown nutty (but not bitter) taste and a hearty yet soft crumb that sliced neatly.

We first do this by substituting bread flour for all-purpose flour. Thanks to the boost in gluten development from its extra protein, we are able to increase the amount of whole-wheat flour from 40 to 50 percent. But to up the percentage even more, we have to soak. A prolonged soaking of the whole-wheat flour accomplishes three things: First and foremost, it softens the grain's bran, thereby preventing the sharp edges from puncturing and deflating the dough. Second, the hydrating effect also prevents the grains from robbing moisture from the dough, which would toughen the crumb. Third, steeping the grains activates the wheat's enzymes, converting some starches into sugars and, in turn, reducing bitterness and coaxing out a sweet flavor. Using a soaker, we can get our whole wheat up to 60 percent, producing a considerably wheatier final product. (See "Soaking Wheat for Better Bread," below.) (In order to keep the dough cool during the kneading process, we refrigerate the soaker overnight. This way, the friction of kneading won't cause the dough's temperature to rise and lead to an overrisen product whose flavor and texture both suffer.)

ADD WHEAT GERM To bring our already wheaty wheat bread up to the next level, we add extra wheat germ, which is removed along with the bran during the milling process for refined flour and is a significant source of not only the whole grain's nutrition but also its sweet flavor. To add even more to the flavor of our bread, we add some honey for a complex sweetness and cut back on the fat, swapping some of the butter for oil, for a hearty yet soft-textured loaf.

USE A BIGA The difference between a good-tasting loaf and one that offers the most robust, well-developed flavor can boil down to the use of a biga. When left to sit overnight, this mixture of flour, water, and yeast develops a full range of unique flavors that give bread even more character. Because we are already soaking the whole-wheat flour overnight, we make our biga at the same time and let it ferment overnight.

IMPLEMENT THE USUAL TRICKS This recipe relies on many of the usual tricks: We turn the dough midway through the first rise in order to remove large gas bubbles and promote even fermentation. We slash the top of the dough before baking to make it easier for the dough to rise suddenly in the oven. And before putting the bread in the oven, we pour boiling water into an empty loaf pan that we positioned on the bottom rack. This supplies steam—a common bread baker's technique that prevents the crust from drying out before the loaves have fully expanded.

PRACTICAL SCIENCE
SOAKING WHEAT FOR BETTER BREAD

Soaking the whole-wheat flour in milk improves both the texture and flavor of our Whole-Wheat Sandwich Bread.

When developing our recipe for whole-wheat bread, our goal was to cram as much whole wheat into the dough as possible to create a seriously wheaty sandwich loaf. Fifty percent whole wheat wasn't enough to get us to this goal—but any more and the bread got too heavy and developed off-flavors. Would giving the whole-wheat flour a long soak before creating the final dough allow us to bump up its amount?

We baked two loaves, each with a 3:2 ratio of whole wheat to refined bread flour. We soaked the whole-wheat flour in the first batch overnight in the milk from our recipe before combining it with the other ingredients. In the second batch, we didn't give the whole-wheat flour any special treatment and proceeded with the recipe as usual.

The texture and flavor of the bread made with the soaked flour were markedly better than those of the loaf in which we didn't soak the whole wheat.

Soaking has a twofold effect on the final loaf. First, it dulls the flour's hard, fibrous bran, blunting its ability to disrupt gluten development and produce a denser crumb. Soaking also activates enzymes in the flour that convert some of the starches into sugars, thereby sweetening the bran's natural bitterness. The technique allowed us to pack our bread with roughly 50 percent more whole wheat than most recipes call for and still create a loaf with earthy-sweet flavor and a soft yet hearty crumb.

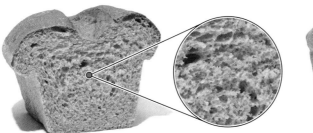

SOAKED FLOUR
Lighter texture, no bitterness

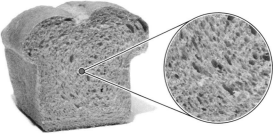

UNSOAKED FLOUR
Dense texture, bitter flavor

These three recipes don't use a sponge but they call for letting the dough rise in the refrigerator so yeast can develop flavor in the dough slowly. This simple idea is applied to recipes that are very different from each other.

NEW YORK–STYLE THIN-CRUST PIZZA
MAKES TWO 13-INCH PIZZAS, SERVING 4 TO 6

If you don't have a baking stone, bake the pizzas on an overturned and preheated rimmed baking sheet. You can shape the second dough round while the first pizza bakes, but don't add the toppings until just before baking. You will need a pizza peel for this recipe. It is important to use ice water in the dough to prevent the dough from overheating while in the food processor. Semolina flour is ideal for dusting the peel; use it in place of bread flour if you have it. The sauce will yield more than needed in the recipe; extra sauce can be refrigerated for up to one week or frozen for up to one month.

DOUGH

3	cups (16½ ounces) bread flour
2	teaspoons sugar
½	teaspoon instant or rapid-rise yeast
1⅓	cups ice water
1	tablespoon vegetable oil
1½	teaspoons salt

SAUCE

1	(28-ounce) can whole tomatoes, drained
1	tablespoon extra-virgin olive oil
1	teaspoon red wine vinegar
2	garlic cloves, minced
1	teaspoon salt
1	teaspoon dried oregano
¼	teaspoon pepper

CHEESE

1	ounce Parmesan cheese, grated fine (½ cup)
8	ounces whole-milk mozzarella, shredded (2 cups)

1. FOR THE DOUGH: Pulse flour, sugar, and yeast in food processor (fitted with dough blade if possible) until combined, about 5 pulses. With food processor running, slowly add water; process until dough is just combined and no dry flour remains, about 10 seconds. Let dough sit for 10 minutes.

2. Add oil and salt to dough and process until dough forms satiny, sticky ball that clears sides of bowl, 30 to 60 seconds. Transfer dough to lightly oiled counter and knead briefly by hand until smooth, about 1 minute. Shape dough into tight ball and place in large, lightly oiled bowl; cover bowl tightly with plastic wrap and refrigerate for at least 24 hours or up to 3 days.

3. FOR THE SAUCE: Process all ingredients in clean bowl of food processor until smooth, about 30 seconds. Transfer to bowl and refrigerate until ready to use.

4. TO TOP AND BAKE THE PIZZA: One hour before baking, adjust oven rack to upper-middle position (rack should be 4 to 5 inches from broiler), set baking stone on rack, and heat oven to 500 degrees. Transfer dough to clean counter and divide in half. With cupped palms, form each half into smooth, tight ball. Place balls of dough on lightly greased baking sheet, spacing them at least 3 inches apart; cover loosely with greased plastic and let sit for 1 hour.

5. Coat 1 ball of dough generously with flour and place on well-floured counter (keep other ball covered). Use fingertips to gently flatten dough into 8-inch disk, leaving 1 inch of outer edge slightly thicker than center. Using hands, gently stretch disk into 12-inch round, working along edges and giving disk quarter turns. Transfer dough to well-floured pizza peel and stretch into 13-inch round. Using back of spoon or ladle, spread ½ cup tomato sauce in thin layer over surface of dough, leaving ¼-inch border around edge. Sprinkle ¼ cup Parmesan evenly over sauce, followed by 1 cup mozzarella. Slide pizza carefully onto baking stone and bake until crust is well browned and cheese is bubbly and beginning to brown, 10 to 12 minutes, rotating pizza halfway through baking. Transfer pizza to wire rack and let cool for 5 minutes before slicing and serving. Repeat step 5 to shape, top, and bake second pizza.

NEW YORK–STYLE THIN-CRUST WHITE PIZZA
MAKES TWO 13-INCH PIZZAS, SERVING 4 TO 6

If you don't have a baking stone, bake the pizzas on an overturned and preheated rimmed baking sheet. You can shape the second dough round while the first pizza bakes, but don't add the toppings until just before baking. You will need a pizza peel for this recipe. It is important to use ice water in the dough to prevent the dough from overheating while in the food processor. Semolina flour is ideal for dusting the peel; use it in place of bread flour if you have it.

DOUGH

3	cups (16½ ounces) bread flour	
2	teaspoons sugar	
½	teaspoon instant or rapid-rise yeast	
1⅓	cups ice water	
1	tablespoon vegetable oil	
1½	teaspoons salt	

WHITE SAUCE

1	cup whole-milk ricotta cheese
¼	cup extra-virgin olive oil
¼	cup heavy cream
1	large egg yolk
4	garlic cloves, minced
2	teaspoons minced fresh oregano
1	teaspoon minced fresh thyme
½	teaspoon salt
¼	teaspoon pepper
⅛	teaspoon cayenne pepper
2	scallions, sliced thin, dark green tops reserved for garnish

CHEESE

1	ounce Pecorino cheese, grated fine (½ cup)
8	ounces whole-milk mozzarella cheese, shredded (2 cups)
½	cup whole-milk ricotta cheese

1. FOR THE DOUGH: Pulse flour, sugar, and yeast in food processor (fitted with dough blade if possible) until combined, about 5 pulses. With food processor running, slowly add water; process until dough is just combined and no dry flour remains, about 10 seconds. Let dough sit for 10 minutes.

2. Add oil and salt to dough and process until dough forms satiny, sticky ball that clears sides of bowl, 30 to 60 seconds. Transfer dough to lightly oiled counter and knead briefly by hand until smooth, about 1 minute. Shape dough into tight ball and place in large, lightly oiled bowl; cover bowl tightly with plastic wrap and refrigerate for at least 24 hours or up to 3 days.

3. FOR THE SAUCE: Whisk all ingredients except scallion greens together in bowl; refrigerate until ready to use.

4. TO TOP AND BAKE THE PIZZA: One hour before baking, adjust oven rack to upper-middle position (rack should be 4 to 5 inches from broiler), set baking stone on rack, and heat oven to 500 degrees. Transfer dough to clean counter and divide in half. With cupped palms, form each half into smooth, tight ball. Place balls of dough on lightly greased baking sheet, spacing them at least 3 inches apart; cover loosely with greased plastic and let sit for 1 hour.

5. Coat 1 ball of dough generously with flour and place on well-floured counter (keep other ball covered). Use fingertips to gently flatten dough into 8-inch disk, leaving 1 inch of outer edge slightly thicker than center. Using hands, gently stretch disk into 12-inch round, working along edges and giving disk quarter turns. Transfer dough to well-floured pizza peel and stretch into 13-inch round. Using back of spoon or ladle, spread half of white sauce in

---

PRACTICAL SCIENCE KEEPING INFLATION DOWN

Cool fermentation results in a thinner crust and more flavor.

The biggest factor contributing to a crust that turns out thick versus thin is the size of the gas bubbles in the dough before it goes into the oven. The more the bubbles expand with carbon dioxide as the dough ferments (or "proofs"), the thicker the final crust. Could a longer rise in the refrigerator fix the problem?

We made two batches of bread dough. We left one to rise at room temperature for four hours and placed the other in the refrigerator for 24 hours. We baked both according to our recipe.

The dough left to rise at room temperature produced a crust that puffed up like focaccia, while the dough that rose in the fridge baked up with smaller bubbles and boasted far more flavor.

Fermentation is a two-phase process: First, the carbohydrates in the dough are converted by the yeast to sugars, alcohol, and acids. Next, these convert to carbon dioxide, expanding the bubbles created in the dough when it was first mixed. At room temperature, the process moves rapidly to the production of carbon dioxide. But in the fridge, the process is slowed way down. With enough time, the complex-tasting sugars, alcohol, and acids form, but very little carbon dioxide gets converted, so the bubbles in the dough stay small and the crust bakes up both thinner and more flavorful.

PUFFY AND BLAND

THIN AND FLAVORFUL

thin layer over surface of dough, leaving ¼-inch border around edge. Sprinkle ¼ cup Pecorino evenly over sauce, followed by 1 cup mozzarella. Dollop ¼ cup ricotta in teaspoon amounts evenly over pizza. Slide pizza carefully onto baking stone and bake until crust is well browned and cheese is bubbly and beginning to brown, 10 to 12 minutes, rotating pizza halfway through baking. Transfer pizza to wire rack and let cool for 5 minutes before slicing and serving. Repeat step 5 to shape, top, and bake second pizza.

✔ WHY THIS RECIPE WORKS

With home ovens that reach only 500 degrees and dough that's impossible to stretch thin, even the savviest cooks can struggle to produce New York–style parlor-quality pizza. We were in pursuit of a New York–style pizza with a perfect crust—thin, crisp, and spottily charred on the exterior; tender yet chewy within. High-protein bread flour gives us a chewy, nicely tanned pizza crust and the right ratio of flour, water, and yeast gives us dough that stretches and retains moisture as it bakes. We knead the dough quickly in a food processor then let it rest in the refrigerator for at least 24 hours to develop its flavors. After we shape and top the pizza, it goes onto a blazing-hot baking stone to cook. Placing the stone near the top of the oven allows the top of the pizza to brown as well as the bottom. In minutes we get a pizza with everything in sync: a thoroughly crisp, browned crust with a slightly chewy texture.

USE HIGH-PROTEIN FLOUR We opt for high-protein bread flour (about 13 percent by weight) in our pizza dough. It's a typical choice when a chewy, nicely tanned crust is the goal, since the proteins both encourage gluten development and brown easily. We add enough water to hydrate the dough at about 63 percent (see concept 38)—enough so it stretches easily without ripping or sticking to our fingers and retains moisture as it bakes. The dough is a little sticky, but we add some extra flour to the exterior as we shape and stretch the dough. We use a food processor to mix the dough. A more conventional stand-mixer method might take 15 to 20 minutes to produce a shiny, elastic dough, but the food processor turns out comparably kneaded dough in less than two minutes. (Though for many bread recipes, we would caution against the rough treatment of a food processor, which can tear apart the strands of gluten that give bread structure and the ability to rise, here the amount of flour used is relatively small. Also, because this is a pizza, we do not need to develop the structure of a dough destined to be a flatbread.)

CHILL THE DOUGH Cool fermentation of the dough not only helps keep the bubbles in the dough smaller and tighter, it creates more flavor via the production of sugar, alcohol, and acids (see "Keeping Inflation Down," page 345).

ADD SUGAR AND OIL Adding oil and sugar to the dough helps to encourage more crunch and color in the crust. (We often sprinkle a spoonful of sugar over poultry skin to help it darken and crisp up in the oven, and there's no reason the same trick can't be used here.) The sugar undergoes both caramelization and the Maillard reaction to produce aromas and brown pigments.

STRETCH BY HAND Forget using a rolling pin. You can flatten and stretch the dough by hand. On a well-floured surface and using your fingertips, gently flatten half of the dough into an 8-inch disk, leaving the outer edge slightly thicker than the center to create a fatter "handle." With your hands, stretch the dough into a 12-inch round, working along the edges and giving the dough quarter turns. Transfer to a well-floured peel and stretch to a 13-inch round.

SHRINK YOUR HEADROOM Home ovens don't get hot enough to produce a deeply browned crust before the interior crumb dries out and toughens. The best solution has always been the hottest setting on the oven dial and a baking stone, which soaks up the radiation heat like a sponge. Following that logic, most recipes call for the stone to be placed as low in the oven as possible, where it gets maximum exposure to the main heating element. But that doesn't really make sense, and we even have an industry clue to prove it: commercial pizza ovens. These wide, shallow chambers quickly reflect heat from the floor back onto the top of the pie as it cooks, preventing the crust from drying out before the toppings have browned. We can't alter the shape of our oven, but we can move the stone up closer to the top to narrow the gap between stone and ceiling. The best position for the stone is really as close to the top of the oven as possible—about 4 inches or so from the ceiling, which leaves just enough headroom to comfortably house the pie.

MAKE AN EASY SAUCE We use a no-cook sauce here—canned tomatoes, garlic, olive oil, and spices pureed in a food processor. Red wine vinegar enhances the tomatoes' bright acidity. We supplement the creamy, stretchy mozzarella with a fistful of sharp, salty, finely grated Parmesan.

TOP WELL We like our thin-crust pizza simply dressed with tomato sauce and shredded mozzarella and Parmesan, but additional toppings are always an option—provided they're prepared correctly and added judiciously. (An overloaded pie will become soggy.) If you're using hearty vegetables, aim for a maximum of 6 ounces per pie, precooked to remove excess moisture. Leafy green vegetables and herbs like spinach and basil are best placed beneath the cheese to protect them or added raw to the fully cooked pie. Meats (no more than 4 ounces per pie) should be precooked and drained to remove excess fat.

CRESCENT ROLLS
MAKES 16 ROLLS

We developed this recipe using lower-protein flour such as Gold Medal or Pillsbury. If using a higher-protein flour such as King Arthur, reduce the flour amount to 3½ cups (17½ ounces). If you don't have a stand mixer, you can mix the dough by hand. To do this, stir the wet and dry ingredients together with a stiff rubber spatula until the dough comes together and looks shaggy. Transfer the dough to a clean counter and knead by hand to form a smooth, round ball, 15 to 25 minutes, adding additional flour, if necessary, to prevent the dough from sticking to the counter. Proceed with the recipe as directed.

16	tablespoons unsalted butter, cut into 16 pieces
¾	cup skim milk
¼	cup (1¾ ounces) sugar
3	large eggs
4	cups (20 ounces) all-purpose flour
1	teaspoon instant or rapid-rise yeast
1½	teaspoons salt
1	large egg white, beaten with 1 teaspoon water

1. Microwave butter, milk, and sugar in 4-cup liquid measuring cup until butter is mostly melted and mixture is warm (110 degrees), about 1½ minutes. Whisk to melt butter and blend in sugar. Beat eggs lightly in medium bowl; add about one-third of warm milk mixture, whisking to combine. When bottom of bowl feels warm, add remaining milk mixture, whisking to combine.

2. Using stand mixer fitted with paddle, mix flour and yeast together on low speed until combined, about 15 seconds. Add egg mixture in steady stream and mix until loose, shiny dough forms (you may also see satiny webs as dough moves in bowl), about 1 minute. Increase speed to medium and beat for 1 minute; add salt slowly and continue beating until stronger webs form, about 3 minutes longer. (Dough will remain loose rather than forming neat, cohesive mass.) Transfer dough to large, lightly greased bowl; cover tightly with plastic wrap and let rise at room temperature until dough doubles in size and surface feels tacky, about 3 hours.

3. Line rimmed baking sheet with plastic. Sprinkle dough with flour (no more than 2 tablespoons) to prevent sticking and press down gently to deflate. Transfer dough to floured counter and press into rough rectangle shape. Transfer rectangle to prepared baking sheet, cover with plastic, and refrigerate for 8 to 12 hours.

4. Transfer dough rectangle to lightly floured counter and line baking sheet with parchment paper. Roll dough into uniform 20 by 13-inch rectangle. Cut dough in half lengthwise, then cut each rectangle into 8 triangles, trimming edges as needed to make uniform triangles. Before rolling crescents, elongate each triangle of dough, stretching it an additional 2 to 3 inches in length. Starting at wide end, gently roll up dough, ending with pointed tip on bottom, and push ends toward each other to form crescent shape. Arrange crescents in 4 rows on prepared baking sheet, wrap baking sheet with plastic, and refrigerate for at least 2 hours or up to 3 days.

5. Remove baking sheet with chilled rolls from refrigerator, unwrap, and slide baking sheet into large clean garbage bag; seal to close. Let crescents rise until they feel slightly tacky and soft and have lost their chill, 45 minutes to 1 hour.

6. Thirty minutes before baking, adjust oven racks to lower-middle and lowest positions, place second rimmed baking sheet on lower rack, and heat oven to 425 degrees. Bring 1 cup water to boil on stovetop. Lightly brush risen crescent rolls with egg-white mixture. Working quickly, place baking sheet with rolls on upper rack, then pour boiling water onto rimmed baking sheet on lower rack and quickly close oven door. Bake for 10 minutes, then reduce oven temperature to 350 degrees and continue baking until tops and bottoms of rolls are deep golden brown, 12 to 16 minutes longer. Transfer rolls to wire rack, let cool for 5 minutes, and serve warm. (Rolls can be placed in zipper-lock bag and stored at room temperature for up to 3 days. Wrapped with aluminum foil before placing in bag, rolls can be frozen for up to 1 month.)

TO MAKE AHEAD: Rolls can be partially baked and frozen until ready to serve. Begin baking rolls as instructed, but let them bake at 350 degrees for only 4 minutes, or until tops and bottoms brown slightly. Remove them from oven and let cool to room temperature. Place partially baked rolls in single layer inside zipper-lock bag and freeze. When ready to serve, defrost rolls at room temperature and place in preheated 350-degree oven for 12 to 16 minutes.

✔ WHY THIS RECIPE WORKS

Crescent rolls from the supermarket are artificial-tasting and stale quickly, but making them at home is time-consuming. We were determined to come up with a recipe for rich, tender, flaky crescent rolls that could fit into an already-hectic holiday cooking schedule. We found that skim milk adds flavor without density, and melted butter and extra eggs enrich the dough. An overnight chill makes the finished rolls crisp and flaky, and the resilient dough can be shaped and refrigerated for three days (or parbaked and frozen for one month), then baked right before serving, for rich, buttery rolls without any fuss.

ADD BUTTER The dough for our crescent rolls differs from rustic bread and pizza doughs—it has a lot of fat. This family of bread dough (which includes American sandwich bread, brioche, and challah) calls for eggs, milk, and butter on top of flour, water, and yeast. With all of that fat, however, the dough can be incredibly sticky and hard to handle. This is why chilling it is essential. (Chilling also gives the gluten time to relax so that you can stretch the dough easily into crescents.)

CHILL WELL Not only is a chilled dough easier to handle, but the texture of the final rolls made from chilled dough is better, too. These rolls are flaky and flavorful with a blistery, snappy crust. The process of retarding (or chilling for a long time) allows acetic acid to build up in the dough, which is responsible for a richer flavor as well as a blistered crust.

STRETCH, CUT, AND ROLL To turn a lump of dough into 16 crescent rolls, first roll the dough into a 20 by 13-inch rectangle. Use a pizza wheel to trim the edges. Cut the dough in half lengthwise, and then cut each length into eight triangles. Elongate each triangle of dough before rolling the crescent, stretching it an additional 2 to 3 inches in length. And then, starting at the wide end, gently roll up the dough, ending with the pointed tip on the bottom.

START IN HOT OVEN We start our crescent rolls in a 425-degree oven for an initial bake, and then lower the oven temperature to 350 degrees just when the rolls are starting to color. Why? This improves the rolls' oven spring, or the dramatic increase in size caused by that initial blast of heat from the oven. The high heat makes the rolls larger and loftier. Lowering the oven temperature allows the rolls to bake through without burning.

YEASTED WAFFLES
MAKES SEVEN 7-INCH ROUND OR
FOUR 9-INCH SQUARE WAFFLES

While the waffles can be eaten as soon as they are removed from the waffle iron, they will have a crispier exterior if rested in a warm oven for 10 minutes. (This method also makes it possible to serve everyone at the same time.) This batter must be made 12 to 24 hours in advance. We prefer the texture of the waffles made in a classic waffle iron, but a Belgian waffle iron will work, though it will make fewer waffles.

1¾	cups milk
8	tablespoons unsalted butter, cut into 8 pieces
2	cups (10 ounces) all-purpose flour
1	tablespoon sugar
1½	teaspoons instant or rapid-rise yeast
1	teaspoon salt
2	large eggs
1	teaspoon vanilla extract

1. Heat milk and butter in small saucepan over medium-low heat until butter is melted, 3 to 5 minutes. Let mixture cool until warm to touch.

2. Meanwhile, whisk flour, sugar, yeast, and salt together in large bowl. Gradually whisk warm milk mixture into flour mixture; continue to whisk until batter is smooth. Whisk eggs and vanilla in small bowl until combined, then add egg mixture to batter and whisk until incorporated. Scrape down bowl with rubber spatula, cover bowl with plastic wrap, and refrigerate for at least 12 hours or up to 24 hours.

3. Adjust oven rack to middle position and heat oven to 200 degrees. Set wire rack in rimmed baking sheet; place in oven. Heat waffle iron according to manufacturer's instructions. Remove batter from refrigerator when waffle iron is hot (batter will be foamy and doubled in size). Whisk batter to recombine (batter will deflate). Bake waffles according to manufacturer's instructions (use about ½ cup for 7-inch round iron and about 1 cup for 9-inch square iron). Transfer waffles to wire rack in pre-heated oven; repeat with remaining batter. Serve.

BLUEBERRY YEASTED WAFFLES

We found that frozen wild blueberries—which are smaller—work best here. Larger blueberries release too much juice, which burns and becomes bitter when it comes in contact with the waffle iron.

After removing waffle batter from refrigerator in step 3, gently fold 1½ cups frozen blueberries into batter using rubber spatula. Bake waffles as directed.

☑ WHY THIS RECIPE WORKS

Raised waffles are barely on the current culinary radar, and that's a shame. They sound old-fashioned and do require an ounce of advance planning, but they are crisp, tasty, and easy to prepare. We wanted to revive this breakfast treat with yeasted waffles that were creamy and airy, tangy and salty, refined and complex. We settled on all-purpose flour, found the right amount of yeast to provide a pleasant tang, and added a full stick of melted butter for rich flavor. Refrigerating the batter overnight keeps the growth of the yeast under control and produces waffles with superior flavor. Even better, now all we have to do in the morning is heat up the iron.

LET RISE OVERNIGHT The concept for yeast waffles is simple enough. Most of the ingredients (flour, salt, sugar, yeast, milk, melted butter, and vanilla) are combined the night before and left to rise on the counter. The next day, eggs and baking soda are added and the batter is baked off. But older recipes call for the batter to be left out at room temperature, which causes the batter to rise and then fall, and turn sour rather than tangy. We find that slowing down the fermentation in the fridge ensures that flavors don't overdevelop. Also, this way we don't need to wait to add the eggs in the morning.

DON'T ADD BUTTERMILK We think buttermilk is the key to great pancakes and waffles made à la minute. (See Best Buttermilk Pancakes recipe, page 360.) Unfortunately, most cooks don't have buttermilk in the fridge and many markets don't even carry it. The good news about this recipe: It works best with regular milk. The yeast provides plenty of tang. Buttermilk would be overkill.

NO BAKING SODA Many older recipes call for baking soda to be added with the eggs just before baking. In our recipe, this isn't necessary. The baking soda is needed for lift in those recipes because the batter is left out overnight, which results in dead yeast in the morning. In our waffles, the yeast has plenty of leavening power the next morning because the batter has been refrigerated; as a result, the baking soda is redundant.

USE A HOT IRON Not all waffle irons are the same—you want to use a hot iron. The best irons produce waffles that are evenly cooked and consistently browned from the beginning to the end of a batch—and in the promised shade of light to dark. Look for models with thick heating coils extending under most of the cooking surface, which helps to ensure uniformly golden waffles that cook efficiently.

Gentle Folding Stops Tough Quick Breads

As we learned in concept 39, yeast breads depend on a well-developed gluten structure to rise properly. Gluten also gives bread its resilient, chewy texture. In contrast, quick breads (such as banana bread), as well as muffins and pancakes, can be ruined by excess development of gluten. That's because tenderness—not chewiness—is the goal.

HOW THE SCIENCE WORKS

Let's start with a definition of quick breads. Unlike yeast breads, which rely on slow fermentation to create rise, quick breads use chemical leaveners, namely, baking powder or baking soda. (For more on the science of chemical leaveners, see concept 42.) When these leaveners are added to a quick-bread batter they create the gases that cause muffins, pancakes, and the like to rise. Because the production of gases begins as soon as these dry leaveners are hydrated, quick breads should be baked immediately and don't require long fermentation, like yeast breads.

Quick breads rely on the same basic mixing method—sometimes (appropriately) called the "quick bread" method. First, the dry ingredients (flour, baking powder and/or baking soda, and salt) are whisked together in one bowl. Next, the wet ingredients (milk or buttermilk, melted butter or oil, sugar, and eggs) are whisked together in another bowl or a large measuring cup. Finally, the wet ingredients are added to the bowl with the dry ingredients. But the important part? How, exactly, and with what force, these mixtures are combined. It's not as simple as a few good strokes with a wooden spoon. Folding—not stirring—is essential.

After all, a rustic yeast bread should be chewy—think about how you can sink your teeth into good bread and pull. In contrast, a quick bread that required a lot of chewing would be considered a failure. Quick breads should be tender, more like cake than bread. The eggs, fats, and sugars in most quick breads have a tenderizing effect. That's because melted fats and oils, the emulsifiers in egg yolks, and dissolved sugars all interfere with the formation of gluten by either preventing or slowing protein unfolding and bonding. But even with eggs, fats, and sugar in the batter, if you overmix a quick bread you will end up with tough results.

Stirring would seem to be a gentle way of mixing the ingredients, but in a wet batter it's enough to begin unfolding the proteins and activate the formation of gluten. It really doesn't require much gluten formation to make a tender quick bread tough. For this reason, quick breads should never be prepared with an electric mixer. Gentle mixing with a rubber spatula (a technique called folding) is key. In fact, it's important to leave some streaks of flour in the batter. If the batter is completely homogeneous, it's likely the batter has been overmixed.

TOUGH QUICK BREADS HAVE TOO MUCH GLUTEN

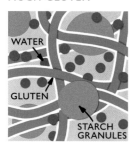

OVERSTIRRED *When water and flour combine in a quick bread batter, gluten begins to form. Too much stirring and the gluten network will overdevelop and cause a tough quick bread.*

TEST KITCHEN EXPERIMENT

Most recipes for quick breads and brownies (which are made by the quick bread method) caution against overmixing the batter, which purportedly leads to tougher baked goods. To avoid overmixing, wet and dry ingredients are gently folded together with a spatula until only a few streaks of dry flour remain. To find out how important this precaution is we designed the following test.

We made three batches of brownies, varying only the mixing technique. For one batch we folded the wet and dry ingredients until they were just combined, with a few streaks of flour remaining. For the second, we folded past this stage until no dry flour remained and the batter had an even, smooth appearance. Finally, we mixed the third sample on low speed in a stand mixer with a whisk attachment for a full five minutes.

THE RESULTS

The differences—even between the two folded samples—were dramatic. While the properly mixed batter baked into compact, tender brownies, the overfolded sample was relatively cakey and tough. The batter prepared in the stand mixer baked up almost twice as tall as the properly folded batter and offered serious resilience. Tasters described these brownies as downright tough and said they lacked the fudgy texture of the properly folded brownies.

THE TAKEAWAY

Whether taking a bite or lining up samples of our three brownies in a row, we could tell: Overmixing gives us tough, not tender, brownies. Why?

Mixing batter or dough leads to gluten formation. Too much mixing leads to a strong gluten network. And a strong gluten network, as we've learned, is what provides structure in a bread, helping to trap gas and ultimately to create chew. The brownies prepared in the stand mixer were twice as tall because extra air had been incorporated into the batter and the strong gluten network was able to trap the air. In a brownie, this is exactly what we don't want. Overmixing means tough, cakey squares instead of tender, fudgy ones.

The easiest way to know when to stop mixing, we've found, is to be sure to leave streaks of flour in your brownie (or cookie, or quick bread) batter. If it's not completely mixed, it's not overmixed, and that's exactly what we do want. We also recommend using a folding—rather than stirring—motion to mix the dry and wet ingredients with the fewest strokes. Scrape a rubber spatula along the bottom and sides of the bowl, turning the mixture over as you go.

HOW MIXING AFFECTS BROWNIE TEXTURE

PERFECTLY MIXED
The brownies that were folded just right, with streaks of flour remaining in the batter, baked up fudgy and tender, just as we like.

FOLDED TOO MUCH
The brownies that we mixed too much by hand were taller, tougher, and noticeably more cakelike.

MIXED TO DEATH
The brownies whipped in a stand mixer were twice as tall, tough, and significantly less chocolaty.

Banana bread, cornbread, and muffins should all have a tender, almost cakey texture. Gluten minimization is key to achieving the proper texture in these baked goods as well as in pancakes (see concept 42). Just how do you minimize gluten? It's mostly what you don't do.

ULTIMATE BANANA BREAD
SERVES 10

Be sure to use very ripe, heavily speckled (or even black) bananas in this recipe. This recipe can be made using five thawed frozen bananas; since they release a lot of liquid naturally, they can bypass the microwaving in step 2 and go directly into the fine-mesh strainer. Do not use a thawed frozen banana in step 4; it will be too soft to slice. Instead, simply sprinkle the top of the loaf with sugar. We developed this recipe using a loaf pan that measures 8½ by 4½ inches; if you use a 9 by 5-inch loaf pan, start checking for doneness five minutes earlier than advised in the recipe. The texture is best when the loaf is eaten fresh, but it can be stored (let cool completely first), covered tightly with plastic wrap, for up to three days.

1¾	cups (8¾ ounces) all-purpose flour
1	teaspoon baking soda
½	teaspoon salt
6	large very ripe bananas (2¼ pounds), peeled
8	tablespoons unsalted butter, melted and cooled
2	large eggs
¾	cup packed (5¼ ounces) light brown sugar
1	teaspoon vanilla extract
½	cup walnuts, toasted and chopped coarse (optional)
2	teaspoons granulated sugar

1. Adjust oven rack to middle position and heat oven to 350 degrees. Spray 8½ by 4½-inch loaf pan with vegetable oil spray. Whisk flour, baking soda, and salt together in large bowl.

2. Place 5 bananas in separate bowl, cover, and microwave until bananas are soft and have released liquid, about 5 minutes. Transfer bananas to fine-mesh strainer over medium bowl and allow to drain, stirring occasionally, for 15 minutes (you should have ½ to ¾ cup liquid).

3. Transfer liquid to medium saucepan and cook over medium-high heat until reduced to ¼ cup, about 5 minutes. Remove pan from heat, stir reduced liquid into bananas, and mash with potato masher until mostly smooth. Whisk in butter, eggs, brown sugar, and vanilla.

4. Pour banana mixture into dry ingredients and stir until just combined, with some streaks of flour remaining. Gently fold in walnuts, if using. Scrape batter into prepared pan. Slice remaining banana diagonally into ¼-inch-thick slices. Shingle banana slices on top of loaf in 2 rows, leaving 1½-inch-wide space down center to ensure even rise. Sprinkle granulated sugar evenly over loaf.

5. Bake until toothpick inserted in center of loaf comes out clean, 55 to 75 minutes. Let loaf cool in pan for 10 minutes, then turn out onto wire rack and let cool for 1 hour before serving.

✓ WHY THIS RECIPE WORKS

Our ideal banana bread is simple enough—a moist, tender loaf that really tastes like bananas. We discovered that doubling the dose of bananas in our favorite test recipe was both a blessing and a curse. The abundance of fruit made for intense banana flavor, but the weight and moisture sank the loaf and gave it a cake-like structure. Looking to add banana flavor without moisture, we experimented with many possible but unsuccessful solutions until we rediscovered the value of the microwave.

SQUEEZE IN MORE BANANAS We wanted maximum banana flavor in our banana bread, but not a dense loaf. To lighten our banana bread, we knew we needed to rid our bananas of some of their moisture. Roasting the

---

PRACTICAL SCIENCE DO THE RIPE THING

Ripe bananas are heavily speckled, with more fructose.

Don't even think of making banana bread with anything less than very ripe, heavily speckled fruit—unless you're fine with a bland loaf. As bananas ripen, their starch converts to sugars at an exponential rate. In lab tests, we found heavily speckled bananas had nearly three times the amount of fructose (the sweetest of the sugars in fruit) of less spotty bananas. (The exact percentage will vary from fruit to fruit.) But the impact of ripeness only goes so far: We found little difference in sweetness between loaves baked with completely black bananas and those made with heavily speckled ones.

1.8% FRUCTOSE = TOO SOON	5.3% FRUCTOSE = JUST RIGHT
A lightly speckled banana has only a little fructose, the sweetest sugar in fruit.	*A heavily speckled banana has a lot more fructose.*

bananas helps drive off moisture but it takes too long and you don't get rid of enough moisture. We tried simmering mashed bananas, as well as dicing and sautéing them. But what worked best? We turned to a technique we use with eggplant that uses the power of the microwave to remove excess moisture. We then reduce the liquid and use that concentrated banana juice in place of some of the dairy in the batter for super banana flavor.

GET THOSE BANANAS RIPE It's important to use very ripe bananas (see "Do the Ripe Thing," opposite). Strategies for speeding ripening in bananas abound, but as we worked our way through over eight cases of fruit while developing this banana bread, we found most of them ineffective. One theory, for example, holds that freezing or roasting underripe bananas in their skins will quickly render them sweet and soft enough for baking. While these methods do turn the bananas black—giving them the appearance of their super-sweet, overripe brethren—they actually do little to encourage the necessary conversion of starch to sugar.

The best way to ripen bananas is to enclose them in a paper bag for a few days. The bag will trap the ethylene gas produced by fruit that hastens ripening, while still allowing some moisture to escape. Since fully ripe fruit emits the most ethylene, placing a ripe banana or other ripe fruit in the bag will speed the process along by a day or two.

TWEAK THE FLAVOR We exchange the typical sugar for light brown sugar, finding that the latter's molasses notes better complement the bananas. A teaspoon of vanilla rounds out the bananas' faintly boozy, rumlike flavor. Don't forget the salt.

REPLACE OIL WITH BUTTER We replace the traditional oil in our banana bread recipe with butter. Butter gives our bread a nutty, rich flavor that we prefer.

SEPARATE, THEN FOLD To make the batter, we combine the wet ingredients (including the brown sugar), and then add them to the bowl with the dry ingredients and fold gently. Gently is the key word here. Make sure that you fold the batter gently enough that flour streaks remain. (And be sure to mash the bananas well before they even hit the dry ingredients.)

TOP WITH MORE BANANAS We slice a sixth banana and shingle it on top of the batter. A final sprinkle of granulated sugar helps the buttery slices to caramelize and gives the loaf an enticingly crisp, crunchy top. To ensure an even rise, place the banana slices along the long sides of the loaf pan and leave a 1½-inch-wide space down the center.

PRACTICAL SCIENCE MAKING BANANAS LAST

Refrigerated bananas turn black but last much longer.

Most people store bananas on the countertop, and we wondered if chilling fruit could slow ripening. To find out, we left 12 pounds of bananas at room temperature for three days until they were perfectly ripe (signified by a firm but yielding texture). We then moved half of the bananas into the refrigerator, leaving the remainder at room temperature.

For the next few days, the bananas were nearly indistinguishable. After four days, however, the room-temperature fruit became markedly soft and mushy, while the refrigerated fruit remained firm, despite blackened skins. We continued to taste the refrigerated bananas after the room-temperature samples had been discarded and were delighted to discover that they lasted an additional five days (so, almost two weeks after purchase) before the flesh became overripe.

The explanation is simple: As a banana ripens, it emits a gas called ethylene that accelerates the ripening process. Cool temperatures slow down the production of ethylene, thereby decelerating ripening. However, refrigeration also causes the cell walls of the peel to break down, releasing enzymes that cause the formation of black-brown pigments. For this reason, keep bananas on the counter until they become speckled; if you're not ready to use the ripe bananas, refrigerate them to prolong their shelf life.

ALL-PURPOSE CORNBREAD
SERVES 6

Before preparing the baking dish or any of the other ingredients, measure out the frozen corn kernels and let them stand at room temperature until needed. When corn is in season, cooked fresh kernels can be substituted for the frozen corn. This recipe was developed with Quaker yellow cornmeal; a stone-ground whole-grain cornmeal will work but will yield a drier and less tender cornbread. We prefer a Pyrex glass baking dish because it produces a nice golden brown crust, but a metal baking pan (nonstick or traditional) will also work.

1½	cups (7½ ounces) all-purpose flour
1	cup (5 ounces) cornmeal
2	teaspoons baking powder
¼	teaspoon baking soda
¾	teaspoon salt
¼	cup packed (1¾ ounces) light brown sugar
¾	cup frozen corn, thawed
1	cup buttermilk
2	large eggs
8	tablespoons unsalted butter, melted and cooled

1. Adjust oven rack to middle position and heat oven to 400 degrees. Spray 8-inch square baking dish with vegetable oil spray. Whisk flour, cornmeal, baking powder, baking soda, and salt in medium bowl until combined; set aside.

2. In food processor or blender, process brown sugar, corn kernels, and buttermilk until combined, about 5 seconds. Add eggs and process until well combined (corn lumps will remain), about 5 seconds longer.

3. Using rubber spatula, make well in center of dry ingredients; pour wet ingredients into well. Begin folding dry ingredients into wet, giving mixture only a few turns to barely combine. Add melted butter and continue folding until dry ingredients are just moistened. Pour batter into prepared baking dish and smooth surface with rubber spatula.

4. Bake until cornbread is deep golden brown and toothpick inserted in center comes out clean, 25 to 35 minutes. Let cool on wire rack for 10 minutes, then invert onto wire rack and turn right side up. Let cool until warm, about 10 minutes longer, before serving. (Leftover cornbread can be wrapped in aluminum foil and reheated in a 350-degree oven for 10 to 15 minutes.)

SPICY JALAPEÑO-CHEDDAR CORNBREAD

Reduce salt to ½ teaspoon. Add ⅜ teaspoon cayenne pepper, 1 seeded and finely chopped jalapeño chile, and ½ cup shredded cheddar cheese to flour mixture and toss well to combine. Reduce brown sugar to 2 tablespoons and sprinkle 2 ounces shredded cheddar cheese over batter in dish just before baking.

BLUEBERRY BREAKFAST CORNBREAD

Reduce salt to ½ teaspoon. Reduce buttermilk to ¾ cup and add ¼ cup maple syrup to food processor along with buttermilk in step 2. Add 1 cup fresh or frozen blueberries with melted butter in step 3. Sprinkle 2 tablespoons granulated sugar over batter in baking dish just before baking.

✔ WHY THIS RECIPE WORKS

Cornbread can be sweet and cakey (the Northern version) or savory and light (the Southern version). We wanted a combination of the two. And most important, we wanted our cornbread to be bursting with corn flavor. The secret was pretty simple: Use corn, not just cornmeal.

<table>
<tr><td>PRACTICAL SCIENCE FREEZING FLOUR</td></tr>
<tr><td>We recommend storing whole-grain flours in the freezer.

Refined flours, including all-purpose, bread, and cake flour, can be stored in airtight containers in your pantry for up to one year. Whole-grain flours such as rye and wheat contain more fat than refined flours and can turn rancid quickly at room temperature. For this reason, we recommend storing these flours in the freezer. In various tests, we found that using flour straight from the freezer inhibited rise and yielded denser baked goods. Therefore, it's important to bring chilled flour to room temperature before baking. To quickly accomplish this, spread the flour in a thin layer on a baking sheet and let it sit for about 30 minutes.</td></tr>
</table>

PUMP UP CORN FLAVOR　For this cornbread, we use degerminated yellow cornmeal—it may not have the best corn flavor, but it is widely available in supermarkets across the country. The best texture comes from using a ratio of 3 parts flour to 2 parts cornmeal—something else that limits the corn flavor in our bread. The solution? We use frozen corn, ground up in the food processor to release its full flavor. With pureed corn in the mix, we need to cut back on the dairy (we prefer the flavor of buttermilk to whole milk). A little brown sugar adds pleasing molasses notes.

DRIZZLE BUTTER　We add the butter to our batter last. This creates subtle streaks of unmixed butter in the batter, but, as the bread bakes, the butter rises to the surface and creates a more deeply browned top crust and a stronger butter flavor. (And we add a lot of butter—a whole stick.)

USE A HOT OVEN　Pouring the batter into a hot skillet is a great way to get a dark brown, crunchy crust. But not everyone has a seasoned cast-iron skillet. We found that using a hot oven allows us to scrape the batter into a square baking pan and still get a decent crust.

BETTER BRAN MUFFINS
MAKES 12 MUFFINS

Dried cranberries or dried cherries may be substituted for the raisins.

1	cup raisins
1	teaspoon water
2¼	cups (5 ounces) All-Bran Original cereal
1¼	cups (6¼ ounces) all-purpose flour
½	cup (2¾ ounces) whole-wheat flour
2	teaspoons baking soda
½	teaspoon salt
1	large egg plus 1 large yolk

2/3	cup packed (4 2/3 ounces) light brown sugar
3	tablespoons molasses
1	teaspoon vanilla extract
6	tablespoons unsalted butter, melted and cooled
1 3/4	cups plain whole-milk yogurt

1. Adjust oven rack to middle position and heat oven to 400 degrees. Spray 12-cup muffin tin with vegetable oil spray. Combine raisins and water in small bowl, cover, and microwave for 30 seconds. Let stand, covered, until raisins are softened and plump, about 5 minutes. Transfer raisins to paper towel–lined plate to cool.

2. Process 1 cup plus 2 tablespoons cereal in food processor until finely ground, about 1 minute. Whisk all-purpose flour, whole-wheat flour, baking soda, and salt in large bowl until combined and set aside. Whisk egg and yolk together in medium bowl until well combined and light-colored, about 20 seconds. Add sugar, molasses, and vanilla to bowl with eggs and whisk until mixture is thick, about 30 seconds. Add melted butter and whisk to combine. Add yogurt and whisk to combine. Stir in processed cereal and remaining 1 cup plus 2 tablespoons unprocessed cereal. Let mixture sit until cereal is evenly moistened (there will still be some small lumps), about 5 minutes.

3. Add wet ingredients to dry ingredients and mix gently with rubber spatula until batter is just combined and evenly moistened (do not overmix). Gently fold raisins into batter. Using ice cream scoop or large spoon, divide batter evenly among prepared muffin cups, dropping batter to form mounds (do not level or flatten batter).

4. Bake until muffins are dark golden and toothpick inserted in center of muffin comes out with few crumbs attached, 16 to 20 minutes, rotating muffin tin halfway through baking. Let muffins cool in tin for 5 minutes, then transfer to wire rack and let cool for 10 minutes before serving.

☑ WHY THIS RECIPE WORKS

Classic bran muffins rely on unprocessed wheat bran, but our supermarket survey showed that few stores carry this specialized ingredient. We wanted to make a moist, hearty muffin redolent of bran's rich, earthy flavor without tracking down unprocessed bran. We accomplish this by using a mixture of pulverized and whole twig bran cereal, adding yogurt, brown sugar, and molasses, and plumping raisins in the microwave.

PICK THE RIGHT CEREAL   Bran is the outer layer of the wheat grain that is removed during milling. Bran cereal can come in various forms, including flakes, buds, and twigs. Here's how they stack up in muffins: Bran flakes are often made with whole wheat in addition to bran and give muffins very little flavor. Small bran buds make dense muffins with almost no bran flavor. Cereal made of bran twigs like All-Bran, however, give muffins the most robust flavor.

CRUSH THE BRAN   The twigs provide a deep bran flavor, but getting them to bend to our will is another matter. Twigs don't easily dissolve in the batter, and pre-soaking them only makes the muffins as dense as hockey pucks. But we find that grinding half of the cereal into a fine powder and leaving the other half in twig form creates muffins with an even, but not heavy, texture. We like mixing all-purpose flour and whole-wheat flour to reinforce the flavor of the bran.

USE YOGURT   We found that more than 6 tablespoons of butter makes these muffins greasy, but we wondered if the dairy might provide additional richness and tenderness. Swapping the milk in most recipes for sour cream was overkill. Buttermilk was an improvement over plain milk, but whole-milk yogurt was the tasters' first choice. And replacing the baking powder with baking soda gives us a coarser crumb that tasters likewise enjoyed.

COMBINE BROWN SUGAR AND MOLASSES   We use both light brown sugar (the classic recipe uses granulated sugar) and molasses to provide malty, caramel sweetness to match with the bran and whole-wheat flour.

PLUMP THE RAISINS   After complaints that the raisins didn't soften enough during baking, we began plumping them in the microwave with a little water. Works like a charm.

FILL THOSE CUPS   For big, hearty muffins, fill the muffin cups to the rim. And for nicely domed tops, mound the batter in the cups and don't level it off.

PRACTICAL SCIENCE   MUFFIN MYTH

You don't need to fill empty muffin cups with water.

We've heard the tip: If you're making a half batch of muffins or cupcakes and thus don't fill all the cups in the pan with batter, you should fill the empty cups with water. Is this really necessary?

Proponents of this practice contend that filling empty cups with water serves two functions: preventing the pan from warping and acting as a "heat sink" to ensure that muffins next to empty cups heat evenly (avoiding stunted growth or spotty browning).

We tested this theory by baking one 12-cup muffin pan completely filled with batter, one pan in which six cups were filled with batter and six with water, and one pan in which six cups were filled with batter and the other six left empty. All muffins had the same height, texture, and color. None of the tins warped.

On reflection, the results made sense: In a full 12-cup muffin tin, all but the two center muffins are directly exposed to the oven's heat on at least one side to no ill effect. If your muffin pan warps, that's a sign that you need to find a better-quality pan.

BLUEBERRY MUFFINS

MAKES 12 MUFFINS

If buttermilk is unavailable, substitute ¾ cup of plain whole-milk or low-fat yogurt thinned with ¼ cup of milk.

LEMON-SUGAR TOPPING

⅓	cup (2⅓ ounces) sugar
1½	teaspoons grated lemon zest

MUFFINS

10	ounces (2 cups) blueberries
1⅛	cups (7¾ ounces) plus 1 teaspoon sugar
2½	cups (12½ ounces) all-purpose flour
2½	teaspoons baking powder
1	teaspoon salt
2	large eggs
4	tablespoons unsalted butter, melted and cooled
¼	cup vegetable oil
1	cup buttermilk
1½	teaspoons vanilla extract

1. FOR THE TOPPING: Stir together sugar and lemon zest in small bowl until combined and set aside.

2. FOR THE MUFFINS: Adjust oven rack to upper-middle position and heat oven to 425 degrees. Spray 12-cup muffin tin with vegetable oil spray. Bring 1 cup blueberries and 1 teaspoon sugar to simmer in small saucepan over medium heat. Cook, mashing berries with spoon several times and stirring frequently, until berries have broken down and mixture is thickened and reduced to ¼ cup, about 6 minutes. Transfer to small bowl and let cool to room temperature, 10 to 15 minutes.

3. Whisk flour, baking powder, and salt together in large bowl. Whisk remaining 1⅛ cups sugar and eggs together in medium bowl until thick and homogeneous, about 45 seconds. Slowly whisk in butter and oil until combined. Whisk in buttermilk and vanilla until combined. Using rubber spatula, fold egg mixture and remaining 1 cup blueberries into flour mixture until just moistened. (Batter will be very lumpy with few spots of dry flour; do not overmix.)

4. Using ice cream scoop or large spoon, divide batter evenly among prepared muffin cups (batter should completely fill cups and mound slightly). Spoon 1 teaspoon cooked berry mixture into center of each mound of batter. Using chopstick or skewer, gently swirl berry filling into batter using figure-8 motion. Sprinkle lemon sugar evenly over muffins.

5. Bake until muffins are golden brown and toothpick inserted in center of muffin comes out with few crumbs attached, 17 to 19 minutes, rotating muffin tin halfway through baking. Let muffins cool in tin for 5 minutes, then transfer to wire rack and let cool for 5 minutes before serving.

✔ WHY THIS RECIPE WORKS

Blueberry muffins should be packed with blueberry flavor and boast a moist crumb. But too often, the blueberry flavor is fleeting, thanks to the fact that the berries in the produce aisle have suffered from long-distance shipping. We wanted blueberry muffins that put the berry flavor at the forefront and would taste great with blueberries of any origin, even the watery supermarket kind. To achieve this goal, we make our own low-sugar blueberry jam and fold our batter rather than using the creaming method. The result? Blueberry muffin success.

USE MORE BERRIES—DIFFERENTLY Adding more blueberries to a muffin batter can make the muffins soggy and heavy. We cook some of the berries down into a jam, evaporating excess moisture and concentrating the flavor. (Commercial jam is too sweet.) Adding this jam to our muffin batter gives us muffins with great texture and pure blueberry flavor. We add some fresh blueberries, too.

MAKE QUICK BREAD Instead of creaming the butter and sugar as if we were making a cake, we fold the batter, as we do for quick breads. This yields a slightly coarser crumb, which we prefer for these muffins. It's important to fold the wet and dry ingredients gently; the batter will be slightly lumpy and have spots of flour.

USE BUTTER AND OIL To achieve the unctuously moist muffins we sought, we examined the fat in the recipe. While the butter contributes tons of flavor, we knew that oil has a propensity for making baked goods moist and tender. Unlike butter, oil contains no water and is able to completely coat flour proteins and restrict them from absorbing liquid to develop gluten. We swapped some butter for oil for a moist, tender texture.

SWIRL IN THAT JAM Add the jam to the batter after it has been mixed and placed in muffin tins. Place 1 teaspoon of cooled berry jam in the center of each batter-filled cup, putting it below the surface. Then, using a chopstick or a skewer, swirl the jam—very gently, using a "figure-eight" motion—to spread berry flavor throughout.

ADD LEMON SUGAR To get a good crust on our muffins, we bake them on the upper-middle rack of a 425-degree oven. We sprinkle lemon-scented sugar on top of the batter just before baking. The oven melts the sugar slightly, which then hardens as it bakes to create an irresistibly crunchy shell.

FLOUR 101

STRUCTURE

Flour, made from wheat, comes in many forms. Whether white or whole wheat, all-purpose or cake, it plays an important role in baked goods, as a thickener in stews and sauces, and as a base for breaded coatings on meat.

BRAN

The bran is the hard outer layer of the wheat kernel and is often removed for the production of refined white flour. It is filled with fiber and a small amount (about 9 percent by weight) of fatty acids; it includes the protein-rich aleurone layer as well.

ENDOSPERM

The endosperm is the large collection of cells in the center of the wheat kernel that store nourishment for the germ. About 80 percent of the endosperm is made up of starch. The endosperm composes about 75 percent of a kernel of wheat and is often the only part of the kernel that is consumed after milling wheatberries. Refined white flour is made only from the endosperm.

GERM (OR EMBRYO)

The germ is the reproductive part of a wheat kernel and is rich in enzymes, fat, and, as a result, flavor. Along with the bran, it is a key component of whole grains.

SIFTING

Sifting flour is a chore, but sometimes it is important. When making a delicate cake like a sponge cake or genoise that requires flour to be folded into beaten eggs and sugar, sifted flour can be added quickly and distributed evenly (because sifting aerates the flour), thereby reducing the risk of deflating the batter.

Sifting reduces the overall amount of flour (in weight) that goes into the recipe. Because of the aeration, 1 cup of sifted cake flour weighs in at about 3 ounces, whereas 1 cup of cake flour measured straight from the bin using the dip-and-sweep method weighs around 4 ounces. As a result, if you don't follow recipe directions regarding sifting, you will end up with way too much (or too little) flour.

To guarantee you're using the proper amount of flour, for recipes that read "1 cup sifted flour," sift the flour directly into a measuring cup set on top of parchment paper and then level off the excess. For recipes reading "1 cup flour, sifted," measure the flour first using the dip-and-sweep method (see page 3) and then sift it. Of course, a scale makes all of this much simpler and more accurate, which is why our baking recipes give both weight and volume. (For more on measuring, see page 4, and on storing, see page 354.)

BUYING

If you bake, you should really keep three flours (all-purpose, cake, and bread) on hand. Why? The protein content varies significantly among the three. Therefore, these flours will absorb water differently—the same amount of water might make a soupy batter with a cup of cake flour but a nice, firm dough with bread flour. Protein content also affects gluten development. More protein leads to more gluten, which, in turn, can translate to coarseness, chewiness, toughness, or crispness. Depending on the recipe, these traits might be desirable or not. But the choices of flour aren't limited to three.

ALL-PURPOSE FLOUR All-purpose is by far the most versatile flour available. Its protein content (10 to 11.7 percent, depending on the brand: King Arthur is close to 11.7 percent, Pillsbury and Gold Medal around 10.5 percent) provides enough structure to make good sandwich bread, yet it's light enough to use for cakes of a medium-to-coarse crumb. We prefer unbleached flour (see "Why Bleach Flour?," page 389). Bleached flours in our tests did not perform as well as the unbleached flours and were sometimes criticized for tasting flat or carrying off-flavors.

CAKE FLOUR Cake flour has a low protein content—about 6 to 8 percent—and thus yields cakes and pastries with less gluten, which translates to a finer, more delicate crumb. We use cake flour for light cakes, such as pound cake, angel food cake, and yellow layer cake. One note: Most cake flour is bleached, which affects the starches in flour so that it can absorb greater amounts of liquid and fat. Most cakes have so much sugar and fat it's very hard to detect any off-notes in the flour caused by the bleaching process. It is possible to approximate 1 cup of cake flour by using 2 tablespoons of cornstarch plus 7/8 cup of all-purpose flour.

BREAD FLOUR This flour has a protein content of about 12 percent to 14 percent, meaning it develops a lot of gluten to provide strong, chewy structure for rustic breads, especially those made with little or no fat. For sandwich breads we prefer using all-purpose flour, which creates a softer crumb.

WHOLE-WHEAT FLOUR Whole-wheat flour is made from all three parts of the wheat kernel—the endosperm as well as the fiber-rich bran, or outer shell, and the tiny, vitamin-packed germ. The presence of the germ and bran in whole-wheat flour makes it not only more nutritious and more flavorful, but more dense and less able to rise. We generally don't like breads or baked goods made with 100 percent whole-wheat flour; they are more dense and can be sour-tasting. Instead, we rely on a combination of all-purpose flour and whole-wheat flour in most recipes.

PASTRY FLOUR Pastry flour is a soft wheat flour with a protein content between that of all-purpose flour and cake flour. It is often used in pie crusts, tart pastry, scones, and other similarly buttery baked goods (such as biscuits and shortbread). While it performs well in these applications, we don't think it's worth stocking pastry flour unless you are a professional baker.

SELF-RISING FLOUR Self-rising flour contains a leavener and is made from a soft flour that brings it closer to cake flour than all-purpose. We've found the convenience of self-rising flour to be pretty minor and recommend using cake flour in recipes that call for self-rising flour and adding the baking powder and salt yourself. The formula is 1½ teaspoons of baking powder and ½ teaspoon of salt for every cup of flour.

Two Leaveners Are Often Better than One

The advent of chemical leaveners, such as baking soda and baking powder, in the 19th century made it easier for cooks to bake at home. No need to rely on fickle yeast in order to make a cake. Chemical leaveners are quick and reliable. But they are also confusing. Some recipes rely on baking powder, some on baking soda, and many on both. Why do you need two leaveners in something as simple as a cookie that doesn't even rise all that much?

HOW THE SCIENCE WORKS

BAKING SODA VS. BAKING POWDER

BAKING SODA *When baking soda and an acidic ingredient interact, they immediately begin to produce carbon dioxide, creating bubbles that help batters and doughs to rise.*

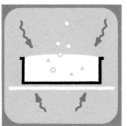

BAKING POWDER *Most baking powder produces bubbles of carbon dioxide a second time—when it is heated in the oven.*

Quick breads, muffins, and biscuits as well as cookies and cakes get their rise from chemical leaveners—baking soda and baking powder—rather than yeast. Chemical leaveners react with acids to produce carbon dioxide, the gas that causes these baked goods to rise.

To do its work, baking soda, which is alkaline, relies on acid in the recipe, provided by ingredients such as buttermilk, sour cream, yogurt, or molasses. When baking soda and an acid interact, they immediately begin to produce carbon dioxide, forming bubbles within the batter or dough. It's important to use the right amount of baking soda in recipes. If you use too little you won't have enough bubbles and the dough won't rise. If you use too much, though, you end up with too much carbon dioxide, which causes the bubbles to get too big. These large bubbles then join up with one another and eventually rise to the top of the dough and burst, resulting in a flat finished product. Also, use more baking soda than can be neutralized by the acidic ingredient and you'll end up with a metallic-tasting, coarse-crumbed quick bread or cake.

Baking powder, on the other hand, is nothing more than baking soda (about one-quarter to one-third of the total makeup) mixed with a dry acid, such as cream of tartar, and double-dried cornstarch. The cornstarch absorbs moisture and keeps the baking soda

and dry acid apart during storage, preventing premature production of the gas. When baking powder becomes wet, the dry acid comes into contact with the baking soda, producing carbon dioxide. Cooks use baking powder rather than baking soda when there is no natural acidity in the batter.

There are two kinds of baking powder. A single-acting baking powder has only one acid combined with the baking soda—a quick-acting acid that begins to work when liquid is added to the batter. A double-acting baking powder (virtually all supermarket brands) has two or more acids added to the baking soda. One of the acids (often sodium aluminum sulfate, also known as alum) begins to work only after the dish is put in the oven, when its temperature has climbed above 120 degrees. We recommend using double-acting baking powder in all recipes—baked goods rise higher since most of the rise with baking powder occurs at oven temperatures. Also, we have found that single-acting baking powder doesn't provide sufficient leavening for doughs with little liquid, such as scones or muffins.

In many of our recipes, we use both baking soda and baking powder because the combination gives better control over how fast gas is released as well as the alkalinity of the dough. Sometimes the recipe contains so much acid that baking soda is added to ensure the baking powder is not neutralized and deactivated by all the acid. Since baking soda relies on the acid from the other ingredients in the recipe, it generally produces more alkaline doughs than baking powder. More alkaline doughs brown faster and have weaker gluten, producing a more tender, porous crumb.

Why does browning occur best in an alkaline environment? An amino acid molecule (like those found in the proteins in flour) has two ends—one is the amino end and one is the acid end. As you might guess, the acid end is acidic, but (as you might not guess) the amino end is alkaline. It's the alkaline end that has to react with the sugar molecules for the Maillard reaction (see concept 2) to occur. In an acidic solution, the alkaline ends are deactivated. In an alkaline environment created by the addition of baking soda, the amino ends thrive and they can react with the sugar to create browning.

TEST KITCHEN EXPERIMENT

Given that double-acting baking powder contains both baking soda and a dry acid—and provides leavening twice during the cooking process (after mixing and during baking)—why would we ever need to include baking soda in the mix? To answer this question, we ran the following experiment: We baked three batches of our Easy Buttermilk Drop Biscuits (page 363)—one leavened with 2 teaspoons of baking powder and ½ teaspoon of baking soda; the second leavened with 2 teaspoons of baking powder alone; the third leavened with 3 teaspoons of baking powder, to roughly equal the leavening power of the first sample. We compared the appearance, flavor, and texture of the biscuits side by side.

THE RESULTS

Interestingly, the biscuits made without baking soda rose just as high as those baked with both leaveners. However, the similarities ended there. The two batches made without baking soda were anemic in color, with smooth tops, while the dual-leavened biscuits were well browned and covered in crispy crags. And the differences weren't merely skin-deep—the biscuits with two leaveners tasted far richer and nuttier. The biscuits made with 3 teaspoons of baking powder didn't rise any higher than the batch made with 2 teaspoons of baking powder but they did have a chemical aftertaste—a sure sign that there was too much leavener.

THE TAKEAWAY

So will baking powder alone provide sufficient leavening to a baked good? In most cases, the answer is yes. But will that baked good look and taste its best? That's another matter entirely. In our buttermilk biscuits, the baking soda (an alkali) is crucial for two reasons. First, it immediately reacts with the buttermilk (an acid) to produce tiny carbon dioxide bubbles that lighten the batter. Second, it neutralizes the batter's acidity to create a more alkaline environment that promotes the Maillard reaction and the creation of hundreds of new flavor compounds, which make the dual-leavened biscuits taste far more complex and interesting.

THE POWER OF BAKING SODA AND POWDER

BAKING POWDER ALONE
The drop biscuits made with only one leavener emerged from the oven smooth and light-colored, with a decidedly bland flavor.

BAKING SODA AND POWDER
The drop biscuits made with both leaveners finished craggy and browned, and had better flavor.

Pancakes are easy but they can be heavy if you don't get them just right. Minimal mixing is important (see concept 41), but the real key is the use of leaveners. What makes this tricky is the use of acidic buttermilk, which reacts with the leaveners to produce bubbles in the batter. Buttermilk can give pancakes great flavor and light, fluffy texture. But if the formula isn't just right, pancakes can be a disaster.

BEST BUTTERMILK PANCAKES

MAKES SIXTEEN 4-INCH PANCAKES, SERVING 4 TO 6

The pancakes can be cooked on an electric griddle. Set the griddle temperature to 350 degrees and cook as directed. The test kitchen prefers a lower-protein all-purpose flour like Gold Medal or Pillsbury for this recipe. If you use an all-purpose flour with a higher protein content, like King Arthur, you will need to add an extra tablespoon or two of buttermilk. Serve with warm maple syrup.

2	cups (10 ounces) all-purpose flour
2	tablespoons sugar
1	teaspoon baking powder
½	teaspoon baking soda
½	teaspoon salt
2	cups buttermilk
¼	cup sour cream
2	large eggs
3	tablespoons unsalted butter, melted and cooled
1–2	teaspoons vegetable oil

1. Adjust oven rack to middle position and heat oven to 200 degrees. Spray wire rack set in rimmed baking sheet with vegetable oil spray; place in oven. Whisk flour, sugar, baking powder, baking soda, and salt together in medium bowl. In second medium bowl, whisk together buttermilk, sour cream, eggs, and melted butter. Make well in center of dry ingredients and pour in wet ingredients; gently stir until just combined (batter should remain lumpy, with few streaks of flour). Do not overmix. Let batter sit for 10 minutes before cooking.

2. Heat 1 teaspoon oil in 12-inch nonstick skillet over medium heat until shimmering. Using paper towels, carefully wipe out oil, leaving thin film of oil on bottom and sides of pan. Using ¼-cup measure, portion batter into pan in 4 places. Cook until edges are set, first side is golden brown, and bubbles on surface are just beginning to break, 2 to 3 minutes. Using thin, wide spatula, flip pancakes and continue to cook until second side is golden brown, 1 to 2 minutes longer. Serve pancakes immediately, or transfer to wire rack in preheated oven. Repeat with remaining batter, using remaining oil as necessary.

✓ WHY THIS RECIPE WORKS

Too often, buttermilk pancakes lack true tang, and they rarely have the light and fluffy texture we desire. We wanted buttermilk pancakes with a slightly crisp, golden crust surrounding a fluffy, tender center with just enough structure to withstand a good dousing of maple syrup. We achieve this with a sour cream substitution, the use of two leaveners, and some techniques to keep the pancakes nice and tender.

START WITH BUTTERMILK When our forebears set out to make pancakes enriched with the sweet tang of buttermilk, they had a built-in advantage: real buttermilk. Instead of using the thinly flavored liquid processed from skim milk and cultured bacteria that passes for buttermilk today, earlier Americans turned to the fat-flecked byproduct of churning cream into butter. The switch from churned buttermilk to cultured buttermilk accounts for the lack of true tang in most modern-day buttermilk pancakes. We have to use other methods to obtain tang.

SUPPLEMENT WITH SOUR CREAM We wanted more tang in our pancakes, but using more buttermilk didn't work. More buttermilk means a greater concentration of acid in the mix, which in turn causes the baking soda to bubble too rapidly. The result: pancakes that over-inflate when they first cook, then collapse like popped balloons, becoming dense and wet by the time they hit the plate. A little sour cream, on the other hand, adds a ton of flavor but doesn't radically affect the consistency of the batter. With the extra fat from the sour cream, we found it best to trim butter back to just 3 tablespoons.

PRACTICAL SCIENCE IS THE PAN READY?

If a pancake is golden brown after one minute, the pan is ready.

The only way to know when the pan is ready for pancakes is to make a test pancake about the size of a half-dollar, or about 1 tablespoon of batter. If after one minute the pancake is blond in color, the pan is not hot enough. If after one minute the pancake is golden brown, the pan is heated correctly. Speeding up the process by heating the pan at a higher temperature will result in a dark, unevenly cooked pancake.

NOT YET

TOO HOT

USE TWO LEAVENERS Both baking soda and powder are essential in our pancakes. Baking soda responds to the acid in the buttermilk, producing carbon dioxide gas that aerates the pancakes, while baking powder reacts to the heat of the pan to release more carbon dioxide. Baking soda likewise helps us to get a nice brown color on the pancakes, boosting flavor through the Maillard reaction.

KEEP IT TENDER Three techniques help us to get our pancakes as tender as possible. First, we use a lower-protein all-purpose flour like Gold Medal or Pillsbury (see "Flour 101," page 357). Second, we fold the batter very minimally (see concept 41). And finally, we let the batter rest for 10 minutes before cooking. Why? Even with minimal mixing, some gluten develops in the pancake batter. During a 10-minute rest, the gluten relaxes and the end result is tender pancakes. Don't worry that the leavening will dissipate. Remember that baking powder is double acting and will provide plenty of lift when the batter hits the hot pan.

MULTIGRAIN PANCAKES

MAKES SIXTEEN 4-INCH PANCAKES, SERVING 4 TO 6

The pancakes can be cooked on an electric griddle. Set the griddle temperature to 350 degrees and cook as directed. Familia brand no-sugar-added muesli is the best choice for this recipe. If you can't find Familia, look for Alpen or any no-sugar-added muesli. (If you can't find muesli without sugar, muesli with sugar added will work; reduce the brown sugar in the recipe to 1 tablespoon.) Mix the batter first and then heat the pan. Letting the batter sit while the pan heats will give the dry ingredients time to absorb the wet ingredients; otherwise, the batter will be runny. Serve with maple syrup or Apple, Cranberry, and Pecan Topping (recipe follows).

2	cups whole milk
4	teaspoons lemon juice
1¼	cups (6 ounces) plus 3 tablespoons no-sugar-added muesli
¾	cup (3¾ ounces) all-purpose flour
½	cup (2¾ ounces) whole-wheat flour
2	tablespoons packed brown sugar
2¼	teaspoons baking powder
½	teaspoon baking soda
½	teaspoon salt
2	large eggs
3	tablespoons unsalted butter, melted and cooled
¾	teaspoon vanilla extract
1–2	teaspoons vegetable oil

1. Adjust oven rack to middle position and heat oven to 200 degrees. Spray wire rack set in rimmed baking sheet with vegetable oil spray; place in oven. Whisk milk and lemon juice together in large measuring cup; set aside while preparing other ingredients.

2. Process 1¼ cups muesli in food processor until finely ground, 2 to 2½ minutes; transfer to large bowl. Add remaining 3 tablespoons unground muesli, all-purpose flour, whole-wheat flour, sugar, baking powder, baking soda, and salt; whisk to combine.

3. Add eggs, melted butter, and vanilla to milk mixture and whisk until combined. Make well in center of dry ingredients; pour in milk mixture and whisk very gently until just combined (batter should remain lumpy with few streaks of flour). Do not overmix. Allow batter to sit while pan heats.

4. Heat 1 teaspoon oil in 12-inch nonstick skillet over medium heat until shimmering. Using paper towels, carefully wipe pan, leaving thin film of oil on bottom and sides of pan. Using ¼-cup measure, portion batter into pan in 4 places. Cook until small bubbles begin to appear evenly over surface, 2 to 3 minutes. Using thin, wide spatula, flip pancakes and cook until second side is golden brown, 1½ to 2 minutes longer. Serve pancakes immediately or transfer to wire rack in preheated oven. Repeat with remaining batter, using remaining oil as necessary.

PRACTICAL SCIENCE HOT STACK

Keep cooked pancakes warm on a cooling rack in the oven.

A tall stack of hot pancakes first thing in the morning just can't be beat. But a 12-inch skillet can turn out only three or four at a time. If you want to cook all of the batter and then sit down with everyone else, you'd better do something to keep those pancakes warm.

What's the best way? We tried several methods, from stacking up the pancakes on a heated plate to covering them with foil to placing the plate of stacked pancakes in a warm oven. All of these methods did the job as far as keeping the pancakes warm. Even by the last batch of pancakes, the temperature reading would hit somewhere between 145 and 150 degrees. But these pancakes were compressed from being stacked, and they steamed from the heat and became very rubbery.

We found that the best method was to spread the pancakes on a large cooling rack placed on a sheet pan (be sure to spray the cooling rack well with vegetable oil spray to save yourself from sticking pancakes). Place the pan and the rack in a 200-degree oven and place your pancakes on the rack in a single layer, uncovered, for up to 20 minutes (otherwise they will start to dry out). The warm oven keeps the pancakes hot enough to melt a pat of butter, and leaving the pancakes uncovered keeps them from becoming soggy.

APPLE, CRANBERRY, AND PECAN TOPPING
SERVES 4 TO 6

We prefer semifirm apples, such as Fuji, Gala, or Braeburn, for this topping. Avoid very tart apples, such as Granny Smith, and soft varieties like McIntosh.

3½   tablespoons unsalted butter, chilled
1¼   pounds apples, peeled, cored, and cut into
      ½-inch pieces
      Pinch salt
1   cup apple cider
½   cup dried cranberries
½   cup maple syrup
1   teaspoon lemon juice
½   teaspoon vanilla extract
¾   cup pecans, toasted and chopped coarse

PRACTICAL SCIENCE BLEMISH-FREE PANCAKES

Splotchy pancakes are all about the way oil heats in the pan.

Why does the first batch of pancakes turn out with brown spots?

We've all experienced the annoying phenomenon of having the first batch of pancakes turn out splotched with brown spots, while subsequent batches come out evenly golden. Here's why: When fresh oil hits a hot pan, the surface tension of the oil causes it to bead together into little droplets, leaving some of the pan bottom without a coating. Since bare metal conducts heat better than oil, when you ladle your batter into the pan, the spots directly in contact with uncoated metal will cook faster than those touching oil. By the time you get to your second batch of pancakes, the oil has undergone chemical changes that make the molecules less prone to clustering. What's more, the first batch of pancakes has absorbed much of the oil, leaving only a thin film that's more likely to be evenly distributed across the pan.

For spot-free pancakes from the get-go, start by applying oil to an unheated pan or griddle. Allow the oil to heat up over medium heat for at least one minute, then use a paper towel to wipe away all but a thin, barely visible layer to prevent sticking. The pancakes should cook up golden brown from the first batch to the last.

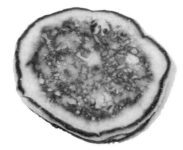

SEEING SPOTS
Tiny droplets of oil that cluster together rather than spread out cause light patches on the first batch of pancakes.

Melt 1½ tablespoons butter in 12-inch skillet over medium-high heat. Add apples and salt; cook, stirring occasionally, until softened and browned, 7 to 9 minutes. Stir in cider and cranberries; cook until liquid has almost evaporated, 6 to 8 minutes. Stir in maple syrup and cook until thickened, 4 to 5 minutes. Add remaining 2 tablespoons butter, lemon juice, and vanilla; whisk until sauce is smooth. Serve with toasted nuts.

✔ WHY THIS RECIPE WORKS

Bland, dense, and gummy, most multigrain pancakes are more about appeasing your diet than pleasing your palate. We wanted flavorful, fluffy, and healthful flapjacks. After testing lots of grains, we found that muesli had all the ingredients and flavor we wanted in one convenient package—raw whole oats, wheat germ, rye, barley, toasted nuts, and dried fruit. But pancakes made with whole muesli are too chewy and gummy. We solve this problem by converting muesli into a flour and combining it with some other flour options, as well as using two leaveners.

MOCK BUTTERMILK   When testing our multigrain pancakes, we found that using buttermilk made them taste too sour, impinging on the flavor of our grains. But if we did away with the buttermilk entirely, we would have to rethink our leaveners. (After all, baking soda needs acid to react.) But what if we simply used a less acidic-tasting blend of milk and lemon juice? That turned out to be the answer. The milk and lemon juice mixture makes for a surprisingly cleaner, richer-tasting pancake with an even lighter texture.

MAKE INSTANT MULTIGRAIN FLOUR   Some multigrain pancake recipes load up on unprocessed grains—great for flavor but bad for texture. To avoid gummy, chewy pancakes, we make our own multigrain "flour" by processing store-bought muesli cereal in a food processor. To give our pancakes a subtle hint of that hearty whole-grain texture, we add a few tablespoons of unprocessed muesli to the batter, too.

USE TWO LEAVENERS   Many chemically leavened pancake recipes include both baking powder and soda—especially when they're bulked up with heavy grains. The combination makes for fail-safe leavening and thorough browning. (After all, baking soda is a browning agent.)

LET THE BATTER REST   To get light, fluffy pancakes, it's important to let the batter rest while the pan heats (a full five minutes). The flour needs this time to absorb all the liquid, thus ensuring that the batter sets up properly. Skip this step and the pancakes will run together in the pan and cook up flat, not to mention misshapen. Properly rested batter will maintain its shape when poured into the pan and will produce tall and fluffy pancakes.

While most biscuits require working cold fat into the flour (see concept 43), you can make biscuits by the quick-bread method: Simply combine melted butter with buttermilk and then add this liquid mixture to the dry mixture.

EASY BUTTERMILK DROP BISCUITS

MAKES 12 BISCUITS

A ¼-cup portion scoop can be used to portion the batter. To refresh day-old biscuits, heat them in a 300-degree oven for 10 minutes.

2	cups (10 ounces) all-purpose flour
2	teaspoons baking powder
½	teaspoon baking soda
1	teaspoon sugar
¾	teaspoon salt
1	cup buttermilk, chilled
8	tablespoons unsalted butter, melted and cooled slightly, plus 2 tablespoons melted

---

PRACTICAL SCIENCE RESTING CLABBERED MILK

Allowing milk and lemon juice to rest is not necessary.

Directions for making a buttermilk substitute by adding lemon juice to milk always call for letting the mixture sit for a while. Can you skip this rest if you're short on time, or is it important?

"Clabbered" milk is widely recommended as a substitute for buttermilk in baked goods. The usual approach is to stir lemon juice into milk (1 tablespoon per cup) and let the mixture sit for 10 minutes to "clabber" (or thicken) before proceeding with the recipe. But after following this method and closely observing what transpired, we discovered that clabbering milk doesn't give it the smooth, thick consistency of buttermilk. Small curds formed almost instantly, but after a 10-minute rest, most of the milk had not thickened at all. And more waiting still didn't give clabbered milk the consistency of buttermilk.

It turns out that when lemon juice is added to milk, the citric acid changes the electrical charge on the dairy's casein proteins, causing them to coagulate tightly into clumps. On the other hand, the *Lactobacillus* bacteria added to milk to produce commercial buttermilk remove some of the sugar molecules bonded to the proteins, allowing them to form a smooth gel that gradually becomes thicker over time.

So, does waiting after treating milk with lemon juice impact its baking properties? To find out, we made multiple batches of biscuits and buttermilk pancakes: one set with clabbered milk that had rested for 10 minutes and one set in which we mixed the milk into the batter immediately after adding the lemon juice. All of the biscuits and pancakes were virtually identical in appearance, flavor, and texture.

Our conclusion: Adding lemon juice to milk simply acidifies it, allowing the leavening in the batter to do its job—the same role played by buttermilk. Since this change happens immediately, you can safely skip the resting time.

---

1. Adjust oven rack to middle position and heat oven to 475 degrees. Line rimmed baking sheet with parchment paper. Whisk flour, baking powder, baking soda, sugar, and salt together in large bowl. Combine buttermilk and 8 tablespoons melted butter in medium bowl, stirring until butter forms small clumps.

2. Add buttermilk mixture to flour mixture and stir with rubber spatula until just incorporated and batter pulls away from sides of bowl. Using greased ¼-cup dry measure and working quickly, scoop level amount of batter and drop onto prepared baking sheet (biscuits should measure about 2¼ inches in diameter and 1¼ inches high). Repeat with remaining batter, spacing biscuits about 1½ inches apart. Bake until tops are golden brown and crisp, 12 to 14 minutes.

3. Brush biscuit tops with remaining 2 tablespoons melted butter. Transfer to wire rack and let cool for 5 minutes before serving.

✔ WHY THIS RECIPE WORKS

We wanted a drop biscuit recipe that would offer a no-nonsense alternative to traditional rolled biscuits, with the same tenderness and buttery flavor. Too many drop biscuits are dense, gummy, and doughy or lean and dry; we wanted a biscuit that could be easily broken apart and eaten piece by buttery piece. Proper leavening and, surprisingly, lumpy butter turned out to be the secret.

USE REGULAR ALL-PURPOSE You don't want a super-soft flour here. Since the dough is not kneaded or rolled, you actually want a little gluten for the structure of your biscuits, and all-purpose flour has more protein than softer flours (see "Flour 101," page 357).

PICK BUTTERMILK Buttermilk provides much-needed flavor in such a basic biscuit recipe. But it does more. Adding buttermilk allows us to likewise add baking soda (along with baking powder). The baking soda reacts with the acid in the buttermilk and gives the biscuits a crisper, browner exterior and fluffier middle.

CLUMP THE BUTTER Usually, properly combining melted butter with buttermilk (or any liquid) requires that both ingredients be at just the right temperature; if they aren't, the melted butter clumps in the cold buttermilk. Since this is supposed to be an easy recipe, we simply use lumpy buttermilk. This may look like a mistake, but it actually mimics the chunks of fat in a classic biscuit recipe (see concept 43). The result is a surprisingly better biscuit, slightly higher and with better texture. It turns out that the water in the lumps of butter turn to steam in the oven, helping create additional height.

Cookies seem so simple. Even kids can make them, right? Wrong. As it turns out, cookie recipes are complex chemical formulas with little room for error. And the simpler the cookie, the bigger the challenge. Texture is the most challenging part of any cookie recipe and is especially important in simple cookies, such as sugar cookies, where there aren't big flavors that might otherwise hide textural imperfections. Understanding how to use baking powder and baking soda is the key to getting texture right in many cookies.

CHEWY SUGAR COOKIES
MAKES ABOUT 24 COOKIES

The final dough will be slightly softer than most cookie dough. For best results, handle the dough as briefly and gently as possible when shaping the cookies. Overworking the dough will result in flatter cookies.

2¼	cups (11¼ ounces) all-purpose flour
1	teaspoon baking powder
½	teaspoon baking soda
½	teaspoon salt
1½	cups (10½ ounces) plus ⅓ cup (2⅓ ounces) sugar
2	ounces cream cheese, cut into 8 pieces
6	tablespoons unsalted butter, melted and still warm
⅓	cup vegetable oil
1	large egg
1	tablespoon whole milk
2	teaspoons vanilla extract

1. Adjust oven rack to middle position and heat oven to 350 degrees. Line 2 baking sheets with parchment paper. Whisk flour, baking powder, baking soda, and salt together in medium bowl. Set aside.

2. Place 1½ cups sugar and cream cheese in large bowl. Place remaining ⅓ cup sugar in shallow dish and set aside. Pour warm butter over sugar and cream cheese and whisk to combine (some small lumps of cream cheese will remain but will smooth out later). Whisk in oil until incorporated. Add egg, milk, and vanilla; continue to whisk until smooth. Add flour mixture and mix with rubber spatula until soft, homogeneous dough forms.

3. Working with 2 tablespoons of dough at a time, roll into balls. Working in batches, roll half of dough balls in sugar to coat and set on prepared baking sheet; repeat with remaining dough balls. Using bottom of greased measuring cup, flatten dough balls until 2 inches in diameter. Sprinkle tops of cookies evenly with sugar remaining in

shallow dish, using 2 teaspoons for each baking sheet. (Discard remaining sugar.)

4. Bake 1 sheet at a time until edges of cookies are set and beginning to brown, 11 to 13 minutes, rotating baking sheet halfway through baking. Let cookies cool on baking sheet for 5 minutes; transfer cookies to wire rack and let cool to room temperature.

CHEWY CHAI-SPICE SUGAR COOKIES

Add ¼ teaspoon ground cinnamon, ¼ teaspoon ground ginger, ¼ teaspoon ground cardamom, ¼ teaspoon ground cloves, and pinch pepper to sugar and cream cheese mixture and reduce vanilla to 1 teaspoon.

CHEWY COCONUT-LIME SUGAR COOKIES

Whisk ½ cup sweetened shredded coconut, chopped fine, into flour mixture in step 1. Add 1 teaspoon finely grated lime zest to sugar and cream cheese mixture and substitute 1 tablespoon lime juice for vanilla.

CHEWY HAZELNUT–BROWNED BUTTER SUGAR COOKIES

Add ¼ cup finely chopped toasted hazelnuts to sugar and cream cheese mixture. Instead of melting butter, heat it in 10-inch skillet over medium-high heat until melted, about 2 minutes. Continue to cook, swirling pan constantly, until butter is dark golden brown and has nutty aroma, 1 to 3 minutes. Immediately pour butter over sugar and cream cheese mixture and proceed with recipe as directed, increasing milk to 2 tablespoons and omitting vanilla.

PRACTICAL SCIENCE THE pH OF COMMON FOODS

The pH of common foods influences the work of leaveners.

The natural levels of acidity in many ingredients can make a significant difference in the finished dish—especially when using chemical leaveners. Here is a chart of the pH values of nine common cooking ingredients, from the least to the most acidic. This data comes from the U.S. Food and Drug Administration.

	pH
Egg White	7.6–8.0
Water	6.9–7.3
Chicken	6.5–6.7
Flour	6.0–6.3
Ground Beef	5.1–6.2
Sugar	5.0–6.0
Buttermilk	4.5
Canned Tomatoes	3.5–4.7
Lemon Juice	2.2–2.4

✔ WHY THIS RECIPE WORKS

Traditional recipes for sugar cookies require obsessive attention to detail. The butter must be at precisely the right temperature and it must be creamed to the proper degree of airiness. Slight variations in measures can result in cookies that spread or become brittle and hard upon cooling. We didn't want a cookie that depended on such a finicky process; we wanted an approachable recipe for great sugar cookies that anyone could make anytime. We melted the butter so our sugar cookie dough could easily be mixed together with a spoon—no more fussy creaming. Replacing a portion of the melted butter with vegetable oil ensured a chewy cookie without affecting flavor. And incorporating an unusual addition, cream cheese, into the cookie dough kept our cookies tender, while the slight tang of the cream cheese made for a rich, not-too-sweet flavor.

MANAGE THE FATS The key to chewy texture is all in the fat. For optimal chew, a recipe must contain saturated and unsaturated fat in approximately a 1:3 ratio. When combined, the two types of fat molecules form a sturdier crystalline structure that requires more force to bite through than the structure formed from a high proportion of saturated fats. This is why we couldn't develop a recipe that called for butter alone (as many of them do). Butter is predominantly—but not entirely—saturated fat, and an all-butter cookie actually contains approximately 2 parts saturated fat to 1 part unsaturated fat. For optimal chew, we needed to reverse this ratio and then some.

This is why we add oil to our recipe, just enough to fix the fat ratio without affecting flavor.

MELT THE BUTTER Because we are using less butter, we melt it rather than cream it. This does three things. First, it eliminates one of the trickier aspects of baking sugar cookies: ensuring that the solid butter is just the right temperature. Second, melted butter aids in our quest for chewiness. When liquefied, the small amount of water in butter mixes with the flour to form gluten, which makes for chewier cookies. Finally, with creaming out of the equation, we no longer need to pull out our stand mixer. We can make these cookies completely by hand.

USE CREAM CHEESE Cream cheese enriches the dough's flavor without adding moisture like other tangy dairy products. Cream cheese contains less than one-third the amount of overall fat of vegetable oil, but most of it is saturated. A modest 2 ounces of cream cheese did not markedly impact the chewy texture of the cookies.

ADD BAKING SODA Cream cheese doesn't just add flavor. It adds acidity. And this allows us to add baking soda. As long as there's an acidic ingredient present, baking soda has all sorts of special powers, including the ability to solve the cookies' other two pesky problems: a slightly humped shape and not enough crackle. Just ½ teaspoon produces cookies that look as good as they taste. (See "Dynamic Duo: Baking Powder + Baking Soda," below).

PRACTICAL SCIENCE DYNAMIC DUO: BAKING POWDER + BAKING SODA

Using both baking powder and baking soda is necessary to produce cookies that spread evenly and have a nice, crackly top.

Many cookie recipes, including our Chewy Sugar Cookies, contain both baking soda and baking powder. Since each is a leavening agent, why do you need both? The answer is that the two work in tandem to create cookies that rise—and spread—to the right degree. Plus in our recipe, baking soda has one more purely aesthetic effect: It creates cookies with an appealingly crackly top.

Baking powder is responsible for lift, since it is engineered to produce most of its gas after the cookies go into the oven, where the dough sets before these bubbles can burst.

But too much lift can mean cookies that turn out humped. Here's where baking soda comes in: As long as there's an acidic ingredient in the dough for it to react with, a small amount of baking soda can even things out. Baking soda raises the pH of dough (baking powder does too, but not as high), weakening gluten. Weaker gluten means less structure and cookies that spread. Goodbye, humped shapes. As for crackly tops, baking soda reacts immediately in the wet dough to produce large bubbles of carbon dioxide that can't all be contained by the weakened dough. Before the cookies can set in the oven, the bubbles rise to the top and burst, leaving fissures in their wake.

The bottom line: For a baker who likes her cookies just so, the use of both baking powder and baking soda can be a potent combo.

HUMPED
Without baking soda, our cookies turn out tall and lumpy.

FLAT
With the addition of baking soda, our cookies spread evenly and have a crackly top.

THIN AND CRISPY OATMEAL COOKIES
MAKES ABOUT 24 COOKIES

Do not use instant or quick oats in this recipe.

1	cup (5 ounces) all-purpose flour
¾	teaspoon baking powder
½	teaspoon baking soda
½	teaspoon salt
14	tablespoons unsalted butter, softened but still cool (60 degrees)
1	cup (7 ounces) granulated sugar
¼	cup packed (1 ¾ ounces) light brown sugar
1	large egg
1	teaspoon vanilla extract
2½	cups (7½ ounces) old-fashioned rolled oats

1. Adjust oven rack to middle position and heat oven to 350 degrees. Line 3 baking sheets with parchment paper. Whisk flour, baking powder, baking soda, and salt together in medium bowl; set aside.

2. Using stand mixer fitted with paddle, beat butter, granulated sugar, and brown sugar at medium-low speed until just combined, about 20 seconds. Increase speed to medium and continue to beat until light and fluffy, about 1 minute longer, scraping down bowl as needed. Add egg and vanilla and beat on medium-low until fully incorporated, about 30 seconds, scraping down bowl as needed. Reduce speed to low, add flour mixture, and mix until just incorporated and smooth, about 10 seconds. With mixer still running on low, gradually add oats and mix until well incorporated, about 20 seconds. Give dough final stir to ensure that no flour pockets remain and ingredients are evenly distributed.

3. Working with 2 tablespoons of dough at a time, roll into balls and place 2½ inches apart on prepared baking sheets. Using fingertips, gently press each dough ball to ¾-inch thickness.

4. Bake 1 sheet at a time until cookies are deep golden brown, edges are crisp, and centers yield to slight pressure when pressed, 13 to 16 minutes, rotating baking sheet halfway through baking. Transfer baking sheet to wire rack and let cookies cool completely.

PRACTICAL SCIENCE
COOL BAKING SHEETS BETWEEN BATCHES

Don't put raw cookie dough onto a hot baking sheet.

While it's tempting to save time by portioning cookie dough onto a baking sheet that has just been removed from the oven, we don't recommend it. The dough begins to melt and spread before it even reaches the oven, which can adversely affect the texture of the cookies. We baked two batches of chocolate chip cookies and sugar cookies, the first using a cool baking sheet and the second using a hot baking sheet that had just been removed from the oven. Both baking sheets were lined with parchment paper. While differences between the two batches of chocolate chip cookies weren't too noticeable, the same couldn't be said of the thinner, more delicate sugar cookies. The sugar cookies baked on the hot baking sheet spread more, had darker bottoms, and were noticeably thinner and crisper around the edges.

Here's our recommendation: After removing baked cookies from the oven and allowing the baking sheet to cool for a few minutes until warm but no longer hot, simply run the baking sheet under cold tap water to cool it down quickly, then wipe it dry. To make the operation even more efficient, line the cookie sheet with parchment paper. As the first batch bakes, load a second piece of parchment with dough. When the cookies come out of the oven, remove them, parchment and all, onto a cooling rack. Once the baking sheet is properly cooled, the next batch will be ready to go.

THIN AND CRISPY COCONUT-OATMEAL COOKIES

Decrease oats to 2 cups and add 1½ cups sweetened shredded coconut to batter with oats.

THIN AND CRISPY ORANGE-ALMOND OATMEAL COOKIES

Beat 2 teaspoons grated orange zest with butter and sugars. Decrease oats to 2 cups and add 1 cup coarsely chopped toasted almonds to batter with oats.

SALTY THIN AND CRISPY OATMEAL COOKIES

We prefer the texture and flavor of a coarse-grained sea salt, such as Maldon or fleur de sel, but kosher salt can be used. If using kosher salt, reduce the amount sprinkled over the cookies to ¼ teaspoon.

Reduce amount of salt in dough to ¼ teaspoon. Lightly sprinkle ½ teaspoon coarse sea salt evenly over flattened dough balls before baking.

✓ WHY THIS RECIPE WORKS

Thin and crispy oatmeal cookies can be irresistible—crunchy and delicate, these cookies really let the flavor of the oats take center stage. But the usual ingredients that give thick, chewy oatmeal cookies great texture—generous amounts of sugar and butter, a high ratio of oats to flour, a modest amount of leavener, eggs, raisins, and nuts—won't all fit in a thin, crispy cookie. We wanted to adjust the standard ingredients to create a crisp, delicate cookie in which the simple flavor of buttery oats really stands out. Scaling back the sugar and fine-tuning our leavening did the trick.

GO WITH OLD-FASHIONED Whole hulled oats are called groats. After being heated to inhibit rancidity, they are further processed, according to the particular style. Steel-cut oats are groats sliced into three or four pieces by steel blades. Old-fashioned or rolled oats are groats steamed and rolled flat or flaked. Quick oats are steel-cut oats steamed and rolled to one third (or less) the thickness of regular rolled oats. And instant oats are very finely cut groats that are rapidly cooked and rolled flat.

When baking, we prefer to use old-fashioned oats for the best texture and flavor. Quick oats can be used in many recipes, in a pinch; their flavor is weaker and the texture of the baked good might be slightly less chewy. We don't recommend baking with instant oats—they are very bland and their powdery texture can negatively impact many baked goods. And never bake with steel-cut oats. The results in anything from scones to cookies can be like aquarium gravel. Steel-cut oats do make a great breakfast, however.

CREAM THE BUTTER Creaming the butter, rather than melting it, tends to make a crisper cookie. When solid butter is mixed with sugar, air is incorporated into the mixture and held there by the crystals of solid fat. This is especially true when they're mixed on medium speed until light and fluffy. This extra air allows the cookies to dry faster in the oven, producing crispier cookies (see concept 46). Limiting the sugar also helps with crispness (the greater the amount of sugar, the chewier the cookie). Using all granulated sugar makes the cookies hard and crunchy, with a one-dimensional, overly sweet flavor. Using light brown sugar in place of some of the granulated aids in the flavor—with subtle caramel notes—without compromising texture.

SPREAD EVEN If the cookies don't spread evenly, the edges end up thinner and crisper than the center, which is thicker and chewier. We wanted to create a dough that would spread evenly, but a liquid-y dough baked up too thin, like lace cookies. We found that using two leaveners, and plenty of each, helped. During baking, large carbon dioxide bubbles created by the baking soda and baking powder (upped from our traditional recipe) caused the cookies to puff up, collapse, and spread out, producing the thin, flat cookies we were looking for.

PRESS, THEN BAKE Pressing the dough balls flat encourages an even spread. Baking the cookies all the way through until they are fully set and evenly browned from center to edge makes them crisp throughout but not tough.

PRACTICAL SCIENCE AVOIDING UNEVEN BAKING

Bake one sheet at a time, and be sure to rotate.

Baking two trays of cookies at a time may be convenient, but it leads to uneven cooking. The cookies on the top tray are often browner around the edges than those on the bottom. If you have two sheets in the oven, switching their position halfway through cooking helps. But for cookies with an especially finicky texture, we find it best to bake the cookies one sheet at a time to ensure the best results. And just because there's just one baking sheet in the oven, don't assume you can walk away. Even the best ovens have hot and cold spots and you must rotate the baking sheet at the halfway mark to ensure even baking. Simply grab the front of the baking sheet and rotate the pan until the cookies that were in the front are now in the back of the oven.

NO ROTATING = UNEVEN BAKING

Layers of Butter Make Flaky Pastry

Butter makes countless baked goods taste great. But butter is also a key factor in creating a flaky texture in biscuits as well as the pastry used in tarts and pies. Knowing how to handle the butter means the difference between biscuits and pastry that are flaky and light and biscuits and pastry that are dense and heavy.

HOW THE SCIENCE WORKS

So how exactly does butter make biscuits and pastry flaky? Butter isn't just fat—it's fat and water. When butter is heated, the water turns to steam. This steam lifts the dough and helps create a flaky texture in biscuits, tart shells, and pie crusts. But for the steam to have a significant effect, the butter must be evenly dispersed in layers throughout the dough. This way, when the butter layers melt, the steam helps separate the super-thin layers of dough into striated flakes.

The challenge, then, is getting the butter evenly dispersed throughout the dough while still leaving it in distinct layers. If the butter becomes fully incorporated (as it does when making a cake, for instance) the flakes won't form. Starting with cold butter is essential but handling the dough is just as important.

Let's start with temperature. Butter begins to soften when it reaches 60 degrees Fahrenheit, begins to melt at 85 degrees, and liquefies completely by 94 degrees. When melted, butter easily works its way into the other ingredients, removing the possibility of forming layers and promoting the formation of flakes in the oven. To keep butter below the melting point while preparing biscuit and pastry doughs, we use a few different methods.

The first technique we will cover in this concept is called lamination. Puff pastry, croissants, and the flaky pastry for many tart doughs all rely on a mathematical phenomenon to achieve their many-layered structure. These so-called laminated pastries, which are made up of alternating layers of dough and fat, are created by repeatedly rolling and folding the dough over itself, typically in thirds (like a business letter). Each set of folds is called a turn, and with each turn the number of layers increases exponentially rather than linearly. Thus, the first turn gives three layers, the next seven, then 19, then 55, and so on. Just six turns creates an astonishing 1,459 layers. This process flattens the butter into thin sheets sandwiched between thin layers of flour. In the oven, the butter melts and steam fills the thin spaces left behind, creating hundreds of flaky, buttery layers.

Next, let's discuss *fraisage*. This French mixing method also creates a dough with thin layers of butter that remain distinct. Fraisage refers to the process of smearing the dough with the heel of your hand, thereby spreading the butter pieces into long, thin streaks between skeletal layers of flour and water. This works especially well in tart dough, giving us a sturdy dough (because the melted butter leaves behind no gaping holes) that won't leak fruit juices. The dough, however, is still flaky.

LAYERING WITH LAMINATION

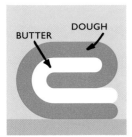

TURN THE DOUGH *When using a technique called lamination, pastry dough is rolled and folded over itself in thirds.*

KEEP ON TURNING *As you continue to turn the dough, the layers of butter and dough multiply exponentially. The result is an incredibly flaky pastry.*

TEST KITCHEN EXPERIMENT

Numerous baked goods (think croissants, pie dough, and biscuits) incorporate super-thin layers of solid butter to develop a flaky texture. To illustrate the importance of getting the butter layers just right, we designed a unique experiment. We started with a traditional rolled and cut biscuit dough and treated the butter three different ways. For the first sample we used the most common method of incorporating butter: We cut cold butter into the flour (using a food processor) until it resembled pebbly pieces. We also made a batch with melted butter and another where we cut thin slices of cold butter and pressed them between well-floured fingers until they resembled nickels. We formed identical doughs with each batch from which we then rolled and cut biscuits.

THE RESULTS

A post-baking lineup told the whole story. The melted-butter biscuits sat squat, dense, and uniform next to the moderately flaky traditional biscuits, both of which paled in comparison to the height and flakiness of the biscuits made with the thin pieces of butter.

THE TAKEAWAY

The key to making flaky biscuits is to get layers of solid fat spread between the layers of dough. This way, the thin layers of fat (butter) will melt when they hit the hot oven. And because butter is part fat and part water, the water turns to steam, filling the now-empty spaces between the dough, and giving rise to flaky layers.

Melted butter, on the other hand, is incapable of forming discrete layers of solid fat between layers of dough; this is why our biscuits made with melted butter turned out dense and flat. Similarly, the standard pebbles of butter can't begin to form layers of fat between layers of dough until they soften enough to spread out. Even when they do start to spread in the oven, the softening pebbles can't spread far enough, forming only small regions of fat that will not give rise to much flakiness at all.

The lesson? If flaky biscuits or pastries are what you desire, be sure to use techniques like lamination or fraisage to get thin, long layers of solid fat in the dough.

HOW YOU HANDLE YOUR BUTTER MAKES BISCUITS FLAKY (OR NOT)

We baked biscuits using butter that we handled in three different ways: melted, cut into flour using a food processor, and pressed between floured fingers until they resembled nickels. The long, thin, nickel-size layers of butter made that batch of biscuits the flakiest of them all.

MELTED BUTTER
The biscuits made with melted butter had no layers of fat and baked up flat and dense.

PEBBLY BUTTER
Small pebbles of butter helped a bit to form the layers of fat that make biscuits flaky.

THIN PIECES OF BUTTER
The nickel-size rounds of butter gave our biscuits perfect flaky layers.

Rolling and folding the dough creates a multilayered structure that generates tremendous rise. Lamination is used in everything from puff pastry and croissants to simple items like biscuits and scones.

FLAKY BUTTERMILK BISCUITS
MAKES 12 BISCUITS

The dough is a bit sticky when it comes together and during the first set of turns. Note that you will use up to 1 cup of flour for dusting the work surface, dough, and rolling pin to prevent sticking. Be careful not to incorporate large pockets of flour into the dough when folding it over. When cutting the biscuits, press down with firm, even pressure; do not twist the cutter.

2½	cups (12½ ounces) all-purpose flour
1	tablespoon baking powder
½	teaspoon baking soda
1	teaspoon salt
2	tablespoons vegetable shortening, cut into ½-inch chunks
8	tablespoons unsalted butter, chilled, lightly floured, and cut into ⅛-inch slices plus 2 tablespoons melted and cooled
1¼	cups buttermilk, chilled

1. Adjust oven rack to lower-middle position and heat oven to 450 degrees. Whisk flour, baking powder, baking soda, and salt together in large bowl.

2. Add shortening to flour mixture; break up chunks with fingertips until only small, pea-size pieces remain. Working with few butter slices at a time, drop butter slices into flour mixture and toss to coat. Pick up each slice of butter and press between well-floured fingertips into flat, nickel-size pieces. Repeat until all butter is incorporated, then toss to combine. Freeze mixture (in bowl) until chilled, about 15 minutes, or refrigerate for about 30 minutes.

3. Spray 24-inch-square area of counter with vegetable oil spray; spread spray evenly across surface with clean kitchen towel or paper towel. Sprinkle ⅓ cup flour across sprayed area, then gently spread flour across work surface with palm to form thin, even coating. Add 1 cup plus 2 tablespoons buttermilk to flour mixture. Stir briskly with fork until ball forms and no dry bits of flour are visible, adding remaining 2 tablespoons buttermilk as needed (dough will be sticky and shaggy but should clear sides of bowl). With rubber spatula, transfer dough onto center of prepared counter, dust surface lightly with flour, and, with floured hands, bring dough together into cohesive ball.

4. Pat dough into approximate 10-inch square, then roll into 18 by 14-inch rectangle about ¼ inch thick, dusting dough and rolling pin with flour as needed. Use bench scraper or thin metal spatula to fold dough into thirds, brushing any excess flour from surface of dough. Lift short end of dough and fold in thirds again to form approximate 6 by 4-inch rectangle. Rotate dough 90 degrees, dusting counter underneath with flour, then roll and fold dough again, dusting with flour as needed.

5. Roll dough into 10-inch square about ½ inch thick. Flip dough over and cut nine 3-inch rounds with floured 3-inch biscuit cutter, dipping cutter back into flour after each cut. Carefully invert and transfer rounds to ungreased baking sheet, spacing them 1 inch apart. Gather dough scraps into ball and roll and fold once or twice until scraps form smooth dough. Roll dough into ½-inch-thick round and cut 3 more 3-inch rounds and transfer to baking sheet. Discard excess dough.

6. Brush biscuit tops with melted butter. Bake, without opening oven door, until tops are golden brown and crisp, 15 to 17 minutes. Let cool on baking sheet for 5 to 10 minutes before serving.

✔ WHY THIS RECIPE WORKS

Truly flaky biscuits have become scarce, while their down-market imitators (think supermarket "tube" biscuits) are alarmingly common. We wanted to achieve a really flaky—not fluffy—biscuit, with a golden, crisp crust surrounding striated layers of tender, buttery dough. While ingredients (lard versus butter, buttermilk versus milk, and so on) influence texture and flavor, we discovered that the secret to the fluffy/flaky distinction is how the ingredients are handled: Flaky butter equals flaky biscuits.

MAKE LARGE FLAKES When we make pie crusts, we usually cut the butter into cubes, and then put them in the food processor along with the other dry ingredients, turning the butter into small pebbles. The pebble shape is ideal for the small, irregular flakes in a pie crust but not for the pronounced layers we need in a biscuit. Instead, we get "flaky" butter by abandoning the food processor, slicing the butter into very thin squares, and—instead of cutting the squares into the flour with a pastry blender—we press each piece onto the flour with our fingers, breaking them into flat, flaky pieces about the size of a nickel. This is exactly what we want for a biscuit; as we roll out the dough we can see the butter develop into long, thin sheets.

ADD SHORTENING Swapping out some butter for some shortening has a tenderizing effect. Why? For one, butter contains 16 to 18 percent water while shortening is all fat. The use of shortening, then, reduces the level of hydration in the biscuits. (Shortening likewise contains a higher amount of unsaturated oil than butter, which has a higher level of saturated fats. The higher level of liquid oil in the room-temperature shortening more effectively coats the protein in the flour, also reducing the level of hydration.) Less hydration means less gluten formation (see concept 38). A weaker gluten network helps to produce a more tender biscuit.

USE TWO LEAVENERS We use both baking soda and baking powder to leaven our biscuits. The baking soda reacts with the acidic buttermilk in the dough, producing carbon dioxide and helping the biscuits to rise immediately. More importantly, if the baking soda was not added to neutralize the acid in the buttermilk, then the acid would reduce the leavening capability of the baking powder. The baking powder adds its leavening power as soon as the biscuits hit the heat of the oven. (See concept 42 for more on leaveners.) Also, the baking soda reacts with the acidic buttermilk to take the edge off of its flavor, which can become almost too tangy.

CHILL WELL Don't let the flakes of butter melt. If they soften and mix with the flour during the series of folds, the result will be biscuits that are short and crumbly instead of crisp and flaky. We don't have the luxury of resting our dough in the refrigerator to firm up the butter because the baking soda in the dough begins reacting the moment the liquid and dry ingredients come together. Chilling the mixing bowl and all of the ingredients (instead of just the butter) before mixing buys us the time needed to complete all of the necessary turns with the cold butter intact.

CREATE A NONSTICK COUNTER Biscuit dough is a Catch-22. It needs to be wet—a dry dough makes a dry biscuit—but it also needs to be rollable. We don't want to scatter too much flour on the surface of the counter, because then the wet dough will absorb the extra flour and no longer be wet. The solution? We give the countertop a quick blast from a can of vegetable oil spray. It helps the flour adhere more evenly to the counter, letting our dough release easily, and without much flour sticking to it.

PRESS, DON'T TWIST To cut the biscuits, flour your biscuit cutter, dipping it back into the flour after each cut. We invert the biscuits onto the baking sheet with the flat underside on top so that they will rise more evenly. Do not twist the biscuit cutter as you cut the dough. Twisting can seal the edges of the biscuit and prevent it from rising. Press gently.

BLUEBERRY SCONES
MAKES 8 SCONES

It is important to work the dough as little as possible—work quickly and knead and fold the dough only the number of times called for or the scones will turn out tough, rather than tender. The butter should be frozen solid before grating. In hot or humid environments, chill the flour mixture and mixing bowls before use. While this recipe calls for two whole sticks of butter, only 10 tablespoons are actually used (see step 1). If fresh berries are unavailable, an equal amount of frozen berries, not thawed, can be substituted. An equal amount of raspberries, blackberries, or strawberries can be used in place of the blueberries. Cut larger berries into ¼- to ½-inch pieces before incorporating. Serve with Homemade Clotted Cream (recipe follows), if desired.

16	tablespoons unsalted butter (2 sticks), frozen
7½	ounces (1½ cups) blueberries
½	cup whole milk
½	cup sour cream
2	cups (10 ounces) all-purpose flour
½	cup (3½ ounces) plus 1 tablespoon sugar
2	teaspoons baking powder
¼	teaspoon baking soda
½	teaspoon salt
1	teaspoon grated lemon zest

1. Adjust oven rack to middle position and heat oven to 425 degrees. Line baking sheet with parchment paper. Remove half of wrapper from each stick of frozen butter. Grate unwrapped ends (half of each stick) on large holes of box grater (you should grate total of 8 tablespoons). Place grated butter in freezer until needed. Melt 2 tablespoons remaining ungrated butter and set aside. Save remaining 6 tablespoons butter for another use. Place blueberries in freezer until needed.

2. Whisk milk and sour cream together in medium bowl; refrigerate until needed. Whisk flour, ½ cup sugar, baking powder, baking soda, salt, and lemon zest together in medium bowl. Add frozen grated butter to flour mixture and toss with fingers until butter is thoroughly coated.

3. Add milk mixture to flour mixture and fold with rubber spatula until just combined. Using spatula, transfer dough to liberally floured counter. Dust surface of dough with flour and with floured hands, knead dough 6 to 8 times, until it just holds together in ragged ball, adding flour as needed to prevent sticking.

4. Roll dough into approximate 12-inch square. Fold dough into thirds like a business letter, using bench scraper or metal spatula to release dough if it sticks to counter. Lift short ends of dough and fold into thirds again to form approximate 4-inch square. Transfer dough to plate lightly dusted with flour and chill in freezer for 5 minutes.

5. Transfer dough to floured counter and roll into approximate 12-inch square again. Sprinkle blueberries evenly over surface of dough, then press down so they are slightly embedded in dough. Using bench scraper or thin metal spatula, loosen dough from counter. Roll dough into cylinder, pressing to form tight log. Arrange log seam side down and press into 12 by 4-inch rectangle. Using sharp, floured knife, cut rectangle crosswise into 4 equal rectangles. Cut each rectangle diagonally to form 2 triangles and transfer to prepared baking sheet.

6. Brush tops with melted butter and sprinkle with remaining 1 tablespoon sugar. Bake until tops and bottoms are golden brown, 18 to 25 minutes. Transfer to wire rack and let cool for at least 10 minutes before serving.

TO MAKE AHEAD: After placing scones on baking sheet in step 5, either refrigerate them overnight or freeze for up to 1 month. When ready to bake, for refrigerated scones, heat oven to 425 degrees and follow directions in step 6. For frozen scones, do not thaw, heat oven to 375 degrees, and follow directions in step 6, extending cooking time to 25 to 30 minutes.

HOMEMADE CLOTTED CREAM
MAKES 2 CUPS

Ultra-pasteurized heavy cream can be substituted but the resulting cream will not be as flavorful and tangy. This recipe can be halved or doubled as needed.

1½	cups pasteurized (not ultra-pasteurized) heavy cream
½	cup buttermilk

Combine cream and buttermilk in jar or measuring cup. Stir, cover, and let stand at room temperature until mixture has thickened to consistency of softly whipped cream, 12 to 24 hours. Refrigerate; cream will continue to thicken as it chills. (Clotted cream can be refrigerated for up to 10 days.)

✓ WHY THIS RECIPE WORKS

For our ultimate blueberry scone recipe, we wanted to bring together the sweetness of a coffeehouse confection, the moist freshness of a muffin, the richness of clotted cream and jam, and the super-flaky crumb of a good biscuit. Increasing the amount of butter and adding enough sugar gave the scones sweetness without making them cloying. Cutting frozen butter into the flour and giving the dough a few folds helped the scones rise. Rolling out the dough, pressing the berries into it, and then rolling it up again before flattening to cut out the scones also contributed to making this our ideal scone recipe.

FOLD THE DOUGH We take a hint from puff pastry, where the power of steam is used to separate super-thin layers of dough into striated flakes. In a standard puff pastry recipe, a piece of dough will be turned, rolled, and folded about five times. With each fold, the number of layers of butter and dough increases exponentially. Upon baking, steam forces the layers apart and then escapes, causing the dough to puff up and crisp. We aren't after the hundreds of layers produced by the standard five-turn puff pastry recipe here, but adding a few quick folds to our recipe allows the scones to gently rise and puff.

GRATE THE BUTTER A good light pastry depends on distinct pieces of butter distributed throughout the dough that melt during baking and leave behind pockets of air. For this to happen, the butter needs to be as cold and solid as possible until baking. The problem with trying to cut butter into the flour with your fingers or a food processor is that the butter gets too warm during the distribution process. We find that freezing sticks of butter and grating them on the large holes of a box grater works best. We start with two sticks of butter, but then, using the wrapper to hold the frozen butter, grate only 4 tablespoons from each.

GET THE FLAVOR RIGHT Too often, berries weigh down scones and impart little flavor. Starting with traditional scone recipes, we increase the amounts of sugar and butter to add sweetness and richness; a combination of whole milk and sour cream lends more richness as well as tang.

ADD BLUEBERRIES Adding the blueberries to the dry ingredients means they get mashed when we mix the dough, but when we add them to the already-mixed dough, they ruin our pockets of butter. The solution is pressing the berries into the dough, rolling the dough into a log, then pressing the log into a rectangle and cutting the scones. You can use fresh or frozen berries.

CREATE A CRISP TOP Brush the tops of the scones with melted butter, and sprinkle them with sugar, before baking to help form a crisp top.

BUTTER 101

STRUCTURE

FAT (OR MILK FAT)
Globules of fat from cream or milk (some of them crystallized) stick together when churned, creating a larger mass, which is kneaded to make the bulk of butter. By law, fat must make up a minimum of 80 percent of the total content of butter. As a result of butter's high level of saturated fat, it is a solid at room temperature, begins to melt at about 85 degrees, and is completely liquefied by 94 degrees. In its solid state, much of the fat occurs as tiny crystals surrounding the droplets of water along with a small amount of protein.

WATER
Butter is 16 to 18 percent water. Butter is one of the few ingredients in the kitchen composed of a water-in-oil emulsion, which is an emulsion of tiny droplets of water suspended in a continuous phase of fat, similar to a classic vinaigrette (see concept 36). A small amount of protein coats the water droplets and keeps them from coalescing unless the butter is completely melted.

MILK SOLIDS
"Milk solids" is the term used to describe everything in butter that isn't water or fat. Milk solids are rich in protein, carbohydrates, vitamins, and minerals, which are all removed when clarifying butter, except for the fat-soluble vitamins. The milk solids represent about 1 percent of the compounds found in butter.

BUYING

You have four basic decisions at the market—salted or unsalted, cultured or uncultured, regular or premium, and whipped or stick.

SALTED OR UNSALTED? In the test kitchen, we use unsalted butter almost exclusively and add our own salt to recipes. Why? First, the amount of salt in salted butter varies from brand to brand—on average ⅓ teaspoon a stick—which makes offering a universal conversion impossible. Second, salted butter almost always contains more water, which can influence gluten development—particularly important in baking. (Biscuits made with salted butter were noticeably mushy.) Third, salt overshadows butter's naturally sweet, delicate flavors; in butter-specific recipes like beurre blanc and buttercream frosting, we found that extra salt to be overwhelming.

CULTURED OR UNCULTURED? The real distinction between premium and regular butters (see description at right) is culturing—the process of fermenting the cream before churning it that builds tangy, complex flavors. Cultured butters are produced by adding certain strains of bacteria that produce unique flavors. That said, these nuances are subtle in most cooked applications, so we save the expensive cultured stuff for spreading on toast.

WHIPPED OR STICK? Whipped butter, made by beating air into butter, makes a creamy spread but isn't always a good alternative to stick butter for cooking. While testers couldn't tell the difference in baked goods, they found the aerated butter "foamy" and "plasticlike" in uncooked applications such as frosting. If you want to use whipped butter, base your substitution on weight, not volume. (Adding air increases the volume, not the weight.) A standard tub of whipped butter weighs 8 ounces, equal to two sticks of butter.

REGULAR OR PREMIUM? While you hear a lot about the higher fat content in premium butters, our tasters had trouble telling the difference, even when tasted plain. Regular unsalted butter contains 81 to 82 percent fat; premium brands have 83 to 86 percent fat. Because higher-fat butter remains solid over a wider temperature range, we like it when making croissant dough and other recipes where rapid softening of the butter would cause problems.

GAUGING BUTTER TEMPERATURE

	TEMPERATURE	METHOD	HOW TO TEST	WHY IT MATTERS
CHILLED	About 35 degrees	Cut into small pieces and freeze until very firm, 10 to 15 minutes.	It should not yield when pressed with a finger and should be cold to the touch.	Cold butter is cut into flour for flaky pie dough.
SOFTENED	60 to 68 degrees	Let refrigerated butter sit at room temperature for 30 to 60 minutes.	At 60 degrees, it should yield to slight pressure and crack when pressed. At 68 degrees, it should bend easily without breaking and give slightly when pressed.	Sugar can be creamed with softened but still cool butter (60 degrees) or completely softened butter (68 degrees) to make different types of cakes (see concepts 46 and 47).
MELTED AND COOLED	85 to 94 degrees	Melt in small saucepan or microwave-safe bowl and let cool for about 5 minutes.	It should be fluid and slightly warm to the touch.	Water in liquefied butter mixes with flour to create chewy cookies.

You can "turn" the dough to create thin layers of butter and flour or you can use a French mixing technique called fraisage to create a similar effect. In this case, you roll the dough but don't fold or turn it. This works well with doughs that must be rolled thin to create a tart or galette—these thin doughs would be tricky to fold.

FREE-FORM FRUIT TART
SERVES 6

Taste the fruit before adding sugar to it; use the lesser amount if the fruit is very sweet, more if it is tart. However much sugar you use, do not add it to the fruit until you are ready to fill and form the tart. Serve with vanilla ice cream or whipped cream.

DOUGH

1½	cups (7½ ounces) all-purpose flour
½	teaspoon salt
10	tablespoons unsalted butter, cut into ½-inch pieces and chilled
4–6	tablespoons ice water

FILLING

1	pound peaches, nectarines, apricots, or plums, halved, pitted, and cut into ½-inch wedges
5	ounces (1 cup) blueberries, raspberries, or blackberries
4–6	tablespoons sugar

1. FOR THE DOUGH: Process flour and salt in food processor until combined, about 5 seconds. Scatter butter over top and pulse until mixture resembles coarse bread crumbs and butter pieces are about size of small peas, about 10 pulses. Continue to pulse, adding water 1 tablespoon at a time, until dough begins to form small curds that hold together when pinched with fingers (dough will be crumbly), about 10 pulses.

2. Turn dough crumbs onto lightly floured counter and gather into rectangular-shaped pile. Starting at farthest end, use heel of hand to smear small amount of dough against counter. Continue to smear dough until all crumbs have been worked. Gather smeared crumbs together in another rectangular-shaped pile and repeat process. Press dough into 6-inch disk, wrap it tightly in plastic wrap, and refrigerate for 1 hour. Before rolling dough out, let it sit on counter to soften slightly, about 10 minutes. (Dough can be wrapped tightly in plastic and refrigerated for up to 2 days or frozen for up to 1 month. If frozen, let dough thaw completely on counter before rolling it out.)

3. Roll dough into 12-inch circle between 2 large sheets of floured parchment paper. (If dough sticks to parchment, gently loosen and lift sticky area with bench scraper and dust parchment with additional flour.) Slide dough, still between parchment sheets, onto rimmed baking sheet and refrigerate until firm, 15 to 30 minutes. (If refrigerated longer and dough is hard and brittle, let stand at room temperature until pliant.)

4. FOR THE FILLING: Adjust oven rack to middle position and heat oven to 375 degrees. Gently toss fruit and 3 to 5 tablespoons sugar together in bowl. Remove top sheet of parchment paper from dough. Mound fruit in center of dough, leaving 2½-inch border around edge of fruit. Being careful to leave ½-inch border of dough around edge of fruit, fold outermost 2 inches of dough over fruit, pleating it every 2 to 3 inches as needed; gently pinch pleated dough to secure, but do not press dough into fruit. Working quickly, brush top and sides of dough with water and sprinkle evenly with remaining 1 tablespoon sugar.

5. Bake until crust is deep golden brown and fruit is bubbling, about 1 hour, rotating baking sheet halfway through baking. Transfer tart with baking sheet to wire rack and let cool for 10 minutes, then use parchment to gently transfer tart to wire rack. Use metal spatula to loosen tart from parchment and remove parchment. Let tart cool on rack until juices have thickened, about 25 minutes; serve slightly warm or at room temperature.

PRACTICAL SCIENCE WHY FRAISAGE MATTERS

Long flaky layers of butter make tart crusts that won't leak.

We found that fraisage—the technique of smearing dough on the counter—was necessary in this recipe. What happens if you omit this key step? Something like the crust on the bottom, which has short flaky layers and is prone to leaking: The dough had lumps of butter that, when melted in the oven, left behind holes that weakened the walls of the crust. The crust on the top has long flaky layers and is far less prone to leaking. The fraisage creates long streaks of butter (rather than lumps) that make for a stable yet tender crust.

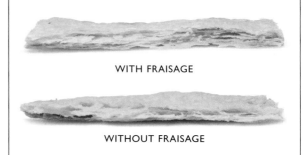

WITH FRAISAGE

WITHOUT FRAISAGE

FREE-FORM SUMMER FRUIT TARTLETS
MAKES 4 TARTLETS

Divide dough into 4 equal portions before rolling out in step 3. Roll each portion into 7-inch circle on parchment paper; stack rounds and refrigerate until firm. Continue with recipe from step 4, mounding one-quarter of fruit in center of dough round, leaving 1½-inch border around edge. Being careful to leave ¼-inch border of dough around edge of fruit, fold outermost 1 to 1¼ inches of dough over fruit. Transfer parchment with tart to rimmed baking sheet. Repeat with remaining fruit and dough. Brush dough with water and sprinkle each tartlet with portion of remaining 1 tablespoon sugar. Bake until crust is deep golden brown and fruit is bubbling, 40 to 45 minutes, rotating baking sheet halfway through baking.

✔ WHY THIS RECIPE WORKS

We wanted a simple take on summer fruit pie, one without the rolling and fitting usually required for a traditional pie or tart. A free-form tart—a single layer of buttery pie dough folded up around fresh fruit—seemed the obvious solution. But without the support of a pie plate, tender crusts are prone to leaking juice, and this can result in a soggy bottom. For our crust, we used a high proportion of butter to flour, which provided the most buttery flavor and tender texture without compromising the structure. We then turned to the French fraisage method to make the pastry sturdy yet flaky.

CREATE STRONG BUT FLAKY DOUGH Using too much butter in our crust results in a weak, leaky crust. Too little and we get a crust that is crackerlike and edging toward tough. We settle on 10 tablespoons for 1½ cups of flour. But just as important as the amount of butter is the mixing method. We tried mixing the dough in a food processor, with a stand mixer, and by hand. We found that the latter two methods mashed the butter into the flour and produced a less flaky crust. Quick pulses with the food processor, however, "cut" the butter into the flour so that it remains in distinct pieces. We mix the butter to be about the size of coarse bread crumbs—just big enough to create the steamed spaces needed for flakiness.

SMEAR THE DOUGH Fraisage is a French method of making pastry and involves smearing the dough with the heel of the hand. This spreads the butter pieces into long streaks between thin layers of flour and water.

DON'T ADD SUGAR OR LEMON We tried adding sugar and lemon juice to the crust dough, but lemon juice made the crust too tender, as acid weakens the gluten structure in dough. Sugar improved the flavor of the crust but was detrimental to the texture, even a small amount making it brittle. We sprinkle sugar on top of the dough before baking instead.

KEEP THE FILLING SIMPLE There is no butter needed in our simple fruit filling. We use just ripe fruit sprinkled with 3 to 5 tablespoons of sugar (depending on the type of fruit and its natural sweetness). Though we prefer a tart made with a mix of stone fruits and berries (our favorite combinations are plums and raspberries, peaches and blueberries, and apricots and blackberries), you can use only one type of fruit if you prefer. Peeling the stone fruit (even the peaches) is not necessary. (For more on sugar and fruit, see concept 49.)

ROLL AND FOLD We roll out the dough to about the height of three stacked quarters (or ³/₁₆ inch). This is thick enough to contain a lot of fruit but thin enough to bake evenly and thoroughly. After mounding the fruit in the center, leaving a 2½-inch border, we lift the dough up and back over the fruit (leaving the center of the tart exposed) and loosely pleat the dough to allow for shrinkage.

USE HOT OVEN, COOL ON A RACK When testing this recipe, we baked it on the center rack of the oven at 350, 375, 400, and 425 degrees. Baking at the lowest temperature took too long; it also dried out the fruit and failed to brown the crust. At too high a temperature, the crust darkened on the folds but remained pale and underdone in the creases, and the fruit became charred. Setting the oven to 375 degrees generates the ideal time and temperature for an evenly baked, flaky tart. The last small but significant step toward a crisp crust is to cool the tart directly on a wire rack; this keeps the crust from steaming itself as it cools.

PRACTICAL SCIENCE STORING BUTTER

Store butter in the freezer for longer than 2½ weeks.

Placed in the back of the fridge where it's coldest (not in the small door compartment), butter will keep for 2½ weeks. In tests we've found that stored any longer it can turn rancid as its unsaturated fatty acids oxidize. For longer storage (up to four months), keep butter in the freezer. Also, since butter quickly picks up odors and flavors, we like to slip the sticks into a zipper-lock bag.

APPLE GALETTE
SERVES 10 TO 12

The most common brands of instant flour are Wondra and Shake & Blend; they are sold in canisters in the baking aisle. The galette can be made without instant flour, using 2 cups of all-purpose flour and 2 tablespoons of cornstarch; however, you might have to increase the amount of ice water. Serve with vanilla ice cream or whipped cream.

DOUGH

1½	cups (7½ ounces) all-purpose flour
½	cup (2½ ounces) instant flour
½	teaspoon salt
½	teaspoon sugar
12	tablespoons unsalted butter, cut into ¼-inch pieces and chilled
7–9	tablespoons ice water

TOPPING

1½	pounds Granny Smith apples, peeled, cored, halved, and sliced ⅛ inch thick
2	tablespoons unsalted butter, cut into ¼-inch pieces
¼	cup (1¾ ounces) sugar
3	tablespoons apple jelly

1. FOR THE DOUGH: Process all-purpose flour, instant flour, salt, and sugar together in food processor until combined, about 5 seconds. Scatter butter over top and pulse until mixture resembles coarse cornmeal, about 15 pulses. Continue to pulse, adding water 1 tablespoon at a time until dough begins to form small curds that hold together when pinched with fingers (dough will be crumbly), about 10 pulses.

2. Turn dough crumbs onto lightly floured counter and gather into rectangular-shaped pile. Starting at farthest end, use heel of hand to smear small amount of dough against counter. Continue to smear dough until all crumbs have been worked. Gather smeared crumbs together in another rectangular-shaped pile and repeat process. Press dough into 4-inch square, wrap it tightly in plastic wrap, and refrigerate for 1 hour. Before rolling dough out, let it sit on counter to soften slightly, about 10 minutes. (Dough can be wrapped tightly in plastic and refrigerated for up to 2 days or frozen for up to 1 month. If frozen, let dough thaw completely on counter before rolling it out.)

3. Adjust oven rack to middle position and heat oven to 400 degrees. Cut piece of parchment paper to measure exactly 16 by 12 inches. Roll dough out over parchment, dusting with flour as needed, until it just overhangs parchment. Trim edges of dough even with parchment. Roll outer 1 inch of dough up to create ½-inch-thick border. Slide parchment with dough onto baking sheet.

4. FOR THE TOPPING: Starting in 1 corner of tart, shingle apple slices into crust in tidy diagonal rows, overlapping them by one-third. Dot with butter and sprinkle evenly with sugar. Bake tart until bottom is deep golden brown and apples have caramelized, 45 minutes to 1 hour, rotating baking sheet halfway through baking.

5. Melt jelly in small saucepan over medium-high heat, stirring occasionally to smooth out any lumps. Brush glaze over apples and let tart cool slightly on sheet for 10 minutes. Slide tart onto large platter or cutting board and slice tart in half lengthwise, then crosswise into square pieces. Serve warm or at room temperature.

PRACTICAL SCIENCE CLARIFYING BUTTER

While we generally use butter as an ingredient, it can also be used as a cooking medium. Here are two ways to do so.

While recipes in this concept rely on the temperature of butter and how the dough is handled to create the right results, there is another option—heat. Many variations on Indian cuisine as well as recipes like baklava rely on butter that has been clarified so it won't brown.

CLARIFIED Clarified butter is butter with the milk solids and water removed. To clarify butter, it is heated to break the emulsion, which causes its different components to separate according to density and chemical makeup. The milk solids turn into a foam at the top, which can be scooped away with a spoon. At the bottom lies a thin layer that includes proteins, phospholipids, and the aqueous layer, which is predominantly water along with some dissolved milk sugar (lactose) and minerals. This milky casein layer can be discarded after the butterfat solidifies as it cools. Clarified butter has a higher smoke point than whole butter and will keep longer in the refrigerator (for three to four weeks) or the freezer (for four to six months) without picking up other flavors and odors.

GHEE Ghee, a butter product used throughout Indian cooking, takes the clarification process a step further by allowing butter to simmer until all the moisture is evaporated and the milk solids begin to brown, giving the butterfat a slightly nutty flavor and aroma. The product can be found in unrefrigerated jars at Indian and Middle Eastern markets, as well as at natural foods stores.

✓ WHY THIS RECIPE WORKS

The French tart known as an apple galette should have a flaky crust and a substantial layer of nicely shingled sweet caramelized apples. But it's challenging to make a crust strong enough to hold the apples and still be eaten out of hand—most recipes create a crust that is tough, crackerlike, and bland. Our ideal galette has the buttery flakiness of a croissant but is strong enough to support a generous layer of caramelized apples. Choosing the right flour, and using fraisage, gives us exactly what we want.

INSTANT FLOUR Even when we used fraisage to make our dough tender and flaky, we found that when using all-purpose flour, it just wasn't tender enough. Switching up the flours—and therefore the protein content of the flour—helped. All-purpose flour has a protein content ranging from 10 to 12 percent. When mixed with water, the proteins (gliadin and glutenin) in flour create a stronger, more elastic protein called gluten (see concept 38). The higher the gluten content, the stronger and tougher the dough. Pastry flour, with a 9 percent protein content, made a big difference. But pastry flour is not widely available. Cake flour, with an 8 percent protein content, turned our crust crumbly, however. (It turns out that cake flour goes through a bleaching process with chlorine gas that affects how its proteins and starch combine with water. As a result, weaker gluten is formed—perfect for a delicate cake but not for a pastry that must be tender and sturdy.) The answer? Instant flour. Instant flour is made by slightly moistening all-purpose flour with water. After being spray-dried, the tiny flour granules look like small clusters of grapes. Since these aggregated flour granules are larger than those of finer-ground all-purpose flour, they absorb less water, making it harder for the proteins to form gluten. Replacing ½ cup of all-purpose with instant flour gives us dough that is tender but sturdy enough to cut neat slices of galette that can be eaten out of hand.

ROLL, TRIM, AND TUCK To make the rectangular pastry, first roll out the dough over a floured piece of parchment paper cut to 16 by 12 inches. Dust with more flour as needed. Trim the dough to fit and then roll up 1 inch of each edge, pinching firmly with your fingers to create a solid border.

SHINGLE AND GLAZE Although any apples will work in this recipe, we prefer Granny Smith. To arrange the apples, start in one corner and shingle to form even rows, overlapping by about one-third. The apples are sugared and dotted with butter. (Apples can be drier than

summer fruits like the ones in our Free-Form Fruit Tart, page 374, and they benefit from some fat as well as some sugar.) Although not all galette recipes call for it, many brush hot-out-of-the-oven tarts with apple jelly. This glaze provides an attractive sheen and helps to reinforce the apple flavor.

USE PARCHMENT AND FAIRLY HOT OVEN This big galette requires a more precise shape than a free-form tart. Using the parchment as a guide (as well as to move the tart around the kitchen) is helpful. We bake the tart at 400 degrees, a temperature that strikes the right balance between intensely caramelized and simply burnt.

Vodka Makes Pie Dough Easy

Whoever coined the phrase "easy as pie" clearly had never made a pie. Yes, the recipe for a pie crust sounds simple to prepare. Mix flour with salt and sugar, cut in fat, add just enough cold water so that the dough sticks together, then roll out and bake. You want a dough that bakes up tender and flaky and is relatively easy to work with. But the reality is that pie dough often bakes up tough and leathery and it's often a pain to work with—cracking and tearing are common problems.

HOW THE SCIENCE WORKS

ADDING ALCOHOL TO PIE DOUGH

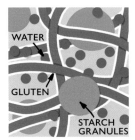

WATER ALONE *In pie dough made with water alone, the water interacts with the flour to form a good deal of gluten, which can cause the dough to be tough.*

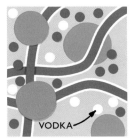

VODKA AND WATER *Gluten does not form in alcohol. Therefore pie dough made with a mixture of vodka and water has less gluten and is much more tender.*

The trouble with pie dough is that it never seems to behave the same way twice. This means that you need to troubleshoot every time you make a pie. And troubleshooting requires experience, so that you can recognize what's going on with that particular dough and then make the proper adjustments. Most modern cooks make pies only a few times a year and can't be expected to troubleshoot at all.

Perfect pie dough has just the right balance of tenderness and structure. The former comes from fat, the latter from long protein chains called gluten that form when flour mixes with water. Too little gluten and the dough won't stick together—but too much and the crust turns tough. We've developed an approach that keeps gluten in check but also allows for an unusually supple dough that's easy to handle and reduces the chances of overworking. Our revolutionary pie dough recipe removes the guesswork by relying on a secret ingredient: It all comes down to alcohol.

You see, gluten forms readily in water. Water hydrates the proteins in flour. This means that the water molecules attach themselves to the proteins through the formation of hydrogen bonds. Hydrogen bonds are weak, electrostatic bonds that hold water molecules onto the surface of the protein molecules, giving the coiled protein molecules flexibility to unravel and bond with each other in order to form strands of gluten. (For more on this, see concept 38.) But gluten won't form in alcohol. The ethyl alcohol in vodka and other liquors does not attach itself in the same way as water. Because of this, it does not hydrate the proteins, and therefore does not aid in gluten formation. By replacing some of the water in our recipe with vodka (which contains 40 percent ethanol and just 60 percent water), we're able to add more liquid to the dough so it stays soft and malleable, but without increasing the danger of the crust turning tough.

But what if you don't have vodka in your pantry—can another 80-proof liquor be used in its place? We baked pie crusts made with rum, whiskey, and gin and compared them side by side with our vodka crust. Surprisingly, the vast majority of our tasters could not distinguish among the different flavors of booze. In fact, they could not taste the alcohol at all. All of the crusts had a clean taste and flaky texture. So if vodka is not your tipple of choice, go ahead and substitute any 80-proof liquor.

TEST KITCHEN EXPERIMENT

While science might provide support for using vodka in pie dough, we weren't going to be convinced of its value until we could see it with our own eyes. To determine whether or not the use of vodka makes a difference in the texture of a flaky pie crust, we baked batches of our Foolproof Pie Dough (page 380)—one with a 1:1 ratio of vodka to water (¼ cup of each), and another with just water (½ cup of water total). To make cross-section comparisons easier, we ditched the pie plates and instead rolled out the dough into large sheets and cut them into 5-inch by 2-inch rectangles, which we baked on a parchment-lined baking sheet. Once the strips of baked pie crust were cool, we balanced them on two small metal cups, like a tightrope, and placed a 250-gram cup of pennies on top of each crust to assess its "toughness."

THE RESULTS

The pie crust made with vodka immediately snapped in two, dropping the cup of pennies, which then spilled out onto the counter. The pie crust made with only water remained intact, however, and kept its pennies balanced for about a minute. Tasters said that the vodka pie crust was much more tender and flaky. The all-water crust was noticeably tougher.

THE TAKEAWAY

Because gluten will not form in the presence of alcohol, the pie crust made with equal parts vodka and water had a much less developed gluten network than the pie crust made with water alone. And less gluten makes for a tender and flaky crust. In addition, using a mixture of vodka and water allows us to add more liquid to the dough to get it to be as malleable and easy to work with as possible without causing excessive toughness.

The lesson? Vodka isn't just for drinking. As a secret ingredient in pie crust, it can both make the pie crust more tender, and the life of the cook trying to roll out the dough easier.

THE POWER OF VODKA: EASY-TO-ROLL, TENDER PIE CRUST

We made two batches of our pie crust, one with the correct ratio of vodka to water, the other with water alone, and then tested the results with a cup of pennies. The flaky vodka dough didn't stand a chance.

VODKA AND WATER
This tender pie crust cracked immediately.

WATER ALONE
This tougher crust held the pennies for a full minute.

Replacing part of the ice water with vodka is the key to creating a well-hydrated dough that is easy to work with. And because the vodka doesn't activate gluten, our dough bakes up flaky. In contrast, most well-hydrated doughs made with just ice water bake up tough and leathery because the extra water activates too much gluten. In addition to the recipes in this concept, pie dough is a key ingredient in Pumpkin Pie (page 184) and Lemon Meringue Pie (page 203).

FOOLPROOF DOUBLE-CRUST PIE DOUGH
MAKES ENOUGH FOR ONE 9-INCH PIE

Vodka is essential to the tender texture of this crust and imparts no flavor—do not substitute water. This dough is moister than most standard pie doughs and will require lots of flour to roll out (up to ¼ cup). A food processor is essential for making this dough—it cannot be made by hand.

2½	cups (12½ ounces) all-purpose flour
2	tablespoons sugar
1	teaspoon salt
12	tablespoons unsalted butter, cut into ¼-inch pieces and chilled
8	tablespoons vegetable shortening, cut into 4 pieces and chilled
¼	cup vodka, chilled
¼	cup ice water

1. Process 1½ cups flour, sugar, and salt together in food processor until combined, about 5 seconds. Scatter butter and shortening over top and continue to process until incorporated and mixture begins to form uneven clumps with no remaining floury bits, about 15 seconds.

2. Scrape down bowl and redistribute dough evenly around processor blade. Sprinkle remaining 1 cup flour over dough and pulse until mixture has broken up into pieces and is evenly distributed around bowl, 4 to 6 pulses.

3. Transfer mixture to large bowl. Sprinkle vodka and ice water over mixture. Stir and press dough together, using stiff rubber spatula, until dough sticks together.

4. Divide dough into 2 even pieces. Turn each piece of dough onto sheet of plastic wrap and flatten each into 4-inch disk. Wrap each piece tightly in plastic and refrigerate for 1 hour. Before rolling dough out, let it sit on counter to soften slightly, about 10 minutes. (Dough can be wrapped tightly in plastic and refrigerated for up to 2 days or frozen for up to 1 month. If frozen, let dough thaw completely on counter before rolling it out.)

FOOLPROOF BAKED PIE SHELL
MAKES ONE 9-INCH PIE SHELL

Vodka is essential to the tender texture of this crust and imparts no flavor—do not substitute water. This dough is moister than most standard pie doughs and will require lots of flour to roll out (up to ¼ cup).

1¼	cups (6¼ ounces) all-purpose flour
1	tablespoon sugar
½	teaspoon salt
6	tablespoons unsalted butter, cut into ¼-inch pieces and chilled
4	tablespoons vegetable shortening, cut into 2 pieces and chilled
2	tablespoons vodka, chilled
2	tablespoons ice water

PRACTICAL SCIENCE HOT-WATER CRUST

Hot-water crust is easy to work with, but it doesn't taste good.

For centuries, pastry dough was used mainly as a cooking receptacle. It wasn't flaky, nor was it all that good. In fact, food historians debate whether it was even consumed. Hot-water crusts are one of the oldest forms of pastry; they were molded around a filling and baked free form, rather than in a pie dish. With a hot-water crust, boiling water is whisked into fat (usually lard) until it forms an emulsion. This lard mixture is then added to flour. The result is an extremely pliable dough that's easy to work with since it doesn't crack or tear.

When we compared a hot-water crust in several recipes (quiche, deep-dish apple pie, and blueberry turnovers) with our Foolproof Pie Dough, we understood why it might not have been eaten in the past. It baked up so tender, some tasters called it "mealy"—the result of both its higher-than-usual fat content and the fact that "precooking" the flour with a hot-water emulsion causes some of its starches to immediately swell with water, making less of the liquid available to form structure-building gluten. While hot-water crust is simple to prepare and easy to work with, stick with our Foolproof Pie Dough if you want pastry worth eating.

HOT-WATER CRUST
Boiling water and fat added to the flour create a nicely pliable dough but a mealy crust.

CLASSIC CRUST
Our favorite pie dough (made with the usual cold water) is both pliable and flaky.

1. Process ¾ cup flour, sugar, and salt together in food processor until combined, about 5 seconds. Scatter butter and shortening over top and continue to process until incorporated and mixture begins to form uneven clumps with no remaining floury bits, about 10 seconds.

2. Scrape down bowl and redistribute dough evenly around processor blade. Sprinkle remaining ½ cup flour over dough and pulse until mixture has broken up into pieces and is evenly distributed around bowl, 4 to 6 pulses.

3. Transfer mixture to medium bowl. Sprinkle vodka and ice water over mixture. Stir and press dough together, using stiff rubber spatula, until dough sticks together.

4. Turn dough onto sheet of plastic wrap and flatten into 4-inch disk. Wrap tightly in plastic and refrigerate for 1 hour. Before rolling dough out, let it sit on counter to soften slightly, about 10 minutes. (Dough can be wrapped tightly in plastic and refrigerated for up to 2 days or frozen for up to 1 month. If frozen, let dough thaw completely on counter before rolling it out.)

5. Adjust oven rack to middle position and heat oven to 425 degrees. Roll dough into 12-inch circle on floured counter. Loosely roll dough around rolling pin and gently unroll it onto 9-inch pie plate, letting excess dough hang over edge. Ease dough into plate by gently lifting edge of dough with 1 hand while pressing into plate bottom with other hand. Leave any dough that overhangs plate in place. Wrap dough-lined pie plate loosely in plastic and refrigerate until dough is firm, about 30 minutes.

6. Trim overhang to ½ inch beyond lip of pie plate. Tuck overhang under itself; folded edge should be flush with edge of pie plate. Crimp dough evenly around edge of pie using your fingers. Wrap dough-lined pie plate loosely in plastic and refrigerate until dough is fully chilled and firm, about 15 minutes, before using.

7. Line chilled pie shell with double layer of aluminum foil, covering edges to prevent burning, and fill with pie weights.

8A. FOR A PARTIALLY BAKED CRUST: Bake until pie dough looks dry and is pale in color, about 15 minutes. Remove weights and foil and continue to bake crust until light golden brown, 4 to 7 minutes longer. Transfer pie plate to wire rack. (Crust must still be warm when filling is added.)

8B. FOR A FULLY BAKED CRUST: Bake until pie dough looks dry and is pale in color, about 15 minutes. Remove weights and foil and continue to bake crust until deep golden brown, 8 to 12 minutes longer. Transfer pie plate to wire rack and let crust cool completely, about 1 hour.

PRACTICAL SCIENCE
HOW TO PREVENT A SOGGY CRUST

We recommend baking pies in a glass pie plate on a preheated baking sheet.

Nobody likes a fruit pie with its bottom crust saturated in fruit juices. We wondered if getting the bottom crust of the pie to heat more rapidly might help prevent fruit juices from soaking through, so we baked two identical cherry pies. We placed one of them directly on the oven rack and the second one on a baking sheet that had been preheated for 15 minutes at 400 degrees.

The bottom crust of the pie baked directly on the oven rack was soaked with cherry juices, while the pie cooked on a preheated baking sheet had a solid, intact bottom crust.

In its raw state, pie dough is made up of cold, solid fat distributed among layers of moist flour. These layers are easily permeated by juices from the cherry filling, which stay in the dough for the duration of baking, producing a soggy crust. The key to protecting the dough is to partially liquefy the solid fat as quickly as possible so that it can better fill the spaces among the particles of flour, creating a watertight barrier and preventing the juices from soaking in. By placing the pie plate on a preheated baking sheet, we are giving the bottom crust a jump start in this liquefying process.

We prefer to use glass pie plates for several reasons. Glass conducts heat poorly but retains and distributes heat very well, so you get more even browning than you do in ceramic or metal, and glass won't react with acidic fillings. (Metal can do this and this becomes a problem if you have leftovers.) Last, glass allows you to lift up the pie plate (with oven mitts, of course) to check the progress of the bottom crust. If it looks underbaked, you can simply put the pie back in the oven.

FOOLPROOF SINGLE-CRUST PIE DOUGH FOR CUSTARD PIES

We like rolling our single-crust dough in fresh graham cracker crumbs because they add flavor and crisp textural appeal to our custard pies.

Crush 3 whole graham crackers to fine crumbs. (You should have about ½ cup crumbs.) Dust counter with graham cracker crumbs instead of flour. Continue sprinkling dough with crumbs, both underneath and on top, as it is being rolled out.

✔ WHY THIS RECIPE WORKS

Pie dough can go wrong so easily: dry dough that is too crumbly to roll out, a flaky but leathery crust, or a tender crust without flakes. We wanted a recipe for pie dough that would roll out easily every time and produce a tender, flaky crust. We found the answer in the liquor cabinet: vodka. While gluten (the protein that makes crust tough) forms readily in water, it doesn't form in ethanol, and vodka is 60 percent water and 40 percent ethanol. Adding ¼ cup of vodka produced a moist, easy-to-roll dough that stayed tender. (The alcohol vaporizes in the oven, so you won't taste it in the baked crust.)

USE TWO FATS Butter contributes rich taste—but also water, which encourages gluten development. For a crust that's both flavorful and tender, we use a 3:2 ratio of butter to shortening, a pure fat with no water.

USE MORE OF THEM We incorporate roughly a third more total fat in our dough than the typical recipe, which coats the flour more thoroughly so less of it can mix with water to form gluten. Also, the extra fat makes the dough more tender. (It makes it taste better, too.)

CREATE LAYERS Traditional recipes process all the flour and fat at once, but we add the flour in two batches. We first process the fat with part of the flour for a good 15 seconds to thoroughly coat it, then give the mixture just a few quick pulses once the remaining flour is added, so less of it gets coated. Besides providing protection against toughness, this approach aids in flakiness by creating two distinct layers of dough—one with gluten and one without.

SHAPE THE DOUGH INTO A ROUND Many bakers struggle to roll dough into an even circle. The first mistake they make is not shaping the dough into a round disk before refrigerating it. Take a minute to shape the dough into a 4-inch disk and you will find it much easier to roll it out into a 12-inch circle.

CHILL DOUGH, FLOUR COUNTER To prevent the dough from sticking to the counter (and to keep the butter from melting), it's best to chill the dough for an hour before attempting to roll it out. If the dough has been refrigerated for longer (it can keep in the fridge for two days or be frozen for four weeks and then defrosted in the fridge) it will be too cold. Let it warm up on the counter for 10 minutes before rolling it out.

ROLL AND TURN Two key pointers to keep in mind when rolling dough: First, always work with well-chilled pastry; otherwise, the dough will stick to the counter and tear. Second, never roll out dough by rolling back and forth over the same section; each time you press on the same spot, more gluten develops that can toughen the dough. Also, rolling back and forth makes it impossible to roll the dough into an even circle. Instead, roll the pin over the dough once, then rotate the dough 90 degrees and roll again. By rolling and rotating the dough you ensure that the dough forms a neat circle and that no part of the dough is getting overworked and tough. We like to use long, tapered French rolling pins; they are gentler on delicate dough than standard rolling pins.

MOVE THE DOUGH To move the dough into the pie plate, place the rolling pin about 2 inches from the top of the dough round. Flip the top edge of the dough over the rolling pin and turn once to loosely roll around the pin. Gently unroll the dough over the plate. Then, lift the dough around the edges and gently press it into the corners of the plate, letting excess dough hang over the edge. For a double-crust pie, roll out the second piece of dough and chill both it and the bottom crust while you make the filling. When you're ready, fill the bottom crust, add the top crust, then trim and flute.

BLUEBERRY PIE
SERVES 8

This recipe was developed using fresh blueberries, but unthawed frozen blueberries will work as well. In step 3, cook half the frozen berries over medium-high heat, without mashing, until reduced to 1¼ cups, 12 to 15 minutes. Use the large holes of a box grater to shred the apple. Grind the tapioca to a powder in a spice grinder or mini food processor.

1	recipe Foolproof Double-Crust Pie Dough (page 380)
30	ounces (6 cups) blueberries
1	Granny Smith apple, peeled, cored, and shredded
¾	cup (5¼ ounces) sugar
2	tablespoons instant tapioca, ground
2	teaspoons grated lemon zest plus 2 teaspoons juice
	Pinch salt
2	tablespoons unsalted butter, cut into ¼-inch pieces
1	large egg white, lightly beaten

1. Roll 1 disk of dough into 12-inch circle on lightly floured counter. Loosely roll dough around rolling pin and gently unroll it onto 9-inch pie plate, letting excess dough hang over edge. Ease dough into plate by gently lifting edge of dough with 1 hand while pressing into plate bottom with other hand. Leave any dough that overhangs plate in place. Wrap dough-lined pie plate loosely in plastic wrap and refrigerate until dough is firm, about 30 minutes.

2. Roll other disk of dough into 12-inch circle on lightly floured counter. Using 1¼-inch round cookie cutter, cut round from center of dough. Cut 6 more rounds from dough, 1½ inches from edge of center hole and equally spaced around center hole. Transfer dough to parchment paper–lined baking sheet; cover with plastic and refrigerate for 30 minutes.

3. Place 3 cups berries in medium saucepan and set over medium heat. Using potato masher, mash berries several times to release juices. Continue to cook, stirring often and mashing occasionally, until about half of berries have broken down and mixture is thickened and reduced to 1½ cups, about 8 minutes; let cool slightly.

4. Adjust oven rack to lowest position, place rimmed baking sheet on rack, and heat oven to 400 degrees.

5. Place shredded apple in clean kitchen towel and wring dry. Transfer apple to large bowl and stir in cooked berries, remaining 3 cups uncooked berries, sugar, tapioca, lemon zest and juice, and salt until combined. Spread mixture in dough-lined pie plate and scatter butter over top.

6. Loosely roll remaining dough round around rolling pin and gently unroll it onto filling. Trim overhang to ½ inch beyond lip of pie plate. Pinch edges of top and bottom crusts firmly together. Tuck overhang under itself; folded edge should be flush with edge of pie plate. Crimp dough evenly around edge of pie using your fingers. Brush surface with beaten egg white.

7. Place pie on heated baking sheet and bake until crust is light golden brown, about 25 minutes. Reduce oven temperature to 350 degrees, rotate baking sheet, and continue to bake until juices are bubbling and crust is deep golden brown, 30 to 40 minutes longer. Let pie cool on wire rack to room temperature, about 4 hours. Serve.

✔ WHY THIS RECIPE WORKS

If the filling in blueberry pie doesn't jell, a wedge can collapse into a soupy puddle topped by a sodden crust. But use too much thickener and the filling can be so dense that it's unpleasantly gluey to eat. We wanted a pie that had a firm, glistening filling full of fresh, bright flavor and still-plump berries. The use of tapioca and a natural pectin, as well as a hot oven, gets us exactly what we want.

USE THE RIGHT THICKENER We prefer using tapioca to cornstarch to thicken the filling of a pie made with juicy fruit, but in order to get the pie to set enough to slice neatly, we have to use a lot of it, and then we end up with a filling that is gluey and dull. (Flour and cornstarch yield a pasty, starchy filling no matter how much, or how little, we use.) We reduce the amount of tapioca and pulverize it in a spice grinder before adding it to the filling so that it doesn't leave any telltale "pearls" in the finished pie.

COOK HALF THE BERRIES Cooking just half of the berries is enough to adequately reduce their liquid and prevent an overly juicy pie. After cooking, we fold the remaining berries in with the cooked, creating a satisfying

combination of intensely flavored cooked fruit and bright-tasting fresh fruit. (This allows us to cut down on the tapioca, as well.)

USE NATURAL PECTIN As we watched the blueberries for our pie bubble away in the pot, we thought about blueberry jam. The secret to the great texture of well-made jam is pectin, a carbohydrate found in fruit. Blueberries are low in natural pectin, so commercial pectin in the form of a liquid or powder is usually added when making blueberry jam. The only downside to commercial pectin is that it needs the presence of a certain proportion of sugar and acid in order to work. Increasing the sugar makes the filling sickeningly sweet. A test with "no sugar needed" pectin set up properly, but this additive

---

PRACTICAL SCIENCE THE APPLE OF MY PIE

Adding a grated apple (and all of its pectin) keeps pie filling thick.

When making our blueberry pie filling, we found that if we used more than 2 tablespoons of tapioca, the texture of the filling took on a gummy consistency we didn't like. But 2 tablespoons or less resulted in a filling that was too loose. Could we solve this problem with pectin, a gentle thickener that occurs naturally in fruit?

As a control, we thickened one pie with 2 tablespoons of tapioca. We then compared it with a second pie thickened with 2 tablespoons of tapioca and a grated apple, which is high in pectin and has a mild flavor. (We hoped that grating the apple would make it less noticeable in the baked pie.)

As expected, the pie thickened with tapioca alone was loose and soupy. But the pie thickened with tapioca plus an apple had a naturally jelled texture that was just right. The apple bits seemed to melt into the berry filling during baking, boosting fruity flavor but leaving no textural sign of their presence.

Pectin is a natural substance, found in fruits and vegetables, that creates structure in a plant by helping to bind its cell walls together. This same substance is used to thicken jams and jellies into a set, but soft, mass. Pectin content varies from fruit to fruit and also within a plant (more pectin is found in the skin of a fruit than in its flesh, for example). Apples are a great source of pectin because they contain high levels of high-methoxyl pectin, the best natural pectin for making gels. By mashing some of the blueberries and grating the apple, we helped to release the pectin from the fruits' cell walls so that it could thicken the pie filling.

ON THE LOOSE
Pie filling thickened without enough tapioca won't firm up. But too much tapioca leads to gumminess.

ALL FIRMED UP
A little tapioca plus a grated apple created a juicy but sliceable filling.

contains lots of natural acid, which compensates for the lack of extra sugar—and its sourness did not appeal. Our solution? Apples. Apples contain a lot of natural pectin. We fold one peeled and grated Granny Smith apple into the berries along with a bit of tapioca. The apple provides enough thickening power to set the pie beautifully, plus it enhances the flavor of the berries without anyone guessing the secret ingredient. (See "The Apple of My Pie," page 383.)

ADD SUGAR, NOT SPICE To our filling we add sugar, of course, and lemon juice and zest. But nothing else. We want the filling to taste like berries, not cinnamon.

MAKE HOLES, NOT A LATTICE To vent the steam from the berries, we found a faster, easier alternative to a lattice top in a cookie cutter, which we use to cut out circles in the top crust.

START HOT We begin baking our pie in a 400-degree oven on a preheated baking sheet (see "How to Prevent a Soggy Crust," page 381) to help jump-start the browning process. After 25 minutes, we lower the heat to 350 degrees and keep baking for another 30 to 40 minutes.

LET IT COOL If you want neat slices of pie, it must cool. The filling will continue to set as the pie cools down to room temperature—a process that will take four hours. If you like to serve warm pie, let it cool fully (so filling sets), then briefly warm the pie in the oven before slicing. But don't overdo it! Leave the pie in a 350-degree oven for 10 minutes—just long enough to warm the pie without causing the filling to loosen.

DEEP-DISH APPLE PIE
SERVES 8

You can substitute Empire or Cortland apples for the Granny Smith apples and Jonagold, Fuji, or Braeburn for the Golden Delicious apples.

I	recipe Foolproof Double-Crust Pie Dough (page 380)
2½	pounds Granny Smith apples, peeled, cored, and sliced ¼ inch thick
2½	pounds Golden Delicious apples, peeled, cored, and sliced ¼ inch thick
½	cup (3½ ounces) plus I tablespoon granulated sugar
¼	cup packed (1¾ ounces) light brown sugar
½	teaspoon grated lemon zest plus I tablespoon juice
¼	teaspoon salt
⅛	teaspoon ground cinnamon
I	large egg white, lightly beaten

1. Roll 1 disk of dough into 12-inch circle on lightly floured counter. Loosely roll dough around rolling pin and gently unroll it onto 9-inch pie plate, letting excess dough hang over edge. Ease dough into plate by gently lifting edge of dough with 1 hand while pressing into plate bottom with other hand. Leave any dough that overhangs plate in place. Wrap dough-lined pie plate loosely in plastic wrap and refrigerate until dough is firm, about 30 minutes. Roll other disk of dough into 12-inch circle on lightly floured counter, then transfer to parchment paper–lined baking sheet; cover with plastic and refrigerate for 30 minutes.

2. Toss apples, ½ cup granulated sugar, brown sugar, lemon zest, salt, and cinnamon together in Dutch oven. Cover and cook over medium heat, stirring often, until apples are tender when poked with fork but still hold their shape, 15 to 20 minutes. Transfer apples and their juices to rimmed baking sheet and let cool to room temperature, about 30 minutes.

3. Adjust oven rack to lowest position, place rimmed baking sheet on rack, and heat oven to 425 degrees. Drain cooled apples thoroughly in colander, reserving ¼ cup of juice. Stir lemon juice into reserved juice.

4. Spread apples in dough-lined pie plate, mounding them slightly in middle, and drizzle with lemon juice mixture. Loosely roll remaining dough round around rolling pin and gently unroll it onto filling. Trim overhang to ½ inch beyond lip of pie plate. Pinch edges of top and bottom crusts firmly together. Tuck overhang under itself; folded edge should be flush with edge of pie plate. Crimp dough evenly around edge of pie using your fingers. Cut four 2-inch slits in top of dough. Brush surface with beaten egg white and sprinkle evenly with remaining 1 tablespoon granulated sugar.

5. Place pie on heated baking sheet and bake until crust is light golden brown, about 25 minutes. Reduce oven temperature to 375 degrees, rotate baking sheet, and continue to bake until juices are bubbling and crust is deep golden brown, 25 to 30 minutes longer. Let pie cool on wire rack until filling has set, about 2 hours; serve slightly warm or at room temperature.

✔ WHY THIS RECIPE WORKS

The problem with deep-dish apple pie is that the apples are often unevenly cooked and the exuded juices leave the apples swimming in liquid, producing a bottom crust that is pale and soggy. Then there is the gaping hole left between the shrunken apples and the top crust, making it impossible to slice and serve a neat piece of pie. We wanted our piece of deep-dish pie to be a towering wedge of tender, juicy apples, fully framed by a buttery, flaky crust. Precooking the apples solved the shrinking problem, helped the apples hold their shape, and prevented a flood of juices from collecting in the bottom of the pie plate, thereby producing a nicely browned bottom crust.

PRECOOK THE APPLES For a deep-dish pie you need a lot of apples. But all those apples make the crust soggy and the filling soupy. Not to mention that when all those apples cook down you're left with a top crust that sits far above the filling. Precooking the apples solves all of these problems—and precooked apples require no thickener, which can dull their flavor. (See "The Incredible Shrinking Apple," below.)

COOK GENTLY Though it's tempting to cook the apples over high heat in order to quickly drive off their liquid, it's not the right choice. Precooked at high heat, the apples in the pie end up mealy and soft. Cooking apples slowly over gentle heat gets rid of excess moisture and actually strengthens the internal structure of the apples, making them better able to hold their shape when baked in the pie. (For more on the science of precooking vegetables, see concept 27.)

USE TWO APPLES, SUGAR, AND SPICE We like tart apples, like Granny Smith and Empire, because of their brash flavor, but used alone their flavor can seem one-dimensional. To achieve a fuller, more balanced flavor, we find it necessary to add a sweeter variety, such as Golden Delicious or Braeburn. Another important factor in choosing the right apple is the texture. Even over the gentle heat of the stovetop, softer varieties such as McIntosh break down readily and turn to mush. With the right combination of apples, heavy flavorings are gratuitous. We add some light brown sugar along with the granulated sugar to heighten the flavor, as well as a pinch of salt and a squeeze of lemon juice (added after stovetop cooking to retain its flavor). We're content with just a hint of cinnamon.

MAKE VENTS IN THE TOP CRUST Apples are a lot less juicy than berries and you've precooked all the filling (not just half), so four vents in the top crust are plenty to allow steam to escape. Brushing the crust with egg white and sprinkling with sugar give the crust a pretty (and tasty) sheen.

START IN A HOT OVEN We begin baking our pie in a hot oven (425 degrees), on a preheated baking sheet set on the lowest rack, in order to help brown up the bottom crust and keep it from becoming soggy. We then turn the temperature down to 375 degrees to finish it off.

PRACTICAL SCIENCE THE INCREDIBLE SHRINKING APPLE

Precooking apples helps them to keep their shape in pie.

When raw apples are used in a deep-dish pie, they shrink to almost nothing, leaving a huge gap between the top crust and filling. Precooking the apples eliminates the shrinking problem and actually helps the apples hold their shape once baked in the pie.

This seems counterintuitive, but here's what happens: When the apples are gently heated, their pectin is converted to a heat-stable form that prevents the apples from becoming mushy when cooked further in the oven. (This process is similar to the phenomenon described in concept 27, where precooking helps roasted vegetables retain their shape and texture.) The key is to keep the temperature of the apples below 140 degrees during this precooking stage. Rather than cooking the apples in a skillet (where they are likely to become too hot), it's best to gently heat the apples and seasonings in a large covered Dutch oven.

PROBLEM
Raw apples shrink away from crust.

SOLUTION
Precook the apples.

Empanadas can be a lot of work. Many recipes braise meat for hours for the filling. Then you have to make the dough, which can be tricky. Then comes filling and shaping all those little empanadas, followed by several rounds of frying. We wanted a simpler approach, so we started with ground beef and decided to bake rather than fry. We decided to make larger empanadas suitable for dinner so there would be less folding and shaping involved. But what about the dough? Could we use what we learned about pie dough to make this dough easier, too?

BEEF EMPANADAS
MAKES 12 EMPANADAS, SERVING 4 TO 6

The alcohol in the dough is essential to the texture of the crust and imparts no flavor—do not substitute. Masa harina can be found in the international foods aisle with other Latin American foods or in the baking aisle with the flour. If you cannot find masa harina, replace it with additional all-purpose flour (for a total of 4 cups).

FILLING

1	slice hearty white sandwich bread, torn into quarters
2	tablespoons plus ½ cup low-sodium chicken broth
1	pound 85 percent lean ground beef
	Salt and pepper
1	tablespoon olive oil
2	onions, chopped fine
4	garlic cloves, minced
1	teaspoon ground cumin
¼	teaspoon cayenne pepper
⅛	teaspoon ground cloves
½	cup minced fresh cilantro
2	Hard-Cooked Eggs (page 21), chopped coarse
⅓	cup raisins, chopped coarse
¼	cup pitted green olives, chopped coarse
4	teaspoons cider vinegar

DOUGH

3	cups (15 ounces) all-purpose flour
1	cup (5 ounces) masa harina
1	tablespoon sugar
2	teaspoons salt
12	tablespoons unsalted butter, cut into ½-inch pieces and chilled
½	cup cold vodka or tequila
½	cup cold water
5	tablespoons olive oil

1. FOR THE FILLING: Process bread and 2 tablespoons broth in food processor until paste forms, about 5 seconds, scraping down sides of bowl as necessary. Add beef, ¾ teaspoon salt, and ½ teaspoon pepper and pulse until mixture is well combined, 6 to 8 pulses.

2. Heat oil in 12-inch nonstick skillet over medium-high heat until shimmering. Add onions and cook, stirring frequently, until beginning to brown, about 5 minutes. Stir in garlic, cumin, cayenne, and cloves; cook until fragrant, about 1 minute. Add beef mixture and cook, breaking meat into 1-inch pieces with wooden spoon, until browned, about 7 minutes. Add remaining ½ cup broth and simmer until mixture is moist but not wet, 3 to 5 minutes. Transfer mixture to bowl and cool for 10 minutes. Stir in cilantro, eggs, raisins, olives, and vinegar. Season with salt and pepper to taste and refrigerate until cool, about 1 hour. (Filling can be refrigerated for up to 2 days.)

3. FOR THE DOUGH: Pulse 1 cup flour, masa harina, sugar, and salt in food processor until combined, about 2 pulses. Add butter and process until homogeneous and dough resembles wet sand, about 10 seconds. Add remaining 2 cups flour and pulse until mixture is evenly distributed around bowl, 4 to 6 quick pulses. Empty mixture into large bowl.

4. Sprinkle vodka and water over mixture. Using hands, mix dough until it forms tacky mass that sticks together. Divide dough in half, then divide each half into 6 equal pieces. Transfer dough pieces to plate, cover with plastic wrap, and refrigerate until firm, about 45 minutes or up to 2 days.

PRACTICAL SCIENCE
THE BEST WAY TO PEEL HARD-COOKED EGGS

Shock eggs in ice water to cool them and make peeling easier.

To find out the best way to peel hard-cooked eggs, we hard-cooked 120 eggs and tested every egg-peeling myth and old wives' tale we could find. Ultimately, while we found that basics like peeling under running water and starting from the fat end (where the air pocket makes it easier to remove the first bit of shell) helped, only one trick guaranteed a nearly perfect peeled egg—shocking the egg in ice water as soon as it is done cooking.

Here's why: As an egg cooks, the layer of protein in the white known as albumin that's closest to the outer shell will slowly bond with it. A hard-cooked egg left at room temperature or even under cold running water will cool relatively slowly, giving the hot albumin plenty of time to form a strong bond with the membrane and shell. Shocking the egg in ice water quickly halts this bonding process. In addition, the sudden cooling causes the cooked egg white to shrink and pull away from the shell, making it much easier to remove the shell without damaging the white. (For more on hard-cooked eggs, see concept 1.)

5. TO ASSEMBLE: Adjust oven racks to upper-middle and lower-middle positions, place 1 rimmed baking sheet on each rack, and heat oven to 425 degrees. While baking sheets are preheating, remove dough from refrigerator. Roll out each dough piece on lightly floured counter into 6-inch circle about ⅛ inch thick, covering each dough round with plastic wrap while rolling remaining dough. Place about ⅓ cup filling in center of each dough round. Brush edges of dough with water and fold dough over filling. Trim any ragged edges. Press edges to seal. Crimp edges of empanadas using fork. (Empanadas can be made through step 5, covered tightly with plastic wrap, and refrigerated for up to 2 days.)

6. TO BAKE: Drizzle 2 tablespoons oil over surface of each hot baking sheet, then return to oven for 2 minutes. Brush empanadas with remaining 1 tablespoon oil. Carefully place 6 empanadas on each baking sheet and cook until well browned and crisp, 25 to 30 minutes, switching and rotating baking sheets halfway through baking. Let empanadas cool on wire rack for 10 minutes and serve.

BEEF EMPANADAS WITH CORN AND BLACK BEAN FILLING

Omit raisins and cook ½ cup frozen corn kernels and ½ cup rinsed canned black beans along with onions in step 2.

✔WHY THIS RECIPE WORKS

As all-in-one meals go, empanadas—the South American equivalent of Britain's pasties, or meat turnovers—are hard to beat: a moist, savory filling encased in a tender yet sturdy crust. But most recipes for empanadas are enormously time-consuming and fussy. We wanted a streamlined recipe that would be hearty enough to stand as a centerpiece on our dinner table. To do this, we enhance our ground chuck with aromatics, spices, and a mixture of chicken broth and bread, and make a few Latin-inspired changes to our Foolproof Pie Dough.

MAKE THE FILLING MOIST Using ground beef is certainly faster than braising and shredding a tough cut, but ground beef can be dry. Using a panade (made with bread and chicken broth), which helps the meat to retain moisture, is the key. (For more on panades, see concept 15.)

BUILD FLAVOR QUICKLY Sautéing the onions and then blooming the garlic and spices (see concept 33) before adding the beef creates a flavor base in just minutes. Punch up the flavors by adding olives, raisins, vinegar, and hard-boiled eggs—salty, sweet, tart, and rich—along with cilantro for a fresh herbal hit.

USE MASA For these empanadas, straight-up pie dough wasn't right. Using our Foolproof Pie Dough as is makes the empanadas seem too much like British pasties. Therefore, we replace some of the flour with masa harina, the dehydrated cornmeal used to make Mexican tortillas and tamales. Though unusual, the cornmeal provides a welcome nutty richness and rough-hewn texture. Even better, less flour means less protein in the dough; less protein means we don't need shortening (to tenderize the dough) and can switch to all butter for better flavor. We keep the vodka (although tequila is just as good).

ROLL, FILL, AND CRIMP To assemble the empanadas, first divide the dough in half, then divide each half into six equal pieces. Roll each piece into a 6-inch round, about ⅛ inch thick. Place ⅓ cup of filling on each round, and brush the edges with water. Fold the dough over the filling, and then crimp the edges using a fork.

OVEN "FRY" Most pastry shells (and empanada crusts) receive an egg wash before baking for a lustrous finish, but we are not the type for cosmetics if they don't improve the flavor and texture. For a crisp crust, we brush the shells with a little oil for the tops to boast shine and crunch. To take care of the underside of the empanadas, we preheat the baking sheet and drizzle the surface with oil. The result is a crust so shatteringly crisp that it almost passes for fried, giving way to a flavorful filling.

PRACTICAL SCIENCE HUMIDITY AND FLOUR

Short-term humidity should not affect flour.

Many baking experts claim that baking on very dry or very humid days can affect flour. We were a little skeptical but thought we'd run some tests while developing our recipe for Foolproof Pie Dough. We constructed a sealed humidity-controlled chamber in which we could simulate various types of weather. We made pie crusts at relative humidities of at least 85 percent (more humid than New Orleans in the wet season) and below 25 percent (drier than Phoenix in midsummer and the average air-conditioned office), leaving the lid to the flour container open for eight hours beforehand. We found that over the course of the test, the flour's weight varied by less than 0.5 percent between the two samples, and after being baked, the crusts were indistinguishable.

If an occasional humid day doesn't make a difference, what about long-term exposure to excess humidity? According to King Arthur Flour Company, flour held in its paper packing bag (even unopened) can gain up to 5 percent of its weight in water after several months in a very humid environment. At this level, humidity might affect baked goods. But this problem is easily avoided by transferring flour to an airtight container (preferably one wide enough to accommodate a 1-cup measure) as soon as you get home.

Less Protein Makes Tender Cakes, Cookies

As we learned in concept 41, too much gluten development can make quick breads tough. The solution is to mix the batter as little as possible to minimize gluten development. But this doesn't work for drier mixtures, such as cookie dough. And in other recipes it may not minimize gluten development sufficiently. Here, the solution starts with the choice of flour.

HOW THE SCIENCE WORKS

BREAD FLOUR VS. CAKE FLOUR

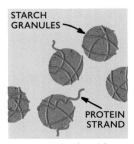

BREAD FLOUR *Bread flour has a good deal of protein and less starch. It is designed to form more gluten, which is necessary when baking chewy breads.*

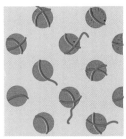

CAKE FLOUR *Cake flour is higher in starch, and lower in protein. When used in baking, it has less of an ability to form gluten than the protein-heavy bread flour.*

While a muffin or quick bread can have some chew, a yellow cake should be really tender. Likewise, while chewiness is fine in many cookies, it is out of place in shortbread, which should have a melt-in-the-mouth texture. In order to create super-tender cakes and cookies, you need to start with less protein. Less protein means a reduction in the production of gluten, which is what gives cakes, cookies, and breads their structure, and which in large amounts can produce a tough end product. Many cake recipes depend on specially milled cake flour, which contains about one-third less protein than all-purpose flour. Other recipes rely on simple techniques to effectively lower the protein content of all-purpose flour.

All-purpose flour has a relatively high protein content of 10 to 12 percent, depending on the brand. (The protein content of King Arthur all-purpose flour is about 11.7 percent while Pillsbury and Gold Medal both contain about 10.5 percent.) Bread flours, which are designed to produce a lot of gluten, necessary to create chewy rustic breads, have even more protein, generally 12 to 14 percent. Cake flour has just 6 to 8 percent protein. (See "Flour 101," page 357.)

Cake flour is made from soft winter wheat, using the inner core of the endosperm, which is easier to mill into a very finely granulated flour. It feels finer than all-purpose flour and this means it can absorb fat and liquid more easily than all-purpose flour, which is made from a mix of hard spring wheat and soft winter wheat. Soft winter wheat is higher in starch and lower in protein and therefore has less of an ability to form gluten.

In addition to containing less protein, cake flour is traditionally bleached with dry bleaches, such as benzoyl peroxide and chlorine gas, so that the starches in the flour can absorb greater amounts of liquid and fat and form thicker batters. Thicker batters hold more air bubbles during baking, producing cakes with a higher volume and finer crumb. Chlorine also weakens gluten, helping to produce a softer, more tender crumb. While bleaching results in a finer crumb, some people can taste an off-flavor when bleached flour is used, owing to the residual chemicals.

A few years ago King Arthur introduced unbleached cake flour. This well-known Vermont miller developed a proprietary technique to mimic the moisture-grabbing abilities of bleached cake flour without the use of any chemicals. In our kitchen tests, we found that their naturally oxidized, unbleached cake flour performed just as well as classic bleached cake flour, with no chemical aftertaste. If you have a choice, we recommend buying unbleached cake flour. That said, most recipes that call for cake flour rely on so much butter and sugar that it is very hard to detect any off-flavor from the bleaching—you have to be looking for it.

TEST KITCHEN EXPERIMENT

We wanted to illustrate the importance of using lower-protein flour for tender baked goods so we did the unthinkable: We made three batches of our Fluffy Yellow Layer Cake (page 390), substituting an equal weight of bread flour for the cake flour. We also baked off three more according to the recipe and had tasters taste them side by side. Finally, we performed a simple stress test by cutting 2 by 8-inch planks from each cake, suspending them between two 4-ounce ramekins, and noting the point at which they cracked under their own weight.

THE RESULTS

Tasters admitted that this was one of the easiest taste tests they'd been asked to perform. Everyone quickly fingered the sample made with bread flour, noting its unpleasant, tough, resilient texture. In contrast, the sample made with cake flour was tender and easily melted in the mouth. The stress test confirmed our tasters' perceptions—the bread flour cake easily supported its own weight for 30 minutes (and likely would have lasted longer if we'd bothered to wait), while the sample with cake flour buckled and crumbled in less than five minutes.

THE TAKEAWAY

This goes to show that paying attention to the protein content of flour is an important step toward minimizing gluten development and creating super-tender baked goods.

THE EFFECT OF PROTEIN LEVELS ON CAKE

BREAD FLOUR
The cake made with high-protein bread flour was tough and resilient. It supported its own weight for 30 minutes.

CAKE FLOUR
The cake made with low-protein cake flour was incredibly tender. It crumbled under its own weight within five minutes.

After all, bread flour has between 12 and 14 percent protein, while cake flour logs in at only 6 to 8 percent protein. Substituting bread for cake flour significantly ups the amount of protein, and therefore the strength of the gluten network in the finished cake. No wonder the Fluffy Yellow Layer Cake made with bread flour was far from tender.

PRACTICAL SCIENCE WHY BLEACH FLOUR?

Bleaching quickly removes the yellow color from flour, makes its proteins less likely to form gluten, and helps its starch absorb more liquid.

We generally prefer unbleached flour in our baked goods. But what is bleaching and why is it done? When flour is first milled, it has a yellowish cast that some consumers find unappealing. Within a few months of milling, however, the yellow pigments, or carotenoids, in all-purpose flour naturally whiten. Because it is expensive to naturally "age" flour, some producers expedite the process chemically. In flours labeled "bleached," benzoyl peroxide or chlorine gas has likely been used to fade the yellow color. Bleaching can leave a faint off-taste that you can pick up in really simple baked goods, such as biscuits. Bleaching also alters the protein and starch structure of the flour, making the proteins less likely to form tough gluten, and the starch more able to absorb more liquid. These traits are desirable in tender baked goods such as cakes or biscuits.

When making cakes that should be tender and delicate, using cake flour is an easy way to reduce the protein content in the batter and thus minimize gluten production.

FLUFFY YELLOW LAYER CAKE WITH CHOCOLATE FROSTING
SERVES 10 TO 12

Bring all the ingredients to room temperature before beginning this recipe. Be sure to use cake pans with at least 2-inch-tall sides. This frosting may be made with milk, semisweet, or bittersweet chocolate; we prefer a frosting made with milk chocolate for this recipe. Cool the chocolate to between 85 and 100 degrees before adding it to the butter mixture.

CAKE

2½	cups (10 ounces) cake flour
1¼	teaspoons baking powder
¼	teaspoon baking soda
¾	teaspoon salt
1¾	cups (12¼ ounces) granulated sugar
1	cup buttermilk, room temperature
10	tablespoons unsalted butter, melted and cooled
3	tablespoons vegetable oil
2	teaspoons vanilla extract
3	large eggs, separated, plus 3 large yolks, room temperature
	Pinch cream of tartar

FROSTING

20	tablespoons (2½ sticks) unsalted butter, softened (68 degrees)
1	cup (4 ounces) confectioners' sugar
¾	cup (2¼ ounces) Dutch-processed cocoa
	Pinch salt
¾	cup light corn syrup
1	teaspoon vanilla extract
8	ounces milk, bittersweet, or semisweet chocolate, melted and cooled

1. FOR THE CAKE: Adjust oven rack to middle position and heat oven to 350 degrees. Grease two 9-inch round cake pans, line with parchment paper, grease parchment, and flour pans. Whisk flour, baking powder, baking soda, salt, and 1½ cups sugar together in large bowl. In medium bowl, whisk together buttermilk, melted butter, oil, vanilla, and egg yolks.

2. Using stand mixer fitted with whisk, whip egg whites and cream of tartar on medium-low speed until foamy,

about 1 minute. Increase speed to medium-high and whip whites to soft billowy mounds, about 1 minute. Gradually add remaining ¼ cup sugar and whip until glossy, stiff peaks form, 2 to 3 minutes. Transfer to bowl and set aside.

3. Add flour mixture to now-empty mixer bowl. With mixer on low speed, gradually pour in butter mixture and mix until almost incorporated (a few streaks of dry flour will remain), about 15 seconds. Scrape down bowl, then beat on medium-low speed until smooth and fully incorporated, 10 to 15 seconds.

4. Using rubber spatula, stir one-third of whites into batter, then add remaining two-thirds of whites and gently fold into batter until no white streaks remain. Divide batter evenly between prepared pans, smooth tops with rubber spatula, and gently tap pans on counter to release air bubbles.

5. Bake cakes until toothpick inserted in center comes out clean, 20 to 22 minutes. Let cakes cool in pans on wire rack for 10 minutes. Remove cakes from pans, discard parchment, and let cool completely, about 2 hours, before frosting. (Cooled cakes can be wrapped tightly in plastic wrap and kept at room temperature for up to 1 day. Wrapped tightly in plastic, then aluminum foil, cakes can be frozen for up to 1 month. Defrost cakes at room temperature before unwrapping and frosting.)

PRACTICAL SCIENCE
PUTTING THE YELLOW IN YOLKS

Bright yellow yolks have everything to do with a hen's diet.

As we developed the recipe for our Fluffy Yellow Layer Cake, we were surprised by the lack of any real yellow color in the cake. A closer look at the standard supermarket eggs we were using provided a clue: The yolks were all relatively pale. When we compared them with yolks from free-range eggs bought fresh at the farmers' market, the contrast was striking. The yolks were much darker. What accounts for the difference in color? It all boils down to the hens' diet. Bright golden yellow yolks show that the hens are well supplied with carotenoids. These substances are found in a wide range of plants that a true free-range hen could find merely by pecking around the farmyard.

Cakes made with light and dark yolks actually tasted the same, the difference was merely aesthetic.

| FARM-FRESH | MASS-PRODUCED |

---

6. FOR THE FROSTING: Process butter, sugar, cocoa, and salt in food processor until smooth, about 30 seconds, scraping down bowl as needed. Add corn syrup and vanilla and process until just combined, 5 to 10 seconds. Scrape down bowl, then add chocolate and process until smooth and creamy, 10 to 15 seconds. (Frosting can be kept at room temperature for up to 3 hours before frosting cake or refrigerated for up to 3 days. If refrigerated, let stand at room temperature for 1 hour before using.)

7. TO ASSEMBLE THE CAKE: Line edges of cake platter with 4 strips of parchment paper to keep platter clean. Place 1 cake layer on prepared platter. Place about 1½ cups frosting in center of cake layer and, using large spatula, spread in even layer right to edge of cake. Place second cake layer on top, making sure layers are aligned, then frost top in same manner as first layer, this time spreading frosting until slightly over edge. Gather more frosting on tip of spatula and gently spread icing onto side of cake. Smooth frosting by gently running edge of spatula around cake and leveling ridge that forms around top edge, or create billows by pressing back of spoon into frosting and twirling spoon as you lift away. Carefully pull out pieces of parchment from beneath cake before serving. (Assembled cake can be refrigerated for up to 1 day. Bring to room temperature before serving.)

✔ WHY THIS RECIPE WORKS

Box mixes are famous for engineering cakes with ultra-light texture. We set out to make an even fluffier cake—one without chemicals and additives. Chiffon cakes are especially weightless, springy, and moist. But unlike butter cakes, they are too light to stand up to a serious slathering of frosting. We decided to blend the two types of cake. To do this, we use whipped egg whites, buttermilk, and a combination of fats for the cake. For the frosting, we use a hefty amount of cocoa powder to keep it tasting like chocolate, and a bit of corn syrup to keep it glossy and smooth.

KNOW HOW BOXED MIXES WORK   Boxed mixes have defined the way many of us look at yellow layer cakes. These mixes rely on a number of chemicals to create volume and tenderness. Emulsifiers like mono- and diglycerides improve the effectiveness of the leaveners so you can get a taller, fluffier cake. Hydrogenated fat guarantees tenderness because it's 100 percent fat while butter is only 80 percent fat (it also contains water, which promotes gluten development). And cake mixes rely on food colorings, too. Don't expect real eggs to do this. (See "Putting the Yellow in Yolks," opposite.) Our goal was to create more height and tenderness with natural ingredients.

MAKE AN EGG FOAM   While reverse creaming (see concept 47) can create a tender cake, it will not create a tall, fluffy cake. For that, we realized we needed to adapt a technique used in cakes such as angel food and chiffon, which rely on egg foams for their height. We use the standard butter-cake ingredients but combine them by the method used to make chiffon cake—combine the dry ingredients, combine the wet ingredients, mix the dry and wet together, then fold in whipped eggs whites. (This is basically the quick-bread method, with the added step of whipping the egg whites and folding them into the batter at the end.) This method gives us a light, delicate cake with just enough heft to stand up to a slathering of frosting.

USE TWO FATS   A cake made with all butter was fluffy, but it didn't have the moisture we wanted. We know that oil, even more than butter, can be a key factor in the moisture level of a cake. (Butter contains between 16 and 18 percent water, which can evaporate in the oven and leave a cake dry.) But after testing a combination of both types of fat, we found that 10 tablespoons of butter plus 3 tablespoons of oil keeps our butter flavor intact and improves the moistness of the cake.

BAKE WITH BUTTERMILK   We began testing this cake with milk but found that switching milk for buttermilk produced a crumb that was slightly porous and so fine it was almost downy. The buttermilk's tang also brings a new flavor dimension to our cake. (But by adding acidic buttermilk, we need to replace some of the baking powder with baking soda to ensure an even rise. See concept 42.)

ADD SUGAR   With the addition of vegetable oil, our cake was moist, but could it be more soft and tender? Sugar is well known for increasing tenderness in cakes by attracting and bonding with water, thus preventing the water from hydrating the proteins in the flour. With less liquid available to them, fewer proteins are able to link together, resulting in weaker gluten. Adding an additional ½ cup of sugar did the trick.

DON'T FORGET COCOA POWDER   We wanted a simple frosting with butter, confectioners' sugar (used because it dissolves better than granulated and keeps frosting smooth), and melted chocolate. We added cocoa powder for more oomph. The cocoa powder remains undetectable, except for its rich flavor. This is because the cocoa butter crystals in cocoa powder blend with the fat in butter to coat and lubricate particles of cocoa powder, helping to mask any grittiness. (See concept 50.)

CORN SYRUP IS KEY   Even confectioners' sugar gives frosting a slightly gritty texture—though it dissolves more easily than granulated sugar, there just isn't much liquid in a butter frosting. We replace some of the confectioners' sugar with corn syrup to help dissolve the sugar.

CHIFFON CAKE

SERVES 12

If your tube pan has a removable bottom, you do not need to line it with parchment. Serve this cake as is or dust with confectioners' sugar.

1½	cups (10½ ounces) sugar
1⅓	cups (5⅓ ounces) cake flour
2	teaspoons baking powder
½	teaspoon salt
7	large eggs (2 whole, 5 separated), room temperature
¾	cup water
½	cup vegetable oil
1	tablespoon vanilla extract
½	teaspoon almond extract
½	teaspoon cream of tartar

1. Adjust oven rack to lower-middle position and heat oven to 325 degrees. Line bottom of 16-cup tube pan with parchment paper but do not grease. Whisk sugar, flour, baking powder, and salt together in large bowl. Whisk in eggs and yolks, water, oil, vanilla, and almond extract until batter is just smooth.

2. Using stand mixer fitted with whisk, whip egg whites and cream of tartar on medium-low speed until foamy, about 1 minute. Increase speed to medium-high and whip until stiff peaks form, 3 to 4 minutes. Using large rubber spatula, fold whites into batter, smearing any stubborn pockets of egg white against side of bowl.

3. Pour batter into prepared pan, smooth top with rubber spatula, and gently tap pan on counter to release air bubbles.

4. Bake cake until skewer inserted in center comes out clean, 55 minutes to 1 hour 5 minutes. If cake has prongs around rim for elevating cake, invert pan on them. If not, invert pan over neck of bottle or funnel so that air can circulate all around it. Let cake cool completely, about 2 hours.

5. Run knife around edge of cake to loosen, then gently tap pan upside down on counter to release cake. Peel off parchment, turn cake right side up onto serving platter, and serve. (Cake can be stored at room temperature for up to 2 days or refrigerated for up to 4 days.)

MOCHA-NUT CHIFFON CAKE

Substitute ¾ cup brewed espresso or strong coffee for water and omit almond extract. Add ½ cup finely chopped toasted walnuts and 1 ounce unsweetened grated chocolate to batter before folding in whites.

LEMON OR LEMON-COCONUT CHIFFON CAKE

Substitute ½ teaspoon baking soda for baking powder, decrease water to ⅔ cup and vanilla to 1 teaspoon, and omit almond extract. Add 3 tablespoons grated lemon zest plus 2 tablespoons juice (3 lemons) along with vanilla in step 1. (For Lemon-Coconut Chiffon Cake, also add ¾ cup sweetened shredded coconut, coarsely chopped, to batter before folding in whites.)

ORANGE OR CRANBERRY-ORANGE CHIFFON CAKE

Substitute 2 tablespoons grated orange zest plus ¾ cup orange juice (2 oranges) for water. Decrease vanilla to 1 teaspoon and omit almond extract. (For Cranberry-Orange Chiffon Cake, also add 1 cup minced cranberries and ½ cup finely chopped toasted walnuts to batter before folding in whites.)

PRACTICAL SCIENCE FLOUR SWAP

Gold Medal and King Arthur flours have different protein levels.

For the sake of standardization, we develop all of our baking recipes requiring all-purpose flour with Gold Medal, the best-selling brand in the United States. The number-two flour brand, Pillsbury, has the same protein content as Gold Medal (about 10.5 percent), and we've found that it performs on par with Gold Medal. However, we know many of our readers keep King Arthur in the pantry. King Arthur all-purpose flour contains 11.7 percent protein—2 percent more than Gold Medal. Protein affects gluten development: The more protein there is, the more gluten will be created during mixing and kneading. Despite the small difference, can the two brands be used interchangeably?

It depends on what you're baking. In tests of recipes with relatively little gluten development, such as cookies, muffins, and biscuits, both flours produced virtually identical batches. But in bread recipes specifically engineered by the test kitchen to use all-purpose flour (not bread flour) to create a tender crumb, such as sandwich bread and challah, the switch mattered. The extra protein in King Arthur produced more gluten when the dough was kneaded, leading to loaves that were gummy and rubbery in comparison to loaves made from Gold Medal. After a few tests, we found an easy fix to bread recipes made with all-purpose flour: Replacing 1 tablespoon of flour per cup with 1 tablespoon of cornstarch made King Arthur behave just like Gold Medal.

CHOCOLATE MARBLE CHIFFON CAKE

Combine ¼ cup cocoa and 2 tablespoons packed dark brown sugar in small bowl, then stir in 3 tablespoons boiling water and mix until smooth. Follow recipe as directed, dividing batter equally into 2 separate bowls at end of step 2. Mix scant ½ cup batter from 1 bowl into cocoa mixture, then partially fold mixture back into same bowl (so that you have 1 bowl of white batter and one of chocolate batter). Sift 3 tablespoons flour over chocolate batter and continue to fold until just mixed. Pour half the white and then half the chocolate batter into the pan; repeat. Do not tap pan on counter before baking. Bake as directed.

✔ WHY THIS RECIPE WORKS

Like the Hollywood stars of the 1920s who were the first to taste Harry Baker's secret-recipe cakes at the Brown Derby, we were delighted by the uniquely light yet full richness and deep flavor of this American invention, which came to be known as the chiffon cake. With the airy height of angel food cake (from using whipped egg whites) and the richness of pound cake (from incorporating egg yolks and oil), this cake seemed like a win-win. And by tweaking the original General Mills recipe, decreasing the flour, increasing the egg yolks, and whipping only some of the egg whites, we succeeded in making it one.

KNOW THE HISTORY The chiffon cake is a cross between angel food and pound cake. It is huge, high, and light as a feather, but also tender and moist, qualities that huge, high cakes typically lack. Chiffon cake was invented by Henry Baker, a Los Angeles insurance salesman turned caterer who had been wholesaling fudge from the kitchen of the apartment that he shared with his aging mother, in 1927. When the cake became a featured attraction at the Brown Derby, then the restaurant of the stars, Baker converted a spare room into his top-secret bakery, with 12 tin hotplate ovens, and personally baked 42 cakes a day. The cakes sold for a remarkable two dollars each to prestigious hostesses and the MGM and RKO studio commissaries.

Baker kept his recipe a secret for 20 years. Finally, having been evicted from his apartment, and fearing memory loss, Baker sold the recipe to General Mills. There ensued considerable testing, but with only a couple of minor changes to the technique and a new name—"chiffon cake"—the cake appeared before the American public in a 1948 pamphlet called "Betty Crocker Chiffon," containing 14 recipes and variations in addition to umpteen icings, fillings, serving ideas, and helpful hints. It was an instant hit and became one of the most popular cakes of the time.

TINKER WITH A CLASSIC We tried the original 1920s recipe and found it too dry and cottony. Using cake flour, with its lower amount of protein and therefore less gluten, is key, but this recipe also simply needs less flour. We reduce the amount of flour used and add an extra egg yolk to help make up for the reduction in the structure of the cake. We also whip only some of the egg whites, adding the rest as is, to keep the structure without causing the cake to spill over the top of the pan.

BEAT THOSE WHITES In the original recipe the directions for beating the egg whites read, "Whip until whites form very stiff peaks. They should be much stiffer than for angel food or meringue. DO NOT UNDER-BEAT." These instructions, with their anxiety-inducing capitalized words, are well taken. If the whites are not very stiff, the cake will not rise properly and the bottom will be heavy, dense, wet, and custardlike. Better to overbeat than underbeat. In fact, if you overwhip the egg whites and they end up dry and "blocky," you can simply smudge and smear any stubborn clumps with the flat side of the spatula to break them up without worrying about deflating the beaten whites, as you would when making an angel food cake. The cream of tartar (see concept 21) helps create an especially stable egg foam.

PRACTICAL SCIENCE BAKING WITH COLD EGGS

In basic cakes, cold eggs are fine. Finicky cakes need 'em warm.

Cake recipes often call for room-temperature eggs, which incorporate into the batter more readily than cold eggs.

We wondered, though, if the difference between room-temperature and cold eggs was so great that it could actually ruin a basic cake recipe. To find out, we conducted a blind tasting of two yellow cakes: one made with room-temperature eggs, the other with eggs pulled straight from the refrigerator. The cake prepared with cold eggs produced a slightly thicker batter and took five minutes longer to bake. The cake made with room-temperature eggs had a slightly finer, more even crumb, but the cold-egg cake was entirely acceptable. Overall, tasters strained to detect differences between the two cakes, so it's fine to use cold eggs in most basic cake recipes.

However, cold eggs can cause problems in finicky cakes, such as angel food, chiffon, and pound cake, which rely on air incorporated into the beaten eggs as a primary means of leavening. In these cases, we found that cold eggs didn't whip nearly as well as room-temperature eggs and the cakes didn't rise properly. As a result, these cakes were too dense when made with cold eggs.

To quickly warm whole eggs, place them in a bowl and cover them with hot—but not boiling—tap water for five minutes. Since it is easier to separate eggs when they are cold, eggs can be separated first and allowed to warm up while the remaining ingredients are assembled. If necessary, the whites or yolks can be placed in a bowl nestled within another bowl filled with warm water to speed up the process.

Using cake flour is one way to reduce the protein level in cookies and bars. But there are other options, especially for cookies where a crumbly, sandy texture is key.

CLASSIC BROWNIES
MAKES 24 BROWNIES

Be sure to test for doneness before removing the brownies from the oven. If underbaked (the toothpick has batter, not just crumbs, clinging to it), the brownies will have a dense and gummy texture; if overbaked (the toothpick comes out completely clean), the brownies will be dry and cakey. To melt the chocolate in a microwave, heat it at 50 percent power for two minutes. Stir the chocolate, add the butter, and continue heating until melted, stirring once every additional minute.

1¼	cups (5 ounces) cake flour
¾	teaspoon baking powder
½	teaspoon salt
6	ounces unsweetened chocolate, chopped fine
12	tablespoons unsalted butter, cut into 6 pieces
2¼	cups (15¾ ounces) sugar
4	large eggs
1	tablespoon vanilla extract
1	cup pecans or walnuts, toasted and chopped coarse (optional)

1. Adjust oven rack to middle position and heat oven to 325 degrees. Make foil sling by folding 2 long sheets of aluminum foil so that they are as wide as 13 by 9-inch baking pan (one 13-inch sheet and one 9-inch sheet). Lay sheets of foil in pan perpendicular to one another, with extra foil hanging over edges of pan. Push foil into corners and up sides of pan, smoothing foil flush to pan. Grease foil and set aside.

2. Whisk flour, baking powder, and salt in medium bowl until combined; set aside.

3. Melt chocolate and butter in medium heatproof bowl set over saucepan of barely simmering water, stirring occasionally, until smooth. Off heat, gradually whisk in sugar. Add eggs, 1 at a time, whisking after each addition, until thoroughly combined. Whisk in vanilla. Add flour mixture in 3 additions, folding with rubber spatula until batter is completely smooth and homogeneous.

4. Transfer batter to prepared pan; spread batter into corners of pan and smooth surface. Sprinkle toasted nuts, if using, evenly over batter. Bake until toothpick inserted in center of brownies comes out with few moist crumbs attached, 30 to 35 minutes, rotating pan halfway through baking. Let brownies cool in pan on wire rack to room temperature, about 2 hours. Remove brownies from pan using foil. Cut brownies into 2-inch squares and serve. (Brownies can be stored at room temperature for up to 3 days.)

✔ WHY THIS RECIPE WORKS

Chewy and chocolaty, brownies should be a simple and utterly satisfying affair. But too often, brownies are heavy, dense, and remarkably low on chocolate flavor. We wanted old-fashioned brownies that had serious chocolate flavor. To get that tender texture and delicate chew, we shelved the all-purpose flour in favor of cake flour; a bit of baking powder further lightened the crumb. Getting the number of eggs just right prevented our brownies from being cakey or dry. Plenty of unsweetened chocolate provided maximum chocolate flavor.

USE UNSWEETENED CHOCOLATE Ounce for ounce, unsweetened chocolate has more chocolate flavor than bittersweet or semisweet chocolate (which are one-third to one-half sugar). Using a hefty amount of unsweetened chocolate gives us brownies that aren't too sweet but have profound chocolate notes. A big dose of vanilla (a full tablespoon) helps reinforce the chocolate flavor. (See "Chocolate 101," page 435.)

ADD CAKE FLOUR Chocolate contains starch, and if you're using a lot of chocolate (which we do here) it can negatively impact the texture of brownies. Switching from the usual all-purpose flour to cake flour (which has a lower protein content) makes the brownies fine-textured (not gritty) and tender. A little baking powder also lightens the texture a bit so they are not overly dense and fudgy.

TOAST THE NUTS If we mix nuts into the batter before baking the brownies, they steam and become soft. Sprinkling the nuts on top just before baking keeps them dry and crunchy; toasting them first makes them even crunchier while also enhancing their flavor.

DON'T OVERBAKE Chocolate flavor really suffers when baked goods are overbaked. Using a 325-degree oven ensures even baking (the edges don't dry out, which can be a problem when making a large tray of brownies, as we are here). Also, don't overbake brownies—you want a toothpick to come out of the brownies with a few moist crumbs still attached.

MAKE A FOIL SLING To make it easier to remove brownies from the baked pan, we line it with two pieces of aluminum foil, which are greased. Once the brownies have cooled, use the foil to lift the entire slab onto a cutting board; remove the foil and cut the brownies into neat squares.

BEST SHORTBREAD
MAKES 16 WEDGES

Use the collar of a springform pan to form the shortbread into an even round. Mold the shortbread with the collar in the closed position, then open the collar, but leave it in place. This allows the shortbread to expand slightly but keeps it from spreading too far. The extracted round of dough in step 2 is baked alongside the rest of the shortbread. The shortbread will keep for up to one week.

½ cup (1½ ounces) old-fashioned rolled oats
1½ cups (7½ ounces) all-purpose flour
¼ cup cornstarch
⅔ cup (2⅔ ounces) confectioners' sugar
½ teaspoon salt
14 tablespoons unsalted butter, chilled and cut into ⅛-inch-thick slices

1. Adjust oven rack to middle position and heat oven to 450 degrees. Pulse oats in spice grinder or blender until reduced to fine powder, about 10 pulses (you should have ¼ to ⅓ cup oat flour). Using stand mixer fitted with paddle, mix oat flour, all-purpose flour, cornstarch, sugar, and salt on low speed until combined, about 5 seconds. Add butter to dry ingredients and continue to mix until dough just forms and pulls away from sides of bowl, 5 to 10 minutes.

2. Place upside-down (grooved edge should be at top) collar of 9- or 9½-inch springform pan on parchment paper–lined baking sheet (do not use springform pan bottom). Press dough into collar in even ½-inch-thick layer, smoothing top of dough with back of spoon. Place 2-inch biscuit cutter in center of dough and cut out center. Place extracted round alongside springform collar on baking sheet and replace cutter in center of dough. Open springform collar, but leave it in place.

3. Bake shortbread for 5 minutes, then reduce oven temperature to 250 degrees. Continue to bake until edges turn pale golden, 10 to 15 minutes longer. Remove baking sheet from oven; turn oven off. Remove springform pan collar; use chef's knife to score surface of shortbread into 16 even wedges, cutting halfway through shortbread. Using wooden skewer, poke 8 to 10 holes in each wedge. Return shortbread to oven and prop door open with handle of wooden spoon, leaving 1-inch gap at top. Allow shortbread to dry in turned-off oven until pale golden in center (shortbread should be firm but giving to touch), about 1 hour.

4. Transfer baking sheet to wire rack; let shortbread cool to room temperature. Cut shortbread at scored marks to separate before serving.

✔ WHY THIS RECIPE WORKS

Often shortbread turns out bland and chalky. We wanted superlative shortbread with an alluring tawny brown crumb and pure, buttery richness. In initial tests, we tinkered with various mixing methods and found that reverse creaming (see concept 47)—mixing the flour and sugar before adding the butter, creating less aeration—yielded the most reliable results. To smooth out an objectionable granular texture, we swapped the white sugar for confectioners' sugar. To curb gluten development, we replaced some of our flour with powdered old-fashioned oats. Crisp and buttery, our shortbread is anything but bland.

MIX WELL At its simplest, shortbread contains just four ingredients—flour, sugar, salt, and butter. But unlike crisp butter cookies, shortbread should have an ultra-fine, sandy texture. It needs to hold together while still being tender and delicate. In traditional recipes, the cold butter is cut into the dry ingredients as if making pie dough. However, we found that beating the cold butter into the dry ingredients (a method called reverse creaming) works best.

USE CONFECTIONERS' SUGAR Granulated sugar won't fully dissolve in this cookie dough—there's not enough liquid, not even an egg. Fine-textured confectioners' sugar gives shortbread a much more delicate crumb.

PICK OATS AND CORNSTARCH The small amount of water in the butter activates the gluten in the flour, which can make shortbread tough. Some recipes use gluten-free rice flour but we found that flavor is sacrificed. Oats contain very few of the proteins necessary for gluten development, plus they have a nice flavor. We grind the oats to a fine meal in a spice grinder or blender and then use them (along with some cornstarch) to replace some of the flour.

GET THE RIGHT SHAPE When baking our shortbread, we had a problem with spreading. As buttery shortbread bakes, it expands, losing its shape as the edges flatten out. We tried baking the dough in a traditional shortbread mold with ½-inch-high sides, but it still widened into an amorphous mass. Needing a substantial barrier to keep its edges corralled, we use a springform pan collar. First, set the closed collar on a parchment-lined baking sheet, then pat the dough into it, cut a hole in the center of the dough with a 2-inch biscuit cutter, and then open the collar to give the cookie about half an inch to spread out.

BAKE HIGH, THEN LOW, THEN OFF We bake our shortbread in an oven that is off for far longer than it is on. After all, early shortbread was made by leaving the dough in a still-warm oven heated only by dying embers. After removing the springform collar, we return our shortbread to a turned-off oven for an hour to let it dry out and finish.

Creaming Butter Helps Cakes Rise

Classic cake recipes begin by creaming softened butter with sugar. Later, the eggs and flavorings are gradually incorporated, and then the dry ingredients are added, alternating with the milk. The goal of this careful process is to ensure that the ingredients are well combined and aerated. Creaming is the first and perhaps most important step if you want the cake to rise high and have a uniform texture.

HOW THE SCIENCE WORKS

Creaming butter and sugar accomplishes two things. First, it makes the butter malleable, allowing other ingredients to be easily blended when the time comes to add them. Second, the tiny sugar crystals act like extra beaters, helping to incorporate air into the butter as it is creamed. Filled with the gas produced by the baking powder and baking soda, these tiny pockets of air expand when baked. This is what gives a cake its lift.

Butter is the preferred fat for cake baking because it is able to form "beta-prime" crystals of fat, which are tiny and needlelike and necessary for trapping and holding the air bubbles whipped inside. But beyond that—butter tastes good. It is the choice fat because of its flavor. Modern vegetable shortening, which is likewise highly effective at trapping and holding air bubbles, does not impart that rich taste. Oil, another fat commonly found in the kitchen, is not often used in cakes that need to be leavened, as oils cannot hold bubbles when whipped like a solid fat. And, finally, lard forms much larger and coarser beta-crystals than butter or shortening do. These crystals are not effective at holding air, rendering lard

unhelpful when trying to bake fine-textured cakes.

Though the act of creaming butter and sugar is easy in itself, it's important to pay careful attention to the temperature of the butter. After all, you can't cream cold butter. It's too firm to admit any air, and it doesn't form the right crystal structure. You also can't cream warm butter. Once the butter starts to melt, which happens around 85 degrees, it likewise won't hold any of those air bubbles because all the crystals have melted. So what temperature is ideal?

Butter that is between 60 and 65 degrees is ready for creaming. This means that it is somewhat softened but still cool. It will yield to slight pressure applied by your finger and will crack when pressed. Since beating warms up the butter, we factor this into the equation. By the time creaming is finished, the butter will have risen to about 68 degrees to help create a cake batter that is light and fluffy.

Proper creaming is essential in recipes without chemical leaveners (like pound cake) or in cakes that demand a tall rise, like a Bundt cake.

WHEN BUTTER
AND SUGAR ARE
COMBINED

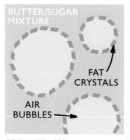

CREAMED *When butter and sugar are whipped together, tiny air bubbles are created and held in place by small fat crystals.*

TEST KITCHEN EXPERIMENT

To determine the importance of butter temperature when creaming butter and sugar for pound cakes, which don't use chemical leaveners to help incorporate air bubbles and provide lift, we devised a simple experiment. We made eight batches of our Classic Pound Cake (page 398): four using stand mixers and four using hand-held mixers. For half of these recipes, we used room-temperature butter (70 degrees) and for the other half we used cool yet still pliable butter (60 degrees), and then compared the results.

THE RESULTS

Whether prepared with a stand mixer or hand-held mixer, the pound cakes made with room-temperature butter produced soft, slick batter that looked shiny and wet. The cakes looked flat and dense. The cakes made with cool butter (and either a stand or hand-held mixer) produced a batter that was light, fluffy, and off-white in color. The finished cakes were nicely domed. Because the ingredients were the same, tasters found that all of the cakes had similar flavor.

THE TAKEAWAY

Temperature matters. When butter is too soft during creaming, the batter will be unable to hold any of the air bubbles produced when whipped. This means that the finished product will be flat and dense.

Butter that is cool (but not cold) is ideal. When creamed, the butter retains its crystal structure as the sugar becomes incorporated, supporting the addition of air bubbles created by the combination of movement and the small, hard sugar crystals. This means that the finished cake will have nice lift and domed shape. This holds true whether you're using a stand mixer or a hand-held mixer.

To make sure that your butter is the correct temperature, remove it from the fridge and leave it on the counter for 30 minutes to one hour. If you're in hurry, cut the butter into chunks, place the chunks in the mixing bowl you plan to use, and wrap a warm towel around the bowl. The butter should be softened in 15 to 30 minutes.

SUCCESSFUL CREAMING IS ALL ABOUT THE BUTTER TEMPERATURE

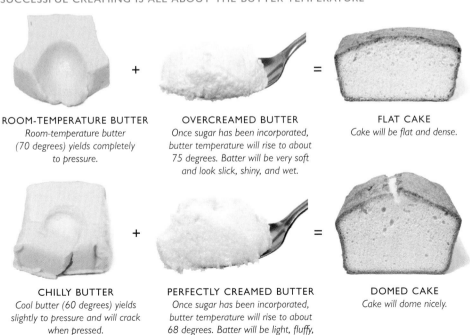

ROOM-TEMPERATURE BUTTER
Room-temperature butter (70 degrees) yields completely to pressure.

OVERCREAMED BUTTER
Once sugar has been incorporated, butter temperature will rise to about 75 degrees. Batter will be very soft and look slick, shiny, and wet.

FLAT CAKE
Cake will be flat and dense.

CHILLY BUTTER
Cool butter (60 degrees) yields slightly to pressure and will crack when pressed.

PERFECTLY CREAMED BUTTER
Once sugar has been incorporated, butter temperature will rise to about 68 degrees. Batter will be light, fluffy, and off-white in color.

DOMED CAKE
Cake will dome nicely.

The key to successful creaming is to start with softened but still cold butter that is about 60 degrees. Beating the butter with some sugar helps aerate it and will ensure cakes rise nicely.

CLASSIC POUND CAKE
SERVES 8

The butter and eggs should be the first ingredients prepared so they have a chance to stand at room temperature and lose their chill while the oven heats, the loaf pan is greased and floured, and the other ingredients are measured. The test kitchen's preferred loaf pan measures 8½ by 4½ inches; if you use a 9 by 5-inch loaf pan, start checking for doneness five minutes earlier than advised in the recipe.

16	tablespoons unsalted butter, cut into 16 pieces and chilled
3	large eggs plus 3 large yolks
2	teaspoons vanilla extract
½	teaspoon salt
1¼	cups (8¾ ounces) sugar
1¾	cups (7 ounces) cake flour

1. Place butter in bowl of stand mixer; let stand at room temperature for 20 to 30 minutes to soften slightly (butter should reach no more than 60 degrees). Using dinner fork, beat eggs, yolks, and vanilla in 4-cup liquid measuring cup until combined. Let egg mixture stand at room temperature until ready to use.

2. Adjust oven rack to middle position and heat oven to 325 degrees. Grease and flour 8½ by 4½-inch loaf pan.

3. Fit stand mixer with paddle and beat butter and salt at medium-high speed until shiny, smooth, and creamy, 2 to 3 minutes, scraping down bowl once. Reduce speed to medium and gradually pour in sugar (this should take about 1 minute). Once all sugar is added, increase speed to medium-high and beat until mixture is light and fluffy, 5 to 8 minutes, scraping down bowl once. Reduce speed to medium and gradually add egg mixture in slow, steady stream (this should take 1 to 1½ minutes). Scrape down bowl, then beat mixture at medium-high speed until light and fluffy, 3 to 4 minutes (batter may look slightly curdled). Remove bowl from mixer and scrape down bowl.

4. Sift flour over butter-egg mixture in 3 additions, folding gently with rubber spatula until combined after each addition. Scrape along bottom of bowl to ensure batter is homogeneous.

5. Pour batter into prepared pan and smooth top with rubber spatula. Bake cake until golden brown and toothpick inserted in center comes out clean, 1 hour 10 minutes to 1 hour 20 minutes. Let cake cool in pan on wire rack for 15 minutes, then invert cake onto wire rack and turn cake right side up. Let cake cool completely on rack, about 2 hours, before serving. (Cake can be stored at room temperature for up to 3 days.)

ALMOND POUND CAKE

Reduce vanilla to 1 teaspoon and add 1½ teaspoons almond extract to eggs along with vanilla. Sprinkle 2 tablespoons sliced almonds over surface of batter just before baking.

POUND CAKE WITH ORANGE ESSENCE

Reduce vanilla to 1 teaspoon and add 1 tablespoon grated then minced orange zest to mixer bowl just after adding eggs in step 3.

CLASSIC POUND CAKE IN A TUBE PAN

Double all ingredients and substitute greased and floured 16-cup tube pan for loaf pan. Bake cake at 350 degrees for 15 minutes, then reduce oven temperature to 325 degrees and continue to bake until cake is golden brown and skewer inserted in center of cake comes out clean, 40 to 45 minutes. Let cake cool in pan on wire rack for 30 minutes, then invert cake onto wire rack and turn cake right side up. Let cake cool completely on rack, about 3 hours, before serving.

✔ WHY THIS RECIPE WORKS

A perfect recipe for pound cake is hard to find. Good-looking pound cakes tend to resemble yellow layer cakes: fluffy, bouncy, and open-textured. Those that taste good often bake up as flat and firm as bricks. We wanted to retool this classic recipe to make it great-tasting and ultra-plush, every time. The first key was starting with chilly 60-degree butter, and making sure the eggs were at the same temperature.

CREAM PROPERLY Pound cake looks so humble that many bakers assume it's simple to prepare. The recipe dates back to the 18th century and originally called for a pound each of flour, sugar, butter, and eggs. Good pound cake should have a fine, even crumb and suedelike texture. Too bad many recipes produce leaden doorstops. To get a good rise, you have to cream the butter properly. That's because traditional recipes contain no leavener— all the rise is provided by air incorporated into the butter and the eggs. Modern recipes often cheat and add baking powder. Sure, the pound cake rises, but now the texture is too light—more like yellow layer cake than pound cake.

START WITH EXTRA-COLD BUTTER Many recipes that call for creaming butter start with softened butter (65 to 67 degrees). Because the butter in this recipe needs to be beaten quite a long time (to work in as much air as possible) you need to start with the butter at a lower temperature—60 degrees is best. For best results, check the temperature of the butter with an instant-read thermometer.

USE CHILLY EGGS Even when the butter is properly creamed, this doesn't mean success is guaranteed. The temperature of the eggs plays a role as well. Too-warm eggs can deflate the batter. And if the eggs are too cold or added too quickly, they are difficult to incorporate and the air is knocked out of the butter by the time you have a smooth batter. After trial and error, we've found that 60 degrees is also the perfect temperature for the eggs in this recipe. (See "Baking with Cold Eggs," page 393.)

ADD EGGS SLOWLY Most cake recipes say to add eggs one at a time, mixing well and scraping the bowl after each addition. Frankly, the pound cake never worked well using this method. The delicate batter just couldn't absorb a whole egg at once yet retain its aeration. Some pound cake recipes require a more extreme method—the eggs are beaten together in a measuring cup then slowly dribbled into the creamed butter and sugar, a process that takes up to five minutes. We discovered that if the beaten

PRACTICAL SCIENCE
LOAF PAN SIZES REALLY MATTER

For a well-domed cake, use the correct size of loaf pan.

Small differences in loaf pan sizes really matter when making pound cake as well as quick breads. Use a pan that's too small and the batter will rise out of the pan. Use a pan that's too big and the cake will bake up with a flat top and the crumb will be dry.

The fact that there's no standard size for a loaf pan makes all of this more important (and trickier) than it seems. "Standard" loaf pans can measure as small as 8 by 4 inches or as large as 10 by 5 inches. The two most common sizes are 8½ by 4½ and 9 by 5. Even this small difference in size can affect the rise and appearance of your baked goods.

When our Classic Pound Cake is baked in the pan size we call for, 8½ by 4½ inches, the cake emerges nicely domed with the classic pound cake fissure through the top. But bake that same batter in a slightly larger 9 by 5-inch pan and it emerges a good inch shorter and with a flat top. Because the batter has more room to spread out in the larger pan, it also bakes up a bit dry.

eggs are added very gradually, they can be incorporated in 60 to 90 seconds, as long as the mixture is beaten a few additional minutes once the last egg is added. This technique results in batter that is more stable and produces much better pound cake that rises higher and has a lighter texture. (See "Add Eggs Slowly to Cake Batters," page 401.)

SIFT THE CAKE FLOUR Lower-protein cake flour helps create a pound cake that is tender. Sifting the flour over the batter makes it easier to incorporate the flour. (For more on flour, see concept 45.)

PRACTICAL SCIENCE THE RIGHT TIME TO SIFT

The timing of when you sift flour (either before or after measuring) can make a noticeable difference in the finished cake.

Does it really matter whether you sift your flour before you measure it or after? In a word: yes. When a recipe calls for "1 cup sifted flour," the flour should be sifted before measuring, whereas "1 cup flour, sifted" should be sifted after measuring. Here's why: A cup of flour sifted before measuring will weigh 20 to 25 percent less than a cup of flour sifted after measuring—a difference that can make a huge impact on the texture of finished baked goods. The best way to make sure you've got the right amount of flour? Weigh it.

Here's what various types of flour weigh, both sifted and unsifted.

TYPE OF FLOUR	WEIGHT OF 1 CUP UNSIFTED	WEIGHT OF 1 CUP SIFTED
All-Purpose	5 ounces	4 ounces
Cake	4 ounces	3.25 ounces
Bread	5.5 ounces	4.5 ounces

TOO LITTLE FLOUR

JUST RIGHT

The cake on the right was made by measuring flour by weight before sifting, as the recipe directed. The one on the left was made by measuring flour by volume after sifting, causing us to use 20 percent less flour by weight and resulting in an overly wet, dense texture.

LEMON BUNDT CAKE
SERVES 12

It is important to pour the glaze over the cake after it has cooled for just 10 minutes and is still warm. Serve this cake as is or dress it up with lightly sweetened berries. The cake has a light, fluffy texture when eaten the day it is baked, but if well wrapped and held at room temperature overnight its texture becomes more dense—like that of pound cake—the following day.

CAKE

3	tablespoons grated lemon zest plus 3 tablespoons juice (3 lemons)
3	cups (15 ounces) all-purpose flour
1	teaspoon baking powder
½	teaspoon baking soda
1	teaspoon salt
¾	cup buttermilk
1	teaspoon vanilla extract
3	large eggs plus 1 large yolk, room temperature
18	tablespoons unsalted butter (2¼ sticks), softened but still cool (60 degrees)
2	cups (14 ounces) granulated sugar

GLAZE

2–3	tablespoons lemon juice
1	tablespoon buttermilk
2	cups (8 ounces) confectioners' sugar

1. FOR THE CAKE: Adjust oven rack to lower-middle position; heat oven to 350 degrees. Spray 12-cup nonstick Bundt pan with baking spray with flour. Mince lemon zest to fine paste (you should have about 2 tablespoons). Combine zest and lemon juice in small bowl; set aside to soften, 10 to 15 minutes.

2. Whisk flour, baking powder, baking soda, and salt in large bowl. Combine lemon juice mixture, buttermilk, and vanilla in medium bowl. In small bowl, gently whisk eggs and yolk to combine. Using stand mixer fitted with paddle, beat butter and sugar on medium-high speed until pale and fluffy, about 3 minutes. Reduce speed to medium and add half of eggs, mixing until incorporated, about 15 seconds. Repeat with remaining eggs and scrape down bowl. Reduce speed to low and add flour mixture in 3 additions, alternating with 2 additions of buttermilk mixture, scraping down bowl as needed. Give batter final stir by hand.

3. Scrape batter into prepared pan and smooth top with rubber spatula. Bake cake until top is golden brown and skewer inserted in center comes out with no crumbs attached, 45 to 50 minutes. Let cake cool in pan on wire rack set over baking sheet for 10 minutes, then invert cake onto rack.

4. FOR THE GLAZE: While cake is baking, whisk 2 tablespoons lemon juice, buttermilk, and sugar together until smooth, adding remaining lemon juice gradually as needed until glaze is thick but still pourable (mixture should leave faint trail across bottom of mixing bowl when drizzled from whisk). Pour half of glaze over warm cake and let cool for 1 hour; pour remaining glaze evenly over top of cake and continue to cool to room temperature, at least 2 hours, before serving.

✔ WHY THIS RECIPE WORKS

Lemons are tart, brash, and aromatic. Why, then, is it so hard to capture their assertive flavor in a straightforward Bundt cake? The flavor of lemon juice is drastically muted when exposed to the heat of an oven, and its acidity can wreak havoc on the delicate nature of baked goods. We wanted to develop a Bundt cake with potent lemon flavor without ruining its texture. To do this, we cream the butter well, add zest, and use a double glaze.

PRACTICAL SCIENCE ALTERNATE INGREDIENTS WHEN MAKING CAKE

The standard method of alternating dry and wet ingredients when making cakes is standard for a good reason.

The mixing method for classic butter cakes is to first cream the butter and sugar, then beat in the eggs, and finally add the flour and liquid components alternately, beginning and ending with the flour. We wondered if this alternation of dry and wet really makes a difference in the cake's texture or if good results could be had without it (and without the extra work).

To find out, we made German chocolate cakes and yellow cakes using four mixing methods: (1) following the standard dry/wet alternation technique, (2) mixing in the wet ingredients followed by the dry, (3) mixing in the dry ingredients followed by the wet, and (4) mixing in dry and wet simultaneously.

The worst cakes were made with the last two methods. These cakes were plagued by dark spots, large holes, and uneven crumbs (coarse in some patches, fine in others)—all signs that the ingredients had not been properly incorporated into the batter. Mixing wet ingredients followed by dry (method 2) yielded better cakes with fewer and smaller holes and more tender and even textures. The standard dry/wet alternation technique (method 1), however, made superior cakes. They had far fewer and smaller holes and evenly fine, soft, tender textures. There are good reasons why this cake-mixing method is widely practiced.

START WITH 1-2-3-4 Many baking recipes are based on simple formulas, mnemonic tools used to pass down recipes through the generations. Bundt cakes commonly fall into the 1-2-3-4 cake category: 1 cup of butter, 2 of cups sugar, 3 cups of flour, 4 eggs (plus 1 cup of milk, a liquid component that sets both layer and Bundt cakes apart from pound cake). We follow this formula—almost. We increase the butter by 2 tablespoons and replace the milk with buttermilk for a lighter, more tender crumb and a nice, mild tang.

CREAM THE BUTTER We tried to create a recipe that eliminated the step of creaming the butter, but that didn't work and gave us rubbery, dense cakes. Creaming is indeed necessary to achieve a light and even crumb. The whipping action aerates the batter, contributing lightness to the final cake. After all, the Bundt cake must be tall, almost statuesque, and chemical leaveners need all the help they can get from properly creamed butter.

USE LEMON JUICE SPARINGLY Desperate to get some good lemon flavor into our cake, we were quickly reminded that playing with acid (as in lemon juice) is no casual affair. (Lemon juice has a pH of about 2.2 to 2.4, even lower than vinegar.) Acids interfere with the formation of gluten, the protein that's so vital to a cake's structure. The more acidic the batter, the less structure in the cake, making the cake literally fall-apart tender. But fragile is not what we're going for here. Instead, we harness the acid's gluten-weakening tendency to produce a slightly more delicate crumb. A modest 3 tablespoons does the trick.

ADD ZEST FOR BIG LEMON FLAVOR To really get the lemon flavor into our cake, we use zest (just the yellow part of the peel; the white pith beneath is very bitter and unpleasant). Three lemons' worth of zest gives us a floral, perfumed lemon flavor that does not go so far as to remind us of furniture polish. We mince the grated zest and then steep it in the lemon juice so that its long stranded texture is not distracting in the baked cake.

PREPARE THE PAN Baking spray works well in our Bundt cake pan. The uniformly blended flour-oil mixture makes it easy to achieve an even coating, and the more solid texture of baking sprays keeps grease from pooling in crevices, which can dull the ridges of a Bundt cake. If you don't have baking spray, a mixture of 1 tablespoon of flour and 1 tablespoon of melted butter can replace it. This does a better job of evenly coating the pan than the usual method of coating the pan with softened butter, then dusting with flour. You need perfectly even coverage in order to ensure that the cake releases from the Bundt pan and no bits get stuck in the pan's crevices.

FINISH WITH A DOUBLE GLAZE For the glaze, we first tried mixing just lemon juice and confectioners' sugar but found that it was too sour and overwhelmed the delicate flavor of the cake. Adding zest made it too floral, butter only muted the flavor, but buttermilk did the trick. Supplementing some of the sour juice with the more mild yet tangy buttermilk smooths out the flavor without dulling the brightness. We apply the first round of glaze while the cake is still warm so it will melt into the cake and then dry into a thin, mottled shellac. We reserve half of the glaze for use once the cake has cooled.

Reverse Cream for Delicate Cakes

While creaming butter and sugar (concept 46) is the first step in most cake recipes, it's not the only option. In recent years, another technique has become popular: reverse creaming. This method is our choice when making a classic yellow layer cake and many kinds of holiday cookies because it minimizes rise and yields cakes and cookies with flat tops, which are perfect for glazing or decorating.

HOW THE SCIENCE WORKS

CREAMING VS. REVERSE CREAMING

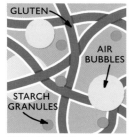

CREAMING *When cake batters begin with the traditional creaming method, there are significant air bubbles incorporated within, and a relatively strong gluten network.*

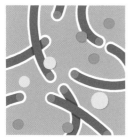

REVERSE CREAMING *When batters begin with reverse creaming, however, there are very few air bubbles and significantly less gluten is formed.*

While creaming, which aerates the butter and sugar and helps to give cakes great rise, is essential in pound cakes (no leaveners added) and in statuesque Bundt cakes, we find this method is not ideal for a layer cake. This is because layer cake recipes always contain at least one chemical leavener, and so getting proper rise is rarely an issue at all. But most of the time you don't even want cake layers to rise all that much. After all, layer cakes contain, well, layers, often multiple layers, which are sandwiched by thick coats of frosting. In the test kitchen, we find that using the creaming method can produce layers that are too tall with a crumb that is too coarse and open to support the layers of the finished cake. Beating all that air into the butter can be superfluous, even detrimental.

So what to do? We prefer to "reverse" the process, using what is also called the "two-stage method." This method was developed by General Mills and Pillsbury in the 1940s and later popularized by Rose Levy Beranbaum in her seminal book *The Cake Bible*, published in 1988. The advent of chlorinated cake flour and modern shortening made this method possible.

Soft, low-protein flour cannot absorb as much liquid as high-protein flours. But low-protein flour that has been bleached with chlorine can hold more liquid (see concept 45). And bleached cake flour is essential for the success of this method because it can hold more water, which is necessary when the weight of the sugar exceeds the weight of the flour. This method of mixing, also known as the high-ratio method because of the high ratio of liquid to flour, produces a more velvety, tender crumb compared with other methods of mixing.

In the two-stage method, the flour, sugar, baking powder, and salt are combined in the mixing bowl and then softened butter is beaten into the dry ingredients, one piece at a time, before the milk and eggs are added in two batches (hence the "two-stage" part of the name). In the test kitchen, however, we don't always find it necessary to add the eggs in two batches, which is why we prefer the name "reverse creaming," highlighting the fact that the flour is added at the outset, not the end of the process. The key element of this technique is that the fat in the softened butter (which should be around 68 degrees) coats the flour and therefore minimizes the development of gluten that begins when the liquid is added (for more on gluten, see concept 38). But just as important, the softened butter contains fewer fat crystals so less air is retained within the batter, which translates to less rise.

And the results? Because this technique does not highly aerate the butter, the cake layers started with reverse creaming end up not quite as tall (perfect for layers of frosting). Because the development of gluten is minimized from the outset, the cakes end up with a crumb that is more delicate and fine, almost velvety smooth and tender, reducing the risk of baking a tough cake. After all, in creaming, flour and milk are added alternately in small batches at the end. The tendency there is to overbeat the batter in order to get it fully incorporated, resulting in an excess of gluten development. The final addition of liquid in reverse creaming happens quickly and requires less beating.

We don't restrict this method to layer cakes alone. Here we explore the use of this alternating technique in crumb cakes, which need to support a layer of buttery crumbs; cupcakes, which can stand up to a thick filling of pastry cream; and sugar cookies that are glazed.

TEST KITCHEN EXPERIMENT

To determine whether the mixing method matters when making a layer cake we compared a simple yellow layer cake mixed two ways. For one batch we used the straightforward creaming method; the other we reverse creamed. We repeated the experiment twice and examined and tasted the results.

THE RESULTS

Holding all ingredients, baking time, and temperature constant, we were able to see that creaming and reverse creaming produce very different products. The cakes mixed by creaming the butter and sugar together first were springy with an open, coarse crumb, while the reverse-creamed cakes baked up extremely tender with a fine crumb and soft, cottony interior.

THE TAKEAWAY

Creaming is a common method used in baking, but it's not always the one we want. Because reverse creaming first mixes the butter with the flour, the fat coats the wheat proteins, preventing them from becoming hydrated, and therefore minimizing the development of gluten. As we learned in concept 38, gluten forms a network in baked goods, giving structure and holding air bubbles within, which contributes to a hefty rise. Without the development of gluten, our reverse-creamed cake did not have as much air trapped within as it baked, resulting in a cake with a fine rather than open crumb. The lack of gluten likewise gives the reverse-creamed cake a much more tender feel in the mouth. Our tasters noticed this immediately. This is why reverse creaming is our go-to method when tenderness is priority number one.

The minimization of gluten development is helpful in more ways than one. Layer cakes are only the beginning. We also choose reverse creaming to make tender but sturdy cupcakes (see Boston Cream Cupcakes, page 407). The denser crumb allows the cupcakes to hold together even when filled with pastry cream. They can be eaten by hand, without crumbling. Reverse creaming also helps us to make butter cookies flat enough to glaze with ease (see Glazed Butter Cookies, page 408). After all, the lack of leaveners along with the lack of air bubbles means that cookies made by reverse creaming don't really rise as they bake and the finished cookies have flat, even tops.

MIXING METHOD MAKES A DIFFERENCE

CREAMING
More rise and open crumb

REVERSE CREAMING
Less rise and finer crumb

Our Fluffy Yellow Layer Cake (page 390) yields an extra-tall, extra-tender cake, but there is another style—what you might call an old-fashioned layer cake. Tenderness is just as important, but the cake is more delicate and richer, and the crumb is particularly fine.

RICH, TENDER YELLOW CAKE WITH BUTTERCREAM FROSTING
SERVES 10 TO 12

Adding the butter pieces to the mixing bowl one at a time prevents the dry ingredients from flying up and out of the bowl.

- ½   cup whole milk, room temperature
- 4   large eggs, room temperature
- 2   teaspoons vanilla extract
- 1¾   cups (7 ounces) cake flour
- 1½   cups (10½ ounces) sugar
- 2   teaspoons baking powder
- ¾   teaspoon salt
- 16   tablespoons unsalted butter, cut into 16 pieces and softened (68 degrees)
- 1   recipe frosting (recipes follow)

1. Adjust oven rack to middle position and heat oven to 350 degrees. Grease two 9-inch round cake pans, line with parchment paper, grease parchment, and flour pans. Whisk milk, eggs, and vanilla together in small bowl.

2. Using stand mixer fitted with paddle, mix flour, sugar, baking powder, and salt on low speed until combined. Add butter, 1 piece at a time, and mix until only pea-size pieces remain, about 1 minute.

3. Add all but ½ cup milk mixture, increase speed to medium-high, and beat until light and fluffy, about 1 minute. Reduce speed to medium-low, add remaining ½ cup milk mixture, and beat until incorporated, about 30 seconds (batter may look slightly curdled). Give batter final stir by hand.

4. Divide batter evenly between prepared pans and smooth tops with rubber spatula. Bake cake until toothpick inserted in centers comes out with few crumbs attached, 20 to 25 minutes. Let cakes cool in pans on wire rack for 10 minutes. Remove cakes from pans, discard parchment, and let cool completely, about 2 hours, before frosting. (Cooled cakes can be wrapped tightly in plastic wrap and kept at room temperature for up to 1 day. Wrapped tightly in plastic, then aluminum foil, cakes can be frozen for up to 1 month. Defrost cakes at room temperature before unwrapping and frosting.)

5. **TO ASSEMBLE THE CAKE:** Line edges of cake platter with 4 strips of parchment paper to keep platter clean. Place 1 cake layer on prepared platter. Place about 1½ cups frosting in center of cake layer and, using large spatula, spread in even layer right to edge of cake. Place second cake layer on top, making sure layers are aligned, then frost top in same manner as first layer, this time spreading frosting until slightly over edge. Gather more frosting on tip of spatula and gently spread icing onto side of cake. Smooth frosting by gently running edge of spatula around cake and leveling ridge that forms around top edge, or create billows by pressing back of spoon into frosting and twirling spoon as you lift away. Carefully pull out pieces of parchment from beneath cake before serving. (Assembled cake can be refrigerated for up to 1 day. Bring to room temperature before serving.)

PRACTICAL SCIENCE   OUT OF CIRCULATION

For even baking, place cakes in the oven side by side.

What's the best way to get a two-layer cake to bake evenly? We baked our Rich, Tender Yellow Cake layers in three positions: side by side on one rack; on two racks with one pan directly above the other; and on two racks with one pan on the top left of the oven and the other on the lower right. Only the cakes on the same rack baked evenly.

The reason is convection (see concept 1)—the hot air currents moving around the oven. In bottom-heating ovens, when cakes are stacked, the bottom one acts as a barrier, creating hot air currents that flow up and over the top cake. The result is an overcooked top cake and an undercooked bottom cake. Results are also uneven in rear-heating ovens or those with top and bottom elements. But when cakes are baked side by side, hot air circulates evenly no matter how your oven heats.

STACKED = UNEVEN
Cakes stacked above each other disrupt heat flow in the oven.

SIDE BY SIDE = EVEN
Cakes kept side by side bake up evenly and brown nicely.

VANILLA BUTTERCREAM FROSTING
MAKES ABOUT 4 CUPS

The whole eggs, whipped until airy, give this buttercream a light, satiny-smooth texture that melts on the tongue.

- 4   large eggs, room temperature
- 1   cup (7 ounces) sugar
- 2   teaspoons vanilla extract
       Pinch salt
- 1   pound unsalted butter (4 sticks), each stick cut into quarters and softened (68 degrees)

1. Combine eggs, sugar, vanilla, and salt in bowl of stand mixer and set bowl over saucepan containing 1 inch of barely simmering water. Whisking gently but constantly, heat mixture until thin and foamy and registers 160 degrees.

2. Fit stand mixer with whisk and whip egg mixture on medium-high speed until light, airy, and cooled to room temperature, about 5 minutes. Reduce speed to medium and add butter, 1 piece at a time. (After adding half of butter, buttercream may look curdled; it will smooth with additional butter.) Once all butter is added, increase speed to high and whip until light, fluffy, and thoroughly combined, about 1 minute. (Frosting can be refrigerated for up to 5 days. Let frosting sit at room temperature until softened, about 2 hours, then, using stand mixer fitted with whisk, whip on medium speed until smooth, 2 to 5 minutes.)

RICH COFFEE BUTTERCREAM FROSTING

Omit vanilla. Substitute 3 tablespoons instant espresso powder in 3 tablespoons warm water and beat dissolved coffee into buttercream after butter has been added.

RICH CHOCOLATE CREAM FROSTING
MAKES ABOUT 3 CUPS

- 1½   cups heavy cream
- 16   ounces semisweet chocolate, chopped fine
- ⅓   cup corn syrup
- 1   teaspoon vanilla extract

Place chocolate in heatproof bowl. Bring heavy cream to boil in small saucepan over medium-high heat, then pour over chocolate. Add corn syrup and let sit, covered, for 5 minutes. Whisk mixture gently until smooth, then stir in vanilla. Refrigerate for 1 to 1½ hours, stirring every 15 minutes, until mixture reaches spreadable consistency.

✔ WHY THIS RECIPE WORKS
We wanted a yellow cake that was moist and tender, with a rich, buttery, eggy flavor and a fine, even crumb. Those cakes made using the classic creaming method—beating the butter and sugar together, then adding the flour and milk-egg mixture alternately to the bowl—gave us disappointing results. Instead of melting in your mouth, these cakes were crumbly, sugary, and a little hard. And they didn't taste of butter and eggs, as all plain cakes ought to, but instead seemed merely sweet. We found that reverse creaming—combining all the dry ingredients in the mixing bowl, then adding the butter, followed by the milk and eggs, in stages—gave us the tender texture and fine crumb we were after.

START WITH CAKE FLOUR   For a delicate cake, you must start with cake flour (see concept 45). Because cake flour contains less protein than all-purpose flour, it produces cake layers with less gluten, which are quite tender.

CHANGE 1-2-3-4   Most yellow cake recipes start with a basic formula of 1 cup of butter, 2 cups of sugar, 3 cups of flour, and 4 eggs—called a 1-2-3-4 cake. After testing, we found that the butter and egg amounts were fine, but we ended up using less sugar and flour, and we reduced the milk, too. The end result is a richer cake with a buttery flavor. More fat also makes the cake especially tender.

LINE PANS WITH PARCHMENT   To ensure easy removal of the cake layer, we grease the pans, line them with rounds of parchment, then grease and flour the parchment. The paper makes it easy to flip the cake layers out of the pan just 10 minutes after they come out of the oven—no need to worry about the hot layers falling apart. The paper peels right off and you can continue to cool the layers to room temperature before frosting them.

MAKE A CLASSIC BUTTERCREAM   Sure, you could mix butter and confectioners' sugar and use that as a base for the frosting, but this kind of quick frosting has a slightly gritty texture and very sweet flavor. We prefer to make a classic buttercream with whole eggs. The eggs, sugar, and vanilla are heated to 160 degrees (to make the eggs safe and unlock their thickening properties) and then whipped until airy before the softened butter is beaten into the mixture. The resulting buttercream has a satiny texture.

NEW YORK–STYLE CRUMB CAKE
SERVES 8 TO 10

Don't be tempted to substitute all-purpose flour for the cake flour, as doing so will make a dry, tough cake. If you can't find buttermilk, you can substitute an equal amount of plain low-fat yogurt. When topping the cake, take care to not push the crumbs into the batter. This recipe can be easily doubled and baked in a 13 by 9-inch baking pan. If doubling, increase the baking time to about 45 minutes.

CRUMB TOPPING

8	tablespoons unsalted butter, melted and still warm
⅓	cup (2⅓ ounces) granulated sugar
⅓	cup packed (2⅓ ounces) dark brown sugar
¾	teaspoon ground cinnamon
⅛	teaspoon salt
1¾	cups (7 ounces) cake flour

CAKE

1¼	cups (5 ounces) cake flour
½	cup (3½ ounces) granulated sugar
¼	teaspoon baking soda
¼	teaspoon salt
6	tablespoons unsalted butter, cut into 6 pieces and softened (68 degrees)
⅓	cup buttermilk
1	large egg plus 1 large yolk
1	teaspoon vanilla extract
	Confectioners' sugar

1. Adjust oven rack to upper-middle position and heat oven to 325 degrees. Cut 16-inch length of parchment paper or aluminum foil and fold lengthwise to 7-inch width. Spray 8-inch square baking dish with vegetable oil spray and fit parchment into dish, pushing it into corners and up sides, allowing excess to hang over edges of dish.

2. FOR THE TOPPING: Whisk butter, granulated sugar, brown sugar, cinnamon, and salt together in medium bowl to combine. Add flour and stir with rubber spatula or wooden spoon until mixture resembles thick, cohesive dough; set aside to cool to room temperature, 10 to 15 minutes.

3. FOR THE CAKE: Using stand mixer fitted with paddle, mix flour, sugar, baking soda, and salt on low speed to combine. With mixer running, add butter 1 piece at a time. Continue beating until mixture resembles moist crumbs, with no visible butter chunks remaining, 1 to 2 minutes. Add buttermilk, egg and yolk, and vanilla and beat on medium-high speed until light and fluffy, about 1 minute, scraping down bowl as needed.

4. Transfer batter to prepared pan. Using rubber spatula, spread batter into even layer. Break apart crumb topping into large pea-size pieces and spread in even layer over batter, beginning with edges and then working toward center. Bake until crumbs are golden and toothpick inserted in center of cake comes out clean, 35 to 40 minutes. Let cool on wire rack for at least 30 minutes. Remove cake from pan by lifting parchment overhang. Dust with confectioners' sugar just before serving.

✔WHY THIS RECIPE WORKS
The original crumb cake was brought to New York by German immigrants; sadly, the bakery-fresh versions have all but disappeared. Most modern recipes use butter cake rather than the traditional yeast dough, which made our job that much easier. The essence of this cake is the balance between the tender, buttery cake and the thick, lightly spiced crumb topping. Starting with our favorite yellow cake recipe, we realized we needed to reduce the amount of butter or the richness would be overwhelming. We wanted our crumb topping to be soft and cookielike, not a crunchy streusel, so we mixed granulated and brown sugars and melted the butter for a doughlike consistency, flavoring the mixture only with cinnamon. Broken into little pieces and sprinkled over the cake batter, our topping held together during baking and made a thick layer of moist crumbs with golden edges that didn't sink into the cake.

CUT BUTTER AND ADD BUTTERMILK Our Rich, Tender Yellow Cake (page 404) is a good base for this crumb cake. But with all those buttery crumbs, we found we wanted a slightly less rich cake as the base. As a result, we cut back on the butter and added more milk to keep the cake from becoming dry, but we then found that the batter became too thin to support the heavy crumbs. We compensated by substituting buttermilk for milk. We also left out an egg white so the cake wouldn't be rubbery.

USE CAKE FLOUR Even though the cake layer has to support a heavy layer of crumbs, don't think about switching to all-purpose flour. Yes, the cake layer will be sturdy but it will also be dry.

MAKE CRUMBS, NOT STREUSEL For really big crumbs you have to make a dough and then break that dough apart by hand. Melted butter, two kinds of sugar, and flour are essential. You need more butter than you do when making streusel—the overall effect is more like cookie dough, with more substance than streusel and less sweetness.

SHAPE AND DISTRIBUTE THE CRUMBS Using both hands, break apart the crumb dough, rolling the broken dough between your thumb and forefinger to form crumbs about the size of large peas. Continue until all the dough has been broken down into crumbs. Sprinkle the crumbs evenly over the cake batter, breaking apart any larger chunks. Spread the crumbs from the outside of the cake toward the center so as to not make the center too heavy.

BAKE IN LOW OVEN Reducing the oven temperature to a gentle 325 degrees, lengthening the baking time, and placing the cake in the upper part of the oven all help to crisp the crumb topping.

BOSTON CREAM CUPCAKES
MAKES 12 CUPCAKES

Bake the cupcakes directly in a greased and floured muffin tin rather than using paper cupcake liners so the chocolate glaze can run down the sides of the cooled cakes.

CUPCAKES

1¾	cups (8¾ ounces) all-purpose flour
1	cup (7 ounces) sugar
1½	teaspoons baking powder
¾	teaspoon salt
12	tablespoons unsalted butter, cut into 12 pieces and softened (68 degrees)
3	large eggs
¾	cup whole milk
1½	teaspoons vanilla extract

CHOCOLATE GLAZE

¾	cup heavy cream
¼	cup light corn syrup
8	ounces bittersweet chocolate, chopped
½	teaspoon vanilla extract
1	recipe Pastry Cream (page 197), cooled

1. FOR THE CUPCAKES: Adjust oven rack to middle position and heat oven to 350 degrees. Spray muffin tin with vegetable oil spray, flour generously, and tap pan to remove excess flour.

2. Using stand mixer fitted with paddle, mix flour, sugar, baking powder, and salt on low speed to combine. With mixer running, add butter, 1 piece at a time, and beat until mixture resembles coarse sand. Add eggs, 1 at a time, and mix until combined. Add milk and vanilla, increase speed to medium, and beat until light and fluffy and no lumps remain, about 3 minutes.

3. Fill muffin cups three-quarters full (do not overfill). Bake until toothpick inserted in center of cupcake comes out clean, 18 to 20 minutes. Let cupcakes cool in pan for 5 minutes, then transfer them to rack to cool completely.

4. FOR THE GLAZE: Heat cream, corn syrup, chocolate, and vanilla in small saucepan over medium heat, stirring constantly, until smooth. Set glaze aside to cool and thicken for 30 minutes.

5. Prepare and fill cupcakes by inserting tip of small knife at 45-degree angle about ⅛ inch from edge of cupcake top and cut all the way around, removing cone of cake. Cut away all but top ¼ inch of cone, leaving only small disk of cake. Fill cupcake with 2 tablespoons pastry cream and top with disk of cake. Set filled cupcakes on wire rack set over parchment paper. Spoon 2 tablespoons glaze over each cupcake, allowing it to drip down sides. Refrigerate until just set, about 10 minutes. (Cupcakes can be refrigerated for up to 2 days; bring to room temperature before serving.)

✓ WHY THIS RECIPE WORKS

We wanted a recipe for Boston cream cupcakes that produced cupcakes with big chocolate flavor and a smooth, creamy center, rather than the artificial, bland flavors characteristic of most Boston cream cupcake recipes. For our recipe, we use the reverse creaming method to achieve tender, close-crumbed cupcakes, then fill them with cream through a cone-shaped hole in the top of the cupcakes. Our chocolate glaze, which clings tightly to the tops of the cupcakes thanks to light corn syrup, covers any evidence of the holes.

REVERSE CREAM We started this recipe with a basic yellow cake, which was a bit too coarsely textured. Instead of the traditional creaming method we use the reverse creaming method, which calls for cutting the butter into the dry ingredients, as is done with biscuit dough. These cupcakes are soft, moist, and tender. The reason? The traditional creaming method, which relies on aerating the butter with the sugar, creates large air pockets that result in a coarser crumb. In the reverse creaming method, the butter coats the flour before the batter is aerated, keeping the cake tender and fine crumbed.

PICK ALL-PURPOSE FLOUR While cake flour is essential when making delicate, tender cake layers, a cupcake should be a bit sturdier—you want to eat a cupcake out of hand without having it fall apart. All-purpose flour adds a bit more structure to the cake portion of this recipe.

MAKE A CONE The real challenge is how to get the pastry cream inside the cupcake. We tried filling a pastry bag with pastry cream and piping it in through a hole in the bottom, but tasters wanted more filling. We tried cutting the top of the cupcake off, scooping out a bit, and then replacing the top, but the scar was obvious. We prefer removing a cone-shaped section of the cake from the top. Once the glaze is applied, the incision becomes invisible.

The reverse creaming method—in which the butter is beaten into the flour and sugar rather than creamed with the sugar—makes for flatter cookies that are easier to decorate. Also, less air in the batter means fewer bubbles in the baked cookies, so they are sturdier and crisper—again, making them perfect for glazing.

GLAZED BUTTER COOKIES
MAKES ABOUT 38 COOKIES

If you cannot find superfine sugar, process granulated sugar in a food processor for 30 seconds. If desired, the cookies can be finished with sprinkles or other decorations immediately after glazing.

COOKIES

2½	cups (12½ ounces) all-purpose flour
¾	cup (5⅔ ounces) superfine sugar
¼	teaspoon salt
16	tablespoons unsalted butter, cut into 16 pieces and softened (68 degrees)
2	tablespoons cream cheese, room temperature
2	teaspoons vanilla extract

GLAZE

1	tablespoon cream cheese, room temperature
3	tablespoons milk
1½	cups (6 ounces) confectioners' sugar

1. FOR THE COOKIES: Using stand mixer fitted with paddle, mix flour, sugar, and salt at low speed until combined, about 5 seconds. With mixer running on low, add butter 1 piece at a time; continue to mix until mixture looks crumbly and slightly wet, 1 to 2 minutes longer. Beat in cream cheese and vanilla until dough just begins to form large clumps, about 30 seconds.

2. Knead dough by hand in bowl, 2 to 3 turns, until it forms large, cohesive mass. Transfer dough to counter and divide it into 2 even pieces. Press each piece into 4-inch disk, wrap disks in plastic wrap, and refrigerate until dough is firm but malleable, about 30 minutes. (Dough can be refrigerated for up to 3 days or frozen for up to 2 weeks; defrost in refrigerator before using.)

3. Adjust oven rack to middle position and heat oven to 375 degrees. Line 2 baking sheets with parchment paper. Working with 1 piece of dough at a time, roll ⅛ inch thick between 2 large sheets of parchment paper; slide rolled dough, still on parchment, onto baking sheet and refrigerate until firm, about 10 minutes.

4. Working with 1 sheet of dough at a time, peel parchment from 1 side of dough and cut into desired shapes using cookie cutters; place cookies 1½ inches apart on prepared sheets. Bake 1 sheet at a time until cookies are light golden brown, about 10 minutes, rotating baking sheet halfway through baking. (Dough scraps can be patted together, chilled, and rerolled once.) Let cookies cool on baking sheet for 3 minutes; transfer cookies to wire rack and let cool to room temperature.

5. FOR THE GLAZE: Whisk cream cheese and 2 tablespoons milk together in medium bowl until combined and no lumps remain. Add confectioners' sugar and whisk until smooth, adding remaining 1 tablespoon milk as needed until glaze is thin enough to spread easily. Using back of spoon, drizzle or spread scant teaspoon of glaze onto each cooled cookie. Allow glazed cookies to dry for at least 30 minutes.

PRACTICAL SCIENCE
STAND VS. HAND-HELD MIXER

We prefer to use stand mixers. But hand-held mixers work, too.

Curious about the performance differences between our favorite hand-held and stand mixers, we conducted side-by-side tests to establish general guidelines for their use. We whipped cream, beat egg whites for meringue, and made cookies, cakes, and buttercream frosting.

Although it took the hand-held mixer 40 to 60 seconds longer than the stand mixer to whip cream and beat egg whites, it did just as good a job (both were fitted with the whisk attachment). When making oatmeal cookie dough, the stand mixer (with the paddle attachment) produced more volume in the batter, but the baked cookies were identical in number, texture, and flavor. Neither mixer had trouble mixing oatmeal and nuts into the stiff dough on low speed.

Our favorite yellow layer cake recipe baked up the same when made with both mixers, although the stand mixer created a slightly more voluminous batter. The same was true with génoise, a cake leavened by whole-egg foam, although the hand-held mixer took nearly twice as long to beat the eggs to the proper volume. For those partial to buttercream frostings, we found that we preferred the hand-held mixer to the stand mixer because it was easier to keep the hot sugar syrup from clinging to the beaters.

Our conclusion? The stand mixer offers greater flexibility and versatility. (Its dough hook is ideal for kneading bread, something a hand-held mixer can't do.) Also, the solid, freestanding base leaves the cook free to accomplish other tasks. We found, however, that with some adjustments for time and technique, the hand-held mixer generally yields baked goods that are identical to those prepared in a stand mixer.

✔ WHY THIS RECIPE WORKS

Baking holiday cookies should be a fun endeavor, but so often it's an exercise in frustration. The dough clings to the rolling pin, it rips and tears as it's rolled out, and moving the dough in and out of the fridge to make it easier to work with turns a simple one-hour process into a half-day project. We wanted a simple recipe that would yield a forgiving, workable dough, producing cookies that would be sturdy enough to decorate yet tender enough to be worth eating. Our first realization was that we had to use enough butter to stay true to the nature of a butter cookie but not so much that the dough became greasy. All-purpose flour had enough gluten to provide structure, while superfine sugar provided a fine, even crumb and a compact, crisp cookie. A surprise ingredient—cream cheese—gave the cookies flavor and richness without altering their texture.

USE SUPERFINE SUGAR Regular granulated sugar makes cookies with a flaky texture and some large holes. In contrast, superfine sugar yields crisp, compact cookies with a fine, even crumb that is preferable for a cookie that will be glazed. There's no leavener in these cookies (you want them flat) and no eggs (which would make them moist and chewy).

ADD CREAM CHEESE We use just enough butter for rich flavor and tenderness. More butter just makes the dough sticky and hard to handle. However, we found that we could supplement the butter with cream cheese. Because it's softer than butter when chilled it makes the dough easier to roll out. And it adds a nice tang.

PICK ALL-PURPOSE FLOUR While holiday glazed cookies should be delicate, cake flour makes overly fragile cookies. All-purpose flour develops enough gluten for cookies to be glazed and decorated without too much worry that they will crumble.

ROLL, THEN CHILL To prevent the dough from sticking to the counter—and to the rolling pin—roll it between two large pieces of parchment. Cold, stiff dough will cut more cleanly than soft dough, so make sure to chill the dough after rolling. Slide the bottom piece of parchment onto a baking sheet to keep the dough flat and then refrigerate it until firm, about 10 minutes.

MINIMIZE SCRAPS Cut shapes close together, starting from the outside and working your way to the middle. When making large and small cookies, alternate cutters as you stamp to use as much dough as possible. While you can reroll this dough once, you want to reduce scraps; if you overwork the dough too much gluten will develop and the cookies will bake up tough. Make sure to chill the dough scraps again before rolling them out a second time.

PEEL AWAY SCRAPS FIRST Use a small spatula to strip away the dough scraps from around the cookies. With excess dough out of the way, it's easier to lift the cookies and transfer them to a baking sheet without marring the shape of the cookies, or stretching the dough.

BAKE ONE SHEET AT A TIME Baking one sheet of cookies at a time ensures even baking. (For more on this, see "Avoiding Uneven Baking," page 367.)

PRACTICAL SCIENCE EXTRA-OLD EXTRACT

Vanilla extract will last indefinitely if stored in a sealed container.

Some people bake enough cookies and cakes to blow through a whole bottle of vanilla extract in just a month, while less enthusiastic bakers may keep the same bottle for years. Does vanilla extract ever go bad or lose potency?

We located three-year-old and 10-year-old bottles of vanilla extract and compared them with a fresh bottle of the same brand in three of our recipes: yellow cupcakes, vanilla frosting, and chocolate chip cookies. Although the older bottles took a bit of effort to open, once the extract was incorporated into recipes, tasters could detect no difference between the old and the new.

Vanilla extract has a minimum alcohol content of 35 percent, which, according to Matt Nielsen of vanilla manufacturer Nielsen-Massey, makes it the most shelf-stable form of vanilla (beans and paste can lose flavor quickly). It will last indefinitely if stored in a sealed container away from heat and light.

WELL PRESERVED
This bottle may look old on the outside, but the extract inside will stay fresh indefinitely.

Sugar Changes Texture (and Sweetness)

Even novice cooks understand that if they add more sugar to a dessert it will become sweeter. But what many fail to realize is that sugar can have a huge effect on texture, too, changing the structure of foods ranging from cookies to frozen desserts.

HOW THE SCIENCE WORKS

SUGAR HOLDS ON TO WATER

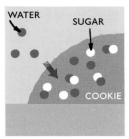

HOLDING ON *Sugar has an affinity for water molecules, holding on to moisture in baked goods while they are in the oven, and even as they cool.*

Sweeteners come in many forms, most of them familiar to the home cook. There is crystalline white table sugar, deep bronze brown sugar, thick, oozy molasses, and the lighter, golden honey. What is less familiar is how sweeteners really work.

Let's begin with structure. Sugar can be a single molecule made up of carbon, hydrogen, and oxygen—like glucose and fructose. Other sugars, like sucrose, are made of two or more molecules (in this case, one glucose and one fructose) tied together with chemical bonds. Table sugar, for example, consists of virtually pure sucrose. (For more information on sugars, see "Sweeteners 101," page 421.)

Sucrose is abundant in many plants, especially fruits. But unlike in fruits, some plants, like potatoes, convert the sucrose they form by photosynthesis into starch. This process is reversible, which explains why some vegetables can become sweeter when stored in the refrigerator. Table sugar is produced from either sugar cane or sugar beets. It is highly water soluble and when dissolved, the sucrose molecules organized within each crystal disperse into the water. Sugar doesn't melt, not in the traditional sense like an ice cube, but instead decomposes when it is brought to temperatures between 320 and 367 degrees.

So how does sugar affect texture in cookies, and even frozen desserts? It has everything to do with moisture. Sucrose is hygroscopic, which means it has an affinity for water molecules.

What happens is this: Because of the nature of the hydrogen and oxygen atoms in both water and sugar, they are electrostatically attracted to each other. When water and sugar are combined, they link together and form hydrogen bonds. It takes a fair amount of heat energy to break these bonds and, as a result, table sugar will hold on to moisture in food. Because of this tendency, sugar can slow the evaporation of moisture from cookies and cakes as they bake, which makes a tremendous difference when it comes to producing moist, tender baked goods.

In addition, when sucrose is heated along with some acid, it breaks back down into two simple sugars, glucose and fructose. When this happens, the result is called an invert sugar. Because fructose does not easily crystallize in the presence of glucose, invert sugars are always viscous liquids. A benefit of invert sugar comes into play when making, for example, chewy cookies (see Test Kitchen Experiment, opposite). Invert sugar is especially hygroscopic, pulling water from wherever it can be found, the best source being the air. Because brown sugar has more invert sugar than granulated sugar, it is our sugar of choice when baking chewy cookies—especially because invert sugar keeps on drawing in moisture even after cookies have been baked, thus helping them to stay chewy as they cool.

Finally, sugar likewise affects the texture of frozen desserts. How? When making frozen desserts, sugar is usually heated with a liquid (cream, water, fruit juice) so that it dissolves. When dissolved, sugar lowers the freezing point of water. This means that a sugar-water mixture freezes at a lower temperature than water alone. And because this mixture freezes at a lower temperature, it is able to become far colder than 32 degrees before beginning to form ice crystals while being made into ice cream. This means that when the ice crystals do form they form very rapidly—and stay very small. And tiny ice crystals translate into ice creams, sherbets, and sorbets that we perceive as smooth and creamy, not icy or grainy.

TEST KITCHEN EXPERIMENT

To show the powerful effect that sugar can have on the texture of a baked good, we ran the following experiment: We made two batches of our Chocolate-Chunk Oatmeal Cookies (page 413), one with brown sugar and the other with granulated white sugar. To isolate this variable, we kept the rest of the ingredients and the baking procedure identical. We repeated the experiment three times.

THE RESULTS

After the cookies had cooled to room temperature, we tasted them for chewiness and then attempted to bend a sample of each batch around a large wooden rolling pin (no easy task for firm, crunchy cookies). The results were clear as day: The brown sugar cookies had serious chew and the flexibility to conform to the curvature of the rolling pin. On the other hand, the cookies made with white sugar were crunchy rather than chewy and quickly snapped when bent.

THE TAKEAWAY

So you want to make some chewy cookies? Using brown sugar is a good start. Our findings confirm the science that sweeteners (like brown sugar) that contain invert sugar help to retard the crystallization of sucrose, therefore holding on to more moisture than white sugar and better maintaining a chewy texture as the cookie cools.

But there are a few other important steps to take for chewy cookies. First, don't be afraid of butter. Many of the cookie recipes that follow rely on melted butter. (Remember that butter is roughly 16 to 18 percent water, and by melting the butter you are encouraging the formation of gluten when the flour is added to the batter.) Second, use a generous amount of dough for each cookie. It's very hard to keep small cookies chewy. Use at least 2 tablespoons of dough (and even more in some cases) for each cookie. Third, don't overbake. Even with brown sugar and melted butter in the mix, if you overbake any of these cookies they will lose their chewy texture. Fourth, be sure to take the cookies out of the oven when they are set around the edges but look a bit underdone in the center. They will continue to firm up as they cool on the baking sheet. Finally, chewy cookies will become less chewy over time. Storing them in an airtight container helps.

THE EFFECT OF SUGAR ON TEXTURE

BROWN SUGAR VS. WHITE SUGAR
The cookie made with brown sugar (left) baked up chewy and easily bent around a rolling pin. The cookie made with white sugar (right) emerged from the oven crisp and dry, and snapped immediately when bent.

The cookie recipes that follow rely on brown sugar, careful baking, and melted butter (in two cases) to create and maintain a good chewy texture. Brown sugar contains invert sugars, which retard the crystallization of sucrose and therefore help the cookies retain moisture as they both bake and cool. Remember to use a generous scoop of dough for each cookie and not to overbake.

BROWN SUGAR COOKIES
MAKES ABOUT 24 COOKIES

Avoid using a nonstick skillet to brown the butter; the dark color of the nonstick coating makes it difficult to gauge when the butter is sufficiently browned. Use fresh, moist brown sugar, as hardened brown sugar will make the cookies too dry. Achieving the proper texture—crisp at the edges and chewy in the middle—is critical to this recipe. Because the cookies are so dark, it's hard to judge doneness by color. Instead, gently press halfway between the edge and center of the cookie. When it's done, it will form an indentation with slight resistance. Check early and err on the side of underdone.

14	tablespoons unsalted butter
2	cups packed (14 ounces) dark brown sugar
¼	cup (1¾ ounces) granulated sugar
2	cups plus 2 tablespoons (10⅔ ounces) all-purpose flour
½	teaspoon baking soda
¼	teaspoon baking powder
½	teaspoon salt
1	large egg plus 1 large yolk
1	tablespoon vanilla extract

1. Melt 10 tablespoons butter in 10-inch skillet over medium-high heat. Cook, swirling pan constantly, until butter is dark golden brown and has nutty aroma, 1 to 3 minutes. Transfer browned butter to large heatproof bowl. Add remaining 4 tablespoons butter and stir until completely melted; set aside for 15 minutes.

2. Meanwhile, adjust oven rack to middle position and heat oven to 350 degrees. Line 2 baking sheets with parchment paper. In shallow baking dish, mix ¼ cup brown sugar and granulated sugar until well combined; set aside. Whisk flour, baking soda, and baking powder together in medium bowl; set aside.

3. Add remaining 1¾ cups brown sugar and salt to bowl with cooled butter; mix until no sugar lumps remain, about 30 seconds. Scrape down bowl; add egg, yolk, and vanilla and mix until fully incorporated, about 30 seconds. Scrape down bowl. Add flour mixture and mix until just

combined, about 1 minute. Give dough final stir to ensure that no flour pockets remain.

4. Working with 2 tablespoons of dough at a time, roll into balls. Roll half of dough balls into sugar mixture to coat. Place dough balls 2 inches apart on prepared baking sheet; repeat with remaining dough balls.

5. Bake 1 sheet at a time until cookies are browned and still puffy and edges have begun to set but centers are still soft (cookies will look raw between cracks and seem underdone), 12 to 14 minutes, rotating baking sheet halfway through baking. Let cookies cool on baking sheet for 5 minutes; transfer to wire rack and let cool to room temperature.

✔ WHY THIS RECIPE WORKS
Simple sugar cookies, while classic, can seem too simple—even dull—at times. We wanted to turn up the volume on the sugar cookie by switching out the granulated sugar in favor of brown sugar. We had a clear vision of this cookie. It would be oversized, with a crackling crisp exterior and a chewy interior. And its flavor would scream "brown sugar." We wanted butter for optimal flavor, but the traditional creaming method (see concept 46) gave us cakey and tender cookies while cutting the butter into the flour produced crumbly cookies. The solution? Melting the butter.

BROWN THE BUTTER Melting the butter is a good start if you want a chewy cookie, but if you brown that butter you develop a range of butterscotch and toffee flavors, too. Adding a full tablespoon of vanilla helps boost the nutty flavors in our cookies without using more brown sugar (which would make them overly sweet). Make sure to use the full ½ teaspoon of salt—you need it to balance the sweetness of these cookies.

LOSE A WHITE Egg whites tend to make cookies cakey—they cause the cookies to puff and dry out. We use a whole egg plus a yolk for richness, leaving out the second white.

USE TWO LEAVENERS The choice of leavener is probably the most confusing part of any cookie recipe (see concept 42). Sugar cookies typically contain baking powder—a mixture of baking soda and a weak acid (calcium acid phosphate) that is activated by moisture and heat. The soda and acid create gas bubbles, which expand cookies and other baked goods. However, many baked goods with brown sugar call for baking soda instead. This is because while granulated sugar is neutral, dark brown sugar can be slightly acidic. But when we used baking soda by itself, the cookies had an open, coarse crumb and craggy top. Tasters loved the craggy top, not the coarse crumb. When we used baking powder by itself, the cookies had a finer, tighter crumb but the craggy top disappeared. After a dozen rounds of testing, we settled on using a combination of both leaveners to moderate the coarseness of the crumb without compromising the craggy tops.

ROLL IN BROWN SUGAR Dark brown sugar is the obvious choice for the dough itself—more butterscotch, brown sugar flavor, and more chewiness because it has more moisture and a little more invert sugar than light brown sugar. Rolling balls of dough in more brown sugar boosts their flavor further. Adding some granulated sugar keeps the brown sugar from clumping.

BAKE ONE SHEET AT A TIME We had hoped to be able to bake two sheets of cookies at a time, but even with rotating and changing tray positions at different times during baking, we could not get two-tray baking to work. Some of the cookies had the right texture, but others were inexplicably dry. Baking one tray at a time allows for even heat distribution and ensures that every cookie has the same texture. It's important not to overbake these cookies. To check cookies for doneness, gently press halfway between the edge and center of the cookie. When the cookie is done, your finger will form an indentation with slight resistance.

PRACTICAL SCIENCE KEEPING COOKIES SOFT

The best way to store chewy cookies is in a zipper-lock bag.

When it comes to storing chewy cookies, too much exposure to air dries them out and causes staling. To find the best method for storing chewy cookies, we baked three types—chocolate chip, molasses spice, and peanut butter—and stored them in the following ways: in a zipper-lock bag with the air pressed out; in a zipper-lock bag with an apple slice; and in a zipper-lock bag with a slice of white sandwich bread thrown in. (The last two help keep brown sugar moist; we wondered if they would do the same for cookies.)

After five days, all three cookie samples exhibited negative traits. The ones simply placed in the bag had become dry on the edges but were still acceptable. Those stored with the apple slice were moist but had begun to pick up the odor and flavor of the apple. The cookies stored with a slice of bread became damp in the areas where the bread touched the cookies. Nestled together in the same bag, the hygroscopic sugar in the cookies attracted some of the water from the bread. In fact, while the cookies became wetter, the bread dried out and became brittle.

Because the bread was providing too much moisture, we wondered if using less bread would produce chewy, rather than soggy, cookies. No such luck. Half- and quarter-slices of bread produced similarly lackluster cookies. Though no longer wet, the cookies didn't seem any fresher than those stored by themselves. So the best way to store cookies is also the simplest: in a zipper-lock bag with the air pressed out. And to return just-baked chewiness to cookies that have been stored for several days, place them on a microwave-safe plate and microwave at full power for 30 seconds.

CHOCOLATE-CHUNK OATMEAL COOKIES WITH PECANS AND DRIED CHERRIES
MAKES ABOUT 16 LARGE COOKIES

We like these cookies made with pecans and dried sour cherries, but walnuts or skinned hazelnuts can be substituted for the pecans and dried cranberries for the cherries. Quick oats used in place of the old-fashioned oats will yield a cookie with slightly less chewiness.

1¼	cups (6¼ ounces) all-purpose flour
¾	teaspoon baking powder
½	teaspoon baking soda
½	teaspoon salt
1¼	cups (3¾ ounces) old-fashioned rolled oats
1	cup pecans, toasted and chopped
1	cup (4 ounces) dried sour cherries, chopped coarse
4	ounces bittersweet chocolate, chopped into chunks about size of chocolate chips
12	tablespoons unsalted butter, softened (68 degrees)
1½	cups packed (10½ ounces) dark brown sugar
1	large egg
1	teaspoon vanilla extract

1. Adjust oven racks to upper-middle and lower-middle positions and heat oven to 350 degrees. Line 2 baking sheets with parchment paper.

2. Whisk flour, baking powder, baking soda, and salt together in medium bowl. In second medium bowl, stir oats, pecans, cherries, and chocolate together.

3. Using stand mixer fitted with paddle, beat butter and sugar at medium speed until no sugar lumps remain, about 1 minute, scraping down bowl as needed. Add egg and vanilla and beat on medium-low until fully incorporated, about 30 seconds, scraping down bowl as needed. Reduce speed to low, add flour mixture, and mix until just combined, about 30 seconds. Gradually add oat mixture; mix until just incorporated. Give dough final stir to ensure that no flour pockets remain and ingredients are evenly distributed.

4. Working with ¼ cup of dough at a time, roll into balls and place 2½ inches apart on prepared baking sheets. Press dough to 1-inch thickness using bottom of greased measuring cup. Bake until cookies are medium brown and edges have begun to set but centers are still soft (cookies will seem underdone and will appear raw, wet, and shiny in cracks), 20 to 22 minutes, switching and rotating baking sheets halfway through baking.

5. Let cookies cool on baking sheets for 5 minutes; transfer cookies to wire rack and let cool to room temperature.

✔ WHY THIS RECIPE WORKS

It's easy to get carried away and overload cookie dough with a crazy jumble of ingredients, resulting in a poorly textured cookie monster. Our ultimate oatmeal cookie would have just the right amount of added ingredients and an ideal texture—crisp around the edges and chewy in the middle. To get the results we wanted, we used brown sugar for moisture and a combination of leaveners. Also, keep a careful eye on the timing to make sure the cookies don't overbake.

MAKING LOADED OATMEAL COOKIES Sure, we like plain oatmeal cookies but here we wanted something special, loaded with flavorful ingredients. Many recipes add too many goodies to the batter. We found that a careful balance of bittersweet chocolate chunks (semisweet is too sweet), pecans (toasting is essential to bring out their flavor), and dried sour cherries (you need something tart) is the way to make a truly great oatmeal cookie. No spices. No coconut. No raisins or dried tropical fruits.

START WITH THE RIGHT OATS When baking we find that old-fashioned oats are far superior to the other choices. Steel-cut oats are great for breakfast but make dry, pebbly cookies. Instant oats will create dense, mealy cookies lacking in good oat flavor. Quick oats are OK, but they taste somewhat bland, and the cookies won't be quite as chewy.

USE ALL BROWN SUGAR We use brown sugar to help add moisture (it is more moist than white sugar). After testing a half-dozen combinations, we found that using all dark brown sugar is best. All light brown sugar is the second best option. In addition to being more moist, the cookies made with brown sugar are chewier than cookies made with granulated, and the brown sugar also gives the cookies a rich, dark color and deep caramel flavor.

PICK TWO LEAVENERS We began making these cookies with baking soda, which made the cookies crisp from the inside out—a problem, since we want a chewy interior and a crisp exterior. When we switched to baking powder, the cookies puffed in the oven and then collapsed, losing their shape and yielding not a hint of crispy exterior. Because we want a combination of crisp edges and chewy centers, we use a combination of baking powder and soda. This pairing produces cookie that are light and crisp on the outside but chewy, dense, and soft in the center. (For more on leaveners, see concept 42.)

PRACTICAL SCIENCE COOKIE SHEET BAKE-OFF

The type of baking sheet that you use (rimmed or rimless) can affect the baking time of your cookies.

Recently, we came across a piece of cookie-baking advice in the 1964 edition of *Joy of Cooking*: Use a flat, unrimmed baking sheet to promote even cooking. To see if this still applied to a modern oven, we made two identical batches of cookies: We baked one on our favorite cookie sheet (its shorter sides boast a slightly raised lip to facilitate handling, but it has no true rim), and the other on our favorite rimmed baking sheet, which features a 1-inch rim on all sides. We baked both batches successively on the same rack in the oven.

How evenly the cookies baked wasn't an issue; both batches came out perfectly pale golden. However, the cookies baked on the rimless pan browned more quickly and finished baking several minutes before those on the rimmed pan. The discrepancy makes sense: Heat rises from the element at the bottom of the oven and circulates in currents to warm the entire chamber. A rimmed baking sheet's raised edges block the hot air currents, diverting them from the cookies to the top of the oven. A rimless baking sheet allows the hot air to immediately sweep over the cookies, which means quicker baking.

Bottom line: No need to rush out and buy a rimless sheet the next time you bake cookies. Just be aware of the type of baking sheet you're using and the timing. We like to check on cookies a minute or two before the timer goes off, just to play it safe.

RIMLESS EDGES = QUICKER BAKING
With no raised edges to block hot air currents, a rimless cookie sheet baked cookies about three minutes faster than a rimmed pan.

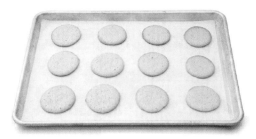

RIMMED EDGES = SLOWER BAKING
After the same amount of time, cookies baked on a rimmed baking sheet, whose edges divert hot air to the top of the oven, were still underdone.

ULTIMATE CHOCOLATE CHIP COOKIES
MAKES ABOUT 16 LARGE COOKIES

Avoid using a nonstick skillet to brown the butter; the dark color of the nonstick coating makes it difficult to gauge when the butter is sufficiently browned. Use fresh, moist brown sugar, as hardened brown sugar will make the cookies too dry.

1¾	cups (8¾ ounces) all-purpose flour
½	teaspoon baking soda
14	tablespoons unsalted butter
¾	cup packed (5¼ ounces) dark brown sugar
½	cup (3½ ounces) granulated sugar
1	teaspoon salt
2	teaspoons vanilla extract
1	large egg plus 1 large yolk
1¼	cups (7½ ounces) semisweet chocolate chips or chunks
¾	cup pecans or walnuts, toasted and chopped (optional)

1. Adjust oven rack to middle position and heat oven to 375 degrees. Line 2 baking sheets with parchment paper. Whisk flour and baking soda together in medium bowl; set aside.

2. Melt 10 tablespoons butter in 10-inch skillet over medium-high heat. Continue cooking, swirling pan constantly, until butter is dark golden brown and has nutty aroma, 1 to 3 minutes. Transfer browned butter to large heatproof bowl. Add remaining 4 tablespoons butter and stir until completely melted.

3. Add brown sugar, granulated sugar, salt, and vanilla to melted butter; whisk until fully incorporated. Add egg and yolk; whisk until mixture is smooth with no sugar lumps remaining, about 30 seconds. Let mixture stand for 3 minutes, then whisk for 30 seconds. Repeat process of resting and whisking 2 more times until mixture is thick, smooth, and shiny. Using rubber spatula, stir in flour mixture until just combined, about 1 minute. Stir in chocolate chips and nuts, if using. Give dough final stir to ensure that no flour pockets remain and ingredients are evenly distributed.

4. Working with 3 tablespoons of dough at a time, roll into balls and place 2 inches apart on prepared baking sheets.

5. Bake 1 sheet at a time until cookies are golden brown and still puffy and edges have begun to set but centers are still soft, 10 to 14 minutes, rotating baking sheet halfway through baking. Transfer baking sheet to wire rack; let cookies cool to room temperature.

PRACTICAL SCIENCE BROWNED BUTTER

Browning your butter adds a nutty, toasted flavor.

Browned butter, or *beurre noisette*, as it is called in French, gives our Ultimate Chocolate Chip Cookies a deep, rich flavor. Beurre noisette translates literally as "hazelnut butter"; as the butter browns, it takes on the flavor and aroma of toasted nuts. Browned butter is used in both baked goods and savory preparations; brightened with lemon juice, it makes a classic, simple "sauce" for fish meunière as well as for vegetables such as asparagus and green beans.

When making browned butter, use a saucepan or skillet with a light-colored interior; the dark color of nonstick or anodized aluminum cookware makes it difficult to judge the color of the butter as it browns. Use medium to medium-high heat, and stir or swirl the butter occasionally so that the milk solids brown evenly; depending on the heat setting and the amount of butter, the process may take as few as three minutes if browning just a couple of tablespoons or as long as 10 minutes if browning a full cup. Finally, if not using the browned butter immediately, transfer it to a bowl; if left in the saucepan or skillet, residual heat can cause it to continue cooking … and then it becomes *beurre noir*.

✔ WHY THIS RECIPE WORKS

Since Nestlé first began printing the recipe for Toll House cookies on the back of chocolate chip bags in 1939, generations of bakers have packed chocolate chip cookies into lunches and taken them to potlucks. But after a few samples, we wondered if this was really the best that a chocolate chip cookie could be. We wanted to refine this recipe to create a moist and chewy chocolate chip cookie with crisp edges and deep notes of toffee and butterscotch to balance its sweetness—in short, a more sophisticated cookie than the standard bake-sale offering. Melting a generous amount of butter before combining it with other ingredients gives us the chewy texture we wanted. We also use a bit more brown sugar than white sugar to enhance chewiness. The resulting cookies are crisp and chewy and gooey with chocolate and boast a complex medley of sweet, buttery, caramel, and toffee flavors.

CHANGE SUGAR Traditionally, Toll House cookies have a 1:1 ratio of brown sugar to white sugar. White sugar granules lend crispness, while brown sugar, which is more hygroscopic (meaning it attracts and retains water, mainly from the air) than white sugar, enhances chewiness. All that moisture sounds like a good thing—but it's too good, in fact. Cookies made with all brown sugar are beyond chewy here. They are so moist they're nearly floppy. We got the best results when we changed the ratio of brown sugar to white sugar to 3:2. This recipe works with light brown sugar, but the cookies will be less full-flavored.

BROWN THE BUTTER, LOSE ONE WHITE As with our Brown Sugar Cookies (page 412), we brown the butter here for flavor. (Melting the butter increases chewiness as well.) Losing an egg white (which makes cookies more cakey) also improves chewiness.

WHISK AND WAIT   After stirring together the butter, sugar, and eggs … wait. After 10 minutes, the sugar will have dissolved and the mixture will turn thick and shiny, like frosting. The finished cookies will emerge from the oven with a slight glossy sheen and an alluring surface of cracks and crags, with a deep, toffeelike flavor. This is because by allowing the sugar to rest in the liquids, more of it dissolves in the small amount of moisture before baking. The dissolved sugar caramelizes more easily and helps to create a cookie with crisp edges and a chewy center (see "For Perfect Cookies, Look to Sugar," right).

BAKE IN A MODERATE OVEN   With caramelization in mind, we bake our cookies in a 375-degree oven—the same as for Toll House cookies. Baking two trays a time may be convenient, but it leads to uneven cooking. The cookies on the top tray are often browner around the edges than those on the bottom, even when rotated halfway through baking. These cookies will finish crisp and chewy, gooey with chocolate, with a complex medley of sweet, buttery, caramel, and toffee flavors. In other words? Perfect.

PRACTICAL SCIENCE
FOR PERFECT COOKIES, LOOK TO SUGAR

Dissolved sugar makes cookies with better flavor and texture.

Crunchy edges, chewy centers, and big butterscotch flavors—that chocolate chip cookie framework sounded pretty sweet to us. As it turns out, perfect cookies have a lot to do with sugar and how it's treated. Sugar that is dissolved in liquid before baking caramelizes more readily than sugar that simply "melts" when exposed to the same amount of heat. What would happen if we rested our cookie batter after we added the sugar to allow more of it to dissolve before going into the oven?

We prepared two batches of our Ultimate Chocolate Chip Cookies. Dough from the first batch went straight from the mixing bowl onto the baking sheet; the other batch rested for 10 minutes (with occasional whisking) after we combined the sugar with the recipe's liquids.

Cookies baked from the rested batter boasted not only richer, deeper flavor but also crisper edges.

Dissolving the sugar in the liquid provided by the melted butter, vanilla, and egg affects both flavor and texture. Dissolved sugar breaks down more quickly from crystalline sucrose into glucose and fructose, which caramelize at a lower temperature to form many new flavor compounds. As the dissolved, caramelized sugar cools, it takes on a brittle structure. In our cookies this brittle texture is more evident at the edges. Why? As the oven burns off moisture from the cookie perimeter, the remaining moisture is retained in the center by the sugar, keeping it chewy.

SUGAR SYRUPS AT WORK   CREAMY FROZEN DESSERTS

When sugar is used in cookies, it is a liquid (dissolved) ingredient in a mixture that is mostly dry ingredients. Sugar behaves differently when heated in a purely liquid medium, as is the case when making frozen desserts. While sugar plays an important role in ice cream (see Vanilla Ice Cream on page 188), its effect on texture is less clear-cut in a recipe with so much fat. However, in sherbets and ices, which contain little or no fat, sugar is the key ingredient that determines the size of the frozen crystals and the overall texture of the dessert.

FRESH ORANGE SHERBET
MAKES ABOUT 1 QUART

If using a canister-style ice-cream machine, be sure to freeze the empty canister at least 24 hours and preferably 48 hours before churning. For self-refrigerating ice cream machines, prechill the canister by running the machine for five to 10 minutes before pouring in the sherbet. For the freshest, purest orange flavor, use freshly squeezed unpasteurized orange juice (either store-bought or juiced at home). Pasteurized fresh-squeezed juice makes an acceptable though noticeably less fresh-tasting sherbet. Do not use juice made from concentrate, which has a cooked and less bright flavor.

1   cup (7 ounces) sugar
1   tablespoon grated orange zest plus 2 cups juice (4 oranges)
⅛   teaspoon salt
3   tablespoons lemon juice
2   teaspoons triple sec or vodka
⅔   cup heavy cream

1. Pulse sugar, orange zest, and salt in food processor until damp, 10 to 15 pulses. With processor running, add orange juice and lemon juice in slow, steady stream; continue to process until sugar is fully dissolved, about 1 minute. Strain mixture through fine-mesh strainer into medium bowl; stir in triple sec, then cover and place in freezer until chilled and mixture registers about 40 degrees, 30 minutes to 1 hour. Do not let mixture freeze.

2. When mixture is chilled, using whisk, whip cream in medium bowl until soft peaks form. Whisking constantly, add juice mixture in steady stream, pouring against edge of bowl. Transfer to ice cream machine and churn until mixture resembles thick soft-serve ice cream, 25 to 30 minutes.

3. Transfer sherbet to airtight container, press firmly to remove any air pockets, and freeze until firm, at least 3 hours. (Sherbet can be frozen for up to 1 week.)

FRESH LIME SHERBET

Substitute lime zest for orange zest, increase sugar to 1 cup plus 2 tablespoons, and omit lemon juice. Substitute ⅔ cup lime juice (6 limes) combined with 1½ cups water for orange juice.

FRESH LEMON SHERBET

Omit orange juice. Substitute lemon zest for orange zest, increase sugar to 1 cup plus 2 tablespoons, and increase lemon juice to ⅔ cup (4 lemons). Combine lemon juice with 1½ cups water before adding to food processor.

FRESH RASPBERRY SHERBET

In-season fresh raspberries have the best flavor, but when they are not in season, frozen raspberries are a better option. Substitute a 12-ounce bag of frozen raspberries for fresh.

Omit orange zest and juice. Cook 15 ounces (3 cups) raspberries with sugar, salt, and ¾ cup water in medium saucepan over medium heat, stirring occasionally, until mixture just begins to simmer, about 7 minutes. Strain through fine-mesh strainer into medium bowl, pressing on solids to extract as much liquid as possible. Add lemon juice and triple sec; cover and place in freezer until chilled and mixture registers about 40 degrees, 30 minutes to 1 hour. Proceed as directed.

✔ WHY THIS RECIPE WORKS

The perfect sherbet recipe is a cross between sorbet and ice cream, containing fruit, sugar, and dairy but no egg yolks. Like its foreign cousin, sorbet, sherbet should taste vibrant and fresh. In the case of sherbet, however, its assertive flavor is tempered by the creamy addition of dairy. Ideally, it is as smooth as ice cream but devoid of ice cream's richness and weight. We began with classic orange sherbet. For bright flavor, we started by combining fruit zest and sugar in a food processor before adding 2 cups of orange juice. A small amount of alcohol ensured the sherbet had a smooth, silky texture, and whipped heavy cream lightened the texture of our frozen dessert. To guarantee sherbet with an even consistency, we prepared it in an ice cream machine and then came up with variations with lime, lemon, and raspberries.

START WITH FRESH FRUIT Commercial rainbow sherbet holds a certain appeal, until you actually taste it. If you want sherbet that tastes like fruit, you need to make it yourself, and you have to start with real fruit. For orange, lime, and lemon flavors, you need the zest (which has a good deal of flavorful oils) as well juice. For raspberry sherbet, you need whole fruit (frozen berries are fine).

ADD SUGAR AND CREAM Sherbet requires sugar and a little cream. There are no eggs. (This is what makes sherbet more refreshing than ice cream.) And the amount of dairy is quite small—less than 1 cup of dairy for a quart of sherbet. (A quart of ice cream has 3 cups of dairy.) We found it best to dissolve the sugar right in the fruit juice to make a concentrated base (no water needed). As for the dairy, we like ⅔ cup of cream—there's less water in cream so it makes the sherbet less icy than versions we tested with half-and-half or milk.

GRIND ZEST AND SUGAR To maximize fruit flavor, we found it best to grind the zest with the sugar in a food processor, then add juice, and strain. Oranges and raspberries need a boost from lemon juice (limes and lemons are fine on their own). We add a pinch of salt to balance sweet and tart flavors.

USE BOOZE You can only add so much sugar before the sherbet becomes too sweet. Unfortunately, that amount of sugar doesn't yield the ideal texture (for more on the role of sugar in frozen desserts, see "Role of Sugar in Freezing," page 189). We tried a variety of tricks used in other recipes to keep the sherbet soft—beaten egg whites, gelatin, and corn syrup—but we ended up preferring a little booze. Like sugar, alcohol lowers the freezing point of the sherbet mixture. In small amounts, you can't taste the alcohol (we use just 2 teaspoons of triple sec or vodka) but it does have a significant effect on texture without affecting sweetness.

WHIP THE CREAM We tried one last refinement—whipping the cream—to make the finished product lighter and smoother. We found it best to chill the strained liquid base (you want to start with a cold mixture whenever making any frozen dessert; see Vanilla Ice Cream, page 188), and then fold the whipped cream into the chilled base right before it goes into the ice cream machine.

CHURN IN A MACHINE An ice cream machine is essential when making sherbet. As with our Vanilla Ice Cream, you need a machine to beat in air and to make the texture lighter and smoother.

Sugar and Time Make Fruit Juicier

Fruit is naturally sweet, so why do so many recipes—everything from fruit salads to fruit crisps—call for so much sugar? While we agree that many recipes go overboard and make the fruit taste too sweet, you can't eliminate the sugar altogether. When fruit is tossed with sugar, it not only changes the flavor of the fruit but it changes its texture, too.

HOW THE SCIENCE WORKS

THE EFFECT OF SUGAR ON FRUIT CELLS

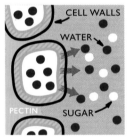

DRAWING WATER OUT
When sugar is added to fruit, the sugar draws water out of the fruit's cells via osmosis.

Fruits, by definition, are the reproductive part of plants, the ones containing all the seeds. Therefore, they are engineered by nature to appeal, enticing animals to eat them and scatter their seeds. When ripe, fruits are often brightly colored, filled with sugar, and smell aggressively good.

The ripening process of fruit is triggered by the release of ethylene, a simple gas produced by the plant when it is ready to ripen. But not all fruits ripen the same way: There are two different methods. One type of fruit, called climacteric fruit, produces a sudden burst of ethylene right when it is ready to ripen. During this process, fruits like bananas, peaches, and pears convert starch to sugar and begin to digest their cell walls, thereby becoming sweeter and softer as they ripen. Most importantly, climacteric fruits continue to ripen in this way even after they are separated from the plant. For this reason most climacteric fruits are harvested before they are ripe, at the firm mature stage, when they are better able to withstand the rigors of shipping and storage. This fruit will continue to ripen and become sweeter after it's brought home from the market. The other type of fruit, called nonclimacteric, produces ethylene only very slowly and does not continue to ripen after being separated from the plant. Nonclimacteric fruits like blueberries, cherries, and oranges do not convert starch to sugar but must receive it from

the parent plant. As a result, nonclimacteric fruits will not get any sweeter after harvesting and should be purchased as ripe as possible to ensure the best quality. (For more on different types of fruit, see Practical Science, opposite.)

The cell structure of fruit is no different from the cell structure of vegetables (see concept 23). But unlike vegetables, to which we often recommend adding salt to release the juices, to fruit we add sugar. Though sugar has one-tenth of the power of salt when it comes to coaxing the fruit to release its liquid, it is effective nonetheless. When added to fruit (which is often chopped, with the skin removed, to maximize surface area) sugar produces osmotic pressure, pulling the moisture out of the fruit's cells.

Why? Sugar is hygroscopic, meaning it has an affinity for water molecules, so it draws out water by osmotic action, then holds on to the water. Sugar has such a lust for water it will even draw moisture out of the air.

When sugar is added to fruit to draw out the juices, this is called maceration. Maceration changes the texture of fruit, making it softer and less waterlogged. Cells filled with water are firm, while those containing less water become flaccid and soft, just like a plant wilts when it becomes dry. The flavor-rich liquid that's created can be used to moisten dishes like fruit salad or berry shortcakes, or it can be discarded to help keep crumbles and pies from becoming a soggy mess.

TEST KITCHEN EXPERIMENT

To see how quickly maceration really works, we ran the following experiment: We sliced 4 ounces of fresh strawberries into ¼-inch pieces, tossed them with 1 tablespoon of granulated sugar, and piled them into the middle of a small cocktail napkin. We then tracked how far the exuded juices traveled on the napkin at five-minute intervals over 15 minutes. We repeated the test three times, averaged the results, and compared them to a control set of strawberry slices that weren't tossed with sugar.

THE RESULTS

The moment the strawberries came in contact with the sugar they started to glisten with moisture and by the five-minute mark they'd saturated almost an inch of the napkin. After another five minutes, the juices traveled an additional ½ inch, and by the 15-minute mark they'd hit the edge of the napkin, registering over 2 inches. By stark comparison, the strawberries that were sliced but not macerated left only a faint damp footprint behind when we removed them after 15 minutes. The berries tossed with sugar were also noticeably softer at the end of the 15-minute test period than the berries that had not been tossed with sugar.

THE TAKEAWAY

Tossing fruit with a little sugar may seem like an insignificant step in a recipe, but our experiment shows that the difference it makes is sizable. The sugar dissolves and draws out juices from the fruit. This process happens quickly—30 minutes, or less, depending on the recipe. The sugar both softens the fruit and creates flavorful juices that can either be used or discarded, depending on the recipe.

THE EFFECT OF SUGAR ON FRUIT

After 15 minutes, the sliced but unsugared strawberries did not lose any liquid.

After 15 minutes, the strawberries macerated in sugar saturated the napkin with juice.

PRACTICAL SCIENCE SELECTED CLIMACTERIC AND NONCLIMACTERIC FRUITS

Different fruits ripen in different ways, but most can be separated into two categories: climacteric and non.

CLIMACTERIC FRUITS
Apples, apricots, avocados, bananas, cantaloupes, peaches, pears, plums, tomatoes, papayas, and mangoes continue to ripen after harvest.

NONCLIMACTERIC FRUITS
Bell peppers, blueberries, cherries, grapefruits, lemons, oranges, grapes, melons, pineapples, raspberries, and strawberries should be purchased only when fully ripe.

We use sugar to draw out moisture from fruit in fruit salads to create a flavorful dressing. Macerating also gives the fruit a more appealing texture.

HONEYDEW, MANGO, AND RASPBERRIES WITH LIME AND GINGER

SERVES 4 TO 6

The optional cayenne adds a bit of heat to this fruit salad.

4	teaspoons sugar
2	teaspoons grated lime zest plus 1 to 2 tablespoons juice
	Pinch cayenne (optional)
3	cups honeydew melon, cut into ½-inch pieces
1	mango, peeled, pitted, and cut into ½-inch pieces (1½ cups)
1–2	teaspoons grated fresh ginger
5	ounces (1 cup) raspberries

Combine sugar, lime zest, and cayenne, if using, in large bowl. Using rubber spatula, press mixture into side of bowl until sugar becomes damp, about 30 seconds. Gently toss honeydew, mango, and ginger to taste with sugar mixture until combined. Let sit at room temperature, stirring occasionally, until fruit releases its juices, 15 to 30 minutes. Gently stir in raspberries. Stir in lime juice to taste, and serve.

PEACHES, BLACKBERRIES, AND STRAWBERRIES WITH BASIL AND PEPPER

SERVES 4 TO 6

Nectarines can be substituted for the peaches.

4	teaspoons sugar
2	tablespoons chopped fresh basil
½	teaspoon pepper
18	ounces peaches, halved, pitted, and cut into ½-inch pieces
10	ounces (2 cups) blackberries
10	ounces strawberries (2 cups), hulled and quartered lengthwise
1–2	tablespoons lime juice

Combine sugar, basil, and pepper in large bowl. Using rubber spatula, press mixture into side of bowl until sugar becomes damp, about 30 seconds. Gently toss fruit with sugar mixture until combined. Let sit at room temperature, stirring occasionally, until fruit releases its juices, 15 to 30 minutes. Stir in lime juice to taste, and serve.

✔ WHY THIS RECIPE WORKS

Most fruit salads betray neither rhyme nor reason regarding the fruit selection or assembly, and the customary heavy sprinkling of sugar seems designed to mask defects in the fruit. We set out to rewrite the rules of fruit salad to bring out the best fruit flavor. We cut the fruit into small, uniform pieces, so the different flavors and textures would come through in each mouthful. To keep each fruit distinct, we also limited the number to three per salad. We found it hard to judge the proper amount of sugar when it was added directly to the salad, so we macerated each fruit in just the amount needed to release the fruits' natural juices; we also balanced the sweetness with fresh lime juice. But first, we mashed the sugar with herbs and zests (in bartending circles, this process is called "muddling") to ensure even flavor distribution.

SKIP THE SYRUP, KEEP THE SUGAR Many classic fruit salads dissolve the sugar in water to make a simple syrup that is then tossed with the fruit. Besides the bother (you have to turn on the stove), the water doesn't improve the flavor of the fruit. We prefer to simply toss the cut fruit with sugar and wait for 15 to 30 minutes. The sugar draws juices out of the fruit and makes a natural syrup that's much more flavorful. The juices moisten the salad and make the fruit taste better.

MUDDLE FLAVORINGS WITH SUGAR Fresh herbs, citrus zest, and spices are nice counterpoints to the fruit in a summer salad. Making the classic syrup does have the advantage of getting these flavors into the fruit; simply tossing these flavorings right into the fruit salad doesn't work as well. To ensure even distribution and/or to make their texture disappear into the salad, we found it best to work these seasonings into the raw sugar. We use the bartending technique of muddling, in which a small wooden dowel with a flattened end is used to mash sugar with herbs or citrus to extract bigger, fresher flavors in alcoholic drinks (think mojitos). Using a flexible rubber spatula, we can apply this technique to our salad.

FINISH WITH LIME JUICE Just before serving we recommend tossing the fruit salad with a little lime juice (1 to 2 tablespoons, depending on the sweetness of the fruit). The acidity balances the sugar and makes the salad taste fresher and brighter.

SWEETENERS 101

BUYING

GRANULATED SUGAR Common granulated sugar starts with either sugar cane or sugar beets. In kitchen tests, we couldn't tell the difference, since the end product, sucrose, is chemically the same, no matter the source.

SUPERFINE SUGAR This finely processed sugar has extra-small crystals that dissolve quickly, making it a must for drinks. Superfine sugar promotes a melt-in-the-mouth texture in delicate cookies such as shortbread.

CONFECTIONERS' SUGAR To prevent clumping, this pulverized sugar contains a small amount of cornstarch, making it ideal for dusting over cakes or dissolving in a quick glaze.

BROWN SUGAR Modern brown sugar is basically granulated sugar with molasses added—6.5 percent for dark brown sugar or 3.5 percent for light brown sugar. Except for certain recipes, we find that light and dark brown sugars are interchangeable, with some slight differences in flavor and texture. Note that natural brown sugars, such as Demerara and turbinado, are derived from sugar cane (like granulated sugar), but they are slightly less processed and thus retain a gentle molasses flavor and larger crystal size.

MOLASSES Molasses is a byproduct of the process by which sugar cane is refined. Depending on when in the process the molasses is extracted, it can be fairly mild or quite strong. Blackstrap molasses is derived late in the refining process and has a harsh flavor we don't like in recipes.

HONEY Honey has a distinct flavor based on the type of plant from which the bees extracted their nectar. Honey contains water as well as fructose and glucose.

CORN SYRUP This modern sweetener is derived from cornstarch and contains glucose along with long chains of glucose molecules that make it very thick (viscous) and keep it from crystallizing like honey or maple syrup. Corn syrup is less sweet than most other sweeteners.

STRUCTURE

Most home kitchens are stocked with a multitude of sweeteners derived from various plant sources. (Honey is an exception since it is "processed" by bees, not humans.) Most natural sweeteners are obtained by either extracting or squeezing them from these plant sources and then purifying the natural sugars. Before examining the differences among these sweeteners, let's first understand their basic chemical composition. Natural sweeteners are based on different types of sugar molecules called mono- and disaccharides, composed of only carbon, hydrogen, and oxygen. Sweet-tasting sugar molecules contain atoms of hydrogen linked to oxygen (called hydroxy groups) attached to a carbon framework in specific three-dimensional shapes that bind with the sweet taste receptors in the mouth. Most sweeteners rely on the following molecules, alone or in combination.

GLUCOSE

Glucose (also known as dextrose) is one of two simple sugar molecules. (The other is fructose.) It is referred to as a monosaccharide. Glucose is found in a variety of living cells, especially fruits and honey. It is also found in corn syrup made from cornstarch. Glucose is only 75 percent as sweet as sucrose.

FRUCTOSE

Fructose is one of two simple sugar molecules. Like glucose, fructose is referred to as a monosaccharide. Like glucose, fructose is found in many fruits as well as honey. Fructose is almost 1.5 times sweeter than sucrose.

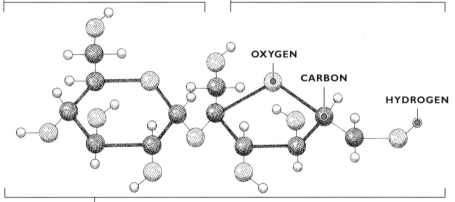

SUCROSE

This complex sugar contains one molecule of glucose bonded to one molecule of fructose, in what is called a disaccharide. Like glucose and fructose, sucrose is produced by green plants during photosynthesis. All sugar derived from cane or beets, including granulated sugar, consists mainly or entirely of sucrose, as does maple syrup.

STORING

GRANULATED SUGAR (as well as superfine and confectioners' sugar) will keep indefinitely in a cool, dry pantry.

BROWN SUGAR must be kept in an airtight container. Over time, brown sugar will dry out. To revive hardened brown sugar, place it in a bowl with a slice of bread, cover the bowl with plastic wrap, and microwave it on high power for 10 to 20 seconds. This should soften the sugar enough to measure it. (It will harden once it cools.) Make sure to pack brown sugar into the cup when measuring it.

HONEY keeps indefinitely but it will crystallize. To return honey to a fluid state, place the open container of honey in a saucepan filled with 1 inch of water and stir over low heat until liquefied.

USING

It is possible to make sweetener substitutions.

TO REPLACE	SUBSTITUTE
1 cup superfine sugar	Grind 1 cup plus 2 teaspoons granulated sugar in food processor for 30 seconds.
1 cup confectioners' sugar	Pulverize 1 cup granulated sugar and 1 teaspoon cornstarch in spice grinder or blender for at least 1 minute. (Do not use food processor.) Strain through fine-mesh strainer before using.
1 cup light brown sugar	Pulse 1 cup granulated sugar with 1 teaspoon molasses in food processor until uniformly blended.
1 cup dark brown sugar	Pulse 1 cup granulated sugar with 2 teaspoons molasses in food processor.

Many crisps, cobblers, crumbles, and shortcakes begin by tossing the fruit with sugar and other flavorings. The idea is to get the fruit to release its juices and help create a saucier texture. Macerating is also a way to get the fruit to release its juices before baking, so you don't end up with a soggy mess.

PEACH CRUMBLE
SERVES 6

Add the lemon juice to taste in step 2 according to the sweetness of your peaches. If ripe peaches are unavailable, you can substitute 3 pounds of frozen peaches, thawed overnight in the refrigerator. If your peaches are firm, you should be able to peel them with a vegetable peeler. If they are too soft and ripe to withstand the pressure of a peeler, you'll need to blanch them in a pot of simmering water for 15 seconds and then shock them in a bowl of ice water before peeling. Serve with vanilla ice cream.

FILLING
- 3½ pounds peaches, peeled, halved, pitted, and cut into ¾-inch wedges
- ⅓ cup (2⅓ ounces) granulated sugar
- 1¼ teaspoons cornstarch
- 3–5 teaspoons lemon juice
- Pinch salt
- Pinch ground cinnamon
- Pinch ground nutmeg

CRUMBLE TOPPING
- 1 cup (5 ounces) all-purpose flour
- 5 tablespoons (2¼ ounces) granulated sugar
- ¼ cup packed (1¾ ounces) brown sugar
- ⅛ teaspoon salt
- 2 teaspoons vanilla extract
- 6 tablespoons unsalted butter, cut into 6 pieces and softened (68 degrees)
- ½ cup sliced almonds

1. Adjust oven racks to lowest and middle positions and heat oven to 350 degrees. Line rimmed baking sheet with parchment paper. Line second rimmed baking sheet with aluminum foil.

2. **FOR THE FILLING:** Gently toss peaches and sugar together in large bowl and let sit for 30 minutes, gently stirring several times. Drain peaches in colander set over large bowl and reserve ¼ cup juices (discard remaining juices). Whisk reserved juices, cornstarch, lemon juice to taste, salt, cinnamon, and nutmeg together in small bowl. Combine peaches and juice mixture in bowl and transfer to 8-inch square baking dish.

3. **FOR THE CRUMBLE TOPPING:** While peaches are macerating, combine flour, ¼ cup granulated sugar, brown sugar, and salt in food processor and drizzle vanilla over top. Pulse to combine, about 5 pulses. Scatter butter pieces and ¼ cup almonds over top and process until mixture clumps together into large, crumbly balls, about 30 seconds, scraping down bowl halfway through processing. Sprinkle remaining ¼ cup almonds over mixture and pulse 2 times to combine. Transfer mixture to parchment-lined baking sheet and spread into even layer (mixture should break up into roughly ½-inch chunks with some smaller, loose bits). Bake on middle rack until chunks are lightly browned and firm, 18 to 22 minutes, rotating baking sheet halfway through baking. (Cooled topping can be stored in airtight container for up to 2 days.)

4. **TO ASSEMBLE AND BAKE:** Grasp edges of parchment paper, slide topping off paper over peaches, and spread into even layer with spatula, packing down lightly and breaking up any very large pieces. Sprinkle remaining 1 tablespoon sugar evenly over top and place dish on foil-lined baking sheet; place on lower rack. Increase oven temperature to 375 degrees and bake until well browned and filling is bubbling around edges, 25 to 35 minutes, rotating baking sheet halfway through baking. Transfer baking dish to wire rack and let cool for at least 15 minutes; serve warm.

PRACTICAL SCIENCE
KEEP YOUR PEACHES OUT OF THE COLD

Unless your peaches are ripe, don't refrigerate them.

Keeping peaches in the fridge might seem like a good way to prolong their shelf life, but unless the fruit is ripe, the cold temperatures can turn their flesh mealy. Storing the fruit at or below 40 degrees deactivates an enzyme that breaks down pectin during ripening. If this happens before the flesh is ripe, the pectin will remain intact and the flesh texture will be mealy. The lesson: Store peaches on the counter.

☑ WHY THIS RECIPE WORKS

A soggy topping and watery, flavorless filling are the norm for the simple, humble peach crumble. The problem is the peaches—you never know just how juicy or how flavorful they will be until you cut them open. We wanted a peach crumble that consisted of fresh-tasting, lightly sweetened peaches topped with a buttery, crisp, and nutty-tasting crumble—no matter how sweet the peaches were (or weren't). Solving the peach problem involved letting peeled, sliced peaches macerate in sugar. The sweetness of the filling was adjusted by adding more or less lemon juice as needed. Baking the topping separately solved the final challenge of getting a crisp, well-browned crust.

MACERATE AND MEASURE Many peaches shed a ton of liquid when baked, causing a soggy crumble that's not nearly crisp enough on top. Our solution is to macerate the sliced peaches for 30 minutes. We then drain the juices and discard all but ¼ cup. We add a little thickener (cornstarch) to the reserved juices, along with the flavorings (lemon juice, salt, cinnamon, and nutmeg), and toss this with the macerated fruit. This way we know just how much juice will be in the baking dish.

MAKE A CRISP CRUMBLE For our crumble we use softened butter rather than melted butter. Melted butter makes a topping that is too sandy. We prefer to make the topping in a food processor. This way, we end up with a cohesive dough, which can be easily broken apart into large chunks that bake up nice and crisp in the oven.

BAKE THE TOPPING FIRST No topping baked on top of steaming fruit will ever become really crisp. Our solution is to bake the topping on a separate baking sheet until lightly browned. We then add the baked topping to the fruit and put the crumble in the oven. A sprinkling of sugar over the crumble topping adds a sweet crunch on top. This method ensures that as soon as the fruit is cooked, the topping will be browned and crisp.

STRAWBERRY SHORTCAKES
SERVES 6

Preparing the fruit first gives it time to release its juices.

FRUIT

2½	pounds strawberries (8 cups), hulled
6	tablespoons (2⅔ ounces) sugar

BISCUITS

2	cups (10 ounces) all-purpose flour
5	tablespoons (2¼ ounces) sugar
1	tablespoon baking powder
½	teaspoon salt
8	tablespoons unsalted butter, cut into ½-inch pieces and chilled
½	cup plus 1 tablespoon half-and-half or milk
1	large egg, lightly beaten, plus 1 large white, lightly beaten
1	recipe Whipped Cream (recipe follows)

1. FOR THE FRUIT: Crush 3 cups strawberries in large bowl with potato masher. Slice remaining 5 cups berries. Stir sliced berries and sugar into crushed berries. Set aside until sugar has dissolved and berries are juicy, at least 30 minutes or up to 2 hours.

2. FOR THE BISCUITS: Adjust oven rack to lower-middle position and heat oven to 425 degrees. Line baking sheet with parchment paper. Pulse flour, 3 tablespoons sugar, baking powder, and salt in food processor until combined. Scatter butter pieces over top and pulse until mixture resembles coarse meal, about 15 pulses. Transfer mixture to large bowl.

3. Whisk half-and-half and whole egg together in bowl, then stir into flour mixture until large clumps form. Turn out onto lightly floured counter and knead lightly until dough comes together (do not overwork dough).

4. Pat dough into 9 by 6-inch rectangle, about ¾ inch thick. Using floured 2¾-inch biscuit cutter, cut out 6 dough rounds. Arrange biscuits on prepared sheet, spaced about 1½ inches apart. Brush tops with egg white and sprinkle evenly with remaining 2 tablespoons sugar. (Unbaked biscuits can be refrigerated, covered with plastic wrap, for up to 2 hours.)

5. Bake until biscuits are golden brown, 12 to 14 minutes, rotating baking sheet halfway through baking. Transfer baking sheet to wire rack and let biscuits cool, about 10 minutes. (Cooled biscuits can be stored at room temperature for up to 1 day. Before assembling, reheat in 350-degree oven for 3 to 5 minutes.)

6. To assemble, split each biscuit in half and place bottoms on individual plates. Spoon portion of berries over each bottom, dollop with whipped cream, and cap with biscuit tops. Serve immediately.

WHIPPED CREAM
MAKES ABOUT 2 CUPS

For lightly sweetened whipped cream, reduce the sugar to 1½ teaspoons.

  1 cup heavy cream, chilled
  1 tablespoon sugar
  1 teaspoon vanilla extract

Using stand mixer fitted with whisk, whip cream, sugar, and vanilla on medium-low speed until foamy, about 1 minute. Increase speed to high and whip until soft peaks form, 1 to 3 minutes. (Whipped cream can be refrigerated in fine-mesh strainer set over small bowl and covered with plastic wrap for up to 8 hours.)

✓ WHY THIS RECIPE WORKS

While some folks like to spoon strawberries over pound cake, sponge cake, or even angel food cake, our idea of strawberry shortcake definitely involves a biscuit. We wanted a juicy strawberry filling and mounds of freshly whipped cream sandwiched in the middle of a lightly sweetened, tender biscuit. Therefore, we enhance the biscuit dough with egg and sugar, and mash a portion of the berries while slicing the rest for a chunky, juicy mixture that won't slide off the biscuits.

PRACTICAL SCIENCE
SECRETS TO FOOLPROOF WHIPPED CREAM

It's best to add sugar early, and keep your cream cold.

When is the best time to add sugar when making whipped cream? The old wives' tale says that you need to add it at the end; otherwise, the cream won't whip properly. We made two batches of whipped cream to find out. We added the sugar at two different points: at the beginning of whipping and at the end. Although both batches whipped to the same volume, there was a difference in texture. When the sugar was added later in the process, the whipped cream had a slightly grainy texture. When added to the cream at the beginning of whipping, however, the granules had dissolved by the time the cream was fully whipped.

While sugar timing doesn't affect the cream's ability to whip up properly, the temperature of the cream does. Whipping the cream introduces air bubbles, whose walls are stabilized by tiny globules of fat. These fat globules hold the air bubbles in place as the whipping continues, forming what eventually becomes light, airy whipped cream. Because heat softens the butterfat in the cream, the liquid fat globules will collapse completely rather than hold together the air bubbles, preventing the cream from whipping up properly. To keep this from happening, it is crucial to use cream straight from the refrigerator. Chilling the bowl and beaters helps, too.

MASH SOME BERRIES Most strawberry shortcakes are made with sliced or quartered berries, which simply slide off the biscuit when you go to eat it. We mash some of the berries and then stir in the sliced berries and sugar. The sugar dissolves after about 30 minutes and you have plenty of thickened, juicy berry puree that will anchor the sliced berries in place.

ENRICH THOSE BISCUITS Yes, you can use regular biscuits to make a shortcake, but we think a true short-cake should be sweet (we add more sugar to the biscuits) and richer (we add an egg and use half-and-half rather than milk). Brushing the biscuits with a beaten egg white and then sprinkling them with sugar gives them a crunchy, appealingly browned top.

USE COLD CREAM The secret to billowy whipped cream is to start with cold cream. If the cream has been well chilled in the refrigerator, it should whip just fine. If your kitchen is warm, chill the mixer bowl and whisk, too. To sweeten the cream, we prefer granulated sugar, added at the outset.

BERRY FOOL
SERVES 6

Blueberries or blackberries can be substituted for the raspberries in this recipe. You may also substitute frozen fruit for fresh, but it will slightly compromise the texture. If using frozen fruit, reduce the amount of sugar in the puree by 1 tablespoon. The thickened fruit puree can be made up to four hours in advance; just make sure to whisk it well in step 4 to break up any clumps before combining it with the whipped cream. For the best results, chill your mixer bowl and whisk before whipping the cream. We like the granular texture and nutty flavor of Carr's Whole Wheat Crackers, but graham crackers or gingersnaps will also work. You will need six tall parfait or sundae glasses for this recipe.

   2 pounds strawberries (6 cups), hulled
  12 ounces (2⅓ cups) raspberries
  ¾ cup (5¼ ounces) sugar
   2 teaspoons unflavored gelatin
   1 cup heavy cream, chilled
  ¼ cup sour cream, chilled
  ½ teaspoon vanilla extract
   4 Carr's Whole Wheat Crackers, crushed fine
      (¼ cup)
   6 sprigs fresh mint (optional)

1. Process half of strawberries, half of raspberries, and ½ cup sugar in food processor until mixture is completely smooth, about 1 minute. Strain berry puree through fine-mesh strainer into large liquid measuring cup (you should have about 2½ cups puree; reserve excess for another use). Transfer ½ cup puree to small bowl and sprinkle gelatin over top; let stand for at least 5 minutes to soften and stir. Heat remaining 2 cups puree in small saucepan over medium heat until it begins to bubble, 4 to 6 minutes. Off heat, stir in gelatin mixture until dissolved. Transfer to medium bowl, cover with plastic wrap, and refrigerate until well chilled, about 2 hours.

2. Meanwhile, chop remaining strawberries into rough ¼-inch pieces. Toss strawberries, remaining raspberries, and 2 tablespoons sugar together in medium bowl. Set aside for 1 hour.

3. Using stand mixer fitted with whisk, whip cream, sour cream, vanilla, and remaining 2 tablespoons sugar on low speed until bubbles form, about 30 seconds. Increase speed to medium and whip until whisk leaves trail, about 30 seconds. Increase speed to high; whip until mixture has nearly doubled in volume and holds stiff peaks, about 30 seconds. Transfer ⅓ cup whipped cream mixture to small bowl; set aside.

4. Remove berry puree from refrigerator and whisk until smooth. With mixer on medium speed, slowly add two-thirds of puree to whipped cream mixture; mix until incorporated, about 15 seconds. Using spatula, gently fold in remaining puree, leaving streaks of puree.

5. Transfer uncooked berries to fine-mesh strainer; shake gently to remove any excess juices. Divide two-thirds of berries evenly among six tall parfait or sundae glasses. Divide creamy berry mixture evenly among glasses, followed by remaining uncooked berries. Top each glass with reserved plain whipped cream mixture. Sprinkle with crushed crackers and garnish with mint sprigs, if using. Serve immediately.

✓ WHY THIS RECIPE WORKS

This traditional British fruit dessert is typically made by folding pureed stewed fruit (usually gooseberries) into pastry cream. Modern fool recipes skip the pastry cream and use whipped cream. Simpler for sure, but with whipped cream the fool ends up too loose and watery. We wanted a dessert with intense fruitiness and rich body—and we wanted to use strawberries and raspberries rather than gooseberries. To do this, we thickened the fruit properly with gelatin and strengthened our whipped cream with sour cream. For even more fruit flavor, we layered the fruit puree and cream base with fresh berries that had been macerated in sugar.

PUREE SOME BERRIES   We tried various methods for thickening the fruit (since we didn't want to lose the ease of whipped cream) and ended up using gelatin to make a thick, sweet puree. The rest of the berries are chopped and macerated so they soften and become more flavorful. We strain off the excess juices to keep the fool from becoming soggy.

SWELL, THEN HEAT THE GELATIN   For the gelatin in the fruit puree, we use a judicious hand. First we add 2 teaspoons of gelatin to some uncooked berry puree to let it soften, and then we combine the softened mixture with some heated puree to help melt and distribute the gelatin. (Most recipes call for the gelatin to be hydrated because adding powdered gelatin directly to hot liquid can cause the exterior of the gelatin granules to hydrate too quickly, making them clump together and preventing the center of the granules from absorbing water.) After sitting for a couple of hours in the refrigerator, the puree thickens to the consistency of loose pie filling—perfect.

BULK UP WHIPPED CREAM   With the gelatin added to our fruit, it could hold its own against the whipped cream, but we wondered if there was an easy way to make the whipped cream itself sturdier and richer. After trying yogurt, mascarpone, crème fraîche, and sour cream, our tasters thought sour cream did the best job—it provided just the right degree of richness along with a mild tang.

BUILD THE LAYERS   We fold some of the gelatin-thickened puree into the some of the whipped cream and then layer that with fresh berries and plain whipped cream. We like a final garnish of some crushed Carr's Whole Wheat Crackers for a little crunch but this is optional.

PRACTICAL SCIENCE   GELATIN VS. PECTIN

Gelatin is our first choice to thicken the berry puree in our fool.

Gelatin might be a newcomer to recipes for fruit fool, but it has long been used to impart a silken texture to desserts ranging from Bavarian crème to mousse. A pure protein derived from animal bones and connective tissues, gelatin changes a liquid into a semisolid state by trapping water and slowing its movement. In contrast to other thickening agents, gelatin begins to melt at body temperature, contributing to a unique sensation in the mouth. These properties work beautifully in our Berry Fool, transforming a thin berry puree into a viscous mixture that lends silkiness to the enriched whipped cream.

Pectin is a carbohydrate that occurs naturally in fruits and vegetables and holds cell walls together like cement. When exposed to heat, sugar, and acid, pectin molecules loosen their grip on the cell walls and bond directly with each other, creating a matrix that traps water in much the same way gelatin molecules do. However, unlike gelatin, pectin requires high temperatures for its thickening action to be reversed. It also proved an unsuitable thickener for the fruit in our fool, requiring so much sugar to work that it turned the berries into jam.

Cocoa Powder Delivers Big Flavor

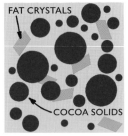

COCOA POWDER *Cocoa powder has a high ratio of cocoa solids, which are responsible for giving big chocolate flavor.*

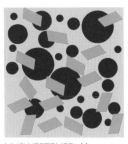

UNSWEETENED *Unsweetened chocolate has a good deal of cocoa solids, but also contains more fat crystals than cocoa powder, and therefore contains less chocolate flavor.*

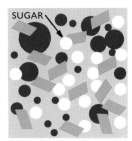

BITTERSWEET *Bittersweet chocolate contains less cocoa solids, and many more fat crystals, as well as sugar, giving it the least chocolate flavor of the three.*

All too often, chocolate cakes, brownies, puddings, and mousses look dark and decadent, but take a bite and the flavor is actually pretty wimpy. This might be because an insufficient amount of chocolate was used. But just as often the culprit is the type of chocolate, not the amount.

HOW THE SCIENCE WORKS

Older dessert recipes generally call for unsweetened chocolate, which contains cocoa butter (the fat that makes chocolate so smooth) and cocoa solids (the compounds that create chocolate flavor). Many newer recipes call for bittersweet chocolate, which is basically unsweetened chocolate with sugar added. These eating chocolates are more highly processed than unsweetened bars and can provide a luscious texture to frostings, but they don't have nearly as much chocolate oomph as unsweetened chocolate. That's why brownies, for instance, are almost always made with unsweetened chocolate.

While we rely on both unsweetened and bittersweet chocolates in our dessert recipes, over the years we have found that cocoa powder is often a key component in creating chocolate recipes that deliver big flavor. We use cocoa in everything from chocolate mousse to chocolate cupcakes. Not only do other recipes rarely call for cocoa powder, but those that do rarely use it correctly.

Why do we like cocoa powder? Cocoa powder is made by removing most of the fat (cocoa butter) from cocoa liquor (produced from fermented cocoa beans), which in effect concentrates the amount of cocoa solids. Ounce for ounce, cocoa powder has more cocoa solids—and thus more chocolate flavor—than any other type of chocolate. But you need to handle the cocoa powder correctly to get the maximum flavor benefit from this potent ingredient.

Cocoa powder contains solid particles of insoluble carbohydrate, fat (about 10 to 12 percent), and a smaller amount of protein, with tiny flavor molecules trapped inside. Some of these flavor molecules come from the cocoa beans, while others are produced during the fermentation and subsequent roasting of the beans. If you simply add cocoa powder to the dry ingredients (as is often the case in cake recipes that call for cocoa powder), you don't get much flavor. The secret to using cocoa powder is to bloom the flavors by pouring hot water over the cocoa. Stirring the cocoa in hot water causes these flavor molecules, which would otherwise remain imprisoned, to burst forth, amplifying overall flavor.

The intensity of this flavor also depends on how the cocoa was produced. Regular cocoa powder produced from fermented, roasted beans has an intense flavor and light color, and is naturally acidic with a pH around 5.7. Dutch-processed, or alkalized, cocoa powder is produced from fermented beans that have been treated with an alkali before or after roasting to raise the pH of the cocoa powder to 6.8 to 7.2. Dutch-processed cocoa powder has a milder, less bitter flavor, but a darker color. (For more on different types of cocoa powder, see "Natural Cocoa and Dutch-Processed Cocoa," page 430.)

TEST KITCHEN EXPERIMENT

We wanted to clear up any confusion about the amount of real chocolate flavor in three common forms of chocolate, so we designed a simple experiment. We made three batches of hot chocolate. For each 8 ounces of hot water, we used 1 ounce of chocolate—cocoa powder, bittersweet bar chocolate, and unsweetened bar chocolate, respectively—and asked 20 tasters to sample them in a blind taste test. Tasters were asked to ignore differences in sugar and fat and focus solely on the intensity of chocolate flavor in each sample.

THE RESULTS

The cocoa powder won hands-down, followed by the unsweetened bar chocolate, and finally the bittersweet bar chocolate. All 20 tasters ranked the hot chocolate made with cocoa powder as the one with the strongest chocolate flavor.

THE TAKEAWAY

Our results correlate directly to the percentage of cocoa solids in each type of chocolate (that is, the more cocoa solids, the more chocolate flavor we noticed), so we did some math to figure out how much unsweetened and bittersweet chocolate we'd need to use in order to have the same intensity of chocolate flavor as we got from the cocoa powder. Cocoa powder is 80 percent cocoa solids, so 1 ounce provides 0.8 ounce of flavorful solids. Our preferred brand of unsweetened chocolate is about 49 percent cocoa solids (the remainder of the bar is made up of fat and emulsifiers) so we would need about 1.63 ounces of it to equal 0.8 ounce of solids. Cocoa solids make up only 21 percent of our winning bittersweet bar chocolate, meaning it would take a whopping 3.8 ounces of it to equal the chocolate flavor in 1 ounce of cocoa powder!

To illustrate our math, we made three more batches of hot chocolate, this time with the adjusted amounts of unsweetened bar chocolate and bittersweet bar chocolate.

Ignoring the varying levels of sugar and fat, tasters found that the level of chocolate flavor was indeed equal across all three samples.

While the fat and sugar found in bittersweet chocolate make it a pleasure to eat straight and can play an important role in imparting a creamy texture to frostings, puddings, and mousses, we now know that to get the most chocolate flavor into baked goods, we have to reach for the cocoa powder.

STACKING UP CHOCOLATE FLAVOR

In order to get the same amount of cocoa solids (0.8 ounces), the source of chocolate flavor, we had to use drastically different amounts of cocoa powder, unsweetened bar chocolate, and bittersweet bar chocolate.

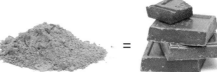

COCOA POWDER	UNSWEETENED BAR CHOCOLATE	BITTERSWEET BAR CHOCOLATE
1 ounce	*1.63 ounces*	*3.8 ounces*

PRACTICAL SCIENCE UNDERSTANDING CACAO PERCENTAGES

When it comes to cooking with chocolate, swapping cacao percentages can make a big difference.

In a recipe specifying a bittersweet or semisweet chocolate, can you substitute a chocolate with a higher cacao percentage (cacao percentage is the combined percentages of cocoa butter and nonfat cocoa solids) than the 60 percent generally used for cooking, making no other adjustments? Not if you expect identical results. First we tasted brownies and pots de crème made with our two top-ranked dark chocolates, Callebaut and Ghirardelli, which have 60 percent cacao, alongside ones made with the same brands' 70 percent cacao offerings.

While all four versions were acceptable, tasters strongly preferred the 60 percent cacao chocolates in these recipes, complaining of dryness and lack of sweetness (and in the case of the pots de crème, a thicker, stiffer consistency) in the versions made with the 70 percent cacao chocolates. Although some tasters noted the "deeper" chocolate flavor of the desserts made with 70 percent cacao chocolates, the problems far outweighed any benefit.

When chocolate manufacturers increase cacao content, they correspondingly decrease the amount of sugar and usually add less cocoa butter. With less sugar and fat, it's no wonder the results were different. If you're baking with 70 percent cacao chocolate and you suspect the recipe was developed with 60 percent cacao chocolate, you can try to add a bit more sugar, but be prepared for some trial and error before obtaining perfection.

Blooming cocoa in hot water—or hot coffee—is the key to bringing out the deep chocolate flavor of this concentrated source of cocoa solids. Cocoa powder is an important ingredient, both for its flavor and for the fact that it contains little fat, which can negatively affect the texture of chewy brownies or sturdy cupcakes. For another recipe that maximizes the flavor of chocolate, see Creamy Chocolate Pudding (page 196).

CHEWY BROWNIES
MAKES 24 BROWNIES

For an accurate measurement of boiling water, bring a full kettle of water to a boil, then measure out the desired amount. For the chewiest texture, it is important to let the brownies cool thoroughly before cutting. If your baking dish is glass, let the brownies cool for 10 minutes, then remove them promptly from the pan (otherwise, the superior heat retention of glass can lead to overbaking). Use high-quality chocolate in this recipe.

⅓	cup (1 ounce) Dutch-processed cocoa
1½	teaspoons instant espresso powder (optional)
½	cup plus 2 tablespoons boiling water
2	ounces unsweetened chocolate, chopped fine
½	cup plus 2 tablespoons vegetable oil
4	tablespoons unsalted butter, melted
2	large eggs plus 2 large yolks
2	teaspoons vanilla extract
2½	cups (17½ ounces) sugar
1¾	cups (8¾ ounces) all-purpose flour
¾	teaspoon salt
6	ounces bittersweet chocolate, cut into ½-inch pieces

1. Adjust oven rack to lowest position and heat oven to 350 degrees. Make foil sling by folding 2 long sheets of aluminum foil so that they are as wide as 13 by 9-inch baking pan (one 13-inch sheet and one 9-inch sheet). Lay sheets of foil in pan perpendicular to one another, with extra foil hanging over edges of pan. Push foil into corners and up sides of pan, smoothing foil flush to pan. Grease foil and set aside.

2. Whisk cocoa, espresso powder, if using, and boiling water together in large bowl until smooth. Add unsweetened chocolate and whisk until chocolate is melted. Whisk in oil and melted butter. (Mixture may look curdled.)

Add eggs, yolks, and vanilla and continue to whisk until smooth and homogeneous. Whisk in sugar until fully incorporated. Whisk together flour and salt in small bowl and then mix into batter with rubber spatula until combined. Fold in bittersweet chocolate pieces.

3. Transfer batter to prepared pan; spread batter into corners of pan and smooth surface. Bake until toothpick inserted in center of brownies comes out with few moist crumbs attached, 30 to 35 minutes, rotating pan halfway through baking. Transfer pan to wire rack and let cool for 1½ hours.

4. Remove brownies from pan using foil. Return brownies to wire rack and let cool completely, about 1 hour. Cut brownies into 2-inch squares and serve. (Brownies can be stored in airtight container at room temperature for up to 3 days.)

PRACTICAL SCIENCE
BAKING BROWNIES WITH A SHINY TOP

Granulated sugar is key for brownies with good shine.

A glossy, crackly top is one of the hallmarks of a great brownie, but achieving it can be elusive. Can the type of sweetener you use help?

We baked three batches of brownies, one sweetened with granulated sugar, another with brown sugar, and a third with brown sugar and corn syrup. Only the brownies made with granulated sugar took on an attractive crackly sheen.

Why? It's all due to what might be deemed "special effects." Whether on its own or in combination with corn syrup, brown sugar forms crystals on the surface of the cooling brownie. Crystals reflect light in a diffuse way, creating a matte effect. The pure sucrose in granulated sugar, on the other hand, forms a smooth, glasslike, noncrystalline surface as it cools that reflects light in a focused way, for a shiny effect. As for the crackly crust, its formation depends on sugar molecules rising to the surface of the batter and drying out during baking. Since both brown sugar and corn syrup contain more moisture than granulated sugar, the surface of brownies made with either of these sweeteners never dries out enough for a crisp crust to form.

BROWN SUGAR = DULL, MATTE FINISH   WHITE SUGAR = SHINY, CRACKLY FINISH

WHY THIS RECIPE WORKS

Brownies are a tricky business; homemade recipes have better fla-
vor, while boxed mixes claim best texture. Our goal was clear: a
homemade brownie with chewiness (and a shiny, crisp, crackly top)
to rival the boxed-mix standard, but flush with a rich, deep, all-
natural chocolate flavor. What it all comes down to is the ratio of
saturated to unsaturated fats.

GO FOR CHEW   Most homemade brownies are either super-rich and fudgy or more cakelike and less rich. The difference between the two styles is simply the ratio of chocolate to flour. Chewy brownies, like the kind you get from a boxed mix, are very hard to make from scratch. We tried all kinds of tricks—everything from using condensed milk and biscuit mix instead of flour to cooking the sugar and butter into a caramel—but nothing worked. We even replaced the granulated sugar with brown sugar, but that only caused us to lose the shiny,

crackly top that we expect from good brownies. (See "Baking Brownies with a Shiny Top," opposite, for more on this phenomenon.)

LOOK TO THE BOX   It turns out that the whole key to the texture of a box brownie resides in the specific types and amounts of fat it includes. To get boxed-mix brownie chew in homemade, we discovered the perfect proportion of liquid to solid fat, without the aid of high-tech fats used by brownie mix makers. It all came down to the magic 1:3 ratio of saturated to unsaturated fat (as opposed to the 2:1 ratio found in homemade brownies made with butter). We balance the saturated fat of butter with unsaturated vegetable oil. To simplify the calculations in our version we chose to eliminate melted chocolate and use cocoa powder, which contains very little fat by comparison.

ADD EXTRA YOLKS   To reduce greasiness, we first tried reducing the overall fat content but found that left

---

PRACTICAL SCIENCE   CHEWY BROWNIES ARE ABOUT THE FAT

The secret to a boxed-mix brownie's chewy texture boils down to one thing: fat—specifically, the ratio of saturated to unsaturated fat.

Fat can be divided into two broad types: saturated and unsaturated. Both types consist of carbon atoms strung together in long chains. In predominantly saturated fats such as shortening (aka partially hydrogenated vegetable oil), beef tallow, and lard, each of these carbon atoms has the maximum number of hydrogen atoms attached to it. The hydrogen acts as a buttress to keep the carbon chains rigid so that they pack together like a box of pencils, forming a fat that is solid even at room temperature. Unsaturated fats, such as vegetable oils, have fewer hydrogen atoms providing support, resulting in carbon chains that don't stick together tightly and a fat that is liquid at room temperature. The right combination of rigid and flexible chains—the shortening system—is what gives box brownies their unique texture.

Boxed brownie mixes already come with the saturated-fat component, which is broken down into tiny, powdery crystals. When a cook then adds unsaturated vegetable oil to this mix, the liquid fat and powdered solid fat combine in a ratio designed to deliver maximum chew.

By using both butter (a predominantly saturated fat) and unsaturated vegetable oil, we were able to approximate the same 1:3 ratio found in commercially engineered specimens to mimic their satisfying chew.

	SATURATED FAT	UNSATURATED FAT
Box Formula	28%	72%
Classic Formula	64%	36%
Our Formula	29%	71%

BOX FORMULA
Besides containing the optimal ratio of different fat types, box brownies make use of highly processed powdered shortening to achieve their chewy texture.

CLASSIC FORMULA
The classic version of brownies is made with all butter (and no vegetable oil) for a high proportion of solid, saturated fat that leads to a tender texture, versus a chewy one.

OUR FORMULA
Our brownies contain a low-tech combo of butter and vegetable oil that creates a chewy texture similar to box brownies, but a far richer taste than shortening ever could.

the brownies dry. We remembered that emulsifiers can help prevent fats from separating (see concept 36) and leaking out during baking. We tried using mayonnaise, which worked surprisingly well, producing brownies with a rich, luxurious texture. But when we dove deeper, we identified the active emulsifier in the mayonnaise as lecithin, a phospholipid that occurs naturally in egg yolks. Rather than using mayonnaise, the simple addition of two extra yolks in exchange for a little oil made greasiness a thing of the past.

BLOOM THE COCOA At this point, our recipe relied on just cocoa. We realized we could replace some of the butter in our recipe with unsweetened chocolate without changing the ratio of fats. We poured boiling water over the cocoa to bloom its flavor and added a little instant espresso for intensity. We then whisked in the chocolate until melted.

END WITH CHUNKS OF CHOCOLATE Only chocolate that is melted and incorporated into the batter actually affects the ratio of fats in the mix. Therefore, for even more chocolate flavor, we incorporate chocolate chunks into the mixed batter. Because they don't melt until the batter starts baking, they have no effect on texture. The final results are as close to a boxed-mix texture as any home cook could produce without the benefits of industrial processing: chewy, fudgy bars with gooey pockets of melted chocolate that evoke images of bake sales past, but with complex flavor and just enough adult flourish to lift them out of the realm of child's fare.

EASY CHOCOLATE CAKE
SERVES 8

Any high-quality dark, bittersweet, or semisweet chocolate will work in this recipe. Instead of confectioners' sugar, the cake can be served with Whipped Cream (page 424).

1½	cups (7½ ounces) all-purpose flour
1	cup (7 ounces) sugar
½	teaspoon baking soda
¼	teaspoon salt
½	cup (1½ ounces) Dutch-processed cocoa
2	ounces bittersweet chocolate, chopped fine
1	cup brewed coffee, hot
⅔	cup mayonnaise
1	large egg, room temperature
2	teaspoons vanilla extract
	Confectioners' sugar (optional)

1. Adjust oven rack to middle position and heat oven to 350 degrees. Grease 8-inch square baking pan, line with parchment paper, grease parchment, and flour pan.

2. Whisk flour, sugar, baking soda, and salt together in large bowl. In separate bowl, combine cocoa and chocolate. Pour hot coffee over cocoa mixture and let sit, covered, for 5 minutes. Gently whisk mixture until smooth, let cool slightly, then whisk in mayonnaise, egg, and vanilla. Stir mayonnaise mixture into flour mixture until combined.

PRACTICAL SCIENCE NATURAL COCOA AND DUTCH-PROCESSED COCOA

The difference between natural cocoa and Dutch-processed cocoa all comes down to the pH. Our preference? Dutched.

To understand a cocoa label, it's necessary to know how cocoa is made. Cocoa beans grow on a tropical evergreen (*Theobroma cacao*). Once picked, the white beans are fermented, turning them dark and developing a characteristic aroma. The dried beans are then cracked open and the nibs separated from the shells and roasted to bring out flavors. The nibs contain about 55 percent cocoa butter, and when they are ground up and heated they form a thick liquid called chocolate liquor, the basis of most chocolate products.

To make cocoa powder, much of the cocoa butter must be removed from the chocolate liquor, leaving a dry powder. The final fat content is indicated by the numbers on the cocoa label. For example, a 10/12 cocoa contains 10 percent to 12 percent cocoa butter, whereas a 22/24 cocoa contains 22 percent to 24 percent cocoa butter and is therefore higher in fat. (Premium brands tend to have higher cocoa butter percentages, while mass-market Hershey's and Nestlé cocoas belong to the 10/12 category.)

Without any further processing, the cocoa is still naturally acidic and, after being finely ground, sifted, and packaged, is marketed as "natural cocoa" powder. During the early 19th century, a Dutch inventor named Conrad van Houten developed a process called Dutching that has been used for over a century by most European companies to make Dutch-processed or alkalized cocoa. To Dutch cocoa, an alkaline solution, usually potassium carbonate, is added to the chocolate liquor as it is refined. The alkali raises the pH of cocoa, from around 5.7 to 7.2. Raising the pH has the effect of darkening the color of the cocoa, mellowing its sometimes harsh flavor, and improving its solubility in liquids.

Most European cocoas are Dutch-processed, whereas most American ones are natural. In most cases, the two types of cocoa are interchangeable, though in recipes for baked goods such as cakes that rely on baking soda or baking powder for some or all of their leavening, it is best to use the type of cocoa that the recipe specifies since the cocoa's acidity may affect the leavener's effectiveness. In general, we prefer the rounder, less harsh flavor of Dutch-processed cocoa powder and use it in most of our recipes.

3. Scrape batter into prepared pan and smooth top with rubber spatula. Bake cake until toothpick inserted in center comes out with few crumbs attached, 30 to 35 minutes.

4. Let cake cool in pan on wire rack, 1 to 2 hours. Dust with confectioners' sugar, if using, cut into squares, and serve straight from pan; alternatively, turn cake out onto serving platter, dust with confectioners' sugar, if using, and serve.

✓ WHY THIS RECIPE WORKS

This easy wartime cake made with just a few ingredients (flour, sugar, cocoa powder, baking soda, vanilla, and mayonnaise, a stand-in for butter and eggs) had a lot of good things going for it, but chocolate flavor wasn't one of them. Our first order of business was deepening the chocolate flavor. We achieved this by blooming the cocoa powder and adding a bit of melted chocolate, too. A surprising ingredient helped to hold everything together and keep the cake moist.

REMEMBER WAR RATIONS   When ingredients like butter and fresh eggs were scarce during World War II, cooks came up with cakes that worked without them—often using mayonnaise. These recipes lived on long after rationing ended because they are so easy (just dump and stir) and the results are so moist. That's because mayonnaise contains lecithin, an emulsifier that helps keep the oil in the mayonnaise suspended in micro-droplets. These small droplets aid the oil's ability to coat the flour's protein particles, leading to a supremely tender cake. In fact, when we tried replacing the mayonnaise with butter and an egg, or oil and an egg, the cake was less moist and the crumb was not as velvety. We did like the extra egg paired with the mayonnaise, which gave the cake a richer flavor and springier texture.

ADD SOME BITTERSWEET CHOCOLATE   While we loved the texture of the original cake, we did want more chocolate flavor. We found that we couldn't increase the amount of cocoa powder; when we did, the cake became dry and chalky. But we could add a few ounces of bittersweet chocolate.

BLOOM FLAVORS WITH HOT COFFEE   Cocoa powder contains solid particles of fat and protein with tiny flavor molecules trapped inside. Dissolving the cocoa in hot water causes these flavor molecules, which would otherwise remain imprisoned, to burst forth, amplifying overall flavor. We found that using a cup of coffee was even more effective. The roasted notes of the coffee reinforce the nutty, roasted notes in the chocolate.

ULTIMATE CHOCOLATE CUPCAKES WITH GANACHE FILLING
MAKES 12 CUPCAKES

Use a high-quality bittersweet or semisweet chocolate for this recipe. Though we highly recommend the ganache filling, you can omit it for a more traditional cupcake.

FILLING

2	ounces bittersweet chocolate, chopped fine
¼	cup heavy cream
1	tablespoon confectioners' sugar

CUPCAKES

3	ounces bittersweet chocolate, chopped fine
⅓	cup (1 ounce) Dutch-processed cocoa
¾	cup brewed coffee, hot
¾	cup (4⅛ ounces) bread flour
¾	cup (5¼ ounces) sugar
½	teaspoon salt
½	teaspoon baking soda
6	tablespoons vegetable oil
2	large eggs
2	teaspoons distilled white vinegar
1	teaspoon vanilla extract
1	recipe Creamy Chocolate Frosting (recipe follows)

1. FOR THE FILLING: Microwave chocolate, cream, and sugar in medium bowl until mixture is warm to touch, about 30 seconds. Whisk until smooth, then transfer bowl to refrigerator and let sit until just chilled, no longer than 30 minutes.

2. FOR THE CUPCAKES: Adjust oven rack to middle position and heat oven to 350 degrees. Line 12-cup muffin tin with paper or foil liners. Place chocolate and cocoa in medium heatproof bowl. Pour hot coffee over mixture and let sit, covered, for 5 minutes. Whisk mixture gently until smooth, then transfer to refrigerator to cool completely, about 20 minutes.

3. Whisk flour, sugar, salt, and baking soda together in medium bowl. Whisk oil, eggs, vinegar, and vanilla into cooled chocolate mixture until smooth. Add flour mixture and whisk until smooth.

4. Using ice cream scoop or large spoon, divide batter evenly among prepared muffin cups. Place 1 slightly rounded teaspoon ganache filling on top of each portion of batter. Bake cupcakes until set and just firm to touch, 17 to 19 minutes. Let cupcakes cool in muffin tin on wire rack until cool enough to handle, about 10 minutes. Lift each cupcake from tin, set on wire rack, and let cool completely before frosting, about 1 hour. (Unfrosted cupcakes can be stored at room temperature for up to 1 day.)

5. TO FROST: Spread 2 to 3 tablespoons frosting over each cooled cupcake and serve.

CREAMY CHOCOLATE FROSTING
MAKES ABOUT 2¼ CUPS

The melted chocolate should be cooled to between 85 and 100 degrees before being added to the frosting. If the frosting seems too soft after adding the chocolate, chill it briefly in the refrigerator and then rewhip it until creamy.

- ⅓ cup (2⅓ ounces) sugar
- 2 large egg whites
   Pinch salt
- 12 tablespoons unsalted butter, cut into 12 pieces and softened (68 degrees)
- 6 ounces bittersweet chocolate, melted and cooled
- ½ teaspoon vanilla extract

1. Combine sugar, egg whites, and salt in bowl of stand mixer and set bowl over saucepan filled with 1 inch of barely simmering water. Whisking gently but constantly, heat mixture until slightly thickened, foamy, and registers 150 degrees, 2 to 3 minutes.

2. Fit stand mixer with whisk and beat mixture on medium speed until consistency of shaving cream and slightly cooled, 1 to 2 minutes. Add butter, 1 piece at a time, until smooth and creamy. (Frosting may look curdled after half of butter has been added; it will smooth with additional butter.) Once all butter is added, add cooled melted chocolate and vanilla; mix until combined. Increase speed to medium-high and beat until light, fluffy, and thoroughly combined, about 30 seconds, scraping down beater and sides of bowl with rubber spatula as necessary.

TO MAKE AHEAD: Frosting can be made up to 1 day in advance and refrigerated in airtight container. When ready to frost, warm frosting briefly in microwave until just slightly softened, 5 to 10 seconds. Once warmed, stir until creamy.

✓ WHY THIS RECIPE WORKS

A chocolate cupcake Catch-22 befalls bakery and homemade confections alike: If the cupcakes have decent chocolate flavor, their structure is too crumbly for out-of-hand consumption. Conversely, if the cakes balance moisture and tenderness without crumbling, the cake and frosting are barely palatable, with the chocolate flavor hardly registering at all. We wanted moist, tender (but not crumbly) cupcakes capped with just enough creamy, not-too-sweet frosting. We got them by using bread flour and reducing the amount of chocolate to strengthen the batter, but upping the chocolate flavor through blooming and replacing butter with oil. A ganache center and Swiss meringue frosting seal the chocolate lover's deal.

DON'T MAKE CRUMBLY CUPCAKES Most cupcakes sacrifice flavor for appearance. We decided to start with our favorite chocolate layer cake recipe, made with cocoa powder, bittersweet chocolate, buttermilk, and brewed coffee. Divided into muffin tins, the batter baked up into delicious cupcakes that literally fell apart in our hands. For a dessert eaten out of hand, and not with a fork, we needed more structure, and therefore more gluten.

MAXIMIZE CHOCOLATE FLAVOR We reduced the amount of cocoa powder in our recipe tests because cocoa powder contains no gluten-forming proteins and works to dilute the flour. We then used less chocolate, in an attempt to cut back on the fat, which was making the cupcakes so tender. We got rid of the dairy in our cake recipe and used more brewed coffee, which helped amp up the chocolate (and reduce the negative impact dairy has on chocolate flavor). We bloomed the cocoa by pouring the hot coffee over the cocoa powder and chopped chocolate. After all of this, we succeeded in making a very chocolaty but dry cupcake.

CHANGE TO OIL Replacing butter with oil adds moisture. Oil, after all, is 100 percent fat, while butter contains around 16 to 18 percent water, which can evaporate in the oven, leaving the cupcakes dry. Oil likewise improved the chocolate flavor a bit more, because the milk solids in butter can mute chocolate flavors.

PICK BREAD FLOUR We began our testing with all-purpose flour but wondered if bread flour, with more gluten, might allow us to use more cocoa and chocolate. It did, giving us a less crumble-prone but not tough cupcake with big chocolate flavor.

MAKE A GANACHE CENTER Adding a teaspoon of cooled ganache onto the cupcakes before baking was the ticket for even bigger chocolate flavor. The ganache sinks in the batter during baking, providing a rich, truffle-like center to the cupcakes, otherwise known as chocolate nirvana.

RECONSIDER THE FROSTING We decided to abandon the super-sweet, grainy classic frosting made by whipping together softened butter and confectioners' sugar. Instead, we choose cooked buttercream—the Swiss meringue variety, where egg whites and granulated sugar are heated over a double boiler, then whipped with knobs of softened butter. The result is utterly silky and decadent, without the weight and greasiness of other rich frostings.

DARK CHOCOLATE MOUSSE
SERVES 6 TO 8

When developing this recipe, we used Callebaut Intense Dark Chocolate and Ghirardelli Bittersweet Chocolate Baking Bar, which each contain about 60 percent cacao. If you want to use a chocolate with a higher percentage of cacao, see our variation, Premium Dark Chocolate Mousse. If you choose to make the mousse a day in advance, let it sit at room temperature for 10 minutes before serving. Serve with Whipped Cream (page 424) and chocolate shavings, if desired.

8	ounces bittersweet chocolate, chopped fine
5	tablespoons water
2	tablespoons Dutch-processed cocoa
1	tablespoon brandy
1	teaspoon instant espresso powder
2	large eggs, separated
1	tablespoon sugar
⅛	teaspoon salt
1	cup plus 2 tablespoons heavy cream, chilled

1. Melt chocolate, water, cocoa, brandy, and espresso in medium heatproof bowl set over saucepan filled with 1 inch of barely simmering water, stirring frequently until smooth. Remove from heat.

2. Whisk egg yolks, 1½ teaspoons sugar, and salt together in medium bowl until mixture lightens in color and thickens slightly, about 30 seconds. Pour melted chocolate into egg-yolk mixture and whisk until combined. Let cool until just warmer than room temperature, 3 to 5 minutes.

3. Using stand mixer fitted with whisk, whip egg whites at medium-low speed until foamy, about 1 minute. Add remaining 1½ teaspoons sugar, increase speed to medium-high, and whip until soft peaks form, about 1 minute. Using whisk, stir about one-quarter of whipped egg whites into chocolate mixture to lighten it; gently fold in remaining egg whites with rubber spatula until few white streaks remain.

4. In now-empty bowl, whip cream on medium speed until it begins to thicken, about 30 seconds. Increase speed to high and whip until soft peaks form, about 15 seconds more. Using rubber spatula, fold whipped cream into mousse until no white streaks remain. Spoon mousse into 6 to 8 individual serving dishes. Cover with plastic wrap and refrigerate until set and firm, at least 2 hours or up to 24 hours. Serve.

PREMIUM DARK CHOCOLATE MOUSSE

This recipe is designed to work with a boutique chocolate that contains a higher percentage of cacao than our master recipe.

Replace bittersweet chocolate (containing about 60 percent cacao) with equal amount of bittersweet chocolate containing 62 to 70 percent cacao. Increase water to 7 tablespoons, increase eggs to 3, and increase sugar to 3 tablespoons, adding extra 2 tablespoons to chocolate mixture in step 1.

PRACTICAL SCIENCE
SMOOTHLY MELTED CHOCOLATE

Adding more liquid can reverse seizing chocolate.

Seizing describes the nearly instantaneous transformation of chocolate from a fluid state to a stiff, grainy one. When chocolate is melted, its ingredients—mainly cocoa solids, sugar, and cocoa butter—disperse evenly, creating a fluid mass. But if even a tiny amount of moisture is introduced, the liquid and the sugar will form a syrup which cements the cocoa particles together, creating grainy clumps. How much liquid it actually takes to trigger this reaction depends mostly on the amount of chocolate and its sugar content. (Even in the absence of sugar, however, such as in unsweetened chocolate, the cocoa particles will cling together if liquid is introduced.) Surprisingly, the addition of more liquid can actually reverse the seizing and bring the chocolate back to a fluid state.

Reversing the reaction means adding just enough water (or other liquid such as milk) to dissolve most of the sugar and disperse the cocoa particles in the seized chocolate clumps. The water will still dilute the chocolate slightly, so it can no longer reliably be used for baking. Use it instead for making chocolate sauce or hot chocolate or drizzling on cookies.

To prevent seizing, follow these guidelines: In recipes that contain no liquid, take great care not to let any moisture into the chocolate. In recipes that do contain liquids such as melted butter, liqueur, or water, always melt the chocolate along with these ingredients to keep the cocoa and sugar particles sufficiently wet.

If your chocolate does seize, add boiling water to it, 1 teaspoon at a time, and stir vigorously after each addition until the chocolate is smooth.

SEIZED UP   SATINY SMOOTH

CHOCOLATE-RASPBERRY MOUSSE

Chambord is our preferred brand of raspberry-flavored liqueur for this recipe. Serve the mousse with fresh raspberries, if desired.

Reduce water to 4 tablespoons, omit brandy, and add 2 tablespoons raspberry-flavored liqueur to melted chocolate mixture in step 1.

✔ WHY THIS RECIPE WORKS

Rich, creamy, and dense, chocolate mousse can be delicious but too filling after a few mouthfuls. On the other hand, light and airy mousse usually lacks deep chocolate flavor. We wanted chocolate mousse that had both a light, meltingly smooth texture and a substantial chocolate flavor. To achieve this, we eliminated the butter, reduced the number of eggs, added whipped cream, and played with the ratio of chocolate and water. The result? A light, ethereal mousse chock-full of chocolate.

LOSE THE BUTTER Mousse contains far less dairy than pudding (see page 196) and more chocolate. And it almost always contains whipped egg whites or whipped cream. The challenge with mousse is daunting: You want intense chocolate flavor but you also want a light, airy texture. Of course, mousse must be perfectly smooth, and it must set but without a trace of the bouncy texture that can pass in pudding. To start, we addressed the mousse's dense, heavy texture. Most recipes for chocolate mousse contain butter. Could we do without it? We eliminated the butter and found that our mousse tasted less heavy. It also lost the waxy texture that butter can impart when it resolidifies in the fridge.

LIMIT THE EGGS Some recipes call for as many four eggs but we found that too many egg whites made the texture similar to marshmallows. We lightened the mousse's texture by reducing the number of egg whites. To make up for the lost volume of the eggs, we whipped the cream to soft peaks before adding it to the chocolate. The volume makes the mousse light but not foamy.

ADD MORE CHOCOLATE We maximized the chocolate flavor with a combination of bittersweet chocolate and cocoa powder. And to further deepen the chocolate flavor, we found that a small amount of instant espresso powder, salt, and brandy did the trick.

WATER TO THE RESCUE With all of this added chocolate, our mixture was beginning to seize, giving us a gritty, grainy texture totally unfit for a mousse. We fixed the texture problem with an unlikely ingredient—water. Liquid can cause chocolate to seize, yes. But more important is the liquid-to-solid ratio. With small amounts of liquid, the solids absorb just enough moisture to form a gritty paste. But with more liquid (at least 1 tablespoon for every 2 ounces of chocolate), the dry cocoa solids become fluid. Increasing the water makes the finished product looser and glossier.

PRACTICAL SCIENCE
GETTING THE TEXTURE RIGHT

There are as many different mousse textures as there are mousse recipes. Here's how some of them look.

DENSE
Butter, unwhipped cream, and too much chocolate are often the culprits in heavy, ganachelike mousse.

FLUFFY
Too many whipped egg whites produce an unappealing "marshmallow effect."

PERFECT
Going easy on the egg whites, omitting the butter, and adding a small amount of water yields just the right texture.

CHOCOLATE 101

STRUCTURE

COCOA BEANS
The cacao tree grows in tropical regions around the world and produces large fruits that look like fibrous pods. Each fruit contains about 40 white cocoa beans, which are dried, fermented, and then shipped to a processing plant where they are stripped of their hulls to form cocoa nibs (left).

CHOCOLATE LIQUOR
At the processing plant the nibs are roasted to dark brown seeds and ground into a liquid cocoa mass called chocolate liquor. Chocolate liquor is pure, unsweetened chocolate and is the base ingredient for all chocolate products.

COCOA BUTTER
About 55 percent of chocolate liquor is cocoa butter, a natural, highly unsaturated fat responsible for chocolate's unique texture. Cocoa butter has a very narrow melting range and stays firm up to 92 degrees. Since the temperature inside the human mouth is just a few degrees higher than the melting point of cocoa butter, chocolate melts very slowly. In fact, it seems to melt into—rather than just in—your mouth.

COCOA SOLIDS
Particles of ground cocoa solids are suspended in the cocoa butter and make up the other 45 percent of chocolate liquor. Cocoa solids carry hundreds of flavor compounds we recognize as chocolate. Most of the characteristic chocolate flavor compounds are produced during the fermentation and roasting steps.

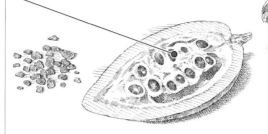

BUYING

UNSWEETENED CHOCOLATE Also called baking chocolate, this is simply pure chocolate liquor that has been cooled and formed into bars. Among bar chocolates, unsweetened has the most intense chocolate flavor.

BITTERSWEET/SEMISWEET CHOCOLATE When sugar is added to chocolate liquor the product is now technically called "dark chocolate," assuming that it still contains at least 35 percent chocolate liquor (most chocolates contain far more). The terms "bittersweet" and "semisweet" are not regulated, although most manufacturers use the former to indicate a product with less sugar. When you see labels that read "70 percent cacao," this means the product contains 70 percent chocolate liquor by weight and the rest is mostly sugar, plus a little emulsifier and/or vanilla.

MILK CHOCOLATE Milk chocolate is similar to bittersweet or semisweet chocolate but with the addition of milk solids, which give this product its unique caramel and butterscotch flavors and soft texture. Most milk chocolate contain less chocolate liquor and more sugar than bittersweet or semisweet chocolates.

WHITE CHOCOLATE White chocolate is technically not chocolate since it contains no cocoa solids. Authentic white chocolate contains at least 20 percent cocoa butter (along with milk solids and sugar), which gives this product its meltingly smooth texture. Note that many brands rely on palm oil in place of some or all of the cocoa butter and can't be labeled "chocolate." If the product is called "white chips" or "white confection," it is made with little or no cocoa butter. That said, since both styles derive their flavor from milk and sugar, not the fat, we find this distinction makes little difference in recipes.

COCOA POWDER Cocoa powder is made by removing most of the cocoa butter from chocolate liquor. The resulting powder is roughly 80 percent cocoa solids and therefore has an intense chocolate flavor. To counter the harsh, acidic flavor of this concentrated form of chocolate, the powder is sometimes treated with an alkaline solution, or "Dutched." We find that Dutch-processed cocoa has a milder, more complex flavor than natural cocoa, which can be harsh and astringent. That said, you can use the two interchangeably in most recipes.

STORING

Never store chocolate in the refrigerator or freezer, as cocoa butter can easily pick up off-flavors from other foods. Wrap chocolate well in plastic wrap and store it in a cool, dark pantry. Milk and white chocolates should keep for six months; dark and unsweetened chocolates will keep for a year. If chocolate is exposed to rapid changes in humidity or temperature, sugar or fat may dissolve and migrate, causing a white film to develop on the surface of the chocolate. This cosmetic condition, known as bloom, does not harm the flavor of the chocolate.

USING

MELTING CHOCOLATE Since chocolate can scorch if overheated, you want to employ gentle heat. The traditional method calls for a double boiler. Place the chopped chocolate in a heatproof bowl set over a pot of barely simmering water. Make sure the water isn't touching the bowl, or the chocolate can overheat. The steam will gently heat the bowl and melt the chocolate. If the recipe also calls for melted butter, you can add the butter to the bowl with the chocolate at the outset.

You can speed up the process with a microwave, but you should use a reduced power setting to reduce the risk of scorching. Place the chopped chocolate in a microwave-safe bowl and microwave for 45 seconds at 50 percent power. Stir the chocolate to help it liquefy and continue to microwave in 15-second intervals as needed. If melting butter, don't add it until the chocolate is almost melted. (If added earlier, the butter will splatter.)

CHOCOLATE SUBSTITUTIONS In a pinch, you can replace some chocolate products with another one.

TO REPLACE	SUBSTITUTE
1 ounce unsweetened chocolate	3 tablespoons cocoa powder + 1 tablespoon butter or oil
1 ounce bittersweet or semisweet chocolate	⅔ ounce unsweetened chocolate + 2 teaspoons granulated sugar

EQUIPPING YOUR KITCHEN

What equipment do you really need to set up a decent home kitchen? The answer depends on what you want to accomplish. Your grandmother probably had a minimum of kitchen gear, yet she was a great cook. In contrast, you probably have friends who own a top-of-the-line kitchen and every gadget imaginable, yet they can't turn out a creditable meal. A well-equipped kitchen won't make you a good cook, but the right tools can help.

The list that follows highlights the gear we find most useful in our test kitchen and the brands that have earned our top ratings. We have not listed specialty items that can be essential for certain recipes (like a springform pan, without which a cheesecake can't be made), nor have we listed "nice-to-have" items like a cleaver for cutting up chicken parts for stock. Start with the items on the following pages and then add more gear depending on the recipes you want to make.

Since cookware and knives are so important, we have included special sections on cookware materials (page 444), the safety of nonstick pans (page 445), and knife basics (page 446).

KNIVES AND MORE	ITEM	WHAT TO LOOK FOR	TEST KITCHEN FAVORITES
	Chef's Knife	• High-carbon stainless steel knife • Thin, curved 8-inch blade • Lightweight • Comfortable grip and nonslip handle	Victorinox Fibrox 8-Inch Chef's Knife (formerly Victorinox Forschner) $29.99
	Paring Knife	• 3- to 3½-inch blade • Thin, slightly curved blade with pointed tip • Comfortable grip	Wüsthof Classic with PEtec 3½-Inch Paring Knife (model #4066) $39.95 BEST BUY: Victorinox Fibrox 3¼-inch Paring Knife $8.95
	Serrated Knife	• 10- to 12-inch blade • Long, somewhat flexible, slightly curved blade • Pointed serrations that are uniformly spaced and moderately sized	Wüsthof Classic 10-Inch Bread Knife $109.95 BEST BUY: Victorinox Fibrox 10¼-Inch Bread Knife $24.95
	Slicing Knife	• Tapered 12-inch blade for slicing large cuts of meat • Oval scallops (called a granton edge) carved into blade • Fairly rigid blade with rounded tip	Victorinox Fibrox 12-Inch Granton Edge Slicing Knife $39.95
	Cutting Board	• Roomy work surface at least 15 by 20 inches • Teak board for minimal maintenance • Durable edge-grain construction (wood grain runs parallel to surface of board)	Proteak Edge Grain Teak Cutting Board $84.99 BEST BUY: OXO Good Grips Carving and Cutting Board $24.99
	Knife Sharpener	• Diamond sharpening material for electric sharpeners • Easy to use and comfortable • Clear instructions	ELECTRIC: Chef'sChoice Model 130 Professional Sharpening Station $149.95 MANUAL: AccuSharp Knife and Tool Sharpener $10.95

POTS AND PANS	ITEM	WHAT TO LOOK FOR	TEST KITCHEN FAVORITES
	Traditional Skillets	• Stainless steel interior, fully clad for even heat distribution • 12-inch diameter and flared sides • Comfortable, ovensafe handle • Cooking surface of at least 9 inches • Good to have smaller (8- or 10-inch) skillets too	All-Clad Stainless 12-Inch Frypan $154.99
	Nonstick Skillets	• Dark, nonstick surface • 12- or 12½-inch diameter, thick bottom • Comfortable, ovensafe handle • Cooking surface of at least 9 inches • Good to have smaller (8- or 10-inch) skillets too	T-Fal Professional Total Non-Stick 12½-Inch Fry Pan $34.99
	Dutch Oven	• Enameled cast iron or stainless steel • Capacity of at least 6 quarts • Diameter of at least 9 inches • Tight-fitting lid • Wide, sturdy handles	Le Creuset 7¼-Quart Round French Oven $279 All-Clad Stainless 8-Quart Stockpot $294.95 BEST BUY: Tramontina 6.5-Quart Cast Iron Dutch Oven $49
	Saucepans	• Large saucepan with 3- to 4-quart capacity and small nonstick saucepan with 2- to 2½-quart capacity • Tight-fitting lids • Pans with rounded corners that a whisk can reach into • Long, comfortable handles that are angled for even weight distribution	LARGE: All-Clad Stainless 4-Quart Saucepan $179.95 BEST BUY: Cuisinart MultiClad Unlimited 4-Quart Saucepan $69.99 SMALL: Calphalon Contemporary Nonstick 2½-Quart Shallow Saucepan $39.95
	Rimmed Baking Sheets	• Light-colored surface (heats and browns evenly) • Thick, sturdy pan • Dimensions of 18 by 13 inches • Good to have at least two	Wear-Ever 13-Gauge Half Size Heavy Duty Sheet Pan by Vollrath (formerly Lincoln Foodservice) $13
	Roasting Pan	• At least 15 by 11 inches • Stainless steel interior with aluminum core for even heat distribution • Upright handles for easy gripping • Light interior for better food monitoring • Fixed V-rack with tall handles	Calphalon Contemporary Stainless Roasting Pan with V-Rack $129.99

HANDY TOOLS	ITEM	WHAT TO LOOK FOR	TEST KITCHEN FAVORITES
	Tongs	• Scalloped edges • Slightly concave pincers • 12 inches in length (to keep your hand far from heat) • Open and close easily	OXO Good Grips 12-Inch Locking Tongs $12.95
	Wooden Spoon	• Slim yet broad bowl • Stain-resistant bamboo • Comfortable handle	SCI Bamboo Wood Cooking Spoon $2.40

HANDY TOOLS	ITEM	WHAT TO LOOK FOR	TEST KITCHEN FAVORITES
	Slotted Spoon	• Deep bowl • Long handle • Enough holes for quick draining	OXO Good Grips Nylon Slotted Spoon $6.99
	All-Around Spatulas	• Head about 3 inches wide and 5½ inches long • 11 inches in length (tip to handle) • Long, vertical slots • Useful to have a metal spatula to use with traditional cookware and a plastic spatula for nonstick cookware	METAL: Wüsthof Gourmet Fish Spatula $34.95 PLASTIC: Matfer Bourgeat Pelton Spatula $11.95
	Rubber Spatula	• Wide, stiff blade with thin edge that's flexible enough to conform to curve of a mixing bowl • Heatproof	Rubbermaid Professional 13½-Inch High Heat Scraper $18.99
	All-Purpose Whisk	• At least 10 wires • Wires of moderate thickness • Comfortable handle • Balanced, lightweight feel	OXO Good Grips 11-Inch Whisk $9.99
	Garlic Press	• Large capacity that holds multiple garlic cloves • Curved plastic handles • Long handle and short distance between pivot point and plunger	Kuhn Rikon Easy-Squeeze Garlic Press $20 BEST BUY: Trudeau Garlic Press $11.99
	Pepper Mill	• At least ½-cup capacity • Wide, unobstructed filler doors • Easy-to-adjust grind settings	Unicorn Magnum Plus Pepper Mill $45
	Can Opener	• Intuitive and easy to attach • Smooth turning motions • Magnet for no-touch lid disposal • Comfortable handle	OXO Good Grips Magnetic Locking Can Opener $21.99
	Vegetable Peeler	• Sharp, carbon steel blade • 1-inch space between blade and peeler to prevent jamming • Lightweight and comfortable	Kuhn Rikon Original 4-Inch Swiss Peeler $3.50
	Grater	• Paddle-style grater • Sharp, extra-large holes and generous grating plane • Rubber-lined feet for stability • Comfortable handle	Rösle Coarse Grater $35
	Rasp Grater	• Sharp teeth (require little effort or pressure when grating) • Maneuverable over round or irregular shapes • Comfortable handle	Microplane Classic 40020 Zester/Grater $14.95

HANDY TOOLS	ITEM	WHAT TO LOOK FOR	TEST KITCHEN FAVORITES
	Rolling Pin	• Moderate weight (1 to 1½ pounds) • 19-inch straight barrel • Slightly textured wooden surface to grip dough for easy rolling	J. K. Adams Plain Maple Rolling Dowel $13.95
	Oven Mitt	• Form-fitting and not overly bulky for easy maneuvering • Machine washable • Flexible, heat-resistant material	Kool-Tek 15-Inch Oven Mitt by KatchAll $44.95 BEST BUY: OrkaPlus Silicone Oven Mitt with Cotton Lining $14.95
	Ladle	• Stainless steel • Handle 9 to 10 inches in length • Hooked handle end for hanging on pot • Pouring rim to prevent dripping	Rösle Ladle with Pouring Rim $29.95
	Colander	• 4- to 7-quart capacity • Metal ring attached to bottom for stability • Many holes for quick draining • Small holes so pasta doesn't slip through	RSVP International Endurance Precision Pierced 5-Quart Colander $32.95
	Fine-Mesh Strainer	• At least 6 inches in diameter (measured from inside edge to inside edge) • Sturdy construction	CIA Masters Collection 6¾-Inch Fine Mesh Strainer $27.50
	Potato Masher	• Solid mashing disk with small holes • Comfortable grip	WMF Profi Plus Stainless Steel Potato Masher $19
	Salad Spinner	• Solid bottom for washing greens in bowl • Ergonomic and easy-to-operate hand pump	OXO Good Grips Salad Spinner $29.99

MEASURING EQUIPMENT	ITEM	WHAT TO LOOK FOR	TEST KITCHEN FAVORITES
	Dry Measuring Cups	• Stainless steel cups (hefty and durable) • Measurement markings that are visible even when cup is full • Evenly weighted and stable • Long handles that are level with rim of cup	Amco Basic Ingredient 4-Piece Measuring Cup Set $11.50
	Liquid Measuring Cups	• Crisp, unambiguous markings that include ¼-and ⅓-cup measurements • Heatproof, sturdy cup with handle • Good to have in a variety of sizes (1, 2, and 4 cups)	Pyrex 2-Cup Measuring Cup $5.99

MEASURING EQUIPMENT	ITEM	WHAT TO LOOK FOR	TEST KITCHEN FAVORITES
	Measuring Spoons	• Long, comfortable handles • Rim of bowl flush with handle for easy "sweeping" off of excess ingredients • Slim design	Cuisipro Stainless Steel Measuring Spoon Set $9.95
	Digital Scale	• Easy-to-read display not blocked by weighing platform • At least 7-pound capacity • Accessible buttons • Gram-to-ounce conversion feature • Roomy platform	OXO Food Scale $49.99 BEST BUY: Soehnle 65055 Digital Scale $34.95
	Instant-Read Thermometer	• Digital model with automatic shut-off • Quick-response readings in 10 seconds or less • Wide temperature range (-40 to 450 degrees) • Long stem that can reach interior of large cuts of meat • Water-resistant	ThermoWorks Splash-Proof Super-Fast Thermapen $89 BEST BUYS: ThermoWorks Super-Fast Pocket Thermometer $19 CDN ProAccurate Quick-Read Thermometer $19.99
	Oven Thermometer	• Clearly marked numbers for easy readability • Hook for hanging or stable base • Large temperature range (up to 600 degrees)	Cooper-Atkins Oven Thermometer (model #24HP) $6
	Kitchen Timer	• Lengthy time range (1 second to at least 10 hours) • Ability to count up after alarm goes off • Easy to use and read	Polder 3-in-1 Clock, Timer, and Stopwatch (model #898–95) $12

ESSENTIAL BAKEWARE	ITEM	WHAT TO LOOK FOR	TEST KITCHEN FAVORITES
	Glass Baking Dish	• Dimensions of 13 by 9 inches • Large enough to hold casseroles and large crisps and cobblers • Handles	Pyrex Bakeware 9 x 13-Inch Baking Dish $12.99
	Metal Baking Pan	• Dimensions of 13 by 9 inches • Straight sides • Nonstick coating for even browning and easy release of cakes and bar cookies • Handles	Baker's Secret 9 x 13-Inch Nonstick Cake Pan $7.49
	Square Baking Pans	• Straight sides • Light gold or dark nonstick surface for even browning and easy release of cakes • Good to have both 9-inch and 8-inch square pans	Williams-Sonoma Nonstick Goldtouch Square Cake Pan $26, 8-inch; $27, 9-inch BEST BUY: Chicago Metallic Gourmetware 8-Inch Nonstick Square Cake Pan $6.99
	Round Cake Pans	• Straight sides • Nonstick coating for even browning and easy release of cakes • Recommend a set of 9-inch and 8-inch pans	Chicago Metallic Professional Lifetime 9-Inch Nonstick Round Cake Pan $12.99

ESSENTIAL BAKEWARE	ITEM	WHAT TO LOOK FOR	TEST KITCHEN FAVORITES
	Pie Plates	• Glass for even browning and easier monitoring • ½-inch rim (makes it easy to shape decorative crusts) • Shallow angled sides prevent crusts from slumping • Good to have two	Pyrex Bakeware 9-Inch Pie Plate $2.99
	Loaf Pans	• Light gold or dark nonstick surface for even browning and easy release • Good to have both 8½ by 4½-inch and 9 by 5-inch pans	Williams-Sonoma 8½ x 4½-Inch Nonstick Goldtouch Loaf Pan $21 BEST BUY: Baker's Secret 9 x 5-Inch Nonstick Loaf Pan $5
	Muffin Tin	• Nonstick surface for even browning and easy release • Wide, extended rims and raised lip for easy handling • Cup capacity of ½ cup	Wilton Avanti Everglide Metal-Safe Nonstick 12-Cup Muffin Pan $13.99
	Cooling Rack	• Grid-style rack with tightly woven, heavy-gauge bars • Should fit inside standard 18 by 13-inch rimmed baking sheet • Dishwasher-safe	CIA Bakeware 12 x 17-Inch Cooling Rack $15.95 BEST BUY: Libertyware Half-Size Sheet Pan Grate $5.25

SMALL APPLIANCES	ITEM	WHAT TO LOOK FOR	TEST KITCHEN FAVORITES
	Food Processor	• 14-cup capacity • Sharp and sturdy blades • Wide feed tube • Should come with basic blades and disks: steel blade, dough blade, shredding/slicing disk	Cuisinart Custom 14-Cup Food Processor $199
	Hand-Held Mixer	• Lightweight model • Slim wire beaters without central post • Digital display • Separate ejector buttons (not part of speed dial) • Variety of speeds NOTE: If you do a lot of baking or want to make bread, you should invest in a stand mixer instead of a hand-held mixer. We recommend the Cuisinart 5.5 Quart Stand Mixer ($299).	Cuisinart Power Advantage 7-Speed Hand Mixer $49.95
	Blender	• Large blades that reach close to the edge and bottom of the jar • Powerful motor (at least 700 watts) • Automatic shut-off to keep motor from overheating • Clear jar to monitor progress	Vitamix 5200 $449 BEST BUY: Breville BBL605XL Hemisphere Control Blender $200

KITCHEN SUPPLIES	ITEM	WHAT TO LOOK FOR	TEST KITCHEN FAVORITES
	Parchment Paper	• Sturdy paper for heavy doughs • Easy release of baked goods • At least 14 inches wide	Reynolds Parchment Paper $3.69
	Plastic Wrap	• Clings tightly and resticks well • Packaging with sharp teeth that aren't exposed (to avoid snags on clothing and skin) • Adhesive pad to hold cut end of wrap	Glad Cling Wrap Clear Plastic $2.59

GRILLING EQUIPMENT	ITEM	WHAT TO LOOK FOR	TEST KITCHEN FAVORITES
	Gas Grill	• Large grilling area (at least 350 square inches) • Built-in thermometer • Two burners for varying heat levels (three are even better) • Attached table • Fat drainage system NOTE: Unless you live in an apartment with no access to outdoor space, you should own either a gas or a charcoal grill. If you choose charcoal, you will want a chimney starter.	Weber Spirit E-210 $399
	Charcoal Grill	• Large grilling area • Deep grill cover to fit large food items (such as a turkey) • Hinged grill grate to tend fire • Ash catcher for easier cleanup	Weber One-Touch Gold 22½-Inch Charcoal Grill $149
	Chimney Starter	• 6-quart capacity • Holes in canister so air can circulate around coals • Sturdy construction • Heat-resistant handle • Dual handle for easy control	Weber Rapidfire Chimney Starter $14.99
	Grill Tongs	• 16 inches in length • Scalloped, not sharp and serrated, edges • Open and close easily • Lightweight • Moderate amount of springy tension	OXO Good Grips 16-Inch Locking Tongs $14.99
	Grill Brush	• Long handle (about 14 inches) • Large woven-mesh detachable stainless steel scrubbing pad	Tool Wizard BBQ Brush $9.99

COOKWARE MATERIALS

REACTIVITY IN COOKWARE

When acidic ingredients are cooked in "reactive" pans (those made of aluminum or unseasoned cast iron), trace amounts of molecules from the metal can leach into the food. These minute amounts are not harmful to consume, but they may impart unwanted metallic flavors.

To determine how noticeable such flavors are, we simmered tomato sauce in an aluminum Dutch oven and in seasoned and unseasoned cast-iron Dutch ovens. We also cooked tomato sauce in a stainless steel Dutch oven. Tasters noticed a strong taste of iron in the sauce from the unseasoned cast-iron pot and a more subtle metallic taste in the sauce from the aluminum pot. The sauces cooked in seasoned cast iron (which has layers of oil compounds protecting the surface) and stainless steel tasted just fine.

We sent samples of each sauce to an independent lab to test for the presence of iron and aluminum. The sauce from the unseasoned cast iron contained nearly 10 times as much iron (108 mg/kg) as the sauce from the seasoned cast-iron pot, which contained only a few more milligrams of iron than the sauce from the stainless steel pot. The sauce from the aluminum pot contained 14.3 mg/kg of aluminum, compared to less than 1 mg/kg in the sauce from the stainless steel pot.

The verdict? Avoid reactive cookware when cooking acidic foods. It can compromise flavor.

Cookware is made from a variety of metals, each with its own pros and cons. The ability of the metal to withstand and conduct heat will determine how well you can brown food, how easily food will burn, and how evenly the heat is distributed. Weight matters too. Buy a lightweight stainless steel pan and your stew meat will stick to the pot. Ease of cleaning can enhance (or detract from) a pan's desirability. Here's what you need to know:

COPPER conducts heat extremely well, but it is expensive, heavy, and tarnishes easily. Copper is also is reactive, leaching into many foods to produce off-colors and flavors. For this reason, copper cookware is usually lined with tin or stainless steel.

THE BOTTOM LINE: Copper looks great but it's not worth the expense.

ALUMINUM is second to copper in conductivity among the metals used for cookware. It is also light and inexpensive and retains heat well, provided it is of sufficient thickness, although the soft metal dents and scratches easily and it can react with acidic ingredients. Anodized aluminum cookware has a harder and less reactive outer surface. But its dark color can make it tricky to monitor the development of fond.

THE BOTTOM LINE: Unless anodized, aluminum is best used in combination with other metals.

CAST IRON heats up slowly but retains heat well. Cast-iron cookware is also inexpensive and lasts a lifetime, but it is heavy, reactive, and must be seasoned before use (unless you buy preseasoned cast-iron cookware, which we recommend). Cast iron is often coated with brightly colored enamel, which is not only attractive but makes the pot nonreactive. Because heavy cast-iron pots retain heat so well, they are perfect for recipes like frying and stewing that require precise temperature control.

THE BOTTOM LINE: Cast iron is great for skillets, and we like enameled cast iron for Dutch ovens.

STAINLESS STEEL is a poor heat conductor. Inexpensive cookware made entirely of thin-gauge stainless steel is prone to hot spots and warping. Stainless steel is, however, nonreactive, durable, and attractive, making it an excellent choice for coating, or "cladding," cookware made from aluminum or copper.

THE BOTTOM LINE: Buy cookware made with stainless steel that is combined with other metals.

CLAD cookware is what we recommend most of the time. The "cladding" label means that it is made from layers of metal that have been bonded under intense pressure and heat. For most clad cookware, these layers form a sandwich with the "filling" made of aluminum and the outer layers made of stainless steel.

THE BOTTOM LINE: Clad cookware heats evenly and quickly, and is easy to care for.

WHAT ABOUT NONSTICK PANS?

You may be wondering about nonstick coatings, which can be applied to cookware made from any of these materials. In general, we reserve nonstick pans for delicate foods, such as fish and eggs, which are prone to sticking. We find that nonstick pans don't brown food as well as conventional pans. Also, there often are no browned bits left in the pan once something like a steak or chicken cutlet has been cooked, and thus nothing for the cook to use in building a pan sauce. (For more on this, see "Don't Use Nonstick Pans for Sauces," right.)

There's been a fair amount of news and concern about the safety of nonstick cookware, which now accounts for more than half of all cookware sales in the United States. What are the issues?

First, the production of nonstick surfaces can pollute the local ground water. This issue directly impacts anyone living near a manufacturing facility where nonstick surfaces are made.

Second, the ingestion of nonstick surfaces (once the coating starts to peel and flake) probably isn't good for you. Maybe the coating just passes through your system, maybe not. In any case, the coating is no longer working if it has started to flake off; you need to throw out the pan and buy another one.

Third, nonstick pans can emit fumes if the surface reaches temperatures in excess of 600 degrees. Manufacturers admit that these fumes can kill small birds and advise against keeping pet birds in the kitchen. These fumes can cause a flulike illness in humans.

So how much of a concern is this? We conducted several kitchen tests in which we exposed both cheap and good-quality nonstick pans to high heat on the stovetop and under the broiler. We wanted to see how hot the cookware would get when used in recipes that call for high heat, like cooking a stir-fry. Using an infrared thermometer gun, we tracked temperatures and found only one way to get the temperature in the pan to 600 degrees: Heat an empty pan over a hot burner and forget about it.

Our recommendation: Never heat any pan, nonstick or otherwise, without first putting some oil in the pan. The oil will smoke at 400 degrees—well before the surface of a nonstick pan will emit dangerous fumes. You will notice the smoking oil and can pull the pan off the heat. This is a good idea when using conventional pans, too.

We continue to use nonstick cookware in the test kitchen, but for anyone who is looking for an alternative, we've found cast iron to be the most effective. Over time, cast-iron pans develop nonstick properties as the oils and fats used in cooking polymerize (the molecules change shape and link up) and essentially fuse with the surface of the pan. How much time? Clearly, the older and more seasoned the pan, the more "nonstick" it will become—as anyone who has been lucky enough to inherit their grandparents' cast-iron skillet will tell you. For the rest of us, it's never too late to start.

NONSTICK PAN
This sauce was nearly indistinguishable from plain water.

STAINLESS STEEL PAN
This sauce acquired a golden-brown color and distinct chicken flavor.

KNIFE BASICS

LIFECYCLE OF
A KNIFE

A sharp edge (top) will make quick work of slicing and chopping. However, even a few minutes of work can make the edge roll over (middle), making the blade feel slightly dull. A quick steeling or sharpening will remove the folded edge and return the knife to its original sharpness. After significant use, the sharp angles on the edge will become rounded and dull (bottom). At this point, the knife needs a new edge, which only an electric sharpener (or whetstone) can provide.

 VERY
SHARP

 SLIGHTLY
DULL

VERY
DULL

Specific knives are designed to perform a variety of tasks, which is why you need several knives. For instance, the serrations on a bread knife "grab" on to craggy surfaces (such as those on crusty bread) much better than the smooth edge of a chef's knife. Likewise, a small paring knife is a much better choice than a large chef's knife when trying to hull strawberries or devein shrimp. For a complete list of the knives we recommend that you own, see "Equipping Your Kitchen" on page 437.

Whichever knife you're using, it should be sharp. Let's say that again. Your knives must be sharp! There are three main reasons to keep your knives sharp.

- Sharp knives are actually less dangerous than dull knives, which are much more likely to slip and end up cutting your hand.
- Sharp knives cut through food more quickly than dull knives. Would you rather take two minutes or five minutes to chop an onion? It may not seem like a big difference, but in a recipe with a lot of vegetable or protein prep those extra minutes can really add up.
- Sharp knives produce food that is more evenly cut than dull knives. A dull blade will yield roughly minced garlic with large hunks, which can burn and impart a harsh flavor to your food. With a sharp knife, you can mince the garlic finer and more evenly, thus producing better-tasting food.

Right from the manufacturer, the blade should be very sharp. Most knife blades are actually shaped like a wedge. The spine (the top of the blade) is thick and helps the cook push the blade through food. The cutting edge is angled to a point. The blades on most European-style knives are angled at about 20 degrees.

So what turns a knife edge dull and what's the best way to remedy the problem? After just a few minutes of use, the edge can roll over, making the blade feel slightly dull. The wedge becomes less effective and the cook needs to supply more energy to push the blade through food. Running the knife blade up and down the steel that came with your knife set can remove the folded edge and return the knife to its original sharpness.

However, most knives used by home cooks are much duller than this. The cook hasn't stopped every few minutes to retool the blade with a steel. As a result, the factory-sharp angles on the edge have become rounded and very dull. At this point, it will take much more effort to use the knife and the edge will bruise food as it cuts. (The blade is also more likely to slip.) The knife needs an entirely new edge. A steel can't do this; you need to regrind the blade and remove some metal. An electric knife sharpener (see page 437) is your best bet for doing this at home.

EMERGENCY INGREDIENT SUBSTITUTIONS

Everybody does it (even though they shouldn't). Here are some tips for doing it well. No one wants to run out to the market for just one ingredient. Perhaps something you've got on hand will do the trick. We tested scores of widely published ingredient substitutions to figure out which ones work under what circumstances and which ones simply don't work. Below is a list of ingredients commonly called for in recipes and the items you are likely to have on hand that will work as substitutions.

TO REPLACE	AMOUNT	SUBSTITUTE			
Whole Milk	1 cup	⅝ cup skim milk + ⅜ cup half-and-half ⅔ cup 1% milk + ⅓ cup half-and-half ¾ cup 2% milk + ¼ cup half-and-half ⅞ cup skim milk + ⅛ cup heavy cream			
Half-and-Half	1 cup	¾ cup whole milk + ¼ cup heavy cream ⅔ cup skim or low-fat milk + ⅓ cup heavy cream			
Heavy Cream	1 cup	1 cup evaporated milk Not suitable for whipping or baking, but fine for soups and sauces.			
Eggs	LARGE	JUMBO	EXTRA-LARGE	MEDIUM	For half of an egg, whisk the yolk and white together and use half of the liquid.
	1	1	1	1	
	2	1½	2	2	
	3	2½	2½	3½	
	4	3	3½	4½	
	5	4	4	6	
	6	5	5	7	
Buttermilk	1 cup	1 cup milk + 1 tablespoon lemon juice or distilled white vinegar Not suitable for raw applications, such as a buttermilk dressing.			
Sour Cream	1 cup	1 cup plain whole-milk yogurt Nonfat and low-fat yogurts are too lean to replace sour cream.			
Plain Yogurt	1 cup	1 cup sour cream			
Cake Flour	1 cup	⅞ cup all-purpose flour + 2 tablespoons cornstarch			
Bread Flour	1 cup	1 cup all-purpose flour Bread and pizza crusts may bake up with slightly less chew.			
Baking Powder	1 teaspoon	¼ teaspoon baking soda + ½ teaspoon cream of tartar (use right away)			
Light Brown Sugar	1 cup	1 cup granulated sugar + 1 tablespoon molasses	Pulse the molasses in a food processor along with the sugar or simply add it along with the other wet ingredients.		
Dark Brown Sugar	1 cup	1 cup granulated sugar + 2 tablespoons molasses			
Confectioners' Sugar	1 cup	1 cup granulated sugar + 1 teaspoon cornstarch, ground in a blender (not a food processor) Works well for dusting over cakes, less so in frostings and glazes.			
Table Salt	1 tablespoon	1½ tablespoons Morton Kosher Salt or fleur de sel OR 2 tablespoons Diamond Crystal Kosher Salt or Maldon Sea Salt Not recommended for use in baking recipes.			
Fresh Herbs	1 tablespoon	1 teaspoon dried herbs			
Wine	½ cup	½ cup broth + 1 teaspoon wine vinegar (added just before serving) OR ½ cup broth + 1 teaspoon lemon juice (added just before serving) Vermouth makes an acceptable substitute for white wine.			
Unsweetened Chocolate	1 ounce	3 tablespoons cocoa powder + 1 tablespoon vegetable oil 1½ ounces bittersweet or semisweet chocolate (remove 1 tablespoon sugar from the recipe)			
Bittersweet or Semisweet Chocolate	1 ounce	⅔ ounce unsweetened chocolate + 2 teaspoons sugar Works well with fudgy brownies. Do not use in a custard or cake.			

FOOD SAFETY

THE BASICS

Food safety sounds scary and in some respects it is. If you don't follow basic sanitation practices, you can make yourself and your family sick. That said, taking a few basic steps will dramatically reduce the risk of food-borne illnesses.

SEPARATE RAW AND COOKED One of the most important rules of food safety is to keep raw and cooked foods separate. Never place cooked food on a plate or cutting board that has come into contact with raw food, or vice versa, and wash any utensil (including a thermometer) that comes in contact with raw food before reusing it. These additional steps will help you avoid cross-contamination.

PUT UP A BARRIER Items that come in contact with both raw and cooked food, like scales and platters, should be covered with aluminum foil or plastic wrap to create a protective barrier. Once the item has been used, the foil—and any bacteria—can be discarded. Similarly, wrapping your cutting board with plastic wrap before pounding meat and poultry will limit the spread of bacteria.

DON'T RINSE RAW MEAT AND POULTRY Avoid rinsing raw meat and poultry, as doing so is likely to spread contaminants around your sink.

SAFER SEASONINGS Though bacteria can't live for more than a few minutes in direct contact with salt (which quickly dehydrates bacteria, leading to death), they can live on the edges of a box or shaker. To avoid contamination, we grind pepper into a small bowl and then mix it with salt (using a ratio of 1 part pepper to 4 parts kosher salt or 2 parts table salt). This way, we can reach into the bowl for seasoning without having to wash our hands every time we touch the meat. Afterward, the bowl goes right into the dishwasher.

DON'T RECYCLE USED MARINADES Used marinade is contaminated with raw meat juices and is therefore unsafe to consume. If you want a sauce to serve with cooked meat, make a little extra marinade and set it aside before adding the rest to the raw meat.

AVOIDING THE DANGER ZONE

Most bacteria thrive between 40 and 140 degrees. Within this "danger zone," bacteria double about every 20 minutes, quickly reaching harmful levels. As a general rule, food shouldn't stay in this zone for more than two hours (one hour if the room temperature is over 90 degrees). Here are some specific steps you should take to avoid letting food spend too much time in the danger zone.

DEFROST IN FRIDGE Defrosting should always be done in the refrigerator, not on the counter, where the temperatures are higher and bacteria can multiply readily. Always place food on a plate or in a bowl while defrosting to prevent any liquid it releases from coming in contact with other foods. Most food will take 24 hours to thaw fully. (Larger items, like whole turkeys, can take far longer. Count on about five hours per pound.)

COUNTERINTUITIVE COOLING
Though it may go against your instincts, don't put hot foods in the fridge immediately after cooking. This will cause the temperature of the refrigerator to rise, potentially making it hospitable to the spread of bacteria. The FDA recommends cooling foods to 70 degrees within the first two hours after cooking and 40 degrees within four hours after that. We stay within these recommendations by cooling food on the countertop for about an hour, until it reaches 80 to 90 degrees (food should be just warm to the touch) before transferring it to the fridge. (See page 101 for details.)

REHEAT RAPIDLY When food is reheated, it should be brought through the danger zone as rapidly as possible—don't let it come slowly to a simmer. Bring leftover sauces, soups, and gravies to a boil and make sure casseroles reach at least 165 degrees, using an instant-read thermometer to determine whether they're at the proper temperature.

KEEP IT COOL

Thermometers are proven assets in limiting the spread of food-borne illness. A refrigerator thermometer will tell you if your fridge and freezer are working properly. Check the temperature of your refrigerator regularly to ensure that it is between 35 and 40 degrees; your freezer should be below 0 degrees.

Here are the recommended storage temperatures for specific foods. Keep in mind that the back of a refrigerator is the coldest. Make sure that raw meat is stored well wrapped and never on shelves that are above other food.

FOOD	TEMPERATURE
Fish and Shellfish	30 to 34 degrees
Meat and Poultry	32 to 36 degrees
Dairy Products	36 to 40 degrees
Eggs	38 to 40 degrees
Produce	40 to 45 degrees

GET IT HOT

The doneness temperatures used throughout this book represent the test kitchen's best assessment of palatability weighed against safety. In most cases, those concerns align. Rare chicken isn't very tasty, or very safe. There are a few notable exceptions, especially as regards ground meat. If safety is your primary concern, you don't want to eat rare burgers.

The USDA has issued a complex set of rules regarding the cooking of meat and poultry.

Here are the basics:
- Cook whole cuts of meat, including pork, to an internal temperature of at least 145 degrees and let rest for at least three minutes.
- Cook all ground meats to an internal temperature of at least 160 degrees.
- Cook all poultry, including ground poultry, to an internal temperature of at least 165 degrees.

If you want more information on food safety, visit www.fsis.usda.gov/factsheets.

CONVERSIONS AND EQUIVALENTS

The recipes in this book were developed using standard U.S. measures. The charts below offer equivalents for U.S. and metric measures. All conversions are approximate and have been rounded up or down to the nearest whole number. For example:

1 teaspoon = 4.929 milliliters, rounded up to 5 milliliters
1 ounce = 28.349 grams, rounded down to 28 grams

VOLUME CONVERSIONS

U.S.	METRIC
1 teaspoon	5 milliliters
2 teaspoons	10 milliliters
1 tablespoon	15 milliliters
2 tablespoons	30 milliliters
¼ cup	59 milliliters
⅓ cup	79 milliliters
½ cup	118 milliliters
¾ cup	177 milliliters
1 cup	237 milliliters
1¼ cups	296 milliliters
1½ cups	355 milliliters
2 cups	473 milliliters
2½ cups	591 milliliters
3 cups	710 milliliters
4 cups (1 quart)	0.946 liter
1.06 quarts	1 liter
4 quarts (1 gallon)	3.8 liters

WEIGHT CONVERSIONS

OUNCES	GRAMS
½	14
¾	21
1	28
1½	43
2	57
2½	71
3	85
3½	99
4	113
4½	128
5	142
6	170
7	198
8	227
9	255
10	283
12	340
16 (1 pound)	454

OVEN TEMPERATURES

FAHRENHEIT	CELSIUS	GAS MARK (IMPERIAL)
225	105	¼
250	120	½
275	135	1
300	150	2
325	165	3
350	180	4
375	190	5
400	200	6
425	220	7
450	230	8
475	245	9

METRIC TEMPERATURES

If you use an oven set to metric or Imperial measures, you will want to refer to the chart on the left when using our recipes. For other temperatures not represented in the chart, use this simple formula:

Subtract 32 degrees from the Fahrenheit reading, then divide the result by 1.8 to find the Celsius reading.

For example, if a recipe says "roast until chicken thighs register 175 degrees," you would convert this Fahrenheit temperature as follows:

175°F − 32 = 143°
143° ÷ 1.8 = 79.44°C, rounded down to 79°C

FURTHER READING

Amendola, Joseph, and Nicole Rees. *Understanding Baking*. Hoboken, NJ: John Wiley & Sons, 2003.

Barham, Peter. *The Science of Cooking*. Berlin: Springer-Verlag, 2001.

Belitz, H.-D., Werner Grosch, and Peter Schieberle. *Food Chemistry*. 4th ed. Berlin: Springer-Verlag, 2009.

Block, Eric. *Garlic and Other Alliums: The Lore and the Science*. Cambridge: The Royal Society of Chemistry, 2010.

Brown, Amy C. *Understanding Food: Principles and Preparation*. 3rd ed. Belmont, CA: Thomson Wadsworth, 2008.

Coultate, Tom. *Food: The Chemistry of Its Components*. 5th ed. Cambridge: The Royal Society of Chemistry, 2009.

Fellows, P. J. *Food Processing Technology: Principles and Practice*. 3rd ed. Boca Raton, FL: CRC Press, 2009.

Figoni, Paula. *How Baking Works*. 3rd ed. Hoboken, NJ: John Wiley & Sons, 2011.

Igoe, Robert S. *Dictionary of Food Ingredients*. 4th ed. Gaithersburg, MD: Aspen Publishers, 2001.

Kamozawa, Aki, and H. Alexander Talbot. *Ideas in Food: Great Recipes and Why They Work*. New York: Clarkson Potter, 2010.

McClements, David Julian. *Food Emulsions: Principles, Practices, and Techniques*. 2nd ed. Boca Raton, FL: CRC Press, 2004.

McGee, Harold. *On Food and Cooking: The Science and Lore of the Kitchen*. New York: Scribner, 2004.

McWilliams, Margaret. *Foods: Experimental Perspectives*. 6th ed. Upper Saddle River, NJ: Prentice Hall, 2008.

Murano, Peter. *Understanding Food Science and Technology*. Belmont, CA: Thomson Wadsworth, 2003.

Myhrvold, Nathan, Chris Young, and Maxime Bilet. *Modernist Cuisine: The Art and Science of Cooking*. Bellevue, WA: The Cooking Lab, 2011.

Nielsen, Suzanne, ed. *Food Analysis*. New York: Springer, 2010.

Owusu-Apenten, Richard. *Introduction to Food Chemistry*. Boca Raton, FL: CRC Press, 2005.

Potter, Jeff. *Cooking for Geeks: Real Science, Great Hacks, and Good Food*. Sebastapol, CA: O'Reilly Media, 2010.

Reineccius, Gary. *Flavor Chemistry and Technology*. 2nd ed. Boca Raton, FL: Taylor and Francis, 2006.

Stauffer, Clyde. *Fats and Oils*. St. Paul: Eagan Press, 1996.

This, Hervé. *Molecular Gastronomy: Exploring the Science of Flavor*. New York: Columbia University Press, 2008.

———. *The Science of the Oven*. New York: Columbia University Press, 2009.

Varnam, Alan, and Jane Sutherland. *Meat and Meat Products: Technology, Chemistry and Microbiology*. London: Chapman & Hall, 1995.

Warriss, Paul. *Meat Science: An Introductory Text*. Oxford: CABI Publishing, 2000.

Wolke, Robert. *What Einstein Told His Cook: Kitchen Science Explained*. New York: W. W. Norton & Co., 2002 .

———. *What Einstein Told His Cook 2: The Sequel: Further Adventures in Kitchen Science*. New York: W. W. Norton & Co., 2005.

RESOURCES–SELECTED SCIENTIFIC JOURNAL ARTICLES

While popular books on cooking science and food science textbooks provide very helpful explanations, the ultimate source of scientific information comes from scholarly review articles and original research papers published in academic journals. While working on this book, I consulted more than 350 scientific papers. These landmark papers were especially helpful.

—GUY CROSBY

MEAT, POULTRY, AND SEAFOOD PREPARATION

Bertram, H., S. Holdsworth, A. Whittaker, and H. Andersen. "Salt Diffusion and Distribution in Meat Studied by 23Na Nuclear Magnetic Resonance Imaging and Relaxometry." *Journal of Agricultural and Food Chemistry* 53 (2005): 7814–7818.

Casey, J., A. Crosland, and R. Patterson. "Collagen Content of Meat Carcasses of Known History." *Meat Science* 12 (1985): 189–203.

Cross, H., M. Stanfield, and E. Koch. "Beef Palatability as Affected by Cooking Rate and Final Temperature." *Journal of Animal Science* 43 (1976): 114–121.

Johnson, I. "Structure and Function of Fish Muscle." *Symposia of the Zoological Society of London* 48 (1981): 71–113.

Jiang, S.-T. "Contribution of Muscle Proteinases to Meat Tenderization." *Proceedings of the National Science Council, ROC* 22 (1998): 97–107.

McCrae, S., and P. Paul. "Rate of Heating as It Affects the Solubilization of Beef Muscle Collagen." *Journal of Food Science* 39 (1974): 18–21.

Offer, G., and J. Trinick. "On the Mechanism of Water Holding in Meat: The Swelling and Shrinking of Myofibrils." *Meat Science* 8 (1983): 245–281.

Oreskovich, D. C., P. J. Bechtel, F. K. McKeith, J. Novakofski, and E. J. Basgall. "Marinade pH Affects Textural Properties of Beef." *Journal of Food Science* 57 (1992): 305–311.

Yusop, S. M., M. G. O'Sullivan, J. F. Kerry, and J. P. Kerry. "Effect of Marinating Time and Low pH on Marinade Performance and Sensory Acceptability of Poultry Meat." *Meat Science* 85 (2010): 657–663.

COOKING WITH CHEESE AND EGGS

Bogenreif, D., and N. Olson. "Hydrolysis of ß-Casein Increases Cheddar Cheese Meltability." *Milchwissenschaft* 50 (1995): 678–682.

Clark, A., G. Kavanagh, and S. Ross-Murphy. "Globular Protein Gelation—Theory and Experiment (Cooking Eggs)." *Food Hydrocolloids* 15 (2001): 383–400.

Lomakina, K., and K. Míková. "A Study of the Factors Affecting the Foaming Properties of Egg White—a Review." *Czech Journal of Food Sciences* 24 (2006): 110–118.

FRUITS, VEGETABLES, CEREAL GRAINS, AND LEGUMES

Brummell, D., et al. "Cell Wall Metabolism during the Development of Chilling Injury in Cold-Stored Peach Fruit: Association of Mealiness with Arrested Disassembly of Cell Wall Pectins." *Journal of Experimental Botany* 55 (2004): 2041–2052.

Kikuchi, K., M. Koizumi, N. Ishida, and H. Kano. "Water Uptake by Dry Beans Observed by Micro-Magnetic Resonance Imaging." *Annals of Botany* 98 (2006): 545–553.

McComber, D., H. Horner, M. Chamberlain, and D. Cox. "Potato Cultivar Differences Associated with Mealiness." *Journal of Agricultural and Food Chemistry* 42 (1994): 2433–2439.

McPherson, A., and J. Jane. "Comparison of Waxy Potato with Other Root and Tuber Starches." *Carbohydrate Polymers* 40 (1999): 57–70.

Micheli, F. "Pectin Methylesterases: Cell Wall Enzymes with Important Roles in Plant Physiology." *Trends in Plant Science* 6 (2001): 414–419.

Stolle-Smits, T., J. Beekhuizen, C. van Dijk, A. G. J. Voragen, and K. Recourt. "Cell Wall Dissolution During Industrial Processing of Green Beans (*Phaseolus vulgaris L.*)." *Journal of Agricultural and Food Chemistry* 43 (1995): 2480–2486.

Waldron, K., M. Parker, and A. Smith. "Plant Cell Walls and Food Quality." *Comprehensive Reviews in Food Science and Food Safety* 2 (2003): 101–119.

BAKING AND CONFECTIONARY SCIENCE

Amend, T., and H.-D. Belitz. "The Formation of Dough and Gluten—A Study by Scanning Electron Microscopy." *Z. Lebensm Unters Forsch* 190 (1990): 401–409.

———. "Gluten Formation Studied by the Transmission Electron Microscope." *Z. Lebensm Unters Forsch* 190 (1990): 184–193.

Campos, R., M. Ollivon, and A. Maragoni. "Molecular Composition Dynamics and Structure of Cocoa Butter." *Crystal Growth & Design* 10 (2010): 205–217.

Wieser, H. "Chemistry of Gluten Proteins." *Food Microbiology* 24 (2007): 115–119.

COOKING METHODS

Aguilera, J., and H. Gloria. "Determination of Oil in Fried Potato Products by Differential Scanning Calorimetry." *Journal of Agricultural and Food Chemistry* 45 (1997): 781–785.

Augustin, J., E. Augustin, R. L. Cutrufelli, S. R. Hagen, and C. Teitzel. "Alcohol Retention in Food Preparation." *Journal of the American Dietetic Association* 92 (1992): 486–488.

Saguy, I., and E. Pinthus. "Oil Uptake During Deep-Fat Frying: Factors and Mechanism." *Food Technology* 49 (1995): 142–150.

CREATING FLAVOR

Ashoor, S., and J. Zent. "Maillard Browning of Common Amino Acids and Sugars." *Journal of Food Science* 49 (1984): 1206–1207.

Kurihara, K. "Glutamate: From Discovery as a Food Flavor to Role as a Basic Taste (Umami)." *American Journal of Clinical Nutrition* 90 (2009): 719S–722S.

Skurray, G., and N. Pucar. "L-Glutamic Acid Content of Fresh and Processed Food." *Food Chemistry* 27 (1988): 177–180.

Randall, W. "Onion Flavor Chemistry and Factors Influencing Flavor Intensity." In *Spices: Flavor Chemistry and Antioxidant Properties*, S. Risch and C.-T. Ho, eds. Washington, D.C.: American Chemical Society, 1997.

INDEX

I

Ice Cream, Vanilla, 188
Indian Curry with Potatoes, Cauliflower, Peas, and
    Chickpeas, 297
Inexpensive Grill-Roasted Beef with Garlic and
    Rosemary, 63
Ingredients
    Butter 101, 373
    Chocolate 101, 435
    Eggs 101, 175
    emergency substitutions, 447
    Fish 101, 33
    Flour 101, 357
    Meat 101, 41
    "101" pages, note about, 15
    Poultry 101, 87
    Salt 101, 113
    Shopping for Beef 101, 141
    Shopping for Pork 101, 149
    substituting, note about, 15
    Sweeteners 101, 421
Invert sugars (concept 48)
    Brown Sugar Cookies, 412
    chewy cookies, 412–16
    Chocolate-Chunk Oatmeal Cookies with Pecans and Dried
        Cherries, 413
    creamy frozen desserts, 416–17
    Fresh Lemon Sherbet, 417
    Fresh Lime Sherbet, 417
    Fresh Orange Sherbet, 416–17
    Fresh Raspberry Sherbet, 417
    how the science works, 410–11
    sugar syrups at work, 416–17
    test kitchen experiment, 411
    Ultimate Chocolate Chip Cookies, 415

J

Juicy Pub-Style Burgers, 139–40
    with Crispy Shallots and Blue Cheese, 140
    with Sautéed Onion and Smoked Cheddar, 140
Julienne, description of, 14

K

Kitchen supplies, ratings of, 443
Kitchen timers, ratings of, 441
Kneading bread (concept 39)
    autolyse at work, 334–37
    how the science works, 332–33
    Olive-Rosemary Bread, 334–35

Kneading bread (concept 39) *(continued)*
    Rustic Dinner Rolls, 336
    test kitchen experiment, 333
Knife basics, 446
Knife sharpeners, ratings of, 437
Knives, ratings of, 437

L

Ladles, ratings of, 440
Lamb
    doneness temperatures, 7
    optimal cooking temperatures, 43
    optimal resting times, 37
    Rack of, Grilled, 45–46
    Rack of, Grilled, with Sweet Mustard Glaze, 46
Lamination
    about, 368
    demonstrating, 370–72
Lasagna, Four-Cheese, 209–10
Leaveners. See Chemical leaveners
Leek(s)
    and Blue Cheese, Deep-Dish Quiche with, 193
    Prosciutto, and Goat Cheese Frittata, 47–48
    and White Wine, Salmon en Cocotte with, 89
Legumes
    Lentil Salad with Hazelnuts and Goat Cheese, 261
    Lentil Salad with Olives, Mint, and Feta, 261
    protein and fiber in, 256
    see also Bean(s)
Lemon
    anatomy 101, 401
    -Basil Salsa Verde, 305
    Browned Butter, 35
    Bundt Cake, 400
    Cheesecake, 185–86
    and Goat Cheese Cheesecake with Hazelnut Crust,
        186
    Meringue Pie, 203
    or Lemon-Coconut Chiffon Cake, 392
    -Parsley Chicken Breasts, Grilled, 131
    and Rosemary Marinade, Grilled Beef Kebabs with,
        127–28
    Sherbet, Fresh, 417
    Triple-Citrus Cheesecake, 186
    Vinaigrette, 316
Lentil
    Salad with Hazelnuts and Goat Cheese, 261
    Salad with Olives, Mint, and Feta, 261
Lime
    -Chipotle Chicken Breasts, Grilled, 131
    -Coconut Sugar Cookies, Chewy, 364
    Sherbet, Fresh, 417
    Triple-Citrus Cheesecake, 186